Fundamental accounting principles

THE WILLARD J. GRAHAM SERIES IN ACCOUNTING
Consulting Editor
ROBERT N. ANTHONY
Harvard University

■ **WILLIAM W. PYLE**

■ **JOHN ARCH WHITE**
Emeritus, The University of Texas at Austin

■ **KERMIT D. LARSON**
The University of Texas at Austin

eighth edition

Fundamental accounting principles

1978

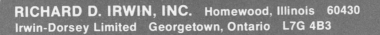

RICHARD D. IRWIN, INC. Homewood, Illinois 60430
Irwin-Dorsey Limited Georgetown, Ontario L7G 4B3

ISBN 0-256-01994-0
Library of Congress Catalog Card No. 77-79382

Printed in the United States of America

5 6 7 8 9 0 K 5 4 3 2 1 0 9

LEARNING SYSTEMS COMPANY—
a division of Richard D. Irwin, Inc.—has developed a
PROGRAMMED LEARNING AID
to accompany texts in this subject area.
Copies can be purchased through your bookstore
or by writing PLAIDS,
1818 Ridge Road, Homewood, Illinois   60430.

Preface

This Eighth Edition of *Fundamental Accounting Principles,* like previous editions, is designed for use in a first-year accounting course at the college and university level. It describes the fundamental concepts and principles that underlie accounting information, shows how accounting data are accumulated, and initiates the student into the effective use of such data. The balance between financial and managerial topics has been carefully reassessed and apportioned with the intent of serving the educational needs of both students who will make accountancy their career and those who will use accounting information in other areas of specialty or in their personal affairs.

In this revision, we have attempted to make several improvements while retaining the important thrust of previous editions, which was and is presenting a flexible and teachable, yet demanding textual base for introductory accounting. Many sections of the book have been rewritten to provide a more understandable, logical flow of discussion. All of the material has been updated wherever appropriate, and the most recent pronouncements of the various authoritative bodies such as the Financial Accounting Standards Board and the Securities and Exchange Commission have been incorporated. To provide space for an expansion of topical coverage in the area of managerial planning and control, some of the more procedural subjects were condensed. Also, the content of some chapters has been rearranged to gain more instructional efficiency. New chapters have been added on accounting for price-level changes and on flexible budgeting. The previous coverage of fixed budgets has been revised to emphasize the preparation of master budgets for several sequential periods; and the income tax chapter has been revised to reflect the most recent changes in the federal income tax laws. To aid the student, each chapter is begun with a set of measurable objectives designed to focus attention on important areas of coverage and on expected student performance. A glossary of important terms has also been added at the end of each chapter.

As in previous editions, the instructor's flexibility in topical and homework assignments has been maximized. Almost any chapter after the fifth may be omitted or abbreviated and, if desired, a minimum of time may be devoted to such subjects as special journals and the voucher system. Although we prefer to teach the course by following the chapter sequence as presented, instructors may substantially alter the sequence of chapter assignments without complicating the student's understanding of the materials that follow. For example, Chapters 13 and 14 may be taught in either the first or second of a two-semester course, since the working papers for the problems of these chapters are included in both the first and second semester booklets of working papers.

The supplementary materials accompanying the text are even more extensive than in previous editions. A workbook of study guides, two booklets of working papers, three practice sets, and a list of problem check figures are available to students. Instructors may obtain a series of ten achievement tests, two final examinations, a booklet of supplementary test questions and short-answer problems, comprehensive solutions manuals for the problems of the text, the practice sets, and the tests, and transparency solutions to each problem in the text plus 35 additional teaching transparencies to be used as aids in classroom presentations.

The booklet of supplementary test questions and short-answer problems, which is new with this edition, allows instructors added flexibility in designing quizzes and examinations that fit their own philosophy and teaching emphasis. The questions and problems are grouped by chapter for ease in preparing pop quizzes.

Three alternate sets of achievement tests and final examinations are available, with each final exam structured into 50 multiple-choice questions and problems that may be graded either electronically or manually. To insure that the examination questions are more than five-answer guessing games, the mistakes students commonly make are anticipated and the resulting wrong answers are provided among the answer choices.

Many adopters of the previous edition and other individuals have contributed to changes in this revision through their criticisms and suggestions. We are indebted to all of them. Special appreciation is due to Russell Andersen, Peat Marwick Mitchell & Co.; Phyllis Barker, Indiana State University; Hugo J. Dallas, El Camino College; Sherman Dearth, William A. Holt, Jeff Hooper, and Lee C. Wilson, Mesa Community College; Al A. Evans, Southwest Missouri State University; Louis H. Gilles, University of South Carolina; Blanca M. Gonzalez, Miami Dade Community College; Carl E. High, New York City Community College; Michael D. Kinsman, University of California, Irvine; Ralph P. Knost, University of Cincinnati; Jack Kramer,

The University of Texas at Austin; Margaret McRae, Arthur Anderson & Co.; Paul W. Parkison, Ball State University; Robert L. Pease, Penn Valley Community College; Joseph E. Rhile, Lake-Sumter Junior College; Marvin J. Slovacek, San Antonio College; Frank F. Silloway, Essex Community College; William P. Thompson, Kennesaw Junior College; Harold O. Wilson, David Lipscomb College; and Robert G. Wrenn, Los Angeles Harbor College.

January 1978   WILLIAM W. PYLE
                                        KERMIT D. LARSON

Contents

Part 1.   Introduction

chapter 1
Accounting, an introduction to its concepts   3

Why study accounting. Accountancy as a profession. The work of an accountant. Accounting and bookkeeping. Focus of this text. Accounting statements. Assets, liabilities, and owner equity. Business entity concept. Cost
principle. Objectivity principle. Continuing-concern concept. The stable-
dollar concept. Accounting principles. Source of accounting principles. The
balance sheet equation. Effects of transactions on the accounting equation.
Realization principle. Important transaction effects.

Part 2.   Processing accounting data

chapter 2
Recording transactions   33

Business papers. Accounts. Accounts commonly used. The ledger. Debit and
credit. Mechanics of double-entry accounting. Transactions illustrating the
rules of debit and credit. The accounts and the equation. Preparing a trial
balance. The proof offered by a trial balance. Standard account form. Need
for a journal. The General Journal. Recording transactions in a General Journal. Posting transaction information. Locating errors. Correcting errors. Bookkeeping techniques.

chapter 3
Adjusting the accounts and preparing the statements   69

Need for adjustments before statements are prepared. Adjusting the accounts.
The adjusted trial balance. Preparing statements from the adjusted trial balance. The adjustment process. Arrangement of the accounts in the ledger.

Disposing of accrued items. Cash and accrual bases of accounting. Classification of balance sheet items. Owner equity on the balance sheet. Arrangement of balance sheet items. Classification of income statement items.

chapter 4
The work sheet and closing the accounts   105

Preparing a work sheet. The work sheet illustrated. Work sheet and the financial statements. Work sheet and adjusting entries. Work sheet and closing entries. Why closing entries are made. Closing entries illustrated. Sources of closing entry information. The accounts after closing. The post-closing trial balance. Matters of terminology. The accounting cycle. Accounting periods; the natural business year.

chapter 5
Accounting for a merchandising concern   141

Revenue from sales. Cost of goods sold. Cost of goods sold, periodic inventory system. Income statement of a merchandising concern. Work sheet of a merchandising concern. Preparing the statements; adjusting entries. Closing entries. Closing entries and the inventory. Other methods. Dispensing with the Adjusted Trial Balance columns. Bases of revenue recognition. Taking the ending inventory. Trade discounts. Debit and credit memoranda. Code numbers as a means of identifying accounts.

chapter 6
Accounting systems   177

Reducing posting labor. Subsidiary ledgers. Posting the sales journals. Controlling accounts. Other columnar journals. Cash Receipts Journal. Posting the Cash Receipts Journal. Posting rule. Sales returns. Accounts payable. The Purchases Journal and its posting. Purchase of assets used in the business. The Cash Disbursements Journal and its posting. Identifying posted amounts. Purchases returns. Proving the ledgers. Sales taxes. Sales invoices as a Sales Journal. The Combined Cash Journal. Speeding the data processing. Electric accounting machines. Automated data processing.

Part 3.   Accounting for assets

chapter 7
Accounting for cash   221

Internal control. Internal control for cash. The voucher system and control. The voucher system and expenses. Recording vouchers. The petty cash fund. Petty cash fund illustrated. Cash over and short. Reconciling the bank balance. Illustration of a bank reconciliation. Other internal control procedures. APPENDIX. Recording vouchers, pen-and-ink system. The unpaid vouchers file. The voucher system, check register. Purchases returns.

chapter 8
Notes and accounts receivable   263

Promissory notes. Calculating interest. Recording the receipt of a note. Dishonored notes receivable. Discounting notes receivable. Payment of a discounted note by its maker. Dishonor of a discounted note. Collecting an out-of-town note. End-of-the-period adjustments. ACCOUNTS RECEIVABLE. Bad debts. Matching bad debt losses with sales. Allowance method of accounting for bad debts. Bad debt recoveries. Other bases for estimating bad debts. Aging accounts receivable. Direct write-off of bad debts.

chapter 9
Inventories and cost of goods sold   297

Matching merchandise costs with revenues. Assigning a cost to the ending inventory. Accounting for an inventory at cost. The principle of consistency. Changing accounting procedures. Items included on an inventory. Elements of inventory cost. Cost or market, the lower. Principle of conservatism. Inventory errors. Perpetual inventories. Periodic and perpetual inventory systems. Estimated inventories.

chapter 10
Plant and equipment   325

Cost of plant and equipment. Nature of depreciation. Productive life of a plant asset. Salvage value. Allocating depreciation. Depreciation on the balance sheet. Balance sheet plant asset values. Recovering the costs of plant assets. Disposal of a plant asset. Depreciation for partial years. Plant asset records. Plant assets of low cost.

chapter 11
Plant and equipment; intangible assets   357

Exchanging plant assets. Exchanging a note for a plant asset. Revising depreciation rates. Repairs and replacements. Betterments. Capital and revenue expenditures. Natural resources. Intangible assets. APPENDIX. The concept of present value.

Part 4. Accounting for equities: Liabilities and partners' equity

chapter 12
Payroll accounting   393

The federal Social Security Act. Withholding employees' federal income taxes. City and state income taxes. Fair Labor Standards Act. Union contracts. Other payroll deductions. Timekeeping. The Payroll Register. Recording the payroll. Paying the employees. Payroll bank account. Employee's Individual Earnings Record. Payroll taxes levied on the employer. Paying the payroll taxes. Accruing taxes and wages. Machine methods.

chapter 13
Current and long-term liabilities   423

Short-term notes payable. End-of-the-period adjustments. Issuing a mortgage to borrow money. Difference between stocks and bonds. Why bonds are issued. Borrowing by issuing bonds. Characteristics of bonds. Issuing bonds. Bonds sold between interest dates. Bond interest rates. Bonds sold at a discount. Bonds sold at a premium. Accrued bond interest expense. Sale of bonds by investors. Redemption of bonds. Convertible bonds. Bond sinking fund. Restriction on dividends due to outstanding bonds. Long-term notes.

chapter 14
Partnership accounting   457

Characteristics of a partnership. Advantages and disadvantages of a partnership. Partnership accounting. Nature of partnership earnings. Division of earnings. Earnings allocated on a stated fractional basis. Division of earnings based on the ratio of capital investments. Salaries and interest as aids in sharing. Partnership financial statements. Addition or withdrawal of a partner. Death of a partner. Liquidations.

Part 5.   Corporation accounting

chapter 15
Corporations: Organization and operation   493

Advantages of the corporate form. Disadvantages of the corporate form. Organizing a corporation. Organization costs. Management of a corporation. Stock certificates and the transfer of stock. Corporation accounting. Corporation owner equity accounts illustrated. Authorization of stock. Selling stock for cash. Exchanging stock for assets other than cash. Par value and minimum legal capital. Stock premiums and discounts. No-par stock. Cash dividends and retained earnings. Dividend policy. Rights of stockholders. Preferred stock. Why preferred stock is issued. Stock values.

chapter 16
Corporations: Additional stock transactions, income,
and retained earnings   529

Stock subscriptions. Sale of stock through subscriptions, with collections in installments. Subscribed stock on the balance sheet. Treasury stock. Purchase of treasury stock. Reissuance of treasury stock. Retirement of stock. Donation of assets by outsiders. Contributed capital in the accounts and on the statements. Retained earnings and dividends. Contributed capital and dividends. Stock dividends. Stock splits. Converting bonds to stock. Appropriation of retained earnings. Comprehensive treatment of equity items. Retained earnings statement. Extraordinary gains and losses. Accounting changes. Prior period adjustments. Comparative single-step income statement. Accounting treatment for corporation income taxes.

chapter 17
Corporations: Stock investments, intercorporate investments, and consolidations   569

Stocks as investments. Classifying investments. Accounting for investments in stock. Parent and subsidiary corporations. Consolidated balance sheets. Earnings of a subsidiary. Consolidated balance sheets at dates after acquisition. Other consolidated statements. Purchase versus a pooling of interests. Who uses consolidated statements. The corporation balance sheet.

Part 6. Financial statements: Interpretation and modifications

chapter 18
Statement of changes in financial position:
Flows of funds and cash   601

Nature of funds and working capital. Sources and uses of funds. Statement of changes in financial position. Preparing a statement of changes in financial position. Determining the change in working capital. Preparing the working paper. Analysis of working capital changes. Extraordinary gains and losses. Broad concept of financing and investing activities. CASH FLOW. Cash flow statement. Preparing a cash flow statement.

chapter 19
Analyzing financial statements   635

Comparative statements. Analysis of working capital. Standards of comparison. Other balance sheet and income statement relations.

chapter 20
Accounting for price-level changes   665

Understanding price-level changes. Construction of a price index. Using price index numbers. Specific versus general price-level indexes. Using price indexes in accounting. General price-level-adjusted (GPLA) accounting. GPLA accounting for assets. Preparing comprehensive GPLA financial statements. GPLA accounting and current values. Current value accounting. Replacement cost accounting. The future of accounting for price-level changes.

Part 7. Managerial accounting for costs

chapter 21
Departmental accounting; responsibility accounting   697

Basis for departmentalization. Departmental gross profits in a merchandising business. Securing departmental information. Income statement showing departmental gross profits. Allocating expenses. Bases for allocating expenses. Mechanics of allocating expenses. Allocating service department expenses. Departmental expense allocation sheet. Eliminating an unprofitable department. Departmental contributions to overhead. Controllable costs and expenses. Responsibility accounting. Joint costs.

chapter 22
Manufacturing accounting   729

Basic difference in accounting. Systems of accounting in manufacturing concerns. Elements of manufacturing costs. Accounts unique to a manufacturing company. Income statement of a manufacturing company. Manufacturing statement. Worksheet for a manufacturing company. Preparing a manufacturing company's work sheet. Preparing statements. Adjusting entries. Closing entries. Inventory valuation problems of a manufacturer.

chapter 23
Cost accounting, job order, and process   759

JOB ORDER COST ACCOUNTING. Job cost sheets. The Goods in Process account. Accounting for materials under a job cost system. Accounting for labor in a job cost system. Accounting for overhead in a job cost system. Overapplied and underapplied overhead. Recording the completion of a job. Recording cost of goods sold. PROCESS COST ACCOUNTING. Assembling costs by departments. Charging costs to departments. Equivalent finished units. Process cost accounting illustrated.

Part 8. Planning and controlling business operations

chapter 24
The master budget: A formal plan for the business   799

The master budget. Benefits from budgeting. The budget committee. The budget period. Preparing the master budget. Preparation of the master budget illustrated.

chapter 25

Cost-volume-profit analysis   823

Cost behavior. Cost assumptions. Break-even point. Break-even graph. Sales
required for a desired net income. Margin of safety. Income from a given
sales level. Other questions. Multi-product break-even point. Evaluating the
results.

chapter 26

Flexible budgets; standard costs   845

Fixed budgets and performance reports. FLEXIBLE BUDGETS. Preparing a
flexible budget. Flexible budget performance report. STANDARD COSTS. Establishing standard costs. Variances. Isolating material and labor variances.
Charging overhead to production. Establishing overhead standards. Overhead variances. Controlling a business through standard costs. Standard costs
in the accounts.

chapter 27

Capital budgeting; managerial decisions   873

Capital budgeting. Accepting additional business. Buy or make. Other costs.
Scrap or rebuild defective units. Process or sell. Deciding the sales mix.

chapter 28

Tax considerations in business decisions   899

Tax planning. Tax evasion and tax avoidance. State and municipal income
taxes. History and objectives of the federal income tax. Synopsis of the federal income tax. Tax effects of business alternatives. Net income and taxable
income. Taxes and the distortion of net income. Entries for the allocation of
taxes.

Index   933

PART 1

Introduction

1
Accounting, an introduction
to its concepts

After studying Chapter 1, you should be able to:

- Tell the function of accounting and the nature and purpose of the information it provides.

- List the main fields of accounting and tell the kinds of work carried on in each field.

- List the accounting concepts and principles introduced and tell the effect of each on accounting records and statements.

- Describe the purpose of a balance sheet and of an income statement and tell the kinds of information presented in each.

- Recognize and be able to indicate the effects of transactions on the elements of an accounting equation.

- Prepare simple financial statements.

- Define or explain the words and phrases listed in the chapter Glossary.

chapter 1

Accounting, an introduction to its concepts

Accounting is a service activity the function of which is to provide quantitative information about economic entities. The information is primarily financial in nature and is intended to be useful in making economic decisions.[1] If the entity for which the information is provided is a business, for example, the information is used by its management in answering questions such as: What are the resources of the business? What debts does it owe? Does it have earnings? Are expenses too large in relation to sales? Is too little or too much merchandise being kept? Are amounts owed by customers being collected rapidly? Will the business be able to meet its own debts as they mature? Should the plant be expanded? Should a new product be introduced? Should selling prices be increased?

In addition, grantors of credit such as banks, wholesale houses, and manufacturers use accounting information in answering such questions as: Are the customer's earning prospects good? What is his debt-paying ability? Has he paid his debts promptly in the past? Should he be granted additional credit?[2] Likewise, governmental units use accounting information in regulating businesses and collecting taxes; labor unions use it in negotiating working conditions and wage agreements; and investors make wide use of accounting data in investment decisions.

---

[1] Accounting Principles Board, "Basic Concepts and Accounting Principles Underlying Financial Statements of Business Enterprises," *APB Statement No. 4* (New York: AICPA, October 1970), par. 9.

[2] Obviously, women as well as men are customers—and students and accountants. In this discussion as in others not referring to a specific person, the pronouns *he, his,* and *him* are used in their generic sense and should be understood to include both men and women.

Why study accounting

Information for use in answering questions like the ones listed is conveyed in accounting reports. If a business owner, manager, banker, lawyer, engineer, or other person is to use these reports effectively, he or she must have some understanding of how their data were gathered and the figures put together. He or she must appreciate the limitations of the data and the extent to which portions are based on estimates rather than precise measurements, and he or she must understand accounting terms and concepts. Needless to say, these understandings are gained in a study of accounting.

Another reason to study accounting is to make it one's lifework—to become a professional accountant. A career in accounting can be very interesting and highly rewarding.

Accountancy as a profession

Over the past half century accountancy as a profession has attained a stature comparable with that of law or medicine. All states license *certified public accountants* or CPAs just as they license doctors and lawyers, and for the same reason—to help ensure a high standard of professional service. Only individuals who have passed a rigorous examination of their accounting and related knowledge, met other education and experience requirements, and have received a license may designate themselves as certified public accountants.

The requirements for the CPA certificate or license vary with the states. In general an applicant must be a citizen, 21 years of age, of unquestioned moral character, and a college graduate with a major concentration in accounting. Also he or she must pass a rigorous three-day examination in accounting theory, accounting practice, auditing, and business law. The three-day examination is uniform in all states and is given on the same days in all states. It is prepared by the American Institute of Certified Public Accountants (AICPA) which is the national professional organization of CPAs. In addition to the examination, many states require an applicant to have two or more years of work experience in the office of a CPA or the equivalent before the certificate is granted. However, some states do not require the work experience and some states permit the applicant to substitute one or more years of experience for the college level education requirement. On this score the AICPA's Committee on Education and Experience Requirements for CPAs has expressed the opinion that at least five years of college study are necessary to obtain the body of knowledge needed to be a CPA; and for those meeting this standard, no previous work experience should be required.[3] However, it will be several years before all states accept this recommendation. In the meantime the interested student can learn the requirements of any state in which he is interested by writing to its state board of accountancy.

------

[3] *Report of the Committee on Education and Experience Requirements for CPAs* (New York, 1969), p. 11.

Accountants are commonly employed in three main fields: (1) in public accounting, (2) in private accounting, or (3) in government.

The work of an accountant

Public-accounting

A public accountant is one who offers his professional services and those of his employees to the public for a fee, in much the same manner as a lawyer or a consulting engineer.

Auditing   The principal service offered by a public accountant is auditing. Banks commonly require an audit of the financial statements of a company applying for a sizable loan, with the audit being performed by a CPA who is not an employee of the audited concern but an independent professional person working for a fee. Companies whose securities are offered for sale to the public generally must also have such an audit before the securities may be sold, and thereafter additional audits must be made periodically if the securities are to continue being traded.

The purpose of an audit is to lend credibility to a company's financial statements. In making the audit the auditor carefully examines the company's statements and the accounting records from which they were prepared to make sure the statements fairly reflect the company's financial position and operating results and were prepared in accordance with generally accepted accounting principles from records kept in accordance with such principles. Banks, investors, and others rely on the information in a company's financial statements in making loans, granting credit, and in buying and selling securities; and they depend on the auditor to verify the dependability of the information the statements contain.

Management advisory services   In addition to auditing, accountants commonly offer management advisory services. An accountant gains from an audit an intimate knowledge of the audited company's accounting procedures and its financial position, and thus is in an excellent position to offer constructive suggestions for improving the procedures and strengthening the position. Clients expect these suggestions as a useful audit by-product, and they also commonly engage certified public accountants to conduct additional investigations for the purpose of determining ways in which their operations may be improved. Such investigations and the suggestions growing from them are known as management advisory services.

Management advisory services include the design, installation, and improvement of a client's general accounting system and any related information system it may have for determining and controlling costs. They also include the application of punched cards, electronics, and other modern machine methods to these systems, plus advice in financial planning, budgeting, forecasting, inventory control – in fact, in all phases of information systems and related matters.

Tax services   In this day of increasing complexity in income and other tax laws and continued high tax rates, few important business decisions are made without consideration being given to their tax effect. A certified public accountant, through training and experience, is well qualified to render important service in this area. The service includes not only the preparation and filing of tax returns but also advice as to how transactions may be completed so as to incur the smallest tax.

Private accounting

When an accountant is employed by a single enterprise, he or she is said to be in private accounting. A small business may employ only one accountant or it may depend upon the services of a public accountant and employ none. A large business, on the other hand, may have more than a hundred employees in its accounting department, working under the supervision of a chief accounting officer, commonly called the *controller,* who is often a CPA. The title, controller, results from the fact that one of the chief uses of accounting data is to control the operations of a business.

The one accountant of the small business and the accounting department of a large concern do a variety of work, including general accounting, cost accounting, budgeting, and internal auditing.

General accounting   Although it is hard to draw a line of demarcation, general accounting has to do primarily with recording transactions and preparing financial and other reports for the use of management, owners, creditors, and governmental agencies. The private accountant may design or help the public accountant design the system used in recording the transactions, and he will supervise the clerical or data processing staff in recording the transactions and preparing the reports.

Cost accounting   The phase of accounting that has to do with collecting, determining, and controlling costs, particularly costs of producing a given product or service, is called cost accounting. Since a knowledge of costs and controlling costs are vital to good management, a large company may have a number of accountants engaged in this activity.

Budgeting   Planning business activities before they occur is called budgeting. The objective of budgeting is to provide management with an intelligent plan for future operations, and after the plan has been put into effect, to provide summaries and reports comparing actual accomplishments with the plan. Many large companies have within their accounting departments a number of people who devote all their time to this phase of accounting.

Internal auditing   In addition to an annual audit by a firm of certified public accountants, many companies maintain a staff of internal auditors who constantly check the records prepared and maintained in each department or company branch. It is the responsibility of these internal auditors to make sure that established accounting procedures and management directives are being followed throughout the company.

Governmental accounting

Furnishing governmental services is a vast and complicated operation in which accounting is just as indispensable as in business. Elected and appointed officials must rely on data accumulated by means of accounting if they are to complete effectively their administrative duties. Accountants are responsible for the accumulation of these data. Accountants also check and audit the millions of income, payroll, and sales tax returns that accompany the tax payments upon which governmental units depend. And finally, federal and state agencies, such as the Interstate Commerce Commission, Securities and Exchange Commission, Federal Power Commission, Federal Communication Commission, and so on, use accountants in many capacities in their regulation of business.

Many people confuse accounting and bookkeeping and look upon them as one and the same — in effect they identify the whole with one of its parts. Actually, bookkeeping is only part of accounting, the record-making part. To keep books is to record transactions, and a bookkeeper is one who records transactions. The work is often routine and primarily clerical in nature. The work of an accountant goes far beyond this, as a rereading of the previous section will show.

Accounting and book-keeping

Accounting is applicable to all types of economic entities such as business concerns, schools, churches, fraternities, and so on. However, this text will focus on accounting for business concerns, of which there are three main types, single proprietorships, partnerships, and corporations. A business owned by one person is called a single proprietorship. When a business is owned by two or more people as partners, the business is a partnership. A corporation is a form of business incorporated under the laws of one of the 50 states or the federal government. Its owners are called shareholders or stockholders because their ownership is represented by shares of stock issued by the corporation.

Focus of this text

As a result of its unique legal characteristics, the corporation is the dominant type of business organization in the United States. These characteristics, which are not possessed by either single proprietorships or partnerships, enable corporations to raise the huge amounts of money required by a General Motors or an American Telephone and Telegraph Company. However, because of the simplicity of the organizational structure of single proprietorships, this text will first describe accounting for this form of business organization. The characteristics of partnerships and corporations and the accounting issues related to these forms of business organizations are described and discussed in subsequent chapters.

Accounting statements are the end product of the accounting process, but a good place to begin the study of accounting. They are used

Accounting statements

to convey to management and interested outsiders a concise picture of the profitability and financial position of a business. The two most important are the income statement and the balance sheet.

The income statement

A company's income statement (see Illustration 1–1) is perhaps more important than its balance sheet, since it shows whether or not the business achieved or failed to achieve its primary objective — earning a "profit" or net income. A net income is earned when revenues exceed expenses, but a net loss is incurred if the expenses exceed the revenues. An income statement is prepared by listing the revenues earned during the period, listing the expenses incurred in earning the revenues, and subtracting the expenses from the revenues to determine if a net income or a net loss was incurred.

Illustration 1–1

Coast Realty		
Income Statement for Year Ended December 31, 19–		
Revenues:		
Commissions earned	$31,450	
Property management fees.......	1,200	
Total revenues		$32,650
Operating expenses:		
Salaries expense	$ 7,800	
Rent expense..........................	2,400	
Utilities expense......................	315	
Telephone expense	560	
Advertising expense	2,310	
Total operating expenses. ..		13,385
Net Income................................		$19,265

Revenues are inflows of cash or other properties received in exchange for goods or services provided to customers. Rents, dividends, and interest earned are also revenues. Coast Realty of Illustration 1–1 had revenue inflows from services which totaled $32,650.

Expenses are goods and services consumed in operating a business or other economic unit. Coast Realty consumed the services of its employees (salaries expense), the services of a telephone company, and so on.

The heading of an income statement tells the name of the business for which it is prepared and the time period covered by the statement. Both bits of information are important, but the time covered is extremely significant, since the items on the statement must be interpreted in relation to the period of time. For example, the item "Commissions earned, $31,450" on the income statement of Illustration 1–1 has little significance until it is known that the amount represents one year's commissions and not the commissions of a week or a month.

The balance sheet

The purpose of a balance sheet is to show the financial position of a business on a specific date, and it is often called a *position statement*. Financial position is shown by listing the *assets* of the business, its *liabilities* or debts, and the *equity of the owner or owners*. The name of the business and the date are given in the balance sheet heading, and it is understood that the item amounts shown are as of the close of business on that day.

Before a business manager, investor, or other person can make effective judgments based on balance sheet information, he or she must gain several concepts and understandings. To illustrate, assume that on August 3, Joan Ball began a new business, called World Travel Agency, and during the day she completed these transactions in the name of the business.

Aug. 3   Invested $18,000 of her personal savings in the business.
   3   Paid $15,000 of the agency's cash for a small office building and the land on which it was built (cost of the building, $10,000, and cost of the land, $5,000).
   3   Purchased *on credit* from Office Equipment Company office equipment costing $2,000. (Purchased on credit means purchased with a promise to pay at a later date.)

A balance sheet reflecting the effects of these transactions appears in Illustration 1–2. It shows that after completing the transactions the agency has four assets, a $2,000 debt, and that its owner has an $18,000 equity in the business.

World Travel Agency
Balance Sheet, August 3, 19–

Assets		Liabilities	
Cash	$ 3,000	Accounts payable	$ 2,000
Office equipment	2,000		
Building	10,000		
Land	5,000	**Owner Equity**	
		Joan Ball, capital	18,000
Total Assets	$20,000	Total Equities	$20,000

Illustration 1–2

Observe that the two sides of the balance sheet are equal. This is where it gets its name. Its two sides must always be equal because one side shows the resources of the business and the other shows who supplied the resources. For example, World Travel Agency has $20,000 of resources (assets) of which $18,000 were supplied by its owner and $2,000 by its creditors. (Creditors are individuals and organizations to whom the business owes debts.)

The assets of a business are, in general, the properties or economic resources owned by the business. They include cash, amounts owed to the business by its customers for goods and services sold to them on

Assets, liabilities, and owner equity

credit (called *accounts receivable*), merchandise held for sale by the business, supplies, equipment, buildings, and land. Assets may also include such intangible rights as those granted by a patent or copyright.

The liabilities of a business are its debts and include amounts owed to creditors for goods and services bought on credit (called *accounts payable*), salaries and wages owed employees, taxes payable, notes payable, and mortgages payable.

Owner equity is the interest of the owner or owners of a business in its assets. When a business is owned by one person, this equity is shown on the balance sheet of the business by listing the person's name, followed by the word *capital,* and then the amount of the equity. The use of the word capital comes from the idea that the owner has furnished the business with resources or "capital" equal to the amount of the equity.

Liabilities are also sometimes called *equities*. An equity is a right, claim, or interest; and a liability represents a claim or right to be paid. Law recognizes this right; and if a business fails to pay its creditors, law gives the creditors the right to force the sale of the assets of the business to secure money to meet creditor claims. Furthermore, if the assets are sold, the creditors are paid first, with any remainder going to the business owner. Obviously, then, by law creditor claims take precedence over those of a business owner.

Since creditor claims take precedence over those of an owner, owner equity in a business is always a residual amount. Creditors recognize this; and when they examine the balance sheet of a business, they are always interested in the share of its assets furnished by creditors and the share furnished by its owner or owners. The creditors' interest in the respective shares results from knowing that if the business must be liquidated and its assets sold, the shrinkage in converting the assets into cash must exceed the equity of the owner or owners before the creditors will lose.

In examining the Illustration 1–2 balance sheet, bear in mind that the $18,000 equity of Joan Ball in this business may not be all the assets she owns. In addition to her equity in the new business she may own a farm, a home, and many personal assets. However, these are not shown on the balance sheet of her business because of the *business entity concept.*

Business entity concept

Under this concept, for accounting purposes, every business is conceived to be and is treated as a separate entity, separate and distinct from its owner or owners and from every other business. Businesses are so conceived and treated because, insofar as a specific business is concerned, the purpose of accounting is to record its transactions and periodically report its financial position and profitability. Consequently, the records and reports of a business should not include either the transactions or assets of another business or the personal assets and transactions of its owner or owners, for to include either distorts the financial position and profitability of the business. For example, the personal automobile of a business owner should not be included among the assets of his business and its gas, oil, and repairs should not be treated as an expense of the business, for to do so distorts the reported financial position and profitability of the business.

In addition to the *business entity concept,* an accounting principle called the *cost principle* should be borne in mind when reading a balance sheet. Under this principle all goods and services purchased are recorded at cost and appear on the statements at cost. For example, if a business pays $50,000 for land to be used in carrying on its operations, the purchase should be recorded at $50,000. It makes no difference if the owner and several competent outside appraisers thought the land "worth" at least $60,000; it cost $50,000 and should appear on the balance sheet at that amount. Furthermore, if five years later, due to booming real estate prices, the land's fair market value has doubled, this makes no difference either. The land cost $50,000 and should continue to appear on the balance sheet at $50,000 even though its estimated market value is twice that.

Cost principle

In applying the *cost principle,* costs are measured on a cash or cash-equivalent basis. If the consideration given for an asset or service is cash, cost is measured at the entire cash outlay made to secure the asset or service. If the consideration is something other than cash, cost is measured at the cash-equivalent value of the consideration given or the cash-equivalent value of the thing received, whichever is more clearly evident.[4]

Why are assets and services recorded at cost and why are the balance sheet amounts for the assets not changed from time to time to reflect changing market values? The *objectivity principle* and the *continuing-concern concept* supply answers to these questions.

The *objectivity principle* supplies the reason transactions are recorded at cost, since it requires that transaction amounts be objectively established. Whims and fancies plus, for example, something like an opinion of management that an asset is "worth more than it cost" have no place in accounting. To be fully useful, accounting information must be based on objective data, and as a rule costs are objective, since they normally are established by a buyer and a seller, each striking the best possible bargain for himself.

Objectivity principle

Balance sheet amounts for assets used in carrying on the operations of a business are not changed from time to time to reflect changing market values because a balance sheet is prepared under the assumption that the business for which it is prepared will continue in opera-

Continuing-concern concept

---

[4] APB, "Accounting for Nonmonetary Transactions," *APB Opinion No. 29* (New York: AICPA, 1973), par. 18.

tion, and as a continuing or going concern the assets are not for sale, in fact cannot be sold without disrupting the business. Therefore, since the assets are for use in the business and are not for sale, their current market values are not particularly relevant. Also, without a sale, their current market values usually cannot be objectively established, as is required by the *objectivity principle*.

The *continuing-concern or going-concern concept* applies in most situations. However, if a business is about to be sold or liquidated, the *continuing-concern concept* and the *cost and objectivity principles* do not apply in the preparation of its statements. In such cases amounts other than costs, such as estimated market values, become more useful and informative.

The stable-dollar concept

In our country all transactions are measured, recorded, and reported in terms of dollars; and in the measuring, recording, and reporting process the dollar has been treated as a stable unit of measure, like a gallon, an acre, or a mile. However, unfortunately the dollar, like other currencies, is not a stable unit of measure. When the general price level (the average of all prices) changes, the value of money (its purchasing power) also changes. For example, during the past 30 years the general price level has approximately doubled, which means that over these years the purchasing power of the dollar has declined from 100 cents to approximately 50 cents.

Nevertheless, although the instability of the dollar is recognized, accountants in their reports continue to add and subtract items acquired in different years with dollars of different sizes. In effect they ignore changes in the size of the measuring unit. For example, assume a company purchased land some years ago for $10,000 and sold it today for $20,000. If during this period the purchasing power of the dollar declined from 100 cents to 50 cents, it can be said that the company is no better off for having purchased the land for $10,000 and sold it for $20,000 because the $20,000 will buy no more goods and services today than the $10,000 at the time of the purchase. Yet, using the dollar to measure both transactions, the accountant reports a $10,000 gain from the purchase and sale.

Since the instability of the dollar as a unit of measure is recognized, the question is should the amounts shown on financial statements be adjusted for changes in the purchasing power of the dollar. Techniques have been devised to convert the historical dollars of statement amounts into dollars of current purchasing power. Such statements are called *price-level-adjusted statements*. Also, by consulting catalogs and securing current prices from manufacturers and wholesalers, it is possible to determine replacement costs for various assets owned, and such costs could be used in preparing financial statements. However, financial statements showing current replacement costs and also price-level-adjusted statements require subjective judgments in their preparation. Consequently, most accountants are of the opinion that the traditional statements based on the *stable-dollar concept* are best for general publication and use. Nevertheless, they also recognize that the information conveyed by traditional statements can be made more useful if accompanied by replacement cost and/or price-level-adjusted information; but more about this in Chapter 20.

From the discussions of the *cost principle*, the *continuing-concern concept*, and *stable-dollar concept*, it should be recognized that in most instances a balance sheet does not show the amounts at which the listed assets can be sold or replaced. Nor does it show the "worth" of the business for which it was prepared, since some of the listed assets may be salable for much more or much less than the dollar amounts at which they are shown.

Accounting principles

A common definition of the word *principle* is: "A broad general law or rule adopted or professed as a guide to action; a settled ground or basis of conduct or practice. . . ." Consequently, generally accepted accounting principles may be described as broad rules adopted by the accounting profession as guides in measuring, recording, and reporting the financial affairs and activities of a business to its owners, creditors, and other interested parties. They consist of a number of concepts, principles, and procedures, the more important of which are first discussed at the points shown in the following list and are referred to again and again throughout this text in order to increase your understanding of the information conveyed by accounting data.

	First Introduced	
	Chapter	Page
Generally Accepted Concepts:		
1. Business entity concept 1		10
2. Continuing-concern concept 1		11
3. Stable-dollar concept.............. 1		12
4. Time-period concept............... 3		69
Generally Accepted Principles:		
1. Cost principle 1		11
2. Objectivity principle................. 1		11
3. Realization principle 1		18
4. Matching principle.................. 3		77
5. Full-disclosure principle........... 8		270
6. Materiality principle 8		282
7. Consistency principle.............. 9		301
8. Conservatism principle............ 9		305

Generally Accepted Procedures:
These specify the ways data are processed and reported and are described and discussed throughout the text.

Source of accounting principles

Generally accepted accounting principles are not natural laws in the sense of the laws of physics and chemistry but man-made rules that depend for their authority upon their general acceptance by the accounting profession. They have evolved from the experience and thinking of members of the accounting profession, aided by such groups as the American Institute of Certified Public Accountants, the Financial Accounting Standards Board, the American Accounting Association, and the Securities and Exchange Commission.

The AICPA has long been influential in describing and defining generally accepted accounting principles. During the years from 1939 to 1959 it published a series of *Accounting Research Bulletins,* which were recognized as expressions of generally accepted accounting principles. In 1959 it established an 18-member Accounting Principles Board (APB) composed of practicing accountants, educators, and representatives of industry, and gave the board authority to issue opinions that were to be regarded by members of the AICPA as authoritative expressions of generally accepted accounting principles. During the years 1962 through 1973 the Board issued 31 such opinions. Added importance was given to these opinions beginning in 1964 when the AICPA ruled that its members must disclose in footnotes to published financial statements of the companies they audit any departure from generally accepted accounting principles as set forth in the *Opinions of the Accounting Principles Board.*

In 1973, after 11 years of activity, the Accounting Principles Board was terminated. Its place was taken by a seven-member Financial Accounting Standards Board (FASB). The seven members, only four of which are required to be CPAs, serve full time, receive salaries, and must resign from accounting firms and other employment. This differs from the Accounting Principles Board, all members of which were CPAs, who served part time, without pay, and continued their affiliations with accounting firms and other employment. The FASB issues *Statements of the Financial Accounting Standards Board* which like the *Opinions of the Accounting Principles Board* must be considered as authorative expressions of generally accepted accounting principles by members of the AICPA. Both the *Statements* and *Opinions* are referred to again and again throughout this text.

The American Accounting Association, an organization with strong academic ties, has also been influential in describing and defining generally accepted accounting principles. It has sponsored a number of research studies and has published many articles dealing with accounting principles. However, its influence has not been as great as the AICPA, since it has no power to impose its views on the accounting profession but must depend upon the prestige of its authors and the logic of their arguments.

The Securities and Exchange Commission (SEC) plays a prominent role in financial reporting. The SEC is an independent quasi-judicial agency of the federal government established to administer the provisions of various securities and exchange acts dealing with the distribution and sale of securities that are widely held. Such securities, to be sold, must be registered with the SEC; and this requires the filing of audited financial statements prepared in accordance with the rules of the SEC. Furthermore, the information contained in the statements must be kept current by filing additional audited annual reports prepared in accordance with the rules of the Commission. The SEC does not appraise the registered securities, but it attempts to safeguard investors by requiring that all material facts affecting the worth of the securities be made public and that no important information be withheld. Its rules carry over into the annual reports of large companies and have contributed to the usefulness of these reports. In a real sense, the SEC should be viewed as the dominant authority in respect to the establishment of accounting principles. However, it has relied on the accounting profession, particularly the AICPA and the FASB, to determine and enforce accepted accounting principles. At the same time it has pressured the accounting profession to reduce the number of acceptable accounting procedures.

The balance sheet equation

As previously stated, a balance sheet is so called because its two sides must always balance; the sum of the assets shown on the balance sheet must equal liabilities plus owner equity. This equality may be expressed in equation form as follows:

Assets = Liabilities + Owner Equity

When balance sheet equality is expressed in equation form, the resulting equation is called the *balance sheet equation*. It is also known as the *accounting equation,* since all double-entry accounting is based on it. And, like any mathematical equation, its elements may be transposed and the equation expressed:

Assets − Liabilities = Owner Equity

The equation in this form illustrates the residual nature of owner equity, an owner's claims are secondary to those of his creditors.

Effects of transactions on the accounting equation

A business transaction is an exchange of goods or services, and business transactions affect the elements of the accounting equation. However, regardless of what transactions a business completes, its accounting equation always remains in balance and its assets always equal the combined claims of its creditors and its owner or owners. This may be demonstrated with the transactions of the law practice of Larry Owen, a service-type business, which follow.

On July 1 Larry Owen began a new law practice by investing $2,500 of his personal cash, which he deposited in a bank account opened in the name of the business, Larry Owen, Attorney. After the investment, the one asset of the new business and the equity of Owen in the business are shown in the following equation:

Assets	=	Owner Equity
Cash, $2,500		Larry Owen, Capital, $2,500

Observe that after its first transaction the new business has one asset, cash, $2,500; and since it has no liabilities, the equity of Owen in the business is $2,500.

To continue the illustration, after the investment, (2) Owen used $600 of the business cash to pay the rent for three months in advance on suitable office space and (3) $1,200 to buy office equipment. These transactions were exchanges of cash for other assets, and their effects on the accounting equation are shown in color in Illustration 1–3. Observe that the equation remains in balance after each transaction.

Illustration 1–3

	Assets			= Owner Equity
	Cash +	Prepaid Rent +	Office Equipment =	Larry Owen, Capital
(1)	$2,500			$2,500
(2)	−600	+$600		
	$1,900	$600		$2,500
(3)	−1,200		+$1,200	
	$ 700 +	$600 +	$1,200 =	$2,500

Continuing the illustration, assume that Owen needed office supplies and additional equipment in the law office, but he felt he should conserve the cash of the law practice. Consequently, he purchased on credit or on account from Alpha Company office equipment costing $300 and office supplies that cost $60. The effects of this transaction (4) are shown in Illustration 1–4. Note that the assets were increased by the purchase, but owner equity did not change because Alpha Company acquired a claim against the assets equal to the increase in the assets. The claim or amount owed Alpha Company is called an account payable.

Illustration 1–4

	Assets				= Liabilities +	Owner Equity
	Cash +	Prepaid Rent +	Office Supplies +	Office Equipment =	Accounts Payable +	Larry Owen, Capital
(1)	$2,500					$2,500
(2)	−600	+600				
	$1,900	$600				$2,500
(3)	−1,200			+$1,200		
	$ 700	$600		$1,200		$2,500
(4)			+$60	+300	+$360	
	$ 700 +	$600 +	$60 +	$1,500 =	$360 +	$2,500

A primary objective of a business is to increase owner equity by earning a profit or a net income. Owen's law practice will accomplish this objective by providing legal services to its clients on a fee basis.

Of course, the practice will earn a net income only if legal fees earned are greater than the expenses incurred in earning the fees. Legal fees earned and expenses incurred affect the elements of an accounting equation. To illustrate their effects, assume that on July 12 Larry Owen completed legal work for a client (transaction 5) and immediately collected $400 in cash for the services rendered; and the same day (transaction 6) he paid the salary of the office secretary for the first two weeks of July, a $250 expense of the business. The effects of these transactions are shown in Illustration 1–5.

	Cash +	Prepaid Rent +	Office Supplies +	Office Equipment =	Accounts Payable +	Larry Owen, Capital
(1)	$2,500					$2,500
(2)	−600	+$600				
	$1,900	$600				$2,500
(3)	−1,200			+$1,200		
	$ 700	$600		$1,200		$2,500
(4)			+$60	+300	+$360	
	$ 700	$600	$60	$1,500	$360	$2,500
(5)	+400					+400
	$1,100	$600	$60	$1,500	$360	$2,900
(6)	−250					−250
	$ 850 +	$600 +	$60 +	$1,500 =	$360 +	$2,650

Assets = Liabilities + Owner Equity

Illustration 1–5

Observe first the effects of the legal fee. The $400 fee is a revenue. A revenue is an inflow of assets from the sale of goods or services. Note that the revenue not only increased the asset cash but also caused a $400 increase in owner equity. Owner equity increased because total assets increased without an increase in liabilities; consequently, Owen's equity in the business increases.

Next observe the effects of paying the secretary's $250 salary, an expense; and note that the effects are opposite those of a revenue. Expenses are goods and services measured at cost that are consumed in the operation of a business. In this instance the business consumed the secretary's services, and when the services were paid for, both the assets and Owen's equity in the business decreased. Owen's equity decreased because cash decreased without an increase in other assets or a decrease in liabilities.

Now note this about earning a net income. A business earns a net income when its revenues exceed its expenses, and the income increases both net assets and owner equity. (Net assets are the excess of assets over liabilities.) Net assets increase because more assets flow into the business from revenues than are consumed and flow out for expenses. Owner equity increases because net assets increase. A net loss has opposite effects.

Realization principle

In transaction 5 the revenue inflow was in the form of cash. However, revenue inflows are not always in cash because the *realization principle* (also called the recognition principle), which governs the recognition of revenue, (1) defines a revenue as an inflow of assets (not necessarily cash) in exchange for goods or services; (2) requires that the revenue be recognized (entered in the accounting records as revenue) at the time, but not before, it is earned (which generally is at the time title to goods sold is transferred or services are rendered); and (3) requires that the amount of revenue recognized be measured by the cash received plus the cash equivalent (fair market value) of any other asset or assets received.

To demonstrate the recognition of a revenue inflow in a form other than cash, assume that on July 19 (transaction 7) Larry Owen completed legal work for a client and sent the client a $750 bill for the services rendered. Also assume that ten days later the client paid in full (transaction 8) for the services rendered. The effects of the two transactions are shown in Illustration 1–6.

						Assets					=	Liabil-ities	+	Owner Equity
	Cash	+	Accounts Receivable	+	Prepaid Rent	+	Office Supplies	+	Office Equipment	=	Accounts Payable	+	Larry Owen, Capital
(1)	$2,500													$2,500
(2)	−600				+$600									
	$1,900				$600									$2,500
(3)	−1,200								+$1,200					
	$ 700				$600				$1,200					$2,500
(4)							+$60		+300		+$360			
	$ 700				$600		$60		$1,500		$360			$2,500
(5)	+400													+400
	$1,100				$600		$60		$1,500		$360			$2,900
(6)	−250													−250
	$ 850				$600		$60		$1,500		$360			$2,650
(7)			+$750											+750
	$ 850		$750		$600		$60		$1,500		$360			$3,400
(8)	+750		−750											
	$1,600	+	0	+	$600	+	$60	+	$1,500	=	$360	+	$3,400

Illustration 1–6

Observe in transaction 7 that the asset flowing into the business was the right to collect $750 from the client, an account receivable. Compare transactions 5 and 7 and note that they differ only as to the type of asset received. Next observe that the receipt of cash (ten days after the services were rendered) is nothing more than an exchange of assets, cash for the right to collect from the client. Also note that the receipt of cash did not affect owner equity because the revenue was recognized in accordance with the *realization principle* and owner equity was increased upon completion of the services rendered.

As a final transaction assume that on July 30 Larry Owen paid Alpha Company $100 of the $360 owed for the equipment and supplies purchased in transaction 4. This transaction reduced in equal amounts both assets and liabilities, and its effects are shown in Illustration 1-7.

	Cash	+	Accounts Receivable	+	Prepaid Rent	+	Office Supplies	+	Office Equipment	=	Accounts Payable	+	Larry Owen, Capital
(1)	$2,500												$2,500
(2)	−600				+$600								
	$1,900				$600								$2,500
(3)	−1,200								+$1,200				
	$ 700				$600				$1,200				$2,500
(4)							+$60		+300		+$360		
	$ 700				$600		$60		$1,500		$360		$2,500
(5)	+400												+400
	$1,100				$600		$60		$1,500		$360		$2,900
(6)	−250												−250
	$ 850				$600		$60		$1,500		$360		$2,650
(7)			+$750										+750
	$ 850		$750		$600		$60		$1,500		$360		$3,400
(8)	+750		−750										
	$1,600		0		$600		$60		$1,500		$360		$3,400
(9)	−100										−100		
	$1,500	+			$600	+	$60	+	$1,500	=	$260		$3,400

Assets = Liabilities + Owner Equity

Illustration 1-7

Look again at Illustration 1-7 and observe that (1) every transaction affected at least two items in the equation and (2) in each case, after the effects were entered in the columns, the equation remained in balance with the sum of the assets equaling the sum of the liabilities plus owner equity. The accounting system you are beginning to study is called a *double-entry system* and is based on the fact that every transaction affects two or more items in an accounting equation such as that in Illustration 1-7 and requires a "double entry" or, in other words, entries in two or more places. Also, the fact that the equation remained in balance after each transaction is important, for this is a proof of the accuracy with which the transactions were recorded.

Important transaction effects

Glossary

Accounting. The art of recording, classifying, reporting, and interpreting the financial data of an organization.

Accounting concept. An abstract idea that serves as a basis in the interpretation of accounting information.

Accounting equation. An expression in dollar amounts of the equivalency of the assets and equities of an enterprise, usually stated: Assets = Liabilities + Owner Equity.

Accounting principle. A broad rule adopted by the accounting profession as a guide in measuring, recording, and reporting the financial affairs and activities of a business.

Account payable. A debt owed to a creditor for goods or services purchased on credit.

Account receivable. An amount receivable from a debtor for goods or services sold on credit.

AICPA. American Institute of Certified Public Accountants, the professional association of certified public accountants in the United States.

APB. Accounting Principles Board, a committee of the AICPA that was responsible for formulating accounting principles.

Asset. A property or economic resource owned by an individual or enterprise.

Audit. A critical exploratory review by a public accountant of the business methods and accounting records of an enterprise, made to enable the accountant to express an opinion as to whether the financial statements of the enterprise fairly reflect its financial position and operating results.

Balance sheet. A financial report showing the assets, liabilities, and owner equity of an enterprise on a specific date.

Bookkeeping. The record-making phase of accounting.

Budgeting. The phase of accounting dealing with planning the activities of an enterprise and comparing its actual accomplishments with the plan.

Business entity concept. The idea that a business is separate and distinct from its owner or owners and from every other business.

Business transaction. An exchange of goods, services, money, and/or the right to collect money.

CPA. Certified public accountant, an accountant who has met legal requirements as to age, education, experience, residence, and moral character and is licensed to practice public accounting.

Continuing-concern concept. The idea that a business is a going concern that will continue to operate, using its assets to carrying on its operations and, with the exception of merchandise, not offering the assets for sale.

Controller. The chief accounting officer of a large business.

Corporation. A business incorporated under the laws of a state or other jurisdiction.

Cost accounting. The phase of accounting that deals with collecting and controlling the costs of producing a given product or service.

Cost principle. The accounting rule that requires assets and services plus any resulting liabilities to be taken into the accounting records at cost.

Creditor. A person or enterprise to whom a debt is owed.

Debtor. A person or enterprise that owes a debt.

Equity. A right, claim, or interest in property.

Expense. Goods or services consumed in operating an enterprise.

FASB. Financial Accounting Standards Board, the seven-member board which replaced the Accounting Principles Board and has the authority to formulate rules governing the practice of accounting.

General accounting. That phase of accounting dealing primarily with recording transactions and preparing financial statements.

Going-concern concept. Another name for continuing-concern concept.

Income statement. A financial statement showing revenues earned by a business, the expenses incurred in earning the revenues, and the resulting net income or net loss.

Internal auditing. A continuing examination of the records and procedures of a business by its own internal audit staff to determine if established procedures and management directives are being followed.

Liability. A debt owed.

Management advisory services. The phase of public accounting dealing with the design, installation, and improvement of a client's accounting system, plus advice on planning, budgeting, forecasting, and all other phases of accounting.

Net assets. Assets minus liabilities.

Net income. The excess of revenues over expenses.

Net loss. The excess of expenses over revenues.

Objectivity principle. The accounting rule requiring that the amounts used in recording transactions be based on objective evidence rather than on subjective judgments wherever possible.

Owner equity. The equity of the owner of a business in the assets of the business.

Partnership. A business owned by two or more people as partners.

Price-level-adjusted statements. Financial statements showing amounts adjusted for changes in the purchasing power of money.

Realization principle. The accounting rule that defines a revenue as an inflow of assets, not necessarily cash, in exchange for goods or services and requires the revenue to be recognized at the time, but not before, it is earned.

Revenue. An inflow of assets, not necessarily cash, in exchange for goods and services sold.

Shareholder. A person or enterprise owning a share or shares of stock in a corporation.

Single proprietorship. A business owned by one individual.

Stable-dollar concept. The idea that the purchasing power of the unit of measure used in accounting, the dollar, does not change.

Tax services. The phase of public accounting dealing with the preparation of tax returns and with advice as to how transactions may be completed in a way as to incur the smallest tax liability.

Questions for class discussion

1. What is the nature of accounting and what is its function?
2. How does a business executive use accounting information?
3. Why do the states license certified public accounts?
4. What is the purpose of an audit? What does a certified public accountant do when he makes an audit?
5. A public accountant may provide management advisory services. Of what does this consist?
6. What do the tax services of a public accountant include beyond preparing tax returns?
7. Differentiate between accounting and bookkeeping.
8. What does an income statement show?
9. As the word is used in accounting, what is a revenue? An expense?
10. Why is the period of time covered by an income statement of extreme significance?
11. What does a balance sheet show?
12. Define (*a*) asset, (*b*) liability, (*c*) equity, and (*d*) owner equity.
13. Why is a business treated as a separate entity for accounting purposes?
14. What is required by the cost principle? Why is such a principle necessary?
15. Why are not balance sheet amounts for the assets of a business changed from time to time to reflect changes in market values?
16. A business shows office stationery on its balance sheet at its $50 cost, although the stationery can be sold for not more than $0.25 as scrap paper. What accounting principle and concept justify this?
17. In accounting, transactions are measured, recorded, and reported in terms of dollars and the dollar is assumed to be a stable unit of measure. Is the dollar a stable unit of measure?
18. What are generally accepted accounting principles?
19. Why are the *Statements* of the Financial Accounting Standards Board and the *Opinions* of the Accounting Principles Board of importance to accounting students?
20. What is the balance sheet equation? What is its importance to accounting students?
21. Is it possible for a transaction to increase or decrease a single liability without affecting any other asset, liability, or owner equity item?
22. In accounting, what does the realization principle require?

Exercise 1–1

On June 30 of the current year the balance sheet of Campus Shop, a single proprietorship showed the following:

Cash .... $ 2,000
Other assets 45,000
Accounts payable.................... 17,000
Jerry Tarr, capital 30,000

On that date Jerry Tarr sold the "Other assets" for $25,000 in preparation for ending and liquidating the business of Campus Shop.

Required:

1. Prepare a balance sheet for the store as it would appear immediately after the sale of the assets.
2. Tell how the store's cash should be distributed in ending the business and why.

Exercise 1–2

Determine:
a. The equity of the owner in a business having $34,500 of assets and $9,300 of liabilities.
b. The liabilities of a business having $26,600 of assets and in which the owner has a $19,400 equity.
c. The assets of a business having $6,300 of liabilities and in which the owner has a $12,400 equity.

Exercise 1–3

A business had the following assets and liabilities at the beginning and at the end of a year:

	Assets	*Liabilities*
Beginning of the year	$60,000	$15,000
End of the year....................	75,000	20,000

Determine the net income or net loss of the business during the year under each of the following unrelated assumptions:

a. The owner of the business had made no additional investments in the business and no withdrawals of assets from the business during the year.
b. During the year the owner made no additional investments in the business but had withdrawn $1,000 per month for personal living expenses.
c. The owner had made no withdrawals but had made a $15,000 additional investment in the business during the year.
d. The owner had withdrawn $1,000 from the business each month to pay personal living expenses and near the year-end had invested an additional $15,000 in the business.

Exercise 1–4

Betty Blake began the practice of dentistry and during a short period completed these transactions:

a. Invested $5,000 in cash and dental equipment having a $500 fair value in a dental practice.
b. Paid the rent on suitable office space for two months in advance, $1,000.
c. Purchased additional dental equipment for cash, $1,500.
d. Completed dental work for a patient and immediately collected $200 cash for the work.
e. Purchased additional dental equipment on credit, $800.
f. Completed $600 of dental work for a patient on credit.
g. Paid the dental assistant's wages, $100.
h. Collected $300 of the amount owed by the patient of transaction (f).
i. Paid for the equipment purchased in transaction (e).

Required:

Arrange the following asset, liability, and owner equity titles in an equation form like Illustration 1–7: Cash; Accounts Receivable; Prepaid Rent; Dental Equipment; Accounts Payable; and Betty Blake, Capital. Then show by additions and subtractions the effects of the transactions on the elements of the equation. Show new totals after each transaction.

Exercise 1–5

Carl Cole began the practice of law on October 1 of the current year, and on October 31 his records showed the following items and amounts. From the information, prepare a month-end balance sheet and an income statement for the month. Head the statements Carl Cole, Attorney. (The October 31 $3,000 amount of Carl Cole's capital is the amount of his capital after it was increased and decreased by the October revenues and expenses shown.)

Cash	$ 500	Carl Cole, capital	$3,000
Accounts receivable	300	Legal fees earned	2,200
Prepaid rent	800	Rent expense	400
Law library	1,600	Salaries expense	500
Accounts payable	200	Telephone expense	100

Problems

Problem 1–1

Ted Sharp owns and operates A-1 Plumbing Service, which had the following assets at the beginning of the current month: cash, $815; plumbing supplies, $1,240; tools, $965; and truck, $2,780. The business owed Plumbing Supply Company $155 for supplies previously purchased. During a short period A-1 Plumbing Service completed these transactions:

a. Paid the rent on the shop space for two months in advance, $200.
b. Purchased tools for cash, $25.
c. Purchased plumbing supplies on credit from Plumbing Supply Company, $150.
d. Completed repair work for a customer and immediately collected $50 cash for the work done.
e. Completed repair work for Gary Hall on credit, $125.
f. Paid Plumbing Supply Company the amount owed at the beginning of the month.

g. Gary Hall paid for the work of transaction (e).
h. Gave tools carried in the accounting records at $100 plus $175 in cash for new tools priced at $275.
i. Purchased plumbing supplies on credit from Plumbing Supply Company, $200.
j. Paid the electric bill for the month, $15.
k. Ted Sharp withdrew $50 cash from the business to pay personal expenses.
l. Paid for the supplies purchased in transaction (c).

Required:

1. Arrange the following asset, liability, and owner equity titles in an equation like Illustration 1–7: Cash; Accounts Receivable; Prepaid Rent; Supplies; Tools; Truck; Accounts Payable; and Ted Sharp, Capital.
2. Enter the beginning assets and liability under the proper titles of the equation. Determine Ted Sharp's beginning equity and enter it.
3. Show by additions and subtractions, as in Illustration 1–7, the effects of the transactions on the elements of the equation. Show new totals after each transaction.

Problem 1–2

Jane Lee, a young lawyer, began the practice of law and completed these transactions during September of the current year.

Sept. 2 Sold a personal investment in General Electric stock for $2,650 and invested $2,500 of the proceeds in a law practice.
2 Rented the furnished office of a lawyer who was retiring, and paid cash for three months' rent in advance, $750.
2 Purchased the law library of the retiring lawyer for $1,750, paying $750 in cash and agreeing to pay the balance within one year.
5 Purchased office supplies for cash, $75.
6 Purchased law books from West Publishing Company on credit, $250.
8 Completed legal work for a client and immediately collected $100 in cash for the work done.
15 Completed legal work for Security Bank on credit, $500.
15 Paid for the law books purchased on credit on September 6.
19 Completed legal work for Coast Realty on credit, $600.
25 Received $500 from Security Bank for the work completed on September 15.
30 Paid the office secretary's salary, $450.
30 Paid the monthly telephone bill, $25.
30 Recognized that one month's rent on the office had expired and become an expense. (Reduce the prepaid rent and the owner's equity.)
30 Took an inventory of unused office supplies and determined that $20 of supplies had been used and had become an expense.

Required:

1. Arrange the following asset, liability, and owner equity titles in an equation like Illustration 1–7: Cash; Accounts Receivable; Prepaid Rent; Office Supplies; Law Library; Accounts Payable; and Jane Lee, Capital.

2. Show by additions and subtractions the effects of each transaction on the items of the equation. Show new totals after each transaction.
3. Prepare a September 30 balance sheet for the law practice. Head the statement Jane Lee, Attorney.
4. Analyze the increases and decreases in the last column of the equation and prepare a September income statement for the law practice.

Problem 1–3

The records of Dr. Sue Cole's dental practice show the following assets and liabilities at the ends of 1977 and 1978:

	December 31	
	1977	1978
Cash	$2,000	$ 400
Accounts receivable..............	7,000	8,500
Dental supplies	500	600
Prepaid insurance	300	500
Prepaid rent.........................	1,200	
Office equipment	4,000	5,000
Land		20,000
Building		45,000
Accounts payable	300	500
Mortgage payable		50,000

During the last week of December 1978, Dr. Cole purchased in the name of the dental practice the building in which she practices. The building and the land it occupies cost $65,000. The practice paid $15,000 in cash and assumed a mortgage liability for the balance. Dr. Cole had to invest an additional $7,500 in the practice to enable it to pay the $15,000. The practice earned a satisfactory net income during 1978, which enabled Dr. Cole to withdraw $1,500 per month from the business for personal use.

Required:

1. Prepare balance sheets for the practice as of the ends of 1977 and 1978. Head the balance sheets Sue Cole, D.D.S.
2. Prepare a calculation to determine the amount of income earned by the dental practice during 1978.

Problem 1–4

Carl Hall graduated from law school in June of the current year and on July 1 began a new law practice by investing $2,000 in cash and law books having a $400 fair value that he had used in college. He then completed these additional transactions:

July 1 Rented the furnished office of a lawyer who was retiring, paying $900 cash for three months' rent in advance.
1 Purchased office supplies for cash, $25.
1 Bought the law library of the retiring lawyer for $2,000, paying $500 cash and agreeing to pay the balance within one year.
2 Purchased insurance protection for one year in advance for cash by paying the premiums on two insurance policies, $120.

July 5 Completed legal work for a client and immediately collected $50 in cash for the work done.
  7 Purchased additional office supplies on credit, $40.
  10 Completed legal work for Western Realty on credit, $600.
  12 Purchased law books from North Publishing Company on credit, $200.
  15 Paid the salary of the office secretary, $300.
  17 Paid for the office supplies purchased on July 7.
  18 Completed legal work for Valley Bank on credit, $400.
  20 Received payment in full for the legal work completed for Western Realty on July 10.
  22 Completed additional legal work for Western Realty on credit, $350.
  27 Received payment in full from Valley Bank for the legal work completed on July 18.
  31 Paid the July telephone bill, $25.
  31 Paid the July utilities expense, $20.
  31 Paid the office secretary's salary, $300.
  31 Recognized that one month's office rent had expired and had become an expense. (Reduce the prepaid rent and owner's equity to record the expense.)
  31 Recognized that one month's prepaid insurance, $10, had expired.
  31 Took an inventory of office supplies and determined that $15 of supplies had been used and had become an expense.

Required:
1. Arrange the following asset, liability, and owner equity titles in an equation like Illustration 1–7: Cash; Accounts Receivable; Prepaid Rent; Prepaid Insurance; Office Supplies; Law Library; Accounts Payable; and Carl Hall, Capital.
2. Show the effects of the transactions on the elements of the equation by recording increases and decreases in the appropriate columns. Indicate an increase with a + and a decrease with a − before the amount. *Do not determine new balances for the items of the equation after each transaction.*
3. After recording the last transaction, determine and insert on the next line the final balance for each item of the equation and determine if the equation is in balance.
4. Prepare a July 31 balance sheet for the law practice. Head the statement Carl Hall, Attorney.
5. Analyze the items in the last column of the equation and prepare a July income statement for the practice.

Problem 1–1A

Alternate problems

  Ted Sharp completed the following transactions within a short period:

a. Sold for $8,200 a personal investment in General Motors stock and deposited $8,000 of the proceeds in a bank account opened in the name of his new business, Sharp TV Service.

b. Purchased for cash the repair supplies, $1,050, tools, $825, and the used truck, $1,100, of a TV repair shop that was going out of business.
c. Paid the rent on the shop space for three months in advance, $600.
d. Purchased additional tools for cash, $150.
e. Purchased additional repair supplies on credit, $250.
f. Gave the old company truck and $3,000 in cash for a new company truck.
g. Completed repair work for Walter Keller and collected $50 cash therefor.
h. Paid for the repair supplies purchased in transaction (e).
i. Completed repair work for Gary Nash on credit, $75.
j. Paid for gas and oil used in the truck, $25.
k. Gary Nash paid in full for the work of transaction (i).
l. Ted Sharp wrote a check on the bank account of the shop to pay a personal expense, $60.

Required:

1. Arrange the following asset, liability, and owner equity items in an equation like in Illustration 1–7: Cash; Accounts Receivable; Prepaid Rent; Supplies; Tools; Truck; Accounts Payable; Ted Sharp, Capital.
2. Show by additions and subtractions, as in Illustration 1–7, the effects of the transactions on the elements of the equation. Show new totals after each transaction.

Problem 1–2A

On October 1 of the current year Jane Lee began the practice of law by investing $1,500 in cash and a law library having a $1,000 fair value, and during a short period she completed the following additional transactions:

Oct. 1 Rented the furnished office of a lawyer who was retiring, and paid three months' rent in advance, $900.
      2 Purchased office supplies for cash, $65.
      5 Purchased law books from West Publishing Company on credit, $150.
      8 Completed legal work for a client and immediately collected $50 cash for the work done.
     14 Completed legal work for Pine Realty on credit, $350.
     15 Paid the salary of the office secretary, $250.
     15 Paid $50 of the amount owed on the law books purchased on October 5.
     20 Completed legal work for Guaranty Bank on credit, $400.
     24 Received $200 from Pine Realty in partial payment for the legal work completed on October 14.
     31 Paid the monthly telephone bill, $20.
     31 Paid the office secretary's salary, $250.
     31 Took an inventory of unused office supplies and determined that $15 of supplies had been used and had become an expense. (Reduce the asset and owner equity.)
     31 Recognized that one month's rent had expired and had become an expense.

Required:

1. Arrange the following asset, liability, and owner equity titles in an equation like Illustration 1–7: Cash; Accounts Receivable; Prepaid Rent; Office Supplies; Law Library; Accounts Payable; Jane Lee, Capital.

2. Show by additions and subtractions the effects of each transaction on the items of the equation. Show new totals after each transaction.
3. Prepare an October 31 balance sheet for the law practice. Head the statement Jane Lee, Attorney.
4. Analyze the increases and decreases in the last column of the equation and prepare an October income statement for the law practice.

Problem 1–3A

Ted Hall began an architectural practice upon graduation from college in 1977, and the records of the practice show the following assets and liabilities of the practice at the ends of 1977 and 1978:

	December 31	
	1977	1978
Cash..	$1,200	$ 400
Accounts receivable	4,000	5,500
Prepaid rent	400	
Drafting supplies......................	300	200
Prepaid insurance.....................	200	300
Office and drafting equipment....	3,500	4,000
Land..		15,000
Building....................................		30,000
Accounts payable......................	600	500
Note payable............................		2,000
Mortgage payable......................		33,000

During the last week of 1978 Mr. Hall purchased in the name of the practice a small office building and moved the practice from rented quarters to the new building. The building and the land it occupies cost $45,000. The practice paid $12,000 in cash and assumed a mortgage liability for the balance. In order for the practice to pay the $12,000, Mr. Hall had to invest an additional $5,000 of his personal funds in the business and borrow in the name of the business $2,000 from Guaranty Bank. To borrow the $2,000, the practice gave the bank a one-year promissory note payable. During 1978 the practice earned a satisfactory net income which enabled Ted Hall to withdraw $1,250 per month from the business for personal use.

Required:

1. Prepare December 31, 1977, and 1978 balance sheets for the business. Head the statements Ted Hall, Architect.
2. Prepare a calculation to show the amount of net income earned by the practice during 1978.

Decision problem 1–1, Quick Delivery Service

Ned Ross dropped out of school at the end of his first college semester but could not find a job. As a result, since he owned a motorcycle having an $800 fair value, he decided to go into business for himself, and he began Quick Delivery Service with no assets other than the motorcycle. He kept no accounting records; and now, at the year-end, has asked you to determine the net income earned by the service since it began operations the last week in January.

You find that the delivery service has a $650, year-end bank balance plus $40 of undeposited cash, and several customers owe the service a total of $150 for packages delivered on credit. Likewise, the service owes $30 for gas and oil purchased through the use of a credit card. The service still owns the motorcycle, but through hard use it has depreciated $200 since the business began operations. In addition to the motorcycle, the service has a new delivery truck that cost $4,200, has depreciated $300 since its purchase, and on which the service owes the finance company $2,500. When the truck was purchased, the service did not have sufficient cash for the down payment, and Ned Ross borrowed $500 from his father. The loan was made to the delivery service, was interest free, and has not been repaid. Finally, since the service has been profitable from its beginning, Ned Ross has withdrawn $100 of its earnings each week (48 weeks) to pay his personal living expenses.

Determine the net income earned by the business during the period of its operations. Present figures to prove your answer. (Hint: Net income increases owner equity.)

Decision Problem 1–2, Boat Dock

Ray Nash has just completed the first summer's operation of a lake-shore concession called Boat Dock at which he rents boats and sells hamburgers, soft drinks, and candy. He began the summer's operations with $3,000 in cash and a five-year lease on a boat dock and a small concession building at the lake. The lease requires a $1,000 annual rent payment, although the concession is open only from May 15 to September 15. On opening day Ray paid the first year's rent and also purchased five boats at $275 each, paying cash. He estimated the boats would have a five-year life, after which he could sell them for $25 each.

During the summer he purchased food, soft drinks, and candy costing $4,250, all of which was paid for by summer's end, excepting food costing $125 which was purchased during the last week's operation. He also paid electric bills, $75, and the wages of a part-time helper, $900; and he withdrew $150 of the earnings of the concession each week for 16 weeks to pay personal living expenses.

He took in $1,500 in boat rentals during the summer and sold $9,800 of food and drinks, all of which was collected in cash, excepting $150 he had not collected from Corona Company for food, drinks, and boat rentals for an employees' party.

When he closed on September 15, he was able to return to the soft drink company several cases of soft drinks for which he received a $35 cash refund. However, he had to take home for consumption by his family a number of candy bars and some hamburger and buns which cost $10 and could have been sold for $25.

Prepare a September 15 balance sheet for the business and an income statement showing the net income earned as a result of the summer's operations. (Hint: A equation like in Illustration 1–7 may be helpful in organizing the data.)

PART 2

Processing accounting data

2
Recording transactions . . .

3
Adjusting the accounts and preparing the
statements . . .

4
The work sheet and closing the accounts . . .

5
Accounting for a merchandising concern . . .

6
Accounting systems

After studying Chapter 2, you should be able to:

- Explain the mechanics of double-entry accounting and tell why transactions are recorded with equal debits and credits.
- State the rules of debit and credit and apply the rules in recording transactions.
- Tell the normal balance of any asset, liability, or owner equity account.
- Record transactions in a General Journal, post to the ledger accounts, and prepare a trial balance to test the accuracy of the recording and posting.
- Define or explain the words and phrases listed in the chapter Glossary.

chapter 2

Recording transactions

Transactions are the raw material of the accounting process, a process which consists of identifying transactions, recording them, and summarizing their effects on periodic reports for the use of management and other decision makers.

Some years ago almost all concerns used pen and ink in recording transactions; but today only small concerns use this method, concerns small enough that their bookkeeping can be done by one person working as bookkeeper a part of his or her day. Larger, modern concerns use electric bookkeeping machines, punched cards, and magnetic tape in recording transactions.

Nevertheless, most students begin their study of accounting by learning a double-entry accounting system based on pen and ink; and there are several reasons for this. First, since accounting reports evolved from and are based on double entry, the effective use of these reports requires some understanding of the system. Second, there is little lost motion from learning the system, since almost everything about it is applicable to machine methods. Primarily the machines replace pen and ink as the recording medium, taking the drudgery out of the recording process. And last, for the student who will start, manage, or own a small business, one small enough to use a pen-and-ink system, the system applies as it is taught.

Business papers Business papers provide evidence of transactions completed and are the basis for accounting entries to record the transactions. For example, when goods are sold on credit, two or more copies of an invoice or sales ticket are prepared. One copy is enclosed with the goods or is delivered to the customer and the other is sent to the accounting department where it becomes the basis for an entry to record the sale. Also, when goods are sold for cash, the sales are commonly "rung up" on a cash register that prints the amount of each sale on a paper tape locked inside the register. At the end of the day, when the proper key is depressed, the register prints on the tape the total cash sales for the day, after which the tape is removed and becomes the basis for an entry to record the sales. Also, when an established business purchases assets, it normally buys on credit and receives an invoice that becomes the basis for an entry to record the purchase. Likewise, when the invoice is paid, a check is issued in its payment and the check or a carbon copy becomes the basis for an entry to record the payment. Obviously then, business papers are the starting point in the accounting process. Furthermore, verifiable business papers, particularly those originating outside the business, are also objective evidence of transactions completed and the amounts at which they should be recorded, as required by the *objectivity principle.*

Accounts

The transactions of a business cause increases and decreases in its assets, liabilities, and owner equity; and a concern using an accounting system based on pen and ink or electric bookkeeping machines uses *accounts* in recording the increases and decreases. A number of accounts are normally required, with a separate account being used for summarizing the increases and decreases in each asset, liability, and owner equity item appearing on the balance sheet and each revenue and expense appearing on the income statement.

In its most simple form an account looks like the letter "T," is called a "T-account," and appears as follows:

(Place for the Name of the Item Recorded in This Account)	
(Left side)	(Right side)

Note that the "T" gives the account a left side, a right side, and a place for the name of the asset, liability, or owner equity item, the increases and decreases in which are recorded therein.

When a T-account is used in recording increases and decreases in an item, the increases are placed on one side of the account and the decreases on the other. For example, if the increases and decreases in the cash of Larry Owen's law practice of the previous chapter are recorded in a T-account, they appear as follows:

Cash			
Investment	2,500	Prepayment of rent	600
Legal fee earned	400	Equipment purchase	1,200
Collection of account receivable	750	Salary payment	250
		Payment on account payable	100

The reason for putting the increases on one account side and the decreases on the other is that this makes it easy to add the increases, then add the decreases, and to subtract the sum of the decreases from the sum of the increases to learn how much of the item recorded in the account the company has, owns, or owes. For example, the increases in the cash of the Owen law practice were:

> Investment $2,500
> Legal fee earned................................   400
> Collection of an account receivable....   750
> Sum of the increases $3,650

And the decreases were:

> Prepayment of office rent .... $ 600
> Equipment purchase................ 1,200
> Salary payment.........................   250
> Payment on account payable   100
> Sum of the decreases...... $2,150

And when the sum of the decreases is subtracted from the sum of the increases,

> Sum of the increases $3,650
> Sum of the decreases..................... 2,150
> Balance of cash remaining $1,500

the subtraction shows the law practice has $1,500 of cash remaining.

Balance of an account

When the increases and decreases recorded in an account are separately added and the sum of the decreases is subtracted from the sum of the increases, the procedure is called determining the *balance* of an account. The balance of an account is the difference between its increases and decreases. It is also the amount of the item recorded in the account that the company has, owns, or owes at the time the balance is determined.

A business uses a number of accounts in recording its transactions. However, the specific accounts used vary from one concern to another, depending upon the assets owned, the debts owed, and the information to be secured from the accounting records. Nevertheless, although the specific accounts vary, the following are common.

Accounts commonly used

Asset accounts

If useful records of a concern's assets are to be kept, an individual account is needed for the increases and decreases in each kind of asset owned. Some of the more common assets for which accounts are maintained are:

Cash   Increases and decreases in cash are recorded in an account called "Cash." The cash of a business consists of money or any media of exchange that a bank will accept at face value for deposit. It includes coins, currency, checks, and postal and bank money orders; and the balance of the Cash account shows both the cash on hand in the store or office and that on deposit in the bank.

Notes receivable   A formal written promise to pay a definite sum of money at a fixed future date is called a promissory note (see the illustration on page 264). When amounts due from others are evidenced by promissory notes, the notes are known as *notes receivable* and are recorded in a Notes Receivable account.

Accounts receivable   Goods and services are commonly sold to customers on the basis of oral or implied promises of future payment. Such sales are known as "sales on credit" or "sales on account"; and the oral or implied promises to pay are known as accounts receivable. Accounts receivable are increased by sales on credit and are decreased by customer payments. Since it is necessary to know the amount currently owed by each customer, a separate record must be kept of each customer's purchases and payments. However, a discussion of the manner in which this separate record is kept is deferred until Chapter 6, and for the present all increases and decreases in accounts receivable are recorded in a single account called Accounts Receivable.

Prepaid insurance   Fire, liability, and other types of insurance protection are normally paid for in advance. The amount paid is called a "premium" and may give protection from loss for from one to five years. As a result, a large portion of each premium is an asset for a considerable time after payment. When insurance premiums are paid, the asset "prepaid insurance" is increased by the amount paid; and the increase is normally recorded in an account called "Prepaid Insurance." Day by day, insurance premiums expire. Consequently, at intervals the insurance policies are examined; the insurance that has expired is calculated; and the balance of the Prepaid Insurance account is reduced accordingly.

Office supplies   Stamps, stationery, paper, pencils, and like items are known as office supplies. They are assets when purchased, and continue to be assets until consumed. As they are consumed, the amounts consumed become expenses. Increases and decreases in the asset "office supplies" are commonly recorded in an account called "Office Supplies."

Store supplies   Wrapping paper, cartons, bags, string, and similar items used by a store are known as store supplies. Increases and decreases in store supplies are recorded in an account of that name.

Other prepaid expenses   Prepaid expenses are items that are assets at the time of purchase but become expenses as they are consumed or used. Prepaid insurance, office supplies, and store supplies are examples. Other examples are prepaid rent, prepaid taxes, and prepaid wages. Each type of prepaid expense is normally accounted for in a separate account which carries the name of the item, the increases and decreases of which are recorded therein.

Equipment   Increases and decreases in such things as typewriters, desks, chairs, and office machines having long lives are commonly recorded in an account called "Office Equipment." Likewise, changes in the amount of counters, showcases, shelves, cash registers, and like items used by a store are recorded in an account called "Store Equipment." And a company that owns and uses such things as lathes, drill presses, and the like records the increases and decreases in these items in an account called "Machinery and Equipment."

Buildings   A building used by a business in carrying on its operations may be a store, garage, warehouse, or factory; but regardless of use, an account called "Buildings" is commonly employed in recording the increases and decreases in the buildings owned by a business and used in carrying on its operations.

Land   An account called "Land" is commonly used in recording increases and decreases in the land owned by a business. Although land and the buildings placed upon it are inseparable in physical fact, it is usually desirable to account for land and its buildings in separate accounts, because buildings depreciate and wear out, but land does not.

Liability accounts

Most companies do not have as many liability accounts as asset accounts; however, the following are common:

Notes payable   Increases and decreases in amounts owed because of promissory notes given to creditors are accounted for in an account called "Notes Payable."

Accounts payable   An account payable is an amount owed to a creditor which resulted from an oral or implied promise to pay. Most accounts payable result from the purchase of merchandise, supplies, equipment, and services on credit. Since it is necessary to know the amount owed each creditor, an individual record must be kept of the purchases from and the payments to each. However, a discussion of the manner in which this individual record is kept is deferred until Chapter 6, and for the present all increases and decreases in accounts payable are recorded in a single Accounts Payable account.

Unearned revenues   The *realization principle* requires that revenue be earned before it is recognized as revenue. Therefore, when a company collects for its products or services before delivery, the amounts collected are unearned revenue. An unearned revenue is a liability that will be extinguished by delivering the product or service paid for in advance. Subscriptions collected in advance by a magazine publisher, rent collected in advance by a landlord, and legal fees collected in advance by a lawyer are examples of unearned revenues.

Upon receipt, the amounts collected are recorded in liability accounts such as Unearned Subscriptions, Unearned Rent, and Unearned Legal Fees. When earned by delivery, the amounts earned are transferred to the revenue accounts, Subscriptions Earned, Rent Earned, and Legal Fees Earned.

Other short-term payables   Wages payable, taxes payable, and interest payable are illustrations of other short-term liabilities for which individual accounts must be kept.

Mortgage payable   A mortgage payable is a long-term debt for which the creditor has a secured prior claim against some one or more of the debtor's assets. The mortgage gives its holder, the creditor, the right to force the sale of the mortgaged assets through a foreclosure if the mortgage debt is not paid when due. An account called "Mortgage Payable" is commonly used in recording the increases and decreases in the amount owed on a mortgage.

Owner equity accounts

Several kinds of transactions affect owner equity, including the investment of the owner, his withdrawals of cash and other assets for personal use, revenues earned, and expenses incurred. In the previous chapter all transactions affecting owner equity were entered in a column under the name of the owner. This simplified the material of the chapter, but made it necessary to analyze the items entered in the column in order to prepare an income statement. Fortunately such an analysis is not necessary. All that is required to avoid it is a number of accounts, a separate one for each owner equity item appearing on the balance sheet and a separate one for each kind of revenue and expense on the income statement. Then as each transaction affecting owner equity is completed, it is recorded in the proper account. Among the accounts required are the following:

Capital account   When a person invests in a business of his own, his investment is recorded in an account carrying his name and the word "Capital." For example, an account called "Larry Owen, Capital" is used in recording the investment of Larry Owen in his law practice. In addition to the original investment, the Capital account is used for any permanent additional increases or decreases in owner equity.

Withdrawals account   Usually a person invests in a business to earn a net income. However, income is earned over a period of time, say a year, and often during this period the business owner finds it necessary to withdraw a portion of the earnings to pay living expenses or for other personal uses. These withdrawals reduce both assets and owner equity; and to record them, an account carrying the name of the business owner and the word "Withdrawals" is used. For example, an account called "Larry Owen, Withdrawals" is used to record the withdrawals of cash and other assets by Larry Owen from his law practice. The Withdrawals account is also known as the "Personal" account or "Drawing" account.

An owner of a small unincorporated business like the Owen law practice often withdraws a fixed amount each week or month for personal living expenses, and often thinks of these withdrawals as a salary. However, in a legal sense they are not a salary because the owner of an unincorporated business cannot enter into a legally binding contract with himself to hire himself and pay himself a salary. Consequently, in law and custom it is recognized that withdrawals by the owner of an unincorporated business for personal living expenses are neither a salary nor an expense of the business, but are withdrawals in anticipation of the net income he expects his business to earn.

Revenue and expense accounts   When an income statement is prepared, it is necessary to know the amount of each kind of revenue earned and each kind of expense incurred during the period covered by the statement; and to accumulate this information, a number of revenue and expense accounts are needed. However, all concerns do not have the same revenues and expenses. Consequently, it is impossible to list all revenue and expense accounts to be encountered. Nevertheless, Revenue from Repairs, Commissions Earned, Legal Fees Earned, Rent Earned, and Interest Earned are common examples of revenue accounts; and Advertising Expense, Store Supplies Expense, Office Salaries Expense, Office Supplies Expense, Rent Expense, Utilities Expense, and Insurance Expense are common examples of expense accounts. It should be noted that the kind of revenue or expense recorded in each above-mentioned account is evident from its title. This is generally true of such accounts.

The ledger

A business may use from two dozen to several thousand accounts in recording its transactions, with each account placed on a separate page in a bound or loose-leaf book, or on a separate card in a tray of cards. If the accounts are kept in a book, the book is called a *ledger;* and if the accounts are kept on cards in a file tray, the tray of cards is a ledger. Actually, as used in accounting, the word ledger means a group of accounts.

Debit and credit

As previously stated, a T-account has a left side and a right side; however, in accounting the left side is called the *debit* side, abbreviated "Dr."; and the right side is called the *credit* side, abbreviated "Cr." Furthermore, when amounts are entered on the left side of an account, they are called *debits,* and the account is said to be *debited;* and when amounts are entered on the right side, they are called credits, and the account is said to be *credited.* Likewise, the difference between the total debits and the total credits recorded in an account is the account balance and may be either a *debit balance* or a *credit balance.* It is a debit balance when the sum of the debits exceeds the sum of the credits and a credit balance when the sum of the credits exceeds the sum of the debits, and an account is said to be *in balance* when its debits and credits are equal.

The words "to debit" and "to credit" should not be confused with "to increase" and "to decrease." To debit means simply to enter an amount on the left side of an account, to credit means to enter an amount on the right side, and either may be an increase or a decrease. This may readily be seen by examining the way in which the investment of Larry Owen is recorded in his Cash and Capital accounts which follow:

Cash	Larry Owen, Capital
Investment 2,500	Investment 2,500

When Owen invested $2,500 in his law practice, both the business cash and Owen's equity were increased. Observe in the accounts that one increase, the increase in cash, is recorded on the left or debit side of the Cash account; while the other increase, the increase in owner equity, is recorded on the right or credit side. The transaction is recorded in this manner because of the mechanics of *double-entry accounting*.

Mechanics of double-entry accounting

The mechanics of double-entry accounting are such that every transaction affects and is recorded in two or more accounts with equal debits and credits. Transactions are so recorded because equal debits and credits offer a means of proving the recording accuracy. The proof is, if every transaction is recorded with equal debits and credits, then the sum of the debits in the ledger must equal the sum of the credits.

The person who first devised double-entry accounting based the system on the accounting equation, $A = L + OE$, and he assigned the recording of increases in assets to the debit sides of asset accounts. He then recognized that the goal of equal debits and credits was possible only if increases in liabilities and owner equity were recorded on the opposite or credit sides of liability and owner equity accounts, or he recognized that if increases in assets were to be recorded as debits, then increases and decreases in all accounts would have to be recorded as follows:

Assets	=	Liabilities	+	Owner Equity		
Debit for Increases	Credit for Decreases	Debit for Decreases	Credit for Increases	Debit for Decreases	Credit for Increases	

From the T-accounts it is possible to formulate rules for recording transactions under a double-entry system. The rules are:

*increase debit
decrease credit*

1. Increases in assets are debited to asset accounts; consequently, decreases must be credited.

*Increase credit
decrease deb.*

2. Increases in liability and owner equity items are credited to liability and owner equity accounts; consequently, decreases must be debited.

At this stage, the beginning student will find it helpful to memorize these rules. He should also note that there are four kinds of owner equity accounts: (1) the Capital account, (2) the Withdrawals account, (3) revenue accounts, and (4) expense accounts. Furthermore, in applying the rules of debit and credit for owner equity, the student should observe these additional points:

1. The original investment of the owner of a business plus any more or less permanent changes in the investment are recorded in his Capital account.
2. Withdrawals of assets for personal use, including cash to pay personal expenses, decrease owner equity and are debited to the owner's Withdrawals account.
3. Revenues increase owner equity and are credited in each case to a revenue account that shows the nature of the revenue earned.
4. Expenses decrease owner equity and are debited in each case to an expense account that shows the nature of the expense incurred.

In addition, the student should also recognize that after a number of transactions are completed, the equity of an owner in his business consists of the credit balance in his Capital account *minus* the debit balance of his Withdrawals account *plus* the credit balances in any revenue accounts and *minus* the debit balances in the expense accounts.

Transactions illustrating the rules of debit and credit

The following transactions of Larry Owen's law practice illustrate the application of debit and credit rules and show how transactions are recorded in the accounts. The number preceding each transaction is used throughout the illustration to identify the transaction as it appears in the accounts. Note that most of the transactions are the same ones used in Chapter 1 to illustrate the effects of transactions on the accounting equation.

1. Larry Owen invested $2,500 in a law practice.
2. He paid three months' office rent in advance, $600.
3. Purchased office equipment for cash, $1,200.
4. Purchased on credit from Alpha Company office supplies, $60, and office equipment, $300.
5. Completed legal work for a client and immediately collected a $400 fee for the services rendered.
6. Paid the secretary's salary for the first two weeks in the month, $250.
7. Signed a contract with Coast Realty to do its legal work on a

fixed-fee basis for $100 per month. The client paid the fee for the first month and a half in advance, $150.

8. Completed legal work on credit for a client and immediately billed him $750 for the services rendered.
9. Paid the secretary's salary for the second two weeks of the month, $250.
10. Larry Owen withdrew $200 from the bank account of the law practice to pay personal living expenses.
11. The client paid the $750 legal fee billed in transaction 8.
12. Paid Alpha Company $100 of the $360 owed for the items purchased on credit in transaction 4.
13. Paid the monthly telephone bill of the office, $30.
14. Paid the July electric bill of the office, $35.

Before a transaction can be recorded, it must be analyzed into its debit and credit elements. The analysis consists of (1) determining what asset, liability, or owner equity items are increased or decreased by the transaction and then (2) applying the rules of debit and credit to determine the debit and credit effects of the increases or decreases. An analysis of each of the following transactions is given in order to demonstrate the process.

1. On July 1 of the current year, Larry Owen invested $2,500 in a new law practice.

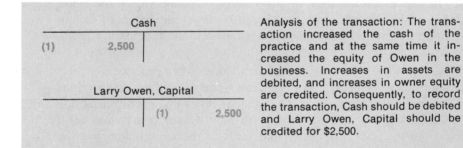

| Cash | | | Analysis of the transaction: The transaction increased the cash of the practice and at the same time it increased the equity of Owen in the business. Increases in assets are debited, and increases in owner equity are credited. Consequently, to record the transaction, Cash should be debited and Larry Owen, Capital should be credited for $2,500. |

```
                    Cash
     _____
     (1)      2,500 |

             Larry Owen, Capital
     _____
                   |  (1)     2,500
```

Analysis of the transaction: The transaction increased the cash of the practice and at the same time it increased the equity of Owen in the business. Increases in assets are debited, and increases in owner equity are credited. Consequently, to record the transaction, Cash should be debited and Larry Owen, Capital should be credited for $2,500.

2. Paid the office rent for three months in advance, $600.

```
                    Cash
     _____
     (1)      2,500 | (2)        600

             Prepaid Rent
     _____
     (2)        600 |
```

Analysis of the transaction: The asset prepaid rent, the right to occupy the office for three months, is increased; and the asset cash is decreased. Increases in assets are debited and decreases are credited. Therefore, to record the transaction, debit Prepaid Rent and credit Cash for $600.

3. Purchased office equipment for cash, $1,200

Cash				Analysis of the transaction: The asset office equipment is increased; and the asset cash is decreased. Debit Office Equipment and credit Cash for $1,200.
(1)	2,500	(2) (3)	600 1,200	

Office Equipment		
(3)	1,200	

4. Purchased on credit from Alpha Company office supplies, $60, and office equipment, $300.

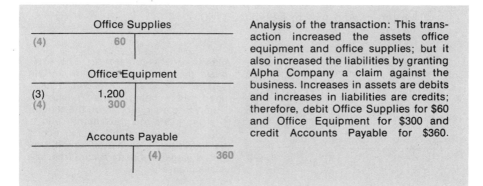

Office Supplies		
(4)	60	

Office Equipment		
(3)	1,200	
(4)	300	

Accounts Payable		
	(4)	360

Analysis of the transaction: This transaction increased the assets office equipment and office supplies; but it also increased the liabilities by granting Alpha Company a claim against the business. Increases in assets are debits and increases in liabilities are credits; therefore, debit Office Supplies for $60 and Office Equipment for $300 and credit Accounts Payable for $360.

5. Completed legal work for a client and immediately collected a $400 fee.

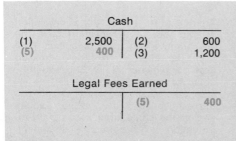

Cash			
(1) (5)	2,500 400	(2) (3)	600 1,200

Legal Fees Earned		
	(5)	400

Analysis of the transaction: This revenue transaction increased both assets and owner equity. Increases in assets are debits, and increases in owner equity are credits. Therefore, Cash is debited; and in order to show the nature of the increase in owner equity and at the same time accumulate information for the income statement, the revenue account Legal Fees Earned is credited.

6. Paid the secretary's salary for the first two weeks of July, $250.

Cash			
(1)	2,500	(2)	600
(5)	400	(3)	1,200
		(6)	250

Office Salaries Expense	
(6)	250

Analysis of the transaction: The secretary's salary is an expense that decreased both assets and owner equity. Debit Office Salaries Expense to decrease owner equity and also to accumulate information for the income statement; and credit Cash to record the decrease in cash.

7. Signed a contract with Coast Realty to do its legal work on a fixed-fee basis for $100 per month. Received the fee for the first month and a half in advance, $150.

Cash			
(1)	2,500	(2)	600
(5)	400	(3)	1,200
(7)	150	(6)	250

Unearned Legal Fees	
(7)	150

Analysis of the transaction: The $150 inflow increased cash, but the inflow is not a revenue until earned. Its acceptance before being earned created a liability, the obligation to do the client's legal work for the next month and a half. Consequently, debit Cash to record the increase in cash and credit Unearned Legal Fees to record the liability increase.

8. Completed legal work for a client on credit and billed him $750 for the services rendered.

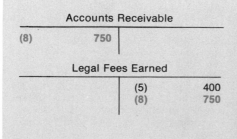

Accounts Receivable	
(8)	750

Legal Fees Earned	
(5)	400
(8)	750

Analysis of the transaction: Completion of this revenue transaction gave the law practice the right to collect $750 from the client, and thus increased assets and owner equity. Consequently, debit Accounts Receivable for the increase in assets and credit Legal Fees Earned to increase owner equity and at the same time accumulate information for the income statement.

9. Paid the secretary's salary for the second two weeks of the month, $250.

Cash			
(1)	2,500	(2)	600
(5)	400	(3)	1,200
(7)	150	(6)	250
		(9)	250

Office Salaries Expense	
(6)	250
(9)	250

Analysis of the transaction: An expense that decreased assets and owner equity. Debit Office Salaries Expense to accumulate information for the income statement and credit Cash.

10. Larry Owen withdrew $200 from the law practice to pay personal expenses.

Cash			
(1)	2,500	(2)	600
(5)	400	(3)	1,200
(7)	150	(6)	250
		(9)	250
		(10)	200

Larry Owen, Withdrawals	
(10)	200

Analysis of the transaction: This transaction reduced in equal amounts both assets and owner equity. Cash is credited to record the asset reduction; and the Larry Owen, Withdrawals account is debited for the reduction in owner equity.

11. The client paid the $750 legal fee billed in transaction 8.

Cash			
(1)	2,500	(2)	600
(5)	400	(3)	1,200
(7)	150	(6)	250
(11)	750	(9)	250
		(10)	200

Accounts Receivable			
(8)	750	(11)	750

Analysis of the transaction: One asset was increased and the other decreased Debit Cash to record the increase in cash, and credit Accounts Receivable to record the decrease in the account receivable, or the decrease in the right to collect from the client.

12. Paid Alpha Company $100 of the $360 owed for the items purchased on credit in transaction 4.

	Cash		
(1)	2,500	(2)	600
(5)	400	(3)	1,200
(7)	150	(6)	250
(11)	750	(9)	250
		(10)	200
		(12)	100

Accounts Payable			
(12)	100	(4)	360

Analysis of the transaction: Payments to creditors decrease in like amounts both assets and liabilities. Decreases in liabilities are debited, and decreases in assets are credited. Debit Accounts Payable and credit Cash.

13. Paid the July telephone bill, $30.
14. Paid the July electric bill, $35.

	Cash		
(1)	2,500	(2)	600
(5)	400	(3)	1,200
(7)	150	(6)	250
(11)	750	(9)	250
		(10)	200
		(12)	100
		(13)	30
		(14)	35

Telephone Expense		
(13)	30	

Heating and Lighting Expense		
(14)	35	

Analysis of the transactions: These expense transactions are alike in that each decreased cash; they differ in each case as to the kind of expense involved. Consequently, in recording them, Cash is credited; and to accumulate information for the income statement, a different expense account, one showing the nature of the expense in each case, is debited.

The accounts and the equation

In Illustration 2–1 the transactions of the Owen law practice are shown in the accounts, with the accounts brought together and classified under the elements of an accounting equation.

Preparing a trial balance

As previously stated, in a double-entry accounting system every transaction is recorded with equal debits and credits so that the equality of the debits and credits in the accounts may be tested as a proof of the recording accuracy. This equality is tested at intervals by preparing a trial balance.

Assets		=	Liabilities		+	Owner Equity	

Cash

(1)	2,500	(2)	600
(5)	400	(3)	1,200
(7)	150	(6)	250
(11)	750	(9)	250
		(10)	200
		(12)	100
		(13)	30
		(14)	35

Accounts Receivable

(8)	750	(11)	750

Prepaid Rent

(2)	600	

Office Supplies

(4)	60	

Office Equipment

(3)	1,200	
(4)	300	

Accounts Payable

(12)	100	(4)	360

Unearned Legal Fees

		(7)	150

Larry Owen, Capital

		(1)	2,500

Larry Owen, Withdrawals

(10)	200	

Legal Fees Earned

		(5)	400
		(8)	750

Office Salaries Expense

(6)	250	
(9)	250	

Telephone Expense

(13)	30	

Heating and Lighting Expense

(14)	35	

Illustration 2–1

A trial balance is prepared by (1) determining the balance of each account in the ledger; (2) listing the accounts having balances, with the debit balances in one column and the credit balances in another (as in Illustration 2–2); (3) adding the debit balances; (4) adding the credit balances; and then (5) comparing the sum of the debit balances with the sum of the credit balances.

Larry Owen, Attorney
Trial Balance, July 31, 19—

	Debit	Credit
Cash	$1,135	
Prepaid rent	600	
Office supplies	60	
Office equipment	1,500	
Accounts payable		$ 260
Unearned legal fees		150
Larry Owen, capital		2,500
Larry Owen, withdrawals	200	
Legal fees earned		1,150
Office salaries expense	500	
Telephone expense	30	
Heating and lighting expense	35	
Totals	$4,060	$4,060

Illustration 2–2

Illustration 2–2 shows a trial balance of Owen's law practice. It was prepared from the accounts in Illustration 2–1. Note that its column totals are equal, or in other words, the trial balance is in balance. When a trial balance is in balance, debits equal credits in the ledger and it is assumed that no errors were made in recording transactions.

The proof offered by a trial balance

If when a trial balance is prepared it does not balance – the two columns are not equal – errors have been made either in recording transactions, in determining the account balances, in copying the balances on the trial balance, or in adding the trial balance columns. On the other hand, if a trial balance balances, it is assumed that no errors have been made. However, a trial balance that balances is not absolute proof of accuracy. Errors may have been made that did not affect the equality of its columns. For example, an error in which a correct debit amount is debited to the wrong account or a correct credit amount is credited to the wrong account will not cause a trial balance to be out of balance. Likewise, an error in which a wrong amount is both debited and credited to the right accounts will not cause a trial balance to be out of balance. Consequently, a trial balance in balance is considered only presumptive proof of recording accuracy.

Standard account form

T-accounts like the ones shown thus far are commonly used in textbook illustration and also in accounting classes for blackboard demonstrations. In both cases their use eliminates details and permits the student to concentrate on ideas. However, although widely used in textbooks and in teaching, T-accounts are not used in business for recording transactions. In recording transactions, accounts like the one in Illustration 2–3 are generally used.

The account of Illustration 2–3 is called a balance column account. It differs from a T-account in that it has columns for specific information about each debit and credit entered in the account. Note that its Debit and Credit columns are placed side by side and that it has a third or Balance column. In this Balance column the account's new balance is entered each time the account is debited or credited; and as

Cash						ACCOUNT NO. 1
DATE	EXPLANATION	FO-LIO	DEBIT	CREDIT	BALANCE	
1978 July 1		G-1	2500 00		2500 00	
1		G-1		600 00	1900 00	
3		G-1		1200 00	700 00	
12		G-1	400 00		1100 00	

Illustration 2–3

a result, the last amount in the column is the account's current balance. For example, on July 1 the illustrated account was debited for the $2,500 investment of Larry Owen, which caused it to have a $2,500 debit balance. It was then credited for $600, and its new $1,900 balance was entered; and on July 3 it was credited again for $1,200, which reduced its balance to $700. Then on July 12 it was debited for $400 and its balance was increased to $1,100.

When a balance column account like that of Illustration 2–3 is used, the heading of the Balance column does not tell whether the balance is a debit balance as, for example, it would normally be for an asset account or a credit balance as it would normally be for a liability. However, this does not create a problem because an account is always assumed to have its normal kind of balance, unless the contrary is indicated in the account. Furthermore, an accountant is expected to know the normal balance of any account. Fortunately this too is not difficult because the balance of an account normally results from recording in it a larger sum of increases than decreases. Consequently, if increases are recorded as debits, the account normally has a debit balance; and if increases are recorded as credits, the account normally has a credit balance. Or, increases are recorded in an account in each of the following classes as shown and its normal balance is:

Type of Account	Increases Are Recorded as—	And the Normal Balance is—
Asset .... Debits		Debit
Contra asset* .... Credits		Credit
Liability .... Credits		Credit
Owner equity:		
Capital .... Credits		Credit
Withdrawals........ Debits		Debit
Revenue............. Credits		Credit
Expense........,.... Debits		Debit
* Explained in the next chapter.		

When an unusual transaction causes an account to have a balance that is opposite from its normal kind of balance, this opposite from normal kind of balance is indicated in the account by entering it in red or entering it in black and encircling the amount. Also when a posting to a balance column account causes the account to have no balance, some bookkeepers place a -0- in the Balance column on the line of the posting. Other bookkeepers and bookkeeping machines write 0.00 in the column to indicate the account does not have a balance.

Need for a journal

It is possible to record transactions by entering debits and credits directly in the accounts, as was done earlier in this chapter. However, when this is done and an error is made, the error is difficult to locate, because even with a transaction having only one debit and one credit, the debit is entered on one ledger page or card and the credit on another, and there is nothing to link the two together.

Consequently, to link together the debits and credits of each transaction and to provide in one place a complete record of each transaction, it is the universal practice in pen-and-ink systems to record all transactions in a *journal* and then to copy the debit and credit information about each transaction from the journal to the ledger accounts. This debit and credit record of each transaction in a journal is important when errors are made, since the journal record makes it possible to trace the debits and credits into the accounts and to see that they are equal and properly recorded.

Each transaction entered in a journal is recorded with a separate *journal entry,* and the process of recording transactions in a journal is called *journalizing transactions.* Also, since transactions are recorded in a journal as the first or original step in their recording and their debit and credit information is copied from the journal to the ledger as a second or last step, a journal is called *a book of original entry* and a ledger *a book of final entry.*

The General Journal

The simplest and most flexible type of journal is a *General Journal.* For each transaction it provides places for recording (1) the transaction date, (2) the names of the accounts involved, (3) an explanation of the transaction, (4) the account numbers of the accounts to which the transaction's debit and credit information is copied, and (5) the transaction's debit and credit effect on the accounts named. A standard ruling for a general journal page with two of the transactions of the Owen law practice recorded therein is shown in Illustration 2–4.

The first entry in Illustration 2–4 records the purchase of supplies and equipment on credit, and three accounts are involved. When a transaction involves three or more accounts and is recorded with a general journal entry, a compound entry is required. A compound

DATE	ACCOUNT TITLES AND EXPLANATION	FO-LIO	DEBIT	CREDIT
1978 July 5	Office Supplies		60 00	
	Office Equipment		300 00	
	Accounts Payable			360 00
	Purchased supplies and equipment on credit.			
12	Cash		400 00	
	Legal Fees Earned			400 00
	Collected a legal fee.			

GENERAL JOURNAL   PAGE /

Illustration 2–4

entry is one involving three or more accounts. The second entry records a legal fee earned.

To record transactions in a General Journal:

1. The year is written in small figures at the top of the first column.
2. The month is written on the first line in the first column. The year and the month are not repeated except at the top of a new page or at the beginning of a new month or year.
3. The day of each transaction is written in the second column on the first line of the transaction.
4. The names of the accounts to be debited and credited and an explanation of the transaction are written in the Account Titles and Explanation column. The name of the account debited is written first, beginning at the left margin of the column. The name of the account credited is written on the following line, indented about one inch. The explanation is placed on the next line, indented about a half inch from the left margin. The explanation should be short but sufficient to explain the transaction and set it apart from every other transaction.
5. The debit amount is written in the Debit column opposite the name of the account to be debited. The credit amount is written in the Credit column opposite the account to be credited.
6. A single line is skipped between each journal entry to set the entries apart.

At the time transactions are recorded in the General Journal, nothing is entered in the Folio column. However, when the debits and credits are copied from the journal to the ledger, the account numbers of the ledger accounts to which the debits and credits are copied are entered in the Folio column.

The process of copying journal entry information and transferring it from the journal to the ledger is called *posting*. Normally, near the end of a day all transactions recorded in the journal that day are posted to the ledger. In the posting procedure, journal debits are copied and become ledger account debits and journal credits are copied and become ledger account credits.

The posting procedures for a journal entry is shown in Illustration 2–5, and it may be described as follows. To post a journal entry:

For the debit:

1. Find in the ledger the account named in the debt of the entry.
2. Enter in the account (*a*) the date of the entry as shown in the journal, (*b*) the page number of the journal from which the entry is being posted, and (*c*) in the Debit column the debit amount. Note the letter "G" preceding the journal page number in the Folio column of the account. The letter indicates that the amount was

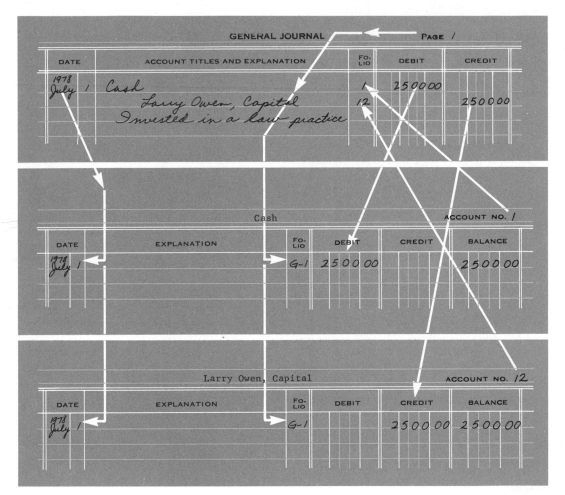

Illustration 2–5

posted from the General Journal. Other journals are introduced in Chapter 6 and each is identified by a letter.

3. Determine the effect of the debit on the account balance and enter the new balance.

4. Enter in the Folio column of the journal the account number of the account to which the amount was posted.

For the credit:

Repeat the foregoing steps, with the exception that the credit amount is entered in the Credit column and has a credit effect on the account balance.

Observe that the last step (Step 4) in the posting procedure for either the debit or the credit of an entry is to insert the account number in the Folio column of the journal. Inserting the account number in the journal Folio column serves two purposes: (1) The account number in the journal and the journal page number in the account act as a cross-reference when it is desired to trace an amount from one record to the other. And, (2) writing the account number in the journal as a last step in posting indicates that posting is completed. If posting is interrupted, the bookkeeper, by examining the journal Folio column, can easily see where posting stopped.

Account numbers and journal page numbers are often called *posting reference numbers*. The reason for this is obvious.

When a trial balance does not balance, an error or errors are indicated. To locate the error or errors, check the journalizing, posting, and trial balance preparation steps in their reverse order. First check the addition of the trial balance columns to see that no error in addition was made. Then check to see that the account balances were correctly copied from the ledger. Then recalculate the account balances. If at this stage the error or errors have not been found, check the posting and then the original journalizing of the transactions.

Locating errors

When an error is discovered in either the journal or the ledger, it must be corrected. Such an error is never erased, for this seems to indicate an effort to conceal something. However, the exact method of correction will vary with the nature of the error and the stage in the accounting procedures at which it is discovered.

Correcting errors

If an error is discovered in a journal entry before the error is posted, it may be corrected by ruling a single line through the incorrect amount or account name and writing in above the correct amount or account name. Likewise, a posted error or an error in posting in which only the amount is wrong may be corrected in the same manner. However, when a posted error involves a wrong account, it is considered best to correct the error with a correcting journal entry. For example, the following journal entry to record the purchase of office supplies was made and posted:

Oct.	14	Office Furniture and Fixtures...................................	15.00	
		Cash..		15.00
		To record the purchase of office supplies.		

Obviously, the debit of the entry is to the wrong account; consequently, the following entry is needed to correct the error:

Oct.	17	Office Supplies	15.00	
		Office Furniture and Fixtures.............................		15.00
		To correct the entry of October 14 in which the Office Furniture and Fixtures account was debited in error for the purchase of office supplies.		

The debit of the second entry correctly records the purchase of supplies, and the credit cancels the error of the first entry. Note the full explanation of the correcting entry. Such an explanation should always be full and complete so that anyone can see exactly what has occurred.

Bookkeeping techniques

Commas and decimal points in dollar amounts

When amounts are entered in a journal or a ledger, commas to indicate thousands of dollars and decimal points to separate dollars and cents are not necessary because the ruled lines accomplish this purpose. However, when statements are prepared on unruled paper, the decimal points and commas are necessary.

Dollar signs

Dollar signs are not used in journals or ledgers but are required on financial reports prepared on unruled paper. On such reports, a dollar sign is placed (1) before the first amount in each column of figures and (2) before the first amount appearing after a ruled line that indicates an addition or a subtraction. Examine Illustration 3–5 on page 83 for examples of the use of dollar signs on a financial report.

Omission of zeros in the cents columns

When an amount to be entered in a ledger or a journal is an amount of dollars and no cents, some bookkeepers will use a dash in the cents column in the place of two zeros to indicate that there are no cents. They feel that the dash is easier and more quickly made than the two zeros. This is a matter of choice in journal and ledger entries. However, on financial reports the two zeros are preferred because they are neater in appearance.

Often in this text, where space is limited, exact dollar amounts are used in order to save space. Obviously, in such cases, neither zeros nor dashes are used to show that there are no cents involved.

Glossary

Account. An accounting device used in recording and summarizing the increases and decreases in a revenue, an expense, asset, liability, or owner equity item.

Account balance. The difference between the increases and decreases recorded in an account.

Account number. An identifying number assigned to an account.

Balance column account. An account having a column for entering the new account balance after each debit or credit is posted to the account.

Book of final entry. A ledger to which amounts are posted.

Book of original entry. A journal in which transactions are first recorded.

Business paper. A sales ticket, invoice, check, or other document arising in and evidence of the completion of a business transaction.

Capital account. An account used to record the more or less permanent changes in the equity of an owner in his business.

Compound journal entry. A journal entry having more than one debit or more than one credit.

Credit. The right-hand side of a T-account.

Debit. The left-hand side of a T-account.

Double-entry accounting. An accounting system in which each transaction affects and is recorded in two or more accounts with equal debits and credits.

Folio column. A column in a journal and in each account for entering posting reference numbers.

General Journal. A book of original entry in which any type of transaction can be recorded.

Journal. A book of original entry in which transactions are first recorded and from which transaction amounts are posted to the ledger accounts.

Journal page number. A posting reference number entered in the Folio column of each account to which an amount is posted and which shows the page of the journal from which the amount was posted.

Ledger. A group of accounts used by a business in recording its transactions.

Mortgage payable. A debt, usually long term, that is secured by a special claim against one or more assets of the debtor.

Normal balance of an account. The usual kind of balance, either debit or credit, that a given account has and which is a debit balance if increases are recorded in the account as debits and a credit balance if increases are recorded as credits.

Posting. Transcribing the debit and credit amounts from a journal to the ledger accounts.

Posting reference numbers. Journal page numbers and ledger account numbers used as a cross-reference between amounts entered in a journal and posted to the ledger accounts.

Promissory note. An unconditional written promise to pay a definite sum of money on demand or at a fixed or determinable future date.

T-account. An abbreviated account form, two or more of which are used in illustrating the debits and credits required in recording a transaction.

Trial balance. A list of accounts having balances in the General Ledger, the debit or credit balance of each account, the total of the debit balances, and the total of the credit balances.

Withdrawals account. The account used to record the withdrawals from a business by its owner of cash or other assets intended for personal use.

Questions for class discussion

1. What is an account? What is a ledger?
2. What determines the number of accounts a business will use?
3. What are the meanings of the following words and terms: (*a*) debit, (*b*) to debit, (*c*) credit, and (*d*) to credit?
4. Does debit always mean increase and credit always mean decrease?
5. A transaction is to be entered in the accounts. How do you determine the accounts in which amounts are to be entered? How do you determine whether a particular account is to be debited or credited?
6. Why is a double-entry accounting system so called?
7. Give the rules of debit and credit for (*a*) asset accounts and (*b*) for liability and owner equity accounts.
8. Why are the rules of debit and credit the same for both liability and owner equity accounts?
9. List the steps in the preparation of a trial balance.
10. Why is a trial balance prepared?
11. Why is a trial balance considered to be only presumptive proof of recording accuracy? What types of errors are not revealed by a trial balance?
12. What determines whether the normal balance of an account is a debit or a credit balance?
13. Can transaction debits and credits be recorded directly in the ledger accounts? What is gained by first recording transactions in a journal and then posting to the accounts?
14. In recording transactions in a journal, which is written first, the debit or the credit? How far is the name of the account credited indented? How far is the explanation indented?
15. What is a compound entry?
16. Are dollar signs used in journal entries? In the accounts?
17. If decimal points are not used in journal entries to separate dollars from cents, what accomplishes this purpose?
18. Define or describe each of the following:
a. Journal.	*e.* Folio column.
b. Ledger.	*f.* Posting.
c. Book of original entry.	*g.* Posting reference numbers.
d. Book of final entry.	
19. Entering in the Folio column of the journal the account number to which an amount was posted is the last step in posting the amount. What is gained by making this the last step?

Exercise 2–1

Prepare the following columnar form. Then (1) indicate the treatment for increases and decreases by entering the words debited and credited in the proper columns. (2) Indicate the normal balance of each kind of account by entering the word debit or credit in the last column of the form.

Kind of Account	Increases	Decreases	Normal Balance
Asset	Dr	CR	Dr
Liability	CR	Dr	CR
Owner's capital	CR	Dr	CR
Owner's withdrawals	Dr	Cr	Dr
Revenue	CR	Dr	CR
Expense	Dr	CR	Dr

Exercise 2–2

Place the following T-accounts on a sheet of ordinary notebook paper: Cash; Accounts Receivable; Shop Supplies; Shop Equipment; Accounts Payable; Ted Moss, Capital; Revenue from Repairs; and Rent Expense. Then record the following transactions by entering debits and credits directly in the T-accounts. Use the transaction letters to identify the amounts in the accounts.

a. Ted Moss opened a TV repair shop, called Moss TV Service, by investing $800 in the business.
b. Paid the rent for one month on the shop space, $100.
c. Purchased shop supplies for cash, $50.
d. Purchased shop supplies, $75, and shop equipment, $200, on credit from Electronics, Inc.
e. Repaired the TV set of a customer and collected $40 cash for the service.
f. Paid Electronics, Inc., $200 of the amount owed it.
g. Repaired the TV set of Ned Brown on credit, $50.
h. Purchased additional shop equipment on credit from Electronics, Inc., $60.
i. Ned Brown paid for the repair work of transaction (g).

Exercise 2–3

After recording the transactions of Exercise 2–2, prepare a trial balance for Moss TV Service. Use the current date.

Exercise 2–4

A careless bookkeeper prepared the following trial balance for Quick Repair Service. It does not balance, and you have been asked to prepare a corrected trial balance. In examining the concern's journal and ledger you discover the following: (1) The debits to the Cash account total $7,625 and the credits total $5,125. (2) A $100 receipt from a customer in payment of his account was not posted to the Accounts Receivable account. (3) A $50 payment to a creditor was entered in the journal but was not posted to any account.

(4) The first two digits in the balance of the Revenue from Services account, as shown on the trial balance prepared by the bookkeeper, were transposed in copying the account balance from the ledger to the trial balance.

QUICK REPAIR SERVICE
Trial Balance, August 31, 19—

Cash.............................		$2,600
Accounts receivable........	$3,400	
Office supplies................		150
Office equipment	1,600	
Accounts payable	450	
Wages payable	100	
David Ross, capital.........	2,650	
Revenue from services		6,500
Rent expense	1,200	
Advertising expense........		50
Totals..................	$9,400	$9,300

Exercise 2–5

Prepare a form on notebook paper having the following three column headings: (1) Error, (2) Amount Out of Balance, and (3) Column Having Larger Total. Then for each of the following errors: (1) list the error by letter in the first column, (2) tell the amount it will cause the trial balance to be out of balance in the second column, and (3) tell in the third column which trial balance column will have the larger total as a result of the error. If an error does not affect the trial balance, write "none" in each of the last two columns.

a. A $25 debit to the Cash account was not posted.
b. A $50 debit to Store Supplies was debited to Store Equipment.
c. A $40 debit to Salaries Expense was debited to the account twice.
d. A $20 debit to Office Supplies was debited to Revenue from Sales.
e. A $45 credit to Accounts Payable was posted as a $54 credit.
f. A $10 debit to Office Supplies was posted as a $100 debit.

Problem 2–1

a. Dale Sims opened a television repair shop and began business by investing cash, $2,500; repair supplies, $450; office equipment, $250; tools, $300; and truck, $2,200. He called his business A-1 TV Service, and during a short period completed these additional transactions:
b. Paid $25 for an advertisement announcing the opening of the shop.
c. Paid the rent for two months in advance on the shop space, $250.
d. Purchased additional office equipment for cash, $175.
e. Purchased additional tools on credit, $150.
f. Traded the old truck and $1,800 in cash for a new truck.
g. Completed repair work for cash, $50.
h. Completed repair work on credit for Walter Rice, $75.
i. Completed repair work for Barry Nash, $125. Accepted $100 in cash and Barry Nash's promise that he would pay the balance in a few days.

j. Paid $100 of the amount owed for the tools purchased on credit in trans-
action (*e*).
k. Barry Nash paid the $25 he owed.
l. Paid the utility bills, $20.
m. Dale Sims withdrew $150 from the business to pay personal expenses.

Required:

1. Open the following T-accounts: Cash; Accounts Receivable; Repair
Supplies; Prepaid Rent; Office Equipment; Tools; Truck; Accounts Payable; Dale Sims, Capital; Dale Sims, Withdrawals; Revenue from Repairs; Advertising Expense; and Utilities Expense.
2. Record the transactions by entering debits and credits directly in the
T-accounts. Use the transaction letters to identify each debit and credit
amount.
3. Prepare a trial balance using the current date.

Problem 2-2

Jane Hall, CPA, completed these transactions during August of the current
year:

Aug. 1 Began a public accounting practice by investing $1,500 in cash and
office equipment having a $1,200 fair value.
 1 Purchased office supplies, $75, and office equipment, $250, from
Sierra Company on credit.
 1 Paid three months' rent in advance on suitable office space, $750.
 5 Completed accounting work for a client and collected $60 cash
therefor.
 11 Paid Sierra Company $125 of the amount owed for the items pur-
chased on August 1.
 12 Paid the premium on an insurance policy, $120.
 15 Completed accounting work for Nevada Company on credit, $350.
 20 Jane Hall withdrew $100 from the accounting practice for personal
expenses.
 23 Completed accounting work for Donner Company on credit, $200.
 25 Received $350 from Nevada Company for the work completed on
August 15.
 31 Paid the August utility bills, $35.

Required:

1. Open the following accounts: Cash; Accounts Receivable; Prepaid Rent;
Prepaid Insurance; Office Supplies; Office Equipment; Accounts Payable;
Jane Hall, Capital; Jane Hall, Withdrawals; Accounting Revenue; and
Utilities Expense. Number the accounts beginning with 1.
2. Prepare general journal entries to record the transactions, post to the ac-
counts, and prepare a trial balance. Head the trial balance Jane Hall, CPA.

Problem 2-3

Ted Darby began a real estate agency called Tahoe Realty, and during a
short period completed these transactions:

a. Began the business by investing $10,000.
b. Purchased a small office building and the office equipment of Apex Realty,

consisting of office equipment, $2,000; building, $18,000; and land, $10,000. Paid $8,000 in cash and signed a mortgage contract to pay the balance.

c. Took his personal automobile, which had a $2,500 fair value, for permanent and exclusive use in the business.

d. Earned and collected a $2,300 commission from the sale of a house.

e. Purchased office supplies, $75, and office equipment, $250, from Office Supply Company on credit.

f. Paid the salary of the office clerk, $300.

g. Completed property management services for Neal Able on credit, $60.

h. Paid Office Supply Company for the items purchased in transaction (e).

i. Received $60 from Neal Able for the services of transaction (g).

j. Purchased additional office supplies on credit, $65.

k. Earned and collected a $2,700 commission from the sale of property.

l. Paid the salary of the office clerk, $300.

m. Paid for newspaper advertising that had appeared, $85.

n. Paid the telephone bill, $25.

o. Ted Darby withdrew $250 from the business for personal expenses.

Required:

1. Open the following T-accounts: Cash; Accounts Receivable; Office Supplies; Office Equipment; Automobile; Land; Building; Accounts Payable; Mortgage Payable; Ted Darby, Capital; Ted Darby, Withdrawals; Commissions Earned; Management Fees Earned; Advertising Expense; Salaries Expense; and Telephone Expense.

2. Record the transactions by entering debits and credits directly in the T-accounts. Use the transaction letters to identify each debit and credit amount.

3. Prepare a trial balance, using the current date.

Problem 2–4

Ann Howe completed these transactions during October of the current year:

Oct. 2   Began the practice of law by investing the law library acquired during her college years. The library had a $600 fair value.

2   Sold 50 shares of AT&T stock, which she had inherited from her grandfather, for $2,400 and deposited $2,000 of the proceeds in a bank account opened in the name of the law practice, Ann Howe, Attorney.

3   Purchased office equipment, $1,500, paying $500 in cash and signing a promissory note payable for the balance.

4   Rented office space, paying $550, the first two months' rent in advance.

5   Paid the premiums on two insurance policies taken out in the name of the law practice, $125.

6   Purchased office supplies, $60, and office equipment, $220, from Office Supply Company on credit.

9   Completed legal work for a client and immediately collected $150 therefor.

12   Completed legal work for Guaranty Bank on credit, $300.

15   Paid the legal secretary's salary, $275.

Oct. 16   Paid Office Supply Company for the items purchased on October 6.
    22   Received $300 from Guaranty Bank for the work completed on the 12th.
    27   Ann Howe wrote a $270 check on the bank account of the law practice to pay the rent on the apartment she occupied.
    30   Completed additional legal work for Guaranty Bank on credit, $200.
    31   Paid $5 interest expense and a $100 installment on the note payable issued on October 3.
    31   Paid the legal secretary's salary, $275.
    31   Paid the October utilities, $40.

Required:

1. Open the following accounts, numbering them beginning with 1: Cash; Accounts Receivable; Prepaid Rent; Prepaid Insurance; Office Supplies; Office Equipment; Law Library; Notes Payable; Accounts Payable; Ann Howe, Capital; Ann Howe, Withdrawals; Legal Fees Earned; Salaries Expense; Utilities Expense; and Interest Expense.
2. Prepare general journal entries to record the transactions, post to the accounts, and prepare a trial balance.

Problem 2–5

Ann Evans graduated from college in June of the current year with a degree in architecture, and during July she completed these transactions:

July 1   Began an architectural practice by investing cash, $1,500.
    1   Rented the furnished office and equipment of an architect who was retiring due to illness, and paid the rent for two months in advance, $800.
    1   Paid the premium on a liability insurance policy giving one year's protection, $120.
    2   Purchased drafting supplies on credit, $30.
    8   Completed a set of plans for a contractor and immediately collected $250 for the job.
    15   Completed and delivered a set of plans to Tahoe Construction Company on credit, $450.
    17   Paid for the drafting supplies purchased on July 2.
    22   Completed architectural work for Lake Realty on credit, $150.
    25   Received $450 from Tahoe Construction Company for the plans delivered on July 15.
    27   Ann Evans withdrew $200 cash from the business to pay personal expenses.
    29   Purchased additional drafting supplies on credit, $45.
    31   Paid blueprinting expense incurred during the month, $75.
    31   Paid the July utility bills, $35.
    31   Recognized that one month's rent had expired and had become an expense. (Make a general journal entry to transfer the amount of the expense from the asset account to the Rent Expense account.)
    31   Recognized that one month's prepaid insurance had expired and had become an expense.
    31   Took an inventory of drafting supplies and determined that supplies costing $25 had been used and had become an expense.

Required:

1. Open the following accounts, numbering them beginning with 1: Cash; Accounts Receivable; Prepaid Rent; Prepaid Insurance; Drafting Supplies; Accounts Payable; Ann Evans, Capital; Ann Evans, Withdrawals; Architectural Fees Earned; Rent Expense; Blueprinting Expense; Utilities Expense; Insurance Expense; and Drafting Supplies Expense.
2. Prepare general journal entries to record the transactions, post to the accounts, and prepare a trial balance headed Ann Evans, Architect.
3. Analyze the trial balance and prepare a July 31 balance sheet and a July income statement for the architectural practice. (The $1,500 trial balance amount of capital for Ann Evans is her July 1 beginning-of-the-month capital. To determine the July 31 balance sheet amount of her capital, remember that the net income increased her equity in the business and her withdrawals decreased it.)

Alternate problems

Problem 2–1A

a. Dale Sims opened a heating and air conditioning service called Sims Air Conditioning Service. He began the business by investing these assets: cash, $1,000; office equipment, $350; tools, $500; and truck, $1,200; and during a short period completed these transactions:
b. Paid the rent for two months in advance on the shop space, $300.
c. Purchased repair supplies on credit, $150.
d. Traded a typewriter carried in the accounting records at $50 for additional tools.
e. Purchased for cash a new typewriter to replace the one traded, $260.
f. Paid for advertising announcing the opening of the shop, $35.
g. Completed repair work for a customer for cash, $60.
h. Completed repair work for George Thomas, $175. Accepted $100 in cash and a promise by Mr. Thomas that he would pay the balance within a short period.
i. Completed repair work for Walter Rice on credit, $85.
j. George Thomas paid the amount owed from transaction (h).
k. Paid $75 of the amount owed for the supplies purchased in transaction (c).
l. Paid the utility bills, $15.
m. Dale Sims withdrew $100 from the business to pay personal expenses.

Required:

1. Open the following T-accounts: Cash; Accounts Receivable; Repair Supplies; Prepaid Rent; Office Equipment; Tools; Truck; Accounts Payable; Dale Sims, Capital; Dale Sims, Withdrawals; Revenue from Repairs; Advertising Expense; and Utilities Expense.
2. Record the transactions by entering debits and credits directly in the accounts. Use the transaction letters to identify each debit and credit amount.
3. Prepare a trial balance using the current date.

Problem 2-2A

Jane Hall received her CPA certificate, and during July of the current year completed these transactions:

July 1 Began a public accounting practice by transferring $2,000 from her savings account to a checking account opened in the name of the practice.
      1 Paid three months' office rent in advance, $675.
      2 Purchased office supplies, $50, and office equipment, $1,200, from Office Outfitters on credit.
      4 Paid the premiums on two insurance policies, $110.
      7 Completed accounting work for a client and immediately collected $75 therefor.
     12 Paid Office Outfitters $1,000 of the amount owed for the items purchased on July 2.
     13 Completed accounting work for Bond Company on credit, $300.
     15 Purchased additional office supplies on credit, $25.
     21 Completed accounting work for Kent Company on credit, $250.
     23 Received $300 from Bond Company for the work completed on July 13.
     26 Jane Hall wrote a check on the bank account of the accounting practice to pay the rent on the apartment in which she lived, $275.
     31 Paid the July utility bills of the accounting office, $30.

Required:

1. Open the following accounts, numbering them beginning with 1: Cash; Accounts Receivable; Prepaid Rent; Prepaid Insurance; Office Supplies; Office Equipment; Accounts Payable; Jane Hall, Capital; Jane Hall, Withdrawals; Accounting Revenue; and Utilities Expense.
2. Prepare general journal entries to record the transactions, post to the accounts, and prepare a trial balance. Head the trial balance Jane Hall, CPA.

Problem 2-3A

Ted Darby owns and operates Darby Real Estate Agency, and on August 1 of the current year a trial balance of the agency's ledger appeared as follows:

DARBY REAL ESTATE AGENCY
Trial Balance, August 1, 19—

Cash	$ 1,190	
Office supplies	145	
Office equipment	2,465	
Automobile.............	2,700	
Land	10,000	
Building	22,000	
Mortgage payable.....		$20,000
Ted Darby, capital....		18,500
Totals............	$38,500	$38,500

The real estate agency completed these transactions during August:

a. Purchased office supplies, $50, and office equipment, $150, on credit.
b. Sold a house and collected a $2,250 commission from the sale.
c. Paid for the items purchased on credit in transaction (*a*).
d. Paid for advertising that had appeared in the local paper, $75.
e. Purchased a typewriter from Office Supply Company on credit, $325.
f. Mr. Darby took the old agency typewriter, carried in the accounting records at $75, home for permanent use of his high school daughter as a practice typewriter.
g. Sold a house and collected a $2,950 commission on the sale.
h. Completed property management services for Albert Pick on credit, $100.
i. Ted Darby withdrew $500 from the business to pay personal expenses.
j. Received $100 from Albert Pick for the services of transaction (*h*).
k. Paid the salary of the office clerk, $550.
l. Gave $3,000 in cash and the old agency car for a new agency car.
m. Paid for advertising that had appeared in the local paper, $50.
n. Paid the August telephone bill, $35.

Required:

1. Open the following T-accounts: Cash; Accounts Receivable; Office Supplies; Office Equipment; Automobile; Land; Building; Accounts Payable; Mortgage Payable; Ted Darby, Capital; Ted Darby, Withdrawals; Commissions Earned; Management Fees Earned; Advertising Expense; Salaries Expense; and Telephone Expense.
2. Enter the August 1 trial balance amounts in the accounts, identifying each amount by writing "Bal." before it.
3. Record the transactions by entering debits and credits directly in the T-accounts. Use the transaction letters to identify the amounts in the accounts.
4. Prepare an August 31 trial balance of the accounts.

Problem 2–4A

Ann Howe finished law school, and during August of the current year completed these transactions:

Aug. 1 Began a law practice by investing $1,800 in cash and a law library having a $700 fair value.
1 Paid two months' rent in advance on suitable office space, $450.
2 Purchased office equipment, $1,350, paying $350 in cash and signing a promissory note payable for the balance.
3 Purchased office supplies, $65, and office equipment, $210, from Office Outfitters on credit.
5 Completed legal work for a client and immediately collected $75 in cash therefor.
8 Paid the premiums on two insurance policies, $135.
14 Completed legal work for Coast Realty on credit, $400.
15 Paid the salary of the legal secretary, $300.
18 Paid Office Outfitters $100 of the amount owed on the items purchased on August 3.

Aug. 24   Received $400 from Coast Realty for the work completed on August 14.

     28   Ann Howe withdrew $300 from the practice to pay personal expenses.

     30   Completed legal work for Security Bank on credit, $250.

     31   Paid the legal secretary's salary, $300.

     31   Paid the August utility bills, $45.

     31   Paid $5 interest expense and a $200 installment on the note payable.

Required:

1. Open the following accounts, numbering them beginning with 1: Cash; Accounts Receivable; Prepaid Rent; Prepaid Insurance; Office Supplies; Office Equipment; Law Library; Notes Payable; Accounts Payable; Ann Howe, Capital; Ann Howe, Withdrawals; Legal Fees Earned; Salaries Expense; Utilities Expense; and Interest Expense.
2. Prepare general journal entries to record the transactions, post to the accounts, and prepare a trial balance, heading it Ann Howe, Attorney.

Decision problem 2–1, Flawless Janitorial Service

Fred Marsh began Flawless Janitorial Service by depositing $1,000 in a bank account opened in the name of the business. From the investment, he made a $500 down payment on a secondhand truck priced at $1,200 and signed a noninterest-bearing note payable for the balance. He also spent $200 for cleaning supplies and paid $75 for newspaper advertising through which he gained a number of customers for his services.

On December 31, 19—, after six months in business, his records showed he had collected $5,150 in cash for services rendered and that customers owed him an additional $200 for services. He had purchased more supplies for cash, $250, which brought the total supplies purchased during the six months to $450; however, supplies that had cost $125 were on hand unused at the period end. He had paid $150 in cash for gas and oil used in the truck, and carbon copies of credit card tickets showed he owed an additional $25 for gas and oil used during the six months. Through cash payments he had reduced the balance owed on the note payable signed at the time the truck was purchased to $400; but through use the truck had worn out and depreciated an amount equal to one fourth of its cost.

Under the assumption the business had a total of $475 of cash on hand and in the bank at the period end, determine the amount of cash Fred had withdrawn from the business. Prepare an income statement for the business showing the net income earned during the six months and a balance sheet as of the period end. (T-accounts should prove helpful in organizing the data.)

Decision problem 2–2, Larry's Lawn Service

Upon graduation from high school last summer, Larry Scott needed a job to earn a portion of his first-year college expenses. He was unable to find anything satisfactory and he decided to go into the lawn care business. He had $250 in his savings account which he used to buy a lawn mower and other lawn care tools; but to haul the tools from job to job, he needed a truck. Consequently, he borrowed $400 from a bank, agreeing to pay $1\frac{1}{4}\%$ interest per month, and used the entire amount to buy a secondhand pickup.

From the beginning he had as much work as he could do, and after two months he repaid the bank loan plus two months' interest; and on September 4 he ended the business after exactly three months' operations. Throughout the summer he had followed the practice of depositing all cash received from customers in the bank, and an examination of his checkbook record showed he had deposited $2,100. In addition he had written checks to pay $40 for repairs to the pickup; $110 for gas, oil, and lubricants used in the truck and mower; and $20 for mower repairs. A notebook in the truck contained copies of credit card tickets that showed he owed $45 for gas and oil and that customers owed him $150 for lawn care services. He estimated that his lawn care equipment had worn out and depreciated an amount equal to one half its cost and the truck had worn out and depreciated an amount equal to one fourth its cost.

Under the assumption that Larry had withdrawn $450 from the business during the summer for spending money and to buy clothes, prepare an income statement showing the results of the summer's operations of the business and a September 4 balance sheet. (T-accounts should prove helpful in organizing the data.)

Decision problem 2–3, Brite Glass Service

Ray Brite lost his job and had no luck finding another. Consequently, he decided to begin a window cleaning service, and on June 1 he took the last $500 of his savings and deposited it in a checking account opened in the name of the business, Brite Glass Service. The same day he signed a one-year promissory note payable having an 8% annual interest rate in order to borrow $3,000 from his brother, and he used the $3,000 to buy a truck needed in carrying on the business. He then ran a series of ads in the local paper; purchased soap, sponges, and other supplies; and went to work.

He did not keep formal accounting records, but business was good from the beginning; and after six months he tried to prepare a set of financial statements to see where the business stood. Following are the results of his efforts:

BRITE GLASS SERVICE

Income Statement for Six Months Ended December 31, 19—

Revenue from cleaning windows		$5,900
Operating expenses:		
Advertising expense	$ 80	
Supplies expense	300	
Gas and oil expense	225	
Salary expense	4,800	
Total operating expenses		5,405
Net Income		$ 495

BRITE GLASS SERVICE
Balance Sheet, December 31, 19—

Assets		*Liabilities*	
Cash......................	$ 995	Note payable	$3,000
Truck	3,000	*Owner Equity*	
		Ray Brite, capital.........	500
Total Assets	$3,995	Total Equities	$3,500

Since the balance sheet did not balance, and he knew it must, he has asked your help. You learn that he has deposited all receipts from his cleaning service in the bank, paid all bills by check, and owes no one other than his brother. By examining his checkbook stubs you learn that he has taken in $5,900 in cash for services rendered and paid out $80 for advertising, $225 for gas and oil used in the truck, and $300 for supplies of which one sixth are on hand and unused. You also learn that the $4,800 of salary expense represents six monthly withdrawals of $800 each which Ray has paid to himself. Also, customers owe the business $275 for work done on credit, and you note that although the truck has depreciated through use, this is not recognized in the statements. Likewise, Ray has not recognized that the business has used his brother's $3,000 for a half of a year and therefore owes six months' interest on the note. After discussing the matter, you and Ray agree that $300 represents a fair amount of expense for six months' wear and tear on the truck.

Prepare a new income statement and balance sheet for the business that reflect the foregoing information.

After studying Chapter 3, you should be able to:

- Explain why the life of a business is divided into accounting periods of equal length and why the accounts of a business must be adjusted at the end of each accounting period.

- Prepare adjusting entries for prepaid expenses, accrued expenses, unearned revenues, accrued revenues, and depreciation.

- Prepare entries to dispose of accrued revenue and expense items in the new accounting period.

- Define each asset and liability classification appearing on a balance sheet, classify balance sheet items, and prepare a classified balance sheet.

- Explain the difference between the cash and accrual bases of accounting.

- Explain the importance of comparability in the financial statements of a business, period after period; and tell how the realization principle and the matching principle contribute to comparability.

- Define or explain the words and phrases listed in the chapter Glossary.

chapter 3

Adjusting the accounts and preparing the statements

The life of a business often spans many years, and its activities go on without interruption over the years. However, taxes based on annual income must be paid governmental units, and the owners and managers of a business must have periodic reports on its financial progress. Consequently, a *time period concept* of the life of a business is required in accounting for its activities; and this concept results in a division of the life of a business into time periods of equal length, called *accounting periods*. Accounting periods may be a month, three months, or a year in length; but *annual accounting periods,* periods one year in length, are the norm.

In the accounting process, an accounting period is an interval over which the transactions of a business are recorded, and at the end of which the recorded data are used in preparing its financial statements. The recording of transactions was discussed in the previous chapter. This chapter deals with end-of-the-period procedures that are necessary before the statements are prepared.

As a rule, at the end of an accounting period, after all transactions are recorded, several of the accounts in a concern's ledger do not show proper end-of-the-period balances for preparing the statements, even though all transactions were correctly recorded. The balances are incorrect for statement purposes, not through error but because of the expiration of costs brought about by the passage of time. For example, the second item on the trial balance of Owen's law practice, as prepared in Chapter 2 and reproduced again as Illustration 3–1, is "Prepaid rent, $600." This $600 represents the rent for three months paid in advance on July 1; but by July 31, $600 is not the balance sheet amount for this asset because one month's rent, or $200, has expired and become an expense and only $400 remains as an asset.

Need for adjustments before statements are prepared

Likewise, a portion of the office supplies as represented by the $60 debit balance in the Office Supplies account has been used, and the office equipment has begun to wear out and depreciate. Obviously, then, the end-of-the-period balances of the Prepaid Rent, Office Supplies, and Office Equipment accounts as they appear on the trial balance simply do not reflect the proper amounts for preparing the July 31 statements. The balance of each and also the balances of the Office Salaries Expense and Legal Fees Earned accounts must be *adjusted* before they will show proper amounts for the July 31 statements.

Larry Owen Attorney
Trial Balance, July 31, 19—

Cash	$1,135	
Prepaid rent.............................	600	
Office supplies	60	
Office equipment......................	1,500	
Accounts payable.....................		$ 260
Unearned legal fees.................		150
Larry Owen, capital		2,500
Larry Owen, withdrawals...........	200	
Legal fees earned.....................		1,150
Office salaries expense	500	
Telephone expense	30	
Heating and lighting expense	35	
Totals............................	$4,060	$4,060

Illustration 3–1

Adjusting the accounts

Prepaid expenses

As the name implies, a prepaid expense is an expense that has been paid for in advance of its use. At the time of payment an asset is acquired that will be used or consumed, and as it is used or consumed, it becomes an expense. For example:

On July 1 the Owen law practice paid three months' rent in advance and thus obtained the right to occupy a rented office for the following three months. On July 1 this right was an asset valued at its $600 cost; but day by day the agency occupied the office; and each day a portion of the prepaid rent expired and became an expense. On July 31 one month's rent, valued at one third of $600, or $200 had expired. Consequently, if the agency's July 31 accounts are to reflect proper asset and expense amounts, the following adjusting entry is required:

incurred expense

July	31	Rent Expense..	200.00	
		Prepaid Rent		200.00
		To record the expired rent.		

Posting the adjusting entry has the following effect on the accounts:

Prepaid Rent				Rent Expense	
July 1	600	July 31	200	July 31	200

After the entry is posted, the Prepaid Rent account with a $400 balance and the Rent Expense account with a $200 balance show proper statement amounts.

To continue, early in July, the Owen law practice purchased some office supplies and placed them in the office for use; and each day the secretary used a portion. The amount used or consumed each day was an expense that daily reduced the supplies on hand. However, the daily reductions were not recognized in the accounts because day-by-day information as to amounts used and remaining was not needed and because bookkeeping labor could be saved if only a single amount, the total of all supplies used during the month, was recorded.

Consequently, if on July 31 the accounts are to reflect proper statement amounts, it is necessary to record the office supplies used during the month. However, to do this, it is first necessary to learn the amount used; and to learn the amount used, it is necessary to count or inventory the unused supplies remaining and to deduct the cost of the supplies remaining from the cost of the supplies purchased. If, for example, $45 of unused supplies remain on hand in the office, then $15 ($60 − $45 = $15) of supplies have been used and have become an expense, and the following entry is required to record this:

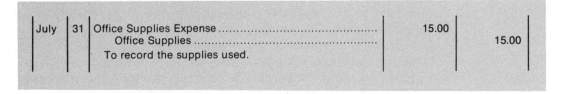

July	31	Office Supplies Expense..	15.00	
		Office Supplies		15.00
		To record the supplies used.		

The effect of the adjusting entry on the accounts is:

Office Supplies				Office Supplies Expense	
July 5	60	July 31	15	July 31	15,

Often, unlike in the two previous examples, items that are prepaid expenses at the time of purchase are both bought and fully consumed within a single accounting period. For example, a company pays its rent in advance on the first day of each month. Each month the amount paid results in a prepaid expense that is entirely consumed before the month's end and before the end of the accounting period. In such cases, it is best to ignore the fact that an asset results from each prepayment, because bookkeeping labor, an end-of-the-accounting-period adjustment, can be saved if each amount paid is recorded as an expense at the time of payment.

Other prepaid expenses that are handled in the same manner as prepaid rent and office supplies are prepaid insurance, store supplies, and factory supplies.

Depreciation

When a business buys a building or an item of equipment, it in effect buys a "quantity of usefulness"; and day by day as the asset is used in carrying on the business operations, a portion of this "quantity of usefulness" is consumed or expires. In accounting, this expiration of a plant asset's "quantity of usefulness" is known as *depreciation*. Depreciation is an expense just like the expiration of prepaid rent is an expense. For example, if a company purchases a machine for $4,500 that it expects to use for four years, after which it expects to receive $500 for the machine in the form of a trade-in allowance on a new machine, the company has purchased a $4,000 quantity of usefulness ($4,500 − $500 = $4,000). Furthermore, this quantity of usefulness expires or the machine depreciates on a straight-line basis at the rate of $1,000 per year [($4,500 − $500) ÷ 4 years = $1,000]. Actually, when depreciation is compared to the expiration of a prepaid expense like rent or insurance, the primary difference is that since it is often impossible to predict exactly how long a plant asset will be used or how much will be received for it at the end of its useful life, the amount it depreciates each accounting period is only an estimate.

Estimating and apportioning depreciation can be simple, as in the foregoing example, or it can become complex. A discussion of more complex situations is unnecessary at this point and is deferred to Chapter 10. However, to illustrate the recording of depreciation, assume that —

On July 31 the Owen law practice estimated its office equipment had depreciated $20 during the month. The depreciation reduced the assets and increased the expenses of the law practice, and to record it the following adjusting entry is required:

July	31	Depreciation Expense, Office Equipment......................	20.00	
		Accumulated Depreciation, Office Equipment		20.00
		To record the July depreciation.		

The effect of the entry on the accounts is:

Office Equipment		Depreciation Expense, Office Equipment	
July 3	1,200	July 31	20
5	300		

Accumulated Depreciation, Office Equipment	
July 31	20

After the entry is posted, the Office Equipment account and its related Accumulated Depreciation, Office Equipment account together show the July 31 balance sheet amounts for this asset; and the Depreciation Expense, Office Equipment account shows the amount of depreciation expense that should appear on the July income statement.

In most cases a decrease in an asset is recorded with a credit to the account in which the asset is recorded. However, note in the accounts that this procedure is not followed in recording depreciation. Rather, depreciation is recorded in a *contra account* such as the Accumulated Depreciation, Office Equipment account. (A contra account is an account the balance of which is subtracted from the balance of an associate account to show a more proper amount for the item recorded in the associated account.)

There are two good reasons for using contra accounts in recording depreciation. First, although based on objective evidence whenever possible, at its best depreciation is only an estimate; and, second, the use of contra accounts better preserves the facts in the lives of plant assets. For example, in this case the asset account, Office Equipment, preserves in the accounts a record of the equipment's cost, and the Accumulated Depreciation, Office Equipment account shows its accumulated depreciation to date.

A better understanding of the latter point, along with an appreciation of why the word "accumulated" is used in the account name, can be gained when it is pointed out that depreciation is recorded at the end of each accounting period in a plant asset's life. As a result, at the end of the third month in the life of the law practice's office equipment, the Office Equipment and its related accumulated depreciation account will look like this:

Office Equipment		Accumulated Depreciation, Office Equipment	
July 3	1,200	July 31	20
5	300	Aug. 31	20
		Sept. 30	20

And the equipment's cost and three months' accumulated depreciation will be shown on its September 30 balance sheet thus:

Office equipment............................ $1,500
　Less accumulated depreciation ....　　60　　$1,440

Accumulated depreciation accounts are sometimes found in ledgers and on statements under titles such as "Allowance for Depreciation, Store Equipment" or the totally unacceptable caption, "Reserve for Depreciation, Office Equipment." However, more appropriate terminology is "Accumulated Depreciation, Store Equipment" and "Accumulated Depreciation, Office Equipment." The "Accumulated" terminology is better because it is more descriptive of the depreciation procedure.

Accrued expenses

Most expenses are recorded during an accounting period at the time they are paid. However, when a period ends there may be a few expenses that have been incurred but have not been paid and recorded because payment is not yet due. These unpaid and unrecorded expenses for which payment is not due are called *accrued expenses*. Earned but unpaid salaries and wages are a common example. To illustrate:

The Owen law practice has a part-time secretary who is paid $25 per day or $125 per week for a week that begins on Monday and ends on Friday. Her wages are due and payable every two weeks on Friday; and during July they were paid on the 12th and 26th and recorded as follows:

Cash			Office Salaries Expense		
July 12	250		July 12	250	
26	250		26	250	

If the calendar for July appears as illustrated and the secretary worked on Monday, Tuesday, and Wednesday, July 29, 30, 31, then at the close of business on Wednesday, July 31, she has earned three days' wages that are not paid and recorded because payment is not due. However, this $75 of earned but unpaid wages is just as much a part of the July expenses as the $500 of wages that have been paid. Furthermore, on July 31, the unpaid wages are a liability. Consequently, if the accounts are to show

JULY						
S	M	T	W	T	F	S
		1	2	3	4	5	6
7	8	9	10	11	12	13
14	15	16	17	18	19	20
21	22	23	24	25	26	27
28	29	30	31			

the correct amount of secretary's wages for July and all liabilities owed on July 31, then an adjusting entry like the following must be made:

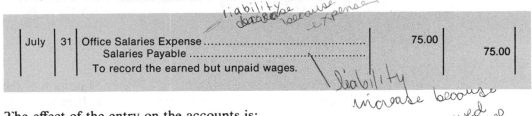

July	31	Office Salaries Expense...	75.00	
		Salaries Payable		75.00
		To record the earned but unpaid wages.		

The effect of the entry on the accounts is:

Office Salaries Expense			Salaries Payable	
July 12	250		July 31	75
26	250			
31	75			

Unearned revenues

An unearned revenue results when payment is received for goods or services in advance of their delivery. For instance, on July 15 Larry Owen entered into an agreement with Coast Realty to do its legal work on a fixed-fee basis for $100 per month, and on that date received $150 in advance for services during the remainder of July and the month of August. The fee was recorded with this entry:

July	15	Cash...... *Accounts Recievable*	150.00	
		Unearned Legal Fees..		150.00
		Received a legal fee in advance.		

Acceptance of the fee in advance increased the cash of the law practice and created for it a liability, the obligation to do Coast Realty's legal work for the next month and a half. However, by July 31 the law practice has discharged $50 of the liability and earned that much income, which according to the *recognition principle* should appear on the July income statement. Consequently on July 31 the following entry is required:

July	31	Unearned Legal Fees..	50.00	
		Legal Fees Earned		50.00
		To record legal fees earned.		

Posting the entry has this effect on the accounts:

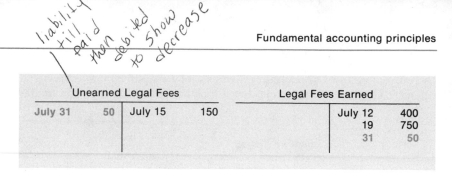

Unearned Legal Fees					Legal Fees Earned	
July 31	50	July 15	150		July 12	400
					19	750
					31	50

The effect of the entry is to transfer the $50 earned portion of the fee from the liability account to the revenue account. It reduces the liability and records as a revenue the $50 that has been earned.

Accrued revenues

An accrued revenue is a revenue that has been earned but has not been collected because payment is not due. For example, assume that on July 15, in addition to the contract with Coast Realty, Larry Owen also entered into an agreement with Guaranty Bank to do its legal work on a fixed-fee basis for $150 per month to be paid monthly. Under this assumption, by July 31 the law practice has earned half of a month's fee, $75, which according to the *realization principle* should appear on its July income statement. Therefore the following entry is required:

July	31	Accounts Receivable	75.00	
		Legal Fees Earned		75.00
		To record legal fees earned.		

Posting the entry has this effect on the accounts:

Accounts Receivable					Legal Fees Earned	
July 19	750	July 29	750		July 12	400
31	75				19	750
					31	50
					31	75

The adjusted trial balance

A trial balance prepared before adjustments is known as an *unadjusted trial balance,* or simply a trial balance. One prepared after adjustments is known as an *adjusted trial balance;* and a July 31 adjusted trial balance for the law practice appears in Illustration 3–2.

Preparing statements from the adjusted trial balance

An adjusted trial balance shows proper balance sheet and income statement amounts; and, consequently, may be used in preparing the statements. When it is so used, the revenue and expense items are arranged into an income statement as an Illustration 3–3 on page 78 and the asset, liability, and owner equity items are arranged into a balance sheet as in Illustration 3–4 on page 79.

Larry Owen, Attorney
Adjusted Trial Balance, July 31, 19—

Cash	$1,135	
Accounts receivable	75	
Prepaid rent	400	
Office supplies	45	
Office equipment	1,500	
Accumulated depreciation, office equipment		$ 20
Accounts payable		260
Salaries payable		75
Unearned legal fees		100
Larry Owen, capital		2,500
Larry Owen, withdrawals	200	
Legal fees earned		1,275
Office salaries expense	575	
Telephone expense	30	
Heating and lighting expense	35	
Rent expense	200	
Office supplies expense	15	
Depreciation expense, office equipment	20	
Totals	$4,230	$4,230

Illustration 3–2

When the statements are prepared from an adjusted trial balance, the income statement is normally prepared first because the net income, as calculated on the income statement, is needed in completing the balance sheet's owner equity section. Observe in Illustration 3–4 how the net income from the income statement is combined with the withdrawals, and the excess of income over withdrawals, $200, is added to Owen's July 1 capital to show the amount of his July 31 equity. The income increased Owen's equity, and the withdrawals reduced it. Consequently, when the excess of the income over the withdrawals is added to the beginning equity, the result is the ending equity.

The adjustment process

The adjustment process described in this chapter arises from recognition that the operation of a business results in a continuous stream of transactions, some of which affect several accounting periods. And, the objective of the adjustment process is to allocate to each accounting period that portion of a transaction's effects applicable to the period. For example, if a revenue like a legal fee is earned over several accounting periods, the adjustment process apportions and credits to each period its fair share. Likewise, if an expense payment like that for rent or insurance benefits several periods, the adjustment process charges a fair share to each benefited period.

The adjustment process is based on two accounting principles, the *recognition principle* and the *matching principle*. The *recognition principle* requires that revenue be assigned to the accounting period in which it is earned, rather than to the period it is collected in cash; and the *matching principle* requires that revenues and expenses be matched. As for matching revenues and expenses, it is recognized

Larry Owen, Attorney
Adjusted Trial Balance, July 31, 19—

Cash	$1,135	
Accounts receivable	75	
Prepaid rent	400	
Office supplies	45	
Office equipment	1,500	
Accumulated depreciation, office equipment		$ 20
Accounts payable		260
Salaries payable		75
Unearned legal fees		100
Larry Owen, capital		2,500
Larry Owen, withdrawals	200	
Legal fees earned		1,275
Office salaries expense	575	
Telephone expense	30	
Heating and lighting expense	35	
Rent expense	200	
Office supplies expense	15	
Depreciation expense, office equipment	20	
Totals	$4,230	$4,230

PREPARING THE INCOME STATEMENT FROM THE ADJUSTED TRIAL BALANCE

Larry Owen, Attorney
Income Statement for Month Ended July 31, 19—

Revenue:		
Legal fees earned		$1,275
Operating expenses:		
Office salaries expense	$575	
Telephone expense	30	
Heating and lighting expense	35	
Rent expense	200	
Office supplies expense	15	
Depreciation expense, office equipment	20	
Total operating expense		875
Net Income		$ 400

Illustration 3-3

PREPARING THE BALANCE SHEET
FROM THE ADJUSTED TRIAL BALANCE

Larry Owen, Attorney
Adjusted Trial Balance, July 31, 19—

Cash	$1,135	
Accounts receivable	75	
Prepaid rent	400	
Office supplies	45	
Office equipment	1,500	
Accumulated depreciation, office equipment		$ 20
Accounts payable		260
Salaries payable		75
Unearned legal fees		100
Larry Owen, capital		2,500
Larry Owen, withdrawals	200	
Legal fees earned		1,275
Office salaries expense	575	
Telephone expense	30	
Heating and lighting expense	35	
Rent expense	200	
Office supplies expense	15	
Depreciation expense, office equipment	20	
Totals	$4,230	$4,230

Larry Owen, Attorney
Balance Sheet, July 31, 19—

Assets

Current Assets:			
Cash		$1,135	
Accounts receivable		75	
Prepaid rent		400	
Office supplies		45	
Total Current Assets			$1,655
Plant and Equipment:			
Office equipment		$1,500	
Less accumulated depreciation		20	
Total Plant and Equipment			1,480
Total Assets			$3,135

Liabilities

Current Liabilities:			
Accounts payable		$ 260	
Salaries payable		75	
Unearned legal fees		100	
Total Liabilities			$ 435

Owner Equity

Larry Owen, capital, July 1, 19—			$2,500
July net income	$400		
Less withdrawals	200		
Excess of income over withdrawals			200
Larry Owen, capital, July 31, 19—			2,700
Total Liabilities and Owner Equity			$3,135

July net income
from the July
income statement

Illustration 3–4

that a business incurs expenses in order to earn revenues; consequently, it is only proper that expenses be matched with (deducted on the income statement from) the revenues they helped to produce.

The basic purpose behind the adjustment process, the *recognition principle,* and the *matching principle* is to make the information on accounting statements comparable from period to period. For example, the Owen law practice paid its rent for three months in advance on July 1 and debited the $600 payment to Prepaid Rent. Then at the end of July it transferred $200 of this amount to its Rent Expense account and the $200 appeared on its July income statement as the July rent expense. At the end of August it will transfer another $200 to rent expense, and at the end of September it will transfer the third $200, with the result that the amounts shown for rent expense on its July, August, and September income statements will be comparable month by month.

An unsatisfactory alternate procedure would be to debit the entire $600 to Rent Expense at the time of payment and permit the entire amount to appear on the July income statement as rent expense for July. However, if this were done, the July income statement would show $600 of rent expense and the August and September statements would show none, and the income statements of the three months would not be comparable. In addition the July net income would be understated $400 and the net incomes of August and September would be overstated $200 each, and a person seeing only the fluctuations in net income might draw an incorrect conclusion.

Arrangement of the accounts in the ledger

Normally the accounts of a business are classified and logically arranged in its ledger. This serves two purposes: (1) it aids in locating any account and (2) it aids in preparing the statements. Obviously, statements can be prepared with the least difficulty if accounts are arranged in the ledger in the order of their statement appearance. This arrangement causes the accounts to appear on the adjusted trial balance in their statement order, which in turn aids in rearranging the adjusted trial balance items into a balance sheet and an income statement. Consequently, the balance sheet accounts beginning with Cash and ending with the owner equity accounts appear first in the ledger. These are followed by the revenue and expense accounts in order of their income statement appearance.

Disposing of accrued items

Accrued expenses

Several pages back the July 29, 30, and 31 accrued wages of the secretary were recorded as follows:

July	31	Office Salaries Expense	75.00	
		Salaries Payable		75.00
		To record the earned but unpaid wages.		

When these wages are paid on Friday, August 9, the following entry is required:

Aug.	9	Salaries Payable	75.00	
		Office Salaries Expense	175.00	
		Cash		250.00
		Paid two weeks' wages.		

The first debit in the second entry cancels the liability for the three days' wages accrued on July 31, and the second debit records the wages of August's first seven working days as an expense of the August accounting period. The credit records the amount paid the secretary.

Accrued revenues

On July 15 Larry Owen entered into an agreement to do the legal work of Guaranty Bank on a fixed-fee basis for $150 per month, and on July 31 the following entry was made to record one-half month's revenue earned under this contract:

July	31	Accounts Receivable	75.00	
		Legal Fees Earned		75.00
		To record legal fees earned.		

And when payment of the first month's fee is received on August 15, the following entry will be made:

Aug.	15	Cash	150.00	
		Accounts Receivable		75.00
		Legal Fees Earned		75.00
		Received legal fees earned.		

The first credit in the August 15 entry records the collection of the fee accrued at the end of July, and the second credit records as revenue the fee earned during the first half of August.

Cash and accrual bases of accounting

For income tax purposes an individual or a business in which inventories are not a factor may report income on either a cash basis or an accrual basis. Under the cash basis no adjustments are made for prepaid, unearned, and accrued items. Revenues are reported as being earned in the accounting period in which they are received in cash; expenses are deducted from revenues in the accounting period in which cash is disbursed in their payment; and as a result, net income is the difference between revenue receipts and expense disbursements.

Under the accrual basis, on the other hand, adjustments are made for accrued and deferred (prepaid and unearned) items. Under this basis revenues are credited to the period in which earned, expenses are matched with revenues, and no consideration is given to when cash is received and disbursed, with the result that net income is the difference between revenues earned and the expenses incurred in earning the revenues.

Needless to say, although the cash basis of accounting is satisfactory for individuals and small concerns in which accrued and deferred items are not important, it is not satisfactory for most concerns since it results in accounting reports that are not comparable from period to period. Consequently, most businesses keep their records on an accrual basis.

Classification of balance sheet items

The balance sheets in the first two chapters were simple ones with few items, and no attempt was made to classify the items. However, a balance sheet with a number of items becomes more useful when its assets and liabilities are classified into significant groups, because a reader of a *classified balance sheet* can better judge the adequacy of the different kinds of assets used in the business. He can also better estimate the probable availability of funds to meet the various liabilities as they become due.

Accountants are not in full agreement as to the best way in which to classify balance sheet items. As a result they are classified in several ways; but a common way classifies assets into (1) current assets, (2) long-term investments, (3) plant and equipment, and (4) intangible assets. It classifies liabilities into (1) current liabilities and (2) long-term liabilities.

Of the four asset classifications listed, only two, current assets and plant and equipment, appear on the balance sheet of Valley Store, Illustration 3–5 on the next page, because the store is small and has no long-term investments and intangible assets.

Current assets

The assets listed on a balance sheet under the current asset caption are primarily those to which current creditors (current liabilities) may look for payment. As presently defined, current assets consist of cash and assets that are reasonably expected to be realized in cash or be sold or consumed within one year or within one operating cycle of the business, whichever is longer. The accounts and notes receivable of Illustration 3–5 are expected to be realized in cash, the merchandise (merchandise inventory) is expected to be sold either for cash or accounts receivable that will be realized in cash, and the prepaid insurance and supplies are to be consumed.

The operating cycle of a business is the average period of time between its acquisition of merchandise or raw materials and the

Valley Store
Balance Sheet, December 31, 1978

Assets

Current Assets:

Cash	$ 1,050	
Notes receivable	300	
Accounts receivable	3,961	
Merchandise inventory	10,248	
Prepaid insurance	109	
Office supplies	46	
Stores supplies	145	
Total Current Assets		$15,859

Plant and Equipment:

Office equipment	$ 1,500		
Less accumulated depreciation	300	$ 1,200	
Store equipment	$ 3,200		
Less accumulated depreciation	800	2,400	
Buildings	$25,000		
Less accumulated depreciation	7,400	17,600	
Land		4,200	
Total Plant and Equipment			25,400
Total Assets			$41,259

Liabilities

Current Liabilities:

Notes payable	$ 3,000	
Accounts payable	2,715	
Wages payable	112	
Total Current Liabilities	$ 5,827	

Long-Term Liabilities:

First mortgage payable, secured by a mortgage on land and buildings	10,000	
Total Liabilities		$15,827

Owner Equity

Samuel Jackson, capital, January 1, 1978	$23,721	
Net income for the year	$ 7,711	
Less withdrawals	6,000	
Excess of income over withdrawals	1,711	
Samuel Jackson, capital, December 31, 1978		25,432
Total Liabilities and Owner Equity		$41,259

Illustration 3–5

realization of cash from the sale of the merchandise or the sale of the products manufactured from the raw materials. In many concerns this interval is less than one year, and as a result these concerns use a one-year period in classifying current assets. However, due to an aging process or other cause, some concerns have an operating cycle longer than one year, for example, distilleries must age some products for several years before the products are ready for sale. Consequently, in such concerns inventories of raw materials, manufacturing supplies, and products being processed for sale are classified as current assets, although the products made from the inventories will not be ready for sale for more than a year.

Such things as prepaid insurance, office supplies, and store supplies are called prepaid expenses. They were purchased for use in the business and will be consumed within a relatively short period of time, and when consumed become expenses; but until consumed they are classified as current assets. The American Institute of Certified Public Accountants through one of its committees said: "Prepaid expenses are not current assets in the sense that they will be converted into cash but in the sense that, if not paid in advance, they would require the use of current assets during the operating cycle."[1] This means that if the prepaid expense items were not already owned, current assets would be required for their purchase during the operating cycle.

The prepaid expenses of a business, as a total, are seldom a major item on its balance sheet. As a result, instead of listing them individually, as in Illustration 3–5, they are commonly totaled and only the total is shown under the caption "Prepaid expenses."

Long-term investments

The second balance sheet classification is long-term investments. Stocks, bonds, and promissory notes that will be held for more than one year appear under this classification. Also, such things as land held for future expansion but not now being used in the business appear here.

Plant and equipment

Plant assets are relatively long-lived assets of a tangible nature that are held for use in the production or sale of other assets or services, for example, items of equipment, buildings, and land. The key words in the foregoing sentence are "long-lived" and "held for use in the production or sale of other assets or services." Land held for future expansion, as mentioned in the previous paragraph, is not a plant asset because it is not being used to produce or sell other assets, goods, or services.

The words "Plant and equipment" are commonly used as a balance sheet caption; but more complete captions are "Property, plant, and equipment" and "Land, buildings, and equipment." However, all three captions are long and unwieldy; and as a result, items of plant and equipment will be called plant assets in this book.

The order in which plant assets are listed within the balance sheet classification is not uniform; however, it is often from the ones of least permanent nature to those of most permanent nature.

---

[1] Committee on Accounting Procedure, "Accounting Research Bulletin No. 43," *Accounting Research and Terminology Bulletins, Final Edition* (New York: AICPA, 1961), p. 20.

Plant assets, with the exception of land, wear out and depreciate through use and the passage of time; and as in Illustration 3–5, they are commonly shown on the balance sheet at cost less accumulated depreciation. The accumulated depreciation is the share of each asset's cost that has been charged off to depreciation expense or the amount the asset has been depreciated from the time of its purchase to the balance sheet date.

Intangible assets

Intangible assets are assets having no physical nature, their value being derived from the rights conferred upon their owner by possession. Goodwill, patents, and trademarks are examples.

Current liabilities

Current liabilities are debts or other obligations that must be paid or liquidated within one year or one operating cycle, and whose payment or liquidation will require the use of current assets. Common current liabilities are notes payable, accounts payable, wages payable, taxes payable, interest payable, and unearned revenues. The order of their listing within the classification is not uniform. Often notes payable are listed as the first current liability because notes receivable are listed first after cash in the current asset section.

Unearned revenues, none of which are shown in Illustration 3–5, result from transactions in which money is received for goods or services to be delivered at a future date. Subscriptions received in advance by a publisher, rent received in advance by a landlord, and payments received for future delivery of merchandise or services are examples. Each is a liability, an obligation to deliver goods or services at a future date. Each is classified as a current liability because current assets will normally be required in its liquidation. For example, payments for future delivery of merchandise will be earned and the obligation for delivery will be liquidated by delivering merchandise, a current asset.

Long-term liabilities

The second main liability classification is long-term liabilities. Liabilities that are not due and payable for a comparatively long period, usually more than one year, are listed under this classification. Common long-term liability items are mortgages payable, bonds payable, and notes payable due more than a year after the balance sheet date.

Owner equity on the balance sheet

The terms owner equity, proprietorship, net worth, and capital are often used synonymously. All four indicate the equity, in the assets, of the owner or owners of a business. Of the four, owner equity, proprietorship, and capital are considered the better terms because the phrase "net worth" seems to indicate that the amount shown is the net or exact "worth" of the owner's equity. Actually the amount shown may or may not be the equity's "worth" because when assets are purchased, they are recorded at cost; and in most cases until sold or consumed in the business operations, cost remains the basis upon which they are accounted for even though their "worth" may change. Thus, if a building lot is bought for $20,000, its purchase is recorded at $20,000 and the lot remains on the records at that amount even though a year later it may be sold for $30,000. The lot remains on the records at $20,000 until sold; and the change in its "worth" along with the resulting change in its owner's "net worth" is not recorded until a sale is completed.

When a business is owned by one person, it is called a single proprietorship and the owner's equity may be reported on the balance sheet as follows:

Owner Equity		
James Gibbs, capital, January 1, 1978		$23,152
Net income for the year $10,953		
Withdrawals... 12,000		
Excess of withdrawals over earnings........		(1,047)
James Gibbs, capital, December 31, 1978		$22,105

The amount of the excess of withdrawals over earnings is enclosed in parentheses in the illustrated owner equity section to show that it is a negative amount. As in this case it is a common practice on financial statements to indicate negative or subtraction items by enclosing them in parentheses.

Arrangement of balance sheet items

The balance sheet of Illustration 1–2 in the first chapter, with the liabilities and owner equity placed to the right of the assets, is called an *account form balance sheet.* Such an arrangement emphasizes that assets equal liabilities plus owner equity. Account form balance sheets are often reproduced on a double page with the assets on the left-hand page and the liabilities and owner equity on the right-hand page.

The balance sheet of Illustration 3–5 is called a *report form balance sheet.* Its items are arranged vertically and better fit a single page. Both forms are commonly used, and neither is preferred.

Classification of income statement items

An income statement, like a balance sheet, is more useful with its items classified. However, the classifications used depend upon the type of business for which the statement is prepared and the nature of its costs and expenses; consequently, a discussion of this is deferred to Chapter 5, after more income statement items are introduced.

Account form balance sheet. A balance sheet with the assets on the left   Glossary
and the liability and owner equity items on the right.

Accounting period. The time interval over which the transactions of a
business are recorded and at the end of which its financial statements are prepared.

Accrual basis of accounting. The accounting basis in which revenues
are assigned to the accounting period in which earned regardless
of whether or not received in cash and expenses incurred in earning the revenues are deducted from the revenues regardless of
whether or not cash has been disbursed in their payment.

Accrued expense. An expense which has been incurred during an accounting period but which has not been paid and recorded because
payment is not due.

Accrued revenue. A revenue that has been earned during an accounting
period but has not been received and recorded because payment
is not due.

Accumulated depreciation. The cumulative amount of depreciation recorded against an asset or group of assets during the entire period
of time the asset or assets have been owned.

Adjusted trial balance. A trial balance showing account balances
brought up to date by recording appropriate adjusting entries.

Adjusting entries. Journal entries made to assign revenues to the period
in which earned and to match revenues and expenses.

Adjustment process. The end-of-the-period process of recording appropriate adjusting entries to assign revenues to the period in
which earned and to match revenues and expenses.

Cash basis of accounting. The accounting basis in which revenues are
reported as being earned in the accounting period received in cash
and expenses are deducted from revenues in the accounting period
in which cash is disbursed in their payment.

Classified balance sheet. A balance sheet with assets and liabilities
classified into significant groups.

Contra account. An account the balance of which is subtracted from
the balance of an associated account to show a more proper
amount for the item recorded in the associated account.

Current asset. Cash or an asset that may reasonably be expected to be
realized in cash or be consumed within one year or one operating
cycle of the business, whichever is longer.

Current liability. A debt or other obligation that must be paid or liquidated within one year or one operating cycle, and the payment or
liquidation of which will require the use of presently classified
current assets.

Depreciation. The expiration of a plant asset's "quantity of usefulness."

Depreciation expense. The expense resulting from the expiration of a plant asset's "quantity of usefulness."

Intangible asset. An asset having no physical existence but having value because of the rights conferred as a result of its ownership and possession.

Matching principle. The accounting rule that all expenses incurred in earning a revenue be deducted from the revenue in determining net income.

Operating cycle of a business. The average period of time between the acquisition of merchandise or materials by a business and the realization of cash from the sale of the merchandise or product manufactured from the materials.

Plant and equipment. Tangible assets having relatively long lives that are used in the production or sale of other assets or services.

Prepaid expense. An asset that will be consumed in the operation of a business, and as it is consumed it will become an expense.

Report form balance sheet. A balance sheet prepared on one page, at the top of which the assets are listed, followed down the page by the liabilities and owner equity.

Time-period concept. The idea that the life of a business is divisible into time periods of equal length.

Unadjusted trial balance. A trial balance prepared after transactions are recorded but before any adjustments are made.

Unearned revenue. Payment received in advance for goods or services to be delivered at a later date.

Questions for class discussion

1. Why are the balances of some of a concern's accounts normally incorrect for statement purposes at the end of an accounting period even though all transactions were correctly recorded?
2. Other than to make the accounts show proper statement amounts, what is the basic purpose behind the end-of-the-accounting-period adjustment process?
3. A prepaid expense is an asset at the time of its purchase or prepayment. When is it best to ignore this and record the prepayment as an expense? Why?
4. What is a contra account? Give an example.
5. What contra account is used in recording depreciation? Why is such an account used?
6. What is an accrued expense? Give an example.
7. How does an unearned revenue arise? Give an example of an unearned revenue.
8. What is the balance sheet classification of an unearned revenue?
9. What is an accrued revenue? Give an example.

10. When the statements are prepared from an adjusted trial balance, why should the income statement be prepared first?
11. The adjustment process results from recognizing that some transactions affect several accounting periods. What is the objective of the process?
12. When are a concern's revenues and expenses matched?
13. Why should the income statements of a concern be comparable from period to period?
14. What is the usual order in which accounts are arranged in the ledger?
15. Differentiate between the cash and the accrual basis of accounting?
16. What is a classified balance sheet?
17. What are the characteristics of a current asset? What are the characteristics of an asset classified as plant and equipment?
18. What are current liabilities? Long-term liabilities?

Exercise 3–1   Class exercises

A company has five office employees who each earn $40 per day for a five-day week that begins on Monday and ends on Friday. They were paid for the week ended December 26, and all five worked full days on Monday, Tuesday, and Wednesday, December 29, 30, and 31. January 1 of the new year was an unpaid holiday and none of the employees worked, but all worked a full day on Friday, January 2. Give in general journal form the year-end adjusting entry to record the accrued wages and the entry to pay the employees on January 2.

Exercise 3–2

Give in general journal form the year-end adjusting entry for each of the following:

a. The Prepaid Insurance account had a $985 debit balance at the end of the accounting period before adjustment for expired insurance. An examination of insurance policies showed that $540 of insurance had expired.
b. The Prepaid Insurance account had an $890 debit balance at the end of the accounting period before adjustment for expired insurance. An examination of insurance policies showed $270 of unexpired insurance.
c. The store supplies account had a $215 debit balance on January 1; store supplies costing $580 were purchased during the year; and a year-end inventory showed $235 of unconsumed store supplies on hand.
d. Four months' property taxes, estimated at $445, have accrued but are unpaid and unrecorded at the accounting period end.
e. Depreciation on store equipment for the accounting period is estimated at $2,775.

Exercise 3–3

Assume that the required adjustments of Exercise 3–2 were not made at the end of the accounting period and tell for each adjustment the effect of its omission on the income statement and balance sheet prepared at that time.

Exercise 3–4

A company paid the $1,800 premium on a three-year insurance policy on August 1, 1978.

a. How many dollars of the premium should appear on the 1978 income statement as an expense?

b. How many dollars of the premium should appear on the December 31, 1978, balance sheet as an asset?

c. Under the assumption that the Prepaid Insurance account was debited for $1,800 in recording the premium payment, give the December 31, 1978, adjusting entry to record the expired insurance.

d. Under the assumption the bookkeeper incorrectly debited the Insurance Expense account for $1,800 in recording the premium payment, give the December 31, 1978, adjusting entry. (Hint: Did the bookkeeper's error change the answers to questions (a) and (b) of this exercise?)

Exercise 3–5

A department store occupies most of the space in the building it owns. However, it also rents space in the building to merchants who sell compatible but not competitive merchandise.

a. A tenant rented space in the store's building on September 1 at $200 per month, paying six months' rent in advance. The store credited Unearned Rent to record the $1,200 received. Give the department store's year-end adjusting entry.

b. Another tenant rented space at $250 per month on October 1. He paid his rent on the first day of October and again on the first day of November; but by December 31 he had not paid his December rent. Give the required year-end adjusting entry.

c. Assume the foregoing tenant paid his rent for December and January on January 2 of the new year. Give the entry to record the receipt of the $500.

Exercise 3–6

Determine the amounts indicated by the question marks in the columns below. The amounts in each column constitute a separate problem.

	(a)	(b)	(c)	(d)
Supplies on hand on January 1	$213	$142	$325	$?
Supplies purchased during the year....	475	537	?	452
Supplies consumed during the year....	?	462	622	395
Supplies remaining at the year-end	238	?	254	204

Problems

Problem 3–1

On December 31, at the end of a yearly accounting period, the following information for adjustments was available:

a. The prepaid insurance account showed these amounts:

Prepaid Insurance

Jan.	1	Balance	65.00
May	1		210.00
Nov.	1		270.00

The January 1 balance represents the unexpired premium on a one-year policy purchased on May 1 of the previous year. The May 1 debit resulted from paying the premium on a one-year policy, and the November 1 debit represents the cost of a three-year policy.

b. The office supplies account showed these amounts:

Office Supplies

Jan.	1	Balance	115.00
Mar.	10	Purchase	155.00
Oct.	5	Purchase	60.00

The December 31 year-end inventory of office supplies showed $95 of unused supplies.

c. The company owns and occupies a building that was completed and occupied for the first time on April 1 of the current year. The company had previously occupied rented quarters. The building cost $192,000, has an estimated 40-year useful life, and is not expected to have any salvage value at the end of its life.

d. The company rents portions of the space in its building to two tenants. Tenant A agreed beginning on September 1 to rent a small amount of space at $100 per month, and on that date paid six months' rent in advance. The $600 was credited to the Unearned Rent account.

e. Tenant B pays $150 rent per month on the space he occupies. During the months of June through November he paid his rent each month on the first day of the month, and the amounts paid were credited to Rent Earned. However, he has recently experienced financial difficulties and has not yet paid his rent for December.

f. The company has two office employees who earn $24 and $36 per day, respectively. They are paid each Friday for a workweek that begins on Monday. They were paid last Friday and have worked on Monday and Tuesday, December 30 and 31 of this week.

Required:
Prepare adjusting journal entries for each of the units of information.

Problem 3–2
A trial balance of the ledger of Resort Realty at the end of its annual accounting period appeared as follows:

RESORT REALTY
Trial Balance, December 31, 19—

Cash	$ 3,145	
Prepaid insurance	380	
Office supplies	335	
Office equipment	2,975	
Accumulated depreciation, office equipment		$ 615
Automobile	3,645	
Accumulated depreciation, automobile	625	1,150
Accounts payable	3020	75
Unearned management fees		450
Marie Sloan, capital		6,140
Marie Sloan, withdrawals	9,000	
Sales commissions earned		17,460
Office salaries expense	4,500	
Advertising expense	565	
Rent expense	1,200	
Telephone expense	145	
Totals	$25,890	$25,890

Required:

1.   Open the accounts of the trial balance plus these additional accounts: Accounts Receivable; Office Salaries Payable; Management Fees Earned; Insurance Expense; Office Supplies Expense; Depreciation Expense, Office Equipment; and Depreciation Expense, Automobile. Enter the trial balance amounts in the accounts.

2.   Use the following information to prepare and post adjusting entries:
   a.   An examination of insurance policies showed $315 of insurance expired at the period end.
   b.   An inventory of unused office supplies showed $115 of supplies on hand.
   c.   The year's depreciation on the office equipment was estimated at $300 and (*d*) on the automobile at $625.
   e.   and (*f*) Resort Realty has just begun to offer property management services and has signed two contracts with clients. In the first contract (*e*) it agreed to manage an apartment building for a $60 monthly fee payable at the end of each quarter. The contract was signed on October 15, and two and a half months' fees have accrued. In the second contract (*f*) it agreed to manage an office building beginning on November 1. The contract called for a $150 monthly fee, and the client paid the fees for the first three months in advance at the time the contract was signed. The amount paid was credited to the Unearned Management Fees account.
   g.   The part-time office employee is paid weekly, and on December 31 four days' wages at $17.50 per day have accrued.

3.   Prepare an adjusted trial balance, an income statement, and a classified balance sheet.

Problem 3–3

A trial balance of Chevron Moving and Storage Company's ledger at the end of its annual accounting period carried these items:

CHEVRON MOVING AND STORAGE COMPANY
Trial Balance, December 31, 19—

Cash	$ 2,460	
Accounts receivable	680	
Prepaid insurance	1,340	
Office supplies	210	
Office equipment	1,540	
Accumulated depreciation, office equipment		$ 320
Trucks	13,800	
Accumulated depreciation, trucks		2,630
Buildings	38,300	
Accumulated depreciation, buildings		10,900
Land	8,000	
Accounts payable		875
Unearned storage fees		685
Mortgage payable		20,000
Ted Davis, capital		18,490
Ted Davis, withdrawals	8,400	
Revenue from moving services		42,995
Storage fees earned		2,960
Office salaries expense	5,200	
Truck drivers' wages expense	18,410	
Gas, oil, and repairs expense	1,515	
Totals	$99,855	$99,855

Required:

1. Open the accounts of the trial balance and these additional accounts: Wages Payable; Insurance Expense; Office Supplies Expense; Depreciation Expense, Office Equipment; Depreciation Expense, Trucks; and Depreciation Expense, Buildings. Enter the trial balance amounts in the accounts.

2. Use this information to prepare and post adjusting journal entries:
   a. An examination of insurance policies showed $915 of insurance expired.
   b. An office supply inventory showed $55 of unused office supplies on hand at the period end.
   c. Estimated depreciation of office equipment, $130; (d) trucks, $2,875; and (e) buildings, $2,100.
   f. The company credits the storage fees of customers who pay in advance to the Unearned Storage Fees account. Of the $685 credited to this account during the year, $385 had been earned by the year-end.
   g. Accrued storage fees earned but unrecorded in the accounts and uncollected at the year-end totaled $140.
   h. There were $285 of earned but unpaid truck drivers' wages at the year-end.

3. After posting the adjusting journal entries, prepare an adjusted trial balance, an income statement, and a classified balance sheet.

Problem 3–4

At the end of its annual accounting period, after all transactions were recorded, the following trial balance was taken from the ledger of Heavenly Trailer Park:

HEAVENLY TRAILER PARK
Trial Balance, December 31, 19—

Cash	$ 2,590	
Prepaid insurance	615	
Office supplies	125	
Office equipment	1,250	
Accumulated depreciation, office equipment		$ 325
Building and improvements	65,000	
Accumulated depreciation, building and improvements		7,200
Land	90,000	
Accounts payable		215
Unearned rent		500
Mortgage payable		120,000
Margret Martin, capital		24,070
Margret Martin, withdrawals	12,000	
Rent earned		33,350
Wages expense	5,120	
Utilities expense	340	
Telephone expense	180	
Property taxes expense	1,840	
Interest expense	6,600	
Totals	$185,660	$185,660

Required:

1. Open the accounts of the trial balance plus these: Accounts Receivable; Wages Payable; Property Taxes Payable; Interest Payable; Insurance Expense; Office Supplies Expense; Depreciation Expense, Office Equipment; and Depreciation Expense, Building and Improvements.
2. Use the following information to prepare and post adjusting journal entries:
    a. An examination of insurance policies showed $450 of insurance expired.
    b. An inventory of office supplies showed $40 of unused supplies on hand.
    c. Estimated depreciation on office equipment, $110; and (*d*) on the building and improvements, $2,150.
    e. The concern follows the practice of crediting the Unearned Rent account for rents paid in advance by tenants, and an examination revealed that one half of the $500 balance of this account had been earned by the year-end.
    f. A tenant is two months in arrears with his rent payments, and this $100 of accrued revenue was unrecorded at the time the trial balance was prepared.
    g. The one employee, a gardner and general handy man, works a five-day week at $20 per day. He was paid last week but has worked four days this week, December 28, 29, 30, and 31, for which he has not been paid.
    h. Two months' property taxes, totaling $300, have accrued but are unpaid and unrecorded.

    i.   Thirty days' interest on the mortgage, $600, has accrued but is unpaid and unrecorded.

3.   After posting the adjusting entries, prepare an adjusted trial balance, an income statement, and a classified balance sheet.

Problem 3–5

    The 1978 and 1979 balance sheets of a company showed the following asset and liability amounts at the end of each year:

	December 31	
	1978	*1979*
Prepaid insurance	$200	$500
Interest payable.............................	100	300
Unearned property management fees..	400	200

    The concern's records showed the following amounts of cash disbursed and received for these items during 1979:

Cash disbursed to pay insurance premiums.... $1,700
Cash disbursed to pay interest.................... 1,400
Cash received for managing property............ 2,100

Required:

    Present calculations to show the amounts to be reported on the 1979 income statement for (*a*) insurance expense, (*b*) interest expense, and (*c*) property management fees earned.

Problem 3–1A

Alternate problems

    The following information for adjustments was available on December 31, at the end of the annual accounting period. Prepare an adjusting journal entry for each unit of information.

a.   An examination of insurance policies showed the following three policies:

Policy No.	Date of Purchase	Life of Policy	Cost
21221-003	November 1 of previous year	3 years	$240
A-1234567	May 1 of current year	3 years	180
565656565	June 1 of current year	1 year	120

    Prepaid Insurance was debited for the cost of each policy at the time of its purchase.

b.   The Office Supplies account had an $85 balance at the beginning of the year, $390 of office supplies were purchased during the year, and an inventory of unused supplies on hand at the year-end totaled $75.

c.   The two office employees each earn $30 per day and are paid each Friday for a workweek that begins on Monday. This year December 31 falls on Thursday and both employees worked Monday, Tuesday, Wednesday, and Thursday.

d.   The company owns a building that it completed and occupied for the first time on May 1 of the current year. The building cost $168,000, has an estimated 40-year life, and is not expected to have any salvage value at the end of that time.

e. The company occupies most of the space in its building, but it also rents space to two tenants. One tenant agreed beginning on November 1 to rent a small amount of space at $150 per month, and on that date he paid six months' rent in advance. The amount paid was credited to the Unearned Rent account.

f. The second tenant whose rent is also $150 per month paid his rent on the first of each month August through November, and the amounts paid were credited to Rent Earned. However, he has not paid his December rent, although he has said on several occasions that he would do so the next day.

Problem 3–2A

Desert Realty operates with annual accounting periods that end each December 31. At the end of the current year, after all transactions were recorded, the following trial balance was taken from its ledger:

DESERT REALTY
Trial Balance, December 31, 19—

Cash	$ 3,145	
Prepaid insurance	380	
Office supplies	335	
Office equipment	2,975	
Accumulated depreciation, office equipment		$ 615
Automobile	3,645	
Accumulated depreciation, automobile		1,150
Accounts payable		75
Unearned management fees		450
Marie Sloan, capital		6,140
Marie Sloan, withdrawals	9,000	
Sales commissions earned		17,460
Office salaries expense	4,500	
Advertising expense	565	
Rent expense	1,200	
Telephone expense	145	
Totals	$25,890	$25,890

Required:

1. Open the accounts of the trial balance plus these additional ones: Accounts Receivable; Office Salaries Payable; Management Fees Earned; Insurance Expense; Office Supplies Expense; Depreciation Expense, Office Equipment; and Depreciation Expense, Automobile. Enter the trial balance amounts in the accounts.

2. Use the following information to prepare and post adjusting entries:
   a. Insurance expired during the year, $260.
   b. An office supplies inventory showed $120 of unused office supplies on hand at the year-end.

c. Estimated depreciation of office equipment, $295; and (d) of automobile, $575.

e. Before departing on a world tour, a client entered into a contract with Desert Realty for the management of her apartment building. She paid the management fee for six months in advance, beginning on November 1, and the amount paid, $450, was credited to the Unearned Management Fees account.

f. On December 1 Desert Realty entered into a contract and began managing a small office building for a $50 monthly fee. The contract specified that payments for this service were to be made quarterly with the first payment becoming due on March 1 of next year.

g. The part-time office employee is paid every two weeks, and on December 31 she has earned $90 of wages that are unpaid and unrecorded because payment is not due.

3. Prepare an adjusted trial balance, an income statement, and a classified balance sheet.

Problem 3–3A

The following trial balance was taken from the ledger of Pace Moving and Storage Company at the end of its annual accounting period:

PACE MOVING AND STORAGE COMPANY
Trial Balance, December 31, 19—

Cash	$ 2,460	
Accounts receivable	680	
Prepaid insurance	1,340	
Office supplies	210	
Office equipment	1,540	
Accumulated depreciation, office equipment		$ 320
Trucks	13,800	
Accumulated depreciation, trucks		2,630
Buildings	38,300	
Accumulated depreciation, buildings		10,900
Land	8,000	
Accounts payable		875
Unearned storage fees		685
Mortgage payable		20,000
Ted Davis, capital		18,490
Ted Davis, withdrawals	8,400	
Revenue from moving services		42,995
Storage fees earned		2,960
Office salaries expense	5,200	
Truck drivers' wages expense	18,410	
Gas, oil, and repairs expense	1,515	
Totals	$99,855	$99,855

Required:

1. Open the accounts of the trial balance plus these additional accounts: Wages Payable; Insurance Expense; Office Supplies Expense; Deprecia-

tion Expense, Office Equipment; Depreciation Expense, Trucks; and Depreciation Expense, Buildings. Enter the trial balance amounts in the accounts.

2. Use this information to prepare and post adjusting journal entries:
   - a. An examination of insurance policies showed $840 of insurance expired.
   - b. An inventory of office supplies showed $45 of unused supplies on hand at the year-end.
   - c. Estimated depreciation of office equipment, $115; (d) trucks, $2,450; and (e) buildings, $1,800.
   - f. The company follows the practice of crediting the storage fees of customers who pay in advance to the Unearned Storage Fees account. Of the amount credited to this account during the year, $415 had been earned by the year-end.
   - g. There were accrued storage fees earned but unrecorded in the accounts and uncollected at the year-end that totaled $110.
   - h. There were $225 of accrued truck drivers' wages at the year-end.
3. After posting the adjusting entries, prepare an adjusted trial balance, an income statement, and a classified balance sheet.

Problem 3–4A

An inexperienced bookkeeper prepared the first of the following income statements but he forgot to adjust the accounts before its preparation. However, the oversight was discovered, and the second correct statement was prepared. Analyze the two statements and prepare the adjusting journal entries that were made between their preparation. Assume that one fourth of the additional property management fees resulted from recognizing accrued management fees and three fourths resulted from previously recorded unearned fees that were earned by the time the statements were prepared. (You will need only general journal paper for the solution of this problem. You may use the paper provided for Problems 3–4 or 3–4A or for any other unassigned problem.)

SUN VALLEY REALTY

Income Statement for Year Ended December 31, 19 –

Revenues:

Commissions earned......................		$29,450
Property management fees earned....		2,110
Total revenues........................		$31,560
Operating expenses:		
Rent expense	$2,750	
Salaries expense	7,080	
Advertising expense	1,235	
Utilities expense..........................	485	
Telephone expense.......................	515	
Gas, oil, and repairs expense	620	
Total operating expenses..........		12,685
Net Income		$18,875

SUN VALLEY REALTY
Income Statement for Year Ended December 31, 19—

Revenues:

Commissions earned		$29,450
Property management fees earned		2,590
Total revenues		$31,040

Operating expenses:

Rent expense	$3,000	
Salaries expense	7,200	
Advertising expense	1,280	
Utilities expense	485	
Telephone expense	515	
Gas, oil, and repairs expense	635	
Office supplies expense	240	
Insurance expense	325	
Depreciation expense, office equipment	410	
Depreciation expense, automobile	915	
Taxes expense	130	
Total operating expenses		15,135
Net Income		$15,905

Problem 3–5A

Dale Sells, a realtor, has always kept his accounting records on a cash basis; and at the end of 1979 he prepared the following cash basis income statement:

DALE SELLS, REALTOR
Income Statement for Year Ended December 31, 1979

Revenues	$39,800
Expenses	21,200
Net Income	$18,600

In preparing the income statement, the following amounts of accrued and deferred items were ignored at the ends of 1978 and 1979:

	End of	
	1978	1979
Prepaid expenses	$1,130	$ 950
Accrued expenses	2,515	2,950
Accrued revenues	1,260	1,430
Unearned revenues	1,610	1,490

Required:

Assume that the 1978 prepaid and unearned items became expenses or were earned in 1979, the ignored 1978 accrued items were either received in cash or were paid in 1979, and prepare a condensed 1979 accrual basis income statement for Dale Sells.

Decision problem 3–1, Cactus Realty

Dale Alder is a real estate agent who owns and operates Cactus Realty. He collects a 6% commission on the selling price of each property he sells. During the second quarter of this year he had five houses listed with his agency, of which he successfully sold four. The fifth (No. 5 in the following list) was sold by a rival agent. Mr. Alder's normal business expenses include operating an automobile, advertising, and office expenses. The car used in the business cost $5,720 one year ago. Mr. Alder operates the car 50% for business and 50% for personal use. He expects to get $2,000 for the car when he trades it in on a new one in two years.

Since individual houses are named and described in the agency's advertising, it is easy to keep a record of advertising expense by houses. A record of the five houses listed during the second quarter, the dates on which they were first listed, advertising expense by months on each, and dates of sale follow:

House	Sales Price	Date Listed	Advertising Expense by Months			Date Sold
			April	May	June	
1	$45,000	March 29	$ 75	$ 90		May 11
2	28,500	April 1	95	60	$ 85	June 21
3	38,000	April 7	25			April 12
4	31,500	May 15		40	55	June 20
5	42,500	April 10	95	80	75	
			$290	$270	$215	

Other expenses incurred were:

Expenses	April	May	June	Total
Gas, oil, and normal car maintenance* ...	$ 85	$ 70	$ 75	$ 230
Office rent...	225	225	225	675
Secretary's salary	500	500	500	1,500
Office supplies consumed....................	15	20	15	50
Telephone	45	50	60	155
Totals......................................	$870	$865	$875	$2,610

* Amounts shown are all expenses incurred in operating the automobile each month.

Prepare an income statement showing the agency's net income for the second quarter. Answer these questions: (*a*) Is it possible to prepare monthly income statements for the agency; and if so, discuss any difficulties that would be encountered? (*b*) Is it possible to prepare an income statement showing the net income from the sale of each house; and if so, discuss any difficulties that would be encountered?

On April Fools' Day of the current year Ted Nash rented shop space and began a business called Ted's TV Service. He has not kept any formal accounting records, but he has kept an accurate check stub record of cash receipts and disbursements since beginning the business. The record shows: **Decision problem 3–2, Ted's TV Service**

Receipts:
Cash investment	$10,000	
Received from customers for services rendered	22,400	32,400

Disbursements:
Shop rent	$ 2,000	
Shop equipment	3,600	
Truck	4,800	
Repair parts and supplies	2,850	
Insurance premiums	380	
Advertising	300	
Utilities	255	
Helper's wages	5,350	
Ted Nash for personal use	9,000	28,535
Cash balance, December 31, 19–		$ 3,865

Ted wants to know how much his business has earned during its first nine months, and he would like for you to prepare an income statement and a year-end balance sheet. You ask a number of questions and learn that the shop equipment and truck were paid for on the day he began business. Ted estimates the shop equipment will have a ten-year life, after which it will be worthless. He plans to drive the truck three years, and he thinks he will get a $1,200 trade-in allowance on a new truck when he trades the truck in after three years. The shop space rents for $200 per month on a five-year lease that required payment of the first and last months' rent in advance. Ted has a $240 unpaid invoice for shop supplies delivered yesterday, and an inventory shows a total of $485 of unused shop supplies on hand. The insurance premiums were on two policies taken out on April 1. The first is a one-year policy that cost $80, and the second is a three-year policy that cost $300. There are $50 of accrued wages owed the helper, and customers owe $315 for services they have received.

June Knott purchased Gypsy Trailer Park on October 1 of the current year and has operated it three months without keeping formal accounting records. However, she has deposited all receipts in the bank and kept an accurate check stub record of all payments, an analysis of which follows: **Decision problem 3–3, Gypsy Trailer Park**

	Receipts	*Payments*
Investment	$20,000	
Purchased Gypsy Trailer Park:		
Land... $36,500		
Buildings and improvements 60,000		
Office equipment................................ 1,500		
Total $98,000		
Less mortgage assumed 80,000		
Cash paid......................................		$18,000
Insurance premiums...............................		960
Office supplies purchased.........................		120
Wages paid...		1,550
Utilities paid...		165
Property taxes paid................................		1,540
Personal withdrawals of cash by owner		1,800
Trailer space rentals collected...................	7,875	
Totals...	$27,875	$24,135
Balance of cash		3,740
Totals...	$27,875	$27,875

Ms. Knott wants you to prepare an accrual basis income statement for the three months she has owned the trailer park and also a December 31 end of the three-month period balance sheet. A few questions on your part reveal the following:

The buildings and improvement were estimated to have 30 years of remaining useful life when purchased, and at the end of that time will have to be wrecked. It is estimated that the sale of salvaged materials will just pay the wrecking costs and the cost of clearing the site. The office equipment is in good condition. When she purchased it, Ms. Knott estimated she would use it for five years and would then trade it in on new equipment of a like nature. She thought $300 was a fair estimate of what she would receive for the old equipment when traded in at the end of the five-year period.

The $960 payment for insurance was for a policy taken out on October 1 and giving protection for three years beginning on that date. Ms. Knott estimates that one fourth of the office supplies have been used. She also says that the one employee earns $25 per day for a five-day week that ends on Friday. The employee was paid on Friday, December 27, and has worked on Monday and Tuesday, December 30 and 31, for which he has not been paid. The property tax payment represents one year's taxes paid on November 15 for a tax year beginning on October 1, the day Ms. Knott purchased the trailer park.

Included in the $7,875 trailer space rentals is $300 received from a tenant who paid his rent for four months in advance beginning on December 1. Also, two tenants have not paid their December rent. The total amount due from both is $150.

The mortgage requires the payment of 7½% interest annually on the beginning principal balance and a $4,000 annual payment on the principal.

After studying Chapter 4, you should be able to:

- Explain why a work sheet is prepared and be able to prepare a work sheet for a service-type business.

- Explain why it is necessary to close the revenue and expense accounts at the end of each accounting period.

- Prepare entries to close the temporary proprietorship accounts of a service business and prepare a post-closing trial balance to test the accuracy of the end-of-the-period adjusting and closing procedures.

- List the steps in the accounting cycle in the order in which they are completed.

- Define or explain the words and phrases listed in the chapter Glossary.

chapter 4

The work sheet and closing the accounts

In the accounting procedures described in the previous chapter, at the end of an accounting period, as soon as all transactions were recorded, recall that (1) adjusting entries were entered in the journal and posted to the accounts and (2) then an adjusted trial balance was prepared and used in making an income statement and balance sheet. Furthermore, for a small business these are satisfactory procedures. However, if a company has more than a very few accounts and adjustments, errors in adjusting the accounts and in preparing the statements are less apt to be made if an additional step is inserted in the procedures. The additional step is the preparation of a work sheet. A work sheet is a tool of the accountant upon which he (1) achieves the effect of adjusting the accounts before entering the adjustments in the accounts, (2) sorts the adjusted account balances into columns according to whether they are used in preparing the income statement or balance sheet, and (3) calculates and proves the mathematical accuracy of the net income.

A work sheet is prepared solely for the accountant's use. It is not given to the owner or manager of the business for which it is prepared but is retained by the accountant. Normally it is prepared with a pencil, which makes changes and corrections easy as its preparation progresses; and after it is completed, the accountant uses it in preparing the income statement and balance sheet and in making adjusting and closing entries. (Closing entries are discussed later in this chapter.)

Preparing a work sheet

The Owen law practice of the previous chapters does not have sufficient accounts or adjustments to warrant use of a work sheet. However, since its transactions and adjustments are familiar, they may be used to illustrate the preparation of a work sheet.

During July, the Owen law practice completed a number of transactions; and on July 31, after these transactions were recorded but *before any adjusting entries were prepared and posted,* a trial balance of its ledger appeared as in Illustration 4–1.

Notice that the illustrated trial balance is an *unadjusted trial balance.* The accounts have not been adjusted for expired rent, supplies consumed, depreciation, and so forth. Nevertheless, this unadjusted trial balance is the starting point in preparing a work sheet, and it is entered in the first two money columns of the work sheet form.

Larry Owen, Attorney
Trial Balance, July 31, 19–

Cash	$1,135	
Prepaid rent	600	
Office supplies	60	
Office equipment	1,500	
Accounts payable		$ 260
Unearned legal fees		150
Larry Owen, capital		2,500
Larry Owen, withdrawals	200	
Legal fees earned		1,150
Office salaries expense	500	
Telephone expense	30	
Heating and lighting expense	35	
Totals	$4,060	$4,060

Illustration 4–1

**The work
sheet
illustrated**

Note that the work sheet shown in Illustration 4–2 has five pairs of money columns and that the first pair is labeled "Trial Balance." In this first pair of columns is copied the unadjusted trial balance of the Owen law practice. Often when a work sheet is prepared, the trial balance is prepared for the first time in its first two money columns.

The second pair of work sheet columns is labeled "Adjustments," and the adjustments are entered in these columns. In the work sheet shown in Illustration 4–2 the adjustments are, with one exception, the same as those for which adjusting journal entries were prepared and posted in the previous chapter, prior to the preparation of the statements. The one exception is the last one, (*e*), in which the two adjustments affecting the Legal Fees Earned account are combined into one compound adjustment because both result in credits to the same account.

Note that the adjustments on the illustrated work sheet are keyed together with letters. When a work sheet is prepared, after it and the accounting statements are completed, the adjusting entries still have to be entered in the journal and posted to the ledger. At that time the key letters help identify each adjustment's related debits and credits. Explanations of the adjustments on the illustrated work sheet are:

Adjustment (*a*): To adjust for the rent expired.
Adjustment (*b*): To adjust for the office supplies consumed.
Adjustment (*c*): To adjust for depreciation of the office equipment.

Larry Owen, Attorney

Work Sheet for Month Ended July 31, 19--

ACCOUNT TITLES	TRIAL BALANCE Dr.	TRIAL BALANCE Cr.	ADJUSTMENTS Dr.	ADJUSTMENTS Cr.	ADJUSTED TRIAL BALANCE Dr.	ADJUSTED TRIAL BALANCE Cr.	INCOME STATEMENT Dr.	INCOME STATEMENT Cr.	BALANCE SHEET Dr.	BALANCE SHEET Cr.
Cash	1,135 00				1,135 00				1,135 00	
Prepaid rent	600 00			(a)200 00	400 00				400 00	
Office supplies	60 00			(b) 15 00	45 00				45 00	
Office equipment	1,500 00				1,500 00				1,500 00	
Accounts payable		260 00				260 00				260 00
Unearned legal fees		150 00	(e) 50 00			100 00				100 00
Larry Owen, capital		2,500 00				2,500 00				2,500 00
Larry Owen, withdrawals	200 00				200 00				200 00	
Legal fees earned		1,150 00		(e)125 00		1,275 00		1,275 00		
Office salaries expense	500 00		(d) 75 00		575 00		575 00			
Telephone expense	30 00				30 00		30 00			
Heating & lighting expense	35 00				35 00		35 00			
	4,060 00	4,060 00								
Rent expense			(a)200 00		200 00		200 00			
Office supplies expense			(b) 15 00		15 00		15 00			
Depr. expense, office equip.			(c) 20 00		20 00		20 00			
Accum. depr., office equip.				(c) 20 00		20 00				20 00
Salaries payable				(d) 75 00		75 00				75 00
Accounts receivable			(e) 75 00		75 00				75 00	
			435 00	435 00	4,230 00	4,230 00	875 00	1,275 00	3,355 00	2,955 00
Net Income							400 00			400 00
							1,275 00	1,275 00	3,355 00	3,355 00

Illustration 4-2

Adjustment (*d*): To adjust for the accrued secretary's salary.
Adjustment (*e*): To adjust for the unearned and accrued revenue.

Each adjustment on the Owen law practice work sheet required
that one or two additional account names be written in below the
original trial balance. These accounts did not have balances when
the trial balance was prepared and, consequently, were not listed in the
trial balance. Often, when a work sheet is prepared, the effects of the
adjustments are anticipated; and any additional accounts required are
provided without amounts in the body of the trial balance.

When a work sheet is prepared, after the adjustments are entered
in the Adjustments columns, the columns are totaled to prove the
equality of the adjustments.

The third set of work sheet columns is labeled "Adjusted Trial
Balance." In preparing a work sheet each amount in the Trial Balance
columns is combined with its adjustment in the Adjustments columns
if there is an adjustment and is entered in the Adjusted Trial Balance
columns. For example, in Illustration 4–2 the Prepaid Rent account
has a $600 debit balance in the Trial Balance columns. This $600 debit
is combined with the $200 credit in the Adjustments columns to give
the Prepaid Rent account a $400 debit balance in the Adjusted Trial
Balance columns. Rent Expense has no balance in the Trial Balance
columns, but it has a $200 debit in the Adjustment columns. Therefore,
no balance combined with a $200 debit gives Rent Expense a $200
debit in the Adjusted Trial Balance columns. Cash, Office Equipment,
and several other accounts have trial balance amounts but no adjustments. As a result, their trial balance amounts are carried unchanged
into the Adjusted Trial Balance columns. Notice that the result of
combining the amounts in the Trial Balance columns with the amounts
in the Adjustments columns is an adjusted trial balance in the Adjusted
Trial Balance columns.

After the amounts in the Trial Balance columns are combined with
the amounts in the Adjustments columns and carried to the Adjusted
Trial Balance columns, the Adjusted Trial Balance columns are added
to prove their equality. Then, after equality is proved, the amounts in
these columns are sorted to the proper Balance Sheet or Income Statement columns according to the statement on which they will appear.
This is an easy task that requires only two decisions: (1) is the item to
be sorted a debit or a credit and (2) on which statement does it appear.
As to the first decision, an adjusted trial balance debit amount must
be sorted to either the Income Statement debit column or the Balance
Sheet debit column and a credit amount must go into either the Income
Statement credit or Balance Sheet credit column. In other words,
debits remain debits and credits remain credits in the sorting process.
As to the second decision, it is only necessary in the sorting process
to remember that revenues and expenses appear on the income statement and assets, liabilities, and owner equity items go on the balance
sheet.

After the amounts are sorted to the proper columns, the columns are totaled; and at this point, the difference between the debit and credit totals of the Income Statement columns is the net income or loss. The difference is the net income or loss because revenues are entered in the credit column and expenses in the debit column. If the credit column total exceeds the debit column total, the difference is a net income; and if the debit column total exceeds the credit column total, the difference is a net loss. In the illustrated work sheet, the credit column total exceeds the debit column total, and the result is a $400 net income.

On the Owen law practice work sheet, after the net income is determined in the Income Statement columns, it is added to the total of the Balance Sheet credit column. The reason for this is that with the exception of the balance of the Capital account, the amounts appearing in the Balance Sheet columns are "end-of-the-period" amounts. Therefore, it is necessary to add the net income to the Balance Sheet credit column total to make the Balance Sheet columns equal. Adding the income to this column has the effect of adding it to the Capital account.

Had there been a loss, it would have been necessary to add the loss to the debit column. This is because losses decrease owner equity, and adding the loss to the debit column has the effect of subtracting it from the Capital account.

Balancing the Balance Sheet columns by adding the net income or loss is a proof of the accuracy with which the work sheet has been prepared. When the income or loss is added in the Balance Sheet columns and the addition makes these columns equal, it is assumed that no errors were made in preparing the work sheet. However, if the addition does not make the columns equal, it is proof that an error or errors were made. The error or errors may have been either mathematical or an amount may have been sorted to a wrong column.

Although balancing the Balance Sheet columns with the net income or loss is *a* proof of the accuracy with which a work sheet was prepared, it is not an absolute proof. These columns will balance even when errors have been made if the errors are of a certain type. For example, an expense carried into the Balance Sheet debit column or an asset carried into the debit column of the income statement section will cause both of these columns to have incorrect totals. Likewise, the net income will be incorrect. However, when such an error is made, the Balance Sheet columns will balance, but with the incorrect amount of income. Therefore, when a work sheet is prepared, care must be exercised in sorting the adjusted trial balance amounts into the correct Income Statement or Balance Sheet columns.

As previously stated, the work sheet is a tool of the accountant and is not for management's use or publication. However, as soon as it is completed, the accountant uses it in preparing the income statement and balance sheet that are given to management. To do this

Work sheet and the financial statements

the accountant rearranges the items in the work sheet's Income Statement columns into a formal income statement and rearranges the items
in the Balance Sheet columns into a formal balance sheet.

**Work sheet
and adjusting
entries**

Entering the adjustments in the Adjustments columns of a work
sheet does not get these adjustments into the ledger accounts. Consequently, after the work sheet and statements are completed, adjusting entries like the ones described in the previous chapter must still
be entered in the General Journal and posted. The work sheet makes
this easy, however, because its Adjustments columns provide the
information for these entries, and all that is needed is an entry for
each adjustment appearing in the columns.

As for the adjusting entries for the work sheet of Illustration 4–2,
they are the same as the entries given in the previous chapter, with
the exception of the entry for adjustment (e). Here a compound entry
having a $50 debit to Unearned Legal Fees, a $75 debit to Accounts
Receivable, and a $125 credit to Legal Fees Earned is used.

**Work sheet
and closing
entries**

In addition to adjusting entries, the work sheet is also an information
source for *closing entries,* which are entries made to clear and close
the revenue and expense accounts. These accounts are cleared in the
sense that their balances are transferred to another account, and they
are closed in the sense that they have zero balances after closing entries
are posted.

**Why closing
entries are
made**

The revenue and expense accounts are cleared and closed at the
end of each accounting period by transferring their balances to a summary account, called Income Summary, where the balances are summarized. Their summarized amount, which is the net income or loss
for the period, is then transferred on to the owner's Capital account.
These transfers are necessary because:

a. Revenues actually increase owner equity and expenses decrease it.
b. However, throughout an accounting period these increases and
    decreases are accumulated in revenue and expense accounts rather
    than in the owner's Capital account.
c. As a result, closing entries are necessary at the end of each ac-
    counting period to transfer the net effect of these increases and
    decreases out of the revenue and expense accounts and on to the
    owner's Capital account.

In addition, closing entries also cause the revenue and expense accounts to begin each new accounting period with zero balances. This
too is necessary because:

a. An income statement reports the revenues and expenses incurred
    during *one* accounting period and is prepared from information
    recorded in the revenue and expense accounts.

b. Consequently, these accounts must begin each new accounting period with zero balances if their end-of-the-period balances are to reflect just *one* period's revenues and expenses.

At the end of July, after its work sheet and statements were prepared and its adjusting entries posted but before its accounts were cleared and closed, the owner equity accounts of Owen's law practice had balances as shown in Illustration 4–3 below. (An account's Balance column heading as a rule does not tell the nature of an account's balance. However, in Illustration 4–3 and in the illustrations immediately following, the nature of each account's balance is shown by means of a color overprint as an aid to the student.)

Observe in Illustration 4–3 that Owen's Capital account shows only its $2,500 July 1 balance. This is not the amount of Owen's equity on July 31; closing entries are required to make this account show the July 31 equity.

Note also the third account in Illustration 4–3, the Income Summary account. This account is used only at the end of the accounting period in summarizing and clearing the revenue and expense accounts.

Closing entries illustrated

Larry Owen, Capital

Date		Explanation	Debit	Credit	Balance
July	1			2,500	2,500

Larry Owen, Withdrawals

Date		Explanation	Debit	Credit	Balance
July	26		200		200

Income Summary

Date		Explanation	Debit	Credit	Balance

Legal Fees Earned

Date		Explanation	Debit	Credit	Balance
July	12			400	400
	19			750	1,150
	31			125	1,275

Office Salaries Expense

Date		Explanation	Debit	Credit	Balance
July	12		250		250
	26		250		500
	31		75		575

Telephone Expense

Date		Explanation	Debit	Credit	Balance
July	31		30		30

Heating and Lighting Expense

Date		Explanation	Debit	Credit	Balance
July	31		35		35

Rent Expense

Date		Explanation	Debit	Credit	Balance
July	31		200		200

Office Supplies Expense

Date		Explanation	Debit	Credit	Balance
July	31		15		15

Depreciation Expense, Office Equipment

Date		Explanation	Debit	Credit	Balance
July	31		20		20

Illustration 4–3

Closing revenue accounts

Before closing entries are posted, revenue accounts have credit balances; consequently, to clear and close a revenue account an entry debiting the account and crediting Income Summary is required.

The Owen law practice has only one revenue account, and the entry to close and clear it is:

July	31	Legal Fees Earned	1,275.00	
		Income Summary...		1,275.00
		To clear and close the revenue account.		

Posting the entry has this effect on the accounts:

Legal Fees Earned

Date		Explanation	Debit	Credit	Balance
July	12			400	400
	19			750	1,150
	31			125	1,275
	31		1,275		-0-

Income Summary

Date		Explanation	Debit	Credit	Balance
July	31			1,275	1,275

Note that the entry (1) clears the revenue account of its balance, transferring the balance to the credit side of the Income Summary account; and (2) causes the revenue account to begin the new accounting period with a zero balance.

Closing expense accounts

Before closing entries are posted, expense accounts have debit balances; consequently, to clear and close a concern's expense accounts, a compound entry debiting the Income Summary account and crediting each individual expense account is required. Owen law practice has six expense accounts, and the compound entry to clear and close them is:

July	31	Income Summary..	875.00	
		Office Salaries Expense..		575.00
		Telephone Expense..		30.00
		Heating and Lighting Expense................................		35.00
		Rent Expense..		200.00
		Office Supplies Expense...		15.00
		Depreciation Expense, Office Equipment................		20.00
		To close and clear the expense accounts.		

Posting the entry has the effect shown in Illustration 4–4. Note again that the effect is a dual one: (1) it clears the expense accounts of their balances by transferring the balances in a total to the debit side of the Income Summary account, and (2) it causes the expense accounts to begin the new period with zero balances.

Closing the Income Summary account

After a concern's revenue and expense accounts are cleared and their balances transferred to the Income Summary account, the bal-

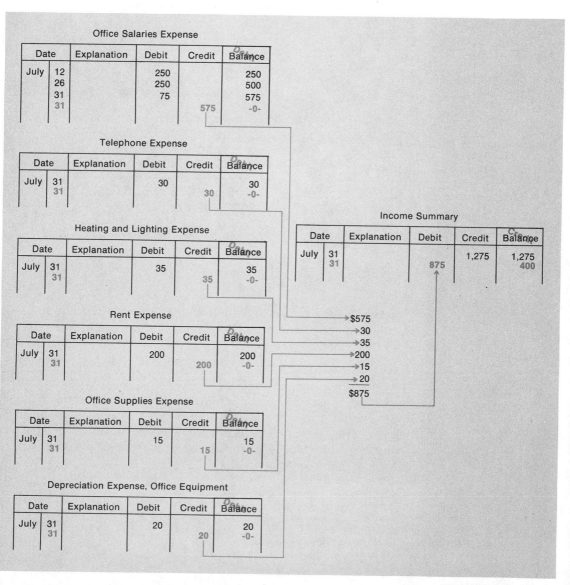

Illustration 4–4

ance of the Income Summary account is equal to the net income or loss. When revenues exceed expenses, there is a net income and the Income Summary account has a credit balance. On the other hand, when expenses exceed revenues, there is a loss and the account has a debit balance. But, regardless of the nature of its balance, the Income Summary account is cleared and its balance, the amount of net income or loss, is transferred to the Capital account.

The Owen law practice earned $400 during July; consequently, after its revenue and expense accounts are cleared, its Income Summary account has a $400 credit balance, which is transferred to the Larry Owen, Capital account with an entry like this:

July	31	Income Summary..	400.00	
		Larry Owen, Capital...		400.00
		To clear and close the Income Summary account.		

Posting this entry has the following effect on the accounts:

	Income Summary					Larry Owen, Capital			
Date	Debit	Credit	Balance		Date	Debit	Credit	Balance	
July 31		1,275	1,275		July 1		2,500	2,500	
31	875		400		31		400	2,900	
31	400		-0-						

Observe that the entry clears the Income Summary account, transferring the balance of the account, the amount of the net income in this case, to the Capital account.

Closing the Withdrawals account

At the end of an accounting period the debit balance of the Withdrawals account shows the amount the owner's equity was reduced during the period by withdrawals of cash and other assets for personal use, and this debit balance is transferred to the Capital account with an entry like this:

July	31	Larry Owen, Capital..	200.00	
		Larry Owen, Withdrawals..		200.00
		To close and clear the Withdrawals account.		

Posting the entry has this effect on the accounts:

Larry Owen, Withdrawls				Larry Owen, Capital			
Date	Debit	Credit	Balance	Date	Debit	Credit	Balance
July 26	200		200	July 1		2,500	2,500
31		200	-0-	31		400	2,900
				31	200		2,700

After the entry clearing and closing the Withdrawals account is posted, observe that the two reasons for making closing entries are accomplished: (1) all revenue and expense accounts have zero balances and (2) the net effect of the period's revenue, expense, and withdrawal transactions on the owner's equity is shown in his Capital account.

After adjusting entries have been posted, information for the closing entries may be taken from the individual revenue and expense accounts; however, the work sheet provides this information in a more convenient form. For example, if the Owen law practice work sheet on page 107 is examined, it will be seen that every account having a'balance extended into the Income Statement debit column has a debit balance in the ledger and must be credited in closing. Now compare the amounts in this column with the compound closing entry on page 112 and observe how the column amounts and their account titles are a source of information for the entry. Observe also that if the work sheet is used as an information source for the entry, it is not even necessary to add the entry's individual credit amounts in order to learn the amount of the debit, because the debit amount can be taken from the work sheet column total.

Sources of closing entry information

In addition, observe also that the work sheet's Income Statement credit column is a convenient information source for the entry that clears and closes the revenue account.

At this stage, after both adjusting and closing entries have been posted, the Owen law practice accounts appear as in Illustration 4–5 on pages 116, 117, and 118. Observe in the illustration that the asset, liability, and the owner's Capital accounts show their end-of-the-period balances. Observe also that the revenue and expense accounts have zero balances and are ready for recording the new accounting period's revenues and expenses.

The accounts after closing

Cash — ACCOUNT NO. 1

DATE	EXPLANATION	FOLIO	DEBIT	CREDIT	BALANCE
1978 July 1		G-1	2 500 00		2 500 00
1		G-1		600 00	1 900 00
3		G-1		1 200 00	700 00
12		G-1	400 00		1 100 00
12		G-1		250 00	850 00
15		G-1	150 00		1 000 00
26		G-2		250 00	750 00
26		G-2		200 00	550 00
29		G-2	750 00		1 300 00
30		G-2		100 00	1 200 00
31		G-2		30 00	1 170 00
31		G-2		35 00	1 135 00

Accounts Receivable — ACCOUNT NO. 2

DATE	EXPLANATION	FOLIO	DEBIT	CREDIT	BALANCE
1978 July 19		G-2	750 00		750 00
29		G-2		750 00	– 0 –
31		G-3	75 00		75 00

Prepaid Rent — ACCOUNT NO. 3

DATE	EXPLANATION	FOLIO	DEBIT	CREDIT	BALANCE
1978 July 1		G-1	600 00		600 00
31		G-3		200 00	400 00

Office Supplies — ACCOUNT NO. 4

DATE	EXPLANATION	FOLIO	DEBIT	CREDIT	BALANCE
1978 July 5		G-1	60 00		60 00
31		G-3		15 00	45 00

Office Equipment — ACCOUNT NO. 5

DATE	EXPLANATION	FOLIO	DEBIT	CREDIT	BALANCE
1978 July 3		G-1	1 200 00		1 200 00
5		G-1	300 00		1 500 00

Accumulated Depreciation, Office Equipment — ACCOUNT NO. 6

DATE	EXPLANATION	FOLIO	DEBIT	CREDIT	BALANCE
1978 July 31		G-3		20 00	20 00

Illustration 4–5

Accounts Payable — ACCOUNT NO. 7

DATE	EXPLANATION	FO-LIO	DEBIT	CREDIT	BALANCE
1978 July 5		G-1		3 6 0 00	3 6 0 00
30		G-2	1 0 0 00		2 6 0 00

Salaries Payable — ACCOUNT NO. 8

DATE	EXPLANATION	FO-LIO	DEBIT	CREDIT	BALANCE
1978 July 31		G-3		7 5 00	7 5 00

Unearned Legal Fees — ACCOUNT NO. 9

DATE	EXPLANATION	FO-LIO	DEBIT	CREDIT	BALANCE
1978 July 15		G-1		1 5 0 00	1 5 0 00
31		G-3	5 0 00		1 0 0 00

Larry Owen, Capital — ACCOUNT NO. 10

DATE	EXPLANATION	FO-LIO	DEBIT	CREDIT	BALANCE
1978 July 1		G-1		2 5 0 0 00	2 5 0 0 00
31		G-3		4 0 0 00	2 9 0 0 00
31		G-3	2 0 0 00		2 7 0 0 00

Larry Owen, Withdrawals — ACCOUNT NO. 11

DATE	EXPLANATION	FO-LIO	DEBIT	CREDIT	BALANCE
1978 July 26		G-2	2 0 0 00		2 0 0 00
31		G-3		2 0 0 00	- 0 -

Income Summary — ACCOUNT NO. 12

DATE	EXPLANATION	FO-LIO	DEBIT	CREDIT	BALANCE
1978 July 31		G-3		1 2 7 5 00	1 2 7 5 00
31		G-3	8 7 5 00		4 0 0 00
31		G-3	4 0 0 00		- 0 -

Legal Fees Earned — ACCOUNT NO. 13

DATE	EXPLANATION	FO-LIO	DEBIT	CREDIT	BALANCE
1978 July 12		G-1		4 0 0 00	4 0 0 00
19		G-2		7 5 0 00	1 1 5 0 00
31		G-3		1 2 5 00	1 2 7 5 00
31		G-3	1 2 7 5 00		- 0 -

Illustration 4–5
(*continued*)

Office Salaries Expense   ACCOUNT NO. 14

DATE	EXPLANATION	FO-LIO	DEBIT	CREDIT	BALANCE
1978 July 12		G-1	2 5 0 00		2 5 0 00
26		G-2	2 5 0 00		5 0 0 00
31		G-3	7 5 00		5 7 5 00
31		G-3		5 7 5 00	- 0 -

Telephone Expense   ACCOUNT NO. 15

DATE	EXPLANATION	FO-LIO	DEBIT	CREDIT	BALANCE
1978 July 31		G-2	3 0 00		3 0 00
31		G-3		3 0 00	- 0 -

Heating and Lighting Expense   ACCOUNT NO. 16

DATE	EXPLANATION	FO-LIO	DEBIT	CREDIT	BALANCE
1978 July 31		G-2	3 5 00		3 5 00
31		G-3		3 5 00	- 0 -

Rent Expense   ACCOUNT NO. 17

DATE	EXPLANATION	FO-LIO	DEBIT	CREDIT	BALANCE
1978 July 31		G-3	2 0 0 00		2 0 0 00
31		G-3		2 0 0 00	- 0 -

Office Supplies Expense   ACCOUNT NO. 18

DATE	EXPLANATION	FO-LIO	DEBIT	CREDIT	BALANCE
1978 July 31		G-3	1 5 00		1 5 00
31		G-3		1 5 00	- 0 -

Depreciation Expense, Office Equipment   ACCOUNT NO. 19

DATE	EXPLANATION	FO-LIO	DEBIT	CREDIT	BALANCE
1978 July 31		G-3	2 0 00		2 0 00
31		G-3		2 0 00	- 0 -

**Illustration 4–5
(concluded)**

It is easy to make errors in adjusting and closing the accounts. Consequently, after all adjusting and closing entries are posted, a new trial balance is prepared to retest the equality of the accounts. This new, after-closing trial balance is called a *post-closing trial balance,* and for Owen's law practice appears as in Illustration 4–6.

The post-closing trial balance

Compare Illustration 4–6 with the accounts having balances in Illustration 4–5. Note that only asset, liability, and the owner's Capital accounts have balances in Illustration 4–5, and that these are the only accounts that appear on the post-closing trial balance of Illustration 4–6. The revenue and expense accounts have been cleared and have zero balances at this point.

Larry Owen, Attorney Post-Closing Trial Balance, July 31, 19–		
Cash	$1,135	
Accounts receivable	75	
Prepaid rent	400	
Office supplies	45	
Office equipment	1,500	
Accumulated depreciation, office equipment		$ 20
Accounts payable		260
Salaries payable		75
Unearned legal fees		100
Larry Owen, capital		2,700
Totals	$3,155	$3,155

Illustration 4–6

Temporary proprietorship accounts

Revenue and expense accounts plus the Income Summary and Withdrawals accounts are called *temporary proprietorship accounts* because in a sense the items recorded in these accounts are only temporarily recorded therein. To appreciate this, recall that all revenue, expense, and withdrawal transactions increase or decrease owner equity. However, the owner's Capital account is not debited and credited in recording such transactions. Rather, the debit and credit effects of these transactions are first accumulated in the revenue, expense, and withdrawals accounts, after which their summarized effect is transferred to the owner's Capital account. Consequently, the items recorded in these accounts are in a sense only temporarily recorded therein because through closing entries their debit and credit effects are transferred out and on to the owner's Capital account at the end of each accounting period.

Matters of terminology

Real and nominal accounts

Balance sheet accounts are commonly called *real accounts,* presumably because the items recorded in these accounts exist in objective form. Likewise, income statement accounts are called *nominal accounts* because items recorded in these accounts exist in name only.

Working papers

As an aid in their work, accountants prepare numerous memoranda, analyses, notes, and informal papers that serve as a basis for the more formal reports given to management or to their clients. These analyses, notes, and memoranda are called "working papers" and are invaluable tools of the accountant. The work sheet of this chapter is a so-called working paper. Others are discussed later in this text.

The accounting cycle

The life of a business is divided into accounting periods; and each period is a recurring accounting cycle, beginning with transactions recorded in a journal and ending with a post-closing trial balance. All steps in the cycle have now been discussed, and a knowledge of accounting requires that each step be understood and its relation to the others seen. The steps in the order of their occurrence are:

1. *Journalizing* .... Analyzing and recording transactions in a journal.
2. *Posting* .... Copying the debits and credits of journal entries into the ledger accounts.
3. *Preparing a trial balance* ...... Summarizing the ledger accounts and testing the recording accuracy.
4. *Preparing a work sheet* .... Gaining the effects of the adjustments before entering the adjustments in the accounts. Then sorting the account balances into balance sheet and income statement accounts and finally determining and proving the income or loss.
5. *Preparing the statements* .... Rearranging the work sheet information into a balance sheet and an income statement.
6. *Adjusting the ledger accounts* .... Preparing adjusting journal entries from information in the Adjustments columns of the work sheet and posting the entries in order to bring the account balances up to date.

7. *Closing the temporary*
   proprietorship accounts .... Preparing and posting entries to close the temporary proprietorship accounts and transfer the net income or loss to the Capital account.

8. *Preparing a post-closing*
   trial balance .... Proving the accuracy of the adjusting and closing procedure.

In order to illustrate the entire accounting cycle, textbooks commonly have problems and illustrations in which a business operates with accounting periods one month in length, and the business is assumed to close its accounts and begin a new cycle of operations each month. In actual practice, however, few business concerns close their accounts each month; most operate with annual accounting periods and close their accounts once each year. **Accounting periods; the natural business year**

Any accounting period of 12 consecutive months is known as a *fiscal year.* A fiscal year or annual accounting period may coincide with the calendar year or it may follow the *natural business year.* The natural business year of a company begins and ends when the company's business activity is at its lowest point. For example, in department stores the natural business year begins February 1, after Christmas and the January sales, and ends the following January 31. When accounting periods follow the natural business year, the books are closed when inventories are at their lowest point and business activity is at its lowest ebb.

Accounting cycle. The accounting steps that recur each accounting period in the life of a business and which begin with the recording of transactions and proceed through posting the recorded amounts, preparing a trial balance, preparing a work sheet, preparing the financial statements, preparing and posting adjusting and closing entries, and preparing a post-closing trial balance. **Glossary**

Calendar year. A year that begins on January 1 and ends on December 31.

Closing entries. Entries made to close and clear the revenue and expense accounts and to transfer the amount of the net income to the owner's Capital account.

Closing procedures. The preparation and posting of closing entries and the preparation of the post-closing trial balance.

Fiscal year. A period of any 12 consecutive months used as an accounting period.

Income Summary account. The account used in the closing procedures to summarize the amounts of revenues and expenses, and from which the amount of the net income or loss is transferred to the owner's Capital account.

Natural business year. Any 12 consecutive months used by a business as an accounting period, at the end of which the activities of the business are at their lowest point.

Nominal accounts. The income statement accounts.

Post-closing trial balance. A trial balance prepared after closing entries are posted.

Real accounts. The balance sheet accounts.

Temporary proprietorship accounts. The revenue, expense, Income Summary and Withdrawals accounts.

Working papers. The memoranda, analyses, and other informal papers prepared by accountants and used as a basis for the more formal reports given to clients.

Work sheet. A working paper used by an accountant to bring together in an orderly manner the information used in preparing the financial statements and the adjusting and closing entries.

Questions for class discussion

1. A work sheet is a tool of the accountant upon which he accomplishes three tasks. What are these tasks?

2. Is it possible to complete the statements and adjust and close the accounts without preparing a work sheet? What is gained by preparing a work sheet?

3. At what stage in the accounting process is a work sheet prepared?

4. From where are the amounts that are entered in the Trial Balance columns of a work sheet obtained?

5. Why are the adjustments in the Adjustments columns of a work sheet keyed together with letters?

6. What is the result of combining the amounts in the Trial Balance columns with the amounts in the Adjustments columns of a work sheet?

7. Why must care be exercised in sorting the items in the Adjusted Trial Balance columns to the proper Income Statement or Balance Sheet columns?

8. In extending the items in the Adjusted Trial Balance columns of a work sheet, what would be the result of extending: (*a*) an expense into the Balance Sheet debit column; (*b*) a liability into the Income Statement credit column; and (*c*) a revenue into the Balance Sheet debit column? Would each of these errors be automatically detected on the work sheet? Which would be automatically detected? Why?

9. Why are revenue and expense accounts called "temporary proprietorship accounts"?

10. What two purposes are accomplished by recording closing entries?

11. What accounts are affected by closing entries? What accounts are not affected?
12. Explain the difference between adjusting and closing entries.
13. What is the purpose of the Income Summary account?
14. Why is a post-closing trial balance prepared?
15. An accounting student listed the item, "Depreciation expense, building, $1,800," on his post-closing trial balance. What did this indicate?

Exericse 4–1   Class exercises

The balances of the following alphabetically arranged accounts appeared in the Adjusted Trial Balance columns of a work sheet. Copy the account numbers in a column on a sheet of note paper and beside each number indicate by letter the income statement or balance sheet column to which the account's balance would be sorted in completing the work sheet. Use the letter *a* to indicate the Income Statement debit column, *b* to indicate the Income Statement credit column, *c* to indicate the Balance Sheet debit column, and *d* to indicate the Balance Sheet credit column.

1. Accounts Payable.
2. Accounts Receivable.
3. Accumulated Depreciation, Repair Equipment.
4. Advertising Expense.
5. Cash.
6. Earl Gage, Capital.

7. Earl Gage, Withdrawals.
8. Prepaid Insurance.
9. Rent Expense.
10. Repair Equipment
11. Repair Supplies
12. Revenue from Repairs.
13. Wages Expense.

Exercise 4–2

The following item amounts are from a work sheet's Adjustments columns. From the information prepare adjusting journal entries. Use December 31 of the current year as the date.

	Adjustments	
	Debit	Credit
Prepaid insurance		(a) 360
Office supplies..................................		(b) 180
Accumulated depreciation, office equipment		(c) 115
Accumulated depreciation, delivery equipment		(d) 2,210
Office salaries expense........................ (e)	30	....
Truck drivers' wages........................ (e)	265	....
Insurance expense, office equipment .... (a)	65	....
Insurance expense, delivery equipment........... (a)	295	....
Office supplies expense........................ (b)	180	....
Depreciation expense, office equipment .... (c)	115	....
Depreciation expense, delivery equipment .... (d) 2,210		....
Salaries and wages payable........................	....	(e) 295
Totals................................	3,160	3,160

Exercise 4–3

Copy the following T-accounts and their end-of-the-accounting-period balances on a sheet of note paper. Below the accounts prepare entries to close the accounts. Post the entries to the T-accounts.

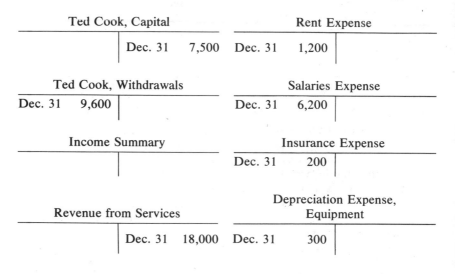

Ted Cook, Capital		Rent Expense	
	Dec. 31 7,500	Dec. 31 1,200	

Ted Cook, Withdrawals		Salaries Expense	
Dec. 31 9,600		Dec. 31 6,200	

Income Summary		Insurance Expense	
		Dec. 31 200	

Revenue from Services		Depreciation Expense, Equipment	
	Dec. 31 18,000	Dec. 31 300	

Exercise 4–4

The following items appeared in the Income Statement columns of a December 31 work sheet prepared for Carl Dale, an attorney. Under the assumption that Mr. Dale withdrew $12,000 from the business during the accounting period of the work sheet, prepare entries to close his revenue, expense, Income Summary, and withdrawals accounts.

	Income Statement	
	Debit	*Credit*
Legal fees earned		26,000
Office salaries expense	9,000	
Rent expense......................................	2,400	
Insurance expense................................	300	
Office supplies expense	200	
Depreciation expense, office equipment....	400	
	12,300	26,000
Net Income.......................................	13,700	
	26,000	26,000

Exercise 4–5

Following is a list of trial balance accounts and their balances. To save you time, the balances are in one- and two-digit numbers; however, to increase your skill in sorting adjusted trial balance amounts to the proper work sheet columns, the accounts are listed in alphabetical order.

TRIAL BALANCE ACCOUNTS AND BALANCES

Accounts payable	$ 2	Paul Parry, withdrawals	$ 2
Accounts receivable	4	Prepaid insurance	3
Accumulated depreciation,		Revenue from services	19
shop equipment	3	Shop equipment	10
Advertising expense	1	Shop supplies	4
Cash	5	Unearned revenue	3
Notes payable	2	Utilities expense	2
Paul Parry, capital	10	Wages expense	8

Required:

1. Prepare a work sheet form on ordinary notebook paper and enter the trial balance accounts and amounts on the work sheet in their alphabetical order.
2. Complete the work sheet using the following information:
   a. Estimated depreciation on shop equipment, $2.
   b. Expired insurance, $1.
   c. Unused shop supplies on hand per inventory, $1.
   d. An examination showed that $2 of the amount listed as unearned revenue had been earned by the work sheet date.
   e. Accrued wages payable, $1.

Problem 4–1   Problems

A trial balance of the ledger of Ted's Fixit Shop at the end of its annual accounting period carried these items:

TED'S FIXIT SHOP
Trial Balance, December 31, 19—

Cash	$ 975	
Prepaid insurance	240	
Repair supplies	1,425	
Repair equipment	7,215	
Accumulated depreciation, repair equipment		$ 1,050
Accounts payable		260
Ted Hall, capital		4,535
Ted Hall, withdrawals	8,200	
Revenue from repairs		21,135
Wages expense	6,860	
Rent expense	1,800	
Advertising expense	265	
Totals	$26,980	$26,980

Required:

1. Enter the trial balance amounts in the Trial Balance columns of a work sheet and complete the work sheet using the following information:
   a. Expired insurance, $185.

    b. An inventory of repair supplies showed $310 of unused supplies on hand.

    c. Estimated depreciation of repair equipment, $725.

    d. Wages earned by the one employee but unpaid on the trial balance date, $80.

2. From the work sheet prepare an income statement and a balance sheet.

3. From the work sheet prepare adjusting journal entries and compound closing entries.

Problem 4–2

A trial balance of the ledger of Jeff's Janitorial Service at the end of its annual accounting period carried these items:

JEFF'S JANITORIAL SERVICE
Trial Balance, December 31, 19—

Cash	$ 580	
Accounts receivable	515	
Cleaning supplies	645	
Prepaid insurance	720	
Cleaning equipment	3,235	
Accumulated depreciation, cleaning equipment		$ 1,470
Trucks	7,895	
Accumulated depreciation, trucks		2,115
Accounts payable		165
Unearned janitorial revenue		200
Jefferson Jack, capital		6,940
Jefferson Jack, withdrawals	12,000	
Janitorial revenue		25,695
Wages expense	8,650	
Advertising expense	335	
Gas, oil, and repairs expense	1,110	
Garage rent expense	900	
Totals	$36,585	$36,585

Required:

1. Enter the trial balance on a work sheet form and complete the work sheet using the following information:

    a. The year-end cleaning supplies inventory showed $125 of unused cleaning supplies on hand.

    b. Expired insurance for the year, $515.

    c. Estimated depreciation of cleaning equipment, $345; and (*d*) of trucks, $1,225.

    e. During December, Jeff's Janitorial Service entered into two contracts to provide cleaning services on a fixed-fee basis. The first contract, on which services began on December 1, called for a $100 monthly fee. The customer paid for the first two months' service in advance, and the amount paid was credited to the Unearned Janitorial Revenue account. The second contract called for a $150 monthly fee payable after services are rendered. One half of a month's services had been rendered on this contract by December 31, but the amount earned was unrecorded at the time the trial balance was prepared.

f. Wages totaling $125 had accrued by the trial balance date but were unpaid and unrecorded.

g. The $335 balance in the Advertising Expense account resulted from $235 in payments to the local paper for advertising that had appeared and $100 for ball-point pens with advertising imprinted thereon. The pens were to be given to customers and prospective customers in the new year.

2. Prepare an income statement and a classified balance sheet from the work sheet.

3. Prepare adjusting and closing entries from the work sheet.

Problem 4-3

(*Covers two accounting cycles*)

On June 1 of the current year Jane Reed began a new business she called Desert Realty, and during the month she completed these transactions:

June 1   Invested $2,000 in cash and an automobile having a $5,000 fair value in the real estate agency.

     1   Rented furnished office space and paid one month's rent, $300.

     1   Paid the premium on a one-year insurance policy, $360.

     3   Purchased office supplies for cash, $100.

   12   Paid the biweekly salary of the office secretary, $250.

   18   Sold a building lot and collected a $1,050 commission.

   26   Paid the biweekly salary of the office secretary, $250.

   30   Paid for gas and oil used in the agency's car, $75.

   30   Paid the monthly telephone bill, $45.

Required work for June:

1. Open the following accounts: Cash; Prepaid Insurance; Office Supplies; Automobile; Accumulated Depreciation, Automobile; Salaries Payable; Jane Reed, Capital; Jane Reed, Withdrawals; Income Summary; Commissions Earned; Rent Expense; Salaries Expense; Gas, Oil, and Repairs Expense; Telephone Expense; Insurance Expense; Office Supplies Expense; and Depreciation Expense, Automobile.

2. Prepare and post journal entries to record the June transactions.

3. Prepare a trial balance in the Trial Balance columns of a work sheet form and complete the work sheet using the following information:

    a. One month's insurance has expired.

    b. An inventory shows $75 of unused office supplies remaining.

    c. Estimated depreciation on the automobile, $100.

    d. Accrued but unpaid salary of the secretary, $50.

4. Prepare a June income statement and a June 30 classified balance sheet.

5. From the work sheet prepare and post adjusting and closing journal entries.

6. Prepare a post-closing trial balance.

During July the following transactions were completed by the real estate agency:

July 1   Paid the July rent on the office space, $300.

     3   Sold a house and collected a $2,900 commission.

     3   Withdrew $1,000 from the business to pay personal expenses.

    10   Paid the secretary's biweekly salary, $250.
    14   Purchased additional office supplies for cash, $40.
    24   Paid the biweekly salary of the office secretary, $250.
    31   Paid the July telephone bill, $35.
    31   Paid for gas and oil used in the agency car during July, $70.

Required for July:

1. Prepare and post journal entries to record the July transactions.
2. Prepare a trial balance in the Trial Balance columns of a work sheet and complete the work sheet using the following information:
   a.   One month's insurance has expired.
   b.   An inventory shows $95 of unused office supplies remaining.
   c.   Estimated depreciation on the automobile, $100.
   d.   Accrued but unpaid salary of the secretary, $125.
3. Prepare a July income statement and a July 31 classified balance sheet.
4. Prepare and post adjusting and closing journal entries.
5. Prepare a post-closing trial balance.

Problem 4–4

A trial balance of the ledger of Golden Alleys carried these items at the end of its annual accounting period:

GOLDEN ALLEYS
Trial Balance, December 31, 19 –

Cash	$ 1,985	
Bowling supplies	1,775	
Prepaid insurance	810	
Bowling equipment	36,565	
Accumulated depreciation, bowling equipment		$ 9,640
Mortgage payable		10,000
Randy Owens, capital		14,850
Randy Owens, withdrawals	12,000	
Bowling revenue		38,500
Salaries expense	13,655	
Advertising expense	750	
Equipment repairs expense	420	
Rent expense	3,000	
Utilities expense	1,135	
Taxes expense	220	
Interest expense	675	
Totals	$72,990	$72,990

The accounts of Golden Alleys with their end-of-the-period balances are reproduced in the booklet of working papers that accompanies this text, and a trial balance of the bowling alley's ledger is reproduced on a work sheet form provided there.

Required:

1. If the working papers are being used, complete the work sheet provided for the solution of this problem, using the information that follows. If the

working papers are not being used, enter the trial balance on a work sheet form and complete the work sheet.

   a. Bowling supplies inventory, $590.

   b. Expired insurance, $515.

   c. Estimated depreciation of bowling equipment, $3,740.

   d. Accrued salaries that are unpaid and unrecorded, $295.

   e. The lease contract on the space occupied by the bowling alley calls for an annual rental equal to 8% of the annual bowling revenue, with $250 payable monthly on the first day of each month. The $250 was paid each month and debited to the Rent Expense account.

   f. Personal property taxes amounting to $110 have accrued on the bowling equipment but are unpaid and unrecorded.

   g. Interest, $125, has accrued on the mortgage but is unpaid and unrecorded.

2. Prepare an income statement and a classified balance sheet.

3. Prepare adjusting and closing journal entries.

4. Post the adjusting and closing entries and prepare a post-closing trial balance. (If the working papers are not being used, omit this last requirement.)

Problem 4–5

   The ledger accounts of Village Delivery Service showing account balances as of the end of its annual accounting period appear in the booklet of working papers that accompanies this text and a trial balance of the ledger is reproduced on a work sheet form provided there. The trial balance carries these items:

VILLAGE DELIVERY SERVICE

Trial Balance, December 31, 19–

Cash	$ 2,775	
Accounts receivable	455	
Prepaid insurance	720	
Office supplies	245	
Office equipment	2,460	
Accumulated depreciation, office equipment		$ 470
Delivery equipment	10,790	
Accumulated depreciation, delivery equipment		3,150
Accounts payable		290
Unearned delivery service revenue		450
Betty Lee, capital		9,855
Betty Lee, withdrawals	10,400	
Delivery service revenue		38,935
Office rent expense	600	
Telephone expense	245	
Office salaries expense	5,060	
Truck drivers' wages	16,320	
Gas, oil, and repairs	2,180	
Garage rent expense	900	
Totals	$53,150	$53,150

Required:

1. If the working papers are being used, complete the work sheet provided for the solution of this problem, using the following information. If the working papers are not being used, enter the trial balance on a work sheet form and complete the work sheet.

   a. Insurance expired on the office equipment, $60; and on the delivery equipment, $420.

   b. An inventory shows $125 of unused office supplies on hand.

   c. Estimated depreciation on office equipment, $125; and (d) on delivery equipment, $2,125.

   e. Three stores entered into contracts with Village Delivery Service in which they agreed to pay a fixed fee for having packages delivered. Two of the stores made advance payments on their contracts, and the amounts paid were credited to Unearned Delivery Service Revenue. An examination of their contracts shows that $250 of the $450 / paid in advance was earned by the accounting period end. The contract of the third store provides for a $100 monthly fee to be paid at the end of each month's service. It was signed on December 15, and a half month's revenue has accrued but is unrecorded.

   f. Office salaries, $60; and truck driver's wages, $320, have accrued.

2. Prepare an income statement and a classified balance sheet.

3. Prepare adjusting and closing journal entries.

4. Post the adjusting and closing entries to the accounts and prepare a post-closing trial balance. (Omit this requirement if the working papers are not in use.)

Alternate Problems

Problem 4–2A

The following trial balance was taken from the ledger of Radiant Janitorial Service at the end of its annual accounting period:

RADIANT JANITORIAL SERVICE
Trial Balance, December 31, 19—.

Cash	$ 550	
Accounts receivable	310	
Prepaid insurance	525	
Prepaid garage rent	150	
Cleaning supplies	815	
Cleaning equipment	2,750	
Accumulated depreciation, cleaning equipment		$ 1,410
Trucks	6,680	
Accumulated depreciation, trucks		3,790
Accounts payable		110
Unearned janitorial revenue		225
Randy Hale, capital		6,435
Randy Hale, withdrawals	8,600	
Janitorial revenue		18,245
Wages expense	8,650	
Garage rent expense	400	
Gas, oil, and repairs expense	785	
Totals	$30,215	$30,215

Required:

1. Enter the trial balance amounts in the Trial Balance columns of a work sheet form and complete the work sheet using the following information:
   a. Expired insurance, $395.
   b. The cleaning service rents garage and equipment storage space. At the beginning of the accounting period three months' rent was prepaid as shown by the debit balance in the Prepaid Garage Rent account. Rents for the months April through November were paid on the first day of each month and debited to the Garage Rent Expense account. The December rent was unpaid on the trial balance date.
   c. An inventory of cleaning supplies showed $145 of cleaning supplies on hand.
   d. Estimated depreciation on cleaning equipment, $320, and (e) on the trucks, $845.
   f. On November 1 the janitorial service contracted to clean the office of Desert Insurance Agency for $75 per month. The insurance agency paid in advance for three months' service, and the amount paid was credited to the Unearned Janitorial Revenue account. The janitorial service also entered into a contract and began cleaning the office of Cactus Realty on December 15. By the month-end a half month's revenue, $50, had been earned on this contract but it was unrecorded.
   g. Employees' wages amounting to $115 had accrued but were unrecorded on the trial balance date.
2. From the work sheet prepare an income statement and a classified balance sheet.
3. Prepare adjusting and closing entries from the work sheet.

Problem 4–3A

(Covers two accounting cycles)

On June 2 Jane Reed opened a real estate office she called Desert Realty, and during June she completed these transactions:

June 2 Invested $1,500 in cash and an automobile having a $4,500 fair value in the real estate agency.
2 Rented furnished office space and paid one month's rent, $275.
2 Purchased office supplies for cash, $115.
3 Paid the biweekly salary of the office secretary, $200.
15 Paid the premium on a one-year insurance policy, $360.
27 Paid the biweekly salary of the office secretary, $200.
27 Sold a house and collected a $3,200 commission.
30 Paid the June telephone bill, $40.
30 Paid for gas and oil used in the agency car during June, $85.

Required work for June:

1. Open the following accounts: Cash; Prepaid Insurance; Office Supplies; Automobile; Accumulated Depreciation, Automobile; Salaries Payable; Jane Reed, Capital; Jane Reed, Withdrawals; Income Summary; Commissions Earned; Rent Expense; Salaries Expense; Gas, Oil, and Repairs Expense; Telephone Expense; Insurance Expense; Office Supplies Expense; and Depreciation Expense, Automobile.
2. Prepare and post journal entries to record the transactions.

3. Prepare a trial balance in the Trial Balance columns of a work sheet form and complete the work sheet using the following information:
   a. One half of a month's insurance has expired.
   b. An inventory shows $85 of unused office supplies remaining.
   c. Estimated depreciation on the automobile, $90.
   d. Accrued but unpaid salary of the secretary, $20.
4. Prepare a June income statement and a June 30 classified balance sheet.
5. From the work sheet prepare and post adjusting and closing journal entries.
6. Prepare a post-closing trial balance.

During July the real estate agency completed these transactions:

July 1 Paid the July rent on the office space, $275.
     4 Purchased additional office supplies for cash, $35.
   11 Paid the biweekly salary of the office secretary, $200.
   14 Sold a building lot and collected an $800 commission.
   15 Withdrew $1,200 from the business to pay personal expenses.
   25 Paid the biweekly salary of the office secretary, $200.
   31 Paid for gas and oil used in the agency car during July, $80.
   31 Paid the July telephone bill, $35.

Required work for July:

1. Prepare and post journal entries to record the transactions.
2. Prepare a trial balance in the Trial Balance columns of a work sheet form and complete the work sheet using the following information:
   a. One month's insurance has expired.
   b. An inventory of office supplies shows $95 of unused supplies remaining.
   c. Estimated depreciation on the automobile, $90.
   d. Accrued but unpaid secretary's salary, $80.
3. Prepare a July income statement and a July 31 classified balance sheet.
4. Prepare and post adjusting and closing journal entries.
5. Prepare a post-closing trial balance.

Problem 4–4A

The ledger accounts of Golden Alleys showing account balances as of the end of its annual accounting period appear in the booklet of working papers that accompanies this text and a trial balance of the ledger is reproduced on a work sheet form provided there. The trial balance has these items:

GOLDEN ALLEYS
Trial Balance, December 31, 19—

Cash	$ 1,985	
Bowling supplies	1,775	
Prepaid insurance	810	
Bowling equipment	36,565	
Accumulated depreciation, bowling equipment		$ 9,640
Mortgage payable		10,000
Randy Owens, capital		14,850
Randy Owens, withdrawals	12,000	
Bowling revenue		38,500
Salaries expense	13,655	
Advertising expense	750	
Equipment repairs expense	420	
Rent expense	3,000	
Utilities expense	1,135	
Taxes expense	220	
Interest expense	675	
Totals	$72,990	$72,990

Required:

1. If the working papers are being used, complete the work sheet provided for the solution of this problem, using the information that follows. If the working papers are not being used, enter the trial balance on a work sheet form and complete the work sheet.
    a. Total of the inventory of unused bowling supplies, $550.
    b. Insurance expired, $540.
    c. Estimated depreciation of bowling equipment, $3,875.
    d. Accrued but unpaid and unrecorded salaries, $315.
    e. The lease contract for the space occupied by the bowling alley calls for an annual rental equal to 10% of the annual bowling revenue, with $250 payable monthly on the first day of each month. The $250 was paid each month and debited to the Rent Expense account.
    f. Accrued but unpaid and unrecorded personal property taxes on the bowling equipment, $85.
    g. The mortgage debt was incurred on June 1, and interest on the debt is at the rate of 9% annually or $75 per month. The mortgage contract calls for the payment of $225 interest each three months in advance. Interest payments of $225 each were made in advance on June 1, September 1, and December 1.
2. Prepare an income statement and a classified balance sheet.
3. Prepare adjusting and closing journal entries.
4. Post the adjusting and closing entries and prepare a post-closing trial balance. (If the working papers are not being used, omit this last requirement.)

Problem 4–5A

A trial balance of the Village Delivery Service ledger at the end of its annual accounting period has these balances:

VILLAGE DELIVERY SERVICE
Trial Balance, December 31, 19—

Cash	$ 2,775	
Accounts receivable	455	
Prepaid insurance	720	
Office supplies	245	
Office equipment	2,460	
Accumulated depreciation, office equipment		$ 470
Delivery equipment	10,790	
Accumulated depreciation, delivery equipment		3,150
Accounts payable		290
Unearned delivery service revenue		450
Betty Lee, capital		9,855
Betty Lee, withdrawals	10,400	
Delivery service revenue		38,935
Office rent expense	600	
Telephone expense	245	
Office salaries expense	5,060	
Truck drivers' wages	16,320	
Gas, oil, and repairs	2,180	
Garage rent expense	900	
Totals	$53,150	$53,150

The accounts of Village Delivery Service with their end-of-the-period balances are reproduced in the booklet of working papers that accompanies this text, and its trial balance is reproduced on a work sheet form provided there.

Required:

1. If the working papers are being used, complete the work sheet provided for the solution of this problem, using the information that follows. If the working papers are not being used, enter the trial balance on a work sheet form and complete the work sheet.

   a. The delivery service entered into contracts with three stores during November and December in which it agreed to deliver packages for each store for a fixed fee. The contract of one store, signed on December 10, provides for a $90 monthly fee, payable on the tenth of each month after service is rendered. On December 31, $60, two thirds of the first month's fee, has been earned but is unrecorded. The other two stores made advance payments on their contracts, and the delivery service credited the amounts paid to its Unearned Delivery Service Revenue account. An examination of the contracts of these stores shows that $175 of the $450 paid has been earned by the accounting period end.

   b. Insurance expired on the office equipment, $50; and on the delivery equipment, $510.

   c. An inventory shows $100 of unused office supplies on hand.

   d. Estimated depreciation on office equipment, $150; and (*e*) on delivery equipment, $2,350.

   f. Unrecorded copies of credit card invoices show that the service owes $135 for gas and oil used in the company trucks during December.

    g.   Office salaries, $50, and truck drivers' wages, $300, have accrued but are unrecorded.

2. Prepare an income statement and a classified balance sheet.
3. Prepare adjusting and closing journal entries.
4. Post the adjusting and closing entries to the accounts and prepare a post-closing trial balance. (Omit this requirement if the working papers are not being used.)

Yesterday, in the midst of preparing financial statements for his real estate agency, Jack Moss became angry with his bookkeeper and fired him. Today, Jack is sorry because in leaving the bookkeeper evidently took the work sheet and year-end balance sheet on which he was working. At the time of the fracas Jack was examining the income statement, which he now has. He has also prepared a trial balance of his ledger accounts, and he wants you to use his trial balance and the income statement to prepare adjusting and closing entries and a year-end classified balance sheet. Jack tells you that his agency has two contracts to provide property management services. In the first the agency agreed to manage an office building beginning on November 1 for a $140 monthly fee. The client paid the first three months' fees in advance at the time the contract was signed. The second contract provides for the management of an apartment building for a $50 monthly fee payable at the end of each quarter. The contract was signed on October 15, and two and a half months' fees have accrued. Jack's trial balance and income statement carry these items:

Decision problem 4–1, Jack Moss Realty

JACK MOSS REALTY

Trial Balance, December 31, 19—

Cash	$ 1,640	
Prepaid insurance	515	
Office supplies	295	
Office equipment	2,240	
Accumulated depreciation, office equipment		$ 920
Automobile	5,790	
Accumulated depreciation, automobile		1,150
Unearned property management fees		420
Jack Moss, capital		5,315
Jack Moss, withdrawals	12,400	
Sales commissions earned		25,840
Office salaries expense	6,400	
Rent expense	1,800	
Advertising expense	1,030	
Telephone expense	360	
Gas, oil, and repairs expense	1,175	
Totals	$33,645	$33,645

JACK MOSS REALTY
Income Statement for Year Ended December 31, 19—

Revenues:

Sales commissions earned	$25,840	
Property management fees earned	405	
Total revenues		$26,245

Operating expenses:

Office salaries expense	$ 6,450	
Rent expense	1,800	
Advertising expense	1,030	
Telephone expense	360	
Gas, oil, and repairs expense	1,340	
Insurance expense	385	
Office supplies expense	215	
Depreciation expense, office equipment	325	
Depreciation expense, automobile	1,200	
Total operating expenses		13,105
Net Income		$13,140

Decision problem 4–2, Bob's TV Service

On January 1 of this year Bob Litton opened Bob's TV Service; and now, at the year-end, he has asked your help in determining the results of the first year's operations and his year-end financial position. He feels he has done a lot of work, but the bank has begun to dishonor his checks, his creditors are dunning him and he is unable to pay, and he just cannot understand why he is in such a position.

You find his accounting records, such as they are, have been kept by his wife, who has had no formal training in record keeping. However, she has prepared the following statement of cash receipts and disbursements for your inspection:

BOB'S TV SERVICE
Cash Receipts and Disbursements For Year Ended December 31, 19—

Receipts:

Investment	$ 5,000	
From customers for services	32,295	$37,295

Disbursements:

Rent expense	$ 1,950	
Repair equipment	4,000	
Insurance	420	
Service truck	4,350	
Repair parts and supplies	5,900	
Wages	20,740	37,360
Bank overdraft		$ (65)

You find no errors in the statement and you learn these additional facts:

1. Mrs. Litton has a list of customers who owe a total of $450 for TV repair work done on credit.
2. The lease contract for the shop space runs for five years and requires rent payments of $150 per month, with payment of the first and last months' rent in advance. All required payments were made on time.
3. The repair equipment cost $4,000 and has an estimated eight-year useful life, after which it will be valueless.
4. The premiums of two insurance policies were paid on January 1. One premium was for $60 and gave protection for one year. The other premium purchased three years' protection.
5. The service truck item consists of an $800 down payment and 12 $200 monthly installment payments made in purchasing the truck used in making service calls, plus $1,150 paid for gas, oil, and minor repairs to the truck. The truck cost $5,600 and will be driven four years, after which it is estimated that it will have a $1,200 trade-in value on a new truck.
6. In addition to the $5,900 of repair parts and supplies paid for during the year, creditors are dunning the service for $550 for parts and supplies purchased and delivered but not paid for. An inventory shows $1,250 of unused parts and supplies on hand.
7. The $20,740 of wages consists of $7,740 paid the shop's one employee plus $250 per week withdrawn by Mr. Litton for personal expenses. In addition, $60 is owed the one employee for wages earned since the last payday.

Prepare an income statement showing the results of the first year's operations of Bob' TV service and prepare a classified balance sheet showing its financial position as of the year-end.

Decision problem 4–3, Pay and Take Cleaners

During his second year in college, Jerry Brill, as the only heir, inherited Pay and Take Cleaners upon the death of his father. He immediately dropped out of school and took over management of the business. At the time he took over, Jerry recognized he knew little about accounting, but he reasoned that if the cash of the business increased, it was doing OK. Therefore, he was pleased as he watched the balance of the concern's cash grow from $2,550 when he took over at the beginning of the year to $7,700 at the end of the year. Furthermore, at the year-end he reasoned that since he had withdrawn $15,000 from the business to buy a new car and pay personal expenses, the business had earned $20,150 during the year. He arrived at the $20,150 by adding the $5,150 increase in cash to the $15,000 he had withdrawn from the business, and he was shocked when he received the following income statement and learned the business had earned less than the amounts he had withdrawn.

After mulling over the statement for several days, he has asked you to explain how in a year in which the cash increased $5,150 and he had withdrawn $15,000, the business could have earned only $13,950. In examining the accounts of the business you note that accrued salaries and wages payable at the beginning of the year were $110, but had increased to $440 at the year's end. Also, the balance of the Cleaning Supplies account had decreased $180 between the beginning and end of the year and the balance of the Prepaid Insurance account had decreased $240. However, except for the changes in

PAY AND TAKE CLEANERS
Income Statement for Year Ended December 31, 19—

Cleaning revenue earned..............................		$47,945
Operating expenses:		
Salaries and wages expense........................	$26,250	
Cleaning supplies expense..........................	760	
Insurance expense....................................	985	
Depreciation expense, cleaning equipment....	1,250	
Depreciation expense, building	4,200	
Property taxes expense	550	
Total operating expenses		33,995
Net Income...		$13,950

these three accounts, the change in cash, and the changes in the accumulated depreciation accounts, there were no other changes in the balances of the company's asset and liability accounts during the year. Back your explanation with a calculation accounting for the increase in cash.

Close revenue accounts &
expense accounts
to Income Summary
Close Income Summary
to Capital account
Close withdrawls
to capital account

After studying Chapter 5, you should be able to:

■ Explain the nature of each item entering into the calculation of cost of goods sold and be able to calculate cost of goods sold and gross profit from sales.

■ Prepare a work sheet and the financial statements for a merchandising business using a periodic inventory system.

■ Prepare entries to close the temporary proprietorship accounts of a merchandising business and to put the new inventory in the accounts.

■ Explain the three bases of revenue recognition and tell when the use of each is appropriate.

■ Define or explain the words and phrases listed in the chapter Glossary.

chapter 5

Accounting for a merchandising concern

The accounting records and reports of the Owen law practice, as described in previous chapters, are those of a service enterprise. Other service enterprises are laundries, taxicab companies, barber and beauty shops, theaters, and golf courses. Each performs a service for a commission or fee, and the net income of each is the difference between fees or commissions earned and operating expenses.

A merchandising concern, on the other hand, whether a wholesaler or retailer, earns revenue by selling goods or merchandise, and a net income results when revenue from sales exceeds the cost of the goods sold plus operating expenses, as the following condensed income statement shows:

XYZ Store
Condensed Income Statement

Net Revenue from sales...........	$100,000
Less cost of goods sold.....	60,000
Gross profit from sales	$ 40,000
Less operating expenses....	25,000
Net Income......................	$ 15,000

The store of the illustrated income statement sold for $100,000 goods that cost $60,000, and thereby earned a $40,000 gross profit from sales, from which it subtracted $25,000 of operating expenses to show a $15,000 net income.

Gross profit from sales, as shown on the illustrated income statement, is the "profit" before operating expenses are deducted; and accounting for the factors that enter into its calculation differentiates the accounting of a merchandising concern from that of a service enterprise.

Gross profit from sales is determined by subtracting the cost of whatever goods were sold from the revenue resulting from their sale; but before the subtraction can be made, both revenue from sales and cost of goods sold must be determined.

Revenue from sales

Revenue from sales consists of gross proceeds from merchandise sales less returns, allowances, and discounts. It is commonly reported on an income statement as follows:

Kona Sales Company
Income Statement for Year Ended December 31, 19—

Revenue from sales:		
Gross sales......................................		$78,750
Less: Sales returns and allowances....	$650	
Sales discounts......................	750	1,400
Net sales..		$77,350

Gross sales

The item, Gross sales, $78,750, on the illustrated partial income statement is the total cash and credit sales made by the company during the year. Cash sales were "rung up" on a cash register as each sale was completed, and at the end of each day the register total showed the amount of that day's cash sales, which was recorded with an entry like this:

Nov.	3	Cash...	205.00	
		Sales..		205.00
		To record the day's cash sales.		

In addition an entry like this was used to record credit sales:

Nov.	3	Accounts Receivable...	45.00	
		Sales..		45.00
		Sold merchandise on credit.		

As a result, at the year-end the $78,750 credit balance of the company's Sales account showed the total of its cash and credit sales for the year.

Sales returns and allowances

In most stores a customer is permitted to return any unsatisfactory merchandise he has purchased; or he is sometimes allowed to keep the unsatisfactory goods and is given an allowance or an amount off its sales price. Either way, returns and allowances result from dissatisfied customers; consequently, it is important for management to know the amount of such returns and allowances and their relation to sales. Information as to returns and allowances is supplied by the Sales Returns and Allowances account when each return or allowance is recorded as follows:

Nov.	4	Sales Returns and Allowances.....................................	20.00	
		Accounts Receivable (or Cash).............................		20.00
		Customer returned unsatisfactory merchandise.		

Sales discounts

When goods are sold on credit, the terms of payment are always made definite so there will be no misunderstanding as to the amount and time of payment. The terms normally appear on the invoice or sales ticket and are part of the sales agreement. Exact terms granted usually depend upon the custom of the trade. In some trades it is customary for invoices to become due and payable ten days after the end of the month in which the sale occurred. Invoices in these trades carry terms, "n/10 EOM." In other trades invoices become due and payable 30 days after the invoice date and carry terms of "n/30." This means that the net amount of the invoice is due 30 days after the invoice date.

When credit periods are long, creditors usually grant discounts, called *cash discounts,* for early payments. This practice reduces the amount invested in accounts receivable and tends to decrease losses from uncollectible accounts. When discounts for early payment are granted, they are made part of the credit terms and appear on the invoice as, for example, "Terms: 2/10, n/60." Terms of 2/10, n/60 mean that the *credit period* is 60 days but that the debtor may deduct 2% from the invoice amount if payment is made within 10 days after the invoice date. The ten-day period is known as the *discount period.*

Since at the time of a sale it is not known if the customer will pay within the discount period and take advantage of a cash discount, normally sales discounts are not recorded until the customer pays. For example, on November 12, Kona Sales Company sold $100 of merchandise to a customer on credit, terms 2/10, n/60, and recorded the sale as follows:

Nov.	12	Accounts Receivable	100.00	
		Sales		100.00
		Sold merchandise, terms 2/10, n/60.		

At the time of the sale the customer had a choice. He could receive credit for paying the full $100 by paying Kona Sales Company $98 any time before November 22. Or he could wait 60 days, until January 11, and pay the full $100. If he elected to pay by November 22 and take advantage of the cash discount, Kona Sales Company would record the receipt of the $98 as follows:

Nov.	22	Cash..	98.00	
		Sales Discounts...	2.00	
		Accounts Receivable...		100.00
		Received payment for the November 12 sale less the discount.		

Sales discounts are accumulated in the Sales Discounts account until the end of an accounting period when their total appears on the income statement as a deduction from gross sales. This is logical, since a sales discount is an "amount off" the regular price of goods that is granted for early payment, and as a result reduces revenue from sales.

Cost of goods sold

An automobile dealer or an appliance store, both of which make a limited number of sales each day, can easily refer to their records at the time of each sale and record the cost of the car or appliance sold. A drugstore, on the other hand, would find this difficult. For instance, if a drug or grocery store sells a customer a tube of toothpaste, a box of aspirin, and a magazine, it can easily record with a cash register the sale of these items at marked selling prices; but it would be difficult to maintain records that would enable it to also "look up" and record as "cost of goods sold" the costs of the items sold. As a result, stores such as drug, grocery, and others selling a volume of low-priced items make no effort to record the cost of the goods sold at the time of each sale. Rather, they wait until the end of an accounting period, take a physical inventory, and from the inventory and their accounting records determine at one time the cost of all goods sold during the period.

The end-of-the-period inventories taken by drug, grocery, hardware, or like stores in order to learn the cost of the goods they have sold are called *periodic inventories;* and the system used by such stores in accounting for cost of goods sold is known as a *periodic inventory system.* Such a system is described and discussed in this chapter. The system used by a car or appliance dealer to record the cost of each car or appliance sold depends on a *perpetual inventory record* of cars or appliances in stock, and as a result is known as a *perpetual inventory system of accounting for goods on hand and sold.* It is discussed in Chapter 9.

As previously said, a store using a periodic inventory system makes no effort to determine and record the cost of items sold as they are sold. Rather, it waits until the end of an accounting period and determines at one time the cost of all the goods it sold during the period. And to do this, it must have information as to (1) the cost of the merchandise it had on hand at the beginning of the period, (2) the cost of the merchandise it purchased during the period, and (3) the cost of the unsold goods on hand at the period end. With this information a store can, for example, determine the cost of the goods it sold during a period as follows:

Cost of goods on hand at beginning of period $10,000
Cost of goods purchased during the period 65,000
Goods available for sale during the period $75,000
Unsold goods on hand at the period end 15,000
Cost of goods sold during the period $60,000

The store of the calculation had $10,000 of merchandise at the beginning of the accounting period, and during the period it purchased an additional $65,000. Consequently, it had available and could have sold $75,000 of merchandise. However, $15,000 of this merchandise was on hand unsold at the period end; therefore, the cost of the goods it sold during the period was $60,000.

A reexamination of the foregoing calculation will show that three factors enter into calculating cost of goods sold: (1) the cost of the goods on hand at the beginning, (2) the cost of the goods purchased, and (3) the cost of the unsold goods on hand at the end. The sum of the first two is the amount of goods that were for sale, and by subtracting the last, the cost of the unsold goods on hand at the end, cost of goods sold is determined.

Merchandise inventories

The merchandise on hand at the beginning of an accounting period is called the *beginning inventory* and that on hand at the end is the *ending inventory*. Furthermore, since accounting periods follow one after another, the ending inventory of one period always becomes the beginning inventory of the next.

When a periodic inventory system is in use, cost of goods on hand at the end of an accounting period, the ending inventory, is determined by (1) counting the items on the shelves in the store and in the stockroom, (2) multiplying the count for each kind of goods by its cost, and (3) adding the costs of the different kinds.

After the cost of the ending inventory is determined in this manner, it appears on the income statement as a subtraction in the cost of goods sold section. Also, by means of a closing entry, it is posted to an

Cost of goods sold, periodic inventory system

account called *Merchandise Inventory*, where it remains throughout the succeeding accounting period as a record of the inventory at the end of the period ended and the beginning of the succeeding period.

It should be emphasized at this point that, other than to correct errors, entries are made in the Merchandise Inventory account only at the end of each accounting period; the entries are closing entries; and furthermore, since some goods are soon sold and other goods purchased, the account does not long show the amount of goods on hand. Rather, as soon as goods are sold or purchased, the account balance becomes a historical record of the amount of goods that were on hand at the end of the last period and the beginning of the new period.

Cost of merchandise purchased

When a periodic inventory system is in use, cost of merchandise purchased is determined by subtracting from purchases any discounts, returns, and allowances and then adding any freight charges on the goods purchased. However, before examining this calculation it is best to see how the amounts involved are accumulated.

Under a periodic inventory system, when merchandise is bought for resale, its cost is debited to an account called *Purchases*, as follows:

Nov.	5	Purchases...	1,000.00	
		Accounts Payable		1,000.00
		Purchased merchandise on credit, invoice dated November 2, terms 2/10, n/30.		

The Purchases account has as its sole purpose the accumulation of the cost of all merchandise bought for resale during an accounting period. The account does not at any time show whether the merchandise is on hand or has been disposed of through sale or other means.

If a credit purchase like that in the entry just given is subject to a cash discount, payment within the discount period results in a credit to *Purchases Discounts*, as in the following entry:

Nov.	12	Accounts Payable	1,000.00	
		Purchases Discounts...		20.00
		Cash..		980.00
		Paid for the purchase of November 5 less the discount.		

When purchase discounts are involved, it is important that every invoice on which there is a discount be paid within the discount period, so that no discounts are lost. On the other hand, good cash management requires that no invoice be paid until the last day of its discount period. Consequently, to ensure that no discount is lost for lack of payment within the discount period but that no invoice is paid before the end of the discount period, every invoice must be filed in such a way that it automatically comes to the attention of the company treasurer or other disbursing officer on the last day of its discount period. A simple way to do this is to provide a file with 31 folders, one for each day in a month. Then after an invoice is recorded, it is placed in the file folder of the last day of its discount period. For example, if an invoice is dated November 2, with terms of 2/10, n/30, the last day of its discount period is November 12, and such an invoice would be filed in folder number 12. Then on November 12 this invoice, together with any other invoices in the same folder, would be removed and paid or refiled for payment on a later date.

Sometimes merchandise received from suppliers is not acceptable and must be returned or, if kept, is kept only because the supplier grants an allowance or reduction in its price. When merchandise is returned, the purchaser "gets his money back"; but from a managerial point of view more is involved. Buying merchandise, receiving and inspecting it, deciding that the merchandise is unsatisfactory, and returning it is a costly procedure that should be held to a minimum; and the first step in holding it to a minimum is to know the amount of returns and allowances. Therefore, to make this information available to management, returns and allowances on purchases are commonly recorded in an account called *Purchases Returns and Allowances,* as follows:

Nov.	14	Accounts Payable	65.00	
		Purchases Returns and Allowances		65.00
		Returned defective merchandise.		

When an invoice is subject to a cash discount and a portion of the goods listed on the invoice is returned before the invoice is paid, the discount applies to just the goods purchased and kept. For example, if $500 of merchandise is purchased, terms 2/10, n/60, and $100 of the goods are returned before the invoice is paid, the discount applies only to the $400 of goods purchased and kept.

Sometimes a manufacturer or wholesaler pays freight, express, or other transportation costs on merchandise he sells and the total cost of the goods to the purchaser is the amount paid the manufacturer or wholesaler. Other times the purchaser must pay transportation costs; and when he does, such charges are a proper addition to the cost of the goods purchased and may be recorded with a debit to the Purchases account. However, more complete information is obtained if such costs are debited to an account called *Freight-In,* as follows:

Nov.	24	Freight-in...	22.00	
		Cash..		22.00
		Paid express charges on merchandise purchased.		

When freight or express charges are involved, it is important that the buyer and seller understand which party is responsible for the transportation costs. Normally, in quoting a price, the seller makes this clear. He may quote a price of, say $400, FOB factory. FOB factory means free on board or loaded on board the means of transportation at the factory free of loading charges, and the buyer pays transportation costs from there. Likewise, FOB destination means the seller will pay transportation costs to the destination of the goods.

Sometimes, when terms are FOB factory, the seller will prepay the transportation costs as a service to the buyer, adding the amount on the invoice and increasing its total. In such a case, if a cash discount is involved, the discount does not apply to the transportation charges.

When an income statement is prepared at the end of an accounting period, the balances of the Purchases, Purchases Returns and Allowances, Purchases Discounts, and Freight-In accounts are combined on it as follows to show the cost of the merchandise purchased during the period:

Purchases		$48,650	
Less: Purchases returns and allowances	$275		
Purchases discounts........................	550	825	
Net purchases..		$47,825	
Add: Freight-in		1,100	
Cost of goods purchased			$48,925

Cost of goods sold

The last item in the foregoing calculation is the cost of the merchandise purchased during the accounting period, and it is combined on the income statement with the beginning and ending inventories to arrive at cost of goods sold as follows:

Cost of goods sold:			
Merchandise inventory, January 1, 19—			$ 7,750
Purchases...	$48,650		
Less: Purchases returns and allowances....	$275		
Purchases discounts	550	825	
Net purchases		$47,825	
Add: Freight-in		1,100	
Cost of goods purchased......................................			48,925
Goods available for sale			$56,675
Merchandise inventory, December 31, 19—			8,950
Cost of goods sold...			$47,725

Inventory losses

Under a periodic inventory system the cost of any merchandise lost through shrinkage, spoilage, or shoplifting is automatically included in cost of goods sold. For example, assume a store lost $500 of merchandise to shoplifters during a year. This caused its year-end inventory to be $500 less than it otherwise would have been, since these goods were not available for inclusion in the year-end count; and since the year-end inventory was $500 smaller because of the loss, the cost of the goods the store sold was $500 greater.

Many stores are troubled with shoplifting; and although under a periodic inventory system the cost of such losses is automatically included in cost of goods sold, it is often important to know their extent. Consequently, a way to estimate shoplifting losses is described in Chapter 9.

Income statement of a merchandising concern

A classified income statement for a merchandising concern has (1) a revenue section, (2) a cost of goods sold section, and (3) an operating expenses section. The first two have already been discussed in this chapter, but note in Illustration 5–1 how they are brought together to show gross profit from sales.

Observe also in Illustration 5–1 how operating expenses are classified as either "Selling expenses" or "General and administrative expenses." Selling expenses include expenses of storing and preparing goods for sale, promoting sales, actually making sales, and if there is not a delivery department separate from the selling departments, the expenses of delivering goods to customers. General and administrative expenses include the general office, accounting, personnel, and credit and collection expenses.

Sometimes an expenditure should be divided or prorated part to selling expenses and part to general and administrative expenses. Kona Sales Company divided the rent on its store building in this manner, as an examination of Illustration 5–1 will reveal. However, it did not prorate its insurance expense because the amount involved was so small the company felt the extra exactness did not warrant the extra work.

When an expense such as rent or heating and lighting is not prorated, it is a common practice to classify the expense as either a general and administrative expense or as a selling expense depending upon whether the office or the store occupies the greater amount of space. For example, if selling activities occupy more space than the office and rent is not prorated, it is only fair to classify it as a selling expense.

Work sheet of a merchandising concern

A concern selling merchandise, like a service-type company, uses a work sheet in bringing together the end-of-the-period information needed in preparing its income statement, balance sheet, and adjusting and closing entries. Such a work sheet, that of Kona Sales Company, is shown in Illustration 5–2.

Note in Illustration 5–2 that the merchandising accounts are stressed

Kona Sales Company
Income Statement for Year Ended December 31, 19—

Revenue:			
Gross sales			$78,750
Less: Sales returns and allowances		$ 650	
Sales discounts		750	1,400
Net sales			$77,350
Cost of goods sold:			
Merchandise inventory, January 1, 19—		$ 7,750	
Purchases	$48,650		
Less: Purchases returns and allowances	$275		
Purchases discounts	550	825	
Net purchases	$47,825		
Add: Freight-in	1,100		
Cost of goods purchased		48,925	
Goods available for sale		$56,675	
Merchandise inventory, December 31, 19—		8,950	
Cost of goods sold			47,725
Gross profit from sales			$29,625
Operating expenses:			
Selling expenses:			
Sales salaries expense	$ 8,200		
Rent expense, selling space	4,800		
Advertising expense	900		
Freight-out and delivery expense	1,350		
Store supplies expense	425		
Depreciation expense, store equipment	775		
Total selling expenses		$16,450	
General and administrative expenses:			
Office salaries expense	$ 3,100		
Rent expense, office space	600		
Insurance expense	65		
Office supplies expense	125		
Depreciation expense, office equipment	160		
Total general and administrative expenses		4,050	
Total operating expenses			20,500
Net Income			$ 9,125

Illustration 5–1

by the use of color. This is done because the remainder of the accounts receive the same work sheet treatment as do the accounts of a service-type concern; and since this was fully discussed in Chapter 4, only the treatment of the merchandising accounts needs consideration here.

Trial Balance columns

The Trial Balance columns of Kona Sales Company's work sheet, Illustration 5–2, show the balances of the company's accounts as of December 31, 19—. The account balances were taken from the company's ledger on that date and indicate that—

1. The January 1 beginning-of-the-year inventory was $7,750.
2. Sales totaling $78,750 were made during the year.

Kona Sales Company
Work Sheet for Year Ended December 31, 19—

Account Titles	Trial Balance Dr.	Trial Balance Cr.	Adjustments Dr.	Adjustments Cr.	Adjusted Trial Balance Dr.	Adjusted Trial Balance Cr.	Income Statement Dr.	Income Statement Cr.	Balance Sheet Dr.	Balance Sheet Cr.
Cash	2,400				2,400				2,400	
Accounts receivable	3,300				3,300				3,300	
Merchandise inventory	7,750				7,750		7,750	8,950	8,950	
Prepaid insurance	195			(a) 65	130				130	
Store supplies	590			(b) 425	165				165	
Office supplies	185			(c) 125	60				60	
Store equipment	7,910				7,910				7,910	
Accumulated depreciation, store equipment		3,200		(d) 775		3,975				3,975
Office equipment	1,590				1,590				1,590	
Accumulated depreciation, office equipment		250		(e) 160		410				410
Accounts payable		1,700				1,700				1,700
George Nelson, capital		14,095				14,095				14,095
George Nelson, withdrawals	4,800				4,800				4,800	
Sales		78,750				78,750		78,750		
Sales returns and allowances	650				650		650			
Sales discounts	750				750		750			
Purchases	48,650				48,650		48,650			
Purchases returns and allowances		275				275		275		
Purchase discounts		550				550		550		
Freight-in	1,100				1,100		1,100			
Sales salaries expense	8,200				8,200		8,200			
Rent expense, selling space	4,800				4,800		4,800			
Advertising expense	900				900		900			
Freight-out and delivery expense	1,350				1,350		1,350			
Office salaries expense	3,100				3,100		3,100			
Rent expense, office space	600				600		600			
	98,820	98,820								
Insurance expense			(a) 65		65		65			
Store supplies expense			(b) 425		425		425			
Office supplies expense			(c) 125		125		125			
Depreciation expense, store equipment			(d) 775		775		775			
Depreciation expense, office equipment			(e) 160		160		160			
			1,550	1,550	99,755	99,755	79,400	88,525	29,305	20,180
Net Income							9,125			9,125
							88,525	88,525	29,305	29,305

Illustration 5–2

3. Customers returned $650 of goods they purchased.
4. Sales discounts totaling $750 were granted during the year.
5. The year's purchases of merchandise amounted to $48,650.
6. Merchandise purchases totaling $275 were returned.
7. Purchases discounts totaling $550 were taken during the year.
8. Freight charges totaling $1,100 were paid on goods purchased.

Adjustments columns and Adjusted Trial Balance columns

Generally none of the merchandising accounts require adjustments. Consequently, no adjustments appear opposite these accounts in the Adjustments columns and the unadjusted trial balance amounts are carried directly into the Adjusted Trial Balance columns.

Income Statement columns

In any company the accounts that appear on its income statement are those the balances of which are carried into the Income Statement columns of its work sheet; and in a merchandising concern these are the (1) revenue, (2) cost of goods sold, and (3) operating expense accounts. (The work sheet treatment of the operating expense accounts was discussed in Chapter 4 and needs no further consideration here.)

Revenue accounts   The Sales account is the primary revenue account of a merchandising concern. It is credited throughout each accounting period for the selling price of goods sold, and always reaches the end of the period with a credit balance, which is carried into the work sheet's Income Statement credit column.

Sales returns and allowances and sales discounts are in effect negative sales; and although the Sales Returns and Allowances and Sales Discounts accounts are classified as revenue accounts, they are really negative revenue accounts. Throughout each accounting period they are debited for returns, allowances, and discounts and both reach the period end with debit balances which are carried into the Income Statement debit column, where in effect the returns, allowances, and discounts are subtracted from the sales when the debit column total is subtracted from the credit column total in arriving at net income.

Cost of goods sold accounts   When a work sheet is prepared for a company selling merchandise, (1) the debit balances of its Merchandise Inventory, Purchases, and Freight-In accounts are carried into the Income Statement debit column; (2) the credit balances of the Purchases Returns and Allowances and Purchases Discounts accounts are carried into the Income Statement credit column; after which (3) the dollar amount of the ending inventory is entered directly in both the Income Statement credit column and Balance Sheet debit column.

It is easy to understand why the balances of the Merchandise Inventory, Purchases, and Freight-In accounts are carried into the Income Statement debit column—the balances are debit balances and they enter into the calculation of the net income. Likewise, it is easy to understand why the credit balances of the Purchases Returns and Allowances and Purchases Discounts accounts are carried into the Income Statement credit column — they are in effect subtractions from Purchases in the debit column. However, the reasons for the work sheet treatment of the ending inventory are not so apparent and require the following explanations:

First: Note that there are two inventories to be dealt with on the work sheet of a company selling merchandise — the beginning-of-the-period inventory and the end-of-the-period inventory.

Second: At the end of a period, before closing entries are posted, it is the beginning inventory amount that appears in the accounts as the debit balance of the Merchandise Inventory account; and it is this beginning inventory amount that is entered in the Trial Balance debit column opposite the account title, Merchandise Inventory, and is carried into the Adjusted Trial Balance and Income Statement debit columns.

Third: Before closing entries are posted, the dollar amount of the ending inventory does not appear in any account. As was explained earlier, the ending inventory is determined at the end of each period by counting the items of unsold merchandise on hand, multiplying the count for each kind by its cost, and adding the dollar amounts of the several kinds to determine the number of dollars of inventory.

Fourth: As soon as the number of dollars of ending inventory is determined, it is entered directly on the work sheet in both the Income Statement credit column and the Balance Sheet debit column. It is thus entered for three reasons: (1) After the other income statement items (including the operating expenses) have been carried into the Income Statement columns, it is necessary to enter the amount of the ending inventory if the difference between the two columns is to equal the net income or loss. (2) Entering the ending inventory in the Income Statement credit column puts this amount on the work sheet in position to become part of one of the closing entries and thus be taken into the accounts as the historical record of the inventory on hand at the end of the period. (Closing entries for a company selling merchandise are discussed in more detail later.) And finally, (3) since the amount of the ending inventory is an end-of-the-period asset, entering it in the Balance Sheet debit column puts this item in position to be added to the other end-of-the-period assets and to appear on the balance sheet.

Completing the work sheet

After the various income statement and balance sheet amounts of a company selling merchandise are sorted and entered in the proper columns of its work sheet, the columns are totaled and the work sheet is completed in the usual way.

Preparing the statements; adjusting entries

As in a service-type concern, the work sheet of a company selling merchandise is a tool for bringing together information needed in preparing the financial statements. The income statement is prepared from information in the Income Statement columns, the balance sheet from the Balance Sheet columns, and no essentially new techniques are required in the preparation of either.

Likewise, no new techniques are required in preparing and posting adjusting entries. Each adjustment in the work sheet's Adjustments columns requires an adjusting entry that is journalized and posted in the usual manner.

Closing entries

The Income Statement columns of its work sheet provide the information needed by a merchandising concern in making its closing entries, just as in a service enterprise. Furthermore, an examination of the following closing entries and the work sheet of Illustration 5–2,

Dec.	31	Income Summary...	79,400.00	
		Merchandise Inventory		7,750.00
		Sales Returns and Allowances...............................		650.00
		Sales Discounts...		750.00
		Purchases..		48,650.00
		Freight-In..		1,100.00
		Sales Salaries Expense......................................		8,200.00
		Rent Expense, Selling Space...............................		4,800.00
		Advertising Expense...		900.00
		Freight-Out and Delivery Expense.........................		1,350.00
		Office Salaries Expense......................................		3,100.00
		Rent Expense, Office Space................................		600.00
		Insurance Expense...		65.00
		Store Supplies Expense......................................		425.00
		Office Supplies Expense		125.00
		Depreciation Expense, Store Equipment.................		775.00
		Depreciation Expense, Office Equipment................		160.00
		To remove the beginning inventory from the accounts and to close the temporary proprietorship accounts having debit balances.		
	31	Merchandise Inventory	8,950.00	
		Sales	78,750.00	
		Purchases Returns and Allowances	275.00	
		Purchases Discounts...	550.00	
		Income Summary...		88,525.00
		To put the ending inventory into the accounts and to close the temporary proprietorship accounts having credit balances.		
	31	Income Summary..	9,125.00	
		George Nelson, Capital..		9,125.00
		To close the Income Summary account.		
	31	George Nelson, Capital..	4,800.00	
		George Nelson, Withdrawals		4,800.00
		To close the Withdrawals account.		

from which they were prepared, will show these closing entries are prepared in the same way as are those of a service-type company. In both types of companies the Income Summary account is debited for the work sheet's Income Statement debit column total and each account having an item in the column is credited. Then, each account having an item in the Income Statement credit column is debited and the Income Summary account is credited for the column total. And so on, as was explained in Chapter 4.

Although there is nothing essentially new about the closing entries of a merchandising concern, their effect on the Merchandise Inventory account should be observed.

Closing
entries
and the
inventory

Before closing entries were posted, the Merchandise Inventory account of Kona Sales Company showed in its $7,750 debit balance the amount of the company's beginning-of-the-period inventory, as follows:

											Merchandise Inventory													ACCOUNT NO. 114

DATE	EXPLANATION	FO-LIO	DEBIT	CREDIT	BALANCE
1978 Dec. 31		63	7 7 5 0 00		7 7 5 0 00

Then, when the first closing entry was posted, its $7,750 credit to the Merchandise Inventory account had the effect of clearing the beginning inventory from the account, as follows:

											Merchandise Inventory													ACCOUNT NO. 114

DATE	EXPLANATION	FO-LIO	DEBIT	CREDIT	BALANCE
1978 Dec. 31		63	7 7 5 0 00		7 7 5 0 00
1979 Dec. 31		77		7 7 5 0 00	- 0 -

After this, when the second closing entry was posted, its $8,950 debit to Merchandise Inventory put back into the account the amount of the ending inventory, as follows, where the amount remains throughout the succeeding year as the debit balance of the account and as a historical record of the amount of inventory on hand at the end of 1979 and the beginning of 1980.

DATE	EXPLANATION	FO-LIO	DEBIT	CREDIT	BALANCE
1978 Dec. 31		63	7 7 5 0 00		7 7 5 0 00
1979 Dec. 31		77		7 7 5 0 00	- 0 -
31		77	8 9 5 0 00		8 9 5 0 00

Merchandise Inventory — ACCOUNT NO. 114

Other methods

There are several ways to handle the beginning and ending inventories in the end-of-the-period procedures. However, all have the same objectives, which are: (1) to remove the beginning inventory amount from the Merchandise Inventory account and charge it to Income Summary and (2) to enter the ending inventory amount in the inventory account and credit it to Income Summary. These objectives may be achieved with closing entries as explained in this chapter or, for example, adjusting entries to accomplish the same objectives may be used. Either method is satisfactory, but most accountants prefer to use closing entries because the amounts debited and credited to Income Summary in the closing entries may be taken directly from the work sheet, which cannot be done if adjusting entries are used.

Dispensing with the Adjusted Trial Balance columns

Thus far, because using such columns makes learning easier, all illustrated work sheets have had Adjusted Trial Balance columns. However, the experienced accountant commonly omits these columns from his work sheet in order to reduce the time and effort required in its preparation. When he does so, after he has entered the adjustments in the Adjustments columns, he combines the adjustment amounts with the trial balance amounts and sorts the combined amounts directly into the Income Statement and Balance Sheet columns in a single operation. In other words, he simply eliminates the adjusted trial balance from his work sheet.

Bases of revenue recognition

The Accounting Principles Board has ruled that revenue is realized and in most cases should be recognized in the accounting records upon the completion of a sale or when services have been performed and are billable.[1] This is known as the *sales basis for revenue recognition*. Under it a sale is considered to be completed when assets such as cash or the right to collect cash within a short period of time are received in exchange for goods sold.

Theoretically revenue is earned throughout the entire performance of a service or throughout the whole process of securing goods for

---

[1] Accounting Principles Board, "Omnibus Opinion—1966," *APB Opinion No. 10* (New York: AICPA, December 1966), par. 12.

sale, taking a customer's order, and delivering the goods.[2] Yet, until all steps are completed and there is a right to collect the sale price, the requirements of the *objectivity principle* are not fulfilled and revenue is not recognized.

An exception to the required use of the sales basis is made for installment sales when payments are to be made over a relatively long period of time and there is considerable doubt as to the amounts that ultimately will be collected. Such sales, when collection of the full sales price is in doubt, may be accounted for on a cash basis.[3]

When the *cash basis of revenue recognition* is used in accounting for an installment sale, the amount of revenue from the sale recognized in an accounting period is related to the portion of the total installment sale price collected in cash during the period. For example, if one fourth of the full sale price is collected in a given year, normally one fourth of the revenue, one fourth of the cost of the goods sold, and one fourth of the expenses directly related to the sale are recognized in that year.

Sometimes the sales basis completely fails in causing revenue to be recognized in the period in which it is earned. For example, large construction jobs often take two or more years to complete. Consequently, if a construction firm has only a few jobs in process at any time and it recognizes revenue on a sales basis (upon the completion of each job), it may have a year in which no jobs are completed and no revenue is recognized even though the year is one of heavy activity. As a result, construction firms may and do recognize revenue on a *percentage-of-completion basis,* which is a second exception to the required use of the sales basis.

When revenue is recognized on a percentage-of-completion basis, both the revenue from a job and its percent of completion are related to construction costs expended. For example, if 20% of the total estimated construction costs for a job are incurred in a given year, then 20% of the work on the job is assumed to have been completed in that year and 20% of the job's contract price is recognized in the year's revenue.

Space does not permit a full discussion of the cash basis and the percentage-of-completion basis of revenue recognition. This must be reserved for a more advanced text.

As previously stated, when a periodic inventory system is in use, the dollar amount of the ending inventory is determined by (1) counting the items of unsold merchandise remaining in the store at the accounting period end, (2) multiplying the count for each kind of item

Taking the ending inventory

---

[2] APB, "Basic Concepts and Accounting Principles Underlying Financial Statements of Business Enterprises," *APB Statement No. 4* (New York: AICPA, October 1970), par. 149.

[3] APB, "Omnibus Opinion—1966," par. 12.

by its cost, and (3) adding the costs for all the items. The first step, counting the items, is called taking an inventory.

Counting unsold merchandise at the end of an accounting period is often a difficult task; and unless great care is exercised, items may be omitted from the count or they may be counted more than once. Because of this, inventories are commonly taken at night, on holidays, and on weekends; or the store is closed for business in order to take the inventory.

A store's salesclerks who are familiar with the store and its merchandise are usually best equipped to make an inventory count. Before the count is started, the merchandise should be straightened and arranged in an orderly fashion on the shelves and in the showcases. Items are less apt to be counted twice or omitted if prenumbered inventory tickets like the one shown in Illustration 5–3 are used in

INVENTORY TICKET no.	786
Item	
Quantity counted	
Sales price	$
Cost price	$
Purchase date	
Counted by	
Checked by	

Illustration 5–3

making the count. If inventory tickets are used, at the start of the count a sufficient number of tickets, at least one for each type of product on hand, is issued to each department in the store. When the inventory count is made, a clerk counts the quantity of each product and from the count and the price tag attached to the merchandise fills in the information on the inventory ticket. The clerk then initials the ticket and attaches it to the counted items. A department head or other responsible person usually examines and recounts a sufficient proportion of the items to ensure an accurate count. In each department, after the clerks complete the count, the department is examined for uncounted items. At this stage, inventory tickets are attached to all counted items. Consequently, any products without tickets attached are uncounted. After all items are counted and tickets attached, the tickets are removed and sent to the accounting department for completion of the inventory. To ensure that no ticket is lost or left attached to merchandise, all the prenumbered tickets issued are accounted for when the tickets arrive in the accounting department.

In the accounting department, the information on the tickets is copied on inventory summary sheets and the sheets are completed by multiplying the number of units of each product by its unit cost. This gives the dollar amount of each product on hand, and the total for all products is the amount of the inventory.

A trade discount is a deduction (often as much as 40% or more) **Trade** from a list or catalog price and is used in determining the actual price **discounts** of the goods to which it applies. Such discounts are discussed here primarily to distinguish them from the cash discounts described earlier in this chapter.

Trade discounts are commonly used by manufacturers and wholesalers to avoid republication of catalogs when selling prices change. If selling prices change, catalog prices can be adjusted by merely issuing a new list of discounts to be applied to the catalog prices. Trade discounts are also used to offer different prices to different classes of customers. For example, a manufacturer might offer to sell to wholesalers at 40% off catalog list prices and at the same time offer to sell to retailers at 30% off list prices.

Trade discounts are not entered in the accounts by either party to a sale. For example, if a manufacturer sells on credit an item listed in its catalog at $100, less a 40% trade discount, it will record the sale as follows:

Dec.	10	Accounts Receivable	60.00	
		Sales		60.00
		Sold merchandise on credit.		

The buyer will also enter the purchase in his records at $60, and if a cash discount is involved, say 2% off for payment in ten days, it applies only to the amount of the purchase, $60.

Merchandise purchased that does not meet specifications on **Debit and** delivery, goods received in damaged condition, goods received that **credit** were not ordered, goods received short of the amount ordered and **memoranda** billed, and invoice errors are matters for adjustment between the buyer and seller. In some cases the buyer can make the adjustment, and in others the adjustment is a subject for negotiation between the buyer and the seller. When there are invoice errors or when goods are received that were not ordered, the purchasing firm may make the adjustment. If it does, it must notify the seller of its action, and commonly it does this by sending a *debit memorandum* or a *credit memorandum.*

A debit memorandum is a business form on which are space for the name and address of the concern to which it is directed and the printed words, "WE DEBIT YOUR ACCOUNT," followed by space for typing in the reason for the debit. A credit memorandum carries the words, "WE CREDIT YOUR ACCOUNT." To illustrate the use of a debit memorandum, assume a buyer of merchandise discovers an invoice error that reduces the invoice total by $10. For such an error the buyer notifies the seller with a debit memorandum reading: "WE DEBIT YOUR ACCOUNT to correct a $10 error on your November 17 invoice." In this case the buyer sends a debit memorandum because the correction reduces the amount recorded in the seller's account, an account payable to the buyer, and to reduce an account payable requires a debit. In recording the purchase, the buyer normally marks the correction on the invoice, attaches a copy of the debit memorandum to show that the seller has been notified, and then debits Purchases and credits Accounts Payable for the corrected amount.

Some adjustments, such as damaged merchandise or merchandise that does not meet specifications, normally require negotiations between the buyer and the seller. In such cases the buyer may debit Purchases for the full invoice amount and enter into negotiations with the seller for a return or a price adjustment. If the seller agrees to the return or adjustment, the seller notifies the buyer with a credit memorandum. A credit memorandum is used because the return or adjustment reduces the amount of the buyer's account, an account receivable on the books of the seller, and to reduce an account receivable requires a credit.

From this discussion it can be seen that a debit or a credit memorandum may originate with either party to a transaction. The memorandum gets its name from the action of the originator. If the originator debits, the originator sends a debit memorandum; and if the originator credits, a credit memorandum is sent.

Code numbers as a means of identifying accounts

The account numbering scheme used in the chapters before this has been a simple one in which the accounts have been numbered consecutively. Such a scheme is satisfactory in a small business. However, in a larger more complicated accounting system, account numbers commonly become code numbers that not only identify accounts but also tell their statement classifications. For example, in one numbering system three-digit numbers with each digit having a significant meaning are used. In this system the first digit in each account number tells the major balance sheet or income statement classification of the account to which it is assigned. For example, account numbers with first digits of 1, numbers 111 to 199, are assigned to asset accounts, and liability accounts are assigned numbers with the first digits of 2, numbers 211 to 299. When this system is used, main balance sheet and income statement account classifications may be assigned the following numbers:

111 to 199 are assigned to asset accounts.
211 to 299 are assigned to liability accounts.
311 to 399 are assigned to owner equity accounts.
411 to 499 are assigned to sales or revenue accounts.
511 to 599 are assigned to cost of goods sold accounts.
611 to 699 are assigned to operating expense accounts.
711 to 799 are assigned to other revenue and expense accounts.

When accounts are assigned code numbers having several digits, all of the digits have a significant meaning. In the system under discussion where the first digit indicates the main balance sheet or income statement classification, the second and third digits further classify the account. For example, the second digits under each of the following main classifications indicate the subclassification shown:

111 to 199. Asset accounts
    111 to 119. Current asset accounts (second digits of 1)
    121 to 129. Long-term investment accounts (second digits of 2)
    131 to 139. Plant asset accounts (second digits of 3)
    141 to 149. Intangible asset accounts (second digits of 4)

211 to 299. Liability accounts
    211 to 219. Current liability accounts (second digits of 1)
    221 to 229. Long-term liability accounts (second digits of 2)

611 to 699. Operating expense accounts
    611 to 629. Selling expense accounts (second digits of 1 and 2)
    631 to 649. Delivery expense accounts (second digits of 3 and 4)
    651 to 669. General administrative expense accounts (second digits of 5 and 6)

The third digit in each number further classifies the account. For example, in the system under discussion, all selling expense accounts, which have account numbers with first digits of 6 and second digits of 1 and 2, are further classified as follows:

611 to 699. Operating expense accounts
    611 to 629. Selling expense accounts
        611. Sales salaries expense (third digit of 1)
        612. Advertising expense (third digit of 2)
        613. Depreciation expense, store equipment (third digit of 3)

Account code number. An identifying number assigned to an account and used as the account's posting reference number.

Cash basis of revenue recognition. The recognition of revenue at the time cash is received for the goods or services sold.

Cash discount. A deduction from the invoice price of goods allowed if payment is made within a specified period of time.

Credit memorandum. A memorandum sent to notify its recipient that the business sending the memorandum has in its records credited the account of the recipient.

Credit period. The agreed period of time for which credit is granted and at the end of which payment is expected.

Credit terms. The agreed terms upon which credit is granted in the sale of goods or services.

Debit memorandum. A memorandum sent to notify its recipient that the business sending the memorandum has in its records debited the account of the recipient.

Discount period. The period of time in which a cash discount may be taken.

EOM. An abbreviation meaning end of month.

Freight-in. Transportation charges on merchandise purchased for resale.

FOB. The abbreviation for "free on board," which is used to denote that goods purchased are placed on board the means of transportation at a specified geographic point free of any loading and transportation charges to that point.

General and administrative expenses. The general office, accounting, personnel, and credit and collection expenses.

Gross profit from sales. Net sales minus cost of goods sold.

Inventory ticket. A form attached to counted items in the process of taking an inventory.

List price. The catalog or other listed price from which a trade discount is deducted in arriving at the invoice price for goods.

Merchandise inventory. The unsold merchandise on hand at a given time.

Percentage-of-completion basis of revenue recognition. The recognition of revenue from a long-term construction contract by allocating it to the accounting periods required in completing the contract on the basis of the percentage of work completed in each accounting period.

Periodic inventory system. An inventory system in which periodically, at the end of each accounting period, the cost of the unsold goods on hand is determined by counting units of each product on hand, multiplying the count for each product by its cost, and adding costs of the various products.

Perpetual inventory system. An inventory system in which an individual record is kept for each product stocked of the units on hand at the beginning, the units purchased, the units sold, and the new balance of the product on hand after each purchase or sale.

Purchases discounts. Discounts taken on merchandise purchased for resale.

Sales basis of revenue recognition. The recognition of revenue in the accounting period in which sales of goods or services are completed.

Sales discounts. Discounts given on sales of merchandise.

Selling expenses. The expenses of preparing and storing goods for sale, promoting sales, making sales, and if a separate delivery department is not maintained, the expenses of delivering goods to customers.

Trade discount. The discount that may be deducted from a catalog list price to determine the invoice price of goods.

Questions for
class discussion

1. What is gross profit from sales?
2. May a concern earn a gross profit on its sales and still suffer a loss? How?
3. Why should a concern be interested in the amount of its sales returns and allowances?
4. Since sales returns and allowances are subtracted from sales on the income statement, why not save the effort of this subtraction by debiting all such returns and allowances directly to the Sales account?
5. What is a cash discount? If terms are 2/10, n/60, what is the length of the credit period? What is the length of the discount period?
6. How and when is cost of goods sold determined in a store using a periodic inventory system?
7. Which of the following are debited to the Purchases account of a grocery store: (a) the purchase of a cash register; (b) the purchase of a roll of wrapping paper; (c) the purchase of advertising space in a newspaper; and (d) the purchase of a case of tomato soup?
8. If a concern may return for full credit all unsatisfactory merchandise purchased, why should it be interested in controlling the amount of its returns?
9. When applied to transportation terms, what do the letters FOB mean? What does FOB destination mean?
10. At the end of an accounting period, which inventory, the beginning inventory or the ending, appears on the trial balance?
11. Why is the amount of the ending inventory entered in the work sheet's Income Statement credit column? Why is it entered in the Balance Sheet debit column?

12. What effect do closing entries have on the Merchandise Inventory account?

13. At what point in the earning process is revenue recognized under the sales basis of revenue recognition? Under the cash basis? Under the percentage-of-completion basis?

14. Why are inventory tickets used in taking a physical inventory?

15. During a year a company purchased merchandise costing $220,000. What was the company's cost of goods sold if there were: (a) no beginning or ending inventories? (b) a beginning inventory of $28,000 and no ending inventory? (c) a $25,000 beginning inventory and a $30,000 ending inventory? and (d) no beginning inventory and a $15,000 ending inventory?

16. In counting the merchandise on hand at the end of an accounting period, a clerk failed to count, and consequently omitted from the inventory, all the merchandise on one shelf. If the cost of the merchandise on the shelf was $100, what was the effect of the omission on (a) the balance sheet and (b) the income statement?

17. Suppose that the omission of the $100 from the inventory (Question 16) was not discovered. What would be the effect on the balance sheet and income statement prepared at the end of the next accounting period?

18. Distinguish between cash discounts and trade discounts. Is the amount of a trade discount on merchandise purchased credited to the Purchases Discounts account?

19. When a debit memorandum is issued, who debits, the originator of the memorandum or the company receiving it?

20. When a three-digit account numbering system like the one described in this chapter is in use, which digit of an account's number is the most significant?

Class exercises   **Exercise 5–1**

Campus Shop purchased merchandise having a $2,000 invoice price, terms 2/10, n/60, from a manufacturer and paid for the goods within the discount period. (a) Give without dates or explanations the journal entries made by Campus Shop to record the purchase and payment and (b) the journal entries made by the manufacturer to record the sale and collection. (c). If Campus Shop borrowed sufficient money at 7½% interest on the last day of the discount period to pay this invoice, how much did it save by borrowing to take advantage of the discount?

Exercise 5–2

The following items, with expenses condensed to conserve space, appeared in the Income Statement columns of Campus Shop's December 31, 1979, work sheet. Use the information to prepare a 1979 income statement for the shop.

	Income Statement	
	Debit	Credit
Merchandise inventory	10,000	9,000
Sales		60,000
Sales returns and allowances	500	
Sales discounts	1,000	
Purchases	34,500	
Purchases returns and allowances		300
Purchases discounts		700
Freight-in	1,500	
Selling expenses	8,000	
General and administrative expenses	6,000	
	61,500	70,000
Net income	8,500	
	70,000	70,000

Exercise 5-3

Part 1. Assume that Campus Shop of Exercise 5-2 is owned by Jane Reed and prepare entries to close the shop's revenue, expense, and Income Summary accounts.

Part 2. Rule a balance column Merchandise Inventory account on notebook paper; and under the date, December 31, 1978, enter the $10,000 beginning inventory of Exercise 5-2 as its balance. Then post to the account the portions of the closing entries that affect the account. (Post first the credit that removes the beginning inventory from the account.)

Exercise 5-4

Copy the following tabulation and fill in the missing amounts. Indicate a loss by placing a minus sign before the amount. Each horizontal row of figures is a separate problem situation.

Sales	Beginning Inventory	Net Purchases	Ending Inventory	Cost of Goods Sold	Gross Profit	Expenses	Net Income or Loss
85,000	30,000	40,000	?	55,000	?	20,000	?
90,000	15,000	?	25,000	50,000	?	25,000	15,000
125,000	30,000	?	20,000	?	55,000	35,000	20,000
?	20,000	70,000	15,000	?	40,000	35,000	?
100,000	20,000	65,000	?	60,000	?	25,000	?
70,000	10,000	?	15,000	40,000	?	?	10,000
?	20,000	50,000	10,000	?	40,000	?	-5,000
85,000	?	50,000	15,000	?	30,000	?	10,000

Exercise 5-5

Following is a list of trial balance accounts and balances from the ledger of Top Shop. To simplify the problem and to save time, the balances are in numbers of not more than two digits. However, in order to increase your skill in sorting adjusted trial balance amounts to the proper Income Statement and Balance Sheet columns of a work sheet, the accounts are listed in alphabetical order.

Trial Balance Acccounts and Balances

Accounts payable	$ 1	Merchandise inventory	$ 4
Accounts receivable	3	Prepaid insurance	3
Accumulated depreciation,		Purchases	10
store equipment	3	Purchases discounts	1
Advertising expense	4	Salaries expense	5
Cash	2	Sales	30
Freight-in	1	Sales returns	2
Jedd Lee, capital	13	Store equipment	9
Jedd Lee, withdrawals	2	Store supplies	3

Required:

Prepare a work sheet form on ordinary notebook paper and copy the trial balance accounts and amounts on the work sheet without changing their alphabetical arrangement. Then complete the work sheet using the following information:

a. Estimated depreciation on store equipment, $1.
b. Ending merchandise inventory, $2.
c. Expired insurance, $2.
d. Accrued salaries payable, $3.
e. Ending inventory of store supplies, $1.

Problems

Problem 5–1

Prepare general journal entries to record the following transactions:

Oct. 1 Purchased merchandise on credit, terms 2/10, n/30, $800.
1 Paid $40 for freight charges on the foregoing shipment of merchandise.
5 Sold merchandise on credit, terms 2/10, 1/15, n/60, $500.
8 Purchased on credit a new typewriter for office use, terms n/10 EOM, $350.
9 Purchased merchandise on credit, invoice dated October 9, terms 2/10, n/60, $785.
11 Received a $35 credit memorandum for merchandise purchased on October 9 and returned for credit.
12 Sold merchandise for cash, $45.
15 Purchased office supplies on credit, terms n/10 EOM, $85.
16 Received a credit memorandum for unsatisfactory office supplies purchased on October 15 and returned, $25.
17 Sold merchandise on credit, terms 2/10, 1/15, n/60, $315.
18 Issued a credit memorandum to the customer of October 17 who returned $65 of the merchandise he had purchased.
19 Paid for the merchandise purchased on October 9, less the return and the discount.

Oct. 20   The customer who purchased merchandise on October 5 paid for his purchase of that date less the applicable discount.

27   Received payment for the merchandise sold on October 17, less the the return and applicable discount.

31   Paid for the merchandise purchase on October 1.

Problem 5–2

(If the working papers that accompany this text are not used, omit this problem.)

Varsity Shop's year-end work sheet has been completed through the Adjusted Trial Balance columns, and the Adjusted Trial Balance, Income Statement, and Balance Sheet columns are reproduced in the booklet of working papers with the adjusted trial balance amounts entered in the Adjusted Trial Balance columns.

Required:

1.   Sort the work sheet's adjusted trial balance amounts into the proper Income Statement and Balance Sheet columns, enter the ending inventory amount, $15,130, in the Income Statement credit column and Balance Sheet debit column, and complete the work sheet.
2.   From the work sheet prepare a classified income statement.
3.   Prepare compound closing entries from the work sheet.
4.   Post those portions of the closing entries that affect the Merchandise Inventory account. Post first the credit that clears the beginning inventory from the account.

Problem 5–3

The following trial balance was taken from the ledger of Western Handcrafts at the end of its annual accounting period:

WESTERN HANDCRAFTS
Trial Balance, December 31, 19 —

Cash	$ 710	
Merchandise inventory	14,665	
Store supplies	670	
Prepaid insurance	470	
Store equipment	8,865	
Accumulated depreciation, store equipment		$ 3,340
Accounts payable		4,110
Lee Davis, capital		20,805
Lee Davis, withdrawals	6,000	
Sales		69,225
Sales returns and allowances	725	
Sales discounts	1,225	
Purchases	42,540	
Purchases returns and allowances		385
Purchases discounts		210
Freight-in	885	
Sales salaries expense	12,560	
Rent expense	7,200	
Advertising expense	925	
Utilities expense	635	
Totals	$98,075	$98,075

Required:

1. Copy the trial balance onto a work sheet form and complete the work using the following information:
   a. Ending inventory of store supplies, $210.
   b. Expired insurance, $355.
   c. Estimated depreciation of store equipment, $980.
   d. Accrued sales salaries payable, $215.
   e. Ending merchandise inventory, $13,115.—
2. Prepare an income statement complete through the calculation of gross profit on sales.
3. Prepare compound closing entries from the work sheet.
4. Open a Merchandise Inventory account and enter the $14,665 beginning inventory amount as its balance. Then post the portions of the closing entries that affect the account, posting first the credit that clears the beginning inventory from the account.

Problem 5–4

The following trial balance was taken from the ledger of Hobby Shop at the end of its annual accounting period:

HOBBY SHOP

Trial Balance, December 31, 19 –

Cash	$ 1,215	
Merchandise inventory	13,135	
Store supplies	565	
Office supplies	155	
Prepaid insurance	590	
Store equipment	8,440	
Accumulated depreciation, store equipment		$ 320
Office equipment	1,490	
Accumulated depreciation, office equipment....		265
Accounts payable		2,590
Mary Neal, capital		17,815
Mary Neal, withdrawals	10,400	
Sales		75,810
Sales returns and allowances	810	
Purchases	40,980	
Purchases returns and allowances		315
Purchases discounts		785
Freight-in	720	
Sales salaries expense	8,455	
Rent expense, selling space	5,400	
Advertising expense	785	
Office salaries expense	4,160	
Rent expense, office space	600	
Totals	$97,900	$97,900

Required:

1. Enter the trial balance on a work sheet form and complete the work sheet using the following information:

a. Ending store supplies inventory, $135; and (b) ending office supplies inventory, $60.
c. Expired insurance, $440.
d. Estimated depreciation on store equipment, $875; and (e) on office equipment, $145.
f. Accrued sales salaries, $110; and accrued office salaries, $30.
g. The Hobby Shop charges 10% of its total rent expense to the office and the remainder to selling space; and its lease contract calls for a total annual rent equal to 9% of its annual net sales with minimum monthly payments of $500 each month. The store had made all of its $500 monthly payments during the year but it has not recorded the additional accrued rent.
h. Ending merchandise inventory, $14,360.
2. Prepare a classified income statement.
3. Prepare compound closing entries.
4. Open a merchandise inventory account and enter the $13,135 beginning inventory amount as its balance. Then post those portions of the closing entries that affect this account.

Problem 5–5

The following trial balance was taken from the ledger of Eastgate Shop at the end of its annual accounting period:

EASTGATE SHOP
Trial Balance, December 31, 19—

Cash	$ 1,350	
Merchandise inventory	12,995	
Store supplies	715	
Office supplies	225	
Prepaid insurance	545	
Office equipment	1,850	
Accumulated depreciation, office equipment		$ 645
Store equipment	8,780	
Accumulated depreciation, store equipment		2,135
Accounts payable		1,540
Jane Hult, capital		14,610
Jane Hult, withdrawals	10,400	
Sales		75,960
Sales returns and allowances	960	
Purchases	38,480	
Purchases returns and allowances		365
Purchases discounts		915
Freight-in	570	
Sales salaries expense	8,245	
Rent expense, selling space	4,320	
Advertising expense	575	
Delivery expense	240	
Heating and lighting expense	885	
Office salaries expense	4,555	
Rent expense, office space	480	
Totals	$96,170	$96,170

Required:

1. The booklet of working papers that accompany this text has the Eastgate Shop's trial balance entered on the work sheet form provided for the solution of this problem. If the booklet is being used, complete the work sheet using the following information. If the booklet is not being used, enter the trial balance on a work sheet form and complete the work sheet.

    a. Store supplies inventory, $180; and (b) office supplies inventory, $75.
    c. Expired insurance, $415.
    d. Estimated depreciation on office equipment, $215; and (e) on store equipment, $970.
    f. Accrued sales salaries payable, $165; and accrued office salaries payable, $45.
    g. Eastgate Shop charges 10% of its rent expense to the office and the balance to selling space; and its lease contract calls for a total annual rent equal to 8% of its annual net sales with a minimum of $400 per month to be paid monthly. The monthly payments have been made but the additional accrued rent has not been recorded.
    h. Ending merchandise inventory, $14,450.

2. Prepare a classified income statement and a classified balance sheet.
3. Prepare compound closing entries.
4. Open a Merchandise Inventory account and enter the $12,995 beginning inventory amount as its balance. Then post the portions of the closing entries that affect this account.

Alternate problems

Problem 5–1A

Prepare general journal entries to record the following transactions:

Oct. 1 Purchased merchandise on credit, invoice dated October 1, terms 1/10, n/30, $700.

4 Sold merchandise for cash, $55.

6 Purchased office equipment on credit, terms n/10 EOM, $385.

8 Purchased merchandise on credit, invoice dated October 8, terms 2/10, n/60, $485.

8 Paid $40 freight charges on the foregoing purchase of merchandise.

12 Received a $35 credit memorandum for merchandise purchased on October 8 and returned for credit.

13 Sold merchandise on credit, terms 2/10, 1/15, n/60, $300.

15 Purchased office supplies on credit, terms n/10 EOM, $165.

16 Sold merchandise on credit, terms 2/10, 1/15, n/60, $295.

17 Received a credit memorandum for unsatisfactory office supplies purchased on October 15 and returned for credit, $30.

18 Issued a $45 credit memorandum to the customer who purchased merchandise on October 16 and returned a portion for credit.

18 Paid for the merchandise purchased on October 8, less the return and the discount.

26 Received payment for the merchandise sold on October 16, less the return and the applicable discount.

Oct. 28 The customer of October 13 paid for his purchase of that date, less the applicable discount.

31 Paid for the merchandise purchased on October 1.

Problem 5–2A

(*If the working papers that accompany this text are not used, omit this problem.*)

The Pro Shop's year-end work sheet, completed through the Adjusted Trial Balance columns, is reproduced on page 110 in the booklet of working papers.

Required:

1. Sort the work sheet's adjusted trial balance amounts into the proper Income Statement and Balance Sheet columns, enter the $15,655 ending inventory amount in the Income Statement credit and Balance Sheet debit columns, and complete the work sheet.
2. From the work sheet prepare an income statement that is complete through the calculation of gross profit from sales.
3. Prepare compound closing entries from the work sheet.
4. Post the portions of the closing entries that affect the Merchandise Inventory account. Post first the credit that clears the beginning inventory from the account.

Problem 5–3A

The following trial balance was taken from the ledger of Lee's Boutique at the end of its annual accounting period:

LEE'S BOUTIQUE
Trial Balance, December 31, 19 —

Cash	$ 1,125	
Merchandise inventory	14,665	
Store supplies	635	
Prepaid insurance	450	
Store equipment	9,890	
Accumulated depreciation, store equipment		$ 3,210
Accounts payable		2,225
Lee Davis, capital		17,045
Lee Davis, withdrawals	9,000	
Sales		74,415
Sales returns and allowances	310	
Sales discounts	1,145	
Purchases	41,320	
Purchases returns and allowances		435
Purchases discounts		790
Freight-in	565	
Sales salaries expense	11,435	
Rent expense	6,000	
Advertising expense	815	
Utilities expense	765	
Totals	$98,120	$98,120

Required:

1. Enter the trial balance on a work sheet form and complete the work sheet using the following information:
   a. Ending store supplies inventory, $170.
   b. Expired insurance, $325.
   c. Estimated depreciation on store equipment, $910.
   d. Accrued sales salaries payable, $165.
   e. Ending merchandise inventory, $15,990.
2. Prepare an income statement complete through the calculation of gross profit from sales.
3. From the work sheet prepare compound closing entries.
4. Open a Merchandise Inventory account and enter the $14,665 beginning inventory amount as its balance. Then post the portions of the closing entries that affect this account, posting first the credit that clears the beginning inventory from the account.

Problem 5–4A

The following trial balance was taken from the ledger of Creative Crafts at the end of its annual accounting period:

CREATIVE CRAFTS
Trial Balance, December 31, 19 —

Cash	$ 975	
Merchandise inventory	13,135	
Store supplies	575	
Office supplies	160	
Prepaid insurance	585	
Store equipment	9,835	
Accumulated depreciation, store equipment		$ 3,370
Office equipment	1,775	
Accumulated depreciation, office equipment		750
Accounts payable		4,145
Mary Neal, capital		20,550
Mary Neal, withdrawals	5,400	
Sales		68,320
Sales returns and allowances	1,510	
Purchases	40,235	
Purchases returns and allowances		515
Purchases discounts		245
Freight-in	915	
Sales salaries expense	12,230	
Rent expense, selling space	4,950	
Advertising expense	830	
Office salaries expense	4,235	
Rent expense, office space	550	
Totals	$97,895	$97,895

Required:

1. Copy the trial balance amounts into the Trial Balance columns of a work sheet form and complete the work sheet using the following information:

a. Ending store supplies inventory, $145; and (b) ending office supplies inventory, $45.

c. Expired insurance, $390.

d. Estimated depreciation on store equipment, $990; and (e) on office equipment, $215.

f. Accrued sales salaries, $205; and accrued office salaries, $45.

g. Creative Crafts allocates one tenth of its rent expense to the office and the remainder to selling space. Rent for the month of December had accrued but was unpaid and unrecorded on the trial balance date.

h. Ending merchandise inventory, $12,120.

2. Prepare a classified income statement for the shop.

3. Prepare compound closing entries.

4. Open a Merchandise Inventory account and enter the $13,135 beginning inventory amount as its balance. Then post the portions of the closing entries that affect this account, posting first the credit that clears the beginning inventory from the account.

On January 2 of the current year Bob Moore opened a feed store, Bob's Feed and Seed, by investing $3,000 in cash and a $7,000 inventory of merchandise. During the year he paid out $26,000 to creditors for merchandise and $14,000 for operating expenses. He also withdrew $9,500 in cash from the business for personal use, and at the year-end he prepared the following balance sheet for the business:

Decision problem 5–1, Bob's Feed and Seed

BOB'S FEED AND SEED
Balance Sheet, December 31, 19–

Cash	$ 1,500	Accounts payable (for	
Accounts receivable	6,500	merchandise)	$ 5,500
Merchandise inventory	8,500	Bob Moore, capital	11,000
Total Assets	$16,500	Total Equities	$16,500

Based on the information given, prepare an income statement showing the results of the first year's operation of the business. Support your income statement with schedules showing your calculations of net income, cost of goods sold, and sales.

The accountant delivered the 1979 financial statements of Lakeside Sales to the concern's owner, David Mack, just before closing time yesterday. Mr. Mack took the statements home with him last night to examine but was unable to do so because of unexpected guests, and this morning he inadvertently left the 1979 income statement at home when he came to work. However, he has the store's 1978 and 1979 balance sheets which show the following in condensed form:

Decision problem 5–2, Lakeside Sales

	1978	1979
Cash	$ 2,300	$ 3,100
Accounts receivable	5,300	4,800
Merchandise inventory	10,400	11,200
Store equipment (net after depreciation)	6,200	5,400
Total Assets	$24,200	$24,500
Accounts payable (for merchandise)	$ 4,200	$ 4,700
Accrued wages payable	100	300
David Mack, capital	19,900	19,500
Total Equities	$24,200	$24,500

He also has the store's 1979 record of cash receipts and disbursements which shows:

	Receipts	Payments
Collections of accounts receivable	$85,100	
Payments of:		
Accounts payable		$51,000
Wages of employees		8,200
Other operating expenses		9,300
David Mack, withdrawals		15,800

Under the assumption that Lakeside Sales makes all purchases and sales of merchandise on credit, prepare a 1979 accrual basis income statement for the store based on the information given.

Decision problem 5–3, Colors Unlimited

Elmer Woods worked in the bank in Heavenly Valley for 23 years, until his aunt died, leaving him $50,000. After sitting around for a year, doing little aside from watching his bank balance dwindle, he opened a retail paint store six months ago, calling it Colors Unlimited. At the time he began business, Heavenly Valley had no such store, and it appeared to Mr. Woods that such a venture would be profitable.

He began business by transferring $25,000 from his savings account to a checking account opened in the name of the business. He immediately bought for cash store equipment costing $4,000, which he expected to use for ten years, after which it would be worn out and valueless. He also bought a stock of merchandise costing $15,000, which he paid for with cash; and he paid the rent for six months in advance on the store building, $1,500.

He estimated that like stores in neighboring communities marked their goods for sale at prices averaging 40% above cost. In other words, an item costing $10 was marked for sale at $14. In order to get his store off to a good start, he decided to mark his merchandise for sale at 35% above cost, and he thought this would still leave him a net income equal to 10% on the cost of goods sold.

Since Heavenly Valley is a farming community, Mr. Woods granted liberal credit terms, telling his creditworthy customers to pay "when the crops are in." His suppliers granted Mr. Woods the normal 30-day credit period on merchandise purchased.

Today, December 1, six months after opening his store, Mr. Woods has come to you for advice. He thinks business has been excellent. He has paid his suppliers for all purchases when due and owes only for the purchases, $8,500, made during the last 30 days and for which payment is not due. He has replaced his inventory four times during the six months, and an income statement he has prepared shows $21,000 gross profit and a $6,800 net income. However, you note that he has not charged any depreciation on his equipment. He says he has a full stock of merchandise which cost $15,000 and his customers owe him $20,500. In addition to the rent paid in advance, he has paid all his other expenses, $12,700, with cash.

Nevertheless, Mr. Woods doubts the validity of his own gross profit and net income figures, since he started business with $25,000 in cash and now has only $800 in the bank and owes $8,500 for merchandise purchased on credit.

Did Mr. Woods actually meet his profit expectations? If so, explain to him the apparent paradox of adequate income and a declining cash balance. Back your explanation with a six months' income statement, a December 1 balance sheet, and a statement accounting for the $800 December 1 cash balance.

**After studying Chapter 6, you
should be able to:**

- Explain how columnar journals save posting labor.
- Tell the kind of transaction recorded in each columnar journal described.
- Explain how a controlling account and its subsidiary ledger operate and give the rule for posting to a subsidiary ledger and its controlling account.
- Record transactions in and post from the columnar journals described.
- Tell how the accuracy of the account balances in the Accounts Receivable and Accounts Payable Ledgers is proved and be able to make such a proof.
- Describe how data is processed in a large business.
- Define or explain the words and phrases listed in the chapter Glossary.

chapter 6

Accounting systems

An accounting system consists of the business papers, records, and reports plus the procedures that are used in recording transactions and reporting their effects. Operation of an accounting system begins with the preparation of a business paper, such as an invoice or check, and includes the capture of the data entered on this paper and its flow through the recording, classifying, summarizing, and reporting steps of the system. Actually an accounting system is a data processing system, and it is now time to introduce more efficient ways of processing data.

The General Journal described in previous chapters is a flexible journal in which it is possible to record any transaction. However, since each debit and credit entered in such a journal must be posted individually, using a General Journal to record all the transactions of a business results in the expenditure of too much posting labor.

Reducing posting labor

Several ways have been devised to reduce this labor. One takes advantage of the fact that like transactions always result in debits and credits to the same accounts. For example, all sales on credit are alike in that they result in debits to Accounts Receivable and credits to Sales. Consequently, if advantage is taken of this and a company's credit sales for, say, a month are recorded in a Sales Journal like Illustration 6–1, labor is saved by waiting until the end of the month, totaling the sales recorded in the journal, and debiting Accounts Receivable and crediting Sales for the total.

The journal of Illustration 6–1 is called a *columnar journal* because it has columns for recording the date, the customer's name, invoice number, and the amount of each charge sale. Only charge sales can be recorded in it, and they are recorded daily with the information about each sale being placed on a separate line. Normally the information

Sales Journal

Date		Account Debited	Invoice Number	F	Amount
Oct.	1	James Henry...	307	✓	200.00
	7	Albert Smith..	308	✓	100.00
	12	John Wright..	309	✓	150.00
	15	Paul Roth	310	✓	225.00
	22	Sam Moore...	311	✓	125.00
	25	Frank Booth	312	✓	50.00
	28	Sam Moore...	313	✓	175.00
	31	Total—Accounts Receivable, Dr.; Sales, Cr...			1,025.00

Illustration 6–1

is taken from the sales ticket or invoice prepared at the time of the sale. However, before discussing the journal further, the subject of *subsidiary ledgers* must be introduced.

Subsidiary ledgers

The one Accounts Receivable account used thus far does not readily tell how much each customer bought and paid for or how much each customer owes. As a result, a business selling on credit must maintain additional accounts receivable, one for each customer, to provide this information. These individual customer accounts are in addition to the Accounts Receivable account used thus far and are normally kept in a book or file tray, called a *subsidiary ledger,* that is separate and distinct from the book or tray containing the financial statement accounts. Also, to distinguish the two, the book or tray containing the customer accounts is called the *Accounts Receivable Ledger,* while the one that contains the financial statement accounts is known as the *General Ledger.*

Posting the sales journals

When customer accounts are placed in a subsidiary ledger, a Sales Journal is posted as in Illustration 6–2. In the posting procedure the individual sales recorded in the journal are posted each day to the proper customer accounts in the Accounts Receivable Ledger. These daily postings keep the customer accounts up to date, which is important in granting credit, because when a customer asks for credit, the person responsible for granting it should know the amount currently owed by the customer, as well as his promptness in meeting past obligations. The source of this information is the customer's account; and if the account is not up to date, an incorrect decision may be made.

Note the check marks in the Sales Journal's Folio column. They indicate that the sales recorded in the journal were individually posted to the customer accounts in the Accounts Receivable Ledger. Check marks rather than account numbers are used because the customer accounts commonly are not numbered. Rather, as an aid in locating

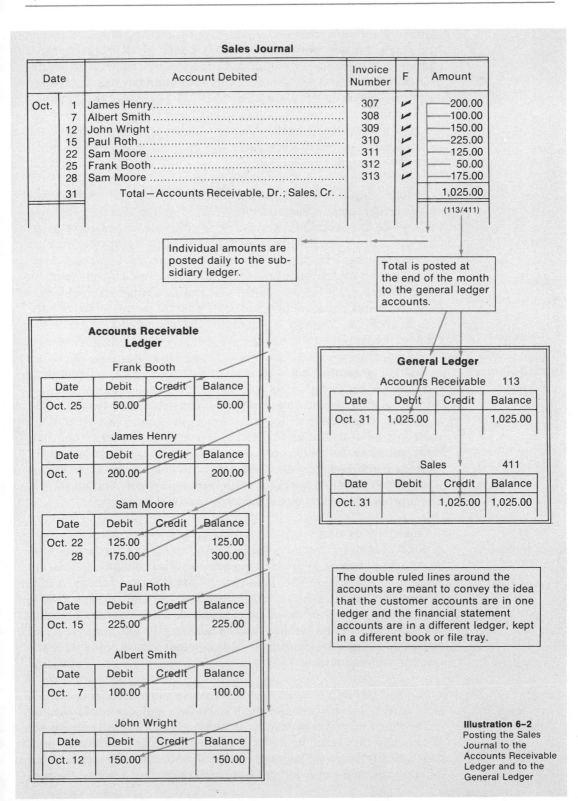

Sales Journal

Date		Account Debited	Invoice Number	F	Amount
Oct.	1	James Henry...	307	✓	200.00
	7	Albert Smith	308	✓	100.00
	12	John Wright	309	✓	150.00
	15	Paul Roth...	310	✓	225.00
	22	Sam Moore	311	✓	125.00
	25	Frank Booth	312	✓	50.00
	28	Sam Moore	313	✓	175.00
	31	Total — Accounts Receivable, Dr.; Sales, Cr. ..			1,025.00
					(113/411)

Individual amounts are posted daily to the subsidiary ledger.

Total is posted at the end of the month to the general ledger accounts.

Accounts Receivable Ledger

Frank Booth

Date	Debit	Credit	Balance
Oct. 25	50.00		50.00

James Henry

Date	Debit	Credit	Balance
Oct. 1	200.00		200.00

Sam Moore

Date	Debit	Credit	Balance
Oct. 22	125.00		125.00
28	175.00		300.00

Paul Roth

Date	Debit	Credit	Balance
Oct. 15	225.00		225.00

Albert Smith

Date	Debit	Credit	Balance
Oct. 7	100.00		100.00

John Wright

Date	Debit	Credit	Balance
Oct. 12	150.00		150.00

General Ledger

Accounts Receivable   113

Date	Debit	Credit	Balance
Oct. 31	1,025.00		1,025.00

Sales   411

Date	Debit	Credit	Balance
Oct. 31		1,025.00	1,025.00

The double ruled lines around the accounts are meant to convey the idea that the customer accounts are in one ledger and the financial statement accounts are in a different ledger, kept in a different book or file tray.

Illustration 6–2
Posting the Sales Journal to the Accounts Receivable Ledger and to the General Ledger

individual accounts, they are alphabetically arranged in the Accounts Receivable Ledger, with new accounts being added in their proper alphabetical positions as required. Consequently, numbering the accounts is impractical, since many numbers would have to be changed each time new accounts are added.

In addition to the daily postings to customer accounts, at the end of the month the Sales Journal's Amount column is totaled and the total is debited to Accounts Receivable and credited to Sales. The credit records the month's revenue from charge sales, and the debit records the resulting increase in accounts receivable.

Before going on, note again in Illustration 6–2 that the individual customer accounts in the subsidiary Accounts Receivable Ledger do not replace the Accounts Receivable account described in previous chapters but are in addition to it. The Accounts Receivable account of previous chapters must still be maintained in the General Ledger where it serves three functions: (1) it shows the total amount owed by all customers; (2) it helps keep the General Ledger a balancing ledger in which debits equal credits; and (3) it offers a means of proving the accuracy of the customer accounts in the subsidiary Accounts Receivable Ledger.

Controlling accounts

When a company maintains an Accounts Receivable account in its General Ledger and puts its individual customer accounts in a subsidiary ledger, the Accounts Receivable account is said to control the subsidiary ledger and is called a *controlling account*. The extent of the control is such that after all posting is completed, if no errors were made, the sum of all of the customer account balances in the subsidiary Accounts Receivable Ledger will equal the balance of the Accounts Receivable controlling account in the General Ledger. This equality is also a proof of the sum of the customer account balances.

Other columnar journals

Only sales on credit may be recorded in a Sales Journal. As a result, if a merchandising company takes full advantage of the laborsaving benefits of columnar journals, it must use several columnar journals in addition to a Sales Journal. These are a Cash Receipts Journal, a Purchases Journal, a Cash Disbursements Journal, and perhaps others. Also, and regardless of the columnar journals used, there are always a few miscellaneous transactions plus adjusting, closing, and correcting entries that cannot be recorded in any columnar journal, and for these a General Journal must be provided.

Cash Receipts Journal

A Cash Receipts Journal designed to save the maximum of posting labor through posting column totals must be a multicolumn journal. A multicolumn journal is necessary because although all cash receipts are alike in that they result in debits to Cash, they differ as to sources and, consequently, as to the accounts credited when cash is received from different sources. For example, if the cash receipts of a mercantile concern are classified as to sources, they normally fall into three groups: (1) cash from charge customers in payment of their accounts, (2) cash from cash sales, and (3) cash from miscellaneous sources. Note in the Cash Receipts Journal of Illustration 6–3 how a special column is provided for entering the credits resulting when cash is received from each of these sources. Also, note the special columns for the debits to Sales Discounts and to Cash.

Cash from charge customers

When cash received from a charge customer in payment of his account is recorded in a columnar Cash Receipts Journal like Illustration 6–3, the customer's name is entered in the Account Credited column; the amount credited to his account is entered in the Accounts Receivable credit column; and the debits to Sales Discounts and Cash are entered in the journal's last two columns.

Give close attention to the Accounts Receivable credit column. Observe that (1) only credits to customer accounts are entered in this column; (2) the individual credits are posted daily to the customer accounts in the subsidiary Accounts Receivable Ledger; and (3) the column total is posted at the month end to the credit of the Accounts Receivable controlling account. This is the normal recording and posting procedure when controlling accounts and subsidiary ledgers are used. When such accounts and ledgers are used, transactions are normally entered in a journal column, the individual amounts are posted to the subsidiary ledger accounts, and the column total is posted to the controlling account.

Cash sales

In an average company, cash sales are "rung up" each day on one or more cash registers and their total is recorded by means of a journal entry at the end of the day. All of these entries are alike; all have repetitive debits to Cash and repetitive credits to Sales.

When cash sales are recorded in a Cash Receipts Journal like that of Illustration 6–3, the repetitive debits to Cash are entered in the Cash debit column and a special column headed "Sales credit" is provided for the repetitive credits to Sales. By entering each day's cash sales in this column, the cash sales of a month may be posted at the month's end in a single amount, the column total. (Although cash sales are normally recorded daily from the cash register reading, the cash sales of Illustration 6–3 are recorded only once each week in order to shorten the illustration.)

At the time daily cash sales are recorded in the Cash Receipts Journal, some bookkeepers, as in Illustration 6–3, place a check mark in the Folio column to indicate that no amount is individually posted from that line of the journal. Other bookkeepers use a double check (⩗⩗) to distinguish amounts not posted from amounts posted to customer accounts.

Cash Receipts Journal

Date		Account Credited	Explanation	F	Other Accounts Credit	Accts. Rec. Credit	Sales Credit	Sales Disc. Debit	Cash Debit
Oct.	6	Sales...................	Cash sales...........	✓			400.00		400.00
	10	James Henry........	Invoice, 10/1.......	✓		200.00		4.00	196.00
	13	Sales...................	Cash sales...........	✓			390.00		390.00
	17	Albert Smith.........	Invoice, 10/7........	✓		100.00		2.00	98.00
	18	Notes Payable......	Note to bank........	211	1,000.00				1,000.00
	20	Sales...................	Cash sales...........	✓			450.00		450.00
	20	John Wright.........	Invoice, 10/12......	✓		150.00		3.00	147.00
	25	Paul Roth	Invoice, 10/15	✓		225.00		4.50	220.50
	27	Sales...................	Cash sales...........	✓			398.50		398.50
	31	Totals........			1,000.00	675.00	1,638.50	13.50	3,300.00
					(✓)	(113)	(411)	(413)	(111)

Individual amounts in the Other Accounts credit and Accounts Receivable credit columns are posted daily.

Total is not posted.

Totals posted at the end of the month.

Accounts Receivable Ledger

James Henry

Date	Debit	Credit	Balance
Oct. 1	200.00		200.00
10		200.00	-0-

Paul Roth

Date	Debit	Credit	Balance
Oct. 15	225.00		225.00
25		225.00	-0-

Albert Smith

Date	Debit	Credit	Balance
Oct. 7	100.00		100.00
17		100.00	-0-

John Wright

Date	Debit	Credit	Balance
Oct. 12	150.00		150.00
20		150.00	-0-

General Ledger

Cash   111

Date	Debit	Credit	Balance
Oct. 31	3,300.00		3,300.00

Accounts Receivable   113

Date	Debit	Credit	Balance
Oct. 31	1,025.00		1,025.00
31		675.00	350.00

Notes Payable   211

Date	Debit	Credit	Balance
Oct. 18		1,000.00	1,000.00

Sales   411

Date	Debit	Credit	Balance
Oct. 31		1,025.00	1,025.00
31		1,638.50	2,663.50

Sales Discounts   413

Date	Debit	Credit	Balance
Oct. 31	13.50		13.50

Illustration 6–3
Posting the Cash Receipts Journal to the Accounts Receivable Ledger and to the General Ledger

Miscellaneous receipts of cash

Most cash receipts come from customer collections and cash sales. However, cash is occasionally received from other sources such as, for example, the sale for cash of an unneeded plant asset, or a promissory note is given to a bank in order to borrow money. For miscellaneous receipts such as these the Other Accounts credit column is provided in the Cash Receipts Journal.

As previously stated, the individual items in the Cash Receipts Journal's Accounts Receivable column are posted daily as credits to the customer accounts named in the Account Credited column. These items must be posted daily so that the accounts receivable ledger accounts show for each customer the current amount owed.

Posting the Cash Receipts Journal

In an average company, the items in the Other Accounts credit column are few and are posted to a variety of general ledger accounts. As a result, postings are less apt to be omitted if these items are also posted daily. Furthermore, if the individual items in both the Other Accounts and the Accounts Receivable columns are posted daily, only the column totals remain to be posted at the end of the month.

The amounts in the Accounts Receivable, Sales, Sales Discounts, and Cash columns are posted as column totals at the end of the month. However, since the transactions recorded in any journal must result in equal debits and credits to general ledger accounts, the debit and credit equality in a columnar journal such as the Cash Receipts Journal is proved by *crossfooting* or cross adding the column totals before they are posted.

To *foot* a column of figures is to add it; and to crossfoot the Cash Receipts Journal the debit column totals are added together, the credit column totals are added together, and the two sums are compared for equality. For example, if the debit column totals of the Cash Receipts Journal in Illustration 6–3 are added and the credit column totals are added, the two sums appear as follows:

Debit Columns		Credit Columns	
Sales discounts debit............ $	13.50	Other accounts credit............	$1,000.00
Cash debit	3,300.00	Accounts receivable credit:....	675.00
		Sales credit.........................	1,638.50
Total	$3,313.50	Total.........................	$3,313.50

And since the sums are equal, the debits in the journal are assumed to equal the credits.

After the debit and credit equality is proved by crossfooting, the totals of the last four columns are posted as indicated in each column heading. As for the Other Accounts column, since the individual items in this column are posted daily, the column total is not posted. This posting procedure is demonstrated in Illustration 6–3.

Posting items daily from the Other Accounts column with a delayed posting of the offsetting totals causes the General Ledger to be out of balance throughout the month. However, this is of no consequence because the offsetting totals are posted before a trial balance is prepared.

The Cash Receipts Journal's Folio column is used only for daily postings from the Other Accounts and Accounts Receivable columns. The account numbers appearing in the Folio column indicate items posted to the General Ledger from the Other Accounts column; and the check marks indicate either that an item like a day's cash sales was not posted or that an item was posted to the subsidiary Accounts Receivable Ledger. Note in Illustration 6–3 the check mark below the Other Accounts column. The check mark indicates that when the journal was posted, this column total was not posted. The account numbers of the accounts to which the Accounts Receivable, Sales, Sales Discounts, and Cash column totals of Illustration 6–3 were posted are indicated in parentheses below each column.

Posting rule   Posting to a subsidiary ledger and its controlling account from two journals has been demonstrated, and a rule to cover all such postings can now be given. The rule is: *In posting to a subsidiary ledger and its controlling account, the controlling account must be debited periodically for an amount or amounts equal to the sum of the debits to the subsidiary ledger and it must be credited periodically for an amount or amounts equal to the sum of the credits to the subsidiary ledger.*
The periodic postings to the controlling account bring its balance up to date and provide a proof of the subsidiary ledger accounts. The proof is that if no errors were made, after all posting is completed, the balance of the controlling account will equal the sum of the account balances in the subsidiary ledger.

Sales returns   A company having only a few sales returns may record them in a General Journal with an entry like the following:

Oct.	17	Sales Returns and Allowances......................................	412	17.50	
		Accounts Receivable – George Ball	113/✔		17.50
		Returned defective merchandise.			

The debit of the entry is posted to the Sales Returns and Allowances account; and the credit is posted to both the Accounts Receivable controlling account and to the customer's account. Note the account number and the check, 113/✔, in the Folio column on the credit line. This indicates that both the Accounts Receivable controlling account in the General Ledger and the George Ball account in the Accounts Receivable Ledger were credited for $17.50. Both were credited because the balance of the controlling account in the General Ledger will not equal the sum of the customer account balances in the subsidiary ledger unless both are credited.

Companies having sufficient sales returns can save posting labor by recording them in a special Sales Returns and Allowances Journal like that of Illustration 6–4. This is in keeping with the idea that a company can design and use a special journal for any class of like transactions in which there are within the class sufficient transactions to warrant the journal. When a Sales Returns and Allowances Journal is used to record returns, the individual amounts entered in the journal are posted daily to the credit of each affected customer account. At the end of the month, the journal total is posted to both the debit of the Sales Returns and Allowances account and the credit of the Accounts Receivable controlling account.

Sales Returns and Allowances Journal

Date		Account Credited	Explanation	Credit Memo No.	F	Amount
Oct.	7	Robert Moore	Defective mdse............	203	✓	10.00
	14	James Warren...........	Defective mdse............	204	✓	12.00
	18	T. M. Jones...............	Not ordered.................	205	✓	6.00
	23	Sam Smith	Defective mdse............	206	✓	18.00
	31	Sales Returns and Allow., Dr.; Accounts Rec., Cr.				46.00
						412/113

Illustration 6–4

As with accounts receivable, the one Accounts Payable account used thus far does not show how much is owed each creditor. One way to secure this information is to maintain an individual account for each creditor in a subsidiary Accounts Payable Ledger controlled by an Accounts Payable controlling account in the General Ledger. If maintained, the controlling account, subsidiary ledger, and columnar journal techniques demonstrated thus far with accounts receivable apply to accounts payable. The only difference is that a Purchases Journal and a Cash Disbursements Journal are used in recording most of the transactions affecting the accounts. However, this difference is not great, since these journals operate in the same manner as the journals described thus far.

Accounts payable

A one-money-column Purchases Journal is very similar to the Sales Journal previously described and operates in the same manner. The information recorded in the journal usually includes the date of each entry, the creditor's name, the invoice date, terms, and the amount of the purchase. This information is recorded from approved purchase invoices; and its use, in the main, is apparent. The invoice date and the terms together indicate the date on which payment is due.

The Purchases Journal and its posting

Purchases Journal

Date	Account Credited	Date of Invoice	Terms	F	Amount
Oct. 3	Horn Supply Company	10/2	n/30	✔	350.00
5	Acme Mfg. Company	10/5	2/10, n/30	✔	200.00
13	Wycoff & Company	10/10	n/30	✔	150.00
20	Smith and Company	10/19	2/10, n/30	✔	300.00
25	Acme Mfg. Company	10/24	2/10, n/30	✔	100.00
29	H. A. Green Company	10/28	2/10, n/60	✔	225.00
31	Total—Purchases, Dr.; Accounts Payable, Cr.				1,325.00
					(511/212)

Individual amounts are posted daily.

Total is posted at the end of the month.

Accounts Payable Ledger

Acme Mfg. Company

Date	Debit	Credit	Balance
Oct. 5		200.00	200.00
15	200.00		-0-
25		100.00	100.00

H. A. Green Company

Date	Debit	Credit	Balance
Oct. 29		225.00	225.00

Horn Supply Company

Date	Debit	Credit	Balance
Oct. 3		350.00	350.00

Smith and Company

Date	Debit	Credit	Balance
Oct. 20		300.00	300.00

Wycoff & Company

Date	Debit	Credit	Balance
Oct. 13		150.00	150.00

General Ledger

Accounts Payable   212

Date	Debit	Credit	Balance
Oct. 31		1,325.00	1,325.00

Purchases _Inventory DR._   511

Date	Debit	Credit	Balance
Oct. 12	25.00		25.00
31	1,325.00		1,350.00

Illustration 6–5
Posting the
Purchases
Journal

The one-money-column Purchases Journal is posted in the same manner as a Sales Journal: (1) the individual amounts in the Amount column are posted daily to the subsidiary Accounts Payable Ledger and (2) the column total is debited at the end of the month to the Purchases account and credited to the Accounts Payable controlling account. This posting is demonstrated in Illustration 6–5.

Purchase of assets used in the business

When a Purchases Journal like the one just described is used, only purchases of merchandise may be recorded in it because its Amount column total is debited to the Purchases account and purchases of assets other than merchandise do not affect this account. However, every company must purchase assets for use in the business; and when these assets are no longer needed, they may be sold. If the purchase or sale is for cash, the transaction is recorded in one of the cash journals. But if the purchase or sale is on credit, the transaction must be recorded in either the General Journal or, in cases where assets are purchased and such a journal is used, a multicolumn Purchases Journal.

A general journal entry to record the purchase of an asset used in the business appears as follows:

Oct.	29	Office Supplies	119	23.75	
		Accounts Payable—Ace Supply Co.	212/✔		23.75
		Bought office supplies on credit.			

A multicolumn journal for recording the purchase of both merchandise and assets used in the business is shown in Illustration 6–6. Note that it has one credit column and three debit columns; more debit columns could be added. The credit column is used to record the amounts credited to each creditor's account. These amounts are posted daily to the individual creditor accounts in the Accounts Payable Ledger, and the column total is credited to the controlling account at the end of the month. The items purchased are recorded in the debit columns and are posted in the column totals at the end of the month.

Purchases Journal

Date		Account Credited	F	Accts. Pay-able Credit	Pur-chases Debit	Store Sup-plies Debit	Office Sup-plies Debit
Oct.	2	Marsh Wholesale Company.........		154.10	154.10		
	2	Office Supply Company		18.75			18.75
	3	Dole and Dole..........................		127.60	99.50	28.10	

Illustration 6–6

The Cash Disburse- ments Journal and its posting

The Cash Disbursements Journal, like the Cash Receipts Journal, has columns that make it possible to post repetitive debits and credits in column totals. The repetitive debits and credits of cash payments are debits to the Accounts Payable controlling account and credits to both Purchases Discounts and Cash. In most companies the purchase of merchandise for cash is not common; therefore, a Purchases column is not needed and a cash purchase is recorded as on line 2 of Illustration 6–7.

Observe that the Cash Disbursements Journal of Illustration 6–7 has a column headed "Check No." In order to gain control over cash disbursements, all such disbursements (excepting petty cash disbursements, which are discussed in Chapter 7) should be made by check. The checks should be prenumbered by the printer, and they should be entered in the journal in numerical order with each check's number in the column headed "Check No." This makes it possible to scan the numbers in the column for omitted checks. When a Cash Disbursements Journal has a column for check numbers, it is often called a Check Register.

A Cash Disbursements Journal or Check Register like Illustration 6–7 is posted as follows. The individual amounts in the Other Accounts column are posted daily to the debit of the general ledger accounts named in the Account Debited column; and the individual amounts in the Accounts Payable column are posted daily to the subsidiary Accounts Payable Ledger to the debit of the creditors named in the Account Debited column. At the end of the month, after the column totals are crossfooted to prove their equality, the Accounts Payable column total is posted to the debit of the Accounts Payable controlling account; the Purchases Discounts column total is posted to the credit of the Purchases Discounts account; and the Cash column total is posted to the credit of the Cash account. Since the items in the Other Accounts column are posted individually, this column total is not posted.

Identifying posted amounts

When several journals are posted to ledger accounts, it is necessary to indicate in the account Folio column before each posted amount the journal as well as the page number of the journal from which the amount was posted. The journal is indicated by using its initial or initials. Because of this, items posted from the Cash Disbursements Journal carry the initial "D" before their journal page numbers in the Folio columns. Likewise, items from the Cash Receipts Journal carry the letter "R," those from the Sales Journal carry the initial "S," items from the Purchases Journal carry the initial "P," and from the General Journal, the letter "G."

Purchases returns

A company having sufficient purchases returns and allowances may use a Purchases Returns and Allowances Journal similar to the Sales Returns and Allowances Journal previously illustrated. However, if

Cash Disbursements Journal

Date	Ch. No.	Payee	Account Debited	F	Other Accounts Debit	Accts. Pay. Debit	Pur. Disc. Credit	Cash Credit
Oct. 3	105	L. & N. Railroad...	Freight in	514	18.50			18.50
12	106	East Sales Co	Purchases	511	25.00			25.00
15	107	Acme Mfg. Co	Acme Mfg. Co	✓		200.00	4.00	196.00
15	108	Jerry Hale	Salaries Expense...	611	86.00			86.00
20	109	Horn Supply Co...	Horn Supply Co.....	✓		75.00		75.00
29	110	Smith and Co......	Smith and Co........	✓		300.00	6.00	294.00
31		Totals........			129.50	575.00	10.00	694.50
					(✓)	(212)	(513)	(111)

Individual amounts in the Other Accounts debit column and Accounts Payable debit column are posted daily.

Totals posted at the end of the month.

Accounts Payable Ledger

Acme Mfg. Company

Date	Debit	Credit	Balance
Oct. 5		200.00	200.00
15	200.00		-0-
25		100.00	100.00

H. A. Green Company

Date	Debit	Credit	Balance
Oct. 29		225.00	225.00

Horn Supply Company

Date	Debit	Credit	Balance
Oct. 3		350.00	350.00
20	75.00		275.00

Smith and Company

Date	Debit	Credit	Balance
Oct. 20		300.00	300.00
29	300.00		-0-

Wycoff & Company

Date	Debit	Credit	Balance
Oct. 13		150.00	150.00

General Ledger

Cash   111

Date	Debit	Credit	Balance
Oct. 31	3,300.00		3,300.00
31		694.50	2,605.50

Accounts Payable   212

Date	Debit	Credit	Balance
Oct. 31		1,325.00	1,325.00
31	575.00		750.00

Purchases   511

Date	Debit	Credit	Balance
Oct. 12	25.00		25.00
31	1,325.00		1,350.00

Purchases Discounts   513

Date	Debit	Credit	Balance
Oct. 31		10.00	10.00

Freight-In   514

Date	Debit	Credit	Balance
Oct. 3	18.50		18.50

Salaries Expense   611

Date	Debit	Credit	Balance
Oct. 15	86.00		86.00

Illustration 6–7
Posting the Cash Disbursements Journal

it has only a few such returns and allowances, it will record them with a general journal entry like the following:

Oct.	8	Accounts Payable—Medford Mfg. Company........	212/✓		
		Purchases Returns and Allowances	512	32.00	
		Returned defective merchandise.			32.00

Proving the ledgers

Periodically, after all posting is completed, the General Ledger and the subsidiary ledgers are proved. The General Ledger is normally proved first by preparing a trial balance; and if the trial balance balances, the accounts in the General Ledger, including the controlling accounts, are assumed to be correct. The subsidiary ledgers are then proved, commonly by preparing schedules of accounts receivable and accounts payable. A schedule of accounts payable, for example, is prepared by listing with their balances the accounts in the Accounts Payable Ledger having balances. The balances are totaled; and if the total is equal to the balance of the Accounts Payable controlling account, the accounts in the Accounts Payable Ledger are assumed to be correct. Illustration 6–8 shows a schedule of the creditor accounts having balances in the Accounts Payable Ledger of Illustration 6–7. Note that the schedule total is equal to the balance of the Accounts Payable controlling account in the General Ledger of Illustration 6–7. A schedule of accounts receivable is prepared in the same way as a schedule of accounts payable; and if its total is equal to the balance of the Accounts Receivable controlling account, the accounts in the Accounts Receivable Ledger are also assumed to be correct.

Hawaiian Sales Company
Schedule of Accounts Payable, December 31, 19—

Acme Mfg. Company.................................	$100
H. A. Green Company................................	225
Horn Supply Company	275
Wycoff & Company	150
Total Accounts Payable.....................	$750

Illustration 6–8

Instead of a formal schedule to prove the accounts in a subsidiary ledger, an adding machine list may also be used. For example, the balances of the accounts in the Accounts Payable Ledger may be proved by listing on an adding machine the balance of each account in the ledger, totaling the list, and comparing the total with the balance of the Accounts Payable controlling account. A similar list may be used to prove the accounts in the Accounts Receivable Ledger.

Many cities and states require retailers to collect sales taxes from their customers and periodically remit these taxes to the city or state treasurer. When a columnar Sales Journal is used, a record of taxes collected can be obtained by adding special columns in the journal as shown in Illustration 6–9.

In posting a journal like Illustration 6–9, the individual amounts in the Accounts Receivable column are posted daily to customer accounts in the Accounts Receivable Ledger and the column total is posted at

		Sales Journal				
Date	Account Debited	Invoice Number	F	Accounts Receivable Debit	Sales Taxes Payable Credit	Sales Credit
Dec. 1	D. R. Horn	7–1698		103.00	3.00	100.00

Illustration 6–9

the end of the month to the Accounts Receivable controlling account. The individual amounts in the Sales Taxes Payable and Sales columns are not posted. However, at the end of the month the total of the Sales Taxes Payable column is credited to the Sales Taxes Payable account and the total of the Sales column is credited to Sales.

A concern making cash sales upon which sales taxes are collected may add a special Sales Taxes Payable column in its Cash Receipts Journal.

To save labor, many companies do not enter charge sales in a Sales Journal. These companies post each sales invoice total directly to the customer's account in a subsidiary Accounts Receivable Ledger. Copies of the invoices are then bound in numerical order in a binder; and at the end of the month, all the invoices of that month are totaled on an adding machine and a general journal entry is made debiting the Accounts Receivable account and crediting Sales for the total. In effect, the bound invoice copies act as a Sales Journal. Such a procedure eliminates the labor of entering each invoice in a Sales Journal and is known as direct posting of sales invoices.

Since each is a separate book, columnar journals like the ones described thus far make it possible for several people to work on the accounting records at the same time. However, in a small business, one in which all the bookkeeping is done by one person, the separate books are inconvenient because the bookkeeper must put aside one book and pick up another each time a different kind of transaction is to be recorded. As a result and to avoid this inconvenience, small con-

Combined

Cash		Sales Discounts	Purchases Discounts	Date	Ch. No.	Account Titles and Explanations
Debit	Credit	Debit	Credit			
....	....	....	....	Oct. 4	.,....	,Lee Gage..
....	....	....	....	7	......	Sales Returns and Allowances—Lee Gage..
1,345.00	....	....	....	11	......	Cash sales, week ended 10/11................
490.00	....	10.00	....	14	......	Lee Gage, Invoice 10/4, less return ....
5,000.00	....	....	....	17	......	˙Notes Payable ....
....	....	....	....	21	......	Olympia Company ....
....	600.00	....	....	31	345	Rent Expense.....................................
....	1,470.00	....	30.00	31	346	Olympia Company ....
6,835.00	2,070.00	10.00	30.00	·31	......	Totals.....................
(111)	(111)	(413)	(513)			

Illustration 6–10

cerns often use a Combined Cash Journal like that shown in Illustration 6–10. Such a journal provides in one book the columns of all the journals described thus far, and it can be used to record any kind of transaction.

The first entry in the illustrated journal records a credit sale. Such a sale is recorded by entering the customer's name in the Account Titles and Explanations column and the amount of the sale in both the Accounts Receivable debit and Sales credit columns. The customer must be named in the entry so that the amount of the sale may be posted to his account in the subsidiary Accounts Receivable Ledger. No explanation is required because the customer's name and the amounts in the proper columns indicate the nature of the transaction.

The second entry records a returned sale, and both the Sales Returns and Allowances account and the customer are named in the Account Titles and Explanations column. Both are named because the amount of the return must be posted to the Sales Returns and Allowances account in the General Ledger and also to the customer's account in the Accounts Receivable Ledger.

Observe that the third entry has only an explanation in the Account Titles and Explanations column. Only an explanation is needed because the entry amounts are posted in the month-end column totals, rather than as individual amounts.

The remainder of the entries in the illustrated journal record in turn the receipt of cash from a customer in payment of his account, a bank loan, a credit purchase, an expense, and the payment of an account payable. After examining the entries, note these rules for recording transactions in and posting from a Combined Cash Journal. (1) Other than for closing entries, only one line is used to record each transaction. (2) If in recording a transaction an amount must be entered in one or more of the Other General Ledger Accounts columns, the Accounts Receivable columns, or the Accounts Payable columns,

Cash Journal

Folio	Other General Ledger Accounts		Accounts Receivable		Accounts Payable		Purchases	Sales	Inv. No.
	Debit	Credit	Debit	Credit	Debit	Credit	Debit	Credit	
✔			525.00					525.00	878
412/✔	25.00			25.00					.....
✔								1,345.00	.....
✔				500.00					.....
211		5,000.00							.....
✔						1,500.00	1,500.00		.....
612	600.00								.....
✔					1,500.00				.....
	625.00	5,000.00	525.00	525.00	1,500.00	• 1,500.00	1,500.00	1,870.00	.....
	(✔)	(✔)	(113)	(113)	(212)	(212)	(511)	(411)	

the affected account or accounts must be named in the Account Titles and Explanations column. (3) Any amounts entered in the Other General Ledger Accounts columns are posted as individual amounts to the accounts named, and the column totals are not posted. (4) Any amounts entered in the Accounts Receivable and Accounts Payable columns are posted as individual amounts to the subsidiary ledger accounts of the customers and creditors, and the column totals are posted to the controlling accounts. (5) All other amounts entered in the journal are posted in the month-end column totals; but before the month-end postings are made it is important that the columns be cross-footed to prove the equality of the debits and credits in the journal.

A Combined Cash Journal is normally specially designed to fit the needs of the company using it. The illustrated journal has 12 amount columns. When space is available, additional columns are often provided, with an additional column being provided for each kind of transaction of which there are a sufficient number to warrant posting the amounts as a column total.

Speeding the data processing

Columnar journals speed the processing of accounting data, and if a business is small, they may serve its needs very well. However, they are pen-and-ink records, and on a per transaction basis any pen-and-ink record is time consuming and costly. Consequently, when a business has sufficient transactions to warrant their use, it will employ electric accounting machines or computers to reduce unit costs and further speed its data processing.

Electric accounting machines

There are many electric accounting machines in use, some designed for a single task and others for a multiplicity of tasks. No effort will be made to describe all the available machines. In fact only one machine will be discussed, and it for purposes of showing how such machines reduce labor and speed the processing of accounting data.

Illustration 6–11 shows an electric accounting machine which can be used for sales accounting, cash receipts, cash disbursements, accounts payable, payroll, and other accounting applications. No attempt will be made to describe the machine's operation in each of these applications. However, when used in sales accounting, as an example, the machine will produce the invoice for each charge sale, post to the customer's account, update the statement to be sent the customer at

Illustration 6–11

the end of the month, and enter the sale in the Sales Journal, all in one operation. Furthermore, it is as proficient in other applications.

In sales accounting the current page of the Sales Journal is placed in the machine at the time the operator begins processing a group of sales transactions. In Illustration 6–11 the Sales Journal sheet is on the tray at the back of the machine. Next, after putting the Sales Journal sheet in the machine, the operator will for each charge sale place in the machine's carriage a blank invoice form, the customer's account from the subsidiary Accounts Receivable Ledger, and the statement to be mailed to the customer at the end of the month. After this, the operator picks up in the machine from the customer's account the amount of the customer's previous balance. The operator then types the customer's name, address, terms, and so forth on the invoice plus a list of the commodities sold. For each commodity this consists of a description, the number of units sold, and the unit price. After listing units and unit price for a commodity, the operator depresses a key and the machine multiplies units by unit price and prints the extension. After listing all items, the operator presses another key and the machine totals the invoice and prints the total on the invoice, makes the entry in the Sales Journal, and spaces over and enters the sale and the new balance on the customer's account and on the month-end statement. After this the carriage returns automatically and opens for the removal of the invoice, customer's account, and statement. It also spaces the Sales Journal sheet up one line and is ready for recording the next sale.

In addition, when the operator completes the processing of a day's sales, the machine will print out the dollar total of the invoices processed, which is the day's debit to the Accounts Receivable controlling account. Also, it will print out the total credit to Sales and, if any, the credit to Sales Taxes Payable. Furthermore, if the sales were entered in the machine by departments, it will break down the sales credit into totals by departments.

Automated data processing is the processing of data without human intervention through the use of a computer, with a computer being a complex electronic machine that is capable of:

1. Accepting and storing data.
2. Performing arithmetic operations on the data.
3. Comparing units of the data and making yes-or-no decisions.
4. Sorting and rearranging the data and preparing reports therefrom.

Data are entered into a computer by means of an electric typewriter, previously prepared punched cards, reels of magnetic tape, and in other ways, some of which are described later. Inside the computer each alphabetical letter or numerical digit of data becomes a combination of electrical or magnetic states that a computer can manipulate with the speed of light. Consequently, if of sufficient size, a computer can do millions of additions, subtractions, multiplications, and divisions per second, all without computer error in a predetermined sequence according to instructions stored in the machine.

For this discussion an understanding of what goes on inside a computer is not required. It is only necessary to recognize that a computer is a machine that can do nothing without a previously prepared set of instructions, called a *program*, being entered and stored in the computer. However, with a properly prepared program, a computer will accept data, store and process the data, and produce the processed results, often in seconds, in the form of a report displayed on a TV-like screen, or typed out on an electric typewriter at the rate of approximately 10 characters per second, or printed by a line printer at upwards to 800 lines of 120-character type per minute.

The program

A computer program is a set of coded instructions specifying each operation a computer is to perform. It is entered into the machine by means of punched cards or magnetic tape before the processing of a batch of data is begun and may contain from a few to several thousand detailed instructions like the following from a program for processing customers' orders for merchandise.

Program Instructions for Processing Customers' Orders

1. For the first item on the customer's order, compare the quantity ordered with the quantity on hand as shown by inventory data stored in the computer.
   a. If the quantity ordered is not on hand:
      (1) Prepare a back order notifying the customer that the goods are not available but will be shipped as soon as a new supply is received.
      (2) Go to the next item on the customer's order.
   b. If the quantity on hand is greater than the amount ordered:
      (1) Deduct the amount ordered from the amount on hand.
      (2) Prepare shipping documents for the goods.
      (3) Compare the amount of the item remaining after filling the customer's order with the reorder point for the item.
         (a) If the amount remaining is greater than the reorder point:
            1. Go to the next item on the customer's order.
         (b) If the amount remaining is less than the reorder point:
            1. Compute the amount to be purchased and prepare documents for the purchase.
            2. Go to the next item on the customer's order.

In addition to these instructions, a program for processing customer orders would also have instructions for preparing the invoices, recording the sales, and updating the customer accounts. However, the listed instructions are sufficient to show the ability of a computer to make yes-or-no decisions.

Yes-or-no decisions

The ability to compare numbers and make yes-or-no decisions makes it possible for a computer to process data containing exceptions, such as in the processing of customers' orders. However, it should be observed that the computer does not really make decisions. It only makes a comparison in each case, after which it processes the data one way or another, depending upon the result of the comparison. Also, for a computer to do this, a person called a programmer must first design a program for the computer to follow. In designing the program, the programmer must determine in advance what exceptions can occur; he must then devise a set of yes-or-no questions that will isolate each exception, and he must tell the computer how to process each exception. Finally, after all this, the computer can follow through the program's maze of decisions and alternate instructions, rapidly and accurately. However, if it encounters an exception not anticipated in the program, it is helpless and can only process the exception incorrectly or stop.

The ability to accept and store a program and then to race through its maze of yes-or-no decisions and alternate instructions is what distinguishes a computer from an electronic calculator. To appreciate this, electronic calculators exist that can do an addition, a multiplication, or division in one millionth of a second, in other words at about the speed of a fast computer. Yet, with all this speed, such a calculator cannot be operated much faster than a mechanical calculator, since without a program it must depend upon a person to push its keys telling it what to do.

Inputting data

Computers operate either *off line* or *on line*. In off-line operation the program and the basic data for a job, say the program for processing customers' orders and the required inventory data, are removed from the computer after all of a day's orders are processed. The program for a new job and a new set of data are then entered and the new job is processed. This is called batch processing and may result in customers' orders being processed daily, the payroll being run each week, financial statements being prepared monthly, and the processing of other jobs on a time-available basis. Because transactions are processed in batches, off-line operation is usually less expensive than on-line operation and is used when an immediate processing or an immediate computer response is not required. Also, off-line processing may be used in operating the computer at night with on-line operation during the day.

In on-line processing a single program is kept in the computer along with its required data. Input devices then enter new data into the computer on a continuous basis. For example, in some large department stores the cash registers are connected to and enter information directly into the store's computer; and in addition to cash sales, the registers are used as follows in recording charge sales: After the customer selects merchandise for purchase, the salesperson uses the customer's plastic credit card to print the customer's name on a blank sales ticket. He or she then places the sales ticket in the Forms Printer of the cash register and records the sale in the same way as a cash sale. The register prints all pertinent information on the sales ticket and totals it. Then in order to finalize the sale, controls within the register require that the salesperson depress the proper register keys to record the customer's account number, and by this final act the salesperson, in effect, posts the sale to the customer's account. He or she does not actually post to the account. Rather, from the information entered with the cash register's keys, the store's computer will update the customer's account and produce the customer's month-end statement, ready for mailing without further bookkeeping labor.

Another example of on-line operation is found in supermarkets, where each item of merchandise is imprinted with a machine-readable price tag similar to Illustration 6–12. At one of the store's checkout stands each item of merchandise selected by a customer is passed over an optical scanner in the counter top or an optical scanner in a wand is passed over each item's price tag. This actuates the cash register and eliminates the need for handkeying information into the register. It also transmits the sales information to a computer which updates the store's inventory records and prepares orders to a central warehouse to restock any item in low supply. Also, at closing time the computer prints out detailed summaries of the day's sales and item inventories and thus provides management with up-to-the-minute information that could not otherwise be obtained.

Illustration 6–12

Other examples of on-line operations are found in banks and in factories. However, all have the same results, they reduce human labor, create more accurate records, and provide management with both better and more up-to-date reports. Furthermore, when there are sufficient transactions, they do the work at less cost per transaction.

Time sharing

Computer service companies provide computer service to many concerns on a time-sharing basis, using computers that are capable of working on many jobs simultaneously. In providing such service, the computer service company installs an input-output device on the premises of a subscriber to its service. The input-output device is connected to the service company's computer through wires leased from the phone company, and the subscriber uses the input-output device to input data into the service company's computer where it is held in storage until processing time is available, usually within a few seconds. The computer then processes the data and transmits the results to the subscriber. For this service the subscriber pays a monthly fee plus a charge for the computer time used.

Through time sharing a growing number of concerns are using computers, even very small businesses. For example, a dentist or a physician practicing alone is a very small business, yet an increasing number of such dentists and physicians are having their accounts receivable and customer billing done by computer service companies. And, in the future more companies will make use of computers through time sharing and otherwise. Consequently, today's accounting student must learn about computers and their operation.

Accounting system. The business papers, records, reports, and pro- Glossary
cedures used by a business in recording transactions and reporting
their effects.

Accounts Payable Ledger. A subsidiary ledger having an account for
each creditor.

Accounts Receivable Ledger. A subsidiary ledger having an account for
each customer.

Automated data processing. The processing of data without human intervention.

Check Register. A book of original entry for recording payments by
check.

Columnar journal. A book of original entry having columns for entering specific data about each transaction of a group of like transactions.

Combined Cash Journal. A columnar book of original entry in which
all the transactions of a business can be recorded.

Computer. A complex electronic machine used to process data and
prepare reports.

Controlling account. A general ledger account that controls the accounts in a subsidiary ledger.

Crossfoot. To add the column totals of a journal or a report.

Foot. To add a column of figures.

General Ledger. A ledger containing the financial statement accounts
of a business.

Off-line processing of data. Processing data in batches with a new program and a new set of data being placed in the computer for each
batch.

On-line processing of data. Processing data of one kind on a continuous
basis using input devices such as cash registers or optical scanners
to enter new data as it arises.

Program. A set of computer instructions for processing data.

Schedule of accounts payable. A list of creditor account balances with
the total.

Schedule of accounts receivable. A list of customer account balances
with the total.

Special journal. A columnar book of original entry for recording one kind of transaction.

Subsidiary ledger. A group of accounts other than general ledger accounts which show the details underlying the balance of a controlling account in the General Ledger.

Time-sharing. The sharing of computer processing time.

Questions for class discussion

1. How do columnar journals save posting labor?
2. How do columnar journals take advantage of the fact that for any single class of transactions either the debit or the credit of each transaction is always to the same account?
3. What functions are served by the Accounts Receivable controlling account?
4. Why should sales to charge customers and receipts of cash from charge customers be recorded and posted daily?
5. A company has the following numbers of accounts with balances:

   a. Asset accounts including the Accounts Receivable account but not the individual customer accounts 25
   b. Customer accounts 500
   c. Liability accounts including the Accounts Payable account but not the individual creditor accounts 10
   d. Creditor accounts 20
   e. Owner equity accounts including income statement accounts 20

   Total 575

   How many items appear on the trial balance of this company? What in addition to a trial balance is used to prove the account balances of this company?
6. How is a schedule of accounts payable prepared? How is it used to prove the balances of the creditor accounts in the Accounts Payable Ledger? What may be substituted for a formal schedule?
7. How is the equality of a controlling account and its subsidiary ledger accounts maintained?
8. Describe how copies of a company's sales invoices may be used as a Sales Journal.
9. After all posting is completed, the balance of the Accounts Receivable controlling account does not agree with the sum of the balances in the Accounts Receivable Ledger. If the trial balance is in balance, where is the error apt to be?
10. How is a multicolumn journal crossfooted? Why is a multicolumn journal crossfooted?
11. How is it possible to tell from which journal a particular amount in a ledger account was posted?
12. When a general journal entry is used to record a returned charge sale, the credit of the entry must be posted twice. Does this cause the trial balance to be out of balance? Why or why not?

13. Both credits to customer accounts and credits to miscellaneous accounts are individually posted from a Cash Receipts Journal like that of Illustration 6–3. Why not place both kinds of credits in the same column and thus save journal space?

Class exercises

Exercise 6–1

A concern uses a Sales Journal, a Purchases Journal having one money column, a Cash Receipts Journal, a Cash Disbursements Journal, and a General Journal. List the following transactions by letter and opposite each letter give the name of the journal in which each transaction should be recorded.

a. Purchased merchandise on credit.
b. Purchased office supplies on credit.
c. Purchased office equipment for cash.
d. Returned merchandise purchased on credit.
e. Sold merchandise for cash.
f. Sold merchandise on credit.
g. Gave a customer credit for merchandise purchased on credit and returned.
h. A customer paid for merchandise previously purchased on credit.
i. Paid a creditor.
j. Paid sales salaries.
k. Recorded adjusting and closing entries.

Exercise 6–2

At the end of November the Sales Journal of Ace Company showed the following sales on credit:

SALES JOURNAL

Date		Account Debited	Invoice Number	F	Amount
Nov.	2	Jerry Marsh......................................	345		300.00
	9	Dale Evans......................................	346		250.00
	16	Ted Bates......................................	347		200.00
	27	Jerry Marsh......................................	348		100.00
	30	Total			850.00

The company had also recorded the return of merchandise with the following entry.

Nov.	18	Sales Returns and Allowances	50.00	
		Accounts Receivable – Ted Bates..........		50.00
		Customer returned merchandise.		

Required:

1. On a sheet of notebook paper open a subsidiary Accounts Receivable Ledger having a T-account for each customer listed in the Sales Journal.

Post to the customer accounts the entries of the Sales Journal and also the portion of the general journal entry that affects a customer's account.

2. Open a General Ledger having T-accounts for Accounts Receivable, Sales, and Sales Returns and Allowances. Post the sales journal total and the portions of the general journal entry that affect these accounts.

3. Prove the subsidiary ledger accounts with a schedule of accounts receivable.

Exercise 6–3

Cole Company, a company that posts its sales invoices directly and then binds the invoices to make them into a Sales Journal, had the following sales during October:

Oct.	3	John Fox.........	$ 800
	6	Gary Ball........	1,100
	11	Jerry Dale	1,600
	18	Gary Ball........	2,200
	21	Jerry Dale.......	700
	27	Walter Scott	1,500
		Total	$7,900

Required:

1. On a sheet of notebook paper open a subsidiary Accounts Receivable Ledger having a T-account for each customer with an invoice bound in the Sales Journal. Post the invoices to the subsidiary ledger.

2. Give the general journal entry to record the end-of-the-month total of the Sales Journal.

3. Open an Accounts Receivable controlling account and a Sales account and post the general journal entry.

4. Prove the subsidiary Accounts Receivable Ledger with a schedule of accounts receivable.

Exercise 6–4

A company that records credit sales in a Sales Journal and records sales returns in its General Journal made the following errors. List each error by letter, and opposite each letter tell when the error will be discovered:

a. Correctly recorded a $75 sale in the Sales Journal but posted it to the customer's account as a $750 sale.

b. Made an addition error in totaling the Amount column of the Sales Journal.

c. Posted a sales return recorded in the General Journal to the Sales Returns and Allowances account and to the Accounts Receivable account but did not post to the customer's account.

d. Posted a sales return to the Accounts Receivable account and to the customer's account but did not post to the Sales Returns and Allowances account.

e. Made an addition error in determining the balance of a customer's account.

Exercise 6–5

Following are the condensed journals of a merchandising concern. The journal column headings are incomplete in that they do not indicate whether the columns are debit or credit columns.

Required:

1. Prepare T-accounts on a sheet of ordinary notebook paper for the following general ledger and subsidiary ledger accounts. Separate the accounts of each ledger group as follows:

General Ledger Accounts
Cash
Accounts Receivable
Prepaid Insurance
Store Equipment
Notes Payable
Accounts Payable
Sales
Sales Returns
Sales Discounts
Purchases
Purchases Returns
Purchases Discounts

Accounts Receivable Ledger Accounts
Customer A
Customer B
Customer C

Accounts Payable Ledger Accounts
Company One
Company Two
Company Three

2. Without referring to any of the illustrations showing complete column headings for the journals, post the following journals to the proper T-accounts.

SALES JOURNAL

Account	Amount
Customer A	1,000
Customer B.........	1,500
Customer C	2,000
Total.........	4,500

PURCHASES JOURNAL

Account	Amount
Company One.....	1,200
Company Two.....	1,400
Company Three...	1,600
Total	4,200

GENERAL JOURNAL

....	...			
	...	Sales Returns...	200.00	
		Accounts Receivable — Customer C.......		200.00
	...	Accounts Payable — Company Three............	300.00	
		Purchases Returns..............................		300.00

CASH RECEIPTS JOURNAL

Account	Other Accounts	Accounts Receivable	Sales	Sales Discounts	Cash
Customer A...................	....	1,000	....	20	980
Cash Sales...................	....	....	1,450	....	1,450
Notes Payable...............	2,000	....	....	....	2,000
Cash Sales...................	....	....	1,650	....	1,650
Customer C..................	....	1,500	....	30	1,470
Store Equipment.............	150	....	....	....	150
	2,150	2,500	3,100	50	7,700

CASH DISBURSEMENTS JOURNAL

Accounts	Other Accounts	Accounts Payable	Purchases Discounts	Cash
Prepaid Insurance....................................	100	....	....	100
Company Two	....	1,400	28	1,372
Company Three	....	1,300	26	1,274
Store Equipment	500	....	....	500
	600	2,700	54	3,246

Problems

Problem 6-1

Valley Sales Company completed the following transactions:

Oct. 2 Sold merchandise to Carl Bates on credit, Invoice No. 671, $850. (Terms of all credit sales are 2/10, n/60.)

3 Received merchandise and an invoice dated October 2, terms 2/10, n/60, from Alpha Company, $1,150.

4 Borrowed $2,500 from Security Bank by giving a note payable.

5 Purchased store equipment on credit from Store Outfitters, terms n/10 EOM, $545.

6 Sold merchandise on credit to Dale Hall, Invoice No. 672, $600.

8 Received a credit memorandum from Store Outfitters for unsatisfactory store equipment returned, $135.

9 Received merchandise and an invoice dated October 6, terms 2/10, n/60, from Western Company, $1,285.

11 Sold merchandise on credit to Walter Nash, Invoice No. 673, $750.

12 Received an $833 check from Carl Bates in payment of the October 2 sale.

12 Issued Check No. 922 to Alpha Company in payment of its October 2 invoice, less the discount.

13 Received a credit memorandum from Western Company for unsatisfactory merchandise received on October 9 and returned, $85.

15 Issued Check No. 923 to Desert Realty in payment of one month's rent on the store building, $500.

15 Issued Check No. 924, payable to Payroll, in payment of sales salaries for the first half of the month, $550.

15 Cash sales for the first half of the month, $2,115. (Cash sales are normally recorded daily from the cash register readings; however, they are recorded only twice in this problem in order to shorten the problem.)

15 *Post to the customer and creditor accounts and also post any amounts that should be posted as individual amounts to the general ledger accounts.*

16 Issued Check No. 925 to Western Company in payment of the October 6 invoice, less the return and the discount.

17 Sold merchandise on credit to Carl Bates, Invoice No. 674, $700.

20 Received a $735 check from Walter Nash in payment of the October 11 sale.

Oct. 21   Received merchandise and an invoice dated October 18, terms 2/10, n/60 from Alpha Company, $900.

    22   Sold unneeded store equipment for cash at cost, $35.

    24   Received merchandise and an invoice dated October 22, terms 2/10, n/60 from Beta Company, $615.

    27   Received a $686 check from Carl Bates in payment of the October 17 sale.

    27   Sold merchandise to Walter Nash on credit, Invoice No. 675, $495.

    28   Issued Check No. 926 to Alpha Company in payment of the October 18 invoice, less the discount.

    31   Issued Check No. 927, payable to Payroll, in payment of sales salaries for the last half of the month, $550.

    31   Cash sales for the last half of the month, $2,295.

    31   *Post to the customer and creditor accounts and post any amounts that should be posted as individual amounts to the general ledger accounts.*

    31   *Total the journals and make the month-end postings.*

Required

1. Open the following general ledger accounts: Cash; Accounts Receivable; Store Equipment; Notes Payable; Accounts Payable; Sales; Sales Discounts; Purchases; Purchases Returns and Allowances; Purchases Discounts; Sales Salaries Expense; and Rent Expense.
2. Open the following accounts receivable ledger accounts: Carl Bates; Dale Hall; and Walter Nash.
3. Open the following accounts payable ledger accounts: Alpha Company; Beta Company; Store Outfitters; and Western Company.
4. Prepare a Sales Journal, Purchases Journal, Cash Recepits Journal, Cash Disbursements Journal, and General Journal like the ones in this chapter.
5. Enter the transactions in the journals and post when instructed to do so.
6. Prepare a trial balance of the General Ledger and prove the subsidiary ledgers with schedules of accounts receivable and accounts payable.

Problem 6–2

Nevada Company completed these transactions during February of the current year:

Feb.   2   Sold merchandise on credit to John Rice, $1,250. (Terms of all credit sales are 2/10, n/60. Number sales invoices beginning with 758.)

    2   Sold merchandise on credit to Fred Able, $1,100.

    3   Received merchandise and an invoice dated January 31, terms 2/10, n/60, from Case Company, $2,800.

    4   Issued Check No. 522 to *The Morning Sun* for advertising, $185.

    5   Received office equipment and an invoice dated February 3, terms n/10 EOM, from office Equipment Company, $650.

    7   Cash sales for the first week of February, $1,200.

    7   *Post to the customer and creditor accounts and also post any amounts that should be posted as individual amounts to the general ledger accounts. (Normally such items are posted daily; but to*

shorten the problem, you are asked to post them only once each week.)

Feb. 9 Sold unneeded office equipment at cost for cash, $140.

10 Sold merchandise on credit to Tom Moss, $800.

10 Received merchandise and an invoice dated February 6, terms 1/10, n/60, from Taylor Company, $1,850.

10 Sent Check No. 523 to Case Company in full of the invoice of January 31, less the discount.

12 Received a check from John Rice in full payment of the sale of February 2, less the discount.

12 Received a check from Fred Able in full payment of the sale of February 2, less the discount.

14 Cash sales for the week ended February 14, $1,450.

14 *Post to the customer and creditor accounts and also post any amounts that should be posted as individual amounts to the general ledger accounts.*

15 Sold merchandise on credit to Tom Moss, $900.

15 Issued Check No. 524, payable to Payroll, in payment of the sales salaries for the first half of the month, $600. Cashed the check and paid the employees.

17 Issued a credit memorandum to Tom Moss for defective merchandise purchased on February 15 and returned, $150.

18 Received a credit memorandum for defective office equipment purchased on February 5 and returned, $50.

18 Sold merchandise on credit to Fred Able, $1,300.

18 Received merchandise and an invoice dated February 15, terms 2/10, n/30, from New Company, $3,500.

20 Received a check from Tom Moss in full of the sale of February 10, less the discount.

21 Cash sales for the week ended February 21, $1,550.

21 *Post to the customer and creditor accounts and also post any amounts that should be posted as individual amounts to the general ledger accounts.*

22 Received merchandise and an invoice dated February 18, terms 1/10, n/60, from Taylor Company, $1,250.

22 Received merchandise and an invoice dated February 18, terms 2/10, n/60, from Case Company, $2,650.

23 Received a credit memorandum from New Company, $350. The merchandise covered by the memorandum did not meet specifications and had been returned.

24 Received a check from Tom Moss in full of the invoice of February 15, less the return and the discount.

24 Sent New Company Check No. 525 in full of the invoice of February 15, less the return and the discount.

25 Sold merchandise on credit to John Rice, $1,175.

27 Borrowed $5,000 from the United States National Bank by giving a 60-day, 7% note payable.

28 Sent Case Company Check No. 526 in full of the invoice of February 18, less the discount.

28 Issued Check No. 527 payable to Payroll for sales salaries, $600. Cashed the check and paid the employees.

Feb. 28   Cash sales for the week ended February 28, $1,225.   *ck / sales*

   28   *Post to customer and creditor accounts and also post any amounts*
          that should be posted as individual amounts to the general ledger
          accounts.

   28   *Crossfoot the journals and make the month-end postings.*

Required:

1.   Open the following general ledger accounts: Cash; Accounts Receivable;
      Office Equipment; Notes Payable; Accounts Payable; Sales; Sales Re-
      turns and Allowances; Sales Discounts; Purchases; Purchases Returns
      and Allowances; Purchases Discounts; Advertising Expense; and Sales
      Salaries Expense.
2.   Open the following accounts receivable ledger accounts: Fred Able; Tom
      Moss; and John Rice.
3.   Open the following accounts payable ledger accounts: Case Company;
      New Company; Office Equipment Company; and Taylor Company.
4.   Prepare a Sales Journal, Purchases Journal, Cash Receipts Journal,
      Cash Disbursements Journal, and General Journal similar to the ones
      illustrated in this chapter. Enter the transactions in the journals and post
      when instructed to do so.
5.   Prepare a trial balance of the General Ledger and prove the subsidiary
      ledgers with schedules of accounts receivable and accounts payable.

Problem 6–3

   Carson Company completed the following transactions:

Feb. 2   Issued Check No. 654 to Valley Realty in payment of the February
           rent, $350.
      2   Sold merchandise on credit to Gary Nash, Invoice No. 889, $500.
           (Terms of all credit sales are 2/10, n/60.)
      3   Sold merchandise on credit to Ted Lee, Invoice No. 890, $315.
      4   Received merchandise and an invoice dated February 2, terms 2/10,
           n/60, from Best Company, $1,500.
      6   Issued a credit memorandum to Ted Lee for defective merchandise
           sold on February 3 and returned for credit, $65.
      7   Cash sales for the first week of February, $975.
      7   *Post to the customer and creditor accounts and also post any*
           amounts that should be posted as individual amounts to the general
           ledger accounts. (Normally such items are posted daily; but to
           shorten the problem, you are asked to post them only once each
           week.)
      9   Issued Check No. 655 to *The News* for advertising, $125.
     10   Purchased office equipment on credit from Western Company, terms
           n/10 EOM, $450.
     11   Issued Check No. 656 to Best Company in full of its invoice of
           February 2, less the discount.
     12   Received a check from Gary Nash in full of the sale of February 2,
           less the discount.
     13   Received a check from Ted Lee in full of the February 3 sale, less
           the return and discount.
     14   Cash sales for the week ended February 14, $850.

Feb. 14 *Post to the customer and creditor accounts and also post any amounts that should be posted as individual amounts to the general ledger accounts.*

16 Received a credit memorandum for defective office equipment purchased on February 10 and returned for credit, $35.

17 Sold merchandise on credit to Ted Lee, Invoice No. 891, $635.

18 Received merchandise and an invoice dated February 15, terms 2/10, n/60, from Dale Company, $860.

21 Cash sales for the week ended February 21, $900.

21 *Post to the customer and creditor accounts and also post any amounts that should be posted as individual amounts to the general ledger accounts.*

23 Received a credit memorandum from Dale Company for unsatisfactory merchandise received on February 18 and returned for credit, $110.

24 Received merchandise and an invoice dated February 20, terms 2/10, n/60, from Best Company, $535.

25 Issued Check No. 657 to Dale Company in payment of its February 15 invoice, less the return and discount.

26 Sold merchandise on credit to Gary Nash, Invoice No. 892, $495.

28 Cash sales for the last week of February, $1,215.

28 *Post to the customer and creditor accounts and also post any amounts that should be posted as individual amounts to the general ledger accounts.*

28 *Foot and crossfoot the journal and make the month-end postings.*

Required:

1. Open the following general ledger accounts: Cash; Accounts Receivable; Office Equipment; Accounts Payable; Sales; Sales Returns and Allowances; Sales Discounts; Purchases; Purchases Returns and Allowances; Purchases Discounts; Rent Expense; and Advertising Expense.

2. Open these accounts receivable ledger accounts: Ted Lee and Gary Nash.

3. Open these accounts payable ledger accounts: Best Company; Dale Company; and Western Company.

4. Prepare a Combined Cash Journal similar to the one illustrated in this chapter, record the transactions in the journal, and post when instructed to do so.

5. Prepare a trial balance of the General Ledger and prove the subsidiary ledgers with schedules of accounts receivable and accounts payable.

Problem 6–4

(If the working papers that accompany this text are not being used, omit this problem.)

It is the last week of June and you have just taken over the accounting work of Western Company, a concern operating with annual accounting periods that end each May 31. The company's previous accountant has journalized the company's transactions through Saturday, June 23, and has posted all items that should be posted as individual amounts, as an examination of the company's journals and ledgers in the booklet of working papers will reveal.

Western Company completed these transactions during the last week of June:

June 25   Douglas Murphy, the proprietor of Western Company, used Check No. 723 to withdraw $500 from the business for personal expenses.

      25   Sold merchandise on credit to Roy Ness, Invoice No. 716, $700. (The terms of all credit sales are 2/10, n/60.)

      26   Purchased store equipment on credit from Lee Supply Company, terms n/10 EOM, $365.

      26   Received a check from Alan Hall in full of the June 16 sale, less the normal 2% discount.

      27   Received merchandise and an invoice dated June 25, terms 2/10, n/60, from Pace Company, $1,250.

      27   Issued Check No. 724 to Clark Company in payment of its June 17 invoice, less the discount.

      30   Issued Check No. 725 to Gary Beal, the company's only sales employee, in payment of his salary for the last half of June plus some overtime, $350.

      30   Issued Check No. 726 to Northern Service Company to pay the June gas and electric bill, $130.

      30   Cash sales for the last half of June, $2,120. (Such sales are usually recorded daily but are recorded only three times in this problem in order to reduce the repetitive transactions.)

Required for June:

1. Record the transactions of the last week of June.
2. Post to customer and creditor accounts and also post any amounts that should be posted as individual amounts to the general ledger accounts. Normally these amounts are posted daily, but they are posted only twice each month in this problem in order to simplify it.)
3. Foot and crossfoot the journals and make the month-end column-total postings.
4. Prepare a June 30 trial balance and prove the subsidiary ledgers with schedules of accounts receivable and accounts payable.
5. Double rule the date and amount columns of the journals so that they may be used to record the July transactions.

Western Company completed these transactions in July:

July 2   Issued Check No. 727 to Apex Realty in payment of the July rent, $500.

      3   Received a check from John Long in full of the June 23 sale, less the discount.

      5   Received a check from Roy Ness in full of the June 25 sale, less the discount.

      5   Issued Check No. 728 to Pace Company in full of its invoice of June 25, less the discount.

      6   Sold a local church a roll of wrapping paper (store supplies) at cost for cash, $10.

      7   Sold merchandise on credit to Alan Hall, Invoice No. 717, $500.

      9   Received merchandise and an invoice dated July 6, terms 2/10, n/60, from Acme Company, $1,150.

July 10 Issued Check No. 729 to Lee Supply Company to pay for the store equipment purchased on June 26.

11 Sold merchandise on credit to John Long, Invoice No. 718, $650.

12 Received merchandise and an invoice dated July 10 from Clark Company, terms 2/10, n/60, $875.

14 Issued Check No. 730 to Gary Beal in payment of his salary for the first half of July plus some overtime, $355.

14 Cash sales for the first half of July were $2,865.

14 *Post to the customer and creditor accounts and also post any amounts that should be posted as individual amounts to the general ledger accounts.*

16 Issued Check No. 731 to Acme Company in payment of its invoice of July 6, less the discount.

16 Received a $125 credit memorandum from Clark Company for defective merchandise received on July 12 and returned.

17 Received a check from Alan Hall in full of the July 7 sale, less the discount.

20 Issued Check No. 732 to Clark Company in payment of its invoice of July 10, less the return and the discount.

21 Received a check from John Long in full of the July 11 sale, less the discount.

22 Sold merchandise on credit to Ted Reed, Invoice No. 719, $835.

24 Sold merchandise on credit to Roy Ness, Invoice No. 720, $780.

26 Received merchandise and an invoice dated July 23, terms 2/10, n/60, from Clark Company, $1,045.

31 Issued Check No. 733 to Northern Service Company to pay the July gas and electric bill, $145.

31 Issued Check No. 734 to Gary Beal in payment of his salary for the last half of July, $320.

31 Cash sales for the last half of July were $2,645.

31 *Post to the customer and creditor accounts and also post any amounts that should be posted as individual amounts to the general ledger accounts.*

31 *Foot and crossfoot the journals and make the month-end postings.*

Required for July:

1. Record the July transactions and post at the points indicated.
2. Prepare a July 31 trial balance and prove the subsidiary ledgers with schedules of accounts receivable and accounts payable.

Alternate problems

Problem 6–1A

Reno Sales Company completed the following transactions:

Oct. 1 Received merchandise and an invoice dated September 30, terms 2/10, n/60, from Western Company, $975.

1 Issued Check No. 516 to Carson Realty in payment of the October rent, $600.

4 Received merchandise and an invoice dated October 1, terms 2/10, n/60, from Beta Company, $1,050.

5 Purchased store equipment on credit from Store Outfitters, terms n/10 EOM, $350.

Oct. 6 Received a $125 credit memorandum from Western Company for unsatisfactory merchandise received on October 1 and returned.

    9 Issued Check No. 517 to Western Company in payment of its September 30 invoice, less the return and discount.

   10 Received a $25 credit memorandum from Store Outfitters for unsatisfactory store equipment purchased on October 5 and returned.

   10 Sold merchandise on credit to Dale Hall, Invoice No. 905, $550. (Terms of all sales are 2/10, n/60.)

   11 Sold merchandise on credit to Walter Nash, Invoice No. 906, $800.

   11 Issued Check No. 518 to Beta Company in payment of its October 1 invoice, less the discount.

   14 Received merchandise and an invoice dated October 10, terms 1/10, n/30, from Alpha Company, $775.

   15 Cash sales for the first half of the month, $2,165. (Cash sales are normally recorded daily from the cash register readings; however, they are recorded only twice in this problem in order to shorten the problem.)

   15 *Post to the customer and creditor accounts and also post any amounts that should be posted as individual amounts to the general ledger accounts.*

   18 Sold merchandise on credit to Carl Bates, Invoice No. 907, $865.

   19 Sold merchandise on credit to Dale Hall, Invoice No. 908, $650.

   20 Received a $539 check from Dale Hall in payment of the October 10 sale.

   21 Received a $784 check from Walter Nash in payment of the October 11 sale.

   23 Sold store equipment at cost for cash, $25.

   24 Received merchandise and an invoice dated October 21, terms 2/10, n/60, from Beta Company, $950.

   25 Borrowed $2,000 from First State Bank by giving a note payable.

   28 Sold merchandise on credit to Walter Nash, Invoice No. 909, $565.

   29 Received a $637 check from Dale Hall in payment of the October 19 sale.

   31 Issued Check No. 519 to Beta Company in payment of its October 21 invoice, less the discount.

   31 Issued Check No. 520, payable to Payroll, in payment of the monthly sales salaries, $1,250.

   31 Cash sales for the last half of the month, $2,230.

   31 *Post to the customer and creditor accounts and also post any amounts that should be posted as individual amounts to the general ledger accounts.*

   31 *Total the journals and make the month-end postings.*

Required:

1. Open the following general ledger accounts: Cash; Accounts Receivable; Store Equipment; Notes Payable; Accounts Payable; Sales; Sales Discounts; Purchases; Purchases Returns and Allowances; Purchases Discounts; Sales Salaries Expense; and Rent Expense.

2. Open the following subsidiary accounts receivable ledger accounts: Carl Bates; Dale Hall; and Walter Nash.

3. Open these subsidiary accounts payable ledger accounts: Alpha Company; Beta Company; Store Outfitters; and Western Company.

4. Prepare a Sales Journal, Purchases Journal, Cash Receipts Journal, Cash Disbursements Journal, and General Journal similar to the ones illustrated in this chapter.
5. Enter the transactions in the journals and post when instructed to do so.
6. Prepare a trial balance of the General Ledger and prove the subsidiary ledgers with schedules of accounts receivable and accounts payable.

Problem 6–2A

Globe Company completed these transactions during February of the current year:

Feb. 2 Received merchandise and an invoice dated January 30, terms 2/10, n/60, from Case Company, $1,535.

     3 Purchased office equipment from Office Equipment Company, terms n/10 EOM, $585.

     3 Sold merchandise on credit to Tom Moss, Invoice No. 617, $950. (Terms of all credit sales are 2/10, n/60.)

     4 Sold merchandise on credit to John Rice, Invoice No. 618, $1,150.

     5 Received merchandise and an invoice dated February 3, terms 1/10, n/60, from New Company, $1,690.

     6 Received a credit memorandum from Case Company for unsatisfactory merchandise received from it on February 2 and returned, $135.

     7 Received a credit memorandum from Office Equipment Company for office equipment received on February 3 and returned, $60.

     7 Cash sales for the first week of February, $1,445.

     7 *Post to the customer and creditor accounts and also post any amounts that should be posted as individual amounts to the general ledger accounts. (Normally such items are posted daily; but to shorten the problem, you are asked to post them only once each week.)*

     9 Sent Case Company Check No. 312 in payment of its invoice of January 30, less the return and discount.

   11 Sold merchandise on credit to Fred Able, Invoice No. 619, $1,710.

   12 Received a check from Tom Moss in payment of the sale of February 3, less the discount.

   13 Received a check from John Rice in payment of the sale of February 4, less the discount.

   14 Received merchandise and an invoice dated February 11, terms 2/10, n/60, from Taylor Company, $1,850.

   14 Issued Check No. 313, payable to Payroll, in payment of the sales salaries for the first half of the month, $815. Cashed the check and paid the employees.

   14 Cash sales for the week ended February 14, $1,395.

   14 *Post to the customer and creditor accounts and also post any amounts that should be posted as individual amounts to the general ledger accounts.*

   16 Issued a $160 credit memorandum to Fred Able for defective merchandise sold on February 11 and returned.

   17 Received merchandise and an invoice dated February 14, terms 2/10, n/60, from Taylor Company, $1,450.

Feb. 18   Received merchandise and an invoice dated February 16, terms 1/10, n/60, from New Company, $435.

   18   Sold merchandise on credit to Tom Moss, Invoice No. 620, $650.

   21   Received a check from Fred Able in payment of the sale of February 11, less the return and discount.

   21   Sent Taylor Company Check No. 314 in payment of its invoice of February 11, less the discount.

   21   Cash sales for the week ended February 21, $1,425.

   21   *Post to the customer and creditor accounts and also post any amounts that should be posted as individual amounts to the general ledger accounts.*

   24   Sent Taylor Company Check No. 315 in payment of its invoice of February 14, less the discount.

   25   Borrowed $4,000 by giving Valley National Bank a 60-day, 6% promissory note payable.

   26   Sold merchandise on credit to Fred Able, Invoice No. 621, $915.

   27   Sold merchandise on credit to John Rice, Invoice No. 622, $1,085.

   28   Issued Check No. 316 to *The Gazette* for advertising expense, $375.

   28   Issued Check No. 317 payable to Payroll for sales salaries, $815. Cashed the check and paid the employees.

   28   Received a check from Tom Moss in payment of the February 18 sale, less the discount.

   28   Cash sales for the last week of the month, $1,345.

   28   *Post to the customer and creditor accounts and also post any amounts that should be posted as individual amounts to the general ledger accounts.*

   28   *Make the month-end postings from the journals.*

Required:

1.   Open the following general ledger accounts: Cash; Accounts Receivable; Office Equipment; Notes Payable; Accounts Payable; Sales; Sales Returns and Allowances; Sales Discounts; Purchases; Purchases Returns and Allowances; Purchases Discounts; Advertising Expense; and Sales Salaries Expense.

2.   Open the following accounts receivable ledger accounts: Fred Able; Tom Moss; and John Rice.

3.   Open the following accounts payable ledger accounts: Case Company; New Company; Office Equipment Company; and Taylor Company.

4.   Prepare a Sales Journal; a Purchases Journal; a Cash Receipts Journal; a Cash Disbursements Journal; and a General Journal similar to the ones illustrated in this chapter.

5.   Enter the transactions in the journals and post when instructed to do so.

6.   Prepare a trial balance and prove the subsidiary ledgers with schedules of accounts receivable and payable.

Problem 6–3A

Surfside Company completed these transactions during February of the current year:

Feb. 1   Received merchandise and an invoice dated January 30, terms 2/10, n/60, from Dale Company, $1,385.

Feb. 3 Issued Check No. 567 to *The Star* for advertising, $115.

4 Sold merchandise on credit to Ted Lee, Invoice No. 862, $750. (Terms of all credit sales are 2/10, n/60.)

5 Received a credit memorandum from Dale Company for defective merchandise received on February 1 and returned for credit, $135.

6 Cash sales for the week ended February 6, $1,045.

6 *Post to the customer and creditor accounts and also post any amounts that should be posted as individual amounts to the general ledger accounts. (Normally such items are posted daily; but to shorten the problem, you are asked to post them only once each week.)*

8 Issued Check No. 568 to Dale Company in payment of its invoice of January 30, less the return and discount.

9 Sold merchandise on credit to Gary Nash, Invoice No. 863, $570.

10 Purchased office equipment on credit from Western Company, terms n/10 EOM, $345.

11 Issued a credit memorandum to Gary Nash for defective merchandise purchased on February 9 and returned, $70.

13 Received a check from Ted Lee in full of the February 4 sale, less the discount.

13 Cash sales for the week ended February 13, $990.

13 *Post to the customer and creditor accounts and also post any amounts that should be posted as individual amounts to the general ledger accounts.*

15 Issued Check No. 569 to Lake Realty for one month's rent on the space occupied by the business, $400.

16 Received a $55 credit memorandum from Western Company for defective office equipment purchased on February 10 and returned.

17 Received merchandise and an invoice dated February 15, terms 2/10, n/60, from Best Company, $1,000.

19 Received a check from Gary Nash in full of the February 9 sale, less the return and discount.

21 Cash sales for the week ended February 21, $1,120.

21 *Post to the customer and creditor accounts and post any amounts that should be posted as individual amounts to the general ledger accounts.*

23 Received merchandise and an invoice dated February 21 from Dale Company, terms 2/10, n/60, $785.

24 Sold merchandise on credit to Gary Nash, Invoice No. 864, $635.

25 Issued Check No. 570 to Best Company in payment of its invoice of February 15, less the discount.

26 Sold merchandise on credit to Ted Lee, Invoice No. 865, $590.

28 Cash sales for the week ended February 28, $1,015.

28 *Post to the customer and creditor accounts and also post any amounts that should be posted as individual amounts to the general ledger accounts.*

28 *Foot and crossfoot the journal and make the month-end postings.*

Required:

1. Open the following general ledger accounts: Cash; Accounts Receivable; Office Equipment; Accounts Payable; Sales; Sales Returns and Al-

lowances; Sales Discounts; Purchases; Purchases Returns and Allowances; Purchases Discounts; Rent Expense; and Advertising Expense.
2. Open these accounts receivable ledger accounts: Ted Lee and Gary Nash.
3. Open these accounts payable ledger accounts: Best Company; Dale Company; and Western Company.
4. Prepare a Combined Cash Journal similar to the one illustrated in this chapter, record the transactions in the journal, and post when instructed to do so.
5. Prepare a trial balance of the General Ledger and prove the subsidiary ledgers with schedules of accounts receivable and accounts payable.

Problem 6–4A

(*If the working papers that accompany this text are not being used, omit this problem.*)

Assume that Western Company operates with annual accounting periods that end each May 31, that it is the last week of June, and you have just taken over the company's accounting work. The company's previous accountant has journalized its transactions of the first part of June and has posted all entry portions that should have been posted as individual amounts, as an examination of the company's journals and ledgers in the booklet of working papers will reveal.

The company completed these transactions during the last week of June:

June 25 Received merchandise and an invoice dated June 22, terms 2/10, n/60, from Acme Company, $900.
  25 Sold merchandise on credit to Alan Hall, Invoice No. 716, $850. (The terms of all credit sales are 2/10, n/60.)
  25 Received a check from Alan Hall in full of the June 16 sale, less the normal 2% discount.
  26 Purchased store supplies on credit from Lee Supply Company, terms n/10 EOM, $85.
  27 Issued Check No. 723 to Clark Company in payment of its June 17 invoice, less the discount.
  28 Douglas Murphy, the proprietor, issued Check No. 724 to himself to withdraw $150 from the business to pay personal expenses.
  30 Issued Check No. 725 to Public Service Company to pay the June gas and electric bill, $115.
  30 Issued Check No. 726 to Gary Beal, the company's only sales employee, to pay his salary for the last half of June plus some overtime, $345.
  30 Cash sales for the last half of June, $2,715. (Such sales are usually recorded daily, but they are recorded only three times in this problem in order to reduce the repetitive transactions.)

Required for June:
1. Record the transactions of the last week of June.
2. Post the customer and creditor accounts and also post any amounts that should be posted as individual amounts to the general ledger accounts. (Normally these amounts are posted daily, but they are posted only twice each month in this problem in order to simplify it.)
3. Foot and crossfoot the journals and make the month-end column-total postings.

4. Prepare a June 30 trial balance and prove the subsidiary ledgers with schedules of accounts receivable and payable.
5. Double rule the date and amount columns of the journals so that they may be used to record the July transactions.

The company completed these transactions in July:

July 2 Issued Check No. 727 to Apex Realty in payment of the July rent, $500.
2 Issued Check No. 728 to Acme Company in payment of its June 22 invoice, less the discount.
3 Received a check from John Long in full of the June 23 sale, less the discount.
5 Received a check from Alan Hall in full of the June 25 sale, less the discount.
6 Sold merchandise on credit to Roy Ness, Invoice No. 717, $650.
7 Received merchandise and an invoice dated July 5, terms 2/10, n/60, from Pace Company, $450.
9 Sold the local Y.M.C.A. a roll of wrapping paper (store supplies) at cost for cash, $15.
10 Issued Check No. 729 to Lee Supply Company to pay for the items purchased on June 26.
11 Received merchandise and an invoice dated July 9 from Clark Company, terms 2/10, n/60, $750.
12 Sold merchandise on credit to John Long, Invoice No. 718, $950.
14 Issued Check No. 730 to Pace Company to pay its invoice of July 5, less the discount.
14 Issued Check No. 731 to Gary Beal in payment of his salary for the first half of July, $320.
14 Cash sales for the first half of July were $2,765.
14 *Post to the customer and creditor accounts and also post any amounts that should be posted as individual amounts to the general ledger accounts.*
16 Received a check from Roy Ness in full of the July 6 sale, less the discount.
19 Issued Check No. 732 to Clark Company in full of its July 9 invoice, less the discount.
21 Received a check from John Long in full of the July 12 sale, less the discount.
23 Sold merchandise on credit to Ted Reed, Invoice No. 719, $865.
24 Sold merchandise on credit to Roy Ness, Invoice No. 720, $985.
26 Received merchandise and an invoice dated July 23, terms 2/10, n/60, from Pace Company, $915.
29 Received a credit memorandum from Pace Company for defective merchandise received on July 26 and returned, $95.
31 Issued Check No. 733 to Gary Beal in payment of his salary for the last half of July, $320.
31 Issued Check No. 734 to Public Utility Company to pay the July gas and electric bill, $110.
31 Cash sales for the last half of July were $2,820.
31 *Post to the customer and creditor accounts and also post any amounts that should be posted as individual amounts to the general ledger accounts.*
31 *Foot and crossfoot the journals and make the month-end postings.*

Required for July:

1. Record the transactions and post at the points indicated.
2. Prepare a July 31 trial balance and prove the subsidiary ledgers with schedules of accounts receivable and accounts payable.

Bob Beach went to work for Asbury Company in its Phoenix Branch upon graduation from college, and at the beginning of last year he was made branch manager. Upon taking over the branch he recognized that his accounting knowledge was limited, but he reasoned that if the branch's cash increased, the branch was making satisfactory progress. Consequently, he watched with enthusiasm the growth of the branch's cash balance from $3,200 when he took over to $22,400 at the end of his first year as manager; and when he received the following income statement covering the year's operations, he was shocked to learn the branch has operated with a $1,500 loss.

Decision problem 6–1, Asbury Company, Phoenix Branch

ASBURY COMPANY, PHOENIX BRANCH
Income Statement for Year Ended December 31, 19—

Sales		$340,000
Cost of goods sold		238,000
Gross profit from sales		$102,000
Operating expenses:		
Salaries expense	$90,000	
Advertising expense	2,500	
Supplies expense	500	
Depreciation expense, equipment	3,000	
Depreciation expense, building........	7,500	
Total operating expenses..........		103,500
Net Loss.......................................		$ (1,500)

As branch accountant, you have been called on to explain to Mr. Beach how it is possible for the branch to suffer a loss during a period in which there was such a gratifying increase in its cash. In your explanation, account for the change in the cash balance. Assume that the number of dollars the branch had invested in supplies was the same at the beginning and end of the period. However, its accounts receivable decreased $8,300, its merchandise inventory decreased $3,600, and its accounts payable decreased $1,200 during the period. Also there were $800 of earned but unpaid salaries at the beginning of the period and $300 at the end. The advertising expense was incurred and paid for during the period.

Walter Collins, the proprietor of Universal Sales, and his employees spent most of the afternoon on December 31, 1979, preparing for the annual inventory to be taken the next day. However, their efforts were wasted because the entire inventory was destroyed in a fire after closing hours that night. Fortunately the accounting records were in a fireproof vault and were used to

Decision problem 6–2, Universal Sales

prepare the following 1978 and 1979 unadjusted trial balances of the concern's General Ledger:

UNIVERSAL SALES

Trial Balances, December 31, 1978, and 1979

	December 31, 1978		December 31, 1979	
Cash.................................. $	2,190		$ 5,440	
Accounts receivable	7,510		8,410	
Merchandise inventory..........	14,785		15,645	
Store supplies......................	670		710	
Prepaid insurance.................	715		695	
Store equipment...................	11,850		14,750	
Accumulated depreciation, store equipment		$ 2,985		$ 3,245
Accounts payable.................		2,130		1,985
Walter Collins, capital...........		23,155		31,210
Walter Collins, withdrawals ...	9,600		12,000	
Sales..................................		108,440		111,630
Sales returns and allowances...	915		980	
Purchases	67,345		67,980	
Purchases returns and allowances		760		810
Purchases discounts		1,210		1,225
Sales salaries expense...........	15,230		15,560	
Rent expense	6,000		6,000	
Advertising expense	790		815	
Utilities expense..................	1,080		1,120	
Totals	$138,680	$138,680	$150,105	$150,105

As the insurance adjuster, you have been called upon to estimate the inventory loss. You learn that 1978 and 1979 were normal years in which no significant changes in operating policies were made. Prepare a report with figures to support your estimate of the concern's December 31, 1979, inventory.

PART 3

Accounting for assets

7
Accounting for cash . . .

8
Notes and accounts receivable . . .

9
Inventories and cost of goods sold . . .

10
Plant and equipment . . .

11
Plant and equipment; intangible assets

After studying Chapter 7, you should be able to:

- Explain why internal control procedures are needed in a large concern and state the broad principles of internal control.

- Describe internal control procedures to protect cash from cash sales, cash received through the mail, and cash disbursements.

- Tell how a petty cash fund operates and be able to make entries in a Petty Cash Record and the entries required to reimburse a petty cash fund.

- Explain why the bank balance of cash and the book balance of cash are reconciled and be able to prepare such a reconciliation.

- Tell how recording invoices at net amounts helps to gain control over cash discounts taken and be able to account for invoices recorded at net amounts.

- Define or explain the words and phrases listed in the chapter Glossary.

chapter 7

Accounting for cash

Cash has universal usefulness, small bulk for high value, and no convenient identification marks by which ownership may be established; consequently, in accounting for cash, the procedures for protecting it from fraud and theft are very important. These procedures are called *internal control procedures*. Internal control procedures apply to all assets owned by a business and to all phases of its operations, but they are most important where cash is involved.

In a small business the owner-manager commonly controls the entire operation through his personal supervision and his direct participation in the affairs and activities of the business. For example, he commonly buys all the assets, goods, and services bought by the business, personally hires and closely supervises all employees, negotiates all contracts, and signs all checks. As a result, when he signs checks, for example, he knows from personal contact and observation that the assets, goods, and services for which the checks are in payment were received by the business. However, as a business grows it becomes increasingly difficult to maintain this personal contact, and at some point it becomes necessary for a manager to delegate responsibilities and rely for control on internal control procedures rather than personal contact.

The methods and procedures adopted by a business to control its operations are collectively known as a *system of internal control*. In a properly designed system the procedures encourage adherence to prescribed managerial policies; promote operational efficiencies; protect the business assets from waste, fraud, and theft; and ensure accurate and reliable accounting data.

Internal control procedures vary from company to company,

Internal control

depending on such factors as the nature of the business and its size. However, some broad principles of internal control are as follows:[1]

Responsibilities should be clearly established

Good internal control necessitates that responsibilities be clearly established. Furthermore, in a given situation or for a given task, one person should be made responsible. When responsibility is shared and something goes wrong, it is difficult to determine who was at fault. For example, when two salesclerks share the same cash drawer and there is a shortage, it is normally impossible to tell which clerk is at fault. Each will tend to blame the other, and neither can prove that the responsibility is not his. In such a situation each clerk should be assigned a separate cash drawer or one of the clerks should be given responsibility for making all change.

Adequate records should be maintained

Good records provide a means of control by placing responsibility for the care and protection of assets, but poor records invite laxity and often theft. When a company has poor accounting control over its assets, dishonest employees soon become aware of this and are quick to take advantage.

Assets should be insured and employees bonded

Assets should be covered by adequate casualty insurance, and employees who handle cash and negotiable assets should be bonded. Bonding not only provides a means for recovery if a loss occurs but it also tends to prevent losses, since a bonded employee is less apt to take assets for his personal use if he knows he must deal with a bonding company when the shortage is revealed.

Record keeping and custody should be separated

A fundamental principle of internal control requires that the person who has access to or is responsible for an asset should not maintain the accounting record for that asset. When this principle is observed, the custodian of an asset, knowing that a record of the asset is being kept by another person, is not apt to either misappropriate the asset or waste it; and the record keeper, who does not have access to the asset, has no reason to falsify his record. Furthermore, if the asset is to be misappropriated and the theft concealed in the records, collusion is necessary.

Responsibility for related transactions should be divided

Responsibility for a divisible transaction or a series of related transactions should be divided between individuals or departments in

---

[1] AICPA, *Internal Control* (New York, 1959), p. 6.

such a manner that the work of one acts as a check on that of another. This does not mean there should be duplication of work. Each employee or department should perform an unduplicated portion. For example, responsibility for placing orders, receiving the merchandise, and paying the vendors should not be given to one individual or department. To do so is to invite laxity in checking the quality and quantity of goods received, and carelessness in verifying the validity and accuracy of invoices. It also invites the purchase of goods for an employee's personal use and the payment of fictitious invoices.

Mechanical devices should be used whenever practicable

Cash registers, check protectors, time clocks, and mechanical counters are examples of control devices that should be used whenever practicable. A cash register with a locked-in tape makes a record of each cash sale, a check protector by perforating the amount of a check into its face makes it almost impossible to change the amount, and a time clock registers the exact time an employee arrived on the job and when he departed.

A good system of internal control for cash should provide adequate procedures for protecting both cash receipts and cash disbursements, and in these procedures three basic principles should always be observed. First, there should be a separation of duties so that the people responsible for handling cash and for its custody are not the same people who keep the cash records. Second, all cash receipts should be deposited in the bank, intact, each day. Third, all payments should be made by check. The one exception to the last principle is that small disbursements may be made in cash from a petty cash fund. Petty cash funds are discussed later in this chapter.

Internal control for cash

The reason for the first principle is that a division of duties necessitates collusion between two or more people if cash is to be embezzled and the theft concealed in the accounting records. The second, requiring that all receipts be deposited intact each day, prevents an employee from making personal use of the money for a few days before depositing it. And, requiring that all receipts be deposited intact and all payments be made by check provides a separate and external record of all cash transactions that may be used to prove the company's own records.

The exact procedures used to achieve control over cash vary from company to company and depend upon such things as company size, number of employees, cash sources, and so on; consequently, the procedures described below are only illustrative of some that are in use.

Cash from cash sales

Cash sales should be rung up on a cash register at the time of each sale. To help ensure that correct amounts are rung up, each register should be so placed that customers can see the amounts rung up, and the clerks should be required to ring up each sale before wrapping the merchandise. Also, each cash register should have a locked-in tape on which the amount of each sale and total sales are printed by the register.

Good cash control, as previously stated, requires a separation of custody for cash from record keeping for cash; and for cash sales this separation begins with the cash register. The salesclerk who has access to the cash in the register should not have access to its locked-in tape. At the end of each day the salesclerk is usually required to count the cash in the register and to turn the cash and its count over to an employee in the cashier's office. The employee in the cashier's office, like the salesclerk, has access to the cash and should not have access to the register tape or other accounting records. A third employee, commonly from the accounting department, removes the tape from the register, compares its total with the cash turned over to the cashier's office, and uses the tape's information as a basis for the entry recording cash sales. This employee who has access to the register tape does not have access to the cash and therefore cannot take any. Likewise, since the salesclerk and the employee from the cashier's office do not have access to the cash register tape, they cannot take cash without the shortage being revealed.

Cash received through the mail

Control of cash coming in through the mail begins with a mail clerk who opens the mail and makes a list in triplicate of the money received. The list should give each sender's name, the purpose for which the money was sent, and the amount. One copy of the list is sent to the cashier with the money, the second copy goes to the book-keeper, and the third copy is kept by the mail clerk. The cashier deposits the money in the bank, and the bookkeeper records the amounts received in the Cash Receipts Journal. Then, if the bank balance is reconciled (discussed later) by a fourth person, errors or fraud by the mail clerk, the cashier, or bookkeeper will be detected. Errors will be detected because the cash deposited and the records of three people must agree; and fraud is impossible, unless there is collusion. The mail clerk must report all receipts or customers will question their account balances. The cashier must deposit all receipts because the bank balance must agree with the bookkeeper's cash balance. The bookkeeper and the person reconciling the bank balance do not have access to cash and, therefore, have no opportunity to withhold any.

Cash disbursements

It is important to gain control over cash from sales and cash received through the mail. However, most large embezzlements have not involved cash receipts but have been accomplished through the payment of fictitious invoices. Consequently, procedures for controlling cash disbursements are equally as important and sometimes more important than those for cash receipts.

To gain control over cash disbursements, all disbursements should be made by check, excepting those from petty cash. If authority to sign checks is delegated to some person other than the business owner, that person should not have access to the accounting records. This helps prevent a fraudulent disbursement being made and concealed in the accounting records.

In a small business the owner-manager usually signs checks and normally knows from personal contact and observation that the items for which the checks pay were received by the business. However, this is impossible in a large business, and in a large business internal control procedures must be substituted for personal contact. These procedures tell the person who signs checks that the obligations for which the checks pay are proper obligations, properly incurred, and should be paid. Often these procedures take the form of a *voucher system*.

A voucher system helps gain control over cash disbursements by providing a routine which (1) permits only designated departments and individuals to incur obligations that will result in cash disbursements; (2) establishes procedures for incurring such obligations and for their verification, approval, and recording; and (3) permits checks to be issued only in payment of properly verified, approved, and recorded obligations. Furthermore, every obligation must be recorded at the time it is incurred and every purchase is treated as an independent transaction, complete in itself, even though a number of purchases may be made from the same company during a month or other billing period.

The voucher system and control

When a voucher system is in use, control over cash disbursements begins with the incurrence of obligations that will result in cash disbursements. Only specified departments and individuals are authorized to incur such obligations, and the kind each may incur is limited. For example, in a large store only the purchasing department may incur obligations by purchasing merchandise, small assets, and supplies. However, to gain control, the purchasing-receiving-and-paying procedures are divided among several departments, which are commonly the departments requesting that merchandise or other assets be purchased, the purchasing department, the receiving department, and the accounting department. It is also necessary to coordinate and control the responsibilities of these departments with business papers, a list of which follows; and an explanation of each paper with its use will show how a large concern may gain control over cash disbursements resulting from the purchase of merchandise.

Business Paper	Prepared by the—	Sent to the—
1. Purchase requisition	Selling department manager desiring that merchandise be purchased	Purchasing department, with a copy to the accounting department
2. Purchase order	Purchasing department	Vendor, with a copy to the accounting department
3. Invoice	Company selling the merchandise	Accounting department
4. Receiving report	Receiving department	Accounting department, with a copy to the purchasing and requisitioning departments
5. Invoice approval form	Accounting department	Attached to invoice in the accounting department
6. Voucher	Accounting department	Cashier's department with other business papers attached

Purchase requisition

The department managers in a large store cannot be permitted to place orders directly with supply sources because if each manager were permitted to deal directly with wholesalers and manufacturers, the amount of merchandise purchased and the resulting liabilities could not be controlled. Therefore, in order to gain control over purchases and resulting liabilities, department managers are commonly required to place all orders through the purchasing department. In such cases the function of the several department managers in the purchasing procedure is to inform the purchasing department of their needs. Each manager performs this function by preparing in triplicate and signing a business paper called a purchase requisition on which he or she lists the merchandise needs of his or her department. The original and a duplicate copy of the purchase requisition are sent to the purchasing department. The third copy is retained by the requisitioning department as a check on the purchasing department.

Purchase order

A purchase order is a business form used by the purchasing department in placing an order with a manufacturer or wholesaler. It authorizes the supplier to ship the merchandise ordered and takes the place of a typewritten letter placing the order. On receipt of a purchase requisition from a selling department, the purchasing department prepares four or more copies of the purchase order. The copies are distributed as follows:

Copy 1   Copy 1, the original copy, is sent to the supplier as a request to purchase and as authority to ship the merchandise listed.

Copy 2   Copy 2, with a copy of the purchase requisition attached, is sent to the accounting department where it will ultimately be used in approving the invoice of the purchase for payment.

Copy 3   Copy 3 is sent to the department issuing the requisition to acknowledge the requisition and tell the action taken.

Copy 4   Copy 4 is retained on file by the purchasing department.

Invoice

An invoice is an itemized statement of goods bought and sold. It is prepared by the seller or *vendor,* and to the seller it is a sales invoice. However, when the same invoice is received by the buyer or *vendee,* it becomes a purchase invoice to the buyer. In the purchasing procedure, upon receipt of a purchase order, the manufacturer or wholesaler receiving the order ships the ordered merchandise to the buyer and mails a copy of the invoice covering the shipment. The goods are delivered to the buyer's receiving department, and the invoice is sent directly to the buyer's accounting department.

Receiving report

Most large companies maintain a special department assigned the duty of receiving all merchandise or other assets purchased. As each shipment is received, counted, and checked, the receiving department prepares four or more copies of a receiving report. On this report are listed the quantity, description, and condition of the items received. The original copy is sent to the accounting department; the second copy to the department that requisitioned the merchandise; the third copy is sent to the purchasing department; and the fourth copy is retained on file in the receiving department. The copies sent to the purchasing and requisitioning departments act as notification of the arrival of the goods.

Invoice approval form

When the receiving report arrives in the accounting department, the accounting department has in its possession copies of the —

1. Requisition listing the items requisitioned.
2. Purchase order that lists the merchandise ordered.
3. Invoice showing quantity, description, unit price, and total of the goods shipped by the seller.
4. Receiving report that lists quantity and condition of the items received.

With the information of these papers, the accounting department is in position to approve the invoice for entry on the books and ultimate payment. In approving the invoice, the accounting department checks and compares the information on all the papers. To facilitate the checking procedure and to ensure that no step is omitted, an invoice approval form is commonly used. This may be a separate business paper that is attached to the invoice, or the information shown in Illustration 7–1 may be stamped directly on the invoice with a rubber stamp.

INVOICE APPROVAL FORM

Purchase Order Number _____

Requisition Check _____

Purchase Order Check _____

Receiving Report Check _____

Invoice Check

    Price Approval _____

    Calculations _____

    Terms _____

Approved for Payment:

    _____

Illustration 7–1

As each step in the checking procedure is completed, the clerk making the check initials the invoice approval form. Initials in each space on the form indicate:

1. Requisition Check .... The items on the invoice agree with the requisition and were requisitioned.
2. Purchase Order Check .... The items on the invoice agree with the purchase order and were ordered.
3. Receiving Report Check ..... The items on the invoice agree with the receiving report and were received.
4. Invoice Check:
        Price Approval............... The invoice prices are the agreed prices.
        Calculations................... The invoice has no mathematical errors.
        Terms.......................... The terms are the agreed terms.

The voucher

When a voucher system is in use, after the invoice is checked and approved, a voucher is prepared. A voucher is a business paper on which a transaction is summarized, its correctness certified, and its recording and payment approved. Vouchers vary somewhat from company to company; but in general they are so designed that the invoice, bill, or other documents from which they are prepared are attached to and folded inside the voucher. This makes for ease in filing. The inside of a voucher is shown in Illustration 7–2 and the outside in Illustration 7–3. The preparation of a voucher is a simple task requiring only that a clerk enter the required information in the proper blank spaces on a voucher form. The information is taken from the invoice and its supporting documents. After the voucher is completed, the invoice and its supporting documents are attached to and folded inside the voucher. The voucher is then sent to the desk of the chief clerk or auditor who makes an additional check, approves the accounting distribution (the accounts to be debited), and approves the voucher for recording.

After being approved and recorded, a voucher is filed until its due date, when it is sent to the office of the company cashier or other dis-

Voucher No. __767__

VALLEY SUPPLY COMPANY
Eugene, Oregon

Date __Oct. 1, 19--__
Pay to __A.B. Seay Wholesale Company__
City __Salem__   State __Oregon__

For the following: (attach all invoices and supporting papers)

Date of Invoice	Terms	Invoice Number and Other Details	Amount
Sept. 30, 19--	2/10, n/60	Invoice No. C-11756 Less Discount Net Amount Payable	800.00 16.00 784.00

Payment Approved

M. O. Neal
Auditor

**Illustration 7–2
Inside of a
voucher**

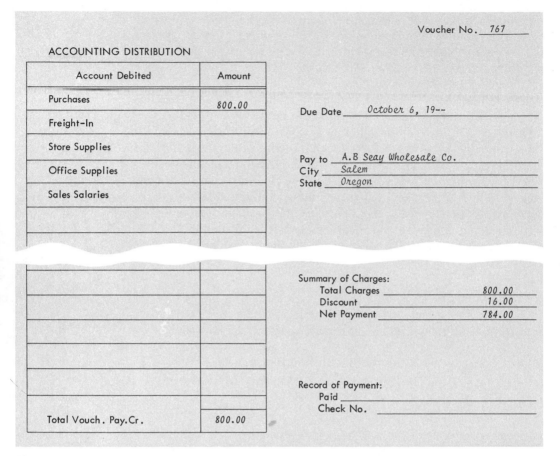

Voucher No. _767_

ACCOUNTING DISTRIBUTION

Account Debited	Amount
Purchases	800.00
Freight-In	
Store Supplies	
Office Supplies	
Sales Salaries	

Due Date _October 6, 19--_

Pay to _A.B Seay Wholesale Co._
City _Salem_
State _Oregon_

Total Vouch. Pay.Cr.	800.00

Summary of Charges:
Total Charges _____ 800.00
Discount _____ 16.00
Net Payment _____ 784.00

Record of Payment:
Paid _____
Check No. _____

**Illustration 7–3
Outside of a
voucher**

bursing officer for payment. Here the person responsible for issuing checks depends upon the approved voucher and its signed supporting documents to verify that the obligation is a proper obligation, properly incurred, and should be paid. For example, the purchase requisition and purchase order attached to the voucher confirm that the purchase was authorized, the receiving report discloses that the items were received, and the invoice approval form verifies that the invoice was checked for errors. As a result, there is little chance for fraud, unless all the documents were stolen and the signatures forged, or there was collusion.

The voucher system and expenses

Under a voucher system, in order to gain control over cash disbursements, every obligation that will result in a cash disbursement must be approved for payment and recorded as a liability at the time it is incurred. This includes all expenses. As a result, for example, when the monthly telephone bill is received, it is verified and any long-distance calls are approved, a voucher is then prepared, and the telephone bill is attached to and folded inside the voucher. The voucher is then recorded in the same way as a voucher for the purchase of merchandise, with the only difference being that the recording entry results in a debit to Telephone Expense rather than to Purchases. A check is then issued in payment of the voucher.

Requiring that an expense payment be approved and recorded as a voucher payable at the time it is incurred helps ensure that every expense payment is approved when information for its approval is available. Often invoices, bills, and statements for such things as equipment repairs are received weeks after the work is done; and if no record of the repairs exist, it is difficult at that time to determine whether the invoice or bill is a correct statement of the amount owed. Also, if no records exist, it is possible for a dishonest employee to arrange with an outsider for more than one payment of an obligation, for payment of excessive amounts, and for payment for goods and services not received, all with kickbacks to the dishonest employee.

Recording vouchers

Normally a company large enough to use a voucher system will use bookkeeping machines or punched cards, magnetic tape, and a computer in recording its transactions. Consequently, for this reason and also because the primary purpose of this discussion is to describe the control techniques of a voucher system, a pen-and-ink system of recording vouchers is not described here. However, such a system is described in the Appendix at the end of this chapter.

The petty cash fund

A basic principle in controlling cash disbursements is that all such disbursements be made by check. However, an exception to this rule is made for petty cash disbursements because every business must make many small payments for items such as postage, express charges, collect telegrams, and small items of supplies. If each such payment is made by check, many checks for immaterial amounts are written, which is both time consuming and expensive. Therefore, to avoid writing checks for small amounts, a petty cash fund is established, and such payments are made from this fund.

When a petty cash fund is established, an estimate is made of the total small payments likely to be disbursed during a short period, usually not more than a month. A check is drawn and debited to the Petty Cash account for an amount slightly in excess of this estimate; the check is cashed; and the money is turned over to a member of the office staff who is designated *petty cashier* and who is responsible for the petty cash and for making payments therefrom.

The petty cashier usually keeps the petty cash in a locked box in the office safe. As each disbursement is made, a *petty cash receipt,* Illustration 7–4, is signed by the person receiving payment and is entered in the *Petty Cash Record* (Illustration 7–6) and then placed with the remaining money in the petty cashbox. Under this system,

```
No. 1479                                    $ 1.65

            RECEIVED OF PETTY CASH
                         DATE  Nov. 3          19 --

       FOR  Collect telegram


       CHARGE TO Miscellaneous General Expenses
                                    ACCOUNT

       APPROVED BY                    RECEIVED BY
              CaB.                         Bob Tone
       TOPS—FORM 3008
```

Illustration 7–4   *Courtesy Tops Business Forms*

the petty cashbox should always contain paid petty cash receipts and money equal to the amount of the fund.

Each disbursement reduces the money and increases the sum of the receipts in the petty cashbox. When the money is nearly exhausted, the fund is reimbursed. To reimburse the fund, the petty cashier presents the receipts for petty cash payments to the company cashier who stamps each receipt "paid" so that it may not be reused, retains the receipts, and gives the petty cashier a check for their sum. When this check is cashed and the proceeds returned to the petty cashbox, the money in the box is restored to its original amount and the fund is ready to begin anew the cycle of its operations.

Petty cash fund illustrated

To avoid writing numerous checks for small amounts, a company established a petty cash fund, designating one of its office clerks, Mae Fox, petty cashier. A check for $35 was drawn, cashed, and the proceeds turned over to this clerk. The entry to record the check is shown in Illustration 7–5. The effect of the entry was to transfer $35 from the regular Cash account to the Petty Cash account.

The Petty Cash account is debited when the fund is established but is not debited or credited again unless the size of the fund is

Cash Disbursements Journal

Date	Ch. No.	Payee	Account Debited	F	Other Accts. Debit	Cash Credit
Nov. 1	58	Mae Fox, Petty Cashier	Petty Cash...............		35.00	35.00

Illustration 7–5

changed. If the fund is exhausted and reimbursements occur too often, the fund should be increased. This results in an additional debit to the Petty Cash account and a credit to the regular Cash account for the amount of the increase. If the fund is too large, part of its cash should be returned to general cash.

During the first month of the illustrated fund's operation, the following petty cash payments were made:

Nov.	3	Collect telegram	$ 1.65
	7	Purchased paper clips	0.50
	12	Express on purchases	3.75
	18	Postage on sale	3.80
	19	Dinner for employee working overtime	3.60
	20	Purchased postage stamps	10.00
	21	Express on purchases	2.80
	27	Repair of typewriter	7.50
		Total	$33.60

As each amount was disbursed, a petty cash receipt was signed by the person receiving payment. Each receipt was then recorded in the Petty Cash Record and placed in the petty cashbox. The Petty Cash Record with the paid receipts entered is shown in Illustration 7–6.

Usually, as in this illustration, the Petty Cash Record is a supplementary record and not a book of original entry. A book of original entry is a journal or register from which postings are made. A supplementary record is one in which information is summarized but not posted. Rather, the summarized information is used as a basis for an entry in a regular journal or register, which is posted.

To continue the illustration, on November 27, after the last of the listed payments was made, only $1.40 in money remained in the fund. The petty cashier recognized that this would probably not cover another payment, so she gave her $33.60 of paid petty cash receipts to the company cashier in exchange for $33.60 check to replenish the fund. On receiving the check, she ruled and balanced her Petty Cash Record (see Illustration 7–6), entered the amount of the replenishing check, cashed the check, and was ready to begin anew payments from the fund.

The reimbursing check was recorded in the Cash Disbursements Journal with the second entry of Illustration 7–7. Information for this entry was secured from a summarization of the entries in the Petty Cash Record. Commonly, as previously stated, the Petty Cash Record is a supplementary record and not a book of original entry; therefore, if petty cash payments are to get to the ledger accounts, an entry like the second one in Illustration 7–7 is required.

Observe the debits in the second entry in Illustration 7–7. All are to accounts affected by payments from the fund. Note that such an entry is necessary to get debits into the accounts for amounts paid

Petty Cash Record

Date	Explanation	Receipt No.	Receipts	Payments	Distribution of Payments			Miscellaneous Payments	
					Postage	Freight-In	Misc. General Expense	Account	Amount
Nov. 1	Established fund (Ch. No. 58)......		35.00	......	......	......	......	......	......
3	Collect telegram........	1	......	1.65	......	......	1.65	......	......
7	Purchased paper clips	2	......	.50	......	......	......	Office supplies.....	.50
12	Express on purchases............	3	......	3.75	......	3.75	......	......	......
18	Postage on sale............	4	......	3.80	......	......	......	Delivery expense...	3.80
19	Overtime meals............	5	......	3.60	......	......	3.60	......	......
20	Purchased postage stamps...........	6	......	10.00	10.00	......	......	......	......
21	Express on purchases...........	7	......	2.80	......	2.80	......	......	......
27	Repair of typewriter........	8	......	7.50	......	......	7.50	......	......
27	Totals........		35.00	33.60	10.00	6.55	12.75	......	4.30
	Balance........		......	1.40	......	......	......	......	......
	Totals........		35.00	35.00	......	......	......	......	......
Nov. 27	Balance........		1.40	......					
27	Replenished fund (Ch. No. 106)..		33.60	......					

Illustration 7–6

Cash Disbursements Journal

Date	Ch. No.	Payee	Account Debited	F	Other Accts. Debit	Cash Credit
Nov. 1	58	Mae Fox, Petty Cashier	Petty Cash		35.00	35.00
Nov. 27	106	Mae Fox, Petty Cashier	Postage.................... Freight-In .... Misc. Gen. Expenses. Office Supplies .... Delivery Expense.......		10.00 6.55 12.75 .50 3.80	33.60

Illustration 7–7

from a petty cash fund. Consequently, petty cash must be reimbursed at the end of each accounting period, as well as at any time the money in the fund is low. If the fund is not reimbursed at the end of each accounting period, the asset petty cash is overstated and the expenses and assets of the petty cash payments are understated on the financial statements.

Occasionally, at the time of a petty cash expenditure a petty cashier will forget to secure a receipt, and by the time the fund is reimbursed, will have forgotten the expenditure. This causes the fund to be short. If at reimbursement time the petty cash fund is short and no errors or omitted entries can be found, the shortage is entered in the Petty Cash Record as a payment in the Miscellaneous Payments column. It is then recorded as an expense in the reimbursing entry with a debit to the Cash Over and Short account discussed in the next section.

Cash over and short

Regardless of care exercised in making change, customers are sometimes given too much change or are shortchanged. As a result, at the end of a day the actual cash from a cash register is commonly not equal to the cash sales "rung up" on the register. When this occurs and, for example, actual cash as counted is $557 but the register shows cash sales of $556, the entry in general journal form to record sales and the overage is:

Nov.	23	Cash..	557.00	
		Cash Over and Short.............................		1.00
		Sales		556.00
		Day's cash sales and overage.		

If, on the other hand, cash is short, the entry in general journal form to record the sales and shortage is:

Nov.	24	Cash...	621.00	
		Cash Over and Short..	4.00	
		Sales		625.00
		Day's cash sales and shortage.		

Over a period of time cash overages should about equal cash shortages. However, customers are more prone to report instances in which they are given too little change; therefore, amounts of cash short are apt to be greater than amounts of cash over, and the Cash Over and Short account normally reaches the end of the accounting period with a debit balance. When it does so, the balance represents an expense, which may appear on the income statement as a separate item in the general and administrative expense section. Or if the amount is small, it may be combined with other miscellaneous expenses and appear as part of the item, miscellaneous expenses. When Cash Over and Short reaches the end of the period with a credit balance, the balance represents revenue and normally appears on the income statement as part of the item, miscellaneous revenues.

Reconciling the bank balance

Once each month banks furnish a commercial depositor a statement of its account. The statement shows: (1) the amount on deposit at the beginning of the month, (2) checks and any other amounts deducted from the account, (3) deposits and any other amounts added to the account, and (4) the account balance at the end of the month, according to the records of the bank. If all receipts are deposited and all payments are made by check, the bank statement becomes a device for proving the depositor's cash records. A bank statement is shown in Illustration 7–8.

Banks commonly mail a depositor's bank statement, and included in the envelope with the statement are the depositor's *canceled checks* and any debit or credit memoranda that have affected the account. The checks returned are the ones the bank has paid during the month. They are called "canceled checks" because they are canceled by stamping or punching to show that they have been paid. During any month, in addition to the checks the depositor has drawn, the bank may deduct from the depositor's account amounts for service charges, printing checks, items deposited that are uncollectible, and for errors. The bank notifies the depositor of each such deduction with a debit memorandum. A copy of the memorandum is always included with the monthly statement. The bank may also add amounts to the depositor's account for errors and for amounts collected for the depositor. A credit memorandum is used to notify of any additions.

Need for reconciling the bank balance

Normally, when the bank statement arrives, the balance of cash as shown by the statement does not agree with the balance shown by the depositor's accounting records. Consequently, in order to prove the accuracy of both the depositor's records and those of the bank, it is necessary to reconcile and account for any differences between the two balances.

MERCHANT'S NATIONAL BANK
Eugene, Oregon

STATEMENT OF ACCOUNT

BALANCE BROUGHT FORWARD		STATEMENT OF BALANCE		CHECKS RETURNED
Date	Balance	Date	Balance	
9/30/78	1,578.00	10/31/78	1,753.00	9

Valley Company
10th and Pine Sts.
Eugene, Oregon

CHECKS IN DETAIL			DEPOSITS		DATE		BALANCE	
DM	3 00				10	1	1575	00
	55 00				10	2	1520	00
	120 00	200 00			10	5	1200	00
			240	00	10	6	1440	00
	25 00	75 00	150	00	10	10	1490	00
			180	00	10	18	1670	00
	10 00	50 00			10	23	1610	00
		135 00	100	00	10	25	1575	00
		DM 20 00			10	28	1555	00
			CM 198	00	10	30	1753	00

If no error is reported within ten days this account will be considered correct.

Illustration 7–8

Numerous things may cause the bank statement balance to differ from the depositor's book balance of cash. Some are:

1. *Outstanding Checks.* These are checks that have been drawn by the depositor and deducted on the depositor's records but have not reached the bank for payment and deduction.
2. *Unrecorded Deposits.* Concerns often make deposits at the end of each business day, after the bank has closed. These deposits are made in the bank's night depository and are not recorded by the bank until the next business day. Consequently, if a deposit is placed in the night depository the last day of the month, it does not appear on the bank statement for that month.

3. *Charges for Service and Uncollectible Items*. A bank often deducts amounts from a depositor's account for services rendered and for items deposited that it is unable to collect. Insufficient funds checks are the most common of the latter. The bank notifies the depositor of each such deduction with a debit memorandum. If the item is material in amount, the memorandum is mailed to the depositor on the day of the deduction. Furthermore, in a well-managed company, each such deduction is recorded on the day the memorandum is received. However, occasionally there are unrecorded amounts near the end of the month.

4. *Collections*. Banks often act as collecting agents for their depositors, collecting for a small fee promissory notes and other items. When an item such as a promissory note is collected, the bank usually adds the proceeds to the depositor's account and sends a credit memorandum as notification of the transaction. As soon as the memorandum is received, it should be recorded. Occasionally, there are unrecorded amounts near the end of the month.

5. *Errors*. Regardless of care and systems of internal control for automatic error detection, both the bank and the depositor make errors that affect the bank balance. Occasionally, these errors are not discovered until the balance is reconciled.

Steps in reconciling the bank balance

The steps in reconciling the bank balance are:

1. Compare the deposits listed on the bank statement with deposits shown in the accounting records. Note any discrepancies and discover which is correct. List any errors or unrecorded items.

2. When canceled checks are returned by the bank, they are in a stack in the order in which the bank paid them and also in the order of their listing on the bank statement. While the checks are in this order, compare each with its bank statement listing. Note any discrepancies or errors.

3. Rearrange the returned checks in numerical order, the order in which they were written. Secure the previous month's reconciliation and determine if any checks outstanding at the end of the previous month are still outstanding. If there are any, list them. Also, see that any deposits that were unrecorded by the bank at the end of the previous month have been recorded.

4. Insert among the canceled checks any bank memorandum according to their dates. Compare each check with its entry in the Cash Disbursements Journal or Check Register. Note for correction any discrepancies, and list any unpaid checks or unrecorded memorandum.

5. Prepare a reconciliation of the bank statement balance with the

book balance of cash. Such a reconciliation is shown in Illustration 7–9.
6. Determine if any debits or credits appearing on the bank statement are unrecorded in the books of account. Make journal entries to record them.

To illustrate a bank reconciliation assume that Valley Company found the following when it attempted to reconcile its bank balance of October 31. The bank balance as shown by the bank statement was $1,753, and the cash balance according to the accounting records was $1,373. Check No. 124 for $150 and Check No. 126 for $200 were outstanding and unpaid by the bank. A $145 deposit, placed in the bank's night depository after banking hours on October 31, was unrecorded by the bank. Among the returned checks was a credit memorandum showing the bank had collected a note receivable for the company on October 30, crediting the proceeds, $200 less a $2 collection fee, to the company account. Also returned with the bank statement was a $3 debit memorandum for checks printed by the bank and an NSF (not sufficient funds) check for $20. This check had been received from a customer, Frank Jones, on October 25, and had been included in that day's deposit. The collection of the note, the return of the NSF check, and the check printing charge were unrecorded on the company books. The statement reconciling these amounts is shown in Illustration 7–9.

Illustration of a bank reconciliation

Valley Company
Bank Reconciliation as of October 31, 19—

Book balance of cash		$1,373	Bank statement balance	$1,753
Add:			Add:	
Proceeds of note less			Deposit of 10/31	145
collection fee		198		$1,898
		$1,571		
Deduct:			Deduct:	
NSF check of Frank Jones	$20		Outstanding checks:	
Check printing charge	3	23	No. 124 ... $150	
			No. 126 ... 200	350
Reconciled balance		$1,548	Reconciled balance	$1,548

Illustration 7–9

A bank reconciliation helps locate any errors made by either the bank or the depositor; discloses any items which have been entered on the company books but have not come to the bank's attention; and discloses items that should be recorded on the company books but are unrecorded on the date of the reconciliation. For example, in the reconciliation illustrated, the reconciled cash balance, $1,548, is the true cash balance. However, at the time the reconciliation is completed,

Valley Company's accounting records show a $1,373 book balance. Consequently, entries must be made to adjust the book balance, increasing it to the true cash balance. This requires three entries, the first in general journal form is:

Nov.	2	Cash..	198.00	
		Collection Expense	2.00	
		Notes Receivable		200.00
		To record the proceeds and collection charge of a note collected by the bank.		

This entry is self-explanatory. The bank collected a note receivable, deducted a collection fee, and deposited the difference to the Valley Company account. The entry increases the amount of cash on the books, records the collection expense, and reduces notes receivable. The second entry is:

Nov.	2	Accounts Receivable—Frank Jones.............................	20.00	
		Cash...		20.00
		To charge back the NSF check received from Frank Jones.		

This entry records the NSF check returned as uncollectible. The check was received from Jones in payment of his account and was deposited as cash. The bank, unable to collect the check, deducted $20 from the Valley Company account, making it necessary for the company to reverse the entry made when the check was received. After recording the returned check, the company will endeavor to collect the $20 from Jones. If after all legal means of collection have been exhausted and the company is still unable to collect, the amount will be written off as a bad debt.

The third entry debits the check printing charge to Miscellaneous General Expenses and in general journal form is:

Nov.	2	Miscellaneous General Expenses...............................	3.00	
		Cash...		3.00
		Check printing charge.		

Other internal control procedures

Internal control procedures apply to every phase of a company's operations from purchases through sales, cash receipts, cash disbursements, and the control of plant assets. Many of these procedures are discussed in later chapters. However, the way in which a company can gain control over purchases discounts can be discussed here where there is time and space for problems illustrating the technique.

Recall that thus far the following entries in general journal form have been used in recording the receipt and payment of an invoice for merchandise purchased:

Nov.	2	Purchases	1,000.00	
		Accounts Payable—Able Company.........................		1,000.00
		Purchased merchandise, terms 2/10, n/60.		
	12	Accounts Payable—Able Company.............................	1,000.00	
		Purchases Discounts...		20.00
		Cash..		980.00
		Paid the invoice of November 2.		

The invoice of these entries was recorded at its gross, $1,000, amount, and this is the way in which invoices are recorded in many companies. However, well-managed companies follow the practice of taking all offered cash discounts; and in many of these companies invoices are recorded at their net, after discount amounts. For example, if a company that records invoices at net amounts purchases merchandise having a $1,000 invoice price, terms 2/10, n/60, on receipt of the goods it deducts the offered $20 discount from the gross invoice amount and records the purchase with these debits and credits:

Nov.	2	Purchases	980.00	
		Accounts Payable—Able Company.........................		980.00
		Purchased merchandise on credit.		

If the invoice for this purchase is paid within the discount period (all invoices should be so paid), the check register entry to record the payment has a debit to Accounts Payable and a credit to Cash for $980. However, if payment is not made within the discount period and the discount is lost, an entry like the following must be made in the General Journal when the invoice is paid:

Dec.	31	Discounts Lost...	20.00	
		Accounts Payable—Able Company.........................		20.00
		To record the discount lost.		

A check for the full $1,000 invoice amount is then drawn, recorded, and mailed to the creditor.

Advantage of the net method

When invoices are recorded at gross amounts, the amount of discounts taken is deducted from the balance of the Purchases account on the income statement to arrive at the cost of merchandise purchased. However, when invoices are recorded at gross amounts, if through oversight or carelessness discounts are lost, the amount of discounts lost does not appear in any account or on the income statement and may not come to the attention of management. On the other hand, when purchases are recorded at net amounts, the amount of discounts taken does not appear on the income statement; but the amount of discounts lost is called to management's attention through the appearance on the income statement of the expense account, Discounts Lost, as in the condensed income statement of Illustration 7–10.

XYZ Company
Income Statement for Year Ended December 31, 19—

Sales...	$100,000
Cost of goods sold	60,000
Gross profit from sales............................	$ 40,000
Operating expenses.................................	28,000
Income from operations	$ 12,000
Other revenues and expenses:	
Discounts lost	(150)
Net Income	$ 11,850

Illustration 7–10

Of the two methods, recording invoices at their net amounts probably supplies management with the more valuable information, the amount of discounts lost through oversight, carelessness, or other cause. It also gives management better control over the work of the people responsible for taking cash discounts; because if discounts are lost, someone must explain why. As a result, few discounts are lost through carelessness.

APPENDIX

Recording vouchers, pen-and-ink system

When a voucher system is in use, an account called Vouchers Payable replaces the Accounts Payable account described in previous chapters, and for every transaction that will result in a cash disbursement, a voucher is prepared and credited to this account. For example, when merchandise is purchased, the voucher covering the transaction is recorded with a debit to Purchases and a credit to Vouchers Payable. Likewise, when a plant asset is purchased or an expense is incurred, the voucher of the transaction is recorded with a debit to the proper plant asset or expense account and a credit to Vouchers Payable.

In a pen-and-ink system, vouchers are recorded in a Voucher Register similar to Illustration 7A–1. Such a register has a Vouchers Payable credit column and a number of debit columns. The exact debit columns vary from company to company, but merchandising concerns always provide a Purchases debit column. Also, in all companies, so long as space is available, special debit columns are provided for transactions that occur frequently, because posting labor can be saved by placing their amounts in columns and posting only the column totals. In addition to the columns for frequent transactions, an Other Accounts debit column is provided for transactions that do not occur often.

In recording vouchers in a register like that of Illustration 7A–1, all information about each voucher entered in the register, with the exception of that entered in the columns used in recording the voucher's payment, is entered as soon as the voucher is approved for recording. The information as to payment date and the number of the paying check is entered later as each voucher is paid.

In posting a Voucher Register like that in Illustration 7A–1, the columns are first totaled and crossfooted to prove their equality. The Vouchers Payable column total is then credited to the Vouchers Payable account; the totals of the Purchases, Freight-In, Sales Salaries Expense, Advertising Expense, Delivery Expense, and Office Salaries Expense are debited to these accounts; and none of the individual amounts in these columns are posted. However, the individual amounts in the Other Accounts column are posted as individual amounts and the column total is not posted.

The unpaid vouchers file

When a voucher system is in use, some vouchers are paid as soon as they are recorded, while others must be filed until payment is due. As an aid in taking cash discounts, vouchers for which payment is not due are generally filed in an unpaid vouchers file under the dates on which they are to be paid.

In a voucher system, the file of unpaid vouchers takes the place of a subsidiary Accounts Payable Ledger. Actually, the file is a subsidiary ledger of amounts owed creditors. Likewise, the Vouchers Payable account is in effect a controlling account controlling the unpaid vouchers file. Consequently, after posting is completed at the end of a month, the balance of the Vouchers Payable account should equal the sum of the unpaid vouchers in the unpaid vouchers file. This is verified each month by preparing a schedule or an adding machine list of the unpaid vouchers in the file and comparing its total with the balance of the Vouchers Payable account. In addition the unpaid vouchers in the file are compared with the unpaid vouchers shown in the Voucher Register's record of payments column. Since the number of each paying check and the payment date are entered in the Voucher Register's payments column as each voucher is paid, the vouchers in the register without check numbers and payment dates should be the same as those in the unpaid vouchers file.

The voucher system check register

In a pen-and-ink voucher system, checks drawn in payment of vouchers are recorded in a simplified Check Register. It is simplified because under a voucher system no obligation is paid until a voucher covering the payment is prepared and recorded, and no check is drawn except in payment of a specific voucher. Consequently, all checks drawn result in debits to Vouchers Payable and credits to Cash, unless a discount must be recorded, and then there are credits to both

Page 32   **Voucher**

Date 19—		Voucher No.	Payee	When and How Paid		Vouch-ers Payable Credit		Pur-chases Debit		Freight-in Debit		
				Date	Check No.							
Oct.	1	767	A. B. Seay Co.	10/6	733	800	00	800	00			1
	1	768	Daily Sentinel	10/9	744	53	00					2
	2	769	Seaboard Supply Co.	10/12	747	235	00	155	00	10	00	3
	6	770	George Smith	10/6	734	85	00					4
	6	771	Frank Jones	10/6	735	95	00					5
	6	772	George Roth	10/6	736	95	00					6
	30	998	First National Bank	10/30	972	505	00					33
												34
	30	999	Pacific Telephone Co.	10/30	973	18	00					35
	31	1000	Tarbell Wholesale Co.			235	00	235	00			36
	31	1001	Office Equipment Co.	10/31	974	195	00					37
	31		Totals			5,079	00	2,435	00	156	00	38
						(213)		(511)		(514)		39
												40
												41

Illustration 7A–1

Purchases Discounts and to Cash. Such a register is shown in Illustration 7A–2. Note that it has columns for debits to Vouchers Payable and credits to Purchases Discounts and to Cash. In posting, all amounts entered in these columns are posted in the column totals.

A Check Register like that shown in Illustration 7A–2 is used when vouchers are recorded at gross amounts, because when vouchers are so recorded, a column must be provided for the discounts taken when the vouchers are paid. However, when vouchers are recorded at net amounts, such a column is not needed because discounts are deducted before vouchers are recorded, rather than when they are paid. Consequently, when vouchers are recorded at net amounts, the Check Register used needs only one money column. The column is commonly headed "Vouchers Payable, Debit; Cash, Credit," and at the end of a month its total is debited to Vouchers Payable and credited to Cash.

Purchases returns

Occasionally an item must be returned after the voucher recording its purchase has been prepared and entered in the Voucher Register. In such cases the return may be recorded with a general journal entry similar to the following:

Nov.	5	Vouchers Payable	15.00	
		Purchases Returns and Allowances		15.00
		Returned defective merchandise.		

Register Page 32

	Sales Salaries Expense Debit		Adver- tising Expense Debit		Delivery Expense Debit		Office Salaries Expense Debit		Other Accounts Debit		
									Account Name	Folio	Amount Debit
1											
2			53	00							
3									Store Supplies	117	70 00
4							85	00			
5	95	00									
6	95	00									
33									Notes Payable	211	500 00
34									Interest Expense	721	5 00
35									Telephone Expense	655	18 00
36											
37									Office Equipment	134	195 00
38	740	00	115	00	358	00	340	00			935 00
39	(611)		(612)		(615)		(651)				(✓)
40											
41											

Check Register

Date 19–		Payee	Voucher No.	Check No.	Vouchers Payable Debit	Purchases Discounts Credit	Cash Credit
Oct.	1	C. B. & Y. RR Co.	765	728	14.00		14.00
	3	Frank Mills	766	729	73.00		73.00
	3	Ajax Wholesale Co.	753	730	250.00	5.00	245.00
	4	Normal Supply Co.	747	731	100.00	2.00	98.00
	5	Office Supply Co.	763	732	43.00		43.00
	6	A. B. Seay Co.	767	733	800.00	16.00	784.00
	6	George Smith	770	734	85.00		85.00
	6	Frank Jones	771	735	95.00		95.00
	30	First National Bank	998	972	505.00		505.00
	30	Pacific Telephone Co.	999	973	18.00		18.00
	31	Office Equipment Co.	1001	974	195.00		195.00
	31	Totals			6,468.00	28.00	6,440.00
					(213)	(512)	(111)

Illustration 7A–2

In addition to the entry, a reference to the entry is made in the Payments columns of the Vouchers Register, on the upper half of the line for the voucher on which the return is made. The reference is made small enough so that the check number of the paying check and the date of the voucher's payment can be entered on the same line. Also, the amount of return is deducted on the voucher and the credit memorandum and other documents verifying the return are attached to the voucher. Then, when the voucher is paid, a check is drawn for its corrected amount.

<table>
<tr><td valign="top">

Glossary

</td><td>

Bank reconciliation. An analysis explaining the difference between an enterprise's book balance of cash and its bank statement balance.

Cash Over and Short account. An account in which are recorded cash overages and cash shortages arising from making change.

Canceled checks. Checks paid by the bank and canceled by punching or stamping.

Discounts lost. Cash discounts offered but not taken.

Gross method of recording invoices. Recording invoices at their gross amounts, their before deducting offered cash discount amounts.

Internal controls system. The methods and procedures adopted by a business to control its operations and protect its assets from waste, fraud, and theft.

Invoice. A document listing items sold, together with prices, the customer's name, and the terms of sale.

Invoice approval form. A document used in checking an invoice and approving it for recording and payment.

Net method of recording invoices. Recording invoices at their net amounts, the after deducting offered cash discount amounts.

Outstanding checks. Checks that have been written, recorded, and sent or given to payees but have not been received by the bank, paid, and returned.

Purchase order. A business form used in placing an order for the purchase of goods from a vendor.

Purchase requisition. A business form used within a business to ask the purchasing department of the business to buy needed items.

Receiving report. A form used within a business to notify the proper persons of the receipt of goods ordered and of the quantities and condition of the goods.

Reconcile. To account for the difference between two amounts.

Vendee. The purchaser of something.

Vendor. The individual or enterprise selling something.

</td></tr>
</table>

Voucher. A business paper used in summarizing a transaction and approving it for recording and payment.

Voucher Register. A book of original entry in which approved vouchers are recorded.

Voucher system. An accounting system used to control the incurrence and payment of obligations requiring the disbursement of cash.

---

1. Internal control procedures are important in every business, but at what stage in the development of a business do they become critical?

Questions for class discussion

2. Name some of the broad principles of internal control.
3. Why should the person who keeps the record of an asset be a different person from the one responsible for custody of the asset?
4. Why should responsibility for a sequence of related transactions be divided among different departments or individuals?
5. In a small business it is sometimes impossible to separate the functions of record keeping and asset custody, and it is sometimes impossible to divide responsibilities for related transactions. What should be substituted for these control procedures?
6. What is meant by the phrase "all receipts should be deposited intact"? Why should all receipts be deposited intact on the day of receipt?
7. Why should a company's bookkeeper not be given responsibility for receiving cash for the company nor the responsibility for signing checks or making cash disbursements in any other way?
8. In purchasing merchandise in a large store, why are the department managers not permitted to deal directly with the sources of supply?
9. What are the duties of the selling department managers in the purchasing procedures of a large store?
10. Tell (*a*) who prepares, (*b*) who receives, and (*c*) the purpose of each of the following business papers:

   a. Purchase requisition.
   b. Purchase order.
   c. Invoice.
   d. Receiving report.
   e. Invoice approval form.
   f. Voucher.

11. Do all companies need a voucher system? At what approximate point in a company's growth would you recommend the installation of such a system?
12. When he issues a check in a large business, the disbursing officer usually cannot know from personal contact that the assets, goods, or services for which the check pays were received by the business or that their purchase was properly authorized. However, if the company has an internal control system, he can depend on the system. Exactly what documents does he depend on to tell him the purchase was authorized and properly made and the goods were actually received?
13. Why are some cash payments made from a petty cash fund? Why are not all payments made by check?
14. What is a petty cash receipt? When a petty cash receipt is prepared, who signs it?

15. Explain how a petty cash fund operates.
16. Why must a petty cash fund be reimbursed at the end of each accounting period?
17. What are two results of reimbursing the petty cash fund?
18. Is the Petty Cash Record a book of original entry?
19. What is a bank statement? What kind of information appears on a bank statement?
20. What is the meaning of the phrase "to reconcile"?
21. Why are the bank statement balance of cash and the depositor's book balance of cash reconciled?
22. What valuable information becomes readily available to management when invoices are recorded at net amounts? Is this information readily available when invoices are recorded at gross amounts?

Class exercises   **Exercise 7–1**

A company established a $25 petty cash fund on September 5. Two weeks later, on September 19, there were $1.75 in cash in the fund and receipts for these expenditures: postage, $6.50; freight-in, $7.25; miscellaneous general expenses, $5; and office supplies, $4.50. (*a*) Give in general journal form the entry to establish the fund and (*b*) the entry to reimburse it on September 19. (*c*) Assume that since the fund was exhausted so quickly, it was not only reimbursed on September 19 but also increased in size to $50. Give the entry to reimburse and increase the fund to $50.

Exercise 7–2

A company established a $50 petty cash fund on October 3. On November 30 there were $23 in cash in the fund and receipts for these expenditures: freight-in, $9.75; miscellaneous general expenses, $8.50; and office supplies, $7.75. The petty cashier could not account for the $1 shortage in the fund. Give in general journal form (*a*) the entry to establish the fund and (*b*) the November 30 entry to reimburse the fund and reduce it to $25.

Exercise 7–3

Southside Shop deposits all receipts intact on the day received and makes all payments by check; and on November 30, after all posting was completed, its Cash account showed a $1,510 debit balance; but its November 30 bank statement showed only $1,299 on deposit in the bank on that day. Prepare a bank reconciliation for the shop, using the following information:

a. Outstanding checks, $200.
b. Included with the November canceled checks returned by the bank was a $4 debit memorandum for bank services.
c. Check No. 512, returned with the canceled checks, was correctly drawn for $24 in payment of the telephone bill and was paid by the bank on November 7, but it had been erroneously entered in the Cash Disbursements Journal and debited to the Telephone Expense account as though it were for $42.
d. The November 30 cash receipts, $425, were placed in the bank's night

depository after banking hours on that date and were unrecorded by the bank at the time the November bank statement was mailed.

Exercise 7–4

Give in general journal form any entries that Southside Shop should make as a result of having prepared the bank reconciliation of the previous exercise.

Exercise 7–5

Sage Company incurred $7,000 of operating expenses in October, a month in which its sales were $25,000. The company began October with a $13,000 merchandise inventory and ended the month with a $14,000 inventory. During the month it purchased merchandise having a $16,000 invoice price, all of which was subject to a 2% discount for prompt payment. The company took advantage of the discounts on $11,000 of the purchases; but through an error in filing it did not earn and could not take the discount on a $5,000 invoice paid on October 30.

Required:

1. Prepare an October income statement for the company under the assumption that it records invoices at gross amounts.
2. Prepare a second income statement for the company under the assumption that it records invoices at net amounts.

Problem 7–1

Problems

David Earl established a petty cash fund for his business and appointed Ted Kane, an office employee, petty cashier. During the fund's first month these transactions were completed:

Nov. 3 Drew a $50 check, No. 410, payable to Ted Kane, petty cashier, and delivered the check and Petty Cash Record to Ted Kane.

5 Paid Parcel Delivery Service $4.50, the COD delivery charges on merchandise purchased for resale.

7 Gave Mrs. Earl, wife of the owner of the business, $5 from petty cash for lunch money.

10 Purchased postage stamps, $6.50.

14 Paid Parcel Delivery Service $4.75, the COD delivery charges on merchandise purchased for resale.

17 Paid the delivery truck driver of Delux Cleaners $3.50 upon delivery of a suit Mr. Earl had dropped off at the cleaners to be cleaned and pressed.

21 Paid $7.50 for minor repairs to an office typewriter.

23 Purchased several small items of office supplies, $5.25.

25 Paid Parcel Delivery Service $6.25, the COD delivery charges on merchandise purchased for resale.

28 Paid $5 from petty cash to have the office windows washed.

30 Drew Check No. 485 to reimburse the fund for the expenditures and a $0.75 shortage.

Required:

Prepare a Petty Cash Record and a Cash Disbursements Journal similar to the ones illustrated in this chapter and record the transactions. Balance and rule the Petty Cash Record before entering the replenishing check. Skip one line between the checks entered in the Cash Disbursements Journal.

Problem 7-2

Cactus Sales completed these transactions involving petty cash during December of the current year:

Dec. 3   Drew Check No. 215 to establish a $25 petty cash fund. Appointed June Hill, one of the office employees, petty cashier.
     4   Paid National Delivery Service $5.75, the COD delivery charges on merchandise purchased for resale.
     7   Paid Offset Press $8 for printing advertising circulars.
     8   Paid a high school boy $3 for delivering the advertising circulars to prospective customers in the neighborhood.
    11   Purchased postage stamps, $6.50.
    11   Drew Check No. 228 to reimburse the petty cash fund; and because the fund had been so rapidly exhausted, made the check sufficiently large to increase the size of the fund to $50.
    14   Paid $4.50 COD delivery charges on merchandise purchased for resale.
    17   Purchased postage stamps, $13.
    18   The owner of the business, Ted Kern, signed a petty cash receipt and took $2 from the petty cash fund for coffee money.
    20   Paid $5 for minor repairs to an office typewriter.
    23   Paid $2.75 for a collect telegram.
    26   Paid $6.25 COD delivery charges on merchandise purchased for resale.
    31   Drew Check No. 262 to reimburse the fund at the end of the accounting period. There was $15 in cash in the fund, and the cashier could not account for the shortage.

Required:

Record the transactions in a Petty Cash Record and, where required, in a Cash Disbursements Journal similar to the ones illustrated in this chapter. Balance and rule the Petty Cash Record at the time of each reimbursement. Skip a line between entries in the Cash Disbursement Journal to set them apart.

Problem 7-3

A concern completed these petty cash transactions during December of the current year:

Dec. 2   Appointed one of the office employees, Joan Dean, petty cashier. Drew Check No. 672 for $25, cashed the check, and turned the proceeds along with the Petty Cash Record over to the newly appointed cashier.
     4   Purchased postage stamps, $6.50.
     5   Paid $5 to have the office windows washed.
     8   Purchased carbon paper and paper clips, $3.50.

Dec. 9   Paid $3.25 COD delivery charges on merchandise purchased for
          resale.
     10   Paid $5 for minor repairs to an office chair.
     10   Drew Check No. 691 to reimburse the petty cash fund; and because
          it had been so rapidly exhausted, made the check sufficiently large
          to increase the size of the fund to $50.
     12   Gave Mrs. Dale Nash, wife of the owner of the business, $10 from
          petty cash for cab fare and lunch money.
     15   Paid $4.75 COD delivery charges on merchandise purchased for
          resale.
     17   Dale Nash, the owner of the business, signed a petty cash receipt
          and took $1 from the fund for coffee money.
     18   Purchased postage stamps, $13.
     21   Paid $2.75 for a collect telegram.
     27   Paid $6.25 COD delivery charges on merchandise purchased for
          resale.
     28   Paid $7.50 for repairs to an office typewriter.
     31   After paying for the typewriter repairs Joan Dean had $3 in cash in
          her petty cash fund and she could not account for the shortage.
          Consequently, she prepared a petty cash receipt for the amount of
          the shortage, had it approved by Mr. Nash, and recorded it in her
          Petty Cash Record. She then exchanged her paid and approved
          petty cash receipts for a $47 check, No. 745, to replenish the fund.

Required:

1. Prepare a Petty Cash Record and a Cash Disbursements Journal similar
    to the ones illustrated in this chapter and open the following T-accounts:
    Cash; Petty Cash; Office Supplies; Dale Nash, Withdrawals; Freight-In;
    Postage; Miscellaneous General Expenses; and Cash Over and Short.
2. Enter the transactions in the Petty Cash Record and, where required, in
    the Cash Disbursements Journal. Balance and rule the Petty Cash Record
    after each reimbursement. Skip a line between entries in tne Cash Dis-
    bursements Journal to set them apart. Post the cash disbursement journal
    entries.

Problem 7–4

The following information was available to reconcile Monroe Company's
November 30 book balance of cash with its bank statement balance of that
date:

a. After all posting was completed on November 30, the company's Cash
      account had a $1,989 debit balance but its bank statement showed a
      $2,615 balance.
b. Checks No. 721 for $102 and No. 726 for $197 were outstanding on the
      October 31 bank reconciliation. Check No. 726 was returned with the
      November canceled checks, but Check No. 721 was not.
c. In comparing the canceled checks returned with the bank statement with
      the entries in the Cash Disbursements Journal, it was found that Check
      No. 801 for the purchase of office equipment was correctly drawn for
      $258 but was entered in the Cash Disbursements Journal as though it
      were for $285. It was also found that Check No. 835 for $125 and Check

No. 837 for $50, both drawn in November, were not among the canceled checks returned with the statement.

d. A credit memorandum enclosed with the bank statement indicated that the bank had collected a $1,000 noninterest-bearing note for the concern, deducted a $5 collection fee, and had credited the remainder to the concern's account.

e. A debit memorandum with a $126 NSF check received from a customer, David Green, attached was among the canceled checks returned.

f. Also among the canceled checks was a $5 debit memorandum for bank services. None of the memoranda had been recorded.

g. The November 30 cash receipts, $542, were placed in the bank's night depository after banking hours on that date and their amount did not appear on the bank statement.

Required:

1. Prepare a bank reconciliation for the company.
2. Prepare entries in general journal form to adjust the company's book balance of cash to the reconciled balance.

Problem 7–5

Phoenix Company reconciled its bank balance on November 30 with two checks, No. 808 for $262 and No. 813 for $93 outstanding. The following information is available for the December 31 reconciliation:

Phoenix Company 1475 North Main Street		Statement of account with THE FIRST NATIONAL BANK	
Date	Checks and Other Debits	Deposits	Balance
Dec. 1	Balance brought forward		1,834.00
2	262.00		1,572.00
3	225.00	223.00	1,570.00
5	306.00		1,264.00
6	846.00		418.00
12		945.00	1,363.00
15	51.00 117.00		1,195.00
22		649.00	1,844.00
28	321.00	748.00	2,271.00
30	240.00 NSF		2,031.00
31	3.00 SC	498.00 CM	2,526.00
Code: CM Credit Memorandum DM Debit Memorandum		NSF Not sufficient funds check SC Service charge	

FROM THE CASH RECEIPTS JOURNAL			FROM THE CASH DISBURSEMENTS JOURNAL		
Date		Cash Debit	Check Number		Cash Credit
Dec. 3		223.00	814		306.00
12		945.00	815		225.00
22		649.00	816		846.00
28		748.00	817		51.00
31		319.00	818		117.00
31		2,884.00	819		312.00
			820		129.00
			821		163.00
					2,149.00

FROM THE GENERAL LEDGER
Cash

Date		Explanation	F	Debit	Credit	Balance
Nov.	30	Balance	✔			1,479.00
Dec.	31		R-9	2,884.00		4,363.00
	31		D-9		2,149.00	2,214.00

Check No. 819 was correctly drawn for $321 in payment for store equipment purchased; however, the bookkeeper misread the amount and entered it in both the Other Accounts debit and Cash credit columns of the Cash Disbursements Journal as though it were for $312. The bank paid and deducted the correct amount.

The NSF check was received from a customer, Jerry Mays, in payment of his account. Its return was unrecorded. The credit memorandum resulted from a $500 note which the bank had collected for the company, deducted a $2 collection fee, and deposited the balance in the company's account. The collection was not recorded.

Required:

1. Prepare a bank reconciliation for Phoenix Company.
2. Prepare in general journal form the entries needed to bring the company's book balance of cash into agreement with the reconciled balance.

Problem 7–6

(This problem is based on information in the Appendix to this chapter.)
Lake Company completed these transactions involving vouchers payable:

Nov. 1　Recorded Voucher No. 911 payable to Dale Company for merchandise having a $750 invoice price, invoice dated October 28, terms FOB destination, 2/10, n/30.

　　 5　Recorded Voucher No. 912 payable to Hill Company for merchandise having a $1,150 invoice price, invoice dated November 3, terms FOB factory, 2/10, n/60. The vendor had prepaid the freight charges, $50, adding the amount to the invoice and bringing its total to $1,200.

Nov. 6 Received a credit memorandum for merchandise having a $250 invoice price. The merchandise was received on November 1, Voucher No. 911, and returned for credit.

13 Issued Check No. 910 in payment of Voucher No. 912.

15 Recorded Voucher No. 913 payable to Payroll for sales salaries, $450, and office salaries, $250. Issued Check No. 911 in payment of the voucher. Cashed the check and paid the employees.

18 Recorded Voucher No. 914 payable to Office Outfitters for the purchase of office equipment having a $300 invoice price, terms n/10 EOM.

22 Recorded Voucher No. 915 payable to *The News* for advertising expense, $125. Issued Check No. 912 in payment of the voucher.

25 Recorded Voucher No. 916 payable to Bell Company for merchandise having an $850 invoice price, invoice dated November 22, terms FOB factory, 2/10, n/60. The vendor had prepaid the freight charges, $30, adding the amount to the invoice and bringing its total to $880.

27 Discovered that Voucher No. 911 had been filed in error for payment on the last day of its credit period rather than on the last day of its discount period, causing the discount to be lost. Issued Check No. 913 in payment of the voucher, less the return.

30 Recorded Voucher No. 917 payable to Payroll for sales salaries, $450, and office salaries, $250. Issued Check No. 914 in payment of the voucher. Cashed the check and paid the employees.

Required:

Assume that Lake Company records vouchers at gross amounts. (*a*) Prepare a Voucher Register, a Check Register, and a General Journal and record the transactions. (*b*) Prepare a Vouchers Payable account and post those portions of the journal and register entries that affect the account. (*c*) Prove the balance of the Vouchers Payable account by preparing a schedule of unpaid vouchers.

Problem 7-7

(*This problem is based on information in the Appendix to this chapter.*)

Required:

Assume that Lake Company of Problem 7-6 records vouchers at net amounts. (*a*) Prepare a Voucher Register, a Check Register, and a General Journal and record the transactions of Problem 7-6, applying these special instructions in recording the November 27 transactions:

Nov. 27 Discovered that Voucher No. 911 had been filed in error for payment on the last day of its credit period rather than on the last day of its discount period. Made a general journal entry debiting Discounts Lost and crediting Vouchers Payable to record the discount lost. Issued Check No. 913 in payment of the voucher as adjusted for the return and the discount lost.

(b) Prepare a Vouchers Payable account and post those journal and register entry portions that affect the account. (c) Prove the balance of the Vouchers Payable account by preparing a schedule of unpaid vouchers.

Problem 7–1A

B. A. Lee, owner of Lee Sales and Service, established a petty cash fund on the advice of his accountant, and during the fund's first month the following transactions were completed:

Nov. 3 Drew Check No. 633, payable to Ned Kern, petty cashier, and cashed the check and delivered the $50 proceeds and the Petty Cash Record to the newly appointed petty cashier.
       5 Purchased postage stamps with $13 from the fund.
       8 Paid National Parcel Service $4.25 COD delivery charges on merchandise purchased for resale.
      10 Paid $8 for minor repairs to an office typewriter.
      13 Paid the delivery truck driver of Top Laundry $3.50 upon the delivery of a package of shirts Mr. Lee had left at the laundry and asked that they be delivered at the office.
      17 Paid National Parcel Service $3.75 COD delivery charges on merchandise purchased for resale.
      18 Gave Mrs. Lee, wife of the proprietor, $5 for cab fare and other personal expenses.
      23 Paid Quick Delivery Service $2.50 to deliver merchandise to a customer.
      27 Paid $2.25 for a collect telegram.
      30 Drew Check No. 710 to reimburse the fund for expenditures and a $1.25 shortage that the petty cashier could not explain.

Required:

Prepare a Petty Cash Record and a Cash Disbursements Journal similar to the ones illustrated in this chapter and record the transactions. Balance and rule the Petty Cash Record before entering the replenishing check. Skip a line between the entries in the Cash Disbursements Journal.

Problem 7–2A

A company established a petty cash fund and appointed one of its office employees, Abby Todd, petty cashier. It then completed these transactions.

Dec. 1 Drew Check No. 889 for $30 to establish the fund and delivered the proceeds of the check and the Petty Cash Record to the new petty cashier.
       3 Paid $5.25 COD delivery charges on merchandise purchased for resale.
       5 Purchased postage stamps, $13.
       6 Paid $6 for minor repairs to an office desk.
       8 Purchased carbon paper and paper clips, $4.50.
       8 Drew Check No. 915 to replenish the petty cash fund; and because

the fund has been so rapidly exhausted, made the check large enough to increase the size of the fund to $50.

Dec. 10   Paid $5 to have the office windows washed.

14   Paid $2.25 for a collect telegram.

17   Paid $3.50 COD delivery charges on merchandise purchased for resale.

20   Paid City Delivery Service $2.50 to deliver merchandise to a customer.

23   Purchased postage stamps, $13.

24   Paid $4.75 COD delivery charges on merchandise purchased for resale.

27   Paid City Delivery Service $3.25 to deliver merchandise to a customer.

31   In reimbursing the petty cash fund at the end of the accounting period, the petty cashier found she had only $15 in money in the fund and she could not account for the shortage. Drew Check No. 998 to reimburse the fund for the shortage and expenditures.

Required:

Record the transactions in a Petty Cash Record and, where required, in a Cash Disbursements Journal similar to the ones illustrated in this chapter. Balance and rule the Petty Cash Record at the time of each reimbursement. Skip a line after each entry in the Cash Disbursements Journal to set the entries apart.

Problem 7–4A

The following information was available to reconcile Abbott Company's book and bank statement balances of cash as of December 31:

a.   The December 31 cash balance according to the accounting records was $2,782, and the bank statement balance for that date was $2,653.

b.   Two checks, No. 722 for $103 and No. 726 for $93, were outstanding on November 30 when the book and bank statement balances were last reconciled. Check No. 726 was returned with the December canceled checks but Check No. 722 was not.

c.   Check No. 803 for $79 and Check No. 805 for $73, both written and entered in the Cash Disbursements Journal in December, were not among the canceled checks returned.

d.   When the December checks were compared with entries in the Cash Disbursements Journal, it was found that Check No. 751 had been correctly drawn for $183 in payment for store supplies but was entered in the Cash Disbursements Journal in error as though it were drawn for $138.

e.   Two debit memoranda and a credit memorandum were included with the returned checks and were unrecorded at the time of the reconciliation. The credit memorandum indicated that the bank had collected a $500 note receivable for the company, deducted a $2 collection fee, and credited the balance to the company's account. One of the debit memoranda was for $32 and had attached to it a NSF check in that amount that had been received from a customer, Dale Hill, in payment of his account. The second debit memorandum was for a special printing of checks and was for $16.

f. The December 31 cash receipts, $789, had been placed in the bank's night depository after banking hours on that date and did not appear on the bank statement.

Required:

Prepare (*a*) a December 31 bank reconciliation for the company and (*b*) the entries in general journal form required to adjust the company's book balance of cash to the reconciled balance.

Problem 7–5A

Coolair Company reconciled its book and bank statement balances of cash on October 31 with two checks outstanding, No. 713 for $275 and No. 716 for $142. The following information was available for the November 30 reconciliation:

Coolair Company 17th and High Streets	Statement of account with UNITED STATES NATIONAL BANK		
Date	Checks and Other Debits	Deposits	Balance
Nov. 1	Balance brought forward		1,912.00
2	275.00		1,637.00
3	218.00	312.00	1,731.00
5	302.00		1,429.00
9	737.00		692.00
12	75.00 132.00		485.00
14		551.00	1,036.00
18	284.00		752.00
21		512.00	1,264.00
28	343.00	472.00	1,393.00
29	43.00 NSF		1,350.00
30	3.00 SC	995.00 CM	2,342.00
Code: CM Credit Memorandum DM Debit Memorandum		NSF Not sufficient funds check SC Service charge	

FROM THE CASH RECEIPTS JOURNAL				FROM THE CASH DISBURSEMENTS JOURNAL			
Date			Cash Debit	Check Number			Cash Credit
Nov. 3			312.00	718			218.00
14			551.00	719			320.00
21			512.00	720			75.00
28			472.00	721			737.00
30			247.00	722			132.00
30			2,094.00	723			136.00
				724			284.00
				725			343.00
				726			53.00
							2,298.00

FROM THE GENERAL LEDGER

CASH

Date		Explanation	F	Debit	Credit	Balance
Oct.	31	Balance	✔			1,495.00
Nov.	30		R-8	2,094.00		3,589.00
	30		D-9		2,298.00	1,291.00

Check No. 719 was correctly drawn for $302 in payment for office equipment; however, the bookkeeper misread the amount and entered it in both the Other Accounts debit and Cash credit columns of the Cash Disbursements Journal as though it were for $320.

The NSF check was received from a customer, Willie Hale, in payment of his account. Its return is unrecorded. The credit memorandum resulted from a $1,000 note collected for Coolair Company by the bank. The bank had deducted a $5 collection fee. The collection is not recorded.

Required:

1. Prepare a November 30 bank reconciliation for the company.
2. Prepare in general journal form the entries needed to adjust the book balance of cash to the reconciled balance.

Problem 7–6A

(*This problem is based on information in the Appendix to this chapter.*)
   Mesa Company completed these transactions involving vouchers payable:

Oct. 2   Recorded Voucher No. 751 payable to Tipton Company for merchandise having $950 invoice price, invoice dated September 28, terms FOB factory, 2/10, n/30. The vendor had prepaid the freight, $45, adding the amount to the invoice and bringing its total to $995.

     4   Recorded Voucher No. 752 payable to *The Times* for advertising expense, $110. Issued Check No. 748 in payment of the voucher.

     5   Received a credit memorandum for merchandise having a $150 invoice price. The merchandise had been received from Tipton Company on October 2 and returned for credit.

     9   Recorded Voucher No. 753 payable to Lake Realty for one month's rent on the space occupied by the store, $500. Issued Check No. 749 in payment of the voucher.

   11   Recorded Voucher No. 754 payable to Beta Supply Company for store supplies, $65, terms n/10 EOM.

   14   Recorded Voucher No. 755 payable to Phoenix Company for merchandise having a $1,250 invoice price, invoice dated October 11, terms FOB factory, 2/10, n/60. The vendor had prepaid the freight charges, $50, adding the amount to the invoice and bringing its total to $1,300.

   15   Recorded Voucher No. 756 payable to Payroll for sales salaries, $600, and office salaries $275. Issued Check No. 750 in payment of the voucher. Cashed the check and paid the employees.

   18   Recorded Voucher No. 757 payable to West Company for merchandise having a $750 invoice price, invoice dated October 15, terms 2/10, n/60, FOB factory. The vendor had prepaid the freight charges,

$35, adding the amount to the invoice and bringing its total to $785.

Oct. 21   Issued Check No. 751 in payment of Voucher No. 755.

26   Recorded Voucher No. 758 payable to Phoenix Company for merchandise having a $1,500 invoice price, invoice dated October 22, terms FOB factory, 2/10, n/60. The vendor had prepaid the freight charges, $70, adding the amount to the invoice and bringing its total to $1,570.

28   Discovered that Voucher No. 751 had been filed in error for payment on the last day of its credit period rather than on the last day of its discount period, causing the discount to be lost. Issued Check No. 752 in payment of the voucher.

31   Recorded Voucher No. 759 payable to Payroll for sales salaries, $600, and office salaries, $275. Issued Check No. 753 in payment of the voucher. Cashed the check and paid the employees.

Required:

1. Assume that Mesa Company records vouchers at gross amounts, and prepare a Voucher Register, a Check Register, and a General Journal and record the transactions.
2. Prepare a Vouchers Payable account and post those entry portions that affect the account.
3. Prove the balance of the Vouchers Payable account by preparing a schedule of vouchers payable.

Problem 7–7A

Required:

1. Under the assumption that Mesa Company of Problem 7–6A records vouchers at net amounts, prepare a Voucher Register, a Check Register, and a General Journal and record the transactions of Problem 7–6A, applying these special instructions in recording the October 28 transactions:

Oct. 28   Discovered that Voucher No. 751 had been filed in error for payment on the last day of its credit period rather than the last day of its discount period. Made a general journal entry debiting Discounts Lost and crediting Vouchers Payable to record the discount lost. Issued Check No. 752 in payment of the voucher as adjusted for the return and the discount lost.

2. Prepare a Vouchers Payable account and post those entry portions that affect the account.
3. Prove the balance of the Vouchers Payable account by preparing a schedule of unpaid vouchers.

Miss Emma, the bookkeeper at Dawson's Department Store, will retire next week after over 40 years with the company, having been hired by the father of the store's present owner. She has always been a very dependable employee, and as a result has been given more and more responsibilities over the years. Actually, for the past 15 years she has "run" the store's office, **Decision problem 7–1, Dawson's Department Store** keeping the books, verifying invoices, and issuing checks in their payment, which in the absence of the store's owner, George Dawson, she could sign. In addition, at the end of each day the store's salesclerks turn over their daily cash receipts to Miss Emma, who after counting the money and comparing the amounts with the cash register tapes, which she is responsible for removing from the cash registers, makes the Cash Receipts Journal entry to record cash sales and then deposits the money in the bank. She also reconciles the bank balance each month with her book balance of cash.

Mr. Dawson, the store's owner, realizes he cannot expect a new bookkeeper to accomplish as much in a day as Miss Emma does; and since the store is not large enough to warrant more than one office employee, he recognizes he must take over some of Miss Emma's duties when she retires. He already places all orders for merchandise and supplies and closely supervises all employees and does not want to add more to his duties than necessary.

Discuss the foregoing situation from an internal control point of view, pointing out which of Miss Emma's tasks should be taken over by Mr. Dawson and which can be assigned to the new bookkeeper with safety.

Decision problem 7–2, Palace Theater

Gary Hale owns and operates Palace Theater, acting as both its manager and its projectionist. The theater has not been too profitable of late; and this morning at breakfast, while discussing ways to cut costs, his wife suggested that he discharge the theater's doorman whose job is to collect and destroy the tickets sold by the cashier, and that he permit the cashier to collect an admission from each patron without issuing a ticket. This, Mrs. Hale pointed out, would result in a double savings, the wages of the doorman and, also, since there would be no one to take up tickets, rolls of prenumbered tickets would not have to be purchased. Mr. Hale said he could not do this unless Mrs. Hale would take over the cashier's job.

Discuss the wife's suggestion and her husband's counter proposal from an internal control point of view. You may assume the cashier is a college student and that cashiers change frequently, since the job interferes with dating.

Decision problem 7–3, Central Supply Company

Earl Lee, manager of Central Supply Company, thought something was wrong with the amount of purchases discounts appearing on the following annual income statement of his company:

CENTRAL SUPPLY COMPANY
Income Statement for Year Ended December 31, 19—

Sales			$515,000
Cost of goods sold:			
Merchandise inventory, January 1, 19—		$ 38,000	
Purchases	$350,000		
Less purchases discounts	4,000		
Cost of goods purchased		346,000	
Goods available for sale		$384,000	
Merchandise inventory, December 31, 19—....		41,000	
Cost of goods sold			343,000
Gross profit on sales			$172,000
Operating expenses			137,000
Net Income			$ 35,000

Mr. Lee knew that every supplier from whom the concern purchased merchandise offered a 2% discount for payment within ten days, and that it was the policy of the concern to pay every invoice within the discount period. Yet when he analyzed the relation between the amount of purchases discounts appearing on the income statement and the amount of goods purchased during the year, he could see that discounts taken were considerable less than 2% of purchases. He recognized that there is never a precise matching between purchases and purchases discounts due to the fact that some goods are purchased near the end of a year and are not paid for until the next year, but he knew that this could not account for the discrepancy in this case. He also knew that the system used by his company in recording purchase invoices and their payment showed only discounts taken during a year and not discounts missed and lost. He also dimly recalled from his one accounting course that there was another way to record invoices that would cause the amount of any discounts lost to appear on the income statement as an expense of the period of the loss.

Describe the system Mr. Lee dimly recalls, giving in general journal form the entries to record the purchase on December 12 of merchandise having a $1,500 invoice price, terms 2/10, n/60, and payment of the invoice on the last day of its discount period. Also give the required entries to pay the invoice under the assumption that it is not paid until the end of its credit period. Then explain why the dimly recalled system offers better control over the people responsible for taking all offered discounts. Finally, recast Central Supply Company's income statement as it would appear if the company had recorded invoices at net amounts. In preparing the statement, assume that the difference between the amount of discounts taken by the company and 2% of its purchases represents discounts lost.

After studying Chapter 8, you should be able to:

- Calculate interest on promissory notes and the discount on notes receivable discounted.

- Prepare entries to record the receipt of a promissory note and its payment or dishonor.

- Prepare entries to record the discounting of a note receivable and its payment by the maker or its dishonor.

- Prepare entries accounting for bad debts both by the allowance method and the direct write-off method.

- Explain the full-disclosure principle and the materiality principle.

- Define or explain the words and phrases listed in the chapter Glossary.

chapter 8

Notes and accounts receivable

Companies selling merchandise on the installment plan commonly take promissory notes from their customers. Likewise when the credit period is long, as in the sale of farm machinery, promissory notes are often required. Also, creditors frequently ask for promissory notes from customers who are granted additional time in which to pay their past-due accounts. In all these situations creditors prefer notes to accounts receivable because the notes may be readily turned into cash before becoming due by discounting or selling them to a bank. Likewise, notes are preferred because if a lawsuit is needed to collect, a note represents written acknowledgment by the debtor of both the debt and its amount. Also, notes are preferred because they generally earn interest.

Promissory notes

A promissory note is an unconditional promise in writing to pay on demand or at a fixed or determinable future date a definite sum of money. In the note shown in Illustration 8–1 Hugo Brown promises to pay Frank Black or his order a definite sum of money at a fixed future date. Hugo Brown is the *maker* of the note; Frank Black is the *payee*. To Hugo Brown the illustrated note is a *note payable,* a liability; and to Frank Black the same note is a *note receivable,* an asset.

The illustrated Hugo Brown note bears interest at 7%. Interest is a charge for the use of money. To a borrower, interest is an expense; to a lender, it is a revenue. A note may be interest bearing or it may be noninterest bearing. If a note bears interest, the rate or the amount of interest must be stated on the note.

Calculating interest

Unless otherwise stated, the rate of interest on a note is the rate charged for the use of the principal for one year. The formula for calculating interest is:

$$\begin{array}{ccc} \text{Principal} & \text{Annual} & \text{Time of the} \\ \text{of the} \;\times\; \text{rate of} \;\times\; \text{note expressed} = \text{Interest} \\ \text{note} & \text{interest} & \text{in years} \end{array}$$

For example, interest on a $1,000, 7%, one-year note is calculated:

$$\$1,000 \times \frac{7}{100} \times 1 = \$70$$

In business, most note transactions involve a period less than a full year, and this period is usually expressed in days. When the time of a note is expressed in days, the actual number of days elapsing, not including the day of the note's date but including the day on which it falls

$ 1,000.00	Eugene, Oregon	March 9, 19--

Thirty days _____ after date _____ I _____ promise to pay to

the order of _____ Frank Black

One thousand and no/100--dollars

for value received with interest at ___ 7%

payable at ___ First National Bank of Eugene, Oregon

Hugo Brown

Illustration 8–1

due are counted. For example, a 90-day note, dated July 10, is due on October 8. This October 8 due date, called the *maturity date*, is calculated as follows:

Number of days in July	31
Minus the date of the note	10
Gives the number of days the note runs in July	21
Add the number of days in August	31
Add the number of days in September	30
Total through September 30	82
Days in October needed to equal the time of the note, 90 days, also the maturity date of the note—October	8
Total time the note runs in days	90

Occasionally, the time of a note is expressed in months. In such cases, the note matures and is payable in the month of its maturity on the same day of the month as its date. For example, a note dated July 10 and payable three months after date is payable on October 10.

In calculating interest, business executives usually consider a year to have just 360 days. This simplifies most interest calculations. It makes the interest calculation on a 90-day, 7%, $1,000 note as follows:

$$\text{Principal} \times \text{Rate} \times \frac{\text{Exact days}}{360} = \text{Interest}$$

or

$$\$1,000 \times \frac{7}{100} \times \frac{90}{360} = \text{Interest}$$

or

$$\$\cancel{1,000} \times \frac{7}{\cancel{100}} \times \frac{\cancel{90}}{\cancel{360}} = \frac{35}{2} = \$17.50$$

Notes receivable are recorded in a single Notes Receivable account. Each note may be identified in the account by writing the name of the maker in the Explanation column on the line of the entry recording its receipt or payment. Only one account is needed because the individual notes are on hand; and the maker, rate of interest, due date, and other information may be learned by examining each note.

A note received at the time of a sale is recorded as follows:

Dec.	5	Notes Receivable	650.00	
		Sales		650.00
		Sold merchandise, terms six-month, 6% note.		

Recording the receipt of a note

When a note is taken in granting a time extension on a past-due account receivable, the creditor usually attempts to collect part of the past-due account in cash. This reduces the debt and requires the acceptance of a note for a smaller amount. For example, Symplex Company agrees to accept $232 in cash and a $500, 60-day, 6% note from Joseph Cook in settlement of his $732 past-due account. When Symplex receives the cash and note, the following entry in general journal form is made:

Oct.	5	Cash..	232.00	
		Notes Receivable	500.00	
		Accounts Receivable—Joseph Cook		732.00
		Received cash and a note in settlement of an account.		

Observe that this entry changes the form of $500 of the debt from an account receivable to a note receivable.

When Cook pays the note, this entry in general journal form is made:

Dec.	4	Cash	505.00	
		Notes Receivable		500.00
		Interest Earned		5.00
		Collected the Joseph Cook note.		

Look again at the last two entries. If Symplex Company uses columnar journals, the entry of December 4 would be recorded in its Cash Receipts Journal and two lines would be required, one line for the credit to Interest Earned and a second line for the credit to Notes Receivable. Likewise, the October 5 transaction would be recorded with two entries, one in the Cash Receipts Journal for the money received and a second entry in the General Journal for the note. Nevertheless, to simplify the illustrations, general journal entries are shown here. Furthermore, beginning at this point and continuing through the remainder of this text, almost all entries will be shown in general journal form. The student should realize that the entries would be made in a Cash Receipts Journal or other appropriate journal if in use.

Dishonored notes receivable

Occasionally, the maker of a note either cannot or will not pay his note at maturity. When a note's maker refuses to pay at maturity, the note is said to be *dishonored*. Dishonoring a note does not relieve the maker of his obligation, and every legal means should be made to collect. However, collection may require lengthy legal proceedings.

The balance of the Notes Receivable account should show only the amount of notes that have not matured. Therefore, a dishonored, past-due note should be removed from the Notes Receivable account and charged back to the account of its maker. For example, Symplex Company holds a $700, 6%, 60-day note of George Jones. At maturity, Mr. Jones dishonors the note. To remove the dishonored note from its Notes Receivable account, the company makes the following entry:

Oct.	14	Accounts Receivable—George Jones	707.00	
		Interest Earned		7.00
		Notes Receivable		700.00
		To charge the account of George Jones for his dishonored $700, 6%, 60-day note.		

Charging a dishonored note back to the account of its maker serves two purposes. It removes the amount of the note from the Notes Receivable account, leaving in the account only notes that have not matured; and it records the dishonored note in the maker's account. The second purpose is important because if in the future the maker of the dishonored note again applies for credit, his account will show all past dealings, including the dishonored note.

Observe in the entry charging back the dishonored note of George Jones that the Interest Earned account is credited for interest earned even though it was not collected. The reason for this is that Jones owes both the principal and the interest, and his account should reflect the full amount owed.

As previously stated, a note receivable is preferred to an account receivable because the note can be turned into cash before maturity by discounting or selling it to a bank. In discounting a note, the owner endorses and delivers the note to the bank in exchange for cash. The bank holds the note to maturity and then collects its maturity value from the maker.

Discounting notes receivable

To illustrate the discounting of a note receivable, assume that on May 28 Symplex Company received a $1,200, 60-day, 6% note dated May 27 from John Owen. It held the note until June 2 and then discounted it at its bank at 7%. Since the maturity date of this note is July 26, the bank must wait 54 days after discounting the note to collect from Owen. These 54 days are called the *discount period* and are calculated as follows:

Time of the note in days..........................		60
Less time held by Symplex Company:		
Number of days in May.....................	31	
Less the date of the note.................	27	
Days held in May	4	
Days held in June	2	
Total days held...............................		6
Discount period in days................		54

At the end of the discount period the bank expects to collect the *maturity value* of this note from Owen; and as is customary, it bases its discount on the maturity value of the note, which is calculated as follows:

Principal of the note	$1,200.00
Interest on $1,200 for 60 days at 6%	12.00
Maturity value	$1,212.00

In this case the bank's discount rate, or the rate of interest it charges for lending money, is 7%; consequently, in discounting the note, it will deduct 54 days' interest at 7% from the note's maturity value and will give Symplex Company the remainder. The remainder is called the *proceeds of the note,* and the amount of interest deducted is known as *bank discount.* The amount of bank discount and the proceeds are calculated as follows:

Maturity value of the note............................	$1,212.00
Less interest on $1,212 for 54 days at 7%.........	12.73
Proceeds..	$1,199.27

Observe in this case that the proceeds, $1,199.27, are $0.73 less than the $1,200 principal amount of the note. Consequently, Symplex will make this entry in recording the discount transaction:

June	2	Cash...	1,199.27	
		Interest Expense...	.73	
		Notes Receivable Discounted..............................		1,200.00
		Discounted the John Owen note for 54 days at 7%.		

In recording the transaction, Symplex in effect offsets the $12 of interest it would have earned by holding the note to maturity against the $12.73 discount charged by the bank and records only the difference, the $0.73 excess of expense.

In the situation just described the principal of the discounted note exceeded the proceeds. However, in many if not most cases the proceeds exceed the principal; and when this happens, the difference is credited to Interest Earned. For example, suppose that instead of discounting the John Owen note on June 2, Symplex held the note and discounted it on June 26. If the note is discounted on June 26 at 7%, the discount period is 30 days, the discount is $7.07, and the proceeds of the note are $1,204.93, calculated as follows:

Maturity value of the note............................	$1,212.00
Less interest on $1,212 at 7% for 30 days.........	7.07
Proceeds..	$1,204.93

And since the proceeds exceed the principal, the transaction is recorded as follows:

June	26	Cash...	1,204.93	
		Interest Earned...		4.93
		Notes Receivable Discounted..............................		1,200.00
		Discounted the John Owen note for 30 days at 7%.		

Contingent liability

A person or company discounting a note is ordinarily required to endorse the note, because an endorsement, unless it is restricted,[1] makes the endorser contingently liable for payment of the note. The *contingent liability* depends upon the note's dishonor by its maker. If the maker pays, the endorser has no liability. However, if the maker defaults, the endorser's contingent liability becomes an actual liability and the endorser must pay the note for the maker.

Observe the credit to Notes Receivable Discounted in the two entries just illustrated. Since contingent liabilities may become actual liabilities, they affect the credit standing of the one contingently liable. Consequently, when a note is discounted, the contingent liability should appear in the accounts and on the balance sheet of the person or company contingently liable. In discounting the John Owen note, Symplex Company made itself contingently liable for paying the note, and the use of the Notes Receivable Discounted account causes this contingent liability to appear in its accounts. If Symplex Company has $500 of other notes receivable, posting either of the illustrated entries will cause its Notes Receivable and Notes Receivable Discounted accounts to appear as follows:

Notes Receivable		Notes Receivable Discounted	
(Owen note) 1,200			(Owen note) 1,200
(Hall note) 500			

If a balance sheet is prepared before the maturity date of the discounted note, the balances of both the Notes Receivable and Notes Receivable Discounted accounts may appear on it as follows:

Current Assets:		
Cash		$ 2,500
Notes receivable	$1,700	
Less notes receivable discounted	(1,200)	500
Accounts receivable		4,000
Merchandise inventory		48,000
Total Current Assets		$55,000

Showing "Notes receivable discounted" on the balance sheet as a subtraction from "Notes receivable" indicates the contingent liability to a balance sheet reader. The contingent liability may also be shown by means of a footnote. If Symplex Company followed this practice, it would show the amount of its notes receivable in the current asset

---

[1] A restricted endorsement is one in which the endorser states in writing that he will not be liable for payment.

section of its balance sheet at $500 followed by an asterisk or other indication of a footnote. It would then place a footnote at the bottom of the balance sheet saying, for example: "Symplex Company is contingently liable for $1,200 of notes receivable discounted."

Full-disclosure principle

The balance sheet disclosure of contingent liabilities due to discounted notes receivable is required under the *full-disclosure principle.* Under this principle it is held that financial statements and their accompanying footnotes and other explanatory materials should disclose fully and completely all relevant data of a material nature relating to the financial position and operating results of the company for which they are prepared. This does not necessarily mean that the information should be detailed, for details can at times obscure. It simply means that all information necessary to an appreciation of the company's position be reported in a readily understandable manner and that nothing of a significant nature be withheld.

Full disclosure is not limited to information in the ledger accounts. For example, any of the following would be considered relevant and should be disclosed by means of footnotes or explanatory paragraphs attached to the statements.

Contingent liabilities   In addition to discounted notes, a company that is contingently liable due to possible additional tax assessments, pending lawsuits, or product guarantees should disclose this on its statements.

Long-term commitments under a contract   If the company has signed a long-term lease requiring a material annual payment, this should be disclosed even though the liability does not appear in the accounts. Also, if the company has pledged certain of its assets as security for a loan, this should be revealed.

Accounting methods used   Whenever there are several acceptable accounting methods that may be followed, a company should report in each case the method used, especially when a choice of methods can materially affect reported net income. For example, a company should report by means of footnotes or notes accompanying its statements the inventory method or methods used, depreciation methods, method of recognizing revenue under long-term construction contracts, and the like.[2]

Payment of a discounted note by its maker

When a note is discounted, the bank will, if possible, collect the note from the maker at maturity. If the maker pays, it is only necessary for the company that discounted the note to remove the contingent liability from its books. If, for example, John Owen pays the note of the pre-

---

[2] APB, "Disclosure of Accounting Policies," *APB Opinion No. 22* (New York: AICPA, April 1972), pars. 12 and 13.

vious section, which was discounted by Symplex Company, the company will make the following entry:

July	29	Notes Receivable Discounted	1,200.00	
		Notes Receivable		1,200.00
		To remove the contingent liability of the John Owen note.		

Posting the entry has this effect on the accounts:

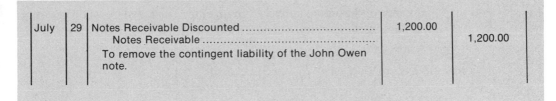

Notes Receivable		Notes Receivable Discounted	
(Owen note) 1,200	(Owen note) 1,200	(Owen note) 1,200	(Owen note) 1,200
(Hall note) 500			

Observe that the entry removes the amount of the note from both the Notes Receivable and Notes Receivable Discounted accounts.

If it is able to do so, a bank always collects a discounted note directly from the maker; and the one who discounted it will not hear from the bank if the note is paid at maturity. However, according to law, if a discounted note is dishonored, the bank must by the end of the next business day notify each endorser of the note if it is to hold the endorsers liable on the note. To notify the endorsers, the bank will normally protest the dishonored note. To protest a note, the bank prepares and mails by the end of the next business day a *notice of protest* to each endorser. A notice of protest is a statement, usually attested by a notary public, that says the note was duly presented to the maker for payment and payment was refused. The cost of protesting a note is called a *protest fee,* and the bank will look to the one who discounted a dishonored note for payment of both the note's maturity value and the protest fee.

Dishonor of a discounted note

For example, suppose that instead of paying the $1,200 note previously illustrated, John Owen dishonored it. In such a situation the bank would notify Symplex Company immediately of the dishonor by mailing a notice of protest and a letter asking payment of the note's maturity value plus the protest fee. If the protest fee is, say $5, Symplex must pay the bank $1,217; and in recording the payment, Symplex will charge the $1,217 to the account of John Owen, as follows:

July	27	Accounts Receivable-John Owen...............................	1,217.00	
		Cash...		1,217.00
		To charge the account of Owen for the maturity value of his dishonored note plus the protest fee.		

The dishonor changed Symplex's contingent liability to an actual liability, and payment of the dishonored note ended both the actual liability and the contingent liability. The entry just illustrated records payment of the actual liability, but an entry must also be made to cancel the contingent liability. It is:

July	27	Notes Receivable Discounted...................................	1,200.00	
		Notes Receivable		1,200.00
		To cancel the contingent liability on the dishonored note of John Owen.		

Of course, upon receipt of the $1,217, the bank will deliver to Symplex the dishonored note. Symplex Company will then make every legal effort to collect from Owen, not only the maturity value of the note and protest fee but also interest on the maturity value and protest fee from the date of dishonor until the date of final settlement. However, it may not be able to collect, and after exhausting every legal means to do so, it may have to write the account off as a bad debt. Normally in such cases no additional interest is taken onto the books before the write-off.

Although dishonored notes commonly have to be written off as bad debts, some are also eventually paid by their makers. For example, if 30 days after dishonor, John Owen pays the maturity value of his dishonored note, the protest fee, and interest at 6% on both for 30 days beyond maturity, he will pay:

Maturity value....................................	$1,212.00
Protest fee	5.00
Interest on $1,217 at 6% for 30 days	6.09
Total......................................	$1,223.09

And Symplex will record receipt of his money as follows:

Aug.	25	Cash..	1,223.09	
		Interest Earned		6.09
		Accounts Receivable-John Owen..........................		1,217.00
		Dishonored note and protest fee collected with interest.		

Collecting an out-of-town note

A promissory note is a *negotiable instrument;* and a negotiable instrument is a document to which title is readily changed, usually by endorsement and delivery, but sometimes by delivery only. Negotiable instruments readily pass from hand to hand without question because negotiable instrument laws have been written to encourage this. No effort will be made here to go into the legal aspects of negotiable instruments. That is reserved for a course in business law. For the purpose of this discussion, it is sufficient to point out that a *holder in due course* of a negotiable instrument, or one who under certain circumstances receives a negotiable instrument from a holder in due course, has the legal right to collect the instrument without proving the existence of a debt. A holder in due course is one who gives something of value for a negotiable instrument before maturity without knowledge of defects in the title of previous holders.

These legal aspects sometimes cause a problem in collecting notes. The holder of a note will not part with it without receiving payment, since he does not wish to part with the evidence of indebtedness. Likewise, the maker will not pay his note without gaining possession of it, because he must pay again if the original holder transfers the note, even after receiving payment, to a holder in due course or to one with the same rights.

No problem is involved in collecting a note when both parties to the transaction live in the same city. The holder can present the note directly to its maker for payment. However, when the parties live in different cities, a problem does arise in the exchange of cash for possession of a note. This problem is usually overcome by using a bank as an agent to collect an out-of-town note. To illustrate, Symplex Company of Eugene, Oregon, holds the $1,000, 6%, 60-day note of Sam Small of Longview, Washington. When the note nears maturity, Symplex delivers the note to its Eugene bank for collection. The Eugene bank forwards the note to a Longview, Washington, correspondent bank, and the Longview bank notifies Sam Small that it has the note for collection. When Small pays the Longview bank, he receives possession of the note. The Longview bank transmits the proceeds of the note to the Eugene bank, and the Eugene bank credits the proceeds, less a collection fee, to the Symplex Company bank account.

Only one entry is needed to record the collection of an out-of-town note through a bank. This is made when the bank notifies that it has credited the proceeds less the collection fee. No entry is made when the note is delivered to the bank for collection. At that time it is not known if the note will be paid or dishonored. Until the note is paid, there is no change in the relationship of the parties. For example, when the Sam Small note is paid, the bank notifies Symplex that it has deposited the proceeds less the collection fee to Symplex's bank account. Symplex then makes the following entry:

Oct.	17	Cash...	1,006.00	
		Collection Expense	4.00	
		Notes Receivable		1,000.00
		Interest Earned		10.00
		Proceeds of the Sam Small note less collection charge.		

End-of-the-
period
adjustments

Notes receivable usually earn interest: and if any such notes are out-standing at the accounting period end, their accrued interest should be calculated and recorded. For example, on December 11 a company accepted a $3,000, 60-day, 6% note from a customer in granting an extension on a past-due account. If the company's accounting period ends on December 31, by then $10 interest has accrued on this note and should be recorded with this adjusting entry:

Dec.	31	Interest Receivable...	10.00	
		Interest Earned		10.00
		To record accrued interest on a note receivable.		

The adjusting entry causes the interest earned to appear on the income statement of the period in which it was earned. It also causes the interest receivable to appear on the balance sheet as a current asset.

Collecting interest previously accrued

When the note is collected, the transaction may be recorded as follows:

Feb.	9	Cash...	3,030.00	
		Interest Earned		20.00
		Interest Receivable...		10.00
		Notes Receivable		3,000.00
		Received payment of a note and its interest.		

The entry's credit to Interest Receivable records collection of the interest accrued at the end of the previous period.

ACCOUNTS RECEIVABLE

Most of the problems encountered in recording transactions with customers have already been discussed. However, the matter of *bad debts* and a few miscellaneous matters need attention.

Bad debts

When goods and services are sold on credit, there are almost always a few customers who do not pay. The accounts of such custo-mers are called bad debts and are a loss and an expense of selling on credit.

It might be asked: Why do merchants sell on credit if bad debts result? The answer is, of course, that merchants sell on credit in order to increase total sales and profits. Merchants are willing to take a reasonable loss from bad debts in order to increase sales and profits. Therefore, bad debt losses are an expense of selling on credit, an expense incurred in order to increase sales. Also, if the requirements of the *matching principle* are met, bad debt losses must be matched against the sales they helped produce.

A bad debt loss results from an error in judgment, an error in granting credit and making a sale to a customer who will not pay. Consequently, a bad debt loss is incurred at the moment credit is granted and a sale is made to such a customer. Of course the merchant making such a sale does not know at the time of the sale that he has incurred a loss. Actually, he normally will not be sure of the loss for as much as a year or more, after he has exhausted every means of collecting. Nevertheless, final recognition a year or so later does not change the time of the loss — the loss occurred at the moment of the sale.

Matching bad debt losses with sales

When it is recognized that a bad debt loss occurs at the moment of a sale to a customer who will not pay and that a merchant cannot be sure the customer will not pay until a year or more after the sale, it follows that if bad debt losses are matched with the sales they helped produce, they must be matched on an estimated basis. The allowance method of accounting for bad debts does just that.

Under the allowance method of accounting for bad debts, an estimate is made at the end of each accounting period of the total bad debts that are expected to result from the period's sales, and an allowance is provided for the resulting loss. This has two advantages: (1) the estimated loss is charged to the period in which the revenue is recognized, and (2) the accounts receivable appear on the balance sheet at their estimated realizable value, a more informative balance sheet amount.

Allowance method of accounting for bad debts

Estimating bad debts

In making the year-end estimate of bad debts that are expected to result from the year's sales, companies commonly assume that "history will repeat." For example, over the past several years Alpha Company has experienced bad debt losses equal to one half of 1% of its charge sales, and during the past year its charge sales were $300,000. Consequently, if history repeats, Alpha Company can expect $1,500 of bad debt losses to result from the year's sales ($300,000 × 0.005 = $1,500).

Recording the estimated bad debts loss

Under the allowance method of accounting for bad debts, the estimated bad debts loss is recorded at the end of each accounting period with a work sheet adjustment and an adjusting entry. For example, Alpha Company will record its $1,500 estimated bad debts loss with a work sheet adjustment and an adjusting entry like the following:

Dec.	31	Bad Debts Expense..	1,500.00	
		Allowance for Doubtful Accounts...........................		1,500.00
		To record the estimated bad debts.		

The debit of this entry causes the estimated bad debts loss to appear on the income statement of the year in which the sales were made; and as a result, the estimated $1,500 expense of selling on credit is matched with the $300,000 of revenue it helped to produce.

Bad debt losses normally appear on the income statement as an administrative expense rather than as a selling expense because granting credit is usually not a responsibility of the sales department. Therefore, since the sales department is not responsible for granting credit, it should not be held responsible for bad debt losses. The sales department is usually not given responsibility for granting credit because it is feared the sales department would at times be swayed in its judgment of a credit risk by its desire to make a sale.

Bad debts in the accounts

If at the time its bad debts adjusting entry is posted, Alpha Company has $20,000 of accounts receivable, its Accounts Receivable and Allowance for Doubtful Accounts accounts will show these balances:

Accounts Receivable		Allowance for Doubtful Accounts	
Dec. 31 20,000			Dec. 31 1,500

The bad debts adjusting entry reduces the accounts receivable to their estimated realizable value. However, note that the credit of the entry is to the contra account, Allowance for Doubtful Accounts, rather than to the Accounts Receivable controlling account.

It is necessary to credit the estimated bad debts loss to the contra account rather than the Accounts Receivable account because at the time of the adjusting entry it is not known for certain just which customers will fail to pay. (The total loss from bad debts can be estimated from past experience, but the exact customers who will not pay cannot be known until every means of collecting from each has been exhausted.) Consequently, since the bad accounts are not identifiable at the time the adjusting entry is made, they cannot be removed from the subsidiary Accounts Receivable Ledger, and the Allowance for Doubtful Accounts account must be credited instead of the controlling account. The allowance account must be credited because to credit the controlling account without removing the bad accounts from the subsidiary ledger would cause the controlling account balance to differ from the sum of the balances in the subsidiary ledger.

Allowance for doubtful accounts on the balance sheet

When the balance sheet is prepared, the balance of the Allowance for Doubtful Accounts account is subtracted thereon from the balance of the Accounts Receivable account to show the amount that is expected to be realized from the accounts, as follows:

Current Assets:		
Cash...		$11,300
Accounts receivable...............................	$20,000	
Less allowance for doubtful accounts....	(1,500)	18,500
Merchandise inventory		67,200
Prepaid expenses		1,100
Total Current Assets.........................		$98,100

Writing off a bad debt

When an allowance for doubtful accounts is provided, accounts deemed uncollectible are written off against this allowance. For example, after spending a year trying to collect, Alpha Company finally concluded the $100 account of George Vale was uncollectible and made the following entry to write it off:

Jan.	23	Allowance for Doubtful Accounts...................................	100.00	
		Accounts Receivable—George Vale		100.00
		To write off an uncollectible account.		

Posting the entry had this effect on the accounts:

Accounts Receivable				Allowance for Doubtful Accounts			
Dec. 31	20,000	Jan. 23	100	Jan. 23	100	Dec. 31	1,500

Two points should be observed in the entry and accounts. First, although bad debts are an expense of selling on credit, the Allowance for Doubtful Accounts account rather than an expense account is debited in the write-off. The allowance account is debited because the expense was recorded at the end of the period in which the sale occurred. At that time, the loss was foreseen, and the expense was recorded in the estimated bad debts adjusting entry.

Second, although the write-off removed the amount of the account receivable from the ledgers, it did not affect the estimated realizable amount of Alpha Company's accounts receivable, as the following tabulation shows:

	Before Write-off	After Write-off
Accounts receivable	$20,000	$19,900
Less allowance for doubtful accounts	1,500	1,400
Estimated realizable accounts receivable	$18,500	$18,500

Bad debts written off seldom equal the allowance provided

The uncollectible accounts from a given year's sales seldom, if ever, exactly equal the allowance provided for their loss. If accounts written off are less than the allowance provided, the allowance account reaches the end of the year with a credit balance. On the other hand, if accounts written off exceed the allowance provided, the allowance account reaches the period end with a debit balance, which is then eliminated with the new bad debts adjusting entry. In either case no harm is done if the allowance provided is approximately equal to the bad debts written off and is neither continually excessive nor insufficient.

Often when the addition to the allowance for doubtful accounts is based on a percentage of sales, the passage of several accounting periods is required before it becomes apparent the percentage is either too large or too small. In such cases when it becomes apparent the percentage is incorrect, a change in the percentage should be made.

Bad debt recoveries

Frequently an error in judgment is made in regard to a customer's ability to pay his past-due account. As a result, accounts written off as uncollectible are later sometimes collected in full or in part. If an account is written off as uncollectible and later the customer pays part or all of the amount previously written off, the payment should be shown in the customer's account for future credit action. It should be shown because when a customer fails to pay and his account is written off, the customer's credit standing is impaired; and later when the customer pays the amount previously written off, the payment helps restore the credit standing. When an account previously written off as a bad debt is collected, two entries are made. The first reinstates the customer's account and has the effect of reversing the original write-off. The second entry records the collection of the reinstated account.

For example, if George Vale, whose account was written off by Alpha Company (page 277) on January 23, pays in full on August 15, the entries in general journal form to record the bad debt recovery are:

Aug.	15	Accounts Receivable—George Vale	100.00	
		Allowance for Doubtful Accounts..........................		100.00
		To reinstate the account of George Vale written off on January 23.		
	15	Cash..	100.00	
		Accounts Receivable—George Vale		100.00
		In full of account.		

In this case George Vale paid the entire amount previously written off. Sometimes after an account is written off the customer will pay a portion of the amount owed. The question then arises, should the entire balance of his account be returned to accounts receivable or just the amount paid? The answer is a matter of judgment. If it is thought the customer will pay in full, the entire amount owed should be returned to accounts receivable. However, only the amount paid should be returned if it is thought that no more will be collected.

Other bases for estimating bad debts

As previously explained, the relationship between charge sales and past bad debt losses is often used in estimating losses from uncollectible accounts. Too, when the proportion of credit sales to cash sales remains about the same, total sales rather than charge sales may be used. Likewise, in companies where about the same percentage of accounts receivable prove uncollectible each year, a percentage of the year-end balance of the Accounts Receivable account may be set up as the estimated bad debts expense.

Aging accounts receivable

In estimating bad debt losses, many companies age their accounts receivable. This consists of preparing a schedule of accounts receivable with the accounts listed and their balances entered in columns according to age, as in Illustration 8–2. After such a schedule is prepared, responsible and experienced executives of the sales and credit departments examine each account listed thereon and from experience and

Schedule of Accounts Receivable by Age					
Customer's Name	Not Due	1 to 30 Days Past Due	31 to 60 Days Past Due	61 to 90 Days Past Due	Over 90 Days Past Due
Charles Abbot	45.00				
Frank Allen	53.00				
George Arden			14.00		
Paul Baum					27.00

Illustration 8–2

by judgment decide which are probably uncollectible. Normally, most of the accounts on the schedule are current and not past due; these are examined for possible losses but receive less scrutiny than past-due accounts. The older accounts are more apt to prove uncollectible; these receive the greatest attention. After decisions are made as to which accounts are probably uncollectible, the allowance for doubtful accounts is adjusted to provide for them.

To illustrate this adjustment, assume that a company has $60,000 of accounts receivable at the end of an accounting period and in aging these accounts its executives estimate that accounts totaling $1,950 are probably uncollectible. Assume further that the company has a $250 credit balance in its allowance account. Under these assumptions the company will make the following adjusting entry to increase the balance of the allowance account to the amount needed to provide for the estimated uncollectible accounts:

Dec.	31	Bad Debts Expense...	1,700.00	
		Allowance for Doubtful Accounts..........................		1,700.00
		To increase the allowance for doubtful accounts to $1,950.		

The $1,700 credit of the illustrated entry increases the balance of the allowance account to the $1,950 needed to provide for the estimated bad debts. If it had been assumed that the allowance account had a $150 debit balance before adjustment, rather than the assumed $250 credit balance, it would have been necessary to increase the entry amounts to $2,100 ($150 + $1,950) in order to bring the account balance up to the required amount.

Aging accounts receivable and increasing the allowance for doubtful accounts to an amount sufficient to provide for the accounts deemed uncollectible has two things in its favor. (1) When accounts receivable are aged, an excessive or an inadequate provision for bad debts in one period is automatically adjusted in the next; and as a result, the balance of the allowance account never builds up to an excessive amount, as sometimes happens when it is increased each period by a percent of sales. (2) The aging method also normally provides a better balance sheet figure than does the percent of sales method, a figure closer to realizable value. However, the aging method may not as closely match revenues and expenses as the percent of sales method.

Direct write-off of bad debts

Since the allowance method of accounting for bad debts better fulfills the requirements of the *matching principle,* it is the method that should be used in most cases. However, under certain circumstances another method, called the *direct write-off method,* may be used. Under the direct write-off method, when it is decided that an account is uncollectible, it is written off directly to the Bad Debts Expense account with an entry like this:

Nov.	23	Bad Debts Expense..	52.50	
		Accounts Receivable—Dale Hall		52.50
		To write off the uncollectible account.		

The debit of the entry charges the bad debt loss directly to the current year's Bad Debts Expense account, and the credit removes the balance of the account from the subsidiary ledger and controlling account.

If an account previously written off directly to the Bad Debts Expense account is later collected in full, the following entries in general journal form are used to record the bad debt recovery.

Mar.	11	Accounts Receivable—Dale Hall	52.50	
		Bad Debts Expense...		52.50
		To reinstate the account of Dale Hall previously written off.		
	11	Cash...	52.50	
		Accounts Receivable—Dale Hall		52.50
		In full of account.		

The entry to reinstate the Dale Hall account assumes collection in the year following the write-off and that the Bad Debts Expense account has a debit balance from other write-offs during the year. If the account has no balance from other write-offs and no write-offs are expected, the credit of the entry could be to a revenue account called, for example, Bad Debt Recoveries.

Direct write-off mismatches revenues and expenses

Since a bad debt loss occurs at the moment of a sale to a customer who will not pay but the bad debt cannot be identified until as much as a year or more later when every effort to collect has failed, it follows that the direct write-off method commonly mismatches revenues and expenses. It mismatches revenues and expenses because the revenue from a bad debt sale appears on the income statement of one year while the expense of the loss is deducted on the income statement of the following or a later year.

When direct write-off is permissible

Although the direct write-off method commonly fails in fulfilling the requirements of the *matching principle,* it may still be used in situations where its use does not materially affect reported net income. For example, it may be used in a store where substantially all sales are for cash and bad debt losses from a few charge sales are immaterial in relation to total sales and net income. In such a store the use of direct write-off comes under the accounting *principle of materiality*.

The principle of materiality

Under the accounting *principle of materiality* it is held that a strict adherence to any accounting principle, in this case the *matching principle,* is not required when adherence is relatively difficult or expensive and the lack of adherence does not materially affect reported net income. Or in other words, failure to adhere is permissible when the failure does not produce an error or misstatement sufficiently large as to influence a financial statement reader's judgment of a given situation.

Glossary

Aging accounts receivable. Preparing a schedule listing accounts receivable by the number of days each account has been unpaid.

Allowance for doubtful accounts. The estimated amount of accounts receivable that will prove uncollectible.

Allowance method of accounting for bad debts. The accounting procedure whereby an estimate is made at the end of each accounting period of the portion of the period's credit sales that will prove uncollectible, and an entry is made to charge this estimated amount to an expense account and to an allowance account against which actual uncollectible accounts can be written off.

Bad debt. An uncollectible account receivable.

Bank discount. The amount of interest a bank deducts in lending money.

Contingent liability. A potential liability that may become an actual liability if certain events occur.

Direct write-off method of accounting for bad debts. The accounting procedure whereby uncollectible accounts are written off directly to an expense account.

Discount period of a note. The number of days for which a note is discounted.

Discounting a note receivable. Selling a note receivable to a bank or other concern.

Dishonoring a note. Refusing to pay a promissory note on its due date.

Full-disclosure principle. The accounting rule requiring that financial statements and their accompanying notes disclose all information of a material nature relating to the financial position and

operating results of the company for which the statements are
prepared.

Holder in due course. One who gives something of value for a negotiable instrument before maturity and without knowledge of any
defect in the title of the previous holder.

Maker of a note. One who signs a note and promises to pay it at maturity.

Materiality principle. The accounting rule that a strict adherence to
any accounting principle is not required when adherence is relatively difficult or expensive and lack of adherence will not materially affect reported net income.

Maturity date of a note. The date on which a note and any interest are
due and payable.

Maturity value of a note. Principle of the note plus any interest due on
the note's maturity date.

Negotiable instrument. A document to which ownership is readily
changed, usually by endorsement and delivery, but sometimes by
delivery only.

Notes receivable discounted. The amount of notes receivable that have
been discounted or sold.

Notice of protest. A document that gives notice that a promissory note
was presented for payment on its due date and payment was refused.

Payee of a note. The one to whom a promissory note is made payable.

Proceeds of a discounted note. The maturity value of a note minus any
interest deducted because of its being discounted before maturity.

Protest fee. The fee charged for preparing and issuing a notice of protest.

Questions for
class
discussion

1. Why does a business prefer a note receivable to an account receivable?
2. Define:

a. Promissory note.	*g.* Discount period of a note.
b. Payee of a note.	*h.* Maker of a note.
c. Maturity date.	*i.* Principal of a note.
d. Dishonored note.	*j.* Maturity value.
e. Notice of protest.	*k.* Contingent liability.
f. Holder in due course.	*l.* Protest fee.

3. What are the due dates of the following notes: (*a*) a 90-day note dated
   June 10, (*b*) a 60-day note dated May 13, and (*c*) a 90-day note dated
   November 12?
4. Distinguish between bank discount and cash discount.
5. If the following accounts and balances appear in a ledger:

Notes Receivable		Notes Receivable Discounted	
Bal. 8,500			Bal. 5,200

    a. How many dollars of notes receivable are in the hands of the company?

    b. How many dollars of notes have been discounted?

    c. What is the contingent liability of the company?

6. What does the full-disclosure principle require in a company's accounting statements?

7. At what point in the selling-collecting procedures of a company does a bad debt loss occur?

8. In estimating bad debt losses it is commonly assumed that "history will repeat." How is this assumption used in estimating bad debt losses?

9. A company had $484,000 of charge sales in a year. How many dollars of bad debt losses may the company expect to experience from these sales if its past bad debt losses have averaged one fourth of 1% of charge sales?

10. What is a contra account? Why are estimated bad debt losses credited to a contra account rather than to the Accounts Receivable controlling account?

11. Classify the following accounts: (*a*) Accounts Receivable, (*b*) Allowance for Doubtful Accounts, and (*c*) Bad Debts Expense.

12. Explain why writing off a bad debt against the allowance account does not reduce the estimated realizable amount of a company's accounts receivable.

13. Why does the direct write-off method of accounting for bad debts commonly fail in matching revenues and expenses?

14. What is the essence of the accounting principle of materiality?

Class exercises

Exercise 8–1

    Prepare general journal entries to record these transactions:

Mar. 3 Accepted a $600, 60-day, 7% note dated this day from Earl Kane in granting a time extension on his past-due account.

May 2 Earl Kane dishonored his note when presented for payment.

Dec. 31 After exhausting all legal means of collecting, wrote off the account of Earl Kane against the allowance for doubtful accounts.

Exercise 8–2

    Prepare general journal entries to record these transactions:

June 7 Sold merchandise to Jerry Hill, $1,200, terms 2/10, n/60.

Aug. 12 Received $200 in cash and a $1,000, 60-day, 6% note dated August 10 in granting a time extension on the amount due from Jerry Hill.

    16 Discounted the Jerry Hill note at the bank at 7%.

Oct. 14 Since notice protesting the Jerry Hill note had not been received, assumed it paid and canceled the discount liability.

Exercise 8–3

Prepare general journal entries to record these transactions:

Aug. 15   Accepted a $1,500, 60-day, 6% note dated August 13 from Dale
           Ball in granting a time extension on his past-due account.
     25   Discounted the Dale Ball note at the bank at 6%.
Oct. 13   Received notice protesting the Dale Ball note. Paid the bank the
           maturity value of the note plus a $5 protest fee and canceled the
           discount liability.
Nov. 11   Received payment from Dale Ball of the maturity value of his dis-
           honored note, the protest fee, and interest at 6% on both for 30
           days beyond maturity.

Exercise 8–4

On July 6 Tri-City Sales sold Robert Todd merchandise having a $1,500
catalog list price, less a 20% trade discount, 2/10, n/60. Todd was unable to
pay and was granted a time extension on receipt of his 60-day, 6% note for
the amount of the debt, dated September 10. Tri-City Sales held the note
until October 16, when it discounted the note at its bank at 6%. The note
was not protested. Answer these questions:

a.   How many dollars of trade discount were granted on the sale?
b.   How many dollars of cash discount could Todd have earned?
c.   What was the maturity date of the note?
d.   How many days were in the discount period?
e.   How much bank discount was deducted by the bank?
f.   What were the proceeds of the discounted note?
g.   What was the last entry made by Tri-City Sales in recording the trans-
     actions of this sale and ultimate payment by Todd?

Exercise 8–5

On December 31, at the end of its annual accounting period, a company
estimated it would lose as bad debts an amount equal to one fourth of 1%
of its $648,000 of charge sales made during the year, and it made an ad-
dition to its allowance for doubtful accounts equal to that amount. On the
following May 10 it decided the $110 account of Albert Lee was uncollectible
and wrote it off as a bad debt. Two months later, on July 10, Mr. Lee unex-
pectedly paid the amount previously written off. Give the required entries in
general journal form to record these transactions.

Exercise 8–6

At the end of each year a company ages its accounts receivable and increases its allowance for doubtful accounts by an amount sufficient to provide
for the estimated uncollectible accounts. At the end of last year it estimated
it would not be able to collect $3,400 of its total accounts receivable. (*a*)
Give the entry to increase the allowance account under the assumption it had
a $150 credit balance before the adjustment. (*b*) Give the entry under the as-
sumption the allowance account had a $225 debit balance before the adjust-
ment.

Problems

Problem 8–1

Prepare entries in general journal form to record these transactions:

Jan.   3   Accepted $200 in cash and a $1,000, 60-day, 6½% note from Carl Moss in granting a time extension on his past-due account.

Feb. 28   Sent the Carl Moss note to Security Bank for collection.

Mar. 6   Received a credit memorandum from Security Bank for the maturity value of the Carl Moss note, less a $4 collection fee.

      10   Accepted an $1,800, 60-day, 6% note from Ted Lee in granting a time extension on his past-due account. The note was dated March 8.

      14   Discounted the Ted Lee note at the bank at 7%.

May 11   Since notice protesting the Ted Lee note had not been received, assumed that it had been paid and canceled the discount liability.

      15   Accepted a $2,400, 60-day 6% note dated May 12 from Gary Nash in granting a time extension on his past-due account.

June 11   Discounted the Gary Nash note at the bank at 7%.

July 12   Received notice protesting the Gary Nash note. Paid the bank the maturity value of the note plus a $5 protest fee and canceled the discount liability.

Aug. 10   Accepted a $600, 60-day, 7% note from Fred Ball in granting a time extension on his past-due account.

Oct.   9   Fred Ball dishonored his note when it was presented for payment.

Dec. 26   Decided the accounts of Gary Nash and Fred Ball were uncollectible and wrote them off against the allowance for doubtful accounts.

Problem 8–2

Prepare entries in general journal form to record these transactions:

Dec.   7   Accepted $300 in cash and a $2,500, 60-day, 6% note dated this day from Ned Ross in granting a time extension on his past-due account.

Dec. 31   Made an adjusting entry to record the accrued interest on the Ned Ross note.

      31   Made an adjusting entry to increase the allowance for doubtful accounts by an amount equal to one third of 1% of the year's $864,000 of charge sales.

Feb.   5   Received payment from Ned Ross of the maturity value of his $2,500 note.

Mar. 2   Accepted a $2,000, 60-day, 6% note from John Ellis in granting a time extension on his past-due account. The note was dated March 1.

       7   Discounted the John Ellis note at the bank at 7%.

May   1   Received notice protesting the John Ellis note. Paid the bank the maturity value of the note plus a $4 protest fee and canceled the discount liability.

      31   Received payment from John Ellis of the maturity value of his dishonored note, the protest fee, and interest on both for 30 days beyond maturity at 6%.

June 10 Decided the $425 account of Walter Sears was uncollectible and wrote it off as a bad debt.

July   8 Accepted a $1,200, 90-day, 6% note dated July 6 from Harold Jones in granting a time extension on his past-due account.

Aug.   5 Discounted the Harold Jones note at the bank at 7%.

    27 Walter Sears unexpectedly paid the $425 account written off on June 10.

Oct.   7 Since notice protesting the Harold Jones note had not been received, assume it paid and canceled the discount liability.

Dec. 28 Decided the $2,150 account of Gary Hill was uncollectible and wrote it off as a bad debt.

Problem 8–3

Prepare entries in general journal form to record these transactions:

Nov. 25 Accepted an $1,800, 60-day, 6% note dated this day in granting a time extension on the past-due account of Earl Larr.

Dec. 31 Made an adjusting entry to record the accrued interest on the Earl Larr note.

Jan. 24 Received payment of the maturity value of the Earl Larr note.

    25 Accepted $265 in cash and a $1,500, 60-day, 6% note from Ted Hall in granting a time extension on his past-due account.

Mar. 24 Sent the Ted Hall note to Security Bank for collection.

    29 Security Bank returned the dishonored note of Ted Hall.

Apr.   5 Accepted an $800, 60-day, 6% note dated April 3 from Carl Jacks in granting a time extension on his past-due account.

     9 Discounted the Carl Jacks note at the bank at 7%.

June   6 Since notice protesting the Carl Jacks note had not been received, assumed it paid and canceled the discount liability.

     8 Accepted a $1,200, 60-day, 6% noted dated June 7 in granting a time extension on the past-due account of Larry Moss.

July   7 Discounted the Larry Moss note at the bank at 7%.

Aug.   7 Received a notice protesting the Larry Moss note. Paid the bank the maturity value of the note plus a $3 protest fee and canceled the discount liability.

Oct.   6 Received payment from Larry Moss of the maturity value of his dishonored note plus the protest fee and interest on both at 6% for 60 days beyond maturity.

Dec. 27 Decided the dishonored note of Ted Hall was uncollectible and wrote its maturity value off against the allowance for doubtful accounts.

Problem 8–4

Prepare entries in general journal form to record these transactions:

Dec. 16 Accepted $220 in cash and a $3,000, 60-day 6% note dated this day in granting a time extension on the past-due account of Jerry Neal.

    31 Made an adjusting entry to increase the allowance for doubtful accounts an amount equal to one fourth of 1% of the year's $868,000 of charge sales.

Dec. 31 Made an adjusting entry to record the accrued interest on the Jerry Neal note.

Jan. 21 Discounted the Jerry Neal Note at the bank at 7%.

Feb. 15 Received notice protesting the Jerry Neal note. Paid the bank the maturity value of the note plus a $5 protest fee and canceled the discount liability.

Apr. 15 · Received payment from Jerry Neal of the maturity value of his dishonored note, the protest fee, and interest on both for 60 days beyond maturity at 6%.

20 Accepted a $2,400, 90-day, 6% note dated this day in granting a time extension on the past-due account of Fred Ball.

June 19 Discounted the Fred Ball note at the bank at 7%.

July 23 Since notice protesting the Fred Ball note had not been received, assumed it paid and canceled the discount liability.

Aug. 1 Accepted $2,100, 60-day, 6% note dated July 30 in granting a time extension on the past-due account of Joel Kane.

5 Discounted the Joel Kane note at the bank at 7%.

Sept. 29 Received a notice protesting the Joel Kane note. Paid the bank the maturity value of the note plus a $5 protest fee and canceled the discount liability.

Dec. 27 Wrote off the uncollectible account of Joel Kane against the allowance for doubtful accounts.

Problem 8–5

A company's Allowance for Doubtful Accounts had a $115 credit balance on December 31, at the end of last year. On that day and during the current year it completed these transactions:

Dec. 31 Provided an addition to its allowance for doubtful accounts equal to one fourth of 1% of the year's $864,000 of charge sales.

31 Closed the Bad Debts Expense account.

Feb. 12 Learned of the bankruptcy of Larry Vale and made a claim on his receiver in bankruptcy for the $340 owed by Mr. Vale for merchandise purchased on credit during the previous year.

Mar. 10 Learned that Earl Hill had gone out of business, leaving no assets to attach. Wrote off his $215 account as a bad debt.

May 15 Accepted $285 in cash and an $800, 60-day, 6% note dated May 13 in granting Harold Kane a time extension on his past-due account.

28 Discounted the Harold Kane note at the bank at 7%.

July 15 Received notice protesting the Harold Kane note. Paid the bank the maturity value of the note plus a $4 protest fee and canceled the discount liability.

Aug. 10 Earl Hill paid $100 of the amount written off on March 10. In a letter accompanying the payment, he said his finances had improved and he expected to pay the balance owed in the near future.

Oct. 5 Received $85 from Larry Vale's receiver in bankruptcy. A letter accompanying the payment said that no more would be paid. Recorded receipt of the $85 and wrote off the remaining amount owed.

20 Decided the account of Harold Kane was uncollectible and wrote it off as a bad debt.

Dec. 20 Made a compound entry to write off these accounts: James Wells, $395; Robert Bell, $480; and Terry Neal, $380.

   31 Made an addition to the allowance for doubtful accounts equal to one fourth of 1% of the year's $964,000 of charge sales.

   31 Closed the Bad Debts Expense account.

Required:

1. Open accounts for Allowance for Doubtful Accounts and Bad Debts Expense. Enter the $115 credit balance in the allowance account. Prepare general journal entries to record the transactions and post the portions affecting the two accounts.

2. Prepare an alternate bad debts adjusting entry for the second December 31 of the problem under the assumption that rather than providing an addition to its allowance account equal to one fourth of 1% of charge sales, the company aged its accounts, estimated that $2,110 of accounts were probably uncollectible, and increased its allowance to provide for them.

Problem 8–1A   Alternate

   Prepare entries in general journal form to record these transactions: problems

Jan. 5 Sold merchandise to Terry Blue, terms: $315 in cash and a $750, 60-day, 6% note.

Mar. 3 Sent the Terry Blue note to Security Bank for collection.

   8 Received a $754 credit memorandum from Security Bank, the proceeds of the Terry Blue note less a $3.50 collection charge.

   11 Accepted an $1,800, 60-day, 6% note dated March 9 in granting a time extension on the past-due account of Jerry Drake.

   15 Discounted the Jerry Drake note at the bank at 7%.

May 9 Received notice protesting the Jerry Drake note. Paid the bank the maturity value of the note plus a $5 protest fee and canceled the discount liability.

July 7 Received payment from Jerry Drake of the maturity value of his dishonored note, the protest fee, and interest on both for 60 days beyond maturity at 6%.

   14 Accepted $445 in cash and a $1,200, 90-day, 6% note dated July 13 in granting a time extension on the past-due account of Ted Cross.

Sept. 11 Discounted the Ted Cross note at the bank at 7%.

Oct. 15 Since notice protesting the Ted Cross note had not been received, assume it paid and canceled the discount liability.

   17 Accepted an $800, 30-day, 6% note dated October 16 from Ned Small in granting a time extension on his past-due account.

   31 Discounted the Ned Small note at the bank at 6%.

Nov. 16 Received notice protesting the Ned Small note. Paid the bank the maturity value of the note plus a $3.50 protest fee and canceled the discount liability.

Dec. 28 Wrote off the uncollectible account of Ned Small against the allowance for doubtful accounts.

Problem 8–2A

Prepare entries in general journal form to record these transactions:

Dec. 1 Accepted an $1,800, 60-day, 6% note dated this day in granting a time extension on the past-due account of Lee Ross.

31 Made an adjusting entry to record the accrued interest on the Lee Ross note.

31 Made an adjusting entry to increase the allowance for doubtful accounts by an amount equal to one third of 1% of the year's $825,000 of charge sales.

Jan. 10 Discounted the Lee Ross note at the bank at 7%.

31 Received notice protesting the Lee Ross note. Paid the bank the maturity value of the note plus a $5 protest fee and canceled the discount liability.

Mar. 11 Received payment from Lee Ross of the maturity value of his dishonored note, the protest fee, and interest on both at 6% for 40 days beyond maturity.

Apr. 4 Accepted a $2,700, 60-day, 6% note dated April 1 in granting a time extension on the past-due account of Dale Parr.

7 Discounted the Dale Parr note at the bank at 7%.

June 2 Received notice protesting the Dale Parr note. Paid the bank the maturity value of the note plus a $5 protest fee and canceled the discount liability.

July 3 Accepted $235 in cash and a $1,600, 90-day, 6% note dated July 2 in granting a time extension on the past-due account of Carl Lane.

Aug. 31 Discounted the Carl Lane note at the bank at 7%.

Oct. 2 Since notice protesting the Carl Lane note had not been received, assume it paid and canceled the discount liability.

Dec. 27 Judged the Dale Parr account uncollectible and wrote it off as a bad debt.

Problem 8–3A

Prepare entries in general journal form to record these transactions:

Dec. 15 Accepted $450 in cash and a $2,400, 60-day, 6% note dated December 13 from Allen Hall in granting a time extension on his past-due account.

31 Made an adjusting entry to record the accrued interest on the Allen Hall note.

Jan. 12 Discounted the Allen Hall note at the bank at 7%.

Feb. 13 Received notice protesting the Allen Hall note. Paid the bank the maturity value of the note plus a $4 protest fee and canceled the discount liability.

Mar. 16 Received payment from Allen Hall of the maturity value of his dishonored note, the protest fee, and interest on both at 6% for 30 days beyond maturity.

18 Sold Ned Otis merchandise on terms of $235 in cash and a $1,200, 90-day, 6% note dated this day.

June 14 Sent the Ned Otis note to the bank for collection.

18 The bank returned the Ned Otis note because it had been dishonored.

June 18 Accepted a $1,500, 60-day, 6% note dated June 17 from Lee Moss in granting a time extension on his past-due account.

Aug. 12 Sent the Lee Moss note to the bank for collection.

17 Received a $1,512 credit memorandum from the bank, the proceeds of the Lee Moss note less a collection charge.

20 Accepted a $1,400, 60-day, 6% note dated this day from Carl Fry in granting a time extension on his past-due account.

Oct. 19 Carl Fry dishonored his note when presented for payment.

Dec. 6 Learned of the bankruptcy of Ned Otis and wrote off his account and the account of Carl Fry against the allowance for doubtful accounts.

Problem 8–4A

Prepare entries in general journal form to record these transactions:

Nov. 25 Accepted $545 in cash and a $1,600, 90-day, 6% note dated this day from Dale Byrd in granting a time extension on his past-due account.

Dec. 31 Made an adjusting entry to record the accrued interest on the Dale Byrd note.

Jan. 18 Discounted the Dale Byrd note at the bank at 7%.

Feb. 24 Received notice protesting the Dale Byrd note. Paid the bank the maturity value of the note plus a $5 protest fee and canceled the discount liability.

Mar. 3 Sold merchandise to Walter Dent, terms: $185 in cash and a $1,200, 90-day, 6% note dated this day.

9 Discounted the Walter Dent note at the bank at 7%.

June 4 Since notice protesting the Walter Dent note had not been received, assumed it paid and canceled the discount liability.

8 Accepted a $1,250, 60-day, 6% note dated June 6 from Lee Fox in granting a time extension on his past-due account.

Aug. 2 Sent the Lee Fox note to the bank for collection.

8 Received a $1,259 credit memorandum from the bank, the proceeds of the Lee Fox note less the collection charge.

10 Accepted $2,400, 60-day, 6% note from Ned Poe in granting a time extension on his past-due account. The note was dated August 9.

Sept. 2 Discounted the Ned Poe note at the bank at 7%.

Oct. 9 Received notice protesting the Ned Poe note. Paid the bank the maturity value of the note plus a $4 protest fee and canceled the discount liability.

Dec. 7 Received payment from Ned Poe of the maturity value of his dishonored note, the protest fee, and interest on both at 6% for 60 days beyond maturity.

27 Wrote off the Dale Byrd account against the allowance for doubtful accounts.

Problem 8–5A

A company completed these transactions during a 15-month period:

Oct. 12 Sold merchandise to Ted Post, $985, terms 2/10, n/60.

Dec. 17 Accepted $185 in cash and an $800, 60-day, 6% note dated De-

cember 16 in granting a time extension on the past-due account of
Ted Post.

Dec. 31 Recorded the accrued interest on the Ted Post note.
     31 An examination showed a $115 credit balance in the Allowance for
         Doubtful Accounts account. Provided an addition to the allowance
         equal to one fourth of 1% of the year's $776,000 of charge sales.
     31 Closed the Bad Debts Expense account.
Jan. 9 Discounted the Ted Post note at Security Bank at 7%.
Feb. 8 Learned of the bankruptcy of Jerry Nash and made a claim on his
         receiver in bankruptcy for the $480 owed by Mr. Nash for mer-
         chandise purchased during the previous year.
     15 Received notice protesting the Ted Post note. Paid the bank the
         maturity value of the note plus a $4 protest fee and canceled the
         discount liability.
Apr. 11 After making every effort to collect, decided the $335 account of
         Lee Wolf was uncollectible and wrote if off as a bad debt.
Aug. 15 Lee Wolf walked into the store and paid $135 of the amount written
         off in April. He said that his financial position had improved and
         that he expected to pay the balance of his account within a short
         time.
Oct. 15 Decided the dishonored note of Ted Post was uncollectible and
         wrote off his account as a bad debt.
     20 Received $120 from Jerry Nash's receiver in bankruptcy. A letter
         accompanying the payment said that no more would be paid. Made
         an entry to record receipt of the cash and to write off the remainder
         owed.
Dec. 22 Made a compound entry to write off the account of Larry Baker,
         $375, and the account of Jerry Davis, $560.
     31 Provided an addition to the allowance for doubtful accounts equal
         to one fourth of 1% of the year's $852,000 of charge sales.
     31 Closed the Bad Debts Expense account.

Required:

1. Open an Allowance for Doubtful Accounts account and a Bad Debts Ex-
    pense account. Enter the $115 credit balance in the allowance account and
    prepare general journal entries to record the transactions. Post those en-
    try portions that affect the two accounts.
2. Prepare an alternate bad debts adjusting entry for the second December 31
    of the problem under the assumption that rather than providing an addi-
    tion to the allowance account equal to one fourth of 1% of charge sales,
    the company aged its accounts, estimated that $1,970 of accounts were
    probably uncollectible, and increased its allowance to provide for them.

**Decision
problem 8–1,
embezzlement**

When his CPA arrived early in January to begin the annual audit, Walter
Morse, the owner of Canyon Sales, asked him to give special attention to the
accounts receivable. Two things caused this request: (1) During the previous
week Mr. Morse had encountered Charles Berg, a former customer, on the
street, and had asked him about his account which had recently been written
off as uncollectible. Mr. Berg had indignantly replied that he had paid his $255

account in full, and he later produced canceled checks endorsed by Canyon Sales to prove it. (2) The income statement prepared for the quarter ended the previous December 31 showed an unusually large volume of sales returns. The bookkeeper who had prepared the statement was a new employee, having begun work on October 1, after being hired on the basis of out-of-town letters of reference. In addition to doing all the record keeping, the bookkeeper also acts as cashier, receiving and depositing the cash from both cash sales and that received through the mail.

In the course of his investigation, the auditor prepared from the company's records the following analysis of the accounts receivable for the period October 1 through December 31:

	Arne	Berg	Cary	Dent	Eads	Fish	Glen
Balance, October 1	$210	$125	$345	$250	$130	$545	$410
Sales	695	130	530		660	420	575
Total	$905	$255	$875	$250	$790	$965	$985
Collections	(510)		(395)		(410)	(490)	(615)
Returns	(85)	(45)	(40)		(80)	(60)	(25)
Bad debts written off		(210)		(250)			
Balance, December 31	$310	-0-	$440	-0-	$300	$415	$345

The auditor communicated with all charge customers and learned that although their account balances as of December 31 agreed with the amounts shown in the company's records, the individual transactions did not. They reported credit purchases totaling $3,435 during the three-month period and $85 of returns for which credit had been granted. Correspondence with Mr. Dent, the customer whose $250 account had been written off, revealed that he had become bankrupt and his creditor claims had been settled by his receiver in bankruptcy at $0.22 on the dollar. The checks had been mailed by his receiver on October 30, and all had been paid and returned by the bank, properly endorsed by the recipients.

Under the assumption the bookkeeper has embezzled cash from the company, determine the total amount he has taken and attempted to conceal with false accounts receivable entries. Account for the deficiency by listing the concealment methods used and the amount he attempted to conceal with each method. Also outline an internal control system that will help protect the company's cash from future embezzlement. Assume the company is small and can have only one office employee who must do all the bookkeeping.

Al Nevin has operated Sport Shop for five years and has been aggressive in expanding its business. Three years ago he liberalized the shop's credit policy in an effort to increase sales. Sales have increased, but now Al is concerned with the effects of the more liberal credit policy. Bad debts written off (the store uses the direct write-off method) have increased materially in the last two years, and now Al wonders if the sales increase justifies the substantial bad debt losses which he is certain have resulted from the more liberal credit policy.

An examination of the shop's income statements, bad debts losses, and accounts receivable for the five years revealed:

Decision problem 8–2, Sport Shop

	1st Year	2d Year	3d Year	4th Year	5th Year
Credit sales	$100,000	$110,000	$150,000	$180,000	$200,000
Cost of goods sold	60,000	66,200	89,900	108,300	120,100
Gross profit from sales	$ 40,000	$ 43,800	$ 60,100	$ 71,700	$ 79,900
Expenses other than bad debts	30,000	32,900	45,200	53,800	60,000
Income before bad debts	$ 10,000	$ 10,900	$ 14,900	$ 17,900	$ 19,900
Bad debts written off	100	440	750	2,340	2,400
Net Income	$ 9,900	$ 10,460	$ 14,150	$ 15,560	$ 17,500
Bad debts by year of sales	$ 400	$ 330	$ 1,950	$ 2,160	$ 2,800

The last line in the tabulation results from reclassifying bad debt losses by the years in which the sales that resulted in the losses were made. Consequently, the $2,800 of fifth-year losses includes $1,610 of estimated bad debts that are still in the accounts receivable.

Prepare a schedule showing in columns by years: income before bad debt losses, bad debts incurred, and net income. Then below the net income figures show for each year bad debts written off as a percentage of sales followed on the next line by bad debts incurred as a percentage of sales. Also prepare a report for Mr. Nevin answering his concern about the new credit policy and recommending any changes you consider desirable in his accounting for bad debts.

**After studying Chapter 9,
you should be able to:**

■ Calculate the cost of an inventory based on (*a*) specific invoice prices, (*b*) weighted-average cost, (*c*) Fifo, and (*d*) Lifo.

■ Explain the income tax effect of the use of Lifo.

■ Tell what is required by the accounting principle of consistency and why the application of this principle is important.

■ Tell what is required of a concern when it changes its accounting procedures.

■ Tell what is required by the accounting principle of conservatism.

■ Explain the effect of an inventory error on the income statements of the current and succeeding years.

■ Tell how a perpetual inventory system operates.

■ Estimate an inventory by the retail method and by the gross profit method.

■ Define or explain the words and phrases listed in the chapter Glossary.

chapter 9

Inventories and cost of goods sold

A merchandising business earns revenue by selling merchandise, and for such a concern the phrase *merchandise inventory* is used to describe the aggregate of the items of tangible personal property it holds for sale. As a rule the items are sold within a year or one cycle; consequently, the inventory is a current asset, usually the largest current asset on a merchandising concern's balance sheet.

An AICPA committee said: "A major objective of accounting for inventories is the proper determination of income through the process of matching appropriate costs against revenues."[1] The matching process referred to is one with which the student is already somewhat familiar. For inventories, it consists of determining how much of the cost of the goods that were available for sale during a period should be deducted from the period's revenue from sales and how much should be carried forward as inventory to be matched against a future period's revenue.

Matching merchandise costs with revenues

The cost of the goods that were for sale during an accounting period may be determined from the accounting records by adding to the cost of the beginning inventory the cost of goods purchased during the period. But, since most concerns do not keep a record of the cost of the goods sold during a period, normally cost of goods sold cannot be determined from accounting records but must be ascertained by separating cost of goods for sale into cost of goods sold and cost of goods unsold.

In separating goods available for sale into its components of goods sold and goods not sold, the key problem is that of assigning a cost to the goods not sold or to the ending inventory. However, it should be

---

[1] Committee on Accounting Procedures, "Accounting Research Bulletin No. 43," *Accounting Research and Terminology Bulletins, Final Edition* (New York: AICPA, 1961), p. 28.

constantly borne in mind that the procedures for assigning a cost to the ending inventory are also the means of determining cost of goods sold, because whatever portion of the cost of goods for sale is assigned to the ending inventory, the remainder goes into cost of goods sold.

Assigning a cost to the ending inventory

Assigning a cost to the ending inventory normally involves two problems: (1) determining the quantity of each product on hand and (2) pricing the products.

The quantity of unsold merchandise on hand at the end of an accounting period is usually determined by a physical inventory. Physical inventories and the way in which such inventories are taken were discussed in Chapter 5; consequently, it is only necessary to repeat that in a physical inventory the unsold merchandise is counted, weighed, or otherwise measured to determine the units, pounds, gallons, board feet, or other measure of each product on hand.

After an inventory is counted, weighed, or otherwise measured, the units are priced. Generally, inventories are priced at cost. However, a departure from cost is sometimes necessary when goods have been damaged or have deteriorated. Likewise, a departure from cost is sometimes necessary when replacement costs for inventory items are less than the amounts actually paid for the items when they were purchased.[2] These points are discussed later in this chapter.

Accounting for an inventory at cost

Pricing an inventory at cost is not difficult when costs remain fixed. However, when identical items were purchased during an accounting period at different costs, a problem arises as to which costs apply to the ending inventory and which apply to the goods sold. There are at least four commonly used ways of assigning costs to goods in the ending inventory and to goods sold. They are: (1) specific invoice prices; (2) weighted average cost; (3) first-in, first-out; and (4) last-in, first-out. Each is a *generally accepted accounting procedure.*

To illustrate the four, assume that a company has on hand at the end of an accounting period 12 units of Article X. Also, assume that the company began the year and purchased Article X during the year as follows:

Jan. 1	Beginning inventory	10 units @	$100 =	$1,000
Mar. 13	Purchased	15 units @	108 =	1,620
Aug. 17	Purchased	20 units @	120 =	2,400
Nov. 10	Purchased	10 units @	125 =	1,250
	Total	55 units		$6,270

---

[2] APB, "Basic Concepts and Accounting Principles Underlying Financial Statements of Business Enterprises," *APB Statement No. 4* (New York: AICPA, October 1970), par. 183.

Specific invoice prices

When it is possible to identify each item in an inventory with a specific purchase and its invoice, specific invoice prices may be used to assign costs to the inventory and to the goods sold. For example, if for purposes of illustration it is assumed that 6 of the 12 unsold units of Article X were from the November purchase and 6 were from the August purchase, costs are assigned to the inventory and goods sold by means of specific invoice prices as follows:

Total cost of 55 units available for sale		$6,270
Less ending inventory priced by means of specific invoices:		
6 units from the November purchase at $125 each	$750	
6 units from the August purchase at $120 each..............	720	
12 units in ending inventory..		1,470
Cost of goods sold..		$4,800

Weighted average

Under this method prices for the units in the beginning inventory and in each purchase are weighted by the number of units in the beginning inventory and in each purchase and are averaged to find the weighted average cost per unit as follows:

```
10 units @ $100 = $1,000
15 units @   108 =   1,620
20 units @   120 =   2,400
10 units @   125 =   1,250
55                 $6,270

$6,270 ÷ 55 = $114, weighted average cost per unit
```

After the weighted average cost per unit is determined, this average is used to assign costs to the inventory and the units sold as follows:

Total cost of 55 units available for sale	$6,270
Less ending inventory priced on a weighted average cost basis:	
12 units at $114 each	1,368
Cost of goods sold..	$4,902

First-in, first-out

In a merchandising business clerks are instructed to sell the oldest merchandise first. Consequently, when this instruction is followed, merchandise tends to flow out on a first-in, first-out basis. When first-in, first-out is applied in pricing an inventory, it is assumed that costs follow this pattern, and as a result, the cost of the last items received are assigned to the ending inventory and the remaining costs are assigned to goods sold. When first-in, first-out, or *Fifo* as it is often called from its first letters, is used, costs are assigned to the inventory and to the goods sold as follows:

Total cost of 55 units available for sale............................		$6,270
Less ending inventory priced on a basis of Fifo:		
10 units from the November purchase at $125 each........	$1,250	
2 units from the August purchase at $120 each	240	
12 units in the ending inventory.....................................		1,490
Cost of goods sold...		$4,780

Last-in, first-out

Under this method of inventory pricing, commonly called *Lifo,* the costs of the last goods received are matched with revenue from sales. The theoretical justification for this is that a going concern must at all times keep a certain amount of goods in stock; consequently, when goods are sold, replacements are purchased. Thus it is a sale that causes the replacement of goods; and if costs and revenues are matched, replacement costs should be matched with the sales that induced the acquisitions.

Under Lifo, costs are assigned to the 12 remaining units of Article X and to the goods sold as follows:

Total cost of 55 units available for sale....................		$6,270
Less ending inventory priced on a basis of Lifo:		
10 units in the beginning inventory at $100 each....	$1,000	
2 units from the first purchase at $108 each.........	216	
12 units in the ending inventory...........................		1,216
Cost of goods sold..		$5,054

Notice that this method of matching costs and revenue results in the final inventory being priced at the cost of the oldest 12 units.

Tax effect on Lifo

During periods of rising prices Lifo offers a tax advantage to its users. This advantage arises because when compared with other commonly used methods the application of Lifo results in assigning greatest amounts of costs to goods sold. This in turn results in the smallest reported net incomes and income taxes.

The use of Lifo is not limited to concerns in which goods are actually sold on a last-in, first-out basis. A concern may choose Lifo even though it actually sells goods on a first-in, first-out basis, or on an average basis, as in the case of an oil dealer who pumps new purchases of oil into a storage tank before exhausting his old inventory.

Comparison of methods

In a stable market where prices remain unchanged, the inventory pricing method is of little importance, because when prices are unchanged over a period of time, all methods give the same cost figures. However, in a changing market where prices are rising or falling, each method may give a different result. This may be seen by comparing the costs for the units in the ending inventory and for the units of Article X sold as calculated by the several methods discussed. These costs are:

	Ending Inventory	Cost of Units Sold
Based on specific invoice prices	$1,470	$4,800
Based on weighted average	1,368	4,902
Based on Fifo..........................	1,490	4,780
Based on Lifo..........................	1,216	5,054

Each of the four pricing methods is recognized as a generally accepted accounting procedure for assigning costs to the ending inventory and cost of goods sold, and arguments can be advanced for the use of each. Specific invoice prices exactly match costs and revenues but are of practical use only for relatively high-priced items of which only a few units are kept in stock and sold. Weighted average costs tend to smooth out price fluctuations. The use of Fifo causes the last costs incurred to be assigned to the ending inventory, and thus provides an inventory valuation for the balance sheet that most closely approximates the current replacement cost of the inventory. The use of Lifo causes last costs incurred to be assigned to cost of goods sold, and therefore results in a better matching of current costs with revenues. However, since the method used commonly affects the amounts of reported ending inventory, cost of goods sold, and net income, the *full-disclosure principle* requires that a company show in its statements by means of footnotes or other manner the pricing method used.[3]

Look again at the table of costs for Article X and note that a com-pany can change its reported net income for an accounting period simply by changing its inventory pricing method. However, the change would violate the accounting *principle of consistency* and would make a comparison of the company's inventory and income with previous periods more or less meaningless.

The principle of consistency

As with inventory pricing, more than one generally accepted method or procedure has been derived in accounting practice to account for an

[3] APB, "Disclosure of Accounting Policies," *APB Opinion No. 22* (New York: AICPA, April 1972), pars. 12 and 13.

item or an activity. In each case one method may be considered better for one enterprise, while another may be considered more satisfactory for a concern operating under different circumstances. Nevertheless, while recognizing the validity of different accounting procedures under varying circumstances, the accounting *principle of consistency* requires a consistent application by a company of any selected accounting method or procedure, period after period. As a result of this principle, and in the absence of clear indication to the contrary, a reader of a company's financial statements may assume that in keeping its records and in preparing its statements the company used the same principles and procedures that it used in previous years. Only on the basis of this assumption can meaningful comparisons be made of the data in a company's statements year after year.

Changing accounting procedures

In achieving comparability, the *principle of consistency* does not require that a method or procedure once chosen can never be changed. Rather, if upon additional consideration a company decides that a different acceptable method or procedure from the one in use will better serve its needs, a change may be made. However, when such a change is made, the *full-disclosure principle* requires that the nature of the change, justification for the change, and the effect of the change on net income be disclosed in notes accompanying the statements.[4]

Items included on an inventory

A concern's inventory should include all goods owned by the business and held for sale, regardless of where the goods may be located at the time of the inventory. In the application of this rule, there are generally no problems with respect to most items. For most items all that is required is to see that they are counted, that nothing is omitted, and that nothing is counted more than once. However, goods in transit from a manufacturer or wholesaler, goods sold but not delivered, goods on consignment, and obsolete and damaged goods do require special attention.

When goods are in transit on the inventory date, the purchase should be recorded and the goods should appear on the purchaser's inventory if ownership has passed to the purchaser. The general rule as to the passing of ownership is: if the buyer is responsible for paying the freight charges, ownership passes as soon as the goods are loaded aboard the means of transportation; if the seller is to pay the freight charges, ownership passes when the goods arrive at their destination.

Goods on consignment are goods shipped by their owner (known as the consignor) to another person or firm (called the consignee) who is to sell the goods for the owner. Consigned goods belong to the consignor and should appear on the consignor's inventory.

Damaged goods and goods that have deteriorated or become obsolete should not be placed on the inventory if they are not salable. If

---

[4] APB, "Accounting Changes," *APB Opinion No. 20* (New York: AICPA, July 1971), par. 17.

such goods are salable but at a reduced price, they should be placed on the inventory at a conservative estimate of their realizable value (sale price less the cost of making the sale). This causes the accounting period in which the goods are damaged, deteriorated, or become obsolete to suffer the resultant loss.

The AICPA's Committee on Accounting Procedure said: "As applied to inventories, cost means in principle the sum of the applicable expenditures and charges directly or indirectly incurred in bringing an article to its existing condition and location."[5] Therefore, the cost of an inventory item includes the invoice price, less the discount, plus any additional incidental costs necessary to put the goods into place and condition for sale. The additional incidental costs include import duties, freight and transportation, storage, insurance while being stored or transported, plus any other applicable costs, such as those incurred during an aging process.

Elements of inventory cost

If incurred, any of the foregoing enter into the cost of an inventory. However, in pricing an inventory, most concerns do not take into consideration the incidental costs of acquiring merchandise. They price the inventory on the basis of invoice prices only, and treat all incidental costs of acquiring goods as expenses of the period in which incurred.

Although not correct in theory, treating incidental costs as expenses of the period in which incurred is commonly permissible and often best. In theory a share of each incidental cost should be assigned to every unit purchased, thus causing a portion of each to be carried forward in the inventory to be matched against the revenue of the period in which the inventory is sold. However, the expense of computing costs on such a precise basis usually outweighs any benefit from the extra accuracy. Consequently, when possible, most concerns take advantage of the accounting principle of materiality and treat such costs as expenses of the period in which incurred.

Over the years the traditional rule for pricing inventory items has been "the lower of cost or market," with "cost" being the price that was paid for an item when it was purchased and "market" being the price that would have to be paid to purchase or replace the item on the inventory date. The use of this rule gained its wide acceptance because it placed an inventory on the balance sheet at a conservative figure, the lower of what the inventory cost or its replacement cost on the balance sheet date.

Cost or market, the lower

The argument advanced to support the use of lower of cost or market was that if the replacement cost of an inventory item had declined, then its selling price would probably have to be reduced, and since this might result in a loss, the loss should be anticipated and

---

[5] *Accounting Research and Terminology Bulletins, Final Edition*, p. 28.

taken in the year of the price decline. It was a good argument. However, since selling prices do not always exactly and quickly follow cost prices, the application of the rule often resulted in misstating net income in the year of a price decline and again in the succeeding year. For example, suppose that a firm purchased merchandise costing $1,000; marked it up to a $1,500 selling price; and sold one half of the goods. The gross profit on the goods sold would be calculated as follows:

Sales.......................... $750
Cost of goods sold 500
Gross profit on sales.... $250

However, if the $500 replacement cost of the unsold goods had declined to $450 on the inventory date, an income statement based upon the traditional application of cost or market would show:

Sales $750
Cost of goods sold:
  Purchases...................... $1,000
    Less ending inventory   450   550
Gross profit on sales........................ $200

The $450 would be a conservative balance sheet figure for the unsold goods. However, if these goods were sold at their full price early in the following year, the $450 inventory figure would have the erroneous effect of deferring $50 of income to the second year's income statement as follows:

Sales.......................... $750
Cost of goods sold:
  Beginning inventory.... 450
Gross profit on sales...... $300

Merchants are prone to be slow in marking down goods; they normally try to sell merchandise at its full price if possible. Consequently, the illustrated situation was not uncommon. For this reason the lower of cost or market rule has been modified as follows for situations in which replacement costs are below actual costs.[6]

1. Goods should be placed on an inventory at cost, even though replacement cost is lower, if there has not been and there is not expected to be a decline in selling price.

---

[6] Ibid., pp. 30 and 31.

2. Goods should at times be placed on an inventory at a price below cost but above replacement cost. For example, suppose the cost of an item that is normally bought for $20 and sold for $30 declines from $20 to $16, and its selling price declines from $30 to $27. The normal profit margin on this item is one third of its selling price. If this normal margin is applied to $27, the item should be placed on the inventory at two thirds of $27, or at $18. This is below cost but above replacement cost. .

3. At times, goods should be placed on an inventory at a price below replacement cost. For example, assume that the goods described in the preceding paragraph can only be sold for $18.50 and that the disposal costs are estimated at $3. In this case the goods should be placed on the inventory at $15.50, a price below their replacement cost of $16.

Principle of conservatism

Decisions based on estimates and opinions as to future events affect financial statements. Financial statements are also affected by the selection of accounting procedures. The *principle of conservatism* holds that the accountant should be conservative in his estimates and opinions and in his selection of procedures, choosing those that neither unduly understate nor overstate the situation.

Something called balance sheet conservatism was once considered the "first" principle of accounting, the objective being to place every item on the balance sheet at a conservative figure. This in itself was commendable; but it was often carried too far and resulted not only in the misstatement of asset values but also in unconservative income statements. For example, as previously shown, when prices are falling, the blind application of the unmodified lower of cost or market rule to inventories may result in a conservative balance sheet figure for inventories; but it may also result in an improper deferring of net income and in inaccurate income statements. Consequently, accountants recognize that balance sheet conservatism does not outweigh other factors. They favor practices that result in a fair statement of net income period after period.

Inventory errors

An error in determining the end-of-the-period inventory will cause misstatements in cost of goods sold, gross profit, reported net income, the current assets, and owner equity. Also, since the ending inventory of one period is the beginning inventory of the next, the error will carry forward and cause misstatements in the succeeding period's cost of goods sold, gross profit, and reported net income. Furthermore, since the amount involved in an inventory is often large, the error and misstatements can be material without being readily apparent.

To illustrate the effects of an inventory error, assume that in each of the years 1978, 1979, and 1980 a company had $100,000 in sales. If the company maintained a $20,000 inventory throughout the period and made $60,000 in purchases in each of the years, its cost of goods sold each year was $60,000 and its annual gross profits were $40,000. However, assume the company incorrectly calculated its December 31, 1978, inventory at $18,000 rather than $20,000. The error would have the effects shown in Illustration 9–1.

Observe in Illustration 9–1 that the $2,000 understatement of the December 31, 1978, inventory caused a $2,000 overstatement in 1978 cost of goods sold and a $2,000 understatement in gross profit and net income. Also, since the ending inventory of 1978 became the beginning inventory of 1979, the error caused an understatement in the 1979 cost of goods sold and a $2,000 overstatement in gross profit and net income. However, by 1980 the error had no effect.

In Illustration 9–1 the December 31, 1978, inventory is understated. Had it been overstated, it would have caused opposite results — the 1978 net income would have been overstated and the 1979 income understated.

	1978		1979		1980	
Sales		$100,000		$100,000		$100,000
Cost of goods sold:						
Beginning inventory	$20,000		$18,000*		$20,000	
Purchases	60,000		60,000		60,000	
Goods for sale	$80,000		$78,000		$80,000	
Ending inventory	18,000*		20,000		20,000	
Cost of goods sold		62,000		58,000		60,000
Gross profit		$ 38,000		$ 42,000		$ 40,000
* Should have been $20,000.						

Illustration 9–1

It has been argued that a mistake in taking a year-end inventory is not too serious, since the error it causes in reported net income the first year is exactly offset by an opposite error in the second. However, such reasoning is unsound because it fails to consider that management, creditors, and owners base many important decisions on fluctuations in reported net income. Consequently, such mistakes should be avoided, and they may be avoided if care is exercised and procedures such as those outlined in Chapter 5 are used in taking an inventory.

Perpetual inventories

Concerns selling a limited number of products of relatively high value often keep perpetual or book inventories. Also, concerns that use computers in processing their accounting data commonly keep such records.

A perpetual or book inventory based on pen and ink makes use of a subsidiary record card for each product in stock. On these individual cards, one for each kind of product, the number of units received is recorded as units are received; the number of units sold is recorded as units are sold; and after each receipt or sale, the balance remaining on hand is recorded. (An inventory record card for Product Z is shown in

Illustration 9–2.) At any time, each perpetual inventory card tells the balance on hand of any one product; and the total of all cards is the amount of the inventory.

The January 10 sale on the card of Illustration 9–2 indicates that the inventory of which this card is a part is kept on a first-in, first-out basis. Observe that this sale is recorded as being from the oldest units in stock. Perpetual inventories may also be kept on a last-in, first-out basis. When this is done, each sale is recorded as being from the last units received in stock, until these are exhausted, then sales are from the next to last, and so on.

Item _Product Z_   Location in stock room ___Bin 8___

Maximum ___25___   Minimum___5___

Date	Received			Sold			Balance		
	Units	Cost	Total	Units	Cost	Total	Units	Cost	Balance
1/1							10	10.00	100.00
1/5				5	10.00	50.00	5	10.00	50.00
1/8	20	10.50	210.00				5	10.00	
							20	10.50	260.00
1/10				3	10.00	30.00	2	10.00	
							20	10.50	230.00

Illustration 9–2

When a concern keeps perpetual inventory records, it normally also makes a once-a-year physical count of each kind of goods in stock in order to check the accuracy of its book inventory records.

Perpetual inventories not only tell the amount of inventory on hand at any time but they also aid in controlling the total amount invested in inventory. Each perpetual inventory card may have on it the maximum and minimum amounts of that item that should be kept in stock. By keeping the amount of each item within these limits, an oversupply or an undersupply of inventory is avoided.

Periodic and perpetual inventory systems

A system of inventory accounting like that described in Chapter 5 is normally based upon periodic, physical inventories and is known as a periodic inventory system. As was explained in Chapter 5, cost of goods sold is determined under such a system by adding cost of goods purchased to beginning inventory and subtracting the ending inventory.

When such a system is used, an inventory is necessary in order to determine ending goods on hand and cost of goods sold.

Under a perpetual inventory system, cost of goods sold during a period, as well as the ending inventory, may be determined from the accounting records without a physical inventory. Under such a system an account called "Merchandise" takes the place of and is used for recording the information entered in the periodic inventory system accounts, "Purchases" and "Merchandise Inventory." The "Merchandise" account is a controlling account that controls the numerous perpetual inventory cards described in previous paragraphs.

When merchandise is purchased by a concern using a perpetual inventory system, the acquisition is recorded as follows:

Jan.	8	Merchandise...	210.00	
		Accounts Payable — Blue Company		210.00
		Purchased merchandise on credit.		

In addition to the entry debiting the purchase to the Merchandise account, entries are also made on the proper perpetual inventory cards in the Received columns to show the kinds of merchandise bought. (See Illustration 9–2.)

When a sale is made, since the inventory cards show the cost of each item sold, it is possible to record both the sale and the cost of the goods sold. For example, if goods that according to the inventory cards cost $30 are sold for $50, cost of goods sold and the sale may be recorded as follows:

Jan.	10	Accounts Receivable — George Black...........................	50.00	
		Cost of Goods Sold...	30.00	
		Sales		50.00
		Merchandise...		30.00
		Sold merchandise on credit.		

In addition to the credit in this entry to the Merchandise account for the cost of the goods sold, the costs of the items sold are also deducted in the Sold columns of the proper inventory cards.

Note the debit to the Cost of Goods Sold account in the entry just given. If this account is debited at the time of each sale for the cost of the goods sold, the debit balance of the account will show at the end of the accounting period the cost of all goods sold during the period.

Note also the debit and the credit to the Merchandise account as they appear in the two entries just given. If this account is debited for the cost of merchandise purchased and credited for the cost of merchandise sold, at the end of an accounting period its debit balance will show the cost of the unsold goods on hand, the ending inventory.

Retail method

Good management requires that income statements be prepared more often than once each year, usually monthly or quarterly; and inventory information is necessary for these statements. However, taking a physical inventory in a retail store is both time consuming and expensive. Consequently, many retailers use the so-called *retail inventory method* to estimate inventories for monthly or quarterly statements. These monthly or quarterly statements are called *interim* or "in between" statements, since they are prepared in between the regular year-end statements.

Estimating an ending inventory by the retail method   When the retail method is used to estimate an end-of-an-interim-period inventory, a store's records must show the amount of inventory it had at the beginning of the period both *at cost* and *at retail*. At cost for an inventory means just that, while "at retail" means the dollar amount of the inventory at the marked selling prices of the inventory items.

In addition to the beginning inventory, the records must also show the amount of goods purchased during the period both at cost and at retail plus the net sales at retail. The last item is easy; it is the balance of the Sales account less returns and discounts. Then, with this information the interim inventory is estimated as follows: (Step 1) The amount of goods that were for sale during the period both at cost and at retail is first computed. Next, (Step 2) "at cost" is divided by "at retail" to obtain a cost ratio. Then, (Step 3) sales (at retail) are deducted from goods for sale (at retail) to arrive at the ending inventory (at retail). And finally, (Step 4) the ending inventory at retail is multiplied by the cost ratio to reduce it to a cost basis. These calculations are shown in Illustration 9–3.

Estimated inventories

		At Cost	At Retail
(Step 1)	Goods available for sale:		
	Beginning inventory	$20,500	$ 34,500
	Net purchases	39,500	65,500
	Good available for sale	$60,000	$100,000
(Step 2)	Cost ratio: $60,000 ÷ $100,000 = 60%)		
(Step 3)	Deduct sales at retail		70,000
	Ending inventory at retail		$ 30,000
(Step 4)	Ending inventory at cost ($30,000 × 60%)	$18,000	

Illustration 9–3

The essence of Illustration 9–3 is: (1) This store had $100,000 of goods (at marked selling prices) for sale during the period. (2) These goods cost 60% of the $100,000 total amount at which they were marked for sale. (3) The store's records (its Sales account) showed that $70,000 of these goods were sold, leaving $30,000 of merchandise unsold and presumably in the ending inventory. Therefore, (4) since cost in this store is 60% of retail, the estimated cost of this ending inventory is $18,000.

An ending inventory calculated as in Illustration 9–3 is an estimate arrived at by deducting sales (goods sold) from goods for sale. Inventories estimated in this manner are satisfactory for interim statements, but for year-end statements, or at least once each year, a store should take a physical inventory.

Using the retail method to reduce a physical inventory to a cost basis
Items for sale in a store normally have price tickets attached that show selling prices. Consequently, when a store takes a physical inventory, it commonly takes the inventory at the marked selling prices of the inventoried items. It then reduces the dollar total of this inventory to a cost basis by applying its cost ratio. It does this because the selling prices are readily available and the application of the cost ratio eliminates the need to look up the invoice price of each inventoried item.

For example, assume that the store of Illustration 9–3, in addition to estimating its inventory by the retail method, also takes a physical inventory at the marked selling prices of the inventoried goods. Assume further that the total of this physical inventory is $29,600. Under these assumptions the store may arrive at a cost basis for this inventory, without having to look up the cost of each inventoried item, simply by applying its cost ratio to the $29,600 inventory total as follows:

$$\$29,600 \times 60\% = \$17,760$$

The $17,760 cost figure for this store's ending physical inventory is a satisfactory figure for year-end statement purposes. It is also acceptable to the Internal Revenue Service for tax purposes.

Inventory shortage   An inventory determined as in Illustration 9–3 is an estimate of the amount of goods that should be on hand; but since it is arrived at by deducting sales from goods for sale, it does not reveal any actual shortages due to breakage, loss, or theft. However, the amount of such shortages may be determined by first estimating an inventory as in Illustration 9–3 and then taking a physical inventory at marked selling prices.

For example, by means of the Illustration 9–3 calculations, it was estimated the store of this discussion had a $30,000 ending inventory at retail. However, in the previous section it was assumed that this same store took a physical inventory and had only $29,600 of merchandise on hand. Therefore, if this store should have had $30,000 of goods in its ending inventory as determined in Illustration 9–3, but had only $29,600 when it took a physical inventory, it must have had a $400 inventory shortage at retail or a $240 shortage at cost ($400 × 60% = $240).

Markups and markdowns   The calculation of a cost ratio is often not as simple as that shown in Illustration 9–3, because many stores not only have a *normal markup* (often called a *markon*) that they apply to items purchased for sale but also make *additional markups* and *markdowns*. A normal markup or markon is the normal amount or percentage that is applied to the cost of an item to arrive at its selling price. For example, if a store's normal markup is 50% on cost and it applies this normal markup to an item that cost $10, it will mark the item for sale at $15. Normal markups appear in the calculation of a store's cost ratio as the difference between net purchases at cost and at retail.

Additional markups are markups made in addition to normal markups. Stores commonly give goods of outstanding style or quality such additional markups, because they can get a higher than normal price for such goods. They also commonly mark down for a clearance sale any slow-moving merchandise.

When a store using the retail inventory method makes additional markups and markdowns it must keep a record of them. It then uses the information in calculating its cost ratio and in estimating an interim inventory as in Illustration 9–4.

	At Cost	At Retail
Goods available for sale:		
Beginning inventory	$18,000	$27,800
Net purchases	34,000	50,700
Additional markups		1,500
Goods available for sale	$52,000	$80,000
Cost ratio: $52,000 ÷ $80,000 = 65%		
Sales at retail		$54,000
Markdowns		2,000
Total sales and markdowns		$56,000
Ending inventory at retail ($80,000 less $56,000)		$24,000
Ending inventory at cost ($24,000 × 65%)	$15,600	

Illustration 9–4

Observe in Illustration 9–4 that the store's $80,000 of goods for sale at retail were reduced $54,000 by sales and $2,000 by markdowns, a total of $56,000. (To understand the markdowns, visualize this effect of a markdown: The store had an item for sale during the period at $25. The item did not sell, and to move it the manager marked its price down from $25 to $20. By this act he reduced the amount of goods for sale in the store at retail by $5, and by a number of such markdowns during the year goods for sale at retail in the store of Illustration 9–4 were reduced $2,000.) Now back to the calculations of Illustration 9–4. The store's $80,000 of goods for sale were reduced $54,000 by sales and $2,000 by markdowns, leaving an estimated $24,000 ending inventory at retail. Therefore, since "cost" is 65% of "retail," the ending inventory at "cost" is $15,600.

Observe in Illustration 9–4 that markups enter into the calculation of the cost ratio but markdowns do not. It has long been customary in using the retail inventory method to add additional markups but to ignore markdowns in computing the percentage relation between goods for sale at cost and at retail. The justification for this was and is that a more conservative figure for the ending inventory results, a figure that approaches "cost or market, the lower." A further discussion of this phase of the retail inventory method is reserved for a more advanced text.

Gross profit method

Often retail price information about beginning inventory, purchases, and markups is not kept. In such cases the retail inventory method cannot be used. However, if a company knows its normal gross profit margin or rate; has information at cost in regard to its beginning inventory, net purchases, and freight-in; and knows the amount of its sales and sales returns, the company can estimate its ending inventory by the gross profit method.

For example, on March 27, the inventory of a company was totally destroyed by a fire. The company's average gross profit rate during the past five years has been 30% of net sales, and on the date of the fire the company's accounts showed the following balances:

Sales..................................	$31,500
Sales returns	1,500
Inventory, January 1, 19—	12,000
Net purchases.....................	20,000
Freight-in	500

With this information the gross profit method may be used to estimate the company's inventory loss for insurance purposes. The first step in applying the method is to recognize that whatever portion of each dollar of net sales was gross profit, the remaining portion was cost of goods sold. Consequently, if the company's gross profit rate averaged 30%, then 30% of each dollar of net sales was gross profit and 70% was cost of goods sold, and the 70% is used in estimating the inventory and inventory loss as follows:

Goods available for sale:		
Inventory, January 1, 19—		$12,000
Net purchases..	$20,000	
Add freight-in	500	20,500
Goods available for sale..		$32,500
Less estimated cost of goods sold:		
Sales..	$31,500	
Less sales returns	(1,500)	
Net sales	$30,000	
Estimated cost of goods sold (70% × $30,000)		(21,000)
Estimated March 27 inventory and inventory loss		$11,500

Illustration 9–5

To understand Illustration 9–5, recall that in a normal situation an ending inventory is subtracted from goods for sale to determine cost of goods sold. Then observe in Illustration 9–5 that the opposite subtraction is made, estimated cost of goods sold is subtracted from goods for sale to arrive at the estimated ending inventory.

In addition to its use in insurance cases, as in this illustration, the gross profit method is also commonly used by accountants in checking on the probable accuracy of a physical inventory taken and priced in the normal way.

Glossary

Conservatism principle. The rule that an accountant should be conservative in his estimates and opinions and in his selection of procedures.

Consignee. One to whom something is consigned or shipped.

Consignor. One who consigns or ships something to another person or enterprise.

Consistency principle. The accounting rule requiring a consistent application of a selected accounting method or procedure, period after period.

Fifo inventory pricing. The pricing of an inventory under the assumption that the first items received were the first items sold.

Gross profit inventory method. A procedure for estimating an ending inventory in which an estimated cost of goods sold based on past gross profit rates is subtracted from the cost of goods available for sale to arrive at an estimated ending inventory.

Interim statements. Financial statements prepared in between the regular annual statements.

Inventory cost ratio. The ratio of goods available for sale at cost to goods available for sale at retail prices.

Lifo inventory pricing. The pricing of an inventory under the assumption that the last items received were the first items sold.

Lower-of-cost-or-market pricing of an inventory. The pricing of inventory at the lower of what each item actually cost or what it would cost to replace each item on the inventory date.

Markdown. A reduction in the marked selling price of an item.

Markon. The normal percentage of its cost that is added to the cost of an item to arrive at its selling price.

Markup. An addition to the marked selling price of an item.

Normal markup. A phrase meaning the same as markon.

Periodic inventory system. An inventory system in which inventories and cost of goods sold are based on periodic physical inventories.

Perpetual inventory system. An inventory system in which inventories and cost of goods sold are based on book inventory records.

Retail inventory method. A method for estimating an ending inventory based on the ratio of the cost of goods for sale at cost and cost of goods for sale at marked selling prices.

Specific invoice inventory pricing. The pricing of an inventory where each inventory item can be associated with a specific invoice and be priced accordingly.

Weighted-average-cost inventory pricing. An inventory pricing system in which the units in the beginning inventory of a product and in each purchase of the product are weighted by the number of units in the beginning inventory and in each purchase to determine a weighted average cost per unit of the product, and after which this weighted average cost is used to price the ending inventory of the product.

Questions for class discussion

1. It has been said that cost of goods sold and ending inventory are opposite sides of the same coin? What is meant by this?
2. Give the meanings of the following when applied to inventory:
   a. First-in, first-out.
   b. Fifo.
   c. Last-in, first-out.
   d. Lifo.
   e. Cost.
   f. Market.
   g. Cost or market, the lower.
   h. Perpetual inventory.
   i. Physical inventory.
   j. Book inventory.
3. If prices are rising, will the "Lifo" or the "Fifo" method of inventory valuation result in the higher gross profit?
4. May a company change its inventory pricing method at will?
5. What is required by the accounting principle of consistency?
6. If a company changes one of its accounting procedures, what is required of it under the full-disclosure principle?
7. Of what does the cost of an inventory item consist?
8. Why are incidental costs commonly ignored in pricing an inventory? Under what accounting principle is this permitted?
9. What is meant when it is said that inventory errors "correct themselves"?
10. If inventory errors "correct themselves," why be concerned when such errors are made?
11. What is required of an accountant under the principle of conservatism?
12. Give the meanings of the following when applied in the retail method of estimating an inventory: (a) at cost, (b) at retail, (c) cost ratio, (d) normal markup, (e) markon, (f) additional markup, and (g) markdown.

Exercise 9–1

A concern began a year and purchased Product Z as follows:

Jan. 1	Beginning inventory....	10 units @ $ 9.20 = $	92	⟩ 90
Feb. 5	Purchased	40 units @ 10.00 =	400	
June 8	Purchased	20 units @ 10.60 =	212	— 10
Aug. 3	Purchased	30 units @ 11.20 =	336	10
Dec. 9	Purchased	20 units @ 11.00 =	220	10
	Total	120 units	$1,260	

Required:

Under the assumption the ending inventory consisted of 30 units, 10 from each of the last three purchases, determine the share of the $1,260 cost of the units for sale that should be assigned to the ending inventory and to goods sold under each of the following assumptions: (*a*) costs are assigned on the basis of specific invoice prices, (*b*) costs are assigned on a weighted average cost basis, (*c*) costs are assigned on the basis of Fifo, and (*d*) costs are assigned on the basis of Lifo.

Exercise 9–2

A company had $80,000 of sales during each of three consecutive years, and it purchased merchandise costing $50,000 during each of the years. It also maintained a $10,000 inventory from the beginning to the end of the three-year period. However, it made an error that caused its December 31, end-of-year-one, inventory to appear on its statements at $11,000, rather than the correct $10,000.

Required:

1. State the actual amount of the company's gross profit in each of the years.
2. Prepare a comparative income statement like the one illustrated in this chapter to show the effect of this error on the company's cost of goods sold and gross profit for each of Year 1, Year 2, and Year 3.

Exercise 9–3

During an accounting period a company sold $78,000 of merchandise at marked retail prices. At the period end the following information was available from its records:

	At Cost	At Retail
Beginning inventory....	$15,000	$21,000
Net purchases	55,000	74,000
Additional markups		5,000
Markdowns...............		2,000

19,570 ending

Use the retail method to estimate the store's ending inventory at cost.

Exercise 9–4

Assume that in addition to estimating its ending inventory by the retail method, the store of Exercise 9–3 also took a physical inventory at the marked selling prices of the inventory items. Assume further that the total of this physical inventory at marked selling prices was $19,500. Then (a) determine the amount of this inventory at cost and (b) determine the store's inventory shrinkage from breakage, theft, or other cause at retail and at cost.

Exercise 9–5

On January 1 a company had a $17,000 inventory at cost. During the first quarter of the year it purchased $65,000 of merchandise, returned $500, and paid freight charges on merchandise purchased totaling $3,500. During the past several years the company's gross profit on sales has averaged 35%. Under the assumption the company had $100,000 of sales during the first quarter of the year, use the gross profit method to estimate its end of the first quarter inventory.

Problems

Problem 9–1

A company began a year with 20 units of a product that cost $60 each, and it made successive purchases of the product as follows:

Jan. 15   60 units @ $75 each.
May 10   50 units @ $80 each.
Aug. 17   30 units @ $90 each.
Nov. 30   40 units @ $85 each.

Required:

1. Prepare a calculation showing the number and total cost of the units for sale during the year.
2. Under the assumption the company had 50 of the units in its December 31, end-of-the-year inventory, prepare calculations showing the portions of the total cost of the units for sale during the year that should be assigned to the ending inventory and to the units sold (a) first on a Fifo basis, (b) then on a Lifo basis, and (c) finally on a weighted average cost basis.

Problem 9–2

Alpha Company incurred $50,000 of operating expenses last year in selling 850 units of its Product X at $200 per unit. It began the year and purchased the product as follows:

January 1 inventory .... 100 units @ $121 each
Purchases:
    January 28.............. 300 units @   120 each
    April 29 .... 200 units @   125 each
    July 27................... 300 units @   129 each
    December 2............ 100 units @   132 each

Required:

Prepare a comparative income statement for the company showing in adjacent columns the net incomes earned from the sale of the product under the assumptions the company priced its ending inventory on the basis of: (a) Fifo, (b) Lifo, and (c) weighted average cost.

Problem 9–3

The inventory record for Item ABC showed these transactions:

Jan. 1 Balance 5 units costing $5 each.
    2 Received 10 units costing $5.40 each.
    6 Sold 3 units.
  10 Sold 8 units.
  14 Received 8 units costing $6 each.
  18 Sold 3 units.
  28 Sold 4 units.

Required:

1. Assume the perpetual inventory record card for Item ABC is kept on a Fifo basis and enter the beginning balance and transactions on the card.
2. Assume the perpetual inventory record for Item ABC is kept on a Lifo basis and enter the beginning balance and transactions on a second card.
3. Assume the four units sold on January 28 were sold on credit at $8 each to Glen Eads and give the entry to record the sale and the cost of goods sold on a Lifo basis.

Problem 9–4

Ski Shop takes a year-end physical inventory at marked selling prices and by the retail inventory method reduces the total to a cost basis for statement purposes. It also estimates its year-end inventory by the retail method and by a comparison determines the amount of any inventory shortage. At the end of last year the following information from the store's records and from its physical inventory was available:

	At Cost	At Retail
January 1 beginning inventory	$ 18,500	$ 28,450
Purchases	143,880	217,180
Purchases returns........................	1,180	1,820
Additional markups		4,190
Markdowns..............................		2,110
Sales......................................		220,120
Sales returns		1,830
December 31 physical inventory....		27,200

Required:

1. Prepare an estimate of the store's year-end inventory at cost.
2. Use the store's cost ratio to reduce the amount of its year-end physical inventory to a cost basis.
3. Prepare a schedule showing the amount of the inventory shortage at cost and at retail.

Problem 9–5

The Clothes Tree suffered a disastrous fire during the night of April 27, and everything except its accounting records, which were in a fireproof vault, was destroyed. As an insurance adjuster, you have been called upon to determine the store's inventory loss. The following information is available from its accounting records for the period, January 1 through April 27:

Merchandise inventory, January 1, at cost $23,400
Purchases... 63,520
Purchases returns 1,260
Freight-in 660
Sales 94,730
Sales returns... 2,230

The accounting records also show that the store's gross profit rate has averaged 34% over the past four years.

Required:

Use the gross profit method to prepare an estimate of the store's inventory loss.

Problem 9–6

Part 1. Able Company's records provide the following information for the year ended last December 31:

	At Cost	At Retail
Year's sales		$221,560
Sales returns		2,345
January 1 inventory	$ 21,540	32,950
Purchases.................	146,490	219,735
Purchases returns	980	1,470
Additional markups.....		5,785
Markdowns		1,285

Required:

Use the retail method to prepare a calculation estimating Able Company's December 31, year-end inventory.

Part 2. Best Company wants an estimate of its June 30 inventory. The following information is available from its accounting records:

January 1 inventory at cost .... $ 42,850
Purchases........................... 123,900
Purchases returns 1,200
Freight-in 2,680
Sales 189,900
Sales returns....................... 3,400
Average gross profit rate........ 32%

The gross profit rate is an average for the past five years. The remaining figures are for the six-month period, January 1 through June 30.

Required:

Use the gross profit method and prepare a calculation estimating Best Company's June 30 inventory.

Problem 9–7

Mesa Sales sold 1,000 units of its Product 2XY in each of three successive years at the following weighted average prices:

Year 1, 1,000 units @ $115 per unit.... $115,000
Year 2, 1,000 units @   133 per unit....   133,000
Year 3, 1,000 units @   138 per unit....   138,000

It began the three-year period with 200 units of the product, costing $50 each, in its inventory; and it ended each of the years with 200 units in the inventory. Also, it made successive purchases of the product as follows:

YEAR ONE		YEAR THREE	
200 units @ $55............	$11,000	200 units @ $70............	$14,000
200 units @ 50............	10,000	400 units @ 65............	26,000
300 units @ 60............	18,000	200 units @ 65............	13,000
300 units @ 65............	19,500	200 units @ 75............	15,000
1,000	$58,500	1,000	$68,000

YEAR TWO	
500 units @ $60............	$30,000
300 units @ 70............	21,000
200 units @ 70............	14,000
1,000	$65,000

Required:

1. Set up three comparative income statements for the company, one for each year, on four-column paper. (If the working papers that accompany this text are in use, these statements are already set up there.)
2. In the first two columns of each statement show sales, cost of goods sold, and gross profit under the assumption the company priced its inventories on a Fifo basis, and in the second two columns show sales, cost of goods sold, and gross profit under the assumption the company priced its inventories on a Lifo basis.
3. Answer these questions: (*a*) Which inventory pricing method results in the smaller annual incomes for the company? (*b*) Which better synchronizes costs and revenues?

Problem 9–1A   *Alternate problems*

A concern began a year with 300 units of Product A in its inventory that cost $50 each, and it made successive purchases of the product as follows:

Mar.   1   400 units @ $60 each.
June 10   500 units @ $70 each.
Aug. 29   400 units @ $80 each.
Nov. 15   400 units @ $60 each.

Required:

1. Prepare a calculation showing the number and total cost of the units that were for sale during the year.
2. Assume the concern had 500 of the units in its December 31, year-end inventory and prepare calculations showing the portions of the total costs of the units for sale during the year that should be assigned to the ending

inventory and to cost of goods sold (*a*) first on a Fifo bases, (*b*) then on a Lifo basis, and finally (*c*) on a weighted average cost basis.

Problem 9–2A

Last year Omega Company sold 8,500 units of its product at $10 per unit. It incurred marketing costs of $2 per unit in selling the 8,500 units, and it began the year and made successive purchases of the product as follows:

January 1, beginning inventory.... 1,000 units costing $5.60 per unit
Purchases:

January 29	....	1,000 units costing $6.00 per unit
March 15	....	3,000 units costing $6.20 per unit
July 12	....	4,000 units costing $6.50 per unit
November 3	....	1,000 units costing $7.00 per unit

Required:

Prepare a comparative income statement for the company showing in adjacent columns the net incomes earned from the sale of the product under the assumptions the company priced its ending inventory on the basis of: (*a*) Fifo, (*b*) Lifo, and (*c*) weighted average cost.

Problem 9–3A

The perpetual inventory record card for Article XYZ showed the following beginning balance and transactions during January of this year:

Jan. 1 Balance 12 units costing $6 each.
    4 Received 20 units costing $7 each.
    9 Sold 10 units.
   15 Sold 15 units.
   19 Received 20 units costing $8 each.
   24 Sold 5 units.
   29 Sold 16 units.

Required:

1. Under the assumption the concern keeps its records on a Fifo basis, enter the beginning balance and the transactions on a perpetual inventory record card like the one illustrated in this chapter.
2. Under the assumption the concern keeps its inventory records on a Lifo basis, enter the beginning inventory and the transactions on a second inventory record card.
3. Assume the 16 units sold on January 29 were sold on credit to Glen Eads at $12.50 each, and prepare a general journal entry to record the sale and cost of goods sold on a Lifo basis.

Problem 9–4A

Hobby Shop takes a year-end physical inventory at marked selling prices and uses the retail method to reduce the inventory total to a cost basis for statement purposes. It also uses the retail method to estimate the amount of inventory it should have at the end of a year, and by comparison determines any inventory shortage due to shoplifting or other cause. At the end of last year its physical inventory at marked selling prices totaled $20,950, and the following information was available from its records:

	At Cost	At Retail
January 1 inventory	$12,210	$ 18,100
Purchases..................	83,385	119,900
Purchases returns	1,415	1,950
Additional markups.....		2,450
Markdowns		1,530
Sales		117,340
Sales returns.............		1,870

Required:

1. Use the retail method to estimate the shop's year-end inventory at cost.
2. Use the retail method to reduce the shop's year-end physical inventory to a cost basis.
3. Prepare a schedule showing the inventory shortage at cost and at retail.

Problem 9–5A

On Monday morning, June 14, the manager of Smart Shop unlocked the store to learn that thieves had broken in over the weekend and stolen the store's entire inventory. The following information for the period, January 1 through June 13, was available to establish the amount of loss:

January 1 merchandise inventory at cost	$ 32,500
Purchases.................................	92,310
Purchases returns	415
Freight-in................................	560
Sales	139,875
Sales returns.............................	1,375

Required:

Under the assumption the store had earned an average 32% gross profit on sales during the past five years, prepare a statement showing the estimated loss.

Problem 9–6A

Part 1. Charles Company's records provided the following information for the year ended December 31:

	At Cost	At Retail
January 1 beginning inventory....	$ 23,830	$ 31,350
Purchases	162,116	229,590
Purchases returns.....................	2,210	3,160
Additional markups		4,700
Markdowns............................		1,170
Sales....................................		228,240
Sales returns		2,880

Required:

Prepare an estimate of the concern's December 31 inventory by the retail method.

Part 2. David Company wants an estimate of its March 31, end-of-the-first quarter inventory. Its January 1 beginning inventory at cost was $38,750. During the last five years its gross profit rate has averaged 34%, and the following information as to purchases and sales for the first quarter is available from its accounting records:

Purchases.............. $ 91,400
Purchases returns   850
Freight-in.............. 1,130
Sales 144,640
Sales returns.......... 2,140

Required:

Use the gross profit method to prepare an estimate of the company's March 31 inventory.

Decision problem, 9–1, Boot Center

Boot Center suffered extensive smoke and water damage and a small amount of fire damage on October 3. The store carried adequate insurance, and the insurance company's claims adjuster appeared the same day to inspect the damage. After completing his survey, the adjuster agreed with Al Berg, the store's owner, that the inventory could be sold to a company specializing in fire sales for about one fifth of its cost. The adjuster offered Mr. Berg $20,-000 in full settlement for the damage to the inventory. He suggested that the offer be accepted and said he had authority to deliver at once a check for that amount. He also pointed out that a prompt settlement would provide funds to replace the inventory in time for the store to participate in the Christmas shopping season.

Mr. Berg felt the loss might exceed $20,000, but he recognized that a time-consuming count and inspection of each item in the inventory would be required to establish the loss more precisely; and he was reluctant to take the time for the inventory, since he was anxious to get back into business before the Christmas rush,. the season making the largest contribution to his annual net income. Yet he was also unwilling to take a substantial loss on the insurance settlement; so he asked for and received a one-day period in which to consider the insurance company offer, and he immediately went to his records for the following information:

		At Cost	At Retail
a.	January 1 inventory	$ 29,150	$ 46,800
	Purchases, January 1 through October 3..............	172,350	277,900
	Net sales, January 1 through October 3..............		280,100

b. On March 1 the remaining inventory of winter footwear was marked down from $12,000 to $9,000, and placed on sale in the annual end-of-winter sale. Two thirds of the shoes were sold; the markdown on the remaining sale shoes was canceled. (A markdown cancellation is subtracted from a markdown, and a markup cancellation is subtracted from a markup.)

c. In May a special line of imported shoes proved popular, and 84 high-styled pairs were marked up from their normal $30 retail price to $35 per pair. Sixty pairs were sold at this higher price, and on July 15 the markup on the remaining 24 pairs was canceled and they were returned to their regular $30 per pair price.

d. Between January 1 and October 3 markdowns totaling $1,400 were taken on several odd lots of shoes.

Recommend whether or not you think Mr. Berg should take the insurance company's offer. Back your recommendation with figures.

Budget Furniture Store has been in operation for six years, during which it has earned a 34% average gross profit on sales. However, night before last, June 2, it suffered a disastrous fire that destroyed its entire inventory; and Fred Arne, the store's owner, has filed a $49,600 inventory loss claim with the store's insurance company. When asked on what he based his claim, he replied that during the day before the fire he had marked every item in the store down 20% in preparation for the annual summer clearance sale, and during the marking down process he had taken an inventory of the merchandise in the store. Furthermore, he said, "It's a big loss, but every cloud has a silver lining, because I am giving you fellows (the insurance company) the benefit of the 20% markdown in filing this claim."

When it was explained to Mr. Arne that he had to back his loss claim with more than his word as to the amount of the loss, he produced the following information from his pre-sale inventory and accounting records, which fortunately were in a fireproof vault and were not destroyed in the fire.

Decision problem 9–2, Budget Furniture Store

1. The store's accounts were closed on December 31, of last year.
2. After posting was completed, the accounts showed the following June 2 balances:

Merchandise inventory, January 1 balance .... $ 43,250
Purchases 116,400
Purchases returns...................................... 1,225
Freight-in 2,940
Sales... 186,710
Sales returns 4,210

3. Mr. Arne's pre-fire inventory totaled $62,000 at pre-markdown prices.

From the information given, present figures to show the amount of loss suffered by Mr. Arne. Also, show how he arrived at the amount of his loss claim. Can his pre-sale inventory be used to substantiate the actual amount of his loss? If so, use the pre-sale inventory figure to substantiate the actual loss.

After studying Chapter 10, you should be able to:

- ■ Tell what is included in the cost of a plant asset.

- ■ Calculate depreciation by the (*a*) straight-line, (*b*) units-of-production, (*c*) declining-balance, and (*d*) sum-of-the-years'-digits methods.

- ■ Explain how accelerated depreciation defers income taxes.

- ■ Explain how the cost of a plant asset is recovered through the sale of the asset's product or service.

- ■ Prepare entries to record the purchase and disposal of plant assets under the situations described in the chapter.

- ■ Define or explain the words and phrases listed in the Glossary.

chapter 10

Plant and equipment

Assets that are used in the production or sale of other assets or services and that have a useful life longer than one accounting period are called *plant and equipment* or *fixed assets*. The phrase "fixed assets" has been used in accounting literature for many years in referring to items of plant and equipment, and it was once commonly used as a balance sheet caption. However, as a caption it is rapidly disappearing from published balance sheets, being replaced by the more descriptive "plant and equipment" or the more complete "property, plant, and equipment" or by "land, buildings, and equipment."

Its use in the production or sale of other assets or services is the characteristic that distinguishes a plant asset from an item of merchandise or an investment. An office machine or a factory machine held for sale by a dealer is merchandise to the dealer. Likewise, land purchased and held for future expansion but presently unused is classified as a long-term investment. Neither is a plant asset until put to use in the production or sale of other assets or services. However, standby equipment for use in case of a breakdown or for use during peak periods of production is a plant asset. Also, when equipment is removed from service and held for sale, it ceases to be a plant asset.

A productive or service life longer than one accounting period distinguishes an item of plant and equipment from an item of supplies. An item of supplies may be consumed in a single accounting period; and if consumed, its cost is charged to the period of consumption. The productive life of a plant asset, on the other hand, is longer than one period. It contributes to production for several periods; and as a result of the *matching principle*, its cost must be allocated to these periods in a systematic and rational manner.[1]

---

[1] APB, "Basic Concepts and Accounting Principles Underlying Financial Statements of Business Enterprises," *APB Statement No. 4* (New York: AICPA, October 1970), par. 159.

Cost of plant and equipment

The cost of an item of plant and equipment includes all normal and reasonable expenditures necessary to get the asset in place and ready to use. For example, the cost of a factory machine includes its invoice price, less any discount for cash, plus freight, unpacking, and assembling costs. Cost also includes any special concrete base or foundation, electrical or power connections, and adjustments needed to place the machine in operation. In short, the cost of a plant asset includes all normal, necessary, and reasonable costs incurred in getting the asset in place and ready to produce.

A cost must be normal and reasonable as well as necessary if it is to be properly included in the cost of a plant asset. For example, if a machine is damaged by being dropped in unpacking, repairs should not be added to its cost but should be charged to an expense account. Likewise, a fine paid for moving a heavy machine on city streets without proper permits is not part of the cost of the machine; although if secured, the cost of the permits would be.

After being purchased but before being put to use, a plant asset must sometimes be repaired, reconditioned, or remodeled before it meets the needs of the purchaser. In such a case the repairing, remodeling, or reconditioning expenditures are part of its cost and should be charged to the asset account. Furthermore, depreciation charges should not begin until the asset is ready for use.

When a plant asset is constructed or manufactured by a concern for its own use, cost includes material and labor costs plus a reasonable amount of overhead or indirect expenses such as heat, lights, power, and depreciation on the machinery used in constructing or manufacturing the asset. Cost also includes architectural and design fees, building permits, and insurance during construction. Insurance during construction is included because it is necessary to get the asset ready to produce or be used. Needless to say, insurance on the same asset after it has been placed in production is an expense.

When land is purchased for a plant or building site, its cost includes the amount paid for the land plus real estate commissions, escrow and legal fees, fees for examining and insuring the title, and any accrued property taxes paid by the purchaser. Cost also includes expenditures for surveying, clearing, grading, draining, and landscaping. All are part of the cost of the land. Furthermore, any assessments incurred at the time of purchase or later for such things as the installation of streets, sewers, and sidewalks should be debited to the Land account since they add a more or less permanent value to the land.

Land purchased as a building site sometimes has an old building that must be removed. In such cases the entire purchase price, including the amount paid for the to-be-removed building, should be charged to the Land account. Also, the cost of removing the old building, less any amounts recovered through the sale of salvaged materials, should be charged to this account.

Land used as a building site is assumed to have an unlimited life and is therefore not subject to depreciation. However, buildings and land improvements such as driveways, parking lots, fences, and lighting systems are subject to depreciation. Consequently, land, building, and land improvement costs should not be recorded in the same account. At least two accounts should be used, one for land and a second for buildings and land improvements; but three accounts, one for land, a second for buildings, and a third for land improvements, would be better.

Often land, buildings, and equipment are purchased together for one lump sum. When this occurs, the purchase price must be apportioned among the assets on some fair basis, since some of the assets depreciate and some do not. A fair basis may be tax-assessed values or appraised values. For example, assume that land independently appraised at $30,-000 and a building appraised at $70,000 are purchased together for $90,000. The cost may be apportioned on the basis of appraised values as follows:

	Appraised Value	Percent of Total	Apportioned Cost
Land	$ 30,000	30%	$27,000
Building	70,000	70%	63,000
Totals....	$100,000	100%	$90,000

When a plant asset is purchased, in effect a quantity of usefulness that will contribute to production throughout the life of the asset is acquired. However, since the life of any plant asset (other than land) is limited, this quantity of usefulness is also limited and will in effect be consumed by the end of the asset's service life. Consequently, depreciation, as the term is used in accounting, is nothing more than the expiration of a plant asset's quantity of usefulness, and the recording of depreciation is a process of allocating and charging the cost of this usefulness to the accounting periods that benefit from the asset's use.

Nature of depreciation

For example, when a company purchases an automobile to be used by one of its salespersons, it in effect purchases a quantity of usefulness, a quantity of transportation for the salesperson. The cost of this quantity of usefulness is the cost of the car less whatever will be received for it when sold or traded in at the end of its service life. And, recording depreciation on the car is a process of allocating the cost of this usefulness to the accounting periods that benefit from the car's use. Note that it is not the recording of physical deterioration nor recording the decline in the car's market value.

The foregoing is in line with the pronouncements of the AICPA's Committee on Accounting Procedure which described depreciation as follows:

The cost of a productive facility is one of the costs of the services it renders during its useful economic life. Generally accepted accounting principles require that this cost be spread over the expected useful life of the facility in such a way as to allocate it as equitably as possible to the periods during which services are obtained from the use of the facility. This procedure is known as depreciation accounting, a system of accounting which aims to distribute the cost or other basic value of tangible capital assets, less salvage (if any), over the estimated useful life of the unit . . . in a systematic and rational manner. It is a process of allocation, not of valuation.[2]

Productive life of a plant asset

The service life of a plant asset is the period of time it will be used in producing or selling other assets or services. This may not be the same as the asset's potential life. For example, typewriters have a potential six- or eight-year life; however, if a company finds from a production-cost view that it is wise to trade its old typewriters on new ones every three years, in this company typewriters have a three-year service life. Furthermore, in this business the cost of new typewriters less their trade-in value, in other words the cost of their quantity of usefulness should be charged to depreciation expense over this three-year period.

At the time of purchase a plant asset's service life must be predicted so that its depreciation may be allocated to the several periods in which it will be used. Predicting or estimating service life is sometimes difficult because several factors are often involved. Wear and tear and the action of the elements determine the useful life of some assets. However, two additional factors, *inadequacy* and *obsolescence,* often need be considered. When a business acquires plant assets, it should acquire assets of a size and capacity to take care of its foreseeable needs. However, a business often grows more rapidly than anticipated; and in such cases plant assets may become too small for the productive demands of the business long before they wear out. When this happens, inadequacy is said to have taken place. Inadequacy cannot easily be predicted. Obsolescence, like inadequacy, is also difficult to foretell because the exact occurrence of new inventions and improvements normally cannot be predicted; yet new inventions and improvements often cause an asset to become obsolete and make it wise to discard the obsolete asset long before it wears out.

A company that has previously used a particular type of asset may estimate the service life of a new asset of like kind from past experience. A company without previous experience with a particular asset must depend upon the experience of others or upon engineering studies and judgment. The Internal Revenue Service publishes information giving estimated service lives for hundreds of new assets. Many business executives refer to this information in estimating the life of a new asset.

---

[2] Committee on Accounting Procedure, "Accounting Research Bulletin No. 43," *Accounting Research and Terminology Bulletins, Final Edition* (New York: AICPA, 1961), p. 76.

When a plant asset has a salvage value, the cost of its quantity of usefulness is the asset's cost minus its salvage value. The salvage value of a plant asset is the portion of its cost that is recovered at the end of its service life. Some assets such as typewriters, trucks, and automobiles are traded in on similar new assets at the end of their service lives. The salvage values of such assets are their trade-in values. Other assets may have no trade-in value and little or no salvage value. For example, at the end of its service life, some machinery can be sold only as scrap metal. **Salvage value**

When the disposal of a plant asset involves certain costs, as in the wrecking of a building, the salvage value is the net amount realized from the sale of the asset. The net amount realized is the amount received for the asset less its disposal cost. Often in the case of a machine the cost to remove the machine will equal the amount that can be realized from its sale. In such a case the machine has no salvage value.

Many methods of allocating a plant asset's total depreciation to the several accounting periods in its service life have been suggested and are used. Four of the more common are the *straight-line method,* the *units-of-production method,* the *declining-balance method,* and the *sum-of-the-years'-digits method.* Each is a *generally accepted accounting method.* **Allocating depreciation**

Straight-line method

When the straight-line method is used, the cost of the asset minus its estimated salvage value is divided by the estimated number of accounting periods in the asset's service life. The result is the estimated amount the asset depreciates each period. For example, if a machine costs $550, has an estimated service life of five years, and an estimated $50 salvage value, its depreciation per year by the straight-line method is $100 and is calculated as follows:

$$\frac{\text{Cost} - \text{Salvage}}{\text{Service life in years}} = \frac{\$550 - \$50}{5} = \$100$$

Note that the straight-line method allocates an equal share of an asset's total depreciation to each accounting period in its life.

Units-of-production method

The primary purpose of recording depreciation is to charge each accounting period in which an asset is used with a fair share of its depreciation. The straight-line method charges an equal share to each period; and when plant assets are used about the same amount in each accounting period, this method rather fairly allocates total depreciation. However, in some lines of business the use of certain plant assets varies greatly from accounting period to accounting period. For example, a contractor may use a particular piece of construction equipment for a month and then not use it again for many months. For such an asset, since use and contribution to revenue may not be uniform from period to period, the units-of-production method often better meets the requirements of the *matching principle* than does the straight-line method.

When the units-of-production method is used in allocating depreciation, the cost of an asset's quantity of usefulness is divided by the estimated units of product it will produce during its entire service life. This division gives depreciation per unit of product. Then the amount the asset depreciates in any one accounting period is determined by multiplying the units of product produced in that period by depreciation per unit. Units of product may be expressed as units of product or in any other unit of measure such as hours of use or miles driven. For example, a delivery truck costing $6,000 is estimated to have a $2,000 salvage value. If it is also estimated that during the truck's service life it will be driven 50,000 miles, the depreciation per mile, or the depreciation per unit of product, is $0.08 and is calculated as follows:

$$\frac{\text{Cost} - \text{Salvage value}}{\substack{\text{Estimated units of} \\ \text{production}}} = \substack{\text{Depreciation per} \\ \text{unit of product}}$$

or

$$\frac{\$6,000 - \$2,000}{50,000 \text{ miles}} = \$0.08 \text{ per mile}$$

If these estimates are correct and the truck is driven 20,000 miles during its first year, depreciation for the first year is $1,600. This is 20,000 miles at $0.08 per mile. If the truck is driven 15,000 miles in the second year, depreciation for the second year is 15,000 times $0.08, or $1,200.

Declining-balance method

The Internal Revenue Code permits depreciation methods for tax purposes which result in higher depreciation charges during the early years of a plant asset's life. These methods are also used in preparing financial reports to investors. The declining-balance method is one of these. Under the declining-balance method, depreciation of up to twice the straight-line rate, without considering salvage value, may be applied each year to the declining book value of a new plant asset having an estimated life of three years or more. If this method is followed and twice the straight-line rate is used, the amount charged each year as depreciation expense on a plant asset is determined by (1) calculating a straight-line depreciation rate for the asset; (2) doubling this rate; and then (3) at the end of each year in the asset's life, applying this doubled rate to the asset's remaining book value. (The book value of a plant asset is its cost less accumulated depreciation; it is the value shown for the asset on the books.)

If this method is used to charge depreciation on a $10,000 new asset that has an estimated five-year life and no salvage value, these steps are followed: (Step 1) A straight-line depreciation rate is calculated by dividing 100% by five (years) to determine the straight-line annual depreciation rate of 20%. Next (Step 2) this rate is doubled; and then (Step 3) annual depreciation charges are calculated as in the following table:

Year	Annual Depreciation Calculation	Annual Depreciation Expense	Remaining Book Value
1st year....	40% of $10,000	$4,000.00	$6,000.00
2d year.....	40% of 6,000	2,400.00	3,600.00
3d year.....	40% of 3,600	1,440.00	2,160.00
4th year....	40% of 2,160	864.00	1,296.00
5th year....	40% of 1,296	518.40	777.60

Under the declining-balance method the book value of a plant asset never reaches zero; consequently, when the asset is sold, exchanged, or scrapped, any remaining book value is used in determining the gain or loss on disposal.

In passing it should be observed that if an asset has a salvage value, the asset may not be depreciated beyond its salvage value. For example, if instead of no salvage value the foregoing $10,000 asset has an estimated $1,000 salvage value, depreciation for its fifth year is limited to $296, the amount required to reduce the asset's book value to its salvage value.

Declining-balance depreciation results in what is called *accelerated depreciation* or higher depreciation charges in the early years of a plant asset's life. The sum-of-the-years'-digits method has a like result.

Sum-of-the-years'-digits method

Under the sum-of-the-years'-digits method the years in an asset's service life are added and their sum becomes the denominator of a series of fractions used in allocating total depreciation to the periods in the asset's service life. The numerators of the fractions are the years in the asset's life in their reverse order.

For example, if the sum-of-the-years'-digits method is used in allocating depreciation on a machine costing $7,000, having an estimated five-year life and an estimated $1,000 salvage value, the sum of the years' digits in the asset's life is calculated:

$$1 + 2 + 3 + 4 + 5 = 15$$

and then annual depreciation charges are calculated as follows:

Year	Annual Depreciation Calculation	Annual Depreciation Expense
1st year .... 5/15 of $6,000		$2,000
2d year .... 4/15 of 6,000		1,600
3d year .... 3/15 of 6,000		1,200
4th year .... 2/15 of 6,000		800
5th year .... 1/15 of 6,000		400
Total depreciation $6,000		

When a plant asset has a long life, the sum of the years' digits in its life may be calculated by using the formula: $SYD = n\left(\dfrac{n+1}{2}\right)$. For example, sum of the years' digits for a five-year life is: $5\left(\dfrac{5+1}{2}\right) = 15$.

When either declining-balance or sum-of-the-years'-digits depreciation is used and accounting periods do not coincide with the years in an asset's life, additional calculations are necessary if depreciation is to be properly charged. For example, assume that the machine for which sum-of-the-years'-digits depreciation was calculated above is placed in use on April 1 and the annual accounting periods of the company owning the machine end on December 31. Under these assumptions the machine will be in use three fourths of a year during the first accounting period in its life; and as a result, this period should be charged with $1,500 depreciation ($2,000 × ¾ = $1,500). Likewise, the second accounting period should be charged with $1,700 depreciation [(¼ × $2,000) + (¾ × $1,600) = $1,700], and like calculations should be used for the remaining periods in the asset's life.

The reducing charge methods (both the declining-balance and the sum-of-the-years'-digits method) are advocated by many accountants who claim that their use results in a more equitable "use charge" for long-lived plant assets than other methods. These accountants point out, for example, that as assets grow older, repairs and maintenance increase. Therefore, when smaller amounts of depreciation computed by a reducing charge method are added to increasing repair costs, a more equitable total expense charge to match against revenue results. Also, they point out that as an asset grows older, in some instances its ability to produce revenue is reduced. For example, rentals from an apartment building are normally higher in the earlier years of its life but will decline as the building becomes less attractive and less modern. Certainly in such cases the requirements of the *matching principle* are better met with heavier depreciation charges in the earlier years and lighter charges in the later years of the asset's life.

The foregoing are sound reasons for the use under applicable conditions of reducing charge or accelerated depreciation. However, a tax reason rather than sound accounting theory is probably more responsible for the increase in their popularity. The tax reason is that accelerated depreciation normally results in deferring income taxes from the early years of a plant asset's life until its later years. Taxes are deferred because accelerated depreciation causes larger amounts of depreciation to be charged to the early years, which results in smaller amounts of income and income taxes in these years. However, the taxes are only deferred because offsetting smaller amounts of depreciation are charged in later years, which results in larger amounts of income and taxes in these years. Nevertheless, through accelerated depreciation a company does have the "interest-free" use of the deferred tax dollars until the later years of a plant asset's life.

In presenting information about the plant assets of a business, the *full-disclosure principle* requires and the Accounting Principles Board has ruled that both the cost of such assets and their accumulated depreciation be shown in the statements by major classes, and that a general description of the depreciation method or methods used be given in a balance sheet footnote or other manner.[3] In complying with this requirement, the plant assets of a concern may be shown on its balance sheet or in a schedule accompanying the balance sheet as follows:

Depreciation on the balance sheet

Plant Assets:	Cost	Accumulated Depreciation	Book Value	
Store equipment	$ 12,400	$1,500	$10,900	
Office equipment.....	3,600	450	3,150	
Building	72,300	7,800	64,500	
Land	15,000	....	15,000	
Totals.................	$103,300	$9,750		$93,550

When plant assets are thus shown and the depreciation methods described, a much better understanding can be gained by a balance sheet reader than if only information as to undepreciated cost is given. For example, $50,000 of assets with $40,000 of accumulated depreciation are quite different from $10,000 of new assets. Yet the net undepreciated cost is the same in both cases. Likewise, the picture is different if the $40,000 of accumulated depreciation resulted from the application of an accelerated depreciation method rather than if straight-line depreciation was used.

Financial statement readers who have never studied accounting sometimes mistakenly think that the amounts shown on a balance sheet as accumulated depreciation represent funds accumulated to

---

[3] Accounting Principles Board, "Omnibus Opinion—1967," *APB Opinion No. 12* (New York: AICPA, December 1967), par. 5.

buy new plant assets when present assets wear out and must be discarded. However, an informed reader recognizes that accumulated depreciation represents that portion of an asset's cost that has been charged off to depreciation expense during its life. Such a reader also knows that accumulated depreciation accounts are contra accounts having credit balances that cannot be used to buy anything. Furthermore, an informed reader knows that if a concern has cash with which to buy assets, it is shown on the balance sheet as a current asset "Cash."

Balance sheet plant asset values

From the discussion thus far students should recognize that the recording of depreciation is not primarily a valuing process, rather it is a process of allocating the costs of plant assets to the several accounting periods that benefit from their use. Furthermore, they should recognize that because the recording of depreciation is an allocating process rather than a valuing process, balance sheets show for plant assets unallocated costs or undepreciated costs rather than market values.

The fact that balance sheets show undepreciated costs rather than market values seems to disturb many beginning accounting students. It should not. When a balance sheet is prepared, normally the company for which it is prepared has no intention of selling its plant assets; consequently, the market values of these assets may be of little significance. The student should recognize that when a balance sheet is prepared, it is under the assumption the company for which it is prepared is a going concern that will continue in business long enough to recover the costs of its plant assets through the sale of its products.

The assumption that a company is a going concern that will continue in business long enough to recover its plant asset costs through the sale of its products is known in accounting as the *continuing- or going concern concept.* It provides the justification for carrying plant assets on the balance sheet at cost less accumulated depreciation, in other words at the share of their cost applicable to future periods. It is also the justification for carrying at cost such things as stationery imprinted with the company name, though salable only as scrap paper. In all such instances the intention is to use the assets in carrying on the business operations. They are not for sale, so it is pointless to place them on the balance sheet at market or realizable values, whether these values are greater or less than book values.

Recovering the costs of plant assets

A company that earns a profit or breaks even (neither earns a profit nor suffers a loss) eventually recovers the cost of its plant assets through the sale of its products. This is best explained with a condensed income statement like that of Illustration 10–1. Even Steven Company broke even during the year of the illustrated income statement; but in breaking even it also recovered $5,000 of the cost of its plant assets through the sale of its products. It recovered the $5,000 because of the $100,000 that flowed into the company from sales only $95,000 flowed out to pay for goods sold, rent, and salaries. No funds flowed out for depreciation expense; and as a result, the company recovered this $5,000 portion of the cost of its plant assets through the sale of its products. Furthermore, if the company remains in business for the life of its plant assets, either breaking even or earning a profit, it will recover their entire cost in this manner.

Even Steven Company
Income Statement for Year Ended December 31, 19—

Sales....................................		$100,000
Cost of goods sold..................	$60,000	
Rent expense..........................	10,000	
Salaries expense.....................	25,000	
Depreciation expense..............	5,000	
Total.............................		100,000
Net Income.............................		$ 0

Illustration 10–1

At this point students commonly ask, "Where is the recovered $5,000?" The answer is that the company may have the $5,000 in the bank. However, the funds may also have been spent to increase merchandise inventory, to buy additional equipment, to pay off a debt, or they may have been withdrawn by the business owner. In short, the funds may still be in the bank or they may have been used for any purpose for which a business uses funds, and only an examination of its balance sheets as of the beginning and end of the year will show this.

Sooner or later a plant asset wears out, becomes obsolete, or becomes inadequate; and when this occurs, the asset is discarded, sold, or traded in on a new asset. (Trade-ins are discussed in the next chapter.) The entry to record the disposal will vary with the nature of the disposal; however, in all cases the asset's cost and its accumulated depreciation are removed from the accounts.

Disposal of a plant asset

Discarding a plant asset

When an asset's accumulated depreciation is equal to its cost, the asset is said to be fully depreciated; and if a fully depreciated asset is discarded, the entry to record the disposal is:

Jan.	7	Accumulated Depreciation, Machinery	1,500.00	
		Machinery...		1,500.00
		Discarded a fully depreciated machine.		

Although often discarded, sometimes a fully depreciated asset is kept in use. In such situations the asset's cost and accumulated depreciation should not be removed from the accounts but should remain on the books until the asset is sold, traded, or discarded. Otherwise the accounts do not show its continued existence. However, no additional depreciation should be recorded, since the reason for recording depreciation is to charge an asset's cost to depreciation expense, and in no case can the expense exceed the asset's cost.

Sometimes an asset is discarded before being fully depreciated. For example, suppose an error was made in estimating the service life of a $1,000 machine and it becomes worthless and is discarded after having only $800 of depreciation recorded against it. In such a situation there is a loss and the entry to record the disposal is:

Jan.	10	Loss on Disposal of Machinery...................................	200.00	
		Accumulated Depreciation, Machinery	800.00	
		Machinery..		1,000.00
		Discarded a worthless machine.		

Selling a plant asset

When a plant asset is sold, it may be sold at book value or at a gain or loss. If the selling price exceeds the asset's book value, there is a gain; and if the price is less than book value, there is a loss. To illustrate the possibilities, assume that a machine which cost $5,000 and which had been depreciated $4,000 is sold. If the machine is sold for its $1,000 book value, the entry to record the sale is:

Jan.	4	Cash...	1,000.00	
		Accumulated Depreciation, Machinery	4,000.00	
		Machinery..		5,000.00
		Sold a machine at book value.		

If the machine is sold at a price in excess of its book value, say, for $1,200, there is a $200 gain and the entry to record the sale is:

Jan.	4	Cash...	1,200.00	
		Accumulated Depreciation, Machinery.........................	4,000.00	
		Machinery..		5,000.00
		Gain on the Sale of Plant Assets............................		200.00
		Sold a machine at a price in excess of book value.		

However, if the machine is sold for $750, there is a $250 loss and the entry to record the sale is:

Jan.	4	Cash..	750.00	
		Loss on the Sale of Plant Assets................................	250.00	
		Accumulated Depreciation, Machinery	4,000.00	
		Machinery...		5,000.00
		Sold a machine at a price below book value.		

Discarding a damaged plant asset

Occasionally, before the end of its service life, a plant asset is wrecked in an accident or destroyed by fire; and in such cases a loss normally occurs. For example, if an uninsured machine that cost $900 and has been depreciated $400 is totally destroyed in an accident such as a fire, the entry to record the loss is:

Jan.	3	Loss from Fire..	500.00	
		Accumulated Depreciation, Machinery	400.00	
		Machinery...		900.00
		To record the accidental destruction of machinery.		

If the loss is partially covered by insurance, the money, say $350, received from the insurance company is debited to Cash; the loss is less; and the entry to record the smaller loss is:

Jan.	3	Cash..	350.00	
		Loss from Fire	150.00	
		Accumulated Depreciation, Machinery	400.00	
		Machinery...		900.00
		To record the destruction of machinery and the receipt of insurance compensation.		

Depreciation for partial years

In most of the illustrations thus far it has been assumed that assets were purchased and discarded at either the beginning or end of an accounting period. This seldom occurs. Business executives normally buy assets when needed and sell or discard these assets when they are no longer usable or needed; and the purchases and sales are normally made without regard for time. Because of this, depreciation must often be calculated for partial years. For example, a truck costing $4,600 and having an estimated five-year service life and a $600 estimated salvage value is purchased on October 8, 1974. If the yearly accounting period ends on December 31, depreciation for three months must be recorded on this truck on that date. Three months are three twelfths of a year. Consequently, the three months' depreciation is calculated:

$$\frac{\$4,600 - \$600}{5} \times \frac{3}{12} = \$200$$

In this illustration, depreciation is calculated for a full three months, even though the asset was purchased on October 8. Depreciation is an estimate; therefore, calculation to the nearest full month is usually sufficiently accurate. This means that depreciation is usually calculated for a full month on assets purchased before the 15th of the month. Likewise, depreciation for the month in which an asset is purchased is normally disregarded if the asset is purchased after the middle of the month.

The entry to record depreciation for three months on the truck purchased on October 8 is:

Dec.	31	Depreciation Expense, Delivery Trucks........................	200.00	
		Accumulated Depreciation, Delivery Trucks		200.00
		To record depreciation for three months on the delivery truck.		

On December 31, 1975, and at the end of each of the following three years, a journal entry to record a full year's depreciation on this truck is required. The entry is:

Dec.	31	Depreciation Expense, Delivery Trucks........................	800.00	
		Accumulated Depreciation, Delivery Trucks		800.00
		To record depreciation for one year on the delivery truck.		

After the December 31, 1978, depreciation entry is recorded, the accounts showing the history of this truck appear as follows:

Delivery Trucks		Accumulated Depreciation Delivery Trucks	
Oct. 8, '74 4,600		Dec. 31, '74 200	
		Dec. 31, '75 800	
		Dec. 31, '76 800	
		Dec. 31, '77 800	
		Dec. 31, '78 800	

If this truck is disposed of during 1979, two entries must be made to record the disposal. The first records 1979 depreciation to the date of disposal, and the second records the actual disposal. For example, assume that the truck is sold for $900 on June 24, 1979. To record the disposal, depreciation for six months (depreciation to the nearest full month) must first be recorded. The entry for this is:

June	24	Depreciation Expense, Delivery Trucks............................	400.00	
		Accumulated Depreciation, Delivery Trucks		400.00
		To record depreciation for one-half year on the		
		delivery truck.		

After making the entry to record depreciation to the date of sale, a second entry to record the actual sale is made. This entry is:

June	24	Cash..	900.00	
		Accumulated Depreciation, Delivery Trucks	3,800.00	
		Delivery Trucks...		4,600.00
		Gain on the Sale of Plant Assets............................		100.00
		To record the sale of a delivery truck.		

Plant asset records

Business concerns commonly divide their plant assets into functional groups and provide separate asset and accumulated depreciation accounts for each group. For example, a store will normally provide an Office Equipment account and an Accumulated Depreciation, Office Equipment account, as well as a Store Equipment account and an Accumulated Depreciation, Store Equipment account. In short, the store will normally have a separate plant asset account and a separate accumulated depreciation account for each functional group of assets it owns. Furthermore, income tax regulations require that any business reporting a deduction from income for depreciation or a gain or a loss on a plant asset sale must be able to substantiate such items with detailed records. No specific kind of records is required, but normally each general ledger plant asset account and its related accumulated depreciation account become controlling accounts controlling detailed subsidiary records. For example, the Office Equipment account and the Accumulated Depreciation, Office Equipment account control a subsidiary ledger having a separate record for each individual item of office equipment. Likewise, the Store Equipment account and its related Accumulated Depreciation, Store Equipment account become controlling accounts controlling a subsidiary store equipment ledger. Often these subsidiary ledger records are kept on plant asset record cards.

To illustrate these plant asset records, assume that a concern's office equipment consists of just one desk and a chair. The general ledger record of these assets is maintained in the Office Equipment controlling account and the Accumulated Depreciation, Office Equipment controlling account. Since in this case there are only two assets, only two subsidiary record cards are needed. The general ledger and subsidiary ledger record of these assets appear as in Illustration 10–2.

Office Equipment				ACCOUNT NO. 132	
DATE	EXPLANATION	FO-LIO	DEBIT	CREDIT	BALANCE
1976 July 2	Desk and chair	G-1	5 3 3 00		5 3 3 00

Accumulated Depreciation, Office Equipment				ACCOUNT NO. 132A	
DATE	EXPLANATION	FO-LIO	DEBIT	CREDIT	BALANCE
1976 Dec. 31		G-23		2 1 00	2 1 00
1977 Dec. 31		G-42		4 2 00	6 3 00
1978 Dec. 31		G-65		4 2 00	1 0 5 00

Plant Asset
No. 132-1

SUBSIDIARY PLANT ASSET AND DEPRECIATION RECORD

Item _Office chair_

General Ledger
Account _Office Equipment_

Description _Office chair_

Mfg. Serial No. _____

Purchased
from _Office Equipment Co._

Where Located _Office_

Person Responsible for the Asset _Office Manager_

Estimated Life _12 years_ Estimated Salvage Value _$4.00_

Depreciation per Year _$6.00_ per Month _$0.50_

Date	Explanation	F	Asset Record			Depreciation Record		
			Dr.	Cr.	Bal.	Dr.	Cr.	Bal.
July 2, '76		G1	76.00		76.00			
Dec. 31, '76		G23					3.00	3.00
Dec. 31, '77		G42					6.00	9.00
Dec. 31, '78		G65					6.00	15.00

Final Disposition of the Asset _____

Illustration 10–2

```
                                              Plant Asset
                                              No. 132-2

        SUBSIDIARY PLANT ASSET AND DEPRECIATION RECORD
                                    General Ledger
Item  Desk                          Account  Office Equipment
Description  Office desk

                                    Purchased
Mfg. Serial No.                     from   Office Equipment Co.
Where Located     Office
Person Responsible for the Asset   Office Manager
Estimated Life  12 years   Estimated Salvage Value $25.00
Depreciation per Year $36.00  per Month   $3.00
```

Date	Explanation	F	Asset Record			Depreciation Record		
			Dr.	Cr.	Bal.	Dr.	Cr.	Bal.
July 2, '76		G1	457.00		457.00			
Dec. 31, '76		G23					18.00	18.00
Dec. 31, '77		G42					36.00	54.00
Dec. 31, '78		G65					36.00	90.00

Final Disposition of the Asset

Illustration 10–2
(continued)

Observe at the top of the cards the plant asset numbers assigned to these two items of office equipment. In each case the assigned number consists of the number of the Office Equipment account, 132, followed by the asset's number. These numbers are stenciled on or otherwise attached to the items of office equipment as a means of identification and to increase control over the items. The remaining information on the record cards is more or less self-evident. Note how the balance of the general ledger account, Office Equipment, is equal to the sum of the balances in the asset record section of the two subsidiary ledger cards. The general ledger account controls this section of the subsidiary ledger. Observe also how the Accumulated Depreciation, Office Equipment account controls the depreciation record section of the cards. The disposition section at the bottom of the card is used to record the final disposal of the asset. When the asset is discarded, sold, or exchanged, a notation telling of the final disposition is entered here. The card is then removed from the subsidiary ledger and filed for future reference.

Plant assets of low cost

Because individual plant asset records are expensive to keep, many concerns establish a minimum, say $50 or a $100, and do not keep such records for assets costing less than the minimum. Rather, they charge the cost of such assets directly to an expense account at the time of purchase; and if about the same amount is expended for such assets each year, this is acceptable under the *materiality principle*.

Glossary

Accelerated depreciation. Any depreciation method resulting in greater amounts of depreciation expense in the early years of a plant asset's life and lesser amounts in later years.

Declining-balance depreciation. A depreciation method in which up to twice the straight-line rate of depreciation, without considering salvage value, is applied to the remaining book value of a plant asset to arrive at the asset's annual depreciation charge.

Deferred income tax. Amounts of income tax the incurrence of which is delayed or put off until later years due to accelerated depreciation or other cause.

Fixed asset. A plant asset.

Going-concern concept. Another name for the continuing-concern concept.

Inadequacy. The situation where a plant asset does not produce enough product to meet current needs.

Internal Revenue Code. The codification of the numerous revenue acts passed by Congress.

Obsolescence. The situation where because of new inventions and improvements, an old plant asset can no longer produce its product on a competitive basis.

Office Equipment Ledger. A subsidiary ledger having a record card for each item of office equipment owned.

Salvage value. The share of a plant asset's cost recovered at the end of its service life through a sale or as a trade-in allowance on a new asset.

Service life. The period of time a plant asset is used in the production and sale of other assets or services.

Store Equipment Ledger. A subsidiary ledger having a record card for each item of store equipment owned.

Straight-line depreciation. A depreciation method that allocates an equal share of the total estimated amount a plant asset will be depreciated during its service life to each accounting period in that life.

Sum-of-the-years'-digits depreciation. A depreciation method that allocates depreciation to each year in a plant asset's life on a fractional basis. The denominator of the fractions used is the sum-of-the years' digits in the estimated service life of the asset, and the numerators are the years' digits in reverse order.

1. What are the characteristics of an asset classified as a plant asset?
2. What is the balance sheet classification of land held for future expansion? Why is such land not classified as a plant asset?
3. What in general is included in the cost of a plant asset?
4. A company asked for bids from several machine shops for the construction of a special machine. The lowest bid was $12,500. The company decided to build the machine for itself and did so at a total cash outlay of $10,000. It then recorded the machine's construction with a debit to Machinery for $12,500, a credit to Cash for $10,000, and a credit to Gain on the Construction of Machinery for $2,500. Was this a proper entry? Discuss.
5. As used in accounting, what is the meaning of the term depreciation?
6. Is it possible to keep a plant asset in such an excellent state of repair that recording depreciation is unnecessary?
7. A company has just purchased a machine that has a potential life of 15 years. However, the company's management believes that the development of a more efficient machine will make it necessary to replace the machine in eight years. What period of useful life should be used in calculating depreciation on this machine?
8. A building estimated to have a useful life of 30 years was completed at a cost of $85,000. It was estimated that at the end of the building's life it would be wrecked at a cost of $1,000 and that materials salvaged from the wrecking operation would be sold for $2,000. How much straight-line depreciation should be charged on the building each year?
9. Define the following terms as used in accounting for plant assets:
   a. Trade-in value.   c. Book value.   e. Inadequacy.
   b. Market value.   d. Salvage value.   f. Obsolescence.
10. When straight-line depreciation is used, an equal share of the total amount a plant asset is to be depreciated during its life is assigned to each accounting period in that life. Describe a situation in which this may not be a fair basis of allocation. Name a more fair basis for the situation described.
11. What is the sum-of-the-years' digits in the life of a plant asset that will be used for 12 years?
12. Does the recording of depreciation cause a plant asset to appear on the balance sheet at market value? What is accomplished by recording depreciation?
13. What is the essence of the going-concern concept of a business?
14. Explain how a concern that breaks even recovers the cost of its plant assets through the sale of its products? Where are the funds thus recovered?
15. Does the balance of the account, Accumulated Depreciation, Machinery, represent funds accumulated to replace the machinery as it wears out? Tell in your own words what the balance of such an account represents?

Exercise 10–1

A machine was purchased for $2,000, terms 2/10, n/60, FOB shipping point. The manufacturer prepaid the freight charges, $110, adding the amount to the invoice and bringing its total to $2,110. The machine required a special concrete base and power connections costing $285, and $270 was paid a millwright to assemble the machine and get it into operation. In moving the machine onto its concrete base, it was dropped and damaged. The damages cost $70 to repair, and after being repaired, $30 of raw materials were consumed in adjusting the machine so it would produce a satisfactory product. The adjustments were normal for this type of machine and were not the result of its having been damaged. The product produced while the adjustments were being made was not salable. Prepare a calculation to show the cost of this machine for accounting purposes.

Exercise 10-2

Three machines were purchased for $8,400 at an auction sale of a bankrupt company's machinery. The purchaser paid $400 to transport the machines to his factory. Machine No. 1 was twice as big and weighed twice as much as Machine No. 2. Machines 2 and 3 were approximately equal in size and weight. The machines had the following appraised values and installation costs:

	Machine No. 1	Machine No. 2	Machine No. 3
Appraised values	$5,000	$4,000	$3,000
Installation costs ...	300	200	150

Determine the cost of each machine for accounting purposes.

Exercise 10-3

A machine was installed in a factory at a $15,800 cost. Its useful life was estimated at five years or 50,000 units of product with an $800 trade-in value. During its second year the machine produced 12,000 units of product. Determine the machine's second-year depreciation with depreciation calculated in each of the following ways: (a) straight-line basis, (b) units-of-production basis, (c) declining-balance basis at twice the straight-line rate, and (d) sum-of-the-years'-digits basis.

Exercise 10-4

A machine cost $2,000 installed and was estimated to have a four-year life and a $200 trade-in value. Use declining-balance depreciation at twice the straight-line rate to determine the amount of depreciation to be charged against the machine in each of the four years of its life.

Exercise 10-5

A machine was installed on January 4, 19—, at a total cost of $6,000. A full year's depreciation on a straight-line basis was charged against the machine on December 31, at the end of each of the first four years in its life under the assumption it would have a five-year life and no salvage value. The machine was disposed of on March 31, during its fifth year. (a) Give the entry to record the partial year's depreciation on March 31, and give the entry to record the disposal under each of the following unrelated assumptions; (b) the machine was sold for $1,000; (c) it was sold for $850; and (d) the machine was totally destroyed in a fire and the insurance company settled the insurance claim for $750.

Problem 10–1

Part 1. A machine costing $5,200, having a four-year life, and an estimated $400 salvage value was installed in a factory. The factory management estimated the machine would produce 60,000 units of product during its life. It actually produced the following numbers of units: Year 1, 11,000; Year 2, 18,000; Year 3, 16,000; and Year 4, 15,000.

Required:

1. Prepare a calculation showing the number of dollars of this machine's cost that should be charged to depreciation over its four-year life.
2. Prepare a form with the following column headings:

Year	Straight Line	Units of Production	Declining Balance	Sum-of-the-Years' Digits

Then show the depreciation for each year and the total depreciation for the machine under each depreciation method. Use twice the straight-line rate for the declining-balance method.

Part 2. A secondhand machine was purchased for $2,280 on January 2. The next day it was repaired and repainted at a cost of $270 and was installed on a new concrete base that cost $210. It was estimated the machine would be used for three years and would then have a $360 salvage value. Depreciation was to be charged on a straight-line basis. A full year's depreciation was charged on December 31, at the end of the first year of the machine's use; and on July 2, in its second year of use, the machine was retired from service.

Required:

1. Prepare general journal entries to record the purchase of the machine, the cost of repairing and repainting it, and its installation. Assume cash was paid in each case.
2. Prepare entries to record depreciation on the machine on December 31 and on July 2.
3. Prepare entries to record the retirement of the machine under each of the following unrelated assumptions: (*a*) the machine was sold for $1,600; (*b*) it was sold for $1,500; and (*c*) it was destroyed in a fire and the insurance company paid $1,250 in full settlement of the loss claim.

Problem 10–2

A concern purchased four machines during 1978 and 1979. Machine No. 1 was placed in use on June 27, 1978. It cost $25,750 installed, had an estimated six-year life and a $1,750 salvage value, and was depreciated on a straight-line basis. Machine No. 2 was placed in use on August 10, 1978, and was depreciated on a units-of-production basis. It cost $17,500 installed, and it was estimated it would produce 80,000 units of product during its ten-year life, after which it would have an estimated $1,500 salvage value. It produced 2,800 units during 1978, 8,200 during 1979, and 7,800 during 1980. Machines 3 and 4 were purchased from a bankrupt firm for $42,000 on August 30, 1979, and were placed in use on the following October 3. Machine No. 3 was depreciated on a declining-balance basis at twice the straight-line rate, and sum-of-the-years'-digits depreciation was used for Machine No. 4. Additional information about these machines follows:

Machine Number	Appraised Value	Salvage Value	Estimated Life	Installation Cost
3............	$30,000	$600	8 years	$800
4............	45,000	900	6 years	900

Required:

1. Prepare a form with the following columnar headings:

Machine Number	Amount to Be Charged to Depreciation	1978 Depreciation	1979 Depreciation	1980 Depreciation

Enter the machine numbers in the first column and complete the information opposite each machine's number. Total the columns.
2. Prepare entries to record the purchase of Machines 3 and 4 and for their installation. Assume cash was paid for the installation on the day the machines were placed in use.
3. Prepare an entry to record the 1980 depreciation on the four machines.

Problem 10–3

On August 3, 1978, a company made a lump-sum purchase of two machines at a bankruptcy sale. The machines cost $27,300 and were placed in use on August 30, 1978. This additional information about the machines is available:

Machine Number	Appraised Value	Salvage Value	Estimated Life	Installation Cost	Depreciation Method
1.........	$15,000	$ 500	4 years	$ 800	Sum-of-the-years' digits
2.........	20,000	1,500	4 years	1,200	Declining balance

The machines were depreciated at the ends of 1978, 1979, and 1980. Machine No. 2's depreciation was calculated at twice the straight-line rate. During the first week in January 1981, the company decided to replace the machines, and on January 10 it sold them in separate sales for cash, Machine No. 1 for $3,000, and Machine No. 2 for $3,700.

Required:

1. Prepare a form with the following headings:

Machine Number	1978 Depreciation	1979 Depreciation	1980 Depreciation	1981 Depreciation	1982 Depreciation

Fill in the machine numbers in the first column and the amounts of depreciation in the remaining columns.

2. Prepare general journal entries to record the purchase of the machines, their installation, the depreciation for each year they were in use, and their sale. Assume cash was paid and received in all transactions and the installation charges were paid for on the day the machines were put in use.

Problem 10–4

Store A and Store B are identical in almost all respects. Both opened their doors for business on January 2 of last year with equipment costing $30,000, having a ten-year life, and $5,000 salvage value; neither added to its equipment during the year; and both purchased merchandise as follows:

Jan.   2........... 100 units @ $100 each.
Mar. 15........... 200 units @   96 each.
July   7........... 300 units @ 110 each.
Oct. 12........... 200 units @ 116 each.
Dec. 15........... 100 units @ 120 each.

At the year-end, before recording depreciation, their records showed the following revenues and expenses:

	Store A	Store B
Sales...................	$135,000	$135,000
Salaries expense....	18,000	18,000
Rent expense........	9,000	9,000
Other expenses.....	1,000	1,000

However, Store A used declining-balance depreciation at twice the straight-line rate, while Store B chose straight-line depreciation. Also, Store A priced its 150-unit ending inventory on a Lifo basis, while Store B used Fifo for its 150-unit inventory.

Required:

1. Prepare an income statement for each store showing last year's results.
2. Prepare a schedule accounting for the difference in their net incomes.

Problem 10–5

Bargain Mart completed these transactions involving plant assets:

1979
Jan.   3   Purchased on credit from Store Equipment Company an Econ Scale priced at $265. The serial number of the scale was B-23452, its service life was estimated at ten years with a trade-in value of $25, and it was assigned plant asset No. 132–1.
Apr.   7   Purchased on credit from Store Equipment Company a Regal cash register priced at $323. The serial number of the register was 3–32564, its service life was estimated at eight years with a trade-in value of $35, and it was assigned plant asset No. 132–2.
Dec. 31   Recorded the 1979 depreciation on the store equipment.
1980
Oct. 28   Sold the Regal cash register to Ted Beal for $250 cash.
Oct. 28   Purchased a new Accurate cash register on credit from Beta Equipment Company for $360. The serial number of the register was

XXX-12345, its service life was estimated at ten years with a trade-in value of $48, and it was assigned plant asset No. 132–3.

Dec. 31   Recorded the 1980 depreciation on the store equipment.

Required:

1. Open general ledger accounts for Store Equipment and for Accumulated Depreciation, Store Equipment. Prepare a subsidiary plant asset record card for each item of equipment purchased.
2. Prepare general journal entries to record the transactions and post to the proper general ledger and subsidiary ledger accounts.
3. Prove the December 31, 1980, balances of the Store Equipment and Accumulated Depreciation, Store Equipment accounts by preparing a list showing the cost and accumulated depreciation on each item of store equipment owned by Bargain Mart on that date.

Problem 10–6

Eaton Company was organized early in January of the current year; and in making your audit of the company's records at the end of the year, you discover that the company's bookkeeper has debited an account called "Land, Buildings, and Equipment" for what he thought was the cost of the company's new factory. The account has a $821,950 debit balance made up of the following items:

Cost of land and an old building on the land purchased as the site of the company's new factory (appraised value of the land, $80,000, and of the old building, $10,000)	$ 84,600
Attorney's fees resulting from land purchase	500
Escrow fees connected with the land purchase	300
Cost of removing old building from plant site	1,800
Surveying and grading plant site	2,800
Cost of retaining wall and the placing of tile to drain the site	1,200
Cost of new building (The contract price was $381,900; however, the contractor accepted $79,400 in cash and 30 bonds having a $300,000 par value. The company had purchased the bonds as a temporary investment at the start of construction for $300,000. The market value of the bonds on the day they were given to the contractor was $302,500.)	379,400
Architect's fee for planning building	23,100
Cost of paving parking lot	8,600
Lights for parking lot	400
Landscaping	2,700
Machinery (including the $800 cost of a machine dropped and made useless while being unloaded from a freight car)	312,500
Fine and permit to haul heavy machinery on city streets. The company was cited for hauling machinery without a permit. It then secured the permit. (Fine, $200; cost of permit, $50)	250
Cost of hauling machinery on city streets	3,000
Cost of replacing damaged machine	800
Total	$821,950

In auditing the company's other accounts it was discovered that the bookkeeper had credited the $300 proceeds from the sale of materials salvaged from the old building removed from the plant site to an account called "Miscellaneous Revenues." He had also credited this account for $50 from the sale of the wrecked machine.

An examination of the payroll records showed that an account called "Superintendence" had been debited for the plant superintendent's $15,000 salary for the ten-month period, March 1 through December 31. From March 1 through August 31 the superintendent had supervised construction of the factory building. During September, October, and November he had supervised installation of the factory machinery. The factory began manufacturing operations on December 1.

Required:

1. Prepare a form having the following four column headings: Land, Land Improvements, Buildings, and Machinery. List the items and sort their amounts to the proper columns. Show a negative amount in parentheses. Total the columns.
2. Under the assumption that the company's accounts had not been closed, prepare an entry to remove the foregoing item amounts from the accounts in which they were incorrectly entered and record them in the proper accounts.
3. The company closes its books annually on December 31. Prepare the entry to record the partial year's depreciation on the plant assets. Assume the building and land improvements are estimated to have 30-year lives and no salvage values and that the machinery is estimated to have a 12-year life and a salvage value equal to 10% of its cost.

Problem 10–1A   Alternate problems

Part 1. A machine costing $7,200 was installed in a factory. Its useful life was estimated at four years, after which it would have a $600 salvage value; and it was estimated the machine would produce 132,000 units of product during its life. It actually produced the following numbers of units: Year 1, 30,000; Year 2, 35,000; Year 3, 34,000; and Year 4, 33,000.

Required:

1. Prepare a calculation to show the total number of dollars of this machine's cost that should be charged to depreciation during its four-year life.
2. Prepare a form with the following column headings:

Year	Straight Line	Units of Production	Declining Balance	Sum-of-the-Years' Digits

Then enter on the form the depreciation for each year and the total depreciation on the machine under each depreciation method. Use twice the straight-line rate for declining-balance depreciation.

Part 2. A secondhand delivery truck was purchased for $2,795 cash on March 18, 1978. The next day $150 was paid for building special racks and shelves in the truck, and the same day $195 was paid Service Garage for minor repairs to the truck's motor and for a new set of tires. The repairs were priced at $35, and the tires at $172. However, a $12 trade-in allowance was received on the truck's old tires. Prepare general journal entries to record the purchase of the truck, payment for racks and shelves, and payment for the new tires and motor repairs.

Part 3. At the time of its purchase it was estimated the truck of Part 2 would be driven 30,000 miles, after which it would have a $440 trade-in value. The truck was driven 9,000 miles during the remaining months of 1978, and between January 1 and July 12, 1979, the truck was driven an additional 7,000 miles. On the latter date it was retired from service. Give the entries to record the 1978 and 1979 depreciation. Also, give the entries to record the truck's retirement under each of the following unrelated assumptions: (*a*) The truck was sold on July 12, 1979, for $1,750. (*b*) The truck was totally destroyed in a wreck, and the insurance company paid $1,450 in full settlement of the loss claim.

Problem 10–2A

A company purchased four machines during 1978 and 1979 and has used four ways to allocate depreciation on the machines. Information about the machines follow:

Machine Number	*Placed in Use on*	*Cost*	*Estimated Life*	*Salvage Value*	*Depreciation Method*
1	Oct. 5, 1978	$ 6,150	8 years	$ 550	Straight line
2	July 2, 1978	19,500	8 years	1,500	Sum-of-the-years' digits
3	Mar. 29, 1979	35,000	60,000 units	2,000	Units of production
4	June 28, 1979	?	10 years	2,000	Declining balance at twice the straight-line rate

Machine No. 3 produced 7,000 units of product in 1979 and 9,300 in 1980. Machine No. 4 had an invoice price of $29,500, 2/10, n/60, FOB point of shipment. The invoice was paid on the last day of the discount period June 29, but the company had to borrow $15,000 on a 60-day, 8% note in order to do so. The loan was repaid on August 28. Freight charges on Machine No. 4 were $215, and the machine was placed on a special concrete base that cost $460. It was assembled and installed by the company's own employees. Their wages during the installation period were $415. Payments for the freight charges, the concrete base, and the employees' wages were made on June 30.

Required:

1. Prepare a form with the following columnar headings:

Machine Number	Amount to Be Charged to Depreciation	1978 Depreciation	1979 Depreciation	1980 Depreciation

Enter the machine numbers in the first column and complete the information opposite each machine's number. Total the columns.
2. Prepare entries to record all transactions involving the purchase of Machine No. 4, including the note transactions.
3. Prepare an entry to record the December 31, 1980, depreciation.

Problem 10–3A

On March 16, 1978, a company made a lump-sum purchase of two machines from another company that was going out of business. The machines cost $48,600 and were placed in use on April 4, 1978. This additional information about the machines is available:

Machine Number	Appraised Value	Salvage Value	Estimated Life	Installation Cost	Depreciation Method
1.........	$24,000	$1,200	4 years	$ 600	Sum-of-the-years' digits
2.........	30,000	2,000	4 years	1,000	Declining balance at twice the straight-line rate

The machines were depreciated at the ends of 1978, 1979, and 1980; and during the first week in January 1981, the company decided to sell and replace them. Consequently, on January 12, 1981, it sold Machine No. 1 for $4,000, and on January 14 it sold Machine No. 2 for $4,500.

Required:

1. Prepare a form with the following columnar headings:

Machine Number	1978 Depreciation	1979 Depreciation	1980 Depreciation	1981 Depreciation	1982 Depreciation

Enter the machine numbers in the first column and the amounts of depreciation in the remaining columns.

2. Prepare general journal entries to record the purchase of the machines, their installation, the depreciation for each year they were in use, and their sale. Assume cash was paid and received in all transactions and the installation charges were paid for on the day the machines were put in use.

Problem 10–4A

Stores X and Y are identical in almost all respects. Both began business one year ago, on January 2, with equipment that cost $25,000 each, and which has an estimated ten-year life and a $5,000 salvage value. Neither store added to its equipment during the year and each purchased merchandise as follows:

Jan.   2   100 units @ $150 each.
Feb. 27   100 units @   160 each.
Apr.   5   300 units @   164 each.
Aug. 25   200 units @   176 each.
Nov. 17   100 units @   180 each.

At the year-end, on December 31, before recording depreciation, their records showed the following revenues and expenses:

	Store X	Store Y
Sales...................	$175,000	$175,000
Salaries expense....	20,000	20,000
Rent expense........	12,000	12,000
Other expenses.....	4,000	4,000

However, Store X used declining-balance depreciation at twice the straight-line rate, while Store Y chose straight-line depreciation. Also, Store X priced its 110-unit ending inventory on a Lifo basis, while Store Y used Fifo for its 110-unit inventory.

Required:

1. Prepare an income statement for each store showing last year's results.
2. Prepare a schedule accounting for the difference in their net incomes.

Problem 10–5A

Monroe Company completed the following plant asset transactions:

1979

Jan. 7   Purchased on credit from Quicko, Inc., a Quicko calculator, $550. The serial number of the machine was X2X345. Its service life was estimated at eight years with a $70 trade-in value. It was assigned plant asset number 132–1.

      9   Purchased on credit from Office Outfitters an Accurate typewriter for $380. The machine's serial number was MMM-0156, and it was assigned plant asset number 132–2. Its service life was estimated at four years with a $44 trade-in value.

Dec. 31   Recorded the 1979 depreciation on the office equipment.

1980

June 3   Sold the Accurate typewriter for $200 cash.

      4   Purchased on credit for $415 from Speedy Typewriter Company a Speedy typewriter. The machine's serial number was MO7781, and it was assigned plant asset number 132–3. Its service life was estimated at four years with a $55 trade-in value.

Dec. 31   Recorded the 1980 depreciation on the office equipment.

Required:

1. Open an office Equipment account and an Accumulated Depreciation, Office Equipment account plus subsidiary plant asset record cards as needed.
2. Prepare general journal entries to record the transactions. Post to the general ledger accounts and subsidiary record cards.
3. Prove the December 31, 1980, balances of the Office Equipment and Accumulated Depreciation, Office Equipment accounts by preparing a schedule showing the cost and accumulated depreciation of each plant asset owned by the company on that date.

Decision problem 10–1, Echo Company

Echo Company earns more than a half million dollars each year, and it has just invested $88,000 in new machinery that will increase its earnings $45,000 per year before depreciation on the new machinery and income taxes on the extra earnings. The new machinery is expected to have a four-year life and an $8,000 salvage value.

Explain which depreciation method is best from a net income point of view for the company to use. Back your answer with calculations to show the number of extra dollars the company will earn by using the "best method" rather than straight-line depreciation. In making your calculations, assume that income taxes take one half of the company's before-tax earnings and that it can invest any deferred tax dollars to earn a 5% after-tax return, compounded annually. Also, to simplify the problem, assume that income taxes must be paid on the first day of January following the year of incurrence.

Last week you went to work for a local accounting firm and today you are working on your first audit, a company that has been organized just one year; and in examining the company's plant asset accounts, you find the following debits and credits in an account called Land and Buildings:

Decision problem 10–2, first audit

Debits

Jan.	3	Cost of land and buildings acquired for new plant site............	$ 50,000
	10	Attorney's fee for title search	500
	27	Cost of wrecking old building on plant site.........................	5,000
Feb.	1	Six months' liability and fire insurance on new building.........	1,500
June	30	Payment to building contractor on completion of building......	225,250
July	1	Architect's fee for new building	13,500
	3	City assessment for street improvements	3,500
	14	Cost of landscaping new plant site....................................	2,000
			$301,250

Credits

Jan.	25	Proceeds from sale of salvaged materials from old building....	$ 1,000
July	3	Refund of one month's insurance premium..........................	250
Dec.	31	Depreciation at 2½% per year	3,750
	31	Balance..	296,250
			$301,250

In consultation with the senior accountant in charge of the audit, you learn that 40 years is a reasonable life expectancy for a building of the type involved and that it is reasonable to assume that there will be no salvage value at the end of the building's life. He also tells you to prepare a schedule with columns headed Date, Description, Total Amount, Land, Buildings, and Other Accounts and to enter the items found in the Land and Buildings account on the schedule, distributing the amounts to the proper columns. He suggests that you show credits on your schedule by enclosing the amounts in parentheses; and finally he suggests that since the accounts have not been closed, you draft any required correcting entry or entries. Assume that an account called Depreciation Expense, Land and Buildings was debited in recording the $3,750 of depreciation.

Red Rock, Inc., a large corporation, is about to invest $200,000 in new machinery to add a new product to its line. The new machinery is expected to have a four-year life and a $20,000 salvage value; and you, the company's

Decision problem 10–3, Red Rock, Inc.

accountant, have prepared the following statement showing the expected results from the sale of the new machinery's product. The statement is based on
the assumption that the new machinery will be depreciated on a straight-line
basis and that the company must pay out 50% of its before-tax earnings in state
and federal income taxes.

RED ROCK, INC.
Expected Results from Sale of New Product

	Year 1	Year 2	Year 3	Year 4	Totals
Sales.....................................	$375,000	$375,000	$375,000	$375,000	$1,500,000
All costs other than depre- ciation and income taxes.........	250,000	250,000	250,000	250,000	1,000,000
Income before depreciation and income taxes	$125,000	$125,000	$125,000	$125,000	$ 500,000
Depreciation expense	45,000	45,000	45,000	45,000	180,000
Income before income taxes	$ 80,000	$ 80,000	$ 80,000	$ 80,000	$ 320,000
Income taxes	40,000	40,000	40,000	40,000	160,000
Net Income	$ 40,000	$ 40,000	$ 40,000	$ 40,000	$ 160,000

When the company president examined your statement, he said he knew
that regardless of how calculated, the company could charge off no more than
$180,000 of depreciation on the new machinery during its four-year life. Fur-
thermore, he said he could see that this would result in $320,000 of earnings
before taxes for the four years, $160,000 of income taxes, and $160,000 of net
income, regardless of how depreciation was calculated. Nevertheless, he continued that he had been talking to a friend on the golf course a few days back
and the friend had tried to explain the tax advantage of using declining-balance
depreciation. He said he did not understand all the friend had tried to tell him;
and as a result he would like for you to prepare an additional statement like
the one already prepared, but based on declining-balance depreciation at
twice the straight-line rate. He said he would also like a written explanation of
the tax advantage the company would gain through the use of declining-balance
depreciation, with a dollar estimate of the amount the company would gain in
this case. Prepare the information for the president. (In making your estimate,
assume the company can earn a 6% after-tax return, compounded annually on
any deferred taxes. Also, to simplify the problem, assume that the taxes must
be paid the first day of January following their incurrence.)

After studying Chapter 11, you should be able to:

- Prepare entries to record the exchange of plant assets under accounting rules and under income tax rules and tell which rules should be applied in any given exchange.

- Explain the concept of present value and apply the concept in the exchange of a long-term noninterest-bearing note for a plant asset.

- Make the calculations and prepare the entries to account for revisions in depreciation rates.

- Make the calculations and prepare the entries to account for plant asset repairs and betterments.

- Prepare entries to account for wasting assets and for intangible assets.

- Define or explain the words and phrases listed in the chapter Glossary.

chapter 11

Plant and equipment; intangible assets

Some of the problems met in accounting for property, plant, and equipment were discussed in the previous chapter. Additional problems involving plant assets and some of the accounting problems encountered with intangible assets are examined in this chapter.

Some plant assets are sold at the ends of their useful lives; but others, such as machinery, automobiles, and office equipment, are commonly exchanged for new up-to-date assets of a like nature. In such exchanges a trade-in allowance is normally received on the old asset, with the balance being paid in cash; and the Accounting Principles Board has ruled that in recording the exchanges a material book loss should be recognized in the accounts but a book gain should not.[1] (A book loss is experienced when the trade-in allowance received is less than the book value of the traded asset, and a book gain results from a trade-in allowance that exceeds the book value of the traded asset.)

Exchanging plant assets

Recognizing a material book loss

To illustrate the recognition of a material book loss on an exchange of plant assets, assume that a machine which cost $18,000 and had been depreciated $15,000 was traded in on a new machine having a $21,000 cash price. A $1,000 trade-in allowance was received, and the $20,000 balance was paid in cash. Under these assumptions the book value of the old machine is $3,000, calculated as follows:

Cost of old machine	$18,000
Less accumulated depreciation	15,000
Book value	$ 3,000

---

[1] APB, "Accounting for Nonmonetary Transactions," *APB Opinion No. 29* (New York: AICPA, May 1973), par. 22.

And since the $1,000 trade-in allowance resulted in a $2,000 loss on the exchange, the transaction should be recorded as follows:

Jan.	5	Machinery..	21,000.00	
		Loss on Exchange of Machinery................................	2,000.00	
		Accumulated Depreciation, Machinery	15,000.00	
		Machinery..		18,000.00
		Cash..		20,000.00
		Exchanged old machine and cash for a new machine of like purpose.		

The $21,000 debit to Machinery puts the new machine in the accounts at its cash price, the debit to Loss on Exchange of Machinery records the loss, and the old machine is removed from the accounts with the $15,000 debit to accumulated depreciation and the $18,000 credit to Machinery.

Nonrecognition of a book gain

When cash is given and there is a book gain on an exchange of plant assets, the Accounting Principles Board has ruled that the new asset should be taken into the accounts at an amount equal to the book value of the traded-in asset plus the cash given. This results in the non-recognition of the gain. For example, assume that in acquiring the $21,-000 machine of the previous section a $4,500 trade-in allowance, rather than a $1,000 trade-in allowance, was received, and the $16,500 balance was paid in cash. A $4,500 trade-in allowance would result in a $1,500 gain on the exchange, calculated as follows:

```
Trade-in allowance....................... $4,500
Less book value of old machine ....  3,000
Book gain ................................. $1,500
```

However, according to the APB, in recording this exchange, the book gain should not be recognized in the accounts. Rather, the gain should be absorbed into the cost of the new machine by taking the new machine into the accounts at an amount equal to the sum of the book value of the old machine plus the cash given. This is $19,500 in this case and is calculated as follows:

```
Book value of old machine........... $ 3,000
Cash given in the exchange ......... 16,500
Cost basis for the new machine.... $19,500
```

And the transaction should be recorded as follows:

Jan.	5	Machinery	19,500.00	
		Accumulated Depreciation, Machinery	15,000.00	
		Machinery		18,000.00
		Cash		16,500.00
		Exchanged old machine and cash for a new machine of like purpose.		

Observe that the $19,500 recorded amount for the new machine is equal to its cash price less the $1,500 book gain on the exchange ($21,000 − $1,500 = $19,500); or in other words the $1,500 book gain was absorbed into the amount at which the new machine was recorded. The $19,500 is called the *cost basis* of the new machine and is the amount that is used in recording depreciation on the machine or any gain or loss on its sale.

The APB bases its ruling that gains on plant asset exchanges should not be recognized on the opinion that ". . . revenue should not be recognized merely because one productive asset is substituted for a similar productive asset but rather should be considered to flow from the production and sale of the goods or services to which the sub-stituted productive asset is committed."[2] In other words the APB is of the opinion that any gain from a plant asset exchange should be taken in the form of increased net income resulting from smaller depreciation charges on the asset acquired. In this case depreciation calculated on the recorded $19,500 cost basis of the new machine is less than if cal-culated on the machine's $21,000 cash price.

Tax rules and plant asset exchanges

Income tax rules and accounting principles are in agreement on the treatment of gains on plant asset exchanges but do not agree on the treatment of losses. According to the Internal Revenue Service, when an old asset is traded in on a new asset of like purpose, either a gain or a loss on the exchange must be absorbed into the cost of the new ma-chine. This cost basis then becomes for tax purposes the amount that must be used in calculating depreciation on the new asset or any gain or loss on its sale or exchange. Consequently, for tax purposes the cost basis of an asset acquired in an exchange for an old asset of like purpose is the sum of the book value of the old asset plus the cash given, and it makes no difference whether there is a gain or a loss on the exchange.

As a result of the difference between accounting principles and tax rules, if a loss on a plant asset exchange is recorded as such at the time of the exchange, two sets of depreciation records must be kept through-

---

[2] Ibid., par. 16.

out the life of the new asset, one for determining net income for accounting purposes and the other for determining the depreciation deduction for tax purposes. Keeping two sets of records is obviously more costly than keeping one. Yet, when an exchange results in a material loss, the loss should be recorded and the two sets of records kept. On the other hand, when an exchange results in an immaterial loss, it is permissible under the accounting principle of materiality to avoid the two sets of records by putting the new asset on the books at its cost basis for tax purposes.

For example, an old typewriter that cost $200 and upon which $140 of depreciation had been recorded was traded in at $35 on a new $250 typewriter, with the $215 difference being paid in cash. In this case the old typewriter's book value is $60; and if it was traded at $35, there was a $25 book loss on the exchange. However, the $25 loss is an immaterial amount, and the following method, called the income tax method, may be used in recording the exchange:

Jan.	7	Office Equipment	275.00	
		Accumulated Depreciation, Office Equipment	140.00	
		Office Equipment		200.00
		Cash		215.00
		Traded an old typewriter and cash for a new typewriter.		

The $275 amount at which the new typewriter is taken into the accounts by the income tax method is its cost basis for tax purposes and is calculated as follows:

Book value of old typewriter ($200 less $140).............. $ 60
Cash paid ($250 less the $35 trade-in allowance) 215
Income tax basis of the new typewriter $275

Not recording the loss on this exchange and taking the new typewriter into the accounts at its cost basis for income tax purposes violates the ruling of the APB that a loss on a plant asset exchange should be recorded. However, when there is an immaterial loss on an exchange, as in this case, the violation is permissible under the accounting principle of materiality, because under the *principle of materiality* an adherence to any accounting principle, including rulings of the APB, is not required when the cost to adhere is proportionally great and the lack of adherence does not materially affect reported periodic net income. In this case failing to record the $25 loss on the exchange would not materially affect the average company's statements. On the other hand, recording the loss and thereafter keeping two sets of depreciation records would be costly.

When a relatively high-cost plant asset is purchased, particularly if the credit period is long, a note is sometimes given in making the purchase. If the amount of the note is approximately equal to the cash price for the asset and the interest on the note is at approximately the prevailing rate, the transaction is recorded as follows:

Exchanging a note for a plant asset

Feb.	12	Store Equipment..	4,500.00	
		Notes Payable..		4,500.00
		Exchanged a $4,500, one-year, 7% note payable for a refrigerated display case.		

A note given in exchange for a plant asset has two elements, which may or may not be stipulated in the note. They are: (1) a dollar amount equivalent to the bargained cash price of the asset and (2) an interest factor to compensate the supplier for the use of the funds that otherwise would have been received in a cash sale. Consequently, when a note is exchanged for a plant asset and the face amount of the note approximately equals the cash price of the asset and the note's stipulated interest rate is at or near the prevailing rate, the asset may be recorded at the face amount of the note as in the previous illustration. However, if no interest rate is stated, or the interest rate is unreasonable, or the face amount of the note materially differs from the cash price for the asset, the asset should be recorded at its cash price or at the *present value* of the note, whichever is more clearly determinable.[3] In such a situation to record the asset at the face amount of the note would cause the asset, the liability, and interest expense to be misstated. Furthermore, the misstatements could be material in case of a long-term note.

(At this point students who are unfamiliar with the concept of present value, mentioned in the previous paragraph, should turn to the Appendix at the end of this chapter and familiarize themselves with the concept before attempting to go further into the discussion of this section.)

To illustrate a situation in which a note having no interest rate stated is exchanged for a plant asset, assume that on January 2, 1978, a noninterest-bearing, five-year, $10,000 note payable is exchanged for a factory machine, the cash price of which is not readily determinable. If the prevailing rate for interest on the day of the exchange is 7%, the present value of the note on that day is $7,130 [based on the fifth amount in the 7% column of Table 11A–1 in the Appendix at the end of this chapter ($10,000 × 0.713 = $7,130)], and the exchange should be recorded as follows:

---

[3] APB, "Interest on Receivables and Payables," *APB Opinion No. 21* (New York: AICPA, August 1971), pars. 8 and 12.

1978					
Jan.	2	Factory Machinery	7,130.00		
		Discount on Notes Payable	2,870.00		
		Long-Term Notes Payable.....................................		10,000.00	
		Exchanged a five-year, noninterest-bearing note for a machine.			

The $7,130 debit amount in the entry is the present value of the note on the day of the exchange. It is also the cost of the machine and is the amount to be used in calculating depreciation and any future loss or gain on the machine's sale or exchange. The entry's notes payable and discount amounts together measure the liability resulting from the transaction, and they should appear on a balance sheet prepared immediately after the exchange as follows:

Long-Term Liabilities:
    Long-term notes payable.. $10,000
        Less unamortized discount based on the 7% interest
          rate prevailing on the date of issue................................ 2,870 $7,130

The $2,870 discount is the interest element of the transaction, and Column 3 of Illustration 11–1 shows the portions of the $2,870 that should be amortized and charged to interest expense at the ends of each of the five years in the life of the note. The first year's amortization entry is:

1978					
Dec.	31	Interest Expense	499.00		
		Discount on Notes Payable		499.00	
		To amortize a portion of the discount on our long-term note.			

The $499 amortized is interest at 7% on the note's $7,130 value on the day it was exchanged for the machine. [The $499 is rounded to the nearest full dollar, as are all the Column 3 amounts ($7,130 × 7% = $499.10).]

Posting the amortization entry causes the note to appear on the December 31, 1978, balance sheet as follows:

Long-Term Liabilities:
    Long-term notes payable.. $10,000
        Less unamortized discount based on the 7% interest
          rate prevailing on the date of issue................................ 2,371 $7,629

Year	Beginning-of-the-Year Carrying Amount	Discount to Be Amortized Each Year	Unamortized Discount at the End of the Year	End-of-the-Year Carrying Amount
1978	$7,130	$499	$2,371	$ 7,629
1979	7,629	534	1,837	8,163
1980	8,163	571	1,266	8,734
1981	8,734	611	655	9,345
1982	9,345	655*	–0–	10,000

* Adjusted for rounding.   **Illustration 11–1**

Compare the net amount at which the note is carried on the December 31, 1978, balance sheet with the net amount shown for the note on the balance sheet prepared on its date of issue; and observe that the *carrying amount* increased $499 between the two dates, which is the amount of discount amortized and charged to interest expense at the end of 1978.

At the end of 1979 and each succeeding year the remaining amounts of discount shown in Column 3 of Illustration 11–1 should be amortized and charged to interest expense. This will cause the carrying amount of the note to increase each year by the amount of discount amortized that year and to reach $10,000, the note's maturity value, at the end of the fifth year. Payment of the note may then be recorded as follows:

1983 Jan.	2	Long-Term Notes Payable...	10,000.00	
		Cash..		10,000.00
		Paid our long-term noninterest-bearing note.		

Now return to Illustration 11–1. Each end-of-the-year carrying amount in the last column is determined by subtracting the end-of-the-year unamortized discount from the $10,000 face amount of the note. For example, $10,000 − $2,371 = $7,629. Each beginning-of-the-year carrying amount is the same as the previous year's end-of-the-year amount. The amount of discount to be amortized each year is determined by multiplying the beginning-of-the-year carrying amount by the 7% interest rate prevailing at the time of the exchange. For example, $7,629 × 7% = $534 (rounded). Each end-of-the-year amount of unamortized discount is the discount remaining after subtracting the discount amortized that year. For example, $2,870 − $499 = $2,371.

Revising depreciation rates

An occasional error in estimating the useful life of a plant asset is to be expected. Furthermore, when such an error is discovered, it is corrected by spreading the cost of the asset's remaining quantity of usefulness over its remaining useful life.[4] For example, seven years ago a machine was purchased at a cost of $10,500. At that time the machine was estimated to have a ten-year life with a $500 salvage value. Therefore, it was depreciated at the rate of $1,000 per year [($10,500 − $500) ÷ 10 = $1,000]; and it began its eighth year with a $3,500 book value, calculated as follows:

Cost	$10,500
Less seven years' accumulated depreciation....	7,000
Book value...	$ 3,500

If at the beginning of its eighth year the estimated number of years remaining in this machine's useful life is changed from three to five years with no change in salvage value, depreciation for each of the machine's remaining years should be recalculated as follows:

$$\frac{\text{Book value} - \text{Salvage value}}{\text{Remaining useful life}} = \frac{\$3,500 - \$500}{5 \text{ years}} = \$600 \text{ per year}$$

And an entry like the following should be used to record depreciation at the end of the machine's eighth and each succeeding year to retirement:

Dec.	31	Depreciation Expense, Machinery...............................	600.00	
		Accumulated Depreciation, Machinery		600.00
		To record depreciation at the revised rate.		

If depreciation is charged at the rate of $1,000 per year for the first seven years of this machine's life and $600 per year for the next five, depreciation expense is overstated during the first seven years and understated during the next five. However, if a concern has many plant assets, the lives of some will be underestimated and the lives of others will be overestimated at the time of purchase; consequently, such errors will tend to cancel each other out with little or no effect on the income statement.

Repairs and replacements

Repairs and replacements fall into two groups: (1) ordinary repairs and replacements and (2) extraordinary repairs and replacements.

Ordinary repairs and replacements

Expenditures for ordinary repairs and replacements are necessary to maintain an asset in good operating condition. A building must be painted and its roof repaired or a machine must be reconditioned and

---

[4] APB, "Accounting Changes," *APB Opinion No. 20* (New York: AICPA, July 1971), par. 31.

small parts replaced. Any expenditures to maintain a plant asset in its normal good state of repair are considered ordinary repairs and replacements. Ordinary repairs and replacements are a current expense and should appear on the current income statement as a deduction from revenues.

Maintenance costs such as those for cleaning, lubricating, and adjusting machinery are also a current expense and are accounted for in the same way as ordinary repairs. Often such costs are combined with ordinary repairs for accounting purposes.

Extraordinary repairs and replacements

Extraordinary repairs and replacements are major repairs and replacements made, not to keep an asset in its normal good state of repair but to extend its useful life beyond that originally estimated. As a rule, the cost of such repairs and replacements should be debited to the repaired asset's accumulated depreciation account under the assumption they make good past depreciation, add to the asset's useful life, and benefit future periods. For example, a machine was purchased for $8,000 and depreciated under the assumption it would last eight years and have no salvage value. As a result, at the end of the machine's sixth year its book value is $2,000, calculated as follows:

Cost of machine	$8,000
Less six years' accumulated depreciation	6,000
Book value	$2,000

If at the beginning of the machine's seventh year it is given a major overhaul that extends its estimated useful life three years beyond the eight originally estimated, the $2,100 cost of the repairs should be recorded with an entry like the following:

Jan.	12	Accumulated Depreciation, Machinery	2,100.00	
		Cash (or Accounts Payable)		2,100.00
		To record extraordinary repairs.		

In addition, depreciation for each of the five years remaining in the machine's life should be calculated as follows:

Book value before extraordinary repairs	$2,000
Extraordinary repairs	2,100
Total	$4,100
Annual depreciation expense for remaining years ($4,100 ÷ 5 years)	$ 820

And, if the machine remains in use for five years after the major overhaul, the five annual $820 depreciation charges will exactly write off its new book value, including the cost of the extraordinary repairs.

Betterments

A betterment may be defined as the replacement of an existing asset or asset portion with an improved or superior asset or portion, usually at a cost materially in excess of the replaced item. Replacing the manual controls on a machine with automatic controls, removing an old motor and replacing it with a larger, more powerful one, and replacing a wood shingle roof with a tile roof are illustrations of betterments. Usually a betterment results in a better, more efficient, or more productive asset, but not necessarily one having a longer life.

When a betterment is made, its cost should be debited to the improved asset's account and depreciated over the remaining service life of the asset. Also, the cost and applicable depreciation of the replaced asset or portion should be removed from the accounts. For example, if the motor on a machine is replaced with a faster more powerful one, the cost of the new motor should be debited to the Machinery account and the cost and applicable depreciation on the old motor should be removed from the accounts.

Capital and revenue expenditures

A *revenue expenditure* is one that should appear on the current income statement as an expense and a deduction from the period's revenues. Expenditures for ordinary repairs, rent, and salaries are examples.

Expenditures for betterments and for extraordinary repairs that lengthen the estimated life of an asset should appear on the balance sheet as increases in asset book values; and as a result, they are examples of what are called *capital expenditures* or balance sheet expenditures that benefit future periods.

Obviously, care must be exercised to distinguish between capital and revenue expenditures when transactions are recorded; for if errors are made, such errors often affect a number of accounting periods. For instance, an expenditure for a betterment initially recorded in error as an expense overstates expenses in the year of the error and understates net income. Also, since the cost of a betterment should be depreciated over the remaining useful life of the bettered asset, depreciation expense of future periods is understated and net income is overstated.

Natural resources

Natural resources such as standing timber, mineral deposits, and oil reserves are known as wasting assets. The distinguishing characteristic of wasting assets is that in their natural state they represent inventories that will be converted into a product by cutting, mining, or pumping. Standing timber, for example, is an inventory of uncut lumber. When it is cut and sawed, it becomes a product to be sold; and one of the costs of the product is the cost of the standing timber from which it was manufactured. However, until cut, it is a noncurrent asset commonly shown on the balance sheet under a caption such as "Timberlands." Or if a mineral deposit or oil reserve, it is commonly shown as "Mineral deposits" or "Oil reserves."

Natural resources are accounted for at cost, and appear on the balance sheet at cost less accumulated *depletion*. The amount such assets are depleted each year by cutting, mining, or pumping is commonly calculated on a "units-of-production" basis. For example, if a mine having an estimated 500,000 tons of available ore is purchased for $500,000, the depletion charge per ton of ore mined is $1. Furthermore, if 85,000 tons are mined during the first year, the depletion charge for the year is $85,000 and is recorded as follows:

Dec.	31	Depletion of Mineral Deposit..	85,000.00	
		Accumulated Depletion, Mineral Deposit		85,000.00
		To record depletion of ore body resulting from mining 85,000 tons of ore.		

On the balance sheet prepared at the end of the first year the mine should appear at its $500,000 cost less $85,000 accumulated depletion. If all of the 85,000 tons of ore are sold by the end of the first year, the entire $85,000 depletion charge reaches the income statement as the depletion cost of the ore mined and sold. However, if a portion of the 85,000 tons remains unsold at the year-end, the depletion cost of the unsold ore is carried forward on the balance sheet as part of the cost of the unsold ore inventory, a current asset.

Often machinery must be installed or a building constructed in order to exploit a natural resource. The costs of such assets should be recorded in plant and equipment accounts, and should be depreciated over the life of the natural resource with annual depreciation charges that are in proportion to the annual depletion charges. For example, if a machine having a ten-year life is installed in a mine that will be depleted in six years, the machine should be depreciated over the six-year period. Furthermore, if one eighth of the mine's ore is removed during the first year, one eighth of the machine's total depreciation should be recorded as one of the costs of the ore mined.

Intangible assets

Intangible assets have no physical existence; rather, they represent certain legal rights and economic relationships which are beneficial to the owner. Their value is derived from the rights conferred by ownership and possession. Patents, copyrights, leaseholds, goodwill, trademarks, and organization costs are examples. Notes and accounts receivable are also intangible in nature, but these appear on the balance sheet as current assets rather than under the intangible assets classification.

Intangible assets are accounted for at cost and should appear on the balance sheet in the intangible asset section at cost or at that portion of cost not previously written off. Normally the intangible asset section follows on the balance sheet immediately after the plant and equipment section. Intangibles should be systematically amortized or written off to expense accounts over their estimated useful lives, which in no case should exceed 40 years.[5] Amortization is a process similar to the recording of depreciation.

Patents

Patents are granted by the federal government to encourage the invention of new machines and mechanical devices. A patent gives its owner the exclusive right to manufacture and sell a patented machine or device for a period of 17 years. When patent rights to a previously developed successful machine or mechanical device are purchased, all costs of acquiring the rights may be debited to an account called "Patents." Also the costs of a successful lawsuit in defense of a patent may be debited to this account.

Although a patent gives its owner exclusive rights to the patented device for 17 years, its cost should be amortized or written off over a shorter period if its useful or economic life is estimated to be less than 17 years. For example, if a patent costing $25,000 has an estimated useful life of only ten years, the following adjusting entry is made at the end of each year in the patent's life to write off one tenth of its cost.

Dec.	31	Patents Written Off...	2,500.00	
		Patents		2,500.00
		To write off one tenth of patent costs.		

The entry's debit causes $2,500 of patent costs to appear on the annual income statement as one of the costs of the patented product manufactured. The credit directly reduces the balance of the Patents account. Normally, patents are written off directly to the Patents account as in this entry.

Research and development costs

Business concerns spend billions of dollars each year on research and new product development, and these expenditures are vital to our country's economic growth. However, the accounting treatment for such expenditures in the years prior to 1975 was not uniform. Some companies charged all research and development costs to expense accounts in the year incurred. Others treated such costs as an intangible asset to be amortized over the lives of successful new products

---

[5] APB, "Intangible Assets," *APB Opinion No. 17* (New York: AICPA, August 1970), par. 29.

developed. Consequently, as a result of the lack of uniformity, the Financial Accounting Standards Board (FASB) has ruled[6] that all research and development costs not directly reimbursable by government agencies or others shall be charged to expense accounts in the accounting period incurred.

Copyrights

A copyright is granted by the federal government and gives its owner the exclusive right to publish and sell a musical, literary, or artwork during the life of the composer, author, or artist and for 50 years thereafter. Many copyrights have value for a much shorter time, and their costs should be amortized over the shorter period. Often the only cost of a copyright is the fee paid the Copyright Office; and since this is nominal, it is commonly charged directly to an expense account.

Leaseholds

Property is rented under a contract called a *lease*. The person or company owning the property and granting the lease is called the *lessor*, the person or company securing the right to possess and use the property is called the *lessee*, and the rights granted the lessee under the lease are called a *leasehold*.

Some leases require no advance payment from the lessee but do require monthly rent payments. In such cases a Leasehold account is not needed and the monthly payments are debited to a Rent Expense account. Sometimes a long-term lease is so drawn that the last year's rent must be paid in advance at the time the lease is signed. When this occurs, the last year's advance payment is debited to the Leasehold account where it remains until the last year of the lease, at which time it is transferred to Rent Expense.

Often a long-term lease, one running 20 or 25 years, becomes very valuable after a few years because its required rent payments are much less than current rentals for identical property. In such cases the increase in value of the lease should not be entered on the books since no extra cost was incurred in acquiring it. However, if the property is subleased and the new tenant makes a cash payment for the rights under the old lease, the new tenant should debit the payment to a Leasehold account and amortize or write it off as additional rent expense over the remaining life of the lease.

Leasehold improvements

Long-term leases often require the lessee to pay for any alterations or improvements to the leased property, such as new partitions and store fronts. Normally the costs of the improvements are debited to an

---

[6] Financial Accounting Standards Board, "Accounting for Research and Development Costs," *FASB Statement No. 2* (Stamford, Conn., 1974), par. 12.

account called Leasehold Improvements; and since the improvements become part of the property and revert to the lessor at the end of the lease, their cost should be amortized over the life of the lease or the life of the improvements, whichever is shorter. The amortization entry commonly has a debit to Rent Expense and a credit to Leasehold Improvements.

Goodwill

When a concern so conducts its affairs that its customers are convinced their future dealings with the company will be as completely satisfactory as in the past, when the customers always return to transact with the concern the kind of business it conducts, and when its customers' good reports tend to bring in new customers, that concern is said to have goodwill.

The foregoing is a common description of goodwill; but it is not sufficiently broad for accounting purposes. In accounting, *a business is said to have goodwill when its rate of expected future earnings is greater than the rate of earnings normally realized in its industry.* Above-average earnings and the existence of goodwill may be demonstrated as follows with Companies A and B, both of which are in the same industry:

	Company A	Company B
Net assets (other than goodwill)...........	$100,000	$100,000
Normal rate of return in this industry....	10%	10%
Normal return on net assets.................	$ 10,000	$ 10,000
Actual net income earned....................	10,000	15,000
Earnings above average	$ 0	$ 5,000

Company B has an above-average earnings rate for its industry and is said to have goodwill. Its goodwill, as with any concern, may be the result of excellent customer relations, the location of the business, manufacturing efficiency, monopolistic privileges, good employee relations, superior management, or a combination of these factors. However, regardless of what created the goodwill, a prospective investor would normally be willing to pay more for Company B than for Company A if he felt the extra earnings rate would continue. Thus, goodwill is an asset having value and it can be sold.

Accountants are in general agreement that goodwill should not be recorded unless it is bought or sold. This normally occurs only when a business is purchased in its entirety or when a new combination of partners takes over an existing partnership. When either of these events occurs, the goodwill of a business may be valued in many ways. Examples of three follow:

1. The buyer and seller may place an arbitrary value on the goodwill of a business being sold. For instance, a seller may be willing to sell a business having an above-average earnings rate for $115,000 and a buyer may be willing to pay that amount; and if they both agree that the net assets of the business other than its goodwill have a $100,000 value, they are arbitrarily valuing the goodwill at $15,000.
2. Goodwill may be valued at some multiple of that portion of expected earnings which is above average. For example, if a company is expected to have $5,000 each year in above-average earnings, its goodwill may be valued at, say, four times that portion of its earnings which are above average or at $20,000. In this case it may also be said that the goodwill is valued at four years' above-average earnings; but regardless of how it is said, this too is placing an arbitrary value on the goodwill.
3. The portion of a concern's earnings which is above average may be capitalized in order to place a value on its goodwill. For example, if a business is expected to continue to have $5,000 each year in earnings that are above average and the normal rate of return on invested capital in its industry is 10%, the excess earnings may be capitalized at 10% and a $50,000 value may be placed on its goodwill ($5,000 ÷ 10% = $50,000). Note that this values the goodwill at the amount that must be invested at the normal rate of return in order to earn the extra $5,000 each year ($50,000 × 10% = $5,000). It is a satisfactory method if the extra earnings are expected to continue indefinitely. However, since this may not happen, the extra earnings are often capitalized at a rate higher than the normal rate of the industry, say in this case, at twice the normal rate or at 20%. If in this case the extra earnings are capitalized at 20%, the goodwill is valued at $25,000 ($5,000 ÷ 20% = $25,000).

There are other ways to value goodwill; but like the three just described, in a final analysis goodwill is always valued at the price a seller is willing to take and a buyer is willing to pay.

Trademarks and trade names

Proof of prior use of a trademark or trade name is sufficient under common law to prove ownership and right of use. However, both may be registered at the Patent Office at a nominal cost for the same purpose. The cost of developing a trademark or trade name through, say, advertising should be charged to an expense account in the period or periods incurred. However, if a trademark or trade name is purchased, its cost should be amortized as explained in the next section.

Amortization of intangibles

Some intangibles, such as patents, copyrights, and leaseholds, have determinable lives based on a law, contract, or the nature of the asset;

and the costs of such assets should be amortized by systematic charges to income over the shorter of the term of their existence or the period expected to be benefited by their use. Other intangibles, such as goodwill, trademarks, and trade names, have indeterminable lives. However, the Accounting Principles Board is of the opinion that the value of any intangible will eventually disappear; that a reasonable estimate of the period of usefulness of such assets should be made; and that their costs should be amortized by systematic charges to income over the periods estimated to be benefited by their use, which in no case should exceed 40 years. The APB designated the use of straight-line amortization unless another method could be shown to be superior.

APPENDIX

The concept of present value

As a rule a business will not invest $1 today unless it expects to get back somewhat more than $1 at a later date, with the "somewhat more" being earnings or interest on the investment. Likewise, if a business makes an investment today that will return $1 a year from now, the $1 to be received a year hence has a *present value* that is somewhat less than $1. How much less depends upon how much the business expects to earn on its investments. If it expects to earn, say, a 10% annual return, the expectation of receiving $1 a year hence has a present value of $0.909. This can be verified as follows: $0.909 invested today to earn 10% annually will earn $0.0909 in one year, and when the $0.0909 earned is added to the $0.909 invested—

Investment.....	$0.909
Earnings........	0.0909
Total	$0.9999

the investment plus the earnings equal $0.9999, which rounds to the $1 expected.

Likewise, the present value of $1 to be received two years hence is $0.826 if a 10% compound annual return is expected. This also can be verified as follows: $0.826 invested to earn 10% compounded annually will earn $0.0826 the first year it is invested, and when the $0.0826 earned is added to the $0.826 invested—

Investment........................	$0.826
First year earnings.............	0.0826
End-of-year-one amount	$0.9086

the investment plus the first year's earnings total $0.9086. And during the second year this $0.9086 will earn $0.09086, which when added to the end-of-the-first-year amount—

End-of-year-one amount $0.9086
Second year earnings 0.09086
End-of-year-two amount $0.99946

equals $0.99946, which rounds to the $1 expected at the end of the second year.

Present value tables

The present value of $1 to be received any number of years in the future can be calculated by using the formula, $1/(1 + i)^n$, with i being the interest rate and n the number of years to the expected receipt. However, the formula need not be used, since tables showing present values computed with the formula at various interest rates are readily available. Table 11A–1, with its amounts rounded to either three or

Present Value of $1 at Compound Interest

Periods Hence	3%	3½%	4%	6%	7%	8%	10%	12%	14%	15%
1	0.9709	0.9662	0.9615	0.943	0.935	0.926	0.909	0.893	0.877	0.870
2	0.9426	0.9335	0.9246	0.890	0.873	0.857	0.826	0.797	0.769	0.756
3	0.9151	0.9019	0.8890	0.840	0.816	0.794	0.751	0.712	0.675	0.658
4	0.8885	0.8714	0.8548	0.792	0.763	0.735	0.683	0.636	0.592	0.572
5	0.8626	0.8420	0.8219	0.747	0.713	0.681	0.621	0.567	0.519	0.497
6	0.8375	0.8135	0.7903	0.705	0.666	0.630	0.565	0.507	0.456	0.432
7	0.8131	0.7860	0.7599	0.665	0.623	0.584	0.513	0.452	0.400	0.376
8	0.7894	0.7594	0.7307	0.627	0.582	0.540	0.467	0.404	0.351	0.327
9	0.7664	0.7337	0.7026	0.592	0.544	0.500	0.424	0.361	0.308	0.284
10	0.7441	0.7089	0.6756	0.558	0.508	0.463	0.386	0.322	0.270	0.247
11	0.7224	0.6849	0.6496	0.572	0.475	0.429	0.351	0.287	0.237	0.215
12	0.7014	0.6618	0.6246	0.497	0.444	0.397	0.319	0.257	0.208	0.187
13	0.6810	0.6394	0.6006	0.469	0.415	0.368	0.290	0.229	0.182	0.163
14	0.6611	0.6178	0.5775	0.442	0.388	0.341	0.263	0.205	0.160	0.141
15	0.6419	0.5969	0.5553	0.417	0.362	0.315	0.239	0.183	0.140	0.123
16	0.6232	0.5767	0.5339	0.394	0.339	0.292	0.218	0.163	0.123	0.107
17	0.6050	0.5572	0.5134	0.371	0.317	0.270	0.198	0.146	0.108	0.093
18	0.5874	0.5384	0.4936	0.350	0.296	0.250	0.180	0.130	0.095	0.081
19	0.5703	0.5202	0.4746	0.331	0.277	0.232	0.164	0.116	0.083	0.070
20	0.5537	0.5026	0.4564	0.312	0.258	0.215	0.149	0.104	0.073	0.061

Table 11A–1

four decimal places, is such a table. (Three or four decimal places would not be sufficiently accurate for some uses, but will suffice here.)

Observe in Table 11A–1 that the first amount in the 10% column is the 0.909 used in the previous section to introduce the concept of present value. The 0.909 in the 10% column means that the expectation of receiving $1 a year hence when discounted for one period, in this case one year, at 10%, has a present value of $0.909. Then note that the second amount in the 10% column is the $0.826 previously used, which means that the expectation of receiving $1 two years hence, discounted at 10%, has a present value of $0.826.

Using present values in investment decisions

Whether or not an investment is a wise one depends upon a number of factors, including the risks involved and whether or not the expected returns justify the risks. Normally the risks are judged and a rate of return is demanded that will justify the anticipated risks. The expected returns are then discounted at this rate to determine whether or not the investment will earn the required return. For example, a company has an opportunity to invest $20,000 in a project, the risks of which it feels justify a 12% compound return. The investment will return $10,000 at the end of the first year, $9,000 at the end of the second year, $8,000 at the end of the third year, and nothing thereafter. Will the project return the original investment plus the 12% demanded? The calculations in Illustration 11A–1 indicate that it will. In Illustration 11A–1

Years Hence	Expected Returns	Present Value of $1 at 12%	Present Value of Expected Returns
1	$10,000	0.893	$ 8,930
2	9,000	0.797	7,173
3	8,000	0.712	5,696
Total present value of the returns			$21,799
Less investment required			20,000
Excess over 12% demanded			1,799

Illustration 11A–1

the expected returns in the second column are multiplied by the amounts in the third column to determine the present values in the last column; and since the total of the present values exceeds the required investment by $1,799, the project will return the $20,000 investment, plus a 12% return thereon, and $1,799 extra.

In Illustration 11A–1 the present value of each year's return was separately calculated, after which the present values were added to determine their total. Separately calculating the present value of each of several returns from an investment is necessary when the returns are unequal, as in this example. However, in cases where the periodic returns are equal, there are shorter ways of calculating the sum of their present values. For instance, suppose a $3,500 investment will return $1,000 at the end of each year in its five-year life, and an investor wants to know the present value of these returns discounted at 12%. In this case the periodic returns are equal, and a short way to determine their total present value at 12% is to add the present values of $1 at 12% for periods one through five (from Table 11A–1), as follows—

$$
\begin{array}{r}
0.893 \\
0.797 \\
0.712 \\
0.636 \\
\underline{0.567} \\
\underline{\underline{3.605}}
\end{array}
$$

and then to multiply $1,000 by the total. The $3,605 result ($1,000 × 3.605 = $3,605) is the same as would be obtained by calculating the present value of each year's return and adding the present values. However, although the result is the same either way, the method demonstrated here requires four fewer multiplications.

Present value of $1 received periodically for a number of periods

Table 11A–2 is based on the idea demonstrated in the previous paragraph, the idea that the present value of a series of equal returns to be received at periodic intervals is nothing more than the sum of the present values of the individual returns. Note the amount on the table's fifth line in the 12% column. It is the same 3.605 amount arrived at in

Present Value of $1 Received Periodically for a Number of Periods

Periods Hence	3%	3½%	4%	6%	7%	8%	10%	12%	14%	15%
1	0.971	0.966	0.962	0.943	0.935	0.926	0.909	0.893	0.877	0.870
2	1.914	1.900	1.886	1.833	1.808	1.783	1.736	1.690	1.647	1.626
3	2.829	2.802	2.775	2.673	2.624	2.577	2.487	2.402	2.322	2.283
4	3.717	3.672	3.630	3.465	3.387	3.312	3.170	3.037	2.914	2.855
5	4.580	4.515	4.452	4.212	4.100	3.993	3.791	3.605	3.433	3.352
6	5.417	5.329	5.242	4.917	4.767	4.623	4.355	4.111	3.889	3.784
7	6.230	6.115	6.002	5.582	5.389	5.206	4.868	4.564	4.288	4.160
8	7.020	6.874	6.733	6.210	5.971	5.747	5.335	4.968	4.639	4.487
9	7.786	7.608	7.435	6.802	6.515	6.247	5.759	5.328	4.946	4.772
10	8.530	8.317	8.111	7.360	7.024	6.710	6.145	5.650	5.216	5.019
11	9.253	9.002	8.761	7.887	7.499	7.139	6.495	5.988	5.453	5.234
12	9.954	9.663	9.385	8.384	7.943	7.536	6.814	6.194	5.660	5.421
13	10.635	10.303	9.986	8.853	8.358	7.904	7.103	6.424	5.842	5.583
14	11.296	10.921	10.563	9.295	8.746	8.244	7.367	6.628	6.002	5.724
15	11.938	11.517	11.118	9.712	9.108	8.560	7.606	6.811	6.142	5.847
16	12.561	12.094	11.652	10.106	9.447	8.851	7.824	6.974	6.265	5.954
17	13.166	12.651	12.166	10.477	9.763	9.122	8.022	7.120	6.373	6.047
18	13.754	13.190	12.659	10.828	10.059	9.372	8.201	7.250	6.467	6.128
19	14.324	13.710	13.134	11.158	10.336	9.604	8.365	7.366	6.550	6.198
20	14.878	14.212	13.590	11.470	10.594	9.818	8.514	7.469	6.623	6.259

Table 11A–2

the previous section by adding the first five present values of $1 at 12%. All the amounts shown in Table 11A–2 could be arrived at by adding amounts found in Table 11A–1. However, there would be some slight variations due to rounding.

When available, Table 11A–2 is used to determine the present value of a series of equal amounts to be received at periodic future intervals. For example, what is the present value of a series of ten $1,000 amounts, with one $1,000 amount to be received at the end of each of ten successive years, discounted at 8%? To determine the answer, go down the 8% column to the amount opposite ten periods (years in this case). It is 6.710, and $6.71 is the present value of $1 to be received annually at the ends of each of ten years, discounted at 8%. Therefore, the present value of the ten $1,000 amounts is 1,000 times $6.71 or is $6,710.

Discount periods less than a year in length

In the examples thus far the discount periods have been measured in intervals one year in length. Often discount periods are based on intervals shorter than a year. For instance, although interest rates on corporation bonds are usually quoted on an annual basis, the interest on such bonds is normally paid semiannually. As a result, a calculation involving the present value of the interest to be received on such bonds must be based on interest periods six months in length.

To illustrate a calculation based on six-month interest periods, assume an investor wants to know the present value of the interest he will receive over a period of five years on some corporation bonds. The bonds have a $10,000 par value and interest is paid on them every six months at a 7% annual rate. Since interest at a 7% annual rate is at the rate of $3\frac{1}{2}$% per six-month interest period, the investor will receive $10,000 times $3\frac{1}{2}$% or $350 in interest on these bonds at the end of each six-month interest period. In five years there are ten such periods. Therefore, if these ten receipts of $350 each are to be discounted at the interest rate of the bonds, to determine their present value, go down the $3\frac{1}{2}$% column of Table 11A–2 to the amount opposite ten periods. It is 8.317, and the present value of the ten $350 semiannual receipts is 8.317 times $350 or is $2,910.95.

Glossary

Amortize. To periodically write off as an expense a share of the cost of an asset, usually an intangible asset.

Betterment. The replacement of an existing asset or asset portion with an improved or superior asset or portion.

Book value. The carrying amount for an item in the accounting records. When applied to a plant asset, it is the cost of the asset minus its accumulated depreciation.

Capital expenditure. An expenditure that increases net assets.

Carrying amount. The amount at which an item is carried in the accounting records. In the case of a noninterest-bearing note, it is the face amount of the note less unamortized discount.

Copyright. An exclusive right granted by the federal government to publish and sell a musical, literary, or art work for a period of years.

Depletion. The amount a wasting asset is depleted through cutting, mining, or pumping.

Extraordinary repairs. Major repairs that extend the life of a plant asset beyond the number of years originally estimated.

Goodwill. That portion of the value of a business due to its ability to earn a rate of return greater than the average in its industry.

Income tax rules. Rules governing how income for tax purposes and income taxes are to be calculated.

Intangible asset. An asset having no physical existence but having value due to the rights resulting from its ownership and possession.

Lease. The contractural right to possess and use property under the terms of a lease contract.

Leasehold. Property held under the terms of a lease contract.

Leasehold improvements. Improvements to leased property made by the lessee.

Lessee. An individual granted possession of property under the terms of a lease contract.

Lessor. The individual or enterprise that has granted possession and use of property under the terms of a lease contract.

Ordinary repairs. Repairs made to keep a plant asset in its normal good operating condition.

Patent. An exclusive right granted by the federal government to manufacture and sell a given machine or mechanical device for a period of years.

Present value. The estimated worth today of an amount of money to be received at a future date.

Present value table. A table showing the present value of one amount to be received at various future dates when discounted at various interest rates.

Revenue expenditure. An expenditure that should be deducted from current revenue on the income statement.

---

1. When should a loss on the exchange of a plant asset be recorded? When is it permissible to absorb a loss into the cost basis of the new plant asset? Should a gain on a plant asset exchange be recorded as such?

Questions for class discussion

2. When plant assets of like purpose are exchanged, what determines the cost basis of the newly acquired asset for federal income tax purposes?
3. When the loss on an exchange of plant assets is immaterial in amount, what advantage results from taking the newly acquired asset into the records at the amount of its cost basis for tax purposes?
4. When an old plant asset is traded in at a book loss on a new asset of like purpose, the loss is not recognized for tax purposes. In the end this normally does not work a financial hardship on the taxpayer. Why?
5. What is the essence of the accounting principle of materiality?
6. If at the end of four years it is discovered that a machine that was expected to have a five-year life will actually have an eight-year life, how is the error corrected?
7. Distinguish between ordinary repairs and replacements and extraordinary repairs and replacements.
8. How should ordinary repairs to a machine be recorded? How should extraordinary repairs be recorded?
9. What is a betterment? How should a betterment to a machine be recorded?
10. Distinguish between revenue expenditures and capital expenditures.
11. What are the characteristics of an intangible asset?
12. In general, how are intangible assets accounted for?
13. Define (a) lease, (b) lessor, (c) leasehold, and (d) leasehold improvement.
14. In accounting, when is a business said to have goodwill?

Class exercises

Exercise 11–1

A machine that cost $4,500 and had $3,200 of accumulated depreciation recorded against it was traded in on a new machine of like purpose having a $5,000 cash price. A $1,000 trade-in allowance was received, and the balance was paid in cash. Determine (a) the book value of the old machine, (b) the cash given in the exchange, (c) the book loss on the exchange, (d) the cost basis of the new machine for income tax purposes, and (e) the annual straight-line depreciation on the new machine for tax purposes under the assumption it will have an estimated six-year life and a $800 trade-in value.

Exercise 11–2

A machine that cost $4,000 and which had been depreciated $2,500 was disposed of on January 4. Give without explanations the entries to record the disposal under each of the following unrelated assumptions:

a. The machine was sold for $1,750 cash.
b. The machine was sold for $600 cash.
c. The machine was traded in on a new machine of like purpose having a $4,500 cash price. A $1,750 trade-in allowance was received, and the balance was paid in cash.
d. A $600 trade-in allowance was received for the machine on a new machine of like purpose having a $4,500 cash price. The balance was paid in cash, and the loss was considered material.
e. Transaction (d) was recorded by the income tax method because the loss was considered immaterial.

Exercise 11–3

On January 1, 1978, a company exchanged a $5,000, two-year, noninterest-bearing note payable for a machine having a cash price that was not readily determinable. Under the assumption that the market rate for interest on the day of the exchange was 6%, prepare (*a*) the entry to record the exchange and (*b*) the December 31, 1978, entry to amortize a portion of the discount on the note payable. (*c*) Show how the note should appear on the December 31, 1978, balance sheet. Prepare entries to record (*d*) the December 31, 1979, amortization of the remainder of the discount and (*e*) the January 1, 1980, entry to pay the note.

Exercise 11–4

A machine that cost $12,000 was depreciated on a straight-line basis for six years under the assumption it would have an eight-year life and a $2,000 trade-in value. At that point it was recognized that the machine had four years of remaining useful life, after which it would have an estimated $1,500 trade-in value. (*a*) Determine the machine's book value at the end of its sixth year. (*b*) Determine the amount of depreciation to be charged against the machine during each of the remaining years in its life.

Exercise 11–5

A company owns a building that appeared on its balance sheet at the end of last year at its original $246,000 cost less $205,000 accumulated depreciation. The building has been depreciated on a straight-line basis under the assumption it would have a 30-year life and no salvage value. During the first week in January of the current year, major structural repairs were completed on the building at a $64,000 cost. The repairs did not improve the building's usefulness but they did extend its expected life for 10 years beyond the 30 years originally estimated. (*a*) Determine the building's age on last year's balance sheet date. (*b*) Give the entry to record the cost of the repairs. (*c*) Determine the book value of the building after its repairs were recorded. (*d*) Give the entry to record the current year's depreciation.

Exercise 11–6

Six years ago a company purchased for $1,000,000 the mineral rights to an ore body containing 1,000,000 tons of ore. The company invested an additional $1,000,000 in mining machinery designed to exhaust the mine in ten years. During the first five years the mine produced 500,000 tons of ore that were sold at a profit. During the sixth year 100,000 tons of ore were mined; but due to technological changes in the manufacturing processes of the customers to whom the ore was normally sold, there was little demand for the ore and it was sold at a $1 per ton loss.

Required:

Under the assumption that the remaining 400,000 tons of ore can be mined and sold at a $1 per ton loss during the next four years and there is no prospect of ever doing better, recommend whether the mine should be closed and the loss stopped or it should be continued in operation at a loss. Cite figures to back your recommendation.

Exercise 11–7

On January 1, 1978, a company paid $90,000 for an ore body containing 900,000 tons of ore, and it installed machinery costing $150,000, having an estimated 12-year life and no salvage value, and capable of removing the entire ore body in 10 years. The company began mining operations on April 1, and it mined 60,000 tons of ore during the remaining nine months of the year. Give the entries to record the December 31, 1978, depletion of the ore body and the depreciation of the mining machinery.

Problems

Problem 11–1

A company completed these transactions involving the purchase and operation of delivery trucks.

1976
July   7   Paid cash for a new truck, $5,700 plus $285 state and city sales taxes. The truck was estimated to have a four-year life and a $1,500 salvage value.
       10   Paid $315 for special racks and shelves installed in the truck. The racks and shelves did not increase the truck's estimated trade-in value.
Dec. 31   Recorded straight-line depreciation on the truck.
1977
June 26   Paid $410 to install an air conditioning unit in the truck. The unit increased the truck's estimated trade-in value $50.
Dec. 31   Recorded straight-line depreciation on the truck.
1978
May 29   Paid $55 for repairs to the truck's rear bumper damaged when the driver backed into a loading dock.
Dec. 31   Recorded straight-line depreciation on the truck.
1979
Aug. 26   Traded the old truck and $3,885 in cash for a new truck. The new truck was estimated to have a three-year life and a $1,600 trade-in value, and the invoice for the exchange showed these items:

Price of the truck................. $6,200
Trade-in allowance granted .... (2,500)
Balance $3,700
State and city sales taxes.......   185
Balance paid in cash............. $3,885

The loss on the exchange was considered immaterial, and the income tax method was used to record the exchange.
       29   Paid $465 for special shelves and racks installed in the truck.
Dec. 31   Recorded straight-line depreciation on the new truck.

Required:

Prepare general journal entries to record the transactions.

Problem 11-2

A company completed the following transactions involving machinery:

Machine No. 133-5 was purchased on May 2, 1972, at an installed cost of $3,500. Its useful life was estimated at five years with a $500 trade-in value. Straight-line depreciation was recorded on the machine at the ends of 1972 and 1973; and on January 5, 1974, it was traded in on Machine No. 133-23. A $2,000 trade-in allowance was received, the loss was considered immaterial, and the income tax method was used to record the exchange.

Machine No. 133-23 was purchased on January 5, 1974, at an installed cost of $4,300, less the trade-in allowance received for Machine No. 133-5. Its life was estimated at five years with a $600 trade-in value. Sum-of-the-years'-digits depreciation was recorded on the machine on each December 31 of its life, and it was sold on October 7, 1978, for $800.

Machine No. 133-25 was purchased on January 9, 1974, at an installed cost of $6,400. Its useful life was estimated at four years, after which it would have a $400 salvage value. Declining-balance depreciation at twice the straight-line rate was recorded on the machine on each December 31 of its life, and it was traded in on Machine No. 133-30 on January 4, 1978. A $900 trade-in allowance was received.

Machine No. 133-30 was purchased on January 4, 1978, at an installed cost of $7,000 less the trade-in allowance received on Machine No. 133-25. It was estimated the new machine would produce 12,000 units of product during its life, after which it would have a $500 trade-in value. It produced 2,500 units of product in 1978 and 500 additional units in 1979 before its sale for $4,000 on June 3, 1979.

Required:

Prepare general journal entries to record: (1) the purchase of each machine, (2) the depreciation recorded on the first December 31 of each machine's life, and (3) the disposal of each machine. (Treat the entries for the first two machines as one series of transactions and those of the next two machines as an unrelated second series. Only one entry is needed to record the exchange of one machine for another.)

Problem 11-3

Prepare general journal entries to record the following transactions. Use straight-line depreciation.

1974

Jan. 10   Purchased and placed in operations Machine No. 133-8 at an $18,000 installed cost. The machine's useful life was estimated at six years with no salvage value.

Dec. 31   Recorded depreciation on the machine.

1975

Mar. 14   After a little over 14 months of satisfactory use, Machine No. 133-8 was cleaned, inspected, oiled, and adjusted by a factory representative at a cost of $215.

Dec. 31   Recorded depreciation on Machine No. 133-8.

1976

June 28   Added a new device to Machine No. 133-8 at a $700 cost. The device did not change the machine's expected life nor change its zero salvage value but it did increase its output by one fourth.

Dec. 31   Recorded depreciation on the machine.
1977
Dec. 31   Recorded depreciation on the machine.
1978
Jan.   9   Repaired and completely overhauled Machine No. 133–8 at a
               $4,000 cost, consisting of $400 for ordinary repairs and $3,600
               for extraordinary repairs. The extraordinary repairs were expected
               to extend the machine's expected useful life for two years beyond
               the six years originally expected but were not expected to change
               its zero salvage value.
Dec. 31   Recorded depreciation on the machine.
1979
July   9   Machine No. 133–8 was destroyed in a fire. The insurance company
               settled the loss claim for $5,000.

Problem 11–4

On January 2, 1976, a company gave its own $12,000, noninterest-bearing,
four-year note payable in exchange for a machine the cash price of which was
not readily determinable. The market rate for interest on such notes on the
day of the exchange was 8% annually.

Required:

1. Prepare a form with the following columnar headings and calculate and
    fill in the required amounts for the four years the note is outstanding.
    Round all amounts to the nearest full dollar.

Year	Beginning-of-the-Year Carrying Amount	Discount to Be Amortized Each Year	Unamortized Discount at the End of the Year	End-of-the-Year Carrying Amount

2. Prepare general journal entries to record: (a) the acquisition of the ma-
    chine, (b) the discount amortized at the end of each year, and (c) the pay-
    ment of the note on January 2, 1980.
3. Show how the note should appear on the December 31, 1978, balance
    sheet.

Problem 11–5

Part 1. Five years ago Parkway Opticians leased space in a building for
a period of 15 years. The lease contract calls for $7,200 annual rental pay-
ments on each January 1 throughout the life of the lease, and also provides
that the lessee must pay for all additions and improvements to the leased
property. The recent construction of a shopping center across the street has
made the location more valuable, and on December 20 Parkway Opticians
subleased the space to The Optical Shop for the remaining ten years of the
lease, beginning on the next January 1. The Optical Shop paid $30,000 for
the privilege of subleasing the property and in addition agreed to assume and
pay the building owner the $7,200 annual rental charges. During the first ten
days after taking possession of the leased space, The Optical Shop remodeled
the shop front of the leased space at a $10,000 cost. The remodeled shop front

is estimated to have a life equal to the remaining life of the building, 20 years, and was paid for on January 12.

Required:

Prepare entries in general journal form to record: (*a*) The Optical Shop's payment to sublease the shop space, (*b*) its payment of the annual rental charge to the building owner, and (*c*) payment for the new shop front. Also, prepare the adjusting entries required at the end of the first year of the sublease to amortize (*d*) a proper share of the $30,000 cost of the sublease and (*e*) a proper share of the shop front cost.

Part 2. On March 12 of the current year Hardrock Mine paid $800,000 for mineral land estimated to contain 4,000,000 tons of recoverable ore. It installed machinery costing $120,000, having a 12-year life and no salvage value, and capable of exhausting the mine in 10 years. The machinery was paid for on July 5, three days after mining operations began. During the first six months' operations the company mined 165,000 tons of ore.

Required:

Prepare entries to record (*a*) the purchase of the mineral land, (*b*) the installation of the machinery, (*c*) the first six months' depletion under the assumption that the land will be valueless after the ore is mined, and (*d*) the first six months' depreciation on the machinery.

Problem 11–6

Thomas Nye wishes to buy an established business and is considering Companies A and B, both of which have been in business for exactly five years, during which time Company A has reported an average annual net income of $11,835 and Company B has reported an average of $14,250. However, the incomes are not comparable, since the companies have not used the same accounting procedures. Current balance sheets of the companies show these items:

	Company A	Company B
Cash	$ 6,700	$ 8,200
Accounts receivable	51,600	58,500
Allowance for doubtful accounts	(3,200)	-0-
Merchandise inventory	71,300	86,100
Store equipment	28,800	25,600
Accumulated depreciation, store equipment	(24,000)	(16,000)
Total Assets	$131,200	$162,400
Current liabilities	$ 62,400	$ 68,900
Owner equity	68,800	93,500
Total Liabilities and Owner Equity	$131,200	$162,400

Company A has used the allowance method in accounting for bad debts and has added to its allowance each year an amount equal to 1% of sales. However, this seems excessive, since an examination shows only $1,500 of its accounts that are probably uncollectible. Company B, on the other hand, has used the direct write-off method but has been slow to write off bad debts, and an examination of its accounts shows $3,000 of accounts that are probably uncollectible.

During the past five years Company A has priced its inventories on a Lifo basis with the result that its current inventory appears on its balance sheet at an amount that is $12,000 below replacement cost. Company B has used Fifo, and its ending inventory appears at approximately its replacement cost.

Both companies have assumed eight-year lives and no salvage value in depreciating equipment; however, Company A has used sum-of-the-years'-digits depreciation, while Company B has used straight line. Mr. Nye is of the opinion that straight-line depreciation has resulted in Company B's equipment appearing on its balance sheet at approximately its fair market value and that it would have had the same result for Company A.

Mr. Nye is willing to pay what he considers fair market value for the assets of either business, not including cash, but including goodwill measured at four times average annual earnings in excess of 15% on the fair market value of the net tangible assets. He defines net tangible assets as all assets other than goodwill, including accounts receivable, minus liabilities. He will also assume the liabilities of the purchased business, paying its owner the difference between total assets purchased and the liabilities assumed.

Required:

Prepare the following schedules: (a) a schedule showing the net tangible assets of each company at their fair market values according to Mr. Nye, (b) a schedule showing the revised net incomes of the companies based on Fifo inventories and straight-line depreciation, (c) a schedule showing the calculation of each company's goodwill, and (d) a schedule showing the amount Mr. Nye would pay for each business.

Alternate
problems

Problem 11–1A

Prepare general journal entries to record these transactions involving the purchase and operation of a secondhand truck:

1976
Jan.   8   Purchased for $3,850 cash a secondhand delivery truck having an estimated three years of remaining useful life and an $800 trade-in value.
        9   Paid Service Garage for the following:

Minor repairs to the truck's motor....	$ 32
New tires for the truck...................	218
Gas and oil.................................	9
Total	$259

Dec. 31   Recorded straight-line depreciation on the truck.
1977
Jan.   4   Paid $550 to install a hydraulic loader on the truck. The loader increased the truck's trade-in value to $850.
June 27   Paid Service Garage for the following:

Minor repairs to the truck's motor $22
New battery for the truck 38
Gas and oil 8
        Total $68

Nov. 3   Paid $55 for repairs to the hydraulic loader damaged when the
          driver backed into a loading dock.
Dec. 31   Recorded straight-line depreciation on the truck.
1978
Jan. 11 Paid Service Garage $350 to overhaul the truck's motor, replacing
          its bearings and rings and extending the truck's life one year beyond
          the original three years planned. However, it was also estimated
          that the extra year's operation would reduce the truck's trade-in
          value to $650.
Dec. 31   Recorded straight-line depreciation on the truck.
1979
July   7 Traded the old truck on a new one having a $5,600 cash price.
          Received a $1,200 trade-in allowance, and paid the balance in cash.

Problem 11–2A

A company completed the following transactions involving machinery:

Machine No. 133–51 was purchased on April 1, 1972, at an installed cost
of $5,400. Its useful life was estimated at four years with a $600 trade-in
value. Straight-line depreciation was recorded on the machine at the ends of
1972 and 1973, and on July 2, 1974, it was traded on Machine No. 133–85.
A $3,000 trade-in allowance was received, and the balance was paid in cash.

Machine No. 133–85 was purchased on July 2, 1974, at an installed cost
of $7,000, less the trade-in allowance received on Machine 133–51. The new
machine's life was estimated at five years with a $700 trade-in value. Sum-of-
the-years'-digits depreciation was recorded on each December 31 of its life,
and on January 4, 1979, it was sold for $1,000.

Machine No. 133–72 was purchased on January 5, 1974, at an installed
cost of $5,000. Its useful life was estimated at five years, after which it
would have a $500 trade-in value. Declining-balance depreciation at twice
the straight-line rate was recorded on the machine at the ends of 1974, 1975,
1976, and 1977; and on September 26, 1978, it was traded on Machine No.
133–99. A $400 trade-in allowance was received, the balance was paid in cash,
the loss was considered immaterial, and the income tax method was used to
record the transaction.

Machine No. 133–99 was purchased on September 26, 1978, at a $5,900
installed cost, less the trade-in allowance received on Machine No. 133–72.
It was estimated the new machine would produce 90,000 units of product
during its useful life, after which it would have a $600 trade-in value. Units-
of-production depreciation was recorded on the machine for the last three
months of 1978, a period in which it produced 6,000 units of product. Between
January 1 and October 12, 1979, the machine produced 16,000 more units,
and on the latter date it was sold for $4,000.

Required:

Prepare general journal entries to record (*a*) the purchase of each machine,
(*b*) the depreciation recorded on the first December 31 of each machine's

life, and (c) the disposal of each machine. Treat the entries for the first two machines as one series of transactions and those of the next two machines as an unrelated second series. Only one entry is needed to record the exchange of one machine for another.

Problem 11–3A

Part 1. On January 7, 1971, a company purchased and placed in operation a machine estimated to have a ten-year life and no salvage value. The machine cost $15,000 and was depreciated on a straight-line basis. On January 3, 1975, a $600 device that increased its output by one fourth was added to the machine. The device did not change the machine's estimated life nor its zero salvage value. During the first week of January 1978, the machine was completely overhauled at a $4,500 cost (paid for on January 9). The overhaul added three additional years to the machine's estimated life but did not change its zero salvage value. On June 27, 1979, the machine was destroyed in a fire and the insurance company settled the loss claim for $5,000.

Required:

Prepare general journal entries to record: (a) the purchase of the machine, (b) the 1971 depreciation, (c) the addition of the new device, (d) the 1975 depreciation, (e) the machine's overhaul, (f) the 1978 depreciation, and (g) the insurance settlement.

Part 2. A company purchased Machine A at a $12,400 installed cost on January 5, 1973, and depreciated it on a straight-line basis at the ends of 1973, 1974, 1975, and 1976 under the assumption it would have a ten-year life and a $2,400 salvage value. After more experience and before recording 1977 depreciation, the company revised its estimate of the machine's remaining years downward from six years to four and revised the estimate of its salvage value downward to $2,000. On April 2, 1979, after recording 1977, 1978, and part of a year's depreciation for 1979, the company traded in Machine A on Machine B, receiving a $4,000 trade-in allowance. Machine B cost $15,300, less the trade-in allowance, the loss was considered immaterial, the balance was paid in cash, and the income tax method was used to record the exchange. Machine B was depreciated on a straight-line basis on December 31, 1979, under the assumption it would have a six-year life and $2,300 salvage value.

Required:

Prepare entries to record (a) the purchase of Machine A, (b) its 1973 depreciation, (c) its 1977 depreciation, (d) the exchange of the machines, and (e) the 1979 depreciation on Machine B.

Problem 11–4A

A company exchanged an $8,000, noninterest-bearing, four-year note payable on January 2, 1976, for a machine the cash price of which was not readily determinable. The market rate for interest on such notes on the day of the exchange was 8% annually.

Required:

1. Prepare a form with the following columnar headings and calculate and fill in the required amounts for the four years the note is outstanding. Round all dollar amounts to the nearest whole dollar.

Year	Beginning-of-the-Year Carrying Amount	Discount to Be Amortized Each Year	Unamortized Discount at the End of the Year	End-of-the-Year Carrying Amount

2. Prepare general journal entries to record (*a*) the acquisition of the machine; (*b*) the discount amortized at the end of each year, and (*c*) the payment of the note on January 2, 1980.
3. Show how the note should appear on the December 31, 1977, balance sheet.

Problem 11–5A

Part 1. Eight years ago A. Merchant leased a store building for a 20-year period. The lease contract requires a $9,000 annual rental payment on each January 1 throughout the life of the lease, and it requires the lessee to pay for all improvements to the leased property. Due to traffic pattern changes the lease has become more valuable, and on December 19 Mr. Merchant subleased the property for the remaining 12 years of the lease, beginning on January 1, to Allied Shops. Allied Shops paid Mr. Merchant $24,000 for his rights under the lease, and it also agreed to pay the annual rental charges directly to the building owner. In addition, during the first two weeks of January it remodeled the store front on the leased building at a $9,600 total cost, paying the contractor on January 14. The remodeled store front was estimated to have a life equal to the remaining life of the building, 24 years.

Required:

Prepare general journal entries to record Allied Shops payments for the sublease, the annual rental charge, and the new store front. Also, prepare the end-of-the-year adjusting entries to amortize portions of the sublease cost and the cost of the store front.

Part 2. On March 2, 19—, Redimix Company paid $200,000 for land containing an estimated 1,000,000 cubic yards of gravel suitable for preparing concrete. The gravel was to be removed by stripping, and the company estimated that it would cost $20,000 to return the land to a condition that would meet governmental safety and ecological standards, after which the land could be sold for its rehabilitation cost. The company installed machinery costing $160,000 (paid for on June 27), having a ten-year life and no salvage value, and capable of exhausting the site in eight years. During the first six months of operations, ending December 31, the company removed 60,000 yards of gravel.

Required:

Prepare general journal entries to record (*a*) the purchase of the land, (*b*) the installation of the machinery, (*c*) the first six months' depreciation, and (*d*) the first six months' depletion.

<table>
<tr><td>Decision
problem 11–1,
junior
accountant</td><td>In helping to verify the records of a concern being audited by the public accounting firm for which you work as a junior accountant, you find the following entries:</td></tr>
</table>

1979				
Oct.	20	Cash..	8,500.00	
		Loss from Fire	3,500.00	
		Accumulated Depreciation, Machinery	9,000.00	
		Machinery		21,000.00
		Received payment of fire loss claim.		
Nov.	15	Cash..	24,000.00	
		Factory Land		24,000.00
		Sold unneeded factory land.		

An investigation revealed that the first entry resulted from recording an $8,500 check from an insurance company in full settlement of a loss claim resulting from the destruction of a machine in a small plant fire on September 29, 1979. The machine had originally cost $18,000, was put in operation on January 5, 1975, and had been depreciated on a straight-line basis at the ends of each of the first four years in its life under the assumption it would have an eight-year life and no salvage value. During the first week of January 1979, the machine had been overhauled at a $3,000 cost. The overhaul did not increase the machine's capacity nor change its zero salvage value. However, it was expected that the overhaul would lengthen the machine's service life two years beyond the eight originally expected.

The second entry resulted from recording a check received from selling a portion of a tract of land. The tract was adjacent to the company's plant and had been purchased the year before. It cost $32,000, and $3,000 was paid for clearing and grading it. Both amounts had been debited to the Factory Land account. The land was to be used for storing raw materials; but after the grading was completed, it was obvious the company did not need the entire tract, and it was pleased when it received an offer from a purchaser who was willing to pay $18,000 for the east half or $24,000 for the west half. The company decided to sell the west half, and it recorded receipt of the purchaser's check with the entry previously given.

Were any errors made in recording the transactions described here? If so, describe the errors and in each case give an entry or entries that will correct the account balances under the assumption the 1979 revenue and expense accounts have not been closed.

<table>
<tr><td>Decision
problem 11–2,
Jane Holt</td><td>Jane Holt plans to buy an established business, and she has narrowed her list to three choices, Companies A, B, and C. All three have been in business for exactly four years and have reported average annual net incomes as fol-</td></tr>
</table>

lows: Company A, $13,125; Company B, $11,912; and Company C, $20,970. However, since they have used different accounting methods, their reported incomes are not comparable, nor are their current balance sheets which show these items:

	Company A	Company B	Company C
Cash	$ 9,800	$ 12,500	$ 19,400
Accounts receivable	82,500	93,400	97,600
Allowance for doubtful accounts	(6,500)	(1,800)	-0-
Merchandise inventory	94,700	75,600	92,100
Equipment	27,500	30,000	26,000
Accumulated depreciation, equipment	(17,000)	(17,712)	(10,400)
Building	110,000	98,000	105,000
Accumulated depreciation, building	(11,000)	(9,800)	-0-
Land	20,000	20,000	20,000
Goodwill			2,500
Total Assets	$310,000	$300,188	$352,200
Current liabilities	$ 80,000	$ 95,000	$ 85,000
Mortgage payable	85,000	80,000	90,000
Owner equity	145,000	125,188	177,200
Total Liabilities and Owner Equity	$310,000	$300,188	$352,200

Company A has added an amount to its allowance for doubtful accounts each year equal to one half of 1% of sales. These amounts seem to have been excessive, since an analysis shows just $2,000 of the company's accounts receivable that are probably uncollectible. Company B has been more conservative, and its allowance is approximately equal to its uncollectible accounts. Company C has used the direct write-off method in accounting for bad debts; but it has always been slow to recognize a bad debt, and an examination shows accounts totaling $8,500 that are probably uncollectible.

Company B has accounted for its inventories on a Lifo basis; and as a result its current inventory appears on its books as an amount that is $15,000 below replacement cost. Companies A and C have used Fifo, and their inventories are stated at amounts near replacement costs.

The three companies have not added to their plant assets since beginning operations, and all three have assumed ten-year lives and no salvage values in recording depreciation on equipment. However, Company A has used sum-of-the-years'-digits depreciation, Company B has used declining balance at twice the straight-line rate, and Company C has used straight line.

The buildings of the companies are of concrete construction and are comparable in most respects. Companies A and B have recorded straight-line depreciation on their buildings, assuming 40-year lives and no salvage values. However, since its building is of concrete construction and "will last forever," Company C has taken no depreciation on its building.

Ms. Holt is of the opinion that if all three companies had used straight-line depreciation for both buildings and equipment, the resulting book values would approximate market values.

The goodwill on Company C's balance sheet resulted from capitalizing advertising costs during the company's first year in business.

In purchasing a business, Ms. Holt will buy its tangible assets, including the accounts receivable but not including cash; and she will pay what she thinks is fair market value. She will assume the liabilities of the business and will pay for goodwill measured at four times average annual earnings in excess of a 10% return on net tangible assets, based on first-in, first-out inventories and straight-line depreciation.

Prepare schedules showing (a) the net tangible assets of each company based on first-in, first-out inventories and straight-line depreciation; (b) corrected average net incomes based on first-in, first-out inventories and straight-line depreciation; (c) the calculation of each company's goodwill; and (d) the price Ms. Holt will pay for each company.

PART 4

Accounting for equities: Liabilities and partners' equity

12
Payroll accounting . . .
13
Current and long-term liabilities . . .
14
Partnership accounting

After studying Chapter 12, you should be able to:

- State which payroll taxes are withheld from employees' wages and which are levied on employers.

- Calculate an employee's gross pay and the various deductions from the pay.

- Prepare a Payroll Register and make the entries to record its information and to pay the employees.

- Explain the operation of a payroll bank account.

- Calculate and prepare the entry to record the payroll taxes levied on an employer.

- Define or explain the words and phrases listed in the chapter Glossary.

chapter 12

Payroll accounting

A liability is a legal obligation requiring the future payment of an asset, the future performance of a service, or the creation of another liability. In accounting for liabilities, the *cost principle* applies and each liability is accounted for at the cost of the asset or service received in exchange for the liability incurred.

An employer incurs a number of liabilities as a result of state and federal programs that are financed by payroll taxes, and an understanding of the records needed in accounting for these taxes and the resulting liabilities requires some understanding of the laws and programs that affect payrolls. Consequently, the more pertinent of these are discussed in the first portion of this chapter before the subject of payroll records is introduced.

The federal Social Security Act provides for a number of programs, two of which materially affect payroll accounting. These are (1) a federal old-age and survivors' benefits program with medical care for the aged and (2) a joint federal-state unemployment insurance program. **The federal Social Security Act**

Federal old-age and survivors' benefits program

The Social Security Act provides that a qualified worker in a covered industry who reaches the age of 62 and retires shall receive monthly retirement benefits for the remainder of his or her life, and in addition certain medical benefits after reaching 65. It further provides benefits for the family of a worker covered by the act who dies either before or after reaching retirement age and benefits for covered workers who become disabled. The benefits in each case are based upon the average earnings of the worker during the years of his or her employment in covered industries.

No attempt will be made here to list or discuss the requirements to be met by a worker or the worker's family to qualify for benefits. In general, any person who works for an employer covered by the act for a sufficient length of time qualifies himself or herself and family. All companies and individuals who employ one or more persons and are not specifically exempted are covered by the law.

Funds for the payment of old-age, survivors,' and medical benefits under the Social Security Act come from payroll taxes. These taxes are imposed under a law called the Federal Insurance Contributions Act and are often called "F.I.C.A. taxes." They are also often called "old-age benefit taxes" or just "social security taxes." These F.I.C.A. taxes are imposed in like amounts on both covered employers and their employees. At this writing the act provides for a 1977 tax on both employers and their employees amounting to 5.85% on the first $16,500 paid each employee. It also provides for rate increases as follows:

Years	Tax on Employees	Tax on Employers
1978 through 1980	6.05%	6.05%
1981 through 1985	6.30%	6.30%
1986 through 2010	6.45%	6.45%
2011 and after.......................	7.45%	7.45%

The act also provides for annual cost-of-living adjustments in the amount of wages subject to F.I.C.A. taxes. For example, in 1975 only the first $14,100 of wages paid were subject to F.I.C.A. taxes, and wages above $14,100 were tax exempt. The tax-exempt point was increased to $15,300 in 1976 and to $16,500 in 1977, and it will increase again each year as the cost of living and average wages earned increase.

The amount of wages subject to F.I.C.A. taxes is almost certain to change each year and, if history is any indication, Congress will change the rates listed above (probably increasing them) before they become effective. Consequently, since changes are almost certain, you are asked to use an assumed F.I.C.A. tax rate of 6% on the first $17,500 of wages paid each employee each year in solving the problems at the end of this chapter. The assumed 6% rate is used because it makes calculations easy and because any rate that is correct in, say 1978, may not be correct for the remaining years this text will be used.

The Federal Insurance Contribution Act in addition to setting rates requires that an employer:

1. Withhold from the wages of each employee each payday an amount of F.I.C.A. tax calculated at the current rate. The withholding to continue each payday during the year until the tax-exempt point is reached.

2. Pay a payroll tax equal to the amount withheld from the wages of all employees.
3. Periodically remit both the amounts withheld from the employees' wages and the employer's tax to the Internal Revenue Service. (Times of payment are discussed later in this chapter.)
4. Within one month after the end of each calendar quarter, file a tax information return known as Employer's Quarterly Federal Tax Return, Form 941. (See Illustration 12–1.)
5. Furnish each employee before January 31 following each year a Withholding Tax Statement, Form W–2, which tells the employee the amounts of his wages that were subject to F.I.C.A. and federal income taxes and the amounts of such taxes withheld. (A W–2 Form is shown in Illustration 12–2.)
6. Furnish the Internal Revenue Service copies of all the W–2 Forms given the employees.
7. Keep a record for four years for each employee that shows among other things wages subject to F.I.C.A. taxes and the taxes withheld. (The law does not specify the exact form of the record; but most employers keep individual employee earnings records similar to the one shown later in this chapter.)

Observe that the Employer's Quarterly Federal Tax Return, Form 941 (Illustration 12–1) actually has two parts. (It is perforated between the two listings of the employer's name and is designed to be torn into two parts at this point.) On the first part, labeled Schedule A, the employer reports each employee's social security number, name, and his wages subject to F.I.C.A. taxes. This schedule is sent to the Social Security Administration by the Internal Revenue Service. The Social Security Administration posts the information as to each employee's wages to his social security record where it becomes the basis for determining the employee's retirement and survivors' benefits.

On the second part the employer reports (1) the total wages subject to withholding, (2) employees' federal income taxes withheld, (3) total wages subject to F.I.C.A. taxes (item 14), and (4) the combined amount of the employees' and the employer's F.I.C.A. taxes. The combined employees' and employer's F.I.C.A. taxes are shown in this case as the final amount for item 14 where it says $4,000 multiplied by $11.7\% =$ TAX, $468. The 11.7% is the sum of the 5.85% 1977 F.I.C.A. tax withheld from the employees' wages and the 5.85% 1977 tax levied on the employer.

Joint federal-state unemployment insurance program

The federal government participates with the states in a joint federal-state unemployment insurance program. Within this joint program each state has established and now administers its own unemployment insurance program under which it pays unemployment benefits to its

Form **941**
(Rev. April 1976)
Department of the Treasury
Internal Revenue Service

Employer's Quarterly Federal Tax Return

Schedule A—Quarterly Report of Wages Taxable under the Federal Insurance Contributions Act—FOR SOCIAL SECURITY

List for each nonagricultural employee the WAGES taxable under the FICA which were paid during the quarter. If you pay an employee more than $15,300 in a calendar year, report only the first $15,300 of such wages. In the case of "Tip Income," see instructions on page 4. IF WAGES WERE NOT TAXABLE UNDER THE FICA, MAKE NO ENTRIES IN ITEMS 1 THROUGH 9 AND 14 THROUGH 18.

SSA Use Only

F ☐ 2 ☐ U ☐ E ☐
S ☐ 1 ☐ L ☐ T ☐
X ☐ 0 ☐ V ☐ A ☐

1. Total pages of this return including this page and any pages of Form 941a ▶ **1**	2. Total number of employees listed ▶ **3**	3. (First quarter only) Number of employees (except household) employed in the pay period including March 12th ▶ **3**

4. EMPLOYEE'S SOCIAL SECURITY NUMBER	5. NAME OF EMPLOYEE (Please type or print)	6. TAXABLE FICA WAGES Paid to Employee in Quarter (Before Deductions) Dollars	Cents	7. TAXABLE TIPS REPORTED (See page 4) Dollars	Cents
000 00 0000 ▼		▼ Dollars	Cents		
123 12 1234	James Jay Nash	1,300	00		
345 34 3456	Robert Dale Robert	1,300	00		
567 56 5678	Mary Jane Smith	1,400	00		

If you need more space for listing employees, use Schedule A continuation sheets, Form 941a.
Totals for this page—Wage total in column 6 and tip total in column 7 ⟶ **4,000** | **00**

8. TOTAL WAGES TAXABLE UNDER FICA PAID DURING QUARTER. $ **4,000.00**   ◁
(Total of column 6 on this page and continuation sheets.) Enter here and in item 14 below.

9. TOTAL TAXABLE TIPS REPORTED UNDER FICA DURING QUARTER. $ **None**   ◁
(Total of column 7 on this page and continuation sheets.) Enter here and in item 15 below. (If no tips reported, write "None.")

Employer's name, address, employer identification number, and calendar quarter. (If not correct, please change)

Name (as distinguished from trade name)
John K. Jones
Trade name, if any
▶ Jones Corner Market
Address and ZIP code
1212 Main Street, Mesa, Arizona 85201

Date quarter ended
March 31, 1977
Employer Identification No.
12 123123

Entries must be made both above and below this line; if address different from previous return, check here ☐

Name (as distinguished from trade name)
John K. Jones
Trade name, if any
▶ Jones Corner Market
Address and ZIP code
1212 Main Street, Mesa, Arizona 85201

Date quarter ended
March 31, 1977
Employer Identification No.
12 123123

T		FP
FF		I
FD		TOT

10. Total Wages And Tips Subject to Withholding Plus Other Compensation . . . . . ⟶	4,000	00
11. Total Income Tax Withheld From Wages, Tips, Annuities, Gambling, etc. (See instructions) .	516	00
12. Adjustment For Preceding Quarters Of Calendar Year		
13. Adjusted Total Of Income Tax Withheld . . . . ⟶	516	00
14. Taxable FICA Wages Paid (Item 8) . . $ **4,000** . . multiplied by 11.7% = TAX	468	00
15. Taxable Tips Reported (Item 9) . . . $ .... multiplied by 5.85% = TAX		
16. Total FICA Taxes (Item 14 plus Item 15)	468	00
17. Adjustment (See instructions)		
18. Adjusted Total Of FICA Taxes . . . . ⟶	468	00
19. Total Taxes (Item 13 plus Item 18)	984	00
20. TOTAL DEPOSITS FOR QUARTER (INCLUDING FINAL DEPOSIT MADE FOR QUARTER) AND OVERPAYMENT FROM PREVIOUS QUARTER LISTED IN SCHEDULE B (See instructions on page 4)	984	00

Note: If undeposited taxes at the end of the quarter are $200 or more, the full amount must be deposited with an authorized commercial bank or a Federal Reserve bank in accordance with instructions on the reverse of the Federal tax deposit form. This deposit must be entered in Schedule B and included in item 20.

21. Undeposited Taxes Due (Item 19 Less Item 20—This Should Be Less Than $200). Pay To Internal Revenue Service And Enter Here . . . .

22. If Item 20 is More Than Item 19, Enter Excess Here ▶ $ ....   And Check If You Want It ☐ Applied to Next Return, Or ☐ Refunded.

23. If not liable for returns in the future, write "FINAL" (See instructions) ▶   Date final wages paid ▶

Under penalties of perjury, I declare that I have examined this return, including accompanying schedules and statements, and to the best of my knowledge and belief it is true, correct, and complete.

Date April 27, 1977   Signature *John K. Jones*   Title (Owner, etc.) Owner

Form 941 (4-76)

218-245-1

Illustration 12–1

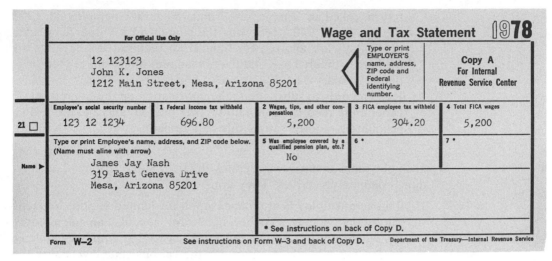

For Official Use Only		Wage and Tax Statement	1978
12 123123 John K. Jones 1212 Main Street, Mesa, Arizona 85201		Type or print EMPLOYER'S name, address, ZIP code and Federal identifying number.	Copy A For Internal Revenue Service Center

	Employee's social security number	1 Federal income tax withheld	2 Wages, tips, and other compensation	3 FICA employee tax withheld	4 Total FICA wages
21 ☐	123 12 1234	696.80	5,200	304.20	5,200

	Type or print Employee's name, address, and ZIP code below. (Name must aline with arrow)	5 Was employee covered by a qualified pension plan, etc.?	6 *	7 *
Name ▶	James Jay Nash 319 East Geneva Drive Mesa, Arizona 85201	No		

* See instructions on back of Copy D.

Form **W–2**   See instructions on Form W–3 and back of Copy D.   Department of the Treasury—Internal Revenue Service

Illustration 12–2

unemployed workers. The federal government through the Social Security Administration approves the state programs and pays a portion of their administrative expenses.

The federal money for administering the state programs is raised by a tax imposed under a law called the Federal Unemployment Tax Act. This act levies a payroll tax on employers of one or more people. Note that the tax is imposed on employers only; employees pay nothing; and also that the money from this tax is used for administrative purposes and not to pay benefits.

Historically, in 1935 when the Federal Unemployment Tax Act was first passed, only one state had an unemployment insurance program; consequently, at that time Congress passed certain sections of the Social Security Act and the Federal Unemployment Tax Act with two purposes in view. The first was to induce the individual states to create satisfactory unemployment insurance programs of their own, and the second was to provide funds to be distributed to the states for use in administering the state programs. These acts were successful in accomplishing their first purpose, all states immediately created unemployment programs; and today the acts remain in effect for their second purpose, to provide funds to be distributed to the states, and also to retain a measure of federal control over the several state programs.

The Federal Unemployment Tax Act   At this writing the Federal Unemployment Tax Act requires employers of one or more employees during 1978 to—

1. Pay an excise tax equal to 0.7% of the first $6,000 in wages paid each employee. (Times of payment are discussed later in this chapter.)
2. On or before January 31 following the end of each year, file a tax

return, called an "Employer's Annual Federal Unemployment Tax Return, Form 940," reporting the amount of tax due. (Ten additional days are allowed for filing if all required tax deposits are made on a timely basis and the full amount of tax due is paid on or before January 31.)

3. Keep records to substantiate the information on the tax return. (In general the records required by other payroll laws and the regular accounting records satisfy this requirement.)

State unemployment insurance programs   While the various state unemployment insurance programs differ in some respects, all have three common objectives. They are:

1. To pay unemployment compensation for limited periods to unemployed individuals. (To be eligible for benefits, an unemployed individual must have worked for a tax-paying employer covered by the law of his state. In general the various state laws cover employers of from one to four or more employees who are not specifically exempted.)
2. To stabilize employment by covered employers. (In all states this is accomplished by a so-called merit-rating plan. Under a merit-rating plan an employer who provides steady employment for his employees gains a merit rating that substantially reduces his state unemployment tax rate.)
3. To establish and operate employment facilities that assist unemployed individuals in finding suitable employment and assist employers in finding employees.

All states support their unemployment insurance programs by placing a payroll tax on employers; a few states place an additional tax on employees. The basic rate in most states is 2.7% of the first $6,000 paid each employee, and an employer can gain a merit rating that will reduce this basic rate to as little as 0.5% in some states and to zero in others. An employer gains a merit rating by not laying his employees off during a slack season to draw unemployment benefits. And, to most employers such a rating offers an important tax savings. For example, an employer with just ten employees who each earn $6,000 or more per year can save $1,320 of state unemployment taxes each year by gaining a merit rating that reduces his state unemployment tax rate to 0.5%.

The states vary as to required unemployment tax reports, but in general all require a tax return and payment of the required tax within one month after the end of each calendar quarter. Also, since the benefits paid an eligible unemployed individual are based upon his earnings, the tax return must usually name each employee and tell his wages.

In addition to reports and payment of taxes, all states require employers to maintain certain payroll records. These vary from state to state; but in general require, among other things, a payroll record for each pay period showing the pay period dates, hours worked, and taxable earnings of each employee. An individual earnings record for each employee is also commonly required, and each earnings record generally must show about the same information required by social security laws. In addition, information as to (1) the date an employee was hired, rehired, or reinstated after a layoff; (2) the date the employee quit, was discharged, or laid off; and (3) the reason for termination is also commonly required.

With few exceptions, employers of one or more persons are required to calculate, collect, and remit to the federal government the income taxes of their employees. Historically, although the present federal income tax law first became effective in 1913, it applied to only a few individuals having high earnings, and it was not until World War II that income taxes were levied on the great masses of wage earners. At that time Congress recognized that many individual wage earners could not be expected to save sufficient money with which to pay their income taxes once each year. Consequently, Congress instituted a system of pay-as-you-go withholding of taxes each payday at their source. This pay-as-you-go withholding of employee income taxes requires an employer to act as a tax collecting agent of the federal government.

Withholding employees' federal income taxes

The federal income tax to be withheld from an employee's wages is determined by his wages and the number of his income tax exemptions, which for payroll purposes are called withholding allowances. At this writing each exemption or withholding allowance exempts from income tax $750 of the employee's yearly earnings. An employee is allowed one exemption for himself, additional exemptions if he or his wife are over 65 or blind, and an exemption for each dependent. Every covered employee is required to furnish his employer an employee's withholding allowance certificate, called a Form W–4, Illustration 12–3, showing the exemptions to which he is entitled.

Form **W-4**	**Employee's Withholding Allowance Certificate**
(Rev. May 1977)	(Use for Wages Paid After May 31, 1977)
Department of the Treasury Internal Revenue Service	This certificate is for income tax withholding purposes only. It will remain in effect until you change it. If you claim exemption from withholding, you will have to file a new certificate on or before April 30 of next year.

Type or print your full name		Your social security number
James Jay Nash		123 12 1234

Home address (number and street or rural route)	Marital Status	[X] Single ☐ Married
319 East Geneva Drive		☐ Married, but withhold at higher Single rate
City or town, State, and ZIP code		Note: *If married, but legally separated, or spouse is a nonresident alien, check the single block.*
Mesa, Arizona 85201		

1 Total number of allowances you are claiming 1

2 Additional amount, if any, you want deducted from each pay (if your employer agrees) . . . . $

3 I claim exemption from withholding (see instructions). Enter "Exempt" . . . .

Under the penalties of perjury, I certify that the number of withholding exemptions and allowances claimed on this certificate does not exceed the number to which I am entitled. If claiming exemption from withholding, I certify that I incurred no liability for Federal income tax for last year and that I anticipate that I will incur no liability for Federal income tax for this year.

Signature ▶ *James Jay Nash*   Date ▶ August 10 , 19 76

Illustration 12–3

Most employers use a wage bracket withholding table similar to the one shown in Illustration 12–4 in determining federal income taxes to be withheld from employee's gross earnings. The illustrated table is for married employees and is applicable when a pay period is one week. Different tables are provided for single employees and for biweekly, semimonthly, and monthly pay periods; and somewhat similar tables are available for determining F.I.C.A. tax withholdings.

Determining the federal income tax to be withheld from an employee's gross wages is quite easy when a withholding table is used.

MARRIED Persons — WEEKLY Payroll Period

And the wages are—		And the number of withholding allowances claimed is—										
At least	But less than	0	1	2	3	4	5	6	7	8	9	10 or more
		The amount of income tax to be withheld shall be—										
$135	$140	$16.40	$13.60	$10.70	$ 7.80	5.40	$ 2.90	$ .50	$0	$0	$0	$0
140	145	17.40	14.60	11.70	8.80	6.20	3.80	1.30	0	0	0	0
145	150	18.40	15.60	12.70	9.80	7.10	4.60	2.20	0	0	0	0
150	160	19.90	17.10	14.20	11.30	8.40	5.90	3.50	1.00	0	0	0
160	170	21.90	19.10	16.20	13.30	10.40	7.60	5.20	2.70	.30	0	0
170	180	23.90	21.10	18.20	15.30	12.40	9.50	6.90	4.40	2.00	0	0
180	190	25.60	23.10	20.20	17.30	14.40	11.50	8.60	6.10	3.70	1.20	0
190	200	27.30	24.80	22.20	19.30	16.40	13.50	10.60	7.80	5.40	2.90	.50
200	210	29.00	26.50	24.10	21.30	18.40	15.50	12.60	9.80	7.10	4.60	2.20
210	220	30.70	28.20	25.80	23.30	20.40	17.50	14.60	11.80	8.90	6.30	3.90
220	230	32.40	29.90	27.50	25.00	22.40	19.50	16.60	13.80	10.90	8.00	5.60
230	240	34.10	31.60	29.20	26.70	24.30	21.50	18.60	15.80	12.90	10.00	7.30
240	250	35.80	33.30	30.90	28.40	26.00	23.50	20.60	17.80	14.90	12.00	9.10
250	260	37.50	35.00	32.60	30.10	27.70	25.20	22.60	19.80	16.90	14.00	11.10
260	270	39.20	36.70	34.30	31.80	29.40	26.90	24.50	21.80	18.90	16.00	13.10
270	280	41.70	38.40	36.00	33.50	31.10	28.60	26.20	23.70	20.90	18.00	15.10
280	290	44.20	40.60	37.70	35.20	32.80	30.30	27.90	25.40	22.90	20.00	17.10
290	300	46.70	43.10	39.50	36.90	34.50	32.00	29.60	27.10	24.70	22.00	19.10
300	310	49.20	45.60	42.00	38.60	36.20	33.70	31.30	28.80	26.40	23.90	21.10
310	320	51.70	48.10	44.50	40.90	37.90	35.40	33.00	30.50	28.10	25.60	23.10
320	$330	$54.20	$50.60	$47.00	$43.40	$39.80	$37.10	$34.70	$32.20	$29.80	$27.30	$24.90
330	340	56.70	53.10	49.50	45.90	42.30	38.80	36.40	33.90	31.50	29.00	26.60
340	350	59.20	55.60	52.00	48.40	44.80	41.20	38.10	35.60	33.20	30.70	28.30
350	360	62.00	58.10	54.50	50.90	47.30	43.70	40.10	37.30	34.90	32.40	30.00
360	370	64.80	60.80	57.00	53.40	49.80	46.20	42.60	39.00	36.60	34.10	31.70
370	380	67.60	63.60	59.50	55.90	52.30	48.70	45.10	41.50	38.30	35.80	33.40
380	...	70.40	...	...	...	...	...	...	...	...	...	...

Illustration 12–4
Wage bracket
withholding table

First the employee's wage bracket is located in the first two columns. Then the amount to be withheld is found on the line of the wage bracket in the column showing the exemption allowances to which the employee is entitled. The column heading numbers refer to the number of exemption allowances claimed by an employee on his Form W–4.

In addition to determining and withholding income tax from each employee's wages every payday, employers are required to —

1. Periodically remit the withheld taxes to the Internal Revenue Service. (Times of remittance are discussed later.)
2. Within one month after the end of each quarter, file a report show-

ing the income taxes withheld. This report is the Employer's Quarterly Federal Tax Return, Form 941, discussed previously and shown in Illustration 13–1. It is the same report required for F.I.C.A. taxes.

3. On or before January 31 following each year, give each employee a Withholding Statement, Form W–2, which tells the employee (1) his total wages for the preceding year, (2) wages subject to F.I.C.A. taxes, (3) income taxes withheld, and (4) F.I.C.A. taxes withheld. A copy of this statement must also be given to each terminated employee within 30 days after his last wage payment.

4. On or before January 31 following the end of each year, send the Internal Revenue Service copies of all W–2 forms given employees.

City and state income taxes

In addition to deducting employees' federal income taxes, employers in many cities and in three fourths of the states must also deduct employees' city and state income taxes. When this is necessary, the city and state taxes are handled much the same as federal income taxes.

Fair Labor Standards Act

The Fair Labor Standards Act, often called the Wages and Hours Law, sets minimum hourly wages and maximum hours of work per week for employees, with certain exceptions, of employers engaged either directly or indirectly in interstate commerce. The law at this writing sets a $2.30 per hour minimum wage for employees in most occupations and sets a maximum 40-hour workweek. However, although the act sets a maximum 40-hour workweek, it does not prohibit an employee from working longer hours but provides that if an employee covered by the act works more than 40 hours in one week, he must be paid for the hours in excess of 40 at his regular pay rate plus an overtime premium of at least one half his regular rate. This gives an employee an overtime rate of at least one and one half times his regular hourly rate. The act also requires employers to maintain records for each covered employee similar to the employee's individual earnings record of Illustration 12–9.

Union contracts

Although the Wages and Hours Law requires covered employers to pay time and one half for hours worked in excess of 40 in any one week, employers commonly operate under contracts with their employees' union that provide even better terms. For example, union contracts often provide for time and one half for work in excess of eight hours in any one day, time and one half for work on Saturdays, and double time for Sundays and holidays. When an employer is under such a union contract, since the contract terms are better than those of the Wages and Hours Law, the contract terms take precedence over the law.

In addition to specifying working hours and wage rates, union contracts often provide for the collection of employees' union dues by the employer. Such a requirement commonly provides that the employer shall deduct dues from the wages of each employee and remit the amounts deducted to the union. The employer is usually required to remit once each month and to report the name and amount deducted from each employee's pay.

Other payroll deductions

In addition to the payroll deductions discussed thus far, employees may individually authorize additional deductions, such as:

1. Deductions to accumulate funds for the purchase of U.S. savings bonds.
2. Deductions to pay health, accident, hospital, or life insurance premiums.
3. Deductions to repay loans from the employer or the employees' credit union.
4. Deductions to pay for merchandise purchased from the company.
5. Deductions for donations to charitable organizations such as Boy Scouts, Girl Scouts, Community Chest, or Red Cross.

Time- keeping

Compiling a record of the time worked by each employee is called *timekeeping*. In an individual company the method of compiling such a record depends upon the nature of the business and the number of its employees. In a very small business timekeeping may consist of no more than pencil notations of each employee's working time made in a memorandum book by the manager or owner. On the other hand, in a larger company a time clock or several time clocks are often used to record on clock cards each employee's time of arrival and departure. When time clocks are used, they are placed at the entrances to the office, store, or factory, and a rack for clock cards is provided beside each clock. At the beginning of each payroll period a clock card for each employee similar to Illustration 12–5 is placed in a rack at the entrance to be used by the employee. Each day as the employee enters the plant, store, or office, he takes his card from the rack and places it in a slot in the time clock. This actuates the clock to stamp the date and arrival time on the card. The employee then returns the card to the rack and proceeds to his place of work. Upon leaving the plant, store, or office at noon or at the end of the day, the procedure is repeated. The employee takes the card from the rack, places it in the clock, and stamps the time of departure. As a result, at the end of a pay period the card shows the hours the employee was on the job.

The Payroll Register

Each pay period the information as to hours worked as compiled on clock cards or otherwise is summarized in a Payroll Register. A pen-and-ink form of such a register is shown in Illustration 12–6. A Payroll Register for use with a bookkeeping machine would be similar. The Illustration 12–6 register is for a weekly pay period and shows the payroll data for each employee on a separate line. The column headings and the data recorded in the columns are in the main self-explanatory.

The columns under the heading "Daily Time" show hours worked each day by each employee. The total of each employee's hours is entered in the column headed "Total Hours." If hours worked include overtime hours, these are entered in the column headed "O.T. Hours."

The column headed "Reg. Pay Rate" is for the hourly pay rate of each employee. Total hours worked multiplied by the regular pay rate equals regular pay; overtime hours multiplied by the overtime premium rate equals overtime premium pay; and regular pay plus overtime premium pay is the gross pay of each employee.

Under the heading "Deductions," the amounts withheld from each employee's gross pay for social security or F.I.C.A. taxes are shown in the column marked "F.I.C.A. Taxes." These amounts are determined by multiplying the gross pay of each employee by the F.I.C.A. tax rate in effect. In this and the remaining illustrations of this chap-

Courtesy Simplex Time Recorder Co.   **Illustration 12–5**

| | | Daily Time | | | | | | | | Earnings | | | |
| | | | | | | | | | | | | | | |
Employee	Clock Card No.	M	T	W	T	F	S	S	Total Hours	O.T. Hours	Reg. Pay Rate	Reg- ular Pay	O.T. Pre- mium Pay	Gross Pay
Robert Austin	105	8	8	8	8	8			40		3.40	136.00		136.00
Charles Cross	97	8	8	8	8	8			40		5.00	200.00		200.00
John Cruz	89	0	8	8	8	8	8		40		4.00	160.00		160.00
Howard Keife	112	8	8	8	8	8	8		48	8	4.00	192.00	16.00	208.00
Lee Miller	95	8	8	8	8	0			32		4.00	128.00		128.00
Dale Sears	53	8	8	8	8	8	4		44	4	7.50	330.00	15.00	345.00
Totals												1,146.00	31.00	1,177.00

Payroll
Week ended

Illustration 12–6

ter it is assumed that the rate is 6% on the first $17,500 paid each employee.

Observe in the F.I.C.A. Taxes column of Illustration 12–6 that there is no F.I.C.A. deduction for the last employee, Dale Sears. This is because Sear's cumulative earnings for the year have previously passed the assumed $17,500 tax-exempt point and therefore his wages are assumed to be no longer subject to tax. (See the discussion for Illustration 12–10 on page 410.)

As previously stated, the income tax withheld from each employee depends upon his gross pay and exemptions. This amount is commonly determined by the use of a wage bracket withholding table; and when determined, it is entered in the column headed "Federal Income Taxes."

The column headed "Hosp. Ins." shows the amounts withheld from employees' wages to pay hospital insurance premiums for the employees and their families. The total withheld from all employees is a current liability of the employer until paid to the insurance company.

As previously stated, union contracts commonly require the employer to withhold union dues and to periodically remit the amounts withheld to the union. The total withheld for employees' union dues is a current liability until paid to the union. The column marked "Union Dues" in the illustrated Payroll Register is for this deduction.

Additional columns may be added to the Payroll Register for deductions that occur sufficiently often to warrant special columns. For example, a company that regularly deducts amounts from its employees' pay for U.S. savings bonds may add a special column for this deduction.

Register
December 18, 1978

	Deductions				Payment		Distribution		
F.I.C.A. Taxes	Federal Income Taxes	Hosp. Ins.	Union Dues	Total Deduc-tions	Net Pay	Check No.	Sales Salaries	Office Salaries	Repair Service Salaries
8.16	18.15	6.00		32.31	103.69	893		136.00	
12.00	18.40	8.00	3.00	41.40	158.60	894			200.00
9.60	13.30	8.00	2.50	33.40	126.60	895	160.00		
12.48	15.50	8.00	2.50	38.48	169.52	896	208.00		
7.68	6.15	8.00	2.50	24.33	103.67	897	128.00		
	44.80	8.00		52.80	292.20	898		345.00	
49.92	116.30	46.00	10.50	222.72	954.28		496.00	481.00	200.00

An employee's gross pay less his total deductions is his net pay and is entered in the column headed "Net Pay." The total of this column is the amount to be paid the employees. The numbers of the checks used in paying the employees are entered in the column headed "Check No."

The three columns under the heading "Distribution" are for sorting the various salaries into kinds of salary expense. Here each employee's gross salary is entered in the proper column according to the type of his work. The column totals then tell the amounts to be debited to the salary expense accounts.

Recording the payroll

Generally a Payroll Register such as the one shown in Illustration 12–6 is a supplementary memorandum record. As a supplementary record, its information is not posted directly to the accounts but is first recorded with a general journal entry, which is then posted. The entry to record the payroll shown in Illustration 12–6 is:

Dec.	18	Sales Salaries Expense	496.00	
		Office Salaries Expense	481.00	
		Repair Service Salaries Expense	200.00	
		F.I.C.A. Taxes Payable		49.92
		Employees' Federal Income Taxes Payable		116.30
		Employees' Hospital Insurance Premiums Payable		46.00
		Employees' Union Dues Payable		10.50
		Accrued Payroll Payable		954.28
		To record the payroll of the week ended December 18.		

The debits of this entry are taken from the Payroll Register's distribution column totals, and they charge the employees' gross earnings to the proper salary expense accounts. The credits to F.I.C.A. Taxes Payable, Employees' Federal Income Taxes Payable, Employees' Hospital Insurance Premiums Payable, and Employees' Union Dues Payable record these amounts as current liabilities. The credit to Accrued Payroll Payable records as a liability the amount to be paid the employees.

Paying the employees

Almost every business pays its employees with checks. In a company having but few employees these checks are often drawn on the regular bank account. When this is done, each check is recorded in either a Check Register or a Cash Disbursements Journal. Since each check results in a debit to the Accrued Payroll Payable account, posting labor may be saved by adding an Accrued Payroll Payable debit column to the Check Register or Cash Disbursements Journal. For example, assume that a firm uses a Check Register like that described in Chapter 6. If a firm uses such a register and adds an Accrued Payroll debit column, the entries to pay the employees of the Illustration 12–6 payroll will appear somewhat like those in Illustration 12–7.

									Check Register	
Date		Check No.	Payee	Account Debited	F	Other Ac- counts Debit	Accts. Pay. Debit	Accr. Payroll Pay. Debit	Pur. Dis. Credit	Cash Credit
Dec.	18	893	Robert Austin	Accrued Payroll				103.69		103.69
	18	894	Charles Cross	"				158.60		158.60
	18	895	John Cruz	"				126.60		126.60
	18	896	Howard Keife	"				169.52		169.52
	18	897	Lee Miller	"				103.67		103.67
	18	898	Dale Sears	"				292.20		292.20

Illustration 12–7

Although not required by law, most employers furnish each employee an earnings statement each payday. The objective of such a statement is to inform the employee and give him a record of hours worked, gross pay, deductions, and net pay that may be retained. The statement usually takes the form of a detachable paycheck portion that is removed before the check is cashed. A paycheck with a detachable portion showing deductions is reproduced in Illustration 12–8.

Payroll bank account

A business with many employees normally makes use of a special payroll bank account in paying its employees. When such an account is used, one check for the amount of the payroll is drawn on the

Robert Austin	40		3.40	136.00		136.00	8.16	18.15	6.00		32.31	103.69
Employee	Total Hours	O.T. Hours	Reg. Pay Rate	Reg-ular Pay	O.T. Prem. Pay	Gross Pay	F.I.C.A. Taxes	In-come Taxes	Hosp. Ins.	Union Dues	Total Deduc-tions	Net Pay

STATEMENT OF EARNINGS AND DEDUCTIONS FOR EMPLOYEE'S RECORDS—DETACH BEFORE CASHING CHECK

THE EUGENE MANUFACTURING COMPANY
2590 Chula Vista Street · Eugene, Oregon

No. 893

PAY TO THE ORDER OF _Robert Austin_ _____ DATE _December 18, 1978_ $ _103.69_

--One-hundred-and-three dollars and sixty-nine cents----------------------------

EUGENE MANUFACTURING COMPANY

James R. Morris

Merchants National Bank
Eugene, Oregon

Illustration 12–8

regular bank account and deposited in the special payroll bank account, after which individual payroll checks are drawn on this special account. Because only one check for the payroll is drawn on the regular bank account each payday, use of a special payroll bank account simplifies reconciliation of the regular bank account, since it may be reconciled without considering the payroll checks outstanding, and there may be many of these. Likewise, when the payroll bank account is separately reconciled, only the outstanding payroll checks need be considered.

A company using a special payroll bank account completes the following steps in paying its employees:

1. First, it records the information shown on its Payroll Register in the usual manner with a general journal entry similar to the one illustrated on page 405. This entry causes the sum of the employees' net pay to be credited to the liability account Accrued Payroll Payable.
2. Next, a single check payable to Payroll Bank Account for the amount of the payroll is drawn and entered in the Check Register. This results in a debit to Accrued Payroll Payable and a credit to Cash.
3. Then this check is endorsed and deposited in the payroll bank account. This transfers an amount of money equal to the payroll from the regular bank account to the special payroll bank account.
4. Last, individual payroll checks are drawn on the special payroll bank account and delivered to the employees. These pay the em-

ployees and, as soon as all employees cash their checks, exhaust the funds in the special account.

A special Payroll Check Register may be used in connection with a payroll bank account. However, most companies do not use such a register but prefer to enter the payroll check numbers in their Payroll Register, making it act as a Check Register.

Employee's Individual Earnings Record

An Employee's Individual Earnings Record, Illustration 12–9, provides for each employee in one record a full year's summary of his working time, gross earnings, deductions, and net pay. In addition it accumulates information that—

1. Serves as a basis for the employer's state and federal payroll tax returns.
2. Tells when an employee's earnings have reached the tax-exempt points for F.I.C.A. and state and federal unemployment taxes.
3. And supplies data for the Withholding Statement, Form W–2, which must be given to the employee at the end of the year.

The payroll information on an Employee's Individual Earnings Record is taken from the Payroll Register. The information as to earnings, deductions, and net pay is first recorded on a single line in the Payroll Register, from where it is posted each pay period to the earnings record. Note the last column of the record. It shows an employee's cumulative earnings and is used to determine when the earnings

EMPLOYEE'S INDIVIDUAL EARNINGS RECORD

Employee's Name _Robert Austin_   S.S. Acct. No. _307-03-2195_   Employee No. _105_

Home
Address _111 South Greenwood_   Notify in Case
of Emergency _Margaret Austin_   Phone
No. _964-9834_

Employed _June 7, 1974_   Date of
Termination _____   Reason _____

Date of
Birth _June 6, 1954_   Date
Becomes 65 _June 6, 2019_   Male (X) Married (X) Number of   Pay
Female ( ) Single ( ) Exemptions _1_ Rate _$3.40 hr._

Occupation _Clerk_   Place _Office_

Date		Time Lost		Time Wk.		Reg. Pay	O.T. Prem. Pay	Gross Pay	F.I.C.A. Taxes	Federal In-come Taxes	Hosp. Ins.	Union Dues	Total De-duc-tions	Net Pay	Check No.	Cumu-lative Pay
Per. Ends	Paid	Hrs.	Rea-son	Total	O.T. Hours											
1/5	1/5			40		136.00		136.00	8.16	18.15	6.00		32.31	103.69	173	136.00
1/12	1/12			40		136.00		136.00	8.16	18.15	6.00		32.31	103.69	201	272.00
1/19	1/19			40		136.00		136.00	8.16	18.15	6.00		32.31	103.69	243	408.00
1/26	1/26	4	Sick	36		122.40		122.40	7.34	14.90	6.00		28.24	94.16	295	530.40
2/2	2/2			40		136.00		136.00	8.16	18.15	6.00		32.31	103.69	339	666.40
2/9	2/9			40		136.00		136.00	8.16	18.15	6.00		32.31	103.69	354	802.40
2/16	2/16			40		136.00		136.00	8.16	18.15	6.00		32.31	103.69	397	938.40
2/23	2/23			40		136.00		136.00	8.16	18.15	6.00		32.31	103.69	446	1,074.40
12/18	12/18			40		136.00		136.00	8.16	18.15	6.00		32.31	103.69	893	6,812.00

Illustration 12–9

reach the tax-exempt points and are no longer subject to the various payroll taxes.

Under the previous discussion of the Federal Social Security Act, it was pointed out that F.I.C.A. taxes are levied in like amounts on both employed workers and their employers. A covered employer is required by law to deduct from his employees' pay the amounts of their F.I.C.A. taxes; but in addition, he must himself pay a tax equal to the sum of his employee's F.I.C.A. taxes. Commonly, the tax levied on the employer is recorded at the same time the payroll to which it relates is recorded. Also, since both the employees' and employer's F.I.C.A. taxes are reported on the same tax return and are paid in one amount, the liabilities for both are normally recorded in the same F.I.C.A. Taxes Payable account.

Payroll taxes levied on the employer

As previously explained, although F.I.C.A. taxes are levied on both covered employers and their employees, employers only are required to pay federal and, usually, state unemployment taxes. Most employers record all three of these payroll taxes with one general journal entry that is normally made at the time the payroll to which the taxes relate is recorded. For example, the entry to record the employer's payroll taxes on the payroll of Illustration 12–6 is:

Dec.	18	Payroll Taxes Expense...	57.06	
		F.I.C.A. Taxes Payable		49.92
		State Unemployment Taxes Payable......................		5.67
		Federal Unemployment Taxes Payable		1.47
		To record the employer's payroll taxes.		

The $57.06 debit of the entry records as an expense the sum of the payroll taxes incurred by the employer as a result of the payroll. The $49.92 credit to F.I.C.A. Taxes Payable is equal to and matches the total deducted from the employees' pay for F.I.C.A. taxes. The $5.67 credit to State Unemployment Taxes Payable is based on the assumption the employer's state tax rate is 2.7% of the first $6,000 paid each employee. In the illustrative payroll it is assumed that the employees have cumulative earnings prior to this pay period and earnings subject to the various taxes as shown in Illustration 12–10.

If the employees have prior cumulative earnings as listed in Illustration 12–10, then four employees have earned in excess of $6,000 and their pay is assumed, as in the majority of states, to be exempt from state unemployment taxes. One employee has previously earned $5,950 and only the first $50 of his earnings are subject to the tax, and the wages of the remaining employee are taxable in full. Consequently, the $5.67 credit to State Unemployment Taxes Payable in the entry recording the employer's payroll taxes resulted from multiplying $210 of wages subject to the tax by the assumed 2.7% rate.

Employees' Cumulative Earnings through the Last Pay Period and Earnings Subject to the Various Taxes

Employees	Earnings through Last Pay Period	Earnings This Pay Period	Earnings Subject to—	
			F.I.C.A. Taxes	State and Federal Unemployment Taxes
Robert Austin.....	$ 6,676	$136	$136	
Charles Cross	10,216	200	200	
John Cruz..........	3,780	160	160	$160
Howard Keife	8,112	208	208	
Lee Miller	5,950	128	128	50
Dale Sears	17,508	345		
Totals.......		$1,177	$832	$210

Illustration 12–10

As the law is presently amended, an employer's federal unemployment tax is also based on the first $6,000 in wages paid each employee. Therefore the $1.47 federal unemployment tax liability recorded in the illustrated journal entry resulted from multiplying $210 by the 0.7% rate.

Paying the payroll taxes

Federal income and the F.I.C.A. taxes withheld each payday from the employees' pay plus the F.I.C.A. tax imposed on the employer are current liabilities until paid to the United States Treasury Department. The normal method of payment is to deposit the amounts due to the credit of the United States Treasury in a bank authorized to accept such deposits. The depositing procedure results in a punched card which the bank mails to the Internal Revenue Service. On receipt of the card the Internal Revenue Service gives the depositor credit for paying the amount deposited, and the depositor reports on his tax return that he has paid the taxes through a federal deposit or deposits.

Required times of payment depend on the amounts involved. If the sum of the F.I.C.A. taxes plus the employees' income taxes is less than $200 for a quarter, the taxes may be paid when the employer files his Employer's Quarterly Tax Return, Form 941. This return is due on April 30, July 31, October 31, and January 31 following the end of each calendar quarter, and a check for the taxes, if less than $200, may be attached to the return or the taxes may be deposited in a federal depository bank at the time the return is filed. The check or the deposit is recorded in the same manner as a check paying any other liability.

If the taxes exceed $200 in a quarter, after each payday the employer must total the amount of his employees' income and F.I.C.A. taxes withheld since the beginning of the quarter plus his own employer's F.I.C.A. tax. This total, less any deposits already made during the quarter, is the employer's F.I.C.A. and income tax liability. Then (1) if on any of the 7th, 15th, 22d, and last day of any month in the quarter this tax liability reaches $2,000 or more, the entire amount must be deposited to the credit of the United States Treasury within three banking days thereafter. (2) If as of the last day of the first or second month of a quarter the tax liability is less than $2,000 but more than $200, the amount must be deposited on or before the 15th day of the next month. For the last month in the quarter a deposit of less than $2,000 does not have to be made until the end of the next month, or it may be remitted with the quarterly tax return.

A deposit of F.I.C.A. and withheld employees' income taxes in a federal depository bank pays these taxes. Consequently, if at the time an employer files his Employer's Quarterly Tax Return, Form 941, he has paid the taxes reported on the return by means of deposits, he needs only to mail the return to the Internal Revenue Service, and no accounting entries are required.

In most states, when state unemployment taxes are less than $100 per month, they may be paid quarterly. If they exceed $100 per month, some states require monthly payments. This is somewhat similar to the federal procedures; therefore, most employers account for state unemployment taxes in the same manner as F.I.C.A. and employee income taxes.

An employer's federal unemployment tax for the first three quarters of a year must be deposited in a federal depository bank by the last day of the month following each quarter (i.e., on April 30, July 31, and October 31). However, no deposit is required if the tax due for a quarter plus the undeposited tax for previous quarters are $100 or less. The tax for the last quarter of a year plus the undeposited tax for previous quarters must either be deposited or paid on or before January 31 following the end of the tax year. If the Employer's Annual Federal Unemployment Tax Return is filed on or before that date, a check for the last quarter's tax and any undeposited tax for previous quarters may be attached to the form.

Payroll taxes are levied on wages actually paid; consequently, there is no legal liability for taxes on accrued wages. Nevertheless, both wages and the employer's payroll taxes on the wages are from a theoretical viewpoint expenses of the accounting period in which the wages are earned; and if the income statement is to show all expenses of an accounting period, both accrued wages and the accrued taxes on the wages should be recorded at the end of the period.

Accruing taxes and wages

To illustrate the entry for accruing wages and taxes on the wages, assume that (1) a company's accounting period ends on June 30, (2) its last pay period ended on June 26, and (3) the company employees worked on June 28, 29, and 30 and earned sales salaries of $750 and office salaries of $250 during the three days. The adjusting entry to record these accrued wages and payroll taxes is:

June	30	Sales Salaries Expense	750.00	
		Office Salaries Expense	250.00	
		Payroll Taxes Expense	94.00	
		F.I.C.A. Taxes Payable		60.00
		State Unemployment Taxes Payable		27.00
		Federal Unemployment Taxes Payable		7.00
		Accrued Payroll Payable		1,000.00
		To record the accrued payroll.		

The $94 debit to Payroll Taxes Expense is the sum of the F.I.C.A., federal unemployment, and state unemployment taxes levied on the employer. The amount is based on the assumptions that all the wages were subject to taxes at a 6% F.I.C.A. tax rate, a 0.7% federal unemployment rate, and a 2.7% state unemployment rate.

Although payroll taxes on accrued wages are theoretically an expense of the accounting period in which the wages are earned, often such accrued taxes are not material in amount. Consequently, many companies apply the *materiality principal* and do not accrue such taxes.

Machine methods

Manually prepared pen-and-ink records like the ones described in this chapter are found in many small concerns, and very satisfactorily meet their needs. However, concerns having many employees commonly use machines in their payroll work. The machines vary but are usually designed to take advantage of the fact that each pay period much the same information must be entered for each employee in the Payroll Register, on his earnings record, and on his paycheck. The machines take advantage of this and simultaneously print the information in all three places in one operation.

Glossary

Clock card. A card used by an employee to record the time of his or her arrival at his or her place of work and the time of departure.

Federal depository bank. A bank authorized to receive as deposits amounts of money payable to the federal government.

Federal unemployment tax. A tax levied by the federal government and used to pay a portion of the costs of the joint federal-state unemployment programs.

FICA taxes. Federal Insurance Contributions Act taxes, otherwise known as social security taxes.

Gross pay. The amount of an employee's pay before any deductions.

Individual earnings record. A record of an employee's hours worked, gross pay, deductions, net pay, and certain personal information about the employee.

Merit rating. A rating granted an employer by a state, which is based on whether or not the employer's employees have experienced periods of unemployment. A good rating reduces the employer's unemployment tax rate.

Net pay. Gross pay minus deductions.

Payroll bank account. A special bank account into which at the end of each pay period the total amount of an employer's payroll is deposited and on which the employees' payroll checks are drawn.

Payroll tax. A tax levied on the amount of a payroll or on the amount of an employee's gross pay.

State unemployment tax. A tax levied by a state, the proceeds from which are used to pay benefits to unemployed workers.

Timekeeping. Making a record of the time each employee is at his or her place of work.

Withholding allowance. An amount of an employee's annual earnings not subject to income tax.

Wage bracket withholding table. A table showing the amounts to be withheld from employees' wages at various levels of earnings.

---

1. What are F.I.C.A. taxes? Who pays these taxes and for what purposes are the funds from F.I.C.A. taxes used?
2. Company A has one employee from whose pay it withholds each week $3.75 of federal income tax and $5.76 of F.I.C.A. tax. Company B has 200 employees from whose pay it withholds each week over $2,000 of employee F.I.C.A. and federal income taxes. When must each of these companies remit these amounts to the Internal Revenue Service?
3. What benefits are paid to unemployed workers from funds raised by the Federal Unemployment Insurance Act? Why was this act passed?
4. Who pays federal unemployment insurance taxes? What is the tax rate?
5. What are the objectives of state unemployment insurance laws? Who pays state unemployment insurance taxes?
6. What is a state unemployment merit rating? Why are such merit ratings granted?
7. What determines the amount that must be deducted from an employee's wages for federal income taxes?
8. What is a wage bracket withholding table? Use the wage bracket withholding table in Illustration 12–4 to find the income tax to be withheld from the wages of a married employee with three exemptions who earned $187 in a week.
9. What does the Fair Labor Standards Act require of a covered employer?
10. How is a clock card used in recording the time an employee is on the job?
11. How is a special payroll bank account used in paying the wages of employees?
12. At the end of an accounting period a firm's special payroll bank account has a $262.35 balance because the payroll checks of two employees have

Questions for class discussion

not cleared the bank. Should this $262.35 appear on the firm's balance sheet? If so, where?

13. What information is accumulated on an employee's individual earnings record? Why must this information be accumulated? For what purposes is the information used?

14. What payroll taxes are levied on the employer? What taxes are deducted from the wages of an employee?

Class exercises

Exercise 12-1

A married employee of a company subject to the Fair Labor Standards Act worked 44 hours during the week ended January 7. His pay rate is $3.50 per hour, and his wages are subject to no deductions other than F.I.C.A. and federal income taxes. He claims three income tax exemptions. Calculate his regular pay, overtime premium pay, gross pay, F.I.C.A. tax deduction at an assumed 6% rate, income tax deduction (use the wage bracket withholding table of Illustration 12-4), total deductions, and net pay.

Exercise 12-2

On January 6, at the end of its first weekly pay period in the year, the column totals of a company's Payroll Register showed that its sales employees had earned $1,450 and its office employees had earned $550. The employees were to have F.I.C.A. taxes withheld at an assumed 6% rate plus $210 of federal income taxes, $40 of union dues, and $80 of hospital insurance premiums. Calculate the amount of F.I.C.A. taxes to be withheld and give the general journal entry to record the Payroll Register.

Exercise 12-3

Give the general journal entry to record the employer's payroll taxes resulting from the Exercise 12-2 payroll. Assume the company has a merit rating that reduces its state unemployment tax rate of 0.8% of the first $6,000 paid each employee.

Exercise 12-4

The following information as to earnings and deductions for the pay period ended December 20 was taken from a company's payroll records:

Employees' Names	Gross Pay	Earnings to End of Previous Week	Federal Income Taxes	Hospital Insurance Deductions
June Abbot.....	$100	$ 3,240	10.90	$ 5.25
John Cotton....	150	5,880	14.20	7.50
Fred Greene...	150	8,110	20.20	5.25
Walter Nash ...	325	17,508	43.40	7.50
	$725		88.70	$25.50

Required:

1. Calculate the employees' F.I.C.A. tax withholdings at an assumed 6% rate on the first $17,500 paid each employee. Also calculate total F.I.C.A. taxes withheld, total deductions, and net pay.
2. Prepare a general journal entry to record the payroll information. Assume all employees work in the office.
3. Prepare a general journal entry to record the employer's payroll taxes resulting from the payroll. Assume a state unemployment tax rate of 1% on the first $6,000 paid each employee.

Problem 12–1   Problems

On January 6, at the end of the first weekly pay period of the year, the column totals of a company's Payroll Register indicated its sales employees had earned $2,000 and its office employees had earned $500. The employees were to have F.I.C.A. taxes withheld from their wages at an assumed 6% rate plus $225 federal income taxes, $110 group insurance deductions, and $50 of union dues.

Required:

1. Calculate the total of the F.I.C.A. Taxes Payable column in the Payroll Register, and prepare a general journal entry to record the register information.
2. Prepare a general journal entry to record the employer's payroll taxes resulting from the payroll. Assume the company has a merit rating that reduces its state unemployment tax rate to 1.2% of the first $6,000 paid each employee.
3. Under the assumption the company uses a payroll bank account and special payroll checks in paying its employees, give the check register entry (Check No. 815) to transfer funds equal to the payroll from the regular bank account to the payroll bank account.
4. Answer this question: After the check register entry is made and posted, are additional debit and credit entries required to record the payroll checks and pay the employees?

Problem 12–2

A company's payroll records provided the following information for the weekly pay period ended December 18:

Employees' Names	Clock Card No.	Daily Time							Pay Rate	Federal Income Taxes	Medi-cal Insur-ance	Union Dues	Earnings to End of Previous Week
		M	T	W	T	F	S	S					
Roy Andrews	11	8	8	8	8	8	4	0	7.50	48.40	6.00	3.00	$17,540
Jerry Dale..........	12	8	8	8	8	8	0	0	7.50	36.20	6.00	3.00	17,400
Ray Lewis..........	13	8	8	8	8	8	0	0	3.50	11.70	6.00	2.50	3,960
Helen Mohr........	14	8	8	8	8	8	0	0	5.00	29.00	6.00		10,135
Mary Page	15	8	8	8	8	8	4	0	3.00	16.40			5,940

Required:

1. Enter the relevant information in the proper columns of a Payroll Register and complete the register using a F.I.C.A. tax rate of 6% on the first $17,500 paid each employee. Assume the company is subject to the Fair Labor Standards Act and that the first two employees are shop workers, the third is a salesperson, and the last two work in the office.

2. Prepare a general journal entry to record the payroll register information.

3. Make the check register entry (Check No. 234) to transfer funds equal to the payroll from the regular bank account to the payroll bank account under the assumption the company uses special payroll checks and a payroll bank account in paying its employees. Assume the first payroll check is numbered 668 and enter the payroll check numbers in the Payroll Register.

4. Prepare a general journal entry to record the employer's payroll taxes resulting from the payroll. Assume the company has a merit rating that reduces its state unemployment tax rate to 2% of the first $6,000 paid each employee.

Problem 12–3

A company subject to the Fair Labor Standards Act accumulated the following payroll information for the weekly pay period ended December 15:

Employees' Names	Clock Card No.	Daily Time M	T	W	T	F	S	S	Pay Rate	Income Tax Exemptions	Medical Insurance	Union Dues	Earnings to End of Previous Week
Paul Baer...........	22	8	8	8	8	8	0	0	4.50	3	7.00	2.00	$ 9,000
Frank Clift	23	8	8	8	8	8	4	0	7.00	2	7.00	3.00	17,200
Dale Duff...........	24	8	8	8	8	8	0	0	7.00	4	7.00	3.00	5,872
June Nash.........	25	8	8	8	9	9	0	0	4.00	2	7.00		3,600

Required:

1. Enter the relevant information in the proper columns of a Payroll Register and complete the register using a F.I.C.A. tax rate of 6% of the first $17,500 paid each employee. Use the wage bracket withholding table of Illustration 12–4 to determine the federal income tax to be withheld from the wages of each employee. Assume all employees are married and the first one is a salesperson, the second two work in the shop, and the last one works in the office.

2. Prepare a general journal entry to record the payroll register information.

3. Make the check register entry to transfer funds equal to the payroll from the regular bank account to the payroll bank account (Check No. 567) under the assumption the company uses special payroll checks and a payroll bank account in paying its employees. Assume the first payroll check is numbered 444 and enter the payroll check numbers in the Payroll Register.

4. Prepare a general journal entry to record the employer's payroll taxes resulting from the payroll. Assume the company has a merit rating that reduces its state unemployment tax rate to 1.8% of the first $6,000 paid each employee.

Problem 12–4

A company has four employees to each of whom it pays $700 per month on the last day of each month. On June 1 the following accounts and balances appeared in its ledger:

a. F.I.C.A. Taxes Payable, $336. (Since the company's F.I.C.A. and employees' income taxes exceed $200 per month, the balance of this account represents the liability for both the employer and employees' F.I.C.A. taxes for the May 31 payroll only.)
b. Employees' Federal Income Taxes Payable, $295 (liability for May only).
c. Federal Unemployment Taxes Payable, $98 (liability for first five months of the year).
d. State Unemployment Taxes Payable, $84 (liability for April and May).
e. Employees' Group Insurance Payable, $80 (liability for April and May).

During June and July the company completed the following payroll related transactions:

June 12 Issued Check No. 755 payable to Security Bank, a federal depository bank authorized to receive F.I.C.A. and employee income tax payments from employers. The check was for $631 and was in payment of the May F.I.C.A. and employee income taxes.

30 Prepared a general journal entry to record the June Payroll Register which had the following column totals:

F.I.C.A. Taxes	Federal Income Taxes	Group Insurance Deductions	Total Deductions	Net Pay	Office Salaries	Shop Wages
$168	$295	$40	$503	$2,297	$700	$2,100

June 30 Issued Check No. 828 payable to Payroll Bank Account in payment of the June payroll. Endorsed the check, deposited it in the payroll bank account, and issued payroll checks to the employees.

30 Prepared a general journal entry to record the employer's payroll taxes resulting from the June payroll. The company has a merit rating that reduces its state unemployment tax rate to 1.5% of the first $6,000 paid each employee.

July 14 Issued Check No. 883 payable to Security Bank. The check was in payment of the June F.I.C.A. and employee income taxes.

14 Issued Check No. 884 payable to Apex Insurance Company. The check was in payment of the April, May, and June employee group insurance premiums.

14 Issued Check No. 885 to the State Tax Commission for the April, May, and June state unemployment taxes. Mailed the check along with the second quarter tax return to the State Tax Commission.

31 Issued Check No. 915 payable to Security Bank. Since the tax liability exceeded $100, the check was in payment of the employer's federal unemployment taxes for the first two quarters of the year.

31 Mailed to the Internal Revenue Service the Employer's Quarterly Tax Return reporting the F.I.C.A. taxes and the employees' federal income tax deductions for the second quarter of the year.

Required:

Prepare the necessary general journal and check register entries to record the transactions.

Alternate
problems

Problem 12–1A

On January 8, at the end of the first weekly pay period of the year, the column totals of a company's Payroll Register indicated its sales employees had earned $1,850, its office employees had earned $510, and its delivery employees $240. The employees were to have F.I.C.A. taxes withheld from their wages at an assumed 6% rate plus $280 federal income taxes, $90 group insurance deductions, and $32 of union dues.

Required:

1. Calculate the total of the F.I.C.A. Taxes Payable column in the Payroll Register, and prepare a general journal entry to record the register information.
2. Prepare a general journal entry to record the employer's payroll taxes resulting from the payroll. Assume the company has a merit rating that reduces its state unemployment tax rate to 1.5% of the first $6,000 paid each employee.
3. Under the assumption the company uses special payroll checks and a payroll bank account in paying its employees, give the check register entry (Check No. 745) to transfer funds equal to the payroll from the regular bank account to the payroll bank account.
4. Answer this question: After the check register entry is made and posted, are additional debit and credit entries required to record the payroll checks and pay the employees?

Problem 12–2A

The following information was taken from a company's payroll records for the weekly pay period ended December 20:

Employees' Names	Clock Card No.	Daily Time							Pay Rate	Federal Income Taxes	Medical Insurance	Union Dues	Earnings to End of Previous Week
		M	T	W	T	F	S	S					
June Agnew	14	8	8	8	8	8	0	0	5.00	33.50	5.00		10,135
Dale Hall...........	15	8	8	8	8	8	6	0	3.00	20.45			5,920
John Koop	16	8	8	8	8	8	0	0	4.25	12.40	6.50	2.00	3,500
Carl Lee	17	8	8	8	8	8	0	0	7.25	36.90	6.50	2.50	17,340
Roy Page...........	18	8	8	8	8	8	2	0	7.00	33.70	6.50	2.50	15.250

Required:

1. Enter the relevant information in the proper columns of a Payroll Register and complete the register using a F.I.C.A. tax rate of 6% on the first $17,500 paid each employee. Assume the company is subject to the Fair

Labor Standards Act; and assume the first two employees work in the office, the third is a salesperson, and the last two work in the shop.

2. Prepare a general journal entry to record the payroll register information.
3. Assume the company uses special payroll checks drawn on a payroll bank account in paying its employees, and make the check register entry (Check No. 202) to transfer funds equal to the payroll from the regular bank account to the payroll bank account. Also assume the first payroll check is No. 653 and enter the payroll check numbers in the Payroll Register.
4. Prepare a general journal entry to record the employer's payroll taxes resulting from the payroll. Assume the concern has a merit rating that reduces its state unemployment tax rate to 0.8% of the first $6,000 paid each employee.

Problem 12–3A

The following information for the weekly pay period ended December 17 was taken from the records of a company subject to the Fair Labor Standards Act:

Employees' Names	Clock Card No.	Daily Time							Pay Rate	Income Tax Exemptions	Medical Insurance	Union Dues	Earnings to End of Previous Week
		M	T	W	T	F	S	S					
Mary Alt............	21	8	8	8	8	8	4	0	4.50	2	6.50		9,840
Harry Bray.........	22	8	8	8	8	8	0	0	4.00	3	6.50		3,650
Jerry Hamm	23	8	8	8	8	8	8	0	6.50	4	6.50	2.00	17,380
Alex Hunt..........	24	8	8	8	8	8	0	0	5.50	2	6.50	2.00	5,860

Required:

1. Enter the relevant information in the proper columns of a Payroll Register and complete the register using a F.I.C.A. tax rate of 6% on the first $17,500 paid each employee. Use the wage bracket withholding table of Illustration 12–4 to determine the federal income taxes to be withheld from the wages of the employees. Assume that all employees are married and that the first employee works in the office, the second is a salesperson, and the last two work in the shop.
2. Prepare a general journal entry to record the payroll register information.
3. Make the check register entry (Check No. 789) to transfer funds equal to the payroll from the regular bank account to the payroll bank account. Assume the first payroll check is numbered 901 and enter the payroll check numbers in the Payroll Register.
4. Prepare a general journal entry to record the employer's payroll taxes resulting from the payroll. Assume the company has a merit rating that reduces its state unemployment tax rate to 1.2% of the first $6,000 paid each employee.

Problem 12–4A

A company has three employees to each of whom it pays $900 per month on the last day of each month. On June 1 the following accounts and balances appeared in its ledger:

F.I.C.A. taxes payable (liability for the employer's and employees'
  taxes resulting from the May 31 payroll) $324.00
Employees' federal income taxes payable (liability for the May 31
  payroll deductions) 275.00
Federal unemployment taxes payable (liability for first five months
  of the year) 94.50
State unemployment taxes payable (liability for April and May) 108.00
Employees' group insurance payable (liability for April and May) 84.00

During June and July the company completed the following payroll related
transactions:

June 14 Issued Check No. 816 payable to Guaranty Bank, a federal depository bank authorized to accept F.I.C.A. and employee income tax
payments from employers. The check was for $599 and was in pay-
ment of the May F.I.C.A. and employee income taxes.

June 30 Prepared a general journal entry to record the June Payroll Register.
The register had the following column totals:

Gross pay $2,700
Employees' F.I.C.A. taxes payable   162
Employees' federal income taxes payable   275
Group insurance deductions   42
Total deductions   479
Net pay 2,221
Sales salaries 1,800
Office salaries   900

30 Issued Check No. 863 payable to Payroll Bank Account in payment
of the June payroll. Endorsed the check, deposited it in the payroll
bank account, and issued payroll checks to the employees.

30 Prepared a general journal entry to record the employer's payroll
taxes resulting from the June 30 payroll. Due to a merit rating the
company's state unemployment tax rate was 2% of the first $6,000
paid each employee, and no employee had earned that amount.

July 15 Issued Check No. 911 payable to Guaranty Bank. The check was in
payment of the June F.I.C.A. and employee income taxes.

15 Issued Check No. 912 to the State Tax Commission for the April,
May, and June state unemployment taxes. Mailed the check along
with the second quarter tax return to the State Tax Commission.

20 Issued Check No. 933 payable to Security Insurance Company. The
check was in payment of the April, May, and June employee group
insurance premiums.

31 Issued Check No. 989 payable to Guaranty Bank. The company's
federal unemployment tax for the second quarter plus the undeposited federal unemployment tax for the first quarter exceeded
$100; consequently, this check was in payment of the tax for the
first two quarters.

31 Mailed the Internal Revenue Service the Employer's Quarterly Tax
Return, Form 941, reporting the F.I.C.A. taxes and the employees'
federal income tax deductions for the second quarter.

Required:

Prepare the necessary general journal and check register entries to record the transactions.

Joy Toy Company has 200 regular employees, all earning in excess of $6,000 per year. The company's plant and office are located in a state in which the maximum unemployment tax rate is 2.7% of the first $6,000 paid each employee. However, the company has an excellent past unemployment record and a merit rating that reduces its state unemployment tax rate to 0.5% of the first $6,000 paid each employee.

Decision problem 12–1, Joy Toy Company

The company has recently received an order for Christmas toys from a large chain of department stores. The order should be very profitable and will probably be repeated each year. In filling the order Joy Toy Company can stamp out the parts for the toys with present machines and employees. However, it will have to add 40 women to its work force for 40 hours per week for 10 weeks to assemble the toys and pack them for shipment.

The company can hire these women and add them to its own payroll or it can secure the services of 40 women through Handy Girls, Inc., a company in the business of supplying temporary help. If the temporary help is secured through Handy Girls, Inc., Joy Toy Company will pay Handy Girls, Inc., $4.25 per hour for each hour worked by each person supplied. The people will be employees of Handy Girls, Inc., and it will pay their wages and all taxes on the wages. On the other hand, if Joy Toy Company employs the women and places them on its payroll, it will pay them $3 per hour and will also pay the following payroll taxes on their wages: F.I.C.A. tax, 6% (assumed rate); federal unemployment tax, 0.7% on the first $6,000 paid each employee; state unemployment tax, 2.7% on the first $6,000 paid each employee. (The state unemployment tax rate will be 2.7% because if the company hires the temporary people and terminates them each year after ten weeks, it will lose its merit rating.)

Should Joy Toy Company place the temporary help on its own payroll or should it secure their services through Handy Girls, Inc.? Justify your answer.

After studying Chapter 13, you should be able to:

- Prepare entries to record transactions involving short-term notes payable.
- Explain the difference between a share of stock and a bond.
- State the advantages and disadvantages of securing capital by issuing bonds.
- Explain how bond interest rates are established.
- Use present value tables to calculate the premium or discount on a bond issue.
- Prepare entries to account for bonds issued between interest dates at par.
- Prepare entries to account for bonds sold on their date of issue at par, at a discount, and at a premium.
- Explain the purpose and operation of a bond sinking fund and prepare entries to account for the operation of such a fund.
- Define or explain the words and phrases listed in the chapter Glossary.

chapter 13

Current and long-term liabilities

A business normally has several different kinds of liabilities, which are classified as either *current liabilities* or *long-term liabilities*. Current liabilities are debts or other obligations the liquidation of which is reasonably expected to require the use of existing current assets or the creation of other current liabilities.[1] Accounts payable, short-term notes payable, wages payable, payroll and other taxes payable, and unearned revenues are common examples of current liabilities. Long-term liabilities are obligations that will not require the use of existing current assets in their liquidation, generally because they are not to be paid or liquidated within one year or one operating cycle. Common long-term liabilities are mortgages payable, bonds payable, and long-term notes payable.

Accounts payable, wages payable, payroll and other taxes payable, unearned revenues, and the accounting procedures applicable to these liabilities were described in previous chapters along with the procedures applicable when a note is given to secure a plant asset. Consequently, this chapter is devoted to some additional transactions involving notes payable plus the procedures applicable to mortgages payable and bonds payable.

Short-term notes payable

Short-term notes payable often arise in gaining an extension of time in which to pay an account payable, and they frequently arise in borrowing from a bank.

Note given to secure a time extension on an account

A note payable may be given to secure an extension of time in which to pay an account payable. For example, Brock Company cannot pay

---

[1] APB, "Basic Concepts and Accounting Principles Underlying Financial Statements of Business Enterprises," *APB Statement No. 4* (New York: AICPA, October 1970), par. 198.

its past-due, $600 account with Ajax Company, and Ajax Company has agreed to accept Brock Company's 60-day, 7%, $600 note in granting an extension on the due date of the debt. Brock Company will record the issuance of the note as follows:

Aug.	23	Accounts Payable—Ajax Company.............................	600.00	
		Notes Payable..		600.00
		Gave a 60-day, 7% note to extend the due date on an account payable.		

Observe that the note does not pay the debt; it merely changes it from an account payable to a note payable. Ajax Company should prefer the note to the account because in case of default and a lawsuit to collect, the note improves its legal position, since the note is written evidence of the debt and its amount.

When the note becomes due, Brock Company will give Ajax Company a check for $607 and record the payment of the note and its interest with an entry like this:

Oct.	22	Notes Payable...	600.00	
		Interest Expense	7.00	
		Cash...		607.00
		Paid our note with interest.		

Borrowing from a bank

In lending money, banks distinguish between *loans* and *discounts*. With either a loan or a discount, the bank lends money. However, in case of a loan, the bank collects interest when the loan is repaid; while in case of a discount, it deducts interest at the time the loan is made. To illustrate loans and discounts, assume that H. A. Green wishes to borrow approximately $2,000 for 60 days at the prevailing $7\frac{1}{2}\%$ rate of interest.

A loan   In a loan transaction the bank will lend Green $2,000 in exchange for a signed promissory note. The note will read: "Sixty days after date I promise to pay $2,000 with interest at $7\frac{1}{2}\%$," and Green will record the transaction as follows:

Sept.	10	Cash...	2,000.00	
		Notes Payable..		2,000.00
		Gave the bank a 60-day, $7\frac{1}{2}\%$ note.		

When the note and interest are paid, Green makes this entry:

Nov.	9	Notes Payable..	2,000.00	
		Interest Expense	25.00	
		Cash...		2,025.00
		Paid our 60-day, $7\frac{1}{2}$% note.		

Observe that in a loan transaction the interest is paid at the time the loan is repaid.

A discount If, contrary to the situation described in the previous paragraphs, it is the practice of Green's bank to deduct interest at the time a loan is made, the bank will discount Green's $2,000 note. If it discounts the note at $7\frac{1}{2}$% for 60 days, it will deduct from the face amount of the note 60 days' interest at $7\frac{1}{2}$%, which is $25, and will give Green the difference, $1,975. The $25 of deducted interest is called *bank discount,* and the $1,975 are the *proceeds* of the discounted note. Green will record the transaction as follows:

Sept.	10	Cash...	1,975.00	
		Interest Expense	25.00	
		Notes Payable..		2,000.00
		Discounted our $2,000 note payable at $7\frac{1}{2}$%.		

When the note matures, Green is required to pay the bank just the face amount of the note, $2,000, and Green will record the transaction like this:

Nov.	9	Notes Payable..	2,000.00	
		Cash...		2,000.00
		Paid our discounted note payable.		

Since interest is deducted in a discount transaction at the time the loan is made, the note used in such a transaction must state that only the principal amount is to be repaid at maturity. Such a note may read: "Sixty days after date I promise to pay $2,000 with no interest," and is commonly called a noninterest-bearing note. However, banks are not in business to lend money interest free; and interest is paid in a discount transaction; but since it is deducted at the time the loan is made, the note used must state that no additional interest is to be collected at maturity. Nevertheless, interest is collected in a discount transaction and at a rate slightly higher than in a loan transaction at the same stated interest rate. For example, in this instance Green paid $25 for the use of $1,975 for 60 days, which was at an effective interest rate just a little in excess of $7\frac{1}{2}$% on the $1,975 received.

End-of-the period adjustments

Accrued interest expense

Interest accrues daily on all interest-bearing notes; consequently, if any notes payable are outstanding at the end of an accounting period, their accrued interest should be calculated and recorded. For example, a company gave its bank a $4,000, 60-day, 7½% note on December 16 to borrow that amount of money. If the company's accounting period ends on December 31, by then 15 days' or $12.50 interest has accrued on this note and may be recorded with this adjusting entry:

Dec.	31	Interest Expense..	12.50	
		Interest Payable..		12.50
		To record accrued interest on a note payable.		

The adjusting entry causes the $12.50 accrued interest to appear on the income statement as an expense of the period benefiting from 15 days' use of the money. It also causes the interest payable to appear on the balance sheet as a current liability.

When the note matures in the next accounting period, its payment may be recorded as follows:

Feb.	14	Notes Payable..	4,000.00	
		Interest Payable..	12.50	
		Interest Expense...	37.50	
		Cash..		4,050.00
		Paid a $4,000 note and its interest.		

The $12.50 debit to Interest Payable in the entry records payment of the interest accrued at the end of the previous period.

Discount on notes payable

When a note payable is discounted at a bank, interest based on the principal of the note is deducted and this interest is normally recorded as interest expense. Furthermore, since most such notes run for 30, 60, or 90 days, the interest is usually an expense of the period in which it is deducted. However, when the time of a note extends beyond a single accounting period, an adjusting entry is required. For example, on December 11, 1978, a company discounted at 7½% its own $6,000, 60-day, noninterest-bearing note payable and recorded the transaction as follows:

1978				
Dec.	11	Cash...	5,925.00	
		Interest Expense	75.00	
		Notes Payable...		6,000.00
		Discounted our noninterest-bearing, 60-day note at 7½%.		

If this company operates with accounting periods that end each December 31, 20 days' interest on this note, or $25 of the $75 of discount, is an expense of the 1978 accounting period and 40 days' interest or $50 is an expense of 1979. Consequently, if revenues and expenses are matched, the company must make the following December 31, 1978, adjusting entry:

1978				
Dec.	31	Discount on Notes Payable	50.00	
		Interest Expense		50.00
		To set up as a contra liability the interest applicable to 1979.		

The adjusting entry removes from the Interest Expense account the $50 of interest that is applicable to 1979, leaving in the account the $25 that is an expense of 1978. The $25 then appears on the 1978 income statement as an expense, and the $50 appears on the 1978 balance sheet where, if this is the only note the company has outstanding, it is deducted from notes payable as follows:

```
Current Liabilities:
    Notes payable........................................ $6,000
        Less discount on notes payable............    50    $5,950
```

Putting discount on notes payable on the balance sheet as a contra liability results in showing as a liability on the balance sheet date the amount of money received in discounting the note plus the accrued interest on the note to the balance sheet date. In this example $5,925 was received in discounting the note and accrued interest on the note to December 31 amounts to $25, which together total $5,950, and which is the amount actually owed the bank on December 31.

The $50 interest set out as discount on notes payable in the previous paragraphs becomes an expense early in 1979. Consequently, sooner or later it must be taken from the Discount on Notes Payable account and returned to the Interest Expense account. Accountants commonly make this return with a *reversing entry* that is made as the last step in the end-of-the-accounting-period work and is dated the first day of the new accounting period. Such a reversing entry appears as follows:

1979					
Jan.	1	Interest Expense		50.00	
		Discount on Notes Payable			50.00
		To reverse the adjusting entry that set out discount on notes payable.			

Observe that the reversing entry is debit for credit and credit for debit the reverse of the adjusting entry it reverses, and that is where it gets its name. Also, observe that it returns the $50 interest to the expense account so that it will appear on the 1979 income statement as an expense without further ado.

Issuing a mortgage to borrow money

When a business needs money for a long-term purpose such as to purchase costly plant assets or to construct a new building, it may obtain the money by placing a mortgage on some or all of its plant assets. A mortgage actually involves two legal documents. The first is a kind of promissory note called a *mortgage note,* which is secured by a second legal document called a *mortgage* or a *mortgage contract.* In the mortgage note the mortgagor, the one who mortgages property, promises to repay the money borrowed. The mortgage or mortgage contract commonly requires the mortgagor to keep the mortgaged property in a good state of repair, carry adequate insurance, pay the interest on the mortgage note, and, often, make payments to reduce the mortgage liability. In addition it normally grants the mortgage holder the right to foreclose in case the mortgagor fails in any of the required duties. In a foreclosure a court takes possession of the mortgaged property for the mortgage holder and may order its sale. If the property is sold, the proceeds go first to pay court costs and the claims of the mortgage holder, after which any money remaining is paid to the former owner of the property.

A loan secured by a mortgage is recorded as follows:

Feb.	1	Cash		40,000.00	
		Mortgage Payable			40,000.00
		Borrowed by placing a 20-year, 7½% mortgage on the plant.			

As previously stated, in addition to paying interest, a mortgage contract commonly requires the mortgagor to make periodic payments to reduce the mortgage debt. For example, if the foregoing mortgage requires semiannual interest payments plus semiannual $1,000 payments to reduce the mortgage debt, the following entry is used to record the first semiannual payments:

Aug,	1	Mortgage Payable	1,000.00	
		Interest Expense	1,500.00	
		Cash..		2,500.00
		Paid the interest and the first semiannual payment on the mortgage principal.		

On a mortgage such as this the balance of the mortgage debt at the beginning of each interest period is normally used in calculating the period's mortgage interest. Likewise, at the end of each year the portion of the mortgage debt to be paid with current assets during the next year becomes a current liability for statement purposes, with the balance of the debt remaining a long-term liability.

Difference between stocks and bonds

The phrase "stocks and bonds" commonly appears on the financial pages of newspapers and is often heard in conversations. However, before beginning a study of bonds, the difference between a share of stock and a bond should be clearly understood. A share of stock (discussed in more detail beginning in Chapter 15) represents an equity or ownership right in a corporation. For example, if a person owns 1,000 of the 10,000 shares of common stock[2] a corporation has outstanding, the person has an equity in the corporation measured at $\frac{1}{10}$ of the corporation's total owner equity and has a right to $\frac{1}{10}$ of the corporation's earnings. If on the other hand a person owns a $1,000, 8%, 20-year bond issued by a corporation,[3] the bond represents a debt or a liability of the corporation, and its owner has two rights: (1) the right to receive 8% or $80 interest each year the bond is outstanding and (2) the right to be paid $1,000 when the bond matures 20 years after its date of issue.

Why bonds are issued

A corporation in need of long-term funds may secure the funds by issuing additional shares of stock or by selling bonds. Each has its advantages and disadvantages. Stockholders are owners, and issuing additional stock spreads ownership, control of management, and earnings over more shares. Bondholders, on the other hand, are creditors and do not share in either management or earnings. However, bond interest must be paid whether there are any earnings or not; otherwise the bond-

---

[2] When a corporation has outstanding only one kind of stock, it is usually called common stock.

[3] The federal government and other governmental units, such as cities, states, and school districts also issue bonds. However, the discussions in this chapter are limited to the bonds of corporations.

holders may foreclose and take the assets pledged for their security. Nevertheless, when long-term funds are needed, bonds are often issued because issuing bonds, rather than additional stock, will result in increased earnings for the owners (the common stockholders) of the issuing corporation.

To illustrate, assume a corporation with 200,000 shares of common stock outstanding needs $1,000,000 to expand its operations. The corporation's management estimates that after the expansion the company can earn $600,000 annually before bond interest, if any, and corporation income taxes; and it has proposed two plans for securing the needed funds. Plan No. 1 calls for issuing 100,000 additional shares of the corporation's common stock at $10 per share, which will increase the total outstanding shares to 300,000. Plan No. 2 calls for the sale at par of $1,000,000 of 8% bonds. Illustration 13–1 shows how the plans will affect the corporation's earnings.

	Plan 1	Plan 2
Earnings before bond interest and income taxes	$600,000	$600,000
Deduct bond interest expense............................		(80,000)
Income before corporation income taxes	$600,000	$520,000
Deduct income taxes (assumed 50% rate)	(300,000)	(260,000)
Net Income	$300,000	$260,000
Plan 1 income per share (300,000 shares)	$1.00	
Plan 2 income per share (200,000 shares)		$1.30

Illustration 13–1

Corporations are subject to state and federal income taxes, which together may take as much as 50% of the corporation's before-tax income. However bond interest expense is a deductible expense in arriving at income subject to taxes. Consequently, when the combined state and federal tax rate is 50%, as in Illustration 13–1, the tax reduction from issuing bonds equals one half the annual interest on the bonds. In other words, the tax savings in effect pays one half the interest cost of the bonds.

Borrowing by issuing bonds

When a large corporation wishes to borrow 25, 50, 100 or more millions of dollars, it will normally borrow by issuing bonds. Bonds are issued because few banks or insurance companies are able or willing to make a loan of such size, and bonds enable the corporation to divide the loan among many lenders.

Borrowing by issuing bonds is in many ways similar to borrowing by giving a mortgage. Actually in many cases the only real difference is that a number of bonds, often in denominations of $1,000, are issued in the place of a single mortgage note. For all practical purposes each bond is a promissory note, promising to pay a definite sum of money to its holder, or owner of record, at a fixed future date. Like promissory notes, bonds bear interest; and like a mortgage note, they are often secured by a mortgage. However, since bonds may be owned and transferred during their lives by a number of people, they differ from promissory notes in that they do not name the lender.

When a company issues bonds secured by a mortgage, it normally sells the bonds to an investment firm, known as the *underwriter,* which in turn resells the bonds to the public. In addition to the underwirter, the company issuing bonds selects a trustee to represent the bond-holders. In most cases the trustee is a large bank or trust company to which the company issuing the bonds executes and delivers the mortgage contract that acts as security for the bonds. It is the duty of the trustee to see that the company fulfills all the pledged responsibilities of the mortgage contract, or as it is often called the *deed of trust.* It is also the duty of the trustee to foreclose if any pledges are not fulfilled.

Over the years corporation lawyers and financiers have created a wide variety of bonds, each with different combinations of characteristics. For example, bonds may be *serial bonds* or *sinking fund bonds.* When serial or term bonds are issued, portions of the issue become due and are paid in installments over a period of years, as in the case of a corporation that issues $5,000,000 of serial bonds with the provision that beginning five years after the date of issuance $500,000 of the bonds become due and are to be paid each year until all are paid. Sinking fund bonds differ in that they are paid at maturity from a sinking fund created for that purpose. Sinking funds are discussed in more detail later in this chapter.

Character-istics of bonds

Bonds may also be either *registered bonds* or *coupon bonds.* Ownership of registered bonds and changes in ownership are registered or recorded with the issuing corporation, which offers some protection from loss or theft; and interest payments are usually made by checks mailed to the registered owners. Coupon bonds secure their name from the interest coupons attached to each bond. Each coupon calls for payment on the interest payment date of the interest due on the bond to which it is attached. The coupons are detached as they become due and are deposited with a bank for collection. Often ownership of a coupon bond is not registered. Such unregistered bonds are payable to bearer or are bearer paper, and ownership is transferred by delivery. Sometimes bonds are registered as to principal with interest payments by coupons.

Bonds also may be secured or unsecured. Unsecured bonds are called *debentures* and depend upon the general credit standing of their issuing corporation for security. Only financially strong companies are able to sell unsecured bonds or bonds that are not secured by a mortgage.

Issuing bonds   When a corporation issues bonds, the bonds are printed and the deed of trust is drawn and deposited with the trustee of the bondholders. At that point a memorandum describing the bond issue is commonly entered in the Bonds Payable account. Such a memorandum might read, "Authorized to issue $8,000,000 of 7½%, 20-year bonds dated January 1, 19—, and with interest payable semiannually on each July 1 and January 1." As in this case, bond interest is usually payable semiannually.

After the deed of trust is deposited with the trustee of the bondholders, all or a portion of the bonds may be sold. If all are sold at their par value, also called their *face amount,* an entry like this is made to record the sale:

Jan.	1	Cash..	8,000,000.00	
		Bonds Payable...		8,000,000.00
		Sold bonds at par on their interest date.		

When the semiannual interest is paid on these bonds, the transaction is recorded as follows:

July	1	Bond Interest Expense	300,000.00	
		Cash...		300,000.00
		Paid the semiannual interest on the bonds.		

And when the bonds are paid at maturity, an entry like this is made:

Jan.	1	Bonds Payable..	8,000,000.00	
		Cash...		8,000,000.00
		Paid bonds at maturity.		

Bonds sold between interest dates   Sometimes bonds are sold on their date of issue, which is also their interest date, as in the previous illustration. More often they are sold after their date of issue and between interest dates. In such cases, when bonds are sold between interest dates, it is customary to charge and collect from the purchasers the interest that has accrued on the bonds since the previous interest payment and to return this accrued interest to the purchasers on the next interest date. For example, assume that on March 1, a corporation sold at par $100,000 of 7½% bonds on which interest is payable semiannually on each January 1 and July 1. (Small dollar amounts are used in order to conserve space.) The entry to record the sale between interest dates is:

Mar.	1	Cash..	101,250.00	
		Bond Interest Expense		1,250.00
		Bonds Payable...		100,000.00
		Sold $100,000 of bonds on which two months'		
		interest has accrued.		

At the end of four months, on the July 1 semiannual interest date, the purchasers of these bonds are paid a full six months' interest. This payment includes four months' interest earned by the bondholders after March 1 and the two months' accrued interest collected from them at the time the bonds were sold. The entry to record the payment is:

July	1	Bond Interest Expense	3,750.00	
		Cash..		3,750.00
		Paid the semiannual interest on the bonds.		

After both of these entries are posted, the Bond Interest Expense account has a $2,500 debit balance and appears as follows:

	Bond Interest Expense		
July 1 (Payment)	3,750.00	Mar. 1 (Accrued interest)	1,250.00

The $2,500 debit balance is the interest on the $100,000 of bonds at $7\frac{1}{2}\%$ for the four months from March 1 to July 1.

Beginning students often think it strange to charge bond purchasers for accrued interest when bonds are sold between interest dates, and to return this accrued interest in the next interest payment. However, this is the custom, all bond transactions are "plus accrued interest"; and there is a good reason for the practice. For instance, if a corporation sells portions of a bond issue to different purchasers on different dates during an interest period without collecting the accrued interest, it must keep records of the purchasers and the dates on which they bought bonds. Otherwise it cannot pay the correct amount of interest to each. However, if it charges each buyer for accrued interest at the time of the purchase, it need not keep records of the purchasers and their purchase dates, since it can pay a full period's interest to all purchasers for the period in which they bought their bonds and each receives the interest he or she has earned and gets back the accrued interest paid at the time of the purchase.

Bond interest rates

At this point students who are not sure of their understanding of the concept of present value should turn back to the Appendix beginning on page 372 and review this concept before going further into this chapter.

A corporation issuing bonds specifies in the deed of trust and on each bond the interest rate it will pay. This rate is called the *contract rate*. It is usually stated on an annual basis, although bond interest is normally paid semiannually; and it is applied to the par value of the bonds to determine the dollars of interest the corporation will pay. For example, a corporation will pay $70 each year in two semi-annual installments of $35 each on a $1,000, 7% bond on which interest is paid semiannually.

Although the contract rate establishes the amount of interest a corporation will pay, it is not necessarily the rate of interest the corporation will incur in issuing bonds. The rate of interest it will incur depends upon what lenders consider their risks to be in lending to the corporation and upon the current *market rate* for bond interest. The market rate for bond interest is the rate borrowers are willing to pay and lenders are willing to take for the use of money at the level of risk involved. It fluctuates from day to day at any level of risk as the supply and demand for loanable funds fluctuate. It goes up when the demand for bond money increases and the supply decreases, and it goes down when the supply increases and the demand decreases.

A corporation issuing bonds usually offers a contract rate of interest equal to what it estimates the market will demand on the day the bonds are to be issued. If its estimate is correct, and the contract rate and market rate coincide on the day the bonds are issued, the bonds will sell at par, their face amount, and the corporation will record the sale as shown on page 432. However, since bonds must be printed and a deed of trust drawn, a number of days always elapse between the day the interest rate estimate is made and the day the bonds are sold. Consequently, when bonds are sold, their contract rate seldom coincides with the market rate; and as a result, bonds usually sell either at a premium or at a discount.

Bonds sold at a discount

When a corporation offers to sell bonds carrying a contract rate below the prevailing market rate, the bonds will sell, but only at a discount. Investors can get the market rate of interest elsewhere for the use of their money, so they will buy the bonds only at a price that will yield the prevailing market rate on the investment. What price will they pay and how is it determined? The price they will pay is the *present value* of the expected returns from the investment and is determined by discounting these returns at the current market rate for bond interest.

To illustrate how bond prices are determined, assume that on a day when the market rate for bond interest is 8%, a corporation offers to sell and issue bonds having a $100,000 par value, a ten-year life, and on which interest is to be paid semiannually at a 7% annual rate.[4] In exchange for current dollars a buyer of these bonds will gain two monetary rights:

1. The right to receive $100,000 at the end of the bond issue's ten-year life.
2. The right to receive $3,500 in interest at the end of each six-month interest period throughout the ten-year life of the bonds.

Since both are rights to receive money in the future, to determine their present value, the amounts to be received are discounted at the prevailing market rate of interest. If the prevailing market rate is 8% annually, it is 4% semiannually; and in ten years there are 20 semi-annual periods. Consequently, using the last number in the 4% column on Table 11A–1 on page 373 to discount the first amount and the last number in the 4% column on Table 11A–2 on page 375 to discount the series of $3,500 amounts, the present value of the rights and the price an informed buyer will offer for the bonds is:

Present value of $100,000 to be received 20 periods hence, dis-
counted at 4% per period ($100,000 × 0.4564)............................ $45,640
Present value of $3,500 to be received periodically for 20 periods,
discounted at 4% ($3,500 × 13.590).. 47,565
Present value of the bonds.. $93,205

If the corporation accepts the $93,205 offer for its bonds and sells them on their date of issue, it will record the sale with an entry like this:

Jan	1	Cash..	93,205.00	
		Discount on Bonds Payable	6,795.00	
		Bonds Payable..		100,000.00
		Sold bonds at a discount on their date of issue.		

If the corporation prepares a balance sheet on the day the bonds are sold, it may show the bonds in the long-term liability section as follows:

Long-Term Liabilities:
First mortgage, 7% bonds payable, due January 1,
1988 .... $100,000
Less unamortized discount based on the 8%
market rate for bond interest prevailing on the
date of issue.. 6,795 $93,205

---

[4] The spread between the contract rate and the market rate of interest on a new bond issue is seldom more than a fraction of a percent. However, a spread of a full percent is used here to simplify the illustrations.

On a balance sheet any unamortized discount on a bond issue is deducted from the par value of the bonds to show the amount at which the bonds are carried on the books, called the *carrying amount*.

Amortizing the discount

The corporation of this discussion received $93,205 for its bonds, but in ten years it must pay the bondholders $100,000. The difference, the $6,795 discount, is a cost of using the $93,205 that was incurred because the contract rate of interest on the bonds was below the prevailing market rate. It is a cost that must be paid when the bonds mature. However, since each semiannual interest period in the life of the bond issue benefits from the use of the $93,205, it is only fair that each should bear a fair share of this cost.

The accounting procedure for dividing a discount and charging a fair share to each period in the life of the applicable bond issue is called *amortizing* a discount. A simple method of amortizing a discount is the *straight-line method,* a method in which an equal portion of the discount is amortized each interest period. If this method is used to amortize the $6,795 discount of this discussion, the $6,795 is divided by 20, the number of interest periods in the life of the bond issue, and $339.75 ($6,795 ÷ 20 = $339.75) of discount is amortized at the end of each interest period with an entry like this:

July	1	Bond Interest Expense	3,839.75	
		Discount on Bonds Payable		339.75
		Cash...		3,500.00
		To record payment of six months' interest and amortization of $\frac{1}{20}$ of the discount.		

The amortization of $339.75 of discount each six months will completely write off the $6,795 of discount by the end of the issue's ten-year life. It also increases the amount of bond interest expense recorded each six months to the sum of the $3,500 paid the bondholders and the discount amortized.

Straight-line amortization is easy to understand and has long been used. However, the APB has ruled that it may now be used only in situations where the results do not materially differ from those obtained through use of the so-called interest method described in the following paragraphs.[5] The APB favors the interest method because it results in a constant rate of interest on the carrying amount of a bond issue, while the straight-line method results in a decreasing rate when a discount is amortized and an increasing rate when a premium is amortized.

---

[5] APB, "Interest on Receivables and Payables," *APB Opinion No. 21* (New York: AICPA, August 1971), par. 15.

When the interest method is used in amortizing a bond discount, the interest expense to be recorded each period is determined by applying a constant rate of interest to the beginning-of-the-period carrying amount of the bonds. The constant rate applied is the market rate prevailing at the time the bonds were issued. The amount of discount amortized each period is then determined by subtracting the amount of interest to be paid the bondholders from the interest expense to be recorded. Illustration 13–2, with amounts rounded to full dollars, shows the interest expense to be recorded, the discount to be amortized, and so forth, when the interest method of amortizing a discount is applied to the bond issue of this discussion. In examining Illustration 13–2, note these points:

Pe-riod	Beginning of-Period Carrying Amount	Interest Expense to Be Recorded	Interest to Be Paid the Bondholders	Discount to Be Amortized	Unamortized Discount at End of Period	End-of-Period Carrying Amount
1	$93,205	$3,728	$3,500	$228	$6,567	$93,433
2	93,433	3,737	3,500	237	6,330	93,670
3	93,670	3,747	3,500	247	6,083	93,917
4	93,917	3,757	3,500	257	5,826	94,174
5	94,174	3,767	3,500	267	5,559	94,441
6	94,441	3,778	3,500	278	5,281	94,719
7	94,719	3,789	3,500	289	4,992	95,008
8	95,008	3,800	3,500	300	4,692	95,308
9	95,308	3,812	3,500	312	4,380	95,620
10	95,620	3,825	3,500	325	4,055	95,945
11	95,945	3,838	3,500	338	3,717	96,283
12	96,283	3,851	3,500	351	3,366	96,634
13	96,634	3,865	3,500	365	3,001	96,999
14	96,999	3,880	3,500	380	2,621	97,379
15	97,379	3,895	3,500	395	2,226	97,774
16	97,774	3,911	3,500	411	1,815	98,185
17	98,185	3,927	3,500	427	1,388	98,612
18	98,612	3,944	3,500	444	944	99,056
19	99,056	3,962	3,500	462	482	99,518
20	99,518	3,982*	3,500	482	-0-	100,000

* Adjusted to compensate for accumulated rounding of amounts.

Illustration 13–2

1. The bonds were sold at a $6,795 discount, which when subtracted from their face amount gives a beginning of Period 1 carrying amount of $93,205.
2. The interest expense amounts result from multiplying each beginning-of-the-period carrying amount by the 4% semiannual market rate prevailing when the bonds were issued. For example, $93,205 × 4% = $3,728 and $93,433 × 4% = $3,737.
3. Interest to be paid bondholders each period is determined by multiplying the par value of the bonds by the contract rate of interest.
4. The discount to be amortized each period is determined by sub-

tracting the amount of interest to be paid the bondholders from the amount of interest expense.

5. The unamortized discount at the end of each period is determined by subtracting the discount amortized from the unamortized discount at the beginning of the period.

6. The end-of-the-period carrying amount for the bonds is determined by subtracting the end-of-the-period amount of unamortized discount from the face amount of the bonds. For example, at the end of Period 1: $100,000 − $6,567 = $93,433.

When the interest method is used in amortizing a discount, the periodic amortizing entries are like the entries used with the straight-line method, excepting as to the amounts. For example, the entry to pay the bondholders and amortize a portion of the discount at the end of the first interest period of the issue of Illustration 13–2 is:

July	1	Bond Interest Expense	3,728.00	
		Discount on Bonds Payable		228.00
		Cash..		3,500.00
		To record payment of the bondholders and amortization of a portion of the discount.		

Similar entries, differing only in the amounts of interest expense recorded and discount amortized, are made at the end of each interest period in the life of the bond issue.

Bonds sold at a premium

When a corporation offers to sell bonds carrying a contract rate of interest above the prevailing market rate for the risks involved, the bonds will sell at a premium. Buyers will bid up the price of the bonds, going as high, but no higher than a price that will return the current market rate of interest on the investment. What price will they pay? They will pay the present value of the expected returns from the investment, determined by discounting these returns at the prevailing market rate for bond interest. For example, assume that on a day the current market rate for bond interest is 6%, a corporation offers to sell bonds having a $100,000 par value and a ten-year life with interest to be paid semiannually at a 7% annual rate. An informed buyer of these bonds will discount the expectation of receiving $100,000 in ten years and the expectation of receiving $3,500 semiannually for 20 periods at the current 6% market rate as follows:

Present value of $100,000 to be received 20 periods hence, discounted at 3% per period ($100,000 × 0.5537)	$ 55,370
Present value of $3,500 to be received periodically for 20 periods, discounted at 3% ($3,500 × 14.878)	52,073
Present value of the bonds	$107,443

And the informed investor will offer the corporation $107,443 for its bonds. If the corporation accepts and sells the bonds on their date of issue, say, May 1, 1978, it will record the sale as follows:

May	1	Cash...	107,443.00	
		Premium on Bonds Payable......................................		7,443.00
		Bonds Payable...		100,000.00
		Sold bonds at a premium on their date of issue.		

It may then show the bonds on a balance sheet prepared on the day of the sale as follows:

Long-Term Liabilities:
First mortgage, 7% bonds payable, due May 1, 1988 .... $100,000
Add unamortized premium based on the 6% market
rate for bond interest prevailing on the date of issue...___7,443___ $107,443

On a balance sheet any unamortized premium on bonds payable is added to the par value of the bonds to show the carrying amount of the bonds, as illustrated.

Amortizing the premium

Although the corporation discussed here received $107,443 for its bonds, it will have to repay only $100,000 to the bondholders at maturity. The difference, the $7,443 premium, represents a reduction in the cost of using the $107,443, which should be amortized over the life of the bond issue in such a manner as to lower the recorded bond interest expense. If the $7,443 premium is amortized by the interest method, Illustration 13–3 shows the amounts of interest expense to be recorded each period, the premium to be amortized, and so forth.

Observe in Illustration 13–3 that the premium to be amortized each period is determined by subtracting the interest to be recorded from the interest to be paid the bondholders.

Based on Illustration 13–3, the entry to record the first interest payment and premium amortization is:

Nov.	1	Bond Interest Expense	3,223.00	
		Premium on Bonds Payable	277.00	
		Cash..		3,500.00
		To record payment of the bondholders and amortization of a portion of the premium.		

Period	Beginning-of-Period Carrying Amount	Interest Expense to Be Recorded	Interest to Be Paid the Bondholders	Premium to Be Amortized	Unamortized Premium at End of Period	End-of-Period Carrying Amount
1......	$107,443	$3,223	$3,500	$277	$7,166	$107,166
2......	107,166	3,215	3,500	285	6,881	106,881
3......	106,881	3,206	3,500	294	6,587	106,587
4......	106,587	3,198	3,500	302	6,285	106,285
5......	106,285	3,189	3,500	311	5,974	105,974
6......	105,974	3,179	3,500	321	5,653	105,653
7......	105,653	3,170	3,500	330	5,323	105,323
8......	105,323	3,160	3,500	340	4,983	104,983
9......	104,983	3,149	3,500	351	4,632	104,632
10......	104,632	3,139	3,500	361	4,271	104,271
11......	104,271	3,128	3,500	372	3,899	103,899
12......	103,899	3,117	3,500	383	3,516	103,516
13......	103,516	3,105	3,500	395	3,121	103,121
14......	103,121	3,094	3,500	406	2,715	102,715
15......	102,715	3,081	3,500	419	2,296	102,296
16......	102,296	3,069	3,500	431	1,865	101,865
17......	101,865	3,056	3,500	444	1,421	101,421
18......	101,421	3,043	3,500	457	964	100,964
19......	100,964	3,029	3,500	471	493	100,493
20......	100,493	3,007*	3,500	493	-0-	100,000

* Adjusted to compensate for accumulated rounding of amounts.

Illustration 13–3

Note how the amortization of the premium results in a reduction in the amount of interest expense recorded. Similar entries having decreasing amounts of interest expense and increasing amounts of premium amortized are made at the ends of the remaining periods in the life of the bond issue.

Accrued bond interest expense

Often when bonds are sold the bond interest periods do not coincide with the issuing company's accounting periods. In such cases it is necessary at the end of each accounting period to make an adjustment for accrued interest. For example, it was assumed that the bonds of Illustration 13–3 were issued on May 1, 1978, and interest was paid on these bonds on November 1 of that year. If the accounting periods of the corporation issuing these bonds end each December 31, on December 31, 1978, two months' interest has accrued on these bonds, and the following adjusting entry is required:

Dec.	31	Bond Interest Expense	1,071.67	
		Premium on Bonds Payable	95.00	
		Bond Interest Payable		1,166.67
		To record two months' accrued interest and amortize one third of the premium applicable to the interest period.		

Two months are one third of a semiannual interest period; consequently, the bond interest and premium amortized in the entry are each one third of the amounts applicable to the second interest period in the life of the bond issue. Similar entries will be made on each December 31 throughout the life of the issue; however, the amounts will differ, since in each case they will apply to a different interest period.

When the interest is paid on these bonds on May 1, 1979, an entry like this is required:

May	1	Bond Interest Expense	2,143.33	
		Bond Interest Payable	1,166.67	
		Premium on Bonds Payable	190.00	
		Cash..		3,500.00
		Paid the interest on the bonds, a portion of which was previously accrued, and amortized four months' premium.		

A purchaser of a bond may not hold it to maturity but may sell it after a period of months or years to a new investor at a price which is determined by the market rate for bond interest on the day of the sale. The market rate for bond interest on the day of the sale determines the price because the new investor can get this current rate elsewhere for the use of his money. Therefore, he will discount the right to receive the bond's face amount at maturity and the right to receive its interest for the remaining periods in its life at the current market rate to determine the price he will pay for the bond. As a result, since bond interest rates may vary greatly over a period of months or years, a bond that originally sold at a premium may later sell at a discount, and vice versa.

Sale of bonds by investors

Bonds are commonly issued with the provision that they may be redeemed at the issuing corporation's option, usually upon the payment of a redemption premium. Such bonds are known as *callable bonds*. Corporations commonly insert redemption clauses in deeds of trust because if interest rates decline, it may be advantageous to call and redeem outstanding bonds and issue in their place new bonds paying a lower interest rate.

Redemption of bonds

Not all bonds have a provision giving their issuing company the right to call. However, even though the right is not provided, a company may secure the same effect by purchasing its bonds on the open market and retiring them. Often such action is wise when a company has funds available and its bonds are selling at a price below their carrying amount. For example, a company has outstanding on their interest date $1,000,000 of bonds on which there is $12,000 unamortized premium. The bonds are selling at 98½% of par value, and the company decides to buy and retire one tenth of the issue. The entry to record the purchase and retirement is:

Apr.	1	Bonds Payable..	100,000.00	
		Premium on Bonds Payable......................................	1,200.00	
		Gain on the Retirement of Bonds		2,700.00
		Cash...		98,500.00
		To record the retirement of bonds.		

The retirement resulted in a $2,700 gain in this instance because the bonds were purchased at a price $2,700 below their carrying amount. A paragraph back the statement was made that the bonds were selling at 98½% of par value. Bond quotations are commonly made in this manner. For example, a bond may be quoted for sale at 101¼. This means the bond is for sale at 101¼% of its par value, plus accrued interest, of course, if applicable.

Convertible bonds

To make an issue more attractive, bond owners may be given the right to exchange their bonds for a fixed number of shares of the issuing company's common stock. Such bonds are known as convertible bonds. They offer investors initial investment security; and if the issuing company prospers and the market value of its stock goes up, an opportunity to share in the prosperity by converting their bonds to stock. Conversion is always at the bondholders' option and is not exercised except when to do so is to their advantage. Converting bonds to shares of stock is discussed further in Chapter 16.

Bond sinking fund

Because of their fixed return and greater security, bonds appeal to a portion of the investing public. Security is usually important to bond investors. A corporation issuing bonds may offer investors a measure of security by placing a mortgage on certain of its assets. Often it will give additional security by agreeing in its deed of trust to create a *bond sinking fund,* which is a fund of assets accumulated to pay the bondholders at maturity.

When a corporation issuing bonds agrees to create a bond sinking fund, it normally agrees to create the fund by making periodic cash deposits with a sinking fund trustee. It is the duty of the trustee to safeguard the cash, to invest it in good sound securities, and to add the interest or dividends earned to the sinking fund. Generally, when the bonds become due, it is also the duty of the sinking fund trustee to sell the sinking fund securities and to use the proceeds to pay the bondholders.

When a sinking fund is created, the amount that must be deposited periodically in order to provide enough money to retire a bond issue at maturity will depend upon the net rate of compound interest that can be earned on the invested funds. The rate is a compound rate because earnings are continually reinvested by the sinking fund trustee to earn an additional return, and it is a net rate because the trustee commonly deducts the fee for its services from the earnings.

To illustrate the operation of a sinking fund, assume a corporation issues $1,000,000 of ten-year bonds and agrees to deposit with a sinking fund trustee at the end of each year in the issue's life sufficient cash to create a fund large enough to retire the bonds at maturity. If the trustee is able to invest the funds in such a manner as to earn a 7% net return, $72,378 must be deposited each year and the fund will grow to maturity (in rounded dollars) as shown in Illustration 13–4.

End of Year	Amount Deposited	Interest Earned on Fund Balance	Balance in Fund after Deposit and Interest
1	$72,378	-0-	$ 72,378
2	72,378	$ 5,066	149,822
3	72,378	10,488	232,688
4	72,378	16,288	321,354
5	72,378	22,495	416,227
6	72,378	29,136	517,741
7	72,378	36,242	626,361
8	72,378	43,845	742,584
9	72,378	51,981	866,943
10	72,378	60,679*	1,000,000

* Adjusted for rounding.

Illustration 13–4

When a sinking fund is created by periodic deposits, the entry to record the amount deposited each year appears as follows:

Dec.	31	Bond Sinking Fund	72,378.00	
		Cash...		72,378.00
		To record the annual sinking fund deposit.		

Each year the sinking fund trustee invests the amount deposited, and each year it collects and reports the earnings on the investments. The earnings report results in an entry to record the sinking fund income. For example, if $72,378 is deposited at the end of the first year in the sinking fund, the accumulation of which is shown in Illustration 13–4, and 7% is earned, the entry to record the sinking fund earnings of the second year is:

Dec.	31	Bond Sinking Fund...	5,066.00	
		Sinking Fund Earnings...		5,066.00
		To record the sinking fund earnings.		

Sinking fund earnings appear on the income statement as financial revenue in the "Other revenues and expenses section."

The assets resulting from sinking fund earnings, as well as sinking fund deposits and sinking fund investments, in other words, the items making up a sinking fund, are the property of the company creating the fund and should appear on its balance sheet in the long-term investments section.

When bonds mature, it is usually the duty of the sinking fund trustee to convert the fund's investments into cash and pay the bondholders. Normally the sinking fund securities, when sold, produce either a little more or a little less cash than is needed to pay the bondholders. If more cash than is needed is produced, the extra cash is returned to the corporation; and if less cash is produced than is needed, the corporation must make up the deficiency. For example, if the securities in the sinking fund of a $1,000,000 bond issue produce $1,001,325 when converted to cash, the trustee will use $1,000,000 to pay the bondholders and will return the extra $1,325 to the corporation. The corporation will then record the payment of its bonds and the return of the extra cash with an entry like this:

Jan.	3	Cash..	1,325.00	
		Bonds Payable..	1,000,000.00	
		Bonds Sinking Fund.................................		1,001,325.00
		To record payment of our bonds and the return of extra cash from the sinking fund.		

Restriction on dividends due to outstanding bonds

If a corporation disburses in dividends to its stockholders all assets acquired each year through earnings and pays out still more assets in sinking fund deposits, it may find itself within a few years without sufficient assets, particularly current assets, to operate and unable either to pay dividends or make sinking fund deposits. To prevent this, a deed of trust may restrict the dividends a corporation may pay while its bonds are outstanding. Commonly the restriction provides that the corporation may pay dividends in any year only to the extent that the year's earnings exceed sinking fund requirements.

Long-term notes

When bond interest rates are temporarily unfavorable and funds are available from several large banks or insurance companies, often long-term notes maturing in two, three, or more years are issued with the intention of refinancing the debt at maturity by issuing bonds. Also, in some instances, in order to avoid the costs of issuing bonds and dealing with several thousand bondholders, long-term notes maturing in 10, 20, or more years are issued instead of bonds.

Long-term notes are often secured by mortgages, and those maturing in ten or more years may provide for periodic payments to reduce the amounts owed. Consequently, long-term notes take on the characteristics of both mortgages and bonds. Ordinarily they differ only in that they may be placed with several lenders, normally at the current market rate of interest, which causes their present value at issuance to equal their maturity value. As a result, they are normally issued at par and receive the same accounting treatment as mortgages or bonds issued at par.

Bond. A type of long-term note payable issued by a corporation or a   **Glossary**
political subdivision.

Bond discount. The difference between the par value of a bond and the price at which it is issued when issued at a price below par.

Bond premium. The difference between the par value of a bond and the price at which it is issued when issued at a price above par.

Bond sinking fund. A fund of assets accumulated to pay a bond issue at maturity.

Callable bond. A bond that may be called in and redeemed at the option of the corporation or political subdivision that issued it.

Carrying amount of a bond issue. The par value of a bond issue less any unamortized discount or plus any unamortized premium.

Common stock. The stock of a corporation when it issues only one kind of stock.

Contract rate of bond interest. The rate of interest to be paid the bondholders.

Convertible bond. A bond that may be converted into shares of its issuing corporation's stock at the option of the bondholder.

Coupon bond. A bond having coupons that are detached by the bondholder to collect interest on the bond.

Debenture bond. An unsecured bond.

Deed of trust. The contract between a corporation and its bondholders governing the duties of the corporation in relation to the bonds.

Face amount of a bond. The bond's par value.

Market rate of bond interest. The current bond interest rate that borrowers are willing to pay and lenders are willing to take for the use of their money.

Mortgage. A lien or prior claim to an asset or assets given by a borrower to a lender as security for a loan.

Mortgage contract. A document setting forth the terms under which a
mortgage loan is made.

Par value of a bond. The face amount of the bond, which is the amount
the borrower agrees to repay at maturity and the amount on which
interest is based.

Registered bond. A bond the ownership of which is registered with the
issuing corporation or political subdivision.

Reversing entries. Entries made at the end of an accounting period to
reverse certain of the period's adjusting entries.

Serial bonds. An issue of bonds that will be repaid in installments over
a period of years.

Share of stock. One proportionate equity in a corporation.

Sinking fund. A fund of assets accumulated for some purpose.

Sinking fund bonds. Bonds which are to be paid at maturity from funds
accumulated in a sinking fund.

**Questions
for class
discussion**

1. Define (*a*) a current liability and (*b*) a long-term liability.
2. What distinction do banks make between loans and discounts?
3. Distinguish between bank discount and cash discount.
4. What two legal documents are involved when a company borrows by
    giving a mortgage? What is the purpose of each?
5. What is the primary difference between a share of stock and a bond?
6. What is a deed of trust? What are some of the provisions commonly con-
    tained in a deed of trust?
7. Define or describe: (*a*) registered bonds, (*b*) coupon bonds, (*c*) serial
    bonds, (*d*) sinking fund bonds, (*e*) callable bonds, (*f*) convertible bonds,
    and (*g*) debenture bonds.
8. Why does a corporation issuing bonds between interest dates charge and
    collect accrued interest from the purchasers of the bonds?
9. As it relates to a bond issue, what is the meaning of "contract rate of
    interest"? What is the meaning of "market rate for bond interest"?
10. What determines bond interest rates?
11. Convertible bonds are very popular with investors. Why?
12. If a $1,000 bond is sold at $98\frac{1}{4}$, at what price is it sold? If a $1,000 bond
    is sold at $101\frac{1}{2}$, at what price is it sold?
13. If the quoted price for a bond is $97\frac{3}{4}$, does this include accrued interest?
14. What purpose is served by creating a bond sinking fund?
15. How are bond sinking funds classified for balance sheet purposes?

Class exercises   **Exercise 13–1**

On December 16 of the current year a company borrowed from two different banks.

Part 1. At the first bank it borrowed $8,000 by giving a 60-day, $7\frac{1}{2}\%$ note payable.

Part 2. From the second bank it borrowed by discounting its $8,000, non-interest-bearing note for 60 days at $7\frac{1}{2}\%$.   6.00

Required:

Prepare general journal entries for each loan to record: (*a*) the issuance of the note, (*b*) the required year-end adjusting entry, (*c*) the reversing entry if needed, and (*d*) the entry to pay the note.

Exercise 13–2

On May 1 of the current year a corporation sold at par plus accrued interest $2,000,000 of its 7.2% bonds. The bonds were dated January 1 of the current year, with interest payable on each July 1 and January 1. (*a*) Give the entry to record the sale. (*b*) Give the entry to record the first interest payment. (*c*) Set up a T-account for Bond Interest Expense and post the portions of the entries that affect the account. Answer these questions: (*d*) How many months' interest were accrued on these bonds when they were sold? (*e*) How many months' interest were paid on July 1? (*f*) What is the balance of the Bond Interest Expense account after the entry recording the first interest payment is posted? (*g*) How many months' interest does this balance represent? (*h*) How many months' interest did the bondholders earn during the first interest period?

Exercise 13–3

On April 1 of the current year a corporation sold $1,000,000 of its 7.4%, ten-year bonds. The bonds were dated April 1 of the current year, with interest payable on each October 1 and April 1. Give the entries to record the sale at $98\frac{1}{4}$ and the first semiannual interest payment under the assumption that $335 of discount was amortized.

Exercise 13–4

On November 1 of the current year a corporation sold $1,000,000 par value of its 7.5%, ten-year bonds. The bonds were dated November 1 of the current year, with interest payable on each May 1 and November 1. (*a*) Give the entry to record the sale of the bonds at 101. (*b*) Give the entry to record the accrued interest on the bonds on the first December 31 that they were outstanding under the assumption that $300 of premium was to be amortized during the first interest period of the bonds. (*c*) Give the entry to pay the bondholders on the following May 1.

Exercise 13–5

A corporation sold $1,000,000 of its $7\frac{1}{2}\%$, ten-year bonds at $99\frac{1}{4}$ on their date of issue, January 1, 19—. Five years later, on January 1, after the bond interest for the period had been paid and 40% of the total discount on the issue had been amortized, the corporation purchased $100,000 par value of the bonds on the open market at $98\frac{1}{4}$ and retired them. Give the entry to record the retirement.

Problems

Problem 13–1

Prepare general journal entries to record these transactions:

Apr. 1 Gave $1,500 cash and a $6,000, 7%, 120-day note to purchase store equipment.

May 14 Borrowed money at the bank by discounting our own $3,000 note payable for 60 days at 7%.

July 13 Paid the note discounted at the bank on May 14.

       30 Paid the $6,000 note of the April 1 transaction.

Aug. 31 Purchased merchandise on credit from Acme Company, invoice dated August 29, terms 2/10, n/60, $2,400.

Nov. 1 Gave Acme Company a $2,400, 7½%, 90-day note dated this day to secure a time extension on our past-due account.

Dec. 1 Borrowed money at Security Bank by discounting our own $4,000 note payable for 90 days at 7½%.

      31 Made an adjusting entry to record the accrued interest on the note given Acme Company on November 1.

      31 Made an adjusting entry to remove from the Interest Expense account the interest applicable to next year on the note discounted on December 1.

      31 Made a reversing entry dated January 1 to return to the Interest Expense account the interest on the note discounted at Security Bank on December 1.

Jan. 30 Paid the note given Acme Company on November 1.

Mar. 1 Paid the note discounted at Security Bank on December 1.

Problem 13–2

Part 1. A corporation completed these bond transactions:

1979

Jan. 1 Sold $1,000,000 of its own 6.7%, ten-year bonds dated January 1, 1979, with interest payable on each June 30 and December 31. The bonds sold for $978,702, a price that would yield the buyers a 7% annual return on their investment.

June 30 Paid the semiannual interest on the bonds and amortized a portion of the discount calculated by the interest method.

Dec. 31 Paid the semiannual interest on the bonds and amortized a portion of the discount calculated by the interest method.

Required:

Prepare general journal entries to record the transactions. Round the amounts of discount amortized each interest period to the nearest whole dollar.

Part 2. A corporation completed these bond transactions:

1979

May 1 Sold $1,000,000 of its own 7.2%, ten-year bonds dated May 1, 1979, with interest payable on each November 1 and May 1. The bonds sold for $1,014,232, a price to yield the buyers a 7% annual return.

Nov. 1   Paid the semiannual interest on the bonds and amortized a portion of the premium calculated by the interest method.

Dec. 31   Made an adjusting entry to record the accrued interest on the bonds and amortize one third of the amount of premium applicable to the second interest period of the bond issue.

1980

May 1   Paid the semiannual interest on the bonds and amortized the remainder of the premium applicable to the second interest period of the issue.

Required:

Prepare general journal entries to record the transactions. Round all amounts of premium amortized to the nearest whole dollar.

Problem 13–3

Part 1. A corporation completed these bond transactions:

1979

Jan. 1   Sold $1,000,000 par value of its own 6.8%, ten-year bonds at a price to yield the buyers a 7% annual return. The bonds were dated January 1, 1979, with interest payable on each June 30 and December 31.

June 30   Paid the semiannual interest on the bonds and amortized a portion of the discount calculated by the interest method.

Dec. 31   Paid the semiannual interest on the bonds and amortized a portion of the discount calculated by the interest method.

Required:

Prepare general journal entries to record the transactions. Round all dollar amounts to the nearest whole dollar.

Part 2. A corporation completed these bond transactions.

1979

Apr. 1   Sold $1,000,000 par value of its own 7.4%, ten-year bonds at a price to yield the buyers a 7% annual return. The bonds were dated April 1, 1979, with interest payable on each October 1 and April 1.

Oct. 1   Paid the semiannual interest on the bonds and amortized a portion of the premium calculated by the interest method.

Dec. 31   Made an adjusting entry to record the accrued interest on the bonds and to amortize one half of the amount of premium applicable to the second interest period of the bond issue.

1980

Apr. 1   Paid the semiannual interest on the bonds and amortized the remainder of the premium applicable to the second interest period of the issue.

Required:

Prepare general journal entries to record the transactions. Round all dollar amounts to the nearest whole dollar.

Problem 13–4

Prepare general journal entries to record the following bond transactions of a corporation. Round all dollar amounts to the nearest full dollar.

1976

Oct. 1 Sold $4,000,000 par value of its 7.1%, ten-year bonds at a price to yield the buyers a 7% annual return. The bonds were dated October 1, 1976, with interest payable each April 1 and October 1.

Dec. 31 Made an adjusting entry to record the accrued interest on the bonds and to amortize one half the premium applicable to the first interest period of the issue. The interest method was used in calculating the premium amortized.

1977

Apr. 1 Paid the semiannual interest on the bonds and amortized the remainder of the premium applicable to the first interest period.

Oct. 1 Paid the semiannual interest on the bonds and amortized the premium applicable to the second interest period.

1980

Apr. 1 After recording the entry paying the semiannual interest on the bonds on this date and amortizing a portion of the premium, the carrying amount of the bonds on the corporation's books was $4,020,700, and it purchased one tenth of the bonds at 98 and retired them.

Problem 13–5

A corporation deposited a deed of trust with the trustee of its bondholders on December 10, 1976, which authorized it to issue $3,000,000 of 7.2%, four-year bonds dated January 1, 1977, with interest payable annually on each December 31 throughout the life of the issue. (Four years are an unrealistically small number of years for a bond issue, and annual interest payments are not common; however, by using four years and annual interest payments, all entries for a bond issue and a bond sinking fund may be required without requiring too many repetitive entries.)

In the deed of trust the corporation agreed to create a bond sinking fund by depositing with a trustee $685,800 at the end of each year in the life of the bond issue. It was assumed the sinking fund investments would earn approximately 6% net and the fund would grow to maturity as follows:

End of—	Amount Deposited	Interest Earned on Fund Balance	Balance in Fund after Deposit and Interest
1977	$685,800	-0-	$ 685,800
1978	685,800	$ 41,130	1,412,730
1979	685,800	84,720	2,183,250
1980	685,800	130,950	3,000,000

After depositing the deed of trust, the corporation completed these transactions:

1977

Jan. 1 Sold the entire issue for $3,020,500 cash, a price to yield the buyers a 7% annual return on the investment.

Dec. 31 Paid the annual interest on the bonds and amortized a portion of the premium based on the following information:

	1977	1978	1979	1980
Beginning of the period carrying amount...	$3,020,500	$3,015,900	$3,011,000	$3,005,700
Interest to be paid the bondholders...........	216,000	216,000	216,000	216,000
Interest expense to be recorded................	211,400	211,100	210,700	210,300
Premium to be amortized	4,600	4,900	5,300	5,700
End-of-the-period carrying amount............	3,015,900	3,011,000	3,005,700	3,000,000

    31 Made the first annual sinking fund deposit.

1978
Dec. 31 Paid the annual interest on the bonds and amortized a portion of the premium.
    31 Received the sinking fund trustee's report showing the sinking fund has earned $41,130.
    31 Made the second annual sinking fund deposit.

1979
Dec. 31 Paid the annual interest on the bonds and amortized a portion of the premium.
    31 Received the sinking fund trustee's report showing the sinking fund had earned $84,625, an amount slightly less than was anticipated the fund would earn. However, it was not enough to warrant a change in the deposit required of the corporation.
    31 Made the third annual sinking fund deposit.

1980
Dec. 31 Paid the interest on the bonds and amortized a portion of the premium.
    31 Received the sinking fund trustee's report showing the fund had earned $131,540.
    31 Made the fourth sinking fund deposit.

1981
Jan. 9 Received a report from the sinking fund trustee showing the bonds had been paid in full. Attached to the report was a check for the excess earnings of the sinking fund.

Required:
Prepare general journal entries to record the transactions.

Problem 13–1A   **Alternate**
Prepare general journal entries to record these transactions: **problems**

Mar. 5 Purchased merchandise on credit from Monroe Company, invoice dated March 3, terms 2/10, n/60, $4,000.
May 2 Borrowed money at Guaranty Bank by discounting our own $6,000 note payable for 60 days at 7%.
    8 Gave Monroe Company $1,000 cash and a $3,000, 60-day, 7% note to secure an extension on our past-due account.
July 1 Paid the note discounted at Guaranty Bank on May 2.
    7 Paid the note given Monroe Company on May 8.

Nov. 1   Borrowed money at Guaranty Bank by discounting our own $8,000 note payable for 90 days at 7½%.

Dec. 1   Borrowed money at Security Bank by giving a $4,000, 60-day, 7½% note payable.

     31   Made an adjusting entry to remove from the Interest Expense account the interest applicable to next year on the note discounted at Guaranty Bank on November 1.

     31   Made an adjusting entry to record the accrued interest on the note given Security Bank on December 1.

     31   Made a reversing entry dated January 1 to return to the Interest Expense account the interest on the note discounted at Guaranty Bank.

Jan. 30   Paid the note discounted at Guaranty Bank on November 1.

     30   Paid the note given Security Bank on December 1.

Problem 13–2A

Part 1. Prepare general journal entries to record the following bond transactions of a corporation. Round all dollar amounts to the nearest whole dollar.

1979

Jan.   1   Sold $1,000,000 of its own 7.9% ten-year bonds dated January 1, 1979, with interest payable on each June 30 and December 31. The bonds sold for $993,205, a price to yield the buyers an 8% annual return.

June 30   Paid the semiannual interest on the bonds and amortized a portion of the discount calculated by the interest method.

Dec. 31   Paid the semiannual interest on the bonds and amortized a portion of the discount calculated by the interest method.

Part 2. Prepare general journal entries to record the following bond transactions of a corporation. Round all dollar amounts to the nearest full dollar.

1979

Nov. 1   Sold $1,000,000 of its own 8.1%, ten-year bonds dated November 1, 1979, with interest payable on each May 1 and November 1. The bonds sold for $1,006,795, a price to yield the buyers an 8% annual return.

Dec. 31   Made an adjusting entry to record the accrued interest on the bonds and to amortize one third of the premium applicable to the first interest period of the bond issue calculated by the interest method.

1980

May   1   Paid the semiannual interest on the bonds and amortized the remainder of the premium applicable to the first interest period.

Nov. 1   Paid the semiannual interest on the bonds and amortized a portion of the premium.

Problem 13–3A

Part 1. Prepare general journal entries to record the following bond transactions of a corporation. Round all dollar amounts to the nearest full dollar.

1979
Jan. 1   Sold $1,000,000 par value of its own 8.2%, ten-year bonds at a price to yield the buyers an 8% annual return. The bonds were dated January 1, 1979, with interest payable on each June 30 and December 31.
June 30   Paid the semiannual interest on the bonds and amortized a portion of the premium calculated by the interest method.
Dec. 31   Paid the semiannual interest on the bonds and amortized a portion of the premium calculated by the interest method.

   Part 2.   Prepare general journal entries to the record the following transactions of a corporation. Round all dollar amounts to the nearest whole dollar.

1979
Nov. 1   Sold $1,000,000 par value of its own 7.8%, ten-year bonds dated November 1, 1979, at a price to yield the buyers an 8% annual return. Interest was payable on the bonds on each May 1 and November 1.
Dec. 31   Made an adjusting entry to record the accrued interest on the bonds and to amortize one third of the discount applicable to the first interest period calculated by the interest method.
1980
May 1   Paid the semiannual interest on the bonds and amortized the remainder of the discount applicable to the first interest period.
Nov. 1   Paid the semiannual interest on the bonds and amortized the portion of the discount applicable to the second interest period.

Problem 13–4A
   Prepare general journal entries to record the following bond transactions of a corporation. Round all dollar amounts to the nearest whole dollar.

1976
Sept. 1   Sold $2,000,000 par value of its own 8.1%, ten-year bonds at a price to yield the buyers an 8% annual return. The bonds were dated September 1, 1976, with interest payable on each March 1 and September 1.
Dec. 31   Made an adjusting entry to record the accrued interest on the bonds and to amortize two thirds of the premium applicable to the first interest period of the issue. The interest method was used in calculating the premium amortized.
1977
Mar. 1   Paid the semiannual interest on the bonds and amortized the remainder of the premium applicable to the first interest period.
Sept. 1   Paid the semiannual interest on the bonds and amortized the premium applicable to the second interest period of the issue.
1979
Sept. 1   After recording the entry paying the semiannual interest on the bonds on this date and amortizing a portion of the premium, the carrying amount of the bonds on the corporation's books was $2,010,500, and it purchased one tenth of the bonds at 98¼ and retired them.

Problem 13–5A

A corporation deposited a deed of trust with the trustee of its bondholders on December 14, 1976, which authorized it to issue $4,000,000 of 6.8%, four-year bonds dated January 1, 1977, with interest payable annually on each December 31 throughout the life of the issue. (Four years are an unrealistically small number of years for a bond issue, and annual interest payments are not common; however, by using four years and annual interest payments, all entries for a bond issue and a bond sinking fund may be required without requiring too many repetitive entries.)

In the deed of trust the corporation agreed to create a bond sinking fund by depositing with a trustee $914,400 at the end of each year in the life of the bond issue. It was assumed the sinking fund investments would earn approximately 6% net and the fund would grow to maturity as follows:

End of—	Amount Deposited	Interest Earned on Fund Balance	Balance in Fund after Deposit and Interest
1977	$914,400	-0-	$ 914,400
1978	914,400	$ 54,800	1,883,600
1979	914,400	113,000	2,911,000
1980	914,400	174,600	4,000,000

After depositing the deed of trust, the corporation completed these transactions:

1977
Jan.   1   Sold the entire issue to an underwriter for $3,973,000 cash, a price that would yield the buyer a 7% annual return on the investment.
Dec. 31   Paid the annual interest on the bonds and amortized a portion of the discount based on the following information:

	1977	1978	1979	1980
Beginning of the period carrying amount	$3,973,000	$3,979,100	$3,985,600	$3,992,600
Interest to be paid the bondholders	272,000	272,000	272,000	272,000
Interest expense to be recorded	278,100	278,500	279,000	279,400
Discount to be amortized	6,100	6,500	7,000	7,400
End-of-the-period carrying amount	3,979,100	3,985,600	3,992,600	4,000,000

       31   Made the first annual sinking fund deposit.
1978
Dec. 31   Paid the annual interest on the bonds and amortized a portion of the discount.
       31   Received the sinking fund trustee's report showing the sinking fund had earned $54,800 during the year.
       31   Made the second annual sinking fund deposit.
1979
Dec. 31   Paid the interest on the bonds and amortized a portion of the discount.
       31   Received the sinking fund trustee's report showing the sinking fund had earned $113,150. (This is a little more than was antici-

pated the fund would earn. However, it is not enough to warrant a change in the deposit required of the corporation.)

Dec. 31 Made the third annual sinking fund deposit.

1980

Dec. 31 Paid the semiannual interest on the bonds and amortized a portion of the discount.

31 Received the sinking fund trustee's report showing the sinking fund had earned $174,675.

31 Made the fourth annual sinking fund deposit.

1981

Jan. 10 Received a report from the sinking fund trustee showing the bonds had been paid in full. Attached to the report was a check for the excess earnings in the sinking fund.

Required:

Prepare general journal entries to record the transactions.

Ownership equity in Sands Corporation is represented by 200,000 shares of outstanding common stock on which the corporation has earned an unsatisfactory average of $0.45 per share during each of the last three years. And, as a result of the unsatisfactory earnings, management of the corporation is planning an expansion that will require the investment of an additional $1,000,000 in the business. The $1,000,000 is to be acquired either by selling an additional 100,000 shares of the company's common stock at $10 per share or selling at par $1,000,000 of 8%, 20-year bonds. Management estimates that the expansion will double the company's before-tax earnings the first year after it is completed and will increase before-tax earnings an additional 25% over that level in the years that follow.

The company's management wants to finance the expansion in the manner that will serve the best interests of present stockholders and they have asked you to determine this for them. In your report express an opinion as to the relative merits and disadvantages of each of the proposed ways of securing the funds needed for the expansion. Attach to your report a schedule showing expected earnings per share of the common stockholders under each method of financing. In preparing your schedule, assume the company presently pays out in state and federal income taxes 50% of its before-tax earnings and that it will continue to pay out the same share after the expansion.

Decision problem 13–1, Sands Corporation

After studying Chapter 14, you should be able to:

- List the characteristics of a partnership and explain the importance of understanding mutual agency and unlimited liability by a person about to become a partner.

- Explain the nature of partnership earnings and be able to make the calculations to divide partnership earnings (*a*) on a stated fractional basis, (*b*) in the partners' capital ratio, and (*c*) through the use of salary and interest allowances.

- Prepare entries for (*a*) the sale of a partnership interest, (*b*) the admission of a new partner by investment, and (*c*) the retirement of a partner by the withdrawal of partnership assets.

- Prepare entries required in the liquidation of a partnership.

- Define or explain the words and phrases listed in the chapter Glossary.

chapter 14

Partnership accounting

A majority of the states have adopted the Uniform Partnership Act to govern the formation and operation of partnerships. This act defines a partnership as "an association of two or more persons to carry on as co-owners a business for profit." A partnership has been further defined as "an association of two or more competent persons under a contract to combine some or all their property, labor, and skills in the operation of a business." And although both of these definitions tell something of its legal nature, a better understanding of a partnership as a form of business organization may be gained by examining some of its characteristics.

A voluntary association

A partnership is a voluntary association into which a person cannot be forced against his will. This is because a partner is responsible for the business acts of his partners, when the acts are within the scope of the partnership; and too, a partner is unlimitedly liable for the debts of his partnership. Consequently, partnership law recognizes it is only fair that a person be permitted to select the people he wishes to join in a partnership, and normally a person will select only financially responsible people in whose judgment he has respect.

Based on a contract

One advantage of a partnership as a form of business organization is the ease with which it may be begun. All that is required is that two or more legally competent people agree to be partners. Their agreement becomes a contract and should be in writing, with all anticipated points of future disagreement covered. However, it is just as binding if only orally expressed.

Limited life

The life of a partnership is always limited. Death, bankruptcy, or anything that takes away the ability of one of the partners to contract automatically ends a partnership. In addition, since a partnership is based on a contract, if the contract is for a definite period, the partnership ends with the period's expiration. If the contract does not specify a time period, the partnership ends when the business for which it was created is completed. Or, if no time is stated and the business for which it was created cannot be completed but goes on indefinitely, the partnership may be terminated at will by any one of the partners.

Mutual agency

Normally there is mutual agency in a partnership. This means that under normal circumstances every partner is an agent of his partnership and can enter into and bind the partnership to any contract within the apparent scope of its business. For example, a partner in a trading business can bind his partnership to contracts to buy merchandise, lease a store building, borrow money, or hire employees, since these are all within the scope of a trading firm. On the other hand, a partner in a law firm, acting alone, cannot bind his partners to a contract to buy merchandise or rent a store building, since these are not within the normal scope of a law firm's business.

Partners among themselves may agree to limit the right of any one or more of the partners to negotiate certain contracts for the partnership. However, although such an agreement is binding on the partners and on outsiders who know of the agreement, it is not binding on outsiders who are unaware of its existence. Outsiders who are unaware of anything to the contrary have a right to assume that each partner has the normal agency rights of a partner.

Mutual agency offers an important reason for care in the selection of partners. Good partners benefit all; but a poor partner can do great damage. Mutual agency plus unlimited liability are the reasons most partnerships have only a few members, with two, three, or four being common numbers of partners.

Unlimited liability

When a partnership is unable to pay its debts, the creditors may satisfy their claims from the personal assets of the partners. Furthermore, if the property of a partner is insufficient to meet his share, the creditors may turn to the assets of the remaining partners who are able to pay. Thus, a partner may be called on to pay all the debts of his partnership and is said to have unlimited liability for its debts.

Unlimited liability may be illustrated as follows: Albert and Bates each invested $5,000 in a store to be operated as a partnership venture, under an agreement to share losses and gains equally. Albert has no property other than his $5,000 investment; Bates owns his own home, a farm, and has sizable savings in addition to his investment. The partners rented store space and bought merchandise and fixtures costing $30,000, paying $10,000 in cash and promising to pay the balance at a later date. However, the night before the store opened the building in which it was located burned and the merchandise and fixtures were totally destroyed. There was no insurance, all the partnership assets were lost, and Albert has no other assets. Consequently, the partnership creditors may collect the full $20,000 of their claims from Bates, although Bates may look to Albert for payment of half at a later date, if Albert ever becomes able to pay.

Advantages and disadvantages of a partnership

Limited life, mutual agency, and unlimited liability are disadvantages of a partnership. Yet, a partnership has advantages over both the single proprietorship and corporation forms of organization. A partnership has the advantage of being able to bring together more money and skills than a single proprietorship, and is much easier to organize than a corporation. Also, it does not have the corporation's governmental supervision nor its extra burden of taxation, and partners may act freely and without the necessity of stockholders' and director's meetings, as in a corporation.

Partnership accounting

Partnership accounting is exactly like that of a single proprietorship except for transactions affecting owner equity. Here, because ownership rights are divided between two or more partners, there must be:

1. A Capital account for each partner.
2. A Withdrawals account for each partner.
3. An accurate measurement and division of earnings among the partners.

As for the separate Capital and Withdrawals accounts, each partner's Capital account is credited, and asset accounts showing the nature of the assets invested are debited in recording the investment of each partner. Likewise, a partner's withdrawals are debited to his Withdrawals account, and in the end-of-the-period closing procedure the Capital account is credited for a partner's share of the net income. Obviously, these procedures are not new, only the added accounts are new, and they need no further consideration here. However, the matter of dividing earnings among partners does need additional discussion.

Nature of partnership earnings

Because, as a member of his partnership, a partner cannot enter into an employer-employee contractual relationship with himself, a partner, like a single proprietor, cannot legally hire himself and pay himself a salary. Law and custom recognize this. Furthermore, law and custom recognize that a partner works for partnership profits and not a salary, and law and custom recognize that a partner invests in a partnership for earnings and not for interest.

Nevertheless, although partners have no legal right to interest on their partnership investments or salaries in payment for their partnership services, it should be recognized that partnership earnings do include a return for services, even though the return is contained within the earnings and is not a salary in a legal sense. Likewise, partnership earnings include a return on invested capital, although the return is not interest in the legal sense of the term.

Furthermore, if partnership earnings are to be fairly shared, it is often necessary to recognize that the earnings do include a return for services and a return on investments. For example, if one partner contributes five times as much capital as another, it is only fair that this be taken into consideration in the method of sharing. Likewise, if the services of one partner are much more valuable than those of another, it is only fair that some provision be made for the unequal service contributions.

Division of earnings

The law provides that in the absence of a contrary agreement, all partnership earnings are shared equally. This means that if partners cannot agree as to the method of sharing, each partner receives an equal share. Partners may agree to any method of sharing; and if they agree as to the method of sharing earnings but say nothing of losses, losses are shared in the same way as earnings.

Several methods of sharing partnership earnings are employed. All attempt in one way or another to recognize differences in service contributions or in investments, when such differences exist. The following three methods will be discussed here:

1. On a stated fractional basis.
2. Based on the ratio of capital investments.
3. Salary and interest allowances and the remainder in a fixed ratio.

Earnings allocated on a stated fractional basis

The easiest way to divide partnership earnings is to give each partner a stated fraction of the total. A division on a fractional basis may provide for an equal sharing if service and capital contributions are equal. An equal sharing may also be provided when the greater capital contribution of one partner is offset by a greater service contribution of another. Or, if the service and capital contributions are unequal, a fixed ratio may easily provide for an unequal sharing. All that is necessary in any case is for the partners to agree as to the fractional share to be given each.

For example, the partnership agreement of Morse and North may provide that each partner is to receive half the earnings; or the agreement may provide for two thirds to Morse and one third to North; or it may provide for three fourths to Morse and one fourth to North. Any fractional basis may be agreed upon as long as the partners feel earnings are thereby fairly shared. For example, assume the agreement of Morse and North provides for a two-thirds and one-third sharing, and earnings for a year are $30,000. After all revenue and expense accounts are closed, if earnings are $30,000, the partnership Income Summary account has a $30,000 credit balance. It is closed, and the earnings are allocated to the partners with the following entry:

Dec.	31	Income Summary..	30,000.00	
		A. P. Morse, Capital..		20,000.00
		R. G. North, Capital..		10,000.00
		To close the Income Summary account and allocate the earnings		

If the business of a partnership is of a nature that earnings are closely related to money invested, a division of earnings based on the ratio of partner's investments offers a fair sharing method. To illustrate this method, assume that Chase, Davis, and Fall have agreed to share earnings in the ratio of their investments. If these are Chase, $50,000, Davis, $30,000, and Fall, $40,000, and if the earnings for the year are $48,000, the respective shares of the partners are calculated as follows: **Division of earnings based on the ratio of capital investments**

Step 1: Chase, capital .... $ 50,000
         Davis, capital   30,000
         Fall, capital.................   40,000
             Total invested $120,000

Step 2: Share of earnings to Chase $\frac{\$50,000}{\$120,000} \times \$48,000 = \$20,000$

         Share of Earnings to Davis $\frac{\$30,000}{\$120,000} \times \$48,000 = \$12,000$

         Share of earnings to Fall $\frac{\$40,000}{\$120,000} \times \$48,000 = \$16,000$

The entry to allocate the earnings to the partners is then:

Dec.	31	Income Summary...	48,000.00	
		T. S. Chase, Capital..		20,000.00
		S. A. Davis, Capital..		12,000.00
		R. R. Fall, Capital..		16,000.00
		To close the Income Summary account and allocate the earnings.		

Sometimes partners' capital contributions are unequal; and sometimes one partner devotes full time to partnership affairs and the other or others devote only part time. Too, in partnerships in which all partners devote full time, the services of one partner may be more valu- **Salaries and interest as aids in sharing** able than the services of another. When these situations occur and, for example, the capital contributions are unequal, the partners may allocate a portion of their net income to themselves in the form of interest, so as to compensate for the unequal investments. Or when service contributions are unequal, they may use salary allowances as a means of compensating for unequal service contributions. Or when investment and service contributions are both unequal, they may use a combination of interest and salary allowances in an effort to share earnings fairly.

For example, Hill and Dale began a partnership business of a kind in which Hill has had experience and could command a $12,000 annual salary working for another firm of like nature. Dale is new to the business and could expect to earn not more than $8,000 working elsewhere. Furthermore, Hill invested $15,000 in the business and Dale invested $5,000. Consequently, the partners agreed that in order to compensate for the unequal service and capital contributions, they will share losses and gains as follows:

1.   A share of the profits equal to interest at 8% is to be allowed on the partners' initial investments.
2.   Annual salary allowances of $12,000 per year to Hill and $8,000 per year to Dale are to be allowed.
3.   The remaining balance of income or loss is to be shared equally.

Under this agreement a first year $22,700 net income would be shared as in Illustration 14–1.

After the shares in the $22,700 net income are determined, the fol-

	Share to Hill	Share to Dale	Income Allocated
Total net income...			$22,700
Allocated as interest:			
Hill (8% on $15,000).......................................	$ 1,200		
Dale (8% on $5,000)..		$ 400	
Total allocated as interest			1,600
Balance of income after interest allowances			$21,100
Allocated as salary allowances:			
Hill...	12,000		
Dale..		8,000	
Total allocated as salary allowances			20,000
Balance of income after interest and salary allowances..			$ 1,100
Balance allocated equally:			
Hill...	550		
Dale..		550	
Total allocated equally............................			1,100
Balance of income.............................			-0-
Shares of the Partners...	$13,750	$8,950	

Illustration 14–1

lowing entry may be used to close the Income Summary account and carry the net income shares to the partners' Capital accounts. Observe in the entry that the credit amounts may be taken from the first two column totals of the computation of Illustration 14–1.

Dec.	31	Income Summary...	22,700.00	
		Robert Hill, Capital..		13,750.00
		William Dale, Capital..		8,950.00
		To close the Income Summary account and allocate the earnings.		

In a legal sense, partners do not work for salaries, nor do they invest in a partnership to earn interest; they invest and work for earnings. Consequently, when a partnership agreement provides for salaries and interest, the partners should understand that the salaries and interest are not really salaries and interest but are only a means of sharing losses and gains.

In the illustration just completed the $22,700 net income exceeded the salary and interest allowances of the partners; but Hill and Dale would use the same method to share a net income smaller than their salary and interest allowances, or to share a loss. For example, assume that Hill and Dale earned only $9,600 in a year. A $9,600 net income would be shared by the partners as in Illustration 14–2.

The Illustration 14–2 items enclosed in parentheses are negative items. It is common practice in accounting to show negative items in

	Share to Hill	Share to Dale	Income Allocated
Total net income			$ 9,600
Allocated as interest:			
Hill (8% on $15,000)......................................	$ 1,200		
Dale (8% on $5,000)..		$ 400	
Total allocated as interest......................			1,600
Balance of income after interest allowances.......			$ 8,000
Allocated as salary allowances:			
Hill	12,000		
Dale		8,000	
Total allocated as salary allowances			20,000
Balance of income after interest and salary allowances (a negative amount)			($12,000)
Balance allocated equally:			
Hill	(6,000)		
Dale		(6,000)	
Total allocated equally			(12,000)
Balance of income			-0-
Shares of the Partners	$ 7,200	$2,400	

Illustration 14–2

red or encircled or to show them enclosed in parentheses as in this illustration.

A net loss would be shared by Hill and Dale in the same manner as the foregoing $9,600 net income; the only difference being that the loss-and-gain-sharing procedure would begin with a negative amount of income, in other words a net loss, and the amount allocated equally would be a larger negative amount.

Partnership financial statements

In most respects partnership financial statements are like those of a single proprietorship. However, one common difference is that the net income allocation is often shown on the income statement, at the end of the statement following the reported net income. For example, an income statement prepared for Hill and Dale might show in its last portion the allocation of the $9,600 net income of Illustration 14–2 as in Illustration 14–3:

Hill and Dale
Income Statement for Year Ended December 31, 19—

Sales...		$123,400

~~~~~~

Net Income..		$ 9,600
Allocation of net income to the partners:		
Robert Hill:		
Interest at 8% on investment..............................	$ 1,200	
Salary allowance..	12,000	
Total..	$13,200	
Less one half the remaining deficit..............	(6,000)	
Share of the net income.................................		$ 7,200
William Dale:		
Interest at 8% on investment..............................	$ 400	
Salary allowance..	8,000	
Total..	$ 8,400	
Less one half the remaining deficit..............	(6,000)	
Share of the net income.................................		2,400
Net Income Allocated...		$ 9,600

Illustration 14–3

Addition or withdrawal of a partner

A partnership is based on a contract between specific individuals. Consequently, an existing partnership is ended when a partner withdraws or a new partner is added. A partner may sell his or her partnership interest and withdraw from a partnership or a partner may withdraw his or her partnership equity, taking partnership cash or other assets. Likewise a new partner may join an existing partnership by purchasing an interest from one or more of its partners or by investing cash or other assets in the business.

Sale of a partnership interest

Assume that Abbott, Burns, and Camp are equal partners in a $15,000 partnership that has no liabilities and the following assets and equities:

Assets		Equities	
Cash	$ 3,000	Abbott, capital	$ 5,000
Other assets	12,000	Burns, capital	5,000
		Camp, capital	5,000
Total Assets...	$15,000	Total Equities...	$15,000

Camp's equity in this partnership is $5,000. If Camp sells this equity to Davis for $7,000, Camp is selling a $5,000 interest in the partnership assets. The entry on the partnership books to transfer the equity is:

Feb.	4	Camp, Capital...	5,000.00	
		Davis, Capital...		5,000.00
		To transfer Camp's equity in the partnership assets to Davis.		

After this entry is posted, the accounting equation that shows the assets and equities of the new partnership is:

Assets		Equities	
Cash	$ 3,000	Abbott, capital	$ 5,000
Other assets	12,000	Burns, capital	5,000
		Davis, capital	5,000
Total Assets...	$15,000	Total Equities...	$15,000

Two points should be noted in regard to this transaction. First, the $7,000 Davis paid Camp is not recorded in the partnership books. Camp sold and transferred a $5,000 equity in the partnership assets to Davis. The entry that records the transfer is a debit to Camp, Capital and a credit to Davis, Capital for $5,000. Furthermore, the entry is the same whether Davis pays Camp $7,000 or $70,000. The amount is paid directly to Camp. It is a side transaction between Camp and Davis and does not affect partnership assets.

The second point to be noted is that Abbott and Burns must agree to the sale and transfer if Davis is to become a partner. Abbott and Burns cannot prevent Camp from selling the interest to Davis. On the other hand, Camp cannot force Abbott and Burns to accept Davis as a partner. If Abbott and Burns agree to accept Davis, a new partnership is formed and a new contract with a new loss-and-gain-sharing ratio must be drawn. If Camp sells to Davis and either Abbott or Burns refuses to accept Davis as a partner, under the common law the old partnership must be liquidated and Davis receives only the liquidation rights of Camp. However, under the Uniform Partnership Act, which is rapidly replacing the common law, Davis gets Camp's share of partnership gains and losses and Camp's share of partnership assets if the firm is liquidated, but Davis gets no voice in the management of the firm until admitted as a partner.

Investing in an existing partnership

Instead of purchasing the equity of an existing partner, an individual may gain an equity in a partnership by investing assets in the business, with the invested assets becoming the property of the partnership rather than the property of one of its partners. For example, assume that the partnership of Evans and Gage has assets and equities as follows:

Assets		Equities	
Cash	$ 3,000	Evans, capital	$20,000
Other assets	37,000	Gage, capital	20,000
Total Assets	$40,000	Total Equities	$40,000

Also, assume that Evans and Gage have agreed to accept Hart as a partner with a one-half interest in the business upon his investment of $40,000. The entry to record Hart's investment is:

Mar.	2	Cash	40,000.00	
		Hart, Capital		40,000.00
		To record the investment of Hart.		

After the entry is posted the assets and equities of the new partnership appear as follows:

Assets		Equities	
Cash	$43,000	Evans, capital	$20,000
Other assets	37,000	Gage, capital	20,000
		Hart, capital	40,000
Total Assets	$80,000	Total Equities	$80,000

Before continuing it should be said that, although Hart has a one half equity in the assets of the business, he does not necessarily have a right to one half of its net income. The sharing of losses and gains is a separate matter on which the partners must agree, and the agreed method may bear no relation to their capital ratio.

A bonus to the old partners

Sometimes when a partnership earns an exceptionally high net income year after year, its partners may require an incoming partner to give a bonus for the privilege of joining the firm and sharing in its high earnings. For example, Judd and Kirk operate a partnership business, sharing its exceptionally large earnings equally. Judd has a $38,000 equity in the business and Kirk has a $32,000 equity, and they have agreed to allow Lee a one third equity and a one third share of the partnership's earnings upon the investment of $50,000. Lee's equity is determined with a calculation like this:

Equities of the existing partners ($38,000 + $32,000)	$ 70,000
Investment of the new partner....................................	50,000
Total equities in the new partnership.........................	$120,000
Equity of Lee (⅓ of total)	$ 40,000

And the entry to record Lee's investment is:

May	15	Cash...	50,000.00	
		Lee, Capital...		40,000.00
		Judd, Capital		5,000.00
		Kirk, Capital		5,000.00
		To record the investment of Lee.		

The $10,000 difference between the $50,000 invested by Lee and the $40,000 credited to his Capital account is a bonus which is shared by Judd and Kirk in their loss and gain sharing ratio. A bonus is always shared by the old partners in their loss and gain sharing ratio, and this is only fair because the bonus is a form of compensation given for the privilege of receiving a portion of the exceptional profits formally shared exclusively by the old partners.

Bonus to the new partner

Sometimes the members of an existing partnership may be very anxious to bring a new partner into their firm, because the business may need additional cash or the new partner may have exceptional abilities or business contacts that will increase profits. In such a situation the old partners may be willing to give the new partner a larger equity in the business than the amount of his or her investment. For example,

Moss and Owen are partners with Capital account balances of $30,000 and $18,000 respectively and sharing losses and gains in a 2 to 1 ratio. The partners are anxious to have Pitt join their partnership and will allow him a one-fourth equity in the firm if he will invest $12,000. If Pitt accepts, his equity in the new firm is calculated as follows:

Equities of the existing partners ($30,000 + $18,000)....	$48,000
Investment of the new partner	12,000
Total equities in the new partnership........................	$60,000
Equity of Pitt (¼ of total)	$15,000

And the entry to record Pitt's investment is:

June	1	Cash...	12,000.00	
		Moss, Capital..	2,000.00	
		Owen, Capital...	1,000.00	
		Pitt, Capital		15,000.00
		To record the investment of Pitt.		

Note that Pitt's bonus is contributed by the old partners in their loss and gain sharing ratio, which is normal. Also remember that Pitt's one fourth equity does not necessarily entitle him to one fourth of the earnings of the business, since the sharing of losses and gains is a separate matter for agreement by the partners.

Withdrawal of a partner

The best practice in regard to withdrawals is for partners to provide in advance, in their partnership contract, the procedure to be followed when a partner withdraws from the partnership. When such a procedure is agreed on in advance, it commonly provides for an audit of the accounting records and a revaluation of the partnership assets. The revaluation just prior to a retirement is very desirable because it places all assets on the books at current values and causes the retiring partner's Capital account to reflect the current value of his equity. Often, if a partnership agreement provides for an audit and asset revaluation when a partner retires, it also provides that the retiring partner is to withdraw assets equal to the book amount of his revalued equity.

For example, assume that Blue is retiring from the partnership of Smith, Blue, and Short. The partners have always shared losses and gains in the ratio of Smith, one half; Blue, one fourth; and Short, one fourth. Their partnership agreement provides for an audit and asset revaluation upon the retirement of a partner, and their balance sheet just prior to the audit and revaluation shows the following assets and equities:

Assets		Equities	
Cash	$11,000	Smith, capital	$22,000
Merchandise inventory	16,000	Blue, capital	10,000
Equipment..................... $20,000		Short, capital..............	10,000
Less accum. depr 5,000	15,000		
Total Assets	$42,000	Total Equities	$42,000

The audit and appraisal indicate the merchandise inventory is overvalued by $4,000 and that due to market changes the partnership equipment should be valued at $25,000 with accumulated depreciation of $8,000. The entries to record these revaluations are:

Oct.	31	Smith, Capital..	2,000.00	
		Blue, Capital...	1,000.00	
		Short, Capital	1,000.00	
		Merchandise inventory		4,000.00
		To revalue the inventory.		
	31	Equipment	5,000.00	
		Accumulated Depreciation Equipment....................		3,000.00
		Smith, Capital...		1,000.00
		Blue, Capital...		500.00
		Short, Capital		500.00
		To revalue the equipment.		

Note in the illustrated entries that losses and gains are shared in the partners' loss-and-gain-sharing ratio. Losses and gains from asset revaluations are always shared by partners in their loss-and-gain-sharing ratio, and the fairness of this is easy to see when it is remembered that if the partnership did not terminate, such losses and gains would sooner or later be reflected on the income statement.

After the entries revaluing the partnership assets are recorded, a balance sheet will show these revalued assets and equities for Smith, Blue, and Short:

Assets		Equities	
Cash	$11,000	Smith, capital	$21,000
Merchandise inventory.....	12,000	Blue, capital	9,500
Equipment..................... $25,000		Short, capital..............	9,500
Less accum. depr 8,000	17,000		
Total Assets	$40,000	Total Equities	$40,000

After the revaluation, if Blue withdraws from the partnership and takes assets equal to his revalued equity, the entry to record his withdrawal is:

Oct.	31	Blue, Capital..	9,500.00	
		Cash..		9,500.00
		To record the withdrawal of Blue.		

In withdrawing, Blue does not have to take cash in settlement of his equity. He may take any combination of assets to which the partners agree, or he may take the new partnership's promissory note. Also, the withdrawal of Blue creates a new partnership; and consequently, a new partnership contract and a new loss-and-gain-sharing ratio are required.

Partner withdraws taking assets of less value than his book equity

Sometimes when a partner retires, the remaining partners may not wish to have the assets revalued and the new values recorded. In such cases the partners may agree, for example, that the assets are overvalued; and due to the overvalued assets, the retiring partner should in settlement of his equity take assets of less value than the book value of his equity. Sometimes, too, when assets are not overvalued, the retiring partner may be so anxious to retire that he is willing to take less than the current value of his equity just to get out of the partnership or out of the business.

When a partner retires taking assets of less value than his equity, he is in effect leaving a portion of his book equity in the business. In such cases, the remaining partners divide the unwithdrawn equity portion in their loss-and-gain-sharing ratio. For example, assume that Black, Brown, and Green are partners sharing gains and losses in a 2:2:1 ratio. Their assets and equities are:

Assets		Equities	
Cash	$ 5,000	Black, capital	$ 6,000
Merchandise	9,000	Brown, capital	6,000
Store equipment	4,000	Green, capital	6,000
Total Assets	$18,000	Total Equities....	$18,000

Brown is so anxious to withdraw from the partnership that he is willing to retire if permitted to take $4,500 in cash in settlement for his equity. Black and Green agree to the $4,500 withdrawal, and Brown retires. The entry to record the retirement is:

Mar.	4	Brown, Capital..	6,000.00	
		Cash..		4,500.00
		Black, Capital...		1,000.00
		Green, Capital		500.00
		To record the withdrawal of Brown.		

In retiring, Brown did not withdraw $1,500 of his book equity. This is divided between Black and Green in their loss-and-gain-sharing ratio. The loss-and-gain-sharing ratio of the original partnership was Black, 2; Brown, 2; and Green, 1. Therefore in the original partnership, Black and Green shared in a 2 to 1 ratio; and the unwithdrawn book equity of Brown is shared by Black and Green in this ratio.

Partner withdraws taking assets of greater value than his book equity

There are two common reasons for a partner receiving upon retirement assets of greater value than his book equity. First, certain of the partnership assets may be undervalued; and second, the partners continuing the business may be so anxious for the retiring partner to withdraw that they are willing for him to take assets of greater value than his book equity.

When assets are undervalued or unrecorded and the partners do not wish to change the recorded values, the partners may agree to permit a retiring member to withdraw assets of greater value than his book equity. In such cases the retiring partner is, in effect, withdrawing his own book equity and a portion of his partners' equities. For example, assume that Jones, Thomas, and Finch are partners sharing gains and losses in a 3:2:1 ratio. Their assets and equities are:

Assets		Equities	
Cash	$ 5,000	Jones, capital.............	$ 9,000
Merchandise	10,000	Thomas, capital	6,000
Equipment...............	3,000	Finch, capital	3,000
Total Assets	$18,000	Total Equities....	$18,000

Finch wishes to withdraw from the partnership; Jones and Thomas plan to continue the business. The partners agree that certain of their assets are undervalued, but they do not wish to increase the recorded values. They further agree that if current values were recorded, the asset total would be increased $6,000 and the equity of Finch would be increased $1,000. Therefore, the partners agree that $4,000 is the proper value for Finch's equity and that he may withdraw that amount in cash. The entry to record the withdrawal is:

May	7	Finch, Capital...	3,000.00	
		Jones, Capital..	600.00	
		Thomas, Capital...	400.00	
		Cash..		4,000.00
		To record the withdrawal of Finch.		

Death of a partner

A partner's death automatically dissolves and ends a partnership, and his estate is entitled to receive the amount of his equity. The partnership contract should contain provisions for settlement in case a partner dies, and one provision should provide a method for ascertaining the current value of the deceased partner's equity. This requires at least: (a) an immediate closing of the books to determine earnings since the end of the previous accounting period and (b) a method for determining and recording current values for the assets. Upon a partner's death and after the current value of the deceased partner's equity is determined, the remaining partners and the deceased partner's estate must agree to a disposition of the equity. They may agree to its sale to the remaining partners or to an outsider, or they may agree to the withdrawal of assets in settlement. Entries for both of these procedures have already been discussed.

Liquidations

When a partnership is liquidated, its business is ended, the assets are converted into cash, the creditors are paid, the remaining cash is distributed to the partners, and the partnership is dissolved. Although many combinations of circumstances occur in liquidations, only three are discussed here.

All assets realized before a distribution, assets are sold at a profit

A partnership liquidation under this assumption may be illustrated with the following example. Ottis, Skinner, and Parr have operated a partnership for a number of years, sharing losses and gains in a 3:2:1 ratio. Due to several unsatisfactory conditions, the partners decide to liquidate as of December 31. On that date the books are closed, the income from operations is transferred to the partners' Capital accounts, and the condensed balance sheet shown in Illustration 14–4 is prepared.

Ottis, Skinner, and Parr
Balance Sheet, December 31, 19—

Assets		Equities	
Cash	$10,000	Accounts payable	$ 5,000
Merchandise inventory	15,000	Ottis, capital	15,000
Other assets	25,000	Skinner, capital	15,000
		Parr, capital	15,000
Total Assets	$50,000	Total Equities	$50,000

Illustration 14–4

In any liquidation the business always ends and the assets are sold. Normally, either a gain or a loss results from the sale of each group of assets. These losses and gains are called "losses and gains from realization" and are shared by the partners in their loss-and-gain-sharing ratio. If Ottis, Skinner, and Parr sell their merchandise inventory for $12,000 and their other assets for $34,000, the sales and the gain allocation are recorded as follows:

Jan.	12	Cash	12,000.00	
		Loss or Gain from Realization	3,000.00	
		Merchandise Inventory		15,000.00
		Sold the inventory at a loss.		
	15	Cash	34,000.00	
		Other Assets		25,000.00
		Loss or Gain from Realization		9,000.00
		Sold the other assets at a profit		
	15	Loss or Gain from Realization	6,000.00	
		Ottis, Capital		3,000.00
		Skinner, Capital		2,000.00
		Parr, Capital		1,000.00
		To allocate the net gain from realization to the partners in their 3:2:1 loss-and-gain-sharing ratio.		

Careful notice should be taken of the last journal entry. In a partnership termination when assets are sold at a loss or gain, the loss or gain is allocated to the partners in their loss-and-gain-sharing ratio. Often students, in solving liquidation problems, attempt to allocate the assets to the partners in their loss-and-gain-sharing ratio. Obviously this is not correct; it is not assets but losses and gains that are shared in the loss-and-gain-sharing ratio.

After partnership assets are sold and the gain or loss allocated, the partnership cash exactly equals the combined equities of the partners and creditors. This point is illustrated for Ottis, Skinner, and Parr in the balance sheet of Illustration 14–5.

Ottis, Skinner, and Parr
Balance Sheet, January 15, 19—

Assets		Equities	
Cash	$56,000	Accounts payable	$ 5,000
		Ottis, capital	18,000
		Skinner, capital	17,000
		Parr, capital	16,000
Total Assets	$56,000	Total Equities	$56,000

Illustration 14–5

After partnership assets are realized and the gain or loss shared, entries are made to distribute the realized cash to the proper parties. Since creditors have first claim, they are paid first. After the creditors are paid, the remaining cash is divided among the partners. Each partner has the right to cash equal to his equity or, in other words, cash equal to the balance of his Capital account. The entries to distribute the cash of Ottis, Skinner, and Parr are:

Jan.	15	Accounts Payable	5,000.00	
		Cash		5,000.00
		To pay the claims of the creditors.		
	15	Ottis, Capital	18,000.00	
		Skinner, Capital	17,000.00	
		Parr, Capital	16,000.00	
		Cash		51,000.00
		To distribute the remaining cash to the partners according to their Capital account balances.		

Notice that after losses and gains are shared and the creditors are paid, each partner receives liquidation cash equal to the balance remaining in his Capital account. The partners receive these amounts because a partner's Capital account balance shows his equity in the one partnership asset, cash.

All assets realized before a distribution, assets sold at a loss, each partner's Capital account is sufficient to absorb his share of the loss

In a partnership liquidation, the assets are sometimes sold at a net loss. For example, if contrary to the assumptions of the previous illustration, the merchandise inventory of Ottis, Skinner, and Parr is sold

for $9,000 and the other assets for $13,000, the entries to record the
sales and loss allocation are:

Jan.	12	Cash...	9,000.00	
		Loss or Gain from Realization....................................	6,000.00	
		Merchandise Inventory..		15,000.00
		Sold the inventory at a loss.		
	15	Cash...	13,000.00	
		Loss or Gain from Realization....................................	12,000.00	
		Other Assets...		25,000.00
		Sold the other assets at a loss.		
	15	Ottis, Capital..	9,000.00	
		Skinner, Capital...	6,000.00	
		Parr, Capital...	3,000.00	
		Loss or Gain from Realization.............................		18,000.00
		To allocate the loss from realization to the partners in their loss-and-gain-sharing ratio.		

After these entries are recorded, a new partnership balance sheet
appears as in Illustration 14–6. The balance sheet shows the equities

Ottis, Skinner, and Parr
Balance Sheet, January 15, 19–

Assets		Equities	
Cash........................	$32,000	Accounts payable........	$ 5,000
		Ottis, capital..............	6,000
		Skinner, capital..........	9,000
		Parr, capital...............	12,000
Total Assets	$32,000	Total Equities	$32,000

Illustration 14–6

in the partnership cash, and the following entries are required to
distribute the cash to the proper parties:

Jan	15	Accounts Payable	5,000.00	
		Cash...		5,000.00
		To pay the partnership creditors.		
	15	Ottis, Capital	6,000.00	
		Skinner, Capital...	9,000.00	
		Parr, Capital...	12,000.00	
		Cash		27,000.00
		To distribute the remaining cash to the partners according to the balances of their Capital accounts.		

Notice again that after realization losses are shared and creditors are paid, each partner receives cash equal to his Capital account balance.

All assets realized before a distribution, assets sold at a loss, a partner's Capital account is not sufficient to cover his share of the loss

Sometimes a partner's share of realization losses is greater than the balance of his Capital account. In such cases the partner whose share of losses is greater than his capital balance must, if he can, cover the deficit by paying cash into the partnership. For example, assume contrary to the previous two illustrations that Ottis, Skinner, and Parr sell their merchandise for $3,000 and the other assets for $4,000. The entries to record the sales and the loss allocation are:

Jan.	12	Cash..	3,000.00	
		Loss or Gain from Realization	12,000.00	
		Merchandise Inventory··		15,000.00
		Sold the inventory at a loss.		
	15	Cash..	4,000.00	
		Loss or Gain from Realization	21,000.00	
		Other Assets..		25,000.00
		Sold the other assets at a loss.		
	15	Ottis, Capital	16,500.00	
		Skinner, Capital..	11,000.00	
		Parr, Capital..	5,500.00	
		Loss or Gain from Realization		33,000.00
		To record the allocation of the loss from realization to the partners in their loss-and-gain-sharing ratio.		

After the entry allocating the realization loss is posted, the Capital account of Ottis has a $1,500 debit balance and appears as follows:

Ottis, Capital

Date		Explanation	F	Debit	Credit	Balance
Dec.	31	Balance				15,000.00
Jan.	15	Share of loss from realization		16,500.00		1,500.00

Since the partnership agreement provides that Ottis is to take one half the losses or gains, and since his Capital account balance is not large enough to absorb his loss share in this case, he must, if he can, pay $1,500 into the partnership to cover his full share of the losses. If he is able to pay, the following entry is made:

Jan.	15	Cash...	1,500.00	
		Ottis, Capital		1,500.00
		To record the additional investment of Ottis to cover his share of realization losses.		

After the $1,500 is received from Ottis, the partnership has $18,500 in cash; and the following entries are made to distribute it to the proper parties:

Jan.	15	Accounts Payable	5,000.00	
		Cash...		5,000.00
		To pay the partnership creditors.		
	15	Skinner, Capital..	4,000.00	
		Parr, Capital...	9,500.00	
		Cash...		13,500.00
		To distribute the remaining cash to the partners according to the balances of their Capital accounts.		

Often when a partner's share of partnership losses exceeds his Capital account balance, he is unable to make up the deficit. In such cases, since each partner has unlimited liability, the deficit must be borne by the remaining partner or partners. For example, assume that contrary to the previous illustration, Ottis is unable to pay in the $1,500 necessary to cover the deficit in his Capital account. If Ottis is unable to pay, the deficit that he is unable to make good must be shared by Skinner and Parr in their loss-and-gain-sharing ratio. In the original loss-and-gain-sharing agreement, the partners shared losses and gains in the ratio of Ottis, 3; Skinner, 2; and Parr, 1. Therefore, Skinner and Parr shared in a 2 to 1 ratio; and the $1,500 that Ottis's share of the losses exceeded his Capital account balance is apportioned between them in this ratio. Normally the defaulting partner's deficit is transferred to the Capital accounts of the remaining partners. This is accomplished for Ottis, Skinner, and Parr with the following entry:

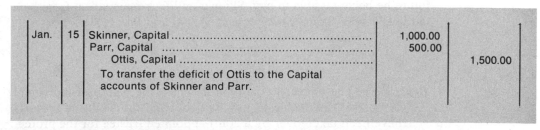

Jan.	15	Skinner, Capital..	1,000.00	
		Parr, Capital	500.00	
		Ottis, Capital		1,500.00
		To transfer the deficit of Ottis to the Capital accounts of Skinner and Parr.		

After the deficit is transferred, the Capital accounts of the partners appear as in Illustration 14–7.

Ottis, Capital

Date		Explanation	F	Debit	Credit	Balance
Dec.	31	Balance				15,000.00
Jan.	15	Share of loss from realization		16,500.00		(1,500.00)
	15	Deficit to Skinner and Parr			1,500.00	–0–

Skinner, Capital

Date		Explanation	F	Debit	Credit	Balance
Dec.	31	Balance				15,000.00
Jan.	15	Share of loss from realization		11,000.00		4,000.00
	15	Share of Ottis's deficit		1,000.00		3,000.00

Parr, Capital

Date		Explanation	F	Debit	Credit	Balance
Dec.	31	Balance				15,000.00
Jan.	15	Share of loss from realization		5,500.00		9,500.00
	15	Share of Ottis's deficit		500.00		9,000.00

Illustration 14–7

After the deficit is transferred, the $17,000 of liquidation cash is distributed with the following entries:

Jan.	15	Accounts Payable	5,000.00	
		Cash..		5,000.00
		To pay the partnership creditors.		
	15	Skinner, Capital...	3,000.00	
		Parr, Capital	9,000.00	
		Cash..		12,000.00
		To distribute the remaining cash to the partners according to their Capital account balances.		

It should be understood that the inability of Ottis to meet his loss share at this time does not relieve him of liability. If at any time in the future he becomes able to pay, Skinner and Parr may collect from him the full $1,500. Skinner may collect $1,000 and Parr, $500.

Glossary

Bankruptcy. The financial condition in which the bankrupt individual or business is unable to pay its debts and the bankrupt's assets have been taken over by a court-appointed trustee for the protection of the creditors.

Deficit. A negative amount of an item.

Liquidation. The winding up of a business by converting its assets to cash and distributing the cash to the proper parties.

Mutual agency. The legal situation in a partnership whereby each partner is an agent of the partnership and is able to bind the partnership to contracts within the normal scope of the partnership business.

Partnership. An association of two or more persons to carry on a business as co-owners for profit.

Partnership contract. The document setting forth the agreed terms under which the members of a partnership will conduct the partnership business.

Unlimited liability. The legal situation in a partnership which makes each partner responsible for paying all the debts of the partnership if his or her partners are unable to pay a share.

Questions for class discussion

1. Hill and Dale are partners. Hill dies and his son claims the right to take his father's place in the partnership. Does he have this right? Why?
2. Ted Hall cannot legally enter into a contract. Can he become a partner?
3. If a partnership contract does not state the period of time the partnership is to exist, when does the partnership end?
4. What is the meaning of the term "mutual agency" as applied to a partnership?
5. Jack and Jill are partners in the operation of a store. Jack without consulting Jill enters into a contract for the purchase of merchandise for resale by the store. Jill contends that she did not authorize the order and refuses to take delivery. The vendor sues the partners for the contract price of the merchandise. Will the firm have to pay? Why?
6. Would your answer to Question 5 differ if Jack and Jill were partners in a public accounting firm?
7. May partners limit the right of a member of their firm to bind their partnership to contracts? Is such an agreement binding (*a*) on the partners and (*b*) on outsiders?
8. What is the meaning of the term "unlimited liability" when it is applied to members of a partnership?
9. Kennedy, Porter, and Foulke have been partners for three years. The partnership is dissolving, Kennedy is leaving the firm, and Porter and Foulke plan to carry on the business. In the final settlement Kennedy places a $45,000 salary claim against the partnership. His contention is that since he devoted all of his time for three years to the affairs of the partnership, he has a claim for a salary of $15,000 for each year. Is his claim valid? Why?
10. The partnership agreement of Martin and Tritt provides for a two-thirds, one-third sharing of income but says nothing of losses. The operations for a year result in a loss. Martin claims the loss should be shared equally since the partnership agreement said nothing of sharing losses. Do you agree?

11. A, B, and C are partners with Capital account balances of $6,000 each. D gives A $7,500 for his one-third interest in the partnership. The bookkeeper debits A, Capital and credits D, Capital for $6,000. D objects. He wants his Capital account to show a $7,500 balance, the amount he paid for his interest. Explain why D's Capital account is credited for $6,000.

12. After all partnership assets are converted to cash and all creditor claims paid, the remaining cash should equal the sum of the balances of the partners' Capital accounts. Why?

13. J, K, and L are partners. In a liquidation J's share of partnership losses exceeds his Capital account balance. He is unable to meet the deficit from his personal assets, and the excess losses are shared by his partners. Does this relieve J of liability?

Class exercises

Exercise 14–1

Larr and More began a partnership by investing $6,000 and $8,000, respectively; and during its first year the partnership earned $21,000.

Required:

1. Prepare a schedule with the following columnar headings:

Ways of Sharing	Larr's Share	More's Share

2. Then complete the tabulation by listing the following ways of sharing by letter in the first column and then opposite each letter showing the share of each partner in the $21,000 net income.
    a. The partners failed to agree on a method of sharing income.
    b. The partners had agreed to share income in their investment ratio.
    c. The partners had agreed to share by allowing a $9,000 per year salary allowance to Larr, a $7,000 per year salary allowance to More, plus 10% interest on investments, and the balance equally.

Exercise 14–2

Assume the partners of Exercise 14–1 agreed to share losses and gains by allowing yearly salary allowances of $9,000 to Larr and $7,000 to More, 10% interest on their investments, and the balance equally. (a) Determine the shares of Larr and More in a $16,400 first-year net income. (b) Determine the partners' shares in a first-year $2,600 net loss.

Exercise 14–3

Marsh, Nalley, and Owen have equities of $7,500 each in a partnership. With the consent of Nalley and Owen, Marsh is selling his equity to Parr for $1 in cash and a bag of peanuts. Give the entry to record the sale as of October 10.

Exercise 14–4

Oak and Ash are partners with Capital account balances of $30,000 and $35,000 and sharing losses and gains in a 3 to 2 ratio. On October 5 Elm is to invest $25,000 and join the partnership. Give the entry for the admission of Elm under each of these unrelated assumptions: (a) Elm is to receive an equity equal to his investment. (b) Elm is to receive a one-fourth equity in the partnership. (c) Elm is to receive a one-third equity.

Exercise 14–5

White is retiring from the partnership of Red, White, and Blue. The partners have always shared losses and gains in a 2:2:1 ratio; and on White's retirement date they have equities in the partnership as follows: Walter White, $9,000; James Red, $9,000; and Jerry Blue, $6,000.

Required:

1. Under a November 1 date give in general journal form the entries for the retirement of White under each of the following unrelated assumptions:

    a. White retires, taking $9,000 of partnership cash for his equity.
    b. White retires, taking $10,500 of partnership cash for his equity.
    c. White retires, taking $8,100 of partnership cash for his equity.

Exercise 14–6

Abbott, Birch, and Collins formed a partnership with Abbott investing $9,000, Birch, $6,000, and Collins, $3,000. They agreed to share losses and gains equally. Their business lost heavily, and at the end of the year they decided to liquidate. After converting all partnership assets to cash and paying all creditor claims, $6,000 of partnership cash remained.

Required:

Prepare a general journal entry to record the distribution of the correct shares of cash to the partners in final liquidation of their business.

Problem 14–1   Problems

Ted Ames, Jane Boyd, and Ned Cohn invested $15,000, $12,000, and $9,000, respectively, in a partnership. During its first year the firm earned $40,800.

Required:

1. Prepare entries to close the firm's Income Summary account as of December 31 and to allocate the net income to the partners under each of these assumptions:
    a. The partners could not agree as to the method of sharing earnings.
    b. The partners had agreed to share earnings in the ratio of their beginning investments.
    c. The partners had agreed to share income by allowing annual salary allowances of $12,000 to Ames, $14,000 to Boyd, and $10,000 to Cohn; allowing a share of the income equal to 10% interest on the partners' investments; and sharing the remainder equally.
2. Prepare the section of the partners' first-year income statement showing the allocation of the income to the partners under assumption (c).

Problem 14–2

Joan Clay and Mary Dent are in the process of forming a partnership to which Joan will devote one third of her time and Mary will devote full time. They have discussed the following plans for sharing gains and losses.

a. In the ratio of their investments which they have agreed to maintain at $10,000 for Joan and $15,000 for Mary.
b. In proportion to the time devoted to the business.
c. A salary allowance of $1,000 per month to Mary and the balance in their investment ratio.
d. A $1,000 per month salary allowance to Mary, 8% interest on their investments, and the balance equally.

Required:

1. Prepare a schedule with the following columnar headings:

Income- Sharing Plan	$36,000 Net Income		$18,000 Net Income		$6,000 Net Loss	
	Joan	Mary	Joan	Mary	Joan	Mary

2. List the plans by letter in the first column and show opposite each plan the shares of the partners in (a) a year's $36,000 net income, (b) a year's $18,000 net income, and (c) a year's $6,000 net loss.

Problem 14–3

Part 1. Cary, Dyer, and Eads are partners sharing losses and gains in a 2:2:1 ratio. Cary plans to withdraw from the partnership, and on the date of his withdrawal, December 5, the partners' equities in the partnership are Cary, $10,000; Dyer, $14,000; and Eads, $8,500. Dyer and Eads plan to continue the business and its records under a new partnership agreement.

Required:

Prepare general journal entries to record the withdrawal of Cary under each of the following unrelated assumptions:

a. Cary, with the consent of Dyer and Eads, sells his interest to Fry, taking from Fry $2,000 in cash and Fry's personal $10,000 note payable.
b. Cary withdraws, taking $10,000 of partnership cash for his interest.
c. Cary withdraws, taking $10,750 of partnership cash.
d. Cary withdraws, taking $6,000 in cash and delivery equipment carried on the partnership books at $4,000, less $1,500 accumulated depreciation.
e. Cary withdraws, taking $1,500 in cash and a $10,000 note payable of the new partnership.
f. Cary withdraws and transfers his interest to Dyer and Eads, taking Dyer's $7,200 personal note for three fifths of his interest and a $4,800 personal note from Eads for two fifths of his interest.

Part 2. Good and Hess are partners with Capital account balances of $30,000 each. Good devotes full time to partnership affairs but Hess does not; consequently, they share losses and gains in a 3 to 1 ratio. Isley is to invest $40,000 in the firm and become a partner on November 10.

Required:

Prepare a general journal entry to record the investment of Isley under each of these unrelated assumptions: (*a*) Isley is to receive a 40% equity in the partnership. (*b*) Isley is to receive a 35% equity. (*c*) Isley is to receive a 50% equity.

Problem 14 -4

Fox, Grey, and Hogg, who have always shared losses and gains in a 2:2:1 ratio, plan to liquidate their partnership. Just prior to the liquidation their balance sheet appeared as follows:

Fox, GREY, AND HOGG
Balance Sheet, April 15, 19 —

Cash.......................	$ 2,500	Accounts payable	$10,500
Other assets	44,000	John Fox, capital	8,000
		Ned Grey, capital	20,000
		Lee Hogg, capital	8,000
Total Assets....	$46,500	Total Equities	$46,500

Required:

Under the assumption the other assets are sold and the cash is distributed to the proper parties on April 20, give the entries for the sales, the loss or gain allocations, and the distributions if —

a. The other assets are sold for $50,000.
b. The other assets are sold for $31,500.
c. The other assets are sold for $21,500, and the partner with a deficit can and does pay in the amount of his deficit.
d. The other assets are sold for $20,250, and the partners have no assets other than those invested in the business.

Problem 14–5

Lee, May, and Nye are partners. Lee devotes full time to partnership affairs; May and Nye devote very little time; and as a result, they share gains and losses in a 3:1:1 ratio. Of late the business has not been too profitable, and the partners have decided to liquidate. Just prior to the first realization sale, a partnership balance sheet appeared as follows:

LEE, MAY, AND NYE
Balance Sheet, October 31, 19 —

Cash	$ 2,500	Accounts payable........	$ 7,000
Accounts receivable.......	9,500	Walter Lee, capital	6,000
Merchandise inventory...	16,000	Jerry May, capital	12,000
Equipment $12,000		Edward Nye, capital....	12,000
Less accumulated depr. 3,000	9,000		
Total Assets........	$37,000	Total Equities....	$37,000

The assets were sold, the creditors were paid, and the remaining cash was distributed to the partners on the following dates:

Nov. 4   The accounts receivable were sold for $6,500.
        8   The merchandise inventory was sold for $11,000.
     11   The equipment was sold for $5,000.
     12   The creditors were paid.
     12   The remaining cash was distributed to the partners.

Required:

1.   Prepare general journal entries to record the asset sales, the allocation of the realization loss, and the payment of the creditors.
2.   Under the assumption that the partner with a deficit can and does pay in the amount of his deficit on November 12, give the entry to record the receipt of his cash and the distribution of partnership cash to the remaining partners.
3.   Under the assumption that the partner with a deficit cannot pay, give the entry to allocate his deficit to his partners. Then give the entry to distribute the partnership cash to the remaining partners.

Alternate problems

Problem 14–1A

The partnership of Fred Ives, John Jay, and Dale King earned $39,600 during its first year in business, which ended December 31.

Required:

1.   Prepare entries to close the firm's Income Summary account and to allocate the net income to the partners under each of the following assumptions:

a.   The partners could not agree on a method of sharing earnings.
b.   The partners shared earnings in the ratio of their beginning investments which were Ives, $16,000; Jay, $12,000; and King, $8,000.
c.   The partners shared earnings by allowing salary allowances of $1,000 per month to Ives, $1,200 per month to Jay, and $900 per month to King, plus interest at 10% annually on beginning investments, and the balance equally.
2.   Prepare the income statement section showing the allocation of the year's income to the partners under assumption (*c*).

Problem 14–2A

Robert Kemp and Walter Lott are forming a partnership to which Kemp is to devote one half of his time and Lott is to devote full time. They have discussed the following plans for sharing gains and losses:

a.   In the ratio of their investments which are to be $12,000 for Kemp and $8,000 for Lott.
b.   In proportion to the time devoted to the business.
c.   A salary allowance of $1,000 per month to Lott and the balance in the investment ratio.
d.   A salary allowance of $1,000 per month to Lott, 10% interest annually on their investments, and the balance equally.

Required:

1. Prepare a schedule with columnar headings as follows: ·

Income-Sharing Plan	$30,000 Net Income		$15,000 Net Income		$9,000 Net Loss	
	Kemp	Lott	Kemp	Lott	Kemp	Lott

2. List the plans for sharing gains and losses by letter in the first column. Then opposite each plan show the partners' shares in a $30,000 annual net income, a $15,000 net income, and a $9,000 net loss.

Problem 14–3A

Part 1. Mae Beck is withdrawing from the partnership of Beck, Clay, and Dent. The partners have always shared losses and gains in a 2:3:1 ratio; and on Beck's withdrawal date, December 11, they have capital account balances as follows: Mae Beck, $12,000; June Clay, $16,000; and John Dent, $8,000. Clay and Dent plan to continue the business and its records under a new partnership agreement.

Required:

Prepare entries in general journal form to record the withdrawal of Beck under each of the following unrelated assumptions:

a. Beck withdraws from the partnership, taking $2,000 in partnership cash and the note of the new partnership of Clay and Dent for $10,000.
b. Beck withdraws taking $13,600 of partnership cash in full settlement for her equity.
c. Beck withdraws, taking $8,000 in partnership cash and delivery equipment carried on the partnership books at its $4,000 cost less $1,000 of accumulated depreciation.
d. Beck sells her partnership interest to Jane Eddy, with the consent of Clay and Dent, taking from Eddy $5,000 in cash and Eddy's personal $10,000 note.
e. Beck sells and transfers her interest to Clay and Dent, taking from Clay a $10,000 personal note payable for two thirds of her interest and taking $5,000 in cash from Dent for one third of her interest.

Part 2. King and Lear are partners with Capital account balances of $50,000 each and sharing losses and gains in a 3 to 2 ratio. Metz is about to join the firm by investing $50,000. Give the November 15 entry to record the investment of Metz under each of these unrelated assumptions: (*a*) Metz is to receive a one-third equity in the partnership. (*b*) Metz is to receive a one-fourth equity. (*c*) Metz is to receive a 40% equity.

Problem 14–4A

Holt, Ives, and Jay plan to liquidate their partnership. They have always shared losses and gains in a 5:3:2 ratio, and on the day of the liquidation their balance sheet appeared as follows:

HOLT, IVES, AND JAY
Balance Sheet, March 31, 19 –

Cash	$ 3,500	Accounts payable	$13,500
Other assets	45,000	Paul Holt, capital	10,000
		Terry Ives, capital	20,000
		Walter Jay, capital	5,000
Total Assets	$48,500	Total Equities	$48,500

Required:

Prepare general journal entries to record the sale of the other assets and the distribution of the cash to the proper parties under each of the following unrelated assumptions:

a. The other assets are sold for $50,500.
b. The other assets are sold for $30,000.
c. The other assets are sold for $22,000, and the partner with the deficit can and does pay in the amount of his deficit.
d. The other assets are sold for $20,000, and the partners have no assets other than those invested in the business.

Problem 14–5A

Until March 2 of the current year Nye, Poe, and Ray were partners sharing losses and gains in their capital ratio. On that date Nye suffered a heart attack and died. Poe and Ray immediately ended the business operations and prepared the following adjusted trial balance:

NYE, POE, AND RAY
Adjusted Trial Balance, March 2, 19 –

Cash	$ 4,500	
Accounts receivable	10,500	
Allowance for doubtful accounts		$ 500
Supplies inventory	23,000	
Equipment	13,500	
Accumulated depreciation, equipment		3,500
Land	4,500	
Building	50,000	
Accumulated depreciation, building		9,500
Accounts payable		3,000
Mortgage payable		10,000
Lee Nye, capital		30,000
Ned Poe, capital		30,000
Ted Ray, capital		15,000
Lee Nye, withdrawals	1,000	
Ned Poe, withdrawals	1,000	
Ted Ray, withdrawals	1,000	
Revenues		39,000
Expenses	31,500	
Totals	$140,500	$140,500

Required:

1. Prepare March 2 entries to close the revenue, expense, income summary, and withdrawals accounts of the partnership.
2. Assume the estate of Nye agreed to accept the land and building and assume the mortgage thereon in settlement of its claim against the partnership assets, and that Poe and Ray planned to continue the business and rent the building from the estate. Give the March 15 entry to transfer the land, building, and mortgage and to settle with the estate.
3. Assume that in the place of the foregoing the estate of Nye demanded a cash settlement and the business had to be sold to a competitor who gave $68,000 for the noncash assets and assumed the mortgage but not the accounts payable. Give the March 15 entry to transfer the noncash assets and mortgage to the competitor, and give the entries to allocate the loss to the partners and to distribute the partnership cash to the proper parties.

Part 1. The partnership agreement of Ross and Sears provides that income be shared by allowing salary allowances of $15,000 per year to Ross and $12,000 per year to Sears and then sharing any remaining balance equally. At the end of their first year in business, when a work sheet was prepared, it was discovered that the partnership had earned just $20 during the year. Sears suggested that the $20 be given to the janitor as a bonus, thereby increasing expenses for the year and causing the partnership to exactly break even. He further suggested that the partnership could then forget about sharing gains and losses for the first year, since there would be none. If his suggestions are followed, who gains most and how much does he gain?

> Decision problem 14–1, partnership decisions

Part 2. Early this year Charles Galt and Robert Hall formed a partnership to operate a delivery service. Galt invested $7,000 in the business and Hall invested $4,000, and the partners agreed to share losses and gains equally. Business has been bad; the partners have not been able to make any withdrawals; and now, after eight months, they have decided to end business operations and liquidate the partnership, the assets of which consist of $4,000 in cash and a delivery truck that both partners agree is worth $4,000. In discussing the liquidation, Hall says he is willing to take either the cash or the delivery truck for his liquidation rights, and he also says he is willing to flip a coin to see which partner takes the cash and which takes the truck. Galt is unsure of who should take what and why, and he has come to you for advice. Advise him, giving reasons for your advice.

Ned Fry and Roy Lee operate Sport Shack, a sporting goods store, as a partnership enterprise. Fry has a $42,000 equity in the business, and Lee has a $25,500 equity. They share losses and gains by allowing annual salary allowances of $15,000 per year to Fry and $12,000 to Lee, with any remaining balance being shared 60% to Fry and 40% to Lee.

> Decision problem 14–2, Sport Shack

Joe Fry, Ned Fry's son, has been working in the store on a salary basis. He was an outstanding high school and college athlete and has maintained his contacts with coaches and athletes since graduating from college, and thus attracts a great deal of business to the store. Actually, one third of the past three years' sales can be traced directly to Joe's association with the store, and it is reasonable to assume he was instrumental in attracting even more.

Joe is paid $1,000 per month, but feels this is not sufficient to induce him to remain with the firm as an employee. However, he likes his work and would like to remain in the sporting goods business. What he really wants is to become a partner in the business.

His father is anxious for him to remain in the business and proposes the following:

a. That Joe be admitted to the partnership with a 20% equity in the partnership assets.
b. That he, Ned Fry, transfer from his Capital account to that of Joe's one half the 20% interest; that Joe contribute to the firm's assets a 7% note for the other half; and that he, Ned Fry, will guarantee payment of the note and its interest.
c. That losses and gains be shared by continuing the $15,000 and $12,000 salary allowances of the original partners and that Joe be given a $12,000 annual salary allowance, after which any remaining loss or gain would be shared 40% to Ned Fry, 40% to Roy Lee, and 20% to Joe Fry.

Prepare a report to Mr. Lee on the advisability of accepting Mr. Fry's proposal. Under the assumption that net incomes for the past three years have been $37,000, $41,000, and $43,000, respectively, prepare schedules showing (a) how net income was allocated during the past three years and (b) how it would have been allocated had the proposed new agreement been in effect. Also, (c) prepare a schedule showing the partners' capital interests as they would be immediately after the admission of Joe.

Decision problem 14–3, Fox and Poe

Fox and Poe are partners sharing losses and gains as follows:

a. Annual salary allowances of $15,000 to Fox and $18,000 to Poe are allowed.
b. Interest at 6% on the excess of his Capital account balance over that of his partner is allowed the partner having the larger Capital account balance as of the beginning of the year.
c. The remaining net income is divided three fourths to Fox and one fourth to Poe.

The partnership earned $45,000 during the past year, and the partners began the year with Capital account balances of $70,000 for Fox and $60,000 for Poe.

Although the partners consider the year just ended a successful one, Poe is unhappy with his share of the net income. He feels he should have a much larger share, since he spends twice as much time on partnership affairs as Fox. Fox agrees that Poe spends double the time he spends on partnership business and also that Poe is primarily responsible for the 10% compound annual increase in partnership profits each year for the past several years. Consequently, he suggests that the partners change their loss-and-gain-sharing plan. He knows that Poe has $40,000 in two savings accounts on which he is earning interest at 5% annually, so he suggests the following:

a. Poe is to invest an additional $40,000 in the business.
b. Interest at 8% is to be paid the partners on the full amounts of their in- investments, which are to be Fox, $70,000; and Poe, $100,000.
c. Each partner is to get a $5,000 increase in his salary allowance, with the allowances becoming: Fox, $20,000; and Poe, $23,000.
d. Any balance remaining after salary and interest allowances is to be given in full to Poe.

Poe is interested in earning 8% on the $40,000 he now has in the bank, is pleased with the $5,000 increase in his salary allowance, and is impressed with Fox's generosity in giving him any balance over and above the partners' salary and interest allowances. However, before accepting the offer, he has come to you for advice. Advice Poe, backing your advice with profit-sharing schedules where desirable.

PART 5

Corporation accounting

15
Corporations: Organization
and operation . . .
16
Corporations: Additional stock
transactions, income, and
retained earnings . . .
17
Corporations: Stock investments,
intercorporate investments,
and consolidations

After studying Chapter 15, you should be able to:

- **Explain the differences between a corporation and a single proprietorship or a partnership.**

- **State the advantages and disadvantages of the corporate form of business organization and explain how a corporation is organized and managed.**

- **Explain why a distinction is made between contributed capital and retained earnings in corporation accounting.**

- **Record the issuance of par value stock at par or at a premium in exchange for cash or other assets.**

- **Record the issuance of no-par stock with or without a stated value.**

- **Explain the effect of a cash dividend on corporation assets and stockholders' equity and be able to record the declaration and payment of a cash dividend.**

- **State the differences between common stock and preferred stock and explain why preferred stock is issued.**

- **Describe the meaning and significance of par, book, market, and redemption values of corporate stock.**

- **Define or explain the words and phrases listed in the chapter Glossary.**

chapter 15

Corporations: Organization and operation

The three common types of business organizations are single proprietorships, partnerships, and corporations. Of the three, corporations are fewer in number; yet in dollar volume, they transact more business than do the other two combined. Because of their business volume and also because almost every student will at some time either work for or own an interest in a corporation, an understanding of corporations and their accounting is important. And, a start on this understanding may well be made by examining some of the advantages and disadvantages of the corporate form of business organization.

Separate legal entity

From Chief Justice John Marshall's famous (1819) definition and description of a corporation as "an artificial being, invisible, intangible, and existing only in the contemplation of the law" has grown the doctrine that a corporation is a legal entity, separate and distinct from the persons who own it. The owners are called *stockholders or shareholders;* they own the corporation, but they are not the corporation. The corporation in a legal sense is an artificial person, separate and distinct from its owners.

Separate legal entity is the most important characteristic of a corporation, since it gives a corporation all the rights and responsibilities of a person except those only a natural person may exercise, such as the right to vote or marry. Because of its separate legal entity, a corporation may buy, own, and sell property in its own name. It may sue and be sued in its own name. It may enter into contracts with both outsiders and its own shareholders. In short, through its agents, a corporation may conduct its affairs as a legal person with the rights, duties, and responsibilities of a person.

Advantages of the corporate form

creatures of state

493

Lack of stockholders' liability

As a separate legal entity a corporation is responsible for its own acts and its own debts, and its shareholders have no liability for either. From the viewpoint of an investor, this is perhaps the most important advantage of the corporate form.

Ease of transferring ownership rights

Ownership rights in a corporation are represented by shares of stock. And all that is necessary to convey these rights is a transfer of ownership of the shares. Furthermore, since a corporation is a legal entity, the transfer has no effect on the corporation, and a stockholder generally may transfer and dispose of his stock at will.

Continuity of life

The death or incapacity of a stockholder does not affect the life of a corporation. A corporation's life may continue for the time stated in its charter. This period may be of any length permitted by the laws of the state in which the corporation is organized; and at the expiration of the stated time, the charter may normally be renewed and the period extended. Thus a perpetual life is possible for a successful corporation.

No mutual agency

Mutual agency does not exist in a corporation. A corporation stockholder, acting as a stockholder, has no power to bind the corporation to contracts. His participation in the affairs of the corporation is limited to the right to vote in the stockholders' meetings. Consequently, stockholders need not exercise the care of partners in selecting people with whom they associate themselves in the ownership of a corporation.

Ease of capital assembly

Lack of stockholders' liability, lack of mutual agency, and the ease with which an interest may be transferred make it easy for a corporation to assemble large amounts of capital from the combined investments of many stockholders. Actually, a corporation's capital-raising ability is as a rule limited only by the profitableness with which it can employ the funds of its stockholders. This is very different from a partnership. In a partnership, capital-raising ability is always limited by the number of partners and their individual wealth; and the number of partners is in turn usually limited because of mutual agency and unlimited liability.

Disadvantages of the corporate form

Governmental control and supervision

Corporations are created by fulfilling the requirements of a state's corporation laws. Because of this, corporations are said to be "creatures of the state," and as such are subject to much closer state control and supervision than are single proprietorships and partnerships.

In addition, the rights, powers, and duties of corporations, their stockholders, and officials are derived from corporation laws. There would be no objection to this if the laws were simple and easy to understand; but unfortunately, they are notoriously diverse, complicated, and in some cases vague; and as a result the exact rights, duties, and responsibilities of corporations, their directors, and shareholders vary from state to state and are often difficult to define precisely.

Taxation

The greatest disadvantage of the corporate form is usually considered its extra burden of taxes. Corporations as business units are subject to all the taxes of single proprietorships and partnerships; and in addition, they are subject to several taxes not levied on either of the other two. The most important of these are state and federal income taxes which together commonly take 50% of a corporation's income. However, insofar as the owners of a corporation are concerned, the burden does not end here. The income of a corporation is taxed twice: first as corporation income and again as personal income when distributed to the stockholders as dividends. This differs from single proprietorships and partnerships, which as business units are not subject to income taxes, and whose income is taxed only as the personal income of their owners.

Organizing a corporation

A corporation is created by securing a charter from one of the 50 states or the federal government. Federal charters are limited to national banks, savings and loan associations, and quasi-government corporations, such as the Federal Deposit Insurance Corporation. Consequently, most corporations are chartered by the states.

The requirements that must be met in order to secure a corporation charter vary with the states. In general, however, a charter application must be signed by three or more subscribers to the prospective corporation's stock (who are called the "incorporators") and then filed with the proper state official. The application usually must include:

1. The name of the corporation and its legal address within the state.
2. The purpose for which the corporation is organized.
3. The amount of stock authorized and its par value, if any.
4. If there is to be more than one kind of stock, the amount of each.
5. If the stock is to be divided into different kinds or classes, a statement must be made as to the preferences, qualifications, limitations, restrictions, and rights of each class.
6. The names and addresses of the subscribers and the amount of stock subscribed by each.

If the application complies with the law, the charter is issued and the corporation comes into existence. Usually at the first meeting of its stockholders, bylaws to govern the conduct of the corporation's affairs are adopted and a board of directors is elected. The bylaws normally include among other things:

1. The time, place, manner of calling, and rules for conducting meetings of the stockholders and directors.
2. The number, qualifications, duties, powers, and length of office of the directors.
3. The appointment, duties, powers, compensations, and length of office of corporation officers other than directors.
4. Any proper rules and regulations to govern the acts of the directors and officers.

Organization costs

The costs of organizing a corporation, such as legal fees, promoters' fees, and amounts paid the state to secure a charter, are called organization costs and are debited on incurrence to an account called Organization Costs. Theoretically, the sum of these costs represents an intangible asset from which the corporation will benefit throughout its life. Since the life of a corporation is always indeterminable, the period over which it will benefit from being organized is also indeterminable. Nevertheless, a corporation should make a reasonable estimate of the benefit period, which in no case should exceed 40 years, and write off its organization costs over this period.[1] Although not necessarily related to the benefit period, income tax rules permit a corporation to write off organization costs as a tax-deductible expense over a period of not less than five years. Consequently, many corporations adopt five years as the period over which to write off such costs. There is no theoretical justification for this, but it is generally accepted in practice because organization costs are usually immaterial in amount and under the *principle of materiality* the write-off eliminates an unnecessary balance sheet item.

Management of a corporation

Although ultimate control of a corporation rests with its stockholders, this control is exercised indirectly through the election of the board of directors. The individual stockholder's right to participate in management begins and ends with his vote in the stockholders' meeting, where he has one vote for each share of stock owned.

Normally a corporation's stockholders meet once each year to elect directors and transact such other business as is provided in the corporation's bylaws. Theoretically, stockholders owning or controlling the votes of 50% plus one share of a corporation's stock can elect the board and control the corporation. Actually, because many stockholders do not attend the annual meeting, a much smaller percentage is frequently sufficient for control. Commonly, stockholders who do not attend the annual meeting delegate to an agent their voting rights. This is done by signing a legal document called a *proxy,* which gives the agent the right to vote the stock.

---

[1] APB, "Intangible Assets," *APB Opinion No. 17* (New York: AICPA, August 1970), par. 29.

A corporation's board of directors is responsible and has final authority for the direction of corporation affairs; but it may act only as a collective body—an individual director, as a director, has no power to transact corporation business. And, as a rule, although it has final authority, a board will limit itself to establishing policy, delegating the day-by-day direction of corporation business to the corporation's administrative officers whom it selects and elects.

A corporation's administrative officers are commonly headed by a president who is normally the chief executive officer and is directly responsible to the board for managing, controlling, and supervising the corporation's business. To aid the president, many corporations have one or more vice presidents who are vested with specific managerial powers and duties by the president and the directors. In addition, the corporation secretary keeps the minutes of the meetings of the stockholders and directors, and in a small corporation may also be responsible for keeping a record of the stockholders and the changing amounts of their stock interests. The treasurer is custodian of corporation funds.

Illustration 15–1 shows a typical organizational chart of a corporation. Note how the chart's lines of authority extend from the stockholders through the board and on to the administrative officers.

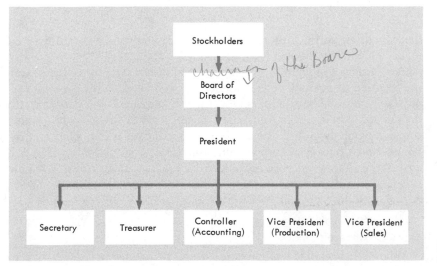

Illustration 15–1
Organization chart

A person invests in a corporation by buying its stock; and when he does so, he receives a stock certificate as evidence of the shares purchased. Usually in a small corporation only one certificate is issued for each block of stock purchased; the one certificate may be for any number of shares. For example, the certificate of Illustration 15–2 is for 50 shares. Large corporations commonly use preprinted 100-share

Stock certificates and the transfer of stock

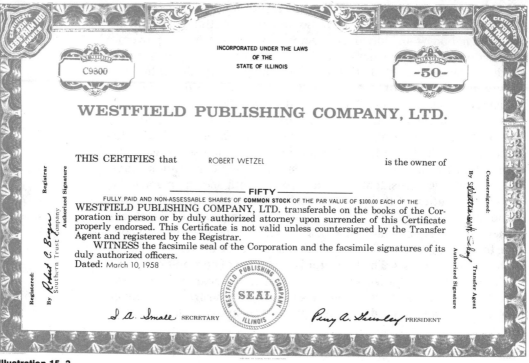

Illustration 15–2

denomination certificates in addition to blank certificates that may be made out for any number of shares.

An owner of stock may transfer at will either part or all the shares represented by a stock certificate. To do so he completes the endorsement on the reverse side of the certificate and sends the certificate to the corporation secretary in a small corporation or to the corporation's transfer agent in a large one. The old certificate is canceled and retained, and a new certificate is issued to the new stockholder. If only a part of the shares represented by the original certificate are sold, a new certificate is also issued to the seller for the number of shares he retained.

Stock certificate book

When it is organized, a corporation must have a supply of stock certificates printed. In a small corporation the certificates often have stubs attached, and the certificates and stubs are bound in a Stock Certificate Book in the manner of a checkbook. As each stock certificate is issued, the name of its owner, the number of shares, and the date of issuance are entered on a blank certificate, and the certificate is signed by the proper corporation officials. At the same time, the name and address of the stock owner, the number of shares, and the date are entered on the certificate stub. The certificate is then removed and delivered to its owner.

When the stock is returned for transfer, the old certificate is marked canceled, attached to its stub in the Stock Certificate Book, and one or more new certificates are issued in its place. Consequently, as a result of these procedures, the Stock Certificate Book of a small corporation contains a current record of the shares owned by each stockholder.

If a small corporation issues more than one kind or class of stock, it uses separate stock certificate books as well as separate stock accounts for each.

Transfer agent and registrar

A large corporation, one whose stock is listed on a major stock exchange, must have a registrar and a transfer agent who are assigned the responsibilities of transferring the corporation's stock, keeping its stockholder records, and preparing the official lists of stockholders for stockholders' meetings and for payment of dividends. Usually registrars and transfer agents are large banks or trust companies.

When the owner of stock in a corporation having a registrar and a transfer agent wishes to transfer his stock to a new owner, he completes the endorsement on the back of his certificate and, usually through a stockbroker, sends the certificate to the transfer agent. The transfer agent cancels the old certificate and issues one or more new certificates which he sends to the registrar. The registrar enters the transfer in the stockholder records and sends the new certificate or certificates to the proper owners.

A corporation's accounting differs from that of an equal-size single proprietorship or partnership only for transactions directly affecting its stockholder equity accounts. Here a difference results because a distinction is always made in corporation accounting between invested capital and capital from earnings retained in the business.

Corporation accounting

No such distinction is made in a single proprietorship or partnership where an owner's investment and changes in his equity resulting from gains and losses are recorded in the same account, the owner's Capital account. However, in a corporation the distinction is made and two kinds of owner equity accounts, (1) *contributed capital accounts* and (2) *retained earnings accounts,* are used in preserving the distinction. The contributed capital accounts, such as the Common Stock account, show amounts invested in or contributed to the corporation by stockholders or others. The retained earnings accounts show earnings retained in the business. The distinction between contributed capital and retained earnings is necessary because in most states a corporation cannot pay a legal dividend unless it has retained earnings.

To demonstrate the use of separate accounts for contributed capital and retained earnings as found in corporation accounting and to contrast their use with the single capital account in a sole proprietorship, assume that on January 5, 1978, a single proprietorship and a corporation having five stockholders were formed. Assume further that $25,000

Corporation owner equity accounts illustrated

was invested in each. In the sole proprietorship the owner, John Ohm, invested the entire amount; and in the corporation five stockholders each bought 500 shares of its $10 par value common stock at $10 per share. Without dates and explanations, general journal entries to record the investments are:

Single Proprietorship		Corporation	
Cash 25,000		Cash 25,000	
John Ohm, Capital	25,000	Common Stock.....	25,000

And after the entries were posted, the owner equity accounts of the two concerns appeared as follows:

Single Proprietorship
John Ohm, Capital

Date	Dr.	Cr.	Bal.
Jan. 5, '78		25,000	25,000

Corporation
Common Stock

Date	Dr.	Cr.	Bal.
Jan. 5, '78		25,000	25,000

To continue the illustration, in a single proprietorship when the Income Summary account is closed, the amount of net income or loss is transferred from the Income Summary account to the owner's Capital account. In a corporation this differs; in a corporation the net income or loss is carried to the Retained Earnings account. For example, if in the two concerns under discussion, each earned $8,000 during the first year and retained the earnings for use in carrying on their operations, after the Income Summary accounts were closed, the owner equity of each would have appeared in its accounts as follows:

Single Proprietorship
John Ohm, Capital

Date	Dr.	Cr.	Bal.
Jan. 5, '78		25,000	25,000
Dec. 31, '78		8,000	33,000

Corporation
Common Stock

Date	Dr.	Cr.	Bal.
Jan. 5, '78		25,000	25,000

Retained Earnings

Date	Dr.	Cr.	Bal.
Dec. 31, '78		8,000	8,000

And the owner equity of each would have appeared on its balance sheet as follows:

Single Proprietorship		Corporation	
Owner Equity		*Stockholders' Equity*	
John Ohm, capital, January 1		Common stock, $10 par	
1978.....................................	$25,000	value, authorized and	
Add net income......................	8,000	issued 2,500 shares	$25,000
John Ohm, Capital, December		Retained earnings...................	8,000
31, 1978.............................	$33,000	Stockholders' Equity...............	$33,000

To continue the illustration, assume that the concerns each lost $11,000 during their second year. If there were no withdrawals in the single proprietorship or additional investments in either concern, the owner equity accounts of each would have appeared at the end of the second year as follows:

Single Proprietorship
John Ohm, Capital

Date	Dr.	Cr.	Bal.
Jan. 5, '78		25,000	25,000
Dec. 31, '78		8,000	33,000
Dec. 31, '79	11,000		22,000

Corporation
Common Stock

Date	Dr.	Cr.	Bal.
Jan. 5, '78		25,000	25,000

Retained Earnings

Date	Dr.	Cr.	Bal.
Dec. 31, '78		8,000	8,000
Dec. 31, '79	11,000		3,000

Observe that the Retained Earnings account of the corporation has a $3,000 debit balance. A corporation is said to have a *deficit* when it has a debit balance in its Retained Earnings account, as in this illustration. A deficit is in effect a negative amount of retained earnings, and in most states a corporation with a deficit cannot pay a legal dividend.

At the end of the second year the owner equity sections on the balance sheets of the two concerns would have appeared as follows:

Single Proprietorship
Owner Equity

John Ohm, capital, January
   1, 1979 .... $33,000
Deduct: Net loss.................... (11,000)
John Ohm, Capital,
December 31, 1979 .... $22,000

Corporation
Stockholders' Equity

Common stock, $10 par
   value, 2,500 shares
   authorized and issued......... $25,000
Deduct: Deficit .... (3,000)
Stockholders' Equity.............. $22,000

During their second year both the corporation and the proprietorship suffered losses, which in each case reduced the equities of their owners to $22,000. Notice in the illustration just given how the $22,000 equity in the corporation is shown by listing the amount of stock and deducting therefrom the $3,000 deficit.

When a corporation is organized, it is authorized in its charter to **Authorization** issue a certain amount of stock. The stock may be of one kind, common **of stock** stock, or both common and preferred stock may be authorized. (Preferred stock is discussed later in this chapter.) However, regardless of whether one or two kinds of stock are authorized, the corporation may issue no more of each than the amount authorized by its charter.

Often a corporation will secure an authorization to issue more stock than it plans to sell at the time of its organization. This enables it to expand at any time in its future through the sale of the additional stock, and without the need of applying to the state for the right to issue more. For example, a corporation needing $300,000 to begin its operations may secure the right to issue $500,000 of stock, but then issue only $300,000, keeping the remainder until a future date when it may wish to sell the stock and expand without applying to the state for the right to issue more stock.

Selling stock for cash

When stock is sold for cash and immediately issued, an entry in general journal form like the following is commonly used to record the sale and issuance:

June	5	Cash..	300,000.00	
		Common Stock..		300,000.00
		Sold and issued 3,000 shares of $100 par value common stock.		

After authorized stock has been sold and issued, it is a common practice to show on the balance sheet both the amount of stock authorized and the amount issued as follows:

Stockholders' Equity
Common stock, $100 par value, 5,000 shares authorized,
   3,000 shares issued... $300,000

Exchanging stock for assets other than cash

Corporations often accept assets other than cash in exchange for their stock. When they do so, the transaction is recorded in somewhat the following manner:

Apr.	3	Machinery	10,000.00	
		Buildings	25,000.00	
		Land...	5,000.00	
		Common Stock...		40,000.00
		Exchanged 400 shares of common stock for machinery, buildings, and land.		

Or another example: A corporation may give shares of its stock to its promoters in exchange for their services in getting the corporation organized. In such a case the corporation receives the intangible asset of being organized in exchange for its stock, and the transaction is recorded as follows:

Apr.	5	Organization Costs..	5,000.00	
		Common Stock...		5,000.00
		Gave the promoters shares of common stock in exchange for their services in getting the corporation organized.		

When a corporation accepts assets other than cash for its stock, the assets are properly recorded at their fair values.

Par value and minimum legal capital

Par value is an arbitrary value a corporation places on a share of its stock at the time it seeks authorization of the stock. Normally a corporation may choose a par value of any amount for its stock; but par values of $100, $50, $25, $10, $5, and $1 are common. Early corporation laws required all stocks to have a par value; but today, all states permit the issuance of stock having no par value.

When a corporation issues par value stock, the par value is printed on each certificate and is used in accounting for the stock. Also, in many states when a corporation issues par value stock, it establishes for itself a *minimum legal capital* equal to the par value of the issued stock. For example, if a corporation issues 1,000 shares of $100 par value stock, it establishes for itself a minimum legal capital of $100,000.

Laws establishing minimum legal capital normally require stockholders in a corporation to invest assets equal in value to minimum legal capital or be liable to the corporation's creditors for the deficiency. In other words, these laws require stockholders to give a corporation par value for its stock or be liable for the deficiency. In addition, when corporation laws set minimum legal capital requirements, they normally also make illegal any payments to stockholders for dividends or their equivalent when these payments reduce stockholder equity below minimum legal capital.

Corporation laws governing minimum legal capital were written in an effort to protect corporation creditors. The authors of these laws reasoned somewhat as follows: A corporation's creditors may look only to the assets of the corporation for satisfaction of their claims. Consequently, when a corporation is organized, its stockholders should provide it with a fund of assets equal to its minimum legal capital. Thereafter, this fund of assets should remain with the corporation and should not be returned to the stockholders in any form until all creditor claims are paid.

Although par value helps establish minimum legal capital and is used in accounting for par value stock, it does not establish a stock's worth nor the price at which a corporation must issue the stock. If purchasers are willing to pay more than par, a corporation may sell and issue its stock at a price above par. Likewise, in some states, if purchasers will not pay par, a corporation may issue its stock at a price below par.

Stock premiums and discounts

Premiums

When a corporation sells and issues stock at a price above the stock's par value, the stock is said to be issued at a premium. For example, if a corporation sells and issues its $10 par value common stock at $12 per share, the stock is sold at a $2 per share premium. Although a premium is an amount in excess of par paid by purchasers of newly issued stock, it is not considered a profit to the issuing corporation. Rather a premium is part of the investment of stockholders who pay more than par for their stock.

In accounting for stock sold at a premium, the premium is recorded separately from the par value of the stock to which it applies. For example, if a corporation sells and issues 10,000 shares of its $10 par value common stock for cash at $12 per share, the sale is recorded as follows:

Dec.	1	Cash...	120,000.00	
		Premium on Common Stock...............................		20,000.00
		Common Stock...		100,000.00
		Sold and issued 10,000 shares of $10 par value		
		common stock at $12 per share.		

When stock is issued in exchange for assets other than cash and the fair value of the assets exceeds the par value of the stock, a premium is recorded. If fair value for the assets cannot be determined within reasonable limits, a price established by recent sales of the stock may be used in recording the exchange. This too may require that a premium be recorded.

When a balance sheet is prepared, stock premium is added to the par value of the stock to which it applies, as in Illustration 15–3.

Stockholders' Equity

Common stock, $10 par value, 25,000 shares authorized,		
20,000 shares issued	$200,000	
Add premium on common stock	30,000	
Total contributed capital		$230,000
Retained earnings..		82,400
Total Stockholders' Equity..		$312,400

Illustration 15–3

Discounts

Stock issued at a price below par is said to be issued at a discount. For example, if a corporation sells and issues its $100 par value stock at $85 per share, the stock is issued at a $15 per share discount. The discount is not considered a loss to the issuing corporation, rather the corporation's stockholders are investing less than minimum legal capital. For this reason, many states prohibit the issuance of stock at a discount. Furthermore, in those states where such stock may be issued at a discount, purchasers of the stock usually become contingently liable to the corporation's creditors for the amount of the discount. Consequently, most investors will not buy such stock.

Since issuing stock at a discount is often illegal, and where legal a discount liability attaches to such shares, and since a corporation is free to establish the par value of its shares at any amount, a discussion of stock discounts is of little practical importance. However, if a corporation issues stock at a discount, the discount is debited to a discount account and is subtracted on the balance sheet from the par value of the stock to which it applies.

At one time all stocks were required to have a par value; but today **No-par** all jurisdictions permit the issuance of so-called no-par stocks or stocks **stock** without par value. The primary advantages claimed for no-par stock are:

1. Since no-par stock does not have a par value, it may be issued at any price without a discount liability attaching.
2. Printing a par value, say $100, on a stock certificate may cause a person lacking in knowledge to believe a share of the stock to be worth $100, when it actually may be worthless. Therefore, eliminating the par value figures helps force such a person to examine the factors that give a stock value, which are earnings, dividends, and future prospects.
3. The use of no-par shares may result in more realistic values being placed on noncash assets acquired in exchange for stock. When par value stock is issued, the law in many instances says the stock may not be issued for less than par value. However, the law can easily be circumvented by issuing the stock in exchange for property other than cash and placing an inflated value on the property, a value equal to the par value of the stock. The use of no-par stock makes such a subterfuge unnecessary and results in more realistic values being placed on assets taken in exchange for stock.

When no-par-value stock is issued, the issuance may be recorded in one of two ways. The choice depends upon the laws of the state of incorporation and the wishes of the board of directors. Some state laws require that a corporation must credit the entire proceeds from the sale of no-par stock to a no-par stock account. In other states, when no-par stock is issued, the board may choose to place a *stated value* on the stock. When a stated value is placed on no-par stock and the stock is sold for more than stated value, the no-par stock account is credited for stated value and the remainder is credited to a contributed capital account called, for instance, "Contributed Capital in Excess of Stated Value of No-Par Stock." To illustrate the two methods of recording no-par stock, assume that a corporation sells and issues 1,000 shares of its authorized no-par common stock at $42 per share.

If the corporation is organized in a state in which the entire amount received from the sale of no-par stock must be credited to a no-par stock account, it will record the sale as follows:

Sept.	20	Cash...	42,000.00	
		No-Par Common Stock..		42,000.00
		Sold and issued 1,000 shares of no-par common stock at $42 per share.		

If the corporation is organized in a state in which the directors may place a stated value on no-par stock, accounting for its sale is similar to accounting for par value stock. For example, if the directors place a stated value of $25 per share on the foregoing stock, its sale and issuance are recorded as follows:

Sept.	20	Cash...	42,000.00	
		No-Par Common Stock..		25,000.00
		Contributed Capital in Excess of Stated Value, No-Par Common Stock..............................		17,000.00
		Sold at $42 per share 1,000 shares of no-par stock having a $25 per share stated value.		

From the entries it is apparent that when a stated value is placed on no-par stock, the accounting treatment for such stock is similar to that for par value stock. However, a sharp distinction should be made between a par value and a stated value; they are not synonymous. A par value is more formal than a stated value. A par value is established by a corporation at the time of its organization. It appears in the corporation's charter and normally can be changed only by a vote of the stockholders and approval of the state. A stated value is more flexible. The directors of a corporation establish a stock's stated value by resolution. Normally, at any time, they may also change it by passing an additional resolution.

As to minimum legal capital requirements for corporations issuing no-par stock, state laws vary. Most states require that the entire amount received by a corporation from the sale of its no-par stock be considered minimum legal capital and as such be made unavailable for dividend payments. A few states permit a corporation issuing no-par stock to establish its minimum legal capital at the stock's stated value and to pay out as "dividends" any amount above stated value received from the sale of such stock.

A dividend is a distribution made to its stockholders by a corporation. Dividends are declared or voted by the board of directors, and courts have generally held that the board is final judge of when, if at all, a dividend should be paid. Dividends may be distributed in cash, other assets, or in a corporation's own stock. Cash dividends are the most common, and are normally stated in terms of so many dollars or cents per share of stock. For example, a corporation may declare a dividend of $1 per share on its outstanding common stock. If it does so, an owner of 100 shares will receive $100.

Since a corporation's stockholders change, a dividend is normally declared on one date to be paid on a future date to the *stockholders of record* (stockholders according to the corporation's records) of a specified third date. For example, a board of directors may declare a dividend on December 28, to be paid on January 31 to the stockholders of record on January 20. Of the three dates involved, December 28 is called the *date of declaration,* January 20 is the *date of record,* and January 31 is the *date of payment.* Declaring a dividend on one date to be paid on a future date gives new purchasers of the stock an opportunity to have their ownership recorded in time to receive the dividend.

A stockholder has no right to a dividend until it is declared by the board of directors. However, as soon as a cash dividend is declared, it becomes a liability of the corporation, normally a current liability, and must be paid. Furthermore, the stockholders have the right to sue and force payment of a cash dividend once it is declared. Since dividends are normally declared on one date to be paid on a future date, two entries are used to record the declaration and payment of each dividend. The first entry, which is made at the time of the declaration, reduces the stockholders' equity and records the liability for the dividend; and the second records its payment. The two entries appear as follows:

Cash dividends and retained earnings

Dec.	28	Retained Earnings..	25,000.00	
		Common Dividend Payable		25,000.00
		To record the declaration of a $1 per share dividend on the 25,000 shares of outstanding common stock.		
Jan.	31	Common Dividend Payable	25,000.00	
		Cash..		25,000.00
		To record payment of the dividend declared on December 28.		

Since a corporation is a legal entity, its earnings belong to the corporation. The stockholders own the corporation, but they have no legal right to its earnings until the board declares a dividend; and the board is the final judge of when such a dividend should be declared. In deciding upon a dividend, the board normally considers both its

Dividend policy

legality and the wisdom of its declaration. Although the answers vary from state to state, generally a legal dividend may be declared if a corporation has retained earnings against which the dividend may be charged. (State laws governing the payment of dividends normally make directors personally liable for repayment to the corporation of a dividend declared and paid in violation of the laws. A director who votes against such a dividend is not held liable; consequently, directors must be careful not to vote for an illegal dividend.)

Some states permit the payment of a "dividend" from amounts received as stock premiums, but others do not. Nevertheless, and regardless of legality, accountants are opposed to calling such a distribution a "dividend," because it is obviously a return of invested capital and should be labeled clearly as such. Calling it a "dividend" might lead an uninformed person to believe the payment was from earnings.

As to the wisdom of a dividend, the directors must decide if the corporation can spare the cash needed for its payment, and when cash is available, if the cash cannot be used to better advantage in expanding the corporation's operations for greater profits in the future. Many large corporations follow the policy of paying out in dividends around 60% of earnings and retaining the balance to finance expansion and growth.

Rights of stock-holders

If a corporation issues only one kind of stock, the stock is known as *common stock*. When individuals buy such stock, they acquire all the specific rights granted by the corporation's charter to its common stockholders; and they also acquire the general rights granted stockholders by the laws of the state in which the corporation is organized. The laws vary, but in general all common stockholders have the following rights:

1. The right to vote in the stockholders' meetings.
2. The right to sell or otherwise dispose of their stock.
3. The right of first opportunity to purchase any additional shares of common stock issued by the corporation. (This is called the common stockholders' *preemptive right*. It gives a common stockholder the opportunity to protect his interest in the corporation. For example, if a stockholder owns one fourth of a corporation's common stock, he has first opportunity to buy one fourth of any new common stock issued. This enables him to maintain his one-fourth interest.)
4. The right to share pro rata with other common stockholders in any dividends declared.
5. The right to share in any assets remaining after creditors are paid if the corporation is liquidated.

Preferred stock

A corporation may issue more than one kind or class of stock. If two classes are issued, one is generally known as common stock and the other as *preferred stock*. Preferred stock is so called because of the preferences granted its owners. These commonly include a preference as to payment of dividends, and may include a preference in the distribution of assets in a liquidation.

A preference as to dividends does not give an absolute right to dividends. Rather if dividends are declared, it gives the preferred stockholders the right to receive their preferred dividend before the common stockholders are paid a dividend. In other words, if dividends are declared, a dividend must be paid the preferred stockholders before a dividend may be paid to the common stockholders. However, if the directors are of the opinion that no dividends should be paid, then neither the preferred nor the common stockholders receive a dividend.

Dividends on the majority of preferred stocks are limited to a fixed maximum amount. For example, a share of $100 par value, 6%, nonparticipating preferred stock has a preference each year to a dividend equal to 6% of its par value, or $6; but the dividend is limited to that amount.

Although dividends on the majority of preferred stocks are limited in amount, dividends on a corporation's common stock are unlimited, except by the earning power of the corporation and the judgment of its board of directors.

While dividends on most preferred stocks are limited to a fixed basic percentage or amount, some preferred stocks have the right under certain circumstances to dividends in excess of a fixed basic percentage or amount. Such preferred stocks are called *participating preferred stocks*. Participating preferred stocks may be fully participating, or their participation may be limited to a fixed amount, depending in each case on the exact terms set forth in the corporation's charter. For example, if a corporation issues fully participating, 6%, $100 par value, preferred stock and $50 par value common stock, the owners of the preferred stock have a preference to a 6% or $6 per share dividend each year. Then, each year, after the common stockholders have received a 6% or $3 per share dividend, the preferred stockholders have a right to participate with the common stockholders in any additional dividends declared. The participation is usually on the basis of the same additional percent-on-par-value-per-share dividend to each kind of stock. For instance, if in this case the common stockholders are paid an additional 2% or $1 per share dividend, the preferred stockholders should receive an additional 2% or $2 per share dividend.

Often when preferred stock is participating, participation is limited. For example, a $100 par value, 5%, preferred stock may be issued with the right to participate in dividends to 10% of its par value. Such a stock has a preference to dividends of 5% each year. It also has a right after the common stockholders receive a 5% dividend to participate in additional dividends until it has received 10%, or $10, per share. Its participation rights end at this point.

In addition to being participating or nonparticipating, preferred stocks are either *cumulative* or *noncumulative.* A cumulative preferred stock is one on which any undeclared dividends accumulate each year until paid. A noncumulative preferred stock is one on which the right to receive dividends is forfeited in any year in which dividends are not declared.

The accumulation of dividends on cumulative preferred stocks does not guarantee their payment. Dividends cannot be guaranteed because earnings from which they are paid cannot be guaranteed. However, when a corporation issues cumulative preferred stock, it does agree to pay its cumulative preferred stockholders both their current dividends and any unpaid back dividends, called *dividends in arrears,* before it pays a dividend to its common stockholders.

In addition to the preferences it receives, preferred stock carries with it all the rights of common stock, unless such rights are specifically denied in the corporation charter. Commonly, preferred stock is denied the right to vote in the stockholders' meetings.

Preferred dividends in arrears on the balance sheet date

A liability for a dividend does not come into existence until the dividend is declared by the board of directors; and unlike interest, dividends do not accrue. Consequently, if on the dividend date a corporation's board fails to declare a dividend on its cumulative preferred stock, the dividend in arrears is not a liability and does not appear on the balance sheet as such. However, if there are preferred dividends in arrears, the *full-disclosure principle* requires that this information appear on the balance sheet, and normally such information is given in a balance sheet footnote. For example, if three years' dividends have been missed, such a footnote might read, "Dividends for the current and two past years are in arrears on the preferred stock." When a balance sheet does not carry such a footnote, a balance sheet reader has the right to assume that all current and back dividends on the preferred stock have been paid.

Why preferred stock is issued

Two common reasons why preferred stock is issued can best be shown by means of an example. Suppose that three persons with a total of $100,000 to invest wish to organize a corporation requiring $200,000 capital. If they sell and issue $200,000 of common stock, they will have to share control with other stockholders. However, if they sell and issue $100,000 of common stock to themselves and sell to outsiders $100,000 of 8%, cumulative preferred stock having no voting rights, they can retain control of the corporation for themselves.

Also, suppose the three promoters expect their new corporation to earn an annual after-tax return of $24,000. If they sell and issue $200,-000 of common stock, this will mean a 12% return; but if they sell and issue $100,000 of each kind of stock, retaining the common for themselves, they can increase their own return to 16%, as follows:

Net after-tax income	$24,000
Preferred dividends at 8%	8,000
Balance to common stockholders (equal to 16% on their $100,000 investment)	$16,000

This is an example of what is known as securing a *leverage* on an investment. The common stockholders secure a leverage, or greater return, on their investment because the dividends on the preferred stock are less than the amount that can be earned through the use of the preferred stockholders' money.

In the example the preferred stock carries a cumulative preference as to dividends. The exact preferences granted in this and every other case always depend on what must be granted to sell the stock. As a rule, nothing is granted beyond what is necessary.

Several values apply to stock. For instance, a stock may have a par value, a book value, a market value, and a redemption value.

Stock values

Par value

Par value is the arbitrary value established for a share of stock in the charter of its issuing corporation and is printed on the face of each stock certificate. Par value does not establish worth, and its main significance is to establish the minimum amount of legal capital.

Book value

The book value of a share of stock measures the equity of the owner of one share of the stock in the assets of its issuing corporation. If a corporation has only one kind of stock, common stock, and all of its authorized shares are outstanding, the book value of all the shares is equal to the sum of the corporation's contributed and retained capital, and the book value of one of the shares is equal to the sum of the contributed and retained capital divided by the number of shares outstanding. For example, consider a corporation that has the following contributed and retained capital:

Common stock, $25 par value, 1,000 shares authorized and issued	$25,000
Retained earnings	6,100
Total Stockholders' Equity	$31,100

The book value of one share of the corporation's common stock is $31,100 divided by 1,000 shares, or $31.10 per share.

When a corporation issues both common and preferred stock and the book value of each is to be determined, it is first necessary to allocate total stockholders' equity between the two classes of stock. Then the equity allocated to the preferred stock is divided by the preferred shares involved and the equity allocated to the common stock is divided by the common shares involved to determine the book value of each.

The allocation of total stockholders' equity between the two classes of stock may be simple or complex, depending upon the liquidation rights granted the preferred stockholders. Preferred stockholders are often given a preference in liquidation to the return of the par value of their shares plus any dividends in arrears. For example, assume a corporation has the following capitalization:

Preferred stock, $100 par value, 7% cumulative and nonparticipating, 1,000 shares authorized and outstanding	$100,000
Common stock, $10 par value, 20,000 shares authorized and outstanding	200,000
Retained earnings	40,000
Total Stockholders' Equity	$340,000

If in this case the preferred stockholders are granted a preference in a liquidation to the par value of their shares plus dividends in arrears and there are no dividends in arrears, the total stockholders' equity is divided as follows:

Total stockholders' equity	$340,000
Less equity allocated to preferred stockholders:	
Par value of outstanding preferred shares	100,000
Equity of common stockholders	$240,000

And the book value of each is:

Preferred stock: $100,000 ÷ 1,000 shares = $100 per share
Common stock: $240,000 ÷ 20,000 shares = $12 per share

When there is a deficit or dividends in arrears, the allocation procedure is the same but the results differ. For example, assume there are two years' dividends in arrears on the preferred stock of a corporation having the following stockholders' equity:

Preferred stock, $100 par value, 7½% cumulative and nonparticipating, 1,000 shares authorized and outstanding	$100,000
Common stock, $10 par value, 50,000 shares authorized and outstanding	500,000
Deficit	(25,000)
Total Stockholders' Equity	$575,000

If in this case the preferred stockholders upon liquidation have a preference to the par value of their shares plus dividends in arrears, total stockholders' equity is allocated as follows:

Total stockholders' equity...		$575,000
Less equity allocated to preferred stockholders:		
Par value of outstanding preferred shares.......................	$100,000	
Dividends in arrears..	15,000	115,000
Equity of common stockholders...		$460,000

And the book value per share is:

> Preferred stock: $115,000 ÷ 1,000 shares = $115 per share
> Common stock: $460,000 ÷ 50,000 shares = $9.20 per share

Corporations in their annual reports to their shareholders often point out the increase that has occurred in the book value of the corporation's shares during a year or other period of time. Book value is also of significance in many contracts. For example, a stockholder may enter into a contract to sell his shares at their book value at some future date. However, book value should not be confused with *liquidation value,* because if a corporation is liquidated, its assets will probably sell at prices quite different from the amounts at which they are carried on the books. Also, book value generally has little bearing upon the market value of stock; and dividends, earning capacity, and future prospects are usually of much more importance. For instance a common stock having a $11 book value may sell for $25 per share if its earnings, dividends, and prospects are good; but it may sell for $5 per share if these factors are unfavorable.

Market value

The market value of a share of stock is the price at which a share can be bought or sold. Market values are influenced by earnings, dividends, future prospects, book value, and general market conditions.

Redemption value

Redemption values apply to preferred stocks. Often corporations issuing preferred stock reserve the right to redeem the stock by paying the preferred stockholders the par value of their stock plus a premium. The amount a corporation agrees to pay to redeem a share of its preferred stock is called the "redemption value" of the stock. Normally, a corporation reserves the right to either redeem or permit the stock to remain outstanding, as it chooses.

Glossary

Book value of a share of stock. The equity represented by one share of stock in the issuing corporation's net assets.

Common stock. Stock of a corporation that has only one class of stock; if there is more than one class, the class that has no preferences relative to the corporation's other classes of stock.

Cumulative preferred stock. Preferred stock on which any undeclared dividends accumulate each year until paid.

Date of declaration. The date on which a corporation's board of directors officially declares a dividend.

Date of payment. The date on which a dividend is actually paid to stockholders.

Date of record. The date on which the stockholders of record are determined for the purpose of deciding who will receive a declared dividend.

Discount on stock. The difference between the par value of stock and the amount below par value contributed by stockholders.

Dividend. A distribution made by a corporation to its stockholders of cash, other assets, or additional shares of the corporation's own stock.

Dividends in arrears. Unpaid back dividends on preferred stock which must be paid before dividends are paid to common stockholders.

Minimum legal capital. An amount, frequently equal to the par value of issued stock, that stockholders must invest in a corporation or be contingently liable to its creditors.

Noncumulative preferred stock. A stock for which the right to receive dividends is forfeited in any year in which dividends are not declared.

No-par stock. A class of stock having no par value.

Organization costs. Cost of bringing a corporation into existence, such as legal fees, promoters' fees, and amounts paid the state to secure a charter.

Participating preferred stock. Preferred stock that has the right to share in dividends above the fixed basic amount or percentage which is preferred.

Par value. An arbitrary value placed on a share of stock at the time the corporation seeks authorization of the stock.

Preemptive right. The right of a common stockholder to have the first opportunity to purchase additional shares of common stock issued by the corporation.

Preferred stock. Stock other than common stock the owners of which are granted certain preferences such as a preference to payment of dividends or in the distribution of assets in a liquidation.

Premium on stock. The amount of capital contributed by stockholders above the stock's par value.

Proxy. A legal document which gives an agent of a stockholder the right to vote the stockholder's shares.

Redemption value of stock. The amount a corporation must pay for the return of a share of preferred stock previously issued by the corporation.

Stated value of no-par stock. An amount, established by a corporation's board of directors, that is credited to the no-par stock account at the time the stock is issued.

Stockholders of record. The persons and/or organizations who are shown in a corporation's records to be the stockholders of the corporation.

---

1. List (*a*) the advantages and (*b*) disadvantages of the corporation form of business organization.

Class
exercises

2. A corporation is said to be a separate legal entity. What is meant by this?
3. What is a proxy?
4. What are organization costs? List several.
5. What are the duties and responsibilities of a corporation's registrar and transfer agent?
6. Why is a corporation whose stock is sold on a stock exchange required to have a registrar and transfer agent? Why is such a corporation required to have both a registrar and a transfer agent?
7. List the rights of common stockholders.
8. What is the preemptive right of common stockholders?
9. Laws place no limit on the amounts partners may withdraw from a partnership. On the other hand, laws regulating corporations place definite limits on the amounts corporation owners may withdraw from a corporation in dividends. Why is there a difference?
10. What is a stock premium? What is a stock discount?
11. Differentiate between discount on stock and discount on a note given to a bank in order to borrow money.
12. Does a corporation earn a profit by selling its stock at a premium? Does it incur a loss by selling its stock at a discount?
13. Why do corporation laws make purchasers of stock at a discount contingently liable for the discount? To whom are such purchasers contingently liable?
14. What is the main advantage of no-par stock?
15. What two kinds of proprietary accounts are used in corporation accounting? Why are the two kinds used?
16. In corporation accounting, what is a deficit?
17. What are the meanings of the following when applied to preferred stock: (*a*) preferred, (*b*) participating, (*c*) nonparticipating, (*d*) cumulative, and (*e*) noncumulative?
18. What are the meanings of the following terms when applied to stock: (*a*) par value, (*b*) book value, (*c*) market value, and (*d*) redemption value?

Exercise 15–1

A corporation sold and issued 1,000 shares of its no-par common stock for $31,500 on February 14. (*a*) Give the entry to record the sale under the assumption the board of directors did not place a stated value on the stock. (*b*) Give the entry to record the sale under the assumption the board placed a $25 per share stated value on the stock.

Exercise 15–2

A corporation has 15,000 shares of $10 par value common stock outstanding. Last year the corporation earned $47,000, after taxes; and on January 16 of this year its board of directors voted a $1 per share dividend on the stock, payable on February 8 to the January 31 stockholders of record. Give the entries to (*a*) close the corporation's Income Summary account at the end of last year and to record (*b*) the dividend declaration and (*c*) its payment. (*d*) Name and give the three dates involved in the dividend declaration and payment.

Exercise 15–3

A corporation has outstanding 2,000 shares of $100 par value, 8% cumulative and nonparticipating preferred stock and 9,000 shares of $25 par value common stock; and during the first four years in its life it paid out the following amounts in dividends: first year, nothing; second year, $19,000; third year, $40,000; and fourth year, $25,000. Determine the total dividends paid to each class of stockholders each year.

Exercise 15–4

Determine the total dividends paid each class of stockholders of the previous exercise under the assumption that rather than being cumulative and nonparticipating, the preferred stock is noncumulative and nonparticipating.

Exercise 15–5

A corporation has outstanding 4,000 shares of $100 par value, 9% cumulative and fully participating preferred stock and 30,000 shares of $10 par value common stock. It has regularly paid all dividends on the preferred stock. This year the board of directors voted to pay out a total of $77,000 in dividends to the two classes of stockholders. Determine the percent on par to be paid each class of stockholders and the dividend per share to be paid each class.

Exercise 15–6

The stockholders' equity section from a corporation's balance sheet appeared as follows:

Stockholders' Equity

Preferred stock, 10% cumulative and nonparticipating,
    $15 par value, 8,000 shares issued and outstanding.................. $120,000
Common stock, $6 par value, 40,000 shares issued and outstanding... 240,000
Retained earnings 72,000

      Total Stockholders' Equity... $432,000

Required:

1. Determine the book value per share of the preferred stock and of the common stock under the assumption there are no dividends in arrears on the preferred stock.
2. Determine the book value per share for each kind of stock under the assumption that two years' dividends are in arrears on the preferred stock.

Problem 15–1   **Problems**

Part 1. Adams, McAlister, and Meeker are contemplating starting a new business. Adams and Meeker will contribute $30,000 each, and McAlister will contribute $20,000.

Required:

1. Prepare the journal entries to record the investments assuming (*a*) the business is organized as a partnership and (*b*) the business is organized as a corporation with $100 par common stock. Adams and Meeker receive 300 shares each, and McAlister receives 200 shares.
2. Prepare the journal entries to close the Income Summary account for both the partnership and corporate forms of business if during the first year the business earns $16,000. Under the partnership, the partners share profits in the ratio of their original capital contributions.
3. Prepare the entries to record the distribution of $12,000 cash to the owners. Under the partnership, the cash is allocated between the partners in the ratio of their capital contributions. Under the corporation, the dividend is declared and paid on the same day.

Part 2. Prepare the required journal entries for each of the following cases:

Case A. Longhorn, Inc., issues 100,000 shares of $10 par value common stock in return for land with a fair value of $1,200,000.

Case B. Longhorn, Inc., issues 100,000 shares of no-par common stock in return for land with a fair value of $1,200,000.

Case C. Same situation as Case B except the board of directors has chosen $10 as the stated value of the common stock.

Problem 15–2

Yukon Company received a charter granting the right to issue 200,000 shares of $1 par value common stock and 10,000 shares of 8%, cumulative and nonparticipating, $50 par preferred stock. It then completed these transactions:

197A
Feb. 19 Issued 45,000 shares of common stock at par for cash.
     22 Gave the corporation's promoters 30,000 shares of common stock for their services in getting the corporation organized. The directors valued the services at $50,000.
Mar. 30 Exchanged 100,000 shares of common stock for the following assets at fair market values: land, $25,000; buildings, $100,000; and machinery, $125,000.

Dec. 31   Closed the Income Summary account. A $25,000 loss was incurred.
197B

Jan. 12   Issued 1,000 shares of preferred stock at par.

Dec. 31   Closed the Income Summary account. A $69,000 net income was earned.

197C

Jan.   5   The board of directors declared an 8% dividend to preferred shares and $0.10 per share to outstanding common shares, payable on January 25 to the January 12 stockholders of record.

Jan. 25   Paid the previously declared dividends.

Required:

1. Prepare general journal entries to record the transactions.
2. Prepare the stockholders' equity section of the corporation's December 31, 197A, balance sheet.
3. Prepare a second stockholders' equity section as of the close of business on January 25, 197C.

Problem 15–3

Greenbriar Company has outstanding 10,000 shares of $10 par value, 7%, preferred stock and 20,000 shares of $10 par value common stock. During a seven-year period the company paid out the following amounts in dividends: 197A, nothing; 197B, $24,000; 197C, nothing; 197D, $31,000; 197E, $18,000; 197F, $30,000; and 197G, $36,000.

Required:

1. Prepare three schedules with columnar headings as follows:

Year	Amount Distributed in Dividends	Total to Preferred	Balance Due Preferred	Total to Common	Dividend per Share Preferred	Dividend per Share Common

2. Complete a schedule under each of the following assumptions, showing for each year the total dollars paid the preferred stockholders, balance due the preferred stockholders, and so on. There were no dividends in arrears for the years prior to 197A.

    a.   The preferred stock is noncumulative and nonparticipating.
    b.   The preferred stock is cumulative and nonparticipating.
    c.   The preferred stock is cumulative and fully participating.

Problem 15–4

Part 1.   Kite Corporation's common stock is selling on a stock exchange today at $7.25 per share, and a just-published balance sheet shows the stockholders' equity in the corporation as follows:

Shareholders' Equity

Preferred stock, 7% cumulative and nonparticipating, $10 par value, 10,000 shares authorized and outstanding	$100,000
Common stock, $5 par value, 50,000 shares authorized and outstanding	250,000
Retained earnings	84,000
Total Shareholders' Equity	$434,000

Required:

Answer these questions: (1) What is the market value of the corporation's common stock? (2) What are the par values of its (*a*) preferred stock and (*b*) common stock? (3) If there are no dividends in arrears, what are the book values of the (*a*) preferred stock and (*b*) common stock? (4) If two years' dividends are in arrears on the preferred stock, what are the book values of the (*a*) preferred stock and (*b*) common stock? (Assume the preferred stock carries the right to the return of par value plus dividends in arrears in a liquidation.)

Part 2. The stockholders' equity sections from three corporation balance sheets follow:

1. Stockholders' Equity:

Cumulative and nonparticipating, $100 par value, 6% preferred stock, authorized and issued 1,000 shares	$100,000
Common stock, $25 par value, 10,000 shares authorized and issued	250,000
Retained earnings	64,000
Total Stockholders' Equity	$414,000

2. Stockholders' Equity:

Preferred stock, $100 par value, 7% cumulative and nonparticipating, 500 shares authorized and issued	$ 50,000*
Common stock, $100 par value, 500 shares authorized and issued	50,000
Retained earnings	6,000
Total Stockholders' Equity	$106,000

* The current year's dividend is unpaid on the preferred stock.

3. Stockholders' Equity:

Cumulative and nonparticipating, $10 par value, 7% preferred stock, 100,000 shares authorized and issued	$1,000,000*
Common stock, $25 par value, 100,000 shares authorized and issued	2,500,000
Total contributed capital	$3,500,000
Deficit	(540,000)
Total Stockholders' Equity	$2,960,000

* Three years' dividends are in arrears on the preferred stock.

Required:

Prepare a schedule showing the book values per share of the preferred and common stock of each corporation under the assumption the preferred stock carries the right to the return of par value plus dividends in arrears in a liquidation.

Problem 15-5

The members of Bahia Corporation's board of directors own all 10,000 outstanding shares of the company's $10 par value common stock. The company needs additional capital for expansion purposes which its owners are unable to supply. Consequently, they are planning to issue at par 1,500 shares of $100 par value, 7% cumulative and nonparticipating, preferred stock to outsiders to gain the needed capital; and they have asked you to prepare a report showing the return to the two classes of stockholders from the following amounts of annual before-tax earnings:

a. $15,000 or a 6% before-tax return on the $250,000 invested.
b. $30,000 or a 12% before-tax return on the $250,000 invested.
c. $40,000 or a 16% before-tax return on the $250,000 invested.
d. $50,000 or a 20% before-tax return on the $250,000 invested.
e. $60,000 or a 24% before-tax return on the $250,000 invested.

Required:

1. Prepare a form with columnar headings as follows:

Before-Tax Earnings	Federal Income Taxes	After-Tax Earnings		Preferred Dividends		Common Dividends	
		Amount	Percent Return on Investment	Total Paid to Preferred	Percent Return on Investment	Total Paid to Common	Percent Return on Investment

2. Enter the amounts of before-tax profit in the first column.
3. Calculate the federal income tax applicable to each level of earnings and enter in the second column. (Corporations are required at this writing to pay a 20% federal income tax on the first $25,000 of their earnings, a 22% tax on the next $25,000 of earnings, and 48% on any earnings over $50,000. Thus, the federal income tax on $60,000 of earnings is 20% of the first $25,000 plus 22% on the second $25,000 plus 48% on the $10,000 which is in excess of $50,000, or a total of $15,300.)
4. Complete the information of the form under the assumption that all after-tax earnings are paid out in dividends.
5. Explain why in this problem at the pretax levels of $30,000 and above, the after-tax rate of return to the common stockholders is greater than the after-tax rate earned by the corporation as a whole.

Alternate problems

Problem 15-1A

Part 1. Prepare the required journal entries to record the following events, assuming (a) the business is organized as a partnership, and (b) the business is organized as a corporation with $100 par common stock.

1. Dilley, Hanes, and Woods organize a new business, with Dilley and Hanes investing $50,000 each, and Woods investing $25,000. Under the corporation form, Dilley and Hanes receive 500 shares each, and Woods receives 250 shares.

2. At the close of the first year's operations, the Income Summary account has a credit balance of $15,000 and must be closed to the appropriate owner equity accounts. Under the partnership alternative, the partners share profits in the ratio of their original capital contributions.
3. Cash in the amount of $10,000 is distributed to the owners. Under the partnership, the cash is allocated between the partners in the ratio of their capital account balances. Under the corporation, the dividend is declared and paid on the same day.

Part 2. Prepare the required journal entries for each of the following cases:

Case A. Lawton Corporation issues 60,000 shares of $20 par value common stock in return for land with a fair value of $1,500,000.

Case B. Lawton Corporation issues 60,000 shares of no-par common stock in return for land with a fair value of $1,500,000.

Case C. Same situation as Case B except the board of directors has chosen $15 as the stated value of the common stock.

Problem 15–2A

Guthrie Corporation received a charter granting it the right to issue 100,000 shares of $5 par value common stock and 20,000 shares of 8%, cumulative and nonparticipating, $50 par preferred stock. It then completed these transactions:

197A
Mar. 2 Issued 16,000 shares of common stock at par for cash.
  30 Issued 2,000 shares of common stock to the corporation's attorneys for their services in getting the corporation organized. The directors placed a $10,000 value on the services.
Apr. 7 Exchanged 60,000 shares of common stock for the following assets at their fair market values: land, $50,000; buildings, $200,000; and machinery, $125,000.
Dec. 31 Closed the Income Summary account. There was a $15,000 loss.
197B
Jan. 15 Issued 1,500 shares of preferred stock at $60 per share.
Dec. 31 Closed the Income Summary account. There was a $86,000 net income.
197C
Jan. 3 The board of directors declared an 8% dividend to preferred shares and $0.15 per share to outstanding common shares, payable on February 5 to the January 15 stockholders of record.
Feb. 5 Paid the dividend previously declared.

Required:

1. Prepare general journal entries to record the transactions.
2. Prepare the stockholders' equity section of the corporation's December 31, 197A, balance sheet.
3. Prepare a second stockholders' equity section as of the close of business on February 5, 197C.

Problem 15–3A

Gateway Company has outstanding 10,000 shares of $10 par value, 9% preferred stock and 30,000 shares of $10 par value common stock. During a seven-year period it paid out the following amounts in dividends: 197A, $5,000; 197B, nothing; 197C, $7,000; 197D, $24,000; 197E, $24,000; 197F, $30,000; and 197G, $54,000. There were no dividends in arrears for the years before 197A.

Required:

1. Prepare three schedules with columnar headings as follows:

Year	Amount Distributed in Dividends	Total to Preferred	Balance Due Preferred	Total to Common	Dividend per Share Preferred	Dividend per Share Common

2. Complete a schedule under each of the following assumptions, showing for each year the total dollars paid the preferred stockholders, balance due the preferred stockholders, and so forth.
   a. The preferred stock is noncumulative and nonparticipating.
   b. The preferred stock is cumulative and nonparticipating.
   c. The preferred stock is cumulative and participating to 10% of its par value.

Problem 15–4A

Part 1. A corporation has had outstanding since it was organized 100,000 shares of $5 par value common stock and 1,000 shares of $100 par value, 7% preferred stock. The current year's and two prior years' dividends have not been paid on the preferred stock. However, the company has recently prospered, and its board of directors wants to know how much cash will be required for dividends if a $0.50 per share dividend is paid on the common stock.

Required:

Prepare a schedule for the board of directors showing the amounts of cash required for dividends to each class of stockholders under each of the following assumptions:

a. The preferred stock is noncumulative and nonparticipating.
b. The preferred stock is cumulative and nonparticipating.
c. The preferred stock is cumulative and fully participating.
d. The preferred stock is cumulative and participating to 9%.

Part 2. The stockholder equity section from a corporation's balance sheet appeared as follows:

Stockholders' Equity

Seven percent cumulative and nonparticipating, $50 par value, preferred stock, authorized and issued 2,000 shares..................	$100,000
Common stock, $50 par value, 5,000 shares authorized and issued...	250,000
Retained earnings	15,000
Total Stockholders' Equity...	$365,000

Required:

Prepare a schedule showing the book values per share of the preferred and common stocks under each of the following assumptions:

1. There are no dividends in arrears on the preferred stock.
2. One year's dividends are in arrears on the preferred stock.
3. Three years' dividends are in arrears on the preferred stock.

Problem 15–5A

All of the 8,000 outstanding shares of Sumrall Corporation's common stock ($25 par) are owned by six individuals. The company needs $300,000 additional capital for expansion purposes, which its owners are unable to supply. Consequently, they are considering the issuance of 3,000 shares of $100 par value, 7% cumulative and nonparticipating, preferred stock to gain the additional capital, and they have asked you to prepare a report showing the return to the two classes of stockholders from the following amounts of annual before-tax earnings:

a. $30,000 or a 6% before-tax return on the $500,000 invested.
b. $60,000 or a 12% before-tax return on the $500,000 invested.
c. $80,000 or a 16% before-tax return on the $500,000 invested.
d. $100,000 or a 20% before-tax return on the $500,000 invested.
e. $120,000 or a 24% before-tax return on the $500,000 invested.

Required:

1. Prepare a form with columnar headings as follows:

Before-Tax Earnings	Federal Income Taxes	After-Tax Earnings		Preferred Dividends		Common Dividends	
		Amount	Percent Return on In-vestment	Total Paid to Preferred	Percent Return on In-vestment	Total Paid to Common	Percent Return on In-vestment

2. Enter the amounts of before-tax profit in the first column.
3. Calculate the federal income tax applicable to each level of earnings and enter in the second column. (Corporations are required to pay at this writing a 20% federal income tax on the first $25,000 of their earnings, a 22% tax on the next $25,000 of earnings, and 48% on any earnings over $50,000. Thus, the federal income tax on $60,000 of earnings is 20% of the first $25,000 plus 22% on the second $25,000 plus 48% on the $10,000 which is in excess of $50,000, or a total of $15,300.)
4. Complete the information of the form under the assumption that all after-tax earnings are paid out in dividends.
5. Explain why in this problem at the $60,000 and above pretax levels, the after-tax rate of return to the common stockholders is greater than the after-tax rate earned by the corporation as a whole.
6. Prepare a calculation to account for the difference between the rate of return to the corporation as a whole at the $100,000 level and the return to the common stockholders at this level.

Decision problem 15–1, Frank Slaton

Frank Slaton plans to withdraw from a professional partnership and reinvest the $20,000 cash he will receive upon his withdrawal. Two securities have been suggested for his consideration: Woodville Corporation common stock and the preferred stock issued by Victoria Company. The companies are similar; both manufacture and sell competing products and both have been in business about the same length of time—four years in the case of Woodville Corporation and five years for Victoria Company. Also, the two companies have about the same amounts of stockholder equity, as the following equity sections from their latest balance sheets show:

WOODVILLE CORPORATION

Common stock, $5 par value, 200,000 shares authorized, 100,000 shares issued	$500,000
Retained earnings	100,000
Total Stockholders' Equity	$600,000

VICTORIA COMPANY

Preferred stock, $100 par value, 7% cumulative and non-participating, 1,000 shares authorized and issued	$100,000*
Common stock, $10 par value, 50,000 shares authorized and issued	500,000
Retained earnings	15,000
Total Stockholders' Equity	$615,000

* The current and two prior years' dividends are in arrears on the preferred stock.

Woodville Corporation did not pay a dividend on its common stock during its first year's operations; however, since then, for the past three years, it has paid a $0.25 per share annual dividend on the stock. The stock is currently selling for $7.80 per share. The preferred stock of Victoria Company, on the other hand, is selling for $91 per share. However, Mr. Slaton favors this stock as an investment. He feels the stock is a real bargain since it is not only selling below its par value but also $30 below book value, and as he says, "Since it is a preferred stock, the dividends are guaranteed." Too, he feels the common stock of Woodville Corporation, selling at 30% above book value and 56% above par value while paying only a $0.25 per share dividend, is overpriced.

a. Is the preferred stock of Victoria Company selling at a price $30 below its book value, and is the common stock of Woodville Corporation selling at a price 30% above book value and 56% above par value?

b. From an analysis of the stockholder equity sections, express your opinion of the two stocks as investments and give the reasons for your opinion.

Decision problem 15–2, Marsha and Nancy

Marsha Clarkson accepted a job ten years ago with a cosmetics firm specializing in the production and sale of facial lotions. After seven years, she quit the company to enter the cosmetics business on her own. Now after three years, although she has little else, she has managed to build a small debt-free single proprietorship organization in which she has a $75,000 equity.

Recently Marsha worked out some rather revolutionary ideas in the area of marketing that she believes will enable her to make dramatic inroads into the market positions of her competitors. However, to carry out her ideas she needs $60,000 additional capital, which she does not have. She finally approached Nancy Gordon, an old friend who has recently inherited several hundred thousand dollars, for a loan. After listening to her friend's ideas, Nancy pointed out that to really exploit the new ideas, much more than $60,000 would be needed.

After discussing the venture for some time, Nancy suggested that instead of a loan she should go into business with Marsha. After more discussion, Marsha accepted her friend's offer, and it was agreed that although Nancy could devote little or no time to the business, she would furnish all its needed capital. It was further agreed that Marsha would devote full time to managing the business; but no agreement was reached as to whether the venture would be organized as a partnership or a corporation.

Write a report to Marsha and Nancy discussing the factors they should consider in choosing between a partnership form of organization for their business or a corporate form.

James Awn and William Allen have operated a stereophonic supply firm, Stereophonic Supply, for a number of years as partners sharing losses and gains in a 3 to 2 ratio. They have entered into an agreement with Francis Lawton to reorganize their firm into a corporation and have just received a charter granting their corporation, Stereo Suppliers, Inc., the right to issue 20,000 shares of $5 par value common stock. On the date of the reoganization, April 9 of the current year, a trial balance of the partnership ledger appears as follows:

Decision problem 15–3, Stereo Suppliers, Inc.

STEREOPHONIC SUPPLY
Trial Balance, April 9, 19—

Cash	$ 5,100	
Accounts receivable	9,300	
Allowance for doubtful accounts		$ 350
Merchandise inventory	42,250	
Store equipment	9,800	
Accumulated depreciation, store equipment		2,100
Buildings	50,000	
Accumulated depreciation, buildings		10,000
Land	12,500	
Accounts payable		5,550
Mortgage payable		35,000
James Awn, capital		45,250
William Allen, capital		30,700
Totals	$128,950	$128,950

The agreement between the partners and Lawton carries these provisions:

1. The partnership assets are to be revalued as follows:
   a. The $300 account receivable of Disco Shop is known to be uncollectible and is to be written off as a bad debt, after which (b) the allow-

ance for doubtful accounts is to be increased to 5% of the remaining accounts receivable.

c. The merchandise inventory is to be written down to $38,000 to allow for damaged and shopworn goods.

d. Insufficient depreciation has been taken on the store equipment; consequently, its book value is to be decreased to $6,500 by increasing the balance of the accumulated depreciation account.

e. The building is to be written up to its replacement cost, $65,000, and the balance of the accumulated depreciation account is to be increased to show the building to be one-fifth depreciated.

2. After the partnership assets are revalued, the assets and liabilities are to be transferred to the corporation in exchange for its stock, with each partner accepting stock at par value for his equity in the partnership.

3. Francis Lawton is to buy any remaining stock for cash at par value.

After reaching the agreement outlined, the three men hired you as accountant for the new corporation. Your first task is to determine the amount of stock each person should receive, and to prepare entries on the corporation's books to record the issuance of stock in exchange for the partnership assets and liabilities and the issuance of stock to Lawton for cash. In addition prepare a balance sheet for the corporation as it should appear after all its stock is issued.

After studying Chapter 16, you should be able to:

- ■ Prepare the entries to record the transactions involving stock subscriptions and explain the effects of subscribed stock on assets and stockholders' equity.

- ■ Record purchases and sales of treasury stock, and describe its effect on stockholders' equity.

- ■ Record stock dividends, and describe their effects on stockholders' equity.

- ■ Explain the financial statement effects of converting bonds to common stock.

- ■ Describe the reasons for appropriations of retained earnings and the required disclosure of such appropriations in the financial statements.

- ■ Describe the nature of extraordinary items, accounting changes, and prior period adjustments, and the appropriate reporting procedures for each.

- ■ Define or explain the words and phrases listed in the chapter Glossary.

chapter 16

Corporations: Additional stock transactions, income, and retained earnings

The organization and management of a corporation and several transactions involving the issuance of stock were discussed in the previous chapter. In this chapter consideration is given to some additional transactions involving stock, as well as the matter of accounting for corporate income and retained earnings.

Often corporations sell their stock for cash and immediately issue the stock. Often, too, especially in organizing a new corporation, stock is sold by means of *subscriptions*. When stock is sold by means of subscriptions, a person wishing to become a stockholder signs a subscription blank or a subscription list for a certain number of shares and agrees to pay for the stock either in one amount or in installments. When the subscription is accepted by the corporation, it becomes a contract; and the corporation acquires an asset, the right to receive payment from the subscriber. At the same time, the corporation's stockholder equity is increased by the amount the subscriber agrees to pay. If the subscription is for common stock, the increase in assets is recorded in an account called *Subscriptions Receivable, Common Stock;* and the increase in stockholder equity is recorded in an account called *Common Stock Subscribed,* and perhaps also in a premium account. The subscriptions receivable and stock subscribed accounts are of a temporary nature. The subscriptions receivable will be turned into cash when the subscribers pay for their stock. Likewise, when

Stock sub-scriptions

payment is completed, the subscribed stock will be issued and will become outstanding stock. Normally subscribed stock is not issued until paid for.

If a corporation receives subscriptions to both common and preferred stock, separate subscriptions receivable and stock subscribed accounts must be kept for each. If the number of subscribers becomes large, the subscriptions receivable accounts often become controlling accounts that control subsidiary Subscribers' Ledgers having an account with each subscriber. The controlling account for each class of subscriptions receivable and its Subscribers' Ledger operate in the same manner as, for example, the Accounts Receivable controlling account and the Accounts Receivable Ledger discussed in a previous chapter.

When unpaid subscriptions exist on the balance sheet date, the intention is normally to collect the amounts within a relatively short period. Therefore, unpaid subscriptions normally appear on the balance sheet as current assets under the title "Subscriptions Receivable, Common Stock" or "Subscriptions Receivable, Preferred Stock."

Sale of stock through subscriptions, with collections in installments

Corporations selling stock through subscriptions may collect the subscriptions in one amount or in installments. To illustrate the sale of stock through subscriptions collected in installments, assume that on June 6, 19—, Northgate Corporation accepted subscriptions to 5,000 shares of its $10 par value common stock at $12 per share, under subscription contracts calling for a 10% down payment to accompany the subscriptions and the balance in two equal installments due in 30 and 60 days.

The subscriptions were recorded with the following entry:

June	6	Subscriptions Receivable, Common Stock......................	60,000.00	
		Premium on Common Stock		10,000.00
		Common Stock Subscribed.................................		50,000.00
		Accepted subscriptions to 5,000 shares of $10 par value common stock at $12 per share.		

Notice that the subscriptions receivable account is debited at the time the subscription is accepted for the sum of the stock's par value and premium; this is the amount the subscribers agree to pay. Notice, too, that the stock subscribed account is credited for par value and that the premium is credited to a premium account at the time the subscriptions are accepted.

Receipt of the down payments and the two installment payments may be recorded with entries like these:

June	6	Cash...	6,000.00	
		Subscriptions Receivable, Common Stock.............		6,000.00
		Collected 10% down payments on the common stock subscribed.		
July	6	Cash...	27,000.00	
		Subscriptions Receivable, Common Stock.............		27,000.00
		Collected the first installment payments on the common stock subscribed.		
Aug.	5	Cash...	27,000.00	
		Subscriptions Receivable, Common Stock.............		27,000.00
		Collected the second installment payments on the common stock subscribed.		

In the series of entries, since the down payments accompanied the subscriptions, the entry to record the receipt of the subscriptions and the entry to record the down payments may be combined.

When stock is sold through subscriptions, the stock is not issued until the subscriptions are paid in full; and as soon as the subscriptions are paid, the stock is issued. The entry to record the issuance of the Northgate common stock appears as follows:

Aug.	5	Common Stock Subscribed.......................................	50,000.00	
		Common Stock..		50,000.00
		Issued 5,000 shares of common stock sold through subscriptions.		

Most subscriptions are collected in full, although not always. Sometimes a subscriber fails to pay; and when this happens, the subscription contract must be canceled. In such a case, if the subscriber has made a partial payment on his contract, the amount paid may be returned. Or, a smaller amount of stock than that subscribed, an amount equal to the partial payment, may be issued. Or, in some states the subscriber's partial payment may be kept by the corporation to compensate for any damages suffered.

In some states a subscriber to stock gains all the rights of a stockholder upon acceptance of his signed subscription contract by the corporation to whose stock he is subscribing. Also, acceptance of such contracts increase a corporation's assets and the equity of the subscribers in the corporation. Consequently, if a corporation prepares a balance sheet after accepting subscriptions to its stock but before the stock is issued, it shows both its issued stock and its subscribed stock on the balance sheet as follows:

Subscribed stock on the balance sheet

Common stock, $10 par value, 25,000 shares authorized,
   20,000 shares issued... $200,000
Unissued common stock subscribed, 5,000 shares.............. 50,000
     Total common stock issued and subscribed.............. $250,000
Add premium on common stock 40,000
   Amount contributed and subscribed by the common
     stockholders $290,000

Treasury stock

Corporations often reacquire shares of their own stock. Sometimes a corporation will purchase its own stock on the open market to be given to employees as a bonus or to be used in acquiring other corporations. Sometimes shares are bought in order to maintain a favorable market for the stock. Regardless, if a corporation reacquires shares of its own stock, such stock is known as *treasury stock*. Treasury stock is a corporation's own stock that has been issued and then reacquired either by purchase or gift. Notice that the stock must be the corporation's own stock; the acquisition of stock of another corporation does not create treasury stock. Furthermore, the stock must have been once issued and then reacquired; only stock issued and reacquired qualifies as treasury stock. The last point distinguishes treasury stock from unissued stock, and the distinction is important because stock once issued at par or above and then reacquired as treasury stock may be legally reissued at a discount without discount liability. Although treasury stock differs from unissued stock in that it may be sold at a discount without discount liability, in other respects it has the same status as unissued stock. Both are equity items rather than assets. Both are subtracted from authorized stock to determine outstanding stock when such things as book values are calculated. Neither receives cash dividends nor has a vote in the stockholders' meetings.

Purchase of treasury stock[1]

When a corporation purchases its own stock, it reduces in equal amounts both its assets and its stockholders' equity. To illustrate this, assume that on May 1 of the current year the condensed balance sheet of Curry Corporation appears as in Illustration 16–1.

If on May 1 Curry Corporation purchases 1,000 shares of its outstanding stock at $11.50 per share, the transaction is recorded as follows:

May	1	Treasury Stock, Common..	11,500.00	
		Cash..		11,500.00
		Purchased 1,000 shares of treasury stock at $11.50 per share.		

---

[1] There are several ways of accounting for treasury stock transactions. This text will discuss the so-called cost basis, which seems to be the most widely used, and it will leave a discussion of other methods to a more advanced text.

Curry Corporation
Balance Sheet, May 1, 19—

Assets		Capital	
Cash	$ 30,000	Common stock, $10 par	
Other assets	95,000	value, authorized and	
		issued 10,000 shares	$100,000
		Retained earnings	25,000
Total Assets	$125,000	Total Capital	$125,000

Illustration 16–1

The debit entry records a reduction in the equity of the stockholders; and the credit records a reduction in assets. Both are equal to the cost of the treasury stock. After the entry is posted, a new balance sheet will show the reductions as in Illustration 16–2.

Notice in the second balance sheet that the cost of the treasury stock appears in the stockholders' equity section as a deduction from common stock and retained earnings. In comparing the two balance sheets, notice that the treasury stock purchase reduces both assets and stockholders' equity by the $11,500 cost of the stock.

Notice also on the second balance sheet that the dollar amount of issued stock remains at $100,000 and is unchanged from the first balance sheet. The amount of *issued stock* is not changed by the purchase of treasury stock. However, the purchase does reduce *outstanding stock*. In Curry Corporation, the purchase reduced the outstanding stock from 10,000 to 9,000 shares.

There is a distinction between issued stock and outstanding stock. Issued stock may or may not be outstanding. Outstanding stock is stock that has been issued and is currently outstanding. Only outstanding stock is effective stock, receives cash dividends, and is given a vote in the meetings of stockholders.

Curry Corporation
Balance Sheet, May 1, 19—

Assets		Capital	
Cash	$ 18,500	Common stock, $10 par	
Other assets	95,000	value, authorized and	
		issued 10,000 shares of	
		which 1,000 are in the	
		treasury	$100,000
		Retained earnings of which	
		$11,500 is restricted by the	
		purchase of treasury	
		stock	25,000
		Total	$125,000
		Less cost of treasury stock	11,500
Total Assets	$113,500	Total Capital	$113,500

Illustration 16–2

Restricting retained earnings by the purchase of treasury stock

When a corporation purchases treasury stock, it transfers corporation assets to its stockholders and thereby reduces both its assets and its stockholders' equity. Consequently, most states place limitations upon treasury stock purchases similar to the limitations they place on dividends. These limitations usually provide that a corporation may purchase treasury stock only to the extent of retained earnings available for dividend charges, after which the retained earnings become restricted and legally unavailable for dividends. This means that (1) only a corporation with retained earnings available for dividends may purchase treasury stock, and (2) it may either purchase treasury stock to the extent of such earnings or it may use the earnings as a basis for dividends, but it may not do both. In other words, a corporation may not purchase treasury stock to the extent of its retained earnings available for dividend charges and then use the same retained earnings again as a basis for the declaration of dividends. Or again, it may not by the purchase of treasury stock transfer corporation assets to its stockholders to the extent of retained earnings available for dividends and then transfer more assets by means of cash dividends.

Notice in Illustration 16–2 how the restriction of retained earnings is shown on the balance sheet. Alternatively, it may be shown by means of a balance sheet footnote. Also, some corporations show the restriction in the accounts. To show such a restriction in the accounts, an entry is made transferring the restricted portion of retained earnings from the Retained Earnings account to an account called, for instance, Retained Earnings Restricted by the Purchase of Treasury Stock. If such an entry is made by Curry Corporation, it appears as follows:

May	1	Retained Earnings...	11,500.00	
		Retained Earnings Restricted by the Purchase of		
		Treasury Stock		11,500.00
		To record the restriction of retained earnings.		

When treasury stock is sold and retained earnings are no longer restricted because of its purchase, the restricted portion of retained earnings is returned to the Retained Earnings account.

Reissuance of treasury stock

When treasury stock is reissued, it may be reissued at cost, above cost, or below cost.

Reissuance at cost

When treasury stock is reissued at cost, the entry to record the transaction is the reverse of the one used to record its purchase. For example, assume that Curry Corporation sells at cost 100 of the 1,000 treasury shares, the purchase of which at $11.50 per share was previously illustrated. The entry to record the sale is:

May	27	Cash...	1,150.00	
		Treasury Stock, Common......................................		1,150.00
		Reissued 100 shares of treasury stock at its $11.50		
		per share cost price.		

Notice that the sale of the 100 shares at cost restores to the corporation the same amount of assets and stockholder equity taken away when these shares were purchased.

Reissuance at a price above cost

Although treasury stock may be sold at cost, it is commonly sold at a price either above or below cost. When sold above cost, the amount received in excess of cost is commonly credited to a contributed capital account called "Contributed Capital, Treasury Stock Transactions." For example, assume that Curry Corporation sells for $12 per share an additional 100 shares of the treasury stock purchased at $11.50. The entry to record the transaction appears as follows:

June	3	Cash...	1,200.00	
		Treasury Stock, Common......................................		1,150.00
		Contributed Capital, Treasury Stock Transactions ...		50.00
		Sold at $12 per share treasury stock that cost		
		$11.50 per share.		

Reissuance at a price below cost

When treasury stock is reissued at a price below cost, the entry to record the sale normally depends upon whether there is contributed capital from previous transactions in treasury stock. If a corporation has such contributed capital, a "loss" on the sale of treasury stock may be debited to the account of this capital. For example, assume that after having sold 100 of its 1,000 treasury shares at $11.50 and 100 at $12, Curry Corporation sells 100 shares at $11. The entry to record the transaction is:

July	7	Cash...	1,100.00	
		Contributed Capital, Treasury Stock Transactions	50.00	
		Treasury Stock, Common......................................		1,150.00
		Sold at $11 per share 100 shares of treasury stock		
		purchased at $11.50.		

If a corporation selling treasury stock below cost does not have sufficient contributed capital from previous treasury stock transactions to absorb the "loss," the "loss" in excess of contributed capital from previous treasury stock sales is normally debited to Retained Earnings. For example, if Curry Corporation sells its remaining 700 shares of treasury stock at $11 per share, the following entry is made to record the transaction:

July	10	Cash..	7,700.00	
		Retained Earnings..	350.00	
		Treasury Stock, Common......................................		8,050.00
		Sold treasury stock purchased at $11.50 per share for $11 per share.		

Retirement of stock

A corporation may purchase shares of its own stock which are not to be held as treasury stock but for immediate retirement, with the shares being permanently canceled upon receipt. Such action is permissible if the interests of creditors and other stockholders are not jeopardized.

When stock is purchased for retirement, all capital items related to the shares being retired are removed from the accounts; and if there is a "gain" on the transaction, it should be credited to contributed capital. On the other hand, a loss should be debited to Retained Earnings.

For example, assume a corporation originally issued its $10 par value common stock at $12 per share, with the premium being credited to Premium on Common Stock. If the corporation later purchased for retirement 1,000 shares of this stock at the price for which it was issued, the entry to record the retirement is:

Apr.	12	Common Stock...	10,000.00	
		Premium on Common Stock	2,000.00	
		Cash...		12,000.00
		Purchased and retired 1,000 shares of common stock at $12 per share.		

If on the other hand the corporation paid $11 per share instead of $12, the entry for the retirement is:

Apr.	12	Common Stock...	10,000.00	
		Premium on Common Stock	2,000.00	
		Cash...		11,000.00
		Contributed Capital from the Retirement of Common Stock...		1,000.00
		Purchased and retired 1,000 shares of common stock at $11 per share.		

Or if the corporation paid $15 per share, the entry for the purchase and retirement is:

Apr.	12	Common Stock..	10,000.00	
		Premium on Common Stock	2,000.00	
		Retained Earnings...	3,000.00	
		Cash..		15,000.00
		Purchased and retired 1,000 shares of common stock at $15 per share.		

Sometimes a corporation will receive a gift or a donation of an asset or assets. For example, as an inducement to locate a plant in a particular city, a corporation may receive a plant site as a gift. Such a donation increases both assets and stockholders' equity by the fair value of the contributed asset. The increase in stockholders' equity is contributed capital, capital contributed by others than the stockholders. **Donation of assets by outsiders**

For example, assume that as an inducement to locate a plant in Circle City, the Circle City Chamber of Commerce donated a plant site to a corporation. The corporation recorded the donation as follows:

Apr.	17	Land..	22,000.00	
		Contributed Capital from Donated Plant Site		22,000.00
		To record the donation of land by Circle City Chamber of Commerce.		

From the discussion thus far it is obvious that numerous accounts are required in recording contributed capital transactions. Actually a separate account is needed for each kind or source of contributed capital. Furthermore, in addition to separate accounts, each kind of contributed capital may be shown on the balance sheet as in Illustration 16–4 on page 545. **Contributed capital in the accounts and on the statements**

Retained earnings, as the name implies, is stockholders' equity that has arisen from retaining assets from earnings in the business. The retained earnings include earnings from normal operations as well as gains from such transactions as the sale of plant assets and investments. **Retained earnings and dividends**

Once retained earnings were commonly called *earned surplus;* but since the word surplus is subject to misinterpretation, the AICPA's Committee on Terminology recommended that its use be discontinued. As a result, the term surplus has almost disappeared from published balance sheets.

In most states a corporation must have retained earnings in order to pay a cash dividend. However, the payment of a cash dividend reduces in equal amounts both cash and stockholders' equity. Consequently, in order to pay a cash dividend, a corporation must have not only a credit balance in its Retained Earnings account but also cash with which to pay the dividend. If cash or assets that will shortly become cash are not available, a board may think it wise to forgo the declaration of a dividend, even though retained earnings exist. Often the directors of a corporation having a large amount of retained earnings will not declare a dividend because all current assets are needed in the operation of the business.

In considering the wisdom of a dividend, a board must recognize that earnings are a source of assets, and while some assets from earnings should probably be paid out in dividends, some should be retained for emergencies, for distribution as dividends in years in which earnings are not sufficient to pay normal dividends, and for use in expanding operations. The last reason is an important one. If a corporation is to expand and grow, it may sell additional stock to secure the assets needed in expansion; however, it may also expand by using assets acquired through earnings. Ford Motor Company is a good example of a company that has made use of the latter method. Less than $100,000 was originally invested in Ford Motor Company, and it has grown to its present size primarily from retaining in the business assets from earnings.

Contributed capital and dividends

Under the laws of some states, contributed capital may not be returned to stockholders as dividends. However, one reason for separate contributed capital accounts is that under the laws of some states, dividends may be debited or charged to certain contributed capital accounts. Seldom may dividends be charged against the par or stated value of the outstanding stock; however, the exact contributed capital accounts to which a corporation may charge dividends depend upon the laws of the state of its incorporation. For this reason it is usually wise for a board of directors to secure competent legal advice before voting to charge dividends to any contributed capital account.

Stock dividends

A stock dividend is a distribution by a corporation of shares of its own common stock to its common stockholders without any consideration being given in return therefor. Usually the distribution is prompted by a desire to give the stockholders some evidence of their interest in retained earnings without distributing cash or other corporation assets which the board of directors thinks it wise to retain in the business. A clear distinction should be made between a cash dividend and a stock dividend. A cash dividend reduces both assets and stockholders' equity. A stock dividend differs in that shares of the corporation's own stock rather than cash are distributed; and such a dividend has no effect on assets, total capital, or the amount of stockholders' equity.

A stock dividend has no effect on corporation assets, total capital, and the amount of stockholders' equity because such a dividend involves nothing more than a transfer of retained earnings to contributed capital. To illustrate this assume that Northwest Corporation has the following capital stock and retained earnings:

Capital Stock and Retained Earnings	
Common stock, $10 par value, authorized 15,000 shares, issued and outstanding 10,000 shares	$100,000
Premium on common stock	8,000
Total contributed capital	$108,000
Retained earnings	35,000
Total contributed capital and retained earnings	$143,000

Assume further that on December 28 the directors of Northwest Corporation declared a 10% or 1,000-share stock dividend distributable on January 20 to the January 15 stockholders of record.

If the fair market value of Northwest Corporation's stock on December 28 is $15 per share, the following entries may be made to record the dividend declaration and distribution:

Dec.	28	Retained Earnings	15,000.00	
		Common Stock Dividend Distributable		10,000.00
		Premium on Common Stock		5,000.00
		To record the declaration of a 1,000-share common stock dividend.		
Jan.	20	Common Stock Dividend Distributable	10,000.00	
		Common Stock		10,000.00
		To record the distribution of a 1,000-share common stock dividend.		

Note that the entries change $15,000 of the stockholders' equity from retained earnings to contributed capital, or as it is commonly said, $15,000 of retained earnings are *capitalized*. Note also that the retained earnings capitalized are equal to the fair market value of the 1,000 shares issued ($15 × 1,000 shares = $15,000).

As previously pointed out, a stock dividend does not distribute funds from retained earnings to the stockholders, nor does it affect in any way the corporation assets. Likewise, it has no effect on total capital and on the individual equities of the stockholders. To illustrate these last points, assume that Johnson owned 100 shares of Northwest Corporation's stock prior to the dividend. The corporation's total contributed and retained capital before the dividend and the book value of Johnson's 100 shares were as follows:

Common stock (10,000 shares) $100,000
Premium on common stock 8,000
Retained earnings 35,000
    Total contributed and retained capital $143,000

$143,000 ÷ 10,000 shares outstanding = $14.30 per share book value
$14.30 × 100 = $1,430 for the book value of Johnson's 100 shares

A 10% stock dividend gives a stockholder one new share for each 10 shares previously held. Consequently, Johnson received ten new shares; and after the dividend, the contributed and retained capital of the corporation and the book value of Johnson's holdings are as follows:

Common stock (11,000 shares) $110,000
Premium on common stock 13,000
Retained earnings 20,000
    Total contributed and retained capital $143,000

$143,000 ÷ 11,000 shares outstanding = $13 per share book value
$13 × 110 = $1,430 for the book value of Johnson's 110 shares

Before the stock dividend, Johnson owned 100/10,000 or 1/100 of the Northwest Corporation stock and his holdings had a $1,430 book value. After the dividend, he owned 110/11,000 or 1/100 of the corporation and his holdings still had a $1,430 book value. In other words, there was no effect on his equity other than that it was repackaged from 100 units into 110. Likewise, the only effect on corporation capital was a permanent transfer to contributed capital of $15,000 in retained earnings. Consequently, insofar as both the corporation and Johnson are concerned, there was no shift in equities or corporation assets.

Why stock dividends are distributed

If a stock dividend has no effect on corporation assets and stockholders' equities other than to repackage the equities into more units, why are such dividends declared and distributed? Insofar as a corporation is concerned, a stock dividend enables it to give its shareholders some evidence of their interest in retained earnings without the necessity of distributing corporation cash or other assets to them. Consequently, stock dividends are often declared by corporations that have used the funds from earnings in expanding and, as a result, do not feel they have sufficient cash with which to pay a cash dividend. Also, if a profitable corporation grows by retaining earnings, the price of its common stock also tends to grow. Eventually, the price of a share may become large enough to prevent some investors from considering purchase of the stock. Thus, corporations may declare stock dividends to keep the price of their shares from growing too large. For this reason, some corporations declare small stock dividends each year.

Many stockholders are interested in receiving a regular flow of cash dividends, and those who are so interested may benefit from stock dividends. Many companies pay a regular amount of cash dividends per share, and when a stock dividend is declared and issued, they may continue to pay the same amount of cash dividends per share. As a consequence, the total amount of cash paid out as dividends will increase. Thus, the receipt of a stock dividend may be followed by an increase in the total amount of cash dividends received by the stockholders.

Amount of retained earnings capitalized

In the entry on page 539, retained earnings equal to the fair market value of the stock to be distributed were capitalized in recording the stock dividend. This is consistent with the rule established by the AICPA's Committee on Accounting Procedure to the effect that small stock dividends (up to 25% of the previously outstanding shares) should be recorded by capitalizing retained earnings equal to the market value of the stock to be distributed. Because some stockholders may (incorrectly) believe that stock dividends involve a distribution of earnings, the committee concluded that the amount of retained earnings capitalized and made unavailable for future dividends should equal the market value of the shares distributed.[2]

A small stock dividend is likely to have only a small impact on the price of the stock. On the other hand, a large stock dividend normally has a pronounced impact, and for this reason is not apt to be perceived as a distribution of earnings. Consequently, in recording a large stock dividend (over 25%), the committee ruled that it is only necessary to capitalize retained earnings to the extent required by law. As a result, in most states a corporation may record a large stock dividend by debiting Retained Earnings and crediting the stock account for the par value of the shares issued.[3]

Stock dividends on the balance sheet

Since a stock dividend is "payable" in stock rather than in assets, it is not a liability to its issuing corporation. Therefore, if a balance sheet is prepared between the declaration and distribution dates of a stock dividend, the amount of the dividend distributable should appear in the contributed capital section. (See Illustration 16-4 on page 545.)

[2] Committee on Accounting Procedure, "Accounting Research Bulletin No. 43," *Accounting Research and Terminology Bulletins, Final Edition* (New York: AICPA, 1961), chap. 7, section B, pars. 10, 13.

[3] Ibid., chap. 7, section B, par. 11.

Stock splits

Sometimes, when a corporation's stock is selling at a high price, the corporation will call it in and issue two, three, four, five, or more new shares in the place of each old share previously outstanding. For example, a corporation having outstanding $100 par value stock selling for $375 a share may call in the old shares and issue to the stockholders two shares of $50 par, or four shares of $25 par, or ten shares of $10 par, or any number of shares of no-par stock in exchange for each $100 share formerly held. This is known as a *stock split* or a *stock split-up*, and its usual purpose is to cause a reduction in the market price of the stock and, consequently, to facilitate trading in the stock.

A stock split has no effect on total stockholders' equity, the equities of the individual stockholders, or on the balances of any of the contributed or retained capital accounts. Consequently, all that is required in recording a stock split is a memorandum entry in the stock account reciting the facts of the split. For example, such a memorandum might read, "Called in the outstanding $100 par value common stock and issued ten shares of $10 par value common stock for each old share previously outstanding." Also, there would be a change in the description of the stock on the balance sheet.

Converting bonds to stock

It was pointed out in Chapter 13 that to make a bond issue more attractive, bondholders may be given the right to exchange their bonds for a fixed number of shares of the issuing company's common stock. Such convertible bonds offer investors initial investment security, and if the issuing company prospers and its stock increases in price, an opportunity to share in the prosperity by converting their bonds to the more valuable stock. Conversion is always at the bondholders' option and therefore does not take place unless it is to their advantage.

When bonds are converted into stock, the conversion changes creditor equity into ownership equity. The generally accepted rule for measuring the contribution for the issued shares is that the carrying amount of the converted bonds becomes the book value of the capital contributed for the new shares. For example, assume that (1) a company has outstanding $1,000,000 of bonds upon which there is $8,000 unamortized discount; (2) the bonds are convertible at the rate of a $1,000 bond for 90 shares of the company's $10 par value common stock; and (3) $100,000 in bonds have been presented on their interest date for conversion. The entry to record the conversion is:

May	1	Bonds Payable..	100,000.00	
		Discount on Bonds Payable		800.00
		Common Stock...		90,000.00
		Premium on Common Stock		9,200.00
		To record the conversion of bonds.		

Note in this entry that the bonds' $99,200 carrying amount sets the accounting value for the capital contributed. Usually when bonds have a conversion privilege, it is not exercised until the stock's market value and normal dividend payments are sufficiently high to make the conversion profitable to the bondholders.

When a corporation expands by retaining assets from earnings, the earnings are invested in plant, equipment, merchandise, and so forth, and are not available for dividends. Some stockholders may not understand this, and upon seeing a large amount of retained earnings reported on the balance sheet, agitate for dividends that cannot be paid because the assets from earnings are invested in the business. Consequently, although the practice is not now common as it once was, some corporations earmark or appropriate retained earnings as a means of informing their stockholders that assets from earnings equal to the appropriations are unavailable for dividends. Retained earnings are appropriated by a resolution passed by the board of directors; and the appropriations are recorded in the accounts and may be reported on the balance sheet as in Illustration 16–3.

Stockholders' Equity		
Common stock, $1 par value, 5,000,000 shares authorized and issued..		$5,000,000
Retained earnings:		
Appropriated retained earnings:		
Appropriated for plant expansion........................... $200,000		
Appropriated for working capital............................ 250,000		
Appropriated for bonded indebtedness................... 75,000		
Total appropriated retained earnings................ $525,000		
Unappropriated retained earnings 350,000		
Total retained earnings		875,000
Total contributed and retained capital		$5,875,000

Illustration 16–3

Appropriated retained earnings are sometimes called "reserves of retained earnings" and may appear on the balance sheet under captions such as "Reserve for plant expansion," "Reserve for working capital," and "Reserve for bonded indebtedness." Such terminology, however, is not preferred.

Appropriations of retained earnings may be voluntarily made or they may be required by contract. Retained earnings appropriated for plant expansion or for working capital are examples of voluntary appropriations since they are made at the discretion of the board of directors. Also, since they are voluntary or discretionary, the board may at any time reverse its judgment and return these or any like appropriations to unappropriated retained earnings.

Illustration of a retained earnings appropriation

To illustrate an appropriation of retained earnings, assume the directors of Deeplake Corporation recognize that in five years their plant will need to be expanded by the construction of a $1,000,000 addition. To finance the expansion, the board discusses the possibility of waiting until the addition is needed and then securing the required funds through the sale of additional stock. They also discuss the possibility of financing the expansion through the annual retention for each of the next five years of $200,000 of assets from earnings. Income in excess of this amount is expected to be earned each year, and the directors decide this is the better plan.

In order each year to retain in the business $200,000 of assets from earnings, the directors recognize it is only necessary to refrain from paying out dividends equal to this amount. However, the board also recognizes that if earnings are retained, the Retained Earnings account and the amount reported on the balance sheet under the caption "Retained earnings" will grow each year and some stockholders may demand more dividends. Consequently, the board decides that in addition to retaining the assets from earnings, it will at the end of each of the succeeding five years vote an appropriation and transfer of $200,000 of retained earnings from the Retained Earnings account to the Retained Earnings Appropriated for Plant Expansion account.

If the board follows through on this plan and votes the yearly appropriations, the entry to record each appropriation is:

Dec.	28	Retained Earnings..	200,000.00	
		Retained Earnings Appropriated for Plant		
		Expansion...		200,000.00
		To record the appropriation of retained earnings.		

This entry reduces the balance of the Retained Earnings account but does not reduce total retained earnings. It merely changes a portion from free, unappropriated retained earnings to appropriated retained earnings.

It should be observed in this situation that the transfer of $200,000 each year from the Retained Earnings account to the Retained Earnings Appropriated for Plant Expansion account does not provide funds for the expansion. Earnings provide the funds; the appropriations do nothing more than inform the stockholders of the board's intention to retain in the business assets from earnings equal to the amount appropriated.

Disposing of an appropriation of retained earnings

The purpose for which an appropriation of retained earnings was made is at times accomplished or passes, and there is no longer a need for the appropriation. When this occurs, the appropriated retained earnings should be returned to the (unappropriated) Retained Earnings account. For example, when bonds mature and are paid and there is no longer a need for an appropriation of retained earnings for bonded indebtedness, the balance of the Retained Earnings Appropriated for Bonded Indebtedness account should be returned to the Retained Earnings account.

In this and previous chapters there have been a number of illustrations showing the balance sheet treatment of stockholder equity items. Rarely, if ever, will all the illustrated items appear on a single balance sheet. However, Illustration 16–4 shows a rather comprehensive stockholder equity section as an aid to the student in dealing with whatever equity items he is called upon to handle. **Comprehensive treatment of equity items**

In Illustration 16–4 the second item is "Capital contributed by preferred stockholders in excess of the par value of their shares, $4,000." This item resulted from preferred stock premiums. At the time the amounts originated they were probably credited to an account called "Premium on Preferred Stock." However, as in Illustration 16–4, it is common practice to show an item such as this on the balance sheet under a more descriptive caption than the name of the account in which it is recorded.

Stockholders' Equity

Preferred stock, $100 par value 7% cumulative and nonparticipating, 2,000 shares authorized, 1,000 shares issued and outstanding	$100,000	
Capital contributed by preferred stockholders in excess of the par value of their shares	4,000	
Total contributed by preferred stockholders		$104,000
Common stock, $10 par value, 50,000 shares authorized, 20,000 shares issued of which 1,000 are in the treasury	$200,000	
Common stock subscribed, 5,000 shares	50,000	
Common stock dividend distributable, 1,900 shares	19,000	
Total common stock issued and to be issued	$269,000	
Capital contributed by common stockholders in excess of the par value of their shares	46,000	
Total contributed and subscribed by common stockholders		315,000
Total capital contributed for shares		$419,000
Other contributed capital:		
Contributed capital from plant site donation	$ 40,000	
Contributed capital from treasury stock transactions	2,000	42,000
Total contributed capital		$461,000
Retained earnings:		
Appropriated for plant expansion	$ 50,000	
Restricted by the purchase of treasury stock	15,000	
Free and unappropriated	181,000	
Total retained earnings		246,000
Total contributed capital and retained earnings		$707,000
Less cost of treasury stock		(15,000)
Total Stockholders' Equity		$692,000

Illustration 16–4

Retained earnings statement

The financial statements prepared for a corporation at the end of each accounting period include a balance sheet, an income statement, a statement of changes in financial position (discussed in Chapter 18), and a statement of retained earnings. On the retained earnings statement are reported the changes in the corporation's retained earnings during the year. Illustration 16–5 shows the retained earnings statement of Westwood Corporation. It was prepared from information in the corporation's accounts which follow the statement.

Westwood Corporation
Statement of Retained Earnings
For Year Ended December 31, 1978

Unappropriated retained earnings:		
Unappropriated retained earnings, January 1, 1978............		$179,000
Additions:		
Net income...		64,400
Total		$243,400
Deductions and appropriations:		
Quarterly cash dividends..	$18,400	
Dividend in common stock..	19,000	
Retained earnings appropriated for plant expansion......	25,000	
Total deductions and appropriations....................		(62,400)
Unappropriated retained earnings, December 31, 1978.......		$181,000
Appropriated retained earnings:		
Appropriated for plant expansion, balance,		
January 1, 1978...	$25,000	
Appropriated during 1978...............................	25,000	
Appropriated for plant expansion, December 31, 1978........		50,000
Total Retained Earnings as of		
December 31, 1978...		$231,000

Illustration 16–5

Retained Earnings

Date	Explanations	Debit	Credit	Balance
Jan. 1, '78	Balance			179,000
Mar. 24, '78	Quarterly dividend	4,600		174,400
June 21, '78	Quarterly dividend	4,600		169,800
Sept. 27, '78	Quarterly dividend	4,600		165,200
Dec. 20, '78	Quarterly dividend	4,600		160,600
Dec. 20, '78	Stock dividend	19,000		141,600
Dec. 20, '78	Appropriation for plant expansion	25,000		116,600
Dec. 31, '78	Net income after taxes		64,400	181,000

Retained Earnings Appropriated for Plant Expansion

Date	Explanations	Debit	Credit	Balance
Dec. 22, '77			25,000	25,000
Dec. 20, '78			25,000	50,000

When the retained earnings statement of Illustration 16–5 is compared with the information shown in the corporation's Retained Earnings and Retained Earnings Appropriated for Plant Expansion accounts, it is apparent the statement is nothing more than a report of the changes recorded in the accounts.

An income statement more clearly displays the results of a company's operations if extraordinary gains and losses are segregated on the statement from the results of ordinary operations of the business, as in Illustration 16–6. *APB Opinion No. 30* requires this segregation and provides the criteria for distinguishing between extraordinary and ordi-

Extraordinary gains and losses

Dale Corporation
Income Statements for Years Ended December 31, 1978, and 1979

	1979	1978
Net sales	$8,500,000	$8,000,000
Cost of goods sold and expenses:		
Cost of goods sold	$6,050,000	$5,650,000
Selling, general, and administrative expenses	540,000	500,000
Interest expense	10,000	10,000
Other expenses	9,000	8,000
Income taxes	916,000	882,000
Total cost of goods sold and expenses	$7,525,000	$7,050,000
Income before extraordinary items and the cumulative effect of an accounting change	$ 975,000	$ 950,000
Extraordinary items:		
Gain on sale of unused land expropriated by the state for a highway interchange, net of $16,700 of applicable income taxes		50,000
Loss from earthquake damage, net of an applicable $22,000 reduction in income taxes	(25,000)	
Cumulative effect on prior years' income (to December 31, 1978) of changing to a different depreciation method	10,000	
Net Income	$ 960,000	$1,000,000
Earnings per common share:		
Income before extraordinary items and the cumulative effect of an accounting change	$1.95	$1.90
Extraordinary items, net of taxes	(0.05)	0.10
Cumulative effect on prior years' income (to December 31, 1978) of changing to a different depreciation method	0.02	
Net Income	$1.92	$2.00

Illustration 16–6

nary items. To qualify as an extraordinary gain or loss, an item must be both unusual in nature and infrequent of occurrence in the environment in which the business operates. Very few items meet both of these criteria. For example, none of the following generally qualify as being extraordinary:

a. Write-down or write-off of assets unless caused by a major casualty, an expropriation, or prohibition under a newly enacted law.
b. Gains or losses from exchange or translation of foreign currencies.

   c. Gains and losses on disposal of a segment of a business.

   d. Other gains and losses from sale or abandonment of property, plant, or equipment unless caused by a major casualty, an expropriation, or prohibition under a newly enacted law.

   e. Effects of a strike, including those against competitors and major suppliers.

   f. Adjustment of accruals on long-term contracts.[4]

The distinction between extraordinary and ordinary items must also be maintained in earnings per share calculations, as indicated in Illustration 16–6. Note that earnings per share statistics must be presented as part of the income statement.[5] The procedures used to calculate earnings per share are examined in a later chapter.

Accounting changes

Changes in accounting methods, such as a change in the method of inventory pricing, or a change in the method of depreciating assets acquired in previous periods, or a change in accounting for long-term construction contracts, can materially affect a company's reported income and financial position. Consequently, under the accounting *principle of consistency* it is held that a company should follow the same accounting methods period after period, but may change if the change is justified and adequate disclosure is made in the financial statements of the period of the change.

Adequate disclosure for an accounting change, such as a change in the depreciation method for assets acquired in previous periods, requires an identification of the assets involved, a description of the change, and the justification therefor in the notes accompanying the financial statements. Also, since a change means that the new method was used in calculating depreciation for the current period, the increase or decrease in the current period's income as a result of the change must be reported in the notes accompanying the statements. Furthermore, since the company's total income for the periods in which the assets were in use would have differed had the new method been in use, this difference, called the cumulative effect of the change, must be determined and reported on the face of the current income statement, as in Illustration 16–6. Finally, if statistics as to net income or earnings per share for prior periods are reported, the effects of the change on these statistics should be shown.[6]

Prior period adjustments

In establishing the treatment for extraordinary items and for ordinary or usual operating items, the APB recognized that certain items, which it called "prior period adjustments," are neither extraordinary items nor ordinary or usual items. The Board concluded that

---

   [4] APB, "Reporting the Results of Operations," *APB Opinion No. 30* (New York: AICPA, 1973), par. 23.

   [5] APB, "Earnings per Share," *APB Opinion No. 15* (New York: AICPA, 1969), pars. 12–13.

   [6] APB, "Accounting Changes," *APB Opinion No. 20* (New York: AICPA, 1971), pars. 18–30.

these prior period adjustments are limited to material adjustments which have all four of these characteristics:[7]

a. Are specifically identified with and directly related to the business activities of a particular prior period;
b. Are not attributable to economic events, including obsolescence, occurring subsequent to the date of the financial statements for such prior period;
c. Depend primarily on decisions or determinations by persons other than management or owners; and
d. Could not reasonably be estimated prior to such decisions or determinations.

Examples of prior period adjustments (provided they have all four characteristics) might be:

a. Nonrecurring adjustments or settlements of income taxes; and
b. Settlements of claims resulting from litigation.

The Board concluded that such prior period adjustments with any related income tax effect should be shown on the retained earnings statement as an adjustment of the opening balance of retained earnings, as in Illustration 16–7.

Smythe Company, Inc. Statement of Retained Earnings For Year Ended December 31, 1979	
Retained earnings, January 1, 1979	$89,000
Adjustments of prior years' income:	
Settlement of lawsuit arising from 1976 accident	(32,000)
Retained earnings, January 1, 1979, as restated	$57,000
Net income for the year	26,000
Total	$83,000
Dividends declared in 1979	(10,000)
Retained Earnings, December 31, 1979	$73,000

(handwritten notes in margin: 250,000 · 75,000 · net inc)

Illustration 16–7

Return again to the income statement of Illustration 16–6 and note that this is a *comparative single-step income statement*. It is a comparative statement because it shows the operating results of two periods in columns side by side. This is a desirable feature that makes it easy for a statement reader to compare the results of the two periods. It is also a single-step income statement because all normal costs and expenses are deducted on it in one step. The income statements illustrated in previous chapters have been multiple-step statements on which cost of goods sold was deducted in a first step, then operating

Comparative single-step income statement

---

[7] APB, "Reporting the Results of Operations," *APB Opinion No. 9* (New York: AICPA, 1969), par. 23.

expenses in a second step, and then income taxes. This treatment for costs and expenses is satisfactory, but the multiple deductions do imply a preferential order for their recovery, when actually there is no preferential order. Consequently, to avoid the implication of a preferential order for the recovery of costs and expenses, the single-step income statement is typically used in published reports. Such statements may show considerable detail, but generally when published for the use of stockholders and the public, they are condensed as in Illustration 16–6.

Accounting treatment for corporation income taxes

Of the three common types of business organizations, only the corporation is subject to paying federal income taxes. Single proprietorships and partnerships as business units are not required to pay federal income taxes and normally are not required to pay state income taxes. The income of single proprietorships and partnerships, whether distributed to the owners or not, is reported on the personal tax returns of the owners.

For a corporation, federal and state income taxes are an expense of doing business. Illustration 16–6 shows how income taxes are included in the income statement among the operating expenses; also, the income tax effects of extraordinary items are separately disclosed in the descriptions of those items. As a result, the extraordinary items are added or subtracted on a net-of-tax basis.

Federal and many state income tax laws require, in general, that corporations estimate the annual income tax liability and make installment payments on the liability during the year. For example, if the taxable income is expected to be earned uniformly throughout the year, the corporation must pay the estimated federal income tax liability in four equal installments which are due on the 15th day of the 4th month, the 6th month, the 9th month, and the 12th month. For example, assume that the Cary Corporation estimates that its federal income tax liability for the 1979 calendar year will be $40,000. The first installment payment will be made on April 15, 1979, and the entry to record the payment will be as follows:

Apr.	15	Federal Income Taxes Expense	10,000.00	
		Cash...		10,000.00
		To record federal income tax installment.		

Similar entries will be made on June 15, September 15, and December 15.

At the end of the year, the actual income tax liability is calculated and any remaining amount to be paid is generally due on the 15th day of the 3rd month after the end of the year. On the work sheet for a corporation, the remaining amount to be paid (or perhaps refunded) is entered as an adjustment in the Adjustment columns; and after the work sheet is completed an adjusting entry is used to record the additional liability. For example, assume that the Cary Corporation calculates its actual tax liability to be $42,000. The adjusting entry to record the $2,000 liability which remains after the installment payments of $40,000 is as follows:

Dec.	31	Federal Income Taxes Expense	2,000.00	
		Federal Income Taxes Payable		2,000.00
		To record remaining tax liability.		

Accounting change. A justified change in accounting methods or **Glossary** principles, the cumulative effect of which must be disclosed on the face of the current income statement.

Appropriated retained earnings. Retained earnings earmarked for a special use as a means of informing stockholders that assets from earnings equal to the appropriations are unavailable for dividends.

Common stock subscribed. Unissued common stock for which the corporation has a contract to issue.

Earned surplus. A synonym for retained earnings, no longer in use.

Extraordinary item. An income statement item that is both unusual in nature and infrequent in occurrence in the environment in which the business operates.

Prior period adjustment. A material adjustment that is reported in the retained earnings statement because it meets a strict set of specific requirements indicating that the item pertains to past periods rather than to the current or future periods.

Small stock dividend. A stock dividend up to 25% of a corporation's previously outstanding shares.

Stock dividend. A distribution by a corporation of shares of its own common stock to its common stockholders without any consideration being received in return therefor.

Stock split. The act of a corporation to call in its stock and to issue more than one new share in the place of each old share previously outstanding.

Stock subscription. An agreement by a person wishing to become a stockholder to buy a certain number of shares.

Treasury stock. Issued stock that has been reacquired by the issuing corporation.

Questions for class discussion

1. What are the balance sheet classifications of the accounts: (a) Subscriptions Receivable, Common Stock and (b) Common Stock Subscribed?
2. What is treasury stock? How is it like unissued stock? How does it differ from unissued stock? What is the legal significance of this difference?
3. General Plastics Corporation bought 1,000 shares of Capital Steel Corporation stock and turned it over to its treasurer for safekeeping. Is this treasury stock? Why or why not?
4. What is the effect of a treasury stock purchase in terms of assets and stockholders' equity? What is the effect on a corporation's assets and stockholders' equity of a treasury stock donation?
5. Distinguish between issued stock and outstanding stock.
6. Why do state laws place limitations on the purchase of treasury stock?
7. What are the effects in terms of assets and stockholders' equity of the declaration and distribution of (a) a cash dividend and (b) a stock dividend?
8. What is the difference between a stock dividend and a stock split?
9. Courts have held that a dividend in the stock of the distributing corporation is not taxable income to its recipients. Why?
10. If a balance sheet is prepared between the date of declaration and the date of distribution of a dividend, how should the dividend be shown if it is to be distributed in (a) cash and (b) stock?
11. While examining a corporation balance sheet, a business executive observed that the various items in the stockholders' equity section really showed sources of assets. Was this observation correct?
12. Explain how earnings increase a corporation's assets and stockholders' equity.
13. Why do accountants feel that the word "surplus" should not be used in published balance sheets as a term to describe a portion of the stockholders' equity?
14. Why are retained earnings sometimes appropriated?
15. Does the appropriation and transfer of retained earnings to retained earnings appropriated for plant expansion provide funds for the expansion? How do such appropriations aid in accumulating funds for a plant expansion?
16. How does a corporation dispose of a retained earnings appropriation such as retained earnings appropriated for plant expansion?

Class exercises

Exercise 16–1

On February 15 Jason Enterprises accepted subscriptions to 100,000 shares of its $1 par value common stock at $1.10 per share. The subscription contracts called for one fifth of the subscription price to accompany each contract as a down payment and the balance to be paid on March 15. Give the entries to record (a) the subscriptions, (b) the down payments, (c) receipt of the remaining amounts due on the subscriptions, and (d) issuance of the stock.

Exercise 16–2

On January 31 the stockholders' equity section of a corporation's balance sheet appeared as follows:

Stockholders' Equity

Common stock, $25 par value, 10,000 shares authorized and issued..	$250,000
Retained earnings	85,000
Total Stockholders' Equity...	$335,000

On the date of the equity section the corporation purchased 1,000 shares of treasury stock at $35 per share. Give the entry to record the purchase and prepare a stockholders' equity section as it would appear immediately after the purchase.

Exercise 16–3

On February 15 the corporation of Exercise 16–2 sold at $37 per share 500 of the treasury shares purchased on January 31, and on March 1 it sold the remaining treasury shares at $32 per share. Give the entries to record the sales.

Exercise 16–4

Pacific Growth Company received a charter and during a short period completed these transactions:

a. Began business by selling and issuing $12,000 of common stock at par for cash.
b. Purchased $10,000 of equipment for cash.
c. Sold and delivered $30,000 of services on credit.
d. Collected $27,000 of accounts receivable.
e. Paid $25,000 of operating expenses.
f. Purchased $7,000 of additional equipment, giving $4,000 in cash and a $3,000 promissory note payable.
g. Closed the Revenue from Services, Operating Expenses, and Income Summary accounts.

Required:

1. Open the following T-accounts on a sheet of ordinary notebook paper: Cash, Accounts Receivable, Equipment, Notes Payable, Common Stock, Retained Earnings, Income Summary, Revenue from Services, and Operating Expenses.
2. Record the transactions directly in the T-accounts.
3. Answer these questions:
    a. Does the corporation have retained earnings?
    b. Does it have any cash?
    c. If the company has retained earnings, why does it not also have cash?
    d. Can the corporation declare a legal cash dividend?
    e. Can it pay the dividend?
    f. In terms of assets, what does the balance of the Notes Payable account represent?
    g. In terms of assets, what does the balance of the Common Stock account represent?

h. In terms of assets, what does the balance of the Retained Earnings account represent?

Exercise 16–5

Stockholders' equity in a corporation appeared as follows on March 5:

Common stock, $10 par value, 100,000 shares authorized, 80,000 shares issued	$800,000
Premium on common stock	64,000
Total contributed capital	$864,000
Retained earnings	110,400
Total Stockholders' Equity	$974,400

On that date, when the stock was selling at $12.50 per share, the corporation's directors voted a 5% stock dividend distributable on April 1 to the March 15 stockholders of record. The dividend's declaration had no apparent effect on the market price of the shares, since they were still selling at $12.50 per share at the close of business on April 1.

Required:

1. Give the entries to record the declaration and distribution of the dividend.
2. Under the assumption that Jerry Jacks owned 100 of the shares on March 5 and received his dividend shares on April 1, prepare a schedule showing the numbers of shares he held on March 5 and April 1, with their total book values and total market values.

Exercise 16–6

Using more modern terminology, rearrange and restate the following stockholders' equity section from Punta Gorda Company's balance sheet. The donated surplus arose from the donation of a plant site.

PUNTA GORDA COMPANY
Capital Stock and Surplus

Common stock, $5 par value, 100,000 shares authorized, 80,000 shares issued			$400,000
Capital surplus:			
Premium on common stock	$ 40,000		
Treasury stock surplus	5,000		
Donated surplus	25,000		
Total capital surplus		$ 70,000	
Earned surplus:			
Appropriated earned surplus:			
Reserve for plant expansion	$100,000		
Unappropriated earned surplus	150,000		
Total earned surplus		250,000	
Total surplus			320,000
Total Capital Stock and Surplus			$720,000

Problem 16–1

Harrison Paper Company completed the following transactions:
a. Received a charter which granted it the right to issue 25,000 shares of $10 par value common stock.
b. Accepted subscriptions to 20,000 shares of stock at $11.25 per share.
c. Received a plant site valued at $10,000 as a donation from the city of Monroe in return for locating its plant in the donor city.
d. Collected the subscriptions of transaction (b) and issued the stock.
e. Gave a contractor 1,000 shares of stock and $50,250 in cash for the erection of a factory building. The contractor had previously agreed to erect the building for $62,000, but accepted the stock and cash in full payment on the building's completion.
f. Paid $125,000 for factory machinery.
g. During the first year's operation sold $585,400 of products for cash and paid $510,200 in operating expenses.
h. Made an adjusting entry to record depreciation of machinery, $12,100, and depreciation of factory building, $1,100. (Debit Operating Expenses, Controlling.)
i. Made an adjusting entry to record state and federal income taxes payable, $30,000.
j. Closed the Sales, Operating Expenses, Controlling, and State and Federal Income Taxes Expense accounts to Income Summary; and then closed the Income Summary account.
k. Declared a $0.10 per share quarterly cash dividend.
l. Declared a stock dividend of one share for each 20 previously held. The stock was selling at $12 per share on the day of the declaration.
m. Paid the cash dividend.
n. Distributed the stock dividend.
o. Purchased 1,000 shares of treasury stock at $12 per share.
p. Sold 500 shares of treasury stock at $12.50 per share.
q. Paid the state and federal income taxes payable.
r. Declared a quarterly cash dividend of $0.10 per share.

Required:

1. Open the following T-accounts: Cash; Subscriptions Receivable, Common Stock; Machinery and Equipment; Accumulated Depreciation, Machinery and Equipment; Buildings; Accumulated Depreciation, Buildings; Land; State and Federal Income Taxes Payable; Cash Dividend Payable; Common Stock; Premium on Common Stock; Common Stock Subscribed; Contributed Capital from Treasury Stock Transactions; Contributed Capital from Plant Site Donation; Retained Earnings; Stock Dividend Distributable; Treasury Stock; Income Summary; Sales; Operating Expenses, Controlling; and State and Federal Income Taxes Expense.
2. Enter the transactions directly in the T-accounts using the transaction letters to identify the amounts in the accounts.
3. Prepare the stockholders' equity section of the concern's balance sheet reflecting the foregoing transactions. (See Illustration 16–4.)

Problem 16–2

The equity sections from the 197A and 197B balance sheets of Hattiesburg Corporation appeared as follows:

Stockholders' Equity
(as of December 31, 197A)

Common stock, $5 par value, 250,000 shares authorized,	
200,000 shares issued..	$1,000,000
Premium on common stock...	200,000
Total contributed capital	$1,200,000
Retained earnings..	975,800
Total Contributed Capital and Retained Earnings	$2,175,800

Stockholders' Equity
(as of December 31, 197B)

Common stock, $5 par value, 250,000 shares authorized,	
219,800 shares issued of which 2,000 are in the treasury	$1,099,000
Premium on common stock..	338,600
Total contributed capital	$1,437,600
Retained earnings..	785,300
Total...	$2,222,900
Less: Cost of treasury stock	21,000
Total Contributed Capital and Retained Earnings	$2,201,900

On February 15, May 17, August 14, and again on November 15, 197B, the board of directors declared $0.15 per share dividends on the outstanding stock. The treasury stock was purchased on July 23. On August 14, while the stock was selling for $12 per share, the corporation declared a 10% stock dividend on the outstanding shares. The new shares were issued on September 15.

Required:

Under the assumption that there were no transactions affecting retained earnings other than the ones given, determine the 197B net income of Hattiesburg Corporation. Present calculations to prove your net income figure.

Problem 16–3

Last October 31, Caribe Corporation had a $211,800 credit balance in its retained earnings account. On that date, the corporation had 100,000 authorized shares of $10 par, common stock of which 60,000 shares had been issued at $12 and were outstanding. It then completed the following transactions:

Nov. 1 The board of directors declared a 20 cents per share dividend on the common stock, payable on December 1 to the November 25 stockholders of record.

Dec. 1 Paid the dividend declared on November 1.

      2 The board declared a 5% stock dividend, distributable on December 30 to the December 22 stockholders of record. The stock was selling at $18 per share, and the directors voted to use this amount in recording the dividend.

   30 Distributed the foregoing stock dividend.

   31 The corporation earned $94,500 during the year.

Jan. 2 The board of directors voted to split the corporation's stock 2 for 1 by calling in the old stock and issuing two $5 par value shares for each old $10 share held. The stockholders voted approval of the split and authorization of 200,000 new $5 par value shares to replace the $10 shares; all legal requirements were met; and the split was completed on February 1.

Required:

1. Prepare general journal entries to record the foregoing transactions and to close the Income Summary account at the year-end. (No entry is required for the split; however, a memorandum reciting the facts would be entered in the Common Stock account.)
2. Under the assumption John Weber owned 500 of the $10 par value shares on October 31 and neither bought nor sold any shares during the period of the transactions, prepare a schedule showing in one column the book value per share of the corporation's stock and in the second column the book value of Weber's shares at the close of business on each of October 31, November 1, December 1, December 30, December 31, and February 1.
3. Prepare three stockholders' equity sections for the corporation, the first showing the stockholders' equity on October 31, the second on December 31, and the third on February 1.

Problem 16–4

On June 27, 197A, and again on December 28, Automart Corporation declared the regular $3 per share semiannual dividend on its preferred stock and a $0.60 per share dividend on its common stock. These were the only dividends declared by the corporation during the year. The December 28 dividends were unpaid on December 31 when the stockholders' equity in the corporation appeared as follows:

Stockholders' Equity

Preferred stock, $100 par value, 6% cumulative and nonparticipating, 5,000 shares authorized, 2,500 shares issued	$250,000	
Add: Premium on preferred stock	12,500	
Amount paid in		$ 262,500
Common stock, $10 par value, 100,000 shares authorized, 60,000 shares issued	$600,000	
Add: Premium on common stock	120,000	
Amount paid in		720,000
Total contributed capital		$ 982,500
Retained earnings		223,000
Total Stockholders' Equity		$1,205,500

During 197B the corporation completed the following stock-related transactions:

Jan. 20 Paid to the January 15 stockholders of record the dividends declared on December 28 of the previous year.

Mar. 15   Accepted subscriptions to 10,000 shares of common stock at $16 per share. Twenty-five percent down payments accompanied the subscription contracts.

Apr. 14   Received the balance due on the common stock subscriptions of March 15 and issued the stock.

June 26   Declared the regular $3 per share semiannual dividend on the preferred stock and a $0.60 per share dividend on the common stock.

July 20   Paid to the July 15 stockholders of record the dividends declared on June 26.

Oct. 24   Declared a 10% common stock dividend distributable on November 20 to the November 15 stockholders of record. The October 24 stock market quotation for Automart Corporation common stock was $16.50 per share, and the board of directors voted to use this quotation in recording the dividend.

Nov. 20   Distributed the stock dividend declared on October 24.

Dec. 29   Declared the regular $3 per share semiannual dividend on the preferred stock and a $0.55 per share dividend on the common stock.

Required:

1. Prepare general journal entries to record the foregoing transactions.

2. Gary Sears purchased 100 shares of Automart Corporation common stock on June 12, 197A, becoming a stockholder of record on June 23. Since becoming a stockholder, he has sold none of his Automart Corporation stock. If he continues to hold this stock until after the December 29, 197B, dividend is paid, will his cash from dividends declared by the corporation during 197B exceed the cash he received from dividends declared by the corporation during 197A? Present figures to prove your answer.

Problem 16–5

At the beginning of the current year Dallas Corporation's stockholders' equity consisted of the following:

Common stock, $25 par value, 15,000 shares authorized, 12,000
    shares issued $300,000
Premium on common stock 45,000
Retained earnings 115,000

      Total Stockholders' Equity... $460,000

During the year the company completed these transactions:

May 10   Accepted as a gift from the city of Irving a plot of land adjacent to the company's plant. The land had a $15,000 fair market value and was to be used in expanding the plant and the company's payroll.

June 15   Purchased 1,000 shares of treasury stock at $40 per share.

23   The directors voted a $0.50 per share cash dividend payable on July 25 to the July 20 stockholders of record.

July 25   Paid the dividend declared on June 23.

Aug. 3   Sold 500 of the treasury shares at $45 per share.

Oct. 12   Sold 500 of the treasury shares at $38 per share.

Dec. 15   The directors voted a $0.50 per share cash dividend payable on January 20 to the January 15 stockholders of record, and they voted a

2% stock dividend distributable on January 30 to the January 20 stockholders of record. The market value of the stock was $40 per share.

Dec. 31 Closed the Income Summary account and carried the company's $31,000 net income to Retained Earnings.

Required:

1. Prepare general journal entries to record the transactions.
2. Prepare a retained earnings statement for the year and the stockholders' equity section of the company's year-end balance sheet.

Problem 16–6

Montgomery Corporation's December 31, 197A, balance sheet carried the following stockholders' equity section:

Common stock, $5 par value, 100,000 shares authorized 80,000 shares issued of which 5,000 are in the treasury...	$400,000	
Premium on common stock.....................................	40,000	
Total capital contributed for shares		$440,000
Retained earnings:		
Appropriated for plant expansion.........................	$ 25,000	
Appropriated and restricted by the purchase of treasury stock..	31,250	
Free and unappropriated	115,300	171,550
Total contributed capital and retained earnings..........		$611,550
Less cost of treasury stock		(31,250)
Total Stockholders' Equity		$580,300

At the end of 197B the corporation's unappropriated Retained Earnings account showed these amounts:

Retained Earnings

Date		Explanation	Debit	Credit	Balance
197B					
Jan.	1	Balance			115,300
May	12	Treasury stock appropriation		31,250	146,550
June	10	Cash dividend (payable July 23)	8,000		138,550
Dec.	15	Cash dividend (payable January 23)	8,000		130,550
	15	Stock dividend (distributable January 23)	28,000		102,550
	15	Plant expansion appropriation	25,000		77,550
	31	Net income		73,400	150,950

The treasury stock was sold on May 12, 197B, at $7 per share, and the June 10 cash dividend was paid on July 23. One new share will be distributed in the stock dividend for each 20 shares held on the record date.

Required:

1. Prepare entries to record the transactions reflected in the Retained Earnings account, and also entries to record the sale of the treasury stock and the payment of the June 10 cash dividend.

2. Prepare a 197B retained earnings statement for the company and also the owner equity section of its December 31, 197B balance sheet.

Alternate problems

Problem 16–1A

Pueblo Corporation received a charter granting the right to issue 50,000 shares of $5 par value common stock. It then completed these transactions:

a. Accepted subscriptions to 15,000 shares of common stock at $5.50 per share.
b. Gave Killeen Corporation 25,000 shares of stock for the following assets: machinery, $35,000; factory building, $85,000; and land, $17,500.
c. Collected the subscriptions of transaction (a) and issued the stock.
d. Purchased additional machinery for cash, $65,000.
e. During its first year sold $628,500 of products for cash and paid $550,300 of operating expenses.
f. Made an adjusting entry to record depreciation on machinery, $10,700, and depreciation on factory building, $2,500. (Debit Operating Expenses, Controlling.)
g. Made an adjusting entry to record state and federal income taxes payable, $25,000.
h. Closed the Sales, Operating Expenses, Controlling, State and Federal Income Taxes Expense, and Income Summary accounts.
i. Declared a $0.10 per share quarterly dividend.
j. Paid the dividend previously declared.
k. Paid the state and federal income taxes payable.
l. Purchased 1,000 shares of treasury stock at $5.75 per share.
m. Sold 500 of the treasury shares at $6 per share.
n. Declared a 10% stock dividend on the outstanding shares. The stock was selling for $6 per share on the day of the declaration.
o. Distributed the stock dividend.
p. Declared a $0.10 per share quarterly cash dividend.
q. The local chamber of commerce purchased and gave to the corporation a plot of land immediately to the west of the present factory building. The land had a fair market value of $15,000 and was to be used in expanding the factory and its payroll.

Required:

1. Open the following T-accounts: Cash; Subscriptions Receivable, Common Stock; Machinery and Equipment; Accumulated Depreciation, Machinery and Equipment; Buildings; Accumulated Depreciation, Buildings; Land; State and Federal Income Taxes Payable; Cash Dividend Payable; Common Stock; Premium on Common Stock; Common Stock Subscribed; Contributed Capital from Treasury Stock Transactions; Contributed Capital from Plant Site Donation; Retained Earnings; Stock Dividend Distributable; Treasury Stock; Income Summary; Sales; Operating Expenses, Controlling; and State and Federal Income Taxes Expense.
2. Enter the transactions directly in the accounts, using the transaction letters to identify the amounts.
3. Prepare the stockholders' equity section of a balance sheet reflecting the foregoing transactions. (See Illustration 16–4.)

Problem 16–2A

On December 31, 197A, Kingsville Corporation had 120,000 shares of $10 par, common stock outstanding and a retained earnings balance of $2,450,-000. During 197B, the board of directors declared cash dividends of $0.25 per outstanding share on each of the following dates: January 30, April 16, July 25, and October 26. During February 197B, the board declared a 5 for 1 stock split, calling in the existing shares and issuing five $2 par shares for each of the old $10 par shares.

On May 17, Kingsville Corporation acquired 60,000 of its outstanding shares, paying $10 per share. And on October 2, the company declared a 5% stock dividend on the outstanding shares to be distributed October 12. At the time of the declaration, the stock was selling for $8 per share.

On December 31, 197B, Kingsville Corporation's retained earnings balance was $2,600,000, including $600,000 which was restricted as a consequence of the purchase of treasury stock.

Required:

Under the assumption that there were no transactions affecting retained earnings other than the ones given, determine the 197B net income of Kingsville Corporation. Present calculations to prove your net income figure.

Problem 16–3A

On September 30, the stockholders' equity of Abacus Company appeared as follows:

Stockholders' Equity

Common stock, $25 par value, 10,000 shares authorized, 8,000 shares issued	$200,000
Premium on common stock	40,000
Total contributed capital	$240,000
Retained earnings	141,600
Total Stockholders' Equity	$381,600

On October 2 the board of directors declared a 40 cents per share cash dividend payable on October 31 to the October 20 stockholders of record. On November 28 the board declared a 10% stock dividend distributable on December 30 to the December 20 stockholders of record. The stock was selling for $50 per share on the day of the declaration, and the board voted to use this price in recording the dividend. The corporation earned $35,200, after taxes, during the year of the foregoing transactions, and on January 8 of the following year the board voted to split the corporation's stock 2½ for 1 by calling in the old stock and issuing 25 shares of $10 par value common stock for each 10 shares of the old $25 par value stock held. The stockholders voted approval of the split and authorization of 25,000 shares of new $10 par value stock to replace the old stock; all legal requirements were met; and the split was completed on February 15.

Required:

1. Prepare general journal entries to record the transactions and to close the Income Summary account. (No entry is needed for the split; however, a memorandum reciting the facts would be entered in the Common Stock account.)

2. Under the assumption that Larry Chambers owned 200 of the $25 par value shares on September 30 and neither bought nor sold any shares during the foregoing period, prepare a schedule showing the book value per share of the corporation's stock in one column and the book value of Chambers' total shares in a second column at the close of business on the following dates: September 30, October 2, October 31, December 30, December 31, and February 15.

3. Prepare the stockholders' equity section of the corporation's balance sheet as of the close of business on December 31, and prepare another equity section as of the close of business on February 15.

Problem 16–4A

On December 31 of last year the stockholders' equity section from Macon Corporation's balance sheet appeared as follows:

Stockholders' Equity

Preferred stock, $100 par value, 6% cumulative and nonparticipating, 2,500 shares authorized, 1,000 shares issued		$100,000
Common stock, $10 par value, 100,000 shares authorized, 50,000 shares issued	$500,000	
Add: Premium on common stock	75,000	
Amount paid in		575,000
Total contributed capital		$675,000
Retained earnings		225,000
Total Stockholders' Equity		$900,000

During the current year the corporation completed the following stock-related transactions:

Mar. 25   Declared the regular semiannual $3 per share dividend on the preferred stock and a $0.50 per share dividend on the common stock.

Apr. 20   Paid to the April 15 stockholders of record the dividends declared on March 25.

30   Accepted subscriptions to 10,000 shares of common stock at $17.50 per share. Ten percent down payments accompanied the subscription contracts.

May 30   Received balance due on April 30 subscriptions and issued the stock.

Sept. 24   Declared the regular semiannual $3 per share dividend on the preferred stock and a $0.50 per share dividend on the common stock.

Oct. 20   Paid to the October 15 stockholders of record the dividends declared on September 24.

Dec. 20   Declared a 10% common stock dividend distributable on January 20 to the January 15 common stockholders of record. The December 20 stock market quotation for Macon Corporation's common stock was $18 per share, and the board of directors voted to use this quotation in recording the dividend.

Dec. 31   Closed the Income Summary account for the year. The year's after-tax net income was $109,000.

Required:

1. Prepare general journal entries to record the foregoing transactions.

2. Under the assumption that Jerry Mozena owns 100 shares of Macon Corporation common stock which he plans to hold until after the distribution

of the stock dividend declared on December 20, (*a*) prepare a calculation of the book value of his 100 shares as of December 31, and (*b*) another calculation of the book value of his total shares after the dividend distribution.

Problem 16–5A

The stockholders' equity in Healy Corporation consisted of the following at the beginning of the current year:

Common stock, $5 par value, 100,000 shares authorized, 50,000 shares issued and outstanding	$250,000
Premium on common stock	25,000
Retained earnings	70,000
Total Stockholders' Equity	$345,000

During the year the company completed these transactions affecting its stockholders' equity:

Apr. 14 Purchased 5,000 shares of treasury stock at $7.50 per share.

May 10 Received as a gift from the city a plot of land adjacent to the company's plant. The land had a $12,500 fair market value and was to be used to expand the company's plant and payroll.

June 23 The directors voted a 10 cents per share cash dividend payable on July 20 to the July 15 stockholders of record.

July 20 Paid the previously declared cash dividend.

Aug. 18 Sold 3,000 of the treasury shares at $8 per share.

Nov. 12 Sold the remaining treasury shares at $7.25 per share.

Dec. 18 The directors voted a 4% stock dividend distributable on January 20 to the January 15 stockholders of record. The stock was selling at $7.50 per share.

Dec. 31 Closed the Income Summary account and carried the company's $28,000 net income to Retained Earnings.

Required:

1. Prepare general journal entries to record the transactions.
2. Prepare a retained earnings statement for the year and the stockholders' equity section of the company's year-end balance sheet.

Ted Rolling purchased 100 shares of Hancock Corporation stock at $15 per share on January 1, 197A, when the corporation had the following stockholders' equity:

Decision problem 16–1, Hancock Corporation

Common stock, $10 par value, 250,000 shares authorized, 200,000 shares issued and outstanding	$2,000,000
Capital contributed by stockholders in excess of the par value of their shares	250,000
Retained earnings	560,000
Total Stockholders' Equity	$2,810,000

Since purchasing the 100 shares, Mr. Rolling has neither purchased nor sold any additional shares of the company's stock; and on December 31 of each year he has received dividends on the shares held as follows: 197A, $66; 197B, $82.50; and 197C, $110.

On June 30, 197A, at a time when its stock was selling for $17.50 per share, Hancock Corporation declared a 10% stock dividend which was distributed one month later. On August 15, 197B, the corporation doubled the number of its authorized shares and split its stock 2 for 1; and on March 27, 197C, it purchased 10,000 shares of treasury stock at $9 per share. The shares were still in its treasury at year-end.

Required:

Under the assumption that Hancock Corporation's stock had a book value of $13.50 per share on December 31, 197A, a book value of $7.20 per share on December 31, 197B, and a book value of $7.70 on December 31, 197C, do the following:

1. Prepare statements showing the nature of the stockholders' equity in the corporation at the end of 197A, 197B, and 197C.
2. Prepare a schedule showing the amount of the corporation's net income for each of 197A, 197B, and 197C, under the assumption that the changes in the company's retained earnings during the three-year period resulted solely from earnings and dividends.

Decision problem 16–2, Big Apple Corporation

On November 3 stockholders' equity in Big Apple Corporation consisted of the following:

Common stock, $10 par value, 150,000 shares authorized, 100,000 shares issued and outstanding	$1,000,000
Capital contributed by the common stockholders in excess of the par value of their shares	150,000
Retained earnings	650,000
Total Stockholders' Equity	$1,800,000

On November 3, when the stock was selling at $20 per share, the corporation's directors voted a 20% stock dividend, distributable on December 1 to the November 25 stockholders of record. The directors also voted an $0.85 per share annual cash dividend, payable on December 20 to the December 15 stockholders of record. The amount of the latter dividend was a disappointment to some stockholders, since the company had for a number of years paid a $1 per share annual cash dividend.

Jack Clifford owned 1,000 shares of Big Apple Corporation stock on November 25, which he had purchased a number of years ago, and as a result he received his dividend shares. He continued to hold all of his shares until after he received the December 20 cash dividend. However, he did note that his stock had a $20 per share market value on November 3, a market value it held until the close of business on November 25, when the market value declined to $17.50 per share.

Give the entries to record the declaration and payment of the dividends involved here, and answer these questions:

a. What was the book value of Clifford's total shares on November 3, and what was the book value on December 1, after he received his dividend shares?

b. What fraction of the corporation did Clifford own on November 3, and what fraction did he own on December 1?

c. What was the market value of Clifford's total shares on November 3, and what was the market value at the close of business on November 25?

d. What did Clifford gain from the stock dividend?

Although Hawkeye Company is a large company with varied operations, its stock has always been held by a few individuals, and the financial statements provided for the stockholders have not been prepared strictly in accordance with generally accepted accounting principles. The most recent income statement and statement of retained earnings are reproduced below:

Decision problem 16–3, Hawkeye Company

HAWKEYE COMPANY
Income Statement
For Year Ended December 31, 197B

Sales		$46,000,000
Cost of goods sold	$21,000,000	
Selling expenses	9,000,000	
Depreciation expense	2,000,000	
Other general and administrative expenses	6,000,000	38,000,000
Income from operations		$ 8,000,000
Other items:		
Gain on settlement of lawsuit, after lengthy appeal process was completed last year, net of $6,000,000 taxes	$18,000,000	
Write-down of obsolete inventory, net of $1,500,000 taxes	(3,000,000)	
Gain on sale of equipment, net of taxes amounting to $1,000,000	2,500,000	17,500,000
		$25,500,000
Income taxes on operating items		3,000,000
Net Income		$22,500,000

HAWKEYE COMPANY
Statement of Retained Earnings
For Year Ended December 31, 197B

Retained earnings, December 31, 197A		$30,000,000
Additions: Net income		22,500,000
		$52,500,000
Deductions:		
Flood loss resulting from broken dam, net of $3,000,000 related reduction in taxes	$8,000,000	
General and administrative expenses incurred during two-month-long strike by company employees, net of related $1,000,000 reduction in taxes	2,000,000	
Dividends declared	3,500,000	13,500,000
Retained earnings, December 31, 197B		$39,000,000

One of Hawkeye Company's stockholders has expressed frustration over the difficulty involved in comparing the financial statements of Hawkeye Company with those of other companies. In particular, the stockholder has questioned the bases used to classify items as operating items, extraordinary items (net of taxes), and as increases or decreases on the statement of retained earnings. To reduce the number of such criticisms, the management of Hawkeye Company has asked you to recast the income statement and statement of retained earnings so that they will be consistent with generally accepted accounting principles. You need not worry about earnings per share calculations, but should pay special attention to the proper classification of items as operating, extraordinary, or corrections of prior periods' income.

After studying Chapter 17, you should be able to:

- State the criteria for classifying stock investments as current assets or as long-term investments.

- Describe the circumstances under which the cost method of accounting for stock investments is used and the circumstances under which the equity method is used.

- Record and maintain the accounts for stock investments according to the cost method and the equity method.

- Prepare consolidated financial statements which include such matters as excess of investment cost over book value and minority interests, and be able to describe the conditions under which consolidated statements should be prepared.

- Explain the differences between the pooling of interests and purchase methods of accounting for corporate combinations.

- Define or explain the words and phrases listed in the chapter Glossary.

chapter 17

Corporations: Stock investments, intercorporate investments, and consolidations

In Chapters 15 and 16, the issues of accounting for corporate stock were approached predominantly from the view of the issuing corporation. In the present chapter that perspective is reversed and accounting for stock is examined from the perspective of the investor. Investors in stock include individuals and a variety of different types of organizations. In fact, corporations frequently invest in the stock of other corporations.

When the stock investor maintains an accounting system and prepares financial statements, several questions arise in regard to how the stock investment should be recorded in the accounts of the investor and reported in the investor's financial statements. For example, how should the stock investment be classified on the balance sheet of the investor? And what should be the basis for recording earnings from the investment on the books of the investor? If the investor is a corporation and the amount of stock owned is so large that the investor controls the activities of the investee, are additional procedures necessary to ensure that the financial statements of the investor will be informative? Questions such as these are answered in this chapter.

Stocks as investments

The stock transactions illustrated thus far have been transactions in which a corporation sold and issued its own stock. Such transactions represent only a very small portion of the daily transactions in stocks. The great daily volume of security sales are transactions between investors, some investors selling and other investors buying, with the transactions taking place through brokers who charge a commission for their services.

Brokers acting as agents for their customers buy and sell stocks and bonds on stock exchanges such as the New York Stock Exchange. Forty million or more shares of stock may be exchanged in a single day on that exchange alone, and each day the prices at which sales occurred are published on the financial pages of many newspapers. Stock prices are quoted on the basis of dollars and $\frac{1}{8}$ dollars per share. For example, a stock quoted at $46\frac{1}{8}$ sold for $46.125 per share, and a stock quoted at $25\frac{1}{2}$ sold for $25.50 per share.

Some securities are not traded in large enough quantities to warrant being listed on an organized stock exchange, and brokers act for their customers to buy and sell such securities in the "over-the-counter" market. Each security in this market is handled by one or more brokers who receive from other brokers offers to buy or sell the security at specific "bid" or "ask" prices. The broker essentially provides a market place for the security, arranging for trades between customers whose "bid" and "ask" prices are consistent.

Classifying investments

Equity securities generally include common, preferred, or other capital stock. Many equity securities are actively traded, so that "sales prices or bid and ask prices are currently available on a national securities exchange or in the over-the-counter market." Such securities are classified as "marketable securities."[1] If, in addition to being marketable, a stock investment is held as "an investment of cash available for current operations,"[2] it is classified as a current asset, and appears on the balance sheet immediately following cash. The stock may be held for a number of years, but this is not important. The important point is that in case of need it may quickly be turned into cash without interfering with the normal operations of the business.

Investments that are not intended as a ready source of cash in case of need are classified as *long-term investments*. They include funds earmarked for a special purpose, such as bond sinking funds, as well as land or other assets owned but not employed in the regular operations of the business. They also include investments in stocks which are not marketable or which, although marketable, are not intended to serve as a ready source of cash. Long-term investments appear on the balance sheet in a classification of their own titled "Long-term investments," which is placed immediately following the current asset section.

Accounting for investments in stock

Most investments in a corporation's stock represent a small percentage of the total amount of stock outstanding. As a consequence, the investor does not exercise a significant influence over the financial

---

[1] FASB, "Accounting for Certain Marketable Securities," *Statement of Financial Accounting Standards No. 12* (New York, 1975), par. 7.

[2] Committee on Accounting Procedure, "Accounting Research Bulletin No. 43," *Accounting Research and Terminology Bulletins, Final Edition* (New York: AICPA, 1961), chap. 3, sec. A, par. 4.

affairs of the corporation. However, in some cases, an investor will buy a large share of the outstanding stock of a corporation in order to influence or control its operations. For example, corporations frequently buy a large share of another corporation's stock in order to influence its activities as well as to receive part of its income.

The method of accounting for stock investments on the books of the investor depends upon whether the investor has the ability to significantly influence the activities of the corporation. If the investor can exercise a significant financial influence, the accounting method used is called the "equity method," and if the investor does not have a significant financial influence, the accounting method used is called the "cost method." The Accounting Principles Board has held that ownership of 20% or more of the voting stock of a corporation is presumptive evidence of the ability to significantly influence its operations.[3] Thus, in general, stock investments of 20% or more are accounted for according to the equity method while investments of less than 20% are accounted for according to the cost method.

The cost method of accounting for stock investments

When less than 20% of a corporation's voting stock is purchased as either a short- or long-term investment, the purchase is recorded at total cost, which includes the commission paid the broker. For example, 1,000 (10%) of American Sales Corporation's 10,000 outstanding common shares were purchased as an investment at $23\frac{1}{4}$ plus a $300 broker's commission. The entry to record the transaction is:

Sept.	10	Investment in American Sales Corporation Stock...........	23,550.00	
		Cash...		23,550.00
		Purchased 1,000 shares of stock for $23,250 plus a $300 broker's commission.		

Observe that nothing is said about a premium or a discount on the American Sales Corporation stock. Premiums and discounts apply only when stock is first issued. They do not apply to sales and purchases between investors. Thus, premiums and discounts are normally recorded only by the corporation which issues the stock. Even if the investor acquires newly issued stock, a premium or discount on the stock is not usually recorded in a separate account.

When less than 20% of a corporation's voting stock is held as either a short- or long-term investment and a dividend is received on the stock, an entry similar to the following is made:

---

[3] APB, "The Equity Method of Accounting for Investments in Common Stock," *APB Opinion No. 18* (New York: AICPA, 1971), par. 17.

Oct.	5	Cash..	1,000.00	
		Dividends Earned..		1,000.00
		Received a $1 per share dividend on the American Sales Corporation stock.		

Dividends on stocks do not accrue; consequently, an end-of-the-accounting-period entry to record accrued dividends is never made. However, if a balance sheet is prepared after a dividend is declared but before it is paid, an entry debiting Dividends Receivable and crediting Dividends Earned may be made. Nevertheless, since dividend earnings are often immaterial and not taxable until received in cash, most companies do not record such dividends until received, and while this is not theoretically correct, it does keep reported and taxable dividends the same.

A dividend in shares of stock is not income, and a debit and credit entry recording it should not be made. However, a memorandum entry or a notation as to the additional shares should be made in the investment account. Also, receipt of the stock does affect the per share cost basis of the old shares. For example, if a 20-share dividend is received on 100 shares originally purchased for $1,500 or at $15 per share, the cost of all 120 shares is $1,500 and the cost per share is $12.50 ($1,500 ÷ 120 shares = $12.50 per share).

When an investment totaling less than 20% of a corporation's stock is sold, normally a gain or a loss is incurred. If the amount received is greater than the original cost of the investment plus the commission on the sale and other costs, there is a gain. For example, if the 1,000 shares of American Sales Corporation common stock, the purchase of which at $23,550 was previously recorded, are sold at $25\frac{3}{4}$ less a commission and taxes on the sale amounting to $315, there is a $1,885 gain, and the transaction is recorded:

Jan.	7	Cash..	25,435.00	
		Investment in American Sales Corporation Stock		23,550.00
		Gain on the Sale of Investments		1,885.00
		Sold 1,000 shares of stock for $25,750 less a $315 commission and other costs.		

If the net amount received for these shares had been less than their $23,550 cost, there would have been a loss on the transaction.

Lower of cost or market

For balance sheet presentation, an investment in stock that is not marketable is accounted for at cost. However, investments in marketable equity securities are divided into two portfolios: (1) those to be shown as current assets, and (2) those to be shown as long-term investments. Then the total current market value of each portfolio is calculated and compared to the total cost of each portfolio. Each portfolio is reported at the lower of cost or market.[4]

In the case of the current asset portfolio, a decline in total market value below the previous balance sheet valuation (or cost) is reported in the income statement as a loss. Subsequent recoveries of market value are reported in the income statement as gains, but market value increases above original cost are not recorded.[5]

In the case of long-term investment portfolios of marketable equity securities, market value declines are reported in the income statement *only* if they appear to be permanent. More often they are not assumed to be permanent in which case the market value decline is disclosed as a separate item in the stockholders' equity section of the balance sheet.[6]

The equity method of accounting for common stock investments

If a corporation acquires 20% or more of another corporation's common stock, the investor is presumed to have a significant financial influence on the investee corporation, and the investment is accounted for according to the equity method. When the stock is acquired, the purchase is recorded at cost just as it is under the cost method. For example, on January 1, 1978, James, Inc., purchased 3,000 shares (30%) of RMS, Inc., common stock for a total cost of $70,650. The entry to record the purchase on the books of James, Inc., is as follows:

Jan.	1	Investment in RMS, Inc.	70,650.00	
		Cash		70,650.00
		Purchased 3,000 shares of common stock for a total cost of $70,650.		

Under the equity method, it is recognized that the earnings of the investee corporation not only increase the net assets of the investee corporation but also increase the investor's equity in the assets. Consequently, under this method, when the investee corporation closes its books and reports the amount of its earnings, the investor takes up its share in its investment account. For example, RMS, Inc., reported net income of $20,000. James, Inc.'s, entry to record its share of these earnings is:

---

[4] FASB, "Accounting for Certain Marketable Securities," *op. cit.*, par. 8.

[5] Ibid., par. 11.

[6] Ibid., par. 11, 21.

Dec.	31	Investment in RMS, Inc..	6,000.00	
		Earnings from Investment in RMS, Inc....................		6,000.00
		To record 30% equity in investee's earnings of $20,000.		

The illustrated entry's debit records the increase in James, Inc.'s equity in RMS, Inc. The credit causes 30% of RMS, Inc.'s net income to appear on James, Inc.'s income statement as earnings from the investment, and James, Inc., closes the earnings to its Income Summary account and on to its Retained Earnings account just as it would close earnings from any investment.

If instead of a net income the investee corporation incurs a loss, the investor debits the loss to an account called Loss from Investment and credits and reduces its Investment in Stock account. It then carries the loss to its Income Summary account and on to its Retained Earnings account.

Dividends paid by an investee corporation decrease the investee's assets and retained earnings and also decrease the investor's equity in the investee. Since, under the equity method, the investor records its equity in the full amount of earnings reported by an investee, the receipt of dividends does not constitute income; instead, dividend receipts from the investee represent a decrease in the equity. For example, RMS, Inc., declared and paid $10,000 in dividends on its common stock. The entry to record James, Inc.'s share of these dividends, which it received on January 9, 1979, is:

Jan.	9	Cash...	3,000.00	
		Investment in RMS, Inc..		3,000.00
		To record receipt of 30% of the $10,000 dividend paid by RMS, Inc.		

Notice that the carrying value of a common stock investment, accounted for by the equity method, changes in reflection of the investor's equity in the undistributed earnings of the investee. For example, after the above transactions have been recorded on the books of James, Inc., the investment account would appear as follows:

Investment in RMS, Inc.

Date	Explanation	Debit	Credit	Balance
Jan. 1, '78	Investment	70,650.00		70,650.00
Dec. 31, '78	Share of earnings	6,000.00		76,650.00
Jan. 9, '79	Share of dividend		3,000.00	73,650.00

When common stock, accounted for by the equity method, is sold, the gain or loss on the sale is determined by comparing the proceeds from the sale with the carrying value of the stock on the date of sale. For example, on January 10, 1979, James, Inc., sold its RMS, Inc., stock for $80,000. The entry to record the sale is as follows:

Jan.	10	Cash...	80,000.00	
		Investment in RMS, Inc.		73,650.00
		Gain on Sale of Investments....................................		6,350.00
		Sold 3,000 shares of stock for $80,000.		

Corporations commonly own and control other corporations. For example, if Corporation A owns more than 50% of the voting stock of Corporation B, Corporation A can elect Corporation B's board of directors and thus control its activities and resources. In such a situation the controlling corporation, Corporation A, is known as the *parent company* and Corporation B is called a *subsidiary*. **Parent and subsidiary corporations**

When a corporation owns all the outstanding stock of a subsidiary, it can take over the subsidiary's assets, cancel its stock, and fuse the subsidiary into the parent company. However, there are often financial, legal, and tax advantages in operating a large business as a parent company controlling one or more subsidiaries rather than as a single corporation. Actually, most large companies are parent corporations owning one or more subsidiaries.

When a business is operated as a parent company with subsidiaries, separate accounting records are kept for each corporation. Also, from a legal viewpoint the parent and each subsidiary is a separate entity with all the rights, duties, and responsibilities of a separate corporation. Nevertheless, investors in the parent company depend on the parent to present financial statements which disclose the financial results of all of the operations under the parent's control, including those of any subsidiaries.

To a limited extent, this disclosure is accomplished through the parent's use of the equity method to account for its investments in other corporations. However, the equity method fails to show all of the individual revenues, expenses, assets, and liabilities of the subsidiary's operations. Therefore, it is usually necessary to develop for a parent and its subsidiaries a set of *consolidated statements* in which the assets and liabilities of all the affiliated companies are combined on a single balance sheet and their revenues and expenses are combined on a single income statement, as though the business were in fact a single company.

Principles of consolidation

When parent and subsidiary balance sheets are consolidated, duplications in items are eliminated so that the combined figures do not **Consolidated balance sheets** show more assets and equities than actually exist. For example, a parent's investment in a subsidiary is evidenced by shares of stock which are carried as an asset in the parent company's records. However, these shares actually represent an equity in the subsidiary's assets. Consequently, if the parent's investment in a subsidiary and the subsidiary's assets were both shown on the consolidated balance sheet, the same resources would be counted twice. To prevent this, the parent's investment and the subsidiary's capital accounts are offset and eliminated in preparing a consolidated balance sheet.

Likewise, a single enterprise cannot owe a debt to itself. This would be analogous to a student borrowing $20 for a date from funds he has saved for next semester's expenses and then preparing a balance sheet showing the $20 as both receivable from himself and payable to himself. To prevent such a double showing, intercompany debts and receivables are also eliminated in preparing a consolidated balance sheet.

Balance sheets consolidated at time of acquisition

When a parent's and a subsidiary's assets are combined in the preparation of a consolidated balance sheet, a work sheet is normally used to effect the consolidation. Illustration 17–1 shows such a work sheet. It was prepared to consolidate the accounts of Parent Company and its subsidiary, called Subsidiary Company, on January 1, 197A, the

Parent Company and Subsidiary Company
Work Sheet for a Consolidated Balance Sheet, January 1, 197A

	Parent Company	Subsidiary Company	Eliminations Debit	Eliminations Credit	Consolidated Amounts
Assets					
Cash	5,000	15,000			20,000
Notes receivable	10,000			(a) 10,000	
Accounts receivable, net	20,000	13,000			33,000
Inventories	45,000	22,000			67,000
Investment in Subsidiary Company	115,000			(b) 115,000	
Buildings and equipment, net	100,000	74,000			174,000
Land	25,000	8,000			33,000
	320,000	132,000			327,000
Equities					
Accounts payable	15,000	7,000			22,000
Notes payable		10,000	(a) 10,000		
Common stock	250,000	100,000	(b) 100,000		250,000
Retained earnings	55,000	15,000	(b) 15,000		55,000
	320,000	132,000	125,000	125,000	327,000

Illustration 17–1

day Parent Company acquired Subsidiary Company through the purchase for cash of all its outstanding $10 par value common stock. The stock had a book value of $115,000 or $11.50 per share, which in this first illustration is the amount Parent Company is assumed to have paid for it. Explanation of the work sheet's two eliminating entries follow:

Entry (a) On the day it acquired Subsidiary Company, Parent Company lent Subsidiary Company $10,000 for use in the subsidiary's operations, taking the subsidiary's note as evidence of the transaction. Since this intercompany debt was in reality a transfer of funds within the organization and did not increase the total assets and total liabilities of the affiliated companies, it is eliminated by means of Entry (a). To understand this entry, recall that the subsidiary's promissory note is represented by a $10,000 debit in Parent Company's Notes Receivable account. Then observe that the first credit in the Eliminations column exactly offsets and eliminates this item. Next, recall that the subsidiary's note appears as a credit in its Notes Payable account, and observe that the $10,000 debit in the Eliminations column completes the elimination of this intercompany debt.

Entry (b) When a parent company invests in a subsidiary by buying the subsidiary's stock, the cost of the investment appears on the parent company's balance sheet as an asset, "Investment in subsidiary." Therefore, in consolidating the assets of a parent and its subsidiary, the parent company's investment in the subsidiary must be eliminated, because to show on the consolidated balance sheet both the subsidiary's assets and the amount of the parent's investment (an equity in these assets) would be to show more resources than actually exist. Also, not only does the parent's investment in the subsidiary represent an equity in the subsidiary's assets but so do the stockholder equity accounts of the subsidiary. Consequently, in consolidating the balance sheets of a parent and its subsidiary, the amount of the parent's investment in the subsidiary is offset against the subsidiary's stockholder equity accounts and both are eliminated.

After the intercompany items are eliminated on a work sheet like Illustration 17–1, the assets of the parent and its subsidiary are combined and carried into the work sheet's last column. Next, the equities in these assets are combined and carried into the column, after which the amounts in the column are used to prepare a consolidated balance sheet like Illustration 17–2.

Parent company does not buy all of subsidiary's stock and does not pay book value

In the situation just described, Parent Company purchased 100% or all of its subsidiary's stock, paying book value for it. Often a parent company purchases less than 100% of a subsidiary's stock, and commonly pays a price either above or below the stock's book value. To illustrate such a situation, assume the parent company of the previous

Parent Company and Subsidiary
Consolidated Balance Sheet, January 1, 197A

Assets

Current Assets:
Cash .... $ 20,000
Accounts receivable, net 33,000
Inventories.. 67,000

Total Current Assets $120,000
Plant and Equipment:
Buildings and equipment, net $174,000
Land 33,000

Total Plant and Equipment 207,000
Total Assets $327,000

Liabilities and Stockholders' Equity

Liabilities:
Accounts payable .... $ 22,000
Stockholders' Equity:
Common stock.. $250,000
Retained earnings.. 55,000

Total Stockholders' Equity....................................... 305,000
Total Liabilities and Stockholders' Equity............. $327,000

Illustration 17–2

illustration purchased for cash only 80% of its subsidiary's stock rather than 100%, and that it paid $13 per share, a price $1.50 above the stock's book value.

These new assumptions result in a more complicated work sheet entry to eliminate the parent's investment and the subsidiary's stockholder equity accounts. The entry is complicated by (1) the minority interest in the subsidiary and (2) the excess over book value paid by the parent company for the subsidiary's stock.

Minority interest When a parent buys a controlling interest in a subsidiary, the parent company is the subsidiary's majority stockholder. However, when the parent owns less than 100% of the subsidiary's stock, the subsidiary has other stockholders who own a minority interest in its assets and share its earnings. Consequently, when there is a minority interest and the stockholder equity accounts of the subsidiary are eliminated on a consolidated work sheet, the interest of the minority stockholders must be set out as on the last line of Illustration 17–3. In this case the minority stockholders have a 20% interest in the subsidiary; consequently, 20% of the balances of the subsidiary's common stock and retained earnings accounts [($100,-000 + $15,000) × 20% = $23,000] is set out on the work sheet as the minority interest.

Excess of investment cost over book value At the time Parent Company purchased 80% of Subsidiary Company's stock, the subsidiary had outstanding 10,000 shares of $10 par value common stock with a book value of $11.50 per share.

Parent Company and Subsidiary Company
Work Sheet for a Consolidated Balance Sheet, January 1, 197A

	Parent Company	Subsidiary Company	Eliminations		Consolidated Amounts
			Debit	Credit	
Assets					
Cash	16,000	15,000			31,000
Notes receivable.................	10,000			(a) 10,000	
Accounts receivable, net	20,000	13,000			33,000
Inventories........................	45,000	22,000			67,000
Investment in Subsidiary					
Company........................	104,000			(b) 104,000	
Buildings and					
equipment, net.................	100,000	74,000			174,000
Land	25,000	8,000			33,000
Excess of cost					
over book value			(b) 12,000		12,000
	320,000	132,000			350,000
Equities					
Accounts payable................	15,000	7,000			22,000
Notes payable		10,000	(a) 10,000		
Common stock...................	250,000	100,000	(b) 100,000		250,000
Retained earnings	55,000	15,000	(b) 15,000		55,000
Minority interest.................				(b) 23,000	23,000
	320,000	132,000	137,000	137,000	350,000

Illustration 17–3

Parent Company paid $13 per share for 8,000 of the shares; conse-
quently, the cost of these shares exceeded their book value by $12,000,
calculated as follows:

Cost of stock (8,000 shares at $13 per share)............. $104,000
Book value (8,000 shares at $11.50 per share)............ 92,000
Excess of cost over book value....................... $ 12,000

Now observe how this excess of cost over book value is set out on the
work sheet in eliminating the parent's investment in the subsidiary and
how it is carried into the Consolidated Amounts column as an asset.

After its completion, the consolidated amounts in the last column of
the work sheet of Illustration 17–3 were used to prepare the consolidated balance sheet of Illustration 17–4. Note the treatment of the
minority interest in the balance sheet. The minority stockholders have
a $23,000 equity in the consolidated assets of the affiliated companies.
Many have argued that this item should be disclosed in the stockholders' equity section. Others believe it should be shown in the long-term
liabilities section. Although both of these alternatives can be found

Parent Company and Subsidiary
Consolidated Balance Sheet, January 1, 197A

Assets

Current Assets:
Cash .... $ 31,000
Accounts receivable, net 33,000
Inventories 67,000
    Total Current Assets $131,000
Plant and Equipment:
Buildings and equipment, net $174,000
Land 33,000
    Total Plant and Equipment 207,000
Goodwill from consolidation 12,000
    Total Assets $350,000

Liabilities and Stockholders' Equity

Liabilities:
Accounts payable .... $ 22,000
Minority interest 23,000
Stockholders Equity:
Common stock $250,000
Retained earnings 55,000
    Total Stockholders' Equity 305,000
    Total Liabilities and Stockholders' Equity $350,000

Illustration 17–4

among audited financial statements, the most often used alternative is to disclose minority interest as a separate item between the liabilities and stockholders' equity sections, as is shown in Illustration 17–4.

Next observe that the $12,000 excess over book value paid by the parent company for the subsidiary's stock appears on the consolidated balance sheet as the asset, "Goodwill from consolidation." When a parent company purchases an interest in a subsidiary, it may pay more than book value for its equity because (1) certain of the subsidiary's assets are carried on the subsidiary's books at less than their fair value; (2) certain of the subsidiary's liabilities are carried at book values which are greater than their fair values; or (3) the subsidiary's earnings prospects are good enough to justify paying more than the sum of the fair (market) values of its assets and liabilities. In this illustration, it is assumed that the book values of Subsidiary Company's assets and liabilities equal their fair values. However, Subsidiary Company's expected earnings justified paying $104,000 for an 80% equity in the subsidiary's net assets (assets less liabilities).

The APB has ruled that where a company pays more than book value because the subsidiary's assets are undervalued or its liabilities are overvalued, the cost in excess of book value should be allocated to those assets and liabilities so that they are restated at their fair values. After the subsidiary's assets and liabilities have been restated to reflect their fair values, any remaining cost in excess of book value should be reported on the consolidated balance sheet as "Goodwill from consolidation."[7]

Occasionally a parent company pays less than book value for its interest in a subsidiary. In such a case, since a "bargain" purchase is very unlikely, the logical reason for a price below book value is that certain of the subsidiary's assets are carried on its books at amounts in excess of fair value. In such a situation the APB has ruled that the amounts at which the overvalued assets are placed on the consolidated balance sheet should be reduced accordingly.[8]

Earnings of a subsidiary

In the years following acquisition, if the operations of a subsidiary are profitable, its net assets and retained earnings increase; and if it pays dividends, the dividends are paid to the parent company and any minority stockholders in proportion to the stockholdings of each. Furthermore, the subsidiary records the transactions that result in earnings, closes its Income Summary account, and records the declaration and payment of dividends just like any other corporation.

A parent generally accounts for its investment in a subsidiary according to the equity method. As a consequence, the parent's recorded net income and Retained Earnings account include the parent's equity in the net income earned by the subsidiary since the date of acquisition. Also, the balance of the parent's Investment in Subsidiary account increases each year by an amount equal to the parent's equity in the subsidiary's earnings less the parent's share of any dividends paid by the subsidiary.

Consolidated balance sheets at dates after acquisition

It should be emphasized that the earnings and dividends of a subsidiary not only affect the balance of the subsidiary's Retained Earnings account but also result in changes in the parent company's account, Investment in Subsidiary. As a result, in the years following acquisition, when consolidated balance sheets are prepared, the amounts eliminated from these accounts change as the account balances change.

For example, Subsidiary Company of this illustration earned $12,500 during the first year after being acquired by Parent Company, and paid out $7,500 in dividends. The earnings less the dividends caused the subsidiary's Retained Earnings account to increase from $15,000 at the beginning of the year to $20,000 at the year-end. Consequently, $20,000 of retained earnings are eliminated on the year-end work sheet to consolidate the balance sheets of the companies (see Illustration 17–5). In examining the work sheet, also observe that the earnings of the subsidiary, less its dividend ($12,500 − $7,500), resulted in a $5,000 increase in the subsidiary's net assets. (To simplify

---

[7] APB, "Business Combinations," *APB Opinion No. 16* (New York: AICPA, 1970), par. 87.

[8] Ibid., par. 91.

Parent Company and Subsidiary Company
Work Sheet for a Consolidated Balance Sheet, December 31, 197A

	Parent Company	Subsidiary Company	Eliminations		Consolidated Amounts
			Debit	Credit	
Assets					
Cash	14,000	10,000			24,000
Notes receivable................	10,000			(a) 10,000	
Accounts receivable, net	27,000	14,000			41,000
Inventories........................	50,000	29,000			79,000
Investment in Subsidiary					
Company.......................	108,000			(b) 108,000	
Buildings and					
equipment, net................	95,000	76,000			171,000
Land	25,000	8,000			33,000
Excess of cost					
over book value			(b) 12,000		12,000
	329,000	137,000			360,000
Equities					
Accounts payable...............	15,000	7,000			22,000
Notes payable		10,000	(a) 10,000		
Common stock....................	250,000	100,000	(b) 100,000		250,000
Retained earnings	64,000	20,000	(b) 20,000		64,000
Minority interest.................				(b) 24,000	24,000
	329,000	137,000	142,000	142,000	360,000

Illustration 17–5

the illustration, it is assumed that the liabilities of both the parent company and the subsidiary were unchanged and that the subsidiary had not paid the note given to Parent Company. It is also assumed that Parent Company earned $31,000 during the year, including the $10,-000 from its investment in Subsidiary Company; and that it paid out $22,000 in dividends and retained the balance for use in expanding its operations. As a result, Parent Company's net assets and Retained Earnings increased $9,000 during the year, as shown in the first column of the illustration.)

To continue the explanation, Parent Company paid $104,000 for 80% of Subsidiary Company's stock and debited that amount to its Investment in Subsidiary Company account. During the year Parent Company increased this account $10,000 by taking up 80% of the subsidiary's earnings and decreased it $6,000 upon receipt of its share of the subsidiary's dividend. As a result, the account had a $108,000 year-end balance, which is the amount eliminated on the work sheet.

Two additional items in Illustration 17–5 require explanations. First, the minority interest set out on the year-end work sheet is greater than on the beginning-of-the-year work sheet (Illustration 17–3). The minority stockholders have a 20% equity in Subsidiary Company, and the $24,000 shown on the year-end work sheet is 20% of the year-end balances of the Subsidiary's Common Stock and Retained Earnings accounts. This $24,000 is $1,000 greater than the beginning-of-the-year minority interest because the subsidiary's retained earnings increased $5,000 during the year and the minority stockholder's share of the increase is 20% or $1,000. Second, the $12,000 amount set out as the excess cost of Parent Company's investment over its book value is, in this illustration, the same on the end-of-the-year work sheet as on the work sheet at the beginning. The AICPA has ruled that such excess cost or "goodwill" should be amortized by systematic charges to income over the accounting periods estimated to be benefited.[9] Similar charges must be recorded by the parent in accounting for its investment according to the equity method. Amortization is not illustrated here because a discussion of the required procedures is beyond the scope of this introduction to consolidations.

After its completion the work sheet of Illustration 17–5 is used to prepare the year-end consolidated balance sheet of the parent company and its subsidiary.

Other consolidated statements

Consolidated income statements and consolidated retained earnings statements are also prepared for affiliated companies. However, preparation of these require procedures a discussion of which must be deferred to an advanced accounting course. Knowledge of the procedures is not necessary to a general understanding of such statements. The reader should recognize that all duplications in items and all profit arising from intercompany transactions are eliminated in their preparation. Also, the amounts of net income and retained earnings which are reported in consolidated statements are equal to the amounts recorded by the parent under the equity method.

Purchase versus a pooling of interests

In the discussion thus far it has been assumed that Parent Company acquired its interest in a subsidiary by purchasing the subsidiary's stock for cash. Other methods of paying for the purchase of a subsidiary include issuing bonds payable or preferred stock. All of these cases are accounted for according to the *purchase method* illustrated thus far. In such cases, it is assumed that the subsidiary's shareholders sold their interest in the subsidiary taking cash, bonds, or shares of the parent company's stock in payment. Even if the parent issues common stock to the subsidiary's shareholders, the combination may be regarded as a purchase/sale transaction.

However, where the parent company issues common stock and certain other criteria are satisfied,[10] the consolidated financial statements are prepared in accordance with the *pooling-of-interests method.* Under the pooling-of-interests method it is assumed that no sale oc-

---

[9] APB, "Intangible Assets," *APB Opinion No. 17* (New York: AICPA, 1970), pars. 27–31.

[10] APB, "Business Combinations," *op. cit.,* pars. 45–49.

curred and that the stockholders of the parent and subsidiary companies pooled or combined their interests to form the consolidated company.

Three important differences in the two methods are:

1. Under the purchase method the parent company records its investment in the subsidiary at the amount of cash given or at the market value of the shares of its stock exchanged for the shares of the subsidiary; but under the pooling-of-interests method the parent company records its investment in the subsidiary at the book value of the subsidiary's net assets, regardless of the market value of the shares given.

2. Under the purchase method only that portion of the subsidiary's net income earned in the year of acquisition after the acquisition date becomes part of the consolidated earnings for the year; but under the pooling-of-interests method the subsidiary's earnings for the entire year in which it was acquired become part of the consolidated earnings for the year, even though the subsidiary was acquired late in the year.

3. Under the purchase method the subsidiary's retained earnings as of the date of acquisition do not become part of the consolidated retained earnings; but under the pooling-of-interests method the retained earnings do become part of the consolidated retained earnings.

Due to the first difference, when a parent company pays more than book value for an interest in a subsidiary and afterwards prepares consolidated statements by the purchase method, it must revalue the subsidiary's assets upward and/or show goodwill from consolidation on the consolidated balance sheet. If the assets are revalued upward, more depreciation must be deducted from revenues on the consolidated income statement; and if goodwill is shown, it must be amortized. Consequently, under the purchase method the extra depreciation and/or the amortization of the goodwill result in less consolidated net income than would result with the pooling-of-interests method, under which neither goodwill nor higher asset values are required. Likewise, since a subsidiary's net income is consolidated from the beginning of the year of acquisition rather than from the date of acquisition, consolidation by the pooling-of-interests method commonly results in more consolidated net income in the year of acquisition. Therefore, it can be seen that significantly different balance sheet and income statement amounts can result from the two methods of consolidation. Nevertheless, the APB has ruled that both methods are acceptable in accounting for business combinations, although not as alternatives in accounting for the same combination.[11] It has further established specific conditions that if met require accounting by the

---

[11] Ibid., pars. 42–43.

pooling-of-interests method, and it has ruled that all other business combinations should be accounted for by the purchase method.

No effort will be made here to discuss further or to illustrate the preparation of financial statements by the pooling-of-interests method. Time and a lack of space require that some things be deferred to an advanced accounting course.

Consolidated statements are of no interest to minority stockholders. Their interests normally go no further than the statements of the subsidiary in which they own stock. Likewise, creditors of a subsidiary and people looking to their legal rights find little of interest in consolidated statements.

Who uses consolidated statements

On the other hand, the stockholders of the parent company, its management, and its board of directors have a very real interest in consolidated statements. The parent company's stockholders benefit from earnings, an increase in assets, and financial strength anywhere in the organization. They likewise suffer from a loss or any weakness. And, the managers and directors of the parent company are responsible for all the resources under their control.

In this and the two previous chapters a number of isolated corporation balance sheet sections have been illustrated. In order to bring all of these together, as well as relevant topics from previous chapters, the consolidated balance sheet of Betco Corporation is shown in Illustration 17–6.

The corporation balance sheet

Note that the only items in Illustration 17–6 that distinguish it as a consolidated balance sheet are (1) the title, (2) goodwill from consolidation, and (3) minority interest. Also, recall that Betco Corporation's investment in the subsidiary's stock was eliminated in the process of preparing the consolidated statement. Thus, the reported investment in Toledo Corporation common stock represents an investment by Betco Corporation *or* by its subsidiary in another (outside) company called Toledo Corporation. Toledo Corporation is not the subsidiary.

Consolidated statements. Financial statements in which the assets and liabilities of all affiliated companies are combined on a single balance sheet and their revenues and expenses are combined on a single income statement as though the businesses were a single company.

Betco Corporation
Consolidated Balance Sheet, December 31, 197A

Assets

Current Assets:

Cash			$ 15,000
Marketable securities			5,000
Accounts receivable		$ 50,000	
Less allowance for doubtful accounts		1,000	49,000
Merchandise inventory			115,000
Subscriptions receivable, common stock			15,000
Prepaid expenses			1,000
Total Current Assets				$200,000

Long-Term Investments:

Bond sinking fund			$ 15,000
Toledo Corporation common stock			5,000
Total Long-Term Investments			20,000

Plant Assets:

Land			$ 28,000
Buildings		$190,000	
Less accumulated depreciation		30,000	160,000
Store equipment		$ 85,000	
Less accumulated depreciation		20,000	65,000
Total Plant Assets			253,000

Intangible Assets:

Goodwill from consolidation		23,000

Deferred Charges:

Unamortized moving costs		4,000
Total Assets		$500,000

Liabilities

Current Liabilities:

Notes payable		$ 10,000	
Accounts payable		14,000	
State and federal income taxes payable		16,000	
Total Current Liabilities			$ 40,000

Long-Term Liabilities:

First 6% real estate mortgage bonds, due in 1990		$100,000	
Less unamortized discount based on the 7% market rate for bond interest prevailing on the date of issue		2,000	98,000
Total Liabilities			$138,000
Minority interest			10,000

Contributed Capital and Retained Earnings

Contributed Capital:

Common stock, $100 par value per share, authorized 2,500 shares, issued 2,000 shares		$200,000	
Unissued common stock subscribed, 250 shares		25,000	
Capital contributed by the stockholders in excess of the par value of their shares		33,000	
Total Contributed Capital			$258,000

Retained Earnings:

Appropriated retained earnings:			
Appropriated for bonded indebtedness	$15,000		
Appropriated for plant expansion	10,000	$ 25,000	
Unappropriated retained earnings		69,000	
Total Retained Earnings			94,000
Contributed Capital and Retained Earnings			352,000
Total Liabilities and Capital			$500,000

Illustration 17–6

Cost method of accounting for stock investments. The investment is recorded at total cost and maintained at that amount; subsequent investee earnings and dividends do not affect the investment account.

Equity method of accounting for stock investments. The investment is recorded at total cost, investor's equity in subsequent earnings of the investee increases the investment account, and subsequent dividends of the investee reduce the investment account.

Long-term investments. Investments, not intended as a ready source of cash in case of need, such as bond sinking funds, land, and certain marketable securities.

Marketable equity securities. Equity securities that are actively traded so that sales prices or bid and ask prices are currently available on a national securities exchange or in the over-the-counter market.

Minority interest. The equity of a subsidiary's shares which are not owned by the parent corporation.

Parent company. A corporation that owns a controlling interest (more than 50% of the voting stock is required) in another corporation.

Pooling of interests. A combination between two corporations in which the stockholders of the two companies combine their interests to form the consolidated company without either stockholder group selling its interest.

Purchase method of acquiring a subsidiary. A combination between two corporations where the shareholders of one company sell their interest, taking cash, bonds, and sometimes shares of the parent company's stock in payment.

Subsidiary. A corporation that is controlled by another (parent) corporation because the parent owns more than 50% of the subsidiary's voting stock.

---

1. What is meant by "marketable securities?"
2. In accounting for common stock investments, when should the cost method be used? When should the equity method be used?
3. Do stock dividends provide income to the investor? How should stock dividends be recorded by the investor?
4. Explain how a stock dividend affects the cost per share owned by the investor.
5. When an investor corporation uses the equity method to account for its investment in another (investee) corporation, what recognition is given by the investor to income or loss reported by the investee corporation? What recognition is given to dividends declared by the investee corporation?
6. What are "consolidated" financial statements?
7. What accounts must be eliminated in preparing a consolidated balance sheet? Why are they eliminated?

Questions for class discussion

8. Why would a parent corporation pay more than book value for the stock of a subsidiary?

9. When a parent pays more than book value for the stock of a subsidiary, how should this additional cost be allocated in the consolidated balance sheet?

10. What is meant by "minority interest?" Where is this item disclosed on a consolidated balance sheet?

11. Consolidated financial statements normally are not expected to provide important information to the creditors of a subsidiary or to the minority interest stockholders. Why is this true?

12. Given a particular corporate combination, does management have the option of selecting which accounting method (pooling-of-interests or purchase) will be used to account for the combination?

13. What are the important differences between the pooling-of-interests method and the purchase method of accounting for a corporate combination?

Class exercises

Exercise 17–1

Give entries in general journal form to record the following events on the books of A Company:

197A
Jan. 10 Purchased 10,000 shares of B Company common stock for $125,-000 plus broker's fee of $3,500. B Company has 100,000 shares of common stock outstanding.

Apr. 15 B Company declared and paid a cash dividend of $0.50 per share.

Dec. 31 B Company announced that net income for the year amounted to $140,000.

197B
Apr. 14 B Company declared and paid a cash dividend of $0.40 per share.

July 9 B Company declared and issued a stock dividend of one additional share for each ten shares already outstanding.

Dec. 26 A Company sold 5,500 shares of B Company for $70,000.

Dec. 31 B Company announced that net income for the year amounted to $75,000.

Exercise 17–2

Give entries in general journal form to record the following events on the books of Jag Company:

197A
Jan. 5 Purchased 10,000 shares of Kay Company for $125,000 plus broker's fee of $3,500. Kay Company has 40,000 shares of common stock outstanding.

Apr. 20 Kay Company declared and paid a cash dividend of $0.50 per share.

Dec. 31 Kay Company announced that net income for the year amounted to $56,000.

197B
Apr. 22 Kay Company declared and paid a cash dividend of $0.40 per share.

July 9 Kay Company declared and issued a stock dividend of one additional share for each ten shares already outstanding.

Dec. 31 Kay Company announced that net income for the year amounted to $30,000.

Dec. 31 Jag Company sold 5,500 shares of Kay Company for $70,000.

Exercise 17–3

On December 31, 197—, Parent Company issued 10,000 shares of common stock in payment for 100% of Subsidiary Company's outstanding stock. On the date of combination, the following information pertained to the two companies:

	Parent Company	Subsidiary Company
Retained earnings	$100,000	$ 60,000
Market price per share of common stock	14	
Book value of net assets		110,000

Required:

1. What is the balance in Parent Company's Investment in Subsidiary Stock account on December 31, 197—, assuming (*a*) the pooling-of-interests method of accounting, and (*b*) the purchase method of accounting?
2. If a consolidated balance sheet was prepared on December 31, 197—, what amount of consolidated retained earnings would be shown assuming (*a*) the pooling-of-interests method of accounting, and (*b*) the purchase method of accounting?

Exercise 17–4

On June 30 Company Y had the following stockholders' equity:

Common stock, $10 par value, 10,000 shares issued and outstanding	$100,000
Retained earnings	25,000
Total Stockholders' Equity	$125,000

On the date of the equity section Company X purchased 8,000 of Company Y's outstanding shares, paying $15 per share, and a work sheet to consolidate the balance sheets of the two companies was prepared. Give the entry made on this work sheet to eliminate Company X's investment and Company Y's stockholder equity account balances.

Exercise 17–5

During the year following its acquisition by Company X (see Exercise 17–4), Company Y earned $5,000, paid out $3,000 in dividends, and retained the balance for use in its operations. Give the entry under these assumptions to eliminate Company X's investment and Company Y's stockholders' equity account balances as of the end of the year.

Problem 17–1

Problems

On January 1, Future Corporation purchased 100,000 shares of Lunar Products Company's common stock at 28¼ plus a 1% broker's commission, paying cash for the investment. On July 1, Lunar Products Company declared and paid a dividend of $0.85 per share; and on December 31, its management announced that net income for the year amounted to $1,500,000. Lunar Products Company's stock is actively traded in the over-the-counter market. However, Future Corporation plans to hold the shares until cash will be needed to pay for a plant expansion that is expected to occur three to five years in the future.

Required:

1. Assuming Lunar Products has 1,000,000 outstanding common shares:
   a. Give the journal entries on the books of Future Corporation to account for its investment during the year; and
   b. State the section of Future Corporation's balance sheet in which the investment should be disclosed.
2. Assuming Lunar Products Company has 300,000 outstanding shares:
   a. State whether the investment should be accounted for as a pooling of interests or as a purchase; and
   b. Give the journal entries on the books of Future Corporation to account for its investment during the year.

Problem 17–2

On January 1, 197A, High Company purchased 8,000 shares (80%) of Low Company's $5 par, common stock for $95,000 cash. On that date, the stockholders' equity accounts of Low Company consisted of Common Stock, $50,000, and Retained Earnings, $60,000. In the two years following acquisition, Low Company reported net income and paid dividends as follows:

	Net Income	Dividends
197A................	$ 40,000	$35,000
197B (loss).......	$(20,000)	-0-

Required:

1. Compute the equities of minority interests to be shown on consolidated balance sheets dated: (*a*) January 1, 197A; (*b*) January 1, 197B; and (*c*) January 1, 197C.
2. In general journal form, prepare the entries to eliminate the investment account and the subsidiary's owner equity accounts, where the entries are to be used in work sheets for consolidated balance sheets on: (*a*) January 1, 197A; (*b*) January 1, 197B; and (*c*) January 1, 197C.

Problem 17–3

Fan Corporation was organized on January 1, 197A, for the purpose of investing in the shares of other companies. Fan Corporation immediately issued 1,000 shares of $100 par, common stock for which it received $100,000 cash. On January 2, 197A, Fan Corporation purchased 5,000 shares (20%) of Breeze Company's outstanding stock at a cost of $100,000. The following transactions and events subsequently occurred:

197A
May 17 Breeze Company declared and paid a cash dividend of $1 per share.
Dec. 31 Breeze Company announced that its net income for the year was $40,000.

197B

June 1 Breeze Company declared and issued a stock dividend of one share for each two shares already outstanding.

Oct. 7 Breeze Company declared and paid a cash dividend of $0.75 per share.

Dec. 31 Breeze Company announced that its net income for the year was $48,000.

197C

Jan. 3 Fan Corporation sold all of its investment in Breeze Company for $112,000 cash.

Part 1. Because Fan Corporation owns 20% of Breeze Company's outstanding stock, Fan Corporation is presumed to have a significant financial influence over Breeze Company.

Required:

1. Give the entries on the books of Fan Corporation to record the above events regarding its investment in Breeze Company.
2. Calculate the cost per share of Fan Corporation's investment, as reflected in the investment account on January 1, 197C.
3. Calculate Fan Corporation's retained earnings balance on January 5, 197C, after a closing of the books.

Part 2. Although Fan Corporation owns 20% of Breeze Company's outstanding stock, a thorough investigation of the surrounding circumstances indicates that Fan Corporation does not have a significant financial influence over Breeze Company, and the cost method is the appropriate method of accounting for the investment.

Required:

1. Give the entries on the books of Fan Corporation to record the above events regarding its investment in Breeze Company.
2. Calculate the cost per share of Fan Corporation's investment, as reflected in the investment account on January 1, 197C.
3. Calculate Fan Corporation's retained earnings balance on January 5, 197C, after a closing of the books.

Problem 17–4

Oakdale Corporation purchased 60% of Monroe Company's stock at $25 per share on January 1, 197A. On that date, Oakdale Corporation had retained earnings of $96,100. Monroe Company had retained earnings of $25,000, and had outstanding 7,500 shares of $10 par, common stock, originally issued at par.

Part 1

Required:

1. Give the elimination entry to be used on a work sheet for a consolidated balance sheet, January 1, 197A.
2. Determine the amount of consolidated retained earnings that should be shown on a consolidated balance sheet, January 1, 197A.

Part 2

During the year ended December 31, 197A, Oakdale Corporation paid cash dividends of $10,000 and earned net income of $20,000 excluding earnings from its investment in Monroe Company. Monroe Company earned net income of $15,000 and paid dividends of $7,000. Except for Oakdale Corporation's Retained Earnings account and the Investment in Monroe Company account, the balance sheet accounts for the two companies on December 31, 197A, are as follows:

	Oakdale Corporation	*Monroe Company*
Cash..	$ 57,000	$ 23,000
Notes receivable........................	10,000	
Merchandise	95,800	33,000
Building (net)	120,000	40,000
Land..	40,000	35,000
Investment in Monroe Company	?	
Total Assets	$?	$131,000
Accounts payable........................	$ 35,000	$ 13,000
Note payable.............................		10,000
Common stock	290,000	75,000
Retained earnings.......................	?	33,000
Total Equities	$?	$131,000

Oakdale Corporation loaned $10,000 to Monroe Company during 197A, for which Monroe Company signed a note. On December 31, 197A, that note had not been repaid.

Required:

1. Calculate the December 31, 197A, balances in Oakdale Corporation's Investment in Monroe Company account and Retained Earnings account.
2. Complete a work sheet to consolidate the balance sheets of the two companies.

Problem 17–5

The following items appeared in the first two columns of a work sheet prepared to consolidate the balance sheets of Company A and Company B on the day Company A gained control of Company B by purchasing 17,000 shares of its $5 par value common stock at $6.50 per share.

At the time Company A acquired control of Company B it took Company B's note in exchange for $10,000 in cash and it sold and delivered $2,000 of equipment at cost to Company B on open account (account receivable). Both transactions are reflected in the accounts on the next page.

Required:

1. Prepare a work sheet to consolidate the balance sheets of the two companies and prepare a consolidated balance sheet.
2. Under the assumption that Company B earned $10,000 during the first year after it was acquired by Company A, paid out $6,000 in dividends, and retained the balance of the earnings in its operations, give the entry to

	Company A	Company B
Assets		
Cash	$ 7,500	$ 11,000
Note receivable, Company B....	10,000	
Accounts receivable, net..........	28,000	24,000
Inventories..............................	42,000	35,000
Investment in Company B	110,500	
Equipment, net........................	80,000	70,000
Buildings, net..........................	85,000	
Land	20,000	
Total Assets	$383,000	$140,000
Equities		
Accounts payable	$ 21,000	$ 10,000
Note payable, Company A........		10,000
Common stock........................	250,000	100,000
Retained earnings	112,000	20,000
Total Equities	$383,000	$140,000

eliminate Company A's investment in the subsidiary and Company B's stockholders' equity accounts at the year's end.

Problem 17–1A

Alternate problems

Waters Company purchased 50,000 shares of Evans Company common stock at 34½ plus 1½% broker's commission on January 2, 197A. Since Evans Company pays a high rate of dividends, the investment was evaluated by Waters Company as a good way of earning some return on excess cash balances until they would be needed in the following year. The Evans Company stock is actively traded in the over-the-counter market.

On July 14, Evans Company declared and paid a dividend of $1.25 per share; and on December 31, its management announced that net income for the year amounted to $468,750.

Required:

1. Assuming Evans Company has 312,500 shares outstanding:
   a. Give the journal entries on the books of Waters Company to account for its investment during the year; and
   b. State the section of Waters Company's December 31, 197A, balance sheet in which the investment should be disclosed.
2. Assuming Evans Company has 250,000 shares outstanding, give the journal entries on the books of Waters Company to account for its investment during 197A.

Problem 17–2A

Island Company purchased 14,000 shares (70%) of Cay Corporation's $10 par, common stock on January 1, 197A. Island Company paid $160,000 cash for the shares. The stockholders' equity accounts of Cay Corporation consisted of Common Stock, $200,000, and Retained Earnings, $90,000, on January 1, 197A. In the two years following acquisition, Cay Corporation reported net income and paid dividends as follows:

	Net Income	Dividends
197A	$50,000	$20,000
197B (loss)	(10,000)	15,000

Required:

1. Compute the equities of minority interests to be shown on consolidated balance sheets dated: (*a*) January 1, 197A; (*b*) January 1, 197B; and (*c*) January 1, 197C.
2. In general journal form, prepare the entries to eliminate the investment account and the subsidiary's owner equity accounts, where the entries are to be used in work sheets for consolidated balance sheets on: (*a*) January 1, 197A; (*b*) January 1, 197B; and (*c*) January 1, 197C.

Problem 17–3A

Flash Company was organized as an investment company on January 1, 197A, and immediately issued 1,500 shares of $80 par, common stock in exchange for $140,000 cash. On January 4, 197A, Flash Company acquired 10,000 shares (20%) of Camera Company's outstanding stock for $140,000. The following transactions and events subsequently occurred.

197A

Apr. 25   Camera Company declared and paid cash dividends of $75,000.
Dec. 31   Camera Company announced that its net income for the year was $90,000.

197B

Apr. 28   Camera Company declared and issued a stock dividend of one share for each five shares already outstanding.
Nov. 12   Camera Company declared and paid cash dividends of $60,000.
Dec. 31   Camera Company announced that its net income for the year was $115,000.

197C

Jan.   4   Flash Company sold all of its Camera Company stock for $145,000.

Part 1. Since Flash Company owns 20% of Camera Company's outstanding stock, Flash Company is presumed to have a significant financial influence over Camera Company, and the equity method is the appropriate method of accounting for the investment.

Required:

1. Give the entries on the books of Flash Company to record the above events regarding its investment in Camera Company.
2. Calculate the cost per share of Flash Company's investment, as reflected in the investment account on January 1, 197C.
3. Calculate Flash Company's retained earnings balance on January 5, 197C, after a closing of the books.

Part 2. Although Flash Company owns 20% of Camera Company's outstanding stock, a thorough investigation of the surrounding circumstances indicates that Flash Company does not have a significant financial influence over Camera Company, and the cost method is the appropriate method of accounting for the investment.

Required:

1. Give the entries on the books of Flash Company to record the above events regarding its investment in Camera Company.
2. Calculate the cost per share of Flash Company's investment, as reflected in the investment account on January 1, 197C.
3. Calculate Flash Company's retained earnings balance on January 6, 197C, after a closing of the books.

Problem 17–5A

The following assets and equities appeared on the balance sheets of Company X and Company Y on the day Company X gained control of Company Y by purchasing 3,600 shares of its $25 par value common stock at $35 per share.

	Company X	Company Y
Assets		
Cash	$ 8,000	$ 12,000
Note receivable, Company Y	5,000	
Accounts receivable, net	37,000	22,000
Inventories	35,000	32,000
Investment in Company Y	126,000	
Equipment, net	75,000	70,000
Buildings, net	100,000	
Land	25,000	
Total Assets	$411,000	$136,000
Equities		
Note payable, Company X		$ 5,000
Accounts payable	$ 24,000	11,000
Common stock	300,000	100,000
Premium on common stock	30,000	5,000
Retained earnings	57,000	15,000
Total Equities	$411,000	$136,000

At the time Company X gained control of Company Y it took Company Y's note in exchange for equipment that cost Company X $5,000 and it also sold and delivered $2,000 of inventory at cost to Company Y on open account (account receivable). Both transactions are reflected in the foregoing accounts.

Required:

1. Prepare a work sheet to consolidate the balance sheets of the two companies and prepare a consolidated balance sheet.
2. Under the assumption Company Y earned $9,600 during the year after it was acquired by Company X, paid out $5,600 in dividends, and retained the balance in its operations, give the entry to eliminate Company X's investment in the subsidiary and Company Y's stockholders' equity accounts at the year's end.

Decision problem 17–1, A confused investor

At the recent stockholders' meeting of Indiana Company, one of the stockholders made the following statements. "I have owned shares of Indiana Company for several years, but am now questioning whether management is telling the truth in the annual financial statements. At the end of 197A, you announced that Indiana Company had just acquired a 30% interest in the outstanding stock of Southern Airlines. You also stated that the 80,000 shares had cost Indiana Company $8,000,000. In the financial statements for 197B, you told us that the investments of Indiana Company were proving to be very profitable, and reported that earnings from all investments had amounted to more than $2.3 million. In the financial statements for 197C, you explained that Indiana Company had sold the Southern Airlines shares during the first week of the year, receiving $9,100,000 cash proceeds from the sale. Nevertheless, the income statement for 197C reports only a $200,000 gain on the sale (before taxes). I realize that Southern Airlines did not pay any dividends during 197B, but it was very profitable. As I recall, it reported net income of $3,000,000 for 197B. Personally, I do not think you should have sold the shares. But, much more importantly, you reported to us that our company gained only $200,000 from the sale. How can that be true if the shares were purchased for $8,000,000 and were sold for $9,100,000?"

Explain to this stockholder why the $200,000 gain is correctly reported.

Decision problem 17–2, Eastern Company

On October 3 of the current year Eastern Company gained control of Western Company through the purchase of 80% of Western Company's outstanding stock. At that time Western Company owed Eastern Company $2,000 for merchandise purchased on credit and $10,000 it had borrowed by giving a promissory note. The condensed October 3 balance sheets of the two companies follow:

EASTERN AND WESTERN COMPANIES
Balance Sheets, October 3, 19—

	Eastern Company	Western Company
Assets		
Cash	$ 5,000	$ 13,000
Notes receivable	10,000	
Accounts receivable, net	32,000	29,000
Inventories	42,000	30,000
Investment in Western Company	96,000	
Equipment, net	75,000	60,000
Buildings, net	80,000	
Land	20,000	
Total Assets	$360,000	$132,000

	Eastern Company	Western Company
Equities		
Accounts payable	$ 30,000	$ 7,000
Notes payable		10,000
Common stock	250,000	100,000
Retained earnings	80,000	15,000
Total Equities	$360,000	$132,000

Prepare a consolidated balance sheet for Eastern Company and its subsidiary. Then write short explanations of why consolidated statements are prepared and the principles of consolidation.

PART 6

Financial statements: Interpretation and modifications

18
Statement of changes in financial position: Flows of funds and cash . . .

19
Analyzing financial statements . . .

20
Accounting for price-level changes

After studying Chapter 18, you should be able to:

- Describe the information that is disclosed in a statement of changes in financial position.

- State three different meanings of the word "funds" and the significance of each meaning in relation to financial statements.

- Describe what is meant by sources and uses of funds and what kinds of transactions qualify as a source or a use.

- Prepare statements of changes in financial position.

- Tell whether or not net income is a source of funds and describe the adjustments that must be made to net income in preparing a statement of changes in financial position.

- Prepare a cash flow statement and describe the information contained therein.

- Explain how cash generated from operations differs from net income generated from operations.

- Define or explain the words and phrases listed in the chapter Glossary.

chapter 18

Statement of changes in financial position: Flows of funds and cash

At the end of an accounting period when financial statements are prepared, the income statement shows how much profit or loss was earned by a business during the period, the retained earnings statement summarizes the changes in its retained earnings, and the balance sheet shows its end-of-the-period financial position. However, for a better understanding of the financing and investing transactions that occurred during the period, more information is needed; and this is supplied by a *statement of changes in financial position,* which as its name implies, summarizes the changes that have occurred in the financial position of the business during the period.

A statement of changes in financial position aids in understanding the financial position of a business by supplying answers to such questions as: How many dollars of funds flowed into the business from operations and how were these funds used? What was the source of the funds used to finance the new plant? For what were the proceeds of the bond issue used? Why were there fewer current assets and more current liabilities at the end of the period than at the beginning? The statement provides information regarding such questions by showing from where a business got funds and how it used them. For this reason it is sometimes called a *statement of sources and uses of funds,* or a *statement of sources and applications of funds,* or simply a *funds statement;* however, the APB recommends that the title "Statement of Changes in Financial Position" be used for published statements.

Business executives use the word "working capital" or sometimes "net working capital" to mean the excess of a concern's current assets over its current liabilities. Working capital is used in this way because the current assets and current liabilities of a business constantly circulate. Short-term credit is used to buy merchandise, which is sold and turned into accounts receivable, which are collected and turned

Nature of funds and working capital

601

into cash, which is used to pay bills so that short-term credit can be used again to buy more merchandise, and so on. Since current assets and current liabilities are constantly circulating, it is only normal to think of that portion of the current assets not immediately needed to pay current debts as liquid resources or available funds. However, business executives recognize that only a portion of these resources can be drawn off at any one time to pay dividends, buy plant assets, pay long-term debt, or for other like purposes. Only a portion can be used because a large share must remain in circulation.

The general public uses the word "funds" to mean cash. In business, however, the word "funds" frequently has a broader meaning which involves economic resources that can be used to acquire assets, pay dividends, reduce debt, and finance similar transactions. Because working capital can be used for these kinds of transactions, the concept of "funds" is often used to mean working capital. However, some financing and investing transactions do not require the use of working capital. For example, the purchase of land and buildings might be financed entirely through the issuance of long-term debt or stock. Thus, although the word "funds" is sometimes used to mean cash, and is often used to mean working capital, a comprehensive list of the sources from which investing transactions are financed would suggest that the concept of "funds" include all financial resources.

Sources and uses of funds

Most statements of changes in financial position are designed to emphasize the increase or decrease in working capital which occurred during the period. From this perspective, transactions that increase working capital are called *sources of funds,* and transactions that decrease working capital are *uses of funds.* If the working capital of a company increases during an accounting period, more funds are generated by its transactions than are used; and if working capital decreases, more funds are used than are generated.

Sources of funds

Some of the more common sources of funds (working capital) are:

Current operations   Funds in the form of cash and accounts receivable flow into a business from sales; and most expenses and goods sold result in outflows of funds. Consequently, funds are increased as a result of normal operations if the inflow from sales exceeds the outflow for expenses and goods sold.

In analyzing funds provided by operations the income statement shows how many dollars of funds were generated by sales. However, although the net income before extraordinary items is the amount revenues exceeded expenses, this figure does not generally represent the net amount of funds from operations because some expenses listed on an income statement, such as depreciation, depletion, and bond discount or premium amortization do not cause either a funds outflow or a funds inflow in the period of the statement.

For example, Rexel Sales Company, Illustration 18–1, experienced a $50,000 funds inflow from sales during the year. It also experienced outflows of $30,000 for goods sold, $8,000 for salaries, and $1,200 for rent; but there was no outflow of working capital for the depreciation expense. Consequently, during this period the company gained funds equal to the sum of its reported net income plus recorded depreciation, or it gained $9,800 plus $1,000 or $10,800 of funds from operations.

Rexel Sales Company
Income Statement for Year Ended December 31, 19—

Sales...		$50,000
Cost of goods sold		30,000
Gross profit from sales.......................		$20,000
Operating expenses:		
Sales salaries expense	$8,000	
Rent expense.................................	1,200	
Depreciation expense, equipment	1,000	10,200
Net Income		$ 9,800

Illustration 18–1

Business executives often speak of depreciation as a source of funds, but it is not. Look again at Illustration 18–1. Sales are the source of funds on this statement. No funds flowed into this company from recording depreciation. In this case, as with every business, the revenues are the source of funds from operations; but since depreciation, unlike most expenses, did not and does not cause a funds outflow in the current period, it must be added to the net income to determine funds from operations.

Long-term liabilities Transactions that increase long-term liabilities increase working capital or are so treated and, therefore, are sources of funds regardless of whether long-term notes, mortgages, or bonds are involved. On the other hand, short-term credit, whether obtained from banks or other creditors, is not a source of funds because short-term credit does not increase working capital. For example, if $10,000 is borrowed for a short period, say six months, both current assets and current liabilities are increased; but since both are increased the same amount, total working capital is unchanged.

Sale of noncurrent assets When a plant asset, long-term investment, or other noncurrent asset is sold for cash or receivables, working capital is increased by the amount of the sale; therefore, such sales are sources of funds.

Sale of capital stock The issuance of stock for cash or current receivables increases current assets; and as a result, such sales are sources of funds. Likewise, an additional investment of current assets by a single proprietor or partner is also a source of funds.

Uses of funds √

Transactions that decrease working capital use funds. A list includes:

.Purchase of noncurrent assets   When noncurrent assets such as plant and equipment or long-term investments are purchased, working capital is reduced; consequently, such purchases are uses of funds.

Payment of noncurrent liabilities   Payment of a long-term debt such as a mortgage, bonds, or a long-term note reduces working capital and is a use of funds. Likewise, a contribution to a debt retirement fund, bond sinking fund, or other special noncurrent fund is also a use of funds.

Capital reductions   The withdrawals of cash or other current assets by a proprietor, the purchase of treasury stock, or the purchase of stock for retirement reduce working capital and are uses of funds.

Declaration of a dividend   The declaration of a dividend which is to be paid in cash or other current assets reduces working capital and is a use of funds. Note that it is the declaration that uses funds. The declaration creates a current liability, dividends payable, and therefore reduces working capital as soon as it is voted by the board of directors. The final payment of a dividend previously declared does not affect working capital because it reduces current assets and current liabilities in equal amounts.

Statement of changes in financial position

The primary reason for preparing a statement of changes in financial position is to summarize and disclose the financing and investing activities of the business during the period. To accomplish this objective, such statements are usually designed so as to explain the increase or decrease in a concern's working capital. This is done by (1) listing on the statement all sources of new working capital, (2) listing the uses made of working capital, and then (3) setting out the difference, which is the net increase or decrease in working capital. Such a statement is shown in Illustration 18–2. Note that it covers a period of time and accounts for the increase or decrease in working capital during the period.

The ability of an enterprise to provide working capital through its operations is an important factor in evaluating its ability to finance new investment opportunities. Consequently, a statement of changes in financial position should separately disclose the amount of funds provided by operations, as in Illustration 18–2. This calculation begins with the amount of the company's net income, exclusive of extraordinary items. To this amount must be added (or deducted) any items recognized in determining the income or loss but which did not require outlays (provide inflows) of working capital. The resulting amount should then be appropriately described as, for example, "Working capital provided by operations," or "Working capital used in operations." (A net loss that exceeds the corrections for items not requiring working capital results in "Working capital used in operations.") The

Delta Company
Statement of Changes in Financial Position
For Year Ended December 31, 1979

Sources of working capital:
  Current operations:
    Net income for 1979*... $12,200
    Add expenses not requiring outlays of working
      capital in the current period:
      Depreciation of buildings and equipment .... _4,500_
        Working capital provided by operations $16,700
  Other sources:
    Sale of common stock... _12,500_
        Total new working capital................................ $29,200
Uses of working capital:
  Purchase of office equipment................................. $ 500
  Purchase of store equipment 6,000
  Addition to building 15,000
  Reduction of mortgage debt 2,500
  Declaration of dividends.. _3,100_
        Total uses of working capital ....   _27,100_
Net Increase in Working Capital .... $ 2,100

  * Delta Company reported no extraordinary items during 1979.   **Illustration 18–2**

effect of extraordinary items on funds is not considered to be part of
funds provided by operations,[1] and the separate disclosure of these
items is discussed later.

Preparing a statement of changes in financial position

A statement of changes in financial position could be prepared by
searching through a concern's current asset and current liability accounts for the transactions that increased or decreased its working
capital. However, this would be time consuming because almost every
transaction completed by a concern affected these accounts and only
a very few of the transactions either increased or decreased its working
capital. Therefore, in preparing a statement of changes in financial
position, it is not the current asset and current liability accounts that
are examined for working capital changes, but rather the noncurrent
accounts. (The noncurrent accounts are the accounts other than the
current asset and current liability accounts.) The noncurrent accounts
are examined because (1) only a few transactions affected these accounts and (2) almost every one either increased or decreased working
capital.

Normally, in making an audit of a company's noncurrent accounts,
the auditor makes a list of the transactions that affected these accounts
during the period under review. This list is then used along with the
company's balance sheets as of the beginning and end of the period to
prepare the statement of changes in financial position. The comparative

---

[1] APB, "Reporting Changes in Financial Position," *APB Opinion No. 19* (New
York: AICPA, 1971), par. 10.

Delta Company
Comparative Balance Sheet
December 31, 1979, and December 31, 1978

Assets

	1979	1978
Current Assets:		
Cash	$ 7,500	$ 4,800
Accounts receivable, net	8,000	9,500
Merchandise inventory	31,500	32,000
Prepaid expenses	1,000	1,200
Total Current Assets	$ 48,000	$ 47,500
Plant and Equipment:		
Office equipment	$ 3,500	$ 3,000
Accumulated depreciation, office equipment	(900)	(600)
Store equipment	26,200	21,000
Accumulated depreciation, store equipment	(5,200)	(4,200)
Buildings	95,000	80,000
Accumulated depreciation, buildings	(10,600)	(8,200)
Land	25,000	25,000
Total Plant and Equipment	$133,000	$116,000
Total Assets	$181,000	$163,500

Liabilities

Current Liabilities:		
Notes payable	$ 2,500	$ 1,500
Accounts payable	16,700	19,600
Dividends payable	1,000	700
Total Current Liabilities	$ 20,200	$ 21,800
Long-Term Liabilities:		
Mortgage payable	$ 17,500	$ 20,000
Total Liabilities	$ 37,700	$ 41,800

Stockholders' Equity

Common stock, $10 par value	$115,000	$100,000
Premium on common stock	8,500	5,000
Retained earnings	19,800	16,700
Total Stockholders' Equity	$143,300	$121,700
Total Liabilities and Stockholders' Equity	$181,000	$163,500

Illustration 18–3

balance sheet of Illustration 18–3 and the following list of transactions that affected the noncurrent accounts of Delta Company were used in preparing the funds statement of Illustration 18–2.

a. Purchased office equipment costing $500 during the year.
b. Purchased store equipment that cost $6,000.
c. Discarded and junked fully depreciated store equipment that cost $800 when new.
d. Added a new addition to the building that cost $15,000.
e. Earned a $12,200 net income during the year. There were no extraordinary items.
f. Delta Company deducted on its 1979 income statement $300 of depreciation on office equipment, (*g*) $1,800 on its store equipment, and (*h*) $2,400 on its building.

i. Made a $2,500 payment on the mortgage.

j. Declared a 5% stock dividend at a time when the company's stock was selling for $12 per share.

k. Sold and issued 1,000 shares of common stock at $12.50 per share.

l. Declared cash dividends totaling $3,100 during the year.

Steps in preparing a statement of changes in financial position

Three steps are involved in preparing a statement of changes in financial position. They are:

1. Determine the increase or decrease in working capital for the period of the statement.
2. Prepare a working paper to account for the changes in the company's noncurrent accounts and in the process set out on the working paper the period's sources and uses of working capital.
3. Use the working paper to prepare the formal statement of changes in financial position.

The 1979 change in Delta Company's working capital is calculated in Illustration 18–4. The calculation is a simple one requiring nothing more than a determination of the amounts of working capital at the beginning and at the end of the period and a subtraction to arrive at the increase or decrease in working capital.

Determining the change in working capital

Working capital, December 31, 1979:		
Current assets	$48,000	
Current liabilities	20,200	
Working capital		$27,800
Working capital, December 31, 1978:		
Current assets	$47,500	
Current liabilities	21,800	
Working capital		25,700
Increase in Working Capital		$ 2,100

Illustration 18–4

Delta Company's sources and uses of funds resulted from simple transactions, and a statement of changes in financial position could be prepared for the company without a working paper. However, the working paper helps to organize the information needed for the statement and also offers a proof of the accuracy of the work.

The working paper for Delta Company's statement of changes in financial position is shown in Illustration 18–5. Such a working paper is prepared as follows:

1. First the amount of working capital at the beginning of the period under review is entered on the first line in the first money column

Preparing the working paper

Delta Company
Working Paper for Statement of Changes in Financial Position
For Year Ended December 31, 1979

	Account Balances 12/31/78	Analyzing Entries Debit	Analyzing Entries Credit	Account Balances 12/31/79
Debits				
Working capital	25,700			27,800
Office equipment	3,000	(a) 500		3,500
Store equipment	21,000	(b) 6,000	(c) 800	26,200
Buildings	80,000	(d) 15,000		95,000
Land	25,000			25,000
Totals	154,700			177,500
Credits				
Accumulated depreciation, office equipment	600		(f) 300	900
Accumulated depreciation, store equipment	4,200	(c) 800	(g) 1,800	5,200
Accumulated depreciation, buildings	8,200		(h) 2,400	10,600
Mortgage payable	20,000	(i) 2,500		17,500
Common stock	100,000		(j) 5,000 (k) 10,000	115,000
Premium on common stock	5,000		(j) 1,000 (k) 2,500	8,500
Retained earnings	16,700	(j) 6,000 (l) 3,100	(e) 12,200	19,800
Totals	154,700			177,500
Sources of working capital:				
Current operations:				
Net income		(e) 12,200		
Depreciation of office equipment		(f) 300		
Depreciation of store equipment		(g) 1,800		
Depreciation of buildings		(h) 2,400		
Other sources:				
Sale of stock		(k) 12,500		
Uses of working capital:				
Purchase of office equipment			(a) 500	
Purchase of store equipment			(b) 6,000	
Addition to building			(d) 15,000	
Reduction of mortgage			(i) 2,500	
Declaration of dividends			(l) 3,100	
Totals		63,100	63,100	

Illustration 18–5

    and the amount of working capital at the end is entered in the last column.

2. Next, the noncurrent balance sheet amounts are entered on the working paper, the amounts or account balances as of the beginning of the period are entered in the first money column and those of the end in the last. Observe that debit items are listed first and are followed by credit items. This is a convenience that places the accumulated depreciation items with the liability and capital amounts.

3. After the noncurrent account balances are entered, the working capital amount and debit items in each column are added; then the credit items are added to be certain that debits equal credits.

4. After the items are added to see that debits equal credits, the phrase "Sources of working capital:" is written on the line following the total of the credit items. Sufficient lines are then skipped to allow for listing all possible fund sources and then the phrase "Uses of working capital:" is written.

5. Next, analyzing entries are entered in the second and third money columns. These entries do two things: (1) they account for or explain the amount of change in each noncurrent account, and (2) they set out the sources and uses of working capital. (The analyzing entries on the illustrated working paper are discussed later in this chapter.)

6. After the last analyzing entry is entered, the working paper is completed by adding the Analyzing Entries columns to determine their equality. The information on the paper as to sources and uses of working capital is then used to prepare the formal statement of changes in financial position.

In passing it should be observed that a funds statement working paper is prepared solely for the purpose of bringing together information as to sources and uses of working capital and its analyzing entries are never entered in the accounts.

Analyzing entries

As previously stated, in addition to setting out sources and uses of funds, the analyzing entries in the working paper also account for or explain the amount of change in each noncurrent account. The change in each noncurrent account is explained with one or more analyzing entries because every transaction that caused an increase or decrease in working capital also increased or decreased a noncurrent account. Consequently, when all increases and decreases in noncurrent accounts are explained by means of analyzing entries, all sources and uses of working capital are set out on the working paper.

The analyzing entries on the working paper of Illustration 18–5 account for the changes in Delta Company's noncurrent accounts and set out its sources and uses of working capital. Explanations of the entries follow:

a. During the year Delta Company purchased new office equipment that cost $500. This required the use of working capital and also caused a $500 increase in the balance of its Office Equipment account. Consequently, analyzing entry (a) has a $500 debit to Office Equipment and a like credit to "Uses of working capital: Purchase of office equipment." The debit accounts for the change in the Office Equipment account, and the credit sets out the use of working capital.

b.   Delta Company purchased $6,000 of new store equipment during the period. This required the use of $6,000 of working capital, and the use is set out with analyzing entry (b). However, note that the $6,000 debit of the entry does not fully account for the change in the balance of the Store Equipment account. Analyzing entry (c) is also needed.

c.   During the period under review Delta Company discarded and junked fully depreciated store equipment that when new had cost $800, and the entry made to record the disposal decreased the company's Store Equipment and related accumulated depreciation accounts by $800. However, the disposal had no effect on the company's working capital. Nevertheless, analyzing entry (c) must be made to account for the changes in the accounts, otherwise all changes in the company's noncurrent accounts will not be explained; and unless all changes are explained, the person preparing the working paper cannot be certain that all sources and uses of funds have been set out on the working paper.

d.   Delta Company used $15,000 to increase the size of its building. The cost of the addition was debited to the Buildings account, and analyzing entry (d) sets out this use of funds.

e.   Delta Company reported a $12,200 net income for 1979, and the income was a source of funds. In the end-of-the-year closing procedures the amount of this net income was transferred from the company's Income Summary account to its Retained Earnings account and helped change the balance of the latter account from $16,700 at the beginning of the year to $19,800 at the year-end. Observe the analyzing entry that sets out this source of funds on the working paper. The entry's debit sets out the net income as a source of funds, and the credit helps explain the change in the Retained Earnings account.

f.   (g), and (h).   On its 1979 income statement Delta Company deducted $300 of depreciation expense on its office equipment, $1,800 on its store equipment, and $2,400 on its building. As previously explained, although depreciation is a rightful deduction from revenues in arriving at net income, any depreciation so deducted must be added to net income in determining working capital from operations. The debits of entries (f), (g), and (h) show the depreciation taken by the company as part of the working capital generated by operations, and the credits of the entries either account for or help account for the changes in the accumulated depreciation accounts.

i.   On June 10 Delta Company made a $2,500 payment on the mortgage on its plant and equipment. The payment required the use of funds, and it reduced the balance of the Mortgage Payable account by $2,500. Entry (i) sets out this use of funds and accounts for the change in the Mortgage Payable account.

j.   At the September board meeting the directors of the company declared a 5% or 500-share stock dividend on a day the company's stock was selling at $12 per share. The declaration and later distribution of this dividend had no effect on the company's working capital. However, it did decrease Retained Earnings $6,000 and increase the Common Stock account $5,000 and Premium on Common Stock $1,000. Entry (*j*) accounts for the changes in the accounts resulting from the dividend.

k. In October the company sold and issued 1,000 shares of its common stock for cash at $12.50 per share. The sale was a source of funds that increased the balance of the company's Common Stock account $10,000 and increased the balance of its Premium on Common Stock account $2,500. Entry (*k*) sets out this source of funds and completes the explanation of the changes in the stock and premium accounts.

l. At the end of each of the first three quarters in the year the company declared a $700 quarterly cash dividend, and on December 22 it declared a $1,000 dividend, payable on the following January 15. The fourth dividend brought the total cash dividends declared during the year to $3,100. Each declaration required the use of working capital, and each reduced the balance of the Retained Earnings account. On the working paper the four dividends are combined and one analyzing entry is made for the $3,100 use of funds. The entry's debit helps account for the change in the balance of the Retained Earnings account, and its credit sets out the use of funds.

After the last analyzing entry is entered on a funds statement working paper, an examination is made to be certain that all changes in the noncurrent accounts listed on the paper have been explained with analyzing entries. To make this examination, the debits and credits in the Analyzing Entries columns opposite each beginning account balance are added to or are subtracted from the beginning balance, and the result must equal the ending balance. For example, the $3,000 beginning debit balance of office equipment plus the $500 debit of analyzing entry (*a*) equals the $3,500 ending amount of office equipment. Likewise, the $21,000 beginning balance of store equipment plus the $6,000 debit and minus the $800 credit equals the $26,200 ending balance for this asset, and so on down the working paper until all changes are accounted for. Then if in every case the debits and credits opposite each beginning balance explain the change in the balance, all sources and uses of working capital have been set out on the working paper and the working paper is completed by adding the amounts in its Analyzing Entries columns.

Preparing the statement of changes in financial position from the working paper

After the working paper is completed, the sources and uses of working capital set out on the bottom of the paper are used to prepare the formal statement of changes in financial position. This is a simple task that requires little more than a relisting of the sources and uses of funds on the formal statement, as a comparison of the items appearing on the statement of Illustration 18–2 with the items at the bottom of the working paper of Illustration 18–5 will show.

A net loss on the working paper

When a concern incurs a net loss, the amount of the loss is debited to its Retained Earnings account in the end-of-the-period closing procedures. Then, when the working paper for a statement of changes in financial position is prepared, the words "Net loss" are substituted for "Net income" in its sources of working capital section, and the amount of the loss is debited to Retained Earnings and credited to "Net loss" on the working paper. After this the loss is placed on the formal statement of changes in financial position as the first monetary item and the expenses not requiring outlays of working capital are deducted therefrom. If the net loss is less than these expenses, the resulting amount is working capital provided by operations. If the net loss exceeds these expenses, the result is working capital used in operations.

Analysis of working capital changes

A statement of changes in financial position accounts for the increase or decrease in a company's working capital by showing sources and uses of working capital. The APB advanced the opinion that the usefulness of such a statement is enhanced if it is accompanied by a tabulation on which the changes in the various elements of the com-

Delta Company
Analysis of Changes in Working Capital Items
For Year Ended December 31, 1979

	Dec. 31, 1979	Dec. 31, 1978	Working Capital Increases	Working Capital Decreases
Current Assets:				
Cash...	$ 7,500	$ 4,800	$2,700	
Accounts receivable, net..............	8,000	9,500		$1,500
Merchandise inventory	31,500	32,000		500
Prepaid expenses	1,000	1,200		200
Total Current Assets...............	$48,000	$47,500		
Current Liabilities:				
Notes payable.............................	$ 2,500	$ 1,500		1,000
Accounts payable	16,700	19,600	2,900	
Dividends payable........................	1,000	700		300
Total Current Liabilities	$20,200	$21,800		
Working Capital.............................	$27,800	$25,700		
			$5,600	$3,500
Net Increase in Working Capital				2,100
			$5,600	$5,600

Illustration 18–6

pany's working capital are analyzed in appropriate detail.[2] Such a tabulation for Delta Company is shown in Illustration 18–6. Note how the tabulation's final figure ties back to the final figure in Illustration 18–2.

Information for preparing the analysis of changes in working capital is taken from balance sheets as of the beginning and end of the period under review. (Compare the information in Illustration 18–6 with that in Illustration 18–3.) The current asset and current liability items on the analysis and the preparation of the analysis need little discussion. However, students sometimes have difficulty understanding how, for example, an increase in a current liability results in a decrease in working capital. They should not, for when a current liability increases, a larger amount is subtracted from current assets in determining working capital.

Extraordinary gains and losses

Extraordinary gains and losses are set out as special items on a company's income statement as was explained in Chapter 16, and they require special treatment on the statement of changes in financial position and on the working paper for such a statement. For example, Beta Company sold land that it had purchased some years before to expand its plant, but had not used for that or any other purpose. The land cost $15,000 and was sold for $25,000, and no future land purchases or sales were expected. The company paid $2,500 of income taxes on the sale and reported the $7,500 net gain on its income statement as shown in Illustration 18–7.

Beta Company Income Statement for Year Ended December 31, 19—		
Revenue:		
Net sales...		$500,000
Cost and expenses:		
Cost of goods sold	$300,000	
Selling and administrative expenses other than depreciation...	141,000	
Depreciation expense, plant and equipment....................	9,000	
Income taxes..	18,000	468,000
Income before extraordinary gain...........................		$ 32,000
Gain on sale of land held for expansion, net of $2,500 of applicable income taxes...............................		7,500
Net Income		$ 39,500

Illustration 18–7

Since Beta Company, as is common, carried this land as a long-term investment, a noncurrent asset, the sale increased its working capital $22,500 (sale price of land less applicable income taxes). The sale

---

[2] Ibid., par. 12.

also reduced by $15,000 the balance of the account, Land Held for Expansion; and it resulted in a $7,500 after-tax, extraordinary gain that was closed to Income Summary and included in the $39,500 net income carried to Retained Earnings at the end of the accounting period. As a result, the analyzing entries of Illustration 18–8 are required on the company's funds statement working paper to set out working capital generated by the land sale and by normal operations.

	Analyzing Entries	
	Debit	Credit
Land held for expansion		(a) 15,000
Accumulated depreciation, plant and equipment		(b) 9,000
Retained earnings		(a) 39,500
Sources of working capital:		
Current operations:		
Income before extraordinary item	(a) 32,000	
Depreciation expense, plant and equipment	(b) 9,000	
Extraordinary item:		
Sale of land held for expansion	(a) 22,500	
Other sources:		

Illustration 18–8

The working capital generated by the land sale is then shown on the formal statement of changes in financial position as an extraordinary item immediately after the amount of working capital provided by normal operations, as shown in Illustration 18–9.

Sources of working capital:	
Current operations:	
Net income of 197A, exclusive of extraordinary item	$32,000
Add expenses not requiring outlays of working capital	
in the current period:	
Depreciation expense, plant and equipment	9,000
Working capital provided by operations, exclusive of	
extraordinary item	$41,000
Extraordinary item:	
Sale of land held for expansion, net of $2,500 of applicable income	
taxes	22,500
Other sources:	

Illustration 18–9

Broad concept of financing and investing activities

The APB has held that a statement of changes in financial position should be based on a broad concept of the financing and investing activities of a business and it should disclose all important aspects of such activities even though elements of working capital are not directly affected.[3] For example, the acquisition of a building in ex-

---

[3] Ibid., par. 8.

change for a mortgage or the conversion of bonds to stock are transactions that do not directly affect elements of working capital. However, the Board has held that such transactions should be disclosed on the statement of changes in financial position even though working capital is not directly involved. For example, if a building is acquired by issuing a mortgage, the issuance of the mortgage should be disclosed on the statement of changes in financial position as a source of funds, "Mortgage issued to acquire building." Likewise the acquisition of the building should appear as a use of funds, "Building acquired by issuing a mortgage."

CASH FLOW

The statement of changes in financial position usually is designed to explain the changes in working capital which occurred during the period. However, it may be designed to explain the changes in cash.[4] If it is, the descriptive phrases used in the statement should clearly state that the statement is constructed to explain cash flows. For example, "Cash provided by operations" should be used instead of "Working capital provided by operations." The details of preparing such statements according to the requirements of *APB Opinion No. 19* are left to a more advanced book.

One of the most important phases of management's work is to manage a company's money, so that adequate cash is available to meet liabilities, pay dividends, and so on. Also, surplus amounts of money should be kept invested in assets which will contribute income to the company. Therefore, the management of a company will often require cash flow statements to assist in planning and controlling the cash flows of the company. Since published statements of changes in financial position are most often designed to explain working capital, the cash flow statements are often prepared for internal management and do not follow precisely the APB guidelines for published statements of changes in financial position on a cash flow basis. Nevertheless, all cash flow statements are quite similar.

Cash flow statement

A cash flow statement covers a period of time and accounts for the increase or decrease in a company's cash by showing where the company got cash and the uses it made of cash during the period. For example, Royal Supply Company of Illustration 18–10 began the period of the statement with $2,200 of cash. This beginning balance was increased $22,000 by cash from operations and $4,500 by cash from the sale of investments; and it was decreased $12,000 by the withdrawals of the business owner and $6,500 by the purchase of plant assets. In other words, there was an $8,000 net increase in cash during the period.

---

[4] Ibid., par. 11.

Royal Supply Company
Cash Flow Statement
For Year Ended December 31, 19—

Cash balance, January 1, 19—			$ 2,200
Sources of cash:			
Cash generated by operations.......	$22,000		
Sale of investments.....................	4,500		
Total sources of cash............		$26,500	
Uses of cash:			
Withdrawals of owner	$12,000		
Purchase of plant assets	6,500		
Total uses of cash		18,500	
Increase in cash			8,000
Cash balance, December 31, 19—			$10,200

Illustration 18–10

A work sheet similar to that utilized in preparing a statement of changes in financial position is commonly used to analyze the changes in a company's noncash accounts and to bring together the data needed to prepare a cash flow statement. A discussion of this work sheet is deferred to a more advanced text, and a simple analysis based on the difference between the cash basis and the accrual basis of accounting is used here to introduce the subject of cash flow. However, before beginning the analysis a review of the difference between the cash and the accrual bases of accounting is in order.

Under the cash basis of accounting a revenue appears on the income statement of the period in which it is collected in cash, regardless of when earned. For example, if a sale of merchandise is made in November 197A, but the customer does not pay for the goods until January 197B, under the cash basis of accounting the revenue from the sale appears on the 197B income statement. Likewise, under the cash basis of accounting an expense appears on the income statement of the period in which cash is disbursed in its payment, regardless of which accounting period benefited from its incurrence. Consequently, under the cash basis the gain or loss reported for an accounting period is the difference between cash received from revenues and cash disbursed for expenses. The difference is also the amount of cash generated by operations during the period.

Under the accrual basis of accounting all of this differs. Under the accrual basis revenues are credited to the period in which they are earned regardless of when cash is received and expenses are matched with revenues regardless of when cash is disbursed. As a result, under the accrual basis the profit or loss of an accounting period is the difference between revenues earned and the expenses incurred in earning the revenues. Most enterprises of any size use the accrual basis of accounting, and all accounting demonstrated thus far in this text has been accrual basis accounting.

Reexamine the cash flow statement of Illustration 18–10 and note that the cash inflow shown thereon from the sale of investments and the outflow for withdrawals and to buy plant assets need no explanations. However, the inflow of cash from operations does.

Cash flows into a company from sales and it flows out for goods sold and expenses; and although cost of goods sold and expenses are deducted from sales on an accrual basis income statement, the resulting net income figure does not show the amount of cash generated by operations. To determine cash from operations, it is necessary to convert the item amounts on a company's income statement from an accrual basis to a cash basis.

Royal Supply Company's accrual basis income statement appears in Illustration 18–11, and the statement amounts are converted from an accrual basis to a cash basis in Illustration 18–13. The conversion is based on the information in the company's condensed Cash account which is shown in Illustration 18–12. Explanations of the conversion follow.

Preparing a cash flow statement

Royal Supply Company
Income Statement for Year Ended December 31, 19—

Sales, net		$90,000
Cost of goods sold:		
Inventory, January 1, 19—	$10,000	
Purchases, net	55,000	
Goods for sale	$65,000	
Inventory, December 31, 19—	11,000	
Cost of goods sold		54,000
Gross profit from sales		$36,000
Operating expenses:		
Depreciation expense	$ 3,400	
Bad debts expense	300	
Salaries and wages expense	12,500	
Other expenses	3,300	
Total operating expenses		19,500
Net Income		$16,500

Illustration 18–11

Condensation of Royal Supply Company's Cash Account

(Debits)		(Credits)	
Balance, January 1	2,200	Cash purchases of merchandise	200
Cash sales	40,000	Payments to creditors for	
Accounts receivable collections	50,500	merchandise purchased	52,800
Sale of investments	4,500	Salary and wage payments	12,100
		Payments for other expenses	3,400
		Plant asset purchases	6,500
		Withdrawals by owner	12,000
		Balance, December 31	10,200
Total	97,200	Total	97,200

Illustration 18–12

Royal Supply Company
Conversion of Income Statement Amounts from an Accrual to a
Cash Basis For Year Ended December 31, 19—

	Accrual Basis Amounts	Add (deduct)	Cash Basis Amounts
Sales, net	$90,000	$ 500	$90,500
Cost of goods sold	54,000	(1,000)	53,000
Gross profit from sales	$36,000		$37,500
Operating expenses:			
Depreciation expense	$ 3,400	(3,400)	$ -0-
Bad debts expense	300	(300)	-0-
Salaries and wages expense......	12,500	(400)	12,100
Other expenses........................	3,300	100	3,400
Total operating expenses	$19,500		$15,500
Net Income................................	$16,500		
Cash Generated by Operations			$22,000

Illustration 18–13

a. Cash flowed into Royal Supply Company from sales; but the $90,000 sales figure on the company's income statement was not the amount. Rather, cash from goods sold consisted of cash sales, $40,000, plus collections from customers, $50,500, or a total of $90,500, as shown in the condensed Cash account of Illustration 18–12. Consequently, since cash from goods sold was $500 greater than the income statement sales figure, $500 is added to convert the sales figure from an accrual basis to a cash basis.

b. Likewise, the $54,000 cost of goods sold figure on the income statement is not the amount of money that flowed out to pay for goods sold. Rather, the actual cash outflow for merchandise amounted to $53,000, $200 for cash purchases plus $52,800 paid to creditors for merchandise, as shown in the condensed Cash account. Since the cash outflow for the purchase of merchandise was $1,000 less than the accrual basis cost of goods sold figure, $1,000 is subtracted in converting cost of goods sold from an accrual to a cash basis.

c. Since depreciation and bad debts expense did not take cash, the amounts for these items are deducted in converting the income statement amounts to a cash basis.

d. And since the cash paid by Royal Supply Company for salaries and wages was $400 less than the accrual basis income statement amount for this expense and cash disbursed for "other expenses" was $100 more, $400 is deducted and $100 is added in in converting these expenses to a cash basis.

The last figure in Illustration 18–13, the $22,000 of cash generated by operations, is the amount Royal Supply Company would have reported as net income had it kept its books on a cash basis rather than an accrual basis. The $22,000 is also the amount of cash the company got from its operations and the amount that appears on its Illustration 18–10 cash flow statement as cash from this source.

Cash flow statement. A financial statement that accounts for the increase or decrease in a company's cash during a period by showing where the company got cash and the uses it made of cash.

Funds. (*a*) cash; (*b*) working capital; and (*c*) economic resources that can be used to acquire assets, pay dividends, reduce debt, and finance similar transactions.

Net working capital. A synonym for working capital.

Source of funds. Under the working capital concept, a transaction that increases working capital.

Statement of changes in financial position. A financial statement that reports, in a summarized fashion, the financing and investing transactions that occurred during the period, generally indicating their effects on working capital.

Use of funds. Under the working capital concept, a transaction that decreases working capital.

Working capital. The excess of a company's current assets over its current liabilities.

Glossary

---

1. State three different meanings of the word "funds."
2. List several sources of working capital and several uses of working capital.
3. Explain why such expenses as depreciation, amortization of patents, and amortization of bond discount are added to the net income in order to determine working capital provided by operations?
4. Some people speak of depreciation as a source of funds. Why do you think this occurs? Is depreciation a source of funds?
5. On May 14 a company borrowed $30,000 by giving its bank a 60-day, interest-bearing note. Was this transaction a source of working capital?
6. A company began an accounting period with a $90,000 merchandise inventory and ended it with a $50,000 inventory. Was the decrease in inventory a source of working capital?
7. What is shown on a statement of changes in financial position?
8. Why are the noncurrent accounts examined to discover changes in working capital?
9. When a working paper for the preparation of a statement of changes in financial position is prepared, all changes in noncurrent balance sheet accounts are accounted for on the working paper. Why?
10. A company discarded and wrote off fully depreciated store equipment. What account balances appearing on the statement of changes in financial position working paper were affected by the write-off? What analyzing entry was made on the working paper to account for the write-off? If the

Questions for class discussion

write-off did not affect working capital, why was the analyzing entry made on the working paper?

11. Explain why a decrease in a current liability represents an increase in working capital.

12. How is the amount of cash generated by a company's operations determined?

Class exercises

Exercise 18–1

Prepare from the following condensed income statement a list and the total of working capital provided by operations:

TORONTO CORPORATION, LTD.
Income Statement for Year Ended December 31, 19—

Sales...		$800,000
Cost of goods sold		520,000
Gross profit from sales.......................................		$280,000
Operating expenses:		
Salaries and wages (including $1,000 accrued)	$125,000	
Depreciation expense	15,000	
Rent expense	36,000	
Patents written off...	3,000	
Bad debts expense (allowance method)..................	4,000	183,000
Operating income..		$ 97,000
Bond interest expense (including $6,000 accrued and		
$500 of bond discount amortized)		12,500
Net Income		$ 84,500

Exercise 18–2

From the following list of transactions completed by Mississippi Airlines during 197—, prepare a statement of changes in financial position for the year.

a. Mississippi Airlines earned $250,000 net income during 197—.

b. Issued a 5-year note payable in the amount of $300,000 to help pay for a new computerized reservations system. The total cost of the new system ($380,000) was paid in cash.

c. Declared cash dividends totaling $25,000 during the year.

d. Depreciation totaled $140,000 on all depreciable assets.

e. Purchased on-line computer terminals costing $75,000.

f. Purchased miscellaneous fixed assets totaling $84,000.

g. Made mortgage payments of $136,000.

h. Sold and issued 10,000 shares of common stock at $11.30 per share.

Exercise 18–3

The 197A and 197B trial balances of Columbus Company follow. From the information prepare an analysis of changes in working capital items for 197B:

	197A		197B	
Cash...	$ 12,000		$ 10,000	
Notes receivable.............................	3,000		5,000	
Accounts receivable, net	30,000		25,000	
Merchandise inventory	50,000		55,000	
Prepaid expenses	1,000		2,000	
Equipment......................................	100,000		109,000	
Accumulated depreciation, equipment		$ 20,000		$ 25,000
Notes payable		8,000		10,000
Accounts payable		20,000		18,000
Taxes payable		5,000		4,000
Wages payable		1,000		2,000
Mortgage payable (due 1990)................		25,000		25,000
Common stock		100,000		100,000
Retained earnings		17,000		22,000
Totals	$196,000	$196,000	$206,000	$206,000

Exercise 18–4

Jamestown Company's 197A and 197B balance sheets carried the following items:

	December 31	
Debits	*197A*	*197B*
Cash	$ 4,000	$ 5,000
Accounts receivable, net.....................	9,000	8,000
Merchandise inventory	18,000	20,000
Equipment	15,000	19,000
Totals.....................................	$46,000	$52,000

Credits		
Accumulated depreciation, equipment....	$ 3,000	$ 4,000
Accounts payable.............................	5,000	7,000
Taxes payable................................	2,000	1,000
Common stock, $10 par value	25,000	27,000
Premium on common stock.................	5,000	6,000
Retained earnings.............................	6,000	7,000
Totals.....................................	$46,000	$52,000

Required:

Prepare a statement of changes in financial position working paper that is designed to explain the changes in working capital, and prepare the formal statement. Also prepare an analysis of changes in working capital items. Use the following information from the company's 197B income statement and accounts:

a. The company earned $6,000 during 197B.
b. Its equipment depreciated $1,500 in 197B.
c. Equipment costing $4,500 was purchased.

d. Fully depreciated equipment that cost $500 was discarded and its cost and accumulated depreciation were removed from the accounts.

e. Two hundred shares of stock were sold and issued at $15 per share.

f. The company declared $5,000 of cash dividends during the year.

Exercise 18–5

From the following income statement and analysis of the Cash account, both for the same year, prepare a cash flow statement.

JOHANSON COMPANY

Income Statement for Year Ended December 31, 19—

Sales, net		$ 91,000
Cost of goods sold:		
Merchandise inventory, January 1, 19—	$12,000	
Purchases	50,000	
Goods for sale	$62,000	
Merchandise inventory, December 31, 19—	11,000	
Cost of goods sold		51,000
Gross profit from sales		$ 40,000
Operating expenses:		
Salaries and wages expense	$12,000	
Rent expense	9,000	
Depreciation expense, equipment	4,000	
Bad debts expense	1,000	26,000
Net Income		$ 14,000

Cash Account Analysis

Cash balance, January 1, 19—		$ 8,000
Debits:		
Cash sales	$40,000	
Accounts receivable collections	52,000	
Bank loan	5,000	97,000
Total		$105,000
Credits:		
Payments to creditors for merchandise	$51,500	
Salaries and wages paid	11,800	
Rent payments	9,000	
Payment for new equipment purchased	12,200	
Dividends paid	10,000	94,500
Cash balance, December 31, 19—		$ 10,500

Problems

Problem 18–1

Worthington Company's 197A and 197B balance sheets carried these items:

	December 31	
Debits	*197A*	*197B*
Cash	$ 4,300	$ 7,500
Accounts receivable, net......................	10,000	8,000
Merchandise inventory........................	32,000	31,500
Prepaid expenses.............................	1,200	1,000
Equipment	24,000	30,100
Totals....................................	$71,500	$78,100

Credits		
Accumulated depreciation, equipment....	$ 4,800	$ 6,100
Accounts payable.............................	17,900	14,300
Notes payable.................................	1,500	2,500
Mortgage payable.............................	10,000	6,000
Common stock, $10 par value	25,000	30,000
Premium on common stock..................		2,500
Retained earnings.............................	12,300	16,700
Totals....................................	$71,500	$78,100

Required:

Prepare a statement of changes in financial position working paper and a formal statement that are designed to explain the change in working capital. Also prepare an analysis of changes in working capital items. Use the following additional information from the company's 197B income statement and accounting records:

a. Net income for the year, $7,400.
b. The equipment depreciated $2,100 during the year.
c. Fully depreciated equipment that cost $800 was discarded, and its cost and accumulated depreciation were removed from the accounts.
d. Equipment costing $6,900 was purchased.
e. The mortgage was reduced by a $4,000 payment.
f. Five hundred shares of common stock were issued at $15 per share.
g. Cash dividends totaling $3,000 were declared and paid.

Problem 18–2

The 197A and 197B balance sheets of Franklin Corporation carried these items:

	December 31	
Debits	*197A*	*197B*
Cash...............................	$ 12,600	$ 10,200
Accounts receivable, net	32,900	35,100
Merchandise inventory.......	86,400	85,200
Prepaid expenses	1,800	1,500
Office equipment...............	5,600	5,000
Store equipment................	28,300	29,800
Totals	$167,600	$166,800

Credits

Accumulated depreciation, office equipment ....$	2,400	$ 2,600
Accumulated depreciation, store equipment.....	6,500	7,500
Accounts payable..	23,500	22,400
Notes payable	5,000	10,000
Common stock, $10 par value.......................	100,000	110,000
Premium on common stock...........................	5,500	6,500
Retained earnings.......................................	24,700	7,800
Totals	$167,600	$166,800

Required:

Use the following additional information and prepare a statement of changes in financial position working paper and a statement of changes in financial position. They should be designed to explain the change in working capital. Also prepare an analysis of changes in working capital items.

a. The company suffered a $1,900 net loss during 197B.
b. Depreciation expense charged on office equipment during the year, $500; and on store equipment, $1,700.
c. Office equipment carried at its $600 cost less $300 accumulated depreciation was sold at its book value.
d. Store equipment costing $2,200 was purchased.
e. Fully depreciated store equipment that cost $700 was discarded, and its cost and accumulated depreciation were removed from the accounts.
f. Cash dividends totaling $4,000 were declared during the year.
g. A 1,000-share stock dividend was declared and distributed. On the declaration date the company's shares were selling at $11 each.

Problem 18–3

Ray Cameron, as a single proprietor, operates Cameron's Art Shop. At the ends of 197A and 197B, the store's balance sheets carried this information:

	December 31	
Debits	*197A*	*197B*
Cash	$ 6,400	$ 7,100
Accounts receivable, net.............................	17,200	16,800
Merchandise inventory...............................	33,700	36,400
Other current assets...................................	800	500
Store equipment.......................................	8,400	13,100
Totals...	$66,500	$73,900

Credits		
Accumulated depreciation, store equipment .... $	3,200	$ 1,800
Accounts payable.......................................	16,800	14,200
Ray Cameron, capital.................................	46,500	57,900
Totals...	$66,500	$73,900

Ray Cameron's 197B statement showing changes in the proprietor's Capital account carried the following information:

Ray Cameron, capital, January 1, 197B..........		$46,500
Add additional investment		5,000
Total investment		$51,500
Net income per income statement	$12,400	
Less withdrawals.....................................	6,000	
Excess of income over withdrawals		6,400
Ray Cameron, Capital, December 31, 197B....		$57,900

The store equipment accounts showed: (1) $1,200 depreciation expense on store equipment recorded in 197B; (2) store equipment costing $4,800 was purchased; (3) equipment carried on the books on the day of its exchange at its $2,800 cost, less $2,400 accumulated depreciation, was traded on new equipment having a $3,100 cash price, and a $600 trade-in allowance was received; and (4) fully depreciated equipment that cost $200 was junked and its cost and accumulated depreciation were removed from the accounts.

Required:

Prepare a statement of changes in financial position working paper and a formal statement of changes in financial position. Both should be designed to explain the change in working capital. Also prepare an analysis of changes in working capital items.

Problem 18–4

The debit and credit amounts from Coronado Corporation's 197A and 197B balance sheets and its noncurrent accounts follow:

	December 31	
Debits	*197A*	*197B*
Cash...	$ 22,900	$ 18,700
Accounts receivable, net	32,100	30,400
Merchandise inventory:...............................	56,400	55,100
Prepaid expenses	1,700	1,900
Store equipment..	32,800	40,400
Land...	30,000	30,000
Building..	112,500	181,000
Totals	$288,400	$357,500
Credits		
Accumulated depreciation, store equipment....	$ 13,700	$ 16,200
Accumulated depreciation, building...............	20,200	23,600
Accounts payable.......................................	24,600	25,700
Wages payable...	1,800	2,100
Income taxes payable	4,200	4,100
Mortgage interest payable...........................		1,000
Cash dividends payable...............................	7,500	5,000
Mortgage payable.......................................		50,000
Common stock, $10 par value.....................	150,000	150,000
Premium on common stock..........................	15,000	18,000
Stock dividend distributable........................		7,500
Retained earnings......................................	51,400	54,300
Totals	$288,400	$357,500

Store Equipment

Date		Explanation	Debit	Credit	Balance
197B					
Jan.	1	Balance			32,800
Apr.	4	Purchased new equipment	8,700		41,500
	7	Discarded equipment		1,100	40,400

Accumulated Depreciation, Store Equipment

Date		Explanation	Debit	Credit	Balance
197B					
Jan.	1	Balance			13,700
Apr.	7	Discarded equipment	1,100		12,600
Dec.	31	Year's depreciation		3,600	16,200

Land

Date		Explanation	Debit	Credit	Balance
197B					
Jan.	1	Balance			30,000

Building

Date		Explanation	Debit	Credit	Balance
197B					
Jan.	1	Balance			112,500
Mar.	17	Building addition	68,500		181,000

Accumulated Depreciation, Building

Date		Explanation	Debit	Credit	Balance
197B					
Jan.	1	Balance			20,200
Dec.	31	Year's depreciation		3,400	23,600

Mortgage Payable

Date		Explanation	Debit	Credit	Balance
197B					
Mar.	15			50,000	50,000

Common Stock

Date		Explanation	Debit	Credit	Balance
197B					
Jan.	1	Balance			150,000

Premium on Common Stock

Date		Explanation	Debit	Credit	Balance
197B					
Jan.	1	Balance			15,000
Dec.	23	Stock dividend		3,000	18,000

Stock Dividend Distributáble

Date		Explanation	Debit	Credit	Balance
197B					
Dec.	23	Stock dividend		7,500	7,500

Retained Earnings

Date		Explanation	Debit	Credit	Balance
197B					
Jan.	1	Balance			51,400
Dec.	23	Stock dividend	10,500		40,900
	23	Cash dividend	5,000		35,900
	31	Net income		18,400	54,300

Required:

Prepare a statement of changes in financial position working paper and a formal statement of changes in financial position. They should be designed to explain the change in Coronado Corporation's working capital. Also prepare an analysis of changes in working capital items.

Problem 18–5

Cracker Supply's income statement and analysis of its Cash account for the year of the statement follow:

CRACKER SUPPLY
Income Statement for Year Ended December 31, 19—

Sales, net..			$113,500
Cost of goods sold:			
Merchandise inventory, January 1, 19—	$ 21,200		
Purchases, net..	79,500		
Goods available for sale......................................	$100,700		
Merchandise inventory, December 31, 19—	22,300		
Cost of goods sold			78,400
Gross profit from sales.......................................			$ 35,100
Operating expenses:			
Rent expense	$ 6,000		
Salaries and wages	15,900		
Bad debts expense	600		
Depreciation expense, store equipment..................	1,400		
Other operating expenses ..:................................	1,700		
Total operating expenses..............................			25,600
Net Income			$ 9,500

Analysis of Cash Account

Cash balance, January 1, 19—................................		$ 4,300
Debits:		
Cash sale receipts	$ 37,200	
Accounts receivable collections...........................	75,900	
Sale of equipment (at book value)........................	200	
Bank loan..	5,000	118,300
Total..		$122,600
Credits:		
Creditor payments for merchandise.......................	$ 78,300	
Rent payments	6,500	
Salary and wage payments..................................	15,700	
Other expense payments	1,600	
Payment for new store equipment purchased	5,800	
Personal withdrawals by proprietor......................	8,400	116,300
Cash balance, December 31, 19—		$ 6,300

The equipment was sold at book value.

Required:

Prepare a cash flow statement to be used by Cracker Supply's manager in evaluating the investing and financing transactions for the year.

Alternate problems

Problem 18–2A

Camden Company's 197A and 197B balance sheets carried these items:

	December 31	
Debits	*197A*	*197B*
Cash...	$ 11,800	$ 12,700
Accounts receivable, net	33,400	34,900
Merchandise inventory................................	86,700	85,900
Other current assets	1,800	2,000
Office equipment.......................................	6,100	5,400
Store equipment..	27,800	31,700
Totals	$167,600	$172,600

Credits		
Accumulated depreciation, office equipment .... $	2,400	$ 2,500
Accumulated depreciation, store equipment.....	6,500	7,400
Accounts payable.......................................	20,200	19,500
Notes payable	5,000	4,500
Federal income taxes payable	3,300	3,500
Common stock, $5 par value........................	100,000	105,000
Premium on common stock...........................	5,500	8,500
Retained earnings......................................	24,700	21,700
Totals	$167,600	$172,600

An examination of the company's statements and accounts showed:

a. A $15,000 net income was earned in 197B.
b. Depreciation charged on office equipment, $600; and on store equipment, $1,500.
c. Office equipment that had cost $700 and had been depreciated $500 was sold for its book value.
d. Store equipment costing $4,500 was purchased.
e. Fully depreciated store equipment that cost $600 was discarded, and its cost and accumulated depreciation were removed from the accounts.
f. Cash dividends totaling $10,000 were declared during the year.
g. A 1,000-share stock dividend was declared and distributed during the year at a time the company's stock was selling at $8 per share.

Required:

Prepare a statement of changes in financial position working paper and a formal statement of changes in financial position for the company. Also prepare an analysis of changes in working capital items.

Problem 18–3A

The 197A and 197B balance sheets of Sailmaker Company carried the following debit and credit amounts:

	December 31	
Debits	*197A*	*197B*
Cash..	$ 22,300	$ 16,100
Accounts receivable, net	15,600	16,200
Merchandise inventory.....................	51,400	50,200
Prepaid expenses	1,100	1,300
Store equipment..............................	24,300	26,000
Office equipment..............................	4,200	4,400
Land...		20,000
Building...		100,000
Totals	$118,900	$234,200

Credits		
Accumulated depreciation, store equipment.....$	3,600	$ 5,200
Accumulated depreciation, office equipment	1,300	1,400
Accumulated depreciation, building.................		1,200
Accounts payable............................	18,700	17,300
Taxes payable	4,100	4,400
Mortgage payable............................		80,000
Common stock, $10 par value..........	80,000	100,000
Premium on common stock...............		4,000
Retained earnings............................	11,200	20,700
Totals	$118,900	$234,200

An examination of the company's 197B income statement and accounting records showed:

a. A $15,500 net income for the year.

b. Depreciation on store equipment, $2,400; on office equipment, $400; and on the building, $1,200.

c. Store equipment that cost $2,500 was purchased during the year.

d. Fully depreciated store equipment that cost $800 was discarded and its cost and accumulated depreciation were removed from the accounts.

e. Office equipment that cost $500 and had been depreciated $300 was traded in on new office equipment priced at $800. A $300 trade-in allowance was received.

f. During the year the company purchased the building it occupied and had previously rented, paying $40,000 in cash and giving a mortgage for the balance.

g. Two thousand shares of common stock were issued at $12 per share.

h. Cash dividends totaling $6,000 were declared during the year.

Required:

Prepare a statement of changes in financial position working paper and a formal statement of changes in financial position. Both should be designed to explain the changes in working capital. Also prepare an analysis of changes in working capital items.

Problem 18–5A

Last year's income statement and analysis of the Cash account of Frisco-burger Company follow:

FRISCOBURGER COMPANY
Income Statement for Year Ended December 31, 19 –

Sales, net		$125,400
Cost of goods sold:		
Merchandise inventory, January 1, 19 – $15,300		
Purchases, net.. 76,600		
Goods for sale $91,900		
Merchandise inventory, December 31, 19 – 16,700		
Cost of goods sold		75,200
Gross profit from sales		$ 50,200
Operating expenses:		
Salaries and wages....................................	$26,400	
Rent expense	7,200	
Depreciation of store equipment....................	1,800	
Bad debts expense	500	
Store supplies used	600	
Other operating expenses............................	1,300	
Total operating expenses........................		37,800
Net Income		$ 12,400

Analysis of Cash Account

Cash balance, January 1, 19—		$ 3,900
Debits:		
Cash sales	$27,600	
Accounts receivable collections.............................	98,700	
Sale of equipment (at book value).........................	300	
Bank loan..	6,000	132,600
Total		$136,500
Credits:		
Rent payments	$ 7,200	
Payments to creditors for merchandise purchased	75,900	
Payments to creditors for store supplies bought	700	
Salary and wage payments	26,300	
Other expense payments.....................................	1,200	
New store equipment purchased............................	9,800	
Personal withdrawals by the proprietor...................	9,000	130,100
Cash balance, December 31, 19—		$ 6,400

The equipment was sold at book value.

Required:

Prepare a cash flow statement for the year.

At the end of 197B, the accountant of Mason City Produce prepared the following changes in working capital accounts and the statement of changes in financial position and the income statement on the next page for the store's owner, Ralph Mason:

Decision problem 18–1, Mason City Produce

Changes in Working Capital Accounts
For Year Ended December 31, 197B

	Dec. 31, 197A	Dec. 31, 197B	Funds	
			Increases	Decreases
Current Assets:				
Cash......................................	$15,500	$ 3,000		$12,500
Accounts receivable	32,000	38,000	$ 6,000	
Merchandise inventory	25,000	35,000	10,000	
Prepaid expenses	500	1,000	500	
Total current assets........	$73,000	$77,000		
Current Liabilities:				
Notes payable		$ 5,000		5,000
Accounts payable	$25,000	21,000	4,000	
Salaries and wages payable....	2,000	1,000	1,000	
Total current liabilities....	$27,000	$27,000		
Working capital	$46,000	$50,000		
			$21,500	$17,500
Increase in Working Capital				4,000
			$21,500	$21,500

Statement of Changes in Financial Position
For Year Ended December 31, 197B

Working capital was provided by:
Current operations:
    Net income.............................. $30,000
    Add depreciation of plant assets.... 12,000

        Total new funds.................... $42,000
Working capital was used for:
  Purchases of new plant assets.......... $20,000
  Reduction of mortgage.................... 6,000
  Personal withdrawals of proprietor.... 12,000

        Total uses of funds..................   38,000
Increase in Working Capital .... $ 4,000

Comparative Income Statements
Years Ended December 31, 197A, and 197B

	197A		197B
Sales......................................	$250,000		$300,000
Cost of goods sold:			
Inventory, January 1 .... $ 30,000		$ 25,000	
Purchases......................... 150,000		190,000	
Goods for sale.................... $180,000		$215,000	
Inventory, December 31 25,000		35,000	
Cost of goods sold	155,000		180,000
Gross profit from sales.............	$ 95,000		$120,000
Operating expenses:			
Salaries and wages .... $ 69,000		$ 76,000	
Depreciation of plant assets... 9,500		12,000	
Insurance and supplies.......... 1,500		2,000	
Total operating expenses...	80,000		90,000
Net Income	$ 15,000		$ 30,000

When Mr. Mason saw the income statement, he was amazed to learn that his net income had doubled in 197B, and he could not understand how this could happen in a year in which his cash had declined to the point that he had found it necessary in late December to secure a $5,000 short-term bank loan in order to meet his current expenses. His accountant pointed to the statement of changes in financial position by way of explanation, but this statement only confused Mr. Mason further. He could not understand how depreciation could be a source of working capital, while a bank loan was not, and he could not understand how his working capital could increase $4,000 at a time when his cash decreased $12,500.

Explain the points Mr. Mason finds confusing. Attach to your explanation a statement showing the cash generated by his store's 197B operations and a cash flow statement for 197B.

Bill Cunningham owns Yacht World, a sailboat equipment store; and during 1978 he remodeled and replaced $20,000 of the store's fully depreciated equipment with new equipment costing $25,000. However, by the year-end he was having trouble meeting the store's current expenses and had to secure a $6,000 short-term bank loan. As a result he asked his accountant to prepare some sort of a report showing what had happened to the store's funds during the year. The accountant analyzed the changes in the store's 1978 accounts and produced the following funds statement:

Decision problem 18–2, Yacht World

YACHT WORLD
Statement of Changes in Financial Position
For Year Ended December 31, 1978

Sources of working capital:		
Income from operations.........................	$17,700	
Depreciation on store equipment..............	5,000	
Additional investment of proprietor..........	5,000	$27,700
Uses of working capital:		
Purchase of new equipment:		
Cost.. $25,000		
Less mortgage placed on equipment..... 12,500	$12,500	
Personal withdrawals of proprietor...........	12,000	24,500
Net Increase in Working Capital.................		$ 3,200

On reading the report, Mr. Cunningham was dumbfounded by the $3,200 increase in working capital in a year he knew his store's bank balance had decreased by $8,000. Also, he could not understand how depreciation was a source of working capital but the $6,000 bank loan was not. Explain these points to Mr. Cunningham and attach to your explanations any additional or different statement from that prepared by the accountant that you think helps to make your explanation clear.

The following post-closing trial balances were used by the accountant in preparing the store's statement of changes in financial position:

YACHT WORLD
1977–1978 Post-Closing Trial Balances

	Dec. 31, 1977		Dec. 31, 1978	
Cash...	$10,500		$ 2,500	
Accounts receivable.........................	14,300		17,600	
Allowance for doubtful accounts.........		$ 300		$ 500
Merchandise inventory......................	17,400		29,600	
Prepaid expenses............................	500		800	
Store equipment..............................	40,000		45,000	
Accumulated depr., store equipment....		26,000		11,000
Notes payable.................................				6,000
Accounts payable.............................		11,500		10,000
Accrued payables.............................		700		600
Mortgage payable (due 1984–89)........				12,500
Bill Cunningham, capital....................		44,200		54,900
Totals.....................................	$82,700	$82,700	$95,500	$95,500

After studying Chapter 19, you should be able to:

■ Describe comparative financial statements, how they are prepared, and the limitations associated with interpreting them.

■ Prepare common-size comparative statements and interpret them.

■ Explain the importance of working capital in the analysis of financial statements and list the typical ratios used to analyze working capital.

■ Calculate the common ratios used in analyzing the balance sheet and income statement and state what each ratio purports to measure.

■ State the limitations associated with using financial statement ratios and the sources from which standards for comparison may be obtained.

■ Define or explain the words and phrases listed in the chapter Glossary.

chapter 19

Analyzing financial statements

The financial statements of a business are analyzed to determine its overall position and also to find out about certain aspects of that position, such as earnings prospects and debt-paying ability. In making the analysis, individual statement items are in themselves generally not too significant, but relationships between items and groups of items plus changes that have occurred are significant. As a result, financial statement analysis requires that relationships between items and groups of items and changes in items and groups of items be seen.

Comparative statements

Changes in financial statement items can usually best be seen when item amounts for two or more successive years are placed side by side in columns on a single statement. Such a statement is called a *comparative statement,* and each of the financial statements, or portions thereof, may be presented in the form of comparative statements.

In its most simple form a comparative balance sheet consists of the item amounts from two or more of a company's successive balance sheets arranged side by side, so that changes in amounts may be seen. However, such a statement can be improved by also showing in both dollar amounts and in percentages the changes that have occurred. When this is done, as in Illustration 19–1, large dollar and large percentage changes become more readily apparent to the statement reader.

A comparative income statement is prepared in the same manner as a comparative balance sheet. Income statement amounts for two or more successive periods are placed side by side, with dollar and percentage changes in additional columns. Such a statement is shown in Illustration 19–2.

Anchor Supply Company
Comparative Balance Sheet
December 31, 1978, and December 31, 1979

	Years Ended December 31		Amount of Increase or (Decrease) during 1979	Percent of Increase or (Decrease) during 1979
	1979	1978		
Assets				
Current Assets:				
Cash	$ 18,000	$ 90,500	$ (72,500)	(80.1)
Accounts receivable, net	68,000	64,000	4,000	6.3
Merchandise inventory	90,000	84,000	6,000	7.1
Prepaid expenses	5,800	6,000	(200)	(3.3)
Total Current Assets	$181,800	$244,500	$ (62,700)	(25.6)
Long-Term Investments:				
Real estate	$ -0-	$ 30,000	$ (30,000)	(100.0)
Apex Company common stock	-0-	50,000	(50,000)	(100.0)
Total Long-Term Investments	$ -0-	$ 80,000	$ (80,000)	(100.0)
Plant and Equipment:				
Office equipment, net	$ 3,500	$ 3,700	$ (200)	(5.4)
Store equipment, net	17,900	6,800	11,100	163.2
Buildings, net	176,800	28,000	148,800	531.4
Land	50,000	20,000	30,000	150.0
Total Plant and Equipment	$248,200	$ 58,500	$189,700	324.3
Total Assets	$430,000	$383,000	$ 47,000	12.3
Liabilities				
Current Liabilities:				
Notes payable	$ 5,000	$ -0-	$ 5,000	
Accounts payable	43,600	55,000	(11,400)	(20.7)
Taxes payable	4,800	5,000	(200)	(4.0)
Wages payable	800	1,200	(400)	(33.3)
Total Current Liabilities	$ 54,200	$ 61,200	$ (7,000)	(11.4)
Long-Term Liabilities:				
Mortgage payable	$ 60,000	$ 10,000	$ 50,000	500.0
Total Liabilities	$114,200	$ 71,200	$ 43,000	60.4
Capital				
Common stock, $10 par value	$250,000	$250,000	$ -0-	-0-
Retained earnings	65,800	61,800	4,000	6.5
Total Capital	$315,800	$311,800	$ 4,000	1.3
Total Liabilities and Capital	$430,000	$383,000	$ 47,000	12.3

Illustration 19–1

Analyzing and interpreting comparative statements

In analyzing and interpreting comparative data, it is necessary for the analyst to select for study any items showing significant dollar or percentage changes, to determine the reasons for each change, and to determine if possible whether they are favorable or unfavorable. For example, in the comparative balance sheet of Anchor Supply Com-

Anchor Supply Company
Comparative Income Statement
Years Ended December 31, 1978, and 1979

	Years Ended December 31		Amount of Increase or (Decrease) during 1979	Percent of Increase or (Decrease) during 1979
	1979	1978		
Gross sales..	$973,500	$853,000	$120,500	14.1
Sales returns and allowances	13,500	10,200	3,300	32.4
Net sales	$960,000	$842,800	$117,200	13.9
Cost of goods sold..................................	715,000	622,500	92,500	14.9
Gross profit from sales	$245,000	$220,300	$ 24,700	11.2
Operating expenses:				
Selling expenses:				
Advertising expense	$ 7,500	$ 5,000	$ 2,500	50.0
Sales salaries expense.........................	113,500	98,000	15,500	15.8
Store supplies expense........................	3,200	2,800	400	14.3
Depreciation expense, store equipment .	2,400	1,700	700	41.2
Delivery expense	14,800	14,000	800	5.7
Total selling expenses	$141,400	$121,500	$ 19,900	16.4
General and administrative expenses:				
Office salaries expense	$ 41,000	$ 40,050	$ 950	2.1
Office supplies expense	1,300	1,250	50	4.0
Insurance expense	1,600	1,200	400	33.3
Depreciation expense, office equipment.	300	300	-0-	-0-
Depreciation expense, buildings	2,850	1,500	1,350	90.0
Bad debts expense..............................	2,250	2,200	50	2.3
Total general and admin. expenses .	$ 49,300	$ 46,500	$ 2,800	6.0
Total operating expenses.........	$190,700	$168,000	$ 22,700	13.5
Operating income.....................................	$ 54,300	$ 52,300	$ 2,000	3.8
Less interest expense	2,300	1,000	1,300	130.0
Income before taxes................................	$ 52,000	$ 51,300	$ 700	1.4
Income taxes	19,000	18,700	300	1.6
Net Income...	$ 33,000	$ 32,600	$ 400	1.2

Illustration 19-2

pany, Illustration 19–1, the first item, "Cash," shows a large decrease, and at first glance this appears unfavorable. However, when the decrease in "Cash" is considered with the decrease in "Investments" and the increases in "Store equipment," "Buildings," and "Land," plus the increase in "Mortgage payable," it becomes apparent the company has materially increased its plant assets between the two balance sheet dates. Further study reveals the company has apparently constructed a new building on land it has held as an investment until needed in this expansion. Also, it seems the company has paid for its new plant assets by reducing cash, selling its Apex Company common stock, and issuing a $50,000 mortgage.

As an aid in controlling operations, a comparative income statement is usually more valuable than a comparative balance sheet. For example, in Illustration 19–2, "Gross sales" increased 14.1% and "Net sales" increased 13.9%. At the same time, "Sales returns" increased 32.4%, or at a rate more than twice that of gross sales. Returned sales represent wasted sales effort and indicate dissatisfied customers; consequently, such an increase in returns should be investigated, and the reason therefor determined if at all possible. Also, in addition to the large increase in the "Sales returns," it is significant that the rate of increase in "Cost of goods sold" is greater than that of "Net sales." This is an unfavorable trend and should be remedied if at all possible.

In attempting to account for Anchor Supply Company's increase in sales, the increases in advertising and in plant assets merit attention. It is reasonable to expect an increase in advertising to increase sales. It is also reasonable to expect an increase in plant assets to result in a sales increase in a merchandising company or a decrease in cost of goods sold in a manufacturing company.

Calculating percentage increases and decreases

When percentage increases and decreases are calculated for comparative statements, the increase or decrease in an item is divided by the amount shown for the item in the base year. No problems arise in these calculations when positive amounts are shown in the base year. However, when no amount is shown or a negative amount is shown in the base year, a percentage increase or decrease cannot be calculated. For example, in Illustration 19–1 there were no notes payable at the end of 1978 and a percentage change for this item cannot be calculated.

In this text, percentages and ratios are typically rounded to one or two decimal places; however, there is no uniform agreement on this matter. In general, percentages should be carried out at least to the point of assuring that meaningful information is conveyed but not so far that the significance of the relationships tend to become "lost" in the length of the numbers.

Trend percentages

Trend percentages or index numbers are useful in comparing data from a company's financial statements covering a number of years, since trend percentages emphasize changes that have occurred during the period. They are calculated as follows:

1. A base year is selected, and each item amount on the base year statement is assigned a weight of 100%.
2. Then each item from the statements for the years after the base year is expressed as a percentage of its base year amount. To determine these percentages, the item amounts in the years after the base year are divided by the amount of the item in the base year.

For example, if 1974 is made the base year for the following data, the trend percentages for "Sales" are calculated by dividing by $210,000,

	1974	1975	1976	1977	1978	1979
Sales...............	$210,000	$204,000	$292,000	$284,000	$310,000	$324,000
Cost of goods sold	145,000	139,000	204,000	198,000	218,000	229,000
Gross profit..........	$ 65,000	$ 65,000	$ 88,000	$ 86,000	$ 92,000	$ 95,000

the amount shown for "Sales" in each year after the first. The trend percentages for "Cost of goods sold" are found by dividing by $145,000 the amount shown for "Cost of goods sold" in each year after the first. And, the trend percentages for "Gross profit" are found by dividing the amounts shown for "Gross profit" by $65,000. When these divisions are made, the trends for these three items appear as follows:

	1974	1975	1976	1977	1978	1979
Sales	100	97	139	135	148	154
Cost of goods sold.....	100	96	141	137	150	158
Gross profit...........	100	100	135	132	142	146

It is interesting to note in the illustrated trends that while after the second year the sales trend is upward, the cost of goods sold trend is upward at a slightly more rapid rate. This indicates a contracting gross profit rate and should receive attention.

It should be pointed out in a discussion of trends that the trend for a single balance sheet or income statement item is seldom very informative. However, a comparison of trends for related items often tells the analyst a great deal. For example, a downward sales trend with an upward trend for merchandise inventory, accounts receivable, and loss on bad debts would generally indicate an unfavorable situation. On the other hand, an upward sales trend with a downward trend or a slower upward trend for accounts receivable, merchandise inventory, and selling expenses would indicate an increase in operating efficiency.

Common-size comparative statements

The comparative statements shown thus far do not show proportional changes in items except in a general way. Changes in proportions are often shown and emphasized by *common-size comparative statements*.

A common-size statement is so called because its items are shown in common-size figures, figures that are fractions of 100%. For example, on a common-size balance sheet (1) the asset total is assigned a value of 100%; (2) the total of the liabilities and owner equity is also assigned a value of 100%; and then (3) each asset, liability, and owner equity item is shown as a fraction of one of the 100% totals. When a company's balance sheets for more than one year are shown in this manner (see Illustration 19–3), proportional changes are emphasized.

A common-size income statement is prepared by assigning net sales a 100% value and then expressing each income statement item as a percent of net sales. Such a statement is an informative and useful tool

Anchor Supply Company
Common-Size Comparative Balance Sheet
December 31, 1978, and December 31, 1979

	Years Ended December 31		Common-Size Percentages	
	1979	1978	1979	1978
Assets				
Current Assets:				
Cash..........	$ 18,000	$ 90,500	4.19	23.63
Accounts receivable, net..............	68,000	64,000	15.81	16.71
Merchandise inventory	90,000	84,000	20.93	21.93
Prepaid expenses..........	5,800	6,000	1.35	1.57
Total Current Assets..........	$181,800	$244,500	42.28	63.84
Long-Term Investments:				
Real estate..........	$ -0-	$ 30,000		7.83
Apex Company common stock	-0-	50,000		13.05
Total Long-Term Investments.........	$ -0-	$ 80,000		20.88
Plant and Equipment:				
Office equipment, net.........	$ 3,500	$ 3,700	0.81	0.97
Store equipment, net..........	17,900	6,800	4.16	1.78
Buildings, net.........	176,800	28,000	41.12	7.31
Land..........	50,000	20,000	11.63	5.22
Total Plant and Equipment.........	$248,200	$ 58,500	57.72	15.28
Total Assets.........	$430,000	$383,000	100.00	100.00
Liabilities				
Current Liabilities:				
Notes payable.........	$ 5,000	$ -0-	1.16	
Accounts payable.........	43,600	55,000	10.14	14.36
Taxes payable.........	4,800	5,000	1.12	1.31
Wages payable	800	1,200	0.19	0.31
Total Current Liabilities	$ 54,200	$ 61,200	12.61	15.98
Long-Term Liabilities:				
Mortgage payable.........	$ 60,000	$ 10,000	13.95	2.61
Total Liabilities.........	$114,200	$ 71,200	26.56	18.59
Capital				
Common stock, $10 par value.........	$250,000	$250,000	58.14	65.27
Retained earnings.........	65,800	61,800	15.30	16.14
Total Capital.........	$315,800	$311,800	73.44	81.44
Total Liabilities and Capital.........	$430,000	$383,000	100.00	100.00

Illustration 19–3

because when the 100% sales amount is assumed to represent one sales dollar, then the remaining income statement items show how each sales dollar was distributed to costs, expenses, and profit. For example, on the comparative income statement shown in Illustration 19–4, the 1978 cost of goods sold consumed 73.86 cents of each sales dollar. In 1979 cost of goods sold consumed 74.48 cents of each sales dollar. While this increase is apparently small, if in 1979 the proportion of cost of goods sold had remained at the 1978 level, almost $6,000 additional gross profit would have been earned; and if carried through to net income, this would have been a significant amount.

Common-size percentages point out efficiencies and inefficiencies that are otherwise difficult to see, and for this reason are a valuable management tool. To illustrate, sales salaries of Anchor Supply Com-

Anchor Supply Company
Common-Size Comparative Income Statement
Years Ended December 31, 1978, and 1979

	Years Ended December 31		Common-Size Percentages	
	1979	1978	1979	1978
Gross sales	$973,500	$853,000	101.41	101.21
Sales returns and allowances	13,500	10,200	1.41	1.21
Net sales	$960,000	$842,800	100.00	100.00
Cost of goods sold	715,000	622,500	74.48	73.86
Gross profit from sales	$245,000	$220,300	25.52	26.14
Operating expenses:				
Selling expenses:				
Advertising expense	$ 7,500	$ 5,000	0.78	0.59
Sales salaries expense	113,500	98,000	11.82	11.63
Store supplies expense	3,200	2,800	0.33	0.33
Depreciation expense, store equipment	2,400	1,700	0.25	0.20
Delivery expense	14,800	14,000	1.54	1.66
Total selling expenses	$141,400	$121,500	14.72	14.41
General and administrative expenses:				
Office salaries expense	$ 41,000	$ 40,050	4.27	4.75
Office supplies expense	1,300	1,250	0.14	0.15
Insurance expense	1,600	1,200	0.17	0.14
Depreciation expense, office equipment	300	300	0.03	0.04
Depreciation expense, buildings	2,850	1,500	0.30	0.18
Bad debts expense	2,250	2,200	0.23	0.26
Total general and administrative expenses	$ 49,300	$ 46,500	5.14	5.52
Total operating expenses	$190,700	$168,000	19.86	19.93
Operating income	$ 54,300	$ 52,300	5.66	6.21
Less interest expense	2,300	1,000	0.24	0.12
Income before taxes	$ 52,000	$ 51,300	5.42	6.09
Income taxes	19,000	18,700	1.98	2.22
Net Income	$ 33,000	$ 32,600	3.44	3.87

Illustration 19–4

pany took a higher percentage of each sales dollar in 1979 than in 1978. On the other hand, office salaries took a smaller percentage of each 1979 sales dollar. Furthermore, although the loss from bad debts was greater in 1979 than in 1978, loss from bad debts took a smaller proportion of each sales dollar in 1979 than in 1978.

Analysis of working capital

The term *working capital* was defined in Chapter 18 as the excess of a company's current assets over its current liabilities; and when balance sheets are analyzed, working capital always receives close attention. Adequate working capital enables a company to carry sufficient inventories, meet current debts, take advantage of cash discounts, and extend favorable terms to customers. These are desirable. A company that is deficient in working capital and unable to do these things is in a poor competitive position. Its survival may even be threatened, unless its working capital position is improved. Inadequacy of working capital has ended the business lives of many companies whose total assets were far in excess of liabilities.

As previously stated, a company's working capital should be sufficient to enable it to carry adequate inventories, meet current debts, and take advantage of cash discounts. However, the amount of working capital a company has is not a measure of these abilities, and this may be demonstrated as follows with Companies A and B:

	Company A	Company B
Current assets........	$100,000	$20,000
Current liabilities....	90,000	10,000
Working capital......	$ 10,000	$10,000

Companies A and B have the same amounts of working capital. However, Company A's current liabilities are nine times its working capital, while Company B's current liabilities and working capital are equal. As a result, if liabilities are to be paid on time, Company A must experience much less shrinkage and delay in converting its current assets to cash than Company B. As the example shows, the amount of a company's working capital is not a measure of its working capital position, but the relation of its current assets to its current liabilities provides such a measure.

Current ratio

The relation of a company's current assets to its current liabilities is known as its *current ratio.* A current ratio is calculated by dividing current assets by current liabilities. The current ratio of the foregoing Company B is calculated as follows:

$$\frac{\text{Current assets, } \$20,000}{\text{Current liabilities, } \$10,000} = 2$$

After the division is made, the relation is expressed as, for example, Company B's current assets are two times its current liabilities, or Company B has $2 of current assets for each $1 of current liabilities, or simply Company B's current ratio is 2 to 1.

The current ratio is the relation of current assets and current liabilities expressed mathematically. A high current ratio indicates a large proportion of current assets to current liabilities. The higher the ratio, the more liquid is a company's current position, and normally the better it can meet current obligations.

For many years bankers and other credit grantors measured a credit-seeking company's debt-paying ability by whether or not it had a 2 to 1 current ratio. Today most credit grantors realize that the 2 to 1 rule of thumb is not an adequate test of debt-paying ability. They realize that whether or not a company's current ratio is good or bad depends upon at least three factors:

1. The nature of the company's business.
2. The composition of its current assets.
3. The turnover of certain of its current assets.

The nature of a company's business has much to do with whether or not its current ratio is adequate. A public utility or a railroad which has no inventories other than supplies and which grants little or no credit can operate on a current ratio less than 1 to 1. On the other hand, because a misjudgment of style can make an inventory of goods for sale almost worthless, a company manufacturing articles in which style is the important sales factor may find a current ratio of much more than 2 to 1 to be inadequate. Consequently, when the adequacy of working capital is studied, consideration must be given to the type of business under review.

Also, in an analysis of a company's working capital, the composition of its current assets should be considered. Normally a company with a high proportion of cash to accounts receivable, merchandise inventory, and other current assets is in a better position to meet quickly its current obligations than is a company with most of its current assets tied up in accounts receivable and merchandise. The company with cash can pay its current debts at once, while the company with accounts receivable and merchandise must often turn these items into cash before it can pay.

Acid-test ratio

An easily calculated check on current asset composition is the *acid-test* ratio, which is also called the *quick ratio* because it is the ratio of "quick assets" to current liabilities. "Quick assets" are cash, notes receivable, accounts receivable, and marketable securities. They are the current assets that can quickly be turned into cash. An acid-test ratio of 1 to 1 is normally considered satisfactory. However, this is a rule of thumb and should be applied with care. The acid-test ratio of Anchor Supply Company as of the end of 1979 is calculated as follows:

Quick Assets:		Current Liabilities:	
Cash.............................	$18,000	Notes payable................	$ 5,000
Accounts receivable.......	68,000	Accounts payable	43,600
		Taxes payable	4,800
		Wages payable	800
Total......................	$86,000	Total......................	$54,200

Acid-test ratio is: $86,000 ÷ $54,200 = 1.59 or is 1.6 to 1

Certain current asset turnovers affect working capital requirements. For example, assume Companies A and B sell the same amounts of merchandise on credit each month. However, Company A grants 30-day terms to its customers, while Company B grants 60 days. Both collect their accounts at the end of the credit periods granted. But as a result of the difference in terms, Company A turns over or collects its accounts twice as rapidly as does Company B. Also, as a result of the more rapid turnover, Company A requires only one half the investment in accounts receivable that is required of Company B and can operate with a smaller current ratio.

Accounts receivable turnover is calculated by dividing net sales for a year by the year-end accounts receivable, and Anchor Supply Company's accounts receivable turnovers for 1978 and 1979 are calculated as follows:

		1979	1978
a.	Net sales for year..	$960,000	$842,800
b.	Year-end accounts receivable	68,000	64,000
	Times accounts receivable were turned over (a ÷ b).......	14.1	13.2

The turnover of 14.1 times in 1979 in comparison to 13.2 in 1978 indicates the company's accounts receivable were collected more rapidly in 1979.

The year-end amount of accounts receivable is commonly used in calculating accounts receivable turnover. However, if year-end accounts receivable are not representative, an average of the year's accounts receivable by months should be used. Also, credit sales rather than the sum of cash and credit sales, and accounts receivable before subtracting the allowance for doubtful accounts should be used. However, information as to credit sales is seldom available in a published balance sheet, and many published balance sheets report accounts receivable at their net amount. Consequently, total sales and net accounts receivable must often be used.

Days' sales uncollected

Accounts receivable turnover is one indication of the speed with which a company collects its accounts. *Days' sales uncollected* is another indication of the same thing. To illustrate the calculation of days' sales uncollected, assume a company had charge sales during a year of $250,000, and that it has $25,000 of accounts receivable at the year-end. In other words, one tenth of its charge sales, or the charge sales made during one tenth of a year, or the charge sales of 36.5 days ($\frac{1}{10} \times 365$ days in a year = 36.5 days) are uncollected. This calculation of days' sales uncollected in equation form appears as follows:

$$\frac{\text{Accounts receivable, \$25,000}}{\text{Charge sales, \$250,000}} \times 365 = 36.5 \text{ days' sales uncollected}$$

Days' sales uncollected takes on more meaning when credit terms are known. According to a rule of thumb, a company's days' sales uncollected should not exceed one and one-third times the days in its credit period when it does not offer discounts and one and one-third times the days in its discount period when it does. If the company, whose days' sales uncollected is calculated in the illustration just given, offers 30-day terms, then 36.5 days is within the rule-of-thumb amount. However, if its terms are 2/10, n/30, its days' sales uncollected seem excessive.

Turnover of merchandise inventory

A company's merchandise turnover is the number of times its average inventory is sold during an accounting period, and a high turnover is considered an indication of good merchandising. Also, from a working capital point of view, a company with a high turnover requires a smaller investment in inventory than one producing the same sales with a low turnover. Merchandise turnover is calculated by dividing cost of goods sold by average inventory. Cost of goods sold is the amount of merchandise at its cost price that was sold during an accounting period; average inventory is the average amount of merchandise, at its cost price, on hand during the period. The 1979 merchandise turnover of Anchor Supply Company is calculated as follows:

$$\frac{\text{Cost of goods sold, \$715,000}}{\text{Average merchandise inventory, \$87,000}} = \text{Merchandise turnover of 8.2 times}$$

The cost of goods sold is taken from the company's 1979 income statement. The average inventory is found by dividing by two the sum of the $84,000, January 1, 1979, inventory and the $90,000, December 31, 1979, inventory. In a company in which beginning and ending inventories are not representative of the inventory normally on hand, a more accurate turnover may be secured by using the average of all the 12 month-end inventories rather than just the beginning- and end-of-the-year inventories.

Standards of comparison

When financial statements are analyzed by computing ratios and turnovers, the analyst must determine whether the ratios and turnovers obtained are good, bad, or just average; and in making the decision he must have some basis for comparison. The following are available:

1. A trained analyst may compare the ratios and turnovers of the company under review with his own mental standards acquired from past experiences.
2. An analyst may calculate for purposes of comparison the ratios and turnovers of a selected group of competitive companies in the same industry as the one whose statements are under review.
3. Published ratios and turnovers such as those put out by Dun & Bradstreet may be secured for comparison.
4. Some local and national trade associations gather data from their members and publish standard or average ratios for their trade or industry. These offer the analyst a very good basis of comparison when available.
5. Rule-of-thumb standards may be used as a basis for comparison.

Of these five standards, the ratios and turnovers of a selected group of competitive companies normally offer the best basis for comparison. Rule-of-thumb standards should be applied with care if erroneous conclusions are to be avoided.

Other balance sheet and income statement relations

Several balance sheet and income statement relations in addition to those having to do with working capital are important to the analyst. Some of the more important are:

Capital contributions of owners and creditors

The share of a company's assets contributed by its owners and the share contributed by creditors are always of interest to the analyst. The owner and creditor contributions of Anchor Supply Company are calculated as follows:

		1979	1978
a.	Total liabilities	$114,200	$ 71,200
b.	Total owner equity	315,800	311,800
c.	Total liabilities and owner equity	$430,000	$383,000
	Creditors' equity (a ÷ c)	26.6%	18.6%
	Owner equity (b ÷ c)	73.4%	81.4%

Creditors like to see a high proportion of owner equity because owner equity acts as a cushion in absorbing losses. The greater the equity of the owners in relation to liabilities, the greater the losses that can be absorbed by the owners before the creditors begin to lose.

From the creditors' standpoint a high percentage of owner equity is desirable. However, if an enterprise can earn a return on borrowed capital that is in excess of the capital's cost, then a reasonable amount of creditor equity is desirable from the owners' viewpoint, with the amount depending upon the stability of the earnings.

Pledged plant assets to long-term liabilities

Companies commonly borrow by issuing a note or bonds secured by a mortgage on certain of their plant assets. The ratio of pledged plant assets to long-term debt is often calculated to measure the security granted to mortgage or bondholders by the pledged assets. This ratio is calculated by dividing the pledged assets' book value by the liabilities for which the assets are pledged. It is calculated for Anchor Supply Company as of the ends of 1978 and 1979 as follows:

		1979	1978
	Buildings, net	$176,800	$28,000
	Land	50,000	20,000
a.	Book value of pledged plant assets	$226,800	$48,000
b.	Mortgage payable	$ 60,000	$10,000
	Ratio of pledged assets to secured liabilities (a ÷ b)	3.8 to 1	4.8 to 1

The usual rule-of-thumb minimum for this ratio is 2 to 1. However, the ratio needs careful interpretation because it is based on the *book value* of the pledged assets, and book value may bear little or no relation to the amount that would be received for the assets in a foreclosure or a liquidation. As a result, estimated liquidation values or foreclosure values are normally a better measure of the protection offered bond or mortgage holders by pledged assets. Too, in a situation in which assets are pledged, the long-term earning ability of the company whose assets are pledged is usually more important to long-term creditors than the pledged assets' book value.

Times fixed interest charges earned

The number of times fixed interest charges were earned is often calculated to measure the security of the return offered to bondholders or a mortgage holder. To make this calculation, the fixed interest charges are added to income before taxes to determine the amount of income before fixed interest charges and income taxes. This amount is available to pay the fixed interest charges and is divided by the amount of the fixed interest charges to determine the number of times the charges were earned. Often the return to a company's long-term creditors is considered secure if the company consistently earns its fixed interest charges two or more times each year.

Rate of return on total assets employed

The return earned on total assets employed is a measure of management's performance. Assets are used to earn a profit, and management is responsible for the way in which they are used; consequently, the return on assets employed is a measure of management's performance.

The return figure used in this calculation should be after-tax income plus interest expense. Interest expense is included because it is a return paid creditors for assets they have supplied. Likewise, if the amount of assets has fluctuated during the year, an average of the beginning- and end-of-the-year assets employed should be used.

The rates of return earned on the average total assets employed by Anchor Supply Company during 1978 and 1979 are calculated as follows:

		1979	1978
	Net income after taxes	$ 33,000	$ 32,600
	Add interest expense	2,300	1,000
a.	Net income plus interest expense	$ 35,300	$ 33,600
b.	Average total assets employed	$406,500	$380,000
	Rate of return on total assets employed (a ÷ b)	8.7%	8.8%

In the case of Anchor Supply Company the change in the rates is not too significant, and it is impossible to tell whether the returns are good or bad without some basis of comparison. The best comparison would be the returns earned by similar-size companies engaged in the same kind of business, or a comparison could be made with the returns earned by this company in previous years. Neither of these is available in this case.

Rate of return on common stockholders' equity

A primary reason for the operation of a corporation is to earn a net income for its common stockholders; and the rate of return on the common stockholders' equity is a measure of the success achieved in this area. Usually an average of the beginning- and end-of-the-year equities is used in calculating the return, and for Anchor Supply Company the 1978 and 1979 calculations are as follows:

		1979	1978
a.	Net income after taxes	$ 33,000	$ 32,600
b.	Average stockholders' equity	313,800	309,000
	Rate of return on stockholders' equity (a ÷ b)	10.5%	10.6%

In the two calculations just illustrated, compare the returns on stock-holders' equity with the returns on total assets employed and note that the return on the stockholders' equity is greater in both years. The greater returns resulted from leverage gained by using borrowed money.

When there is preferred stock outstanding, the preferred dividend requirements must be subtracted from net income to arrive at the common stockholders' share of income to be used in calculating the rate of return on common stockholders' equity.

Earnings per common share

Earnings per common share data are among the most commonly quoted figures on the financial pages of daily newspapers. Such data are used by investors in evaluating the past performance of a business, in projecting its future earnings, and in weighing investment opportunities. Because of the significance attached to earnings per share data by investors and others, the APB concluded that earnings per common share or net loss per common share data should be shown on the face of a published income statement.[1] Also, if there are extraordinary items or accounting changes, per share amounts should be shown (a) for income before extraordinary items and the cumulative effects of accounting changes and (b) for the final net income figure. The Board also held that it may be desirable to present per share data for the extraordinary items and for the cumulative effects of accounting changes, as in Illustration 16–6, which is reproduced here as Illustration 19–5.

The importance of presenting per share data for income before extraordinary items, as well as for the final income figure, is demonstrated in Illustration 19–5. Note that Dale Company earned $0.08 per share less in 1979 than in 1978, but its 1979 earnings from normal operations increased $0.05 per share. In judging a company's earnings trend in a situation such as this, earnings from normal operations are usually more important than the final income figure, since the extraordinary items that contribute to the final figure are nonrecurring.

In Illustration 19–5 it is assumed that Dale Company had 500,000 common shares outstanding during the two-year period and no preferred stock. Consequently, its earnings per share data were determined by dividing each earnings item by 500,000. Had there been preferred stock outstanding, it would have been necessary to subtract the preferred dividend requirements from the income from ordinary operations and from the final income figure before making the divisions.

Many corporations, like the Dale Corporation, have simple capital structures consisting only of common stock and, perhaps, preferred stock which is not convertible into common stock. Other corporations have more complex structures which include preferred stock and bonds that are convertible into common stock at the option of the preferred

---

[1] APB, "Earnings per Share," *APB Opinion No. 15* (New York: AICPA, 1969), par. 12.

Dale Corporation
Income Statements for Years Ended December 31, 1978, and 1979

	1979	1978
Net sales	$8,500,000	$8,000,000
Cost of goods sold and expenses:		
Cost of goods sold	$6,050,000	$5,650,000
Selling, general, and administrative expenses	540,000	500,000
Interest expense	10,000	10,000
Other expenses	9,000	8,000
Income taxes	916,000	882,000
Total cost of goods sold and expenses	$7,525,000	$7,050,000
Income before extraordinary items and the cumulative effect of an accounting change	$ 975,000	$ 950,000
Extraordinary items:		
Gain on sale of unused land expropriated by the state for a highway interchange, net of $16,700 of applicable income taxes		50,000
Loss from earthquake damage, net of an applicable $22,000 reduction in income taxes	(25,000)	
Cumulative effect on prior years' income (to December 31, 1978) of changing to a different depreciation method	10,000	
Net Income	$ 960,000	$1,000,000
Earnings per common share:		
Income before extraordinary items and the cumulative effect of an accounting change	$1.95	$1.90
Extraordinary items, net of taxes	(0.05)	0.10
Cumulative effect on prior years' income (to December 31, 1978) of changing to a different depreciation method	0.02	
Net Income	$1.92	$2.00

Illustration 19–5

stockholders and bondholders; and if conversions should occur, the equity of common stockholders in the company's earnings would undoubtedly change due solely to the conversions. Recognizing this, the APB provided in *Opinion No. 15* specific requirements for calculating and reporting earnings per share for corporations with complex capital structures. However, these requirements are so lengthy and involved that a discussion must be left for an advanced course.

Price-earnings ratio

Price-earnings ratios are commonly used in comparing investment opportunities. A price-earnings ratio is calculated by dividing market price per share by earnings per share; and if a company reports extraordinary items, the price-earnings ratio is usually based on the amount of earnings per share before extraordinary items. For example, if Dale Corporation's common stock sold at $29.25 per share at the end of 1979, the stock's end-of-the-year price-earnings ratio is calculated:

$$\frac{\$29.25 \text{ market price per share}}{\$1.95 \text{ earnings per share}} = 15$$

After the calculation is made, it may be said that the stock had a 15 to 1 price-earnings ratio at the end of 1979, or it may be said that $15 was required at that time to buy $1 of this company's 1979 earnings.

In comparing price-earnings ratios it must be remembered that such ratios vary from industry to industry. For example, in the steel industry a 10 or 12 to 1 price-earnings ratio is normal, while in growth industries, such as photography, 30 to 1 or higher ratios are not uncommon.

Accounts receivable turnover. An indication of how long it takes a company to collect its accounts, calculated by dividing net sales or credit sales by ending or average accounts receivable.   **Glossary**

Acid-test ratio. The relation of quick assets, such as cash, notes receivable, accounts receivable, and marketable securities to current liabilities, calculated as quick assets divided by current liabilities.

Common-size comparative statements. Comparative financial statements in which each amount is expressed as a percentage of a base amount; in the balance sheet, total assets is usually selected as the base amount and is expressed as 100%; in the income statement, net sales is usually selected as the base amount.

Comparative statement. A financial statement with data for two or more successive years placed in columns side by side in order to better illustrate changes in the data.

Current ratio. The relation of a company's current assets to its current liabilities, that is, current assets divided by current liabilities.

Merchandise turnover. The number of times a company's average inventory is sold during an accounting period, calculated by dividing cost of goods sold by average merchandise inventory.

Price-earnings ratio. Market price per share of common stock divided by earnings per share.

Quick ratio. A synonym for acid-test ratio.

Rate of return on common stockholders' equity. Net income after taxes and dividends to preferred stock divided by average common stockholders' equity.

Rate of return on total assets employed. Net income after taxes, plus interest expense, expressed as a percentage of total assets employed during the period.

Times fixed charges earned. An indicator of a company's ability to satisfy fixed charges, calculated as net income before fixed charges and income taxes divided by fixed charges (e.g., interest).

1. Comparative balance sheets often have columns showing increases and decreases in both dollar amounts and percentages. Why is this so?
2. When trends are calculated and compared, what item trends should be compared with the trend of sales?
3. What is meant by "common-size" financial statements?
4. What items are assigned a value of 100% (*a*) on a common-size balance sheet and (*b*) on a common-size income statement?
5. Why is working capital given special attention in the process of analyzing balance sheets?
6. For the following transactions tell which increase working capital, which decrease working capital, and which have no effect on working capital:
    a. Collected accounts receivable.
    b. Borrowed money from the bank by giving a 90-day interest-bearing note.
    c. Declared a cash dividend.
    d. Paid a cash dividend previously declared.
    e. Sold plant assets at their book value.
    f. Sold merchandise at a profit.
7. Why is adequate working capital of importance to a business?
8. List several factors that have an effect on working capital requirements.
9. A company has a 2 to 1 current ratio. List several reasons why this ratio may not be adequate.
10. State the significance of each of the following ratios and turnovers and tell how each is calculated:
    a. Current ratio.
    b. Acid-test ratio.
    c. Turnover of accounts receivable.
    d. Turnover of merchandise inventory.
    e. Rate of return on common stockholders' equity.
    f. Ratio of pledged plant assets to long-term liabilities.
11. How are days' sales uncollected calculated? What is the significance of the number of days' sales uncollected?
12. Why do creditors like to see a high proportion of owner equity?
13. What is the ratio of pledged plant assets to long-term liabilities supposed to measure? Why must this ratio be interpreted with care?
14. What does the rate of return on assets employed tell about management?

Exercise 19–1

Calculate trend percentages for the following items and tell whether the situation shown by the trends is favorable or unfavorable:

	197A	197B	197C	197D	197E
Sales	$200,000	$226,000	$238,000	$248,000	$260,000
Cost of goods sold..................	120,000	144,000	162,000	168,000	180,000
Accounts receivable................	20,000	25,000	27,000	28,000	31,000

Exercise 19–2

Where possible calculate percentages of increase and decrease for the following unrelated items. The parentheses indicate deficit items.

	197B	197A
Equipment, net	$80,000	$60,000
Notes receivable	-0-	3,000
Notes payable.........	10,000	-0-
Retained earnings....	(2,400)	12,000
Cash	10,000	(1,000)

Exercise 19–3

Express the following income statement information in common-size percentages and tell whether the situation shown is favorable or unfavorable.

HARRISON COMPANY
Comparative Income Statement
Years Ended December 31, 197A, and 197B

	197B	197A
Sales	$100,000	$90,000
Cost of goods sold	66,800	59,850
Gross profit from sales	$ 33,200	$30,150
Operating expenses.........	25,100	22,320
Net Income	$ 8,100	$ 7,830

Exercise 19–4

The year-end statements of Great Abaco Company follow:

GREAT ABACO COMPANY
Balance Sheet, December 31, 19—

Assets		Equities	
Cash	$ 6,000	Accounts payable	$ 20,000
Accounts receivable, net..........	24,000	Mortgage payable, secured by	
Merchandise inventory, net......	28,500	a lien on the plant assets.......	35,000
Prepaid expenses....................	1,500	Common stock, $10 par value...	100,000
Plant assets, net	140,000	Retained earnings	45,000
Total Assets	$200,000	Total Equities	$200,000

GREAT ABACO COMPANY
Income Statement for Year Ended December 31, 19—

Sales...		$365,000
Cost of goods sold:		
Merchandise inventory, January 1, 19—	$ 31,500	
Purchases	267,000	
Goods available for sale.......................................	$298,500	
Merchandise inventory, December 31, 19—	28,500	
Cost of goods sold		270,000
Gross profit on sales..		$ 95,000
Operating expenses		74,000
Operating income...		$ 21,000
Mortgage interest expense		2,100
Income before taxes		$ 18,900
Income taxes..		4,900
Net Income		$ 14,000

Required:

Calculate the following: (*a*) current ratio, (*b*) acid-test ratio, (*c*) days' sales uncollected, (*d*) merchandise turnover, (*e*) capital contribution of owners expressed as a percent, (*f*) ratio of pledged plant assets to long-term debt, (*g*) times fixed interest charges earned, (*h*) return on stockholders' equity, and (*i*) earnings per share. (Assume all sales were on credit and the stockholders' equity was $135,000 on January 1.)

Exercise 19–5

Common-size and trend percentages for a company's sales, cost of goods sold, and expenses follow:

COMMON-SIZE PERCENTAGES	197A	197B	197C	TREND PERCENTAGES	197A	197B	197C
Sales	100.0	100.0	100.0	Sales	100.0	95.0	90.0
Cost of goods sold	64.0	63.0	63.0	Cost of goods sold	100.0	93.5	88.6
Expenses	28.0	28.0	27.0	Expenses	100.0	95.0	86.8

Required:

Present statistics to prove whether the company's net income increased, decreased, or remained unchanged during the three-year period represented above.

Problems

Problem 19–1

The year-end statements of Spinaker Company follow:

SPINAKER COMPANY
Income Statement for Year Ended December 31, 19—

Sales		$510,000
Cost of goods sold:		
Merchandise inventory, January 1, 19—	$ 37,800	
Purchases	320,400	
Goods available for sale	$358,200	
Merchandise inventory, December 31, 19—	34,200	
Cost of goods sold		324,000
Gross profit from sales		$186,000
Operating expenses		158,700
Operating income		$ 27,300
Mortgage interest expense		4,200
Income before taxes		$ 23,100
Income taxes		5,100
Net Income		$ 18,000

SPINAKER COMPANY
Balance Sheet, December 31, 19—

Cash	$ 8,600	Accounts payable	$ 23,800
Temporary investments	10,000	Accrued wages payable	1,100
Notes receivable	3,000	Income taxes payable	5,100
Accounts receivable, net	25,500	Mortgage payable, secured by	
Merchandise inventory	34,200	a lien on the plant assets	68,000
Prepaid expenses	1,200	Common stock, $5 par value	100,000
Plant assets, net	170,000	Retained earnings	54,500
Total Assets	$252,500	Total Equities	$252,500

Required:

Calculate the following: (*a*) current ratio, (*b*) acid-test ratio, (*c*) days' sales uncollected, (*d*) merchandise turnover, (*e*) ratio of pledged plant assets to long-term debt (*f*) times fixed interest charges earned, (*g*) return on total assets employed, (*h*) return on stockholders' equity, and (*i*) earnings per share. Assume all sales were on credit, the assets totaled $247,500 on January 1, and the stockholders' equity at the beginning of the year was $145,500.

Problem 19–2

The condensed statements of Fort Dodge Metals follow:

FORT DODGE METALS
Comparative Income Statements
Years Ended December 31, 197A, 197B, and 197C
(in thousands of dollars)

	197A	197B	197C
Sales	$8,000	$9,000	$10,000
Cost of goods sold	5,688	6,480	7,150
Gross profit from sales	$2,312	$2,520	$ 2,850
Selling expenses	$1,216	$1,359	$ 1,500
Administrative expenses	784	855	940
Total expenses	$2,000	$2,214	$ 2,440
Income before taxes	$ 312	$ 306	$ 410
State and federal income taxes	152	149	196
Net Income	$ 160	$ 157	$ 214

FORT DODGE METALS
Comparative Balance Sheets
December 31, 197A, 197B, and 197C
(in thousands of dollars)

	197A	197B	197C
Assets			
Current assets	$ 750	$ 615	$ 696
Long-term investments	50	5	-0-
Plant and equipment	2,400	2,676	2,664
Total Assets	$3,200	$3,296	$3,360

Liabilities and Capital

Current liabilities................................	$ 250	$ 280	$ 290
Common stock....................................	2,000	2,100	2,100
Other contributed capital	50	61	61
Retained earnings	900	855	909
Total Liabilities and Capital	$3,200	$3,296	$3,360

Required:

1. Calculate each year's current ratio.
2. Express the income statement data in common-size percentages.
3. Express the balance sheet data in trend percentages.
4. Comment on any significant relationships revealed by the ratios and percentages.

Problem 19–3

Following are the condensed 197A and 197B statements of Weber Feeds:

WEBER FEEDS
Comparative Income Statements
Years Ended December 31, 197A and 197B

	197B	197A
Sales (all on credit)...	$476,000	$451,000
Cost of goods sold:		
Merchandise inventory, January 1	$ 43,000	$ 41,000
Purchases...	305,600	273,800
Goods for sale	$348,600	$314,800
Merchandise inventory, December 31	56,000	43,000
Cost of goods sold..	$292,600	$271,800
Gross profit from sales	$183,400	$179,200
Operating expenses..	163,400	156,600
Income before Taxes	$ 20,000	$ 22,600

WEBER FEEDS
Comparative Balance Sheets
December 31, 197A and 197B

	197B	197A
Assets		
Cash	$ 14,000	$ 12,000
Accounts receivable...	38,000	44,000
Merchandise inventory	56,000	43,000
Plant assets, net	104,000	102,000
Total Assets	$212,000	$201,000
Liabilities and Stockholders' Equity		
Accounts payable	$ 26,000	$ 28,000
Notes payable...	10,000	6,000
Mortgage payable (due in 1990)	40,000	40,000
Common stock...	100,000	100,000
Retained earnings	36,000	27,000
Total Liabilities and Stockholders' Equity........	$212,000	$201,000

Required:

1. Calculate common-size percentages for sales, cost of goods sold, gross profit from sales, operating expenses, and income before taxes; and calculate the current ratio, acid-test ratio, merchandise turnover, and days' sales uncollected for each of the two years.
2. Comment on the situation shown by your calculations.

Problem 19–4

The condensed comparative statements of Belton Bolt Company follow:

BELTON BOLT COMPANY
Comparative Income Statements
For Years Ended December 31, 197A–197G
(in thousands of dollars)

	197A	197B	197C	197D	197E	197F	197G
Sales.................................	$400	$500	$572	$680	$760	$840	$872
Cost of goods sold	250	310	360	430	515	585	604
Gross profit from sales..............	$150	$190	$212	$250	$245	$255	$268
Operating expenses	100	110	118	138	197	220	238
Income before Taxes................	$ 50	$ 80	$ 94	$112	$ 48	$ 35	$ 30

BELTON BOLT COMPANY
Comparative Balance Sheets
December 31, 197A–197G
(in thousands of dollars)

	197A	197B	197C	197D	197E	197F	197G
Assets							
Cash.................................	$ 20	$ 14	$ 17	$ 15	$ 12	$ 10	$ 4
Accounts receivable, net	40	52	54	62	88	90	92
Merchandise inventory....................	100	118	141	165	204	218	226
Other current assets	2	4	4	6	2	4	2
Long-term investments....................	38	38	38	38	-0-	-0-	-0-
Plant and equipment, net.................	200	198	204	202	446	450	440
Total Assets..........................	$400	$424	$458	$488	$752	$772	$764
Liabilities and Capital							
Current liabilities	$ 50	$ 64	$ 82	$ 90	$140	$156	$159
Long-term liabilities........................	40	38	36	34	182	180	178
Common stock	200	200	200	200	250	250	250
Premium on common stock...............	50	50	50	50	60	60	60
Retained earnings........................	60	72	90	114	120	126	117
Total Liabilities and Capital......	$400	$424	$458	$488	$752	$772	$764

Required:

1. Calculate trend percentages for the items of the statements.
2. Analyze and comment on any situations shown in the statements.

Problem 19–5

A company had $180,000 of current assets, a 3 to 1 current ratio, and a 1½ to 1 quick ratio. It then completed the following transactions:

a. Collected a $2,500 account receivable.
b. Wrote off a $1,000 bad debt against the allowance for doubtful accounts.
c. Borrowed $20,000 by giving its bank a 60-day, 6% note.
d. Bought $10,000 of merchandise on credit. The company uses a perpetual inventory system.
e. Declared a $0.50 per share cash dividend on its 20,000 shares of outstanding common stock.
f. Paid the dividend declared in (e) above.
g. Declared a 1,000-share stock dividend. The stock was selling at $15 per share on the day of the declaration.
h. Distributed the dividend stock of (g) above.
i. Sold for $10,000 merchandise that cost $5,000.

Required:

Prepare a schedule showing the company's current ratio, its acid-test ratio, and the amount of its working capital after each of the foregoing transactions. Round to two decimal places.

Alternate problems

Problem 19–1A

The year-end statements of Rayford Tarp Company follow:

RAYFORD TARP COMPANY
Balance Sheet, December 31, 19—

Cash	$ 12,000	Accounts payable	$ 19,800
Temporary investments	8,000	Accrued wages payable	550
Notes receivable	2,500	Income taxes payable	4,650
Accounts receivable, net	23,000	Mortgage payable, secured by	
Merchandise inventory	36,300	a lien on the plant assets	70,000
Prepaid expenses	1,200	Common stock, $10 par value	100,000
Plant assets, net	168,000	Retained earnings	56,000
Total Assets	$251,000	Total Equities	$251,000

RAYFORD TARP COMPANY
Income Statement for Year Ended December 31, 19—

Sales		$460,000
Cost of goods sold:		
Merchandise inventory, January 1, 19—	$ 33,700	
Purchases	300,100	
Goods available for sale	$333,800	
Merchandise inventory, December 31, 19—	36,300	
Cost of goods sold		297,500
Gross profit from sales		$162,500
Operating expenses		136,850
Operating income		$ 25,650
Mortgage interest expense		4,500
Income before taxes		$ 21,150
Income taxes		4,650
Net Income		$ 16,500

Required:

Calculate the following: (*a*) current ratio, (*b*) acid-test ratio, (*c*) days' sales uncollected, (*d*) merchandise turnover, (*e*) ratio of pledged plant assets to long-term debt, (*f*) times fixed interest charges earned, (*g*) return on total assets employed, (*h*) return on stockholders' equity, and (*i*) earnings per share. Assume all sales were on credit, assets employed at the beginning of the year totaled $249,000, and stockholders' equity at the beginning of the year was $144,000.

Problem 19–2A

The condensed statements of Schwab Technics Company follow:

SCHWAB TECHNICS COMPANY
Comparative Income Statements
Years Ended December 31, 197A, 197B, and 197C
(in thousands of dollars)

	197A	197B	197C
Sales	$5,000	$6,000	$6,500
Cost of goods sold	3,600	4,398	4,745
Gross margin on sales	$1,400	$1,602	$1,755
Selling expenses	$ 700	$ 810	$ 884
Administrative expenses	500	588	637
Total expenses	$1,200	$1,398	$1,521
Income before taxes	$ 200	$ 204	$ 234
State and federal income taxes	90	92	105
Net Income	$ 110	$ 112	$ 129

SCHWAB TECHNICS COMPANY
Comparative Balance Sheets
December 31, 197A, 197B, and 197C
(in thousands of dollars)

Assets	197A	197B	197C
Current assets	$ 400	$ 256	$ 240
Plant and equipment	1,200	1,380	1,440
Total Assets	$1,600	$1,636	$1,680

Liabilities and Capital	197A	197B	197C
Current liabilities	$ 125	$ 131	$ 127
Common stock, $10 par value	1,000	1,000	1,000
Other contributed capital	175	175	175
Retained earnings	300	330	378
Total Liabilities and Capital	$1,600	$1,636	$1,680

Required:
1. Calculate each year's current ratio.
2. Express the income statement data in common-size percentages.
3. Express the balance sheet data in trend percentages.
4. Comment on any significant relationships revealed by the ratios and percentages.

Problem 19–3A

Following are data from the statements of two companies selling similar products:

DATA FROM THE CURRENT YEAR-END BALANCE SHEETS

	Company X	Company Y
Cash	$ 8,500	$ 12,500
Notes receivable	3,500	2,000
Accounts receivable	30,000	40,000
Merchandise inventory	44,000	54,800
Prepaid expenses	1,200	1,200
Plant and equipment, net	165,800	172,500
Total Assets	$253,000	$283,000
Current liabilities	$ 40,000	$ 50,000
Mortgage payable	50,000	50,000
Common stock, $10 par value	100,000	100,000
Retained earnings	63,000	83,000
Total Liabilities and Capital	$253,000	$283,000

DATA FROM THE CURRENT YEAR'S INCOME STATEMENTS

	Company X	Company Y
Sales	$480,000	$550,000
Cost of goods sold	377,200	437,400
Interest expense	3,000	3,500
Net income	16,695	18,060

BEGINNING-OF-THE-YEAR DATA

	Company X	Company Y
Merchandise inventory	$ 38,000	$ 53,200
Total assets	247,000	277,000
Stockholders' equity	155,000	178,200

Required:

1. Calculate current ratios, acid-test ratios, merchandise turnovers, and days' sales uncollected for the two companies. Then state which company you think is the better short-term credit risk and why.
2. Calculate earnings per share, rate of return on total assets employed, and rate of return on stockholders' equity. Then under the assumption that each company's stock can be purchased at book value, state which company's stock you think is the better investment and why.

Problem 19–5A

A company began the month of August with $200,000 of current assets, a $2\frac{1}{2}$ to 1 current ratio, and a $1\frac{1}{4}$ to 1 acid-test ratio. During the month it completed the following transactions:

Aug. 1   Bought $20,000 of merchandise on account. (The company uses a perpetual inventory system.)
     5   Sold for $10,000 merchandise that cost $5,000.
     7   Collected a $2,500 account receivable.
   11   Paid a $10,000 account payable.
   15   Wrote off a $1,500 bad debt against the allowance for doubtful accounts.

Aug. 18 Declared a $1 per share cash dividend on the 10,000 shares of out-
standing common stock.
28 Paid the dividend declared on May 18.
29 Borrowed $10,000 by giving the bank a 60-day, 6% note.
30 Borrowed $25,000 by placing a ten-year mortgage on the plant.
31 Used the $25,000 proceeds of the mortgage to buy additional ma-
chinery.

Required:

Prepare a schedule showing the company's current ratio, acid-test ratio,
and working capital after each of the foregoing transactions. Round to two
decimal places.

As controller of Beaumont Retail Company you have calculated the
following ratios, turnovers, and percentages to enable you to answer questions the directors will ask at their next meeting.

Decision
problem 19–1,
Beaumont
Retail
Company

	197C	*197B*	*197A*
Current ratio	2.91/1	2.47/1	2.09/1
Acid-test ratio	0.88/1	1.07/1	1.48/1
Merchandise turnover	9.5 times	10.1 times	10.5 times
Accounts receivable turnover	6.9 times	7.4 times	8.2 times
Return on stockholders' equity	6.11%	6.51%	6.89%
Return on total assets	6.20%	6.29%	6.52%
Sales to plant assets	4.70/1	4.50/1	4.20/1
Sales trend	124.00	114.00	100.00
Selling expenses to net sales	14.65%	14.85%	15.21%

Using the statistics given, answer each of the following questions and explain how you arrived at your answer.

a. Is it becoming easier for the company to meet its current debts on time
and to take advantage of cash discounts?
b. Is the company collecting its accounts receivable more rapidly?
c. Is the company's investment in accounts receivable decreasing?
d. Are dollars invested in inventory increasing?
e. Is the company's investment in plant assets increasing?
f. Is the stockholders' investment becoming more profitable?
g. Is the company using debt leverage to the advantage of its stockholders?
h. Did the dollar amount of selling expenses decrease during the three-year
period?

Ace Company and Fox Company are competitors; both were organized
about ten years ago; and both have seen their sales increase tenfold during
the ten-year period. However, the tenfold increase is not as good as it sounds
because the costs and selling prices of the items the companies sell have
doubled during the same period. Nevertheless, the sales of the companies have
continued to increase. Both offer the same credit terms; age their accounts receivable to allow for bad debts; and collect their accounts in about the same

Decision
problem 19–2,
Ace Company
and Fox
Company

length of time. Actually about the only real difference in the accounting procedures of the two companies is that Ace Company has since its organization used Lifo in costing its goods sold and Fox Company has used Fifo.

The current ratios of the two companies for the past four years were as follows:

CURRENT RATIOS

	Ace Company	Fox Company
December 31, 197A	3.1 to 1	5.4 to 1
December 31, 197B.....	3.4 to 1	5.8 to 1
December 31, 197C.....	2.8 to 1	6.0 to 1
December 31, 197D	2.6 to 1	6.1 to 1

You are the loan officer of a bank and both companies have come to your bank for 90-day loans. In addition to the current ratios, you note that Ace Company turned its inventory twice as fast as Fox Company in each of 197A and 197B and three times as fast in each of the last two years. You also discover that for each $10,000 of current liabilities the companies have the following amounts of inventory:

	Ace Company	Fox Company
December 31, 197A	$19,000	$44,000
December 31, 197B.....	23,000	49,000
December 31, 197C	16,000	52,000
December 31, 197D	14,000	54,000

Which company do you think is the better short-term credit risk? Back your opinion with computations showing why. Are the inventory turnovers of the two companies comparable? Explain. Which company seems to have the better inventory turnover?

Decision problem 19–3, Adell Davis

Adell Davis has an opportunity to invest in either of two companies, both of which operate locally and in the same line of business. The stock of either company can be bought at its book value, and Adell is undecided which is the better managed company and which is the better investment. Following are data from the financial statements of the companies:

DATA FROM THE CURRENT YEAR-END BALANCE SHEETS

	Eastgate Company	Westgate Company
Cash...	$ 26,000	$ 28,000
Accounts receivable, net....................	64,000	78,500
Merchandise inventory	85,000	102,500
Prepaid expenses.............................	2,000	3,000
Plant and equipment, net...................	320,000	350,000
Total Assets	$497,000	$562,000
Current liabilities............................	$ 75,000	$ 98,000
Mortgage payable	106,000	110,000
Common stock, $10 par value............	200,000	200,000
Retained earnings	116,000	154,000
Total Liabilities and Capital	$497,000	$562,000

DATA FROM THE CURRENT YEAR'S INCOME STATEMENTS

Sales..........................	$1,220,000	$1,395,000
Cost of goods sold	860,500	993,000
Gross profit on sales.... $	359,500	$ 402,000
Operating expenses	280,000	336,000
Operating income........ $	79,500	$ 66,000
Interest expense	10,500	11,000
Income before taxes.... $	69,000	$ 55,000
Income taxes..............	26,600	19,900
Net Income .... $	42,400	$ 35,100

BEGINNING-OF-THE-YEAR DATA

Merchandise inventory .... $	67,000	$ 87,500
Total assets	480,000	550,000
Stockholders' equity........	310,000	360,000

Prepare a report to Adell Davis stating which company you think is the better managed and which company's stock you think is the better investment. Back your report with any ratios, turnovers, and other analyses you think pertinent.

After studying Chapter 20, you should be able to:

■ Describe the effects of inflation on historical financial statements.

■ Explain how price-level changes are measured.

■ Tell how to construct both general and specific price-level indexes.

■ Describe the use of price indexes in general price-level-adjusted accounting.

■ Restate unit-of-money financial statements for general price-level changes.

■ Explain how purchasing power gains and losses arise and how they are computed and integrated into the general price-level-adjusted financial statements.

■ Describe what replacement costs purport to measure and how these costs are currently presented by some companies in reports filed with the Securities and Exchange Commission.

■ State the differences between general price-level-adjusted costs and current values such as exit prices and replacement costs.

■ Define or explain the words and phrases listed in the chapter Glossary.

chapter 20

Accounting for price-level changes

Perhaps all accountants agree that conventional financial statements do in fact provide useful information to persons making economic decisions related to the business firms for which the financial statements are rendered. Nevertheless, many accountants also agree that conventional financial statements fail to adequately account for the impact of price-level changes, and as a general rule, this means a failure to adequately account for the impact of inflation. Indeed, they admit that the failure of conventional financial statements to adequately account for inflation may sometimes even make the statements misleading. That is, the statements may imply certain facts that are inconsistent with the real state of affairs; and as a result, decision makers may be inclined to make decisions that are inconsistent with their intended objectives.

In what ways do conventional financial statements fail to adequately account for inflation? The general problem is that transactions are recorded in terms of the historical number of dollars received or paid and these amounts are not adjusted even though subsequent changes in prices may dramatically change the purchasing power of the dollars received or paid. For example, Old Company purchased ten acres of land for $25,000, and at the end of each accounting period thereafter presented a balance sheet showing "Land, $25,000." Six years later, after inflation of 97% (12% per year, compounded for six years), New Company purchased ten acres of land that was adjacent and nearly identical to Old Company's land. New Company paid $49,250 for the land. In comparing the conventional balance sheets of the two companies, which own identical pieces of property, the following balances are observed:

Balance Sheets

	Old Company	New Company
Land	$25,000	$49,250

Without knowing the details that underlie these balances, a statement reader is likely to conclude that New Company either has more land than does Old Company or that New Company's land is more valuable than is Old Company's. Nevertheless, both companies own ten acres, which are identical in value. The entire difference between the prices paid by the two companies is explained by the 97% inflation between the two purchase dates, that is, $25,000 \times 1.97 = $49,250$.

The failure of conventional financial statements to adequately account for inflation shows up in the income statement as well as the balance sheet. For example, assume that the previous example of Old Company and New Company involved the purchase of machinery instead of land. Also, assume that the machinery is identical except as to age and is being depreciated on a straight-line basis over a ten-year period, with no salvage value. As a result, the annual income statements of the two companies show the following:

	Income Statements	
	Old Company	New Company
Depreciation expense, machinery.........	$2,500	$4,925

Although assets of equal value are being depreciated, the income statements show that New Company's depreciation expense is 97% higher than is Old Company's. And, if all other revenue and expense items are the same, Old Company will appear more profitable than New Company, which is inconsistent with the fact that both companies own the same machines that are subject to the same depreciation factors. Furthermore, although Old Company will appear more profitable, it must pay more income taxes due to the apparent extra profits and also may not recover the full replacement cost of its machinery through the sale of its product.

Some of the procedures used in conventional accounting, such as Lifo inventory pricing and accelerated depreciation, tend to reduce the impact of price-level changes on the income statement. However, they are only partial solutions, since they do not offset the impact on both the income statement and the balance sheet.

Because of these deficiencies in conventional accounting practices, accountants have devoted increasing attention to the possible introduction of alternatives that make comprehensive adjustments for the effects of price-level changes. This chapter discusses the two that have received the greatest attention. The first alternative examined involves adjusting conventional financial statements for changes in the general level of prices. This alternative is called *general price-level-adjusted accounting,* or *GPLA accounting.* Subsequently, consideration is given to *replacement cost accounting,* which is another alternative to conventional reporting practices. Replacement cost accounting makes adjustments for changes in the specific prices of the specific assets, liabilities, and so forth, owned or owed by the company.

In one way or another, all readers of this book have experienced the effects of inflation, which is a general increase in the prices paid for goods and services. Of course, the prices of specific items do not all change at the same rate, and even when most prices are rising, the prices of some goods or services may be falling. For example, consider the following prices of four different items:

Understanding price-level changes

Item	Price/Unit in 1978	Price/Unit in 1979	Percent Change
A	$1.00	$1.30	+30%
B	2.00	2.20	+10%
C	1.50	1.80	+20%
D	3.00	2.70	−10%
Totals	$7.50	$8.00	

What can be said to describe these price changes? One possibility is to state the percentage change in the price per unit of each item, as is shown in Column 4. While this information is very useful for some purposes, it does not show the average effect or impact of the price changes that occurred. A better indication of the average effect would be obtained by determining the average increase in the per unit prices of the four items, as follows: $8.00/$7.50 − 1.00 = 6.7%[1] average increase in per unit prices. However, even this average may fail to indicate the impact of the price changes on most individuals or businesses. It is a good indicator only if the typical individual or business purchased an equal number of units of each item. But what if these items are typically purchased in the following ratio? For each unit of A purchased, 2 units of B are purchased, 5 units of C are purchased, and 1 unit of D is purchased. With a different number of each item being purchased, the impact of changing prices must take into account the typical quantity of each item purchased. Thus, the average change in the price of the A, B, C, D "market basket" would be calculated as follows:

---

[1] Throughout this chapter amounts are rounded to the nearest 1/10 percent or to the nearest full dollar.

Item	Units Purchased	1978 Prices	Units Purchased	1979 Prices
A..............	1 unit × $1.00 = $ 1.00		1 unit × $1.30 = $ 1.30	
B..............	2 units × $2.00 = 4.00		2 units × $2.20 = 4.40	
C..............	5 units × $1.50 = 7.50		5 units × $1.80 = 9.00	
D..............	1 unit × $3.00 = 3.00		1 unit × $2.70 = 2.70	
Totals		$15.50		$17.40

Weighted average price change = $17.40/$15.50 − 1.00 = 12%

It may now be said that the annual rate of inflation in the prices of these four items was 12%. Of course, not every individual and business can be expected to purchase these four items in exactly the same proportion of 1 unit of A, 2 units of B, 5 units of C, and 1 unit of D. As a consequence, the stated 12% inflation rate is only an approximation of the impact of price changes on each buyer. But if these proportions represent the typical buying pattern, the stated 12% inflation rate fairly reflects the inflationary impact on the average buyer.

Construction of a price index

When the total cost of purchasing a given market basket of items is determined for each of several periods, the results can be expressed as a price index. In constructing such an index, one year is arbitrarily selected as the "base" year, and the cost of purchasing the market basket in that year is assigned a value of 100. For example, suppose the cost of purchasing the A, B, C, D market basket in each year is:

```
1973........$ 9.00
1974.......  11.00
1975.......  10.25
1976.......  12.00
1977.......  13.00
1978.......  15.50
1979.......  17.40
```

If 1976 is selected as the base year, then the $12 cost for 1976 is assigned a value of 100. The price-level index number for each of the other years is then calculated and expressed as a percent of the base year's cost. For example, the index number for 1975 is 85 ($10.25/$12.00 × 100 = 85). The index numbers for the remaining years are calculated in the same way, and the entire price index for the years 1973 through 1979 is presented in Illustration 20–1. Having constructed a price index for the A, B, C, D market basket, it is possible to make comparative statements about the cost of purchasing these items in various years. For example, it may be said that the price level in 1979 was 45% (145/100) higher than it was in 1976;

or, the price level in 1979 was 34% (145/108) higher than it was in 1977, and 12% (145/129) higher than it was in 1978. Stated another way, it may be said that $1 in 1979 would purchase the same amount of A, B, C, D as would $0.69 in 1976 (100/145 = 0.69). Also, $1 in 1979 would purchase the same amount of A, B, C, D as would $0.52 in 1973 (75/145 = 0.52).

Year	Calculations of Price Level	Price Index
1973.........	($9.00/$12.00) × 100 =	75
1974.........	($11.00/$12.00) × 100 =	92
1975.........	($10.25/$12.00) × 100 =	85 ✓
1976.........	($12.00/$12.00) × 100 =	100
1977.........	($13.00/$12.00) × 100 =	108
1978.........	($15.50/$12.00) × 100 =	129
1979.........	($17.40/$12.00) × 100 =	145 ✓

Illustration 20–1

Using price index numbers

For accounting purposes, the most important use of a price index is to restate dollar amounts of cost that were paid in some earlier year into the current price level. In other words, a specific dollar amount of cost incurred in a previous year can be restated in terms of the comparable number of dollars that would be incurred if the cost were paid with dollars having the current amount of purchasing power. For example, suppose that $1,000 were paid in 1975 to purchase items A, B, C, D. Stated in terms of 1979 prices, that 1975 cost is $1,000 × (145/85) = $1,706. As another example, if $1,500 were paid for A, B, C, D in 1976, that 1976 cost can be restated in terms of 1979 prices as $1,500 × (145/100) = $2,175.

Note that the 1976 cost of $1,500 correctly states the number of monetary units (dollars) expended for items A, B, C, D in 1976. Also, the 1975 cost of $1,000 correctly states the units of money expended in 1975. And these two costs can be added together to determine the cost for the two years, stated in terms of the historical number of monetary units (units of money) expended. However, in a very important way, the 1975 monetary units do not mean the same thing as do the 1976 monetary units. A dollar (one monetary unit) in 1975 represented a different amount of *purchasing power* than did a dollar in 1976, and both of these dollars represented different amounts of purchasing power than did a dollar in 1979. If one intends to communicate the amount of purchasing power expended or incurred, the historical number of monetary units expended must be adjusted so that they are stated in terms of dollars having the same amount of purchasing power. For example, the total amount of cost incurred during 1975 and 1976 could be stated in terms of the purchasing power of 1976 dollars, or stated in terms of the purchasing power of 1979 dollars. These calculations are presented in Illustration 20–2.

Year Cost Was Incurred	Monetary Units Expended	Adjustment to 1976 Dollars	Historical Cost Stated in 1976 Dollars	Adjustment to 1979 Dollars	Historical Cost Stated in 1979 Dollars
1975	$1,000	1,000 × (100/85)	$1,176	1,176 × (145/100)	$1,706*
1976	1,500	—	1,500	1,500 × (145/100)	2,175
Total cost	$2,500		$2,676		$3,881

* Raised $1 to correct for rounding. An alternative calculation is $1,000 × (145/85) = $1,706.

Illustration 20–2

Specific versus general price-level indexes

Price changes and price-level indexes can be calculated for narrow groups of commodities or services, such as housing construction material costs, or for broader groups of items, such as all construction costs, or for very broad groups of items, such as all items produced in the economy. A *specific price-level index,* such as for housing construction materials, indicates the changing purchasing power of a dollar spent for items in that specific category, that is, to pay for housing construction materials. A *general price-level index,* such as for all items produced in the economy, indicates the changing purchasing power of a dollar, in general. Two general price-level indexes frequently used are the Consumer Price Index (CPI), prepared by the Bureau of Labor Statistics, and the Gross National Product (GNP) Implicit Price Deflator, prepared by the U.S. Department of Commerce.

Using price indexes in accounting

There are at least two important alternatives to conventional financial statements that utilize price indexes to develop comprehensive financial statements. One alternative, called replacement cost accounting, uses specific price-level indexes (along with appraisals and other means) to develop statements that report items such as assets and expenses in terms of their current replacement costs. Additional consideration is given to this alternative later in this chapter.

The other alternative, called general price-level-adjusted (GPLA) accounting, uses general price-level indexes to restate the conventional, unit-of-money financial statements into dollar amounts that represent current, general purchasing power. Most of the proposals for making general price-level-adjusted (GPLA) financial statements have suggested using the GNP Implicit Price Deflator because it is the broadest, most general index of general price-level changes.[2] The following sections of this chapter explain how a general price

[2] See, for example, APB, "Financial Statements Restated for General Price Level Changes," *APB Statement No. 3* (New York: AICPA, 1969), par. 30; and also FASB, "Financial Reporting in Units of General Purchasing Power," *Proposed Statement of Financial Accounting Standards, Exposure Draft* (Stamford, Conn., 1974), par. 35.

index, such as the GNP Implicit Price Deflator, is used to prepare general price-level-adjusted (GPLA) financial statements.

Conventional financial statements disclose revenues, expenses, assets, liabilities, and owners' equity in terms of the historical monetary units that were exchanged at the time the transactions occurred. As such, they are sometimes referred to as "unit-of-money" financial statements.[3] This term is intended to emphasize the difference between conventional financial statements and general price-level-adjusted (GPLA) financial statements; in the latter, the dollar amounts shown are adjusted for changes in the general purchasing power of the dollar.

General price-level-adjusted (GPLA) accounting

Students should understand clearly that the same principles for determining depreciation expense, cost of goods sold, accruals of revenue, and so forth, apply to both unit-of-money statements and GPLA statements; the same generally accepted accounting principles apply to both. The only difference between the two is that GPLA statements reflect adjustments for general price-level changes whereas unit-of-money statements do not. As a matter of fact, GPLA financial statements are prepared by adjusting the amounts appearing on the unit-of-money financial statements.

The effect of general price-level changes on investments in assets depends on the nature of the assets involved. Some assets, called *monetary assets,* represent money or claims to receive a fixed amount of money. The number of dollars owned or to be received is fixed in amount, regardless of changes that may occur in the purchasing power of the dollar. Examples of monetary assets are cash, accounts receivable, notes receivable, and investments in bonds.

GPLA accounting for assets

Because the amount of money owned or to be received from a monetary asset does not change as a consequence of general price-level changes, the (GPLA) balance sheet amount of a monetary asset is not adjusted for general price-level changes. For example, if $200 in cash was owned at the end of 1978, and was held throughout 1979, during which time the general price-level index increased from 150 to 168,[4] the cash would be reported on both the December 31, 1978, and 1979, general price-level-adjusted (GPLA) balance sheets at $200. However, although no balance sheet adjustment is made, it is important to note that the investment in such a monetary asset held during a period of inflation does result in a loss of purchasing power. Since $200 would buy less at the end of 1979 than it would have at

---

[3] FASB, *Proposed Statement,* par. 2.

[4] Observe that these index numbers, and those used in the remaining sections of the chapter, are different from those that were calculated on page 669. Since the earlier calculations were based on only four items (A, B, C, D), that index would not be appropriate to illustrate a general price index, which must reflect the prices of many, many items.

the end of 1978, the reduced amount of purchasing power constitutes a loss. The amount of the loss is calculated as follows:

Monetary asset balance on December 31, 1978............................	$ 200
Adjustment to reflect an equal amount of purchasing power on December 31, 1979: $200 × 168/150	$ 224
Amount of monetary asset balance on December 31, 1979	(200)
General purchasing power loss...	$ 24

Nonmonetary assets are defined as all assets other than monetary assets. The prices at which nonmonetary assets may be bought and sold tend to increase or decrease over a period of time as the general price level increases or decreases, and at approximately the same rate. Consequently, as the general price level changes, investments in nonmonetary assets tend to retain the amounts of purchasing power originally invested. As a result, the reported amounts of nonmonetary assets on GPLA balance sheets are adjusted to reflect changes in the price level that have occurred since the nonmonetary assets were acquired.

For example, if $200 were invested in land (a nonmonetary asset) at the end of 1978, and the investment were held throughout 1979, during which time the general price index increased from 150 to 168, the GPLA balance sheets would disclose the following amounts:

Asset	December 31, 1978, GPLA Balance Sheet	Adjustment to December 31, 1979, Price Level	December 31, 1979, GPLA Balance Sheet
Land $200		$200 × (168/150)	$224

The $224 shown as the investment in land at the end of 1979 has the same amount of general purchasing power as did $200 at the end of 1978; and thus, no change in general purchasing power resulted from holding the land.

GPLA accounting for liabilities and stockholders' equity

The effect of general price-level changes on liabilities depends on the nature of the liability. Most liabilities are monetary items, but some liabilities and stockholders' equity are nonmonetary items.[5]

---

[5] Depending on its nature, preferred stock may be treated as a monetary item. If so, it is an exception to the general rule that stockholders' equity items are nonmonetary items.

Monetary liabilities represent fixed amounts that are owed, with the number of dollars to be paid fixed in amount and not changing regardless of changes in the general price level.

Since monetary liabilities are unchanged in amounts owed even when price levels change, monetary liabilities are not adjusted for price-level changes. However, a company with monetary liabilities outstanding during a period of general price-level change will experience a general purchasing power gain or loss. Assume, for example, that a note payable for $300 was outstanding on December 31, 1978, and remained outstanding throughout 1979, when the general price index increased from 150 to 168. On the GPLA balance sheets for December 31, 1978, and 1979, the note payable would be reported at $300. The general purchasing power gain or loss is calculated as follows:

Monetary liability balance on December 31, 1978	$ 300
Adjustment to reflect an equal amount of purchasing power on December 31, 1979: $300 × (168/150)	$ 336
Amount of monetary liability balance on December 31, 1979	(300)
General purchasing power gain	$ 36

Since $336 at the end of 1979 has the same amount of general purchasing power as $300 had at the end of 1978, and the company can pay off the note with $300, the $36 difference is a gain in general purchasing power realized by the firm. Alternatively, if the general price index had decreased during 1979, the monetary liability would have resulted in a general purchasing power loss.

Nonmonetary liabilities are obligations that are not fixed in amount and therefore tend to change in amount as changes occur in the general price level. For example, product warranties may require that a manufacturer pay for certain product repairs and replacements for a specified period of time after the product is sold. Since the amount of money required to make the repairs or replacements tends to change in response to changes in the general price level, there is no purchasing power gain or loss associated with such warranties. Further, the balance sheet amount of such a nonmonetary liability must be adjusted to reflect changes in the general price index which occurred after the nonmonetary liability came into existence. Stockholder equity items also are, with the possible exception of preferred stock, nonmonetary items, and also must be adjusted for changes in the general price index.

Illustration 20–3 summarizes the impact of general price-level changes on monetary items and nonmonetary items. The illustration indicates what adjustments must be made in preparing a GPLA

Financial Statement Item	When the General Price Level Rises (inflation)		When the General Price Level Falls (deflation)	
	Balance Sheet Adjustment Required	Income Statement Gain or Loss	Balance Sheet Adjustment Required	Income Statement Gain or Loss
Monetary assets.........	No	Loss	No	Gain
Nonmonetary assets...	Yes	None	Yes	None
Monetary liabilities.....	No	Gain	No	Loss
Nonmonetary equities and liabilities..........	Yes	None	Yes	None

Illustration 20–3

balance sheet and what purchasing power gains and losses must be recognized on a GPLA income statement.

Preparing comprehensive GPLA financial statements

The previous discussion of price indexes and of GPLA accounting for assets, liabilities, and stockholders' equity provides a basis for describing the necessary procedures used in preparing comprehensive GPLA financial statements. The unit-of-money financial statements of Delivery Service Company, Illustration 20–4, serve as an illustrative basis for the discussion.

Delivery Service Company was organized on January 1, 1978, at which time $25,000 of the original $30,000 invested in the company

Delivery Service Company
Balance Sheets
For Years Ended December 31, 1978, and 1979

	1978	1979
Cash	$ 8,000	$ 30,000
Land (acquired December 31, 1978)	12,000	12,000
Delivery equipment (acquired January 1, 1978)....	25,000	25,000
Accumulated depreciation...............................	(4,000)	(8,000)
Total Assets..	$41,000	$ 59,000
Note payable (issued July 1, 1978).....................	$ 5,000	$ 5,000
Capital stock (issued January 1, 1978)	30,000	30,000
Retained earnings	6,000	24,000
Total	$41,000	$ 59,000

Delivery Service Company
Income Statement
For Year Ended December 31, 1979

Delivery revenues	$100,000
Depreciation expense......................................	(4,000)
Other expenses	(78,000)
Net Income	$ 18,000

Illustration 20–4

was used to buy delivery trucks. The trucks are being depreciated over five years on a straight-line basis and have a $5,000 salvage value. Assume that since the company was organized, the general price index has changed as follows:

Date	Price Index
December 1977	130
June 1978 (also average for 1978)	140
December 1978	150
Average for 1979	160
December 1979	168

Delivery Service Company's cash balance increased from $8,000 to $30,000 during 1979 and is explained as follows:

Beginning cash balance	$ 8,000
Revenues, earned uniformly throughout the year	100,000
Expenses, paid uniformly throughout the year	(78,000)
Ending cash balance	$ 30,000

Restatement of the balance sheet

In preparing a GPLA balance sheet, the individual account balances are first identified as representing monetary items or nonmonetary items. Since monetary items are fixed amounts that do not change regardless of changes in the price level, the unit-of-money balance of each monetary item is placed on the GPLA balance sheet without adjustment. Each nonmonetary item, on the other hand, must be adjusted for the price-level changes that have occurred since the original transactions giving rise to the item.

The restatement of Delivery Service Company's balance sheet is presented in Illustration 20–5. Observe that the monetary items, Cash and Note Payable, are transferred without adjustment from the unit-of-money column to the price-level-adjusted column. All of the remaining items are nonmonetary and are adjusted. The land was purchased on December 31, 1978, at which time the price level was 150;[6] thus, the historical cost of the land is restated from December 1978 dollars to December 1979 dollars (price index was 168) as follows: $12,000 × 168/150 = $13,440. Since the delivery equipment was purchased on January 1, 1978, which was the same time the capital stock was issued, each of the three account balances, Delivery Equipment, Accumulated Depreciation, and Capital Stock, are

---

[6] Normally, price index numbers are determined for a period of time, such as one quarter or one month, and are not determined for a specific point in time, such as December 31. Thus, the index number for the last quarter of the year, or for December if available, is used to approximate the price level on December 31.

Delivery Service Company
Restatement of Balance Sheet
December 31, 1979

	Unit-of-Money Balances	Restatement Factor from Price Index	GPLA Amounts
Cash	$30,000	–	$30,000
Land	12,000	168/150	13,440
Delivery equipment	25,000	168/130	32,308
Less accumulated depreciation	(8,000)	168/130	(10,338)
Total Assets	$59,000		$65,410
Note payable	$ 5,000	–	$ 5,000
Capital stock	30,000	168/130	38,769
Retained earnings	24,000	(See discussion)	21,641
Total Liabilities and Stockholders' Equity	$59,000		$65,410

Illustration 20–5

restated from January 1978 prices (index number was 130) to December 1979 prices by applying the restatement factor of 168/130.

The retained earnings balance of $24,000 cannot be adjusted in a single step because this balance resulted from more than one transaction. However, the correct, adjusted amount of retained earnings can be determined simply by "plugging" the necessary amount to make the balance sheet balance, as follows:

Total assets, adjusted		$65,410
Less: Note payable	$ 5,000	
Capital stock	38,769	(43,769)
Necessary retained earnings		$21,641

The process of testing the correctness of this restated retained earnings amount is explained later in the chapter.

Students should recognize that Delivery Service Company is a simplified illustration in that only two of its balance sheet amounts (Cash and Retained Earnings) resulted from more than one transaction. In a more complex case, most account balances would reflect several past transactions that took place at different points in time. In such a situation, the adjustment procedures are more detailed. For example, suppose that the $12,000 balance in the Land account resulted from three different purchases of land, as follows:

January 1, 1978, purchased land for	$ 3,000
July 1, 1978, purchased land for	4,000
December 31, 1978, purchased land for	5,000
Total	$12,000

Under this assumption the following adjustments would be required to prepare the GPLA balance sheet, as of December 31, 1979:

	Unit-of-Money Balances	Adjustment Factor from Price Index	Restated to December 31, 1979, General Price Level
Land purchased on:			
January 1, 1978	$ 3,000	168/130	$ 3,877
July 1, 1978	4,000	168/140	4,800
December 31, 1978	5,000	168/150	5,600
Total	$12,000		$14,277

Restatement of the income statement

The general procedure followed in preparing a GPLA income statement is that every individual revenue and expense item in the accounts must be restated from the price index level which existed on the date that item was recorded in units of money to the price index level at the end of the year. The restated amounts are then entered on the GPLA income statement along with the purchasing power gain or loss resulting from holding or owing monetary items.

The calculations to restate the 1979 income statement of Delivery Service Company from units of money to the price-level-adjusted amounts are presented in Illustration 20–6.

Delivery Service Company
Restatement of Income Statement
For Year Ended December 31, 1979

	Unit-of-Money Amounts	Restatement Factor from Price Index	GPLA Amounts
Delivery service revenues	$100,000	168/160	$105,000
Depreciation expense	(4,000)	168/130	(5,169)
Other expenses	(78,000)	168/160	(81,900)
Operating income	$ 18,000		$ 17,931
Purchasing power loss (from Illustration 20–7)			(1,460)
Net Income	$ 18,000		$ 16,471

Illustration 20–6

As previously mentioned, Delivery Service Company's revenues were received and its other expenses were incurred in many transactions that occurred throughout the year. To be completely precise, each of these individual transactions would have to be separately restated. However, because these revenues and expenses occurred in a nearly uniform pattern throughout the year, restating the total revenue and the total other expenses from the average price level during the year (160) to the end-of-year price level (168) is an acceptable approximation procedure.

The unit-of-money amount of depreciation expense on delivery trucks ($4,000) was determined by taking 20% of the $25,000 − $5,000 cost to be depreciated. Since this cost was incurred on January 1, 1978, the restatement of depreciation expense must be based on the price index existing on that date (130) and the index number for the end of 1979 (168).

Purchasing power gain or loss

As was explained, the purchasing power gain or loss experienced by Delivery Service Company and previously shown in Illustration 20–6 stems from the amount of monetary assets held and monetary liabilities owed by the company during the year. During 1979, cash was the only monetary asset held by the company, and the only monetary liability was a $5,000 note payable. The purchasing power gain or loss for these items is calculated in Illustration 20–7.

Delivery Service Company
Calculation of Purchasing Power Gain or Loss
For Year Ended December 31, 1979

	Unit-of-Money Amounts	Restatement Factor from Price Index	Restated to December 31, 1979	Gain or Loss
Cash:				
Beginning balance............	$ 8,000	168/150	$ 8,960	
Delivery revenue receipts..	100,000	168/160	105,000	
Payments for expenses.....	(78,000)	168/160	(81,900)	
Ending balance, adjusted.....			$ 32,060	
Ending balance, actual........	$ 30,000		(30,000)	
Purchasing power loss.........				$ 2,060
Note payable: beginning balance...........................	$ 5,000	168/150	$ 5,600	
Ending balance, actual.....	$ 5,000		(5,000)	
Purchasing power gain.....				(600)
Net purchasing power loss...				$ 1,460

Illustration 20–7

Note in Illustration 20–7 that the purchasing power loss from holding cash must take into account the changes in the cash balance that occurred during the year. First, the beginning cash balance of $8,000 is restated into an equivalent amount of general purchasing power at the end of the year. Since the December 1979 price index was 168 and the December 1978 price index was 150, the balance is restated as follows: $8,000 × 168/150 = $8,960. Next, each cash change is adjusted from the price level that existed at the time the change occurred to the price level that existed at the end of the year. Since cash receipts from revenues occurred throughout the year on a relatively uniform basis, the average price index number for the year (160) is used to approximate the price level in existence when the revenues were received. Thus, the cash received from revenues during the year is restated from the $100,000 units of money received to the equivalent amount of general purchasing power at the end of the year, as follows: $100,000 × 168/160 = $105,000. Cash payments for expenses were also made uniformly throughout the year, so the same index numbers are used to restate the $78,000 units-of-money amount to the equivalent amount of general purchasing power at the end of the year, that is, $78,000 × 168/160 = $81,900. With the initial cash balance and the cash changes restated into end-of-year purchasing power, the adjusted end-of-year amount of purchasing power for cash is $32,060. Since the actual ending cash balance is only $30,000, the $2,060 difference represents a loss in general purchasing power. The $5,000 note payable was issued on July 1, 1978, at which time the price index was 140. Nevertheless, the purchasing power gain associated with this monetary liability is calculated by adjusting the $5,000 from the beginning-of-1979 price level (index number was 150) to the end-of-1979 price level (index number was 168). Since the calculation is being made for the purpose of preparing a 1979 GPLA income statement, only the purchasing power gain arising from inflation during 1979 should be included. The gain associated with the price index change from 140 to 150 occurred during 1978, and would have been included in the GPLA income statement for 1978.

Adjusting the retained earnings balance

The December 31, 1979, adjusted retained earnings balance was previously determined by "plugging" the amount necessary to make liabilities plus stockholders' equity equal to total assets (page 676). Alternatively, if a GPLA balance sheet for December 31, 1978, was available, the adjusted retained earnings balance at that date could be restated to the December 31, 1979, price level, and the GPLA net income for 1979 could be added to determine GPLA retained earnings at December 31, 1979. For example, had GPLA financial statements been prepared for 1978, the $6,000 retained earnings balance in units of money (see Illustration 20–4) would have been adjusted to a December 31, 1978, general price-level amount of $4,616.[7] With this additional information, the adjusted retained balance for December 31, 1979, is calculated as follows:

---

[7] Notice that the $4,616 price-level-adjusted retained earnings on December 31, 1978, is smaller than the $6,000 units-of-money amount. This decrease was caused by the same factors that caused the adjusted net income for 1979 to be less than the units-of-money net income (see Illustration 20–6).

	Restated to December 31, 1978, General Price Level	Factor from Price Index	Restated to December 31, 1979, General Price Level
Retained earnings, December 31, 1978	$4,616	168/150	$ 5,170
GPLA net income for 1979 (see Illustration 20–6)			16,471
Dividends declared during 1979			-0-
Retained earnings, December 31, 1979			$21,641

GPLA accounting and current values

Early in this chapter, the fact that prices do not all change at the same rate was discussed. Indeed, when the general price level is rising, some specific prices may be falling. If this were not so, if prices all changed at the same rate, then GPLA accounting would report current values on the financial statements. For example, suppose that a company purchased land for $50,000 on January 1, 1978, at which time the general price index was 130, and the general price level subsequently increased until December 1979, at which time the general price index was 168. A GPLA balance sheet for this company on December 31, 1979, would report the land at $50,000 × 168/130 = $64,615. If all prices increased at the same rate during that period, then the price of the land would have increased from $50,000 to $64,-615, and the company's GPLA balance sheet would coincidentally disclose the land at its current value.

However, since all prices do not change at the same rate, the current value of the land may differ substantially from the GPLA amount of $64,615. For example, assume that the company obtained an appraisal of the land and determined that its current value on December 31, 1979, was $80,000. The difference between the original purchase price of $50,000 and the current value of $80,000 can be explained as follows:

Unrealized holding gain	$80,000 − $64,615 =	$15,385
Adjustment for general price-level increase	$64,615 − $50,000 =	14,615
		$30,000

In that case, the GPLA balance sheet would report land at $64,615, which is $15,385 ($80,000 − $64,615) less than its current value. This illustrates a very important fact concerning GPLA accounting; that is, GPLA accounting is not a form of current value accounting. Rather, GPLA accounting restates original transaction prices into equivalent amounts of current, *general* purchasing power. Only if current, *specific* purchasing power were the basis of valuation would the balance sheet display current values.

GPLA accounting has been frequently proposed as a means of improving the relevance of accounting information. Proponents of GPLA accounting argue that conventional, unit-of-money financial statements have questionable relevance to decision makers and may even be misleading in a world of persistent, long-run inflation. Since GPLA accounting adjusts for general price-level changes, its proponents believe that GPLA financial statements provide a more meaningful portrayal of a company's past operations and financial position. And, they argue, GPLA accounting is sufficiently objective to allow its practical application without damaging the credibility of financial statements.

Current value accounting

On the other hand, some accountants argue that even GPLA accounting fails to accomplish the necessary objective of communicating to statement readers the economic values that are of most relevance. They would design financial statements so that each item in the statements is measured in terms of that item's current value.

Some arguments for current value accounting conclude that the current liquidation price or "exit value" of an item is the most appropriate basis of valuation for financial statements. However, other arguments, which appear to be having a greater impact on accounting practice, conclude that the price which would have to be paid to replace an item, its *replacement cost,* is the most appropriate basis of financial statement valuation.

Replacement costs on the income statement

Replacement cost accounting

Following the replacement cost approach to accounting, the reported amount of each expense should be the number of dollars required, at the time the expense is incurred, to replace the resources consumed. For example, assume that the annual sales of a company included an item that was sold in May for $1,500 and the item had been acquired on January 1 for $500. Also, suppose that in May, at the time of sale, the cost to replace this item was $700. Then the annual replacement cost income statement would include sales of $1,500 less cost of goods sold of $700. To state this idea in more general terms, whenever an asset is acquired some time prior to its expiration, the historical number of dollars paid for the asset likely will differ from its replacement cost at the time of the expense incurrence (asset expiration), and replacement cost accounting requires that the reported amount of expense be measured at the time of the asset expiration.

The result of measuring expenses in terms of replacement costs is that any revenue that appears in the income statement is matched with the current (at the time of the sale) cost of the resources which were used to earn that revenue. Thus, operating profit is not positive unless revenues are sufficient to replace all of the resources that were consumed in the process of producing those revenues. The operating profit figure is therefore thought to be an important (and improved) basis for evaluating the effectiveness of operating activities.

Replacement costs on the balance sheet

On the balance sheet, replacement cost accounting requires that assets be reported at the amounts that would have to be paid to replace them as of the balance sheet date. Similarly, liabilities should be reported at the amounts that would have to be paid to satisfy the liabilities as of the balance sheet date. Note that this valuation basis is similar to GPLA accounting in that a distinction exists between monetary and nonmonetary assets and liabilities. Monetary assets and liabilities are fixed in amount regardless of price level changes, and therefore need not be adjusted in amount. But all of the nonmonetary items must be evaluated at each balance sheet date to determine the best approximation of replacement cost.

A little reflection on the variety of assets reported on balance sheets will confirm the existence of numerous difficulties in obtaining reliable estimates of replacement costs. In some cases, specific price indexes may provide the most reliable source of replacement cost information. In other cases, where an asset is not new and has been partially depreciated, its replacement cost may be estimated by determining the cost to acquire a new asset of like nature. Depreciation on the old asset is then based on the replacement cost of the new asset. Clearly, the professional judgment of the accountant is an important factor in developing replacement cost data necessary to prepare such financial statements.

The SEC requirement for replacement cost information

Students should not think of replacement cost accounting only as a possible substitute for conventional, unit-of-money financial statements. It is entirely possible for replacement cost information to be presented in addition to the conventional, unit-of-money financial statements. For example, the Securities and Exchange Commission (SEC) has recently begun to require that certain large companies disclose supplemental information on:

... the estimated current replacement cost of inventories and productive capacity at the end of each fiscal year for which a balance sheet is required and the approximate amount of cost of sales and depreciation based on replacement cost for the two most recent full fiscal years.[8]

Consider the SEC requirement more closely.

Replacement cost of inventories   In the case of inventories, replacement cost at the date of the balance sheet must be presented.

---

[8] Securities and Exchange Commission, *Accounting Series Release No. 190* (Washington, D.C., 1976).

Also, if the net realizable value of the inventory happens to be less than replacement cost, the amount of the difference must be disclosed.

Replacement cost of goods sold In respect to cost of goods sold, replacement cost is to be determined at the time the sales were made, not at the end of the year. However, the average cost levels during the year are usually an acceptable means of estimating replacement costs at the time of sale.

Replacement cost of productive capacity According to the staff of the SEC's Division of Corporation Finance and the Office of the Chief Accountant:

. . . productive capacity is a measurement of a company's ability to produce and distribute. The productive capacity of a manufacturer would be measured by the number of units it can presently produce and distribute within a particular time frame; in the case of a telephone company, for example, it would be a measurement of the number of telephone calls it can presently complete within a certain time frame.[9]

Of interest is the fact that the SEC staff excludes land and intangible assets from the list of assets that constitute the productive capacity of a company. Thus, the requirement implies that replacement cost of productive capacity involves the replacement cost of depreciable, tangible assets and amortizable wasting assets such as mineral deposits.

Regarding the replacement cost of productive capacity, both "replacement cost (new)" and "depreciated replacement cost" must be reported. The SEC staff defined these terms as follows:

In the case of depreciable, depletable or amortizable assets, replacement cost (new) and depreciated replacement cost should be distinguished. Replacement cost (new) is the total estimated current cost of replacing total productive capacity at the end of the year while depreciated replacement cost is the replacement cost (new) adjusted for the already expired service potential of such assets.[10]

Annual depreciation on replacement cost of productive capacity The amount of annual depreciation on replacement cost of productive capacity must also be reported. However, it is to be based upon the average replacement cost during the year rather than the ending amount of replacement cost. Also, it must be calculated on the basis of straight-line depreciation or the equivalent, rather than one of the accelerated depreciation methods.

The SEC action requiring companies to report replacement cost information is limited to certain very large companies. Also, the required information is obviously much more limited than would be a complete set of financial statements prepared on a replacement cost

The future of accounting for price-level changes

---

[9] Division of Corporation Finance and the Office of the Chief Accountant, Securities and Exchange Commission, *Staff Accounting Bulletin, Release No. 7* (Washington, D.C., 1976). See also *Staff Accounting Bulletin, Release Nos. 9 and 10.*

[10] Ibid.

basis. For example, there need not be any attempt to present a net income figure on a replacement cost basis, and the only income statement items for which replacement cost information is required are cost of sales and depreciation of productive capacity. However, notwithstanding these limitations, the SEC action represents a major break with the United States tradition of relying on unit-of-money financial statements.

Conventional, unit-of-money financial statements will, no doubt, continue to represent the primary basis of United States accounting in the near future. However, the SEC action is an important step in the direction of improved accounting for price level changes. Whether or not these requirements will eventually be expanded to include a complete set of replacement cost financial statements remains to be seen. Also, the future adoption of GPLA accounting is a possible but not predictable occurrence. Both of these alternatives are being used in some countries. The strength of the calls for expanded usage of them in the United States will probably depend on the extent to which future inflation as well as specific price changes serve to undermine the perceived relevance of conventional reporting methods.

Glossary

Current value accounting. An accounting system that provides financial statements in which current values are reported; different versions of current value are possible, for example, current replacement costs or current exit values.

General price-level-adjusted accounting. An accounting system that adjusts unit-of-money financial statements for changes in the general purchasing power of the dollar.

General price-level index. A measure of the changing purchasing power of a dollar in general; measures the price changes for a broad market basket that includes a large variety of goods and services, for example, the Gross National Product Implicit Price Deflator.

General purchasing power gain or loss. The gain or loss that results from holding monetary assets and/or owing monetary liabilities during a period in which the general price level changes.

Monetary assets. Money or claims to receive a fixed amount of money.

Monetary liabilities. Fixed amounts which are owed, with the number of dollars to be paid fixed in amount and not changing regardless of changes in the general price level.

Price index. A measure of the changes in prices of a particular market basket of goods and/or services.

Productive capacity. A measurement of a company's ability to produce and distribute.

Replacement cost. On the income statement, the numbers of dollars required to replace the resources consumed. On the balance sheet, the amounts that would have to be paid to replace the assets or satisfy the liabilities.

Replacement cost accounting. An accounting system that uses specific price-level indexes (and other means) to develop financial statements that report items such as assets and expenses in terms of their current replacement costs.

Specific price-level index. An indicator of the changing purchasing power of a dollar spent for items in a specific category; includes a much more narrow range of goods and services than does a general price index.

Unit-of-money financial statements. Conventional financial statements which disclose revenues, expenses, assets, liabilities, and owners' equity in terms of the historical monetary units exchanged at the time the transactions occurred.

---

1. Some people argue that conventional financial statements fail to adequately account for inflation. What is the general problem with conventional financial statements that generates this argument?
2. Are there any procedures used in conventional accounting that offset the effects of inflation on financial statements? Give some examples.
3. What is the fundamental difference in the price-level adjustments made under replacement cost accounting and under general price-level-adjusted accounting?
4. Explain the difference between an "average change in per unit prices" and a "weighted average change in per unit prices."
5. What is the significance of the "base" year in constructing a price index? How is the base year chosen?
6. For accounting purposes, what is the most important use of a price index?
7. What is the difference between a specific price-level index and a general price-level index?
8. What is meant by "unit-of-money" financial statements?
9. Define "monetary assets."
10. Explain the meaning of "nonmonetary assets."
11. Define "monetary liabilities" and "nonmonetary liabilities." Give examples of both.
12. If the monetary assets held by a firm exceed its monetary liabilities throughout a period in which prices are rising, which should be recorded on a GPLA income statement—a purchasing power gain or loss? What if monetary liabilities exceed monetary assets during a period in which prices are falling?
13. If accountants preferred to display current values in the financial statements, would they use general price-level-adjusted accounting or replacement cost accounting? Are there any other alternatives?
14. Describe the meaning of "operating profit" under a replacement cost accounting system.
15. "The distinction between monetary assets and nonmonetary assets is

Questions for class discussion

just as important for replacement cost accounting as it is for general price-level-adjusted accounting." Is this statement true? Why?

16. The Securities and Exchange Commission requires that certain large companies report replacement cost information on selected items. What are those items?

Exercises

Solutions to the following exercises and problems should be rounded to the nearest 1/10 percent and to the nearest full dollar.

Exercise 20–1

Market basket No. 1 consists of 3 units of A, 4 units of B, and 2 units of D. Market basket No. 2 consists of 2 units of B, 3 units of C, and 4 units of D. The per unit prices of each item during 197A and during 197B are as follows:

Item	197A Price per Unit	197B Price per Unit
A	$1.00	$0.60
B	3.00	3.10
C	5.00	4.80
D	1.00	1.80

Required:

Compute the annual rate of inflation for market basket No. 1 and for market basket No. 2.

Exercise 20–2

The following total prices of a specified market basket were calculated for each of the years 197A through 197E:

Year	Total Price
197A	$12,000
197B	15,000
197C	19,000
197D	21,000
197E	29,000

Required:

1. Using 197C as the base year, prepare a price index for the five-year period.
2. Convert the index from a 197C base year to a 197E base year.

Exercise 20–3

A company's plant and equipment consisted of equipment purchased during 197A for $150,000, land purchased during 197C for $40,000, and a building purchased during 197E for $260,000. The general price index during these and later years was as follows:

197A 100
197B 110
197C 120

197D................. 130
197E 140
197F 150
197G................. 160

Required:

1. Assuming the above price index adequately represents end-of-year price levels, calculate the amount of each cost that would be shown on a GPLA balance sheet for (*a*) December 31, 197F, and (*b*) December 31, 197G. Ignore any accumulated depreciation.
2. Would the GPLA income statement for 197G disclose any purchasing power gain or loss as a consequence of holding the above assets? If so, how much?

Exercise 20–4

Determine whether the following items are monetary or nonmonetary items.

1. Trade accounts receivable.
2. Petty cash.
3. Notes receivable.
4. Goodwill.
5. Income taxes payable.
6. Retained earnings deficit.
7. Merchandise.
8. Product warranties liability.
9. Common stock subscribed.
10. Prepaid rent.
11. Furniture and fixtures.
12. Common stock.
13. Prepaid fire and casualty insurance.
14. Accounts payable.

Exercise 20–5

Calculate the general purchasing power gain or loss in 197B given the following information:

Time Period	*Price Index*
December 197A............................	100
Average during 197B	120
December 197B	150

a. The Accounts Receivable balance on December 31, 197A, was $500. During 197B, sales on account occurred uniformly throughout the year and amounted to $1,500. Receipts also occurred evenly throughout the year and amounted to $600.
b. Accounts payable amounted to $200 on December 31, 197A. Additional accounts payable amounting to $800 were recorded evenly throughout 197B. None of the accounts were paid.
c. A note payable of $250 was issued during 197A and was repaid on December 30, 197B.

Problems

Problem 20–1

The costs of purchasing a common "market basket" in each of several years are as follows:

Year   Cost of Market Basket

197A $30,000
197B.............. 31,800
197C 34,000
197D.............. 33,800
197E.............. 40,000
197F.............. 42,000
197G 41,200
197H 45,000

Required:

1. Construct a price index using 197E as the base year.
2. Using the index constructed in 1, what was the percent increase in prices from 197F to 197H?
3. Using the index constructed in 1, how many dollars in 197H does it take to have the same purchasing power as $1 in 197B?
4. Using the index constructed in 1, if $14,000 were invested in land during 197A and $17,000 were invested in land during 197E, what would be reported as the total land investment on a GPLA balance sheet prepared in 197G? What would your answer be if the investments were in U.S. long-term bonds rather than in land?

Problem 20–2

The directors of Dew Company have expressed an interest in general price-level-adjusted financial statements and the concepts of purchasing power gains and losses. The price index in December 197A was 120, and in December 197B, it was 140. The average price index during 197B was 128.

The unit-of-money financial statements for Dew Company are presented below. The increase in notes payable during 197B occurred on July 15, at which time the reported price index was 125. The funds derived from the increase in notes payable were used to increase the cash balance. Dew Company purchased the equipment several years ago when the price index was 105.

DEW COMPANY
Balance Sheets
December 31, 197A, and 197B

	197A	*197B*
Cash...	$120,000	$210,000
Accounts receivable	100,000	100,000
Equipment (net of depreciation).............................	80,000	75,000
Total Assets...	$300,000	$385,000
Notes payable	$100,000	$140,000
Capital stock...	100,000	100,000
Retained earnings..	100,000	145,000
Total Liabilities and Stockholders' Equity	$300,000	$385,000

DEW COMPANY
Income Statement
For Year Ended December 31, 197B

Revenues....................		$200,000
Depreciation expense....	$ 5,000	
Other expenses............	150,000	155,000
Net Income.................		$ 45,000

Required:
1. Calculate the purchasing power gain or loss incurred by Dew Company during 197B. You should assume that revenues were received in cash evenly throughout the year and that expenses other than depreciation were paid in cash evenly throughout the year.
2. Prepare a general price-level-adjusted income statement for 197B.

Problem 20–3

Dew Company, for which data were presented in Problem 20–2, was organized at a time when the price index was 105. All of the $100,000 capital stock was issued at that time.

Required:
1. Based on the above information and the data provided in Problem 20–2, prepare a GPLA balance sheet for Dew Company as of December 31, 197B. (The retained earnings balance may be determined simply by "plugging" in the amount that is necessary to make the balance sheet balance.)
2. On Dew Company's GPLA balance sheet on December 31, 197A, retained earnings was reported as $97,144. Assuming that GPLA net income for 197B was $23,332, present a calculation that confirms the retained earnings balance as it is reported on the GPLA balance sheet for December 31, 197B.

Problem 20–4

The 197B income statement of ABC Company and its comparative balance sheets for December 31, 197A, and December 31, 197B, are as follows:

ABC COMPANY
Income Statement
For Year Ended December 31, 197B

Sales revenue		$50,000
Cost of goods sold:		
Beginning inventory...............	$ 7,000	
Purchases	26,000	
Total available merchandise	$33,000	
Ending inventory...................	8,000	25,000
Gross profit.........................		$25,000
Depreciation expense................	$ 2,000	
Other expenses	13,000	15,000
Net Income..........................		$10,000

ABC Company
Balance Sheets
December 31, 197A, and 197B

	197A	197B
Cash	$ 5,000	$ 4,500
Accounts receivable	15,000	20,000
Notes receivable	5,000	5,000
Inventory	7,000	8,000
Building	40,000	40,000
Accumulated depreciation	(2,000)	(4,000)
Land	25,000	25,000
Total Assets	$95,000	$98,500
Accounts payable	$25,000	$20,000
Notes payable	10,000	10,000
Common stock	50,000	50,000
Retained earnings	10,000	18,500
Total Liabilities and Stockholders' Equity	$95,000	$98,500

Selected index numbers from a general price-level index are:

General Price Index

January 197A	110
June 197A (Also average for 197A)	120
December 197A	130
June 197B (Also average for 197B)	140
December 197B	150

Additional information regarding ABC Company is as follows:

a. All sales are on credit and recorded to Accounts Receivable. Cash collections of Accounts Receivable occurred evenly throughout the year.

b. All merchandise purchases were credited to Accounts Payable and cash payments of Accounts Payable occurred evenly throughout the year. The beginning inventory was acquired when the price index was 120.

c. Other expenses ($13,000) were paid in cash evenly throughout the year.

d. Dividends of $1,500 were paid to stockholders in late December 197B.

e. The Building and Land accounts reflect assets that were acquired in January 197A. The outstanding stock was issued on January 1, 197A.

f. The changes during the year in Cash, Accounts Payable, and Accounts Receivable, are as follows:

Cash

Beginning balance	5,000	Payments of accounts	31,000
Receipts from customers	45,000	Other expenses	13,000
		Dividend payments	1,500

Accounts Payable

Cash payments	31,000	Beginning balance	25,000
		Merchandise purchases	26,000

Accounts Receivable

Beginning balance	15,000	Cash receipts	45,000
Credit sales	50,000		

Required:
1. Calculate the purchasing power gain or loss to be reported on the GPLA income statement for 197B.
2. Prepare the GPLA income statement for 197B.
3. Prepare a GPLA balance sheet as of December 31, 197B. (Retained earnings may be determined by "plugging" in the amount necessary to make the balance sheet balance.)
4. Based on the additional information that the GPLA balance sheet on December 31, 197A, disclosed a retained earnings balance of $12,946, calculate the GPLA retained earnings balance on December 31, 197B, so as to confirm the "plugged" amount used in answering Requirement 3.

Problem 20–1A   Alternate
   The costs of purchasing a common "market basket" in each of several   **problems**
years are as follows:

Year	Cost of Market Basket
197A	$41,000
197B	44,000
197C	43,500
197D	48,000
197E	50,000
197F	54,000
197G	57,000
197H	56,000

Required:
1. Construct a price index using 197D as the base year.
2. Using the index constructed in 1, what was the percent increase in prices from 197E to 197H?
3. Using the index constructed in 1, how many dollars in 197H does it take to have the same purchasing power as $1 in 197B?
4. Using the index constructed in 1, if $18,000 were invested in land during 197A and $24,000 were invested in land during 197E, what would be reported as the total land investment on a GPLA balance sheet prepared in 197G? What would your answer be if the investments were in corporate bonds rather than in land?

Problem 20–2A
   The unit-of-money income statement for 197B and December 31, 197A, and 197B, balance sheets of Crafter Company are given below:

CRAFTER COMPANY
Income Statement
For Year Ended December 31, 197B

Commissions revenue....		$120,000
Depreciation expense $15,000		
Other expenses 80,000		95,000
Net Income		$ 25,000

CRAFTER COMPANY
Balance Sheets
December 31, 197A, and 197B

	197A	197B
Cash...	$ 70,000	$100,000
Accounts receivable	30,000	55,000
Equipment (net of depreciation).............................	90,000	75,000
Total Assets..	$190,000	$230,000
Notes payable	$ 50,000	$ 65,000
Capital stock...	130,000	130,000
Retained earnings...	10,000	35,000
Total Liabilities and Stockholders' Equity	$190,000	$230,000

Selected numbers from a general price-level index are as follows:

Price Index

December 197A................	80
Average during 197B	90
September 197B................	95
December 197B	105

The increase in notes payable during 197B occurred on September 10, and the funds derived from the increase in notes payable were used to increase the cash balance. Crafter Company purchased the equipment at a time when the general price index was 62.

Required:

1. Calculate the purchasing power gain or loss incurred by Crafter Company during 197B. You should assume that all commissions were earned evenly throughout the year and were debited to Accounts Receivable. Cash receipts from receivables ($95,000) were also distributed evenly throughout the year, and expenses other than depreciation were paid in cash evenly throughout the year.
2. Prepare a general price-level-adjusted income statement for 197B.

Problem 20–3A

Assume the same facts as were presented in Problem 20–2A. In addition, Crafter Company was organized some time ago when the price index was 59. All of the capital stock ($130,000) was issued at that time.

Required:

1. Based on the above information and the data provided in Problem 20–2A, prepare a GPLA balance sheet for Crafter Company on December 31,

197B. (The retained earnings balance may be determined simply by "plugging" in the amount that is necessary to make the balance sheet balance.)

2. On Crafter Company's GPLA balance sheet on December 31, 197A, retained earnings was reported as a deficit of $10,142.48. Assuming that Crafter Company reported a GPLA net loss for 197B of $1,028, present a calculation that confirms the retained earnings balance as it is reported on the GPLA balance sheet for December 31, 197B.

Diversified Enterprises purchased a plot of land in 197A when the general price index was 94. The land cost $200,000 and was zoned for heavy industrial use. In 197D, the general price index is 118. However, a specific price index for heavy industrial property in the general area of the land in question has risen from 80 in 197A to 140 in 197D.

Decision problem 20–1, Diversified Enterprises

Diversified Enterprises has no intention of building a plant on the property. It is being held only as an investment and will eventually be sold. Some of the employees of Diversified Enterprises have been arguing over the matter of how the land should be presented in the balance sheet at the close of 197D and also over the amount of real economic benefit the company will have obtained from the investment if the land were to be sold immediately. Prepare an analysis which recognizes the alternative balance sheet valuation possibilities and which will help resolve the dispute.

PART 7

Managerial accounting for costs

21
Departmental accounting; responsibility accounting . . .

22
Manufacturing accounting . . .

23
Cost accounting, job order, and process

After studying Chapter 21, you should be able to:

- State the reasons for departmentalization of businesses.

- Describe the differences between manufacturing and merchandising firms and how each records its departmental costs.

- Describe the types of expenses that should be allocated among departments, the bases for allocating such expenses, and the procedures involved in the allocation process.

- Explain the bases for determining profitability of a department and evaluating the department managers.

- Describe the problems associated with allocation of joint costs between departments.

- Define or explain the words and phrases listed in the chapter Glossary.

chapter 21

Departmental accounting; responsibility accounting

A business is departmentalized or divided into departments for managerial purposes, with a manager commonly being placed in charge of each department. Under perfect circumstances, the manager is responsible for both the output of the department and the resources expended in attaining that output. Output may be in units of product manufactured, dollars of sales achieved, or services performed; and resources expended may be goods sold, raw materials consumed, wages paid, depreciation, heat, lights, and so forth. And, ideally the optimum output should be obtained with the most reasonable expenditure of resources.

When a business is divided into departments, if management is to know how well each department is performing, it is necessary for the accounting system to supply information by departments as to resources expended and outputs achieved, and this requires that revenue and expense information be measured and accumulated by departments. However, before going further it should be observed that such information is generally not made public, since it might be of considerable benefit to competitors. Rather, it is for the use of management in controlling operations, appraising performances, allocating resources, and in taking remedial actions. For example, if one of several departments is particularly profitable, perhaps it should be expanded. Or if a department is showing poor results, information as to its revenues, costs, and expenses may point to a proper remedial action.

Basis for departmentalization

In every departmentalized business there are two basic kinds of departments, *productive departments* and *service departments*. In a factory the productive departments are those engaged directly in manufacturing operations, and in a store they are the departments making sales. Departmental divisions in a factory are commonly based on manufacturing processes employed or products or components

697

manufactured. The division in a store is usually based on kinds of goods sold, with each selling or productive department being assigned the sale of one or more kinds of merchandise. In either type of business the service departments, such as the general office, advertising, purchasing, payroll, and personnel departments, assist or perform services for the productive departments.

In addition to dividing a business into productive departments and service departments, it is also recognized that certain departments are *cost centers* and others are *profit centers*. A cost center is a unit of the business that incurs costs (or expenses) but does not directly generate revenues. The productive departments of a factory and such service departments as the general office, advertising, and purchasing departments are cost centers. A profit center differs from a cost center in that it not only incurs costs but also generates revenues. The selling departments of a store are profit centers. In judging departmental efficiencies in the two kinds of centers, the manager of a cost center is judged on his ability to control costs and keep his costs within a satisfactory range. The manager of a profit center, on the other hand, is judged on his ability to generate earnings, which are the excess of revenues over costs.

Departmental gross profits in a merchandising business

In a merchandising concern the managers of the sales departments constantly make decisions that affect the gross profits of their departments, generally with the intention of maximizing such profits. Of course they do not ignore operating expenses, since their ultimate objective is net income; but the factors of gross profit receive a great deal of attention, probably because gross profit is subject to considerable managerial control. It at times can be increased by lowering prices and increasing the volume of goods sold. At other times a larger margin on a smaller volume will increase gross profit.

The gross profit of a department is a function of (1) the number of dollars of goods sold and (2) the markup on the goods. Therefore, management of departmental gross profits depends on the accumulation of information as to sales, purchases, and inventories by departments, so that departmental gross profits may be calculated. The information is gathered in a number of ways; and normally a store's size, the goods it sells, and the number of its departments determine the methods and procedures used. For instance, a store may provide a separate set of merchandising accounts for each of its departments or it may use analysis sheets to accumulate the information necessary to determine gross profits by departments.

If separate merchandising accounts are provided, separate Sales, Sales Returns, Purchases, Purchases Returns, and Merchandise Inventory accounts are provided for each department. However, unless the store has a very limited number of departments, this may cause its ledger to become large and awkward and complicate its end-of-the-period closing procedures. Consequently, rather than separate departmental accounts, many stores use a single store-wide account each for sales, sales returns, purchases, purchases returns, and merchandise inventory; but in addition accumulate a separate supplementary record of sales, purchases, and inventories by departments. This separate supplementary record may be accumulated with electronic equipment on magnetic tapes or analysis sheets may be used.

Analysis sheets

When a store uses departmental analysis sheets, it provides only one undepartmentalized general ledger account for sales, another account for sales returns, another for purchases, and another for purchases returns; and it records its transactions and posts to these accounts as though it were not departmentalized. But in addition to this, each day it also summarizes its merchandise transactions by departments and records the summarized amounts on analysis sheets. For example, a concern using analysis sheets, in addition to recording sales in its usual manner, will total each day's sales by departments and enter the daily totals on a sales analysis sheet like Illustration 21–1. As a result, at the end of a month or other period the column totals of the analysis sheet will show total sales by departments and the grand total of all the sheet's columns should equal the balance of the Sales account.

Departmental Sales Analysis Sheet

Date		Men's Wear Dept.	Boys' Wear Dept.	Shoe Dept.	Leather Goods Dept.	Women's Wear Dept.
May	1	$357.15	$175.06	$115.00	$ 75.25	$427.18
	2	298.55	136.27	145.80	110.20	387.27

Illustration 21–1

When a store uses departmental analysis sheets, it uses one analysis sheet to accumulate sales figures, another analysis sheet for sales returns, another for purchases, and still another for purchases returns; and at the end of the period the several analysis sheets show the store's sales, sales returns, purchases, and purchases returns by departments. If the store then takes inventories by departments, it can calculate gross profits by departments.

Securing departmental information

Modern cash registers enable even a small store to accumulate daily totals for sales and sales returns by departments. Such a store can also use analysis sheets to sort information as to purchases and purchases returns by departments. Larger stores use electric bookkeeping machines, punched inventory tags, and/or cash registers that feed information directly into the store's computer.

Electric bookkeeping machines

Illustration 6–11 on page 194 shows an electric bookkeeping machine. It was explained beginning on page 193 that this machine could be used for sales accounting, purchases, cash receipts, or many other accounting applications; and it was also explained how the machine could, for example, for each charge sale produce the customer's invoice, post to the customer's account, update the customer's month-end statement, and enter the sale in the Sales Journal. In addition to this, the machine will accumulate information as to sales by departments and will print out departmental sales totals after the last sales invoice is prepared each day. When used for recording purchases or returns, it will also accumulate departmental totals for these transactions. Such machines are commonly used by wholesale firms.

Inventory tags

Illustration 21–2 shows a type of pin-punched price tag used by many large department stores. Such tags show the price of an item of merchandise and are an essential part of the inventory control system in a store using them — an inventory control system that makes it easy to accumulate information as to sales and returns by items, colors, sizes, manufacturers, and so forth, as well as in dollar amounts by departments.

Pin-punched price tags get their name from the pin-size holes punched in the tags. These holes carry information in the code arrangement of their punching as to an item's price, size, color, and so on. The machine used to punch the holes also prints the punched information on the tag for visual reading.

When an item of merchandise is sold, the lower half of the tag is removed by the salesperson and retained, and the upper half is left attached to the item sold. At the end of each day the retained tag portions are taken to the accounting department and run through a tag

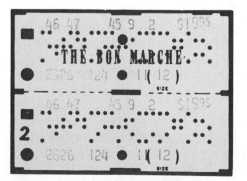

Illustration 21–2

converter, a machine that electronically records each tag's information on computer cards or on paper or magnetic tape. The information on the cards or tape is then fed into a computer that sorts it and produces reports as to sales by departments plus information for inventory control and for updating the inventory records.

When merchandise is returned, the customer is instructed to return with the merchandise the price tag portion left attached at the time of sale. These returned portions are run through the tag converter to produce the cards or tapes used in accumulating information about returns.

Cash registers

Some cash registers capture data on magnetic tape rather than on paper tape, and in large stores the registers are often connected to and enter information directly into the store's computer. All such modern cash registers are capable of doing much more than accumulating sales totals. In addition to printing all of the pertinent information on the sales ticket, the register may automatically initiate entries to record credit sales in the customer's account. Also, if the necessary information on the type of goods sold is entered in the register, it may initiate entries to the appropriate inventory accounts, thereby providing constantly up-to-date inventory account balances.

Income statement showing departmental gross profits

Accumulating information and arriving at a gross profit figure for each selling department in a departmentalized business is not too difficult, as the discussion thus far reveals. However, to go beyond this and arrive at useful net income figures by departments is not so easy; consequently, many concerns make no effort to calculate more than gross profits by departments. Illustration 21–3 shows an income statement prepared for such a concern. The statement sets out departmental gross profits and combines these figures to arrive at a combined gross profit figure, a figure from which the unallocated operating expenses are deducted to arrive at the store's net income.

Observe in Illustration 21–3 that in addition to showing gross profits in dollar amounts, gross profits are also expressed as percentages of net sales. These percentages make departmental comparisons easier.

Allocating expenses

If a concern goes beyond the calculation of departmental gross profits and attempts to arrive at a net income figure for each selling department, it must charge each department with its *direct expenses* and allocate to the departments any *indirect expenses*. The direct expenses of a department are those incurred for the sole benefit of that department; as such, they are easily traced to that department. In other words, little if any doubt exists regarding the decision as to which department should be charged with a direct expense. For example, the salary of an employee who works in only one department is a direct expense of that department.

Valley Haberdashery
Income Statement
For Year Ended December 31, 19—

	Men's Clothing	Boys' Clothing	Shoes	Combined
Revenue from sales:				
Sales	$46,000	$34,000	$20,000	$100,000
Less returns	750	425	350	1,525
Net sales	$45,250	$33,575	$19,650	$ 98,475
Cost of goods sold:				
Inventory, Jan. 1	$ 7,400	$ 4,200	$ 3,350	$14,950
Purchases	30,000	21,700	11,800	63,500
Freight-in	150	125	75	350
Goods for sale	$37,550	$26,025	$15,225	$78,800
Inventory, Dec. 31	8,100	3,500	4,150	15,750
Cost of goods sold	29,450	22,525	11,075	63,050
Gross profits	$15,800	$11,050	$ 8,575	$ 35,425
Gross profit percentages	(34.9%)	(32.9%)	(43.5%)	(36.0%)

Operating expenses:
Selling expenses:
Sales salaries $7,000
Sales commissions 5,000
Advertising 550
Sales supplies used 200
Depreciation of store equipment 700
Total selling expenses $13,450
General and administrative expenses:
Office salaries $3,800
Office supplies used 250
Expired insurance 300
Bad debts 210
Depreciation of office equipment ... 150
Depreciation of building 1,200
Property taxes 900
Total general and administrative expenses 6,810
Total operating expenses 20,260
Net Income .... $ 15,165

Illustration 21–3

Indirect expenses, on the other hand, are incurred for the joint benefit of more than one department; for example, rent, heat, and lights are often indirect expenses. Indirect expenses are not easily traced to the activities of a single department, and considerable doubt may exist regarding the most appropriate allocation of an indirect expense between departments. While the entire amount of a direct expense may be charged directly to the department benefited by its incurrence, an indirect expense can only be allocated on some fair basis such as, for example, the amount of floor space occupied, as in the allocation of janitorial expenses.

When an indirect expense is allocated, portions are assigned to each department, preferably on the basis of benefits received. For example, a jewelry store purchases janitorial services from an outside firm and allocates the cost among its three departments according to the floor space occupied. The cost of janitorial services for a short period is $280 and the amounts of floor space occupied are:

Jewelry department .... 250 sq. ft.
Watch repair department....................... 125
China and silver department................ 500
Total .... 875 sq. ft.

The departmental shares of the janitorial expense are:

Jewelry department: $\frac{250}{875} \times \$280 = \$80$

Watch repair department: $\frac{125}{875} \times \$280 = \$40$

China and silver department: $\frac{500}{875} \times \$280 = \$160$

Students should note that the concepts of "direct" costs or expenses and "indirect" costs or expenses can be usefully applied in a variety of situations in addition to departmental accounting. In general, direct costs are easily traced to or associated with a "cost object." In this chapter, the cost object of significance is the department. However, other cost objects may also be of interest. For example, in manufacturing units of products, the cost object may be a unit of product (see Chapter 22). In that case, costs that can be easily identified with a unit of product may be called "direct costs." Other costs which are perhaps essential to the manufacturing process but which cannot be easily traced to specific units of product would be called "indirect costs."

In the following paragraphs, bases for allocating a representation of indirect expenses are discussed. In the discussions no hard-and-fast rules are given because several factors are often involved in an expense allocation, and the importance of the factors varies from situation to situation. As previously stated, indirect expenses are, by definition, subject to doubt as to how they should be allocated between departments. Judgment rather than hard-and-fast rules is required, and often accountants of equal ability and experience will not agree as to the proper basis for allocating an indirect expense.

Bases for allocating expenses

Wages and salaries

An employee's wages may be either a direct or an indirect expense. If an employee spends all of his time in one department, his wages are a direct expense of the benefited department; but if an employee works in more than one department, his wages become an indirect expense to be allocated between or among the benefited departments. Normally, working time spent in each department is a fair basis for allocating wages.

A supervisory employee at times supervises more than one department, and in such cases the time spent in each department is usually a fair basis for allocating his salary. However, since a supervisory employee is frequently on the move from department to department, the time spent in each is often difficult to measure. Consequently, some companies allocate the salary of such an employee to his departments on the basis of the number of employees in each department, while others make the allocation on the basis of the supervised departments' sales. When a supervisor's salary is allocated on the basis of employees, it is assumed that he is supervising people and the time spent in each department is related to the number of employees in each. When a supervisory employee's salary is allocated on the basis of sales, it is assumed that the time devoted to each department is related to the department's productiveness.

Rent

Rent expense is normally allocated to benefited departments on the basis of the amount and value of the floor space occupied by each. Furthermore, since all customers who enter a store must pass the departments by the entrance and only a fraction of these people go beyond the first floor, ground floor space is more valuable for retail purposes than is basement or upper floor space, and space near the entrance is more valuable than is space in an out-of-the-way corner. Yet since there is no exact measure of floor space values, all such values and the allocations of rent based on such values must depend on judgment. Nevertheless, if good judgment, statistics as to customer traffic, and the opinions of experts who are familiar with current rental values are used, fair allocations can be made.

Advertising

When a store advertises a department's products, if the advertising is effective, people come into the store to buy the products. However, at the same time they also often buy other unadvertised products. Consequently, advertising benefits all departments, even those the products of which are not advertised; and as a result, many stores treat advertising as an indirect expense and allocate it on the basis of sales. When advertising costs are allocated on a sales basis, a department producing one fifteenth of the total sales is charged with one fifteenth of the advertising cost and a department producing one sixth of the sales is charged with one sixth.

Although in many stores advertising costs are allocated to departments on the basis of sales, in others each advertisement is analyzed and the cost of the column inches of newspaper space or minutes of

TV or radio time devoted to the products of a department is charged to the department.

Depreciation

Depreciation on equipment used solely in one department is a direct expense of that department; and if adequate plant asset records are kept, the depreciation applicable to each department may be learned by examining the records. Where adequate records are not maintained, depreciation must be treated as an indirect expense and allocated to the departments on the basis of the value of the equipment in each. When the building is owned, building depreciation is normally allocated like rent.

Taxes and insurance

Taxes and insurance are indirect expenses and are allocated to departments on the basis of the insured and taxable property in each. Taxes and insurance on the building are allocated like rent.

Heating and lighting expense

Heating and lighting expense is usually allocated on the basis of floor space occupied under the assumption that the amount of heat and the number of lights, their wattage, and the extent of their use are uniform throughout the store. Should there be a material variation in lighting, however, further analysis and a separate allocation may be advisable.

Delivery expense

The cost of delivering packages typically depends upon the number, size, and weight of the packages. Usually, it is impossible to consider all three factors in a single allocation basis. Consequently, the most important one is often used. Sometimes all three factors, number, size, and weight, are ignored, and delivery expenses are allocated on a sales basis. Often, too, where the number, size, and weight of packages are closely related to sales, such a basis is fair.

Mechanics of allocating expenses

It would be possible in most cases to analyze each indirect expense incurred and to allocate and charge portions to several departmental expense accounts at the time of incurrence or payment. However, this is seldom done because it involves too many allocations and too much work. Instead, expense amounts paid or incurred, both direct and indirect, are commonly accumulated in undepartmentalized expense accounts until the end of a period, when a *departmental expense allocation sheet* is used to allocate and charge each expense to the benefited departments. A departmental expense allocation sheet is shown in Illustration 21–4 and is discussed in more detail later in this chapter.

Tempe Hardware Company
Departmental Expense Allocation Sheet
Year Ended December 31, 19—

Undepartmentalized Expense Accounts and Service Departments	Bases of Allocation	Expense Account Balances	Allocations of Expenses to Departments					
			General Office Dept.	Purchasing Dept.	Cleaning and Maintenance	Hardware Dept.	Housewares Dept.	Appliances Dept.
Salaries expense	Direct, payroll records	$39,050	$7,250	$6,400	$3,000	$10,200	$ 4,800	$ 7,400
Rent expense	Amount and value of space	7,200	360	360	40	3,200	814	2,426
Advertising expense	Sales	2,070				920	460	690
Insurance expense	Insured property	320	50	30	12	132	24	72
Depreciation expense, equipment	Direct, property records	1,200	200	125	50	350	175	300
Lighting expense	Wattage of lights	226	18	18	5	90	40	55
Heating expense	Floor space	960	48	48	8	424	144	288
Supplies expense	Direct, requisitions	625	102	63	125	133	54	148
Total expenses by departments		$51,651	$8,028	$7,044	$3,240	$15,449	$ 6,511	$11,379
Allocation of service department expenses:								
General office department	Sales		8,028			3,568	1,784	2,676
Purchasing department	Purchases			7,044		3,166	1,761	2,117
Cleaning and maintenance	Floor space				3,240	1,605	545	1,090
Total Expenses Applicable to Selling Departments		51,651				$23,788	$10,601	$17,262

Illustration 21–4

In order that they may sell their products, selling departments must have the services provided by the service departments just as they must have building space, heat, and lights. Therefore, service department operating expenses are in effect indirect expenses of the selling departments; and if departmental net incomes are calculated, the cost of operating each service department should be allocated to the selling departments it serves. The following list shows commonly used bases for these allocations:

Allocating service department expenses

Departments	Expense Allocation Bases
General office department	Number of employees in each department or sales.
Personnel department	Number of employees in each department.
Payroll department	Number of employees in each department.
Advertising department	Sales or amounts of advertising charged directly to each department.
Purchasing department	Dollar amounts of purchases or number of purchase invoices.
Cleaning and maintenance department	Square feet of floor space occupied.

As previously stated, expenses are commonly accumulated in undepartmentalized expense accounts until the end of an accounting period when a departmental expense allocation sheet is used, not only to allocate the accumulated expenses to the benefited departments but also to allocate to the productive departments the costs of operating the service departments, Illustration 21–4 shows such an allocation sheet.

Departmental expense allocation sheet

To prepare an expense allocation sheet, the account names of the to-be-allocated expenses are entered in the sheet's first column along with the names of the service departments. Next, the bases of allocation are entered in the second column, and the account balances are entered in the third. Then, each expense account balance is allocated according to the basis shown, and the allocated portions are entered in the departmental columns. After this the departmental columns are totaled and the service department column totals are allocated in turn to the productive departments.

Upon completion, the amounts in the columns of an expense allocation sheet are available for preparing departmental income statements showing net incomes by departments. Such a statement for the appliance department of the firm of Illustration 21–4 is shown in Illustration 21–5.

The management of a store in which departmental net incomes are calculated is often confronted with a situation in which one or more departments shows a loss. When this occurs, consideration is often given to eliminating the unprofitable department or departments; and when such consideration is given, what are known as escapable and in-

Eliminating an unprofitable department

Tempe Hardware Company
Appliance Department Income Statement
For Year Ended December 31, 19—

Sales		$84,464
Cost of goods sold		59,321
Gross profit from sales		$25,143
Operating expenses:		
Sales salaries expense	$7,400	
Rent expense	2,426	
Advertising expense	690	
Insurance expense	72	
Depreciation expense, equipment	300	
Lighting expense	55	
Heating expense	288	
Supplies expense	148	
General office department expense	2,676	
Purchasing department expenses	2,117	
Cleaning and maintenance expenses	1,090	
Total operating expenses		17,262
Appliance Department Net Income		$ 7,881

Illustration 21–5

escapable expenses are encountered. *Escapable expenses* are those that would end with an unprofitable department's elimination; *inescapable expenses* are those that would continue even though the department were eliminated. For example, Joe M. Hardt Company is contemplating the elimination of its Department A. The company's income statement for the past year, see Illustration 21–6, shows that Department A incurred a $415 net loss for the year. However, an examination of its expenses reveals the following escapable and inescapable expenses.

	Escapable Expenses	Inescapable Expenses
Sales salaries expense	$ 8,200	
Advertising expense	1,225	
Store supplies expense	225	
Depreciation expense, store equipment		$ 320
Rent expense		2,800
Insurance expense (merchandise and equipment)	215	85
Bad debts expense	325	
Share of the general office expenses	550	3,220
Totals	$10,740	$6,425

If Department A is discontinued, its $6,425 of inescapable expenses will have to be borne by Department B; thus until Department A's annual loss exceeds $6,425, Joe M. Hardt Company is better off continuing the unprofitable department.

In considering the elimination of an unprofitable department, aside

Joe M. Hardt Company
Income Statement for Year Ended December 31, 19—

	Department A	Department B	Combined
Sales	$63,150	$94,725	$157,875
Cost of goods sold	46,400	56,550	102,950
Gross profit on sales	$16,750	$38,175	$ 54,925
Operating expenses:			
Selling expenses:			
Sales salaries expense	$ 8,200	$12,400	$ 20,600
Advertising expense	1,225	1,580	2,805
Store supplies expense	225	420	645
Depreciation expense, store equipment	320	630	950
Rent expense	2,800	3,200	6,000
Total selling expenses	$12,770	$18,230	$ 31,000
General and administrative expenses:			
Insurance expense	$ 300	$ 425	$ 725
Bad debts expense	325	435	760
Share of the general office expenses	3,770	5,655	9,425
Total general and administrative expenses	$ 4,395	$ 6,515	$ 10,910
Total operating expenses	$17,165	$24,745	$ 41,910
Net Income or (Loss)	$ (415)	$13,430	$ 13,015

Illustration 21–6

from the fact that some of its expenses cannot be escaped, such a department is often continued because it brings business to other profitable departments. Also, the solution is often one of substituting a more profitable department or endeavor for the unprofitable department.

Departmental contributions to overhead

Many people, particularly department heads whose efficiencies are judged and whose salaries depend on the amounts of "net income" earned by their departments, are critical when such net income figures are used in making decisions as to departmental efficiencies. Their critical attitude arises from the fact that departmental net income figures are always affected by the assumptions made in allocating expenses. Such people often suggest the substitution of what are known as *departmental contributions to overhead* when decisions are to be made as to the efficiencies with which departments have been operated. A department's contribution to overhead is the amount its revenues exceed its direct costs and expenses. Illustration 21–7 is a departmental income statement showing contributions to overhead.

Controllable costs and expenses

Net income figures and contributions to overhead are used in judging departmental efficiencies; but is either a good index of how well a department manager has performed? Many people hold that neither is. These people say that since many expenses entering into the calculation of a department's net income or into its contribution to overhead are beyond the control of the department's manager, neither net in-

Smithfield Men's Store
Income Statement Showing Departmental Contributions
Year Ended December 31, 19—

	Men's Department	Boys' Department	Shoe Department	Combined
Revenue from sales	$100,000	$ 40,000	$ 30,000	$170,000
Cost of goods sold	62,000	24,000	17,000	103,000
Gross profit on sales	$ 38,000	$ 16,000	$ 13,000	$ 67,000
Direct expenses:				
Sales salaries expense	$ 16,500	$ 7,500	$ 6,000	$ 30,000
Advertising expense	900	500	400	1,800
Depreciation expense	700	400	500	1,600
Supplies expense	300	200	100	600
Total direct expenses	$ 18,400	$ 8,600	$ 7,000	$ 34,000
Departmental contribution to overhead	$ 19,600	$ 7,400	$ 6,000	$ 33,000
Contribution percentages	19.6%	18.5%	20.0%	19.4%
Indirect expenses:				
Rent expense				$ 6,000
Heating and lighting expense				800
Taxes and insurance expense				1,200
Expenses of the general office				9,400
Total indirect expenses				$17,400
Net Income				$15,600

Illustration 21–7

come nor contribution to overhead should be used in judging how well the manager has performed. These people are of the opinion that only a departments *controllable costs and expenses* should be used in judging a manager's performance.

A department's controllable costs and expenses are those over which the department's manager has control as to the amounts expended. They are not the same as direct costs and expenses. Direct costs and expenses are easily traced and therefore chargeable to a specific department, but the amounts expended may or may not be under the control of the department's manager. For example, a manager often has little or no control over the amount of equipment assigned to his department and the resulting depreciation expense, but he commonly has some control over the employees and the amount of work they do. Also, he normally has some control over supplies used in his department, but no control over the amount of his own salary.

When controllable costs and expenses are used in judging a manager's efficiency, statistics are prepared showing the department's output and its controllable costs and expenses. The statistics of the current period are then compared with prior periods and with planned levels of output and planned costs and the manager's performance is judged.

The concepts of "controllable costs" and "uncontrollable costs" must be defined with reference to a particular manager and within a definite time period. Without these two reference points, all costs are controllable; that is, all costs are controllable at some level of management if the time period is long enough. For example, a cost such as property insurance may not be controllable at the level of a department manager, but it is subject to control by the executive who is responsible for obtaining insurance coverage for the concern. Likewise the executive responsible for obtaining insurance coverage may not have any control over insurance expense resulting from insurance contracts presently in force; but when a contract expires, the executive is free to renegotiate and thus has control over the long run. Consequently, it is recognized that all costs are subject to the control of some manager at some point in time. Revenues are likewise subject to the control of some manager.

The concept of controllable costs and expenses leads naturally to the idea of responsibility accounting. In responsibility accounting:

Responsibility accounting

a. A determination is made of the person responsible for each activity carried on by the business, and the controllable costs and expenses of each activity are assigned to the person responsible for the activity. Responsibility assignments are normally made at the lowest possible managerial level, under the assumption that the manager nearest the action is in the best position to control its costs. For example, a factory foreman is made responsible for the raw materials and supplies used in his department.

b. The accounting system is then designed to accumulate costs and expenses in such a way that timely reports can be made to each manager of the costs for which he is responsible. Each manager is then judged on his ability to control his costs and keep them within a budgeted range, and no manager is held responsible for a cost over which he has no control. Furthermore, prorations and arbitrary allocations of costs are not made because it is recognized that responsibilities cannot be allocated.

At the lowest levels of management, responsibilities and costs over which control is exercised are limited. Consequently, cost reports to this management level cover only a few costs, usually just those costs over which a manager exercises control. Moving up the management hierarchy, responsibilities and control broaden, and reports to a higher level manager are broader and cover a wider range of costs. However, reports to a higher level manager normally do not contain the details reported to his subordinates. Rather, the details reported to a lower level manager are normally summarized on the report to his superior. The details are summarized for two reasons: (1) the lower level manager is primarily responsible and (2) too many details can confuse. If the higher manager's report contains too much detail, he may have difficulty "seeing the woods because of the trees."

In conclusion it should be said that our ability to produce vast amounts of raw figures mechanically and electronically has far outstripped our ability to use the figures. What is needed is the ability to select those figures that are meaningful for planning and control. This is recognized in responsibility accounting, and every effort is made to get the right figure to the right person at the right time, and the right person is the person who can control the cost or revenue.

Joint costs   Joint costs are encountered in some manufacturing concerns and are introduced here because they have much in common with indirect expenses. A joint cost is a single cost incurred to secure two or more essentially different products. For example, a meat-packer incurs a joint cost when he buys a pig from which he will get bacon, hams, shoulders, liver, heart, hide, pig feet, and a variety of other products in portions which he cannot alter. Likewise, a sawmill incurs joint costs when it buys a log and saws it into unalterable portions of Clears, Select Structurals, No. 1 Common, No. 2 Common, and other grades of lumber. In both cases, as with all joint costs, the problem is one of allocating the costs to the several joint products.

A joint cost may be, but is not commonly, allocated on some physical basis, such as the ratio of pounds, square feet, or gallons of each joint product to total pounds, square feet, or gallons of all joint products flowing from the cost. The reason this method is not commonly used is that the cost allocations resulting from its use may be completely out of keeping with the market values of the joint products, and thus may cause certain of the products to sell at a profit while other products always show a loss. For example, a sawmill bought for $30,000 a number of logs which when sawed produced a million board feet of lumber in the grades and amounts shown in Illustration 21–8.

Observe in Illustration 21–8 that the logs produced 200,000 board feet of No. 3 Common lumber and that this is two tenths of the total lumber produced from the logs. If the No. 3 lumber is assigned two tenths of the $30,000 cost of the logs, it will be assigned $6,000 of the cost ($30,000 × $\frac{2}{10}$ = $6,000); and since this lumber can be sold for only $4,000, the assignment will cause this grade to show a loss. As a result, as in this situation, to avoid always showing a loss on one or more of

Grade of Lumber	Production in Board Feet	Market Price per 1,000 Board Feet	Market Value of Production of Each Grade	Ratio of Market Value of Each Grade to Total
Structural..........................	100,000	$120	$12,000	12/50
No. 1 Common	300,000	60	18,000	18/50
No. 2 Common	400,000	40	16,000	16/50
No. 3 Common	200,000	20	4,000	4/50
	1,000,000		$50,000	

Illustration 21–8

the products flowing from a joint cost, such costs are commonly allocated to the joint products *in the ratio of the market values of the joint products at the point of separation.*

The ratios of the market values of the joint products flowing from the $30,000 of log cost are shown in the last column of Illustration 21–8, and if these ratios are used to allocate the $30,000 cost, the cost will be apportioned between the grades as follows:

Structural:	$30,000 × 12/50 =	$ 7,200
No. 1 Common:	$30,000 × 18/50 =	10,800
No. 2 Common:	$30,000 × 16/50 =	9,600
No. 3 Common:	$30,000 × 4/50 =	2,400
		$30,000

Observe that if the No. 3 Common is allocated a share of the $30,000 joint cost based on market values by grades, it is allocated $2,400 of the $30,000. Furthermore, when the $2,400 is subtracted from the grade's $4,000 market value, $1,600 remains to cover other after-separation costs and provide a profit.

Controllable costs or expenses. Costs over which the manager has control as to the amounts incurred.

Cost center. A unit of a business that incurs costs or expenses but does not directly generate revenues.

Departmental contribution to overhead. The amount by which a department's revenues exceed its direct costs and expenses.

Direct costs or expenses. Costs that are easily traced to or associated with a cost object, for example, costs incurred by a department for the sole benefit of the department.

Escapable expenses. Costs that would end with an unprofitable department's elimination.

Indirect costs or expenses. Costs that are not easily traced to a cost object, for example, costs incurred for the joint benefit of more than one department.

Joint cost. A single cost incurred to secure two or more essentially different products.

Productive departments. In a factory, those departments engaged directly in manufacturing operations, and in a store, those departments making sales.

Profit center. A unit of a business that incurs costs and generates revenues.

Responsibility accounting. An accounting system designed to accumulate controllable costs in timely reports to be given to each manager determined responsible for the costs, and also to be used in judging the performance of each manager.

Service departments. Those departments in either a manufacturing or merchandising firm that assist or perform services for the productive departments.

Uncontrollable cost. A cost the amount of which a specific manager cannot control within a given period of time.

1. Why is a business divided into departments?
2. Differentiate between productive departments and service departments.
3. Name several of a department store's service departments.
4. What are the productive departments of (*a*) a factory and (*b*) a store?
5. What is the purpose of a departmental sales analysis sheet? How is a sales analysis sheet used in determining sales by departments?
6. What is a pin-punched price tag? How is such a tag used in determining sales by departments?
7. Differentiate between direct and indirect expenses.
8. Suggest a basis for allocating each of the following expenses to departments: (*a*) salary of a supervisory employee, (*b*) rent, (*c*) heat, (*d*) electricity used in lighting, (*e*) janitorial services, (*f*) advertising, (*g*) expired insurance, and (*h*) taxes.
9. How is a departmental expense allocation sheet used in allocating expenses to departments?
10. How reliable are the amounts shown as net incomes for the various departments of a store when expenses are allocated to the departments?
11. As the terms are used in departmental accounting, what are (*a*) escapable expenses and (*b*) inescapable expenses?
12. How is a department's contribution to overhead measured?
13. What are controllable costs and expenses? What are uncontrollable costs and expenses?
14. In responsibility accounting, who is the right person to be given timely reports and statistics on a given cost?
15. What is a joint cost? How are joint costs normally allocated?

Exercise 21–1

A company rents for $30,000 per year all the space in a building, which is assigned to its departments as follows:

Department A: 2,000 sq. ft. of first-floor space
Department B: 1,000 sq. ft. of first-floor space
Department C: 600 sq. ft. of second-floor space
Department D: 800 sq. ft. of second-floor space
Department E: 1,600 sq. ft. of second-floor space

The company allocates 60% of the total rent to the first floor and 40% to the second floor, and then allocates the rent of each floor to the departments on that floor on the basis of the space occupied. Determine the rent to be allocated to each department.

Exercise 21–2

A company rents for $7,200 per year all the space in a small building, and it occupies the space as follows:

Department A: 2,500 sq. ft. of first-floor space
Department B: 1,500 sq. ft. of first-floor space
Department C: 4,000 sq. ft. of second-floor space

Determine the rent expense to be allocated to each department under the assumption that first-floor space rents for twice as much as second-floor space in the city in which this company is located.

Exercise 21–3

Thomas Cross works part-time in the men's shoe department and in the men's clothing department of Hawaiian Department Store. His work consists of waiting on customers who enter either department and also in straightening and rearranging merchandise in either department as needed after it has been shown to customers. The store allocates his $4,000 in annual wages to the two departments in which he works. Last year the division was based on a sample of the time Cross spent working in the two departments. To gain the sample, observations were made on several days throughout the year of the manner in which Cross spent his time while at work. Following are the results of the observations:

Observed Manner in Which Employee Spent His Time	*Elapsed Time in Minutes*
Selling in men's shoe department	1,850
Straightening and rearranging merchandise in men's shoe department	350
Selling in men's clothing department	1,425
Straightening and rearranging merchandise in men's clothing department	375
Doing nothing while waiting for a customer to enter one of the selling departments	250

Required:

Prepare a calculation to show the shares of the employee's wages that should be allocated to the departments.

Exercise 21–4

Bearing Company has two service departments, the office department and the purchasing department, and two sales departments, One and Two. During the past year the departments had the following direct expenses: general office department, $3,800; purchasing department, $2,800; Department One, $10,000; and Department Two, $7,000. The departments occupy the following amounts of floor space: office, 600; purchasing, 400; One, 1,200; and Two, 800. Department One had three times as many dollars of sales during the year as did Department Two, and during the year the purchasing department processed twice as many purchase orders for Department One as it did for Department Two.

Required:

Prepare an expense allocation sheet for Bearing Company on which the direct expenses are entered by departments, the year's $6,000 of rent expense is allocated to the departments on the basis of floor space occupied, office department expenses are allocated to the sales departments on the basis of sales, and purchasing department expenses are allocated on the basis of purchase orders processed.

Exercise 21–5

Field's Realty Company has just completed a subdivision containing 15 building lots, of which 10 lots are for sale at $3,000 each and 5 are for sale at $4,000 each. The land for the subdivision cost $12,500, and the company spent $27,500 on street and sidewalk improvements. Assume that the land and improvement costs are to be assigned to the lots as joint costs and determine the share of the costs to assign to a lot in each price class.

Problems

Problem 21–1

This 'N That Company occupies all the space in a two-story building, and it has an account in its ledger called "Building Occupancy" to which it charged the following during the past year:

Depreciation, building..........	$12,000
Interest, building mortgage....	17,500
Taxes, building and land.......	5,400
Heating expenses	1,700
Lighting expense................	600
Cleaning and maintenance	12,000
Total......................	$49,200

The building has 6,000 square feet of floor space on each of its two floors, a total of 12,000 square feet; and the bookkeeper divided the $49,200 by 12,000 and charged the selling departments on each floor with $4.10 of occupancy cost for each square foot of floor space occupied.

Frank Rey, the manager of a second-floor department occupying 2,000 square feet of floor space, saw the $4.10 per square foot, or $8,200 of occupancy cost, charged to his department and complained. He cited a recent real estate board study which showed average rental charges for like space, including heat but not including lights, cleaning, and maintenance, as follows:

Ground-floor space	$4.50 per sq. ft.
Second-floor space..	$3.00 per sq. ft.

Required:

Prepare a computation showing how much building occupancy cost you think should have been charged to Frank Rey's department last year.

Problem 21–2

Horseshoe Supply Company began its operations one year ago with two selling departments and one office department. The year's operating results are:

HORSESHOE SUPPLY COMPANY
Departmental Income Statement for Year Ended December 31, 19—

	Dept. A	Dept. B	Combined
Revenue from sales	$80,000	$50,000	$130,000
Cost of goods sold	52,000	30,000	82,000
Gross profit from sales	$28,000	$20,000	$ 48,000
Direct expenses:			
Sales salaries	$10,500	$ 6,000	$ 16,500
Advertising	900	675	1,575
Store supplies used	400	200	600
Depreciation of equipment	1,075	575	1,650
Total direct expenses	$12,875	$ 7,450	$ 20,325
Allocated expenses:			
Rent expense	$ 4,800	$ 2,400	$ 7,200
Heating and lighting expense	1,200	600	1,800
Share of office department expenses	4,800	3,000	7,800
Total allocated expenses	$10,800	$ 6,000	$ 16,800
Total expenses	$23,675	$13,450	$ 37,125
Net Income	$ 4,325	$ 6,550	$ 10,875

The company plans to open a third selling department which it estimates will produce $30,000 in sales with a 35% gross profit margin and will require the following direct expenses: sales salaries, $4,500; advertising, $450; store supplies, $175; and depreciation of equipment, $350.

A year ago, when operations began, it was necessary to rent store space in excess of requirements. This extra space was assigned to and used by Departments A and B during the year; but when the new department, Department C, is opened it will take one fourth of the space presently assigned to Department A and one sixth of the space assigned to Department B.

The company allocates its general office department expenses to its selling departments on the basis of sales, and it expects the new department to cause a $525 increase in general office department expenses.

The company expects Department C to bring new customers into the store who in addition to buying goods in the new department will also buy sufficient merchandise in the two old departments to increase their sales by 5% each. And, although the old departments' sales are expected to increase, their gross profit percentages are not expected to change. Likewise, their direct expenses, other than supplies, are not expected to change. The supplies used will increase in proportion to sales.

Required:

Prepare a departmental income statement showing the company's expected operations with three selling departments.

Problem 21–3

Humboldt Company is considering the elimination of its unprofitable Department B. The company's income statement for last year appears as follows:

HUMBOLDT COMPANY
Income Statement for Year Ended December 31, 19—

	Dept. A	Dept. B	Combined
Sales	$76,500	$45,900	$122,400
Cost of goods sold	46,750	34,325	81,075
Gross margin on sales	$29,750	$11,575	$ 41,325
Operating expenses:			
Direct expenses:			
Advertising	$ 1,175	$ 895	$ 2,070
Store supplies used	325	215	540
Depreciation of store equipment	850	475	1,325
Total direct expenses	$ 2,350	$ 1,585	$ 3,935
Allocated expenses:			
Sales salaries	$11,050	$ 6,630	$ 17,680
Rent expense	2,625	1,575	4,200
Bad debts expense	380	230	610
Office salaries	2,600	1,560	4,160
Insurance expense	200	150	350
Miscellaneous office expenses	325	200	525
Total allocated expenses	$17,180	$10,345	$ 27,525
Total expenses	$19,530	$11,930	$ 31,460
Net Income (Loss)	$10,220	$ (355)	$ 9,865

If Department B is eliminated:

1. The company has one office clerk who earns $80 per week or $4,160 per year and four salesclerks each of whom earns $85 per week or $4,420 per year. At present the salaries of two and one-half salesclerks are charged to Department A and one and one-half salesclerks to Department B. It is the opinion of management that two salesclerks may be dismissed if Department B is eliminated, leaving only two full-time clerks in Department A, and making up the difference by assigning the office clerk to part-time sales work in the department. It is felt that although the office clerk has not devoted half of his time to the office work of Department B, if he devotes the same amount of time to selling in Department A during rush hours as he has to the office work of Department B, it will be sufficient to carry the load.
2. The lease on the store building is long term and cannot be changed; therefore, the space presently occupied by Department B will have to be used by and charged to Department A. Likewise, Department A will have to make whatever use of Department B's equipment it can, since the equipment has little or no sales value.
3. The elimination of Department B will eliminate the Department B advertising expense, losses from bad debts, and store supplies used. It will also eliminate 80% of the insurance expense, the portion on merchandise, and 25% of the miscellaneous office expenses presently allocated to Department B.

Required:

1. List in separate columns the amounts of Department B's escapable and inescapable expenses.
2. Under the assumption that Department A's sales and gross profit will not be affected by the elimination of Department B, prepare an income statement showing what the company can expect to earn from the operation of Department A after Department B is eliminated.

Problem 21–4

Richard and Kay Carmean own a farm that produces potatoes. Last year after preparing the following income statement Richard remarked to Kay that they should have fed the No. 3 potatoes to the pigs and thus avoided the loss from the sale of this grade.

RICHARD AND KAY CARMEAN
Income from the Production and Sale of Potatoes
For Year Ended December 31, 19 –

	Results by Grades			Combined
	No. 1	No. 2	No. 3	
Sales by grades:				
No. 1, 300,000 lbs. @ $0.045 per lb.............	$13,500			
No. 2, 500,000 lbs. @ $0.04 per lb...............		$20,000		
No. 3, 200,000 lbs. @ $0.03 per lb...............			$6,000	
Combined				$39,500
Costs:				
Land preparation, seed, planting, and cultivating @ $0.01422 per lb.............	$ 4,266	$ 7,110	$2,844	$14,220
Harvesting, sorting, and grading @ $0.01185 per lb.........................	3,555	5,925	2,370	11,850
Marketing @ $0.00415 per lb......................	1,245	2,075	830	4,150
Total costs..	$ 9,066	$15,110	$6,044	$30,220
Net Income or (Loss)	$ 4,434	$ 4,890	$ (44)	$ 9,280

On the foregoing statement Richard and Kay divided their costs among the grades on a per pound basis. They did this because with the exception of marketing costs, their records did not show costs per grade. As to marketing costs, the records did show that $4,020 of the $4,150 was the cost of placing the No. 1 and No. 2 potatoes in bags and hauling them to the warehouse of the produce buyer. Bagging and hauling costs were the same for both grades. The remaining $130 of marketing costs was the cost of loading the No. 3 potatoes into trucks of a potato starch factory that bought these potatoes in bulk and picked them up at the farm.

Required:

Prepare an income statement that will show better the results of producing and marketing the potatoes.

Problem 21-5

Hansen Retail Company has three selling departments, X, Y, and Z, and two service departments, general office and purchasing. At the end of an accounting period its bookkeeper brought together the following information for use in preparing the year-end statements:

SALES, PURCHASES, AND INVENTORIES:

	Dept. X	Dept. Y	Dept. Z
Sales	$95,400	$51,200	$73,400
Purchases	67,900	35,300	41,800
January 1 (beginning) inventory	12,300	8,500	10,200
December 31 (ending) inventory	14,500	9,400	7,300

DIRECT DEPARTMENTAL EXPENSES:

Hansen Retail Company treats salaries, supplies used, and depreciation as direct departmental expenses. The payroll, requisition, and plant asset records showed the following amounts of these expenses by departments:

	Salaries Expense	Supplies Used	Depr. of Equipment
General office	$ 9,345	$ 235	$ 625
Purchasing department	6,160	195	375
Department X	10,360	385	850
Department Y	5,510	215	450
Department Z	8,140	295	500
	$39,515	$1,325	$2,800

INDIRECT EXPENSES:

The concern incurred the following amounts of indirect expenses:

Rent expense	$6,600
Advertising expense	5,500
Expired insurance	750
Heating and lighting expense	1,750
Janitorial expense	2,100

Hansen Retail Company allocates the foregoing expenses to its departments as follows:

a. Rent expense on the basis of the amount and value of floor space occupied. The general office and purchasing departments occupy space in the rear of the store which is not as valuable as space in the front; consequently, $600 of the total rent is allocated to these two departments in proportion to the space occupied by each. The remainder of the rent is divided between the selling departments in proportion to the space occupied. The five departments occupy these amounts of space: General Office, 600 square feet; Purchasing Department, 400 square feet; Department X, 3,000 square feet; Department Y, 1,500 square feet; and Department Z, 1,500 square feet.

b. Advertising expense on the basis of sales.

c. Expired insurance on the basis of equipment book values. The book values of the equipment in the departments are: General Office, $3,500; Purchasing Department, $2,000; Department X, $9,000; Department Y, $5,000; and Department Z, $5,500.

d. Heating and lighting and janitorial expenses on the basis of floor space occupied.

SERVICE DEPARTMENT EXPENSES:

Hansen Retail Company allocates its general office department expenses to its selling departments on the basis of sales, and it allocates purchasing department expenses on the basis of purchases.

Required:

1. Prepare a departmental expense allocation sheet for the concern.
2. Prepare a departmental income statement showing sales, cost of goods sold, expenses, and net incomes by departments and for the entire store.
3. Prepare a second departmental income statement showing departmental contributions to overhead and overall net income.

Problem 21–1A

Alternate problems

Mississippi Department Store has in its ledger an account called "Building Occupancy Costs" to which it charged the following last year:

Building rent $54,000
Lighting expense................. 2,000
Cleaning and maintenance 10,000
        Total....................... $66,000

The store occupies all the space in a building having selling space on three levels — basement level, street level, and second-floor level. Each level has 5,000 square feet of selling space, a total of 15,000 square feet; and the bookkeeper divided the $66,000 of building occupancy cost by 15,000 and charged each selling department with $4.40 of building occupancy cost for each square foot of space occupied.

When Ray Burchette, the manager of a basement-level department having 1,500 square feet of floor space, saw the $4.40 per square foot of building occupancy cost charged to his department, he complained. In this complaint he cited a recent local real estate study which showed average charges for like space, including heat but not including lights and janitorial service, as follows:

Basement-level space........ $2 per sq. ft.
Street-level space............. $6 per sq. ft.
Second-floor-level space.... $4 per sq. ft.

Required:

Prepare a computation showing the amount of building occupancy cost you think should be charged to Ray Burchette's department.

Problem 21–2A

Valley Retail Company began business last year with two selling departments and a general office department. It had the following results for the year:

VALLEY RETAIL COMPANY
Departmental Income Statement for Year Ended December 31, 19—

	Dept. 1	Dept. 2	Combined
Sales	$120,000	$60,000	$180,000
Cost of goods sold	84,000	36,000	120,000
Gross profit from sales	$ 36,000	$24,000	$ 60,000
Direct expenses:			
Sales salaries	$ 12,500	$ 7,200	$ 19,700
Advertising expense	1,125	750	1,875
Store supplies used	600	300	900
Depreciation of equipment	1,025	550	1,575
Total direct expenses	$ 15,250	$ 8,800	$ 24,050
Allocated expenses:			
Rent expense	$ 5,400	$ 3,600	$ 9,000
Heating and lighting expense	1,080	720	1,800
Share of general office expenses	7,000	3,500	10,500
Total allocated expenses	$ 13,480	$ 7,820	$ 21,300
Total expenses	$ 28,730	$16,620	$ 45,350
Net Income	$ 7,270	$ 7,380	$ 14,650

The company plans to add a third selling department which it estimates will produce $40,000 in sales with a 35% gross profit margin. The new department will require the following estimated direct expenses: sales salaries, $4,500; advertising expense, $450; store supplies, $250; and depreciation on equipment, $525.

When the company began its operations, it was necessary to rent a store room having selling space in excess of requirements. This extra space was assigned to and used by Departments 1 and 2 during the year; but when Department 3 is opened, it will take over one third the space presently assigned to Department 1 and one sixth the space assigned to Department 2. The space reductions are not expected to affect the operations or sales of the old departments.

The company allocates its general office department expenses to its selling departments on the basis of sales. It expects the new department to cause a $950 increase in general office department expenses.

The company expects the addition of Department 3 to bring new customers to the store who in addition to buying Department 3 merchandise will also do sufficient buying in the old departments to increase their sales by 5% each. It is not expected that the increase in sales in the old departments will affect their gross profit percentages nor any of their direct expenses other than supplies. It is expected the supplies used will increase in proportion to sales.

Required:

Prepare a departmental income statement showing the company's expected operating results with three departments.

Problem 21–4A

Ed Sample produced and sold a half million pounds of apples last year, and he prepared the following statement to show the results:

ED SAMPLE
Income from the Sale of Apples, Year Ended December 31, 19—

| | Results by Grades | | | Combined |
	No. 1	No. 2	No. 3	
Sales by grades:				
No. 1, 200,000 lbs. @ $0.11 per lb	$22,000			
No. 2, 200,000 lbs. @ $0.07 per lb......		$14,000		
No. 3, 100,000 lbs. @ $0.04 per lb......			$ 4,000	
Combined sales........................				$40,000
Costs:				
Tree pruning and orchard care @				
$0.021 per lb............................	$ 4,200	$ 4,200	$ 2,100	$10,500
Fruit picking, grading, and sorting				
@ $0.0252 per lb........................	5,040	5,040	2,520	12,600
Marketing @ $0.0084 per lb..............	1,680	1,680	840	4,200
Total costs	$10,920	$10,920	$ 5,460	$27,300
Net Income or (Loss)	$11,080	$ 3,080	$ (1,460)	$12,700

Upon completing the statement, Mr. Sample thought a wise course of future action might be to leave the No. 3 apples on the trees to fall off and be plowed under when he cultivated between the trees, and thus avoid the loss from their sale. However, before doing so he consulted you.

When you examined the statement, you recognized that Mr. Sample had divided all his costs by 500,000 and allocated them on a per pound basis. You asked him about the marketing costs and learned that $3,960 of the $4,200 was incurred in placing the No. 1 and No. 2 fruit in boxes and delivering them to the warehouse of the fruit buyer. The cost for this was the same for both grades. You also learned that the remaining $240 was for loading the No. 3 fruit on the trucks of a cider manufacturer who bought this grade of fruit in bulk at the orchard for use in making apple cider.

Required:

Prepare an income statement that will reflect better the results of producing and marketing the apples.

Problem 21–5A

Capital Stores carries on its operations with two service departments, the general office department and the purchasing department, and with three selling departments, A, B, and C. At the end of its annual accounting period the company's accountant prepared the following adjusted trial balance:

CAPITAL STORES
Adjusted Trial Balance, December 31, 19—

Cash	$ 7,875	
Merchandise inventory, Department A	9,300	
Merchandise inventory, Department B	18,200	
Merchandise inventory, Department C	14,500	
Supplies	620	
Equipment	36,940	
Accumulated depreciation, equipment		$ 10,135
Jerry Collingsworth, capital		72,925
Jerry Collingsworth, withdrawals	9,000	
Sales, Department A		52,400
Sales, Department B		104,200
Sales, Department C		68,400
Purchases, Department A	34,400	
Purchases, Department B	79,300	
Purchases, Department C	41,700	
Salaries expense	36,855	
Rent expense	7,500	
Advertising expense	5,625	
Expired insurance	500	
Heating and lighting expense	1,200	
Depreciation of equipment	1,820	
Supplies used	1,125	
Janitorial services	1,600	
Totals	$308,060	$308,060

Required:

1. Prepare a departmental expense allocation sheet for Capital Stores, using the following information:

    a. Capital Stores treats salaries, supplies used, and depreciation of equipment as direct departmental expenses. The payroll, requisition, and plant asset records show the following amounts of these expenses by departments:

	Salaries Expense	Supplies Used	Depr. of Equip- ment
General office	$10,295	$ 145	$ 250
Purchasing department	7,040	130	220
Department A	4,660	275	425
Department B	8,320	315	615
Department C	6,540	260	310
	$36,855	$1,125	$1,820

    b. The company treats the remainder of its expenses as indirect and allocates them as follows:

    (1)   Rent expense on the basis of the amount and value of floor space occupied. The general office occupies 600 square feet, and the purchasing department occupies 400 square feet on a balcony at the rear of the store. This space is not as valuable as space on the main floor; therefore, the store allocates $500 of its rent to these two departments on the basis of space occupied and allocates the remainder to the selling departments on the basis of the main-floor space they occupy. The selling departments occupy main-floor space as follows: Department A, 2,000 square feet; Department B, 3,500 square feet; and Department C, 1,500 square feet.

    (2)   Advertising expense on the basis of sales.

    (3)   Insurance expense on the basis of the book values of the equipment in the departments, which are: general office, $2,500; purchasing, $2,000; Department A, $6,500; Department B, $9,500; and Department C, $4,500.

    (4)   Heating and lighting and janitorial services on the basis of floor space occupied.

   c. The company allocates general office department expenses to the selling departments on the basis of sales, and it allocates purchasing department expenses on the basis of purchases.

2.   Prepare a departmental income statement for the company showing sales, cost of goods sold, expenses, and net incomes by departments and for the entire store. The year-end inventories were Department A, $11,600; Department B, $23,400; and Department C, $13,400.

3.   Prepare a second income statement for the company showing departmental contributions to overhead and overall net income.

    Kevin Langfeld, Larry Fellingham, and John Tomassini entered into a partnership for the purpose of developing and selling a plot of land currently owned by Langfeld. Fellingham invested $52,000 cash in the partnership, Langfeld invested his land at its $60,000 fair market value, and Tomassini invested $8,000; and they agreed to share losses and gains equally. Tomassini was to provide the necessary real estate expertise to make the project a success. The partnership installed streets and water mains costing $60,000 and divided the land into 14 building lots. They priced Lots 1, 2, 3, and 4 for sale at $12,000 each; Lots 5, 6, 7, 8, 9, 10, 11, and 12 at $14,000 each; and Lots 13 and 14 at $16,000 each. The partners agreed that Tomassini could take Lot 13 at cost for his personal use. The remaining lots were sold, and the partnership dissolved. Determine the amount of partnership cash each partner should receive in the dissolution.

Decision problem 21–1, Land Deal Partnership

    The Powerflow Company bookkeeper prepared the following income statement for March of the current year:

Decision problem 21–2, Powerflow Company

POWERFLOW COMPANY
Income Statement for March, 19—

	Motor Department	Compressor Department	Combined
Sales	$40,000	$60,000	$100,000
Cost of goods sold	28,600	42,900	71,500
Gross profit on sales	$11,400	$17,100	$ 28,500
Warehousing expenses	$ 2,950	$ 2,950	$ 5,900
Selling expenses	5,600	6,100	11,700
General and administrative expenses	1,525	1,525	3,050
Total expenses	$10,075	$10,575	$ 20,650
Net Income	$ 1,325	$ 6,525	$ 7,850

The company is a wholesaler of motors and compressors and is organized on a departmental basis. However, the company manager does not feel that the bookkeeper's statement reflects the profit situation in the company's two selling departments and he has asked you to redraft it with any supporting schedules or comments you think desirable. Your investigation reveals the following:

1. The company sold 500 motors and 400 compressors during March. The bookkeeper apportioned cost of goods sold between the two departments on an arbitrary basis. A compressor actually costs the company twice as much as a motor.

2. A motor and a compressor are of approximately the same weight and bulk. However, because there are two styles of motors and three styles of compressors, the company must carry a 50% greater inventory of compressors, than motors.

3. The company occupies its building on the following bases:

	Area of Space	Value of Space
Warehouse	80%	60%
Motor sales office	5%	10%
Compressor sales office	5%	10%
General office	10%	20%

4. Warehousing expenses for March consisted of the following:

Wages expense	$3,000
Depreciation of building	2,000
Heating and lighting expenses	500
Depreciation of warehouse equipment	400
Total	$5,900

The bookkeeper had charged all of the building's depreciation plus all of the heating and lighting expenses to warehousing expenses.

5. Selling expenses for March consisted of the following:

	Motor Department	Compressor Department
Sales salaries	$4,000	$4,500
Advertising	1,500	1,500
Depreciation of office equipment	100	100
Totals	$5,600	$6,100

Sales salaries and depreciation were charged to the two departments on the basis of actual amounts incurred. Advertising was apportioned by the bookkeeper. The company has an established advertising budget based on dollars of sales which it followed rather closely in March.

6. General and administrative expenses for March consisted of the following:

Salaries and wages	$2,800
Depreciation of office equipment	200
Miscellaneous office expenses	50
Total	$3,050

Air Conditioner Sales Corporation wholesales automobile air conditioners for small imported cars. Operations of the company during the past year resulted in the following:

Decision problem 21–3, Air Conditioner Sales Corporation

	Standard	Deluxe
Units sold	900	300
Selling price per unit	$300	$400
Cost per unit	160	210
Sales commission per unit	45	60
Indirect selling and administrative expenses	75	100

Indirect selling and administrative expenses totaled $97,500 and were allocated between the sales of Standard and Deluxe units on the basis of their relative sales volumes. The Standard model produced $270,000 of revenue, and the Deluxe model produced $120,000; thus, the Standard model was assigned 27/39 of the $97,500 of indirect expenses and the Deluxe model was assigned 12/39. After allocating the total indirect expenses to the two models, the indirect expenses per unit were determined by dividing the total by the number of units sold. Hence, the Standard model's cost per unit was $75 and the Deluxe model's cost per unit was $100.

Management of Air Conditioner Sales Corporation is attempting to decide between three courses of action and asks you to evaluate which of the three courses is most desirable. The three alternatives are: (1) through advertising push the sales of the Standard model, (2) through advertising push the sales of the Deluxe model, or (3) do no additional advertising, in which case sales of each model will continue at present levels. The demand for air conditioners is fairly stable, and an increase in the number of units of one model sold will cause an equally large decrease in the sales of the other model. However, through the expenditure of $3,000 for advertising, the company can shift the sale of 150 units of the Standard model to the Deluxe model, or vice versa, depending upon which model receives the advertising attention. Should the company advertise; and if so, which model? Back your position with income statements.

After studying Chapter 22, you should be able to:

- Describe the basic differences in the financial statements of manufacturing companies and merchandising companies.

- Describe the procedures inherent in a general accounting system for a manufacturing company.

- List the different accounts which appear on a manufacturing company's books and state what the accounts represent.

- Explain the purpose of a manufacturing statement, how one is composed, and how the statement is integrated with the primary financial statements.

- Prepare financial statements for a manufacturing company from a work sheet.

- Prepare the closing entries for a manufacturing company.

- Explain the procedures for assigning costs to the different manufacturing inventories.

- Define or explain the words and phrases listed in the chapter Glossary.

chapter 22

Manufacturing accounting

In previous chapters consideration has been given to the accounting problems of service-type and merchandising concerns. In this chapter some problems of manufacturing enterprises are examined.

Manufacturing and merchandising concerns are alike in that both depend for revenue upon the sale of one or more commodities or products. However, they differ in that a merchandising company buys the goods it sells in the finished state in which they are sold, while a manufacturing concern buys raw materials which it manufactures into the finished products it sells. For example, a shoe store buys shoes and sells them in the same form in which they are purchased; but a manufacturer of shoes buys leather, cloth, glue, nails, and dye and turns these items into salable shoes.

The basic difference in accounting for manufacturing and merchandising concerns grows from the idea in the preceding paragraph—the idea that a merchant buys the goods he sells in their finished ready-for-sale state, while a manufacturer must create what he sells from raw materials. As a result the merchant can easily determine the cost of the goods he has bought for sale by examining the debit balance of his Purchases account, but the manufacturer must combine the balances of a number of material, labor, and overhead accounts to determine the cost of the goods he has manufactured for sale.

Basic difference in accounting

To emphasize this difference, the cost of goods sold section from a merchandising concern's income statement is condensed and reproduced at the top of the next page beside that of a manufacturing company.

Notice in the costs of goods sold section from the manufacturing company's income statement that the inventories of goods for sale are called *finished goods inventories* rather than merchandise inventories. Notice too that the "Cost of goods purchased" element of the merchandising company becomes "Cost of goods manufactured (see Manu-

Merchandising Company		Manufacturing Company	
Cost of goods sold:		Cost of goods sold:	
Beginning merchandise inventory	$14,200	Beginning finished goods inventory	$ 11,200
Cost of goods purchased	34,150	Cost of goods manufactured (see Manufacturing Statement)	170,500
Goods available for sale	$48,350	Goods available for sale	$181,700
Ending merchandise inventory	12,100	Ending finished goods inventory	10,300
Cost of goods sold	$36,250	Cost of goods sold	$171,400

facturing Statement)" on the manufacturer's income statement. These differences result because the merchandising company buys its goods ready for sale, while the manufacturer creates its salable products from raw materials.

The words "see Manufacturing Statement" refer the income statement reader to a separate schedule called a manufacturing statement (see page 735) which shows the costs of manufacturing the products produced by a manufacturing company. The records and techniques used in accounting for these costs are the distinguishing characteristics of manufacturing accounting.

Systems of accounting in manufacturing concerns

The accounting system used by a manufacturing concern may be either a so-called general accounting system like the one described in this chapter or a cost accounting system. A general accounting system uses periodic physical inventories of raw materials, goods in process, and finished goods; and it has as its goal the determination of the total cost of all goods manufactured during each accounting period. Cost accounting systems differ in that they use perpetual inventories and have as their goal the determination of the unit cost of manufacturing a product or performing a service. Such systems are discussed in the next two chapters.

Elements of manufacturing costs

A manufacturer takes *raw materials* and by applying *direct labor* and *factory overhead* converts these materials into finished products. Raw materials, direct labor, and factory overhead are the "elements of manufacturing costs."

Raw materials

Raw materials are the commodities that enter directly into and become a part of a finished product. Such items as leather, dye, cloth, nails, and glue are raw materials of a shoe manufacturer. Raw materials are often called *direct materials*. Since direct materials physically become part of the finished product, the cost of direct materials is easily traced to units of product or batches of production, and the direct materials cost of production can be directly charged to units of product or batches of production without the use of arbitrary or highly judgmental cost allocation procedures.

Direct materials are distinguished from *indirect materials* or factory supplies which are such items as grease and oil for machinery, cleaning fluids, and so on. Indirect materials are not easily traced to specific units or batches of production and are accounted for as factory overhead.

The materials of a manufacturer are called "raw materials," even though they may not necessarily be in their natural raw state. For example, leather is manufactured from hides, nails from steel, and cloth from cotton. Nevertheless, leather, nails, and cloth are the raw materials of a shoe manufacturer even though they are the finished products of previous manufacturers.

Direct labor

Direct labor is often described as the labor of those people who work, either with machines or hand tools, directly on the materials converted into finished products. The cost of direct labor can therefore be easily associated with and charged to the units or batches of production to which the labor was applied. In manufacturing, direct labor is distinguished from *indirect labor*. Indirect labor is the labor of superintendents, foremen, millwrights, engineers, janitors, and others who do not work directly on the manufactured products. Indirect labor aids in production; often it makes production possible but it does not enter directly into the finished product. Indirect labor is accounted for as a factory overhead cost.

In a general accounting system, an account called *Direct Labor* is debited each payday for the wages of those workers who work directly on the product. Likewise, each payday, the wages of indirect workers are debited to one or more indirect labor accounts. Also, at the end of each period, the amounts of accrued direct and indirect labor are recorded in the direct and indirect labor accounts by means of adjusting entries. From this it can be seen that a manufacturing company's payroll accounting is similar to that of a merchandising concern. When a cost accounting system is not involved, no new techniques are required and only the new direct and indirect labor accounts distinguish the payroll accounting of a manufacturer from that of a merchant.

Factory overhead

Factory overhead, often called *manufacturing overhead* or *factory burden,* includes all manufacturing costs other than for direct materials and direct labor. Factory overhead may include:

Indirect labor.	Heat, lights, and power.
Factory supplies.	Depreciation of plant and equipment.
Repairs to buildings and equipment.	Patents written off.
Insurance on plant and equipment.	Small tools written off.
Taxes on plant and equipment.	Workmen's compensation insurance.
Taxes on raw materials and work in process.	Payroll taxes on the wages of the factory workers.

Factory overhead does not include selling and administrative expenses. Selling and administrative expenses are not factory overhead because they are not incurred in order to produce the manufactured products. They could be called selling and administrative overhead, but this is not factory overhead.

All factory overhead costs are accumulated in overhead cost accounts which vary from company to company, with the exact accounts depending in each case upon the nature of the company and the information desired. For example, one account called "Expired Insurance on Plant Equipment" may be maintained, or an expired insurance account each for buildings and the different kinds of equipment may be used. But regardless of accounts, overhead costs are recorded in the same ways as are selling and administrative expenses. Some, such as indirect labor and light and power, are recorded in registers or journals as they are paid and are then posted to the accounts. Others, such as depreciation and expired insurance, reach the accounts through adjusting entries.

Accounts unique to a manufacturing company

Because of the nature of its operations, a manufacturing concern's ledger normally contains more accounts than that of a merchandising concern. However, some of the same accounts are found in the ledgers of both, for example, Cash, Accounts Receivable, Sales, and many selling and administrative expenses. Nevertheless, although there are accounts in common, many accounts are unique to a manufacturing company. For instance, accounts such as Machinery and Equipment, Accumulated Depreciation of Machinery and Equipment, Factory Supplies, Factory Supplies Used, Raw Materials Inventory, Raw Material Purchases, Goods in Process Inventory, Finished Goods Inventory, and Manufacturing Summary are normally found only in the ledgers of manufacturing concerns. Some of these accounts merit special attention.

Raw Material Purchases account

When a general accounting system is in use, the cost of all raw materials purchased is debited to an account called Raw Material Purchases. Often a special column is provided in the Voucher Register or other special journal for the debits of the individual purchases, thus making it possible to periodically post these debits in one amount, the column total.

Raw Materials Inventory account

When a general accounting system is in use, the raw materials on hand at the end of each accounting period are determined by a physical inventory; and through a closing entry the cost of this inventory is debited to the Raw Materials Inventory account where it becomes a record of the materials on hand at the end of one period and the beginning of the next.

Goods in Process Inventory account

All manufacturing concerns except those in which the manufacturing process is instantaneous normally have on hand at any time partially processed products called *goods in process* or *work in process*. These are products in the process of being manufactured, products that have received a portion or all of their materials and have had some labor and overhead applied but that are not completed.

In a manufacturing concern using a general accounting system the amount of goods in process at the end of each accounting period is determined by a physical inventory; and through a closing entry the cost of this inventory is debited to the Goods in Process Inventory account where it becomes a record of the goods in process at the end of one period and the beginning of the next.

Finished Goods Inventory account

The finished goods of a manufacturer are the equivalent of a store's merchandise; they are products in their completed state ready for sale. Actually, the only difference is that a manufacturing concern creates its finished goods from raw materials, while a store buys its merchandise in a finished, ready-for-sale state.

In a general accounting system the amount of finished goods on hand at the end of each period is determined by a physical inventory; and through a closing entry the cost of this inventory is debited to the Finished Goods Inventory account as a record of the finished goods at the end of one period and the beginning of the next.

The three inventories — raw materials, goods in process, and finished goods — are current assets for balance sheet purposes. Factory supplies is also a current asset.

Income statement of a manufacturing company

The income statement of a manufacturing company is similar to that of a merchandising concern. To see this, compare the income statement of Kona Sales Company, Illustration 5–1 on page 150, with that of Excel Manufacturing Company, Illustration 22–1 on page 734. Notice that the revenue, selling, and general and administrative expense sections are very similar. However, when the cost of goods sold sections are compared, a difference is apparent. Here the item "Cost of goods manufactured" replaces the "purchases" element, and finished goods inventories take the place of merchandise inventories.

Observe in the cost of goods sold section of Excel Manufacturing Company's income statement that only the total cost of goods manufactured is shown. It would be possible to expand this section to show the detailed costs of the materials, direct labor, and overhead entering into the cost of goods manufactured. However, if this were done, the income statement would be long and unwieldy. Consequently, the common practice is to show only the total cost of goods manufactured on the income statement and to attach a supporting schedule showing

The Excel Manufacturing Company
Income Statement for Year Ended December 31, 19—

Revenue:		
Sales..		$310,000
Cost of goods sold:		
Finished goods inventory, January 1, 19—	$ 11,200	
Cost of goods manufactured (see		
Manufacturing Statement)............................	170,500 ✳	
Goods available for sale..................................	$181,700	
Finished goods inventory, December 31, 19— ...	10,300	
Cost of goods sold		171,400
Gross profit		$138,600
Operating expenses:		
Selling expenses:		
Sales salaries expense................................$18,000		
Advertising expense 5,500		
Delivery wages expense 12,000		
Shipping supplies expense........................... 250		
Delivery equipment insurance expense......... 300		
Depreciation expense, delivery equipment 2,100		
Total selling expenses	$ 38,150	
General and administrative expenses:		
Office salaries expense $15,700		
Miscellaneous general expense 200		
Bad debts expense..................................... 1,550		
Office supplies expense 100		
Depreciation expense, office equipment 200		
Total general and administrative		
expenses..	17,750	
Total operating expenses		55,900
Operating income..		$ 82,700
Financial expense:		
Mortgage interest expense		4,000
Income before state and federal income taxes......		$ 78,700
Less state and federal income taxes................		32,600
Net Income..		$ 46,100
Net income per common share (20,000 shares		
outstanding)		$2.31

Illustration 22–1

the details. This supporting schedule is called a "schedule of the cost of goods manufactured" or a "manufacturing statement."

Manufacturing
statement
The cost elements of manufacturing are raw materials, direct labor, and factory overhead; and a manufacturing statement is normally constructed in such a manner as to emphasize these elements. Notice in Illustration 22–2 that the first section of the statement shows the cost of raw materials used. Also observe the manner of presentation is the same as that used on the income statement of a merchandising company to show cost of goods purchased and sold.

The so-called second section shows the cost of direct labor used in

Excel Manufacturing Company
Manufacturing Statement for Year Ended December 31, 19—

Raw materials:			
Raw materials inventory, January 1, 19—		$ 8,000	
Raw materials purchased	$85,000		
Freight on raw materials purchased	1,500		
Delivered cost of raw materials purchased		86,500	
Raw materials available for use		$94,500	
Raw materials inventory, December 31, 19—		9,000	
Raw materials used			$ 85,500
Direct labor			60,000
Factory overhead costs:			
Indirect labor		$ 9,000	
Supervision		6,000	
Power		2,600	
Repairs and maintenance		2,500	
Factory taxes		1,900	
Factory supplies used		500	
Factory insurance expired		1,200	
Small tools written off		200	
Depreciation of machinery and equipment		3,500	
Depreciation of building		1,800	
Patents written off		800	
Total factory overhead costs			30,000
Total manufacturing costs			$175,500
Add: Goods in process inventory, January 1, 19—			2,500
Total goods in process during the year			$178,000
Deduct: Goods in process inventory, December 31, 19—			7,500
Cost of Goods Manufactured			$170,500

Illustration 22–2

production, and the third section shows factory overhead costs. If overhead accounts are not too numerous, the balance of each is often listed in this third section, as in Illustration 22–2. However, if overhead accounts are numerous, only the total of all may be shown; and in such cases the total is supported by a separate attached schedule showing each cost.

In the last section the calculation of cost of goods manufactured is completed. Here the cost of the beginning goods in process inventory is added to the sum of the manufacturing costs to show the cost of all goods in process during the period. Then, the cost of the goods still in process at the end is subtracted to show cost of the goods manufactured.

The manufacturing statement is prepared from the Manufacturing Statement columns of a work sheet. The items that appear on the statement are summarized in these columns, and all that is required in constructing the statement is a rearrangement of the items into the proper statement order. Illustration 22–3 shows the manufacturing work sheet.

The Excel Manufacturing Company
Manufacturing Work Sheet for Year Ended December 31, 19—

Account Titles	Trial Balance Dr.	Trial Balance Cr.	Adjustments Dr.	Adjustments Cr.	Mfg. Statement Dr.	Mfg. Statement Cr.	Income Statement Dr.	Income Statement Cr.	Balance Sheet Dr.	Balance Sheet Cr.
Cash	11,000								11,000	
Accounts receivable	32,000								32,000	
Allowance for doubtful accounts		300		(a) 1,550						1,850
Raw materials inventory	8,000				8,000	9,000			9,000	
Goods in process inventory	2,500				2,500	7,500			7,500	
Finished goods inventory	11,200						11,200	10,300	10,300	
Office supplies	150			(b) 100					50	
Shipping supplies	300			(c) 250					50	
Factory supplies	750			(d) 500					250	
Prepaid insurance	1,800			(e) 1,500					300	
Small tools	1,300			(f) 200					1,100	
Delivery equipment	9,000								9,000	
Accumulated depreciation of delivery equipment		1,900		(g) 2,100						4,000
Office equipment	1,700								1,700	
Accumulated depreciation of office equipment		200		(h) 200						400
Machinery and equipment	72,000								72,000	
Accumulated depr. of machinery and equipment		3,000		(i) 3,500						6,500
Factory building	90,000								90,000	
Accumulated depreciation of factory building		1,500		(j) 1,800						3,300
Land	9,500								9,500	
Patents	12,000			(k) 800					11,200	
Accounts payable		14,000								14,000
Mortgage payable		50,000								50,000
Common stock, $5 par value		100,000								100,000
Retained earnings		3,660								3,660
Sales		310,000						310,000		
Raw material purchases	85,000				85,000					
Freight on raw materials	1,500				1,500					
Direct labor	59,600		(l) 400		60,000					
Indirect labor	8,940		(l) 60		9,000					

Account	Trial Balance Dr	Adjustments Dr	Adjustments Cr	Manufacturing Dr	Manufacturing Cr	Income Statement Dr	Income Statement Cr	Balance Sheet Dr	Balance Sheet Cr
Supervision	6,000			6,000					
Power expense	2,600			2,600					
Repairs and maintenance	2,500			2,500					
Factory taxes	1,900			1,900					
Sales salaries expense	18,000					18,000			
Advertising expense	5,500					5,500			
Delivery wages expense	11,920	(l) 80				12,000			
Office salaries expense	15,700					15,700			
Miscellaneous general expense	200					200			
Mortgage interest expense	2,000	(m) 2,000				4,000			
	484,560								
	484,560								
Bad debts expense		(a) 1,550				1,550			
Office supplies expense		(b) 100				100			
Shipping supplies expense		(c) 250				250			
Factory supplies used		(d) 500		500					
Factory insurance expired		(e) 1,200		1,200					
Delivery equipment insurance expense		(e) 300				300			
Small tools written off		(f) 200		200					
Depreciation expense, delivery equipment		(g) 2,100				2,100			
Depreciation expense, office equipment		(h) 200				200			
Depreciation of machinery and equipment		(i) 3,500		3,500					
Depreciation of building		(j) 1,800		1,800					
Patents written off		(k) 800		800					
Accrued wages payable			(l) 540						540
Mortgage interest payable			(m) 2,000						2,000
State and federal income taxes expense		(n) 32,600				32,600			
		(n) 32,600	(n) 32,600						
		47,640	47,640	187,000	16,500				
Cost of goods manufactured to Income Statement columns					170,500	170,500			
				187,000	187,000	274,200	320,300	320,300	218,850
Net income						46,100			46,100
						320,300	320,300	264,950	264,950

Illustration 22-3

Work sheet for a manufacturing company

In examining Illustration 22–3, note first that there are no Adjusted Trial Balance columns. These columns are omitted because the experienced accountant commonly omits such columns from his work sheet to save time and effort. How a work sheet without Adjusted Trial Balance columns is prepared and how this saves time and effort were explained in Chapter 5.

To understand the work sheet of Illustration 22–3, recall that a work sheet is a tool with which the accountant —

1. Achieves the effect of adjusting the accounts before entering the adjustments in a journal and posting them to the accounts.
2. Sorts the adjusted account balances into columns according to the financial statement upon which they appear.
3. Calculates and proves the mathematical accuracy of the net income.

With the foregoing in mind, the primary difference between the work sheet of a manufacturing company and that of a merchandising company is an additional set of columns. Insofar as the adjustments are concerned, they are made in the same way on both kinds of work sheets. Also, the mathematical accuracy of the net income is proved in the same way. However, since an additional accounting statement, the manufacturing statement, is prepared for a manufacturing company, the work sheet of such a company has an additional set of columns, the Manufacturing Statement columns, into which are sorted the items appearing on the manufacturing statement.

Preparing a manufacturing company's work sheet

A manufacturing company's work sheet is prepared in the same manner as that of a merchandising concern. First a trial balance of the ledger is entered in the Trial Balance columns in the usual manner. Next, information for the adjustments is assembled, and the adjustments are entered in the Adjustments columns just as for a merchandising company. The adjustments information for the work sheet shown in Illustration 22–3 is as follows:

a. Estimated bad debt losses ½% of sales, or $1,550.
b. Office supplies used, $100.
c. Shipping supplies used, $250.
d. Factory supplies used, $500.
e. Expired insurance on factory, $1,200; and expired insurance on the delivery equipment, $300.
f. The small tools inventory shows $1,100 of usable small tools on hand. As is frequently done, small hand tools are in this case accounted for in the same manner as are supplies.
g. Depreciation of delivery equipment, $2,100.
h. Depreciation of office equipment, $200.
i. Depreciation of factory machinery and equipment, $3,500.
j. Depreciation of factory building, $1,800.
k. Yearly write-off of one seventeenth of the cost of patents, $800.

l. Accrued wages: direct labor, $400; indirect labor, $60; delivery wages, $80. All other employees paid monthly on the last day of each month.

m. One-half year's interest accrued on the mortgage, $2,000.

n. State and federal income taxes expense, $32,600.

After the adjustments are completed, the amounts in the Trial Balance columns are combined with the amounts in the Adjustments columns and are sorted to the proper Manufacturing Statement, Income Statement, or Balance Sheet columns, according to the statement on which they appear.

No new techniques are required in the sorting, just two decisions for each item: First, does the item have a debit balance or a credit balance; and second, on which statement does it appear? The first decision is necessary because a debit item must be sorted to a Debit column and a credit item to a Credit column. As for the second, a work sheet is a tool for sorting items according to their statement appearance; and to properly sort the items it is only necessary to know that asset, liability, and owner equity items appear on the balance sheet and are sorted to the Balance Sheet columns. The finished goods inventory plus the revenue, selling, general and administrative, and financial expense items go on the income statement and are sorted to the Income Statement columns. And finally, the raw material, goods in process, direct labor, and factory overhead items appear on the manufacturing statement and are sorted to the Manufacturing Statement columns.

After the trial balance items with their adjustments are sorted to the proper statement columns, the ending inventory amounts are entered on the work sheet. The raw materials and goods in process inventories appear on the manufacturing statement. Therefore, the ending raw materials and goods in process inventory amounts are entered in the Manufacturing Statement credit and Balance Sheet debit columns. They must be entered in the Manufacturing Statement credit column in order to make the difference between the two columns equal cost of goods manufactured. Likewise, since these inventory amounts represent end-of-the-period assets, they must be entered in the Balance Sheet debit column with the other assets.

The ending finished goods inventory is the equivalent of an ending merchandise inventory and receives the same work sheet treatment. It is entered in the Income Statement credit column and the Balance Sheet debit column. It is entered in the Income Statement credit column so that the net income may be determined; and since it is a current asset, it must also be entered in the Balance Sheet debit column.

After the ending inventories are entered on the work sheet, the Manufacturing Statement columns are added and their difference determined. This difference is cost of the goods manufactured; and after it is determined, it is entered in the Manufacturing Statement credit column to make the two columns equal. Also, it is entered in the Income Statement debit column, the same column in which the balance of the Purchases account of a merchant is entered. After this the work sheet is completed in the usual manner.

Preparing statements

After completion, the manufacturing work sheet is used in preparing the statements and in making adjusting and closing entries. The manufacturing statement is prepared from the information in the work sheet's Manufacturing Statement columns, the income statement from the information in the Income Statement columns, and the balance sheet from information in the Balance Sheet columns. After this the adjusting and closing entries are entered in the journal and posted.

Adjusting entries

The adjusting entries of a manufacturing company are prepared in the same way as those of a merchandising concern. An adjusting entry is entered in the General Journal for each adjustment appearing in the work sheet Adjustments columns. No new techniques are required.

Closing entries

The account balances that enter into the calculation of cost of goods manufactured show manufacturing costs for a particular accounting period and must be closed and cleared at the end of each period. Normally they are closed and cleared through a Manufacturing Summary account, which is in turn closed and cleared through the Income Summary account.

The entries to close and clear the manufacturing accounts of Excel Manufacturing Company are as follows:

Dec.	31	Manufacturing Summary...	187,000.00	
		Raw Materials Inventory..		8,000.00
		Goods in Process Inventory		2,500.00
		Raw Material Purchases		85,000.00
		Freight on Raw Materials......................................		1,500.00
		Direct Labor..		60,000.00
		Indirect Labor...		9,000.00
		Supervision		6,000.00
		Power Expense..		2,600.00
		Repairs and Maintenance		2,500.00
		Factory Taxes...		1,900.00
		Factory Supplies Used..		500.00
		Factory Insurance Expired		1,200.00
		Small Tools Written Off...		200.00
		Depr. of Machinery and Equipment........................		3,500.00
		Depreciation of Building..		1,800.00
		Patents Written Off..		800.00
		To close those manufacturing accounts having debit balances.		
	31	Raw Materials Inventory...	9,000.00	
		Goods in Process Inventory	7,500.00	
		Manufacturing Summary......................................		16,500.00
		To set up the ending raw materials and goods in process inventories and to remove their balances from the Manufacturing Summary account.		

The entries are taken from the information in the Manufacturing Statement columns of the Illustration 22–3 work sheet. Compare the first entry with the information shown in the Manufacturing Statement debit column. Note how the debit to the Manufacturing Summary account is taken from the column total, and how each account having a balance in the column is credited to close and clear it. Also observe that the second entry has the effect of subtracting the ending raw materials and goods in process inventories from the manufacturing costs shown in the work sheet's debit column.

The effect of the two entries is to cause the Manufacturing Summary account to have a debit balance equal to the $170,500 cost of goods manufactured. This $170,500 balance is closed to the Income Summary account along with the other cost and expense accounts having balances in the Income Statement debit column. Observe the following entry which is used to close the accounts having balances in the Income Statement debit column of the Illustration 22–3 work sheet and especially note its last credit.

Dec.	31	Income Summary	274,200.00	
		Finished Goods Inventory		11,200.00
		Sales Salaries Expense		18,000.00
		Advertising Expense		5,500.00
		Delivery Wages Expense		12,000.00
		Office Salaries Expense		15,700.00
		Miscellaneous General Expense		200.00
		Mortgage Interest Expense		4,000.00
		Bad Debts Expense		1,550.00
		Office Supplies Expense		100.00
		Shipping Supplies Expense		250.00
		Delivery Equipment Insurance Expense		300.00
		Depreciation Expense, Delivery Equipment		2,100.00
		Depreciation Expense, Office Equipment		200.00
		State and Federal Income Taxes Expense		32,600.00
		Manufacturing Summary		170,500.00
		To close the income statement accounts having debit balances.		

After the foregoing entry, the remainder of the income statement accounts of Illustration 22–3 are closed as follows:

Dec.	31	Finished Goods Inventory	10,300.00	
		Sales	310,000.00	
		Income Summary		320,300.00
		To close the Sales account and to bring the ending finished goods inventory on the books.		
	31	Income Summary	46,100.00	
		Retained Earnings		46,100.00
		To close the Income Summary account.		

Inventory
valuation
problems of a
manufacturer

In a manufacturing company using a general accounting system, at the end of each period, an accounting value must be placed on the inventories of raw materials, goods in process, and finished goods. No particular problems are encountered in valuing raw materials because the items are in the same form in which they were purchased and a cost or market price may be applied. However, placing a valuation on goods in process and finished goods is generally not so easy because goods in process and finished goods consist of raw materials to which certain amounts of labor and overhead have been added. They are not in the same form in which they were purchased. Consequently, a price paid a previous producer cannot be used to measure their inventory amount. Instead, their inventory amount must be built up by adding together estimates of the raw materials, direct labor, and overhead costs applicable to each item.

Estimating raw material costs applicable to a goods in process or finished goods item is usually not too difficult. Likewise, from its percentage of completion, a responsible plant official can normally make a reasonably accurate estimate of the direct labor applicable to an item. However, estimating factory overhead costs presents more of a problem, which is often solved by assuming that factory overhead costs are closely related to direct labor costs, and this is often a fair assumption. Frequently there is a close relation between direct labor costs and such things as supervision, power, repairs, and so forth. Furthermore, when this relation is used to apply overhead costs, it is assumed that the relation of overhead costs to the direct labor costs in each goods in process and finished goods item is the same as the relation between total factory overhead costs and total direct labor costs for the accounting period.

For example, an examination of the manufacturing statement in Illustration 22–2 will show that Excel Manufacturing Company's total direct labor costs were $60,000 and its overhead costs were $30,000. Or, in other words, during the year the company incurred in the production of all its products $2 of direct labor for each $1 of factory overhead costs, which means that overhead costs were 50% of direct labor cost.

Overhead costs, $30,000 ÷ Direct labor, $60,000 = 50%

Consequently, in estimating the overhead applicable to a goods in process or finished goods item, Excel Manufacturing Company may assume that this 50% overhead rate is applicable. It may assume that if in all its production the overhead costs were 50% of the direct labor costs, then in each goods in process and finished goods item this relationship also exists.

If Excel Manufacturing Company makes this assumption and its goods in process inventory consists of 1,000 units of Item X with each unit containing $3.75 of raw material and having $2.50 of applicable direct labor, then the goods in process inventory is valued as shown in Illustration 22–4.

Product	Estimated Raw Material Cost	Estimated Direct Labor Applicable	Overhead (50% of Direct Labor)	Estimated Total Unit Cost	No. of Units	Estimated Inventory Cost
Item X	$3.75	$2.50	$1.25	$7.50	1,000	$7,500.00

Illustration 22–4

Excel Manufacturing Company may use the same procedure in placing an accounting value on the items of its finished goods inventory.

Glossary

Direct labor. The labor of those people who work directly on materials converted into finished products; in other words, with units of product designated as the cost object, labor that can be easily associated with units of product.

Direct materials. A synonym for raw materials.

Factory overhead. All manufacturing costs other than for direct materials and direct labor.

Finished goods. Products in their completed state, ready for sale; equivalent to a store's merchandise.

Indirect labor. The labor of superintendents, foremen, millwrights, engineers, janitors, and others who do not work directly on the manufactured products, and whose labor therefore cannot be easily associated with specific units of product.

Indirect materials. Commodities that are used in production but that do not enter into and become a part of the finished product, for example, grease and oil for machinery, or cleaning fluid.

Manufacturing overhead. A synonym for factory overhead, also called manufacturing burden.

Manufacturing statement. A financial report showing the costs incurred to manufacture a product or products during a period.

Raw materials. Commodities that enter directly into and become a part of a finished product; therefore, commodities that are easily associated with specific units of product.

Work in process. Products in the process of being manufactured that have received a portion or all of their materials and have had some labor and overhead applied but that are not completed; also called goods in process.

1. Manufacturing costs consist of three elements. What are they?
2. Explain how the income statement of a manufacturing company differs from the income statement of a merchandising company.
3. What are (a) direct labor, (b) indirect labor, (c) direct material, (d) indirect material, and (e) factory overhead costs?
4. Factory overhead costs include a variety of items. List several examples of factory overhead costs.
5. Name several accounts that are often found in the ledgers of both manufacturing and merchandising companies. Name several accounts that are found only in the ledgers of manufacturing companies.
6. What three new inventory accounts appear in the ledger of a manufacturing company?
7. How are the raw material inventories handled on the work sheet of a manufacturing company? How are the goods in process inventories handled? How are the finished goods inventories handled?
8. Which inventories of a manufacturing company receive the same work sheet treatment as the merchandise inventories of a merchandising company?
9. Which inventories of a manufacturing company appear on its manufacturing statement? Which appear on the income statement?
10. What accounts are summarized in the Manufacturing Summary account? What accounts are summarized in the Income Summary account?
11. What are the three manufacturing cost elements emphasized on the manufacturing statement?
12. What account balances are carried into the Manufacturing Statement columns of the manufacturing work sheet? What account balances are carried into the Income Statement columns? What account balances are carried into the Balance Sheet columns?
13. Why is the cost of goods manufactured entered in the Manufacturing Statement credit column of a work sheet and again in the Income Statement debit columns?
14. May prices paid a previous manufacturer for items of raw materials determine the balance sheet value of the items of the raw material inventory? Why? May such prices also determine the balance sheet values of the goods in process and finished goods inventories? Why?
15. Standard Company used an overhead rate of 70% of direct labor cost to apply overhead to the items of its goods in process inventory. If the manufacturing statement of the company showed total overhead costs of $84,700, how much direct labor did it show?

The following items appeared in the Manufacturing Statement and Income Statement columns of Donaldson Equipment Company's year-end work sheet:

	Manufacturing Statement		Income Statement	
	Debit	Credit	Debit	Credit
Raw materials inventory............	13,000	14,000	....	....
Goods in process inventory........	15,000	12,000	....	....
Finished goods inventory...........	....	....	16,000	17,000
Sales......................................	....	....	....	210,000
Raw material purchases.............	44,000	....	....	....
Direct labor............................	52,000	....	....	....
Indirect labor..........................	12,000	....	....	....
Power	5,000	....	....	....
Machinery repairs	2,000	....	....	....
Rent expense, factory building ...	6,000	....	....	....
Selling expenses, controlling.......	....	....	38,000	....
Administrative expenses, controlling.............................			22,000	....
	149,000	26,000	....	....
Cost of goods manufactured.......		123,000	123,000	
	149,000	149,000	199,000	227,000
Net Income.............................			28,000	
			227,000	227,000

Exercise 22–1

From the information just given, prepare a manufacturing statement for Donaldson Equipment Company.

Exercise 22–2

Prepare an income statement for Donaldson Equipment Company.

Exercise 22–3

Prepare compound closing entries for Donaldson Equipment, a corporation.

Exercise 22–4

A company that uses the relation between overhead and direct labor costs to apply overhead to its goods in process and finished goods inventories incurred the following costs during a year: materials, $95,000; direct labor, $80,000; and factory overhead costs, $160,000. (a) Determine the company's overhead rate. (b) Under the assumption the company's $12,500 goods in process inventory had $3,000 of direct labor costs, determine the inventory's material costs. (c) Under the assumption the company's $17,000 finished goods inventory had $5,000 of material costs, determine the inventory's labor cost and overhead costs.

Exercise 22–5

An end-of-the-accounting-period trial balance of Edwards Awning Company follows. To simplify the problem and to save time the trial balance is in numbers of not more than two integers.

EDWARDS AWNING COMPANY
Trial Balance
December 31, 19 —

Cash	$ 4	
Accounts receivable	5	
Allowance for doubtful accounts		$ 1
Raw materials inventory	2	
Goods in process inventory	4	
Finished goods inventory	3	
Factory supplies	3	
Prepaid factory insurance	4	
Factory machinery	23	
Accumulated depreciation, factory machinery		2
Common stock		20
Retained earnings		5
Sales		81
Raw material purchases	15	
Freight on raw materials	1	
Direct labor	12	
Indirect labor	3	
Power	5	
Machinery repairs	2	
Rent expense, factory	8	
Selling expenses, controlling	9	
Administrative expenses, controlling	6	
	$109	$109

Required:

1. Prepare a manufacturing work sheet form on ordinary notebook paper.
2. Copy the trial balance on the work sheet form and complete the work sheet using the following information:
   a. Ending inventories:
      Raw materials, $3.
      Goods in process, $5.
      Finished goods, $2.
      Factory supplies, $1.
   b. Allowance for doubtful accounts, an additional $2.
   c. Expired factory insurance, $1.
   d. Depreciation of factory machinery, $3.
   e. Accrued payroll:
      Direct labor, $4.
      Indirect labor, $2.
      Office salaries, $1. (Debit Administrative Expenses, controlling account.)

Problems   **Problem 22–1**

Following are the items from the Manufacturing Statement columns of Lasater Manufacturing Company's work sheet prepared at the end of last year.

The illustrated columns show the items as they appeared after all adjustments were completed but before the ending work in process inventory was calculated and entered and before the cost of goods manufactured was calculated.

Lasater Manufacturing Company makes a single product called NuBlock. On December 31, at the end of last year, the goods in process inventory consisted of 5,000 units of NuBlock with each unit containing an estimated $0.80 of raw materials and having had an estimated $2 of direct labor applied:

	Manufacturing Statement	
	Debit	Credit
Raw materials inventory..	21,200	19,300
Goods in process inventory	17,800	22,100
Raw materials purchased...	81,400	
Direct labor	100,000	
Indirect labor	16,900	
Factory supervision..	12,000	
Heat, light, and power	8,600	
Machinery repairs..	6,300	
Rent expense, factory...	7,200	
Property taxes, machinery	1,900	
Factory insurance expired	3,300	
Factory supplies used	7,400	
Depreciation expense, factory machinery	16,900	
Small tools written off..	500	
	301,400	41?400
Cost of goods manufactured.....................................		?
	301,400	301,400

Required:

1. Calculate the relation between direct labor and factory overhead costs and use this relation to determine the value of the ending goods in process inventory.
2. After placing a value on the ending goods in process inventory, determine the cost of goods manufactured.
3. Prepare a manufacturing statement for Lasater Manufacturing Company.
4. Prepare entries to close the manufacturing accounts and to summarize their balances in the Manufacturing Summary account.
5. Prepare an entry to close the Manufacturing Summary account.

Problem 22-2

The following items appeared in the Manufacturing Statement and Income Statement columns of a work sheet prepared for Ranger Airparts Company, Inc., on December 31, 19—, at the end of an annual accounting period:

	Manufacturing Statement		Income Statement	
	Debit	Credit	Debit	Credit
Raw materials inventory.............................	12,600	12,100	....	....
Goods in process inventory	14,800	12,900	....	....
Finished goods inventory............................	....	....	16,100	18,800
Sales..	....	....	....	361,500
Raw material purchases.............................	59,000	....	....	....
Discounts on raw material purchases............	....	800	....	....
Direct labor	90,000	....	....	....
Indirect labor	13,800	....	....	....
Factory supervision...................................	12,000	....	....	....
Heat, lights, and power	18,400	....	....	....
Machinery repairs	4,500	....	....	....
Rent expense, factory	7,200	....	....	....
Property taxes, machinery	1,700	....	....	....
Selling expenses, controlling	....	....	30,800	....
Administrative expenses, controlling	....	....	28,900	....
Expired factory insurance..........................	2,400	....	....	....
Factory supplies used	6,100	....	....	....
Depreciation expense, factory machinery	10,500	....	....	....
Small tools written off..............................	400	....	....	....
Patents written off....................................	2,500	....	....	....
State and federal income taxes expense.........	....	....	29,500	....
	255,900	25,800	....	....
Cost of goods manufactured.......................	....	230,100	230,100	....
	255,900	255,900	335,400	380,300
Net Income..			44,900	....
			380,300	380,300

Required:

1. From the information given prepare an income statement and a manufacturing statement for the company.
2. Prepare compound closing entries for the company.

Problem 22–3

Cork Production Company began this year with the following inventories: raw materials, $9,200; goods in process, $10,300; and finished goods, $12,500. The company uses the relation between its overhead and direct labor costs to apply overhead to its inventories of goods in process and finished goods; and at the end of this year its inventories were assigned these costs:

	Raw Materials	Goods in Process	Finished Goods
Material costs	$8,600	$2,800	$ 4,500
Direct labor costs	-0-	3,600	5,600
Overhead costs	-0-	?	7,000
Totals...........	$8,600	?	$17,100

And this additional information was available from the company's records:

Total factory overhead costs incurred during the year .... $ 82,500
Cost of all goods manufactured during the year 198,400

Required:

On the basis of the information given plus any data you can derive from it, prepare a manufacturing statement for Cork Production Company.

Problem 22–4

The December 31, 19—, trial balance of Hull Manufacturing Company's ledger carried the following items:

HULL MANUFACTURING COMPANY
Trial Balance, December 31, 19—

Cash...	$ 32,300	
Accounts receivable	36,200	
Allowance for doubtful accounts...........		$ 200
Raw materials inventory......................	37,100	
Goods in process inventory	34,400	
Finished goods inventory	48,700	
Prepaid factory insurance....................	4,100	
Factory supplies	13,100	
Machinery	227,500	
Accumulated depreciation, machinery....		78,400
Accounts payable...............................		25,300
Common stock		100,000
Retained earnings...............................		94,900
Sales...		692,500
Raw materials purchased.....................	185,100	
Direct labor	159,500	
Indirect labor	36,600	
Heat, lights, and power.......................	13,600	
Machinery repairs	9,400	
Selling expenses, controlling................	81,200	
Administrative expenses, controlling......	72,500	
Totals	$991,300	$991,300

The following adjustments and inventory information was available at the year-end:

a. Allowance for doubtful accounts to be increased to $1,700. (Debit Administrative Expenses, controlling account.)
b. An examination of policies showed $3,100 of factory insurance expired.
c. An inventory of factory supplies showed $9,700 of factory supplies used.
d. Estimated depreciation of factory machinery, $31,300.
e. Accrued direct labor, $500; and accrued indirect labor, $300.
f. Accrued state and federal income taxes payable amount to $37,500.
g. Year-end inventories:
   (1) Raw materials, $36,700.
   (2) Goods in process consisted of 3,200 units of product with each unit containing an estimated $3.65 of materials and having had an estimated $4 of direct labor applied.

(3) Finished goods inventory consisted of 3,000 units of product with each unit containing an estimated $7.50 of materials and having had an estimated $6 of direct labor applied.

Required:

1. Enter the trial balance on a work sheet form and make the adjustments from the information given. Then sort the items to the proper Manufacturing Statement, Income Statement, and Balance Sheet columns.
2. After the Direct Labor and factory overhead accounts have been adjusted and carried into the Manufacturing Statement columns, determine the relation between direct labor and overhead costs and use this relation to determine the overhead applicable to each unit of goods in process and finished goods. Next, calculate the balance sheet values for these inventories, enter the inventory amounts on the work sheet, and complete the work sheet.
3. From the work sheet prepare a manufacturing statement and an income statement.
4. Prepare compound closing entries.

Problem 22–5

A trial balance of Macro Pumps Company's ledger on December 31, 19 —, the end of an annual accounting period, appeared as follows:

MACRO PUMPS COMPANY
Trial Balance, December 31, 19 —

Cash	$ 14,800	
Raw materials inventory	13,700	
Goods in process inventory	12,500	
Finished goods inventory	15,100	
Prepaid factory insurance	3,600	
Factory supplies	6,800	
Factory machinery	168,200	
Accumulated depreciation, factory machinery		$ 31,300
Small tools	4,100	
Patents	6,700	
Common stock		100,000
Retained earnings		16,700
Sales		370,000
Raw material purchases	62,000	
Discounts on raw material purchases		1,200
Direct labor	98,400	
Indirect labor	12,100	
Factory supervision	11,700	
Heat, light, and power	17,900	
Machinery repairs	4,200	
Rent expense, factory	6,000	
Property taxes, machinery	1,700	
Selling expenses, controlling	31,400	
Administrative expenses, controlling	28,300	
Totals	$519,200	$519,200

Additional information:

1. Expired factory insurance, $2,400.
2. Factory supplies used, $5,900.
3. Depreciation of factory machinery, $10,200.
4. Small tools written off, $500.
5. Patents written off, $1,400.
6. Accrued wages payable:
   a. Direct labor, $1,600.
   b. Indirect labor, $700.
   c. Factory supervision, $300.
7. Ending inventories:
   a. Raw materials, $13,200.
   b. Goods in process consisted of 2,500 units of product with each unit containing an estimated $1.10 of raw materials and having had an estimated $2 of direct labor applied.
   c. Finished goods consisted of 2,000 units of product with each unit containing an estimated $2.60 of raw materials and having had an estimated $3.60 of direct labor applied.
8. Estimated state and federal income taxes payable, $30,000.

Required:

1. Enter the trial balance on a work sheet form. Make the adjustments from the information given. Sort the items to the proper Manufacturing Statement, Income Statement, and Balance Sheet columns.
2. After the Direct Labor account and the factory overhead cost accounts have been adjusted and carried into the Manufacturing Statement columns, determine the relation between overhead costs and direct labor cost and use the relation to determine the amount of overhead applicable to each unit of goods in process and finished goods. After overhead applicable to each unit of goods in process and finished goods is determined, calculate the inventory values of the goods in process and finished goods inventories. Enter these inventory amounts on the work sheet and complete the work sheet.
3. From the work sheet prepare a manufacturing statement and an income statement.
4. Prepare closing entries.

Problem 22–1A   Alternate
problems

A work sheet prepared by Zoom Lens Company at the end of last year had the following items in its Manufacturing Statement columns:

| | Manufacturing Statement | |
	Debit	Credit
Raw materials inventory.............................	12,300	13,500
Goods in process inventory........................	14,700	?
Raw material purchases.............................	54,300	
Direct labor...	90,000	
Indirect labor..	35,600	
Heat, lights, and power.............................	16,900	
Machinery repairs...................................	5,200	
Rent expense, factory...............................	12,000	
Property taxes, machiney..........................	3,200	
Expired factory insurance	2,600	
Factory supplies used..............................	6,100	
Depreciation expense, machinery	15,300	
Patents written off	2,100	
	270,300	?
Cost of goods manufactured		?
	270,300	270,300

Zoom Lens Company's work sheet does not show the amount of the ending goods in process inventory and cost of goods manufactured. However, the company makes a single product; and on December 31, at the end of last year, there were 3,000 units of goods in process with each unit containing an estimated $1.05 of materials and having had an estimated $1.50 of direct labor applied.

Required:

1. Calculate the relation between direct labor and factor overhead costs and use this relation to place an accounting value on the ending goods in process inventory.
2. After placing a value on the ending goods in process inventory, prepare a manufacturing statement for the company.
3. Prepare entries to close the manufacturing accounts and to summarize their balances in the Manufacturing Summary account.
4. Prepare an entry to close the Manufacturing Summary account.

Problem 22–2A

The following alphabetically arranged items were taken from the Manufacturing Statement and Income Statement columns of Soccer Manufacturing Company's year-end work sheet:

Advertising	$ 1,200	Goods in process, December 31	$ 7,500
Depreciation, machinery	2,100	Finished goods, January 1	10,500
Depreciation, office equipment	500	Finished goods, December 31	8,400
Depreciation, selling equipment	600	Miscellaneous factory expenses	500
Direct labor	38,800	Office salaries	4,200
Factory supplies used	1,100	Raw material purchases	51,500
Federal income taxes expense	8,100	Rent expense, factory building	4,800
Freight on raw materials	1,500	Rent expense, office space	1,400
Heat and power, factory	2,000	Rent expense, selling space	1,600
Indirect labor	3,500	Repairs to machinery	1,800
Inventories:		Sales	180,100
Raw materials, January 1	9,800	Sales discounts	3,400
Raw materials, December 31	10,100	Sales salaries	17,500
Goods in process, January 31	8,200	Superintendence, factory	7,200

Required:

Prepare an income statement and a manufacturing statement for the company.

Problem 22–3A

Fibre Products Company incurred a total of $217,200 of material, labor, and factory overhead costs in manufacturing its product last year; and of this amount, $93,600 represented factory overhead costs. The company began last year with the following inventories: raw materials, $8,400; goods in process, $14,500; and finished goods, $17,500. It applies overhead to its goods in process and finished goods inventories on the basis of the relation of overhead to direct labor costs; and at the end of last year it assigned the following costs to its inventories:

	Raw Materials	Goods in Process	Finished Goods
Material costs	$9,200	$4,700	$ 5,750
Direct labor costs	-0-	4,800	5,800
Overhead costs	-0-	?	8,700
Totals	$9,200	$?	$20,250

Required:

On the basis of the information given plus any information you can derive from it, prepare a manufacturing statement for Fibre Products Company.

Problem 22–5A

Keel Manufacturing Company prepared the following trial balance at the end of its annual accounting period:

KEEL MANUFACTURING COMPANY
Trial Balance
December 31, 19—

Cash	$ 17,500	
Raw materials inventory	13,300	
Goods in process inventory	15,300	
Finished goods inventory	16,600	
Prepaid factory insurance	4,200	
Factory supplies	6,400	
Factory machinery	175,500	
Accumulated depreciation, factory machinery		$ 28,800
Small tools	3,700	
Patents	4,500	
Common stock		100,000
Retained earnings		34,400
Sales		359,700
Raw material purchases	61,800	
Discounts on raw material purchases		1,000
Direct labor	89,100	
Indirect labor	13,300	
Factory supervision	11,800	
Heat, lights, and power	17,900	
Machinery repairs	4,400	
Rent expense, factory	7,200	
Property taxes, machinery	800	
Selling expenses, controlling	31,400	
Administrative expenses, controlling	29,200	
Totals	$523,900	$523,900

Additional information:

1. Expired factory insurance, $2,200.
2. Factory supplies used, $6,300.
3. Depreciation of factory machinery, $9,900.
4. Small tools written off, $700.
5. Patents written off, $1,300.
6. Accrued wages payable: (*a*) direct labor, $900; (*b*) indirect labor, $500; and (*c*) factory supervision, $200.
7. Ending inventories: (*a*) raw materials, $12,800; (*b*) goods in process consisted of 4,000 units of product with each unit containing an estimated $1.40 of materials and having had an estimated $1 of direct labor applied; and (*c*) finished goods consisted of 3,000 units of product with each unit containing an estimated $1.96 of raw materials and having an estimated $2.40 of direct labor applied.
8. Estimated state and federal income taxes expense, $29,000.

Required:

1. Enter the trial balance on a work sheet form and make the adjustments from the information given. Then sort the items to the proper Manufacturing Statement, Income Statement, and Balance Sheet columns.
2. After the Direct Labor and factory overhead cost accounts have been

adjusted and carried into the Manufacturing Statement columns, determine the relation between direct labor and overhead costs and use this relation to determine the overhead applicable to each unit of goods in process and finished goods. After the amounts of overhead applicable to the units of goods in process and finished goods are determined, calculate the balance sheet values of these inventories, enter these inventory amounts on the work sheet, and complete the work sheet.

3. From the work sheet prepare a manufacturing statement and an income statement.

4. Prepare compound closing entries.

Schwab Airconditioning Company has been in operation for three years, manufacturing and selling a single product. Sales have increased during each of the three years, but profits have not, and the company president, Chuck Schwab, has asked you to analyze the situation and tell him why. Mr. Schwab is primarily a production man and knows nothing about accounting. The company bookkeeper knows a debit from a credit, is an excellent clerk, but has little accounting training.

Decision problem 22–1, Schwab Airconditioning

The company's condensed income statements for the past three years show:

	1st Year	2d Year	3d Year
Sales	$250,000	$350,000	$400,000
Cost of goods sold:			
Finished goods inventory, January 1	$ 0	$ 15,000	$ 45,000
Cost of goods manufactured	165,000	256,000	280,500
Goods for sale	$165,000	$271,300	$325,500
Finished goods inventory, December 31	15,000	45,000	60,000
Cost of goods sold	$150,000	$226,000	$265,500
Gross profit from sales	$100,000	$124,000	$134,500
Selling and administrative expenses	75,000	98,000	108,000
Net Income	$ 25,000	$ 26,000	$ 26,500

Investigation disclosed the following additional information:

a. The company sold 5,000 units of its product during the first year in business, 7,000 during the second year, and 8,000 during the third. All sales were at $50 per unit, and no discounts were granted.

b. There were 500 units in the finished goods inventory at the end of the first year, 1,500 at the end of the second, and 2,000 at the end of the third.

c. The units in the finished goods inventory were priced each year at 60% of their selling price, or at $30 per unit.

Prepare a report to Mr. Schwab which shows (1) the number of units of product manufactured each year, (2) the cost each year to manufacture a unit of product, and (3) the selling and administrative expenses per unit of product sold each year. Also, (4) prepare an income statement showing the correct net income each year, using a first-in, first-out basis for pricing the finished goods inventory. And finally, (5) express an opinion as to why net income has not kept pace with the rising sales volume.

Decision problem 22–2, Patterson's Boat Yard

Several years ago Will Patterson took over the operation of his family's boat yard from his father. Once the shop specialized in manufacturing power boats, but of late years it has turned more and more to building sailboats to the specifications of its customers. However, this business is seasonal in nature, since few people order boats in October, November, December, and January. As a result, things are rather slow around the shop during these months.

Will has tried to increase business during the slow months. However, most prospective customers who come into the shop during these months are shoppers; and when Will quotes a price for a new boat, they commonly decide the price is too high and walk out. Will thinks the trouble arises from his application of a rule established by his father when he ran the shop. The rule is that in pricing a job to a customer, "always set the price so as to make a 10% profit over and above all costs, and be sure that all costs are included."

Will says that in pricing a job, the material and labor costs are easy to figure but that overhead is another thing. His overhead consists of depreciation of building and machinery, heat, lights, power, taxes, and so on, which in total run to $600 per month whether he builds any boats or not. Furthermore, when he follows his father's rule, he has to charge more for a boat built during the slow months because the overhead is spread over fewer jobs. He readily admits that this seems to drive away business during the months he needs business most, but he finds it difficult to break his father's rule, for as he says, "Dad did all right in this business for many years."

Explain with assumed figures to illustrate your point why Will charges more for a boat made in December than for one built in May, a very busy month. Suggest how Will might solve his pricing problem and still follow his father's rule.

Decision problem 22–3, Digital Manufacturing Company

Digital Manufacturing Company had outstanding 6,000 shares of $12 par value common stock on January 1, 197A. The stock was issued at par. The assets and liabilities of the company on that date were as follows:

Cash...	$16,000
Accounts receivable	8,000
Raw materials inventory..................	10,000
Goods in process inventory..............	12,000
Finished goods inventory.................	14,000
Plant and equipment, net.................	34,000
Accounts payable...........................	8,000

During 197A the company paid no dividends, although it earned a 197A net income (ignore income taxes) of $7,500. At the year-end the amounts of the company's accounts receivable, accounts payable, and common stock outstanding were the same as of the beginning of the year. However, its cash decreased $1,500, its raw materials inventory increased by 40%, its goods in process inventory increased by 25%, and its finished goods inventory increased by one half during the year. The net amount of its plant and equipment decreased $5,000 due to depreciation, chargeable four fifths to factory overhead costs and one fifth to general and administrative expenses. The year's direct labor costs were $20,000, and factory overhead costs excluding depreciation were 60% of that amount. Cost of finished goods sold was $50,-000, and all sales were made at prices 50% above cost. Selling expenses were 10%, and general and administrative expenses excluding depreciation were 12% of sales.

Based on the information given and on amounts you can derive therefrom, prepare a manufacturing work sheet for the company.

After studying Chapter 23, you should be able to:

- State the conditions under which job order cost accounting should be used and those under which process cost accounting should be used.

- Describe how costs for individual jobs are accumulated on job cost sheets and how control accounts are charged with the total costs of all jobs.

- Allocate overhead to jobs and distribute any over- or underapplied overhead.

- Describe how costs are accumulated by departments under process costing.

- Explain what an equivalent finished unit is and how equivalent finished units are used in calculating unit costs.

- Prepare a process cost summary.

- Define or explain the words and phrases listed in the chapter Glossary.

chapter 23

Cost accounting, job order, and process

In a general accounting system for a manufacturer, such as that described in the previous chapter, physical inventories are required at the end of each accounting period in order to determine cost of goods manufactured. Furthermore, cost of goods manufactured as determined under such a system is the cost of all goods that were manufactured during the period, and commonly no effort is made to determine unit costs. A cost accounting system differs in that it is based on perpetual inventories and its emphasis is on unit costs and the control of costs.

There are two common types of cost accounting systems: (1) job order cost systems and (2) process cost systems. However, of the two there are an infinite number of variations and combinations. A job order system is described first.

JOB ORDER COST ACCOUNTING

In job order cost accounting a *job* is a turbine, machine, or other product manufactured especially for and to the specifications of a customer. A job may also be a single construction project of a contractor. A *job lot* is a quantity of identical items, such as 500 typewriters, manufactured in one lot as a job or single order; and a *job order cost system* is one in which costs are assembled in terms of jobs or job lots of product.

As previously stated, a job cost system differs from a general accounting system in that its primary objective is the determination of the cost of each job or job lot of product as it is finished. A job cost system also differs in that all inventory accounts used in such a system are perpetual inventory accounts controlling subsidiary ledgers. For example, in a job cost system the purchase and use of all materials are recorded in a perpetual inventory account called Materials which controls a subsidiary ledger having a separate ledger card (Illustration 23–1) for each different kind of material used. Likewise, in a job cost system the Goods in Process and Finished Goods accounts are also perpetual inventory accounts controlling subsidiary ledgers.

MATERIALS LEDGER CARD

Item _Whatsit clip_   Stock No. _C-347_   Location in Storeroom _Bin 137_

Maximum _400_   Minimum _150_   Number to Reorder _200_

	Received				Issued					Balance		
Date	Receiving Report No.	Units	Unit Price	Total Price	Requi- sition No.	Units	Unit Price	Total Price		Units	Unit Price	Total Price
3/1										180	1.00	180.00
3/5					4345	20	1.00	20.00		160	1.00	160.00
3/11					4416	10	1.00	10.00		150	1.00	150.00
3/12	C-114	200	1.00	200.00						350	1.00	350.00
3/25					4713	21	1.00	21.00		329	1.00	329.00

Illustration 23–1

    In addition to perpetual inventory controlling accounts, job cost accounting is also distinguished by the flow of manufacturing costs from the Materials, Factory Payroll, and Overhead Costs accounts into and through the Goods in Process and Finished Goods accounts and on to the Cost of Goods Sold account. The flow is diagrammed in Illustration 23–2 on the next page. An examination of the diagram will show that costs flow through the accounts in the same way materials, labor, and overhead are placed in production in the factory, move on to become finished goods, and finally are sold.

Job cost sheets

    The heart of a job cost system is a subsidiary ledger of _job cost sheets_ called a _Job Cost Ledger._ The cost sheets are used to accumulate costs by jobs. A separate cost sheet is used for each job.

    Observe in Illustration 23–3 how a job cost sheet is designed to accumulate costs. Although this accumulation is discussed in more detail later, it may be summarized as follows. When a job is begun, information as to the customer, job number, and job description is filled in on a blank cost sheet and the cost sheet is placed in the Job Cost Ledger. The job number identifies the job and simplifies the process of charging it with materials, labor, and overhead. As materials are required for the job, they are transferred from the materials storeroom and are used to complete the job. At the same time their cost is charged to the job in the Materials column of the job's cost sheet. Labor used on the job is likewise charged to the job in the Labor column; and when the job is finished, the amount of overhead applicable is entered

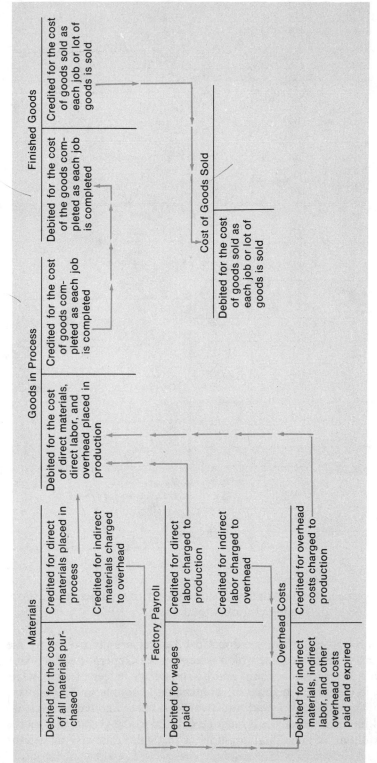

Illustration 23–2
Diagram showing
the flow of costs in
a job cost system

JOB COST SHEET

Customer's Name ___Cone Lumber Company___   Job No. __7452__
Address ___Eugene, Oregon___
Job Description ___10 H.P. electric motor to customer's specifications___

Date   Date   Date
Promised ___4/1___   Started ___3/23___   Completed ___3/29___

| Date | Materials | | Labor | | Overhead Costs Applied | | |
	Requisition No.	Amount	Time Ticket No.	Amount	Date	Rate	Amount
19-- Mar. 23	4698	53.00	C-3422	6.00	3/29	150 per-cent of the direct labor	$123.00
24			C-3478 C-3479	16.00 6.00			
25	4713	21.00	C-4002	16.00			
26			C-4015	16.00	Summary of Costs		
27			C-4032	12.00	Materials _____ $ 74.00		
28			C-4044	10.00	Labor _____ 82.00		
					Overhead _____ 123.00		
					Total Cost of the job _____ 279.00		
	Total	74.00	Total	82.00	Remarks: Completed and shipped 3/29		

Illustration 23-3

in the Overhead Costs Applied column. After this, the cost totals are summarized to determine the job's total cost.

The Goods in Process account

The job cost sheets in the Job Cost Ledger are controlled by the Goods in Process account, which is kept in the General Ledger. And, the Goods in Process account and its subsidiary ledger of cost sheets operate in the usual manner of controlling accounts and subsidiary ledgers. The material, labor, and overhead costs debited to each individual job on its cost sheet must be debited to the Goods in Process account either as individual amounts or in totals. Likewise all credits to jobs on their cost sheets must be credited individually or in totals to the Goods in Process account.

In addition to being a controlling account, the Goods in Process account is a perpetual inventory account operating somewhat as follows: At the beginning of a cost period the cost of any unfinished jobs in process is shown by its debit balance. Throughout the cost period materials, labor, and overhead are placed in production in the factory; and periodically their costs are debited to the account (note the last three debits in the Goods in Process account that follows). Also, throughout the period the cost of each job completed (the sum of the job's material, labor, and overhead costs) is credited to the account as each job is finished. As a result, the account is a perpetual inventory account, and after all entries are posted, the debit balance shows the cost of the unfinished jobs still in process. This current balance is obtained and maintained without having to take a physical count of inventory, except as an occasional means of confirming the account balance. For example, the following Goods in Process account shows a $12,785 March 31 ending inventory of unfinished jobs in process.

Goods in Process

Date		Explanation	Debit	Credit	Balance
Mar.	1	Balance, beginning inventory			2,850
	10	Job 7449 completed		7,920	(5,070)
	18	Job 7448 completed		9,655	(14,725)
	24	Job 7450 completed		8,316	(23,041)
	29	Job 7452 completed		279	(23,320)
	29	Job 7451 completed		6,295	(29,615)
	31	Materials used	17,150		(12,465)
	31	Labor applied	10,100		(2,365)
	31	Overhead applied	15,150		12,785

Accounting for materials under a job cost system

Under a job cost system all materials purchased are placed in a materials storeroom under the care of a storeroom keeper, and are issued to the factory only in exchange for properly prepared material requisitions (Illustration 23–4). The storeroom provides physical control over materials. The requisitions enhance the control and also provide a means of charging material costs to jobs or, in the case of indirect materials, to factory overhead costs. The use of requisitions is described in the next paragraphs.

When a material is needed in the factory, a material requisition is prepared and signed by a foreman, superintendent, or other responsible person. The requisition identifies the material and shows the number of the job or overhead account to which it is to be charged, and is given to the storeroom keeper in exchange for the material. The store-

Illustration 23–4

room keeper collects the requisitions, and then forwards them, in batches, to the accounting department.

Issuing units of material to the factory reduces the amount of that particular material in the storeroom. Consequently, when a material requisition reaches the accounting department, it is first recorded in the Issued column of the materials ledger card of the material issued. This reduces the number of units of that material shown to be on hand. Note the last entry in Illustration 23–1, which records the requisition of Illustration 23–4.

Materials issued to the factory may be used on jobs or for some overhead task, such as machinery repairs. Consequently, after being entered in the Issued columns of the proper materials ledger cards, a batch of requisitions is sorted by jobs and overhead accounts and charged to the proper jobs and overhead accounts. Materials used on jobs are charged to the jobs in the Materials columns of the job cost sheets. (Note the last entry in the Materials column on the cost sheet of Illustration 23–3 where the requisition of Illustration 23–4 is recorded.) Materials used for overhead tasks are charged to the proper overhead accounts in the Overhead Costs Ledger. A company using a job cost system commonly has an Overhead Costs, controlling account in its General Ledger which controls a subsidiary Overhead Costs Ledger having an account for each overhead cost, such as Heating and Lighting or Machinery Repairs. Consequently, a requisition for light bulbs, for example, is charged to the Heating and Lighting account in the subsidiary Overhead Costs Ledger.

Material ledger cards, job cost sheets, and overhead cost accounts are all subsidiary ledger accounts controlled by accounts in the General Ledger. Consequently, in addition to the entries just described, entries must also be made in the controlling accounts. To make these entries, the requisitions charged to jobs and the requisitions charged to overhead accounts are accumulated until the end of a month or other cost period when they are separately totaled; and if, for example, the requisitions charged to jobs during the month total $17,150 and those charged to overhead accounts total $320, an entry like the following is made:

Mar.	31	Goods in Process...	17,150.00	
		Overhead Costs	320.00	
		Materials...		17,470.00
		To record the materials used during March.		

The debit to Goods in Process in the illustrated entry is equal to the sum of the requisitions charged to jobs on the job cost sheets during March. The debit to Overhead Costs is equal to the sum of the requisitions charged to overhead accounts, and the credit to Materials is equal to the sum of all requisitions entered in the Issued columns of the material ledger cards during the month.

Accounting for labor in a job cost system

Time clocks, clock cards, and a Payroll Register similar to those described in an earlier chapter are commonly used in a factory to record the hours and cost of the work of each direct and indirect labor employee. Furthermore, without the complications of payroll taxes, income taxes, and other deductions, the entry to pay the employees is as follows:

Mar.	7	Factory Payroll	2,900.00	
		Cash...		2,900.00
		To record the factory payroll and pay the employees.		

This entry is repeated at the end of each pay period; consequently, at the end of a month or other cost period the Factory Payroll account has a series of debits (see Illustration 23–6) like the debit of this entry, and the sum of these debits is the total amount paid the direct and indirect labor employees during the month.

The clock cards just mentioned are a record of hours worked each day by each employee, but they do not show how the employees spent their time or the specific jobs and overhead tasks on which they worked. Consequently, if the hours worked by each employee are to be charged to specific jobs and overhead accounts, another record called a *labor time ticket* must be prepared. Labor time tickets like the one shown in Illustration 23–5 tell how an employee spent his time while at work.

The time ticket of Illustration 23–5 is a "pen-and-ink" ticket and is suitable for use in a plant in which only a small number of such tickets are prepared and recorded each day. In a plant in which many tickets are prepared, a time ticket that can be made into a punched card similar to Illustration 23–4 would be more suitable.

TIME TICKET _____ C-3422 _____

EMPLOYEE
  name_____ *George Jones* _____
  clock number__ *342* __
JOB
  number__ *7452* _____
  description__ *Armature winding* _____

OVERHEAD ACCOUNT NUMBER_____
TIME/RATE

started	stopped	elapsed	rate	pay
8:00	10:00	2	3.00	6.00

Date: *George Jones*
                                  employee
3/23   *J. Calloway*
                                  foreman

Illustration 23–5
A labor time ticket

Labor time tickets serve as a basis for charging jobs and overhead accounts for an employee's wages. Throughout each day a labor time ticket is prepared each time an employee is changed from one job or overhead task to another. The tickets may be prepared by the worker, his foreman, or a clerk called a timekeeper. If the employee works on only one job all day, only one ticket is prepared. If he works on more than one job, a separate ticket is made for each. At the end of the day all the tickets of that day are sent to the accounting department.

In the accounting department the direct labor time tickets are charged to jobs on the job cost sheets (see the first entry in the Labor column of Illustration 23–3 where the ticket of Illustration 23–5 is recorded); and the indirect labor tickets are charged to overhead accounts in the Overhead Costs Ledger. The tickets are then accumulated until the end of the cost period when they are separately totaled; and if, for example, the direct labor tickets total $10,100 and the indirect labor tickets total $2,500, the following entry is made:

Mar.	31	Goods in Process.....................................	10,100.00	
		Overhead Costs	2,500.00	
		Factory Payroll		12,600.00
		To record the March time tickets.		

The first debit in the illustrated entry is the sum of all direct labor time tickets charged to jobs on the job cost sheets, and the second debit is the sum of all tickets charged to overhead accounts. The credit is the total of the month's labor time tickets, both direct and indirect. Notice in Illustration 23–6 that after this credit is posted, the Factory Payroll account has a $605 credit balance. This $605 is the accrued factory payroll payable at the month's end, and it is also the dollar amount of time tickets prepared and recorded during the days following the end of the March 28 pay period.

Factory Payroll					
Date		Explanation	Debit	Credit	Balance
Mar.	7	Weekly payroll payment	2,900		2,900
	14	Weekly payroll payment	2,950		5,850
	21	Weekly payroll payment	3,105		8,955
	28	Weekly payroll payment	3,040		11,995
	31	Labor cost summary		12,600	(605)

Illustration 23–6

In a job cost system, if the cost of each job is to be determined at the time it is finished, it is necessary to associate with each job the costs of its materials, labor, and overhead. Requisitions and time tickets make possible a direct association of material and labor costs with jobs. However, overhead costs are incurred for the benefit of all jobs and cannot be related directly to any one. Consequently, to associate overhead with jobs it is necessary to relate overhead to, for example, direct labor costs and to apply overhead to jobs by means of a *predetermined overhead application rate*.

Accounting for overhead in a job cost system

A predetermined overhead application rate based on direct labor cost is established by (1) estimating before a cost period begins the total overhead that will be incurred during the period; (2) estimating the cost of the direct labor that will be incurred during the period; then (3) calculating the ratio, expressed as a percentage, of the estimated overhead to the estimated direct labor cost. For example, if a cost accountant estimates that a factory will incur $180,000 of overhead during the year about to begin and that $120,000 of direct labor will be applied to production during the period, and these estimates are used to establish an overhead application rate, the rate is 150% and is calculated as follows:

$$\frac{\text{Next year's estimated overhead costs, \$180,000}}{\text{Next year's estimated direct labor costs, \$120,000}} = 150\%$$

After a predetermined overhead application rate is established, it is used throughout the year to apply overhead to jobs as they are finished. Overhead is assigned to each job, and its cost is calculated as follows: (1) As each job is completed, the cost of its materials is determined by adding the amounts in the Materials column of its cost sheet. Then (2) the cost of its labor is determined by adding the amounts in the

Labor column. Next (3) the applicable overhead is calculated by multiplying the job's total labor cost by the predetermined overhead application rate and is entered in the Overhead Costs Applied column. Finally (4) the job's material, labor, and overhead costs are entered in the summary section of the cost sheet and totaled to determine the cost of the job.

The predetermined overhead application rate is also used to assign overhead to any jobs still in process at the cost period end. Then, the total overhead assigned to all jobs during the period is recorded in the accounts with an entry like this:

Mar.	31	Goods in Process..	15,150.00	
		Overhead Costs		15,150.00
		To record the overhead applied to jobs during March.		

The illustrated entry assumes that the overhead applied to all jobs during March totaled $15,150, and after it is posted the Overhead Costs account appears as in Illustration 23–7.

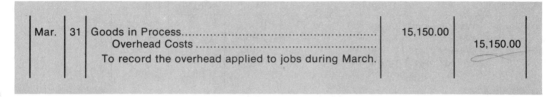

Overhead Costs

Date		Explanation	F	Debit	Credit	Balance
Mar.	31	Indirect materials	G24	320		320
	31	Indirect labor	G24	2,500		2,820
	31	Miscellaneous payments	D89	3,306		6,126
	31	Accrued and prepaid items	G24	9,056		15,182
	31	Applied			15,150	32

Illustration 23–7

In the Overhead Costs account of Illustration 23–7 the actual overhead costs incurred during March are represented by four debits. The first two need no explanation; the third represents the many payments for such things as water, telephone, and so on; while the fourth represents such things as depreciation, expired insurance, taxes, and so forth.

When overhead is applied to jobs on the basis of a predetermined overhead rate based upon direct labor costs as in this discussion, it is assumed that the overhead applicable to a particular job bears the same relation to the job's direct labor cost as the total estimated overhead of the factory bears to the total estimated direct labor costs. This assumption may not be proper in every case. However, when the ratio of overhead to direct labor cost is approximately the same for all jobs, an overhead rate based upon direct labor cost offers an easily calculated and fair basis for assigning overhead to jobs. In those cases in which the ratio of overhead to direct labor cost does not remain the same for all jobs, some other relationship must be used. Often overhead rates based upon the ratio of overhead to direct labor hours or overhead to machine-hours are used. However, a discussion of these is reserved for a course in cost accounting.

When overhead is applied to jobs by means of an overhead application rate based on estimates, the Overhead Costs account seldom, if ever, has a zero balance. At times actual overhead incurred exceeds overhead applied, and at other times overhead applied exceeds actual overhead incurred. When the account has a debit balance (overhead incurred in excess of overhead applied), the balance is known as *underapplied overhead* (see Illustration 23-7); and when it has a credit balance (overhead applied in excess of overhead incurred), the balance is called *overapplied overhead*. Usually the balance is small and fluctuates from debit to credit throughout a year. However, any balance in the account must be disposed of at the end of each year before a new accounting period begins.

If the year-end balance of the Overhead Costs account is material in amount, it is reasonable that it be disposed of by apportioning it among the goods still in process, the finished goods inventory, and cost of goods sold. This has the effect of restating the inventories and goods sold at "actual" cost. For example, assume that at the end of an accounting period, (1) a company's Overhead Costs account has a $1,000 debit balance (underapplied overhead), and (2) the company had charged the following amounts of overhead to jobs during the period: jobs still in process, $10,000; jobs finished but unsold, $20,000; and jobs finished and sold, $70,000. In such a situation the following entry apportions fairly the underapplied overhead among the jobs worked on during the period:

Dec.	31	Goods in Process...	100.00	
		Finished Goods	200.00	
		Cost of Goods Sold...	700.00	
		Overhead Costs		1,000.00
		To clear the Overhead Costs account and charge the underapplied overhead to the work of the accounting period.		

Sometimes when the amount of over- or underapplied overhead is immaterial, all of it is closed to Cost of Goods Sold under the assumption that the major share would be charged there anyway and any extra exactness gained from prorating would not be worth the extra record keeping involved.

When a job is completed, its cost is transferred from the Goods in Process account to the Finished Goods account with an entry like the following which transfers the cost of the job the cost sheet of which appears on page 762.

Overapplied and underapplied overhead

Recording the completion of a job

Mar.	29	Finished Goods	279.00	
		Goods in Process..		279.00
		To transfer the cost of Job No. 7452 to		
		Finished Goods.		

In addition to the entry, and at the same time it is made, the completed job's cost sheet is removed from the Job Cost Ledger, marked "completed," and filed. This is in effect the equivalent of posting a credit to the Job Cost Ledger equal to the credit to the Goods in Process controlling account.

Recording cost of goods sold

When a cost system is in use, the cost to manufacture a job or job lot of product is known as soon as the goods are finished. Consequently, when goods are sold, since their cost is known, the cost can be recorded at the time of sale. For example, if goods costing $279 are sold for $450, the cost of the goods sold may be recorded with the sale as follows:

Mar.	29	Accounts Receivable—Cone Lumber Co.......................	450.00	
		Cost of Goods Sold..	279.00	
		Sales		450.00
		Finished Goods		279.00
		Sold for $450 goods costing $279.		

When cost of goods sold is recorded at the time of each sale, the balance of the Cost of Goods Sold account shows at the end of an accounting period the cost of goods sold during the period.

PROCESS COST ACCOUNTING

A *process* is a step in manufacturing a product, and a *process cost system* is one in which costs are assembled in terms of processes or manufacturing steps.

Process cost systems are found in companies producing cement, flour, or other products the production of which is characterized by a large volume of standardized units manufactured on a more or less continuous basis. In such companies responsibility for completing each step in the production of a product is assigned to a department. Costs are then assembled by departments, and the efficiency of each department is measured by the processing costs incurred in processing the units of product that flow through the department.

Assembling costs by departments

When costs are assembled by departments in a process cost system, a separate goods in process acount is used for the costs of each department. For example, assume a company makes a product from metal that is cut to size in a cutting department, sent to a bending department to be bent into shape, and then on to a painting department to be painted. Such a concern would collect costs in three goods in process accounts, one for each department, and costs would flow through the accounts as in Illustration 23–8.

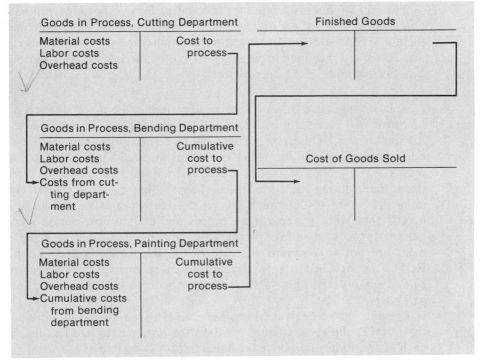

Illustration 23–8

Observe in Illustration 23–8 that each department's material, labor, and overhead costs are charged to the department's goods in process account. (It is assumed there were additional materials charged directly to the bending department.) Observe too how costs are transferred from department to department, just as the product is transferred in the manufacturing procedure. The cost to cut the product in the cutting department is transferred to the bending department; and the sum of the costs in the first two departments is transferred to the third department; and finally the sum of the processing costs in all three departments, which is the cost to make the product, is transferred to finished goods.

Since there are no jobs in a process cost system, accounting for material and labor costs in such a system is much simplified. Material requisitions may be used. However, a consumption report kept by the storeroom keeper and showing the materials issued to each department during a cost period is often substituted. Likewise, labor time tickets may be used; but since most employees spend all their working time **Charging costs to departments** in the same department, an end-of-the-period summary of the payroll records is usually all that is required in charging labor to the departments. And since there are no jobs, there is no need to distinguish between direct and indirect materials and direct and indirect labor. All that is required is that material and labor costs, both direct and indirect, be charged to the proper departments.

The lack of jobs also simplifies accounting for overhead in a process cost system. Since there are no jobs to charge with overhead on completion, predetermined overhead application rates are not required and actual overhead incurred may be charged directly to the goods in process accounts of the departments.

Equivalent finished units

A basic objective of a process cost system is the determination of unit processing costs for material, labor, and overhead in each processing department. This requires that (1) material, labor, and overhead costs be accumulated for each department for a cost period of, say, a month; (2) a record be kept of the number of units processed in each department during the period; and then (3) that costs be divided by units processed to determine unit costs. However, it should be observed that when a department begins and ends a cost period with partially processed units of product, the units completed in the department are not an accurate measure of the department's production. Rather, in such instances production must be measured in terms of *equivalent finished units* and unit costs become *equivalent finished unit costs*.

The idea of an equivalent finished unit is based on the assumption that it takes the same amount of labor, for instance, to one-half finish each of two units of product as it takes to fully complete one, or it takes the same amount of labor to one-third finish each of three units as to complete one. Equivalent finished units are discussed further in the Delta Processing Company illustration that follows.

Process cost accounting illustrated

The process cost system of Delta Processing Company, a company manufacturing a patented home remedy called Noxall, is used to illustrate process cost accounting.

The procedure for manufacturing Noxall is as follows: Material A is finely ground in Delta Processing Company's grinding department, after which it is transferred to the mixing department where Material B is added, and the two materials are thoroughly mixed. The mixing process results in finished product, Noxall, which is transferred on completion to finished goods. All Material A placed in process in the grinding department is placed in process when the grinding process is first begun; but the Material B added in the mixing department is added evenly throughout its process. In other words, a product one-third mixed in the latter department has received one third of its Material B and a product three-fourths mixed has received three fourths. Labor and overhead are applied evenly throughout each department's process.

At the end of the April cost period, after entries recording materials, labor, and overhead were posted, the company's two goods in process accounts appeared as follows:

Goods in Process, Grinding Department

Date		Explanation	Debit	Credit	Balance
Apr.	1	Beginning inventory			4,250
	30	Materials	9,900		14,150
	30	Labor	5,700		19,850
	30	Overhead	4,275		24,125

Goods in Process, Mixing Department

Date		Explanation	Debit	Credit	Balance
Apr.	1	Beginning inventory			3,785
	30	Materials	2,040		5,825
	30	Labor	3,570		9,395
	30	Overhead	1,020		10,415

The production reports prepared by the company's two department foremen give the following information about inventories and goods started and finished in each department during the month:

	Grinding Department	Mixing Department
Units in the beginning inventories of goods in process.............................	30,000	16,000
April 1 stage of completion of the beginning inventories of goods in process...	$\frac{1}{3}$	$\frac{1}{4}$
Units started in process and finished during period................................	70,000	85,000
Total units finished and transferred to next department or to finished goods..	100,000	101,000
Units in the ending inventories of goods in process	20,000	15,000
Stage of completion of ending inventories of goods in process................	$\frac{1}{4}$	$\frac{1}{3}$

After receiving the production reports, the company's cost accountant prepared a process cost summary, Illustration 23–9, for the grinding department. A process cost summary is a report peculiar to a processing company; a separate one is prepared for each processing department and shows: (1) the costs charged to the department, (2) the department's equivalent unit processing costs, and (3) the costs applicable to the department's goods in process inventories and its goods started and finished.

Observe in Illustration 23–9 that a process cost summary has three sections. In the first, headed Costs Charged to the Department, are summarized the costs charged to the department. Information for this section comes from the department's goods in process account. Com-

Delta Processing Company
Process Cost Summary, Grinding Department
For Month Ended April 30, 19—

COSTS CHARGED TO THE DEPARTMENT:

Material requisitioned..	$ 9,900
Labor charged..	5,700
Overhead costs incurred..	4,275
Total processing costs...	$19,875
Goods in process at the beginning of the month...	4,250
Total Costs to Be Accounted for..	$24,125

EQUIVALENT UNIT PROCESSING COSTS:

Material:	Units Involved	Fraction of a Unit Added	Equivalent Units Added
Beginning inventory..	30,000	-0-	-0-
Units started and finished..	70,000	one	70,000
Ending inventory	20,000	one	20,000
			90,000

Equivalent unit processing cost for material: $9,900 ÷ 90,000 = $0.11

Labor and overhead:	Units Involved	Fraction of a Unit Added	Equivalent Units Added
Beginning inventory..	30,000	$\frac{2}{3}$	20,000
Units started and finished..	70,000	one	70,000
Ending inventory	20,000	$\frac{1}{4}$	5,000
			95,000

Equivalent unit processing cost for labor: $5,700 ÷ 95,000 = $0.06
Equivalent unit processing cost for overhead: $4,275 ÷ 95,000 = $0.045

COSTS APPLICABLE TO THE WORK OF THE DEPARTMENT:

Goods in process, one-third processed at the beginning of April:

Costs charged to the beginning inventory of goods in process during previous month...	$4,250	
Material added (all added during March)	-0-	
Labor applied (20,000 × $0.06)...	1,200	
Overhead applied (20,000 × $0.045)...	900	
Cost to process...		$ 6,350

Goods started and finished in the department during April:

Material added (70,000 × $0.11)..	$7,700	
Labor applied (70,000 × $0.06)...	4,200	
Overhead applied (70,000 × $0.045)...	3,150	
Cost to process...		15,050
Total cost of the goods processed in the department and transferred to the mixing department (100,000 units at $0.214 each)*..		$21,400

Goods in process, one-fourth processed at the end of April:

Material added (20,000 × $0.11)..	$2,200	
Labor applied (5,000 × $0.06)	300	
Overhead applied (5,000 × $0.045)	225	
Cost to one-fourth process		2,725
Total Costs Accounted for..		$24,125

* Note that the $0.214 is an average unit cost based on all 100,000 units finished. Other alternatives such as Fifo and Lifo are deferred to a more advanced course.

Illustration 23-9

pare the first section of Illustration 23–9 with the goods in process account of the grinding department shown on the previous page.

The second section of a process cost summary shows the calculation of equivalent unit costs. The information for this section as to units involved and fractional units applicable to the inventories comes from the production report of the department foreman. Information as to material, labor, and overhead costs comes from the first section of the summary.

Notice in the second section of Illustration 23–9 that there are two separate equivalent unit calculations. Two calculations are required because material added to the product and labor and overhead added are not added in the same proportions and at the same stages in the processing procedure of this department. As previously stated, all material is added at the beginning of this department's process, and labor and overhead are added evenly throughout the process. Consequently, the number of equivalent units of material added is not the same as the number of equivalent units of labor and overhead added.

Observe in the calculation of equivalent finished units for materials that the beginning-of-the-month inventory is assigned no additional material. In the grinding department all material placed in process is placed there at the beginning of the process. The 30,000 beginning inventory units were begun during March and were one-third completed at the beginning of April. Consequently, these units received all their material during March when their processing was first begun.

Note also how the $9,900 cost of the material charged to the department in April is divided by 90,000 equivalent units of material to arrive at an $0.11 per equivalent unit cost for material consumed in this department.

Now move on to the calculation of equivalent finished units for labor and overhead and note that the beginning inventory units were each assigned two thirds of a unit of labor and overhead. If these units were one-third completed on April 1, then two thirds of the work done on these units was done in April. Beginning students often have difficulty at this point. In a situation such as this they are apt to assign only an additional one-third unit of labor and overhead when two thirds is required.

Before going further observe that the essence of the equivalent unit calculation for labor and overhead is that to do two thirds of the work on 30,000 units, all the work on 70,000 units, and one fourth the work on 20,000 units is the equivalent of doing all the work on 95,000 units. Consequently, the $5,700 of labor cost and $4,275 of overhead cost charged to the department are each divided by 95,000 to determine equivalent unit costs for labor and overhead.

When a department begins and ends a cost period with partially processed units of product, it is necessary to apportion the department's costs between the units that were in process in the department at the beginning of the period, the units started and finished during the period, and the ending inventory units. This division is necessary to determine the cost of the units completed in the department during the period; and the division and assignment of costs are shown in the third section of the process cost summary.

Notice in the third section of Illustration 23–9 how costs are assigned to the beginning inventory. The first amount assigned is the $4,250 beginning inventory costs. This amount represents the material, labor, and overhead costs used to one-third complete the inventory during March, the previous cost period. Normally, the second charge to a beginning inventory is for additional material assigned to it. However, in the grinding department no additional material costs are assigned the beginning inventory because these units received all of their material when their processing was first begun during the previous month. The second charge to the beginning inventory is for labor. The $1,200 portion of applicable labor costs is calculated by multiplying the number of equivalent finished units of labor used in completing the beginning inventory by the cost of an equivalent finished unit of labor (20,000 equivalent finished units at $0.06 each). The third charge to the beginning inventory is for overhead. The applicable $900 portion is determined by multiplying the equivalent finished units of overhead used in completing the beginning inventory by the cost of an equivalent finished unit of overhead (20,000 × $0.45).

After costs are assigned to the beginning inventory, the procedures used in their assignment are repeated for the units started and finished. Then the cost of the units completed and transferred to finished goods, in this case the cost of the 30,000 beginning inventory units plus the cost of the 70,000 units started and finished, is determined by adding the costs assigned to the two groups. In this situation the total is $21,400 or $0.214 per unit ($21,400 ÷ 100,000 units = $0.214 per unit).

Before going further, notice in the second section of the grinding department's process cost summary that the equivalent finished unit cost for materials is $0.11, for labor is $0.06, and for overhead is $0.045, a total of $0.215. Notice, however, in the third section of the summary that the unit cost of the 100,000 units finished and transferred is $0.214, which is less than $0.215. It is less because costs were less in the department during the previous month and the 30,000 beginning units were one-third processed at these lower costs.

The grinding department's process cost summary is completed by assigning costs to the ending inventory, and after it was completed the accountant prepared the following entry to transfer from the grinding department to the mixing department the cost of the 100,000 units processed in the department and transferred during April. Information for the entry as to the cost of the units transferred was taken from the third section of Illustration 23–9.

Apr.	30	Goods in Process, Mixing Department	21,400.00	
		Goods in Process, Grinding Department.................		21,400.00
		To transfer the cost of the 100,000 units of product transferred to the mixing department.		

Posting the entry had the effect on the accounts shown in Illustration 23–10. Observe that the effect is one of transferring and advancing costs from one department to the next just as the product is transferred and advanced in the manufacturing procedure.

Goods in Process, Grinding Department

Date		Explanation	Debit	Credit	Balance
Apr.	1	Beginning inventory			4,250
	30	Materials	9,900		14,150
	30	Labor	5,700		19,850
	30	Overhead	4,275		24,125
	30	Units to mixing department		21,400	2,725

Goods in Process, Mixing Department

Date		Explanation	Debit	Credit	Balance
Apr.	1	Beginning inventory			3,785
	30	Materials	2,040		5,825
	30	Labor	3,570		9,395
	30	Overhead	1,020		10,415
	30	Units from grinding department	21,400		31,815

Illustration 23–10

After posting the entry transferring to the mixing department the grinding department costs of the units transferred, the cost accountant prepared a process cost summary for the mixing department. Information required in its preparation was taken from the mixing department's goods in process account and production report. The summary appeared as in Illustration 23–11.

Two points in Illustration 23–11 require special attention. The first is the calculation of equivalent finished units. Since the materials, labor, and overhead added in the mixing department are all added evenly throughout the process of this department, only a single equivalent unit calculation is required. This differs from the grinding department, the previous department, where two equivalent unit calculations were required. Two were required because material was not placed in process at the same stage in the processing procedure as were the labor and overhead.

The second point needing special attention in the mixing department

Delta Processing Company
Process Cost Summary, Mixing Department
For Month Ended April 30, 19—

COSTS CHARGED TO THE DEPARTMENT:

Materials requisitioned	$ 2,040
Labor charged	3,570
Overhead costs incurred	1,020
Total processing costs	$ 6,630
Goods in process at the beginning of the month	3,785
Costs transferred from the grinding department (100,000 units at $0.214 each)	21,400
Total Costs to Be Accounted for	$31,815

EQUIVALENT UNIT PROCESSING COSTS:

Materials, labor, and overhead:	Units Involved	Fraction of a Unit Added	Equivalent Units Added
Beginning inventory	16,000	$\frac{3}{4}$	12,000
Units started and finished	85,000	one	85,000
Ending inventory	15,000	$\frac{1}{3}$	5,000
Total equivalent units			102,000

Equivalent unit processing cost for materials: $2,040 ÷ 102,000 = $0.02
Equivalent unit processing cost for labor: $3,570 ÷ 102,000 = $0.035
Equivalent unit processing cost for overhead: $1,020 ÷ 102,000 = $0.01

COSTS APPLICABLE TO THE WORK OF THE DEPARTMENT:

Goods in process, one-fourth completed at the beginning of April:

Costs charged to the beginning inventory of goods in process during previous month	$ 3,785	
Materials added (12,000 × $0.02)	240	
Labor applied (12,000 × $0.035)	420	
Overhead applied (12,000 × $0.01)	120	
Cost to process		$ 4,565

Goods started and finished in the department during April:

Costs in the grinding department (85,000 × $0.214)	$18,190	
Materials added (85,000 × $0.02)	1,700	
Labor applied (85,000 × $0.035)	2,975	
Overhead applied (85,000 × $0.01)	850	
Cost to process		23,715
Total accumulated cost of goods transferred to finished goods (101,000 units at $0.28)		$28,280

Goods in process, one-third processed at the end of April:

Costs in the grinding department (15,000 × $0.214)	$ 3,210	
Materials added (5,000 × $0.02)	100	
Labor applied (5,000 × $0.035)	175	
Overhead applied (5,000 × $0.01)	50	
Cost to one-third process		3,535
Total Costs Accounted for		$31,815

Illustration 23–11

cost summary is the method of handling the grinding department costs transferred to this department. During April, 100,000 units of product with accumulated grinding department costs of $21,400 were transferred to the mixing department. Of these 100,000 units, 85,000 were started in process in the department, finished, and transferred to finished goods. The remaining 15,000 were still in process in the department at the end of the cost period.

Notice in the first section of Illustration 23–11 how the $21,400 of grinding department costs transferred to the mixing department are added to the other costs charged to the department. Compare the information in this first section with the mixing department's goods in process account as it is shown on page 773 and again in Illustration 23–10.

Notice again in the third section of the mixing department's process cost summary how the $21,400 of grinding department costs are apportioned between the 85,000 units started and finished and the 15,000 units still in process in the department. The 16,000 beginning goods in process units received none of this $21,400 charge because they were transferred from the grinding department during the previous month. Their grinding department costs are included in the $3,785 beginning inventory costs.

The third section of the mixing department's process cost summary shows that 101,000 units of product (16,000 beginning inventory units plus 85,000 started and finished) with accumulated costs of $28,280 were completed in the department during April and transferred to finished goods. The cost accountant used the entry on the next page to transfer the accumulated cost of these 101,000 units from the mixing department's goods in process account to the finished goods account.

Goods in Process, Mixing Department

Date		Explanation	Debit	Credit	Balance
Apr.	1	Beginning inventory			3,785
	30	Materials	2,040		5,825
	30	Labor	3,570		9,395
	30	Overhead	1,020		10,415
	30	Units from grinding department	21,400		31,815
	30	Units to finished goods		28,280⌐	3,535

Finished Goods

Date		Explanation	Debit	Credit	Balance
Apr.	30	Units from mixing department	28,280 ◄──── ◄──┘		28,280

Illustration 23–12

Apr.	30	Finished Goods	28,280.00	
		Goods in Process, Mixing Department		28,280.00
		To transfer the accumulated grinding department and mixing department costs of the 101,000 units transferred to Finished Goods.		

Posting the entry had the effect shown in Illustration 23–12.

Cost accounting system. An accounting system based on perpetual inventory records that is designed to emphasize the determination of unit costs and the control of costs.

Equivalent finished units. A measure of production with respect to materials or labor, expressed as the number of units that could have been manufactured from start to finish during a period given the amount of materials or labor used during the period.

Job. A special production order to meet customers' specifications.

Job cost ledger. A subsidiary ledger to the Goods in Process account in which are kept the job cost sheets of unfinished jobs.

Job cost sheet. A record of the costs incurred on a single job.

Job lot. A quantity of identical items manufactured in one lot or single order.

Job order cost system. A cost accounting system in which costs are assembled in terms of jobs or job lots.

Labor time ticket. A record of how an employee's time was spent on the job that serves as the basis for charging jobs and overhead accounts for the employee's wages.

Overapplied overhead. The amount by which overhead applied on the basis of a predetermined overhead application rate exceeds overhead actually incurred.

Predetermined overhead application rate. A rate that is used to charge overhead cost to production; calculated by relating estimated overhead cost for a period to another variable such as estimated direct labor cost.

Process cost system. A cost accounting system in which costs are assembled in terms of steps in manufacturing a product.

Requisition. A document that identifies the materials needed for a certain job and the account to which the materials cost should be charged, and that is given to a storeroom keeper in exchange for the materials.

Underapplied overhead. The amount by which actual overhead incurred

exceeds the overhead applied to production, based on a predetermined application rate and evidenced by a debit balance in the
overhead account.

---

1. Name the two primary types of cost accounting systems and indicate Questions for class discussion which of the two would best fit the needs of a manufacturer who (a) produces special-purpose machines designed to fit the particular needs of
each customer, (b) produces electric generators in lots of 100, and (c)
manufactures copper tubing.

2. Define the following terms in the context of cost accounting:
   a. Job order cost system.
   b. Process cost system.
   c. Job.
   d. Job lot.
   e. Job cost sheet.
   f. Labor time ticket.
   g. Materials requisition.
   h. Process cost summary.

3. The Materials account and the Goods in Process account each serves
   as a control account for a subsidiary ledger. What subsidiary ledgers do
   these accounts control?

4. How is the inventory of goods in process determined in a general accounting system like that described in Chapter 22? How may this inventory be determined in a job cost system?

5. What is the purpose of a job cost sheet? What is the name of the ledger
   containing the job cost sheets of the unfinished jobs in process? What
   account controls this ledger?

6. What business papers are the bases for the job cost sheet entries for (a)
   materials and (b) labor?

7. Refer to the job cost sheet of Illustration 23–3. How was the amount of
   overhead costs charged to this job determined?

8. How is a predetermined overhead application rate established? Why is
   such a predetermined rate used to charge overhead to jobs?

9. Why does a company using a job cost system normally have either overapplied or underapplied overhead at the end of each accounting period?

10. At the end of a cost period the Overhead Costs controlling account has
    a debit balance. Does this represent overapplied or underapplied over-
    head?

11. What are the basic differences in the products and in the manufacturing
    procedures of a company to which a job cost system is applicable as op-
    posed to a company to which a process cost system is applicable?

12. What is an equivalent finished unit of labor? Of materials?

13. What is the assumption on which the idea of an equivalent finished unit
    of, for instance, labor is based?

14. What is the production of a department measured in equivalent finished
    units if it began an accounting period with 8,000 units of product that
    were one-fourth completed at the beginning of the period, started and
    finished 50,000 units during the period, and ended the period with 6,000
    units that were one-third processed at the period end?

15. The process cost summary of a department commonly has three sec-
    tions. What is shown in each section?

Class exercises   **Exercise 23–1**

Part 1. During December 197A, a cost accountant established his company's 197B overhead application rate based on direct labor cost. In setting the rate, he estimated the company would incur $200,000 of overhead costs during 197B and it would apply $160,000 of direct labor to the products that would be manufactured during 197B. Determine the rate.

Part 2. During February 197B, the company of Part 1 began and completed Job No. 619. Determine the job's cost under the assumption that on its completion the job's cost sheet showed the following materials and labor charged to it:

JOB COST SHEET							
Customer's Name _____ Lowview Development _____ Job No. _____ 619							
Job Description _____ 24 Amp. Generator							
	Materials		Labor		Overhead Costs Applied		
Date	Requisition Number	Amount	Time Ticket Number	Amount	Date	Rate	Amount
Feb. 2	1524	68.00	2116	10.00			
3	1527	47.00	2117	20.00			
4	1531	10.00	2122	22.00			

Exercise 23–2

In December 197A, a cost accountant for Jason Company established the following overhead application rate for applying overhead to the jobs that would be completed during 197B:

$$\frac{\text{Estimated overhead costs, } \$147,000}{\text{Estimated direct labor costs, } \$98,000} = 150\%$$

At the end of 197B the company's accounting records showed that $149,-000 of overhead costs had actually been incurred during 197B and $100,000 of direct labor, distributed as follows, had been applied to jobs during the year.

Direct labor on jobs completed and sold.....................................	$ 85,000
Direct labor on jobs completed and in the finished goods inventory...	10,000
Direct labor on jobs still in process	5,000
	$100,000

Required:

1. Set up an Overhead Costs T-account and enter on the proper sides the amounts of overhead costs incurred and applied. State whether overhead was overapplied or underapplied during the year.

2. Give the entry to close the Overhead Costs account and allocate its balance between jobs sold, jobs finished but unsold, and jobs in process.

Exercise 23-3

Franklin Company uses a job cost system in which overhead is charged to jobs on the basis of direct labor cost, and at the end of a year the company's Goods in Process account showed the following:

Goods in Process

Materials	85,000	To finished goods	205,500
Labor	60,000		
Overhead	75,000		

Required:

1. Determine the overhead application rate used by the company under the assumption that the labor and overhead costs actually incurred were the same as the amounts estimated.
2. Determine the cost of the labor and the cost of the overhead charged to the one job in process at the year-end under the assumption it had $5,500 of materials charged to it.

Exercise 23-4

During a cost period a department finished and transferred 56,000 units of product to finished goods, of which 16,000 were in process in the department at the beginning of the cost period and 40,000 were begun and completed during the period. The 16,000 beginning inventory units were three-fourths completed when the period began. In addition to the 56,000 units completed, 12,-000 more units were in process in the department, one-half completed when the period ended.

Required:

Calculate the equivalent units of product completed in the department during the cost period.

Exercise 23-5

Assume the department of Exercise 23-4 had $25,000 of labor charged to it during the cost period of the exercise and that labor is applied in the process of the department evenly throughout the process.

Required:

Calculate the cost of an equivalent unit of labor in the department and the portion of the department's $25,000 labor cost that should be assigned to each of its inventories and to the units started and finished.

Exercise 23-6

Forty-eight thousand units of product were completed in a department and transferred to finished goods during a cost period. Of these 48,000 units, 12,000 were in process and were one-third completed at the beginning of the period and 36,000 units were begun and completed during the period. In addition to the 48,000 units completed, 10,000 more units were in process in the department three-fifths processed at the period end.

Required:

Calculate the equivalent units of material added to the product processed in the department during the period under each of the following unrelated assumptions: (*a*) All material added to the product of the department is added when the department's process is first begun. (*b*) The material added to the product of the department is added evenly throughout the department's process. (*c*) One half the material added in the department is added when the department's process is first begun and the other half is added when the process is three-fourths completed.

Problems

Problem 23–1

A cost accountant for Snell Company estimated before a year began that the company would incur during the year the direct labor cost of 20 persons working 2,000 hours each at an average rate of $3 per hour. The accountant also estimated that the following overhead costs would be incurred during the year:

Indirect labor	$15,750
Superintendence.........................	12,000
Rent of factory building..............	7,200
Heat, lights, and power	4,800
Insurance expense......................	3,400
Depreciation of machinery...........	24,200
Machinery repairs	3,000
Supplies expense........................	1,500
Miscellaneous factory expenses	1,350
Total............................	$73,200

At the end of the year for which the estimates were made the cost records showed the company had actually incurred $73,350 of overhead costs and had completed and sold five jobs which had direct labor costs as follows: Job No. 603, $25,400; Job No. 604, $23,200; Job No. 605, $21,700; Job No. 606, $22,800; and Job No. 607, $24,900. In addition Job No. 608 was in process at the period end and had had $2,500 of direct labor and its share of overhead costs charged.

Required:

Under the assumption the concern used a predetermined overhead application rate based on the foregoing overhead and direct labor estimates, determine: (1) the predetermined application rate used, (2) the total overhead applied to jobs during the year, and (3) the over- or underapplied overhead at the year-end. (4) Under the further assumption that the company considered the amount of its over- or underapplied overhead to be immaterial, give the entry to close the Overhead Costs account.

Problem 23–2

A company completed the following internal and external transactions, among others, during a cost period:

a. Purchased materials on account, $16,000.
b. Paid factory wages, $12,400.
c. Paid miscellaneous factory overhead costs, $800.
d. Material requisitions were used during the cost period to charge materials to jobs. The requisitions were then accumulated until the end of the cost period when they were totaled and recorded with a general journal entry. (Instructions for this entry are given in Item j.) An abstract of the requisitions showed the following materials charged to jobs. (Charge the materials to the jobs by making entries directly in the job T-accounts in the subsidiary Job Cost Ledger.)

Job No. 1........ $ 2,600
Job No. 2........   1,300
Job No. 3........   2,800
Job No. 4........   3,000
Job No. 5........   600
      Total $10,300

e. Labor time tickets were used to charge jobs with direct labor. The tickets were then accumulated until the end of the cost period when they were totaled and recorded with a general journal entry. (Instructions for the entry are given as Item k.) An abstract of the tickets showed the following labor charged to jobs. (Charge the labor to the jobs by making entries directly in the job T-accounts in the Job Cost Ledger.)

Job No. 1........ $2,400
Job No. 2........   1,400
Job No. 3........   2,600
Job No. 4........   2,800
Job No. 5........   400
      Total $9,600

f. Job Nos. 1, 3, and 4 were completed and transferred to finished goods. A predetermined overhead application rate, 150% of direct labor cost, was used to apply overhead to each job upon its completion. (Enter the overhead in the job T-accounts; mark the jobs "completed"; and make a general journal entry to transfer their costs to the Finished Goods account.)
g. Job Nos. 1 and 3 were sold on account for a total of $24,000.
h. At the end of the cost period, charged overhead to the jobs in process at the rate of 150% of direct labor cost. (Enter the overhead in the job T-accounts.)
i. At the end of the cost period made a general journal entry to record: depreciation, factory building, $2,300; depreciation, machinery, $4,100; expired factory insurance, $600; and accrued factory taxes payable, $1,200.
j. Separated the material requisitions into direct material requisitions and indirect material requisitions, totaled each kind, and made a general journal entry to record them. The requisition totals were:

Direct materials...... $10,300
Indirect materials....   2,000
      Total $12,300

k. Separated the labor time tickets into direct labor time tickets and indirect labor time tickets, totaled each kind, and made a general journal entry to record them. The time ticket totals were:

Direct labor...... $ 9,600
Indirect labor....   3,100
        Total $12,700

l. Determined the total overhead assigned to all jobs and made a general journal entry to record it.

Required:

1. Open the following general ledger T-accounts: Materials, Goods in Process, Finished Goods, Factory Payroll, Overhead Costs, and Cost of Goods Sold.
2. Open an additional T-account for each of the five jobs. Assume that each job's T-account is a job cost sheet in a subsidiary Job Cost Ledger.
3. Prepare general journal entries to record the applicable information of Items *a, b, c, f, g, i, j, k,* and *l.* Post the entry portions that affect the general ledger accounts opened.
4. Enter the applicable information of Items *d, e, f,* and *h* directly in the T-accounts that represent job cost sheets.
5. Present statistics to prove the balances of the Goods in Process and Finished Goods accounts.
6. List the general ledger accounts and tell what is represented by the balance of each.

Problem 23–3

If the working papers that accompany this text are not being used, omit this problem.

Lakatos Company manufactures to the special order of its customers a machine called a dynatester. On January 1 the company had a $2,230 materials inventory but no inventories of goods in process and finished goods. However, on that date it began Job No. 1, a dynatester for Farsome Company, and Job No. 2, for Nearsome Company; and during the January cost period it completed the following summarized internal and external transactions:

1. Recorded invoices for the purchase of materials on credit. The invoices and receiving reports carried this information:
   Receiving report No. 1, Material A, 200 units at $11 each.
   Receiving report No. 2, Material B, 300 units at $5 each.
   (*Record the invoices with a single general journal entry and post to the general ledger T-accounts, using the transaction number to identify the amounts in the accounts. Enter the receiving report information on the proper materials ledger cards.*)
2. Materials were requisitioned as follows:
   Requisition No. 1, for Job No. 1, 100 units of Material A.
   Requisition No. 2, for Job No. 1, 120 units of Material B.
   Requisition No. 3, for Job No. 2, 80 units of Material A.
   Requisition No. 4, for Job No. 2, 100 units of Material B.
   Requisition No. 5, for 10 units of machinery lubricant.
   (*Enter the requisition amounts for direct materials on the materials ledger cards and on the job cost sheets. Enter the indirect material*

amount on the proper materials ledger card and debit it to the Indirect Materials account in the subsidiary Overhead Costs Ledger. Assume the requisitions are accumulated until the end of the month and will be recorded with a general journal entry. Instructions for this entry follow in the problem.)

3. Received the following labor time tickets from the timekeeping department:

    Time tickets Nos. 1 through 60 for direct labor on Job No. 1, $1,000.
    Time tickets Nos. 61 through 100 for direct labor on Job No. 2, $800.
    Time tickets Nos. 101 through 120 for machinery repairs, $375.

    (Charge the direct labor time tickets to the proper jobs and charge the indirect labor time tickets to the Indirect Labor account in the subsidiary Overhead Costs Ledger. Assume the time tickets are accumulated until the end of the month for recording with a general journal entry.)

4. Made the following cash disbursements during the month:

    Paid the month's factory payroll, $2,100.
    Paid for miscellaneous overhead items totaling $1,000.

    (Record the payments with general journal entries and post the general ledger accounts. Enter the charge for miscellaneous overhead items in the subsidiary Overhead Costs Ledger.)

5. Finished Job No. 1 and transferred it to the finished goods warehouse. *(The company charges overhead to each job by means of a predetermined overhead application rate based on direct labor costs. The rate is 80%. (1) Enter the overhead charge on the cost sheet of Job No. 1. (2) Complete the cost summary section of the cost sheet. (3) Mark "Finished" on the cost sheet. (4) Prepare and post a general journal entry to record the job's completion and transfer to finished goods.)*

6. Prepared and posted a general journal entry to record both the cost of goods sold and the sale of Job No. 1 to Farsome Company, sale price $5,000.

7. At the end of the cost period, charged overhead to Job No. 2 based on the amount of direct labor applied to the job thus far. *(Enter the applicable amount of overhead on the job's cost sheet.)*

8. Totaled the requisitions for direct materials, totaled the requisitions for indirect materials, and made and posted a general journal entry to record them.

9. Totaled the direct labor time tickets, totaled the indirect labor time tickets, and made and posted a general journal entry to record them.

10. Determined the amount of overhead applied to jobs and made and posted a general journal entry to record it.

Required:

1. Record the transactions as instructed in the narrative.
2. Complete the statements in the book of working papers by filling in the blanks.

Problem 23-4

In the sanding department of a processing concern labor is added to the department's product evenly throughout its processing. During a cost period 50,000 units of product were finished in this department and transferred to finished goods. Of these 50,000 units, 15,000 were in process at the beginning of the period and 35,000 were begun and completed during the period. The

15,000 beginning goods in process units were one-fifth completed when the period began. In addition to the foregoing units, 9,000 additional units were in process and were one-third completed at the period end.

Required:

Under the assumption that $13,800 of labor was charged to the sanding department during the period, determine (1) the equivalent units of labor applied to the department's product, (2) the cost of an equivalent unit of labor, and (3) the shares of the $13,800 that should be charged to the beginning inventory, the units started and finished, and the ending inventory.

Problem 23-5

The product of Rosewell Manufacturing Company is produced on a continuous basis in a single processing department in which material, labor, and overhead are added to the product evenly throughout the manufacturing process.

At the end of the current May cost period, after the material, labor, and overhead costs were charged to the Goods in Process account of the single processing department, the account appeared as follows:

Goods in Process

May	1	Balance	1,362	
	31	Materials	5,325	
	31	Labor	10,863	
	31	Overhead	15,194	
			32,744	

During the cost period the company finished and transferred to finished goods 72,000 units of the product, of which 9,000 were in process at the beginning of the period and 63,000 were begun and finished during the period. The 9,000 that were in process were one-third processed when the period began. In addition to the foregoing units, 8,000 additional units were in process and were one-fourth completed at the end of the cost period.

Required:

1. Prepare a process cost summary for the department.
2. Draft the general journal entry to transfer to Finished Goods the cost of the product finished in the department during the month.

Problem 23-6

Easytime Processing Company manufactures a simple product on a continuous basis in one department. All materials are added in the manufacturing process of this product when the process is first begun. Labor and overhead are added evenly throughout the process.

During the current April cost period the company completed and transferred to finished goods 43,000 units of the product. These consisted of 5,000 units that were in process at the beginning of the period and 38,000 units begun and finished during the period. The 5,000 beginning goods in process units were complete as to materials and four-fifths complete as to labor and overhead when the period began. In addition to the foregoing units, 6,000 additional units were in process at the end of the period, complete as to materials and one-half complete as to labor and overhead.

Since the company has only one processing department, it has only one Goods in Process account. At the end of the period, after entries recording material, labor, and overhead had been posted, the account appeared as follows:

Goods in Process

Apr.	1	Balance	5,333
	30	Materials	27,060
	30	Labor	9,744
	30	Overhead	14,868
			57,005

Required:

Prepare a process cost summary and the entry to transfer to Finished Goods the cost of the product completed in the department during April.

Problem 23–1A

Alternate problems

Late in 197A a cost accountant for Breton Company established the 197B overhead application rate by estimating that the company would assign ten persons to direct labor tasks during 197B and that each person would work 2,000 hours at $3 per hour during the year. At the same time the accountant estimated that the company would incur the following amounts of overhead costs during 197B:

Indirect labor	$20,000
Factory building rent	12,000
Depreciation expense, machinery	15,000
Machinery repairs expense	3,000
Heat, lights, and power	6,000
Factory supplies expense	1,000
Total	$57,000

At the end of 197B the accounting records showed the company had actually incurred $58,560 of overhead costs during the year while completing four jobs and beginning the fifth. The completed jobs were assigned overhead on completion, and the in-process job was assigned overhead at the year-end. The jobs had the following direct labor costs:

Job No. 1 (sold and delivered)	$12,800
Job No. 2 (sold and delivered)	13,000
Job No. 3 (sold and delivered)	14,200
Job No. 4 (in finished goods inventory)	14,000
Job No. 5 (in process, unfinished)	7,000
Total	$61,000

Required:

1. Determine the overhead application rate established by the cost accountant under the assumption it was based on direct labor cost.
2. Determine the total overhead applied to jobs during the year and the amount of over- or underapplied overhead at the year-end.
3. Give the entry to dispose of the over- or underapplied overhead by prorating it between goods in process, the finished goods inventory, and cost of goods sold.

Problem 23–2A

During its first cost period a company completed the following internal and external transactions:

a. Purchased materials on account, $22,000.
b. Paid factory wages, $18,800.
c. Paid miscellaneous factory overhead costs, $3,000.
d. Material requisitions were used during the cost period to charge materials to jobs. The requisitions were then accumulated until the end of the cost period when they were totaled and recorded with a general journal entry. (Instructions for the entry are given in Item *j.*) An abstract of the requisitions showed the following materials charged to jobs. (Charge the materials to the jobs by making entries directly in the job T-accounts in the subsidiary Job Cost Ledger.)

Job No. 1.......	$ 4,000
Job No. 2.......	2,100
Job No. 3.......	3,900
Job No. 4.......	4,300
Job No. 5.......	800
Total....	$15,100

e. Labor time tickets were used to charge jobs with direct labor. The tickets were then accumulated until the end of the cost period when they were totaled and recorded with a general journal entry. (Instructions for the entry are given as Item *k.*) An abstract of the tickets showed the following labor charged to jobs. (Charge the labor to the jobs by making entries directly in the job T-accounts in the Job Cost Ledger.)

Job No. 1.......	$ 3,800
Job No. 2.......	2,200
Job No. 3.......	4,000
Job No. 4.......	3,600
Job No. 5.......	400
Total....	$14,000

f. Job Nos. 1, 3, and 4 were completed and transferred to finished goods. A predetermined overhead application rate, 200% of direct labor cost, was used to apply overhead to each job upon its completion. (Enter the overhead in the job T-accounts; mark the jobs "completed"; and make a general journal entry to transfer their costs to the Finished Goods account.)
g. Job Nos. 1 and 4 were sold on account for a total of $40,000.
h. At the end of the cost period, charged overhead to the jobs in process,

using the 200% of direct labor cost application rate. (Enter the overhead in the job T-accounts.)

i. Made a general journal entry at the end of the cost period to record depreciation on the factory building, $6,000; machinery depreciation, $6,700; expired factory insurance, $1,200; and accrued factory taxes payable, $2,000.

j. Separated the material requisitions into direct material requisitions and indirect material requisitions, totaled each kind, and made a general journal entry to record them. The requisition totals were:

Direct materials $15,100
Indirect materials   4,000
Total $19,100

k. Separated the labor time tickets into direct labor time tickets and indirect labor time tickets, totaled each kind, and made a general journal entry to record them. The time ticket totals were:

Direct labor............ $14,000
Indirect labor..........   5,000
Total $19,000

l. Determined the total overhead assigned to all jobs and made a general journal entry to record it.

Required:

1. Open the following general ledger T-accounts: Materials, Goods in Process, Finished Goods, Factory Payroll, Overhead Costs, and Cost of Goods Sold.
2. Open an additional T-account for each of the five jobs. Assume that each job's T-account is a job cost sheet in a subsidiary Job Cost Ledger.
3. Prepare general journal entries to record the applicable information of Items a, b, c, f, g, i, j, k, and l. Post the entry portions that affect the general ledger accounts opened.
4. Enter the applicable information of Items d, e, f, and h directly in the T-accounts that represent job cost sheets.
5. Present statistics to prove the balances of the Goods in Process and Finished Goods accounts.
6. List the general ledger accounts and tell what is represented by the balance of each.

Problem 23–4A

The Harris Machine Shop is a one department operation in which labor and overhead are added to the department's product evenly throughout the production process. In July, 42,000 units of product were transferred from the shop to finished goods inventory. Included in these 42,000 units were 16,000 units from the June 30 work in process inventory, at which time those units were one-fourth finished. In addition to the beginning inventory, 54,000 units were placed in process during July. On July 31, the units which remained in process were one-half complete. Total overhead costs of the shop incurred during July were $93,600.

Required:

Determine (1) the equivalent units of production in July to be used in applying overhead costs to the product of the shop, (2) the overhead cost of an equivalent unit of production, and (3) the portions of July overhead cost that should be charged to completing the units in beginning inventory, to units started and finished during July, and to the ending inventory.

Problem 23–5A

Two operations, cutting and molding, and two departments are used in the manufacturing procedure of Gorge Manufacturing Company. The procedure is begun in the cutting department and completed in the molding department.

At the beginning of the May cost period there were 5,000 units of product in the cutting department which were three-fifths processed. These units were completed during the period and transferred to the molding department. Also, the processing of 31,000 additional units was begun in the cutting department during the period. Of these 31,000 units, 23,000 were finished and transferred to the molding department. The remaining 8,000 units were in the department in a one-half processed state at the end of the period.

It is assumed that the material, labor, and overhead applied in the cutting department are applied evenly throughout the process of the department.

At the end of the cost period, after entries recording materials, labor, and overhead were posted, the company's Goods in Process, Cutting Department account appeared as follows:

Goods in Process, Cutting Department

May	1	Balance	2,901	
	31	Materials	9,280	
	31	Labor	12,209	
	31	Overhead	6,090	
			30,480	

Required:

1. Prepare a process cost summary for the cutting department.
2. Prepare the journal entry to transfer to the molding department the cost of the goods completed in the cutting department and transferred.

Decision problem 23–1, Rayford Processing

Rayford Processing Company uses a job order cost system in accounting for manufacturing costs, and following are a number of its general ledger accounts with the January 1 balances and some January postings shown. The postings are incomplete. Commonly only the debit or credit of a journal entry appears in the accounts, with the offsetting debits and credits being omitted. Also, the amounts shown represent total postings for the month and no date appears. However, this additional information is available: (1) The company charges jobs with overhead on the basis of direct labor cost, using a 150% overhead application rate. (2) The $17,000 debit in the Overhead Costs account represents the sum of all overhead costs for January other than indirect materials and indirect labor. (3) The accrued factory payroll on January 31 was $3,000.

Materials	
Jan. 1 Bal. 11,000	12,000
15,000	

Factory Payroll	
19,000	Jan. 1 Bal. 2,000

Goods in Process	
Jan. 1 Bal. 6,000	48,000
Materials 10,000	
Labor 16,000	

Cost of Goods Sold	

Finished Goods	
Jan. 1 Bal. 12,000	50,000

Factory Overhead Costs	
17,000	

Copy the accounts on a sheet of paper, supply the missing debits and credits, and tie together the debits and credits of an entry with key letters. Answer these questions: (1) What was the January 31 balance of the Finished goods account? (2) How many dollars of factory labor cost (direct plus indirect) were incurred during January? (3) What was the cost of the goods sold during January? (4) How much overhead was actually incurred during the month? (5) How much overhead was charged to jobs during the month? (6) Was overhead overapplied or underapplied during the month?

The production facility of the Browning Company was nearly destroyed on June 10, 197B, as a consequence of an explosion and fire in the plant. Assets lost in the blaze included all of the inventories. In addition, many of the accounting records were destroyed. In preparation for settlement with the insurance company, you are requested to estimate the amounts of raw materials, goods in process, and finished goods destroyed. Through your investigation, you determined that the company used a job order cost system, and also obtained the following additional information:

Decision problem 23–2, The Browning Company

a. The company's December 31, 197A, balance sheet showed the following inventory amounts: materials, $15,000; goods in process, $21,000; and finished goods, $24,000. The balance sheet also showed a $3,000 liability for accrued factory wages payable.
b. The overhead application rate used by the company was 70% of direct labor cost.
c. Goods costing $81,000 were sold and delivered to customers between January 1 and June 10, 197B.
d. Materials purchased between January 1 and June 10 amounted to $31,000, and $27,000 of direct and indirect materials were issued to the factory during the same period.
e. Factory wages totaling $35,000 were paid between January 1 and June 10, and there were $1,000 of accrued factory wages payable on the latter date.
f. The debits to the Overhead Costs account during the period before the fire totaled $21,000 of which $3,000 was for indirect materials and $5,000 was for indirect labor.

g. The cost of goods finished and transferred to finished goods inventory during the January 1 to June 10 period amounted to $76,000.

h. It was decided that the June 10 balance of the Overhead Costs account should be apportioned between goods in process, finished goods, and cost of goods sold. Between January 1 and June 10 the company had charged the following amounts of overhead to jobs: to jobs sold, $12,740; to jobs finished but unsold, $3,920; and to jobs still in process on June 10, $2,940.

Determine the June 10 inventories of materials, goods in process, and finished goods. (T-accounts may be helpful in organizing the data.)

Decision problem 23-3, Handy Tool Company

Handy Tool Company manufactures a single product, a tool that it sells to distributors who in turn sell to hardware stores. The company uses a job cost system to accumulate costs on job lots of tools. During the past several years it has sold an average of 30,000 of the tools annually at $20 each, using about 80% of its production capacity. Next year's estimated costs for manufacturing the tool, assuming 30,000 units are produced, are $14 per unit and consist of the following:

Materials	$ 4.00
Direct labor	4.00
Manufacturing overhead (150% of direct labor cost)	6.00
Estimated cost per unit	$14.00

The company's overhead application rate was established at 150% two years ago by the accountant who set up its cost system. The same rate was used again last year and proved satisfactory, since sales volume and costs did not materially vary from the previous year. The company had planned to use the 150% rate again next year, and it had estimated next year's overhead costs at $180,000 and direct labor costs for 30,000 units at $120,000. However, although the company's volume and costs have been stable in the recent past, this morning it received an offer from a mail-order company to purchase 6,000 units of its tool at $12.50 each with the mail-order company's name attached. No changes in the tool are required to fit it to the mail-order company's specifications other than affixing the company's name, which will cost 25 cents per unit for additional materials.

The company president can see no point in accepting the order, for, as he says, "Why manufacture and sell something when you lose money on every unit sold?" The sales manager is not sure the new business should be rejected, and he has asked that a further study of costs be made before a final decision is reached.

You have been asked to make the cost study. In your investigation you find that next year's estimated manufacturing overhead consists of $150,000 of what is known as fixed overhead costs plus variable overhead costs of $1 per unit for 30,000 units, which together total $180,000. (Fixed overhead costs are such costs as depreciation of factory building, taxes, insurance, and the like. They receive their name from the fact that their total amounts do not change with a change in the number of units produced but remain fixed. Variable overhead costs are costs that vary with the number of units produced and are for such things as power and indirect materials.)

You also find that selling and administrative expenses consist of $100,000 of fixed expenses plus 50 cents per unit of variable selling and administrative expenses. Acceptance of the mail-order business will not affect fixed costs nor change present variable costs per unit, including material and direct labor costs per unit.

Attach to your report a condensed columnar income statement that shows the revenue, costs, and before-tax income from present business in its first two columns; the revenue, costs, and before-tax income from the new business in the second columns; and the combined results of present and the new business in the third set of columns. In preparing the statement, show as separate amounts the material, direct labor, fixed overhead, variable overhead, fixed selling and administrative, and variable selling and administrative costs for present business, for the new business, and combined.

PART 8

Planning and controlling business operations

24
The master budget: A formal plan for the business . . .

25
Cost-volume-profit analysis . . .

26
Flexible budgets; standard costs . . .

27
Capital budgeting; managerial decisions . . .

28
Tax considerations in business decisions

After studying Chapter 24, you should be able to:

- Explain the importance of budgeting.
- Describe the specific benefits to be derived from budgeting.
- List the sequence of steps involved in preparing a master budget.
- Prepare each budget in a master budget and explain the importance of each budget to the overall budgeting process.
- Integrate the individual budgets into planned financial statements.
- Define or explain the words and phrases listed in the chapter Glossary.

chapter 24

The master budget: A formal plan for the business

The process of managing a business consists of two basic elements: planning and control. If a business is to accomplish the variety of objectives expected of it, management must first carefully plan the activities and events the business should enter and accomplish during future weeks, months, and years. Then, as the activities take place, they must be monitored and controlled so that actual events conform as closely as possible to the plan.

Although the management functions of planning and control are perhaps equally important to insure the long-run success of a business, most business failures are generally said to result from inadequate planning. Countless pitfalls can be avoided if management carefully anticipates the future conditions within which the business will operate and prepares a detailed plan of the activities the business should pursue. Furthermore, the plans for future business activities should be formally organized and preserved. This process of planning future business actions and expressing those plans in a formal manner is called *budgeting*. Correspondingly, a *budget* is a formal statement of future plans. Since the economic or financial aspects of the business are the primary matters of consideration, a budget is usually expressed in monetary terms.

When the plan to be formalized is a comprehensive or overall plan for the business, the resulting budget is called a *master budget*. As an overall plan, the master budget should include specific plans for expected sales, the units of product to be produced, the materials or merchandise to be purchased, the expense payments to be made, the long-term assets to be purchased, and the amount of cash to be borrowed, if any. The planned activities of each subunit of the business should be separately organized and presented within the master budget. Thus, the master budget for a business consists of several subbudgets,

The master budget

all of which articulate or join with each other to form the overall, co-ordinated plan for the business. As finally presented, the master budget typically includes sales, expense, production, equipment, and cash budgets. In addition, the expected impact of the planned future activities may be expressed in terms of a planned income statement for the budget period and a planned balance sheet for the end of the budget period.

Benefits from budgeting

All business managements engage in planning; some planning is absolutely necessary if business activities are to continue. However, a typical characteristic of poor management is sloppy or incomplete planning. On the other hand, if the management plans carefully and formalizes its plans completely enough, that is, if the management engages in a thorough budgeting process, it may expect to obtain the following benefits.

Study, research, and a focus on the future

When a concern plans with sufficient care and detail to prepare a budget, the planning process usually involves thorough study and research. Not only should this result in the best conceivable plans but it should also instill in executives the habit of doing a reasonable amount of research and study before decisions are made. In short, budgeting tends to promote good decision-making processes. In addition, the items of interest to a budgetary investigation lie in the future. Thus, the attention of management is focused on future events and the associated opportunities available to the business. The pressures of daily operating problems naturally tend to take precedence over planning, thereby leaving the business without carefully thought-out objectives. Budgeting counteracts this tendency by formalizing the planning process; it makes planning an explicit responsibility of management.

The basis for evaluating performance

The control function of management requires that performance be evaluated in light of some norms or objectives. On the basis of this evaluation, appropriate corrective actions can be implemented. In evaluating performance, there are two alternative norms or objectives against which actual performance can be compared: (1) past performance or (2) expected (budgeted) performance. Although past performance is sometimes used as the basis of comparison, budgeted performance is generally superior for determining whether actual performance is acceptable or in need of corrective action. Past performance fails to take into account all of the environmental changes that may impact on the performance level. For example, in the evaluation of sales performance, past sales may have occurred under economic conditions that were dramatically different from those that apply to the current sales effort. Economy-wide fluctuations, competitive shifts within the industry, new product line developments, increased or decreased advertizing commitments, and so forth, all tend to invalidate comparisons between past performance and present performance. On the other hand, budgeted (anticipated) performance levels are developed after a research and study process which attempts to take such environmental factors into account. Thus, budgeting provides the benefit of a superior basis for evaluating performance and a more effective control mechanism.

Coordination

Coordination requires that a business be operated as a whole rather than as a group of separate departments. When a budget plan is prepared, each department's objectives are determined in advance, and these objectives are coordinated; for example, the production department is scheduled to produce approximately the number of units the selling department can sell. The purchasing department is to buy raw materials on the basis of production scheduled, and the hiring activities of the personnel department are to take into account budgeted production levels. Obviously, the departments and activities of a business must be closely coordinated if the business operations are to be efficient and profitable. Budgeting provides this coordination.

Communication

In a very small business, adequate communication of business plans might be accomplished by direct contact between the employees. Frequent conversations could perhaps serve as the means of communicating business plans that have been approved by management. However, oral conversations often leave ambiguities and potential confusion if not backed up by documents that clearly state the content of the plans. Further, businesses need not be very large before informal conversations become obviously inadequate. When a budget is prepared, the budget becomes a means of informing the organization not only of plans that have been approved by management but also of budgeted actions management wishes the organization to take during the budget period.

A source of motivation

Since budgeted data provide the standards against which actual performance is evaluated, the budget and the manner in which it is used may significantly affect the attitudes of those who are to be evaluated. If the budgeted level of performance is unrealistic, if the personnel who will be evaluated in terms of the budget are not consulted or involved in preparing the budget, or if the subsequent evaluations of performance are rendered critically without offering the affected employees an opportunity to explain the reasons for performance failures, the whole budgeting process may have a negative impact on the attitudes of the employees. But, if the affected employees are consulted when the budget is prepared, if obtainable objectives are budgeted, and if the subsequent evaluations of performance are made fairly with opportunities provided to explain performance deficiencies, budgeting can be a strongly positive, motivating force in the organization. Budgeted performance levels can provide goals that individuals will attempt to attain or even exceed as they fulfill their responsibilities to the organization.

The budget committee

The task of preparing a budget should not be made the responsibility of any one department; and the budget definitely should not be handed down from above as the "final word." Rather budget figures and budget estimates should be developed from the bottom up. For example, the sales department should have a hand in preparing sales estimates and the production department should have initial responsibility for preparing its own expense budget. Otherwise production and salespeople may say the budget figures are meaningless, as they were prepared by front office personnel who know nothing of sales and production problems.

Nevertheless, the preparation of a budget needs central guidance, and this is commonly supplied by a budget committee of department heads or other high-level executives who are responsible for seeing that budget figures are realistically established and coordinated. If a department submits budget figures that do not reflect proper performance, the figures should be returned to the department with the budget committee's comments. The originating department then either adjusts the figures or defends them. It should not change the figures just to please the committee, since it is important that all parties agree that the figures are reasonable and attainable.

The budget period

Budget periods normally coincide with accounting periods. This means that in most companies the budget period is one year in length. However, in addition to their annual budgets, many companies prepare long-range budgets setting forth major objectives for from three to five or ten years in advance. These long-range budgets are particularly important in planning for major expenditures of capital to buy plant and equipment. Additionally, the financing of major capital projects, for example, by issuing bonds, by issuing stock, by retaining earnings, and so forth, can be anticipated and planned as a part of preparing long-range budgets.

Long-range budgets of two, three, five, and ten years should reflect the planned accomplishment of long-range objectives. Within this context, the annual master budget for a business reflects the objectives that have been adopted for the next year. The annual budget, however, is commonly broken down into quarterly or monthly budgets. Short-term budgets of a quarter or a month are useful yardsticks that allow management to evaluate actual performance and take corrective actions promptly. After the quarterly or monthly results are known, the actual performance is compared to the budgeted amounts in a report similar to that disclosed in Illustration 24–1.

Consolidated Stores, Inc.
Income Statement with Variations from Budget for Month Ended April 30, 19—

	Actual	Budget	Variations
Sales	$63,500	$60,000	$+ 3,500
Less: Sales returns and allowances	1,800	1,700	+ 100
Sales discounts	1,200	1,150	+ 50
Net sales	$60,500	$57,150	$+ 3,350
Cost of goods sold:			
Merchandise inventory, April 1, 19—	$42,000	$44,000	$— 2,000
Purchases, net	39,100	38,000	+ 1,100
Freight-in	1,250	1,200	+ 50
Goods for sale	$82,350	$83,200	$— 850
Merchandise inventory, April 30, 19—	41,000	44,100	— 3,100
Cost of goods sold	$41,350	$39,100	$+ 2,250
Gross profit	$19,150	$18,050	$+ 1,100
Operating expenses:			
Selling expenses:			
Sales salaries	$ 6,250	$ 6,000	$+ 250
Advertising expense	900	800	+ 100
Store supplies used	550	500	+ 50
Depreciation of store equipment	1,600	1,600	
Total selling expenses	$ 9,300	$ 8,900	$+ 400
General and administrative expenses:			
Office salaries	$ 2,000	$ 2,000	
Office supplies used	165	150	$+ 15
Rent	1,100	1,100	
Expired insurance	200	200	
Depreciation of office equipment	100	100	
Total general and administrative expenses	$ 3,565	$ 3,550	$+ 15
Total operating expenses	$12,865	$12,450	$+ 415
Income from Operations	$ 6,285	$ 5,600	$+ 685

Illustration 24–1

Many businesses follow the practice of "continuous" budgeting, and are said to prepare "rolling" budgets. As each monthly or quarterly budget period goes by, these firms revise their entire set of budgets, adding new monthly or quarterly sales, production, expense, equipment, and cash budgets to replace the ones that have elapsed. Thus, at any point in time, monthly or quarterly budgets are available for a full year in advance.

As indicated in the previous discussion, the master budget consists of a number of budgets that collectively express the planned activities of the business. The number and arrangement of the budgets included in the master budget depend on the size and complexity of the business. However, a master budget typically includes:

Preparing the master budget

1. Operating budgets.
   a. Sales budget.
   b. For merchandising companies: Merchandise purchases budget.
   c. For manufacturing companies:
      (1) Production budget (stating the number of units to be produced).
      (2) Manufacturing budget.
   d. Selling expense budget.
   e. General and administrative expense budget.
2. Capital expenditures budget, which includes the budgeted expenditures for new plant and equipment.
3. Financial budgets.
   a. Budgeted statement of cash receipts and disbursements, called the cash budget.
   b. Budgeted income statement.
   c. Budgeted balance sheet.

In addition to these budgets, numerous calculations or schedules may be required to support the information disclosed in these budgets.

Some of the budgets listed above cannot be prepared until other budgets on the list are first completed. For example, the merchandise purchases budget cannot be prepared until the sales budget is available, since the number of units to be purchased depends upon how many units are budgeted to be sold. As a consequence, preparation of the budgets within the master budget must follow a definite sequence, as follows:

First: The sales budget must be prepared first because the operating and financial budgets depend upon information provided by the sales budget.

Second: The remaining operating budgets are prepared next. For manufacturing companies, the production budget must be prepared prior to the manufacturing budget, since the number of units to be manufactured obviously affects the amounts of materials, direct labor, and overhead to be budgeted. Other than this, the budgets for manufacturing costs or merchandise costs, general and administrative expenses, and selling expenses may be prepared in any sequence.

Third: If capital expenditures are anticipated during the budget period the capital expenditures budget is prepared next. This budget usually depends upon long-range sales forecasts more than it does upon the sales budget for the next year.

Fourth: Based upon the information provided in the above budgets, the budgeted statement of cash receipts and disbursements is prepared. If this budget discloses unrealistic disbursements compared to planned receipts, the previous plans may have to be revised.

Fifth: The budgeted income statement is prepared next. If the plans contained in the master budget result in unsatisfactory profits, the entire master budget may be revised to incorporate any corrective measures available to the firm.

Sixth: The budgeted balance sheet for the end of the budget period is prepared last. An analysis of this statement may also lead to revisions in the previous budgets. For example, the budgeted balance sheet may disclose too much debt resulting from an overly ambitious capital expenditures budget, and revised plans may be necessary.

The following sections explain the procedures involved in preparing the budgets that comprise the master budget. Northern Company, a wholesaler of a single product, provides an illustrative basis for the discussion. The September 30, 197A, balance sheet for Northern Company is presented in Illustration 24–2. The master budget for Northern Company is prepared on a monthly basis, with a budgeted balance sheet prepared for the end of each quarter. Also, a budgeted income statement is prepared for each quarter. In the following sections, Northern Company budgets are prepared for October, November, and December, 197A.

Preparation of the master budget illustrated

Northern Company
Balance Sheet, September 30, 197A

Cash	$ 20,000	Accounts payable	$ 58,200
Accounts receivable	42,000	Loan from bank	10,000
Inventory (9,000 units @ $6)	54,000	Accrued income taxes payable (Due	
Equipment*	200,000	October 15, 197A)	20,000
Less accumulated depreciation	(36,000)	Common stock	150,000
		Retained earnings	41,800
Total	$280,000	Total	$280,000

* The equipment is being depreciated on a straight-line basis over ten years. Estimated salvage value is $20,000.

Illustration 24–2

Sales budget

The sales budget, an estimate of goods to be sold and revenue to be derived from sales, is the starting point in the budgeting procedure, since the plans of all departments are related to sales and expected revenue. The sales budget commonly grows from a reconciliation of forecasted business conditions, plant capacity, proposed selling expenses, such as advertising, and estimates of sales. As to sales estimates, since people normally feel a greater responsibility for reaching goals they have had a hand in setting, the sales personnel of a concern is often asked to submit through the sales manager estimates of sales for each territory and department. The final sales budget is then based on these estimates as reconciled for forecasted business conditions, selling expenses, and so forth.

During September 197A, Northern Company sold 7,000 units of product at a price of $10 per unit. After obtaining the estimates of sales personnel and taking into account the economic conditions affecting the market for Northern Company's product, the sales budget (Illustration 24–3) is established for October, November, and December, 197A. Since the purchasing department must base December 197A purchases on estimated sales for January 197B, the sales budget is expanded to include January 197B.

Northern Company
Monthly Sales Budget
October 197A–January 197B

	Budgeted Unit Sales		Budgeted Unit Price		Budgeted Total Sales
September 197A (actual)	7,000	×	$10	=	$ 70,000
October 197A...................	10,000	×	$10	=	$100,000
November 197A................	8,000	×	$10	=	$ 80,000
December 197A................	14,000	×	$10	=	$140,000
January 197B...................	9,000	×	$10	=	$ 90,000

Illustration 24–3

Observe in Illustration 24–3 that the sales budget is more detailed than simple projections of total sales; both unit sales and unit prices are forecasted. Some budgeting procedures are less detailed, expressing the budget only in terms of total sales volume. Also, many sales budgets are far more detailed than the one illustrated. The more detailed sales budgets may show units and unit prices for each of many different products, classified by salesperson and by territory or by department.

Merchandise purchases budget

A variety of sophisticated techniques have been developed to assist management in making inventory purchase decisions. All of these techniques recognize that the number of units to be added to inventory depends upon the budgeted sales volume. Whether a company manufactures or purchases the product it sells, budgeted future sales volume is the primary factor to be considered in most inventory management situations.

The amount of merchandise or materials to be purchased each month is determined as follows:

Budgeted sales for the month	XXX
Add the budgeted end-of-the-month inventory....	XXX
Required amount of available merchandise.........	XXX
Deduct the beginning-of-the-month inventory.....	(XXX)
Inventory to be purchased...............................	XXX

The calculation may be made in either dollars or in units. If the calculation is in units and only one product is involved, the number of dollars of inventory to be purchased may be determined by multiplying units to be purchased by the cost per unit.

After considering the cost of maintaining an investment in inventory and the potential cost associated with a temporary inventory shortage, Northern Company has decided that the number of units in its inventory at the end of each month should equal 90% of the next month's sales. In other words, the inventory at the end of October should equal 90% of the budgeted November sales, the November ending inventory should equal 90% of the expected December sales, and so on. Also, the company's suppliers have indicated that the September 197A per unit cost of $6 can be expected to remain unchanged through January 197B. Based on these factors the company prepared the merchandise purchases budget of Illustration 24–4.

Northern Company
Merchandise Purchases Budget
October, November, December, 197A

	October	November	December
Next month's budgeted sales (in units)	8,000	14,000	9,000
Ratio of inventory to future sales	×90%	×90%	×90%
Desired end-of-the-month inventory	7,200	12,600	8,100
Budgeted sales for the month (in units)	10,000	8,000	14,000
Required units of available merchandise	17,200	20,600	22,100
Deduct beginning-of-the-month inventory	(9,000)	(7,200)	(12,600)
Number of units to be purchased	8,200	13,400	9,500
Budgeted cost per unit	×$6	×$6	×$6
Budgeted cost of merchandise purchases	$49,200	$80,400	$57,000

Illustration 24–4

The calculations in Northern Company's merchandise purchases budget differ slightly from the basic calculation previously given in that the first lines are devoted to determining the desired end-of-each-month inventory. Also, budgeted sales are added to the desired end-of-each-month inventory instead of vice versa, and on the last lines the number of dollars of inventory to be purchased is determined by multiplying units to be purchased by the cost per unit.

It was previously mentioned that some budgeting procedures are designed to provide only the total dollars of budgeted sales. Likewise, the merchandise purchases budget may not state the number of units to be purchased, and may be expressed only in terms of the total cost of merchandise to be purchased. In such situations, it is assumed that there is a constant relationship between sales and cost of goods sold. For example, Northern Company expects that cost of goods sold will equal 60% of sales. (Note that the budgeted sales price is $10 and the budgeted unit cost is $6.) Thus, its cost of purchases can be budgeted in dollars on the basis of budgeted sales, without requiring information on the number of units involved.

Production budgets and manufacturing budgets

Since Northern Company does not manufacture the product it sells, its budget for acquiring goods to be sold is a merchandise purchases budget (Illustration 24–4). If Northern Company had been a manufacturing company, a production budget rather than a merchandise purchases budget would be required. In a production budget the number of units to be produced each month is shown, and for Northern Company such a budget would be very similar to a merchandise purchases budget. It would differ in that the indicated number of units to be purchased each month (see Illustration 24–4) would be described as the number of units to be manufactured each month. Also, it would not show costs, since a production budget is always expressed entirely in terms of units of product and does not include budgeted production costs. Such costs are shown in the manufacturing budget, which is based on the budgeted production volume shown in the production budget.

A manufacturing budget shows the budgeted costs for raw materials, direct labor, and manufacturing overhead. In many manufacturing companies, the manufacturing budget is actually prepared in the form of three subbudgets: a raw materials purchases budget, a direct labor budget, and a manufacturing overhead budget. These budgets show the total budgeted cost of goods to be manufactured during the budget period.

Selling expense budget

The responsibility for preparing a budget of selling expenses typically falls on the vice president, marketing or the equivalent sales manager. Although budgeted selling expenses should affect the expected amount of sales, the typical procedure is to prepare a sales budget first and then to budget selling expenses. Estimates of selling expenses are based on the tentative sales budget and upon the experience of previous periods adjusted for known changes. After the entire master budget is prepared on a tentative basis, it may be decided that the projected sales volume is inadequate. If so, subsequent adjustments in the sales budget would generally require that corresponding adjustments be made in the selling expense budget.

Northern Company's selling expenses consist of commissions paid to sales personnel and a $24,000 per year salary, paid on a monthly basis to the sales manager. Sales commissions amount to 10% of total sales and are paid during the month the sales are made. The selling expense budget for Northern Company is presented in Illustration 24–5.

General and administrative expenses

General and administrative expenses usually are the responsibility of the office manager, who should therefore be charged with the task of

Northern Company
Selling Expense Budget
October, November, December, 197A

	October	November	December	Total
Budgeted sales	$100,000	$80,000	$140,000	$320,000
Sales commission percentage	×10%	×10%	×10%	×10%
Sales commissions	$ 10,000	$ 8,000	$ 14,000	$ 32,000
Salary for sales manager ($24,000/12 = $2,000 per month)	2,000	2,000	2,000	6,000
Total selling expenses	$ 12,000	$10,000	$ 16,000	$ 38,000

Illustration 24–5

preparing the budget for these items. The amounts of some general and administrative expenses may depend upon budgeted sales volume. However, most of these expenses depend more upon other factors such as management policies, inflationary influences, and so forth, than they do upon monthly fluctuations in sales volume. Although interest expense and income tax expense are frequently classified as general and administrative expenses, they generally cannot be budgeted at this point in the budgeting sequence. Interest expense must await preparation of the cash budget, which determines the need for loans, if any. Income tax expense must await preparation of the budgeted income statement, at which time taxable income and income tax expense can be estimated.

General and administrative expenses for Northern Company include administrative salaries amounting to $54,000 per year and depreciation of $18,000 per year on equipment (see Illustration 24–2). The salaries are paid each month as they are earned. Illustration 24–6 shows the budget for these expenses.

Northern Company
General and Administrative Expense Budget
October, November, December, 197A

	October	November	December	Total
Administrative salaries ($54,000/12 = $4,500)	$4,500	$4,500	$4,500	$13,500
Depreciation of equipment ($18,000/12 = $1,500)	1,500	1,500	1,500	4,500
	$6,000	$6,000	$6,000	$18,000

Illustration 24–6

Capital expenditures budget

The capital expenditures or plant and equipment budget lists equipment to be scrapped and additional equipment to be purchased if the proposed production program is carried out. The purchase of additional equipment requires funds; and anticipating equipment additions in advance normally makes it easier to provide the funds.

Also at times estimated production may exceed plant capacity. Budgeting makes it possible to anticipate this and either revise the production schedule or increase plant capacity. Planning plant and equipment purchases is called capital budgeting, and this is discussed in more detail in Chapter 27.

Northern Company does not anticipate any sales or retirements of equipment through December 197A. However, management plans to acquire additional equipment for $25,000 cash near the end of December 197A.

Cash budget

After tentative sales, merchandise purchases, expenses, and capital expenditures budgets have been set, the cash budget is prepared. This budget is important because a company should have at all times enough cash to meet needs but not too much. Too much cash is undesirable because it often cannot be profitably invested. A cash budget requires management to forecast cash receipts and disbursements, and usually results in better cash management. Also, it enables management to arrange well in advance for loans to cover any anticipated inadequacies.

In preparing the cash budget, anticipated receipts are added to the beginning cash balance and anticipated expenditures are deducted. If the resulting cash balance is inadequate, the required additional cash is provided in the budget through planned increases in loans.

Much of the information that is needed to prepare the cash budget can be obtained directly from the previously prepared operating and capital expenditures budgets. However, further investigation and additional calculations may be necessary to determine the amounts to be included.

Illustration 24–7 shows the cash budget for Northern Company. October's beginning cash balance was obtained from the September 30, 197A, balance sheet (Illustration 24–2).

Budgeted sales of Northern Company are shown in Illustration 24–3. An investigation of previous sales records indicates that 40% of Northern Company's sales are for cash. The remaining 60% are credit sales, and customers can be expected to pay for these sales in the month after the sales are made. Thus, the budgeted cash receipts from customers are calculated as follows:

	September	October	November	December
Sales	$70,000	$100,000	$80,000	$140,000
Credit sales percentage	×60%	×60%	×60%	×60%
Accounts receivable, end of month	$42,000	$ 60,000	$48,000	$ 84,000
Cash sales percentage		×40%	×40%	×40%
Cash sales		$ 40,000	$32,000	$ 56,000
Collections of accounts receivable		42,000	60,000	48,000
Total cash receipts		$ 82,000	$92,000	$104,000

Observe in the calculation that the October cash receipts consist of $40,000 from cash sales ($100,000 × 40%) plus the collection of $42,000 of accounts receivable as calculated in the previous column. Also, note that each month's total cash receipts are listed on the second line of Illustration 24–7.

Northern Company
Cash Budget
October, November, December, 197A

	October	November	December
Beginning cash balance	$ 20,000	$ 20,000	$ 22,272
Cash receipts from customers	82,000	92,000	104,000
Total	$102,000	$112,000	$126,272
Cash disbursements:			
Payments for merchandise	$ 58,200	$ 49,200	$ 80,400
Sales commissions (Illustration 24–5)	10,000	8,000	14,000
Salaries: Sales (Illustration 24–5)	2,000	2,000	2,000
Administrative (Illustration 24–6)	4,500	4,500	4,500
Accrued income taxes payable	20,000		
Dividends ($150,000 × 0.02 = $3,000)		3,000	
Interest on loan from bank:			
$10,000 × 0.01 = $100	100		
$22,800 × 0.01 = $228		228	
Purchase of equipment			25,000
Total cash disbursements	$ 94,800	$ 66,928	$125,900
Balance	$ 7,200	$ 45,072	$ 372
Additional loan from bank	12,800		19,628
Repayment of loan from bank		(22,800)	
Ending cash balance	$ 20,000	$ 22,272	$ 20,000
Loan balance, end of month	$ 22,800	$ –0–	$ 19,628

Illustration 24–7

Northern Company's purchases of merchandise are entirely on account, and full payments are made regularly in the month following purchase. Thus, in Illustration 24–7, the cash disbursements for purchases are obtained from the September 30, 197A, balance sheet (Illustration 24–2) and from the merchandise purchases budget (Illustration 24–4), as follows:

September 30, accounts payable equal October payments	$58,200
October purchases equal November payments	49,200
November purchases equal December payments	80,400

Sales commissions and all salaries are paid monthly, and the budgeted cash disbursements for these items are obtained from the selling expense budget (Illustration 24–5) and the general and administrative expense budget (Illustration 24–6).

As indicated in the September 30, 197A, balance sheet (Illustration 24–2), accrued income taxes are paid in October. Estimated income tax expense for the quarter ending December 31 is 40% of net income and is due in January 197B.

Northern Company pays 2% quarterly cash dividends, and the November payment of $3,000 is the planned disbursement for this item. Also, Northern Company has an agreement with the bank whereby additional loans are granted at the end of each month if they are necessary to maintain a minimum cash balance of $20,000 at the end of the month. Interest is paid at the end of each month at the rate of 1% per month; and if the cash balance at the end of a month exceeds $20,000, the excess is used to repay the loans to the bank. Illustration 24–7 indicates that the $10,000 loan from the bank at the end of September was not sufficient to provide a $20,000 cash balance at the end of October and, as a result, the loan was increased by $12,800 at the end of October. The entire loan was repaid at the end of November, and $19,628 was again borrowed at the end of December.

Budgeted income statement

One of the final steps in preparing a master budget is to summarize the effects of the various budgetary plans on the income statement. The necessary information to prepare a budgeted income statement is drawn primarily from the previously prepared budgets or from the investigations that were made in the process of preparing those budgets.

For many companies, the volume of information that must be summarized in the budgeted income statement and the budgeted balance sheet is so large that a working paper must be used to accumulate all of the budgeted transactions and to classify them in terms of their impact on the income statement and/or on the balance sheet. However, the transactions and account balances of Northern Company are few in number, and the budgeted income statement (and balance sheet) can be prepared simply by inspecting the previously discussed budgets and recalling the information that was provided in the related discussions. Northern Company's budgeted income statement is shown in Illustration 24–8.

Budgeted balance sheet

If a work sheet is used to prepare the budgeted income statement and balance sheet, the first two columns of the work sheet are used to list the estimated post-closing trial balance of the period prior to the budget period. Next the budgeted transactions and adjustments are entered in the second pair of work sheet columns in the same manner as end-of-period adjustments are entered on an ordinary work sheet. For example, if the budget calls for sales on account of $250,000, the name of the Sales account is entered on the work sheet in the Account Titles column below the names of the post-closing trial

Northern Company
Budgeted Income Statement for Three Months Ended December 31, 197A

Sales (Illustration 24–3, 32,000 units @ $10)........................		$320,000
Cost of goods sold (32,000 units @ $6)............................		192,000
Gross profit...		$128,000
Operating expenses:		
Sales commissions (Illustration 24–5)..............................	$32,000	
Sales salaries (Illustration 24–5).....................................	6,000	
Administrative salaries (Illustration 24–6)..........................	13,500	
Depreciation on equipment (Illustration 24–6)....................	4,500	
Interest expense (Illustration 24–7)..................................	328	(56,328)
Net income before income taxes.................................		$ 71,672
Income tax expense ($71,672 × 40%)...................................		(28,669)
Net Income...		$ 43,003

Illustration 24–8

balance accounts; and then Sales is credited and Accounts Receivable is debited for $250,000 in the second pair of money columns. After all budgeted transactions and adjustments are entered on the work sheet, the estimated post-closing trial balance amounts in the first pair of money columns are combined with the budget amounts in the second pair of columns and are sorted to the proper Income Statement and Balance Sheet columns of the work sheet. Finally, the information in these columns is used to prepare the budgeted income statement and budgeted balance sheet.

As previously mentioned, the transactions and account balances of Northern Company are few in number, and its budgeted balance sheet, shown in Illustration 24–9 (below), can be prepared simply by inspecting the previously prepared budgets and recalling the related discussions of those budgets.

Northern Company
Budgeted Balance Sheet, December 31, 197A

Assets:		
Cash (Illustration 24–7)...		$ 20,000
Accounts receivable (page 810)..		84,000
Inventory (Illustration 24–4, 8,100 units @ $6)..................		48,600
Equipment (Illustrations 24–2 and 24–7).........................	$225,000	
Less accumulated depreciation (Illustrations 24–2 and 24–6)...	40,500	184,500
Total Assets...		$337,100
Liabilities:		
Accounts payable (Illustration 24–4)...............................	$ 57,000	
Accrued income taxes payable (Illustration 24–8)..............	28,669	
Bank loan payable (Illustration 24–7)..............................	19,628	$105,297
Stockholders' Equity:		
Common stock (Illustration 24–2).....................................	$150,000	
Retained earnings (see discussion)...................................	81,803	231,803
Total Liabilities and Stockholders' Equity..................		$337,100

Illustration 24–9

Observe that the retained earnings balance in Illustration 24–9 is $81,803. This amount was determined as follows:

Retained earnings, September 30, 197A (Illustration 24–2)	$41,800
Net income for three months ended December 31, 197A (Illustration 24–8)	43,003
Total	$84,803
Dividends declared in November, 197A (Illustration 24–7)	(3,000)
Retained earnings, December 31, 197A	$81,803

Glossary

Budget. A formal statement of future plans, usually expressed in monetary terms.

Budgeting. The process of planning future business actions and expressing those plans in a formal manner.

Capital expenditures budget. A listing of the plant and equipment to be purchased if the proposed production program is carried out; also called the plant and equipment budget.

Cash budget. A forecast of cash receipts and disbursements.

Manufacturing budget. A statement of the estimated costs for raw materials, direct labor, and manufacturing overhead associated with producing the number of units estimated in the production budget.

Master budget. A comprehensive or overall plan for the business that typically includes budgets for sales, expenses, production, equipment, cash, and also a planned income statement and balance sheet.

Merchandise purchases budget. An estimate of the units (or cost) of merchandise to be purchased by a merchandising company.

Production budget. An estimate of the number of units to be produced during a budget period.

Rolling budgets. A sequence of revised budgets that are prepared in the practice of continuous budgeting.

Sales budget. An estimate of goods to be sold and revenue to be derived from sales; serves as the usual starting point in the budgeting procedure.

Questions for class discussion

1. What is a budget? What is a master budget?

2. What are the benefits from budgeting?

3. How does the process of budgeting tend to promote good decision making?

4. What are the basic alternative norms or objectives against which actual performance can be compared and evaluated? Which of the two is generally superior?

5. Why should each department be asked to prepare or at least to participate in the preparation of its own budget estimates?

6. What are the duties of the budget committee?

7. What is the normal length of a master budget period? How far in advance are long-range budgets generally prepared?

8. What is meant by the terms "continuous" budgeting and "rolling" budgets?

9. What are the three primary types of budgets that make up the master budget?

10. In comparing merchandising companies and manufacturing companies, what differences show up in the operating budgets?

11. What is the sequence that is followed in preparing the set of budgets that collectively make up the master budget?

12. What is a sales budget? A selling expense budget? A capital expenditures budget?

13. What is the difference between a production budget and a manufacturing budget?

14. What is a cash budget? Why must it be prepared after the operating budgets and the capital expenditures budget?

Class
exercises

Exercise 24–1

The sales budget of Coast Department Store's Department B calls for $8,400 of sales during March. The department expects to begin March with a $6,700 inventory and end the month with a $5,500 inventory. Its cost of goods sold averages 65% of sales.

Required:

Prepare a merchandise purchases budget for Department B showing the amount of goods to be purchased during March.

Exercise 24–2

Simon Company manufactures a product called Zipalls. The company's management estimates there will be 3,800 units of Zipalls in the March 31 finished goods inventory, that 12,500 units will be sold during the year's second quarter, that 16,000 units will be sold during the third quarter, and that 20,000 units will be sold during the fourth quarter. Management also believes the concern should begin each quarter with units in the finished goods inventory equal to 30% of the next quarter's budgeted sales.

Required:

Prepare a production budget showing the units of Zipalls to be manufactured during the year's second quarter and third quarter.

Exercise 24-3

A company has budgeted the following cash receipts and cash disbursements from operations during the second quarter of 197A:

	Receipts	Disbursements
April	$250,000	$170,000
May	90,000	200,000
June	170,000	130,000

According to a credit agreement with the bank, the company promises to maintain a minimum, end-of-month cash balance of $20,000. In return, the bank has agreed to provide the company the right to receive loans up to $100,000 with interest of 12% per year, paid monthly on the last day of the month. If the loan must be increased during the last ten days of a month to provide enough cash to pay bills, interest will not begin to be charged until the end of the month.

The company is expected to have a cash balance of $20,000 and a loan balance of $10,000 on March 31, 197A.

Required:

Prepare a monthly cash budget for the second quarter of 197A.

Exercise 24-4

Using the following information, prepare a cash budget showing expected cash receipts and disbursements for the month of June and the balance expected on June 30.

1. Beginning cash balance on June 1, $33,000.
2. Budgeted sales for June: $250,000; 40% are collected in the month of sale, 50% in the next month, 5% in the following month, and 5% are uncollectible.
3. Sales for May: $300,000.
4. Sales for April: $200,000.
5. Budgeted merchandise purchases for June: $150,000; 50% are paid in month of purchase; 50% are paid in the month following purchase.
6. Merchandise purchased in May: $100,000.
7. Budgeted cash disbursements for salaries in June, $64,000.
8. Depreciation expense in June: $4,000.
9. Other cash expenses budgeted for June: $18,000.
10. Budgeted taxes payable in June: $42,000.
11. Budgeted interest payable on bank loan in June: $2,400.

Exercise 24-5

Based on the information provided in Exercise 24-4 and the additional information which follows, prepare a budgeted income statement for the month of June and a budgeted balance sheet for June 30.

1. Cost of goods sold is 55% of sales.
2. The inventory at the end of May was $45,000.
3. Salaries payable on May 31 was $10,000 and is expected to be $12,000 on June 30.
4. The Equipment account shows a balance of $384,000. On May 31, Accumulated Depreciation had a balance of $92,000.

5. The $2,400 cash payment of interest represents the 1% monthly expense on a bank loan of $240,000.
6. Income taxes payable on May 31 amounted to $42,000, and the income tax rate applicable to the company is 48%.
7. The 5% of sales which prove to be uncollectible are debited to Bad Debts Expense and credited to Allowance for Doubtful Accounts during the year of sale. However, specific accounts that prove to be uncollectible are not written off until the second month after the sale, at which time all accounts not yet collected are so written off.
8. The only balance sheet accounts other than those implied by the previous discussion are Common Stock, which shows a balance of $100,000, and Retained Earnings, which showed a balance of $103,000 on May 31.

Problems

Problem 24–1

Welling Manufacturing Company manufactures a steel product called a "sand tap." Each "sand tap" requires 80 pounds of steel and is produced in a single operation by a stamping process. The concern's management estimates there will be 1,500 units of the product and 50 tons of steel on hand on March 31 of the current year, and that 12,000 units of the product will be sold during the year's second quarter. Management also believes that due to the possibility of a strike in the steel industry, the concern should begin the third quarter with a 150-ton steel inventory and 2,000 finished "sand taps." Steel can be purchased for approximately $480 per ton ($0.24 per pound).

Required:

Prepare a second-quarter production budget and a second-quarter steel purchases budget for the company.

Problem 24–2

During the latter part of February, the owner of Cottonwood Store approached the bank for a $10,000 loan to be made on April 1 and repaid 60 days thereafter with interest at 6%. The owner planned to increase the store's inventory by $10,000 during March and needed the loan to pay for the merchandise during April. The bank's loan officer was interested in Cottonwood Store's ability to repay the loan and asked the owner to forecast the store's May 31 cash position.

On March 1 Cottonwood Store was expected to have a $4,100 cash balance, $28,000 of accounts receivable, and $14,600 of accounts payable. Its budgeted sales, purchases, and cash expenditures for the following three months are as follows:

	March	April	May
Sales	$24,000	$25,000	$23,000
Merchandise purchases	25,500	15,000	14,000
Payroll	2,400	2,400	2,400
Rent	1,000	1,000	1,000
Other cash expenses	1,200	1,100	1,300
Repayment of bank loan			10,100

The budgeted March purchases include the inventory increase. All sales are on account; and past experience indicates 80% is collected in the month following the sale, 15% in the next month, 4% in the next, and the remainder is not collected. Application of this experience to the March 1 accounts receivable balance indicates $22,500 of the $28,000 will be collected during March, $4,000 during April, and $1,000 during May. All merchandise is paid for in the month following its purchase.

Required:

Prepare cash budgets for March, April, and May for Cottonwood Store under the assumption the bank loan will be paid on May 31.

Problem 24–3

Lyndale Company has a cash balance of $25,000 on June 1, 197A. The product sold by the company sells for $25 per unit. Actual and projected sales are:

April, actual	$200,000
May, actual	150,000
June, estimated	250,000
July, estimated	200,000
August, estimated....	180,000

Experience has shown that 50% of the billings are collected in the month of sale, 30% in the second month, 15% in the third month, and 5% will prove to be uncollectible.

All purchases are payable within 15 days. Thus, approximately 50% of the purchases in a month are due and payable in the next month. The unit purchase cost is $16. Lyndale Company's management has established a policy of maintaining an end-of-month inventory of 100 units plus 50% of the next month's unit sales, and the June 1 inventory is consistent with this policy.

Selling and general administrative expenses (excluding depreciation) for the year amount to $360,000 and are distributed evenly throughout the year.

Required:

Prepare a monthly cash budget for June and July, with supporting schedules showing cash receipts from collections of receivables and cash payments for merchandise purchases.

Problem 24–4

Shortly before the end of 197A, XYZ Company's management prepared a budgeted balance sheet for December 31, 197A, as follows:

XYZ Company
Balance Sheet
For December 31, 197A

Cash	$ 5,000	Accounts payable	$ 8,000
Accounts receivable........	15,000	Loan from bank	5,000
Inventory.......................	25,000	Taxes payable (due March	
Equipment	60,000	15, 197B).....................	12,000
Accumulated depreciation	(6,000)	Common stock................	50,000
		Retained earnings............	24,000
Total....................	$99,000	Total....................	$99,000

In the process of preparing a master budget for January, February, and March 197B, the following information has been obtained:

1. The product sold by XYZ Company is purchased for $10 per unit and resold for $15 per unit. Although the inventory level on December 31, 197A, (2,500 units) is smaller than desired, management has established a new inventory policy for 197B whereby the end-of-month inventory should be 80% of the next month's expected sales (in units). Budgeted unit sales are: January, 10,000; February, 9,000; March, 12,000; April, 12,000.

2. Total sales each month are 50% for cash and 50% on account. Of the credit sales, 80% are collected in the first month after the sale and 20% in the second month after the sale. Similarly, 80% of the Accounts Receivable balance on December 31, 197A, should be collected during January and 20% should be collected in February.

3. Merchandise purchased by the company is paid for as follows: 70% in the month after purchase and 30% in the second month after purchase. Similarly, 70% of the Accounts Payable balance on December 31, 197A, will be paid during January and 30% will be paid during February.

4. Sales commissions amounting to 10% of sales are paid each month. Additionally, the salary of the sales manager is $12,000 per year.

5. Repair expenses amount to $500 per month and are paid in cash. General administrative salaries amount to $108,000 per year.

6. The equipment shown in the December 31, 197A, balance sheet was purchased one year ago. It is being depreciated over ten years according to the straight-line method. Regarding new purchases of equipment, management has decided to take a full month's depreciation (rounded to the nearest dollar) during the month the equipment is purchased, and to use straight-line depreciation over ten years, assuming no salvage value. The company plans to purchase additional equipment worth $10,000 in January, $5,000 in February, and $15,000 in March.

7. The company plans to acquire some land in March at a cost of $100,000. The land will not require a cash outlay until the last day of March. Thus, if a bank loan is necessary, the first payment of interest will be due at the end of April.

8. XYZ Company has an arrangement with the bank whereby additional loans are available as they are needed at a rate of 10% per year, paid monthly. If part or all of a loan is repaid during a month, the payment will be made on the last day of the month, along with any interest that is due. XYZ Company has agreed to maintain an end-of-month cash balance of at least $5,000.

9. The income tax rate applicable to the company is 48%. However, tax on the income for the first quarter of 197B will not be paid until April.

Required:

Prepare a master budget for the first quarter of 197B, with the operating budgets, capital expenditures budget, and the cash budget prepared on a monthly basis. The budgeted income statement should show operations for the first quarter, and the budgeted balance sheet should be prepared as of March 31, 197B. The operating budgets included in the master budget should include a sales budget (showing both budgeted unit sales and dollar sales), a merchandise purchases budget, a selling expense budget, and a general and administrative expense budget. Round all amounts to the nearest dollar.

Problem 24–1A

Big Bend Sales Company sells three products that it purchases in their finished ready-for-sale state. The products' March 1 inventories are Product X, 3,900 units; Product Y, 3,750 units; and Product Z, 6,300 units. The company's manager is disturbed because each product's March 1 inventory is excessive in relation to immediately expected sales. Consequently, he has set as a goal a month-end inventory for each product that is equal to one half the following month's expected sales. Expected sales in units for March, April, May, and June are as follows:

Expected Sales in Units

	March	*April*	*May*	*June*
Product X.....	5,000	4,600	5,000	3,800
Product Y.....	2,800	2,800	3,400	3,600
Product Z.....	6,000	5,400	5,200	5,800

Required:

Prepare purchases budgets in units for the three products for each of March, April, and May.

Problem 24–2A

Oceanic Company expects to have a $5,800 cash balance on December 31 of the current year. It also expects to have a $35,200 balance of accounts receivable and $20,900 of accounts payable. Its budgeted sales, purchases, and cash expenditures for the following three months are:

	January	*February*	*March*
Sales......................................	$24,000	$18,000	$27,000
Purchases..............................	14,000	17,300	18,000
Payroll....................................	2,400	2,400	2,800
Rent.......................................	1,000	1,000	1,000
Other cash expenses.................	1,200	1,600	1,400
Purchase of store equipment.......	–	5,000	–
Payment of quarterly dividend	–	–	4,000

All sales are on account; and past experience indicates that 85% will be collected in the month following the sale, 10% in the next month, and 4% in the third month. Notwithstanding these expectations for future sales, an analysis of the December 31 accounts receivable balance indicates that $28,000 of the $35,200 balance will be collected in January, $5,200 in February, and $1,600 in March.

Purchases of merchandise on account are paid in the month following each purchase; likewise, the store equipment will be paid for in the month following its purchase.

Required:

Prepare cash budgets for the months of January, February, and March.

Problem 24–3A

The actual and projected monthly sales of Frantz Company are as follows:

September 197A, actual......... $240,000
October 197A, actual............   160,000
November 197A, estimated....   190,000
December 197A, estimated 230,000
January 197B, estimated........ 210,000

Experience has shown that 40% of the sales are collected in the month of sale, 40% are collected in the first month after the sale, 18% in the second month after the sale, and 2% prove to be uncollectible.

Merchandise purchased by the Frantz Company is paid for ten days after the date of purchase. Thus, approximately one third of the purchases in a month are due and paid for in the next month. Frantz Company pays $25 per unit of merchandise and subsequently sells the merchandise for $50 per unit. Frantz Company always plans to maintain an end-of-month inventory of 250 units plus 60% of the next month's unit sales, and the October 31, 197A, inventory is consistent with this policy.

In addition to cost of goods sold, Frantz Company incurs other operating expenses (excluding depreciation) of $582,000 per year, and they are distributed evenly throughout the year. On October 31, 197A, the company has a cash balance of $40,000.

Required:

Prepare a monthly cash budget for November and December, with supporting schedules showing cash receipts from collections of receivables and cash payments for merchandise purchases. Round all amounts to the nearest dollar.

Fibertool Corporation produces a Product X which requires 4 pounds of fiberglass per unit of X. The owner of Fibertool Corporation is in the process of negotiating with the bank for the approval to make loans as they are needed by the company. One of the important items in their discussion has been the question of how much cash will be needed to pay for purchases of fiberglass. Fibertool Corporation purchases fiberglass on account, and the resulting payables are paid in cash as follows: 60% during the month after purchase and 40% during the second month after purchase. The company plans to manufacture enough units of X to maintain an end-of-month inventory of finished units equal to 70% of the next month's sales, and enough fiberglass is purchased each month to maintain an end-of-month inventory equal to 50% of the next month's production requirements. Budgeted sales (in units) are as follows: February, 4,000; March, 6,000; April, 7,000; and May, 8,000. On January 31, 197A, the following data are available: finished units of Product X on hand, 2,800; pounds of fiberglass on hand, 10,800; Accounts Payable, $140,000 due in February plus $60,000 due in March.

Decision problem 24–1, Fibertool Corporation

In recent months the price of fiberglass has varied substantially, and the owner estimates that during the next few months the price could range from $10 to $15 per pound. You are asked to assist the owner by estimating the cash payments to be made in February, in March, and in April. In preparing your answer, you should prepare separate estimates based on a $10 price and a $15 price.

After studying Chapter 25, you should be able to:

- Describe the different types of cost behavior experienced by a typical company.

- State the assumptions that underlie cost-volume-profit analysis and explain how these assumptions restrict the usefulness of the information obtained from the analysis.

- Calculate a break-even point for a single product company and plot the costs and revenues of a company on a graph.

- Describe some extensions that may be added to the basic cost-volume-profit analysis of break-even point.

- Calculate a composite sales unit for a multiproduct company and a break-even point for such a company.

- Define or explain the words and phrases listed in the chapter Glossary.

chapter 25

Cost-volume-profit analysis

Cost-volume-profit analysis is a means of predicting the effect of changes in costs and sales levels on the income of a business. In its simplest form it involves the determination of the sales level at which a company neither earns a profit nor incurs a loss, in other words, the point at which it breaks even. For this reason it is often called break-even analysis. However, the technique can be expanded to answer additional questions, such as: What sales volume is necessary to earn a desired net income? What net income will be earned if unit selling prices are reduced in order to increase sales volume? What net income will be earned if a new machine that will reduce unit labor costs is installed? What net income will be earned if we change the sales mix? When the technique is expanded to answer such additional questions, the descriptive phrase, "cost-volume-profit analysis," is more appropriate than "break-even analysis."

Cost behavior

Conventional cost-volume-profit analyses require that costs be classified as either fixed or variable. However, when costs are examined, it is recognized that some are definitely fixed in nature, others are recognized to be variable, but still others are neither fixed nor completely variable.

Fixed costs

A fixed cost remains unchanged in total amount over a wide range of production levels. For example, if the factory building is rented for, say, $1,000 per month, this cost remains the same whether the factory operates on a one-shift, two-shift, or an around-the-clock basis. Likewise, the cost is the same whether one hundred units of product are produced in a month, a thousand units are produced, or any other number up to the full capacity of the plant. However, it should be observed that while fixed costs remain the same in total when the level of production changes, fixed costs per unit of product decrease as volume increases. For example, if rent is $1,000 per month and two units of product are produced in a month, the rent cost per unit is $500; but if production is increased to ten units per month, rent cost per unit decreases to $100. Likewise it decreases to $2 per unit if production is increased to 500 units per month.

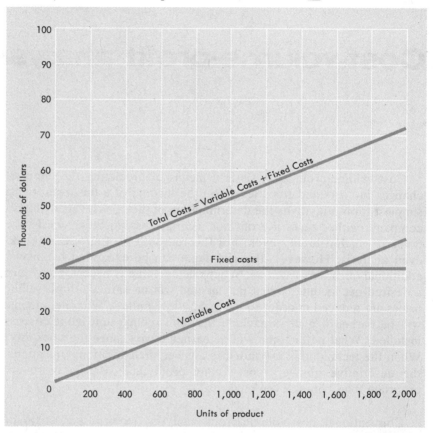

Illustration 25–1

When production volume is plotted on a graph, units of product are shown on the horizontal axis and dollars of cost are shown on the vertical axis. Fixed costs are then expressed as a horizontal line, since the total amount of fixed costs remains constant at all levels of production. This is shown in the Illustration 25–1 graph where the fixed costs remain at $32,000 at all production levels up to 2,000 units of product.

Variable costs

A variable cost changes in total amount as production volume changes. For example, the cost of the material that enters into a product is a variable cost. If material costing $20 is required in the production of one unit of product, material costs are $20 if one unit of product is manufactured, $40 if two units are manufactured, $60 if three units are manufactured, and so on up for any number of units. In other words, the variable cost per unit of production remains constant while the total amount of variable cost changes in direct proportion to changes in the level of production. Variable costs appear on a graph as a straight line that climbs up the graph as the production volume increases, as in Illustration 25–1.

Other costs

Costs are not necessarily either fixed or variable. Some costs are semivariable. They go up with volume but not in the same proportion. Other costs go up in steps, for example, supervisory salaries. Supervisory salaries may be more or less fixed for any production volume from zero to the maximum that can be completed on a one-shift basis. Then if an additional shift must be added to increase production, a whole new group of supervisors must be hired and supervisory salaries go up by a lump-sum amount. They then remain fixed at this level until a third shift is added when they go up another lump sum. In addition to semivariable and "stair step" costs, there are costs that are curvilinear (curved line) in nature. They go up with volume, but when plotted on a graph, they must be plotted as a curved line. For example, people who work the second shift in a factory are generally not as productive as those who work the regular or daytime shift, and people on the third or "graveyard" shift are usually even less productive. Consequently, labor costs will rise more rapidly than volume when such shifts are added. The plotting of curvilinear and "stair step" costs is shown in Illustration 25–2 on the next page.

Conventional cost-volume-profit analysis is based on relationships that can be expressed as straight lines. The lines are then compared in order to answer the questions to which the analysis is applicable. Consequently, the reliability of the answers secured through application of the technique rests on three basic assumptions, which for any one analysis are:

Cost assumptions

1. The per unit selling price is constant. (The selling price per unit will remain the same regardless of production level.)
2. The costs that are classified as "variable" do, in fact, behave as variable costs, that is, the actual (variable) cost per unit of production remains constant.
3. The costs that are classified as "fixed" do, in fact, remain constant over wide changes in the level of production.

When these assumptions are met, costs and revenues may be correctly represented by straight lines. However, the actual behavior of

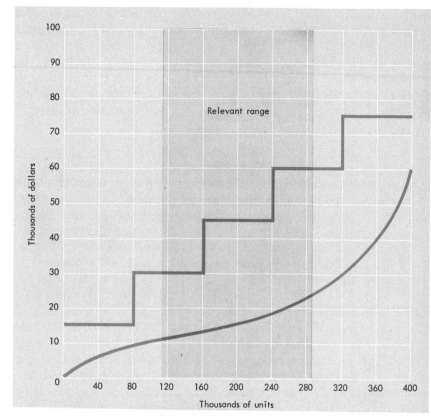

Illustration 25-2

costs and revenues often is not completely consistent with these assumptions, and if the assumptions are violated by significant amounts,
the results of cost-volume-profit analysis will not be reliable. Yet,
there are at least two reasons why these assumptions tend to provide
reliable analyses. First, while individual variable costs may not act in
a truly variable manner, the process of adding such costs together may
offset such violations of the assumption. In other words, the assumption of variable behavior may be satisfied in respect to total variable
costs even though it is violated in respect to individual variable costs.

Second, the assumptions that revenues, variable costs, and fixed
costs can be reasonably represented as straight lines are only intended
to apply over the *relevant range* of operations. The relevant range of
operations, as plotted in Illustration 25-2, is the normal operating
range for the business. It excludes the extremely high and low levels
that are not apt to be encountered. Thus, a specific fixed cost is
expected to be truly fixed only within the relevant range. It may be that
beyond the limits of the relevant range, the fixed cost would not remain constant.

The previous discussion defined variable costs and fixed costs in terms of levels of production activity. However, in cost-volume-profit analysis, the level of activity is usually measured in terms of sales volume, whether stated as sales dollars or number of units sold. Thus, an additional assumption is frequently made that the level of production is the same as the level of sales, or if they are not the same, that the difference will not be enough to materially damage the reliability of the analysis.

It must also be recognized that cost-volume-profit analysis yields approximate answers to questions concerning the interrelations of costs, volume, and profits. So long as management understands that the answers provided are approximations, cost-volume-profit analysis can be a useful managerial tool.

A company's break-even point is the sales level at which it neither earns a profit nor incurs a loss. It may be expressed either in units of product or in dollars of sales. To illustrate its calculation, assume that Alpha Company sells a single product for $100 per unit and incurs $70 of variable costs per unit sold. If the fixed costs involved in selling the product are $24,000, the company breaks even on the product as soon as it sells 800 units or as soon as its sales volume reaches $80,000. This break-even point may be determined as follows:

Break-even point

1. Each unit sold at $100 recovers its $70 variable costs and contributes $30 toward the fixed costs.
2. The fixed costs are $24,000; consequently, 800 units ($24,000 ÷ $30 = 800) must be sold to pay the fixed costs.
3. And 800 units at $100 each produce an $80,000 sales volume.

The $30 amount that the sales price of this product exceeds variable costs per unit is its *contribution margin per unit*. In other words, the contribution margin per unit is the amount that the sale of one unit contributes toward recovery of the fixed costs and then toward a profit.

Also, the contribution margin of a product expressed as a percentage of its sales price is its *contribution rate*. For instance, the contribution rate of the $100 product of this illustration is 30% ($30 ÷ $100 = 30%).

And with contribution margin and contribution rate defined, it is possible to set up the following formulas for calculating a break-even point in units and in dollars:

$$\text{Break-even point in units} = \frac{\text{Fixed costs}}{\text{Contribution margin}}$$

$$\text{Break-even point in dollars} = \frac{\text{Fixed costs}}{\text{Contribution rate}}$$

Application of the second formula to figures for the product of this illustration gives this result:

$$\text{Break-even point in dollars} = \frac{\$24,000}{30\%} = \frac{\$24,000}{0.30} = \$80,000$$

Although the present example comes out evenly, a contribution rate may have to be carried out several decimal places to avoid minor rounding errors when calculating the break-even point in dollars. In solving the exercises and problems at the end of this chapter, for example, calculations of contribution rate should be carried to six decimal places unless the requirements state otherwise. Calculated either way, Alpha Company's break-even point may be proved with an income statement, as in Illustration 25–3. Observe in the illustration

Illustration 25–3

Alpha Company
Income Statement at the Break-Even Point

Sales (800 units @ $100 each)..................		$80,000
Costs:		
Fixed costs...	$24,000	
Variable costs (800 units @ $70 each)....	56,000	80,000
Net Income..		$ -0-

that revenue from sales exactly equals the sum of the fixed and variable costs at the break-even point. Recognizing this will prove helpful in understanding the material that follows in this chapter.

Break-even graph

A cost-volume-profit analysis may be shown graphically as in Illustration 25–4; and when presented in this form, the graph is commonly called a break-even graph or break-even chart. On such a graph the horizontal axis shows units sold, the vertical axis shows both dollars of sales and dollars of costs, and costs and revenues are plotted as straight lines. The illustrated graph shows the break-even point of Alpha Company. A break-even graph is prepared as follows:

1. The line representing fixed costs is plotted at the fixed cost level. Note that it is a horizontal line, since the fixed costs are the same at all sales levels. Actually, the fixed costs line is not essential to the analysis; however, it contributes important information and is commonly plotted on a break-even chart.
2. Next the sales line is projected from the point of zero units and zero dollars of sales to the point of maximum sales shown on the graph. In choosing the maximum number of units to be shown, a better graph results if the number chosen is such that it will cause the break-even point to fall near the center of the graph.
3. Next the variable cost plus fixed cost line is plotted. Note that it begins at the fixed cost level and, as a result, shows total costs at all production levels. At the zero sales level there are no variable costs, only fixed costs. However, at any level above zero sales all the fixed costs are present and so are the variable costs for that

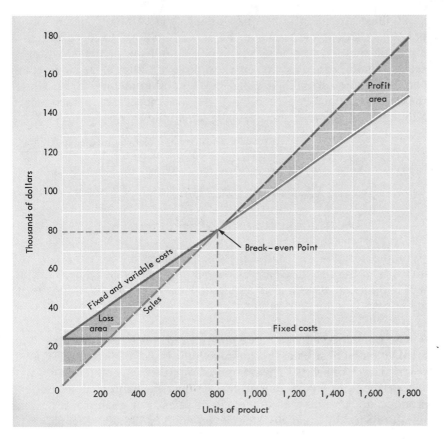

Illustration 25-4

level. Also observe that the variable cost plus fixed cost line intersects the sales line at the break-even point. It intersects at this point because at the break-even point the revenue from sales exactly equals the sum of the fixed and variable costs, in other words, the total costs.

In reading a break-even chart, the vertical distance between the sales line and the total cost line represents a loss to the left of the break-even point and a profit to the right of it. The amount of profit or loss at any given sales level can be determined from the graph by measuring the vertical distance between the sales line and the total cost line at the given level.

A slight extension of the concept behind the break-even calculation will produce a formula that may be used in determining the sales level necessary to produce a desired net income. The formula is:

Sales required for a desired net income

$$\text{Sales at desired income level} = \frac{\underset{\text{costs}}{\text{Fixed}} + \underset{\text{income}}{\text{Net}} + \underset{\text{taxes}}{\text{Income}}}{\text{Contribution rate}}$$

To illustrate the formula's use, assume that Alpha Company of the previous section, the company having $24,000 of fixed costs and a 30% contribution rate has set a $20,000 after-tax income goal for itself. Assume further that in order to have a $20,000 net income, the company must earn $28,500 and pay $8,500 in income taxes. Under these assumptions, $175,000 of sales are necessary to produce a $20,000 net income. This is calculated as follows:

$$\text{Sales at desired income level} = \frac{\overset{\text{Fixed}}{\text{costs}} + \overset{\text{Net}}{\text{income}} + \overset{\text{Income}}{\text{taxes}}}{\text{Contribution rate}}$$

$$\text{Sales at desired income level} = \frac{\$24{,}000 + \$20{,}000 + \$8{,}500}{30\%}$$

$$\text{Sales at desired income level} = \frac{\$52{,}500}{30\%} = \$175{,}000$$

In the formula just given the contribution rate was used as the divisor and the resulting answer was in dollars of sales. The contribution margin can also be used as the divisor; and when it is, the resulting answer is in units of product.

Margin of safety

The difference between a company's current sales and sales at its break-even point, when sales are above the break-even point, is known as its margin of safety. The margin of safety is the amount sales may decrease before a loss is incurred. It may be expressed in units of product, dollars, or as a percentage of sales. For example, if current sales are $100,000 and the break-even point is $80,000, the margin of safety is $20,000 or 20% of sales, calculated as follows:

$$\frac{\text{Sales} - \text{Break-even sales}}{\text{Sales}} = \text{Margin of safety}$$

or

$$\frac{\$100{,}000 - \$80{,}000}{\$100{,}000} = 20\% \text{ margin of safety}$$

Income from a given sales level

Cost-volume-profit analysis goes beyond break-even analysis and can be used to answer other questions. For example, what income will result from a given sales level? To understand the analysis used in answering this question, recall the factors that enter into the calculation of income. When expressed in equation form, they are:

$$\text{Sales} - (\text{Fixed costs} + \text{Variable costs}) = \text{Income}$$

And like any mathematical equation, the factors can be transposed and made to read:

$$\text{Income} = \text{Sales} - (\text{Fixed costs} + \text{Variable costs})$$

In its last form the equation may be used to calculate the income that will result at a given sales level. For example, assume that Alpha Company of the previous illustrations wishes to know what income

will result if its sales level can be increased to $200,000, which would
be 2,000 units of its product at $100 per unit. To determine the an-
swer, recall that the variable costs per unit of this product are $70
and note that the $70 is 0.7 of the product's selling price. Conse-
quently, variable costs for 2,000 units of the product are 0.7 of the
selling price of these units or are $140,000 ($200,000 × 0.7 = $140,-
000). Alpha Company's fixed costs are $24,000. Therefore, if these
known factors are substituted in the equation for determining income,
the equation will read:

$$Income = \$200,000 - [\$24,000 + (0.7 \times \$200,000)]$$
$$Income = \$200,000 - \$164,000$$
$$Income = \$36,000$$

The $36,000 is "before-tax" income; and as a result, if Alpha Com-
pany wishes to learn its after-tax income from the sale of 2,000 units
of its product, it will have to apply the appropriate tax rates to the
$36,000.

A company may wish to know what would happen to its break-even **Other questions**
point if it reduced the selling price of its product in order to increase
sales. Or it might wish to know what would happen if it installed a new
machine that would increase its fixed costs but which would reduce
variable costs. These are two of several possible questions involving
changes in selling prices and costs; and at first glance such changes
seem to violate the basic assumptions on which cost-volume-profit
analysis is based. But this is not true. A constant selling price, truly
variable costs, and truly fixed costs are assumed to hold for any analysis involving the assumed price and costs. However, changes may
be made, and if made, the new price and new costs are assumed to
remain constant for the analyses involving that price and those costs.
The fact that changes can be made in the factors makes it possible to
predict the effect of changes before the changes are actually made.

To illustrate the effect of changes, assume that Alpha Company is
considering the installation of a new machine that will increase the
fixed costs of producing and selling its product from $24,000 to $30,-
000. However, the machine will reduce the variable costs from $70
per unit of product to $60. The selling price of the product will remain
unchanged at $100, and the company wishes to know its break-even
point if the machine is installed. Examination of the costs shows that
the installation will not only increase the company's fixed costs but it
will also change the contribution margin and contribution rate of the
company's product. The new contribution margin will be $40 ($100 −
$60 = $40), and the new contribution rate will be 40% ($40 ÷ $100 =
0.4 or 40%). Consequently, if the machine is installed, the company's
new break-even point will be:

$$\text{Break-even point in dollars} = \frac{\$30,000}{0.4} = \$75,000$$

In addition to their use in determining Alpha Company's break-even point, the new fixed costs and the new contribution rate may be used to determine the sales level needed to earn a desired net income, or to determine the expected income at a given sales level, or to answer other questions the company will want to answer before installing the new machine.

Multi-product break-even point

The break-even point for a company selling a number of products can be determined by using a hypothetical unit made up of units of each of the company's products in their expected sales mix. Such a hypothetical unit is really a composite unit and is treated in all analyses as though it were a single product. To illustrate the use of such a hypothetical unit, assume that Beta Company sells three products, A, B, and C, and it wishes to calculate its break-even point. Unit selling prices for the three products are: Product A, $5; Product B, $8; and Product C, $4. The sales mix or ratio in which the products are sold is 4:2:1, and the company's fixed costs are $48,000. Under these assumptions a composite unit selling price for the three products can be calculated as follows:

```
4 units of Product A @ $5 per unit = $20
2 units of Product B @ $8 per unit =  16
1 unit  of Product C @ $4 per unit =   4
        Selling price of a composite
        unit                          $40
```

Also, if the variable costs of selling the three products are Product A, $3.25; Product B, $4.50; and Product C, $2, the variable costs of a composite unit of the products are:

```
4 units of Product A @ $3.25 per unit = $13
2 units of Product B @ $4.50 per unit =   9
1 unit  of Product C @ $2.00 per unit =   2
        Variable costs of a
        composite unit                  $24
```

With the variable costs and selling price of a composite unit of the company's products calculated, the contribution margin for a composite unit may be determined by subtracting the variable costs of a composite unit from the selling price of such a unit, as follows:

$$\$40 - \$24 = \$16 \text{ contribution margin per composite unit}$$

The $16 contribution margin may then be used to determine the company's break-even point in composite units. The break-even point is:

$$\text{Break-even point in composite units} = \frac{\text{Fixed costs}}{\text{Composite contribution margin}}$$

$$\text{Break-even point in composite units} = \frac{\$48,000}{\$16}$$

Break-even point = 3,000 composite units

The company breaks even when it sells 3,000 composite units of its products. However, to determine the number of units of each product it must sell to break even, the number of units of each product in the composite unit must be multiplied by the number of composite units needed to break even, as follows:

Product A: 4 × 3,000 = 12,000 units
Product B: 2 × 3,000 = 6,000 units
Product C: 1 × 3,000 = 3,000 units

The accuracy of all these computations can be proved by preparing an income statement showing the company's revenues and costs at the break-even point. Such a statement is shown in Illustration 25–5.

Beta Company
Income Statement at the Break-Even Point

Sales:		
Product A (12,000 units @ $5)		$ 60,000
Product B (6,000 units @ $8)		48,000
Product C (3,000 units @ $4)		12,000
Total revenues		$120,000
Costs:		
Fixed costs	$48,000	
Variable costs:		
Product A (12,000 units @ $3.25)	$39,000	
Product B (6,000 units @ $4.50)	27,000	
Product C (3,000 units @ $2.00)	6,000	
Total variable costs	72,000	
Total costs		120,000
Net Income		$ -0-

Illustration 25–5

A composite unit made up of units of each of a company's products in their expected sales mix may be used in answering cost-volume-profit questions in addition to the break-even point. In making all such analyses it is assumed that the product mix remains constant at all sales levels just as the other factors entering into an analysis are assumed to be constant. Nevertheless, this does not prevent changes in the assumed sales mix in order to learn what would happen if the mix were changed. However, problems involving changes in the sales mix require a recomputation of the composite unit selling price and composite unit variable costs for each change in the mix.

Evaluating
the results

Cost-volume-profit analyses have their greatest use in predicting what will happen when changes are made in selling prices, product mix, and the various cost factors. However, in evaluating the results of such analyses, several points should be borne in mind. First, the analyses are used to predict future results. Therefore, the data put into the formulas and on the graphs are assumed or forecasted data. Consequently, the results of the analyses are no more reliable than the data used. Second, cost-volume-profit analyses as presented here are based on the assumption that in any one analysis selling price will remain constant, fixed costs are truly fixed, and variable costs are truly variable. This assumption does not always reflect reality. Therefore, at best the answers obtained through cost-volume-profit analyses are approximations. However, if this is recognized, cost-volume-profit analyses can be useful to management in making decisions.

The cost-volume-profit analyses presented in this chapter are based on the assumption that revenues and costs may be expressed as straight lines; and as pointed out, such an assumption does not always hold. Therefore, it should be noted that cost-volume-profit analyses based on curvilinear relationships are also possible. However, the use of curvilinear relationships takes some rather sophisticated mathematics, and a discussion is deferred to a more advanced text.

Glossary

Break-even point. The sales level at which a company neither earns a profit nor incurs a loss.

Contribution margin per unit. The dollar amount that the sale of one unit contributes toward recovery of fixed costs and then toward a profit.

Contribution rate. The contribution margin per unit expressed as a percentage of sales price.

Cost-volume-profit analysis. A method of predicting the effects of changes in costs and sales level on the income of a business.

Fixed cost. A cost that remains unchanged in total amount over a wide range of production levels.

Margin of safety. The difference between a company's current sales and sales at its break-even point, when sales are above the break-even point.

Relevant range of operations. The normal operating range for the business, which excludes extremely high and low levels of production that are not apt to be encountered.

Sales mix. The ratio in which a company's different products are sold.

Semivariable cost. A cost that changes with production volume but not in the same proportion.

Variable cost. A cost that changes in total amount proportionately with production-level changes.

1. For what is cost-volume-profit analysis used?
2. What is a fixed cost? Name two fixed costs.
3. When there are fixed costs in manufacturing a product and the number of units manufactured is increased, do fixed costs per unit increase or decrease? Why? *yes if you produce more cost less*
4. What is a variable cost? Name two variable costs. *— labor, materials*
5. What is a semivariable cost? *—*
6. The reliability of cost-volume-profit analysis rests upon three basic assumptions. What are they? *page 825*
7. What two factors tend to make it possible to classify costs as either fixed *— unchanged* or variable.
8. What is the break-even point in the sale of a product?
9. A company sells a product for $90 per unit. The variable costs of producing and selling the product are $54 per unit. What is the product's contribution margin per unit? What is its contribution rate?
10. If a straight line is begun at the fixed cost level on a break-even graph and the line rises at the variable cost rate, what does the line show?
11. When a break-even graph is prepared, why are the fixed costs plotted as a horizontal line?
12. What is a company's margin of safety?
13. When we speak of a company's sales mix, what is meant by sales mix?
14. If a company produces and sells more than one product, the reliability of cost-volume-profit analysis depends on an additional assumption in regard to sales mix. What is that assumption?

.60 % | 30/0 % sales | 90. 54 entri | 40. 36

Exercise 25–1

Ranger Company manufactures a single product which it sells for $91 per unit. The variable costs of manufacturing the product are $75 per unit, and the annual fixed costs incurred in manufacturing it are $56,320. Calculate the company's (1) contribution margin, (2) contribution rate, (3) break-even point for the product in units, and (4) break-even point in dollars of sales. The calculation of contribution rate should be carried to six decimal places.

Exercise 25–2

Prepare an income statement for Ranger Company's operations (Exercise 25–1), showing sales, fixed costs, and variable costs at the break-even point. Also, if Ranger Company's fixed costs increased by $7,200, calculate how many additional sales (in dollars) would be necessary to break even.

Exercise 25–3

Assume that Ranger Company of Exercise 25–1 wishes to earn a $32,000 annual after-tax income from the sale of its product, and that it must pay 50% of its income in state and federal income taxes. Calculate (1) the number of units of its product it must sell to earn a $32,000 after-tax income from the sale of the product. (2) Calculate the number of dollars of sales that are needed to earn a $32,000 after-tax income.

Exercise 25–4

The sales manager of Ranger Company (Exercise 25–1) thinks that within two years annual sales of the company's product will reach 5,500 units while the sales price will go up to $96. Variable costs are expected to increase only $2 per unit, and fixed costs are not expected to change. Calculate the company's (1) before-tax income from the sale of these units and (2) calculate its after-tax income from the sale of the units.

Exercise 25–5

X-Ray Company markets Products X and Y which it sells in the ratio of four units of Product X at $3 per unit to each two units of Product Y at $10 per unit. The variable costs of marketing Product X are $2.12 per unit, and the variable costs for Product Y are $5.18 per unit. The annual fixed costs for marketing both products are $16,450. Calculate (1) the selling price of a composite unit of these products, (2) the variable costs per composite unit, (3) the break-even point in composite units, and (4) the number of units of each product that will be sold at the break-even point.

Problems

Problem 25–1

Beaufort Company manufactures a number of products, one of which, Product P, is produced and sold quite independently from the others, and sells for $675 per unit. The fixed costs of manufacturing Product P are $77,700, and the variable costs are $490 per unit. In solving requirements 1 (*b*) and 4 (below), the calculation of a contribution rate should be carried to six decimal places.

Required:

1. Calculate the company's break-even point in the sale of Product P (*a*) in units and (*b*) in dollars of sales.
2. Prepare a break-even graph for Product P. Use 1,000 as the maximum number of units on your graph.
3. Prepare an income statement showing sales, fixed costs, and variable costs for Product P at the break-even point.
4. Determine the sales volume in dollars that the company must achieve to earn a $22,200 after-tax (50% rate) income from the sale of Product P.
5. Determine the after-tax income the company will earn from a $513,000 sales level for Product P.

Problem 25–2

Baytown Company incurred a $4,000 loss last year in selling 4,000 units of its Product A, as the following income statement shows:

Baytown Company
Last Year's Income Statement for Product A

Sales		$100,000
Costs:		
Fixed..	$24,000	
Variable.....................................	80,000	104,000
Net Loss from Sale of Product A....		$ (4,000)

The production manager has pointed out that the variable costs of Product A can be reduced 25% by installing a machine to do a labor operation presently done by hand. However, the new machine will increase fixed costs by $6,400 annually.

Required:

1. Calculate last year's dollar break-even point for Product A.
2. Calculate the dollar break-even point for Product A under the assumption the new machine is installed.
3. Prepare a break-even chart under the assumption the new machine is installed. Use 6,000 as the maximum number of units on your chart.
4. Prepare an income statement showing expected annual results with the new machine installed, no change in the selling price of Product A, and no change in the number of units sold. Assume a 50% income tax rate.
5. Calculate the sales level required to earn a $12,000 per year after-tax income with the new machine installed and no change in the selling price of Product A. Prepare an income statement showing the results at this sales level.

Problem 25-3

Last year Willis Company earned an unsatisfactory 2.5% after-tax return from the sale of 50,000 packages of its Product M at $1 each. The company buys Product M in bulk and packages it for resale. Following are last year's costs for the product:

Costs of bulk Product M (sufficient for 50,000 packages)... $25,000
Packaging materials and other variable packaging costs   5,000
Fixed costs 17,500
Income tax rate 50%

It has been suggested that if the selling price of the product is reduced 10% and a slight change made in its packaging, the number of units sold can be doubled. The packaging change will increase packaging costs 10% per unit, but doubling the sales volume will gain a 5% reduction in the product's bulk purchase price. The packaging and volume changes will not affect fixed costs.

Required:

1. Calculate the dollar break-even points for Product M at the $1 per unit sales price and at $0.90 per unit.
2. Prepare a break-even chart for the sale of the product at each price. Use 100,000 units as the upper limit of your charts.
3. Prepare a condensed comparative income statement showing the results of selling the product at $1 per unit and the estimated results of selling it at $0.90 per unit.

Problem 25-4

Badlands Company sells two products, S and T, which are produced and sold independently. Last year the company sold 8,000 units of each of these products at $120 per unit, earning $105,000 from the sale of each as the following condensed income statement shows:

	Product S	Product T
Sales	$960,000	$960,000
Costs:		
Fixed costs	$150,000	$600,000
Variable costs	600,000	150,000
Total costs	$750,000	$750,000
Income before taxes	$210,000	$210,000
Income taxes (50% rate)	105,000	105,000
Net Income	$105,000	$105,000

Required:

1. Calculate the break-even point for each product in units.
2. Prepare a break-even graph for each product. Use 10,000 as the maximum number of units on each graph.
3. Prepare a condensed income statement showing in separate columns the net income the company will earn from the sale of each product under the assumption that without a change in selling prices, the number of units of each product sold declines to 5,926 units.
4. Prepare a second condensed income statement showing in separate columns the net income the company will earn if the number of units of each product increases 25%.

Problem 25–5

Shiner Company manufactures and sells three products, A, B, and C. Product A sells for $16 per unit, Product B sells for $9 per unit, and Product C sells for $7 per unit. Their sales mix is in the ratio of 3:7:4, and the variable costs of manufacturing and selling the products have been: Product A, $12; Product B, $6; and Product C, $5. The fixed costs of manufacturing the three products are $139,400. A special material called Zefluss has been used in manufacturing both Products A and B; however, a new material called Sulfez has just become available, and if it is substituted for Zefluss, it will reduce the variable cost of manufacturing Product A by $0.75 and Product B by $0.25. However, fixed costs will go up to $144,000 because of special equipment needed to process Sulfez. In solving requirements 1 and 2 (below), calculations of contribution rates should be carried to six decimal places.

Required:

1. Determine the company's break-even point in dollars and the number of units of each product sold at the break-even point under the assumption that Zefluss is used in manufacturing Products A and B. Show all pertinent calculations.
2. Determine the company's break-even point in dollars and the number of units of each product sold at the break-even point under the assumption that the new Sulfez material is used in manufacturing Products A and B. Show all pertinent calculations.

Alternate
problems

Problem 25–1A

Among the products sold by Kennan Company is Product B, which is produced and sold independently from the other products of the company, and which sells for $320 per unit. The fixed costs of selling Product B are $39,000, and the variable costs are $260 per unit.

Required:

1. Calculate the company's break-even point in the sale of Product B (*a*) in units and (*b*) in dollars of sales.
2. Prepare a break-even graph for Product B, using 1,000 as the maximum number of units on the graph.
3. Prepare an income statement showing sales, fixed costs, and variable costs for Product B at the break-even point.
4. Determine the sales volume in dollars required to achieve a $3,000 after-tax (50% rate) income from the sale of Product B.
5. Determine the after-tax income the company will earn from a $313,600 sales level for Product B.

Problem 25–2A

Athens Company lost $1,000 last year in selling 2,000 units of its Product X, as the following income statement shows:

Athens Company
Last Year's Sales of Product X

Sales		$100,000
Costs:		
Fixed..	$26,000	
Variable.....................................	75,000	101,000
Net Loss from Sales of Product X....		$ (1,000)

The company has discovered that if it will install a new machine, it can save enough piece-rate labor and spoiled materials to reduce the variable costs of manufacturing Product X by 20%. However, the new machine will increase fixed costs $2,400 annually.

Required:

1. Calculate last year's dollar break-even point for Product X.
2. Calculate the dollar break-even point under the assumption the new machine is installed.
3. Prepare a break-even chart under the assumption the new machine is installed. Use 3,000 as the maximum number of units on your chart.
4. Prepare an income statement showing expected annual results with the new machine installed, no change in Product X's price, and sales at last year's level. Assume a 50% income tax rate.
5. Calculate the sales level required to earn a $10,000 per year after-tax income with the new machine installed and no change in the selling price of Product X. Prepare an income statement showing the results at this sales level.

Problem 25–3A

Last year Commerce Company sold 20,000 units of its product at $20 per unit. To manufacture and sell the product required $100,000 of fixed manufacturing costs and $20,000 of fixed selling and administrative expenses. Last year's variable costs and expenses per unit were:

Material $8.00
Direct labor (paid on a piece-rate basis) 3.00
Variable manufacturing overhead costs 0.60
Variable selling and administrative expenses 0.40

A new material has just come on the market that will cut the material cost of producing the product in half if substituted for the material presently being used. The substitution will have no effect on the product's quality; but it will give the company a choice in pricing the product. (1) The company can maintain the present per unit price, sell the same number of units, and make an extra $4 per unit profit as a result of the substitution. Or (2) it can reduce the product's price $4 per unit to an amount equal to the material savings, and because of the reduction, increase the number of units sold by 60%. If the latter choice is made, the fixed manufacturing overhead and fixed selling and administrative expenses will not change and the remaining variable costs and expenses will vary with volume.

Required:

1. Calculate the break-even point in dollars for each alternative.
2. Prepare a break-even chart for each. The company's capacity is 40,000 units, and this should be used as the upper limit of your charts.
3. Prepare a comparative income statement showing sales, total fixed costs, and total variable costs and expenses, operating income, income taxes (50% rate), and net income for each alternative.

Problem 25–5A

Spooner Company manufactures and sells three products, X, Y, and Z, which sell for $24 per unit, $20 per unit, and $16 per unit, respectively. Their sales mix is in the ratio of 2:5:8, and the variable costs of manufacturing and selling the products have been: Product X, $16; Product Y, $14; and Product Z, $10. Fixed manufacturing, selling, and administrative costs amount to $488,800.

The management of Spooner Company is considering the possible purchase of a new machine to be used in the manufacture of Products Y and Z. If the machine is purchased, fixed manufacturing costs will increase by $99,200. However, variable costs of Product Y will decrease by $2 per unit and variable costs of Product Z will decrease by $1 per unit.

Required:

1. Determine the company's break-even point in dollars and the number of units of each product sold at the break-even point assuming the new machine is not purchased. Show all pertinent calculations.
2. Determine the company's break-even point in dollars and the number of units of each product sold at the break-even point assuming that the new machine is purchased. Show all pertinent calculations.

**Decision
problem 25–1,
Paper Products
Company**

Paper Products Company produces a high-protein content cattle feed additive at its Waldport plant. The plant produced at near capacity last year with the results shown in the following condensed income statement:

Sales (300,000 lbs.)..	$600,000
Cost of goods manufactured and sold (fixed, $100,000;	
variable, $240,000)	340,000
Gross margin..	$260,000
Selling and administrative expenses (fixed, $80,000;	
variable, $60,000)...	140,000
Income before Taxes	$120,000

Worldwide Company has offered a five-year contract to buy 200,000 pounds of the additive annually at $1.60 per pound for export sales. Delivery on the contract would require a plant addition that would double fixed manufacturing costs. The contract would not affect present fixed and variable selling and administrative expenses. Variable manufacturing costs would vary with volume.

Management is not certain it should enter into the contract, and it has asked for your opinion, including the following:

1. An estimated income statement for the first year following the plant addition, assuming no change in domestic sales.
2. A comparison of break-even sales levels before the plant addition and after the contract expiration. Assume after-contract sales and expense levels, other than fixed manufacturing costs, will be at the same levels as last year.
3. A statement showing net income after the contract expiration but at sales and expense levels of last year, other than fixed manufacturing costs.

Crazy Company manufactures and sells Loops, Scoups, and Dangles. Last year's sales mix for the three products was in the ratio of 6:1:3, with combined sales totaling 12,000 units. Loops sell for $120 each and have a 20% contribution rate. Scoups sell for $100 each and have a 25% contribution rate, and Dangles sell for $90 each and have a 40% contribution rate. The fixed costs of manufacturing and selling the products amounts to $161,214. The company estimates that combined sales of the three products will continue at the 12,000 unit level next year. However, the sales manager is of the opinion that if the company's advertising and sales efforts are slanted further toward Scoups and Dangles during the coming year, with no increases in the amounts of money expended, the sales mix of the three products can be changed to the ratio of 3:3:4.

Should the company change its sales mix through advertising and sales efforts? What effect will the change have on the composite contribution rate of the three products? What effect will it have on the company's break-even point? Back your answers with figures. Calculations of contribution rate should be carried to seven decimal places.

Decision problem 25–2, Crazy Company

Bancroft Company operated at near capacity during 197A, and a 20% annual increase in the demand for its product is expected. As a result the company's management is trying to decide how to meet this demand. Two alternatives are being considered. The first calls for changes that will increase variable

Decision problem 25–3, Bancroft Company

costs to 55% of the selling price of the company's product but will not change fixed costs. The second calls for a capital investment that will increase fixed costs 15% but will not affect variable costs.

Bancroft Company's income statement for 197A provided the following summarized information:

Sales.........................		$450,000
Costs:		
Variable costs	$216,000	
Fixed costs..............	160,000	376,000
Income before Taxes....		$ 74,000

Which alternative do you recommend? Back your recommendation with income statement information and any other data you consider relevant.

After studying Chapter 26, you should be able to:

- State the deficiencies of fixed budgets.
- Prepare flexible budgets and state their advantages.
- State what standard costs represent, how they are determined, and how they are used in the evaluation process.
- Calculate material, labor, and overhead variances, and state what each variance indicates about the performance of a company.
- Explain the relevance of standard cost accounting to the management philosophy known as "management by exception."
- Define or explain the words and phrases listed in the chapter Glossary.

chapter 26

Flexible budgets; standard costs

The development of a master plan for the business was discussed in Chapter 24, and consideration was also given to the importance of controlling subsequent operations. This function of control was recognized as one of the two basic functions of management. In order to control business operations, management must obtain information or feedback regarding how closely actual operations conform to the plans. To the extent possible, the comparison of actual performance with planned performance should be designed so that it directs the attention of management toward the reasons why actual performance differs from planned performance. Flexible budgets and standard costs are important techniques that are used to help management determine why actual performance differs from the plan.

In preparing a master budget as discussed in Chapter 24, the initial step is to determine the expected sales volume for the budget period. All of the subsequent budget procedures are based on this specific estimate of sales volume. The amount of each budgeted cost is based on the assumption that a specific or fixed amount of sales will take place. When a budget is based on a single estimate of sales or production volume, the budget is called a *fixed* or *static budget*. In budgeting the total amount of each cost, a fixed budget gives no consideration to the possibility that the actual sales or production volume may be different from the fixed or budgeted amount.

If a company uses only fixed budgets, the comparison of actual performance with the budgeted performance is presented in a performance report such as that shown in Illustration 26-1.

The budgeted sales volume of Tampa Manufacturing Company is 10,000 units (see Illustration 26-1). Also, to simplify the discussion, production volume is assumed to equal sales volume; and no beginning

Fixed budgets and performance reports

Tampa Manufacturing Company
Fixed Budget Performance Report
For Month Ended November 30, 19—

	Fixed Budget	Actual Performance	Variances
Sales: In units	10,000	12,000	
In dollars	$100,000	$125,000	$25,000 F
Cost of goods sold:			
Raw materials	$ 10,000	$ 13,000	3,000 U
Direct labor	15,000	20,000	5,000 U
Overhead:			
Factory supplies	2,000	2,100	100 U
Utilities	3,000	4,000	1,000 U
Depreciation of machinery	8,000	8,000	—
Supervisory salaries	11,000	11,000	—
Selling expenses:			
Sales commissions	9,000	10,800	1,800 U
Shipping expenses	4,000	4,300	300 U
General and administrative expenses:			
Office supplies	5,000	5,200	200 U
Insurance expense	1,000	1,200	200 U
Depreciation of office equipment	7,000	7,000	—
Administrative salaries	13,000	13,000	—
Total expenses	$ 88,000	$ 99,600	$11,600 U
Income from Operations	$ 12,000	$ 25,400	$13,400 F

F = favorable variance, that is, compared to the budget, the actual cost or revenue contributes to a higher income.
U = unfavorable variance, that is, compared to the budget, the actual cost or revenue contributes to a lower income.

Illustration 26–1

or ending inventory is maintained by the company. In evaluating Tampa Manufacturing Company's operations, management should be interested in answering such questions as: Why is the actual income from operations $13,400 higher than the budgeted amount? Are the prices being paid for each expense item too high? Is the manufacturing department using too much raw material? Is it using too much direct labor? The performance report shown in Illustration 26–1 provides little help in answering questions such as these. Since the actual sales volume was 2,000 units higher than the budgeted amount, it may be assumed that this increase caused total dollar sales and many of the expenses to be higher. But other factors may have influenced the amount of income, and the fixed budget performance report fails to provide management much information beyond the fact that the sales volume was higher than budgeted.

FLEXIBLE BUDGETS

To help answer questions such as those mentioned above, many companies prepare *flexible* or *variable budgets*. In contrast to fixed budgets, which are based on one, fixed amount of budgeted sales or production, flexible budgets recognize that different levels of activity should produce different amounts of cost.

To prepare a flexible budget, each type of cost is examined to determine whether it should be classified as a variable cost or as a fixed cost. Recall from Chapter 25 that the total amount of a variable cost changes in direct proportion to a change in the level of activity, and the total amount of a fixed cost remains unchanged regardless of changes in the level of activity (within the relevant or normal operating range of activity).[1]

Preparing a flexible budget

After each cost item is classified as variable or fixed, each variable cost is expressed as a constant amount of cost per unit of sales (or per sales dollar). Fixed costs are, of course, budgeted in terms of the total amount of each fixed cost that is expected regardless of the sales volume that may occur within the relevant range.

Illustration 26–2 shows how the fixed budget of Tampa Manufacturing Company is reformulated as a flexible budget. Compare the first

Tampa Manufacturing Company
Flexible Budget
For Month Ended November 30, —

	Fixed Budget	Flexible Budget Variable Cost per Unit	Flexible Budget Total Fixed Cost	Flexible Budget for Unit Sales of 12,000	Flexible Budget for Unit Sales of 14,000
Sales: In units	10,000			12,000	14,000
In dollars......................	$100,000	$10.00		$120,000	$140,000
Variable costs:					
Raw materials	$ 10,000	$ 1.00		$ 12,000	$ 14,000
Direct labor.........................	15,000	1.50		18,000	21,000
Factory supplies	2,000	0.20		2,400	2,800
Utilities..............................	3,000	0.30		3,600	4,200
Sales commissions	9,000	0.90		10,800	12,600
Shipping expenses	4,000	0.40		4,800	5,600
Office supplies	5,000	0.50		6,000	7,000
Total variable costs.........	$ 48,000	$ 4.80		$ 57,600	$ 67,200
Contribution margin...............	$ 52,000	$ 5.20		$ 62,400	$ 72,800
Fixed costs:					
Depreciation of machinery.....	$ 8,000		$ 8,000	$ 8,000	$ 8,000
Supervisory salaries..............	11,000		11,000	11,000	11,000
Insurance expense...............	1,000		1,000	1,000	1,000
Depreciation of office equipment	7,000		7,000	7,000	7,000
Administrative salaries	13,000		13,000	13,000	13,000
Total fixed costs.............	$ 40,000		$40,000	$ 40,000	$ 40,000
Income from Operations..........	$ 12,000			$ 22,400	$ 32,800

Illustration 26–2

[1] In Chapter 25, it was recognized that some costs are neither strictly variable nor strictly fixed. However, in the present discussion, it is assumed that all costs can be reasonably classified as being either variable or fixed.

column of Illustration 26-2 with the first column of Illustration 26-1. Notice that seven of the expenses have been reclassified as variable costs, and the remaining five expenses have been reclassified as fixed costs. This classification results from an investigation of each expense incurred by Tampa Manufacturing Company, and the classification should not be misunderstood. It does not mean that these particular expenses are always variable costs in every company. For example, Office Supplies Expense may frequently be a fixed cost, depending upon the nature of the company's operations. Nevertheless, Tampa Manufacturing Company's accountant investigated this item and concluded that the Office Supplies cost behaves as a variable cost.

Observe in Illustration 26-2 that the variable costs of Tampa Manufacturing Company are listed together, totaled, and subtracted from sales. As explained in Chapter 25, the difference between sales and variable costs is identified as the contribution margin. The budgeted amounts of fixed costs are then listed and totaled.

In Illustration 26-2, columns 2 and 3 show the flexible budget amounts which may be applied to any volume of sales that occurs. The last two columns merely illustrate what form the flexible budget takes when the budget amounts are applied to particular sales volumes.

Recall from Illustration 26-1 that Tampa Manufacturing Company's actual sales volume for November 19—, was 12,000 units, or 2,000 units more than the 10,000 units originally forecasted in the master budget. The effect of this sales increase on the income from operations can be determined by comparing the budget for 10,000 units with the budget for 12,000 units (see Illustration 26-2). At a sales volume of 12,000 units, the budgeted income from operations is $22,400, whereas the budget for sales of 10,000 units shows income from operations of $12,000. Thus, if sales volume is 12,000 rather than 10,000 units, management should expect income from operations to be higher by $10,400 ($22,400 − $12,000). In other words, the difference between the $25,400 actual income from operations (see Illustration 26-1) and the $12,000 income from operations shown on the master budget can be analyzed, as follows:

Actual income from operations (12,000 units)	$25,400
Income from operations on master budget (10,000 units)	12,000
Difference to be explained	$13,400
Income from operations:	
On the flexible budget for 12,000 units $22,400	
On the budget for 10,000 units 12,000	
Additional income caused by increase in sales volume	(10,400)
Unexplained difference	$ 3,000

This $3,000 unexplained difference is the amount by which the actual income from operations exceeds budgeted income from operations as shown on the flexible budget for a sales volume of 12,000 units. As management seeks to determine what steps should be taken to control Tampa Manufacturing Company's operations, the next step is to determine what caused this $3,000 unexplained difference. Information to help answer this question is provided by a flexible budget performance report.

A flexible budget performance report is designed to analyze the difference between actual performance and budgeted performance, where the budgeted amounts are based on the actual sales volume or level of activity. The report should serve to direct management's attention toward those particular costs or revenues where actual performance has differed substantially from the budgeted amount.

Flexible budget performance report

The flexible budget performance report for Tampa Manufacturing Company is presented in Illustration 26–3.

Tampa Manufacturing Company
Flexible Budget Performance Report
For Month Ended November 30, 19—

	Flexible Budget	Actual Performance	Variances
Sales (12,000 units)	$120,000	$125,000	$5,000 F
Variable costs:			
Raw materials	$ 12,000	$ 13,000	$1,000 U
Direct labor	18,000	20,000	2,000 U
Factory supplies	2,400	2,100	300 F
Utilities	3,600	4,000	400 U
Sales commissions	10,800	10,800	
Shipping expenses	4,800	4,300	500 F
Office supplies	6,000	5,200	800 F
Total variable costs	$ 57,600	$ 59,400	$1,800 U
Contribution margin	$ 62,400	$ 65,600	$3,200 F
Fixed costs:			
Depreciation of machinery	$ 8,000	$ 8,000	
Supervisory salaries	11,000	11,000	
Insurance expense	1,000	1,200	$ 200 U
Depreciation of office equipment	7,000	7,000	
Administrative salaries	13,000	13,000	
Total fixed costs	$ 40,000	$ 40,200	$ 200 U
Income from operations	$ 22,400	$ 25,400	$3,000 F

F = favorable variance, that is, compared to the budget, the actual cost or revenue contributes to a higher income.
U = unfavorable variance, that is, compared to the budget, the actual cost or revenue contributes to a lower income.

Illustration 26–3

Observe in Illustration 26–3 the $5,000 favorable variance in total dollar sales. Since the actual number of units sold amounted to 12,000 and the budget was also based on unit sales of 12,000, the $5,000 variance must have resulted entirely from a difference between the average price per unit and the budgeted price per unit. Further analysis of the $5,000 variance is as follows:

Average price per unit, actual............................	$125,000/12,000 =	$10.42
Budgeted price per unit....................................	$120,000/12,000 =	10.00
Favorable variance in price per unit.................	$5,000/12,000 =	$ 0.42

Each of the variances in Illustration 26–3 serves to direct management's attention toward the areas in which corrective action may be necessary in controlling Tampa Manufacturing Company's operations. In addition, students should recognize that each of the cost variances can be analyzed in a manner similar to the above discussion of sales. Each of the expenses can be thought of as involving the use of a given number of units of the expense item, and paying a specific price per unit. Following this approach, each of the cost variances shown in Illustration 26–3 might result in part from a difference between the actual price per unit and the budgeted price per unit (a price variance); and they may also result in part from a difference between the actual number of units used and the budgeted number of units to be used (a quantity variance). This line of reasoning, called variance analysis, is discussed more completely in the following section on standard costs.

STANDARD COSTS

In Chapter 23 it was said that there are two basic types of cost systems, job order and process, but a large number of variations of the two. A *standard cost system,* one based on *standard* or *budgeted costs,* is such a variation.

The costs of a job or a process as discussed in Chapter 23 were historical costs, historical in the sense that they had been incurred and were history by the time they were recorded. Such costs are useful; but to judge whether or not they are reasonable or what they should be, management needs a basis of comparison. Standard costs offer such a basis.

Standard costs are the costs that should be incurred under normal conditions in producing a given product or part or in performing a particular service. They are established by means of engineering and accounting studies made before the product is manufactured or the service performed; and once established, they are used to judge the reasonableness of the actual costs incurred when the product or service is produced. Standard costs are also used to place responsibilities when actual costs vary from standard.

Accountants speak of *standard material cost, standard labor cost,* and *standard overhead cost;* and this terminology is used in this chapter; however, it should be observed that standard material, labor, and overhead costs are really budgeted material, labor, and overhead costs.

Great care and the combined efforts of people in accounting, engineering, personnel administration, and other management areas are required in establishing standard costs. Time and motion studies are made of each labor operation in a product's production or in performing a service to learn both the best way to perform the operation and the standard labor time required under normal conditions for performance. Exhaustive investigations are also made of the quantity, grade, and cost of each material required; and machines and other productive equipment are subject to detailed studies in an effort to achieve maximum efficiencies and to learn what costs should be.

However, regardless of care exercised in establishing standard costs and in revising them as conditions change, actual costs incurred in producing a given product or service are apt to vary from standard costs. When this occurs, the difference in total cost is likely to be a composite of several cost differences. For example, the quantity, or the price, or both the quantity and price of the material used may have varied from standard; and the labor time, or the labor price, or both the time and price of labor may have varied. Likewise, overhead costs may have varied.

Establishing standard costs

When actual costs vary from standard costs, the differences are called *variances*. Variances may be favorable or unfavorable. A favorable variance is one in which actual cost is below standard cost, and an unfavorable variance is one in which actual cost is above standard.

When variances occur, they are isolated and studied for possible remedial action and to place responsibilities. For example, if the standard material cost for producing 2,000 units of Product A is $800 but material costing $840 was used in producing the units, the $40 variance may have resulted from paying a price higher than standard for the material, a greater quantity of material than standard may have been used, or there may have been some combination of these causes. The price paid for a material is a purchasing department responsibility; consequently, if the variance was caused by a price greater than standard, responsibility rests with the purchasing department. On the other hand, since the production department is usually responsible for the amount of material used, if a quantity greater than standard was used, responsibility normally rests with the production department. However, if more than a standard amount of material was used because the material was of a grade below standard, causing more than a normal waste, responsibility is back on the purchasing department for buying a substandard grade.

Variances

As previously stated, when variances occur, they are isolated and studied for possible remedial action and to place responsibilities. For example, assume that XL Company has established the following standard costs per unit for its Product Z:

Isolating material and labor variances

Material (1 pound per unit at $1 per pound) $1.00
Direct labor (1 hour per unit at $3 per hour) 3.00
Overhead ($2 per standard direct labor hour).... 2.00
            Total standard cost per unit................... $6.00

Material variances

Assume further that during May, XL Company completed 3,500 units of Product Z, using 3,600 pounds of material costing $1.05 per pound, or $3,780. Under these assumptions the actual and standard material costs for the 3,500 units are:

Actual cost: 3,600 pounds @ $1.05 per pound $3,780
Standard cost: 3,500 pounds @ $1.00 per pound 3,500
            Material cost variance (unfavorable)................. $ 280

Observe that the actual material cost for these units is $280 above their standard cost. This unfavorable material cost variance may be isolated as to causes in the following manner:

QUANTITY VARIANCE:
    Actual units at the standard price..... 3,600 lbs. @ $1.00 = $3,600
    Standard units at the standard price... 3,500 lbs. @ $1.00 = 3,500
        Variance (unfavorable) ....   100 lbs. @ $1.00 = $100

PRICE VARIANCE:
    Actual units at the actual price .... 3,600 lbs. @ $1.05 = $3,780
    Actual units at the standard price..... 3,600 lbs. @ $1.00 = 3,600
        Variance (unfavorable) .... 3,600 lbs. @ $0.05 =   180
            Material cost variance
                (unfavorable)................... $280

The analysis shows that $100 of the excess material cost resulted from using 100 more pounds than standard, and $180 resulted from a unit price $0.05 above standard. With this information management can go to the responsible individuals for explanations.

Labor variances

Labor cost in manufacturing a given part or in performing a service depends on a composite of the number of hours worked (quantity) and the wage rate paid (price). Therefore, when the labor cost for a task varies from standard, it too may be analyzed into a quantity variance and a price variance.

For example, the direct labor standard for the 3,500 units of Product Z is one hour per unit, or 3,500 hours at $3 per hour. If 3,400 hours costing $3.10 per hour were used in completing the units, the actual and standard labor costs for these units are:

> Actual cost: 3,400 hours @ $3.10 per hour..... $10,540
> Standard cost: 3,500 hours @ $3.00 per hour..... 10,500
> Direct labor cost variance (unfavorable) .... $ 40

In this case actual cost is only $40 over standard, but isolating the quantity and price variances involved reveals the following:

QUANTITY VARIANCE:
Standard hours at standard price...... 3,500 hrs. @ $3.00 = $10,500
Actual hours at standard price .... 3,400 hrs. @ $3.00 =   10,200
    Variance (favorable) ....   100 hrs. @ $3.00 = $300

PRICE VARIANCE:
Actual hours at actual price .... 3,400 hrs. @ $3.10 = $10,540
Actual hours at standard price .... 3,400 hrs. @ $3.00 =   10,200
    Variance (unfavorable) .... 3,400 hrs. @ $0.10 =   340
    Direct labor cost variance
    (unfavorable).................. $ 40

The analysis shows a favorable quantity variance of $300, which resulted from using 100 fewer direct labor hours than standard for the units produced. However, this favorable variance was more than offset by a wage rate that was $0.10 above standard.

When a factory or department has workers of various skill levels, it is the responsibility of the foreman or other supervisor to assign to each task a worker or workers of no higher skill level than is required to accomplish the task. In this case an investigation could reveal that workers of a higher skill level were used in producing the 3,500 units of Product Z; hence, fewer labor hours were required for the work. However, because the workers were of higher grade, the wage rate paid them was higher than standard.

When standard costs are used, factory overhead is charged to production by means of a predetermined standard overhead rate. The rate may be based on the relation of overhead to standard labor cost, standard labor hours, standard machine-hours, or some other measure of production. For example, XL Company charges its Product Z with $2 of overhead per standard direct labor hour; and since the direct labor standard for Product Z is one hour per unit, the 3,500 units manufactured in May were charged with $7,000 of overhead.

Charging overhead to production

Before going on, recall that only 3,400 actual direct labor hours were used in producing these units. Then note again that overhead is charged to the units, not on the basis of actual labor hours but on the basis of standard labor hours. Standard labor hours are used because the amount of overhead charged to these units should not be less than standard simply because less than the standard (normal) amount of labor was used in their production. In other words, overhead should not vary from normal simply because labor varied from normal.

Establishing overhead standards

A variable or flexible factory overhead budget is the starting point in establishing reasonable standards for overhead costs. A flexible budget is necessary because the actual production level may vary from the expected level; and when this happens, certain costs vary with production, but others remain fixed. This may be seen by examining XL Company's flexible budget shown in Illustration 26–4.

XL Company
Flexible Overhead Costs Budget
For Month Ended May 31, 19—

	Budget Amounts	Production Levels			
		70%	80%	90%	100%
Production in units...........................	1 unit	3,500	4,000	4,500	5,000
Standard direct labor hours..............	1 unit	3,500	4,000	4,500	5,000
Budgeted factory overhead:					
Fixed costs:					
Building rent............................	$1,000	$1,000	$1,000	$1,000	$1,000
Depreciation, machinery	1,200	1,200	1,200	1,200	1,200
Supervisory salaries..................	1,800	1,800	1,800	1,800	1,800
Totals..............................	$4,000	$4,000	$4,000	$4,000	$4,000
Variable costs:					
Indirect labor............................	$0.40	$1,400	$1,600	$1,800	$2,000
Indirect materials	0.30	1,050	1,200	1,350	1,500
Power and lights.......................	0.20	700	800	900	1,000
Maintenance.............................	0.10	350	400	450	500
Totals..............................	$1.00	$3,500	$4,000	$4,500	$5,000
Total Factory Overhead.....		$7,500	$8,000	$8,500	$9,000

Illustration 26–4

Observe in Illustration 26–4 that XL Company's flexible budget amounts have been used to establish standard costs for four production levels ranging from 70% to 100% of capacity. When actual costs are known, they should be compared with the standards for the level actually achieved and not with the standards at some other level. For example, if the plant actually operated at 70% capacity during May, actual costs incurred at this 70% level should be compared with standard costs at this level and not with costs established for the 80% or 90% levels.

In setting overhead standards, after the flexible overhead budget is prepared, management must determine the expected operating level for the plant. This can be 100% of capacity; but it seldom is since errors in scheduling work, breakdowns, and, perhaps, the inability of the sales force to sell all the product produced commonly reduce the operating level to some point below full capacity.

After the flexible budget is set up and the expected operating level is determined, overhead costs at the expected level are related to, for example, labor hours at this level to establish the standard overhead rate. The rate thus established is then used to charge overhead to production. For example, assume XL Company decided that 80% of capacity is the expected operating level for its plant. The company then arrived at its $2 per direct labor hour overhead rate by dividing the budgeted $8,000 of overhead costs at the 80% level by the 4,000 standard direct labor hours required to produce the product manufactured at this level.

As previously stated, when standard costs are used, overhead is applied to production on the basis of a predetermined overhead rate. Then at the end of a cost period the difference between overhead applied and overhead actually incurred is analyzed and variances are calculated to set out responsibilities for the difference.

Overhead variances

Overhead variances are computed in several ways. A common way divides the difference between overhead applied and overhead incurred into (1) the *volume variance* and (2) the *controllable variance*.

Volume variance

The volume variance is the difference between (1) *the amount of overhead budgeted at the actual operating level achieved during the period* and (2) *the standard amount of overhead charged to production during the period*. For example, assume that during May XL Company actually operated at 70% of capacity, producing 3,500 units of Product Z, which were charged with overhead at the standard rate. Under this assumption the company's volume variance for May is:

VOLUME VARIANCE:
Budgeted overhead at 70% of capacity.. $7,500
Standard overhead charged to production (3,500 standard labor
   hours at the $2 per hour standard rate)...................................... 7,000
     Variance (unfavorable)... $ 500

To understand why this volume variance occurred, reexamine the flexible budget of Illustration 26–4 and observe that at the 80% level the $2 per hour overhead rate may be subdivided into $1 per hour for fixed overhead and $1 per hour for variable overhead. Furthermore, at the 80% (normal) level, the $1 for fixed overhead exactly covers the fixed overhead. However, when this $2 rate is used for the 70% level, and again subdivided, the $1 for fixed overhead will not cover all the fixed overhead because $4,000 is required for fixed overhead and 3,500 hours at $1 per hour equals only $3,500. In other words, at this 70% level the $2 per hour standard overhead rate did not absorb all the overhead incurred; it lacked $500, the amount of the volume variance. Or again, the volume variance resulted simply because the plant did not reach the expected operating level.

An unfavorable volume variance tells management that the plant did not reach its normal operating level; and when such a variance is large, management should investigate the cause or causes. Machine breakdowns, failure to schedule an even flow of work, and a lack of sales orders are common causes. The first two may be corrected in the factory, but the third requires either more orders from the sales force or a downward adjustment of the operating level considered to be normal.

Controllable variance

The controllable variance is the difference between (1) *overhead actually incurred and* (2) *the overhead budgeted at the operating level achieved.* For example, assume that XL Company incurred $7,650 of overhead during May; and since its plant operated at 70% of capacity during the month, its controllable overhead variance for May is:

```
CONTROLLABLE VARIANCE:
  Actual overhead incurred.................................... $7,650
  Overhead budgeted at operating level achieved ....  7,500
            Variance (unfavorable)................................ $   150
```

The controllable overhead variance measures management's efficiency in adjusting controllable overhead costs (normally variable overhead) to the operating level achieved. In this case management failed by $150 to get overhead down to the amount budgeted for the 70% level.

Although the controllable overhead variance measures management's efficiency in adjusting overhead costs to the operating level achieved, an overhead variance report is a more effective means for showing just where management achieved or failed to achieve the budgeted expectations. Such a report for XL Company appears in Illustration 26–5 on the next page.

Combining the volume and controllable variances

The volume and controllable variances may be combined to account for the difference between overhead actually incurred and overhead charged to production. For example, XL Company incurred $7,650 of overhead during May and charged $7,000 to production, and its overhead variances may be combined as follows to account for the difference:

VOLUME VARIANCE:
Overhead budgeted at operating level achieved $7,500
Standard overhead charged to production (3,500 standard
   hours at $2 per hour) 7,000
      Variance (unfavorable) $500

CONTROLLABLE VARIANCE:
Actual overhead incurred.. $7,650
Overhead budgeted at operating level achieved 7,500
      Variance (unfavorable)   150
     Excess of overhead incurred over overhead charged to
      production $650

Controlling a business through standard costs

Business operations are carried on by people, and control of a business is gained by controlling the actions of the people responsible for its revenues, costs, and expenses. When a budget is prepared and standard costs established, control is maintained by taking appropriate action when actual costs vary from standard or from the budget.

Reports like the ones shown in this chapter are a means of calling management's attention to these variations, and a review of the reports is essential to the successful operation of a budget program. However, in making the review, management should practice the control tech-

XL Company
Factory Overhead Variance Report
For Month Ended May 31, 19—

VOLUME VARIANCE:
Normal production level .... 80% of capacity.
Production level achieved...................................... 70% of capacity.
Volume variance .... $ 500 (unfavorable)

CONTROLLABLE VARIANCE

	Budget	Actual	Favorable	Unfavorable
Fixed overhead costs:				
Building rent	$1,000	$1,000		
Depreciation, machinery	1,200	1,200		
Supervisory salaries	1,800	1,800		
Total fixed............................	$4,000	$4,000		
Variable overhead costs:				
Indirect labor................................	$1,400	$1,525		$125
Indirect materials	1,050	1,025	$ 25	
Power and lights..........................	700	750		50
Maintenance.................................	350	350		
Total variable.........................	$3,500	$3,650		
Total controllable variances			$ 25	$175
Net controllable variance (unfavorable)			150	
			$175	$175

Illustration 26–5

nique known as *management by exception.* Under this technique management gives its attention only to the variances in which actual costs are significantly different from standard and it ignores the cost situations in which performance is satisfactory. In other words, management concentrates its attention on the exceptional or irregular situations and pays little or no attention to the normal.

Many companies develop standard costs and apply variance analysis only when dealing with manufacturing costs. In these companies, the master budget includes selling, general, and administrative expenses, but the subsequent process of controlling these expenses is not based upon the establishment of standard costs and variance analysis. However, other companies have recognized that standard costs and variance analysis may help control selling, general, and administrative expenses just as well as manufacturing costs. Students should understand that the previous discussions of material and labor cost variances can easily be adapted to many selling, general, and administrative expenses.

Standard costs in the accounts

Standard costs can be used solely in the preparation of management reports and need not be taken into the accounts. However, in most standard cost systems such costs are taken into the accounts to facilitate both the record keeping and the preparation of reports.

No effort will be made here to go into the record-keeping details of a standard cost system. This is reserved for a course in cost accounting. Nevertheless, when standard costs are taken into the accounts, entries like the following (the data for which are taken from the discussion of material variances on page 852) may be used to take the standard costs into the Goods in Process account and to set out in variance accounts any variances:

May	31	Goods in Process...	3,500.00	
		Material Quantity Variance...	100.00	
		Material Price Variance..	180.00	
		Materials...		3,780.00
		To charge production with 3,600 pounds of material @ $1.05 per pound.		

Variances taken into the accounts are allowed to accumulate in the variance accounts until the end of an accounting period. If at that time the variance amounts are immaterial, they are closed to Cost of Goods Sold as an adjustment of the cost of goods sold. However, if the amounts are large, they may be prorated between Goods in Process, Finished Goods, and Cost of Goods Sold.

Glossary

Controllable variance. The difference between overhead actually incurred and the overhead budgeted at the operating level achieved.

Fixed budget. A budget based on a single estimate of sales or production volume that gives no consideration to the possibility that the actual sales or production volume may be different from the assumed amount.

Flexible budget. A budget that provides budgeted amounts for all levels of production within the relevant range.

Flexible budget performance report. A report designed to analyze the difference between actual performance and budget performance, where the budgeted amounts are based on the actual sales volume or level of activity.

Performance report. A financial report that compares actual cost and/or revenue performance with budgeted amounts and designates the differences between them as favorable or unfavorable variances.

Price variance. A difference between actual and budgeted revenue or cost caused by the actual price per unit being different from the budgeted price per unit.

Quantity variance. The difference between actual cost and budgeted cost caused by the actual number of units used being different from the budgeted number of units.

Standard costs. The costs that should be incurred under normal conditions in producing a given product or part or in performing a particular service.

Static budget. A synonym for fixed budget.

Variable budget. A synonym for flexible budget.

Volume variance. The difference between the amount of overhead budgeted at the actual operating level achieved during the period and the standard amount of overhead charged to production during the period.

---

1. What is a "fixed" or "static" budget?
2. What limits the usefulness of fixed budget performance reports?
3. What is the essential difference between a fixed budget and a flexible budget?
4. What is the initial step in preparing a flexible budget?
5. Is there any sense in which a variable cost may be thought of as being constant in amount? Explain.
6. A particular type of cost may be classified as variable by one company and fixed by another company. Why might this be appropriate?
7. What is meant by contribution margin?
8. What is a flexible budget performance report designed to analyze?
9. In cost accounting, what is meant by a "variance?"
10. A cost variance can be analyzed so as to show that it consists of a price variance and a quantity variance. What is a price variance? What is a quantity variance?

Questions for class discussion

11. What is the purpose of a "standard cost?"
12. Who is usually responsible for a material price variance? Who is generally responsible for a material quantity variance?
13. What is a "predetermined standard overhead rate?"
14. In analyzing the overhead variance, explain what is meant by a "volume variance?"
15. In analyzing the overhead variance, explain what is meant by a "controllable variance?"
16. What is the relationship between standard costs, variance analysis, and "management by exception?"

Class exercises

Exercise 26-1

A company manufactures and sells wooden desks and generally operates eight hours a day, five days per week. On the basis of this general information, classify the following costs as fixed or variable. In those instances where further investigation might reverse your classification, comment on the possible reasons for treating the item in the opposite manner.

a. Wood planks.
b. Nails and glue.
c. Paint.
d. Direct labor.
e. Electricity to run saws.
f. President's salary.
g. Repair expense on saws.
h. Depreciation on saws.
i. Fire insurance on property.
j. Supplies for office.
k. Sales commissions.
l. Packaging expenses.
m. Utilities (gas and water).
n. Shipping expenses.

Exercise 26-2

Cadena Company's fixed budget for the second quarter of 197A is presented below. Recast the budget as a flexible budget and show the budgeted amounts for 8,000 units and 9,000 units of production.

Sales (8,500 units)		$119,000
Cost of goods sold:		
Materials	$22,100	
Direct labor	24,650	
Production supplies	3,400	
Depreciation	2,800	
Plant manager's salary	3,000	(55,950)
Gross profit		$63,050
Selling expenses:		
Sales commissions	$9,860	
Packaging expense	2,550	(12,410)
Administrative expenses:		
Administrative salaries	$ 5,200	
Insurance expense	1,400	
Office rent expense	3,400	
Executive salaries	7,900	(17,900)
Income from Operations		$32,740

Exercise 26–3

Outdoor Furniture Company has just completed 300 units of its deluxe picnic table using 14,500 board feet of lumber costing $3,045. The company's material standards for one unit of this table are 50 board feet of lumber at $0.20 per board foot.

Required:

Isolate the material variances incurred in manufacturing these tables.

Exercise 26–4

Outdoor Furniture Company takes its standard costs into its cost records. As a result, in charging material costs to Goods in Process, it also takes any variances into its accounts.

Required:

1. Under the assumption that the materials used to manufacture the tables of Exercise 26–3 were charged to Goods in Process on March 5, give the entry to charge the materials and to take the variances into the accounts.
2. Under the further assumption that the material variances of Exercise 26–3 were the only variances of the year and were considered immaterial, give the year-end entry to close the variance accounts.

Exercise 26–5

A company has established the following standard costs for one unit of its product:

Material (1 unit @ $5 per unit)............. $ 5
Direct labor (1 hr. @ $3 per hr.)............   3
Factory overhead (1 hr. @ $4 per hr.)   4
      Standard cost $12

The $4 per direct labor hour overhead rate is based on a normal 80% of capacity operating level and the following monthly flexible budget information:

	Operating Levels		
	75%	80%	85%
Budgeted production in units	7,500	8,000	8,500
Budgeted overhead:			
Fixed overhead	$16,000	$16,000	$16,000
Variable overhead..............	15,000	16,000	17,000

During the past month the company operated at 75% of capacity, producing 7,500 units of product with the following overhead costs:

Fixed overhead costs............ $16,000
Variable overhead costs 15,250
    Total overhead costs.... $31,250

Required:

Isolate the overhead variances into a volume variance and a controllable variance.

Problems

Problem 26–1

Craven Company's master (fixed) budget for 197A was based on an expected production and sales volume of 9,200 units, and included the following operating items:

CRAVEN COMPANY
Fixed Budget
For Year Ended December 31, 197A

Sales		$184,000
Cost of goods sold:		
Materials..	$46,000	
Direct labor..	27,600	
Machinery repairs (variable cost)...................	1,380	
Depreciation of plant................................	5,000	
Utilities (40% of which is a variable cost)	9,200	
Supervisory salaries	12,000	(101,180)
Gross profit		$ 82,820
Selling expenses:		
Packaging..	$ 4,600	
Shipping..	6,900	
Sales salary (an agreed-upon, annual salary)....	14,000	(25,500)
General and administrative expenses:		
Insurance expense	$ 3,000	
Salaries..	21,000	
Rent expense	16,000	(40,000)
Income from Operations		$ 17,320

Required:

1. Prepare a flexible budget for the company and show detailed budgets for sales and production volumes of 8,400 units and 10,000 units.
2. A consultant to the company has suggested that developing business conditions in the area are reaching a crossroads, and that the impact of these events on the company could result in a sales volume of approximately 11,300 units. The president of Craven Company is confident that this is within the relevant range of existing production capacity but is hesitant to estimate the impact of such a change on operating income. What would be the expected increase in operating income?
3. In the consultant's report, the possibility of unfavorable business events was also mentioned, in which case production and sales volume for 197A would likely fall to 8,000 units. What amount of income from operations should the president expect if these unfavorable events occur?

Problem 26–2

Refer to the discussion of Craven Company in Problem 26–1. Craven Company's actual statement of income from 197A operations is as follows:

CRAVEN COMPANY
Statement of Income from Operations
For Year Ended December 31, 197A

Sales (10,000 units)..		$190,000
Cost of goods sold:		
Materials..	$45,000	
Direct labor...	31,000	
Machinery repairs......................................	1,000	
Depreciation of plant.................................	5,000	
Utilities (50% of which was a variable cost)....	11,040	
Supervisory salaries	11,700	(104,740)
Gross profit		$ 85,260
Selling expenses:		
Packaging..	$ 4,500	
Shipping..	7,900	
Sales salary	14,000	(26,400)
General and administrative expenses:		
Insurance expense	$ 3,100	
Salaries..	21,500	
Rent expense	16,000	(40,600)
Income from Operations		$ 18,260

Required:

1. Using the flexible budget you prepared for Problem 26–1, present a flexible budget performance report for 197A.
2. Explain the sales variance.

Problem 26–3

Gull Manufacturing Company makes a single product for which it has established the following standard costs per unit:

Material (5 lbs. @ $0.50 per lb.) $2.50
Direct labor (1 hr. @ $3 per hr.) 3.00
Factory overhead (1 hr. @ $3.25 per hr.) 3.25
Total Standard Cost........................ $8.75

The $3.25 per direct labor hour overhead rate is based on a normal, 90% of capacity, operating level and the following flexible budget information:

	Operating Levels		
	80%	90%	100%
Production in units	1,600	1,800	2,000
Standard direct labor hours	1,600	1,800	2,000
Fixed factory overhead	$3,600	$3,600	$3,600
Variable factory overhead......	$2,000	$2,250	$2,500

During March the company operated at 80% of capacity, producing 1,600 units of product which were charged with the following standard costs:

Material (8,000 lbs. @ $0.50 per lb.) .... $ 4,000
Direct labor (1,600 hrs. @ $3 per hr.)........................   4,800
Factory overhead costs (1,600 hrs. @ $3.25 per hr.)   5,200
    Total standard cost....................................... $14,000

Actual costs incurred during March were:

Material (8,100 lbs) .... $ 3,969
Direct labor (1,550 hrs.)   4,805
Fixed factory overhead costs   3,600
Variable factory overhead costs....   2,115
    Total actual costs $14,489

Required:

Isolate the material and labor variances into price and quantity variances and isolate the overhead variance into the volume variance and the controllable variance.

Problem 26–4

Weberville Company has established the following standard costs per unit for the product it manufactures:

Material (4 lbs. @ $1.50 per lb.)....... $ 6.00
Direct labor (3 hrs. @ $3 per hr.) 9.00
Overhead (3 hrs. @ $1.50 per hr.) 4.50
    Total standard cost $19.50

The $1.50 per direct labor hour overhead rate is based on a normal, 85% of capacity, operating level and the following flexible budget information for one month's operations.

	Operating Levels		
	80%	85%	90%
Production in units	1,600	1,700	1,800
Standard direct labor hours	4,800	5,100	5,400
Budgeted factory overhead:			
Fixed costs:			
Rent of factory building........................	$1,800	$1,800	$1,800
Depreciation expense, machinery...........	1,600	1,600	1,600
Taxes and insurance	200	200	200
Supervisory salaries.............................	1,500	1,500	1,500
Total fixed costs	$5,100	$5,100	$5,100
Variable costs:			
Indirect materials	$ 640	$ 680	$ 720
Indirect labor	1,200	1,275	1,350
Power...	320	340	360
Maintenance......................................	240	255	270
Total variable costs	$2,400	$2,550	$2,700
Total factory overhead costs	$7,500	$7,650	$7,800

During May the company operated at 90% of capacity, produced 1,800 units of product, and incurred the following actual costs:

Material (7,250 lbs. @ $1.48 per lb.)	$10,730	
Direct labor (5,300 hrs. @ $3.10 per hr.)	16,430	
Overhead costs:		
Rent of factory building $1,800		
Depreciation expense, machinery.... 1,600		
Taxes and insurance.................... 200		
Supervisory salaries.................... 1,500		
Indirect materials........................ 700		
Indirect labor 1,310		
Power...................................... 355		
Maintenance 300	7,765	
Total costs........................	$34,925	

Required:

1. Isolate the material and labor variances into quantity and price variances and isolate the overhead variance into the volume variance and the controllable variance.
2. Prepare a factory overhead variance report showing the volume and controllable variances.

Problem 26–5

Ranger Company has established the following standard costs for one unit of its product:

Material (3 lbs. @ $1.25 per lb.) $3.75
Direct labor ($\frac{1}{2}$ hr. @ $3 per hr.)..... 1.50
Overhead ($\frac{1}{2}$ hr. @ $2.60 per hr.) 1.30
Total standard cost............. $6.55

The $2.60 per direct labor hour overhead rate is based on a normal, 80% of capacity, operating level, and at this level the company's monthly output is 4,000 units. However, production does vary slightly, and each 1% variation results in a 50-unit increase or decrease in the production level. Following are the company's budgeted overhead costs at the 80% level for one month:

RANGER COMPANY
Budgeted Monthly Factory Overhead at 80% Level

Fixed costs:		
Depreciation expense, building $1,000		
Depreciation expense, machinery.... 800		
Taxes and insurance..................... 200		
Supervision............................... 1,200		
Total fixed costs	$3,200	
Variable costs:		
Indirect materials......................... $ 800		
Indirect labor 480		
Power....................................... 320		
Repairs and maintenance............... 400		
Total variable costs	2,000	
Total overhead costs	$5,200	

During July of the current year the company operated at 70% of capacity and incurred the following actual costs:

Material (10,620 lbs.)	$12,744
Direct labor (1,700 hrs.)	5,185
Depreciation expense, building	1,000
Depreciation expense, machinery	800
Taxes and insurance	200
Supervision	1,200
Indirect materials	725
Indirect labor	400
Power	295
Repairs and maintenance	360
Total costs	$22,909

Required:

1. Prepare a flexible overhead budget for the company showing the amount of each fixed and variable cost at the 70%, 80%, and 90% levels.
2. Isolate the material and labor variances into quantity and price variances and isolate the overhead variance into the volume variance and the controllable variance.
3. Prepare a factory overhead variance report showing the volume and controllable variances.

Alternate problems

Problem 26–1A

In the process of preparing a master budget for 197A, Prichard Company assumed a sales volume of 18,000 units. The resulting budgeted income statement included the following items that comprise income from operations.

PRICHARD COMPANY
Fixed Budget
For Year Ended December 31, 197A

Sales		$315,000
Cost of goods sold:		
Raw materials	$72,000	
Direct labor	41,004	
Factory supplies	4,194	
Depreciation of plant	7,800	
Utilities (of which $6,000 is a fixed cost)	11,796	
Salary of plant manager	18,000	(154,791)
Gross profit		$160,209
Selling expenses:		
Packaging	$37,998	
Sales commissions	25,200	
Shipping	14,202	
Salary of vice president–marketing	14,000	
Promotion (variable)	15,750	(107,150)
General and administrative expenses:		
Depreciation	$ 7,000	
Consultant's fees (annual retainer)	14,500	
Administrative salaries	32,500	(54,000)
Income from Operations		$ (941)

Required:

1. Prepare a flexible budget for the company, showing specific budget columns for sales and production volumes of 20,000 units and 22,000 units.
2. What would be the expected increase in income from operations if sales and production volume were 21,200 units rather than 18,000 units?
3. Although the management of Prichard Company believes that the master budget was a conservative estimate of sales and production volume, it is possible that the level of activity could fall to 16,000 units. What would be the effect on income from operations if this occurs?

Problem 26–2A

Refer to the discussion of Prichard Company in Problem 26–1A. Prichard Company's actual statement of income from 197A operations is as follows:

PRICHARD COMPANY
Statement of Income from Operations
For Year Ended December 31, 197A

Sales (20,000 units)		$390,000
Cost of goods sold:		
Raw materials	$78,000	
Direct labor	49,000	
Factory supplies	4,900	
Depreciation of plant	7,800	
Utilities (of which 50% is a fixed cost)	12,400	
Salary of plant manager	18,000	(170,100)
Gross profit		$219,900
Selling expenses:		
Packaging	$39,000	
Sales commissions	31,200	
Shipping	14,950	
Salary of vice president–marketing	14,000	
Promotion (variable)	18,250	(117,400)
General and administrative expenses:		
Depreciation	$ 7,000	
Consultant's fees	16,300	
Administrative salaries	31,250	(54,550)
Income from Operations		$ 47,950

Required:

1. Using the flexible budget you prepared for Problem 26–1A, present a flexible budget performance report for 197A.
2. Explain the sales variance.

Problem 26–3A

A company has established the following standard costs for one unit of its product:

Material (3 lbs. @ $5 per lb.)	$15.00
Direct labor (3 hrs. @ $3.50 per hr.)	10.50
Overhead (3 hrs. @ $3 per hr.)	9.00
Total standard cost	$34.50

The $3 per direct labor hour overhead rate is based on a normal, 90% of capacity, operating level for the company's plant and the following flexible budget information for April.

	Operating Levels		
	80%	90%	100%
Production in units	800	900	1,000
Direct labor hours..............	2,400	2,700	3,000
Fixed factory overhead	$4,500	$4,500	$4,500
Variable factory overhead....	$3,200	$3,600	$4,000

During April the company operated at 80% of capacity, producing 800 units of product having the following actual costs:

Material (2,350 lbs. @ $5.10 per lb.).................. $11,985
Direct labor (2,500 hrs. @ $3.40 per hr.) 8,500
Fixed factory overhead costs 4,500
Variable factory overhead costs 3,325

Required:

Isolate the material and labor variances into price and quantity variances and isolate the overhead variance into the volume variance and the controllable variance.

Problem 26–4A

Frankford Company has established the following standard costs per unit for the product it manufactures:

Material (4 lbs. @ $0.75 per lb.) .... $ 3.00
Direct labor (2 hrs. @ $3.50 per hr.).... 7.00
Overhead (2 hrs. @ $2.50 per hr.)....... 5.00
   Total standard cost.................. $15.00

The $2.50 per direct labor hour overhead rate is based on a normal, 80% of capacity, operating level and the following flexible budget information for one month's operations.

	Operating Levels		
	75%	80%	85%
Production in units	1,500	1,600	1,700
Standard direct labor hours	3,000	3,200	3,400
Budgeted factory overhead:			
Fixed costs:			
Depreciation, building	$1,200	$1,200	$1,200
Depreciation, machinery.....................	1,700	1,700	1,700
Taxes and insurance	300	300	300
Supervisory salaries..........................	1,600	1,600	1,600
Total fixed costs.........................	$4,800	$4,800	$4,800
Variable costs:			
Indirect materials	$ 750	$ 800	$ 850
Indirect labor.................................	1,500	1,600	1,700
Power..	375	400	425
Maintenance..................................	375	400	425
Total variable costs.....................	$3,000	$3,200	$3,400
Total factory overhead	$7,800	$8,000	$8,200

During August the company operated at 75% of capacity, produced 1,500 units of product, and incurred the following actual costs:

Material (5,900 lbs. @ $0.78 per lb.)		$ 4,602
Direct labor (3,060 hrs. @ $3.45 per hr.)....		10,557
Overhead costs:		
Depreciation expense, building	$1,200	
Depreciation expense, machinery...........	1,700	
Taxes and insurance	300	
Supervisory salaries...........................	1,600	
Indirect materials	735	
Indirect labor.................................	1,560	
Power	385	
Maintenance..................................	340	7,820
Total...		$22,979

Required:

1. Isolate the material and labor variances into price and quantity variances and isolate the overhead variance into the volume variance and the controllable variance.
2. Prepare a factory overhead variance report showing the volume and controllable variances.

Potter Company's manager plans to sell artistic, clay pots for $3 each. Each pot should require 2 pounds of a specially processed clay that the company expects to purchase for $0.50 per pound. The pots ought to be produced at the rate of five pots per direct labor hour, and the company should be able to hire

Decision problem 26–1, Potter Company

the needed laborers for $3.75 per hour. Each pot will be packaged in a cardboard container which weighs one-half pound, and the company will seek to buy cardboard for $0.08 per pound.

If actual sales and production volume range from 80,000 to 120,000 pots, the manager would expect the company to incur administrative and sales personnel salaries of $50,000, depreciation of $10,000, utilities expenses of $9,000, and insurance expense of $6,000.

In 197A, Potter Company actually produced and sold 100,000 pots at $2.90 each. It used 225,000 pounds of clay, purchased at $0.52 per pound. Laborers were paid $3.65 per hour and worked 22,000 hours to produce the pots. Cardboard was purchased for $0.085 per pound and 48,000 pounds were used. All other expenses occurred as planned.

Although the above facts are all available to the manager, he has expressed considerable confusion over the matter of evaluating the operating performance of the company. He recognizes that the actual operating income was different from the expected amount but is not able to sort out which items caused the change. He has also expressed interest in learning the magnitude of the impact of price changes in specific items purchased by the company as well as any other factors that might be of help in evaluating the company's performance. Can you help the manager?

Decision problem 26–2, Machine Products Company

Ray Saul has been an employee of Machine Products Company for nine years, the last seven of which he has worked in the casting department. Eight months ago he was made foreman of the department, and since then has been able to end a long period of internal dissention, high employee turnover, and inefficient operation in the department. Under Ray's supervision the department's production has increased, employee morale has improved, absenteeism has dropped, and for the past two months the department has regularly been beating its standard for the first time in years.

However, a few days ago Jack Payne, an employee in the department, suggested to Ray that the company install new controls on the department's furnace similar to those developed by a competitor. The controls would cost $15,000 installed and would have a ten-year life and no salvage value. They should increase production 10%, reduce maintenance costs $500 per year, and do away with the labor of one person.

Ray's answer to Jack was, "Forget it. We are doing OK now; we don't need the extra production; and besides, jobs are hard to find and if we have to let someone go, who'll it be?"

Do you think standard costs had anything to do with Ray's answer to Jack? Explain. Do you agree with Ray's answer? Should Ray be the person to make a decision such as this? How can a company be sure that suggestions such as Jack's are not lost in the chain of command?

Decision problem 26–3, Rayburn Company

Rayburn Company manufactures Frebolas which have a seasonal demand and which cannot be stored for long periods; consequently, the number of units manufactured varies with the season. In accounting for costs, the company charges actual costs incurred to a goods in process account maintained for the product, which it closes at the end of each quarter to Finished Goods. At the end of last year, which was an average year, the following cost report was prepared for the company manager:

RAYBURN COMPANY
Quarterly Report of Costs for Frebolas
Year Ended December 31, 19 —

	1st Quarter	2d Quarter	3d Quarter	4th Quarter
Materials...	$ 31,200	$ 38,900	$ 15,700	$ 7,900
Direct labor......................................	93,400	116,000	47,000	23,600
Fixed overhead costs	42,000	42,000	42,000	42,000
Variable overhead costs......................	51,200	63,900	25,900	13,000
Total manufacturing costs	$217,800	$260,800	$130,600	$ 86,500
Production in units..............................	40,000	50,000	20,000	10,000
Cost per unit......................................	$5.445	$5.216	$6.530	$8.650

The manager has asked you to explain why unit costs for the product varied from a low of $5.216 in the second quarter to a high of $8.650 in the last quarter, and to suggest a better way to accumulate or allocate costs. The manager feels that the quarterly reports are needed for purposes of control, so attach to your explanation a schedule showing what last year's material, labor, and overhead costs per unit would have been had your suggestion or suggestions been followed for the year.

After studying Chapter 27, you should be able to:

■ Describe the impact of capital budgeting on the operations of a company.

■ Calculate a payback period on an investment and state the inherent limitations of this method.

■ Calculate a rate of return on an investment and state the assumptions on which this method is based.

■ Describe the information obtained by using the discounted cash flow method, the procedures involved in using this method, and the problems associated with its use.

■ Explain the effects of incremental costs on a decision to accept or reject additional business and on a decision whether to make or buy a given product.

■ State the meaning of sunk costs, out-of-pocket costs, and opportunity costs, and describe the importance of each type of cost to capital budgeting decisions such as to scrap or rebuild defective units or to sell a product as is or process it further.

■ Define or explain the words and phrases listed in the chapter Glossary.

chapter 27

Capital budgeting; managerial decisions

A business decision involves choosing between two or more courses of action, with the best choice normally being the one offering the highest return on the investment or the greatest cost savings. Business managers at times make such decisions intuitively and without trying to measure systematically the advantages and disadvantages of each possible choice. Often they make intuitive decisions because they are unaware of any other way to choose; but sometimes the available information is so sketchy or unreliable that systematic measurement is useless. Also, intangible factors such as convenience, prestige, and public opinion are at times more important than the factors that can be reduced to a quantitative basis. Nevertheless, in many situations it is possible to reduce the anticipated consequences of alternative choices to a quantitative basis and measure them systematically. This chapter will examine several.

Planning plant asset investments is called *capital budgeting*. The plans may involve new buildings, new machinery, or whole new projects; but in every case the objective is to earn a satisfactory return on the invested funds; and to accomplish this often requires some of the most crucial and difficult decisions faced by management. The decisions are difficult because they are commonly based on estimates projected well into a future that is at best uncertain; and they are crucial because (1) large sums of money are often involved; (2) funds are committed for long periods of time; and (3) once a decision is made and a project is begun, it may be difficult or impossible to reverse the effects of a poor decision.

Capital budgeting

Capital budgeting involves the preparation of cost and revenue estimates for all proposed projects, an examination of the merits of each, and a choice of those worthy of investment. It is a broad field, and this text must limit its discussion to three ways of comparing investment opportunities. They are the *payback period,* the *return on average investment,* and *discounted cash flows.*

Payback period

Generally an investment in a machine or other plant asset will produce a *net cash flow,* and the payback period for the investment is the time required to recover the investment through this net cash flow. For example, assume that Murray Company is considering several capital investments, among which is the purchase of a machine to be used in manufacturing a new product. The machine will cost $16,000, have an eight-year service life, and no salvage value. The company estimates that 10,000 units of the machine's product will be sold each year, and the sales will result in $1,500 of after-tax net income, calculated as follows:

Annual sales of new product..		$30,000
Deduct:		
Cost of materials, labor, and overhead other than depreciation on the new machine..................................	$15,500	
Depreciation on the new machine......................................	2,000	
Additional selling and administrative expenses	9,500	27,000
Annual before-tax income...		$ 3,000
Income tax (assumed rate, 50%)		1,500
Annual after-tax net income from new product sales..............		$ 1,500

Through annual sales of 10,000 units of the new product, Murray Company expects to gain $30,000 of revenue and $1,500 of net income. The net income will be available to pay back the new machine's cost; but in addition, since none of the funds that flow in from sales flow out for depreciation, so will the amount of the annual depreciation charge. The $1,500 of net income and the $2,000 depreciation charge total $3,500, and together are the *annual net cash flow* expected from the investment. Furthermore, this annual net cash flow will pay back the investment in the new machine in 4.6 years, calculated as follows:

$$\frac{\text{Cost of new machine, \$16,000}}{\text{Annual net cash flow, \$3,500}} = 4.6 \text{ years to recover investment}$$

The answer just given is 4.6 years. Actually, when $16,000 is divided by $3,500, the result is just a little over 4.57; but 4.6 years is close enough for a decision. Remember that the calculation is based on estimated net income and estimated depreciation; consequently, it is pointless to carry the answer to several decimal places.

In choosing investment opportunities, a short payback period is a desirable factor because (1) the sooner an investment is recovered the sooner the funds are available for other uses and (2) a short payback period also means a short "bail-out period" if conditions should change. However, the payback period should never be the only factor considered because it ignores the length of time revenue will continue to be earned after the end of the payback period. For example, one investment may pay back its cost in three years and cease to produce revenue at that point, while a second investment may require five years to pay back its cost but will continue to produce income for another 15 years.

Rate of return on average investment

The rate of return on the average investment in a machine is calculated by dividing the after-tax net income from the sale of the machine's product by the average investment in the machine. For example, Murray Company estimates it will earn a $1,500 after-tax net income from selling the product of the $16,000 machine it proposes to buy. As to average investment, each year depreciation will reduce the book value of the machine $2,000, and the company will recover this amount of its investment through the sale of the machine's product. Consequently, the company may assume it will have $16,000 invested in the machine during its first year, $14,000 during the second, $12,000 during the third, and so on for the machine's eight-year life. Or, in other words, the company may assume it will have an amount equal to the machine's book value invested each year. If it makes this assumption, then the average amount it will have invested during the eight-year life is the average of the machine's book values. This is $9,000 and may be calculated as follows:

Year	Beginning of the Year Book Value	
1	$16,000	
2	14,000	
3	12,000	
4	10,000	$\dfrac{\$72,000}{8} = \$9,000$ average book value and average investment
5	8,000	
6	6,000	
7	4,000	
8	2,000	
Total	$72,000	

In the illustrated calculation the eight yearly book values were averaged to determine average investment. A shorter way to the same answer is to average the book values of the machine's first and last years in this manner:

$$\frac{\$16,000 + \$2,000}{2} = \$9,000$$

And since the answer is the same either way the calculation is made, the shorter calculation is preferable.

After average investment is determined, the rate of return on average investment is calculated, as previously stated, by dividing the estimated annual after-tax net income from the sale of the machine's product by average investment, as follows:

$1,500 ÷ $9,000 = 16⅔% return on average investment

At this point students commonly want to know if 16⅔% is a good investment return. The answer is that it is better than, say, 12%, but not as good as 18%; or in other words, a return is good or bad only when related to other returns. Also, factors other than return, such as risk, are always involved in investment decisions. However, when average investment returns are used in comparing and deciding between capital investments, the one having the least risk, the shortest payback period, and the highest return for the longest time is usually the best.

Rate of return on average investment is easy to calculate and understand, and as a result has long been used in selecting investment opportunities. Furthermore, when the opportunities produce uniform cash flows, it offers a fair basis for selection. However, a comparison of *discounted cash flows* with amounts to be invested offers a better means of selection.

An understanding of discounted cash flows requires an understanding of the concept of present value. This concept was explained in the Appendix following Chapter 11, beginning on page 372, and the explanation should be reviewed at this point by any student who does not fully understand it. The present value tables in that Appendix, on pages 373 and 375, must be used to solve some of the problems which follow the present chapter.

Discounted cash flows

When a business invests in a new plant asset, it expects to secure from the investment a stream of future cash flows, and normally it will not invest unless the flows are sufficient to return the amount of the investment plus a satisfactory return on the investment. For example, will the cash flows from the investment in the machine being considered by Murray Company return the amount of the investment plus a satisfactory return? If Murray Company considers a 10% compound annual return a satisfactory return on its capital investments, it can answer this question with the calculations of Illustration 27–1.

To secure the machine of Illustration 27–1, Murray Company must invest $16,000. However, from the sale of the machine's product it will recapture $2,000 of its investment each year in the form of depreciation; and in addition it will earn a $1,500 annual net income. Or in other words, the company will receive a $3,500 net cash flow from the investment each year for eight years. The first column of Illustration 27–1 indicates that the net cash flows of the first year are received one year hence, and so forth for subsequent years. In other words, the column indicates that the net cash flows are received at

Analysis of Proposed Investment in Machine

Years Hence	Net Cash Flows	Present Value of $1 at 10%	Present Value of Net Cash Flows
1	$3,500	0.909	$ 3,181.50
2	3,500	0.826	2,891.00
3	3,500	0.751	2,628.50
4	3,500	0.683	2,390.50
5	3,500	0.621	2,173.50
6	3,500	0.565	1,977.50
7	3,500	0.513	1,795.50
8	3,500	0.467	1,634.50

Total present value $18,672.50
Amount to be invested 16,000.00
Positive Net Present Value................................ $ 2,672.50

Illustration 27–1

the end of the year. To simplify the discussion of this chapter and the problems at the end of the chapter, the net cash flows of a company's operations are generally assumed to occur at the end of the year. More refined calculations are left for consideration in an advanced course.

The annual net cash flows, shown in the second column of Illustration 27–1, are multiplied by the amounts in the third column to determine their present values, which are shown in the last column. Observe that the total of these present values exceeds the amount of the required investment by $2,672.50. Consequently, if Murray Company considers a 10% compound return satisfactory, this machine will recover its required investment, plus a 10% compound return, and $2,672.50 in addition.

Generally, when the cash flows from an investment such as this, discounted at a satisfactory rate, have a present value in excess of the investment, the investment is a good one and is worthy of acceptance. Also, when several investment opportunities are being compared, and each of them requires the same amount to be invested and has the same risk, the one having the highest positive net present value is the best.

Shortening the calculation

In Illustration 27–1 the present values of $1 at 10% for each of the eight years involved are shown, and it is assumed that each year's cash flow is multiplied by the present value of $1 at 10% for that year to determine its present value. The present values of the eight cash flows are then added to determine their total, which is one way to determine total present value. However, since in this case the cash flows are uniform, there are two shorter ways. One shorter way is to add the eight yearly present values of $1 at 10% and to multiply $3,500 by the total. Another even shorter way is based on Table 11A–2 on page 375. Table 11A–2 shows the present value of $1 to be received periodically for a number of periods. In the case of the Murray Company machine, $3,500 is to be received annually for eight years. Consequently, to determine the present value of these annual receipts discounted at 10%, go down the 10% column of Table 11A–2 to the amount opposite eight periods. It is 5.335. Therefore, the present value of the eight annual $3,500 receipts is $3,500 multiplied by 5.335 or is $18,672.50.

Cash flows not uniform

Present value analysis has its greatest usefulness when cash flows are not uniform. For example, assume a company can choose one capital investment from among Projects A, B, and C. Each requires a $12,000 investment and will produce cash flows as follows:

Years Hence	Annual Cash Flows		
	Project A	Project B	Project C
1	$ 5,000	$ 8,000	$ 1,000
2	5,000	5,000	5,000
3	5,000	2,000	9,000
	$15,000	$15,000	$15,000

Note that all three projects produce the same total cash flow. However, the flows of Project A are uniform, those of Project B are greater in the earlier years, while those of Project C are greater in the later years. Consequently, when present values of the cash flows, discounted at 10% are compared with the required investments, the statistics of Illustration 27–2 result.

	Years Hence	Present Values of Cash Flows Discounted at 10%		
		Project A	Project B	Project C
	1	$ 4,545	$ 7,272	$ 909
	2	4,130	4,130	4,130
	3	3,755	1,502	6,759
Total present values............		$12,430	$12,904	$11,798
Required investments..........		12,000	12,000	12,000
Net Present Values.............		+$ 430	+$ 904	−$ 202

Illustration 27–2

Note that an investment in Project A has a $430 positive net present value, an investment in Project B a $904 positive net present value, and an investment in Project C a $202 negative net present value.

Therefore, if a 10% return is required, an investment in Project C should be rejected, since the investment's net present value indicates it will not earn such a return. Furthermore, as between Projects A and B, other things being equal, Project B is the better investment, since its cash flows have the higher net present value.

Salvage value and accelerated depreciation

The $16,000 machine of the Murray Company example was assumed to have no salvage value at the end of its useful life. Often a machine is expected to have a salvage value, and in such cases the expected salvage value is treated as an additional cash flow to be received in the last year of the machine's life.

Also, in the Murray Company example, depreciation was deducted on a straight-line basis; but in actual practice, an accelerated depreciation method, such as the sum-of-the-years'-digits method, is commonly used for tax purposes. Accelerated depreciation results in larger depreciation deductions in the early years of an asset's life and smaller deductions in the later years, which in turn result in smaller income tax liabilities in the early years and larger ones in later years. However, this does not change the basic nature of a present value analysis. It only results in larger cash flows in the early years and smaller ones in later years, which normally make an investment more desirable.

Selecting the earnings rate

The selection of a satisfactory earnings rate for capital investments is always a matter for top-management decision. Formulas have been devised to aid management; but in many companies the choice of a satisfactory or required rate of return is largely subjective. Management simply decides that enough investment opportunities can be found that will earn, say, a 10% compound return; and this becomes the minimum below which the company refuses to make an investment of average risk.

Whatever the required rate, it is always higher than the rate at which money can be borrowed, since the return on a capital investment must include not only interest but also an additional allowance for risks involved. Therefore, when the rate at which money can be borrowed is around 8%, a required after-tax return of 12% may be acceptable in industrial companies, with a lower rate for public utilities and a higher rate for companies in which investment opportunities are unusually good or the risks are high.

Replacing plant assets

In a dynamic economy, new and better machines are constantly coming on the market. As a result the decision to replace an existing machine with a new and better machine is common. Often the existing machine is in good condition and will produce the required product; but the new machine will do the job with a large savings in operating costs. In such a situation management must decide whether the after-tax savings in operating costs justifies the investment.

The amount of after-tax savings from the replacement of an existing machine with a new machine is complicated by the fact that depreciation on the new machine for tax purposes is based on the book value of the old machine plus the cash given in the exchange. There can be other complications too; consequently, a discussion of the replacement of plant assets is deferred to a more advanced course.

Accepting additional business

Costs obtained from a cost accounting system are average costs and also historical costs. They are useful in product pricing and in controlling operations, but in a decision to accept an additional volume of business they are not necessarily the relevant costs. In such a decision the relevant costs are the additional costs, commonly called the *incremental* or *differential costs*.

For example, a concern operating at its normal capacity, which is 80% of full capacity, has annually produced and sold approximately 100,000 units of product with the following results:

Sales (100,000 units @ $10)		$1,000,000
Materials (100,000 units @ $3.50)	$350,000	
Labor (100,000 units @ $2.20)	220,000	
Overhead (100,000 units @ $1.10)	110,000	
Selling expenses (100,000 units @ $1.40)	140,000	
Administrative expenses (100,000 units @ $0.80)	80,000	900,000
Operating Income		$ 100,000

The concern's sales department reports it has an exporter who has offered to buy 10,000 units of product at $8.50 per unit. The sale to the exporter is several times larger than any previous sale made by the company; and since the units are being exported, the new business will have no effect on present business. Therefore, in order to determine whether the order should be accepted or rejected, management of the company asks that statistics be prepared to show the estimated net income or loss that would result from accepting the offer. It received the following figures based on the average costs previously given:

Sales (10,000 units @ $8.50)		$85,000
Materials (10,000 units @ $3.50)	$35,000	
Labor (10,000 units @ $2.20)	22,000	
Overhead (10,000 units @ $1.10)	11,000	
Selling expenses (10,000 units @ $1.40)	14,000	
Administrative expenses (10,000 units @ $0.80)	8,000	90,000
Operating Loss		$ (5,000)

If a decision were based on these average costs, the new business would likely be rejected. However, in this situation average costs are not relevant. The relevant costs are the added costs of accepting the new business. Consequently, before rejecting the order, the costs of the new business were examined more closely and the following additional information obtained: (1) Manufacturing 10,000 additional units of product would require materials and labor at $3.50 and $2.20 per unit just as with normal production. (2) However, the 10,000 units could be manufactured with overhead costs, in addition to those already incurred, of only $5,000 for power, packing, and handling labor. (3) Commissions and other selling expenses resulting from the sale would amount to $2,000 in addition to the selling expenses already incurred. And (4) $1,000 additional administrative expenses in the form of clerical work would be required if the order were accepted. Based on this added information, the statement of Illustration 27–3 showing the effect of the additional business on the company's normal business was prepared.

	Present Business	Additional Business	Present Plus the Additional Business
Sales	$1,000,000	$85,000	$1,085,000
Materials.....................	$350,000	$35,000	$385,000
Labor..........................	220,000	22,000	242,000
Overhead	110,000	5,000	115,000
Selling expenses..........	140,000	2,000	142,000
Administrative expense	80,000	1,000	81,000
Total	900,000	65,000	965,000
Operating income	$ 100,000	$20,000	$ 120,000

Illustration 27–3

It is obvious from Illustration 27–3 that when present business is charged with all present costs and the additional business is charged only with its incremental or differential costs, accepting the additional business at $8.50 per unit will apparently result in $20,000 additional income before taxes.

Incremental or differential costs always apply to a particular situation at a particular time. For example, adding units to a given production volume might or might not increase depreciation expense. If the additional units require the purchase of more machines, depreciation expense is increased. Likewise, if present machines are used but the additional units shorten their life, more depreciation expense results. However, if present machines are used and their depreciation depends more on the passage of time or obsolescence rather than on use, additional depreciation expense might not result from the added units of product.

Buy or make

Incremental or differential costs are often a factor in a decision as to whether a given part or product should be bought or made. For example, a manufacturer has idle machines upon which he can make Part 417 of his product. This part is presently purchased at a $1.20 delivered cost per unit. The manufacturer estimates that to make Part 417 would cost $0.45 for materials, $0.50 for labor, and an amount of overhead. At this point a question arises as to how much overhead should be charged. If the normal overhead rate of the department in which the part would be manufactured is 100% of direct labor cost, and this amount is charged against Part 417, then the unit costs of making Part 417 would be $0.45 for materials, $0.50 for labor, and $0.50 for overhead, a total of $1.45. At this cost, the manufacturer would be better off to buy the part at $1.20 each.

However, on a short-run basis the manufacturer might be justified in ignoring the normal overhead rate and in charging Part 417 for only the additional overhead costs resulting from its manufacture. Among these additional overhead costs might be, for example, power to operate the machines that would otherwise be idle, depreciation on the machines if the part's manufacture resulted in additional depreciation, and any other overhead that would be added to that already incurred. Furthermore, if these added overhead items total less than $0.25 per unit, the manufacturer might be justified on a short-run basis in manufacturing the part. However, on a long-term basis, Part 417 should be charged a full share of all overhead.

Any amount of overhead less than $0.25 per unit results in a total cost for Part 417 that is less than the $1.20 per unit purchase price. Nevertheless, in making a final decision as to whether the part should be bought or made, the manufacturer should consider in addition to costs such things as quality, the reactions of customers and suppliers, and other intangible factors. When these additional factors are considered small cost differences may become a minor factor.

Other costs

Sunk costs, out-of-pocket costs, and *opportunity costs* are additional costs encountered in managerial decisions.

A sunk cost is a cost resulting from a past irrevocable decision, and is sunk in the sense that it cannot be avoided. As a result, sunk costs are irrelevant in decisions affecting the future.

An out-of-pocket cost is a cost requiring a current outlay of funds. Material costs, supplies, heat, and power are examples. Generally, out-of-pocket costs can be avoided; consequently, they are relevant in decisions affecting the future.

Costs as discussed thus far have been outlays or expenditures made to obtain some benefit, usually goods or services. However, the concept of costs can be expanded to include *sacrifices made to gain some benefit.* For example, if a job that will pay a student $1,200 for working during the summer must be rejected in order to attend summer school, the $1,200 is an opportunity cost of attending summer school.

Obviously, opportunity costs are not entered in the accounting records; but they may be relevant in a decision involving rejected opportunities, such as in a decision to scrap or rebuild defective units of product, where both sunk and opportunity costs are commonly encountered.

Any costs incurred in manufacturing units of product that do not pass inspection are sunk costs and as such should not enter into a decision as to whether the units should be sold for scrap or be rebuilt to pass inspection. For example, a concern has 10,000 defective units of product that cost $1 per unit to manufacture. The units can be sold as they are for $0.40 each, or they can be rebuilt for $0.80 per unit, after which they can be sold for their full price of $1.50 per unit. Should the company rebuild the units or should it sell them in their present form? Obviously, the original manufacturing costs of $1 per unit are sunk costs and are irrelevant in the decision; so based on the information given, the comparative returns from scrapping or rebuilding are:

Scrap or rebuild defective units

	As Scrap	Rebuilt
Sale of defective units	$4,000	$15,000
Less cost to rebuild		(8,000)
Net Return	$4,000	$ 7,000

From the information given, it appears that rebuilding is the better decision, and this is true if the rebuilding does not interfere with normal operations. However, suppose that to rebuild the defective units the company must forgo manufacturing 10,000 new units that will cost $1 per unit to manufacture and can be sold for $1.50 per unit. In this situation the comparative returns may be analyzed as follows:

	As Scrap	Rebuilt
Sale of defective units	$ 4,000	$15,000
Less cost to rebuild the defective units		(8,000)
Sale of new units	15,000	
Less cost to manufacture the new units	(10,000)	
Net Return	$ 9,000	$ 7,000

If the defective units are sold without rebuilding, then the new units can also be manufactured and sold, with a $9,000 return from the sale of both the new and old units, as shown in the first column of the analysis. Obviously this is better than forgoing the manufacture of the new units and rebuilding the defective units for a $7,000 net return.

The situation described here also may be analyzed on an opportunity cost basis as follows: If to rebuild the defective units the company must forgo manufacturing the new units, then the return on the sale of the new units is an opportunity cost of rebuilding the defective units. This opportunity cost is measured at $5,000 (revenue from sale of new units, $15,000, less their manufacturing costs, $10,000 equals the $5,000 benefit that will be sacrificed if the old units are rebuilt); and an opportunity cost analysis of the situation is as follows:

	As Scrap	Rebuilt
Sale of defective units	$4,000	$15,000
Less cost to rebuild the defective units		(8,000)
Less opportunity cost (return sacrificed by not manufacturing the new units)		(5,000)
Net Return	$4,000	$ 2,000

Observe that it does not matter whether this or the previous analysis is made, since either way there is a $2,000 difference in favor of scrapping the defective units.

Process or sell

Sunk costs, out-of-pocket costs, and opportunity costs are also encountered in a decision as to whether it is best to sell an intermediate product as it is or process it further and sell the product or products that result from the additional processing. For example, a company has 40,000 units of Product A that cost $0.75 per unit or a total of $30,000 to manufacture. The 40,000 units can be sold as they are for $50,000 or they can be processed further into Products X, Y, and Z at a cost of $2 per original Product A unit. The additional processing will produce the following numbers of each product, which can be sold at the unit prices indicated:

Product X	10,000 units @ $3
Product Y	22,000 units @ $5
Product Z	6,000 units @ $1
Lost through spoilage	2,000 units (no salvage value)
Total	40,000 units

The net advantage of processing the product further is $16,000, as shown in Illustration 27–4 on the next page.

Note that the revenue available through the sale of the Product A units is an opportunity cost of further processing these units. Also notice that the $30,000 cost of manufacturing the 40,000 units of Product A does not appear in the Illustration 27–4 analysis. This cost is present regardless of which alternative is chosen; therefore it is irrelevant to the decision. However, the $30,000 does enter into a calculation of the net income from the alternatives. For example, if the company

Revenue from further processing:		
Product X, 10,000 units @ $3	$ 30,000	
Product Y, 22,000 units @ $5	110,000	
Product Z, 6,000 units @ $1	6,000	
Total revenue		$146,000
Less:		
Additional processing costs, 40,000 units @ $2	$ 80,000	
Opportunity cost (revenue sacrificed by not selling the Product A units)	50,000	
Total		130,000
Net advantage of further processing		$ 16,000

Illustration 27–4

chooses to further process the Product A units, the gross return from the sale of Products X, Y, and Z may be calculated as follows:

Revenue from the sale of Products X, Y, and Z		$146,000
Less:		
Cost to manufacture the Product A units	$30,000	
Cost to further process the Product A units	80,000	110,000
Gross return from the sale of Products X, Y, and Z		$ 36,000

Deciding the sales mix

When a company sells a combination of products, ordinarily some of the products are more profitable than others, and normally management should concentrate its sales efforts on the more profitable products. However, if production facilities or other factors are limited, an increase in the production and sale of one product may require a reduction in the production and sale of another. In such a situation management's job is to determine the most profitable combination or sales mix for the products and concentrate its efforts in selling the products in this combination.

To determine the best sales mix for its products, management must have information as to the contribution margin of each product, the facilities required to produce and sell each product, and any limitations on these facilities. For example, assume that a company produces and sells two products, A and B. The same machines are used to produce both products, and the products have the following selling prices and variable costs per unit:

	Product A	Product B
Selling price	$5.00	$7.50
Variable costs	3.50	5.50
Contribution margin	$1.50	$2.00

If the amount of production facilities required to produce each product is the same and there is an unlimited market for Product B, the company should devote all its facilities to Product B because of its larger contribution margin. However, if the company's facilities are limited to, say, 100,000 machine-hours of production per month and one machine-hour is required to produce each unit of Product A but two machine-hours are required for each unit of Product B, the answer differs. Under these circumstances, if the market for Product A is unlimited, the company should devote all its production to this product because it produces $1.50 of contribution margin per machine-hour, while Product B produces only $1 per machine-hour.

Actually, when there are no market or other limitations, a company should devote all its efforts to its most profitable product. It is only when there is a market or other limitation on the sale of the most profitable product that a need for a sales mix arises. For example, if in this instance one machine-hour of production facilities are needed to produce each unit of Product A and 100,000 machine-hours are available, 100,000 units of the product can be produced. However, if only 80,000 units can be sold, the company has 20,000 machine-hours that can be devoted to the production of Product B, and 20,000 machine-hours will produce 10,000 units of Product B. Consequently, the company's most profitable sales mix under these assumptions is 80,000 units of Product A and 10,000 units of Product B.

The assumptions in this section have been kept simple. More complicated factors and combinations of factors exist. However, a discussion of these is deferred to a more advanced course.

Glossary

Capital budgeting. Planning plant asset investments; involves the preparation of cost and revenue estimates for all proposed projects, an examination of the merits of each, and a choice of those worthy of investment.

Discounted cash flows. The present value of a stream of future cash flows from an investment, based on an interest rate that gives a satisfactory return on investment.

Incremental cost. An additional cost resulting from a particular course of action.

Opportunity cost. A sacrifice made to gain some benefits; that is, in choosing one course of action, the lost benefit associated with an alternative course of action.

Out-of-pocket cost. A cost requiring a current outlay of funds.

Payback period. The time required to recover the original cost of an investment through net cash flows from the investment.

Rate of return on average investment. The annual, after-tax income from the sale of an asset's product divided by the average investment in the asset.

Sunk cost. A cost incurred as a consequence of a past irrevocable decision and that, therefore, cannot be avoided; hence, irrelevant to decisions affecting the future.

---

1. What is capital budgeting? Why are capital budgeting decisions crucial to the business concern making the decisions?
2. A successful investment in a machine will produce a net cash flow. Of what does this consist?
3. If depreciation is an expense, explain why, when the sale of a machine's product produces a net income, the portion of the machine's cost recovered each year through the sale of its product includes both the net income from the product's sale and the year's depreciation on the machine.
4. Why is a short payback period on an investment desirable?
5. What is the average amount invested in a machine during its life if the machine cost $28,000, has an estimated five-year life, and an estimated $3,000 salvage value?
6. Is a 15% return on the average investment in a machine a good return?
7. Why is the present value of the expectation of receiving $100 a year hence less than $100? What is the present value of the expectation of receiving $100 one year hence, discounted at 12%?
8. What is indicated when the present value of the net cash flows from an investment in a machine, discounted at 12%, exceeds the amount of the investment? What is indicated when the present value of the net cash flows, discounted at 12%, is less than the amount of the investment?
9. What are the incremental costs of accepting an additional volume of business?
10. A company manufactures and sells 250,000 units of product in this country at $5 per unit. The product costs $3 per unit to manufacture. Can you describe a situation under which the company may be willing to sell an additional 25,000 units of the product abroad at $2.75 per unit?
11. What is a sunk cost? An out-of-pocket cost? An opportunity cost? Is an opportunity cost a cost in the accounting sense of the term?
12. Any costs that have been incurred in manufacturing a product are sunk costs. Why are such costs irrelevant in deciding whether to sell the product in its present condition or to make it into a new product through additional processing?

Questions for class discussion

Exercise 27–1

Class exercises

Machine A cost $8,000 and has an estimated four-year life and no salvage value. Machine B cost $12,000 and has an estimated five-year life and a $2,000 salvage value. Under the assumption that the average investment in each machine is the average of its yearly book values, calculate the average investment in each machine.

Exercise 27–2

A company is planning to purchase a machine and add a new product to its line. The machine will cost $20,000, have a four-year life, no salvage value, and will be depreciated on a straight-line basis. The company expects to sell 10,000 units of the machine's product each year with these results:

Sales		$50,000
Costs:		
Materials, labor, and overhead excluding depreciation on the new machine	$26,000	
Depreciation on new machine	5,000	
Selling and administrative expenses	15,000	46,000
Operating income		$ 4,000
Income taxes		2,000
Net Income		$ 2,000

Required:

Calculate (1) the payback period and (2) the return on the average investment in this machine.

Exercise 27–3

After evaluating the risk characteristics of the investment described in Exercise 27–2, the company concludes that it must earn at least a 12% compound return on the investment in the machine. Based on this decision, determine the total present value and net present value of the net cash flows from the machine the company is planning to buy.

Exercise 27–4

A company can invest in each of three projects, A, B, and C. Each project requires a $12,500 investment and will produce cash flows as follows:

Years	Annual Cash Flows		
Hence	Project A	Project B	Project C
1	$ 3,000	$ 5,000	$ 7,000
2	5,000	5,000	5,000
3	7,000	5,000	3,000
	$15,000	$15,000	$15,000

Required:

Under the assumption the company requires a 10% compound return from its investments, determine in which of the projects it should invest.

Exercise 27–5

A company has 10,000 units of Product X that cost $1 per unit to manufacture. The 10,000 units can be sold for $15,000, or they can be further processed at a cost of $7,000 into Products Y and Z. The additional processing will produce 4,000 units of Product Y that can be sold for $2 each and 6,000 units of Product Z that can be sold for $2.25 each.

Required:

Prepare an analysis to show whether the Product X units should be further processed.

Problems

Problem 27-1

A company is planning to add a new product to its line, the production of which will require new machinery costing $45,000 and having a five-year life and no salvage value. This additional information is available:

Estimated annual sales of new product	$150,000
Estimated costs:	
Materials..	30,000
Labor	40,000
Overhead excluding depreciation on new machinery	38,000
Selling and administrative expenses...........................	25,000
State and federal income taxes	50%

Required:

Using straight-line depreciation, calculate (1) the payback period on the investment in new machinery, (2) the rate of return on the average investment, and (3) the net present value of the net cash flows discounted at 12%.

Problem 27-2

A company has an opportunity to invest in either of two projects. Project A requires an investment of $40,000 for new machinery having a five-year life and no salvage value. Project B requires an investment of $35,000 for new machinery having a seven-year life and no salvage value. The products of the projects differ; however, each will produce an estimated $3,000 after-tax profit for the life of the project.

Required:

Calculate the payback period, the return on average investment, and the net present value of the net cash flows from each project discounted at 10%. State which project you think is the better investment and why.

Problem 27-3

Twist'n Fix Company manufactures a small tool that it sells to wholesalers at $3 each. The company manufactures and sells approximately 100,000 of the tools each year, and a normal year's costs for the production and sale of this number of tools are as follows:

Materials..........................	$ 60,000
Direct labor	50,000
Manufacturing overhead.....	75,000
Selling expenses	30,000
Administrative expenses.....	25,000
	$240,000

A mail-order concern has offered to buy 10,000 of the tools at $2.25 each to be marketed under the mail-order concern's trade name. If accepted, the order is not expected to affect sales through present channels.

A study of normal costs and their relation to the new business reveals the following: (*a*) Material costs are 100% variable. (*b*) The per unit direct labor costs for the additional units will be 50% greater than normal since their production will require overtime at time and one half. (*c*) Of a normal year's manufacturing overhead costs, two thirds will remain fixed at any production level from zero to 150,000 units and one third will vary with volume. (*d*) There will be no additional selling costs if the new business is accepted. (*c*) Acceptance of the new business will increase administrative costs $1,500.

Required:

Prepare a comparative income statement that shows (1) in one set of columns the operating results and operating income of a normal year, (2) in the second set of columns the operating results and income that may be expected from the new business, and (3) in the third set of columns the combined results from normal and the expected new business.

Problem 27–4

Ft. Dodge Company is considering a project that requires a $108,000 investment in machinery having a six-year life and a $3,000 salvage value. The project will annually produce $36,500 of income before depreciation on the new machinery and income taxes. The company's state and federal income taxes take 50% of its before-tax income; consequently, with depreciation calculated on a straight-line basis, the project will produce a $9,500 annual after-tax income calculated as follows:

Income before depreciation and income taxes............	$36,500
Depreciation [($108,000 − $3,000) ÷ 6]	17,500
Income before taxes...	$19,000
Income taxes	9,500
Net Income from the Project.................................	$ 9,500

The company refuses to invest in a project that will not earn at least a 14% compound return, and it has been determined that this project will earn such a return. However, it has been pointed out that if the company will depreciate the machinery of the project on a sum-of-the-years'-digits basis, the compound return from the investment can be materially increased.

Required:

1. Calculate the company's net income from the project for each of the six years with depreciation calculated on a sum-of-the-years'-digits basis.
2. With the machinery depreciated on a straight-line basis, calculate the net present value of the net cash flows discounted at 14%.
3. With the machinery depreciated on a sum-of-the-years'-digits basis, calculate the net present value of the net cash flows discounted at 14%.
4. Explain why sum-of-the-years'-digits depreciation increases the desirability of this investment.

Problem 27–5

Straiken Company's sales and costs for its two products last year were:

	Product X	Product Y
Unit selling price	$20	$18
Variable costs per unit	$12	$6
Fixed costs....................	$60,000	$80,000
Units sold	9,000	8,000

Through sales effort the company can change its sales mix. However, sales of the two products are so interrelated that a percentage increase in the sales of one product causes an equal percentage decrease in the sales of the other, and vice versa.

Required:

1. State which of its products the company should push, and why.
2. Prepare a columnar statement showing last year's sales, fixed costs, variable costs, and income before taxes for Product X in the first pair of columns, the results for Product Y in the second set of columns, and the combined results for both products in the third set of columns.
3. Prepare a like statement for the two products under the assumption that the sales of Product X are increased 20%, with a resulting 20% decrease in the sales of Product Y.
4. Prepare a third statement under the assumption that the sales of Product X are decreased 20%, with a resulting 20% increase in the sales of Product Y.

Alternate problems

Problem 27–1A

A company is considering adding a new product to its line, of which it estimates it can sell 20,000 units annually at $10 per unit. To manufacture the product will require new machinery having an estimated five-year life, no salvage value, and costing $60,000. The new product will have a $4 per unit direct material cost and a $2 per unit direct labor cost. Manufacturing overhead chargeable to the new product, other than for depreciation on the new machinery, will be $33,000 annually. Also, $25,000 of additional selling and administrative expenses will be incurred annually in producing and selling the product, and state and federal income taxes will take 50% of the before-taxes profit.

Required:

Using straight-line depreciation, calculate (1) the payback period on the investment in new machinery, (2) the rate of return on the average investment, and (3) the net present value of the net cash flows discounted at 12%.

Problem 27–2A

A company has the opportunity to invest in either of two projects. Project X requires an investment of $56,000 for new machinery having a seven-year life and no salvage value. Project Y requires an investment of $60,000 for new machinery having a five-year life and no salvage value. Sales of the two projects will produce the following estimated annual results:

	Project X		Project Y	
Sales		$130,000		$150,000
Costs:				
Materials	$30,000		$36,000	
Labor	27,000		35,000	
Manufacturing overhead including depreciation on new machinery	38,000		44,000	
Selling and administrative expenses	25,000	120,000	25,000	140,000
Operating income		$ 10,000		$ 10,000
State and federal income taxes		5,000		5,000
Net Income		$ 5,000		$ 5,000

Required:

Calculate the payback period, the return on average investment, and the net present value of the net cash flows from each project discounted at 12%. State which project you think the better investment and why.

Problem 27–3A

Heatransfer Company annually sells at $10 per unit 100,000 units of its product. At the 100,000-unit production level the product costs $9 a unit to manufacture and sell, and at this level the company has the following costs and expenses:

Fixed manufacturing overhead costs..................	$100,000
Fixed selling expenses	50,000
Fixed administrative expenses.........................	60,000
Variable costs and expenses:	
Materials ($2 per unit)	200,000
Labor ($2.50 per unit)	250,000
Manufacturing overhead ($1.50 per unit).........	150,000
Selling expenses ($0.50 per unit)	50,000
Administrative expense ($0.40 per unit)..........	40,000

All the units the company presently sells are sold in this country. However, recently an exporter has offered to buy 10,000 units of the product for sale abroad, but he will pay only $8.90 per unit, which is below the company's present $9 per unit manufacturing and selling costs.

Required:

Prepare an income statement that shows (1) in one set of columns the revenue, costs, expenses, and income from selling 100,000 units of the product in this country; (2) in a second set of columns the additional revenue, costs, expenses, and income from selling 10,000 units to the exporter; and (3) in a third set of columns the combined results from both sources. (Assume that acceptance of the new business will not increase any of the company's fixed costs and expenses nor change any of the variable per unit costs and expenses.)

Problem 27–4A

A company is considering a $75,000 investment in machinery to produce a new product. The machinery is expected to have a five-year life and no salvage value, and annual sales of its product are expected to produce $29,000 of income before depreciation and income taxes. Since state and federal income taxes take 50% of the company's income, with depreciation calculated on a straight-line basis, this means a $7,000 annual after-tax income, calculated as follows:

Income before depreciation and income taxes............	$29,000
Depreciation ($75,000 ÷ 5 years)	15,000
Income before taxes...	$14,000
Income taxes	7,000
Net Income from Sale of Product............................	$ 7,000

The company demands a 15% compound return on such investments, and its controller has calculated that the $75,000 will not earn such a return.

However, in presenting his figures to the company president, he pointed out that the desirability of the investment could be increased by depreciating the machinery on a sum-of-the-years'-digits basis. The president wanted to know why an accounting method would improve the desirability of an investment in machinery.

Required:

1. Calculate the company's net income from the sale of the new product for each of the five years with depreciation calculated by the sum-of-the-years'-digits method.
2. With the machinery depreciated on a straight-line basis, calculate the net present value of the net cash flows discounted at 15%.
3. With the machinery depreciated on a sum-of-the-years'-digits basis, calculate the net present value of the net cash flows discounted at 15%.
4. Explain why sum-of-the-years'-digits depreciation improves the desirability of this investment.

Problem 27–5A

Cross Cutter Company manufactures and sells a machine called a sectioner. Last year the company made and sold 1,400 sectioners, with the following results:

Sales (1,400 units @ $180).....................		$252,000
Costs and expenses:		
Variable:		
Materials..	$55,440	
Labor	45,360	
Factory overhead	37,800	
Selling and administrative expenses	25,200	
Fixed:		
Factory overhead	38,000	
Selling and administrative expenses	24,000	225,800
Income before Taxes.............................		$ 26,200

The state highway department has asked for bids on 150 sectioners almost identical to Cross Cutter Company's machine, the only difference being a counter not presently installed on the Cross Cutter Company sectioner. To install the counter would require the purchase of a new machine costing $1,000, plus $4 per sectioner for additional material and $5 per sectioner for additional labor. The new machine would have no further use after the completion of the highway department contract, but it could be sold for $400. Sale of the additional units would not affect the company's fixed costs and expenses, but all variable costs and expenses, including variable selling and administrative expenses, would increase proportionately with the volume increase.

Required:

1. List with their total the unit costs of the material, labor, and so forth, that would enter into the lowest unit price the company could bid on the special order without causing a reduction in income from normal business.
2. Under the assumption the company bid $159 per unit and was awarded the contract for the 150 special units, prepare an income statement show-

ing (1) in one set of columns the revenues, costs, expenses, and income before taxes from present business; (2) in a second set of columns the revenue, costs, expenses, and income before taxes from the new business; and (3) in a third set of columns the combined results of both the old and new business.

Decision problem 27–1, Coppernic Company

Coppernic Company operates metal alloy producing plants, one of which is located at Selma. The Selma plant no longer produces a satisfactory profit due to its distance from raw material sources, relatively high electric power costs, and lack of modern machinery. Consequently, construction of a new plant to replace the Selma plant is under consideration.

The new plant would be located close to a raw material source and near low-cost hydroelectric power; but its construction would necessitate abandonment of the Selma plant. The company president favors the move; but several members of the board are not convinced the Selma plant should be abandoned in view of the great loss that would result.

You have been asked to make recommendations concerning the proposed abandonment and construction of the new plant. Data developed during the course of your analysis include the following:

Loss from abandoning the Selma Plant. The land, buildings, and machinery of the Selma plant have a $3,800,000 book value. Very little of the machinery can be moved to the new plant. Most will have to be scrapped. Therefore, if the plant is abandoned, it is estimated that only $800,000 of the remaining investment in the plant can be recovered through the sale of its land and buildings, the sale of scrap, and by moving some of its machinery to the new plant. The remaining $3,000,000 will be lost.

Investment in the new plant. The new plant will cost $12,000,000, including the book value of any machinery moved from Selma, and will have a 20-year life. It will also have double the 25,000-ton capacity of the Selma plant, and it is estimated the 50,000 tons of metal alloy produced annually can be sold without a price reduction.

Comparative production costs. A comparison of the production costs per ton at the old plant with the estimated costs at the new plant shows the following:

	Old Plant	New Plant
Raw material, labor, and plant costs (other than depreciation)	$325	$275
Depreciation	18	12
Total costs per ton	$343	$287

The higher per ton depreciation charge of the old plant results primarily from depreciation being allocated to fewer units of product.

Prepare a report analyzing the advantages and disadvantages of the move, including your recommendation. You may assume that the Selma plant can continue to operate long enough to recover the remaining investment in the plant; however, due to the plant's high costs, operation will be at the break-even point. Furthermore, a shortage of skilled personnel would not allow the company to operate both the Selma plant and the new plant. Present any pertinent analyses based on the data given.

Rayburn Company has operated at substantially less than its full plant capacity for several years, producing and selling an average of 65,000 units of its product annually and receiving a per unit price of $12. Its costs at this sales level are:

Direct materials......................................	$266,500
Direct labor	208,000
Manufacturing overhead:	
Variable	81,250
Fixed..	40,000
Selling and administrative expenses:	
Variable	39,000
Fixed..	80,000
Income taxes	50%

After searching for ways to utilize the plant capacity of the company more fully, management has begun to consider the possibility of processing the product beyond the present point at which it is sold. If the product is further processed, it can be sold for $14 per unit. Further processing will increase fixed manufacturing overhead by $16,500 annually, and it will increase variable manufacturing costs per unit as follows:

Materials...	$0.42
Direct labor	0.38
Variable manufacturing overhead............	0.30
Total	$1.10

Selling the further processed product will not affect fixed selling and administrative expenses, but it will increase variable selling and administrative expenses 10%. Further processing is not expected to either increase or decrease the number of units sold.

Should the company further process the product? Back your opinion with a simple calculation and also a comparative income statement showing present results and the estimated results with the product further processed.

Jamestown Company manufactures and sells a common piece of industrial machinery, selling an average of 56,000 units of the machine each year. The company generally earns an after-tax (50% rate) net income of $16 per unit sold. Jamestown Company's production process involves assemblying the several components of the machine, some of which are manufactured by the company and others of which are purchased from a variety of suppliers.

One of the components that has been manufactured by the company is a pump which is also available from other suppliers. Jamestown Company uses special equipment to make the pump, and the equipment has no alternative uses. The equipment has a $42,000 book value, a seven-year remaining life, and is depreciated at the rate of $6,000 per year. In addition to depreciation of the equipment, the costs to manufacture the pump are: direct materials, $2.00; direct labor, $1.60; and variable overhead, $0.40.

One of Jamestown's suppliers has recently offered the company a contract to purchase pumps from the supplier at a delivered cost of $4.26 per unit. If the company decides to purchase the pumps, the special equipment used to manufacture them can be sold for cash at its book value (no profit or loss) and the cash can be invested in other projects that will pay a 12% compound after-tax return, which is the return the company demands on all its capital investments.

Should the company continue to manufacture the pump, or should it sell the special equipment and buy the pump? Back your answer with explanations and computations.

After studying Chapter 28, you should be able to:

- Explain the importance of tax planning.
- Describe the steps an individual must go through to calculate his tax liability, and explain the difference between deductions to arrive at adjusted gross income, deductions from adjusted gross income, and tax credits.
- Calculate the taxable income and net tax liability for an individual.
- State the procedures used to determine the tax associated with capital gains and losses.
- Describe the differences between the calculations of taxable income and tax liability for corporations and for individuals.
- Explain why income tax expenses shown in financial statements may differ from taxes actually payable.
- Define or explain the terms and phrases listed in the chapter Glossary.

chapter 28

Tax considerations
in business decisions

Years ago, when income tax rates were low, management could afford to ignore or dismiss as of minor importance the tax effects of a business decision; but today, when nearly half the income of a business must commonly be paid out in income taxes, this is no longer wise. Today, a successful management must constantly be alert to every possible tax savings, recognizing that it is often necessary to earn two "pre-tax dollars" in order to keep one "after-tax dollar," or that a dollar of income tax saved is commonly worth a two-dollar reduction in any other expense.

When taxpayers plan their affairs in such a way as to incur the small-est possible tax liability, they are engaged in tax planning. Tax planning requires the application of tax laws to the alternate ways in which transactions may be completed, and a choice in each case of the way that will result in the smallest tax liability.

Tax planning

Normally tax planning requires that a tax-saving opportunity be recognized prior to the occurrence of the transaction. Although it is sometimes possible to take advantage of a previously overlooked tax saving, the common result of an overlooked opportunity is a lost opportunity, since the Internal Revenue Service usually deems the original action in a tax situation the final action for tax purposes.

Since effective tax planning requires an extensive knowledge of both tax laws and business procedures, it is not the purpose of this chapter to make expert tax planners of elementary accounting students. Rather, the purpose is to make students aware of the merits of effective tax planning, recognizing that for complete and effective planning, the average student, business executive, or citizen should seek the advice of a certified public accountant, tax attorney, or other person qualified in tax matters.

Tax evasion and tax avoidance

In any discussion of taxes a clear distinction should be drawn between tax evasion and tax avoidance. Tax evasion is illegal and may result in heavy penalties; but tax avoidance is a perfectly legal and profitable activity.

Taxes are avoided by preventing a tax liability from coming into existence. This may be accomplished by any legal means, for example, by the way in which a transaction is completed, or the manner in which a business is organized, or by a wise selection from among the options provided in the Internal Revenue Code. It makes no difference how, so long as the means is legal and it prevents a tax liability from arising.

In contrast, tax evasion involves the fraudulent denial and concealment of an existing tax liability. For example, taxes are evaded when taxable income, such as interest, dividends, tips, fees, or profits from the sale of stocks, bonds, and other assets, is unreported. Taxes are also evaded when items not legally deductible from income are deducted. For example, taxes are evaded when the costs of operating the family automobile are deducted as a business expense, or when charitable contributions not allowed or not made are deducted. Tax evasion is illegal and should be scrupulously avoided.

State and municipal income taxes

Most states and a number of cities levy income taxes, in most cases modeling their laws after the federal laws. However, other than noting the existence of such laws and that they increase the total tax burden and make tax planning even more important, the following discussion is limited to the federal income tax.

History and objectives of the federal income tax

Although the federal government first used an income tax during the War between the States, the history of today's federal income tax dates from the 1913 ratification of the Sixteenth Amendment, which cleared away all questions as to the constitutionality of such a tax. Since its ratification, Congress has passed more than 50 revenue acts and other laws implementing the tax, placing the responsibility for their enforcement in the hands of the Treasury Department acting through the Internal Revenue Service.

The original purpose of the federal income tax was to raise revenue, but over the years this original goal has been expanded to include the following and other nonrevenue objectives:

1. To assist small businesses.
2. To encourage foreign trade.
3. To encourage exploration for oil and minerals.
4. To redistribute the national income.
5. To control inflation and deflation.
6. To stimulate business.
7. To attain full employment.
8. To support social objectives.

Also, just as the objectives have expanded over the years, so have the rates and the number of people required to pay taxes. In 1913 the minimum rate was 1% and the maximum for individuals was 7%. This contrasts with today's minimum 14% rate for individuals and maximum of 70%. Likewise, the total number of tax returns filed each year has grown from a few thousand in 1913 to well over 100,000,000 in recent years.

The following brief synopsis of the federal income tax is given at this point because it is necessary to know something about the federal income tax in order to appreciate its effect on business decisions.

Synopsis of the federal income tax

Classes of taxpayers

Federal income tax law recognizes four classes of taxpayers: individuals, corporations, estates, and trusts. Members of each class must file returns and pay taxes on taxable income.

A business operated as a single proprietorship or partnership is not treated as a separate taxable entity under the law. Rather, a single proprietor must include the income from his business on his individual tax return; and although a partnership must file an information return showing its net income and the distributive shares of the partners, each partner is required to include his share on his individual return. In other words, the income of a single proprietorship or partnership, whether withdrawn from the business or not, is taxed as the individual income of the single proprietor or partners.

The treatment given corporations under the law is different, however. A business operated as a corporation must file a return and pay taxes on its taxable income. Also, if a corporation pays out in dividends some or all of its "after-tax income," its stockholders must report these dividends as income on their individual returns. Because of this, it is commonly claimed that corporation income is taxed twice, once to the corporation and again to its stockholders.

A discussion of the federal income tax as applied to estates and trusts is not necessary at this point and is deferred to a more advanced course.

The individual income tax

The amount of federal income tax individuals must pay each year depends upon their gross income, deductions, exemptions, and tax credits. For those individuals who do not qualify to use the simplified Tax Rate Tables, the typical calculation of the tax liability involves the sequence shown in Illustration 28–1.

To determine the federal income tax liability of an individual, the amounts of gross income, deductions, exemptions, tax credits (if any), and prepayments are listed on forms supplied by the federal government. (For many individuals, simplified Tax Tables automatically

Gross income...	$xx,xxx
Less: Deductions to arrive at adjusted gross income	(xx,xxx)
Adjusted gross income...................................	$xx,xxx
Less: Itemized deductions............................ $x,xxx	
Less: Standard deduction (Zero bracket amount)... (x,xxx)	
Itemized deductions in excess of standard deduction........................... $x,xxx	
Deduction for exemptions .... x,xxx	(x,xxx)
Taxable income...	$xx,xxx
Gross tax liability from tax rate schedule........	$xx,xxx
Less: Tax credits and prepayments................	(xx,xxx)
Net tax payable (or refund)............................	$ xxx

Illustration 28–1

incorporate *some* of the deductions, exemptions, and credits so that fewer of these items must be separately listed.) Then the appropriate calculations (additions, subtractions, and so forth) are performed in accordance with the instructions. The listing of the items on the forms is not precisely the same for all classes of taxpayers and does not always follow the general pattern shown in Illustration 28–1; however, the illustration does show the relation of the items and the basic mathematics required in completing the tax forms.

The items that appear on a tax return as gross income, adjusted gross income, deductions, exemptions, tax credits, and prepayments require additional description and explanation.

Gross income   Income tax law defines income as *all income from whatever source derived, unless expressly excluded by law.* Gross income therefore includes income from operating a business, gains from property sales, dividends, interest, rents, royalties, and compensation for services, such as salaries, wages, fees, commissions, bonuses, and tips. Actually, the answers to two questions are all that is required to determine whether an item should be included or excluded. The two questions are: (1) Is the item income? (2) Is it expressly excluded by law? If an item is income and not specifically excluded, it must be included.

Certain items are recognized as not being income, for example, gifts, inheritances, scholarships, social security benefits, veterans' benefits, workmen's compensation insurance, and in most cases the proceeds of life insurance policies paid upon the death of the insured. These are not income and are excluded.

Other items, such as the first $100 of dividend income and interest on the obligations of the states and their subdivisions are specifically excluded. In the case of the first exclusion, Congress, in partial recognition of the claim that corporation income is "taxed twice," and for other reasons, has so written the law as to permit an individual owner of stock in qualifying domestic corporations to exclude from gross income the first $100 in dividends received on this stock. (On a joint return of a husband and wife, each may exclude $100 for a total of $200. However, to do so husbands and wives who do not live in states with community property laws must each have received $100 in dividends and neither may exclude dividends on stock owned by the other.) In the case of the interest paid on debts of the states and their subdivisions, the Supreme Court has held that a federal income tax on such items effectively amounts to having the power to destroy these governmental units, and consequently violates constitutional guarantees. As a result, interest on the bonds of the states and their subdivisions, with a few exceptions, is excluded from gross income.

Deductions to arrive at adjusted gross income These are generally deductions of a business nature. For example, all ordinary and necessary expenses of carrying on a business, trade, or profession are deductions to arrive at adjusted gross income. To understand this, recognize that under income tax law gross profit from sales (sales less cost of goods sold) is gross income to a merchant, that gross legal fees earned are gross income to a lawyer, and gross rentals from a building are gross income to a landlord. Consequently, the merchant, the lawyer, and the landlord may each deduct all ordinary and necessary expenses of carrying on the business or profession, such as salaries, wages, rent, depreciation, supplies used, repairs, maintenance, insurance, taxes, interest, and so on.

Also, as with the business executive, employees may deduct from gross income certain expenses incurred in connection with their employment if paid by the employees. These include transportation and travel expenses, expenses of an outside salesperson, and moving expenses. Employees who work in more than one place during a day may deduct transportation costs incurred in moving from one place of employment to another during the day. However, as a rule they may not deduct the cost of commuting from home to the first place of employment or from the last place of employment to home, unless their work requires that they carry in their car or truck tools too heavy or bulky to be carried on public transportation. Travel expenses include in addition to transportation expenses, the costs of meals and lodging while away from home overnight on employment connected business. Expenses of outside salespersons are expenses incurred in soliciting orders for an employer while away from the employer's place of business. They include such things as transportation, telephone, stationery, and postage. Moving expenses are expenses incurred by employees (or self-employed individuals) in moving their place of residence upon being transferred by their employer or to take a new job. Certain minimum requirements as to the distance moved and the length of employment in the new location must be met. Commonly an employer reimburses employees for the foregoing expenses. In such cases employees may deduct only that portion of their expenses not reimbursed by the employer; and if the reimbursement exceeds the expenses, employees must include the excess in their gross income.

In addition to the foregoing business expenses, from a tax management point of view, a very important deduction from gross income is the long-term capital gain deduction, which permits under certain circumstances the deduction from gross income of one half the net long-term gains from capital asset sales and exchanges. This is discussed in more detail later in this chapter.

Deductions from adjusted gross income   By legislative grace an individual taxpayer is permitted certain deductions from adjusted gross income. These are of two kinds. The first consists of certain personal expenses, commonly called itemized deductions, and the second is a deduction for exemptions.

In the case of the first kind of deduction, taxpayers have a choice. First, they may choose the standard deduction, which is already incorporated in the tax rates as a "zero bracket amount." In other words, if the taxpayer reports income up to the amount of the standard deduction, the schedules of tax rates will show that zero tax is levied against this amount. The standard deduction, or zero bracket amount, is a flat amount that depends upon the taxpayer's filing status. For 1977 and subsequent years, the standard deduction amounts to $2,200 for a single taxpayer, $3,200 for married taxpayers filing a joint return or for a surviving spouse, or $1,600 for a married taxpayer filing a separate return.

Second, instead of choosing the standard deduction, taxpayers may itemize their allowable deductions and deduct the amount by which the itemized deductions are in excess of the standard deduction. Obviously, taxpayers tend to elect whichever alternative results in the largest deduction. Itemized deductions commonly consist of the taxpayer's personal interest expense, state and local taxes, charitable contributions, casualty losses over $100 for each loss, one half the cost of medical and hospital insurance (but not more than $150 per year), and a medical expense deduction. The medical expense deduction consists of that portion of medical, dental, and hospital expenses in excess of 3% of the taxpayer's adjusted gross income, including the cost of medicines and drugs in excess of 1% of adjusted gross income and including the excess over $150 of the cost of medical and hospital insurance.

In addition to itemized deductions or the standard deduction, a taxpayer is allowed a second kind of deduction, called the deduction for exemptions. For each exemption, the taxpayer may deduct $750 from adjusted gross income, and a taxpayer is allowed one exemption for himself and one for each dependent. Additional exemptions are allowed if the taxpayer is 65 or over or is blind. If a husband and wife file a joint return, each is a taxpayer and they may combine their exemptions.

To qualify as a dependent for whom an exemption may be claimed, the person must meet these tests: (1) be closely related to the taxpayer or have been a member of the taxpayer's household for the entire year; (2) have received over half his or her support from the taxpayer during the year; (3) if married, has not and will not file a joint return with his or her spouse; and (4) had less than $750 of gross income during the year. An exception to the gross income test is granted if the person claimed as a dependent is a child of the taxpayer and under 19 years of age at the end of the tax year or was a full-time student in an educational institution during each of five months of the year. This exception is always of interest to college students because it commonly results in two exemptions for such students, if they qualify in all other respects as a dependent. One exemption may be taken by the parent who claims the student as a dependent and the other exemption may be taken by the student on his own tax return.

Observe in the discussion thus far that there are *deductions to arrive at adjusted gross income* and also *deductions from adjusted gross income*. Furthermore, it is important that each kind be subtracted at the proper point in the tax calculation, because the allowable amounts of some deductions from adjusted gross income are determined by the amount of adjusted gross income.

Federal income tax rates   Federal income tax rates are progressive in nature. By this is meant that each additional segment or bracket of taxable income is subject to a higher rate than the preceding segment or bracket. This may be seen by examining Illustration 28–2 which shows the rates for an unmarried person not qualifying as a head of household and for married persons filing a joint return or qualifying widows or widowers.

The Tax Rate Schedules shown in Illustration 28–2 are used by taxpayers who do not qualify to use simplified Tax Tables, which are discussed later in the chapter. To use the rate schedules of Illustration 28–2, a taxpayer reads down the first two columns of the appropriate schedule until he comes to the bracket of his taxable income. For example, if an unmarried taxpayer's taxable income is $29,000, the taxpayer reads down the proper columns to the bracket "over $28,200 but not over $34,200." The remaining columns then tell him that the tax on $29,000 is $7,590 plus 45% of the excess over $28,200, or is $7,590 + (45% × $800), or is $7,950.

A husband and wife have a choice. They may combine their incomes and use the rate schedule shown for married individuals (Schedule Y) or they may each file a separate return using a rate schedule (not shown) that results in a tax for each somewhat in excess of that shown in Illustration 28–2 for single taxpayers. The phrase "qualified widows and widowers" in the title of Schedule Y refers to surviving spouses who, if they are not remarried and if they have a dependent child, may continue to use Schedule Y for two tax years after the year of their spouse's death.

Also, a person who can qualify as a head of household may use a

Schedule X—Single Taxpayers Not Qualifying for Rates in Schedule Y or Z				Schedule Y—Married Taxpayers Filing Joint Returns and Qualifying Widows and Widowers			
If the amount of taxable income is:		Then the gross income tax liability is:		If the amount of taxable income is:		Then the gross income tax liability is:	
Not over $2,200...		−0−		Not over $3,200...		−0−	
Over—	But not over—		of the amount over—	Over—	But not over—		of the amount over—
$2,200	$2,700	14%	$2,200	$3,200	$4,200	14%	$3,200
$2,700	$3,200	$70+15%	$2,700	$4,200	$5,200	$140+15%	$4,200
$3,200	$3,700	$145+16%	$3,200	$5,200	$6,200	$290+16%	$5,200
$3,700	$4,200	$225+17%	$3,700	$6,200	$7,200	$450+17%	$6,200
$4,200	$6,200	$310+19%	$4,200	$7,200	$11,200	$620+19%	$7,200
$6,200	$8,200	$690+21%	$6,200	$11,200	$15,200	$1,380+22%	$11,200
$8,200	$10,200	$1,110+24%	$8,200	$15,200	$19,200	$2,260+25%	$15,200
$10,200	$12,200	$1,590+25%	$10,200	$19,200	$23,200	$3,260+28%	$19,200
$12,200	$14,200	$2,090+27%	$12,200	$23,200	$27,200	$4,380+32%	$23,200
$14,200	$16,200	$2,630+29%	$14,200	$27,200	$31,200	$5,660+36%	$27,200
$16,200	$18,200	$3,210+31%	$16,200	$31,200	$35,200	$7,100+39%	$31,200
$18,200	$20,200	$3,830+34%	$18,200	$35,200	$39,200	$8,660+42%	$35,200
$20,200	$22,200	$4,510+36%	$20,200	$39,200	$43,200	$10,340+45%	$39,200
$22,200	$24,200	$5,230+38%	$22,200	$43,200	$47,200	$12,140+48%	$43,200
$24,200	$28,200	$5,990+40%	$24,200	$47,200	$55,200	$14,060+50%	$47,200
$28,200	$34,200	$7,590+45%	$28,200	$55,200	$67,200	$18,060+53%	$55,200
$34,200	$40,200	$10,290+50%	$34,200	$67,200	$79,200	$24,420+55%	$67,200
$40,200	$46,200	$13,290+55%	$40,200	$79,200	$91,200	$31,020+58%	$79,200
$46,200	$52,200	$16,590+60%	$46,200	$91,200	$103,200	$37,980+60%	$91,200
$52,200	$62,200	$20,190+62%	$52,200	$103,200	$123,200	$45,180+62%	$103,200
$62,200	$72,200	$26,390+64%	$62,200	$123,200	$143,200	$57,580+64%	$123,200
$72,200	$82,200	$32,790+66%	$72,200	$143,200	$163,200	$70,380+66%	$143,200
$82,200	$92,200	$39,390+68%	$82,200	$163,200	$183,200	$83,580+68%	$163,200
$92,200	$102,200	$46,190+69%	$92,200	$183,200	$203,200	$97,180+69%	$183,200
$102,200	—	$53,090+70%	$102,200	$203,200	—	$110,980+70%	$203,200

Illustration 28–2

rate schedule (not shown) in which the rates fall between those for un-married individuals and those for married couples filing jointly. Generally a head of household is an unmarried or legally separated person who maintains a home in which lives his or her unmarried child or a qualifying dependent.

Regardless of the rate schedule used, it is generally recognized that our federal income tax rates are steeply progressive. Proponents claim that this is only fair, since the taxpayers most able to pay, those with higher incomes, are subject to higher rates. Opponents, on the other hand, claim the high rates stifle initiative. For example, a young unmarried executive with $34,200 of taxable income per year, upon being offered a new job carrying additional responsibilities and a $6,000 salary increase, might turn the new job down, feeling the after-tax increase in pay insufficient to compensate for the extra responsibilities. In this case the executive could keep after federal income taxes just $3,000 or 50% of the increase.

In a situation like that described here, a decision as to whether another dollar of income is desirable or worth the effort depends on the *marginal tax rate* that applies to that dollar. The marginal tax rate is the rate that applies to the next dollar of income to be earned. For example, the highest rate that is applicable to the young executive before taking the new job is 45% on the taxable dollars between $28,200 and $34,200 (see Illustration 28–2). However, if the new job is taken, the marginal rate on the next $6,000 of taxable income goes up to 50%.

Whether or not our progressive income tax rates stifle initiative is probably open to debate. Notwithstanding the progression of marginal tax rates up to 70%, as shown in Illustration 28–2, it should be noted that certain types of income are subject to lesser tax rates. For example, an individual's "personal service income" includes wages, salaries, other compensation for personal services, and certain pensions, annuities, and deferred compensation. Importantly, the maximum tax rate on personal service income is 50%. In terms of Illustration 28–2, this means that for single taxpayers, all personal service income in excess of $40,200 (taxable income) is taxed at a 50% rate. For married taxpayers filing a joint return and certain widows and widowers, all personal service income in excess of $55,200 (taxable income) is taxed at a 50% rate. However, there is no question that the progressive nature of the tax rates causes high-income taxpayers to search for tax-saving opportunities.

Tax credits and prepayments   After an individual's gross income tax liability is computed from the appropriate tax rate schedule, his tax credits, if any, and prepayments are deducted to determine his net tax liability. Tax credits represent direct reductions in the amount of tax liability, that is, a $100 tax credit reduces the tax liability by $100. By comparison, deductions (as discussed earlier) reduce the amount of taxable income, against which is applied the appropriate tax rates to determine the gross tax liability. Thus, a tax credit of $100 is more valuable to the taxpayer than would be a tax deduction of $100. Assuming a marginal tax rate of 30%, an additional tax deduction of $100 effectively reduces the tax liability by $30 ($100 × 30%), whereas a tax credit of $100 reduces the tax liability by $100.

Examples of tax credits include the following. A retired taxpayer with retirement income may receive a "credit for the elderly." A taxpayer who has paid income taxes to a foreign government may be eligible for a "foreign tax credit." A taxpayer who has contributed to a political candidate or party may be eligible for a "political contribution credit." The latter credit is limited to one half the donation with a maximum of $25 on a separate return and $50 on a joint return; and in lieu of the credit, the taxpayer may elect to deduct up to $100 ($200 on a joint return) as an itemized deduction.

Taxpayers also receive a "general tax credit" equal to the larger of (*a*) $35 per exemption, or (*b*) 2% of (taxable income less the zero bracket amount) up to a credit of $180 (2% × $9,000 = $180). However, a married individual filing a separate return must use the $35 per exemption method of calculating the credit. To illustrate the general tax credit calculations, assume married taxpayers with a total of three exemptions filing a joint return. The standard deduction or zero bracket amount is $3,200. Given several alternative levels of taxable income, the general tax credit is calculated as follows:

Taxable Income	Zero Bracket Amount	Taxable Income less Zero Bracket Amount	2% × (Taxable Income less Zero Bracket Amount)	$35 × Number of Exemptions	General Tax Credit
$ 8,000	$3,200	$ 4,800	$ 96	$105	$105
11,000	3,200	7,800	156	105	156
12,200	3,200	9,000	180	105	180
15,000	3,200	11,800	236	105	180

Note that when taxable income less the zero bracket amount exceeds $9,000, the 2% alternative is nevertheless limited to $180.

An "investment tax credit" equal to 10% of the purchase price of certain, qualified property is also available to taxpayers. And taxpayers may also qualify for an "earned income credit" equal to 10% of "earned income" up to $4,000 (10% × $4,000 = $400). "Earned income" consists of wages, professional fees, and certain compensation for personal services. But, as earned income increases from $4,000 to $8,000, the amount of the earned income credit is reduced from $400 to $0.

In addition to tax credits, any prepayments of tax are also deducted in order to determine the net tax liability. Most taxpayers have income taxes withheld from their salaries and wages. Other taxpayers have income that is not subject to withholding and on which they are required to estimate the tax, file an estimated tax return, and pay the estimated amount of the tax on the income in installments in advance. Both the income tax withholdings and the estimated tax paid in advance are examples of tax prepayments that are deducted in determining a taxpayer's net tax liability.

Special tax treatment of capital gains and losses

From a tax-saving point of view, one of the most important features of our federal income tax laws is the special treatment given long-term gains from capital asset sales and exchanges. The usual effect of this special treatment is a tax on net long-term capital gains that is one half, or less than one half, the tax on an equal amount of income from some other source, commonly called "ordinary income." For this reason, whenever possible, tax planners try to cause income to emerge in the form of long-term capital gains rather than as ordinary income.

The Internal Revenue Code defines a capital asset as any item of property except (a) inventories; (b) trade notes and accounts receiv-

able; (c) real property and depreciable property used in a trade or ⚹ *1231 Asset*
business; (d) copyrights, letters, and similar property in the hands of *total cap group*
the creator of the copyrighted works or his donee and certain other *cap gain*
transferees; and (e) any government obligation due within one year and *ordinary loss*
issued at a discount. Common examples of capital assets held by individuals and subject to sale or exchange are stocks, bonds, and a
personal residence.

A gain on the sale of a capital asset occurs when the proceeds of the
sale exceed the *basis* of the asset sold, and a loss occurs when the
asset's basis exceeds the proceeds. The basis of a purchased asset is
generally its cost less any depreciation previously allowed or allowable for tax purposes. Not all capital assets are acquired by purchase;
but rules for determining the basis of an asset acquired other than by
purchase are at times complicated and need not be discussed here.

For tax purposes, a distinction is made between short- and long-
term capital gains and losses. For tax years beginning in 1978 and
thereafter, short-term gains and losses result when capital assets are
held 12 months or less before being sold or exchanged, and long-term
gains and losses result when such assets are held more than 12 months.
Furthermore, under the law, net short-term gains must be reported in
full and are taxed as ordinary income; but only one half the amount of
any excess net long-term capital gains over net short-term capital
losses, if any, must be included in adjusted gross income, and the
maximum tax is limited to 25% of the total of such excess net gains,
if the total does not exceed $50,000 ($25,000 for a married taxpayer
filing a separate return).

For example, if an individual taxpayer has $1,000 of long-term gains, *40%*
no losses, and other income that places these gains in a 36% bracket,
he is required to include only $500 of the gains in adjusted gross in-
come, and to pay only a $180 ($500 × 36% = $180) tax thereon. Con-
sequently, his effective tax rate on the gains is 18% ($180 ÷ $1,000 =
18%), and is one half what it would be if the $1,000 were ordinary
income.

Often a high-income taxpayer's capital gains fall in a tax bracket
where if the tax thereon were calculated as in the preceding paragraph, the effective rate would exceed 25%, but in such cases the tax is
limited to 25% if such gains do not exceed the previously mentioned
$50,000 or $25,000. For example, assume that a taxpayer has $1,000
of long-term capital gains, no losses, and other income that causes these
gains to fall in the 70% bracket. If the taxpayer calculated his tax as
in the foregoing example, the indicated tax resulting from the calculation would be $350 ($500 × 70% = $350), or the effective rate would be
35% ($350 ÷ $1,000 = 35%). Consequently, since this exceeds the
25% maximum, the taxpayer is permitted by law to limit his tax to
25% of the $1,000, or to $250. Note that this is considerably less than
half the $700 tax which would be paid if the $1,000 were ordinary
income.

In the preceding paragraphs the terms "net long-term gains" and "net short-term gains" appear. When long-term gains exceed long-term losses, a net long-term gain results. Likewise, when long-term losses exceed long-term gains, a net long-term loss occurs. Short-term gains and losses are combined in a like manner to arrive at either a net short-term gain or loss.

When an individual's net short-term capital losses exceed his net long-term capital gains, he may deduct up to $3,000 of the excess losses ($1,500 for a married taxpayer filing a separate return) from ordinary income in the year of the loss. However, when net long-term capital losses exceed net short-term capital gains, he may in any one year deduct from ordinary income only one half of the excess losses up to $3,000 ($1,500 for a married taxpayer filing a separate return). A carry-over provision is available to allow deduction in subsequent years of amounts which exceeded the $3,000 or $1,500 limitations.

One last point in regard to real property and depreciable property used in a taxpayer's trade or business (see definition of capital assets in a previous paragraph). Such properties are legally not capital assets; consequently, when sold or exchanged, the excess of losses over gains is fully deductible in arriving at taxable income. However, if such properties are held over 12 months, the excess of gains over losses is eligible for capital gain treatment, except to the extent of certain amounts of depreciation taken after 1961. As to depreciation taken after 1961, there may be a share of the gain equal to a portion or all of this depreciation, depending on the nature of the property and the method of depreciation, which must be treated as ordinary income.

Tax tables   As previously mentioned, not all taxpayers are required to use the Tax Rate Schedules such as those shown in Illustration 28–2. Instead, most individual taxpayers use simplified Tax Tables. The Tax Tables are constructed from the Tax Rate Schedules and both of them incorporate the standard deduction or "zero bracket amount." In addition, the Tax Tables incorporate the number of exemptions claimed by the taxpayer and the general tax credit. Thus, individuals who use the Tax Tables do not have to calculate the deduction for exemptions or the general tax credit. The taxpayer simply has to calculate his "tax table income" and then search through the appropriate Tax Table to determine the gross income tax liability. Depending upon whether the taxpayer takes the standard deduction or chooses to itemize deductions, tax table income is calculated as is shown in Illustration 28–3.

The corporation income tax

For federal tax purposes, the taxable income of a corporation organized for profit is calculated in much the same way as the taxable income of an individual. However, there are important differences, five of which follow:

a.   Instead of the $100 dividend exclusion of an individual, a corpora-

For taxpayers selecting the standard deduction:

Gross income..	$x,xxx
Less: Deductions to arrive at adjusted gross income......	(x,xxx)
Tax table income..	$x,xxx

For taxpayers choosing to itemize deductions:

Gross income..		$x,xxx
Less: Deductions to arrive at adjusted gross income......		(x,xxx)
Adjusted gross income..................................		$x,xxx
Less: Itemized deductions..............................	$x,xxx	
Less: Standard deduction (Zero bracket amount)...................................	(x,xxx)	
Itemized deductions in excess of standard deduction		(xxx)
Tax table income...		$x,xxx

Illustration 28–3

tion may deduct from gross income the first 85% of dividends received from stock it owns in other domestic corporations. This in effect means that only 15% of such dividends are taxed. However, if two corporations qualify as affiliated corporations, which essentially means that one owns 80% or more of the other's stock, then 100% of the dividends received by the investor corporation from the investee corporation may be excluded.

b. The capital gains of a corporation are also treated differently. Recall that the taxable income of individuals must include only 50% of their long-term capital gains in excess of short-term capital losses. Corporations must include 100% of such gains in income. However, just as individuals may calculate an alternative tax of 25% on such gains up to $50,000, a 30% alternative tax rate is available on all such gains accruing to a corporation.

c. A corporation may only offset capital losses against capital gains; and if in any year the offset results in a net capital loss, the loss may not be deducted from other income, but it may be carried back to the three preceding years and forward to the next five years and deducted from any capital gains of those years.

d. The standard deduction and the deduction for exemptions do not apply to a corporation, and a corporation does not have certain other deductions of an individual, such as that for personal medical expenses.

e. In addition, the big difference between the corporation and the individual income tax is that the corporation tax is progressive in just three steps and consists of a *normal tax* and a *surtax,* as follows:

Income Bracket	Normal Tax	Surtax	Total Tax
$0–$25,000	20%	—	20%
$25,001–$50,000	22	—	22
$50,001–	22	26%	48

Tax effects of business alternatives

Alternative decisions commonly have different tax effects. Following are several examples illustrating this.

Form of business organization

The difference between individual and corporation tax rates commonly affects one of the basic decisions a business executive must make, namely, that as to the legal form the business should take. Should it be a single proprietorship, partnership, or corporation? The following factors influence the decision:

a. As previously stated, a corporation is a taxable entity. Its income is taxed at corporation rates, and any portion distributed in dividends is taxed again as individual income to its stockholders. On the other hand, the income of a single proprietorship or partnership, whether withdrawn or left in the business, is taxed as individual income of the proprietor or partners.

b. In addition, a corporation may pay reasonable amounts in salaries to stockholders who work for the corporation, and the sum of these salaries is a tax-deductible expense in arriving at the corporation's taxable income. In a partnership or a single proprietorship on the other hand, salaries of the partners or the proprietor are nothing more than allocations of income.

In arriving at a decision as to the legal form a business should take, a business executive, with the foregoing points in mind, must estimate how he will fare taxwise under each form, and select the best. For example, assume that a business executive is choosing between the single proprietorship and corporate forms, and that he estimates his business will have annual gross sales of $250,000, with cost of goods sold and operating expenses, other than his own salary as manager, of $185,000. Assume further than $45,000 per year is a fair salary for managing such a business and the owner plans to withdraw all profits from the business. Under these assumptions, the business executive will fare taxwise as shown in Illustration 28–4.

Under the assumptions of Illustration 28–4, the business executive will incur the smaller tax and have the larger after-tax income under the single proprietorship form. However, this may not be true in every case. For instance, if he has large amounts of income from other sources, he may find he would incur less tax if the business were organized as a corporation.

Furthermore, in the example just given it is assumed that all profits are withdrawn and none are left in the business for growth. This happens. However, growth is commonly financed through the retention of earnings; and when it is, the relative desirability of the two forms may change. This is because income retained in a business organized as a corporation is not taxed as individual income to its stockholders, but the income of a single proprietorship or partnership is so taxed, whether retained in the business or withdrawn.

Operating results under each form:	Proprietorship		Corporation	
Estimated sales..		$250,000		$250,000
Cost of goods sold and operating expenses other				
than owner-manager's salary............................	$185,000		$185,000	
Salary of owner-manager.......................................	−0−	185,000	45,000	230,000
Before-tax income...		$ 65,000		$ 20,000
Corporation income tax at 20%		−0−		4,000
Net Income...		$ 65,000		$ 16,000
Owner's after-tax income under each form:				
Single proprietorship net income...........................		$ 65,000		
Corporation salary..				$ 45,000
Dividends				16,000
Total individual income..		$ 65,000		$ 61,000
Individual income tax (assuming a joint return with itemized deductions of $8,700 (less the standard deduction of $3,200), a deduction for exemptions of $1,500, and a general tax credit of 2% × $9,000 = $180 under both forms plus a $100 dividend exclusion under the corporation form)		19,364		17,230
Owner's After-Tax Income.......................................		$ 45,636		$ 43,770

Illustration 28–4

For instance, if the business of Illustration 28–4 is organized as a single proprietorship, the tax burden of the owner remains the same whether he withdraws any of his profits or not. But, in case of the corporation, if all $16,000 of the earnings are retained in the business, the owner is required to pay individual income taxes on his $45,000 salary only. This would reduce his annual individual income tax from the $17,230 shown in Illustration 28–4 to $9,656, and would reduce the total tax burden with the corporation form to $13,656 ($4,000 + $9,656), which is $5,708 less than the tax burden under the single proprietorship form.

The foregoing is by no means all of the picture. Other tax factors may be involved. For example, a corporation may incur an extra tax if after it has accumulated $150,000 of retained earnings, it accumulates additional retained earnings beyond the reasonable needs of the business. Also, under present laws a corporation may elect to be taxed somewhat like a single proprietorship, thus eliminating the corporate tax. Furthermore, in a decision as to the legal form a business should take, factors other than taxes are often important, for example, lack of stockholder liability in a corporation.

Dividends and growth

It was pointed out earlier in this chapter that it is normally to a taxpayer's advantage to have income emerge in the form of long-term capital gains rather than as ordinary income. Furthermore, earnings paid out in dividends result in ordinary income to stockholders, but earnings retained in an incorporated business commonly result in its growth and an increase in the value of its stock, which may be turned into long-term capital gains through a later sale of the stock. For this reason it is often to the advantage of the owner of an incorporated business to forego dividends and at a later date, through the sale of the business, to take the profits of his business in the form of long-term gains resulting from growth.

Method of financing

When a business organized as a corporation is in need of additional financing, the owners may supply the corporation whatever funds are needed by purchasing its stock. However, an overall tax advantage may often be gained if instead of purchasing stock, they supply the funds through long-term loans. Insofar as the owners are concerned, beyond the allowable dividend exclusion, it makes no difference on their individual returns whether they report interest or dividends from the funds supplied. However, whether the corporation issues stock or floats a loan usually makes a big difference on its return. Interest on borrowed funds is a tax-deductible expense, but dividends are a distribution of earnings and have no effect on the corporation's taxes. Consequently, if owners lend the corporation funds rather than buy its stock, the total tax liability (their own plus their corporation's) will be reduced. In addition, the repayment of long-term debt always is considered to be a return of capital transaction. The redemption of stock, however, may result in the proceeds being treated as dividend income to the shareholders.

In making financial arrangements such as these, owners must be careful not to overreach themselves in attempting to maximize the interest deduction of their corporation. If they do so and thereby create what is called a "thin corporation," one in which the owners have supplied an unreasonably "thin" portion of capital, the Internal Revenue Service may disallow the interest deductions and require that such deductions be treated as dividends. Furthermore, repayments of "principal" may also be held to be taxable dividends.

Timing transactions

The timing of transactions can be of major importance in tax planning. For example, securities may be held a little longer in order to make the gain on their sale subject to treatment as a long-term capital gain. Or as another example, if a company has several items of real or depreciable property to be sold and some of the sales will result in losses and others in gains, the losses should be taken in one year and the gains in another. The losses and gains should be taken this way because if the losses and gains are both incurred in the same year, they must be offset. However, if the losses are taken in one year and the gains in another, the losses may be deducted in full from other ordinary income, while the gains become eligible in their year for long-term capital gain treatment, at least to the extent they exceed depreciation taken after 1961.

Forms in which related transactions are completed

The tax consequences of related transactions are often dependent upon the forms in which they are completed. For example, the sale of one property at a profit and the immediate purchase of another like property normally results in a taxable gain on the property sold, but an exchange of these properties may result in a tax-free exchange.

351 transfer

A tax-free exchange occurs when like kinds of property are exchanged for each other, or when one or more persons transfer property to a corporation and immediately thereafter are in control of the corporation. Control in such cases is interpreted as meaning that after the transfer the transferring persons (or person) must own at least 80% of the corporation's voting stock plus at least 80% of the total number of shares of all other classes of stock.

At first glance it seems that it should be to anyone's advantage to take a tax-free exchange rather than to pay taxes, but this may not be so. For example, ten years ago a corporation acquired, for $50,000, land then at the edge of the city. Today, due to booming growth, the land is well within the city and has a fair market value of $250,000. Aside from a fully depreciated fence, the land is without improvements, having been used over the years for storage of idle equipment and excess inventory. The corporation plans to move part of its operations to a suburb and has an opportunity to trade the city property for vacant suburban acreage on which it would build a factory. Should it make the trade? From a tax viewpoint, since the new land is not depreciable, the answer is probably, yes, the company should make the tax-free exchange.

However, if the suburban property rather than being vacant consisted of land having a fair market value of $25,000 with a suitable factory building thereon valued at $225,000, the corporation would probably be better off if it sold the city property, paid the tax on its gain, and purchased the suburban factory and its site. The corporation would probably be better off because the gain on the city land would be taxable as a long-term capital gain on which the tax would not exceed $60,000 (30% of [$250,000 − $50,000] = $60,000). However, by purchasing the new factory, the corporation gains the right to deduct the building's $225,000 cost (over its life) in the form of depreciation, an expense deductible in full in arriving at taxable income.

Accounting basis and procedures

With certain exceptions, the accounting basis and procedures used by a taxpayer in keeping his records must also be used in computing his taxable income. Generally, a taxpayer keeps his records on either a cash or accrual basis (see pages 81–82); but regardless of which he uses, the basis and any procedures used must clearly reflect income and be consistently followed.

When inventories are a material factor in calculating income, a taxpayer is required to use the accrual basis in calculating gross profit from sales. Also, plant assets cannot be expensed in the year of purchase but must be depreciated over their useful lives. However, other than for gross profit from sales and depreciation, a taxpayer may use the cash basis in accounting for income and expenses. Furthermore, this is often an advantage, since under the cash basis, a taxpayer can often shift expense payments and the receipt of items of revenue other than from the sale of merchandise from one accounting period to the next and thus increase or decrease his taxable income.

An accrual-basis taxpayer cannot shift income from year to year by timing receipts and payments; however, somewhat of the same thing may be accomplished through a choice of accounting procedures. For example, recognition of income on an installment basis (discussed in Chapter 5) commonly shifts income from one year to another for a merchant making installment sales. Likewise, a contractor may use the percentage-of-completion basis (Chapter 5) to shift construction income from one year to another and to level taxable income over a period of years.

Furthermore, any taxpayer may shift taxable income to future years through a choice of inventory and depreciation procedures. For example, during periods of rising prices the Lifo inventory method results in charging higher costs for goods sold against current revenues, and thus reduces taxable income and taxes. It may be argued that this only postpones taxes since in periods of declining prices the use of Lifo results in lower costs and higher taxes. However, the history of recent years has been one of constantly rising prices; therefore, it may also be argued that Lifo will postpone taxes indefinitely.

Depreciation methods that result in higher depreciation charges in an asset's early years and lower charges in later years, such as the sum-of-the-years'-digits or declining-balance methods, also postpone taxes. And while tax postponement is not as desirable as tax avoidance, postponement does give the taxpayer interest-free use of tax dollars until these dollars must be paid to the government.

Before turning to a new topic, it should be pointed out that the opportunities for tax planning described in these pages are only illustrative of those available. The wise business executive will seek help from his tax consultant in order to take advantage of every tax-saving opportunity.

Net income and taxable income

The taxable income of a business commonly differs from its reported net income. In regard to corporations, one reason for this difference is that net income as reported on the income statement is calculated after subtracting income tax expense, whereas taxable income obviously does not include a deduction for federal income taxes. Taxable income and net income also differ because net income is determined by the application of generally accepted accounting principles, while tax rules are used in determining taxable income, and the rules differ from generally accepted accounting principles on some points. For example:

a. The application of accounting principles requires that dividend income be fully included in the reported net income or, where appropriate, the investment be accounted for according to the equity method. But, for tax purposes, some of the dividends received are excluded from taxable income, and the equity method is not used.

b. For accounting purposes, interest received on state and municipal bonds must be included in net income, but such interest is usually not taxable income.

c. As a rule, unearned income, such as rent collected in advance, is taxable in the year of receipt; however, under an accrual basis of accounting such items are taken into income in the year earned regardless of when received.

d. Accounting principles require an estimate of future costs, such as, for example, costs of making good on guarantees; and accounting principles require a deduction of such costs from revenue in the year the guaranteed goods are sold. However, tax rules do not permit the deduction of such costs until after the guarantor has to make good on his guarantee.

In addition, reported net income commonly differs from taxable income because the taxpayer is permitted by law in some cases to use one method or procedure for tax purposes and a different method or procedure in keeping his accounting records. For example, a taxpayer may elect to use declining-balance depreciation for tax purposes but to use straight-line depreciation in his accounting records.

Some accountants believe the interests of government, business, and the public would better be served if there were more uniformity between taxable income and reported net income. However, since the federal income tax is designed to serve other purposes than raising revenue, it is apt to be some time before this is achieved.

Taxes and the distortion of net income

Sometimes one procedure is elected for tax purposes and an alternative procedure is used in the accounting records, and the two procedures differ only in respect to their timing of expense recognition or revenue recognition. When this occurs, pre-tax net income for the year differs from taxable income, and a problem arises as to how much income tax expense should be deducted each year on the income statement. If the tax liability for each year were deducted as tax expense, the amount of the reported tax expense would not appear to have a meaningful relationship to the amount of pre-tax net income, and the final net income figures might be misleading. Consequently, in cases such as this, the Accounting Principles Board concluded that income taxes should be allocated so that the distortion caused by timing differences between tax accounting procedures and financial accounting procedures will be avoided.[1]

To appreciate the problem involved here, assume that a corporation has installed a $100,000 machine, the product of which will produce a half million dollars of revenue in each of the succeeding four years and $80,000 of income before depreciation and taxes. Assume further that the company must pay income taxes at a 50% rate (round number assumed for easy calculation) and that it plans to use straight-line depreciation in its records but the declining-balance method for tax purposes. If the machine has a four-year life and an $8,000 salvage value, annual depreciation calculated by each method will be as follows:

Year	Straight Line	Declining Balance
1	$23,000	$50,000
2	23,000	25,000
3	23,000	12,500
4	23,000	4,500
Totals	$92,000	$92,000

And since the company has elected declining-balance depreciation for tax purposes, it will be liable for $15,000 of income tax on the first year's income, $27,500 on the second, $33,750 on the third, and $37,750 on the fourth. The calculation of these taxes is shown in Illustration 28–5.

Annual Income Taxes	Year 1	Year 2	Year 3	Year 4	Total
Income before depreciation and income taxes	$80,000	$80,000	$80,000	$80,000	$320,000
Depreciation for tax purposes (declining balance)	50,000	25,000	12,500	4,500	92,000
Taxable income	$30,000	$55,000	$67,500	$75,500	$228,000
Annual Income Taxes (50% of Taxable Income)	$15,000	$27,500	$33,750	$37,750	$114,000

Illustration 28–5

Furthermore, if the company were to deduct its actual tax liability each year in arriving at income to be reported to its stockholders, it would report the amounts shown in Illustration 28–6.

Observe in Illustrations 28–5 and 28–6 that total depreciation,

---

[1] APB, "Accounting for Income Taxes," *APB Opinion No. II* (New York: AICPA, 1967).

Income after Deducting Actual Tax Liabilities	Year 1	Year 2	Year 3	Year 4	Total
Income before depreciation and income taxes...........	$80,000	$80,000	$80,000	$80,000	$320,000
Depreciation per books (straight line)........................	23,000	23,000	23,000	23,000	92,000
Income before taxes..	$57,000	$57,000	$57,000	$57,000	$228,000
Income taxes (actual liability of each year)	15,000	27,500	33,750	37,750	114,000
Remaining income...	$42,000	$29,500	$23,250	$19,250	$114,000

Illustration 28–6

$92,000, is the same whether calculated by the straight-line or the declining-balance method. Also note that the total tax liability for the four years, $114,000, is the same in each case. Then note the distortion of the final income figures in Illustration 28–6 due to the postponement of taxes.

If this company should report successive annual income figures of $42,000, $29,500, $23,250, and then $19,250, some of its stockholders might be misled as to the company's earnings trend. Consequently, in cases such as this the Accounting Principles Board requires that income taxes be allocated so that the distortion caused by the postponement of taxes is removed from the income statement. In essence, *APB Opinion No. 11* requires that—

When a procedure used in the accounting records and an alternative procedure used for tax purposes differ in respect to their timing of expense recognition or revenue recognition, the tax expense deducted on the income statement should not be the actual tax incurred, but the amount that would have resulted if the procedure used in the records had also been used in calculating the tax.

If the foregoing is applied in this case, the corporation will report to its stockholders in each of the four years the amounts of income shown in Illustration 28–7.

In examining Illustration 28–7, recall that the company's tax liabilities are actually $15,000 in the first year, $27,500 in the second, $33,-750 in the third, and $37,750 in the fourth, a total of $114,000. Then

Net Income That Should Be Reported to Stockholders	Year 1	Year 2	Year 3	Year 4	Total
Income before depreciation and income taxes...........	$80,000	$80,000	$80,000	$80,000	$320,000
Depreciation per books (straight line)	23,000	23,000	23,000	23,000	92,000
Income before taxes..	$57,000	$57,000	$57,000	$57,000	$228,000
Income taxes (amounts based on straight-line depreciation)..	28,500	28,500	28,500	28,500	114,000
Net income	$28,500	$28,500	$28,500	$28,500	$114,000

Illustration 28–7

observe that when this $114,000 liability is allocated evenly over the
four years, the distortion of the annual net incomes due to the postponement of taxes is removed from the published income statements.

Entries for the allocation of taxes   When income taxes are allocated as in Illustration 28–7, the tax
liability of each year and the deferred taxes are recorded with an ad-
justing entry. The adjusting entries for the four years of Illustration
28–7 and the entries in general journal form for the payment of the
taxes (without explanations) are as follows: *

Year 1	Income Taxes Expense	28,500.00	
	Income Taxes Payable		15,000.00
	Deferred Income Taxes		13,500.00
Year 1	Income Taxes Payable	15,000.00	
	Cash		15,000.00
Year 2	Income Taxes Expense	28,500.00	
	Income Taxes Payable		27,500.00
	Deferred Income Taxes		1,000.00
Year 2	Income Taxes Payable	27,500.00	
	Cash		27,500.00
Year 3	Income Taxes Expense	28,500.00	
	Deferred Income Taxes	5,250.00	
	Income Taxes Payable		33,750.00
Year 3	Income Taxes Payable	33,750.00	
	Cash		33,750.00
Year 4	Income Taxes Expense	28,500.00	
	Deferred Income Taxes	9,250.00	
	Income Taxes Payable		37,750.00
Year 4	Income Taxes Payable	37,750.00	
	Cash		37,750.00

* To simplify the illustration, it is assumed here that the entire year's tax liability is paid at one time. However, corporations are usually required to pay estimated taxes on a quarterly basis.

In the entries the $28,500 debited to Income Taxes Expense each
year is the amount that is deducted on the income statement in reporting annual net income. Also, the amount credited to Income Taxes
Payable each year is the actual tax liability of that year.

Observe in the entries that since the actual tax liability in each of the
first two years is less than the amount debited to Income Taxes Expense, the difference is credited to Deferred Income Taxes. Then note
that in the last two years, since the actual liability each year is greater
than the debit to Income Taxes Expense, the difference is debited to
Deferred Income Taxes. Now observe in the following illustration of
the company's Deferred Income Taxes account that the debits and
credits exactly balance each other out over the four-year period:

Deferred Income Taxes

Year	Explanation	Debit	Credit	Balance
1			13,500.00	13,500.00
2			1,000.00	14,500.00
3		5,250.00		9,250.00
4		9,250.00		-0-

Adjusted gross income. Gross income minus ordinary and necessary expenses of carrying on a business, trade, or profession, or in the case of an employee, gross income minus expenses incurred in connection with his employment if paid by the employee.

Basis. In general, the cost of a purchased asset less any depreciation previously allowed or allowable for tax purposes.

Capital asset. Any item of property except (1) inventories, (2) trade notes and accounts receivable, (3) real property and depreciable property used in a trade or business, (4) copyrights or similar property, and (5) any government obligation due within one year and issued at a discount.

Capital gain or loss. The difference between the proceeds from the sale of a capital asset and the basis of the asset.

Deferred income taxes. The difference between the income tax expense in the financial statements and the income taxes payable according to tax law, resulting from financial accounting and tax accounting timing differences with respect to expense or revenue recognition.

Gross income. All income from whatever source derived, unless expressly excluded by law.

Head of household. An unmarried or legally separated person who maintains a home in which lives his or her unmarried child or a qualifying dependent.

Marginal tax rate. The rate that applies to the next dollar of income to be earned.

Normal tax on corporations. A tax of 20% on the first $25,000 of taxable income and 22% on taxable income in excess of $25,000.

Standard deduction. A synonym for zero bracket amount.

Surtax on corporations. A tax of 26% on taxable income in excess of $50,000.

Tax avoidance. A legal means of preventing a tax liability from coming into existence.

Tax credit. A direct reduction in the amount of tax liability.

Glossary

Tax evasion. The fraudulent denial and concealment of an existing liability.

Tax planning. Planning the affairs of a taxpayer in such a way as to incur the smallest possible tax liability.

Tax table income. Adjusted gross income of a taxpayer choosing the standard deduction; adjusted gross income less the excess of itemized deductions over the standard deduction for a taxpayer who chooses to itemize deductions.

Zero bracket amount. The amount of income, after subtracting all allowable deductions, that is not subject to tax; for married taxpayers filing jointly and qualifying widows and widowers, $3,200; for married taxpayers filing separately, $1,600; and for an unmarried taxpayer, $2,200.

Questions for class discussion

1. Jackson expects to have $500 of income in a 50% bracket; consequently, which should be more desirable to him: (*a*) a transaction that will reduce his income tax by $100 or (*b*) a transaction that will reduce an expense of his business by $150?

2. Why must a taxpayer normally take advantage of a tax-saving opportunity at the time it arises?

3. Distinguish between tax avoidance and tax evasion. Which is legal and desirable?

4. What are some of the nonrevenue objectives of the federal income tax?

5. What nonrevenue objective is gained by granting a $50,000 surtax exemption to corporations?

6. What questions must be answered in determining whether an item should be included or excluded from gross income for tax purposes?

7. Name several items that are not income for tax purposes.

8. What justification is given for permitting an individual to exclude the first $100 of dividends from domestic corporations from his gross income for tax purposes?

9. For tax purposes, define a capital asset.

10. What is a short-term capital gain? A long-term capital gain?

11. An individual had capital asset transactions that resulted in nothing but long-term capital gains. What special tax treatment may be given these gains?

12. For tax purposes, what is "ordinary income"?

13. Why do tax planners try to have income emerge as a long-term capital gain?

14. Differentiate between the normal tax and the surtax of a corporation.

15. It is often a wise tax decision for the owner of an incorporated business to forgo the payment of dividends from the earnings of his business. Why?

16. Why does the taxable income of a business commonly differ from its net income?

In some of the Exercises and Problems which follow, the taxpayers would
qualify to use the simplified Tax Tables (not provided in the book) rather than
the Tax Rate Schedules. However, to restrict the length of the chapter and to
facilitate student understanding of the underlying concepts, calculations of
individual tax liability should be based on the Tax Rate Schedules shown in
Illustration 28–2 on page 906.

Exercise 28–1

List the letters of the following items and write after each either the word
included or *excluded* to tell whether the item should be included in or excluded
from gross income for federal income tax purposes.

a. A portable TV set having a $100 fair market value which was received as a
    door prize.
b. Tips received while working as a parking lot attendant.
c. Cash inherited from a deceased aunt.
d. Scholarship received from a state university.
e. Social security benefits.
f. Workmen's compensation insurance received as the result of an accident
    while working on a part-time job.
g. Gain on the sale of a personal automobile bought and rebuilt.
h. First $100 of dividends from stock in domestic corporations received by
    an individual.
i. First $850 of $1,000 in dividends on stock in domestic corporations re-
    ceived by a corporation.
j. Interest on a savings account.

Exercise 28–2

During 1978 Kathy Boley furnished more than half the support of her sis-
ter, a college student living in a girls' dormitory. Kathy is unmarried and earned
$26,000 as the employee of an investment brokerage. She had $5,650 of federal income tax and $965 of F.I.C.A. tax withheld from her paychecks. She
also received $100 interest on a savings account and $95 in dividends from a
domestic corporation in which she owned stock. During the year she paid $780
state income tax, $620 interest on the balance owed on a car she purchased,
and gave her church $1,375. Show the calculation of Kathy's taxable income in
the manner outlined in Illustration 28–1. Then using the rate schedule of Illustration 28–2, show the calculation of the net federal income tax payable or
refund due Kathy.

Exercise 28–3

In 1978, a married taxpayer who files a joint return and had no other capital
gains sold for $7,500 a number of shares of stock he had purchased for $5,500.
Use the rate schedule of Illustration 28–2 and determine the amount of federal income tax the taxpayer will have to pay on the gain from this transaction
under each of the following unrelated assumptions:

a. The taxpayer had $41,000 of taxable income from other sources and had
    held the shares four months.

b. The taxpayer had $41,000 of taxable income from other sources and had held the shares for 14 months.

c. The taxpayer had $45,000 of taxable income from other sources and had held the shares six months.

d. The taxpayer had $45,000 of taxable income from other sources and had held the shares for 12 months and one day.

e. The taxpayer had $83,300 of taxable income from other sources (which was not subject to the 50% maximum tax provision) and had held the shares for two months.

f. The taxpayer had $83,300 of taxable income from other sources (which was not subject to the 50% maximum tax provision) and had held the shares for 15 months.

Exercise 28–4

Diane Orr, Margaret Jones, and Michael Crab are unmarried and have three income tax exemptions each. Last year their adjusted gross incomes were: Orr, $20,500; Jones, $21,500; and Crab, $19,800. Their itemized deductions were: Orr, $2,800; Jones, $2,400; and Crab, $2,000. Prepare calculations to show the taxable income of each person.

Exercise 28–5

Gary and Karen Ford had $25,000 of adjusted gross income last year. They are both 37 years old and have two children, ages 7 and 10. Last year their motorcycle having a fair value of $1,350 was stolen from their home and their insurance did not cover the loss. They donated $360 to their church and incurred the following expenses during the year: local property taxes, $700; interest on home mortgage, $940; hospital insurance $290; and uninsured doctor and dentist bills, $810. Prepare a calculation to show the Fords' taxable income on a joint return.

Problems

Problem 28–1

Larry and Janet Steel are married and file a joint tax return. They have no income other than from Hillview Store, a profitable partnership business that Larry and Janet own and which averages $350,000 annually in sales, with a 40% gross profit and $100,000 of operating expenses. The Steels have no dependents, but each year they have $3,000 of itemized deductions and two exemptions. In the past, the Steels have withdrawn $12,000 annually from the business for personal living expenses plus sufficient additional cash to pay the income tax on their joint return.

Larry and Janet think that they can save taxes by reorganizing their business into a corporation beginning with the 1978 tax year. If the corporation is organized, it will issue 1,000 shares of no-par stock, 300 to Larry and 700 to Janet. Also, $15,000 per year is a fair salary for managing such a business, and the corporation will pay that amount to Larry.

Required:

1. Prepare a comparative income statement for the business showing its net income as a partnership and as a corporation.

2. Use the rate schedule of Illustration 28–2 and determine the amount of federal income taxes the Steels will pay for themselves on a joint return and for the business under each of the following assumptions: (a) the business remains a partnership; (b) the business is incorporated, pays Larry Steel a $15,000 salary, but pays no dividends; and (c) the business is incorporated, pays Larry Steel a $15,000 salary, and pays $16,000 in dividends, $4,800 to Larry Steel and $11,200 to Janet Steel. (Each may exclude the first $100 of dividends.)

Problem 28–2

Ajax Corporation is planning an expansion program that will cost $100,000 and will increase its earnings $20,000 annually before interest on the money used in the expansion, if borrowed, and before income taxes. All the outstanding stock of Ajax Corporation is owned by the Kim family, and the family will supply the money to finance the expansion, either investing an additional $100,000 in the corporation by purchasing its unissued stock or lending it $100,000 at 7% interest.

The corporation presently earns in excess of $50,000 annually and pays $20,000 per year to the family in dividends. If the loan is made, the dividends will be reduced by an amount equal to the interest on the loan.

Required:

Present statistics to show whether it would be advantageous for the family to make the loan or to purchase the corporation's stock. No additional dividend exclusions will be gained by issuing the stock.

Problem 28–3

Paul Grudnitski owns all the outstanding stock of Northern Products Company. The corporation is a small manufacturing concern; however, over the years it has purchased and owns stocks costing $85,000 (present market value much higher) which it holds as long-term investments. The corporation has seldom paid a dividend, but it does pay Mr. Grudnitski a $12,000 annual salary as president and manager. Last year the corporation earned $28,000, after its president's salary but before income taxes, consisting of $20,000 in manufacturing income and $8,000 in dividends on its long-term investments.

Mr. Grudnitski has no dependents, but he had $3,250 of itemized deductions last year plus a single $750 exemption deduction. He had no income last year other than his corporation salary and $1,000 in interest from a real estate loan.

Required:

1. Prepare a comparative statement showing for last year the operating income, investment income, total income, share of the dividend income excluded, taxable income, and income tax of the corporation under the (a) and (b) assumptions which follow. (a) The corporation owns the investment stocks and had the operating income just described. (b) The corporation had the operating income described; but instead of owning the investment stocks, over the years it paid dividends (none last year) and Mr. Grudnitski used them to buy the stocks in his own name rather than in the corporation name.
2. Calculate the amounts of individual income tax and corporation income tax incurred by Mr. Grudnitski and the corporation under the (a) assump-

tions, and the amounts that would have been incurred under the (b) assumptions. Also calculate the amount of individual income tax Mr. Grudnitski would have incurred with the business organized as a single proprietorship and the stocks registered in Mr. Grudnitski's name. Under this last assumption remember that the corporation's operating income plus its president's salary equal the operating income of the single proprietorship. Use the rate schedule of Illustration 28–2 in all individual income tax calculations.

Problem 28–4

At a $200,000 cost, ABC Corporation installed a new machine in its plant early in January 197A, so that it could add a new product to its line. It estimated the new machine would have a four-year life, a $16,000 salvage value, and its product would produce $180,000 of income each year before depreciation and income taxes at an assumed 50% rate. The company uses declining-balance depreciation at twice the straight-line rate for tax purposes and straight-line depreciation for its accounting records. It also allocates income taxes in its reports to stockholders.

Required:

1. Prepare a schedule showing 197A, 197B, 197C, 197D, and total net income for the four years from the sale of the new product after deducting declining-balance depreciation and actual income taxes.
2. Prepare a second schedule showing each year's income and total net income after deducting straight-line depreciation and actual income taxes.
3. Prepare a third schedule showing income reported to stockholders with straight-line depreciation and allocated income taxes.
4. Set up a T-account for Deferred Income Tax and show therein the entries that result from allocating the income taxes.

Problem 28–5

Bill and Mary Clark are both 41 years old, have three sons, and file a joint tax return. Their oldest son, Larry, is a junior high school student and earned $600 last year working at odd jobs. The other two sons earned nothing during the year. Mr. and Mrs. Clark had the following cash receipts and disbursements last year:

CASH RECEIPTS

Salary to Bill Clark from his employer, an industrial sales firm, for which Bill is an outside salesman ($30,500 gross income less $4,500 federal income taxes withheld, $965 F.I.C.A. taxes, and $400 for hospital insurance premiums)	$24,635
Dividends from General Motors common stock (jointly owned)	2,310
Interest from savings account owned by Mary Clark	210
Interest from bonds issued by City of Austin, Texas	1,000
Proceeds from sale of IBM common stock which had been acquired 28 months ago at a cost of $8,400 (jointly owned)	10,100

CASH DISBURSEMENTS

Cost of Bill driving from home to business office and back.............	$ 400
Cost of Bill driving from business office to visit customers.............	500
Entertainment of customers while soliciting sales orders................	600
Telephone charges for calls made to customers...........................	50
Contributions to church...	1,020
Local property taxes...	1,000
Contribution to political campaign of State Senator......................	200
Interest on home mortgage	1,450
Uninsured doctor and dentist bills...	1,845
Donation to college from which Bill and Mary graduated..............	500
Advance payment of federal income tax.....................................	525

Required:

Follow the form of Illustration 28–1 and use the rate schedule in Illustration 28–2 to calculate for the Clarks the amount of federal income tax due or to be refunded.

Problem 28–1A   Alternate
                                                                        problems

Wayne Mettlan has operated the Country Store for a number of years with the following average annual results:

COUNTRY STORE
Income Statement for an Average Year

Sales........................		$280,000
Cost of goods sold $165,000		
Operating expenses	85,000	250,000
Net Income		$ 30,000

Mr. Mettlan is unmarried and without dependents and has been operating Country Store as a single proprietorship. He has been withdrawing $12,000 each year to pay his personal living expenses, including $4,250 of charitable contributions, state and local taxes, and other itemized deductions. He has no income other than from Country Store.

Required:

1. Assume that Mr. Mettlan is considering the incorporation of his business beginning with the 1978 tax year and prepare a comparative income statement for the business showing its net income as a single proprietorship and as a corporation. Assume that if he incorporates, Mr. Mettlan will pay $12,000 per year to himself as a salary, which is a fair amount.
2. Use the rate schedule of Illustration 28–2 and determine the amount of federal income tax Mr. Mettlan will have to pay for himself and for his business under each of the following assumptions; (*a*) the business is not incorporated; (*b*) the business is incorporated, pays Mr. Mettlan a $12,000 annual salary as manager, and also pays him $12,000 per year in dividends; and (*c*) the business is incorporated, pays Mr. Mettlan a $12,000 salary, but does not pay any dividends.

Problem 28–2A

Mike and Sue Slick, husband and wife who file a joint return, own all the outstanding stock of Slick Corporation. The corporation has an opportunity to expand, but to do so it will need $50,000 additional capital. The Slicks have the $50,000 and can either lend this amount to the corporation at 7% interest or they can invest the $50,000 in the corporation, taking its presently unissued stock in exchange for the money.

They calculate that with the additional $50,000 the corporation will earn $30,000 annually after paying Mike $15,000 per year as president and manager but before interest on the loan, if made, and before income taxes. They require $20,000 for personal living expenses and their own income taxes. Consequently, if they invest the additional $50,000 in the corporation, they will pay $5,000 per year to themselves in dividends in addition to Mike's salary. But if they lend the corporation the $50,000, they will use the interest on the loan, plus $1,500 in dividends and Mike's salary for their personal expenses.

Required:

Determine whether the loan to the corporation or an investment in its stock is to the best interest of the Slicks.

Problem 28–3A

Norm Youra, Jr., recently inherited the business of his father. The business, Delcon, Inc., is a small manufacturing corporation; however, a share of its assets, $75,000 at cost, consists of blue-chip investment stocks purchased over the years by the corporation from earnings. The father was the sole owner of the corporation at his death, and before his death he had paid himself a $15,000 annual salary for a number of years as president and manager. Over the years the corporation seldom paid a dividend but instead had invested any earnings not needed in the business in the blue-chip stocks previously mentioned. At the father's death the market value of these stocks far exceeded their cost.

Norm's mother is dead, and after Norm graduated from college, the father had no dependents. His tax return for the year before his death showed $16,500 of gross income, consisting of his $15,000 corporation salary plus $1,500 interest from real estate loans. It also showed $3,250 of itemized deductions plus a single $750 exemption deduction. The corporation had earned during the year before the father's death $23,000 from its manufacturing operations plus $10,000 in dividends from its investments, a total of $33,000 after the president's salary but before income taxes.

Required:

1. Prepare a comparative statement showing for the year before the father's death the corporation's operating income, dividend income, total income, share of the dividend income excluded, taxable income, and income tax under the following (*a*) and (*b*) assumptions. (*a*) The corporation owns the investment stocks and had the operating income just described. (*b*) The corporation had the operating income described; but instead of owning the investment stocks, over the years it paid dividends (none last year) and Norm Youra, Sr., used the dividends to buy the stocks in his own name rather than in the corporation name.

2. Calculate the amounts of individual income tax and corporation income tax incurred by Mr. Youra, Sr., and the corporation for the year before Mr. Youra's death under the foregoing (a) assumptions, and the amounts that would have been incurred under the (b) assumptions. Also calculate the amount of individual income tax Mr. Youra would have incurred with the business organized as a single proprietorship and the stocks registered in his own name. Under this last assumption remember that the corporation's operating income plus the salary paid its president equal the operating income of the single proprietorship. Use the rate schedule of Illustration 28–2 in the individual income tax calculations.

Problem 28–4A

Early in January 197A, Uptown Corporation installed a new machine in its plant that cost $280,000 and was estimated to have a four-year life and no salvage value. The machine enabled the company to add a new product to its line that produces $200,000 of income annually before depreciation and income taxes. The company allocates income taxes in its reports to its stockholders, since it uses straight-line depreciation in its accounting records and sum-of-the-years'-digits depreciation for tax purposes.

Required:

1. Prepare a schedule showing 197A, 197B, 197C, 197D, and total net income for the four years after deducting sum-of-the-years'-digits depreciation and actual taxes. Assume a 50% income tax rate.
2. Prepare a second schedule showing each year's net income and the four-year total after deducting straight-line depreciation and actual taxes.
3. Prepare a third schedule showing income reported to stockholders with straight-line depreciation and allocated taxes.
4. Set up a T-account for Deferred Income Tax and show therein the entries that result from allocating the income taxes.

Tedrow Grey and his wife own all the outstanding stock of Ithaca Corporation, a company Tedrow organized several years ago and which is growing rapidly and needs additional capital.

Bob Brown, a friend of the Greys, examined the following comparative income statement, which shows the corporation's net income for the past three years and which was prepared by its bookkeeper, and expressed a tentative willingness to invest $50,000 in the corporation by purchasing a portion of its unissued stock.

Decision problem 28–1, Ithaca Corporation

ITHACA CORPORATION
Comparative Income Statement, 197A, 197B, and 197C

	197A	197B	197C
Sales	$700,000	$750,000	$825,000
Costs and expenses other than depreciation and federal income taxes	$425,000	$450,000	$500,000
Depreciation expense	105,000	110,000	125,000
Income taxes	65,000	70,000	75,000
Total costs and expenses	$595,000	$630,000	$700,000
Net Income	$105,000	$120,000	$125,000

However, before making a final decision, Bob Brown asked permission for his own accountant to examine the accounting records of the corporation. Permission was granted, the examination was made, and the accountant prepared the following comparative income statement covering the past three years.

ITHACA CORPORATION
Comparative Income Statement, 197A, 197B, and 197C

	197A	197B	197C
Sales	$700,000	$750,000	$825,000
Costs and expenses other than depreciation	$425,000	$450,000	$500,000
Depreciation expense*	105,000	110,000	125,000
Total costs and expenses	$530,000	$560,000	$625,000
Income before income taxes	$170,000	$190,000	$200,000
Applicable income taxes	85,000	95,000	100,000
Net Income	$ 85,000	$ 95,000	$100,000

* The corporation deducted $145,000 of depreciation on its 197A tax returns, $160,000 on its 197B returns, and $175,000 on its 197C returns.

Tedrow was surprised at the difference in annual net incomes reported on the two statements and immediately called for an explanation from the accountant who set up the corporation's accounting system and who prepares the annual tax returns of the corporation and the Greys.

Explain why there is a difference between the net income figures on the two income statements. Prepare a statement that will justify the amounts shown on the corporation bookkeeper's statement. Account for the difference in the reported net incomes. Assume a 50% total federal and state income tax rate.

Index

Index

A

Accelerated depreciation, 331, 342, 879
Accepting new or additional business, costs of, 180–81
Account balance, 35, 40, 54
Account form balance sheet, 86–87
Account numbers, 53–54
Accountancy as a profession, 4
Accountants, fields of work of, 5–7
Accounting; *see also other specific topics*
  bookkeeping distinguished, 7
  corporations, 499
  defined, 3, 19
  focus of text, 7
  merchandising concerns, 141–75
  partnerships, 459
  price-level changes, 665–93
  reasons for study of, 4
  service enterprises, 105–138, 141
  stock investments, 570–75
  tax aspects, 915–16
Accounting change, 548, 551
Accounting concepts, 3–30
  defined, 19
Accounting cycle
  defined, 120–21
  steps in, 120–21
Accounting equation, 15, 46
  business transaction as affecting, 15–17
  defined, 20
  double-entry accounting based on, 40

Accounting information, uses of, 3–4
Accounting methods used, disclosure of, 270
Accounting periods, 69, 87, 120–21
Accounting principles, 11–15
  defined, 20
  sources of, 13–15
Accounting Principles Board (APB), 20
  establishment, 14
  membership, 14
  opinions, 14
    No. 10, "Omnibus Opinion—1966," 156–57
    No. 11, "Accounting for Income Taxes," 918–19
    No. 12, "Omnibus Opinion—1967," 333
    No. 15, "Earnings per Share," 548, 649–50
    No. 16, "Business Corporations," 581, 583–84
    No. 17, "Intangible Assets," 368, 496, 583
    No. 18, "The Equity Method of Accounting for Investments in Common Stock," 571
    No. 19, "Reporting Changes in Financial Position," 605, 613–15
    No. 20, "Accounting Changes," 302, 548
    No. 21, "Interest on Receivables and Payables," 361, 436

Accounting Principles Board—*Cont.*
  opinions—*Cont.*
    No. 22, "Disclosure of Accounting Policies," 270, 301
    No. 29, "Accounting for Nonmonetary Transactions," 11, 357–59
    No. 30, "Reporting the Results of Operations," 547–49
  statements
    No. 3, "Financial Statements Restated for General Price Level Changes," 670
    No. 4, "Basic Concepts and Accounting Principles Underlying Financial Statements of Business Enterprises," 3, 157, 298, 325, 423
  termination, 14
Accounting Research Bulletins, 14
  No. 43, 84, 297, 328, 541, 570
Accounting Research and Terminology Bulletins, Final Edition, 84, 297, 303, 328, 541, 570
Accounting statements; *see also specific types*
  defined, 7–8
Accounting systems, 177–218
  defined, 177, 199
Accounts, 34–35; *see also specific types*
  adjusted, 70–76

Accounts—*Cont.*
after closing, 115–19
arrangement in ledger, 80
code numbers to identify, 160–62
commonly used, 35–39
defined, 54
standard costs, 858
standard form, 48–49
variances, 858
Accounts payable, 10, 20, 37
defined, 16
schedule of, 190, 199
Accounts payable account, 185
Accounts payable controlling account, 190
Accounts payable ledger, 185, 190
adding machine list to prove, 190
defined, 199
Accounts receivable, 10, 20, 36, 274–94
aging, 279–80, 282
schedule of, 190, 199, 279–80
uncollectible; *see* Bad debts
Accounts receivable account, functions of, 180
Accounts receivable controlling account, 190
Accounts receivable ledger, 178–80, 190
adding machine list to prove, 190
alphabetical arrangement of, 180
defined, 199
sales invoices posted to, 191
Accounts receivable turnover, 644–45, 651
Accrual basis of accounting, 81–82, 87, 616
taxes, 916
Accrued expense, 87
adjusting accounts for, 74–75
defined, 74
disposition of, 80–81
Accrued revenue, 87
adjusting accounts for, 76
defined, 76
disposition of, 81
Accrued wages and taxes on wages, 411–12
Accumulated depreciation, 333–34
Accumulated depreciation accounts, 74, 87
plant assets, 85
Acid-test ratio, 643–44, 651
Actual performance, 845
Additional markups and markdowns, 310–11

Adjusted gross income for tax purposes, 921
deductions from, 904–5
deductions to arrive at, 903–4
Adjusted retained earnings balance, 679–80
Adjusted trial balance, 76–80, 87, 105, 108
preparing statements from, 76–77
process of adjustment, 77–80
Adjusting entries, 87, 105, 120; *see also* Adjustments
errors in, 115
manufacturing company, 740
merchandising concern, 154
notes payable, 426–28
notes receivable, 274
collecting interest previously accrued, 274
worksheet and, 110
Adjustment process, 77–80, 87
Adjustments; *see also* Adjusting entries
accounts, 70–76
accrual basis, 81–82
accrued expense accounts, 74–75, 80–81
accrued revenue accounts, 76, 81
cash basis, 81–82
depreciation accounts, 72–74
matching principle, 77, 80
need for, 69–70
prepaid expense accounts, 70–72
prior period, 548–49, 551
recognition principle, 77, 80
trial balance, 76–80
unearned revenue accounts, 75–76
worksheet, 152
illustration, 106–9
Advertising expense, allocation of, 704–5
After-tax income, 831, 901
Aging accounts receivable, 279–80, 282
AICPA; *see* American Institute of Certified Public Accountants
Allocating expenses, 701–3
bases for, 703–5
departmental sheet for, 705–8
mechanics of, 705–6
service department expenses, 707
Allowance for doubtful accounts, 276–77, 282
balance sheet, 277
Allowance method of accounting for bad debts, 275–78, 282

American Accounting Association, 14
American Institute of Certified Public Accountants (AICPA), 4, 14, 20
Accounting Principles Board opinions and statements; *see* Accounting Principles Board
Accounting Research Bulletins; *see* Accounting Research Bulletins
Committee on Education and Experience Requirements for CPAs, 4
Internal Control, 222
Amortization, 362–63, 368–72, 376
bond discount, 436–38
bond premiums, 438–40
Amortize; *see* Amortization
Analysis of financial statements, 635–63
Analysis of working capital, 642–46
Analyzing entries in working paper, 609–11
Annual accounting periods, 69
Annual budget, 802
APB; *see* Accounting Principles Board
Appropriated retained earnings, 543–45, 551
Ask prices, 570
Asset accounts, 35–37; *see also* *specific types*
Assets, 9–10
accounting for, 219 ff.; *see also* *specific assets*
defined, 20
GPLA accounting for, 671–74
Audit
defined, 20
purpose, 5
tax returns, 7
Auditing, 5
Automated data processing, 195–99, 231
defined, 199
input-output device, 198
inputting data, 197–98
off-line operations, 197, 199
on-line operations, 197–99
program for, 195–96, 199
time sharing, 198–200
yes or no decisions, 196–97
Average change in per unit prices, 667–68
Average costs, 880
Average inventory; *see* Inventory
Average investment, determination of, 875–76

B

Bad debt expense account, 281
Bad debts, 274–75, 282
  accounts, 276–77
  aging accounts receivable, 279–
    80, 282
  allowance method of account-
    ing for, 275–78, 282
  direct write-off, 280–82
  estimating, 275, 279
    recording, 275–76
  income statement, 276
  matching losses with sales, 275
  recoveries, 278–79
  writing off, 277–78
Bail-out period, 874
Balance column account, 48–49,
  54
Balance sheet, 9–10, 601; see also
    specific types
  accounts, 120
  allowances for doubtful ac-
    counts, 277, 282
  arrangement of items on, 86
  classification of items on, 82–
    86
  common-size comparative, 640
  comparative, 635–36
  corporation, 585–86
  defined, 20
  depreciation, 333–34
  plant asset values, 334
  purpose, 9
  replacement costs on, 682
  stock dividend, 541
  stock subscriptions, 531–32
  worksheet illustration, 109–10
Balance sheet conservatism, 305
Balance sheet equation, 15
Bank balance reconciliation, 236
  defined, 246
  illustration, 239–40
  need for, 237–38
  payroll accounts, 407–8
  steps in, 238–39
Bank charges for service, 238
Bank discount, 268, 282, 425
Bank reconciliation; see Bank
    balance reconciliation
Bank statements; see Bank bal-
    ance reconciliation
Bankruptcy, 458, 478
Basis for tax purposes, 909, 921
Batch processing, 197
Before-tax income, 831
Beginning inventory; see Inven-
    tories
Betterments, 366, 376
Bid prices, 570
Bond quotations, 442
Bond sinking fund, 442–45, 570
Bondholders defined, 429

Bonds; see Corporate bonds
Book of final entry, 50, 55
Book of original entry, 50, 55
Book equity, 470–71, 478
Book gain, 358–59
Book loss, 357–58
Book value, 365–66, 376
  excess of investment cost over,
    578–81
  plant asset, 330
  pledged assets, 647
  stock, 511–14
Bookkeeping
  accounting distinguished, 7
  defined, 20
Bookkeeping machines, 231
Break-even analysis, 823
Break-even graph, 828–29
Break-even point, 827–32, 834
  multiproduct, 832–33
Broad concept of financing and in-
    vesting activities, 614–15
Budget, 799, 814; see also specific
    types
Budget committee, 802
Budget period, 802–3
Budgeted balance sheet, 804–5,
  812–14
Budgeted costs, 850; see also
    Standard costs
Budgeted income statement, 804–
  5, 812
Budgeting, 6, 799, 814
  benefits from, 800–802
  defined, 20
Buildings, 37
Business, primary objective of, 16
Business entity concept, 10–11,
  13, 20
Business organizations
  taxes affected by form of, 912–
    13
  types, 7, 493
Business papers, 33–34, 55, 226
Business transaction
  accounting equation as affected
    by, 15–17
  defined, 15, 20
  recording, 33–67
Buy or make decision, 882

C

Calendar year, 121
Callable bonds, 441, 445
Canceled checks, 236, 246
Capital, 10, 85
Capital account, 38, 41, 55
Capital asset, 908–9, 921
Capital budgeting, 810
  accelerated depreciation, 879
  cash flows not uniform, 878–79

Capital budgeting—Cont.
  defined, 873–74, 886
  discounted cash flows, 874,
    876–77, 886
  earnings rate, selection of, 879
  payback period, 874–75, 886
  present value concept, 876–77
  replacing plant assets, 879–80
  return on average investment,
    874–76, 886
  salvage value, 879
Capital contribution of owners
    and creditors, 646–47
Capital expenditures, 366, 377
Capital expenditures budget, 804,
    809–10, 814
Capital gains and losses, tax treat-
    ment of, 908–10, 921
Capital reductions, 604
Capital stock, sale of, 603
Carrying amount
  bond issues, 436–38, 440, 445
  note, 363, 377
Cash, 9, 36
  accounting for, 221–61
  from charge customers, 181
  internal control for, 223–25
  mail as source, 224
  over and short, 235–36
  over and short account, 246
  protection from fraud and theft,
    221
  receipts deposited intact, 223
Cash basis of accounting, 81–82,
    87, 616
  taxes, 916
Cash basis of revenue recogni-
    tion, 157, 162
Cash budget, 804, 810–12, 814
Cash disbursements, 224–25
Cash disbursements journal, 180,
    185, 406
  posting to, 188–89
Cash discounts, 143, 162, 241
Cash dividend, 507, 538, 541
Cash flow statement, 615–16
  defined, 619
  preparation of, 617–19
Cash receipts, 223–24
Cash receipts journal, 180–83
  cash from charge customers,
    181
  cash sales, 181
  miscellaneous receipts of cash,
    183
  multicolumn, 180–81
  posting to, 181–84
  sales tax column, 191
Cash registers, 699–701
Cash sales, 33–34, 181, 223–24
Catalog price, 159, 162

Certified public accountants
(CPAs), 4
defined, 20
licensing of, 4
state requirements for, 4
Check register, 188–89, 243–45,
406–8
defined, 199
Classified balance sheet, 82, 87
Clock card, 402, 412, 765
Closing entries
accounts after, 115–19
defined, 110, 121
errors in, 119
expense accounts, 112–13
illustrations, 111–15
income summary account, 113–
14
inventory and, 155
manufacturing company, 740–
41
merchandising concern, 154–
55
reasons for making, 110–11
revenue accounts, 112
sources of information for, 110,
115
withdrawals account, 114–15
worksheet and, 110
Closing procedure, 121
Code numbers to identify accounts, 160–62
Collections, 238
Columnar journal, 177, 180
crossfooting, 183
defined, 199
foot, 183
Combined cash journal, 191–93,
199
Commas in dollar amounts, 54
Common-size comparative statements, 639–42, 651
Common-size percentages, 641–
42
Common stock, 429, 445, 501,
508, 514, 570
Common stock subscribed, 529–
30, 551
Comparative single-step income
statement, 549–50
Comparative statements, 635–37
analyzing and interpreting,
636–38
defined, 651
percentage increases and decreases, 638
Compound journal entry, 50–51,
55
Computer defined, 199
Computer processing; see Automated data processing
Conservatism principle, 13, 305,
313

Consigned goods, 302
Consignee, 302, 313
Consignor, 302, 313
Consistency principle, 13, 301–2,
313, 548
Consolidated balance sheets,
575–81
dates after acquisition, 581–83
principles of consolidation,
575–76
time of acquisition, 576–77
Consolidated statements, 575,
583, 586
who uses, 585
Consumer Price Index (CPI), 670
Contingent liabilities
disclosure of, 270
note, 269–70, 282
Continuing-concern concept, 11–
13, 20, 334, 342
Continuous budgeting, 803
Contra accounts, 73
accumulated depreciation, 334
bad debt allowance, 276
defined, 87
depreciation recorded in, 73
Contract rate of bond interest,
434, 445
Contributed capital accounts, 499
Contributed capital and dividends,
538
Contribution margin, 848
Contribution margin per composite unit, 832–34
Contribution margin per unit, 827,
834
Contribution rate, 827, 831, 834
Control, 799–800, 845
standard costs to achieve, 857–
58
Controllable costs and expenses,
709–11, 713
Controllable variance, 855–58
Controller
defined, 20
position and function of, 6
Controlling accounts, 180; see
also specific accounts
accounts payable, 185
defined, 199
posting to, 184
Controlling interest, 578
Conventional financial statements, 671
Convertible bonds, 442, 445
Copyrights, 369, 377; see also
Intangible assets
Corporate bonds, 429, 445
accrued interest expense, 440–
41
amortization of discount or
premium, 436–40

Corporate bonds—Cont.
borrowing by issuance of, 430–
31
characteristics of, 431
converting to stock, 542–43
dividend restrictions due to outstanding, 444
interest rates, 434
issuance of, 432
reasons for issuance of, 429–30
redemption, 441–42
sale on date of issue, 432
sale at discount, 434–38, 445
sale between interest dates,
432–33
sale by investors, 441
sale at premium, 438–40, 445
types, 431
Corporations, 493
accounting, 499
administrative officers, 497
advantages of, 493–94
authorization of stock, 501–2
balance sheet, 585–86
board of directors, 497
bonds issued by; see Corporate
bonds
bylaws, 496
charters, 495
continuity of life, 494
contributed capital, 537
control of, 496–97
defined, 7, 20
disadvantages of, 494–95
donation of assets by outsiders,
537
ease of capital assembly, 494
ease of transferring ownership
rights, 494
government control and supervision, 494–95
income tax, 911–12
lack of stockholders' liability,
494
legal characteristics, 7
management of, 496–97
minimum legal capital, 503, 514
mutual agency lacking, 494
normal tax on, 911, 921
organization of, 495–96
organization costs, 496, 514
owner equity accounts, 499–
501
parent, 575, 587
separate legal entity, 493
stock issued by; see Stock
stockholders of; see Shareholders
subsidiary, 575, 587
surtax on, 911, 921
taxation of, 495
accounting treatment for,
550–51

Correcting entry, 53–54
Correcting errors, 53
Cost; see also specific types
  assembling by departments, 770–71
  inventory; see Inventory
  plant and equipment, 326–27
  replacement below actual, 304–5
Cost of goods manufactured, 729
Cost of goods purchased, 146–48, 729
Cost of goods sold, 144, 148, 297–98, 645
  factors in calculating, 145
  periodic inventory system, 145
  recording of, 770
  replacement cost, 683
Cost of goods sold accounts, 152–53
Cost or market, the lower
  inventory, 303–5, 312–13
  stock investments, 572–73
Cost accounting, 6
  defined, 21
Cost accounting systems, 730, 780
  job order, 759–70, 780–95
  process, 770–95
Cost assumptions, 825–27
Cost basis of plant asset, 359
Cost behavior, 823–26
Cost centers, 698, 713
Cost method of accounting for stock investments, 571–72, 587
Cost principle, 11–13, 21, 393
Cost variance, 852
Cost-volume-profit analysis, 823–42
  defined, 834
  evaluation of results of, 834
Coupon bonds, 431, 445
CPA; see Certified public accountants
Credit, 55
Credit balance, 39
Credit memorandum, 159–60, 162
Credit period, 143, 162
Credit terms, 143, 162
Creditors
  defined, 9, 21
  interest of, 10
Creditors' equity, 646–47
Credits, 39–40
Crossfoot, 183
  defined, 199
Cumulative preferred stock, 510, 514
Current assets, 82–84, 87, 601–2
Current liabilities, 82–83, 85, 87, 423, 601–2

Current operations, 602–3
Current ratio, 642–43, 651
Current value accounting, 681, 684
Current values, 680–81

D

Damaged goods, 302–3
Data processing
  automated, 195–99; see also Automated data processing
  columnar journals to speed, 193
Date of declaration, 507, 514
Date of payment, 507, 514
Date of record, 507, 514
Days' sales uncollected, 645
Death of partner, 472
Debenture bond, 431, 445
Debit, 39–40, 55
Debit balance, 39
Debit and credit rules, 39–41
  transactions illustrating, 41–46
Debit memorandum, 159–60, 162
Debt-paying ability, 643
Debtor defined, 21
Debts, 9–10
Decimal points in dollar amounts, 54
Decision defined, 873
Declining-balance depreciation, 329–33, 342
Deed of trust, 431, 445
Defective units, scrapping or re-building of, 883–84
Deferred income tax, 333, 342, 920–21
Deficit, 477–79
Delivery expense, allocation of, 705
Departmental accounting, 697–711, 713–27
Departmental analysis sheets, 699
Departmental contributions to overhead, 709–10, 713
Departmental expense allocation sheet, 705–8
Departmental gross profits
  income statement showing, 701–2
  merchandising concern, 698–99
Departmental information, methods of securing, 699–701
Departmentalization, 697
  basis for, 697–98
Departments
  assembling of costs by, 770–71
  charging costs to, 771–72
Depletion, 367, 377
Depreciation, 327
  accelerated, 331, 342
  accumulated, 74, 333–34
  adjusting account for, 72–74

Depreciation—Cont.
  allocation of, 329–33, 705
  balance sheet, 333–34
  contra account for, 73
  declining-balance method, 329–33, 342
  defined, 72, 88
  errors, 363–64
  nature of, 327–28
  partial years, 337–39
  replacement cost of productive capacity, 683
  revising rates of, 363–64
  straight-line method, 329, 342
  source of funds, 603
  sum-of-the-year-digits method, 329, 331–33, 342
  units-of-production method, 329–30
Depreciation accounting, 328
Depreciation expenses, 72, 88
Deteriorated goods, 302–3
Differential costs, 880–81
  buy or make decision, 882
Direct costs or expenses, 701–3, 713
Direct labor, 731, 743
Direct labor time tickets, 766
Direct materials, 730–31, 743
Direct write-off of bad debts, 280–82
Discarding plant asset, 335–36
Discount period, 143, 162
  less than one year, 376
  note, 267, 282
Discounted cash flows, 874, 876–77, 886
Discounted notes receivable, 267–68, 282–83
  contingent liability, 269–70, 282
  dishonor, 271–72
  full-disclosure principle, 270, 282–83
  payment by maker, 270–71
  proceeds, 268, 283
Discounts, 424–25; see also specific types
  bonds sold at, 424–38, 445
  lost, 246
  notes payable, 426–28
  stock issued at, 504–5, 514
Dishonored notes receivable, 266–67, 271–72, 282
Disposal of plant asset, 335–37
Dividend restrictions, 444
Dividends, 506–8, 514, 537–38; see also specific types
  contributed capital and, 538
  corporate policy, 507–8
  date of declaration, 507, 514
  date of payment, 507, 514
  date of record, 507, 514

Dividends—*Cont.*
  declaration of, 604
  payment of, 604
  preference as to, 509
  state laws governing, 508
  stock investments, 572
  taxes, 913–14
Dividends in arrears, 510, 514
Dollar signs, 54
Donations by outsiders, 537
Double-entry accounting system,
    19, 33, 40
  defined, 55
  equality of debits and credits,
    40, 46
  mechanics of, 40–41
  proof of accuracy of recording
    under, 40, 46
  rules for recording transactions
    under, 40–41
Drawing account, 39

                    E

Earned surplus, 537, 551
Earnings per common share, 649–
    50
Earnings per share calculations,
    547–48
Earnings rate, selection of, 879
Electric accounting machines,
    193–95
Electric bookkeeping machines,
    33–34, 699–700
Eliminating an unprofitable de-
    partment, 707–9
Employee's individual earnings
    record, 408–9, 412
End-of-the-accounting-period
    adjustment; *see* Adjustments
End-of-the-period balances, 69–
    70
End-of-the-period inventories,
    144
End-of-the-period procedures, 69
Ending inventory; *see* Inventories
Entries; *see specific types*
EOM, 143, 162
Equipment, 37; *see also* Plant and
    equipment
Equity
  defined, 10, 21
  of the owner; *see* Owner equity
Equity method of accounting for
    stock investments, 571, 573–
    75, 587
Equity securities; *see* Stock in-
    vestments
Equivalent finished unit costs,
    772
Equivalent finished units, 772,
    780
Errors
  bank balance, 238

Errors—*Cont.*
  correcting, 53
  depreciation, 363–64
  inventory, 305–6
  locating, 53
Escapable expenses, 708, 713
Exchanging plant assets, 357–61
  material book loss, 357–58
  nonrecognition of book gain,
    358–59
  note for, 361–63
  tax rules, 359–61, 377
Exchanging stock for assets other
    than cash, 502–3
Expected performance, 800–801
Expense accounts, 39, 41
  closing, 112–13
Expenses, 8; *see also specific
    types*
  allocation of, 701–8
  defined, 17, 21
  proration, 149
  voucher system and, 230–31
Extraordinary gains and losses,
    547–48, 551, 613–14
Extraordinary repairs and re-
    placements, 365–66, 377

                    F

Face amount of bonds, 432, 445
Factory burden, 731–32
Factory overhead, 731–32, 743
Factory payroll account, 765
Factory supplies, 731
Fair Labor Standards Act, 401
FASB; *see* Financial Accounting
    Standards Board
Favorable variances, 951
Federal depository banks, 410–
    12
Federal income tax; *see* Taxes
Federal Insurance Contributions
    Act, 394–95
Federal old-age and survivors'
    benefits program, 393–95
Federal Unemployment Tax Act,
    397–98, 412
Feedback, 845
F.I.C.A. taxes, 394–95, 412
  levied on employer, 409–10
  paying, 410–11
Fifo; *see* First-in, first-out method
    of inventory pricing
Financial Accounting Standards
    Board (FASB), 14, 21
  membership, 14
  statements, 14
    No. 2, "Accounting for Re-
      search and Development
      Costs," 369
    No. 12, "Accounting for Cer-
      tain Marketable Securi-
      ties," 570, 573

Financial Accounting Standards
    Board—*Cont.*
  statements—*Cont.*
    Proposed, "Financial Re-
      porting in Units of
      General Purchasing
      Power," 670–71
Financial budgets, 804
Financial statements; *see also
    specific types*
  analysis of, 635–63
  footnotes to, 270
  merchandising concern, 154
  partnership, 464
  preparation of, 120
  worksheet and, 109–10
Finished goods, 733, 743
Finished goods inventories, 729
Finished goods inventory ac-
    count, 733
First-in, first-out method of in-
    ventory pricing, 298–300,
    313
Fiscal year, 121
Fixed assets, 325, 342; *see also*
    Plant and equipment
Fixed budget, 845–46, 859
  performance report and, 845–
    46
Fixed costs, 823–24, 826, 834,
    847–48
Flexible budgets, 845–50, 858–
    71
  defined, 859
  performance report and, 849–
    50, 859
  preparation of, 847–49
Flexible factory overhead budget,
    854
FOB, 162
FOB destination, 148
FOB factory, 148
Folio column, 51–53, 55
Folio letters, identifying posted
    amounts by, 188
Foot, 183, 199
Footnotes, 270
Foreclosure values, 647
Freight-in, 162
Freight-in account, 147–48, 152
Full-disclosure principle, 13, 270,
    282–83, 301–2, 335, 510
  footnotes, use of, 270
Funds defined, 602, 619
Funds statement, 601

                    G

Gains and losses
  capital, 908–10, 921
  exchange of plant assets, 358–
    59
  extraordinary, 547–48, 551,
    613–14

General accounting system, 6, 21, 730, 759

General and administrative expenses, 149, 162, 804, 808-9

General journal
defined, 50, 55
function, 50
posting labor involved, reduction in, 177-78
recording transactions in, 50-51

General ledger, 178-80, 199

General price-level-adjusted (GPLA) accounting, 667, 670-81, 684
assets, 671-74
current values, 680-81
future adoption of, 684
liabilities, 672-74
stockholders' equity, 672-74

General price-level-adjusted (GPLA) balance sheet, 671-72, 675-77

General price-level-adjusted (GPLA) financial statements, 671
preparation of, 674-80

General price-level-adjusted (GPLA) income statement, 677-79

General price-level index, 670, 684

Generally accepted concepts, 13; see also specific concepts

Generally accepted principles, 13; see also specific principles
sources of, 13-15

Generally accepted procedures, 13; see also specific topics

Going-concern concept, 11-13, 21, 334, 342

Goods on consignment, 302

Goods in process, 733

Goods in process account, 762-63

Goods in process inventory account, 733

Goods in transit, 302

Goodwill, 370-72, 377; see also Intangible assets

Governmental accounting, 5, 7

GPLA accounting; see General price-level-adjusted (GPLA) accounting

Gross income for tax purposes, 902-3, 921

Gross method of recording invoices, 241, 246

Gross National Product (GNP) Implicit Price Deflator, 670-71

Gross pay, 403-5, 412

Gross profit from sales, 162
defined, 141
determination of, 142

Gross profit inventory method, 312-13

Gross profits, departmental, 698-99, 701-2

Gross sales, 142

H-I

Head of household, 905-6, 921

Heating and lighting expense, allocation of, 705

Historical costs, 759-95, 850, 880

Holder in due course, 273, 283

Inadequacy, 328, 342

Incidental costs, 303

Income from given sales level, 830-31

Income statement, 8, 601
bad debts, 276
classification of items, 86
common-size comparative, 640-41
comparative, 635, 637
comparative single-step, 549-50
defined, 21
departmental gross profits, 701-2
manufacturing company, 733-34
merchandising concern, 149
multiple step, 549-50
partnership, 464
preparation of, 8
single step, 549-50
work sheet, 152-53
illustration, 109-10

Income summary account
closing, 113-14
defined, 122

Income tax; see Taxes

Income tax expense, 809

Income tax rules, 359-61, 377; see also Taxes

Income tax withholding, 399-401

Incorporators, 495

Incremental costs, 880-81, 886
buy or make decision, 882

Indirect costs or expenses, 701-3, 713

Indirect labor, 731, 743

Indirect labor time tickets, 766

Indirect materials, 731, 743

Individual earnings record, 408-9, 412

Individual income tax, 901-8

Inescapable expenses, 708

Inflation, failure to adequately account for, 665-66

Inputting data, 197-98

Insurance expense, allocation of, 705

Insurance premium, 36

Intangible assets, 10, 82, 85, 367-72; see also specific types
amortization of; see Amortization
defined, 88, 377
value, 367

Interest
calculating, 263-64
corporate bonds, 434
loans, 424-25
notes payable, 425
prevailing rate, 361
rate of, 263

Interest expense, 809

Interest method of amortization, 436-38

Interest receivable, 274

Interim statements, 309, 313

Internal auditing, 6, 21

Internal control principles, 222-23
adequate records, maintenance of, 222
division of responsibilities, 222-23
mechanical devices, use of, 223
recordkeeping and asset custody, separation of, 222
responsibilities, clear establishment of, 222

Internal control procedures, 221, 240-42

Internal controls system, 221, 246
cash, 223-25
vouchers and, 225-30

Internal Revenue Code, 330, 342, 900

Inventories
beginning, 145, 153, 156
ending, 145, 153, 156-59, 298, 309-10
finished goods, 729
periodic, 144-45
perpetual, 144, 306-8
replacement cost of, 682-83
worksheet, 153

Inventory
accounting at cost for, 298-302
assigning cost to, 298
average, 645-46
book, 306-7
changing accounting procedures for, 302
closing entries and, 155
conservatism principle, 305, 313
consistency principle, 301-2, 313
at cost, 309

Inventory — *Cont.*
  cost or market, the lower, 303–5, 312–13
  count of, 158–59
  elements of cost, 303
  errors, 305–6
  estimations, 309–13
  first-in, first-out method, 298–300, 313
  full-disclosure principle, 301–2
  gross profit method, 312–13
  incidental costs, 303
  interim statements, 309, 313
  items included on, 302–3
  last-in, first-out method, 298, 300–301, 313
  matching merchandise costs with revenues, 297–98
  pricing methods, 299–301
    comparison of, 301
  replacement costs below actual costs, 304–5
  at retail, 309
  retail method, 309–12, 314
  specific invoice prices, 298–99, 314
  taking of, 158
  weighted average, 298–99, 314
Inventory cost ratio, 310–11, 313
Inventory losses, 149
Inventory tags, 700–701
Inventory tickets, 158–59, 162
Inventory turnover, 645–46, 651
Inventory valuation problems of manufacturer, 742–43
Investments
  balance sheet, 82, 570
  long-term, 82–84, 570, 587
  stocks and bonds, 569–70
Invoice approval form, 226–28, 246
Invoice terms, 143
Invoices, 226–27, 246
  gross method of recording, 241, 246
  net method of recording, 241–42, 246
Issued stock, 533

J

Job, 759, 780
Job completion, recording of, 769–70
Job cost ledger, 760, 762, 780
Job cost sheets, 760, 762, 780
Job lot, 759, 780
Job order cost accounting, 759–70, 780–95
  flow of manufacturing costs, 760–61
  labor, 765–67
  materials, 763–65
  overhead, 767–69

Job order cost accounting — *Cont.*
  perpetual inventory controlling accounts, 760–61
Job order cost system, 759, 780
Joint costs, 712–13
Joint federal-state unemployment insurance program, 395–99
Journal, 50; *see also specific types*
  defined, 55
  need for, 49–50
Journal entry, 50
  posting of, 51–53
Journal page numbers, 53, 55
Journalizing transactions, 50, 120

K–L

Key letters in work sheet, 106
Labor; *see also specific types*
  job order cost accounting for, 765
Labor time ticket, 765–67, 771, 780
Labor variances, 852–53
  isolating, 851–52
Land, 37, 84
Land, buildings, and equipment, 325–27
Last-in, first-out method of inventory pricing, 298, 300, 313
  tax advantage, 300–301
Lease, 369, 377
Leasehold, 369, 377
Leasehold improvements, 369–70, 377
Ledger, 50; *see also specific types*
  adjusting accounts in, 120
  arrangement of accounts in, 80
  defined, 39, 55
  proving, 190
  subsidiary, 178
Lessee, 369, 377
Lessor, 369, 377
Leverage on an investment, 511
Liabilities, 9–10, 423–55; *see also specific types*
  defined, 21, 393
  GPLA accounting for, 672–74
Liability accounts, 37–38; *see also specific types*
Lifo; *see* Last-in, first-out method of inventory pricing
Liquidation of partnership, 472–79
Liquidation value, 513, 647
List price, 159, 162
Loans, 424–25
  interest on, 424–25
Locating errors, 53
Long-range budgets, 802
Long-term commitments under a contract, disclosure of, 270

Long-term investments, 82–84, 570, 587
Long-term liabilities, 82–83, 85, 423, 603
Long-term notes, 444–45
Lower of cost or market pricing; *see* Cost or market, the lower

M

Machinery and equipment, 37
Magnetic tape, 33, 231, 701
Maker of a note, 263, 283
Management by exception, 858
Management advisory services, 5, 21
Management functions, 799, 845
Managerial decisions, 873–96
Manufacturing accounting, 729–57
  accounts unique to, 732–33
  adjusting entries, 740
  closing entries, 740–41
  income statement, 733–34
  inventory valuation problems, 742–43
  merchandise concerns distinguished, 729–30
  systems of, 730
Manufacturing budgets, 804, 808, 814
Manufacturing costs, 730–32
  flow of, 760–61
Manufacturing overhead, 731–32, 743
Manufacturing statement, 734–35, 743
  worksheet for, 735–40
Margin of safety, 830, 834
Marginal tax rate, 907, 921
Markdowns, 310–13
Market rate of bond interest, 434, 445
Market value of stock, 513
Marketable equity securities, 570, 587
Markon, 310, 313
Markups, 310–13
Master budget, 799–800, 814
  preparation of, 803–5
    illustration of, 805–14
Matching principle, 13, 275, 280–82, 325, 330
  adjustment process based on, 77, 80
  defined, 88
Material; *see also specific types*
  job order cost accounting for, 763–64
Material ledger cards, 764
Material price variance, 858
Material quantity variance, 858
Material requisition; *see* Purchase requisition

Material variances, 852
  isolating, 851–52
Materiality principle, 13, 282–83, 303, 342, 360, 412, 496
Maturity date of a note, 264, 283
Maturity value of a note, 267, 283
Maximum hours of work, 401
Merchandise account, 308
Merchandise inventory, 145–46, 162, 297; *see also* Inventories *and* Inventory
Merchandise inventory account, 152–56, 308
Merchandise purchases budget, 804–7, 814
Merchandising concern
  accounting for, 141–75
  departmental gross profits, 698–99, 701–2
  income statement of, 149
  manufacturing concern distinguished, 729–30
  worksheet for, 149–53
Merit rating plan, 398, 413
Minimum legal capital, 503, 514
Minimum wages, 401
Minority interest, 578, 587
Monetary assets, 671, 674, 684
Monetary liabilities, 673–74, 684
Mortgage, 428–29, 446
Mortgage contract, 428, 446
Mortgage note, 428
Mortgage payable, 38, 55
Multiproduct break-even point, 832–33
Mutual agency, 458, 479, 494

N

Natural business year, 121
  defined, 122
Natural resources, 366–67
Negotiable instruments
  defined, 272, 283
  holder in due course, 273, 283
Net assets, 17, 21
Net cash flow, 874, 877
Net income, 8, 17, 21, 81–82, 709
  distortion of, 917–20
  tax purposes, 916–17
Net loss, 8, 21, 612
Net method of recording invoices, 241, 246
Net pay, 405, 413
Net working capital, 601, 619
Net worth, 85–86
No-par stock, 505–6, 514
Nominal accounts, 120, 122
Noncumulative preferred stock, 510, 514
Noncurrent accounts, 605–6
Noncurrent assets
  purchase of, 604
  sale of, 603

Noncurrent liabilities, payment of, 604
Noninterest-bearing note, 425
Nonmonetary assets, 672, 674
Nonmonetary liabilities, 673–74
Nonparticipating preferred stock, 509
Normal balance of account, 49, 55
Normal markup, 310–11, 313
Normal tax on corporations, 911, 921
Notes; *see* Promissory notes
Notes payable, 37
  adjusting entries, 426–28
  amortization of interest or discount, 362–63
  borrowing from a bank, 424–25
  defined, 263
  discount on, 426–28
  exchange for plant asset, 361–63
  interest on, 425
  short-term, 423–25
  time extension on an account, 423–24
Notes receivable, 36, 263–74, 282–94
  collecting out-of-town, 272–73
  discount period, 267, 282
  discounting, 267–71, 282–83
  dishonored, 266–67, 271–72, 282
  end-of-the-period adjustments, 274
  maturity value, 267, 283
  recording, 264–66
Notice of protest, 271, 283

O

Objectivity principle, 11–13, 21, 34, 157
Obsolescence, 328, 335, 342
Obsolete goods, 302–30
Off-line computer operations, 197, 199
Office equipment, 37
Office equipment ledger, 339–42
Office supplies, 36
On-line computer operations, 197–99
Operating budgets, 804
Operating cycle of business, 82–83
  defined, 88
Opinions of the Accounting Principles Board; *see* Accounting Principles Board
Opportunity costs, 882–86
Ordinary income for tax purposes, 908
Ordinary items, 547–48

Ordinary repairs and replacements, 364–65, 377
Organization costs, 496, 514
Out-of-pocket costs, 882–86
Out-of-town notes, collection of, 272–73
Outstanding checks, 237, 246
Outstanding stock, 533
Over-the-counter securities market, 570
Overapplied overhead, 769, 780
Overhead
  charged to production, 853–54
  establishing standards, 854–55
  job order cost accounting for, 767–69
Overhead cost accounts, 731–32
Overhead costs ledger, 764
Overhead variances, 855–57
Owner equity, 9–10, 83, 85–86, 646–47
  defined, 21
Owner equity accounts, 38–39, 41, 499; *see also specific types*
  illustration of, 499–501

P

Par value, 503–4
  bond, 432, 446
  stock, 511, 514
Parent corporations, 575, 587
Participating preferred stocks, 509, 514
Partnership, 493
  accounting, 459
  addition of partner, 464
  advantages, 459
  bonus to new partner, 467–68
  bonus to old partners, 467
  characteristics of, 457–59
  contract basis, 457, 479
  death of partner, 472
  defined, 7, 21, 457, 479
  disadvantages, 459
  division of earnings, 460
  earnings allocated on stated fractional basis, 460–64
  financial statements, 464
  income statement, 464
  investment in existing, 466–67
  limited life, 458
  liquidations, 472–79
  loss-and-gain ratio, 464, 469, 473
  mutual agency, 458, 479
  nature of earnings of, 459–60
  salaries and interest as aids in sharing, 461–64
  sale of interest in, 465–66
  unlimited liability, 458–59, 479
  voluntary association as basis, 457

Partnership—*Cont.*
  withdrawal of partner, 464,
    468–72
Past performances, 800
Patents, 368, 377; *see also* Intan-
    gible assets
Payback period, 874–75, 886
Paycheck, 406–7
Payee of a note, 263, 283
Paying the employees, 406
Payroll accounting, 393–421, 731
  machine methods, 412
  pen-and-ink methods, 412
Payroll bank account, 406–8, 413
  reconciliation, 407–8
Payroll check register, 408
Payroll deductions, 393–402
Payroll register, 402–5, 765
  recording the payroll, 405–6
Payroll taxes, 393–401, 409–13
  accruing, 411–12
  expense account, 412
  levied on employer, 409–10
  paying, 410–11
Pen-and-ink accounting system,
    33–34, 50, 193, 412
  recording vouchers, 231, 242–
    43
Pen-and-ink ticket, 765
Percentage-of-completion basis of
    revenue recognition, 157, 162
Performance, evaluation of, 800–
    801
Performance reports, 845–46,
    849–50, 859
Periodic inventories; *see* Inven-
    tories
Periodic inventory system, 144,
    307–8, 313
  cost of goods sold, 145
  cost of merchandise purchased,
    146–48
  defined, 162–63
Perpetual inventory; *see* Inven-
    tories
Perpetual inventory controlling
    accounts, 760–61
  goods in process, 762–63
Perpetual inventory record, 144
Perpetual inventory system, 144,
    308, 314
  defined, 163
Petty cash fund, 231–32
  illustration, 232–35
  reimbursement of, 232
Petty cash receipt, 231
Petty cash record, 231, 234
Petty cashier, 231
Physical inventory; *see* Inven-
    tories
Pin-punched price tags, 700–701
Planned performance, 845
Planning, 799–800

Plant and equipment, 82–85, 88,
    325–54
  accumulated depreciation, 85
  balance sheet values, 334
  cost, 326–27
  damaged, discarding of, 337
  depreciation; *see* Depreciation
  discarding, 335–36
  disposal, 335–37
  exchanges of, 357–63
  inadequacy, 328, 347
  low cost, 341–42
  obsolescence, 328, 335, 342
  pledged to long-term liabilities,
    647
  productive life of, 325, 328
  records of, 339–41
  recovering costs of, 334–35
  repairs and replacements, 364–
    66, 377, 879–80
  sale of, 336–37
  salvage value, 329, 342
  supplies distinguished, 325
Pledged plant assets to long-term
    liabilities, 647
Pooling-of-interests method, 583–
    85, 587
Position statement, 9
Post-closing trial balance, 119,
    121–22
Posting, 55, 120
  cash disbursements journal,
    188–89
  cash receipts journal, 181–84
  controlling account, 184
  defined, 51
  double check, 181
  error in, 53
  folio letters to identify items,
    188
  process of, 51–53
  purchases journal, 185–87
  reducing labor involved in, 177–
    78
  rule of, 184
  sales journal, 178–80
  subsidiary ledger, 184
Posting reference numbers, 53, 55
Predetermined overhead applica-
    tion rate, 767–69, 780
Predetermined standard overhead
    rate, 853
Preemptive rights, 508, 514
Preferred stock, 501, 508–11,
    514, 570, 672
  reasons for issuance, 510–11
Premium
  bonds sold at, 438–40, 445
  stock issued at, 504, 515
Prepaid expenses, 36–37, 88
  adjusting account for, 70–72
Prepaid insurance, 36

Present value concept, 361, 372–
    77, 434–35, 438–39
  cash flows not uniform, 878–79
  discount periods less than one
    year, 376
  discounted cash flows, 876–77
  investment decisions, 374–75
  present value tables, 373, 375,
    377
Present value of $1 at compound
    interest, 373
Present value of $1 received peri-
    odically for a number of peri-
    ods, 375
Prevailing rate of interest, 361
Price-earnings ratio, 650–51
Price index
  base year, 668
  construction of, 668–69
  defined, 684
  specific versus general, 670,
    684–85
  use in accounting, 669–71
Price-level-adjusted statements,
    12–13
  defined, 21
Price-level changes, 665–93
  future of accounting for, 683–
    84
  understanding, 667–68
Price tags, pin-punched, 700–701
Price variance, 852–53, 859
Principal of a note, 263–64
Principle defined, 13
Prior period adjustments, 548–49,
    551
Private accounting, 5–6
Proceeds of a discounted note,
    268, 283, 425
Process, 770
Process cost accounting, 770–95
  basic objective of, 772
  illustration, 772–80
Process cost summary, 773–81
Process cost system, 770, 780
Process or sell decision, 884–85
Production budgets, 804, 808, 814
Productive capacity, 684
  replacement cost of, 683
    depreciation on, 683
Productive departments, 697–98,
    713
Productive life of plant assets,
    325, 328
Profit centers, 698, 713
Program, computer, 195–96
  defined, 199
Promissory notes, 37, 55
  defined, 263, 272
  maturity date, 264, 283
  time period of, 264
Property, plant, and equipment,
    325

Proprietorship; *see* Single proprietorships
Protest fee, 271, 283
Proving the ledgers, 190
Proxy, 497, 515
Public accountant defined, 5
Public accounting, 5–6
Punched cards, 33, 231
Purchase method, 576–84, 587
Purchase order, 226–27, 246
Purchase requisition, 226, 246, 763–64, 780
Purchases, 152
  noncurrent assets, 604
Purchases account, 146–48, 308
Purchases discounts, 146–48, 163
Purchases journal, 180, 185
  assets used in business, 187
  merchandise, 187
  one-money-column, 185, 187
  posting to, 185–87
Purchases returns and allowances, 147–48, 152–53, 244
  journal, 188, 190
Purchasing power, 669
  gain or loss, 678–79, 684
  general versus specific, 680–81

Q–R

Quantity variance, 852–853, 859
Quick assets, 643
Quick ratio, 643–44, 651
Rate of return
  common stockholders' equity, 648–49, 651
  total assets employed, 648, 651
Rate of return on average investment, 874–76, 886
Rates of federal income tax, 905–7
Ratios, 642–44, 646, 650–51; *see also specific types*
Raw materials, 730–31, 743
  inventory account, 732
  purchases account, 732
Real accounts, 120, 122
Realization principle, 13, 18–19, 21, 37, 76
Rebuilding defective units, 883–84
Receiving report, 226–27, 246
Recognition principle, 18, 75
  adjustment process based on, 77, 80
Reconcile, 237, 246
Reconciling bank balance; *see* Bank balance reconciliation
Recording transactions, 33–67
Redemption value of stock, 513, 515
Reducing charge depreciation methods, 332–33
Registered bonds, 431, 446

Registers; *see specific types*
Registrar, 499
Reissuance of treasury stock, 534–36
  at cost, 534–35
  at price above cost, 535
  at price below cost, 535–36
Relevant range of operations, 826, 834
Rent expense account, 369
Rent expense allocation, 704
Repairs and replacements, 364
  extraordinary, 365–66, 377
  ordinary, 364–65, 377
Replacement cost, 12–13
  balance sheet, 682
  cost of goods sold, 683
  inventories, 682–83
  productive capacity, 683
    depreciation on, 683
  SEC requirement for information of, 682–83
Replacement cost accounting, 667, 670, 681–83, 685
  operating profit, 681–82
Replacing plant assets, 879–80
Report form balance sheet, 86, 88
Requisition; *see* Purchase requisition
Research and development costs, 368–69
Responsibility accounting, 711–27
  defined, 713–14
Restricted endorsement, 269
Retail inventory method, 309, 314
  estimating ending inventory by, 309–10
  inventory shortage, 310
  markups and markdowns, 310–13
  reducing physical inventory to cost basis, 310
Retained earnings, 537–38
  adjusted balance, 679–80
  amount capitalized, 541
  appropriation of, 543–45, 551
Retained earnings accounts, 499
Retained earnings statement, 546–47, 601
Retirement of stock, 536–37
Return on average investment, 875–76, 886
Revenue, 8
  defined, 17–18, 22
Revenue from sales, 142–44
  defined, 142
Revenue accounts, 39, 41, 152
  closing, 112
Revenue expenditures, 366, 377
Revenue recognition, 18
  bases of, 156–57

Reversing entry, 428, 446
Rolling budgets, 803, 814
Rule-of-thumb standards of comparison, 644–47

S

Salaries
  allocation of, 703–4
  partnership, 461–64
Sales
  on account, 36
  capital stock, 603
  cash, 33–34, 181, 223–24
  credit, 36
  noncurrent assets, 603
  partnership interest, 465–66
  plant asset, 336–37
  required for desired net income, 829–30
  stock for cash, 502
  stock through subscriptions, 530–31
Sales basis for revenue recognition, 156, 163
Sales budget, 804–6, 814
Sales discounts, 143–44, 152, 163
Sales journal, 177–78
  daily posting of account receivable amounts, 191
  posting to, 178–80
  sales invoices instead of, 191
  sales taxes column, 191
Sales mix, 833–34
  determination of most profitable, 885–86
Sales returns and allowances, 142–43, 152, 184–85
Sales returns and allowances journal, 185
Sales taxes, 191
Salvage value, 329, 342, 879
Schedule of accounts payable, 190, 199
Schedule of accounts receivable, 190, 199, 279–80
Scrapping defective units, 883–84
Secured bonds, 431
Securities; *see* Stock *and* Stock investments
Securities and Exchange Commission (SEC), 14–15
  replacement cost information requirement, 682–83
Selling and administrative overhead, 732
Selling expense budget, 804, 808
Selling expenses, 149, 163
Semivariable costs, 825–26, 834
Serial bonds, 431, 446
Service departments, 697–98, 714
Service enterprise accounting, 105–138, 141

Service life of plant asset, 325, 328, 342
Share of stock, 429, 446; see also Stock
Shareholders, 493
  defined, 7, 22, 429
  lack of liability, 494
  meetings, 496
  rights of, 508
Shoplifting losses, 149
Short-term credit, 601-2
Short-term notes payable, 423-25; see also Notes payable
Short-term payables, 38
Shortages in inventory, 310
Shrinkage, 149
Single proprietorships, 85, 493
  defined, 7, 22
  owner equity accounts, 499-501
Sinking fund, 442-44, 446
Sinking fund bonds, 431, 446
Small stock dividend, 541, 551
Social Security Act, 393-99
Sources of funds, 602-3
  defined, 602, 619
Special journal, 200
Specific invoice prices for inventory, 298-99, 314
Specific price-level index, 670, 685
Spoilage, 149
Stable-dollar concept, 12-13, 22
Stair step costs, 826
Standard cost system, 850
Standard costs, 845, 850-71
  accounts, 858
  charging overhead to production, 853-54
  controlling a business through, 857-58
  defined, 859
  establishing overhead standards, 854-55
  establishment of, 851
  isolating material and labor variances, 851-52
  labor variances, 852-53
  material variances, 852
  overhead variances, 855-57
  variances, 851
Standard deduction for taxes, 904, 921
Standard labor cost, 850
Standard material cost, 850
Standard overhead costs, 850
Standards of comparison, 646
State income taxes; see Taxes
State unemployment insurance programs, 398-99, 413
Stated value of no-par stock, 505-6, 515

Statement of changes in financial position, 601-33
  broad concept of financing and investing activities, 614-15
  cash flow, 615-19
  design of, 604-5
  extraordinary gains and losses, 613-14
  function, 601
  noncurrent assets, examination of, 605-6
  preparation of, 605-7
    steps in, 607
  reason for preparing, 604
  working paper for, 607-12
    analyzing entries, 609-11
    net loss on, 612
Statement of sources and applications of funds, 601
Statements; see Financial statements or specific types
Statements of the Accounting Principles Board; see Accounting Principles Board
Statements of the Financial Accounting Standards Board; see Financial Accounting Standards Board
Static budget, 845-46, 859
Stock, 429; see also specific types
  authorization of, 501-2
  book value, 511-14
  certificates of, 497-99
  converting bonds to, 542-43
  exchange for assets other than cash, 502-3
  investments in; see Stock investments
  issued at discount, 504-5, 514
  issued at premium, 504, 515
  market value, 513
  par value, 503-4, 511, 514
  redemption value, 513, 515
  retirement of, 536-37
  sale for cash, 502
  stated value, 505-6, 515
  transfer of, 497-99
  values of, 511-13
Stock brokers, 569-70
Stock certificate, 497-99
Stock certificate book, 498-99
Stock dividends, 538-40, 551
  amount of retained earnings capitalized, 541
  balance sheet, 541
  reasons for distribution, 540-41
Stock exchanges, 570
Stock investments, 569-70
  accounting for, 570-75
  classification of, 570
  cost or market, the lower, 572-73

Stock investments—Cont.
  cost method of accounting, 571-72, 587
  dividends, treatment of, 572
  equity method of accounting, 571, 573-75, 587
  excess of investment cost over book value, 578-81
  long-term, 570, 587
Stock split-up, 542
Stock splits, 542, 551
Stock subscriptions, 529-30, 551
  balance sheet, 531-32
  sale of stock through, 530-31
Stockholders; see Shareholders
Stockholders' equity, 545
  GPLA accounting for, 672-74
Stockholders of record, 507, 515
Store equipment, 37
Store equipment ledger, 339, 342
Store supplies, 36
Straight-line amortization method, 372, 436
Straight-line depreciation, 329, 342, 879
Subbudgets, 799-800
Subscribers' ledgers, 530
Subscriptions; see Stock subscriptions
Subscriptions receivable, common stock, 529-30
Subsidiary corporations, 575, 587
  earnings of, 581
  pooling of interests in, 583-85, 587
  purchase of interest for cash, 576-84, 587
Subsidiary ledgers, 178
  defined, 200
  posting to, 184
  proving, 190
Sum-of-the-years' digits depreciation, 329, 331-33, 342, 879
Sunk costs, 882-85, 887
Supplies and plant and equipment distinguished, 325
Surplus, 537
Surtax on corporations, 911, 921
System of internal controls; see Internal controls system

T

T-accounts, 34-35, 39-40
  defined, 55
  when used or not used, 48
Tax avoidance, 900, 921
Tax evasion, 900, 922
Tax planning, 899, 922
Tax services, 5-6, 22
Tax table income, 911, 922
Taxable income, 916-17

Taxes, 899–930
accounting basis and procedures, 915–16
allocation of, 705
entries for, 920–21
basis, 900, 921
capital gains and losses, 908–10, 921
city income tax, 401, 900
classes of taxpayers, 901
corporation income tax, 495, 911–12
accounting treatment for, 550–51
credits, 907–8, 921
deductions from adjusted gross income, 904–5
deductions to arrive at adjusted gross income, 903–4
dividends and growth, 913–14
federal income tax, 399–401, 901–20
history of, 900–901
rates of, 905–7
synopsis of, 901–16
financing method, effect of, 914
form of business organization affecting, 912–13
gross income, 902–3, 921
individual income tax, 901–8
net income, 916–17
distortion of, 916–20
objectives of federal income tax, 900–901
payroll, 393–401, 409–13
plant asset exchanges, 359–61
prepayments, 907–8
related transactions, 915
returns, audit of, 7
state income tax, 401, 900
tables to calculate, 910–11
taxable income, 916–17
timing of transactions, effect of, 914–15
unemployment tax, 395–99
withholding from employees' salaries, 399–401
zero bracket amount, 904, 922
Taxpayers, classes of, 901
Temporary proprietorship accounts, 119, 122
closing, 121
Three-digit account numbering system, 160–61
Time clocks, 765
Time and motion studies, 851
Time-period concept, 13, 69, 88
Time sharing, 198–200
Timekeeping, 402–3, 413
Times fixed interest charges earned, 647–48, 651
Trade discounts, 159, 163
Trade-in value, 329

Trade-ins; see Exchanging plant assets
Trade names, 371–72
Trademarks, 371–72
Transactions defined, 33
Transfer agent, 499
Transportation costs, 147
Treasury stock, 532, 551
purchase of, 532–34
reissuance of, 534–36
restricting retained earnings by purchase of, 534
Trend percentages, 638–39
Trial balance
adjusted, 76–80, 87, 105, 108
defined, 56
post-closing, 119, 121–22
preparation of, 46–48, 120
proof offered by, 48
unadjusted, 76, 88, 106
unbalanced, 48, 53
worksheet, 150–52
illustration, 108
Trustee
bondholders, 431
sinking fund, 442
Turnover, 646
accounts receivable, 644–45, 651
merchandise inventory, 645–46, 651

U

Unadjusted trial balance, 76, 88, 106
Uncollectible accounts; see Bad debts
Uncollectible items, 238
Uncontrollable costs, 710, 713
Underapplied overhead, 769, 780
Underwriter, 431
Unearned revenues, 37–38, 85, 88
adjusting accounts for, 75–76
Unemployment insurance taxes, 395–99, 413
accruing, 411–12
levied on employers, 409–10
paying, 411
Unfavorable variances, 851
Uniform Partnership Act, 457, 466
Union contracts, 401–2
Unit-of-money financial statements, 671, 674, 682, 684–85
Units-of-production depletion basis, 367
Units-of-production depreciation, 329–30
Unlimited liability, 458–59, 479
Unpaid vouchers file, 243
Unprofitable department, elimination of, 708–9

Unrecorded deposits, 237
Unsecured bonds, 431
Uses of funds, 604
defined, 602, 604, 619

V

Variable budgets, 846, 859; see also Flexible budgets
Variable costs, 823–26, 834
Variance analysis, 850
Variances, 851
accounts, 858
controllable, 855–58
isolation of, 851–52
labor, 851–53
material, 851–52
overhead, 855–57
price, 852–53, 859
quantity, 852–53, 859
volume, 855–57, 859
Vendee, 227, 246
Vendor, 227, 246
Volume-profit analysis, 823–42
Volume variance, 855–57, 859
Voucher, 226, 228–30
defined, 247
recording of, 231, 242–43
unpaid, file of, 243
Voucher register, 242–47
Voucher system, 247
control and, 225–30
expenses and, 230–31
Vouchers payable account, 242

W

W–2 form, 395, 397
Wage bracket withholding table, 400–401, 413
Wages and Hours Law, 401
Wages and salaries, allocation of, 703–4
Wasting assets, 366–67
Weighted average change in per unit prices, 667–68
Weighted average cost inventory pricing, 298–99, 314
Withdrawal of partner, 464, 468–72
Withdrawals account, 38–39, 41, 56
closing, 114–15
Withholding
federal income taxes, 399–401
federal unemployment insurance contributions taxes, 394–95, 400–401
tables, 400–401, 413
Withholding allowance, 399, 413
Work in process, 733, 743
Worksheet
adjusting entries, 110
adjustments on, 106–9, 152
balance sheet, 109–10

Worksheet—*Cont.*
  closing entries, 110
  completion of, 153
  cost of goods sold accounts, 152–53
  defined, 105, 122
  illustration of, 106–9
  income statement, 109–10, 152–53
  key letters, 106
  manufacturing company, 735–40
  merchandising concern, 149–53
  preparation of, 105–6, 120

Worksheet—*Cont.*
  purpose of preparing, 105
  revenue accounts, 152
  tasks achieved by, 105
  trial balance, 108, 150–52
    dispensing with, 156
Working capital, 601–2, 619
  analysis of, 642–46
  analysis of changes in, 612–13
  deficiency in, 642
    determining change in, 607
  sufficiency of, 642
Working papers, 120, 122
  analyzing entries, 609–11

Working papers—*Cont.*
  net loss on, 612
  statement of changes in financial position, 607–12
Write-down or write-off of assets, 547–48
Write-off of bad debt, 277–78
  direct, 280–82

Y–Z

Yes or no decisions, 196–97
Zero bracket amount, 904, 921
Zeros in cents column, 54

This book has been set in 10 and 9 point Times Roman, leaded 2 points. Part and chapter titles are 24 point Venus Bold Extended and chapter numbers are 42 point Venus Bold Extended. The size of the type area is 26 by 49½ picas.